Real-Time Data Analysis Exercises

Up-to-date macro data is a great way to engage in and understand the usefulness of macro variables and their impact on the economy. Real-Time Data Analysis exercises communicate directly with the Federal Reserve Bank of St. Louis's FRED® site, so every time FRED posts new data, students see new data.

End-of-chapter exercises accompanied by the Real-Time Data Analysis icon 🌐 include Real-Time Data versions in **MyEconLab**.

Select in-text exhibits labeled **MyEconLab** Real-Time Data update in the electronic version of the text using FRED data.

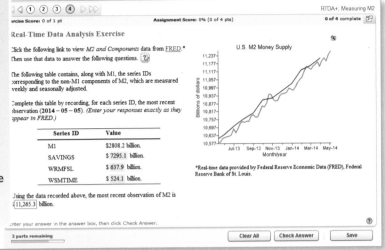

Current News Exercises

Posted weekly, we find the latest microeconomic and macroeconomic news stories, post them, and write auto-graded multi-part exercises that illustrate the economic way of thinking about the news.

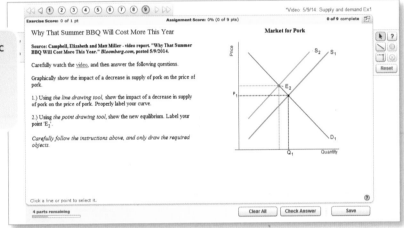

Interactive Homework Exercises

Participate in a fun and engaging activity that helps promote active learning and mastery of important economic concepts.

Pearson's experiments program is flexible and easy for instructors and students to use. For a complete list of available experiments, visit *www.myeconlab.com*.

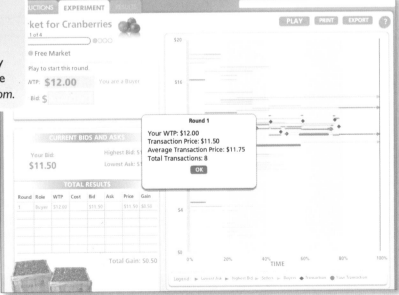

ECONOMICS

Daron Acemoglu
Massachusetts Institute of Technology

David Laibson
Harvard University

John A. List
University of Chicago

PEARSON

Boston Columbus Indianapolis New York San Francisco Hoboken
Amsterdam Cape Town Dubai London Madrid Milan Munich Paris Montréal Toronto
Delhi Mexico City São Paulo Sydney Hong Kong Seoul Singapore Taipei Tokyo

Vice President, Business Publishing: Donna Battista
Executive Acquisitions Editor: Adrienne D'Ambrosio
Executive Development Editor: Mary Clare McEwing
Editorial Assistant: Courtney Turcotte
Vice President, Product Marketing: Maggie Moylan
Director of Marketing, Digital Services and Products: Jeanette Koskinas
Senior Product Marketing Manager: Alison Haskins
Executive Field Marketing Manager: Lori DeShazo
Senior Strategic Marketing Manager: Erin Gardner
Product Testing and Learning Validation: Kathleen McLellan
Team Lead, Program Management: Ashley Santora
Program Manager: Nancy Freihofer
Team Lead, Project Management: Jeff Holcomb
Project Manager: Sarah Dumouchelle
Supplements Project Manager: Andra Skaalrud
Operations Specialist: Carol Melville

Creative Director: Blair Brown
Art Director: Jon Boylan
Vice President, Director of Digital Strategy and Assessment: Paul Gentile
Manager of Learning Applications: Paul DeLuca
Digital Editor: Denise Clinton
Director, Digital Studio: Sacha Laustsen
Digital Studio Manager: Diane Lombardo
Digital Studio Project Manager: Melissa Honig
Digital Content Team Lead: Noel Lotz
Digital Content Project Lead: Courtney Kamauf
Full-Service Project Management and Composition: Diane Kohnen, Ann Francis, S4Carlisle Publishing Services
Interior Designer: Jonathan Boylan
Cover Designer: Jonathan Boylan
Printer/Binder: Courier Kendallville
Cover Printer: Courier Kendallville

Library of Congress Cataloging-in-Publication Data

Acemoglu, Daron.
  Economics / Daron Acemoglu, David Laibson, John A. List. — First Edition.
    pages cm
  Includes bibliographical references and index.
  ISBN-13: 978-0-321-38395-2
  ISBN-10: 0-321-38395-8
  1. Economics. I. Laibson, David I. II. List, John A. III. Title.
  HB171.5.A276 2014
  330—dc23

                                        2013048486

V011
10 9 8 7 6 5 4 3 2

ISBN 10:   0-321-39158-6
ISBN 13: 978-0-321-39158-2

Dedication

With love for Asu, Nina, and Jennifer,
who inspire us every day.

About the Authors

Daron Acemoglu is Elizabeth and James Killian Professor of Economics in the Department of Economics at the Massachusetts Institute of Technology. He has received a B.A. in economics at the University of York, 1989; M.Sc. in mathematical economics and econometrics at the London School of Economics, 1990; and Ph.D. in economics at the London School of Economics in 1992.

He is an elected fellow of the National Academy of Sciences, the American Academy of Arts and Sciences, the Econometric Society, the European Economic Association, and the Society of Labor Economists. He has received numerous awards and fellowships, including the inaugural T. W. Shultz Prize from the University of Chicago in 2004, the inaugural Sherwin Rosen Award for outstanding contribution to labor economics in 2004, Distinguished Science Award from the Turkish Sciences Association in 2006, and the John von Neumann Award, Rajk College, Budapest in 2007.

He was also the recipient of the John Bates Clark Medal in 2005, awarded every two years to the best economist in the United States under the age of 40 by the American Economic Association, and the Erwin Plein Nemmers prize awarded every two years for work of lasting significance in economics. He holds Honorary Doctorates from the University of Utrecht and Bosporus University.

His research interests include political economy, economic development and growth, human capital theory, growth theory, innovation, search theory, network economics, and learning.

His books include *Economic Origins of Dictatorship and Democracy* (jointly with James A. Robinson), which was awarded the Woodrow Wilson and the William Riker prizes, *Introduction to Modern Economic Growth*, and *Why Nations Fail: The Origins of Power, Prosperity, and Poverty* (jointly with James A. Robinson), which has become a *New York Times* bestseller.

David Laibson is the Robert I. Goldman Professor of Economics at Harvard University. He is also a member of the National Bureau of Economic Research, where he is Research Associate in the Asset Pricing, Economic Fluctuations, and Aging Working Groups. His research focuses on the topic of behavioral economics, and he leads Harvard University's Foundations of Human Behavior Initiative. He serves on several editorial boards, as well as the boards of the Health and Retirement Study (National Institutes of Health) and the Pension Research Council (Wharton). He serves on Harvard's Pension Investment Committee and on the Academic Research Council of the Consumer Financial Protection Bureau. He is a recipient of a Marshall Scholarship and a Fellow of the Econometric Society and the American Academy of Arts and Sciences. He is also a recipient of the TIAA-CREF Paul A. Samuelson Award for Outstanding Scholarly Writing on Lifelong Financial Security. Laibson holds degrees from Harvard University (A.B. in Economics, Summa), the London School of Economics (M.Sc. in Econometrics and Mathematical Economics), and the Massachusetts Institute of Technology (Ph.D. in Economics). He received his Ph.D. in 1994 and has taught at Harvard since then. In recognition of his teaching, he has been awarded Harvard's Phi Beta Kappa Prize and a Harvard College Professorship.

John A. List is the Homer J. Livingston Professor in Economics at the University of Chicago, and Chairman of the Department of Economics. List received the Kenneth Galbraith Award, Agricultural and Applied Economics Association, 2010. He is a Member of the American Academy of Arts and Sciences, 2011; Editor, *Journal of Economic Perspectives*; Associate Editor, *American Economic Review*; and Associate Editor, *Journal of Economic Literature*. His research focuses on questions in microeconomics, with a particular emphasis on the use of experimental methods to address both positive and normative issues. Much of his time has been spent developing experimental methods in the field to explore economic aspects of environmental regulations, incentives, preferences, values, and institutions. Recently, he has focused on issues related to the economics of charity, exploring why people give, plus optimal incentive schemes for first-time as well as warm-list donors.

The Pearson Series in Economics

Abel/Bernanke/Croushore
Macroeconomics*

Acemoglu/Laibson/List
Economics*

Bade/Parkin
Foundations of Economics*

Berck/Helfand
The Economics of the Environment

Bierman/Fernandez
Game Theory with Economic Applications

Blanchard
Macroeconomics*

Blau/Ferber/Winkler
The Economics of Women, Men, and Work

Boardman/Greenberg/Vining/Weimer
Cost-Benefit Analysis

Boyer
Principles of Transportation Economics

Branson
Macroeconomic Theory and Policy

Bruce
Public Finance and the American Economy

Carlton/Perloff
Modern Industrial Organization

Case/Fair/Oster
Principles of Economics*

Chapman
Environmental Economics: Theory, Application, and Policy

Cooter/Ulen
Law & Economics

Daniels/VanHoose
International Monetary & Financial Economics

Downs
An Economic Theory of Democracy

Ehrenberg/Smith
Modern Labor Economics

Farnham
Economics for Managers

Folland/Goodman/Stano
The Economics of Health and Health Care

Fort
Sports Economics

Froyen
Macroeconomics

Fusfeld
The Age of the Economist

Gerber
International Economics*

González-Rivera
Forecasting for Economics and Business

Gordon
Macroeconomics*

Greene
Econometric Analysis

Gregory
Essentials of Economics

Gregory/Stuart
Russian and Soviet Economic Performance and Structure

Hartwick/Olewiler
The Economics of Natural Resource Use

Heilbroner/Milberg
The Making of the Economic Society

Heyne/Boettke/Prychitko
The Economic Way of Thinking

Holt
Markets, Games, and Strategic Behavior

Hubbard/O'Brien
Economics*

Money, Banking, and the Financial System*

Hubbard/O'Brien/Rafferty
Macroeconomics*

Hughes/Cain
American Economic History

Husted/Melvin
International Economics

Jehle/Reny
Advanced Microeconomic Theory

Johnson-Lans
A Health Economics Primer

Keat/Young/Erfle
Managerial Economics

Klein
Mathematical Methods for Economics

Krugman/Obstfeld/Melitz
International Economics: Theory & Policy*

Laidler
The Demand for Money

Leeds/von Allmen
The Economics of Sports

Leeds/von Allmen/Schiming
Economics*

Lynn
Economic Development: Theory and Practice for a Divided World

Miller
Economics Today*

Understanding Modern Economics

Miller/Benjamin
The Economics of Macro Issues

Miller/Benjamin/North
The Economics of Public Issues

Mills/Hamilton
Urban Economics

Mishkin
The Economics of Money, Banking, and Financial Markets*

The Economics of Money, Banking, and Financial Markets, Business School Edition*

Macroeconomics: Policy and Practice*

Murray
Econometrics: A Modern Introduction

O'Sullivan/Sheffrin/Perez
Economics: Principles, Applications and Tools*

Parkin
Economics*

Perloff
Microeconomics*

Microeconomics: Theory and Applications with Calculus*

Perloff/Brander
Managerial Economics and Strategy*

Phelps
Health Economics

Pindyck/Rubinfeld
Microeconomics*

Riddell/Shackelford/Stamos/Schneider
Economics: A Tool for Critically Understanding Society

Roberts
The Choice: A Fable of Free Trade and Protection

Rohlf
Introduction to Economic Reasoning

Roland
Development Economics

Scherer
Industry Structure, Strategy, and Public Policy

Schiller
The Economics of Poverty and Discrimination

Sherman
Market Regulation

Stock/Watson
Introduction to Econometrics

Studenmund
Using Econometrics: A Practical Guide

Tietenberg/Lewis
Environmental and Natural Resource Economics
Environmental Economics and Policy

Todaro/Smith
Economic Development

Waldman/Jensen
Industrial Organization: Theory and Practice

Walters/Walters/Appel/Callahan/Centanni/Maex/O'Neill
Econversations: Today's Students Discuss Today's Issues

Weil
Economic Growth

Williamson
Macroeconomics

*denotes MyEconLab titles   Visit www.myeconlab.com to learn more.

Brief Contents

Chapters on the Web

Web chapters are available on MyEconLab.

Contents

CHAPTERS ON THE WEB

Web chapters are available on MyEconLab.

WEB Chapter 1 Financial Decision Making

WEB Chapter 2 Economics of Life, Health, and the Environment

WEB Chapter 3 Political Economy

Preface

We love economics. We marvel at the way economic systems work. When we buy a smartphone, we think about the complex supply chain and the hundreds of thousands of people who played a role in producing an awe-inspiring piece of technology that was assembled from components manufactured across the globe.

The market's ability to do the world's work without anyone being in charge strikes us as a phenomenon no less profound than the existence of consciousness or life itself. We believe that the creation of the market system is one of the greatest achievements of humankind.

We wrote this book to highlight the simplicity of economic ideas and their extraordinary power to explain, predict, and improve what happens in the world. We want students to master the *essential* principles of economic analysis. With that goal in mind, we identify the three key ideas that lie at the heart of the economic approach to understanding human behavior: optimization, equilibrium, and empiricism. These abstract words represent three ideas that are actually highly intuitive.

Our Vision: Three Unifying Themes

The first key principle is that people try to choose the best available option: *optimization*. We don't assume that people always successfully optimize, but we do believe that people try to optimize and often do a relatively good job of it. Because most decision makers try to choose the alternative that offers the greatest net benefit, optimization is a useful tool for predicting human behavior. Optimization is also a useful prescriptive tool. By teaching people how to optimize, we improve their decisions and the quality of their lives. By the end of this course, every student should be a skilled optimizer—without using complicated mathematics, simply by using economic intuition.

The second key principle extends the first: economic systems operate in *equilibrium*, a state in which everybody is simultaneously trying to optimize. We want students to see that they're not the only ones maximizing their well-being. An economic system is in equilibrium when each person feels that he or she cannot do any better by picking another course of action. The principle of equilibrium highlights the connections among economic actors. For example, Apple stores stock millions of iPhones because millions of consumers are going to turn up to buy them. In turn, millions of consumers go to Apple stores because those stores are ready to sell those iPhones. In equilibrium, consumers and producers are simultaneously optimizing and their behaviors are intertwined.

Our first two principles—optimization and equilibrium—are conceptual. The third is methodological: *empiricism*. Economists use *data* to test economic theories, learn about the world, and speak to policymakers. Accordingly, data play a starring role in our book, though we keep the empirical analysis extremely simple. It is this emphasis on matching theories with real data that we think most distinguishes our book from others. We show students how economists use data to answer specific questions, which makes our chapters concrete, interesting, and fun. Modern students demand the evidence behind the theory, and our book supplies it.

For example, we begin every chapter with an empirical question and then answer that question using data. One chapter begins by asking:

Would a smoker quit the habit for $100 a month?

Later in that chapter, we describe how smoking fell when researchers paid smokers to quit. Another chapter opens with the question

Why are you so much more prosperous than your great-great-grandparents were?

Later in that chapter, we demonstrate the central role played by technology in explaining U.S. economic growth and why we are much better off than our relatives a few generations ago.

In our experience, students taking their first economics class often have the impression that economics is a series of theoretical assertions with little empirical basis. By using data, we explain how economists evaluate and improve our scientific insights. Data also make concepts more memorable. Using evidence helps students build intuition, because data move the conversation from abstract principles to concrete facts. Every chapter sheds light on how economists use data to answer questions that directly interest students. Every chapter demonstrates the key role that evidence plays in advancing the science of economics.

Features

All of our features showcase intuitive empirical questions.

- In **Evidence-Based Economics (EBE)**, we show how economists use data to answer the question we pose in the opening paragraph of the chapter. The EBE uses actual data that highlights some of the major concepts discussed within the chapter. This tie-in with the data gives students a substantive look at economics as it plays out in the world around them.

    The questions explored aren't just dry intellectual ideas; they spring to life the minute the student sets foot outside the classroom—*Is Facebook free? Is college worth it? Will free trade cause you to lose your job? Is there value in putting yourself into someone else's shoes? Are tropical and semitropical areas condemned to poverty by their geographies? What caused the recession of 2007–2009? Are companies like Nike harming workers in Vietnam?*

 Evidence-Based Economics

Q: Would a smoker quit the habit for $100 per month?

 At the beginning of this chapter, we posed a question concerning whether *a smoker would quit the habit for $100 a month*. Within the economics literature, an approach that is gaining popularity is to *pay* people to quit smoking. The tools of this chapter can help us begin to think about whether such an incentive can work, and why it might work.

In thinking about such a reward, we have learned that the impact of an increase in income leads to changes in the consumer budget constraint and subsequently the demand for goods and services. To see these tools in action, we return to the shopping-spree example. Exhibit 5.5 shows the mechanics behind the effects of an increase in what we have available to spend.

With that foundation laid, we can return to the question of quitting smoking for a month. Given our economic framework, the very same principle that was at work in the shopping-spree problem applies when considering the smoker's problem. By providing $100 for not smoking, we create a trade-off between the current benefits of smoking and the benefits ob

 Evidence-Based Economics

Q: Why are you so much more prosperous than your great-great-grandparents were?

 The theoretical discussion in the previous section supports the central role of technology in explaining sustained growth. We will now see that empirical evidence also bolsters the conclusion that technology plays a key role.

To evaluate the sources of U.S. economic growth, we follow the same strategy as in the previous chapter. There, we used the aggregate production function and estimates of the physical capital stock and the efficiency units of labor across different countries to evaluate their contributions to cross-country differences in GDP. The only major difference here is that higher-quality U.S. data enable us to conduct the analysis for GDP per

- **Letting the Data Speak** is another feature that analyzes an economic question by using real data as the foundation of the discussion. Among the many issues we explore are such topics as McDonald's and elasticity, fair trade, airline price wars, life expectancy and innovation, living in an interconnected world, and why Chinese authorities have historically kept the yuan undervalued.

Life Expectancy and Innovation

Life expectancy around the world was much lower 70 years ago than it is today.[4] In 1940, child and infant mortality rates were so high and adult diseases, such as pneumonia and tuberculosis, were so deadly (and without any cure) that life expectancy at birth in many nations stood at less than 40 years. For example, the life expectancy at birth of an average Indian was an incredibly low 30 years. In Venezuela, it was 33; in Indonesia, 34; in Brazil, 36. Life expectancy at birth in many Western nations was also low but still considerably higher than the corresponding numbers in the poorer nations. Consider that life expectancy at birth in the United States was 64 years.

In the course of the next three or four decades, this picture changed dramatically. As we saw in the previous chapter, while the gap in life expectancy between rich and poor nations still remains today, health conditions have improved significantly all over the world, particularly before the spread of the AIDS epidemic in sub-Saharan Africa starting in the 1980s. Life expectancy at birth in India in 1999 was 60 years. This was twice as large as the same number in 1940. It was also 50 percent higher than life expectancy at birth in Britain in 1820 (40 years), which had approximately the same GDP per capita as India in 1999. How did this tremendous improvement in health conditions in poor nations take place?

The answer lies in scientific breakthroughs and innovations that took place in the United States and Western Europe throughout the twentieth century. First, there was a wave of global drug innovation, most importantly the development of antibiotics, which produced many products that were highly effective against major killers in developing countries. Penicillin, which provided an effective treatment against a range of bacterial infections, became widely available by the early 1950s. Also important during the same period was the development of new vaccines, including ones against yellow fever and smallpox.

The second major factor was the discovery of DDT (Dichlorodiphenyl trichloroethylene). Although eventually the excess use of DDT as an agricultural pesticide would turn out to be an environmental hazard, its initial use in disease control was revolutionary. DDT allowed a breakthrough in attempts to control one of the major killers of children in relatively poor parts of the world—malaria. Finally, with the establishment and help of the World Health Organization (WHO), simple but effective medical and public health practices, such as oral rehydration and boiling water to prevent cholera, spread to poorer countries.

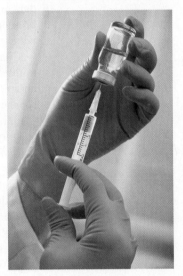

- In keeping with the optimization theme, from time to time we ask students to make a real economic decision or evaluate the consequences of past real decisions in a feature entitled **Choice & Consequence**. We explain how an economist might analyze the same decision. Among the choices investigated are such questions and concepts as the unintended consequences of fixing market prices, the tragedy of the commons, signaling, the power of growth, foreign aid and corruption, and policies that address the problem of banks that are "too big to fail."

The Race to Fish

Imagine that you are a fisherman who owns a private pond fully stocked with 100 bluegill fish. Because you own the property rights to the pond, you are the only one who can fish at the pond. Therefore, you can catch as many bluegill as you want. But you know that in the late spring in 70°F water, the female deposits around 40,000 eggs in a shallow nest near the sandy shore. Two to six days later, the eggs hatch and the male guards the young fry during their first days.

Knowing this, how many fish will you catch?

You will likely not decide to catch all of the bluegill, instead leaving many in the pond to restock your supply for the next season.

Now imagine that this pond is a common pool resource—anyone and everyone can fish from it, and one more fish on another angler's line means one less fish on yours. Would you still be careful to leave a lot of fish in the pond for next season?

Both real-world situations and lab experiments conducted by Nobel Laureate Elinor Ostrom have shown us that you probably wouldn't.[4,5] After all, if you decide to leave, say, 50 fish in the pond, who is to stop another fisherman from catching those fish?

This line of thinking may lead everyone to keep fishing until there is absolutely nothing left. As you just learned, this type of situation is referred to as the *tragedy of the commons*; a dilemma in which multiple individuals acting in their own self-interest deplete a shared limited resource when in the long run it isn't in anyone's best interest to do so.

How might the fishermen in our example prevent this from happening?

Organization

Part I Introduction to Economics lays the groundwork for understanding the economic way of thinking about the world. In *Chapter 1*, we show that the principle of *optimization* explains most of our choices. In other words, we make choices based on a consideration of benefits and costs, and to do this we need to consider trade-offs, budget constraints, and opportunity cost. We then explain that *equilibrium* is the situation in which everyone is simultaneously trying to individually optimize. In equilibrium, there isn't any perceived benefit to changing one's own behavior. We introduce the free-rider problem to show that individual optimization and social optimization do not necessarily coincide.

Because data plays such a central role in economics, we devote an entire chapter—*Chapter 2*—to economic models, the scientific method, empirical testing, and the critical distinction between correlation and causation. We show how economists use models and data to answer interesting questions about human behavior. For the students who want to brush up their graphical skills, there is an appendix on constructing and interpreting graphs, which is presented in the context of an actual experiment on incentive schemes.

Chapter 3 digs much more deeply into the concept of optimization, including an intuitive discussion of marginal analysis. We use a single running example of choosing an apartment, which confronts students with a trade-off between the cost of rent and the time spent commuting. We demonstrate two alternative approaches—optimization in levels and optimization in differences—and show why economists often use the latter (marginal) technique.

Chapter 4 introduces the demand and supply framework via a running example of the market for gasoline. We show how the price of gasoline affects the decisions of buyers, like commuters, and sellers, like ExxonMobil. As we develop the model, we explore how individual buyers are added together to produce a market demand curve and how individual sellers are added together to generate a market supply curve. We then show how buyers and sellers jointly determine the equilibrium market price and the equilibrium quantity of goods transacted in a perfectly competitive market. Finally, we show how markets break down when prices aren't allowed to adjust to equate the quantity demanded and the quantity supplied.

Part II Foundations of Microeconomics anchors Micro with a deeper exploration of the sources of demand and supply. One important thing that we have learned as teachers is that even after a year of economics, most students really have no idea about the underpinnings of the demand and supply curves—specifically, where the curves actually come from. Most textbooks do not illuminate these issues.

When crafting Chapters 5 and 6, our goal was to provide two stand-alone chapters that show students that consumption and production are really two sides of the same coin, "glued" together by the idea of incentives. We gather consumer and producer concepts under their own respective umbrellas, and merge material that is spread out over several chapters in other texts. The goal is to show the commonalities and linkages between consumers' and producers' optimization decisions. With this setup, the student is able to view the whole picture in one place and understand how concepts tie together without flipping back and forth between several chapters.

In *Chapter 5*, we look "under the hood" to show where the demand curve actually comes from. We frame the question of how consumers decide what to buy as "the buyer's problem" and discuss the three key ingredients of tastes and preferences, prices, and the budget set. The discussion is intuitive: once these three pieces are in place, the demand curve naturally falls out. This approach leads fluidly to a discussion of consumer surplus, demand elasticities, and how consumers predictably respond to incentives. In this way, the student can readily see holistically why policymakers and business people should concern themselves with the demand side of economics. For the students who want it, there is an appendix on income and substitution effects, which is presented as an extension of the text.

In *Chapter 6*, we use the same holistic approach, but here we follow a single company (The Wisconsin Cheeseman, which a coauthor worked at for two high school summers) to showcase "the seller's problem." The seller's problem also has three parts: production, costs, and revenues. In thinking through the seller's problem, it is natural to treat these three components together rather than strew them over separate chapters as in other books. They need to be simultaneously considered by the firm when making optimal choices, so why not present them jointly? The running theme of The Wisconsin Cheeseman makes the chapter quite cohesive, and what was once a difficult puzzle to sort through becomes clear when presented under a single continuous example. For the more inquisitive students there is an appendix showing that for firms with different cost structures, economic profits can exist in long-run equilibrium.

Chapter 7 takes an aerial view by considering what happens when we put together the buyers of Chapter 5 and the sellers of Chapter 6 in a perfectly competitive market. The chapter begins by asking: can markets composed of only self-interested people maximize the overall well-being of society? The beauty of economics is on full display in this chapter, as it shows that in a perfectly competitive market, the invisible hand creates harmony between the interests of the individual and those of society. Prices guide the invisible hand and incentivize buyers and sellers, who in turn maximize social surplus by allocating resources efficiently within and across sectors of the economy. The chapter uses Vernon Smith's seminal laboratory experiments to provide the evidence that prices and quantities converge to the intersection of supply and demand.

In *Chapter 8* we first walk through a discussion of the production possibilities curve, comparative advantage, and the gains from trade. We move the discussion from individuals trading with each other to trade between states (an innovation in a principles text) and finally to trade between countries. Students can thus see that the principles motivating them to trade are the same as those motivating states and nations to trade. They develop an understanding that there are sometimes winners and losers in trade, but that overall, the gains from trade are larger than the losses. The key policy issue becomes: can we shift surplus to make trade a win–win for everyone?

If students stopped reading the book at this point, they would be rabid free-market proponents. This is because the beauty of the free market is unparalleled. *Chapter 9* begins a discussion of important cases that frustrate the workings of the invisible hand. When some firms produce, they pollute the air and water. There are some goods that everyone can consume once they are provided, such as national defense. Chapter 9 probes three cases of market failure—externalities, public goods, and common pool resources—and highlights an important link: in all three cases, there is a difference between social and private benefits or social and private costs. The student learns that the invisible hand of Chapter 7 can become "broken" and that government can enact policies in regard to externalities to improve social well-being, provide public goods, and protect common pool resources.

But government intervention can be a two-edged sword, and in *Chapter 10* we ask the question, "How much government intervention is necessary and how much is desirable?" We provide an aerial view of taxation and spending, and study how regulation—the main tool that governments use to deal with the externalities and other market failures of Chapter 10—has its costs and limitations. We see that the trade-off between equity and efficiency represents the nub of the conflict between those who support big government and those who argue for smaller government. The Evidence-Based Economics feature at the end of the chapter tackles the thorny question of the optimal size of government by exploring the deadweight loss of income taxation.

Chapter 11 motivates the importance of factor markets—the inputs that firms use to make their goods and services—by asking if there is discrimination in the labor market. This question is couched within a general discussion about why people earn different wages in the labor market. This approach allows the student to seamlessly transition from being a demander (as in Chapter 5 as a buyer) to being a supplier (of labor). The economics behind the other major factors of production—physical capital and land—naturally follow from the labor discussion. The chapter concludes by showing several interesting data sets measuring whether discrimination exists in labor markets.

Part III Market Structure introduces the alternatives to the perfectly competitive market: monopolies, oligopolies, and monopolistic competition. This section also provides the tools necessary to understand these market structures.

Chapter 12 on monopoly connects the student's thinking to Chapter 6 where the seller's problem was introduced and shows that all of the production and cost concepts learned earlier apply here: production should be expanded until marginal cost equals marginal revenue. To illustrate the "monopolist's problem," we use a running example of the allergy drug Claritin and its 20-year patent to show how a monopoly optimizes. Once again, we use the metaphor of the broken invisible hand to illustrate how a monopoly reallocates resources toward itself and thereby sacrifices social surplus. At this point, the student might wonder why legal market power is ever granted by the government. The opening question, *Can a monopoly ever be good for society?* discusses the other side of the coin by presenting evidence that a monopoly *can* sometimes be good for society.

At this point in the book, we have covered many of the topics that are treated in existing texts. *Chapter 13* is a point of major departure, as we devote an entire chapter to game theory, which is a source of some of the most powerful economic insights. We emphasize that it helps us better understand the world when we place ourselves in the shoes of someone else. In so doing, the student develops a deeper understanding of how to choose a strategy that is a best response to the strategies of others. We apply game theory to many situations, including pollution, soccer, and advertising, to name a few.

In *Chapter 14*, we present the two market structures that fall between the extremes of perfect competition and monopoly: oligopoly and monopolistic competition. We develop the chapter around the motivating question of how many firms are necessary to make a market competitive. Throughout, we emphasize how oligopolist firms and monopolistically competitive firms set their prices and quantities by considering the choices of their competitors. We connect with previous chapters by framing the discussion in terms of the optimization problem of these firms: the "oligopolist's problem" and the "monopolistic competitor's problem." We show how in the short run it is identical to the monopolist's problem and in the long run to the perfectly competitive model.

Part IV Extending the Microeconomic Toolbox provides a selection of special-topic, optional chapters, depending on the individual instructor's course emphasis. We have included these chapters because we feel that too often the student doesn't get to see the myriad of interesting applications that follow from all those months of learning basic economic principles!

Chapter 15 studies trade-offs involving time and risk. The chapter begins by asking how the timing of a reward affects its economic value. We show how compound interest causes an investment's value to grow over time. We also show how to discount future financial flows and how to make financial decisions using the net present value framework. The second half of the chapter discusses probability and risk and explains how to calculate expected value. We apply these ideas to the study of gambling, extended warranties, and insurance.

Why does a new car lose considerable value the minute it is driven off the lot? *Chapter 16* examines markets we are all familiar with—ones in which one side of the market has more information than the other. The chapter examines the informational disparities between buyers and sellers in terms of hidden characteristics (for example, a sick person is more likely to apply for health insurance) and hidden actions (for example, an insured person is more likely to drive recklessly). Along the way, we look at many timely topics such as lemons in the used-car market, adverse selection in the health insurance market, and moral hazard in risk and insurance markets.

In *Chapter 17* we explore situations that students sometimes face: auctions and bargaining. Our optimization theme continues, as we discuss best strategies and bargaining principles in a variety of settings. We explore the four common types of auctions and provide insights into how economics can help the student bid in auctions—from eBay to estate auctions to charity auctions. We then shift gears and examine bargaining situations that affect our lives daily. To show the power of the bargaining model, we present empirical evidence of who in the household determines how money is spent.

Perhaps the most unusual chapter for a principles textbook is *Chapter 18*, which is on social economics. Here we introduce new variants of *homo economicus*. We explore two different areas of human behavior: the economics of charity and fairness and the economics of revenge. We then revisit the concept and origin of preferences—do we take satisfaction from contributing to a charity or from exacting revenge on a perceived enemy? This last chapter drives home the fact that economic principles can be extended to every corner of our world. And it teaches us that we can considerably extend our understanding of the world around us by adding insights from our sister sciences—psychology, history, anthropology, sociology, and political science—to name a few.

Part V Introduction to Macroeconomics provides an introduction to the field. In *Chapter 19* we explain the basic measurement tools. Here we explore the derivation of the aggregate output of the economy, or the gross domestic product (GDP), with the production, expenditure, and income methods, explaining why all these methods are equivalent and lead to the same level of total GDP. We also consider what *isn't* measured in GDP, such as production that takes place at home for one's family. Finally, we discuss the measurement of inflation and the concept of a price index.

In *Chapter 20* we show how income (GDP) per capita can be compared across countries using two similar techniques—an exchange rate method and a purchasing power method. We explain how the aggregate production function links a country's physical capital stock, labor resources (total labor hours and human capital per worker), and technology to its GDP and thus draw the link between income per capita and a country's physical capital stock per worker, human capital, and technology. We then use these tools to investigate the roles of physical capital, human capital, and technology in accounting for the great differences in prosperity across countries.

In **Part VI, Long-Run Growth and Development**, we turn to a comprehensive treatment of growth and development. In *Chapter 21*, we show that economic growth has transformed many countries over the past 200 years. For example, in the United States today, GDP per capita is about 25 times higher than it was in 1820. In this discussion, we explain the "exponential" nature of economic growth, which results from the fact that new growth builds on past growth, and implies that small differences in growth rates can translate into huge differences in income per capita over several decades. We explain how sustained economic growth relies on advances in technology and why different countries have experienced different long-run growth paths. We also emphasize that economic growth does not benefit all citizens equally. For some citizens, poverty is the unintentional by-product of technological progress. For the instructors who want a more in-depth treatment of growth and the determinants of GDP, we present a simplified version of the Solow Model in an optional appendix to the chapter.

Why do some nations not invest enough in physical and human capital, adopt the best technologies, and organize their production efficiently? Put another way, why isn't the whole world economically developed? *Chapter 22* probes this question and considers the fundamental causes of prosperity. We discuss several potential fundamental causes, in particular, geography, culture, and institutions, and argue why the oft-emphasized geographic factors do not seem to account for much of the wide cross-country gaps in economic prosperity.

In **Part VII, Equilibrium in the Macroeconomy**, we discuss three key markets that play a central role in macroeconomic analysis: the labor market, the credit market, and the market for bank reserves. *Chapter 23* begins with the labor market—labor demand and labor supply. We first describe the standard competitive equilibrium, where the wage and the quantity of labor employed are pinned down by the intersection of the labor demand and labor supply curves. We then show how imperfectly flexible wages lead to unemployment. We then use this framework to discuss the many different factors that influence unemployment, including both frictional and structural sources.

Chapter 24 extends our analysis by incorporating the credit market. We explain how the modern financial system circulates funds from savers to borrowers. We describe the different types of shocks that can destabilize a financial system. We look at how banks and other financial intermediaries connect supply and demand in the credit market, and we use banks' balance sheets to explain the risks of taking on short-term liabilities and making long-term investments.

Chapter 25 introduces the monetary system. We begin by explaining the functions of money. The chapter then introduces the Federal Reserve Bank (the Fed) and lays out the basic plumbing of the monetary system, especially the role of supply and demand in the market for bank reserves. We explain in detail the Fed's role in controlling bank reserves and influencing interest rates, especially the interest rate on bank reserves (the federal funds rate). The chapter explains the causes of inflation and its social costs and benefits.

In **Part VIII, Short-Run Fluctuations and Macroeconomic Policy**, we use a modern framework to analyze and explain short-run fluctuations. Our analysis is inclusive and integrative, enabling us to combine the most relevant and useful insights from many different schools of economic thought. We believe that the labor market is the most informative lens through which first-year economics students can understand economic fluctuations. We therefore put the labor market and unemployment at the center of our analysis. In this part of the book, we also extend our discussion of the role of financial markets and financial crises. We present a balanced perspective that incorporates the diverse range of important insights that have emerged in the last century of theoretical and empirical research.

Chapter 26 lays the foundations of this approach, showing how a wide range of economic shocks cause short-run fluctuations and how these can be studied using the labor market. We trace out the impact of technological shocks, shocks to sentiments (including animal spirits), and monetary and financial shocks that work through their impact on the interest rate or by causing financial crises. In each case, we explain how multipliers amplify the impact of the initial shock. We also explain how wage rigidities affect the labor market response to these shocks. We apply our labor market model to both economic contractions and expansions and look at the problems that arise when the economy grows too slowly or too quickly.

Chapter 27 discusses the wide menu of monetary and fiscal policies that are used to partially offset aggregate fluctuations. We describe the most important strategies that have recently been adopted by central banks. We then discuss the role of fiscal policy and provide an analytic toolkit that students can use to estimate the impact of countercyclical expenditures and taxation.

In **Part IX, Macroeconomics in a Global Economy**, we provide a wide-angle view of the global economy and the relationships that interconnect national economies. In *Chapter 28* we show how international trade works, using the key concepts of specialization, comparative advantage, and opportunity cost. We study the optimal allocation of tasks inside a firm and show that firms should allocate their employees to tasks—and individuals should choose their occupations—according to comparative advantage. We then broaden the picture by focusing on the optimal allocation of tasks across countries and show that here, too, the same principles apply. We analyze international flows of goods and services and the financial consequences of trade deficits. We describe the accounting identities that enable economists to measure the rich patterns of globalized trade. We also discuss the critical role of technology transfer.

Chapter 29 studies the determinants of exchange rates—both nominal and real—between different currencies and how they impact the macroeconomy. We describe the different types of exchange rate regimes and the operation of the foreign exchange market. Finally, we study the impact of changes in the real exchange rate on net exports and GDP.

MyEconLab®

MyEconLab is an extraordinary online course management, homework, quizzing, testing, activity, and tutorial resource.

For Instructors

With comprehensive homework, quiz, test, activity, practice, and tutorial options, instructors can manage all their assessment and online activity needs in one place. MyEconLab saves time by automatically grading questions and activities and tracking results in an online gradebook.

Each chapter contains two preloaded homework exercise sets that can be used to build an individualized study plan for each student. These study plan exercises contain tutorial resources, including instant feedback, links to the appropriate chapter section in the eText, pop-up definitions from the text, and step-by-step guided solutions, where appropriate. Within its rich assignment library, instructors will find a vast array of assessments that ask the students to draw graph lines and shifts, plot equilibrium points, and highlight important graph areas, all with the benefit of instant, personalized feedback. This feedback culminates, when needed, with the correct graph output alongside the student's personal answer, creating a powerful learning moment.

After the initial setup of the MyEconLab course for Acemoglu/Laibson/List, there are two primary ways to begin using this rich online environment. The first path requires no further action by the instructor. Students, on their own, can use MyEconLab's adaptive Study Plan problems and tutorial resources to enhance their understanding of concepts. The online gradebook records each student's performance and time spent on the assessments, activities, and the study plan and generates reports by student or chapter.

Alternatively, instructors can fully customize MyEconLab to match their course exactly: reading assignments, homework assignments, video assignments, current news assignments, digital activities, experiments, quizzes, and tests. Assignable resources include:

- Preloaded exercise assignment sets for each chapter that include the student tutorial resources mentioned earlier
- Preloaded quizzes for each chapter
- *Interactive Reading Assignments* in MyEconLab enable educators to encourage core reading by providing an assessment incentive along the way. These short reading segments feature embedded exercises that prompt students to learn actively. These exercises are automatically graded, so educators can integrate assessment into reading assignments quickly and easily.
- Assignable and gradable exercises that are similar to the end-of-chapter questions and problems and numbered exactly as in the book to make assigning homework easier
- *Real-Time Data Analysis Exercises* allow students and instructors to use the very latest data from the Federal Reserve Bank of St. Louis's FRED site. By completing the exercises, students become familiar with a key data source, learn how to locate data, and develop skills in interpreting data.
- In the eText available in MyEconLab, select exhibits labeled MyEconLab Real-Time Data allow students to display a pop-up graph updated with real-time data from FRED.
- *Current News Exercises* provide a turnkey way to assign gradable news-based exercises in MyEconLab. Each week, Pearson scours the news, finds current economics articles, creates exercises around the news articles, and then automatically adds them to MyEconLab. Assigning and grading current news-based exercises that deal with the latest economics events and policy issues have never been more convenient.
- *Econ Exercise Builder* allows you to build customized exercises. Exercises include multiple-choice, graph drawing, and free-response items, many of which are generated algorithmically so that each time a student works them, a different variation is presented.
- Test Item File questions that allow you to assign quizzes or homework that will look just like your exams

MyEconLab grades every problem type (except essays), even problems with graphs. When working homework exercises, students receive immediate feedback, with links to additional learning tools.

- *Experiments in MyEconLab* are a fun and engaging way to promote active learning and mastery of important economic concepts. Pearson's Experiments program is flexible and easy for instructors and students to use.
  - Single-player experiments allow your students to play against virtual players from anywhere at any time as long as they have an Internet connection.
  - Multiplayer experiments allow you to assign and manage a real-time experiment with your class.

    Pre- and post-questions for each experiment are available for assignment in MyEconLab.

    For a complete list of available experiments, visit **www.myeconlab.com**.

- *Digital Interactives* immerse students in a fundamental economic principle, helping them to learn actively. They can be presented in class as a visually stimulating, highly engaging lecture tool, and can also be assigned with assessment questions for grading. Digital Interactives are designed for use in traditional, online, and hybrid courses, and many incorporate real-time data, as well as data display and analysis tools. To learn more, and for a complete list of digital interactives, visit **www.myeconlab.com**.

Learning Catalytics™ is a bring-your-own-device classroom engagement tool that allows instructors to ask students questions utilizing 18 different question types, allowing students to participate in real time during lectures. With Learning Catalytics you can:

- Engage students in real time, using open-ended tasks to probe student understanding.
- Promote student participation using any modern Web-enabled device they already have—laptop, smartphone, or tablet.
- Address misconceptions before students leave the classroom.
- Understand immediately where students are and adjust your lecture accordingly.
- Improve your students' critical-thinking skills.
- Engage with and record the participation of every student in your classroom.

Learning Catalytics gives you the flexibility to create your own questions to fit your course exactly or choose from a searchable question library Pearson has created.

For more information, visit **learningcatalytics.com**.

Customization and Communication MyEconLab in MyLab/Mastering provides additional optional customization and communication tools. Instructors who teach distance-learning courses or very large lecture sections find the MyLab/Mastering format useful because they can upload course documents and assignments, customize the order of chapters, and use communication features such as Document Sharing, Chat, ClassLive, and Discussion Board.

For Students

MyEconLab puts students in control of their learning through a collection of testing, practice, and study tools tied to the online, interactive version of the textbook and other media resources.

In MyEconLab's environment, students practice what they learn, test their understanding, and pursue a personalized and adaptive study plan generated from their performance on sample tests and from quizzes created by their instructor. In Homework or Study Plan mode, students have access to a wealth of tutorial features, including:

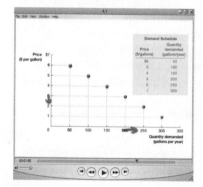

- Instant feedback on exercises that helps students understand and apply the concepts
- Links to the eText to promote reading of the text just when the student needs to revisit a concept or an explanation
- Animations of most of the textbook's exhibits provide step-by-step animation and audio to help students develop intuition in reading and interpreting graphs. The animations are accessible directly from the eText or from the Multimedia Library.
- Step-by-step guided solutions that force students to break down a problem in much the same way an instructor would do during office hours
- Pop-up key term definitions from the eText to help students master the vocabulary of economics
- A graphing tool that is integrated into the various exercises to enable students to build and manipulate graphs to better understand how concepts, numbers, and graphs connect

Additional MyEconLab Resources

- *Enhanced eText*—In addition to the portions of eText available as pop-ups or links, a fully searchable enhanced eText is available for students who wish to read and study in a fully electronic environment. The enhanced eText includes all of the animations and embedded links to all of the end-of-chapter questions and problems, enabling students to read, review, and immediately practice their understanding. The embedded exercises are auto-graded exercises and feed directly into MyEconLab's adaptive Study Plan.
- *Print upgrade*—For students who wish to complete assignments in MyEconLab but read in print, Pearson offers registered MyEconLab users a loose-leaf version of the print text at a significant discount.

MyEconLab and Adaptive Learning MyEconLab's Study Plan is now powered by a sophisticated adaptive learning engine that tailors learning material to meet the unique needs of each student. MyEconLab's new Adaptive Learning Study Plan monitors students' performance on homework, quizzes, and tests and continuously makes recommendations based on that performance.

If a student is struggling with a concept such as supply and demand or having trouble calculating a price elasticity of demand, the Study Plan provides customized remediation activities—a pathway based on personal proficiencies, number of attempts, or difficulty of questions—to get the student back on track. Students will also receive recommendations for additional practice in the form of rich multimedia learning aids such as an interactive eText, Help Me Solve This tutorials, and graphing tools.

The Study Plan can identify a student's potential trouble spots and provide learning material and practice to avoid pitfalls. In addition, students who are showing a high degree of success with the assessment material are offered a chance to work on future topics based on the professor's course coverage preferences. This personalized and adaptive feedback and support ensures that students are optimizing their current and future course work and mastering the concepts, rather than just memorizing and guessing answers. You can learn more about adaptive learning at **http://www.pearsonmylabandmastering .com/northamerica/myeconlab/educators/features/adaptive-learning**.

Dynamic Study Modules, which focus on key topic areas and are available from within MyEconLab, are an additional way for students to obtain tailored help. These modules work by continuously assessing student performance and activity on discrete topics and provide personalized content in real time to reinforce concepts that target each student's particular strengths and weaknesses.

Each Dynamic Study Module, accessed by computer, smartphone, or tablet, promotes fast learning and long-term retention. Because MyEconLab and Dynamic Study Modules help students stay on track and achieve a higher level of subject-matter mastery, more class time is available for interaction, discussion, collaboration, and exploring applications to current news and events. Instructors can register, create, and access all of their MyEconLab courses at **www.pearsonmylab.com**.

Instructor Resources

The **Instructor's Manual** for *Economics* was prepared by James Hornsten of Northwestern University and Rashid Al-Hmoud of Texas Tech University and includes:

- A chapter-by-chapter outline of the text
- Lecture notes highlighting the big ideas and concepts from each chapter
- Teaching Tips on how to motivate the lecture
- Common Mistakes or Misunderstandings students often make and how to correct them
- Short, real-world Alternative Teaching Examples, different from those in the text

Active Learning Exercises, included online and at the end of each Instructor's Manual chapter, were prepared by Timothy Diette of Washington and Lee University and Rashid Al-Hmoud and include:

- 3–5 Active Learning Exercises per chapter that are ideal for in-class discussions and group work

The **Solutions Manual**, prepared by Robert Schwab of the University of Maryland and Bruce Watson of Boston University, includes solutions to all end-of-chapter Questions and Problems in the text. It is available in print and downloadable PDFs.

Three flexible **PowerPoint Presentation** packages make it easy for instructors to design presentation slides that best suit their style and needs:

- Lecture notes with animations of key text exhibits, as well as alternative examples with original static exhibits.
- Exhibits from the text with step-by-step animation
- Static versions of all text exhibits

Each presentation maps to the chapter's structure and organization and uses terminology used in the text. Julia Heath and David Bourne of the University of Cincinnati and Steven Yamarik of California State University, Long Beach created the Lecture PowerPoint presentation. Paul Graf of Indiana University, Bloomington and Eric Nielsen of St. Louis Community College prepared the step-by-step instructions for the animated exhibits.

The **Test Bank** for *Economics* was written by Anuradha Gupta and Julia Paul, and edited and reviewed by Robert Harris of Indiana University–Purdue University Indianapolis; John W. Dawson of Appalachian State University; Phillip K. Letting of Harrisburg Area Community College; Heather Luea of Kansas State University, Todd Fitch of University of California, Berkeley; Gregory Gilpin of Montana State University; Grace O of Georgia State University; Nevin Cavusoglu of James Madison University; and Sang Lee of Southeastern Louisiana University. The Test Bank contains approximately 4,100 multiple-choice, numerical, short-answer, and essay questions. These have been edited and reviewed to ensure accuracy and clarity, and include terminology used in the book. Each question can be sorted by difficulty, book topic, concept covered, and AACSB learning standard to enhance ease of use. The Test Bank is available in Word, PDF, and TestGen formats.

The Test Bank is available in test generator software (TestGen with QuizMaster). TestGen's graphical interface enables instructors to view, edit, and add questions; transfer questions to tests; and print different forms of tests. Instructors also have the option to reformat tests with varying fonts and styles, margins, and headers and footers, as in any word-processing document. Search-and-sort features let the instructor quickly locate questions and arrange them in a preferred order. QuizMaster, working with your school's computer network, automatically grades the exams, stores the results on disk, and allows the instructor to view and print a variety of reports.

Instructor's Resource Center

Instructor resources are available online via our centralized supplements Web site, the Instructor Resource Center (**www.pearsonhighered.com/irc**). For access or more information, contact your local Pearson representative or request access online at the Instructor Resource Center.

Acknowledgments

As the three of us worked on this project, we taught each other a lot about economics, teaching, and writing. But we learned even more from the hundreds of other people who helped us along the way. For their guidance, we are thankful and deeply humbled. Their contributions turned out to be critical in ways that we never imagined when we started, and our own ideas were greatly improved by their insights and advice.

Our reviewers, focus group participants, and class testers showed us how to better formulate our ideas and helped us sharpen our writing. Through their frequently brilliant feedback, they corrected our economic misconceptions, improved our conceptual vision, and showed us how to write more clearly. Their contributions appear in almost every paragraph of this book. All of their names are listed below.

Our research assistants—Alec Brandon, Justin Holz, Josh Hurwitz, Xavier Jaravel, Angelina Liang, Daniel Norris , Yana Peysakhovich, and Jan Zilinsky—played a critical role at every phase of the project, from analyzing data to editing prose to generating deep insights about pedagogical principles that are woven throughout the book. These research assistants played many roles. We learned to trust their instincts on every element of the book, and quickly realized that their contributions were indispensable to the project's success. We are especially indebted to Josh, who has earned our eternal gratitude for many late work nights and for his brilliant editorial and economic insights.

We are grateful to Zick Rubin, who advised us as we started to organize the project and encouraged us as the book developed. We are also deeply thankful to the many inspiring economists who contributed major components of the project. Robert M. Schwab, University of Maryland, Bruce Watson of Boston University, Anuradha Gupta, and Julia Paul contributed extensively to the development of the end-of-chapter questions and problems, which stand out as examples of inspiring pedagogy. James Hornsten, Northwestern University, Timothy Diette, Washington and Lee University, and Rashid Al-Hmoud of Texas Tech University wrote the innovative and intuitive Instructor's Manual and Active Learning Exercises. Julia Heath and David Bourne, University of Cincinnati, Eric Nielsen, St. Louis Community College, Steven Yamarik, California State University, Long Beach and Paul Graf, Indiana University, Bloomington created outstanding PowerPoint slides and animations that illuminate and distill the key lessons of the book. Anuradha Gupta and Julia Paul created the expansive test bank.

Most importantly, we acknowledge the myriad contributions of our editors and all of our amazing colleagues at Pearson. They have marched with us every step of the way. We wouldn't dare count the number of hours that they dedicated to this project–including evenings and weekends. Their commitment, vision, and editorial suggestions touched every sentence of this book. Most of the key decisions about the project were made with the help of our editors, and this collaborative spirit proved to be absolutely essential to our writing. Dozens of people at Pearson played key roles, but the most important contributions were made by Adrienne D'Ambrosio, Executive Acquisitions Editor, Mary Clare McEwing, Executive Development Editor, Nancy Freihofer, Production Manager, Sarah Dumouchelle, Andra Skaalrud, Diane Kohnen, and Ann Francis our Project Managers, Kathleen McLellan, Product Testing and Learner Validation Manager, Lori DeShazo, Executive Field Marketing Manager, Alison Haskins, Senior Product Marketing Manager, Noel Lotz, Digital Content Team Lead, Melissa Honig, Digital Studio Project Manager, and Margaret E. Monahan-Pashall.

We are particularly grateful to Adrienne who has been deeply committed to our project from the first day and has tirelessly worked with us at every key decision. We also wish to thank Denise Clinton, Digital Editor, who first got us started, and Donna Battista, Vice President Product Management, who championed the project along the way. All of these advisers transformed us as writers, teachers, and communicators. This book is a testimony to their perseverance, their dedication, and their brilliant eye for good (and often bad!)

writing. Their commitment to this project has been extraordinary and inspirational. We are profoundly grateful for their guidance and collaboration.

Finally, we wish to thank our many other support networks. Our own professors, who first inspired us as economists and showed, through their example, the power of teaching and the joy that one can take from studying economics. Our parents, who nurtured us in so many ways and gave us the initial human capital that made our entire careers possible. Our kids—Annika, Aras, Arda, Eli, Greta, Mason, Max, and Noah—who sacrificed when our long hours on this book ate into family life. And, most profoundly, we thank our spouses, who have been supportive, understanding, and inspirational throughout the project.

This book is the product of many streams that have flowed together and so many people who have contributed their insights and their passion to this project. We are deeply grateful for these myriad collaborations.

Reviewers

The following reviewers, class test participants, and focus group participants provided invaluable insights.

Adel Abadeer, Calvin College

Ahmed Abou-Zaid, Eastern Illinois University

Temisan Agbeyegbe, City University of New York

Carlos Aguilar, El Paso Community College

Rashid Al-Hmoud, Texas Tech University

Sam Allgood, University of Nebraska, Lincoln

Neil Alper, Northeastern University

Farhad Ameen, Westchester Community College

Catalina Amuedo-Dorantes, San Diego State University

Lian An, University of North Florida

Samuel Andoh, Southern Connecticut State University

Brad Andrew, Juniata College

Len Anyanwu, Union County College

Robert Archibald, College of William and Mary

Ali Arshad, New Mexico Highlands University

Robert Baden, University of California, Santa Cruz

Mohsen Bahmani-Oskooee, University of Wisconsin, Milwaukee

Scott L. Baier, Clemson University

Rita Balaban, University of North Carolina

Mihajlo Balic, Harrisburg Area Community College

Sheryl Ball, Virginia Polytechnic Institute and State University

Spencer Banzhaf, Georgia State University

Jim Barbour, Elon University

Hamid Bastin, Shippensburg University

Clare Battista, California State Polytechnic University, San Luis Obispo

Jodi Beggs, Northeastern University

Eric Belasco, Montana State University

Susan Bell, Seminole State University

Valerie Bencivenga, University of Texas, Austin

Pedro Bento, West Virginia University

Derek Berry, Calhoun Community College

Prasun Bhattacharjee, East Tennessee State University

Benjamin Blair, Columbus State University

Douglas Blair, Rutgers University

John Bockino, Suffolk County Community College

Andrea Borchard, Hillsborough Community College

Luca Bossi, University of Pennsylvania

Gregory Brock, Georgia Southern University

Bruce Brown, California State Polytechnic University, Pomona

David Brown, Pennsylvania State University

Jaime Brown, Pennsylvania State University

Laura Bucila, Texas Christian University

Don Bumpass, Sam Houston State University

Chris Burkart, University of West Florida

Colleen Callahan, American University

Fred Campano, Fordham University

Douglas Campbell, University of Memphis

Cheryl Carleton, Villanova University

Scott Carrell, University of California, Davis

Kathleen Carroll, University of Maryland, Baltimore

Regina Cassady, Valencia College, East Campus

Shirley Cassing, University of Pittsburgh

Nevin Cavusoglu, James Madison University

Suparna Chakraborty, University of San Francisco

Catherine Chambers, University of Central Missouri

Chiuping Chen, American River College

Susan Christoffersen, Philadelphia University

Benjamin Andrew Chupp, Illinois State University

David L. Cleeton, Illinois State University

Cynthia Clement, University of Maryland

Marcelo Clerici-Arias, Stanford University

Rachel Connelly, Bowdoin College

William Conner, Tidewater Community College

Patrick Conway, University of North Carolina

Jay Corrigan, Kenyon College

Antoinette Criss, University of South Florida

Sean Crockett, City University of New York

Patrick Crowley, Texas A&M University, Corpus Christi

Kelley Cullen, Eastern Washington University

Scott Cunningham, Baylor University

Muhammed Dalgin, Kutztown University

David Davenport, McLennan Community College

Stephen Davis, Southwest Minnesota State University

John W. Dawson, Appalachian State University

Pierangelo De Pace, California State University, Pomona

David Denslow, University of Florida

Arthur Diamond, University of Nebraska, Omaha

Timothy Diette, Washington and Lee University

Isaac Dilanni, University of Illinois, Urbana-Champaign

Oguzhan Dincer, Illinois State University

Ethan Doetsch, Ohio State University

Murat Doral, Kennesaw State University

Tanya Downing, Cuesta College

Gary Dymski, University of California, Riverside

Kevin Egan, University of Toledo

Eric Eide, Brigham Young University, Provo

Harold Elder, University of Alabama, Tuscaloosa

Harry Ellis, University of North Texas

Noha Emara, Columbia University

Lucas Engelhardt, Kent State University, Stark

Hadi Esfahani, University of Illinois, Urbana-Champaign

Molly Espey, Clemson University

Jose Esteban, Palomar College

Hugo Eyzaguirre, Northern Michigan University

Jamie Falcon, University of Maryland, Baltimore

Liliana Fargo, DePaul University

Sasan Fayazmanesh, California State University, Fresno

Bichaka Fayissa, Middle Tennessee State University

Virginia Fierro-Renoy, Keiser University

Donna Fisher, Georgia Southern University

Paul Fisher, Henry Ford Community College

Todd Fitch, University of California, Berkeley

Mary Flannery, University of Notre Dame

Hisham Foad, San Diego State University

Mathew Forstater, University of Missouri, Kansas City

Irene Foster, George Mason University

Hamilton Fout, Kansas State University

Shelby Frost, Georgia State University

Timothy Fuerst, University of Notre Dame

Ken Gaines, East-West University

John Gallup, Portland State University

William Galose, Lamar University

Karen Gebhardt, Colorado State University

Gerbremeskel Gebremariam, Virginia Polytechnic Institute and State University

Lisa George, City University of New York

Gregory Gilpin, Montana State University

Seth Gitter, Towson University

Rajeev Goel, Illinois State University

Bill Goffe, State University of New York, Oswego

Julie Gonzalez, University of California, Santa Cruz

Paul Graf, Indiana University, Bloomington

Philip Graves, University of Colorado, Boulder

Lisa Grobar, California State University, Long Beach

Fatma Gunay Bendas, Washington and Lee University

Michael Hammock, Middle Tennessee State University

Michele Hampton, Cuyahoga Community College

Moonsu Han, North Shore Community College

F. Andrew Hanssen, Clemson University

David Harris, Benedictine College

Robert Harris, Indiana University-Purdue University Indianapolis

Julia Heath, University of Cincinnati

Jolien Helsel, Youngstown State University

Matthew Henry, Cleveland State University

Thomas Henry, Mississippi State University

David Hewitt, Whittier College

Wayne Hickenbottom, University of Texas, Austin

Michael Hilmer, San Diego State University

John Hilston, Brevard College

Naphtali Hoffman, Elmira College and Binghamton University

Kim Holder, University of West Georgia

Robert Holland, Purdue University

James A. Hornsten, Northwestern University

Gail Hoyt, University of Kentucky

Jim Hubert, Seattle Central Community College

Scott Hunt, Columbus State Community College

Kyle Hurst, University of Colorado, Denver

Ruben Jacob-Rubio, University of Georgia

Joyce Jacobsen, Wesleyan University

Kenneth Jameson, University of Utah

Andres Jauregui, Columbus State University

Sarah Jenyk, Youngstown State University

Robert Jerome, James Madison University

Deepak Joglekar, University of Connecticut

Paul Johnson, Columbus State University

Ted Joyce, City University of New York

David Kalist, Shippensburg University

Lilian Kamal, University of Hartford

Leonie Karkoviata, University of Houston, Downtown

Kathy Kelly, University of Texas, Arlington

Colin Knapp, University of Florida

Yilmaz Kocer, University of Southern California

Ebenezer Kolajo, University of West Georgia

Janet Koscianski, Shippensburg University

Robert Krol, California State University, Northridge

Daniel Kuester, Kansas State University

Patricia Kuzyk, Washington State University

Sumner La Croix, University of Hawaii

Rose LaMont, Modesto Community College

Carsten Lange, California State University, Pomona

Vicky Langston, Columbus State University

Susan Laury, Georgia State University

Phillip K. Letting, Harrisburg Area Community College

Myoung Lee, University of Missouri, Columbia

Sang Lee, Southeastern Louisiana University

John Levendis, Loyola University

Steven Levkoff, University of California, San Diego

Dennis P. Leyden, University of North Carolina, Greensboro

Gregory Lindeblom, Brevard College

Alan Lockard, Binghamton University

Joshua Long, Ivy Technical College

Linda Loubert, Morgan State University

Heather Luea, Kansas State University

Rita Madarassy, Santa Clara University

James Makokha, Collin County Community College

Liam C. Malloy, University of Rhode Island

Paula Manns, Atlantic Cape Community College

Vlad Manole, Rutgers University

Hardik Marfatia, Northeastern Illinois University

Lawrence Martin, Michigan State University

Norman Maynard, University of Oklahoma

Katherine McClain, University of Georgia

Scott McGann, Grossmont College

Kim Marie McGoldrick, University of Richmond

Shah Mehrabi, Montgomery Community College

Saul Mekies, Kirkwood Community College

Kimberly Mencken, Baylor University

Diego Mendez-Carbajo, Illinois Wesleyan University

Catherine Middleton, University of Tennessee, Chattanooga

Nara Mijid, Central Connecticut State University

Laurie A. Miller, University of Nebraska, Lincoln

Edward Millner, Virginia Commonwealth University

Ida Mirzaie, Ohio State University

David Mitchell, Missouri State University, Springfield

Michael Mogavero, University of Notre Dame

Robert Mohr, University of New Hampshire

Barbara Moore, University of Central Florida

Thaddeaus Mounkurai, Daytona State College

Usha Nair-Reichert, Emory University

Camille Nelson, Oregon State University

Michael Nelson, Oregon State University

John Neri, University of Maryland

Andre Neveu, James Madison University

Jinlan Ni, University of Nebraska, Omaha

Eric Nielsen, St. Louis Community College

Jaminka Ninkovic, Emory University

Chali Nondo, Albany State University

Richard P. Numrich, College of Southern Nevada

Andrew Nutting, Hamilton College

Grace O, Georgia State University

Norman Obst, Michigan State University

Scott Ogawa, Northwestern University

Lee Ohanian, University of California, Los Angeles

Paul Okello, Tarrant County College

Ifeakandu Okoye, Florida A&M University

Alan Osman, Ohio State University

Tomi Ovaska, Youngstown State University

Caroline Padgett, Francis Marion University

Peter Parcells, Whitman College

Cynthia Parker, Chaffey College

Mohammed Partapurwala, Monroe Community College

Robert Pennington, University of Central Florida

Kerk Phillips, Brigham Young University

Goncalo Pina, Santa Clara University

Michael Podgursky, University of Missouri

Greg Pratt, Mesa Community College

Guangjun Qu, Birmingham-Southern College

Fernando Quijano, Dickinson State University

Joseph Quinn, Boston College

Reza Ramazani, Saint Michael's College

Ranajoy Ray-Chaudhuri, Ohio State University

Mitchell Redlo, Monroe Community College

Javier Reyes, University of Arkansas

Teresa Riley, Youngstown State University

Nancy Roberts, Arizona State University

Malcolm Robinson, Thomas More College

Randall Rojas, University of California, Los Angeles

Sudipta Roy, Kankakee Community College

Jared Rubin, Chapman University

Jason C. Rudbeck, University of Georgia

Melissa Rueterbusch, Mott Community College

Mariano Runco, Auburn University at Montgomery

Nicholas G. Rupp, East Carolina University

Steven Russell, Indiana University-Purdue University-Indianapolis

Michael Ryan, Western Michigan University

Ravi Samitamana, Daytona State College

David Sanders, University of Missouri, St. Louis

Michael Sattinger, State University of New York, Albany

Anya Savikhin Samek, University of Wisconsin, Madison

Peter Schuhmann, University of North Carolina, Wilmington

Robert M. Schwab, University of Maryland

Jesse Schwartz, Kennesaw State University

James K. Self, Indiana University, Bloomington

Mark Showalter, Brigham Young University, Provo

Dorothy Siden, Salem State University

Mark V. Siegler, California State University, Sacramento

Timothy Simpson, Central New Mexico Community College

Michael Sinkey, University of West Georgia

John Z. Smith, Jr., United States Military Academy, West Point

Thomas Snyder, University of Central Arkansas

Joe Sobieralski, Southwestern Illinois College

Sara Solnick, University of Vermont

Martha Starr, American University

Rebecca Stein, University of Pennsylvania

Liliana Stern, Auburn University

Adam Stevenson, University of Michigan

Cliff Stone, Ball State University

Mark C. Strazicich, Appalachian State University

Chetan Subramanian, State University of New York, Buffalo

AJ Sumell, Youngstown State University

Charles Swanson, Temple University

Tom Sweeney, Des Moines Area Community College

James Swofford, University of South Alabama

Vera Tabakova, East Carolina University

Emily Tang, University of California, San Diego

Mark Tendall, Stanford University

Jennifer Thacher, University of New Mexico

Charles Thomas, Clemson University

Rebecca Thornton, University of Houston

Jill Trask, Tarrant County College, Southeast

Steve Trost, Virginia Polytechnic Institute and State University

Ty Turley, Brigham Young University

Nora Underwood, University of Central Florida

Mike Urbancic, University of Oregon

Don Uy-Barreta, De Anza College

John Vahaly, University of Louisville

Ross Van Wassenhove, University of Houston

Don Vandegrift, College of New Jersey

Nancy Virts, California State University, Northridge

Cheryl Wachenheim, North Dakota State College

Jeffrey Waddoups, University of Nevada, Las Vegas

Donald Wargo, Temple University

Charles Wassell, Jr., Central Washington University

Matthew Weinberg, Drexel University

Robert Whaples, Wake Forest University

Elizabeth Wheaton, Southern Methodist University

Mark Wheeler, Western Michigan University

Anne Williams, Gateway Community College

Brock Williams, Metropolitan Community College of Omaha

DeEdgra Williams, Florida A&M University

Brooks Wilson, McLennan Community College

Mark Witte, Northwestern University

Katherine Wolfe, University of Pittsburgh

William Wood, James Madison University

Steven Yamarik, California State University, Long Beach

Bill Yang, Georgia Southern University

Young-Ro Yoon, Wayne State University

Madelyn Young, Converse College

Michael Youngblood, Rock Valley College

Jeffrey Zax, University of Colorado, Boulder

Martin Zelder, Northwestern University

Erik Zemljic, Kent State University

Kevin Zhang, Illinois State University

Microeconomics: Flexibility Chart

Core Approach	Emphasis on Long-Run Growth	Emphasis on International
Chapter 1: The Principles and Practice of Economics	**Chapter 1:** The Principles and Practice of Economics	**Chapter 1:** The Principles and Practice of Economics
Chapter 2: Economic Methods and Economic Questions (optional)	**Chapter 2:** Economic Methods and Economic Questions (optional)	**Chapter 2:** Economic Methods and Economic Questions (optional)
Chapter 3: Optimization: Doing the Best You Can (optional)	**Chapter 3:** Optimization: Doing the Best You Can (optional)	**Chapter 3:** Optimization: Doing the Best You Can (optional)
Chapter 4: Demand, Supply, and Equilibrium	**Chapter 4:** Demand, Supply, and Equilibrium	**Chapter 4:** Demand, Supply, and Equilibrium
Chapter 5: Consumers and Incentives	**Chapter 5:** Consumers and Incentives **Chapter 5 Appendix:** Representing Preferences with Indifference Curves	**Section 5.4:** Consumer Surplus (optional) **Section 5.6:** Demand Elasticities (optional)
Chapter 6: Sellers and Incentives	**Chapter 6:** Sellers and Incentives **Chapter 6 Appendix:** When Firms Have Different Cost Structures	**Section 6.4:** Producer Surplus (optional)
Chapter 7: Perfect Competition and the Invisible Hand	**Chapter 7:** Perfect Competition and the Invisible Hand	**Chapter 7:** Perfect Competition and the Invisible Hand
Chapter 8: Trade	**Chapter 11:** Markets for Factors of Production	**Chapter 8:** Trade
Chapter 9: Externalities and Public Goods	**Chapter 12:** Monopoly	**Chapter 9:** Externalities and Public Goods
Chapter 10: The Government in the Economy: Taxation and Regulation	**Chapter 13:** Game Theory and Strategic Play	**Chapter 10:** The Government in the Economy: Taxation and Regulation
Chapter 11: Markets for Factors of Production	**Chapter 14:** Oligopoly and Monopolistic Competition	**Chapter 11:** Markets for Factors of Production (optional)
Chapter 12: Monopoly	**Chapter 8:** Trade	**Chapter 12:** Monopoly
Chapter 13: Game Theory and Strategic Play	**Chapter 9:** Externalities and Public Goods	**Chapter 13:** Game Theory and Strategic Play
Chapter 14: Oligopoly and Monopolistic Competition	**Chapter 10:** The Government in the Economy: Taxation and Regulation	**Chapter 14:** Oligopoly and Monopolistic Competition
Chapter 15: Trade-offs Involving Time and Risk (optional)	**Chapter 15:** Trade-offs Involving Time and Risk (optional)	**Chapter 15:** Trade-offs Involving Time and Risk (optional)
Chapter 16: The Economics of Information (optional)	**Chapter 16:** The Economics of Information (optional)	**Chapter 16:** The Economics of Information (optional)
Chapter 17: Auctions and Bargaining (optional)	**Chapter 17:** Auctions and Bargaining (optional)	**Chapter 17:** Auctions and Bargaining (optional)
Chapter 18: Social Economics (optional)	**Chapter 18:** Social Economics (optional)	**Chapter 18:** Social Economics (optional)

Macroeconomics: Flexibility Chart

Core Approach	Emphasis on Long-Run Growth	Emphasis on International
Chapter 19: The Wealth of Nations: Defining and Measuring Macroeconomic Aggregates	**Chapter 19:** The Wealth of Nations: Defining and Measuring Macroeconomic Aggregates	**Chapter 19:** The Wealth of Nations: Defining and Measuring Macroeconomic Aggregates
Chapter 20: Aggregate Incomes	**Chapter 20:** Aggregate Incomes	**Chapter 20:** Aggregate Incomes
Chapter 21: Economic Growth	**Chapter 21:** Economic Growth	**Chapter 21:** Economic Growth
Chapter 22: Why Isn't the Whole World Developed? (optional)	**Chapter 22:** Why Isn't the Whole World Developed?	**Chapter 22:** Why Isn't the Whole World Developed? (optional)
Chapter 23: Employment and Unemployment	**Chapter 23:** Employment and Unemployment	**Chapter 23:** Employment and Unemployment
Chapter 24: Credit Markets	**Chapter 24:** Credit Markets	**Chapter 24:** Credit Markets
Chapter 25: The Monetary System	**Chapter 25:** The Monetary System	**Chapter 25:** The Monetary System
Chapter 26: Short-Run Fluctuations	**Chapter 26:** Short-Run Fluctuations	**Chapter 26:** Short-Run Fluctuations
Chapter 27: Countercyclical Macroeconomic Policy	**Chapter 27:** Countercyclical Macroeconomic Policy	**Chapter 27:** Countercyclical Macroeconomic Policy
Chapter 28: Macroeconomics and International Trade (optional)	**Chapter 28:** Macroeconomics and International Trade (optional)	**Chapter 28:** Macroeconomics and International Trade
Chapter 29: Open Economy Macroeconomics (optional)	**Chapter 29:** Open Economy Macroeconomics (optional)	**Chapter 29:** Open Economy Macroeconomics

1

The Principles and Practice of Economics

Is Facebook free?

Facebook doesn't charge you a penny, so it's tempting to say, "it's free."

Here's another way to think about it. What do you give up when you use Facebook? That's a different kind of question. Facebook doesn't take your money, but it does take your time. If you spend an hour each day on Facebook, you are giving up some alternative use of that time. You could spend that time playing soccer, watching Hulu videos, napping, daydreaming, or listening to music. There are many ways to use your time. For example, a typical U.S. college student employed 7 hours per week earns almost $4,000 in a year—enough to pay the annual lease on a sports car. A part-time job is just one alternative way to use the time that you spend on Facebook. In your view, what is the best alternative use of your Facebook time? That's the economic way of thinking about the cost of Facebook.

In this chapter, we introduce you to the economic way of thinking about the world. Economists study the choices that people make, especially the costs and benefits of those choices, even the costs and the benefits of Facebook.

CHAPTER OUTLINE

⚙ Economics is the study of people's choices.

⚙ The first principle of economics is that people try to *optimize*: they try to choose the best available option.

⚙ The second principle of economics is that economic systems tend to be in *equilibrium,* a situation in which nobody would benefit by changing his or her own behavior.

⚙ The third principle of economics is *empiricism*—analysis that uses data. Economists use data to test theories and to determine what is causing things to happen in the world.

1.1 The Scope of Economics

Choice—not money—is the unifying feature of all the things that economists study.

Most people are surprised to learn how much ground economics covers. Economists study *all* human behavior, from a person's decision to lease a new sports car, to the speed the new driver chooses as she rounds a hairpin corner, to her decision not to wear a seat belt. These are all choices, and they are all fair game to economists. And they are not all directly related to money. Choice—not money—is the unifying feature of all the things that economists study.

In fact, economists think of almost all human behavior as the outcome of choices. For instance, imagine that Dad tells his teenage daughter that she *must* wash the family car. Though it may not be obvious, the daughter has several options: she can wash it, she can negotiate for an easier chore, she can refuse to wash it and suffer the consequences, or she can move out (admittedly, a drastic response, but still a choice). Obeying one's parents is a choice, though it may not always feel like one.

Economic Agents and Economic Resources

Saying that economics is all about choices is an easy way to remember what economics is. To give you a more precise definition, we first need to introduce two important concepts: *economic agents* and *resource allocation*.

An **economic agent** is an individual or a group that makes choices.

An **economic agent** is an individual or a group that makes choices. Let's start with a few types of individual economic agents. For example, a *consumer* chooses to eat bacon cheeseburgers *or* tofu burgers. A *parent* chooses to enroll her children in public school *or* private school. A *student* chooses to attend his classes *or* to skip them. A *citizen* chooses whether *or* not to vote, and if so, which candidate to support. A *worker* chooses to do her job *or* pretend to work while texting. A *criminal* chooses to hotwire cars *or* mug little old ladies. A *business leader* chooses to open a new factory in Chile *or* China. A *senator* chooses to vote for *or* against a bill. Of course, you are also an economic agent because you make an enormous number of choices every day.

Not all economic agents, however, are individuals. An economic agent can also be a group—a government, an army, a firm, a university, a political party, a labor union, a sports team, a street gang. Sometimes economists simplify their analysis by treating these groups as a single decision maker, without worrying about the details of how the different individuals in the group contributed to the decision. For example, an economist might say that Apple prices the iPhone to maximize its profits, glossing over the fact that hundreds of executives participated in the analysis that led to the choice of the price.

1.1

1.2

1.3

1.4

1.5

1.6

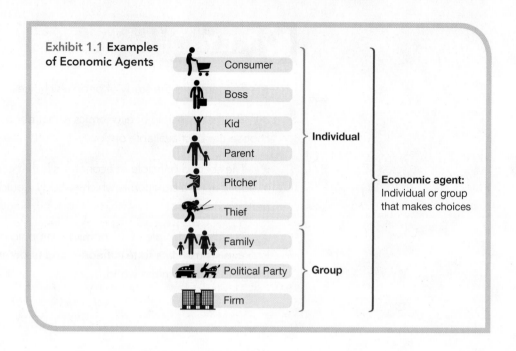

Exhibit 1.1 **Examples of Economic Agents**

Scarce resources are things that people want, where the quantity that people want exceeds the quantity that is available.

Scarcity is the situation of having unlimited wants in a world of limited resources.

The second important concept to understand is that economics studies the allocation of *scarce resources*. **Scarce resources** are things that people want, where the quantity that people want exceeds the quantity that is available. Gold wedding bands, Shiatsu massages, Coach handbags, California peaches, iPhones, triple-chocolate-fudge ice cream, and rooms with a view are all scarce resources. And so are most ordinary things, like toilet paper, subway seats, and clean drinking water. **Scarcity** exists because people have unlimited wants in a world of limited resources. The world does not have enough resources to give everyone *everything* they want. Consider sports cars. If sports cars were given away for free, there would not be enough of them to go around. Instead, sports cars are sold to the consumers who are willing to pay for them.

The existence of a marketplace for sports cars gives economic agents lots of choices. You have 24 hours to allocate each day—this is your daily budget of time. You choose how many of those 24 hours you will allocate to Facebook. You choose how many of those 24 hours you will allocate to other activities, including a job. If you have a job, you also choose whether to spend your hard-earned wages on a sports car. These kinds of decisions determine how scarce sports cars are allocated in a modern economy: to the consumers who are able and willing to pay for them.

Economists don't want to impose our tastes for sports cars, hybrids, electric vehicles, SUVs, or public transportation on you. We are interested in teaching you how to use economic reasoning so that *you* can compare the costs and benefits of the alternative options and make the choices that are best for you.

Definition of Economics

Economics is the study of how agents choose to allocate scarce resources and how those choices affect society.

We are now ready to define economics precisely. **Economics** is the study of how agents choose to allocate scarce resources and how those choices affect society.

As you might have expected, this definition emphasizes *choices*. The definition also takes into account how these choices affect society. For example, the sale of a new sports car doesn't just affect the person driving off the dealer's lot. The sale generates sales tax, which is collected by the government, which in turn funds projects like highways and hospitals. The purchase of the new car also generates some congestion—that's one more car in rush-hour gridlock. And it's another car that might grab the last parking spot on your street. If the new owner drives recklessly, the car may also generate risks to other drivers. The car will also be a source of pollution. Economists study the original choice and its multiple consequences for other people in the world.

Positive Economics and Normative Economics

We now have an idea of what economics is about: people's choices. But what is the reason for studying choices? Part of the answer is that economists are just curious, but that's only a small part of the picture. Understanding people's choices is practically useful for two key reasons. Economic analysis:

1. Describes what people *actually* do (positive economics).
2. Recommends what people *ought* to do (normative economics).

The first application is descriptive and the second is advisory.

Positive Economics Describes What People Actually Do   Descriptions of what people actually do are *objective* statements about the world. Such factual statements can be confirmed or tested with data. For instance, it is a fact that in 2010, 50 percent of U.S. households earned less than $52,000 per year. Describing what has happened or predicting what will happen is referred to as **positive economics** or positive economic analysis.

For instance, consider the prediction that in 2020 U.S. households will save about 5 percent of their income. This forecast can be compared to future data and either confirmed or disproven. Because a prediction is ultimately testable, it is part of positive economics.

Normative Economics Recommends What People Ought to Do   Normative **economics**, the second of the two types of economic analysis, advises individuals and society on their choices. Normative economics is about what people ought to do. Normative economics is almost always dependent on *subjective* judgments, which means that normative analysis depends at least in part on personal feelings, tastes, or opinions. So whose subjective judgments do we try to use? Economists believe that the person being advised should determine the preferences to be used.

For example, if an economist were helping a worker to decide how much to save for retirement, the economist would first ask the worker about her own preferences. Suppose the worker expressed a high degree of patience—"I want to save enough so I can maintain my level of expenditure when I retire." In this case, the economist would recommend a saving rate that achieves the worker's desire for steady consumption throughout her life—about 10 to 15 percent of income for most middle-income families. Here the economist plays the role of engineer, finding the saving rate that will deliver the future level of retirement spending that the worker wants.

The economist does not tell the worker what degree of patience to have. Instead, the economist asks the worker about her preferences and then recommends a saving rate that is best for the worker given her preferences. In the mind of most economists, it is legitimate for the worker to choose any saving rate, as long as she understands the implications of that saving rate for expenditure after retirement.

Normative Analysis and Public Policy   Normative analysis also generates advice to society in general. For example, economists are often asked to evaluate public policies, like taxes or regulations. When public policies have winners and losers, citizens tend to have opposing views about the desirability of the government program. One person's migratory bird sanctuary is another person's mosquito-infested swamp. Protecting a wetland with environmental regulations benefits bird-watchers but harms landowners who plan to develop that land.

When a government policy has winners and losers, economists will need to make some ethical judgments to conduct normative analysis. Economists must make ethical judgments whenever we evaluate policies that make one group worse off so another group can be made better off.

Ethical judgments are usually unavoidable when economists think about government policies, because there are very few policies that make everyone better off. Deciding whether the costs experienced by the losers are justified by the benefits experienced by the winners is partly an ethical judgment. Is it ethical to create environmental regulations that prevent a real estate developer from draining a swamp so he can build new homes? What if

Economics is the study of choice.

Positive economics is analysis that generates objective descriptions or predictions about the world that can be verified with data.

Normative economics is analysis that prescribes what an individual or society ought to do.

Economic agents have divergent views on the future of this swamp. The owner of the property wants to build housing units. An environmentalist wants to preserve the wetland to protect the whooping crane, an endangered species. What should happen?

Microeconomics is the study of how individuals, households, firms, and governments make choices, and how those choices affect prices, the allocation of resources, and the well-being of other agents.

Macroeconomics is the study of the economy as a whole. Macroeconomists study economy-wide phenomena, like the growth rate of a country's total economic output, the inflation rate, or the unemployment rate.

those environmental regulations protect migratory birds that other people value? Are there other solutions to this seemingly unresolvable problem? Should the government try to buy the land from the real estate developer? And if land purchasing is the government's policy, how should society determine the price that the government offers the developer? Should the developer be forced to sell at that price? These public policy questions—which all ask what society *should* do—are normative economic questions.

Microeconomics and Macroeconomics

There is one other distinction that you need to know to understand the scope of economics. Economics can be divided into two broad fields of study, though many economists do a bit of both.

Microeconomics is the study of how individuals, households, firms, and governments make choices, and how those choices affect prices, the allocation of resources, and the well-being of other agents. For example, microeconomists design policies that reduce pollution. Because global warming is partially caused by carbon emissions from coal, oil, and other fossil fuels, microeconomists design policies to reduce the use of these fuels. For example, a "carbon tax" targets carbon emissions. Under a carbon tax, relatively carbon-intensive energy sources—like coal power plants—pay more tax per unit of energy produced than energy sources with lower carbon emissions—like wind farms. Microeconomists have the job of designing carbon taxes and determining how such taxes will affect the energy usage of households and firms. In general, microeconomists are called upon whenever we want to understand a small piece of the overall economy.

Macroeconomics is the study of the economy as a whole. Macroeconomists study economy-wide phenomena, like the growth rate of a country's total economic output, or the percentage increase in overall prices (the inflation rate), or the fraction of the labor force that is looking for work but cannot find a job (the unemployment rate). Macroeconomists design government policies that improve overall, or "aggregate," economic performance.

For example, macroeconomists try to identify the best policies for stimulating an economy that is experiencing a sustained period of negative growth—in other words, an economy in recession. During the 2007–2009 financial crisis, when housing prices were plummeting and banks were failing, macroeconomists had their hands full. It was their job to explain why the economy was contracting and to recommend policies that would bring it back to life.

1.2 Three Principles of Economics

You now have a sense of what economics is about. But you might be wondering what distinguishes it from the other social sciences, including, anthropology, history, political science, psychology, and sociology. All of the social sciences study human behavior, so what sets economics apart?

Economists emphasize three key concepts.

Trying to choose the best feasible option, given the available information, is **optimization**.

1. Optimization: We have explained economics as the study of people's choices. The study of all human choices may initially seem like an impossibly huge topic. And at first glance, choosing a double-bacon cheeseburger at McDonalds does not appear to have much in common with a corporate executive's decision to build a $500 million laptop factory in China. Economists have identified some powerful concepts that unify the enormous range of choices that economic agents make. One such insight is that all choices are tied together by *optimization*: people decide what to do by consciously or unconsciously weighing all of the known pros and cons of the different available options and trying to pick the best feasible option. In other words, people make choices that are motivated by calculations of benefits and costs.

People make choices that are motivated by calculations of benefits and costs.

Equilibrium is the special situation in which everyone is simultaneously optimizing, so nobody would benefit personally by changing his or her own behavior.

Empiricism is analysis that uses data. Economists use data to test theories and to determine what is causing things to happen in the world.

Optimization is the first principle of economics. Economists believe that optimization explains most of our choices, including minor decisions like accepting an invitation to see a movie, and major decisions like deciding whom to marry.

2. Equilibrium: The second principle of economics holds that economic systems tend to be in *equilibrium*, a situation in which no agent would benefit personally by changing his or her own behavior. The economic system is in equilibrium when each agent feels that he or she cannot do any better by picking another course of action. In other words, equilibrium is a situation in which everyone is simultaneously optimizing.

3. Empiricism: The third principle of economics is an emphasis on *empiricism*—analysis that uses data or analysis that is evidence-based. Economists use data to test theories and to determine what is causing things to happen in the world.

1.3 The First Principle of Economics: Optimization

Let's now consider our first principle in more detail. Economics is the study of choices, and economists have a theory about how choices are made. Economists believe that economic agents try to optimize, meaning that economic agents try to choose the best feasible option, given the information that they have. Feasible options are those that are available and affordable to an economic agent. If you have $10 in your wallet and no credit/debit/ATM cards, then a $5 Big Mac is a feasible lunch option, while a $50 filet mignon is not.

The concept of feasibility goes beyond the financial budget of the agent. There are many different constraints that determine what is feasible. For instance, it is not feasible to work more than 24 hours in a day. It is not feasible to attend meetings (in person) in New York and Beijing at the same time.

The definition of optimization also refers to the information available at the time of the choice. For example, if you choose to drive from San Diego to Los Angeles and your car is hit by a drunk driver, you are unlucky but you haven't necessarily failed to optimize. As long as you made your travel plans taking into account the realistic risk of a car crash, then you have optimized. Optimization means that we weigh the potential risks in a decision, not that we perfectly foresee the future. When someone chooses the best feasible option given the information that is available, economists say that the decision maker is being rational or, equivalently, he or she is exhibiting rationality. Rational action does not require a crystal ball, just a logical appraisal of the costs, benefits, and risks associated with each decision.

On the other hand, if you decide to let a friend drive you from San Diego to Los Angeles and you know that your friend has just had a few beers, this is probably a case in which you failed to optimize. It is important to note that the test of optimization is the quality of your decision, and not the outcome. If you arrive at your destination without a crash, that would still (probably) be a suboptimal choice, because you got lucky despite making a bad decision.

In the cases where agents fail to optimize, normative economic analysis can help them realize their mistakes and make better choices in the future.

We devote much of this book to the analysis of optimization. We explain how to optimize, and we discuss lots of evidence that supports the theory that economic agents usually optimize. We also discuss important cases where behavior deviates from optimization. In the cases where agents fail to optimize, normative economic analysis can help them realize their mistakes and make better choices in the future.

Finally, it is important to note that *what* we optimize varies from person to person and group to group. Although most firms try to maximize profits, most economic agents are not

1.1

1.2

1.3

1.4

1.5

1.6

trying to maximize only income. If that were our goal, we'd all work far more than 40 hours per week and we'd keep working well past retirement age. Most households are trying to optimize overall well-being, which requires income, leisure, health, and a host of other factors (like social networks and a sense of purpose in life). Most governments are trying to optimize a complex mix of policy goals. For most economic agents, optimization is not just about how much money we have.

Trade-offs and Budget Constraints

An economic agent faces a **trade-off** when the agent needs to give up one thing to get something else.

To understand optimization, you need to understand trade-offs. **Trade-offs** arise when some benefits must be given up in order to gain others. Think about Facebook. If you spend an hour on Facebook, then you cannot spend that hour doing other things. For example, you cannot work at most part-time jobs at the same time you are editing your Facebook profile.

A **budget constraint** shows the bundles of goods or services that a consumer can choose given her limited budget.

Economists use budget constraints to describe trade-offs. A **budget constraint** is the set of things that a person can choose to do (or buy) without breaking her budget.

Here's an illustration. Suppose that you can do only one of two activities with your free time: work at a part-time job or surf the Web. Suppose that you have 5 free hours in a day (once we take away necessities like sleeping, eating, bathing, attending classes, doing problem sets, and studying for exams). Think of these 5 free hours as your budget of free time. Then your budget constraint would be:

$$5 \text{ hours} = \boxed{\text{Hours surfing the Web}} + \boxed{\text{Hours working at part-time job.}}$$

This budget constraint equation implies that you face a trade-off. If you spend an extra hour surfing the Web, you need to spend one less hour working at a part-time job. Likewise, if you spend an extra hour working at the part-time job, you need to spend one less hour surfing the Web. More of one activity implies less of the other. We can see this in Exhibit 1.2, where we list all of the ways that you could allocate your 5 free hours.

Budget constraints are useful economic tools because they quantify trade-offs. When economists talk about the choice that an economic agent faces, the economist first specifies the budget constraint.

Opportunity Cost

We are now ready to introduce another critical tool in the optimization toolbox: opportunity cost. Our Web surfing example provides an illustration of the concept. The time that we spend on the Web is time that we could have spent in some other way: playing basketball, jogging, daydreaming, sleeping, calling a friend, catching up on e-mail, working on a problem set, working at a part-time job, and so on. You implicitly sacrifice time on these alternative activities when you spend time surfing the Web (unless you secretly use Facebook while you are being paid for a job—in this case, please keep your boss off your friend list).

Try generating your own list of alternative activities that are squeezed out when you surf the Web. Think about the best alternative to Web surfing, and put that at the top; then work down from there. Your list illustrates the concept of opportunity cost; you can either spend

Exhibit 1.2 Possible Allocations of 5 Free Hours (Round Numbers Only)

Each row reports a different way that a person could allocate 5 free hours, assuming that the time must be divided between surfing the Web and working at a part-time job. To keep things simple, the table only reports allocations in round numbers.

Budget	Hours Surfing the Web	Hours at Part-Time Job
5 hours	0 hours	5 hours
5 hours	1 hours	4 hours
5 hours	2 hours	3 hours
5 hours	3 hours	2 hours
5 hours	4 hours	1 hours
5 hours	5 hours	0 hours

1.1

1.2

1.3

1.4

1.5

1.6

a specific hour of your day surfing the Web or on some other activity. In most situations you can't simultaneously do both.

Evaluating trade-offs like this can be difficult because so many options are under consideration. Economists tend to focus on the best alternative activity. We refer to this best alternative activity as the **opportunity cost**. This is what an optimizer is effectively giving up when she surfs the Web.

The importance of opportunity cost is clear once we remember that resources are limited, or scarce. Whenever we do one thing, something else gets squeezed out. When you surf the Web for an hour, some other activity is reduced by an hour, though you may not think about it at the time. You can't write a term paper and update your Facebook page at the same time. Even if you only *postpone* the term paper, something else has got to give when that postponed time comes up. (Studying for the economics final?) Optimization requires that you take account of the opportunity cost of whatever you are doing. In essence, an optimizer always considers how else she could be using her limited resources.

Here's another example to drive home the concept. Assume that your family is taking a vacation over spring break. Your choices are a Caribbean cruise, a trip to Miami, or a trip to Los Angeles. (Assume that they all have the same monetary cost and use the same amount of time.) If your first choice is the cruise and your *second* choice is Miami, then your opportunity cost of taking the cruise is the Miami trip.

The concept of opportunity cost applies to all resources, not just your time budget of 24 hours each day. Suppose that a woodworker has a beautiful piece of maple that can be used to make a sculpture, or a bowl, or a picture frame. (Assume that they all use the same amount of wood and take the same amount of time.) If the woodworker's first choice is the sculpture and the *second* choice is the bowl, then the bowl is the opportunity cost of making the sculpture.

Assigning a Monetary Value to an Opportunity Cost Economists sometimes try to put a monetary value on opportunity cost. Translating benefits and costs into monetary units, like dollars or yen, makes everything easier to analyze. One way to estimate the monetary value of an hour of your time is to analyze the consequences of taking a part-time job or working additional hours at the part-time job you already have.

The opportunity cost of your time is at least the net benefit that you would receive from a job (assuming that you can find one that fits your schedule). Here's why. A part-time job is one item in the long list of alternatives to surfing the Web. If the part-time job is at the top of your list, then it's the best alternative, and the part-time job is your opportunity cost of surfing the Web. What if the part-time job is not at the top of your list, so it's not the best alternative? Then the best alternative is even better than the part-time job, so the best alternative is worth more than the part-time job. To sum up, your opportunity cost is either the net benefit of a part-time job or a value that is even greater than that.

To turn these insights into something quantitative, it helps to note that the median wage for U.S. workers between 16 and 24 years of age was $11.35 per hour in 2013—this data is from the U.S. Bureau of Labor Statistics. However, a job has many attributes *other* than the wage you are paid: unpleasant tasks (like being nice to obnoxious customers), on-the-job training, friendly or unfriendly coworkers, and resumé building, just to name a few.

If we ignore these non-wage attributes, the benefit of an hour of work is just the wage (minus taxes paid). On the other hand, if the positive and negative non-wage attributes don't cross each other out, the calculation is much harder. To keep things simple, we'll focus only on the after-tax wage in the analysis that follows—about $10 per hour for young workers—but we urge you to keep in mind all of the non-wage consequences that flow from a job.

Cost-Benefit Analysis

Let's use opportunity cost to solve an optimization problem. Specifically, we want to compare a set of feasible alternatives and pick the best one. Economists call this process *cost-benefit analysis*. **Cost-benefit analysis** is a calculation that adds up costs and benefits using a common unit of measurement, like dollars. It is used to identify the alternative that has the greatest net benefit, which is equivalent to benefits minus costs.

Opportunity cost is the best alternative use of a resource.

Cost-benefit analysis is a calculation that adds up costs and benefits using a common unit of measurement, like dollars.

1.1

1.2

1.3

1.4

1.5

1.6

To see these ideas in action, suppose that you and a friend are going to Miami Beach from Boston for spring break. The only question is whether you should drive or fly. Your friend argues that you should drive because splitting the cost of a rental car and gas "will only cost $200 each." He tries to seal the deal by pointing out "that's much better than a $300 plane ticket."

To analyze this problem using cost-benefit analysis, you need to list all of the costs and benefits of driving relative to the alternative of flying. You then need to translate those costs and benefits into a common unit of measurement.

From a benefit perspective, driving saves you $100—the difference between driving expenses of $200 and a plane ticket of $300. From a cost perspective, driving costs you an extra 40 hours of time—the difference between 50 hours of round-trip driving time and about 10 hours of round-trip airport/flying time. Spending 40 extra hours traveling is a cost of driving.

But we still don't know whether driving is a good idea or a bad idea, because we haven't yet expressed everything in common units. Suppose the opportunity cost of your time is $10 per hour (slightly below the median wage for U.S. workers between ages 16 and 24). This is the value of your time. Then the net benefit of driving relative to flying is

$$(\$100 \text{ Cost saving}) - (40 \text{ Hours of additional travel time}) \times (\$10/\text{hour})$$
$$= \$100 - \$400 = -\$300.$$

Hence, the net benefit of driving is overwhelmingly negative. An optimizer would choose to fly.

Your decision about travel to Miami is a simple example of cost-benefit analysis, which is a great tool for collapsing all sorts of things down to a net dollar benefit. This book will guide you in making such calculations. If you are making choices as to which house to buy, which job to take, or whether Medicare should pay for heart transplants, cost-benefit analysis can help. Economists are not popular for making some of these "cold-hearted" calculations, but it's nonetheless useful to be able to quantitatively analyze difficult decisions.

To an economist, cost-benefit analysis and optimization are the same thing. When you pick the option with the greatest net benefits—benefits minus costs—you are optimizing. So cost-benefit analysis is useful for *normative* economic analysis. It enables an economist to determine what an individual or a society should do. Cost-benefit analysis also yields many useful positive economic insights. In most cases, cost-benefit analysis correctly predicts the choices made by actual consumers.

Evidence-Based Economics

Q: Is Facebook free?

We can now turn to the question we posed at the beginning of the chapter. By now you know that Facebook has an opportunity cost—the best alternative use of your time. We will now estimate this cost. To do this, we're going to need some data. Whenever you see a section in this textbook titled "Evidence-Based Economics," you'll know that we are using data to analyze an economic question.

In 2013, Web users worldwide spent 250 million hours on Facebook each day. On a per person basis, each of the nearly 1 billion Facebook users allocated an average of 15 minutes per day to the site. College students used Facebook more intensively. The average college student spent about an hour per day on Facebook.

1.1

1.2

1.3

1.4

1.5

1.6

We estimate that the time spent worldwide on Facebook has an *average* opportunity cost of $5 per hour. We generated this estimate with a back-of-the-envelope—in other words, approximate—calculation that averages together every Facebook user's opportunity cost.

Here's how we did the calculation. First, we assume that users in the developed world—which represents wealthy countries such as France, Japan, and the United States—have an opportunity cost of $9 per hour, which is a typical minimum wage in a developed country. Employers are legally required to pay at least the minimum wage, and most workers in developed countries get paid much more than this. Even people who choose not to work still value their time, since it can be used for lots of good things like napping, texting, dating, studying, playing angry birds, and watching movies. It's reasonable to guess that these nonworkers—for instance, students—will also have an opportunity cost of at least the minimum wage.

Second, we assume that Facebook users in the developing world—which represents all countries, except the developed countries—have a relatively lower opportunity cost of time. We assume that Facebook users in the developing countries have an opportunity cost of $1 per hour—for instance, their employment opportunities are far less favorable than those in the developed world.

To evaluate the reasonableness of these estimates, ask yourself this question: "How much would someone need to pay *you* to take away an hour of your free time?" Does your answer correspond more closely to our estimate for the developed world ($9/hour) or the developing world ($1/hour)?

About half of Facebook users live in developed countries and half live in developing countries, so, given our assumptions, the average opportunity cost is $(1/2) \times \$9 + (1/2) \times \$1 = \$5$ per hour. Accordingly, the *total* opportunity cost of time spent on Facebook is calculated by multiplying the total number of hours spent on Facebook each day, by the average opportunity cost of time per hour:

$$\left(\frac{250 \text{ million hours}}{\text{day}} \right) \left(\frac{\$5}{\text{hour}} \right) = \left(\frac{\$1.25 \text{ billion}}{\text{day}} \right).$$

Multiplying this by 365 days per year yields an annualized opportunity cost of over $450 billion. This is an estimate of the cost of Facebook. As you have seen, this is only a crude approximation, since we can't directly observe the opportunity cost of each person's time.

We can also think about this calculation another way. If people had substituted their time on Facebook for work with average pay of $5 per hour, the world economy would have produced about $450 billion more measured output in 2013. This is more than the annual economic output of Austria.

Finally, we can also estimate the opportunity cost of a typical U.S. college student who spends 1 hour per day on Facebook. Assuming that this student's opportunity cost is equal to $10 per hour, the opportunity cost is $3,650 per year.

$$(\$10/\text{hour}) \times (365 \text{ hours/year}) = \$3,650 \text{ per year}.$$

We chose $10 per hour for the opportunity cost, since the median before-tax wage of 16- to 24-year-old U.S. workers was $11.35 per hour in 2013, and such low-income workers don't pay much in taxes.

So far, we have gone through a purely positive economic analysis, describing the frequency of Facebook usage and the trade-offs that this usage implies. None of this analysis, however, answers the related question: Are Facebook and other social networking sites worth it? We've seen that the time spent on sites like these is costly because it has valuable alternative uses. But Facebook users are deriving substantial benefits that may justify this allocation of time. For example, social networking sites keep us up-to-date

Exhibit 1.3 What Could You Buy with $3,650?

Everyone would choose to spend $3,650 in their own particular way. This list illustrates one feasible basket of goods and services. Note that this list includes just the monetary costs. A complete economic analysis would also include the opportunity cost of the time that you'll need to consume them.

	Cost per unit	Number of units	Total cost
Starbucks cappuccino	$4	52 cups	$208
iPhone	$400	1	$400
Roundtrip: NYC to Paris	$1,000	1	$1,000
Hotel in Paris	$250	4 nights	$1,000
Roundtrip: NYC to U.S. Virgin Islands	$300	1	$300
Hotel in Virgin Islands	$180	4 nights	$720
11 iPhone apps	$2	11	$22
Total			**$3,650**

on the activities of our friends and family. They facilitate the formation of new friendships and new connections. And Facebook and similar sites are entertaining.

Because we cannot easily quantify these benefits, we're going to leave that analysis to you. Economists won't tell you what to do, but we will help you identify the trade-offs that you are making in your decisions. Here is how an economist would summarize the normative question that is on the table:

> *Assuming a $10 per hour opportunity cost, the opportunity cost of using Facebook for an hour per day is $3,650 per year. Do you receive benefits from Facebook that exceed this opportunity cost?*

Economists don't want to impose their tastes on other people. In the view of an economist, people who get big benefits from intensive use of Facebook should stay the course. Economists don't want to dictate choices. Instead, we want economic agents to recognize the implicit trade-offs that are being made. Economists are interested in helping people make the best use of scarce resources like budgets of money and time. In many circumstances, people are already putting their resources to best use. Occasionally, however, economic reasoning can help people make better choices.

Question

Is Facebook free?

Answer

No. The opportunity cost of Facebook was $450 billion dollars in 2013.

Data

Facebook usage statistics provided by Facebook.

Caveat

We can only crudely estimate opportunity cost for Facebook's 1 billion worldwide users.

1.4 The Second Principle of Economics: Equilibrium

1.1
1.2
1.3
1.4
1.5
1.6

In most economic situations, you aren't the only one trying to optimize. Other people's behavior will influence what you decide to do. Economists think of the world as a group of economic agents who are interacting and influencing one another's efforts at optimization. Recall that *equilibrium* is the special situation in which everyone is optimizing, so nobody would benefit personally by changing his or her own behavior.

An important clarification needs to accompany this definition. When we say that nobody would benefit personally by changing his or her own behavior, we mean that nobody *believes* they would benefit from such a change. In equilibrium, all economic agents are making their best feasible choices taking into account all of the information they have, including their beliefs about the behavior of others. We could rewrite the definition by saying that in equilibrium, nobody *perceives* that they will benefit from changing their own behavior.

In equilibrium

In equilibrium, everyone is simultaneously optimizing, so nobody would benefit by changing his or her own behavior.

Out of equilibrium

To build intuition—which means understanding—for the concept of equilibrium, consider the length of the regular checkout lines at your local supermarket (ignore the express lines). If any line has a shorter wait than the others, optimizers will choose that line. If any line has a longer wait than the others, optimizers will avoid that line. So the short lines will attract shoppers, and the long lines will drive them away. And it's not just the length of the lines that matters. You pick your line by estimating which line will move the fastest, which incorporates every-thing that you can see, including the number of items in each person's shopping cart. Economists say that "in equilibrium" all of the checkout lines will have roughly the same wait time. When the wait times are expected to be the same, no shopper has an incentive to switch lines. In other words, nobody perceives that they will benefit by changing their behavior.

Here's another example. Suppose the market price of gasoline is $3/gallon and the gasoline market is in equilibrium. Three conditions will need to be satisfied.

1. The amount of gasoline produced by gasoline sellers—oil companies—will equal the amount of gasoline purchased by buyers.
2. Oil companies will only operate wells where they can extract oil and produce gasoline at a cost that is less than the market price of gasoline: $3/gallon.
3. The buyers of gasoline will only use it for activities that are worth at least $3/gallon—like driving to their best friend's wedding—and they won't use it for activities that are worth less than $3/gallon—like visiting their least favorite relatives. When gas prices go up, who in the family can't make it for Thanksgiving?

In equilibrium, both the sellers and the buyers of gasoline are optimizing, given the market price of gasoline. Nobody would benefit by changing his or her behavior.

In this book, we often study the behavior of groups of economic agents. A group could be 2 chess players; or 30 participants in an eBay auction; or millions of investors buying and selling shares on the New York Stock Exchange; or billions of households buying gasoline to fuel their tractors, trucks, mopeds, motorcycles, and cars. In all these cases, we study the equilibrium that emerges when all of these economic agents interact. In other words, we examine these environments using the assumption that everyone is constantly simultaneously optimizing—for instance, at every move in a chess game and during every trade on the New York Stock Exchange. Economists believe that this

1.1

1.2

1.3

1.4

1.5

1.6

equilibrium analysis provides a good description of what actually happens when groups of people interact.

The Free-Rider Problem

Let's use the concept of equilibrium to analyze an economic problem that may interest you: roommates. Assume that five roommates live in a rented house. The roommates can spend some of their free time contributing to the general well-being of the group by throwing away used pizza boxes and soda cans and otherwise cleaning up after themselves. Or they can spend all their free time on activities that only benefit themselves—for instance, watching YouTube videos or listening to Pandora.

It would be beneficial to the group if everyone chipped in and did a little cleaning. But each of the five roommates has an incentive to leave that to others. If one roommate spends 30 minutes doing the dishes, all the other roommates benefit without having to lift a finger. Consequently, rentals with lots of roommates are often a mess.

Lazy roommates are an example of something that economists call the *free-rider problem*. Most people want to let someone else do the dirty work. We would like to be the free riders who don't contribute but still benefit from the investments that others make.

Sometimes free riders get away with it. When there are very few free riders and lots of contributors, the free riders might be overlooked. For example, a small number of people sneak onto public transportation without paying. These turnstile jumpers are such a small group that they don't jeopardize the subway system. But if everyone started jumping turnstiles, the subway would soon run out of cash.

In the subway system, free riding is discouraged by security patrols. In rooming groups, free riding is discouraged by social pressure. Even with these "punishment" techniques, free riding is sometimes a problem because it's not easy to catch the free rider in the act. It's possible to slip over a turnstile in a quiet subway station. It's easy to leave crumbs on the couch when nobody is watching.

A free rider in the New York subway system. Are *you* paying for him to ride the subway?

People's private benefits are often out of sync with the public interest. Jumping the subway turnstile is cheaper than paying for a subway ticket. Watching YouTube is more fun than sweeping up the remains of last night's party. Equilibrium analysis helps us predict the behavior of groups of people and understand why free riding occurs. People sometimes pursue their own private interests and don't contribute *voluntarily* to the public interest. Unfortunately, selfless acts—like those of a war hero—are exceptional, and selfish acts are more common. When people in a group act, each member of the group might do what's best for himself or herself instead of acting in a way that optimizes the well-being of the entire group.

Equilibrium analysis helps us design special institutions—like financial contracts—that reduce or even eliminate free riding. For example, what would happen in the rooming group if everyone agreed to pay $5 per week so the roommates could hire a cleaning service? It would be easier to enforce $5 weekly payments than to monitor compliance with the rule "clean up after yourself, even when nobody is here to watch you." Pizza crumbs don't have name tags. So equilibrium analysis explains why individuals often fail to serve the interest of the group and how the incentive structure can be redesigned to fix these problems.

1.5 The Third Principle of Economics: Empiricism

Economists test their ideas with data. We call such evidence-based analysis, empirical analysis or *empiricism*. Economists use data to determine whether our theories about human behavior—like optimization and equilibrium—match up with *actual* human behavior.

1.1

1.2

1.3

1.4

1.5

1.6

Of course, we want to know if our theories fail to explain what is happening in the world. In that case, we need to go back to the drawing board and come up with better theories. That is how economic science, and science in general, progresses.

Economists are also interested in understanding what is *causing* things to happen in the world. We can illustrate what causation is—and is not—via a simple example. Hot days and crowded beaches tend to occur at the same time of the year. What is the cause and what is the effect here? It is, of course, that hot days *cause* people to go swimming. It is *not* that swimming *causes* the outside air temperature to rise.

But there are other cases when cause and effect are hard to untangle. Does being relatively smart cause people to go to college? Or does going to college cause people to be relatively smart? Or do both directions of causation apply?

We'll come back to the topic of empiricism in general, and causality in particular, in great detail in Chapter 2. Sometimes causes are easy to determine but sometimes identifying cause and effect requires great ingenuity.

1.6 Is Economics Good for You?

Is taking this course good for you? Let's start by thinking about the costs. Though opportunity costs are often hard to see, they are still important. The key opportunity cost of this course is another course that you won't be able to take during the time spent as a student. What other course did economics crowd out? Japanese history? Biochemistry? Russian poetry? If you are taking the two-semester version of this course, then you need to consider the two other courses that economics is crowding out.

Now consider the benefits of an economics education. The benefits come in a few different forms, but the biggest benefit is the ability to apply economic reasoning in your daily life. Whether you are deciding how much to spend on a date, where to go on vacation, or how to keep an apartment with four other roommates clean, economic reasoning will improve the quality of your decisions. These benefits will continue throughout your life as you make important decisions, such as where to invest your retirement savings and how to secure the best mortgage.

> **Learning to make good choices is the biggest benefit you'll realize from learning economics.**

Most decisions are guided by the logic of costs and benefits. Accordingly, you can use positive economic analysis to predict other people's behavior. Economics illuminates and clarifies all human behavior.

We also want you to use economic principles when you give other people advice and when you make your own choices. This is normative economics. Learning how to make good choices is the biggest benefit you'll realize from learning economics. That's why we have built our book around the concept of decision making. Looking at the world through the economic lens puts you at an enormous advantage throughout your life.

We also think that economics is a lot of fun. Understanding people's motivations is fascinating, particularly because there are many surprising insights along the way.

To realize these payoffs, you'll need to connect the ideas in this textbook to the economic activities around you. To make those connections, keep a few tips in mind:

- You can apply economic tools such as trade-offs and cost-benefit analysis to any economic decision. Learn to use them in your own daily decisions. This will help you master the tools and also appreciate their limitations.
- Even if you are not in the midst of making a decision, you will learn a lot of economics by keeping your eyes open when you walk through any environment in which people are using or exchanging resources. Think like an economist the next time you find yourself in a supermarket, a used car dealership, a soccer match, or a poker game.
- The easiest way to encounter economic ideas is to keep up with what's happening in the world. Go online and read a national newspaper like the *New York Times* or the *Wall Street Journal*. News magazines will also do the job. There's even a newsmagazine called *The Economist*, which is required reading for prime ministers

and presidents. Almost every page of any magazine—including *People*, *Sports Illustrated*, and *Vogue*—describes events driven by economic factors. Identifying and understanding these forces will be a challenge. But over time, you'll find that it gets very easy to recognize and interpret the economic story behind every headline.

Once you realize that you are constantly making economic choices, you'll understand that this course is only a first step. You'll discover the most important applications *outside* class and *after* the final exam. The tools of economics will improve your performance in all kinds of situations—making you a better businessperson, a better consumer, and a better citizen. Keep your eyes open and remember that every choice is economics in action.

Summary

⚙ Economics is the study of how agents choose to allocate scarce resources and how those choices affect society. Economics can be divided into two kinds of analysis: positive economic analysis (what people actually do) and normative economic analysis (what people ought to do). There are two key topics within economics: microeconomics (individual decisions and individual markets) and macroeconomics (the total economy).

⚙ Economics is based on three key principles: optimization, equilibrium, and empiricism.

⚙ Choosing the best feasible option, given the available information, is optimization. To optimize, an economic agent needs to consider many issues, including trade-offs, budget constraints, opportunity costs, and cost-benefit analysis.

⚙ Equilibrium is a situation in which nobody would benefit personally by changing his or her own behavior.

⚙ Economists test their ideas with data. We call such evidence-based analysis empirical analysis or empiricism. Economists use data to determine whether our theories about human behavior—like optimization and equilibrium—match actual human behavior. Economists also use data to determine what is causing things to happen in the world.

Key Terms

economic agent *p. 3*
scarce resources *p. 4*
scarcity *p. 4*
economics *p. 4*
positive economics *p. 5*

normative economics *p. 5*
microeconomics *p. 6*
macroeconomics *p. 6*
optimization *p. 6*
equilibrium *p. 7*

empiricism *p. 7*
trade-off *p. 8*
budget constraint *p. 8*
opportunity cost *p. 9*
cost-benefit analysis *p. 9*

Questions

All questions are available in MyEconLab for practice and instructor assignment.

1. Why do we have to pay a price for most of the goods we consume?

2. Many people believe that the study of economics is focused on money and financial markets. Based on your reading of the chapter, how would you define economics?

3. Examine the following statements and determine if they are normative or positive in nature. Explain your answer.

   a. The U.S. automotive industry registered its highest growth rate in 5 years in 2012; U.S. auto sales increased by 13% compared to those in 2011.

   b. The U.S. government should increase carbon taxes to reduce carbon emissions that cause global warming.

4. How does microeconomics differ from macroeconomics? Would the supply of iPhones in the United States be studied under microeconomics or macroeconomics? What about the growth rate of total economic output in the national economy?

5. What does a budget constraint represent? How do budget constraints explain the trade-offs that consumers face?

6. This chapter introduced the idea of opportunity cost.

   a. What is meant by opportunity cost? How are the opportunity costs of various choices compared?

   b. What is the opportunity cost of taking a year after graduating from high school and backpacking across Europe? Are people who do so being irrational?

7. Suppose your New Year's resolution is to get back in shape. You are considering various ways of doing this: you can sign up for a gym membership, walk to work, take the stairs instead of the elevator, or watch your diet. How would you evaluate these options and choose an optimal one?

8. Suppose the market price of corn is $5.50 per bushel. What are the three conditions that will need to be satisfied for the corn market to be in equilibrium at this price?

9. Economists are often concerned with the free-rider problem.

   a. What is meant by free riding? Explain with an example.

   b. Are public parks subject to the free-rider problem? What about keeping city streets clean? Explain your answer.

10. Explain the concept of causation with the help of a simple real-life example.

11. Identify cause and effect in the following examples:

    a. Lower infant mortality and an improvement in nutrition

    b. A surge in cocoa prices and a pest attack on the cocoa crop that year

Problems

All problems are available in MyEconLab for practice and instructor assignment.

1. In an episode of the sitcom *Seinfeld,* Jerry and his friends Elaine and George are waiting to be seated at a Chinese restaurant. Tired of waiting, Elaine convinces the others that they should bribe the *maître d'* to get a table.

   a. What factors should they consider when they are deciding how high to make their bribe?

   b. Jerry, Elaine, and George had tickets for a movie after dinner. How would this have affected the amount that they were willing to pay as a bribe?

   c. The amount that they finally decide to pay is higher than the value of the meal that they would have had. Does this mean that they are being irrational?

   Adapted from: http://yadayadayadaecon.com/clip/10/

2. You are thinking about buying a house. You find one you like that costs $200,000. You learn that your bank will give you a mortgage for $160,000 and that you will have to use all of your savings to make the down payment of $40,000. You calculate that the mortgage payments, property taxes, insurance, maintenance, and utilities would total $950 per month. Is $950 the cost of owning the house?

   What important factor(s) have you left out of your calculation of the cost of ownership?

3. You have 40,000 frequent flier miles. You could exchange your miles for a round-trip ticket to Bermuda over spring break. Does that mean your flight to Bermuda would be free? Explain your reasoning.

4. You have decided that you are going to consume 600 calories of beer and snacks at a party Saturday night. A beer has 150 calories and a snack has 75 calories.

   a. Create a table that shows the various combinations of beer and snacks you can consume. To keep things simple, use only round numbers (e.g., you could choose 1 or 2 beers but not 1.5 beers).

   b. What is the opportunity cost of a beer?

5. There is an old saying that "The proof of the pudding is in the eating," which means that by definition good decisions work out well and poor decisions work out badly. The following scenarios ask you to consider the wisdom of this saying.

   a. Your friends live in a city where it often rains in May. Nonetheless, they plan a May outdoor wedding and have no backup plan if it does rain. The weather turns out to be lovely on their wedding day. Do you think your friends were being rational when they made their wedding plans? Explain.

b. You usually have to see a doctor several times each year. You decided to buy health insurance at the start of last year. It turns out you were never sick last year and never had to go the doctor. Do you think you were being rational when you decided to buy health insurance? Explain.

c. Given your answers to the first two parts of this question, do you agree or disagree that "The proof of the pudding is in the eating?" Explain.

6. Consider the following three statements:

i. You can either stand during a college football game or you can sit. You believe that you will see the game very well if you stand and others sit but that you will not be able to see at all if you sit and others stand. You therefore decide to stand.

ii. Your friend tells you that he expects many people to stand at football games.

iii. An economist studies photos of many college football games and estimates that 75 percent of all fans stand and 25 percent sit.

Which of these statements deals with optimization, which deals with equilibrium, and which deals with empiricism? Explain.

7. The costs of many environmental regulations can be calculated in dollars, but the benefits often are in terms of lives saved (mortality) or decreases in the incidence of a particular disease (morbidity). What does this imply about the cost-benefit analysis of environmental regulations? There is an old saying "You can't put a price on a human life." Do you agree or disagree? Explain.

8. This chapter discussed the free-rider problem. Consider the following two situations in relation to the free-rider concept.

a. The Taft-Hartley Act (1947) allows workers to be employed at a firm without joining the union at their workplace or paying membership fees to the union. This arrangement is known as an open shop. Considering that unions negotiate terms of employment and wages on behalf of all the workers at a firm, why do you think that most unions are opposed to open shops?

b. For your business communication class, you are supposed to work on a group assignment in a team of six. You soon realize that a few of your team members do not contribute to the assignment but get the same grade as the rest of the team. If you were the professor, how would you redesign the incentive structure here to fix this problem?

2 Economic Methods and Economic Questions

Is college worth it?

If you are reading this book, there is a good chance that you are either in college or thinking about taking the plunge. As you know, college is a big investment. Tuition averages almost $2,500 per year at community colleges, almost $5,000 per year at public colleges, and almost $25,000 per year at private colleges. And that's not the only cost. Your time, as we have seen, is worth $10 or more per hour—this time value adds at least $20,000 per year to the opportunity cost of a college education.

As with any other investment, you'd like to know how a college education is going to pay you back. What are the "returns to education," and how would you measure them? In this chapter you'll see that you can answer such questions with models and data.

CHAPTER **OUTLINE**

2.1	EBE	2.2	EBE	2.3
The Scientific Method	**How much more do workers with a college education earn?**	**Causation and Correlation**	**How much do wages increase when an individual is compelled by law to get an extra year of schooling?**	**Economic Questions and Answers**

KEY IDEAS

⚙ A model is a simplified description of reality.

⚙ Economists use data to evaluate the accuracy of models and understand how the world works.

⚙ Correlation does not imply causality.

⚙ Experiments help economists measure cause and effect.

⚙ Economic research focuses on questions that are important to society and can be answered with models and data.

2.1 The Scientific Method

Recall that empiricism—using data to analyze the world—is the third key principle of economics. We explored the first two principles—optimization and equilibrium—in the previous chapter. Empiricism is the focus of this chapter.

Empiricism is at the heart of all scientific analysis. The **scientific method** is the name for the ongoing process that economists, other social scientists, and natural scientists use to:

1. Develop models of the world
2. Test those models with data—evaluating the match between the models and the data

Economists do not expect this process to reveal the "true" model of the world, since the world is vastly complex. However, economists do expect to identify models that are useful in understanding the world. Testing with data enables economists to separate the good models—those that approximately match the data—from the bad models. When a model is overwhelmingly inconsistent with the data, economists try to fix the model or replace it altogether. We believe that this process enables us to find more useful models that help to explain the past and to predict the future with some confidence. In this section, we explain what a model is and how a model can be tested with data.

> The **scientific method** is the name for the ongoing process that economists and other scientists use to (1) develop models of the world and (2) test those models with data.

Models and Data

Everyone once believed that the earth was flat. We now know that it is more like a beach ball than a Frisbee. Yet the flat-earth model is still actively used. Go into a gas station and you'll find only flat road maps for sale. Consult your GPS receiver and you'll also see flat maps. Nobody keeps a globe in the glove compartment.

Flat maps and spherical globes are both models of the surface of the earth. A **model** is a simplified description, or representation, of the world. Because models are simplified, they are not perfect replicas of reality. Obviously, flat maps are not perfectly accurate models of the surface of the earth—they distort the curvature. If you are flying from New York to Tokyo, the curvature matters. But if you are touring around New York City, you don't need to worry about the fact that the earth is shaped like a sphere.

> A **model** is a simplified description, or representation, of the world. Sometimes, economists will refer to a model as a *theory*. These terms are often used interchangeably.

> **All scientific models make predictions that can be checked with data.**

Scientists—and commuters—use the model that is best suited to analyze the problem at hand. Even if a model/map is based on assumptions that are known to be false, like flatness of the earth, the model may still help us to make good predictions and good plans for the

Exhibit 2.1 Flying from New York to Tokyo Requires More Than a Flat Map

This flat map is a model of part of the earth's surface. It treats the world as perfectly flat, which leads the map maker to exaggerate distances in the northern latitudes. It is useful for certain purposes—for instance, learning geography. But you wouldn't want to use it to find the best air route across the Pacific Ocean. For example, the shortest flight path from New York to Tokyo is not a straight line through San Francisco. Instead, the shortest path goes through Northern Alaska! The flat-earth model is well suited for some tasks (geography lessons) and ill-suited for others (intercontinental flight navigation).

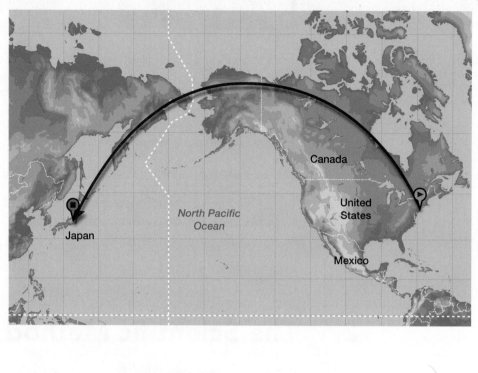

Exhibit 2.2 New York City Subway Map

This is a model of the subway system in New York City. It is highly simplified—for example, it treats New York City as a perfectly flat surface and it also distorts the shape of the city—but it is nevertheless very useful for commuters and tourists.

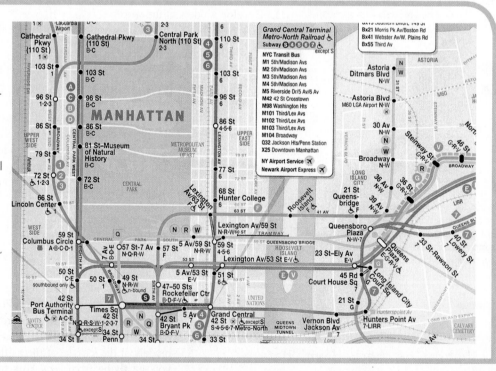

Data are facts, measurements, or statistics that describe the world.

future. It is more important for a model to be simple and useful than it is for a model to be precisely accurate.

All scientific models make predictions that can be checked with **data**—facts, measurements, or statistics that describe the world. Recall from Chapter 1 that economists often describe themselves as empiricists, or say that we practice empiricism, because we use data

Empirical evidence is a set of facts established by observation and measurement.

Hypotheses are predictions (typically generated by a model) that can be tested with data.

to create **empirical evidence**. These terms all boil down to the same basic idea: using data to answer questions about the world and using data to test models. For example, we could test the New York City subway map by actually riding the subway and checking the map's accuracy.

When conducting empirical analysis, economists refer to a model's predictions as **hypotheses**. Whenever such hypotheses are contradicted by the available data, economists return to the drawing board and try to come up with a better model that yields new hypotheses.

An Economic Model

Let's consider an example of an economic model. We're going to study an extremely simple model to get the ball rolling. But even economic models that are far more complicated than this example are also highly simplified descriptions of reality.

All economic models begin with assumptions. Consider the following assumption about the returns to education: *Investing in one extra year of education increases your future wages by 10 percent.* Let's put the assumption to work to generate a model that relates a person's level of education to her wages.

Increasing a wage by 10 percent is the same as multiplying the wage by $1 + 0.10 = 1.10$. The returns-to-education assumption implies that someone with an extra year of education earns 1.10 times as much as she would have earned without the extra year of education. For example, if someone would earn \$15 per hour with 13 years of education, then a 14th year of education will cause her hourly wage to rise to $1.10 \times \$15$, or \$16.50.

Economists use assumptions to derive other implications. For example, the returns-to-education assumption implies that *two* additional years of education will increase earnings by 10 percent twice over—once for each extra year of education—producing a 21 percent total increase.

$$1.10 \times 1.10 = 1.21.$$

Consider another example. *Four* additional years of education will increase earnings by 10 percent four times over, implying a 46 percent total increase.

$$1.10 \times 1.10 \times 1.10 \times 1.10 = (1.10)^4 = 1.46.$$

This implies that going to college would increase a college graduate's income by 46 percent compared to what she would have been paid if she had ended her education after finishing high school. In other words, a prediction—or hypothesis—of the model is that college graduates will earn 46 percent more than high school graduates.

In principle, we can apply this analysis to *any* number of years of education. We therefore have a general model that relates people's educational attainment to their income. The model that we have derived is referred to as the returns-to-education model. It describes the economic payoff of more education—in other words, the "return" on your educational investment. Most economic models are much, much more complex than this. In most economic models, it takes pages of mathematical analysis to derive the implications of the assumptions. Nevertheless, this simple model is a good starting point for our discussion. It illustrates two important properties of all models.

First, *a model is an approximation.* The model does not predict that *everyone* would increase their future wages by *exactly* 10 percent if they obtained an extra year of education. The predicted relationship between education and future wages is an average relationship—it is an approximation for what is predicted to happen for most people in most circumstances. The model overlooks lots of special considerations. For example, the final year of college probably does much more to increase your wages than the second-to-last year of college, because that final year earns you the official degree, which is a key item on your resumé. Likewise, your college major importantly impacts how much you will earn after college. Those who major in economics, for example, tend to earn more than graduates in most other majors. Our simple model overlooks many such subtleties. Just as a flat subway map is only an approximation of the features of a city, the returns-to-education model is only an approximation of the mapping from years of education to wages.

Second, *a model makes predictions that can be tested with data*—in this case, data on people's education and earnings. We are now ready to use some data to actually evaluate the predictions of the returns-to-education model.

Evidence-Based Economics

Q: How much more do workers with a college education earn?

To put the model to the test we need data, which we obtain from the Current Population Survey (CPS), a government data source. This survey collects data on wages, education, and many other characteristics of the general population and is available to anyone who wants to use it. When data are available to the general public, they are called "public-use data."

Exhibit 2.3 summarizes the average annual earnings for our test. The returns-to-education model does not match the data perfectly. The exhibit shows that for 30-year-old U.S. workers with 12 years of education, which is equivalent to a high school diploma, the average yearly salary is $32,941. For 30-year-old U.S. workers with 16 years of education, which is equivalent to graduation from a four-year college, the average salary is $51,780.

If we simply divide these two average wages—college wage over high school wage—the ratio is 1.57.

$$\frac{\text{average salary of 30-year-olds with 16 years of education}}{\text{average salary of 30-year-olds with 12 years of education}} = \frac{\$51,780}{\$32,941} = 1.57.$$

Recall that the returns-to-education model says that each additional year of education raises the wage by 10 percent, so four extra years of education should raise the wage by a factor of $(1.10)^4 = 1.46$.

We can see that the model does not *exactly* match the data. Going from 12 years of education to 16 years is associated with a 57 percent increase in income. However, the model is not far off—the model predicted a 46 percent increase.

Exhibit 2.3 Average Annual Earnings of 30-Year-Old Americans by Education Level (2013 data)

Average annual earnings of 30-year-old Americans show that people who stop going to school after earning their high school diplomas earn $32,941 per year, whereas those who go on to college earn $51,780 per year.

Source: Current Population Survey.

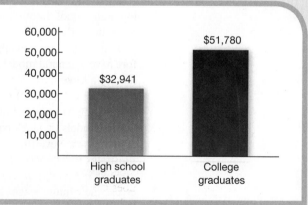

Question

How much more do workers with a college education earn?

Answer

Average wages for a college graduate are 1.57 times higher than average wages for a high school graduate.

Data

Wages from the Current Population Survey (CPS, 2013). Compare average wages for 30-year-old workers with different levels of education.

Caveat

These are averages for a large population of individuals. Each individual's experience will differ.

2.1

2.2

2.3

Means

The **mean**, or **average**, is the sum
of all the different values divided by
the number of values.

You may wonder how the data from the CPS can be used to calculate the wages reported above. We used the concept of the *mean*, or *average*. The **mean** (or **average**) is the sum of all the different values divided by the number of values and is a commonly used technique for summarizing data. Statisticians and other scientists use the terms *mean* and *average* interchangeably.

We can quickly show how the mean works in a small example. Say that there are five people: Mr. Kwon, Ms. Littleton, Mr. Locke, Ms. Reye, and Mr. Shephard, each with a different hourly wage:

$$Kwon = \$26 \text{ per hour,}$$
$$Littleton = \$24 \text{ per hour,}$$
$$Locke = \$8 \text{ per hour,}$$
$$Reye = \$35 \text{ per hour,}$$
$$Shephard = \$57 \text{ per hour.}$$

If we add the five wages together and divide by 5, we calculate a mean wage of $30 per hour.

$$\frac{\$26 + \$24 + \$8 + \$35 + \$57}{5} = \$30.$$

This analysis of a small sample illustrates the idea of calculating a mean, but convincing data analysis in economics relies on using a large sample. For example, a typical economic research paper uses data gathered from thousands of individuals. So a key strength of economic analysis is the *amount* of data used. Earlier we didn't rely on a handful of observations to argue that education raises earnings. Instead, we used data from more than thousands of surveyed 30-year-olds. Using lots of data—economists call them *observations*—strengthens the force of an empirical argument because the researcher can make more precise statements.

To show you how to make convincing empirical arguments, this course uses lots of real data from large groups of people. Credible empirical arguments, based on many observations, are a key component of the scientific method.

Argument by Anecdote

Education is not destiny. There are some people with lots of education who earn very little. There are some people with little education who earn a lot. When we wrote this book, Bill Gates, a *Harvard dropout* who founded Microsoft, was the richest man in the world. Mark Zuckerberg, the Facebook CEO, also dropped out of Harvard.

With these two examples in mind, it is tempting to conclude that dropping out of college is a great path to success. However, it is a mistake to use two anecdotes, or any small sample of people, to try to judge a statistical relationship.

Here's another example of how the amount of data can make a big difference. Exhibit 2.4 plots data from just two people. They are both 30-years-old. As you can see, the exhibit does not reproduce the positive relationship between education and earnings that is plotted in Exhibit 2.3. Instead, it looks as though rising education is associated with *falling* earnings. But the pattern in Exhibit 2.4 is far from shocking given that it plots only two people. Indeed, if you study two randomly chosen 30-year-olds, there is a 25 percent chance that the person with only a high school diploma has higher earnings than the person with a four-year college degree. This fact highlights that there is much more than education that determines your earnings, although getting a college degree will usually help make you money.

When you look at only a small amount of data, it is easy to jump to the wrong conclusion. Keep this warning in mind the next time a newspaper columnist tries to convince you of something by using a few anecdotes. If the columnist backs up her story with data reflecting the experiences of thousands of people, then she has done her job and may deserve to win the argument. But if she rests her case after sharing a handful of anecdotes, remain skeptical. Be doubly skeptical if you suspect that the anecdotes have been carefully

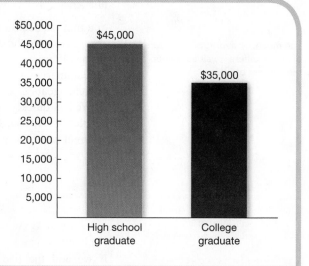

Exhibit 2.4 Annual Earnings for Two 30-Year-Old Americans by Education

Even though Exhibit 2.3 taught us that the average annual earnings of college graduates is 57 percent higher than those of high school graduates, it is not difficult to find specific examples where a high school graduate is actually earning more than a college graduate. Here we learn of one such example: the high school graduate earns $45,000 per year, whereas the college graduate earns $35,000.

selected to prove the columnist's point. Argument by anecdote should not be taken too seriously.

There is one exception to this rule. Argument by example is appropriate when you are contradicting a *blanket* statement. For example, if someone asserts that *every* National Basketball Association (NBA) player has to be tall, just one counterexample is enough to prove this statement wrong. In this case, your proof would be Tyrone Bogues, a 5-foot 3-inch dynamo who played in the NBA for 14 years.

2.2 Causation and Correlation

Using our large data set on wages and years of education, we've seen that on average wages rise roughly 10 percent for every year of additional education. Does this mean that if we could encourage a student to stay in school one extra year, that would *cause* that individual's future wages to rise 10 percent? Not necessarily. Let's think about why this is not always the case with an example.

The Red Ad Campaign Blues

Assume that Walmart has hired you as a consultant. You have developed a hypothesis about ad campaigns: you believe that campaigns using the color red are good at catching people's attention. To test your hypothesis, you assemble empirical evidence from historical ad campaigns, including the color of the ad campaign and how revenue at Walmart changed during the campaign.

Your empirical research confirms your hypothesis! Sales go up 25 percent during campaigns with lots of red images. Sales go up only 5 percent during campaigns with lots of blue images. You race to the chief executive officer (CEO) to report this remarkable result. You are a genius! Unfortunately, the CEO instantly fires you.

What did the CEO notice that you missed?

The red-themed campaigns were mostly concentrated during the Christmas season. The blue-themed campaigns were mostly spread out over the rest of the year. In the CEO's words,

The red colors in our advertising don't cause an increase in our revenue. Christmas causes an increase in our revenue. Christmas also causes an increase in the use of red in our ads. If we ran blue ads in December our holiday season revenue would still rise by about 25 percent.

Does jogging cause people to be healthy? Does good health cause people to jog? In fact both kinds of causation are simultaneously true.

Unfortunately, this is actually a true story, though we've changed the details—including the name of the firm—to protect our friends. We return, in the appendix, to a related story where the CEO was not as sharp as the CEO in this story.

Causation versus Correlation

> **Think of causation as the path from cause to effect.**

Causation occurs when one thing directly affects another through a cause-and-effect relationship.

A **correlation** means that there is a mutual relationship between two things.

People often mistake *causation* for *correlation*. **Causation** occurs when one thing directly affects another. You can think of it as the path from cause to effect: putting a snowball in a hot oven *causes* it to melt.

Correlation means that there is a mutual relationship between two things—as one thing changes, the other changes as well. There is some kind of connection. It *might* be cause and effect, but correlation can also arise when causation is not present. For example, as it turns out students who take music courses in high school score better on their SATs than students who do not take music courses in high school. Some educators have argued that this relationship is causal: more music courses cause higher SAT scores.

Yet, before you buy a clarinet for your younger sibling, you should know that researchers have shown that students who already would have scored high on their SATs are more likely to also have enrolled in music classes. There is something else—being a good student—that causes high SAT scores and enrollment in music. SAT scores and taking music courses are only correlated; if a trombone player's arm were broken and she had to drop out of music class, this would not cause her future SAT scores to fall. When two things are correlated, it suggests that causation may be possible and that further investigation is warranted—it's only the beginning of the story, not the end.

A **variable** is a factor that is likely to change or vary.

Positive correlation implies that two variables tend to move in the same direction.

Negative correlation implies that two variables tend to move in opposite directions. When the variables have movements that are not related, we say that the variables have **zero correlation**.

Correlations are divided into three categories: *positive correlation*, *negative correlation*, and *zero correlation*. Economists refer to some factor, like a household's income, as a **variable**. **Positive correlation** implies that two variables tend to move in the same direction—for example, surveys reveal that people who have a relatively high income are more likely to be married than people who have a relatively low income. In this situation we say that the variables of income and marital status are positively correlated. **Negative correlation** implies that the two variables tend to move in opposite directions—for example, people with a high level of education are less likely to be unemployed. In this situation we say that the variables of education and unemployment are negatively correlated. When two variables are not related, we say that they have a **zero correlation**. The number of friends you have likely has no relation to whether your address is on the odd or even side of the street.

When Correlation Does Not Imply Causality   There are two reasons why we should *not* jump to the conclusion that a correlation between two variables implies a particular causal relationship:

1. Omitted variables
2. Reverse causality

An **omitted variable** is something that has been left out of a study that, if included, would explain why two variables that are in the study are correlated.

An **omitted variable** is something that has been left out of a study that, if included, would explain why two variables are correlated. Recall that the amount of red content in Walmart's ads is positively correlated with the growth rate of Walmart's sales. However, the red color does not necessarily cause Walmart's sales to rise. The arrival of the Christmas season causes Walmart's ads to be red and the Christmas season also causes Walmart's month-over-month sales revenue to rise. The Christmas season is an omitted variable that explains why red ads tend to occur at around the time that sales tend to rise. (See Exhibit 2.5.)

Is there also an omitted variable that explains why education and income are positively correlated? One possible factor might be an individual's tendency to work hard. What if workaholics tend to thrive in college more than others? Perhaps pulling all-nighters to write term papers allows them to do well in their courses. Workaholics *also* tend to earn more money than others because workaholics tend to stay late on the job and work on weekends. Does workaholism cause you to earn more and, incidentally, to graduate from college rather than drop out? Or does staying in college cause you to earn those higher wages? What is cause and what is effect?

Reverse causality occurs when we mix up the direction of cause and effect.

Reverse causality is another problem that plagues our efforts to distinguish correlation and causation. Reverse causality is the situation in which we mix up the

Exhibit 2.5 An Example of an Omitted Variable

The amount of red content in Walmart's ads is positively correlated with the growth of Walmart's revenue. In other words, when ads are red-themed, Walmart's month-over-month sales revenue tends to grow the fastest. However, the redness does not cause Walmart's revenue to rise. The Christmas season causes Walmart's ads to be red and the Christmas season also causes Walmart's sales revenue to rise. The Christmas season is the omitted variable that explains the positive correlation between red ads and revenue growth.

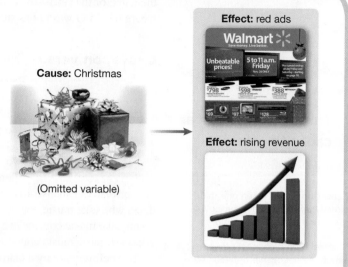

Cause: Christmas

(Omitted variable)

Effect: red ads

Effect: rising revenue

direction of cause and effect. For example, consider the fact that relatively wealthy people tend to be relatively healthy too. This has led some social scientists to conclude that greater wealth causes better health—for instance, wealthy people can afford better healthcare. On the other hand, there may be reverse causality: better health may cause greater wealth. For example, healthy people can work harder and have fewer healthcare expenditures than less healthy people. It turns out that both causal channels seem to exist: greater wealth causes better health and better health causes greater wealth!

In our analysis of the returns to education, could it be that reverse causality is at play: higher wages at age 30 cause you to get more education at age 20? We can logically rule this out. Assuming that you don't have a time machine, it is unlikely that your wage as a 30-year-old causes you to obtain more education in your 20s. So in the returns-to-education example, reverse causality is probably not a problem. But in many other analyses—for example, the wealth-health relationship—reverse causality is a key consideration.

Economists have developed a rich set of tools to determine what is causation and what is only correlation. We turn to some of these tools next.

Experimental Economics and Natural Experiments

An **experiment** is a controlled method of investigating causal relationships among variables.

One method of determining cause and effect is to run an **experiment**—a controlled method of investigating causal relationships among variables. Though you may not read much about economic experiments in the newspaper, headlines for experiments in the field of medicine are common. For example, the Food and Drug Administration (FDA) requires pharmaceutical companies to run carefully designed experiments to provide evidence that new drugs work before they are approved for general public use.

To run an experiment, researchers usually create a treatment (test) group and a control group. Participants are assigned randomly to participate either as a member of the treatment group or as a member of the control group—a process called *randomization*. **Randomization** is the assignment of subjects by chance, rather than by choice, to a treatment group or to a control group. The treatment group and the control group are treated identically, except along a single dimension that is intentionally varied across the two groups. The impact of this variation is the focus of the experiment.

Randomization is the assignment of subjects by chance, rather than by choice, to a treatment group or control group.

If we want to know whether a promising new medicine helps patients with diabetes, we could take 1,000 patients with diabetes and *randomly* place 500 of them into a treatment group—those who receive the new medicine. The other 500 patients would be in the control group and receive the *standard* diabetes medications that are already widely used. Then, we would follow all of the patients and see how their health changes over the next few years. This experiment would test the causal hypothesis that the new drug is better than the old drug.

Now, consider an economics experiment. Suppose that we want to know what difference a college degree makes. We could take 1,000 high school students who cannot afford college, but who want to attend college, and randomly place 500 of them into a treatment group where they had all of their college expenses paid. The other 500 students would be placed in the control group. Then, we would keep track of *all* of the original 1,000 students—including the 500 control group students who weren't able to go to college because they couldn't afford it. We would use periodic surveys during their adult lives to see how the wages in the group that got a college education compare with the wages of the group that did not attend college. This experiment would test the hypothesis that a college education causes wages to rise.

One problem with experimentation is that experiments can sometimes be very costly to conduct. For instance, the college-attendance experiment that we just described would cost tens of millions of dollars, because the researchers would need to pay the college fees for 500 students. Another problem is that experiments do not provide immediate answers to some important questions. For example, learning about how one more year of education affects wages over the entire working life would take many decades if we ran an experiment on high school students today.

Another problem is that experiments are sometimes run poorly. For example, if medical researchers do not truly randomize the assignment of patients to medical treatments, then the experiment may not teach us anything at all. For instance, if patients who go to cutting-edge research hospitals tend to be the ones who get prescribed the newest kind of diabetes medication, then we don't know whether the new medication caused those patients to get better or whether it was some other thing that their fancy hospitals did that actually caused the patients' health to improve. In a well-designed experiment, randomization alone would determine who got the new medicine and who got the old medicine.

When research is badly designed, economists tend to be very skeptical of its conclusions. We say "garbage in, garbage out" to capture the idea that bad research methods invalidate a study's conclusions.

If we don't have the budget or time to run an experiment, how else can we identify cause and effect? One approach is to study historical data that has been generated by a "natural" experiment. A **natural experiment** is an empirical study in which some process—out of the control of the experimenter—has assigned subjects to control and treatment groups in a random or nearly random way.

Economists have found and exploited natural experiments to answer numerous major questions. This methodology can be very useful in providing a more definitive answer to our question at hand: What are you getting from your education?

A **natural experiment** is an empirical study in which some process—out of the control of the experimenter—has assigned subjects to control and treatment groups in a random or nearly random way.

Evidence-Based Economics

Q: How much do wages increase when an individual is compelled by law to get an extra year of schooling?

Many decades ago, compulsory schooling laws were much more permissive, allowing teenagers to drop out well before they graduated from high school. Philip Oreopoulos studied a natural experiment that was created by a change in these compulsory schooling laws.[1] Oreopoulos looked at an educational reform in the United Kingdom in 1947, which increased the minimum school leaving age from 14 to 15. As a result of this change, the fraction of children dropping out of school by age 14 fell by 50 percentage points between 1946 and 1948.

In this way, those kids reaching age 14 before 1947 are a "control group" for those reaching age 14 after 1947. Oreopoulos found that the students who turned 14 in 1948 and were therefore compelled to stay in school one extra year earned 10 percent more on average than the students who turned 14 in 1946.

Natural experiments are a very useful source of data in empirical economics. In many problems, they help us separate correlation from causation. Applied to the returns to education, they suggest that the correlation between years of education and higher income is not due to some omitted variable, but reflects the causal influence of education.

The returns-to-education model thus obtains strong confirmation from the data. Does a 10 percent return to each additional year of education increase your appetite for more years of schooling?

Question	**Answer**	**Data**	**Caveat**
How much do wages increase when an individual is compelled by law to get an extra year of schooling?	On average, wages rise by 10 percent when kids are compelled to stay in school an extra year.	United Kingdom General Household Survey. Compare kids in the United Kingdom who were allowed to drop out of school at age 14 with others who were compelled to stay in school an extra year due to changes in compulsory schooling laws.	Factors other than the change in the compulsory schooling laws might explain why the kids who were compelled to stay in school eventually earned more in the workforce (this is an example of an omitted variable).

2.3 Economic Questions and Answers

Economists like to think about our research as a process in which we pose and answer questions. We've already seen a couple of these questions. For example, in the current chapter, we asked, "How much do wages increase when an individual is compelled by law to get an extra year of schooling?" and in Chapter 1, we asked, "What is the opportunity cost of your time?"

Good questions come in many different forms. But the most exciting economic questions share two properties.

1. *Good questions address topics that are important to individual economic agents and/or to our society.* Economists tend to think about economic research as something that contributes to society's welfare. We try to pursue research that has general implications for human behavior or economic performance. For example, understanding the returns to education is important because individuals invest a lot of resources obtaining an education. The United States spends nearly a tenth of its economic output on education—$1.5 trillion per year. It is useful to quantify the payoffs from all this investment. If the returns to education are very high, society may want to encourage even more educational investment. If the returns to education are low, we should share this important fact with students who are deciding whether or not to stay in school. Knowing the returns to education will help individuals and governments decide how much of their scarce resources to allocate to educational investment.

2. *Good economic questions can be answered.* In some other disciplines, posing a good question is enough. For example, philosophers believe that some of the most important questions don't have answers. In contrast, economists are primarily interested in questions that can be answered with enough hard work and careful reasoning.

Here are some of the economic questions that we discuss in this book. As you look over the set, you will see that these are big questions with significant implications for you and for society as a whole. The rest of this book sets out to discover answers to these questions. We believe the journey will be exhilarating—so let's get started!

Chapter	Questions
1	Is Facebook free?
2	Is college worth it?
3	How does location affect the rental cost of housing?
4	How much more gasoline would people buy if its price were lower?
5	Would a smoker quit the habit for $100 a month?
6	How would an ethanol subsidy affect ethanol producers?
7	Can markets composed of only self-interested people maximize the overall well-being of society?
8	Will free trade cause you to lose your job?
9	How can the Queen of England lower her commute time to Wembley Stadium?
10	What is the optimal size of government?
11	Is there discrimination in the labor market?
12	Can a monopoly ever be good for society?
13	Is there value in putting yourself into someone else's shoes?
14	How many firms are necessary to make a market competitive?
15	Do people exhibit a preference for immediate gratification?
16	Why do new cars lose considerable value the minute they are driven off the lot? Why is private health insurance so expensive?
17	How should you bid in an eBay auction? Who determines how the household spends its money?
18	Do people care about fairness?
19	In the United States, what is the total market value of annual economic production?
20	Why is the average American so much richer than the average Indian?
21	Why are you so much more prosperous than your great-great-grandparents were?
22	Are tropical and semitropical areas condemned to poverty by their geographies?
23	What happens to employment and unemployment if local employers go out of business?
24	How often do banks fail?
25	What caused the German hyperinflation of 1922–1923?
26	What caused the recession of 2007–2009?
27	How much does government spending stimulate GDP?
28	Are companies like Nike harming workers in Vietnam?
29	How did George Soros make $1 billion?
Web Chapter 1	Do investors chase historical returns?
Web Chapter 2	What is the value of a human life?
Web Chapter 3	Do governments and politicians follow their citizens' and constituencies' wishes?

Summary

☼ The scientific method is the name for the ongoing process that economists and other scientists use to (a) develop mathematical models of the world and (b) test those models with data.

☼ Empirical evidence is a set of facts established by observation and measurement, which are used to evaluate a model.

☼ Economists try to uncover causal relationships among variables.

☼ One method to determine causality is to run an experiment—a controlled method of investigating causal relationships among variables. Economists now actively pursue experiments both in the laboratory and in the field. Economists also study historical data that have been generated by a natural experiment to infer causality.

Key Terms

scientific method *p. 21*
model *p. 21*
data *p. 22*
empirical evidence *p. 23*
hypotheses *p. 23*
mean (average) *p. 25*

causation *p. 27*
correlation *p. 27*
variable *p. 27*
positive correlation *p. 27*
negative correlation *p. 27*
zero correlation *p. 27*

omitted variable *p. 27*
reverse causality *p. 27*
experiment *p. 28*
randomization *p. 28*
natural experiment *p. 29*

Questions

All questions are available in MyEconLab for practice and instructor assignment.

1. What does it mean to say that economists use the scientific method? How do economists distinguish between models that work and those that don't?

2. What is meant by empiricism? How do empiricists use hypotheses?

3. What are two important properties of economic models? Models are often simplified descriptions of a real-world phenomenon. Does this mean that they are unrealistic?

4. How is the mean calculated from a series of observations? Suppose 5,000 people bought popsicles on a hot summer day. If the mean of the average number of popsicles bought is 2, how many popsicles were sold that day?

5. How does the sample size affect the validity of an empirical argument? When is it acceptable to use only one example to disprove a statement?

6. Explain why correlation does not always imply causation. Does causation always imply *positive* correlation? Explain your answer.

7. Give an example of a pair of variables that have a positive correlation, a pair of variables that have a negative correlation, and a pair of variables that have zero correlation.

8. What is meant by randomization? How does randomization affect the results of an experiment?

9. This chapter discussed natural and randomized experiments. How does a natural experiment differ from a randomized one? Which one is likely to yield more accurate results?

10. Suppose you had to find the effect of seatbelt rules on road accident fatalities. Would you choose to run a randomized experiment or would it make sense to use natural experiments here? Explain.

Problems

All problems are available in MyEconLab for practice and instructor assignment.

1. This chapter talks about means. The median is a closely related concept. The median is the numerical value separating the higher half of your data from the lower half. You can find the median by arranging all of the observations from lowest value to highest value and picking the middle value (assuming you have an odd number of observations). Although the mean and median are closely related, the difference between the mean and the median is sometimes of interest.

   a. Suppose country A has five families. Their incomes are $10,000, $20,000, $30,000, $40,000, and $50,000. What is the median family income in A? What is the mean income?

   b. Country B also has five families. Their incomes are $10,000, $20,000, $30,000, $40,000, and $150,000. What is the median family income in B? What is the mean income?

   c. In which country is income inequality greater, A or B?

   d. Suppose you thought income inequality in the US had increased over time. Based on your answers to this question, would you expect that the ratio of the mean income in the US to the median income has risen or fallen? Explain.

2. Consider the following situation: your math professor tells your class that the mean score on the final exam is 43. The exam was scored on a total of 100 points. Does this imply that you, too, scored poorly on the exam? Explain.

3. This chapter stressed the importance of using appropriate samples for empirical studies. Consider the following two problems in that light.

   a. You are given a class assignment to find out if people's political leanings affect the newspaper or magazine that they choose to read. You survey two students taking a political science class and five people at a coffee shop. Almost all the people you have spoken to tell you that their political affiliations do not affect what they read. Based on the results of your study, you conclude that there is no relationship between political inclinations and the choice of a newspaper. Is this a valid conclusion? Why or why not?

   b. Your uncle tells you that the newspaper or magazine that people buy will depend on their age. He says that he believes this because, at home, his wife and his teenage children read different papers. Do you think his conclusion is justified?

4. Some studies have found that people who owned guns were more likely to be killed with a gun. Do you think this study is strong evidence in favor of stricter gun control laws? Explain.

5. As the text explains, it can sometimes be very difficult to sort out the direction of causality.

   a. Why might you think that more police officers would lead to lower crime rates? Why might you think that higher crime rates would lead to more police officers?

   b. In 2012, the *New England Journal of Medicine* published research that showed a strong correlation between the consumption of chocolate in a country and the number of Nobel Prize winners in that country. Do you think countries that want to encourage their citizens to win Nobel Prizes should increase their consumption of chocolate?

6. The chapter shows that in general people with more education earn higher salaries. Economists have offered two explanations of this relationship. The human capital argument says that high schools and colleges teach people valuable skills, and employers are willing to pay higher salaries to attract people with those skills. The signaling argument says that college graduates earn more because a college degree is a signal to employers that a job applicant is diligent, intelligent, and persevering. How might you use data on people with two, three, and four years of college education to shed light on this controversy?

7. Maimonides, a twelfth-century scholar, said, "Twenty-five children may be put in the charge of one teacher. If the number in the class exceeds twenty-five but is not more than forty, he should have an assistant to help with the instruction. If there are more than forty, two teachers must be appointed." Israel follows Maimonides's rule in determining the number of teachers for each class. How could you use Maimonides's rule as a natural experiment to study the effect of teacher-student ratios on student achievement?

8. Oregon expanded its Medicaid coverage in 2008. Roughly 90,000 people applied but the state had funds to cover only an additional 30,000 people (who were randomly chosen from the total applicant pool of 90,000). How could you use the Oregon experience to estimate the impact of increased access to healthcare on health outcomes?

9. A simple economic model predicts that a fall in the price of bus tickets means that more people will take the bus. However, you observe that some people still do not take the bus even after the price of a ticket fell.

   a. Is the model incorrect?

   b. How would you test this model?

Appendix

Constructing and Interpreting Graphs

> A well-designed graph summarizes information with a simple visual display—the old adage "a picture is worth a thousand words" might help you understand the popularity of visual images.

As you start to learn economics, it's important that you have a good grasp of how to make sense of data and how to present data clearly in visible form. Graphs are everywhere—on TV, on the Web, in newspapers and magazines, in economics textbooks. Why are graphs so popular?

A well-designed graph summarizes information with a simple visual display—the old adage "a picture is worth a thousand words" might help you understand the popularity of visual images. In this textbook, you will find many graphs, and you will see that they provide a way to supplement the verbal description of economic concepts.

To illustrate how we construct and interpret graphs, we will walk you through a recent study that we have conducted, presenting some data summaries along the way.

A Study About Incentives

Would you study harder for this economics class if we paid you $50 for earning an A? What if we raised the stakes to $500? Your first impulse might be to think "Well, sure . . . why not? That money could buy a new Kindle and maybe a ticket to a Beyoncé concert."

But as we have learned in Chapter 1, there are opportunity costs of studying more, such as attending fewer rock concerts or spending less time at your favorite coffee house chatting with friends. Such opportunity costs must be weighed against the benefits of earning an A in this course. You might conclude that because this question is hypothetical, anyway, there's no need to think harder about how you would behave.

But it might not be as imaginary as you first thought.

Over the past few years, thousands of students around the United States have actually been confronted with such an offer. In fact, Sally Sadoff, Steven Levitt, and John List carried out an experiment at two high schools in the suburbs of Chicago over the past several years in which they used incentives to change students' behavior. Such an experiment allows us to think about the relationship between two *variables*, such as how an increase in a financial reward affects student test scores. And it naturally leads to a discussion of cause and effect, which we have just studied in this chapter: we'll compare causal relationships between variables and consider simple correlations between variables. Both causation and correlation are powerful concepts in gaining an understanding of the world around us.

Experimental Design

There are two high schools in Chicago Heights, and both have a problem with student dropouts. In terms of dropouts, it is not uncommon for more than 50 percent of incoming ninth-graders to drop out before receiving a high school diploma. There are clearly problems in this school district, but they are not unique to Chicago Heights; many urban school districts face a similar problem.

How can economists help? Some economists, including one of the coauthors of this book, have devised incentive schemes to lower the dropout rates and increase academic achievement in schools. In this instance, students were *paid* for improved academic performance.[2]

Let's first consider the experiment to lower the dropout rate. Each student was randomly placed into one of the following three groups:

Control Group: No students received financial compensation for meeting special standards established by experimenters (which are explained below).

Treatment Group with Student Incentives: Students would receive $50 for each month the standards were met.

Treatment Group with Parent Incentives: Students' parents would receive $50 for each month the standards were met.

A student was deemed to have met the monthly standards if he or she:

1. did not have a D or F in any classes during that month,
2. had no more than one unexcused absence during that month,
3. had no suspensions during that month.

Describing Variables

Before we discover how much money these students actually made, let's consider more carefully the variables that we might be interested in knowing. As its name suggests, a variable is a factor that is likely to vary or change; that is, it can take different values in different situations. In this section, we show you how to use three different techniques to help graphically describe variables:

1. Pie charts
2. Bar graphs
3. Time series graphs

Pie Charts

A **pie chart** is a circular chart split into segments, with each showing the percentages of parts relative to the whole.

Understanding pie charts is a piece of cake. A **pie chart** is a circular chart split into segments to show the percentages of parts relative to the whole. Put another way, pie charts are used to describe how a single variable is broken up into different categories, or "slices." Economists often use pie charts to show important economic variables, such as sources of government tax revenue or the targets of government expenditure, which we discuss in Chapter 10.

For example, consider the race of the students in our experiment. In Exhibit 2A.1, we learn that 59 percent of ninth-graders in the experiment are African-American. We therefore differentiate 59 percent of our pie chart with the color blue to represent the proportion of African-Americans relative to all participants in the experiment. We see that 15 percent of the students are non-Hispanic whites, represented by the red piece of the pie. We continue

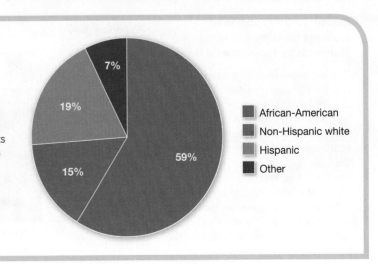

Exhibit 2A.1 Chicago Heights Experiment Participants by Race

The pie segments are a visual way to represent what fraction of all Chicago Heights high school students in the experiment are of the four different racial categories. Just as the numbers add up to 100 percent, so do all of the segments add up to the complete "pie."

African-American
Non-Hispanic white
Hispanic
Other

breaking down participation by race until we have filled in 100 percent of the circle. The circle then describes the racial composition of the participants in the experiment.

Bar Charts

A **bar chart** uses bars of different heights or lengths to indicate the properties of different groups.

Another type of graph that can be used to summarize and display a variable is a bar chart. A **bar chart** uses bars (no surprise there) of different heights or lengths to indicate the properties of different groups. Bar charts make it easy to compare a single variable across many groups. To make a bar chart, simply draw rectangles side-by-side, making each rectangle as high (or as long, in the case of horizontal bars) as the value of the variable it is describing.

For example, Exhibit 2A.2 captures the overall success rates of students in the various experimental groups. In the exhibit we have the **independent variable**—the variable that the experimenter is choosing (which treatment a student is placed in)—on the horizontal or x-axis. On the vertical or y-axis is the **dependent variable**—the variable that is potentially affected by the experimental treatment. In the exhibit, the dependent variable is the proportion of students meeting the academic standards. Note that 100 percent is a proportion of 1, and 30 percent is a proportion of 0.30.

An **independent variable** is a variable whose value does not depend on another variable; in an experiment it is manipulated by the experimenter.

A **dependent variable** is a variable whose value depends on another variable.

We find some interesting experimental results in Exhibit 2A.2. For instance, we can see from the bar graph that 28 percent of students in the Control group (students who received no incentives) met the standards. In comparison, 34.8 percent of students in the Parent Incentive group met the standards. This is a considerable increase in the number of students meeting the standards—important evidence that incentives can work.

Time Series Graphs

A **time series graph** displays data at different points in time.

With pie charts and bar graphs, we can summarize how a variable is broken up into different groups, but what if we want to understand how a variable changes over time? For instance, how did the proportion of students meeting the standards change over the school year? A **time series graph** can do the trick. A time series graph displays data at different points in time.

As an example, consider Exhibit 2A.3, which displays the proportion of students meeting the standards in each month in the Control and Parent Incentive groups. Keep in mind that although there are multiple months and groups, we are still measuring only a single variable—in this case, the proportion meeting the standard. As Exhibit 2A.3 makes clear, the number of students meeting the standard is higher in the Parent Incentive treatment group than in the Control group. But notice that the difference within the Parent Incentive and Control groups changes from month to month. Without a time series, we would not be able to appreciate these month-to-month differences and would not be able to get a sense for how the

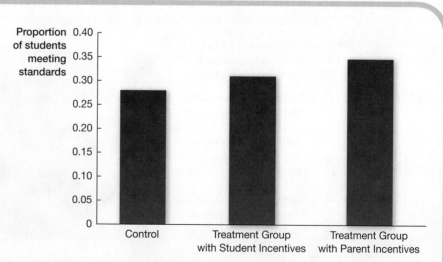

Exhibit 2A.2 Proportion of Students Meeting Academic Standards by Experimental Group

The bar chart facilitates comparing numbers across groups in the experiment. In this case, we can compare how different groups perform in terms of meeting academic standards by comparing the height of each bar. For example, the Parent Incentive group's bar is higher than the Control group's bar, meaning that a higher proportion of students in the Parent Incentives group met the standards than in the Control group.

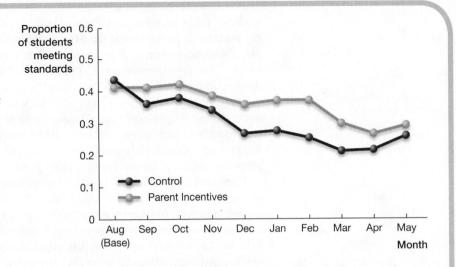

Exhibit 2A.3 Participants Meeting All Standards by Month

The time series graph takes the same information that was in the bar chart, but shows how it changes depending on the month of the school year during the experiment. The points are connected to more clearly illustrate the month-to-month trend. In addition, by using a different color or line pattern, we can represent two groups (Control and Parent Incentives) on the same graph, giving the opportunity to compare the two groups, just as with the bar chart from before.

effectiveness of the incentive varies over the school year. As you read this book, one important data property to recognize is how variables change over time; time series graphs are invaluable in helping us understand how a variable changes over time.

Scatter Plots

A **scatter plot** displays the relationship between two variables as plotted points of data.

You might ask yourself, without such monetary incentives is education worth it? In this chapter we showed you how wages and years of education are related. Another way to show the relationship is with a **scatter plot**. A scatter plot displays the relationship between two variables as plotted points of data. Exhibit 2A.4 shows the relationship between years of education and average weekly income across U.S. states in September of 2013. For example, the point 10.4 years of education and $800 in weekly earnings is from New Jersey. This means that the average years of education for New Jersey adults is 10.4 and the average weekly earnings is $800.

Cause and Effect

We've written a fair amount about causation and correlation in this chapter. Economists are much more interested in the former. Causation relates two variables in an active way—*a* causes *b* if, because of *a*, *b* has occurred.

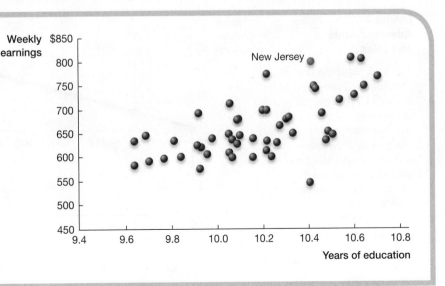

Exhibit 2A.4 Relationship Between Education and Earnings

Each point in Exhibit 2A.4 is the average years of education and the median weekly earnings for one state in the United States. The exhibit is constructed using Current Population Survey (CPS) data from September 2013. The exhibit highlights the positive relationship between years of education and weekly earnings.

For example, we could conclude in our experimental study that paying money for the students' performance *causes* them to improve their academic performance. This would not necessarily be the case if the experiment were not properly implemented—for example, if students were not randomly placed into control and treatment groups. For instance, imagine that the experimenters had placed all of the students who had achieved poorly in the past in the control group. Then the relatively poor performance of the control group might be due to the composition of students who were assigned to the control group, and not to the lack of payment. Any relationship between academic achievement and payment stemming from such an experiment could be interpreted as a correlation because all other things were not equal at the start of the experiment—the control group would have a higher proportion of low achievers than the other groups.

Fortunately, the Chicago Heights Experiment was implemented using the principle of randomization, discussed earlier in this chapter. The experimenters split students into groups randomly, so each experimental group had an equal representation of students and their attributes (variables such as average student intelligence were similar across groups). Because the only possible reason that a student would be assigned to one group instead of another was chance, we can argue that any difference between the groups' academic performance at the end of the experiment was due to the difference the experimental treatment imposed, such as differences in financial incentives.

This means that we can claim that the cause of the difference between the performance of the Student Incentive group and the Control group, for example, is that students in the Student Incentive group were given an incentive of $50 whereas students in the Control group received no incentive for improvement.

Correlation Does Not Imply Causality

Often, correlation is misinterpreted as causation. You should think of correlation between two variables as providing a reason to look for a causal relationship, but correlation should only be considered a first step to establishing causality. As an example, not long ago, a high-ranking marketing executive showed us Exhibit 2A.5 (the numbers are changed for confidentiality reasons). He was trying to demonstrate that his company's retail advertisements were effective in increasing sales: "It shows a clear positive relationship between ads and sales. When we placed 1,000 ads, sales were roughly $35 million. But see how sales dipped to roughly $20 million when we placed only 100 ads?! This proves that more advertisements lead to more sales."

Before discussing whether this exhibit proves causality, let's step back and think about the basic characteristics of Exhibit 2A.5. In such an exhibit we have:

1. The *x*-variable plotted on the horizontal axis, or *x*-axis; in our figure the *x*-variable is the number of advertisements.

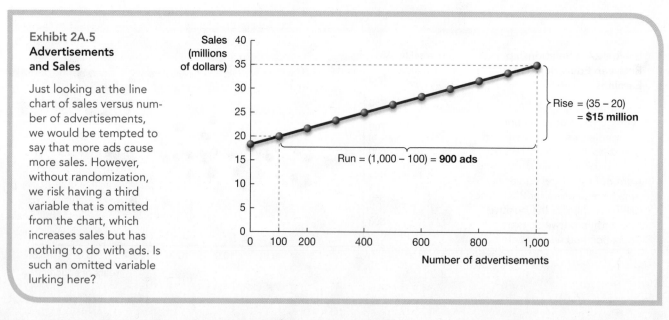

Exhibit 2A.5
Advertisements and Sales

Just looking at the line chart of sales versus number of advertisements, we would be tempted to say that more ads cause more sales. However, without randomization, we risk having a third variable that is omitted from the chart, which increases sales but has nothing to do with ads. Is such an omitted variable lurking here?

2. The *y*-variable plotted on the vertical axis, or *y*-axis; in our figure the *y*-variable is the sales in millions of dollars.

3. The origin, which is the point where the *x*-axis intersects the *y*-axis; both sales and the number of advertisements are equal to zero at the origin.

In the exhibit, the number of advertisements is the independent variable, and the amount of sales is the dependent variable. When the values of both variables increase together in the same direction, they have a positive relationship; when one increases and the other decreases, and they move in opposite directions, they have a negative relationship.

So in Exhibit 2A.5, we find a positive relationship between the two variables. What is the strength of that positive relationship? This is called the slope. The **slope** is the change in the value of the variable plotted on the *y*-axis divided by the change in the value of the variable plotted on the *x*-axis:

$$\text{Slope} = \frac{\text{Change in } y}{\text{Change in } x} = \frac{\text{Rise}}{\text{Run}}.$$

In this example, the increase in the number of advertisements from 100 to 1,000 was associated with an increase in sales from $20 million to $35 million. Thus, the rise, or the change in sales (*y*), is $15 million and the run, or change in *x*, is 900. Because both are rising (moving in the same direction), the slope is positive:

$$\text{Slope} = \frac{\$35,000,000 - \$20,000,000}{1000 \text{ ads} - 100 \text{ ads}} = \frac{\$15,000,000}{900 \text{ ads}} = \$16,667 \text{ per ad.}$$

Thus, our exhibit implies that one more advertisement is associated with $16,667 more in sales. But, does this necessarily mean that if the retailer increases the number of advertisements by one, this will cause sales to increase by $16,667?

Unfortunately, no. While it is tempting to interpret the sales increasing with ads as a causal relationship between the two variables, because the number of advertisements was not randomly determined with an experiment, we cannot be sure that this relationship is causal. In this case, the marketing executive forgot to think about *why* they so drastically increased their advertisement volume to begin with! They did so because of the holiday season, a time when sales would presumably have been high anyway.

So, after some further digging (we spare you the details), what the data actually say is that the retailer placed more ads during times of busy shopping (around Thanksgiving and in December), but that is exactly when sales were high—because of the holiday shopping season. Similar to what happened in the Walmart red/blue ad example in this chapter, once we recognize such seasonal effects and take them into account, the causal relationship between ads and sales disappeared!

This example shows that you should be careful when you connect a few points in a graph. Just because two variables move together (a correlation), they are not necessarily related in a causal way. They could merely be linked by another variable that is causing them both to increase—in this case, the shopping season.

To see the general idea of what is happening more clearly, let's instead graph the quantity of ice cream produced versus the number of monthly drownings in the United States. Using data across months in 2011, we constructed Exhibit 2A.6. In Exhibit 2A.6, we see that in months when ice cream production is relatively high, there are a lot of drownings. Likewise, in months when there is relatively little ice cream production, there are many fewer drownings. Does this mean that you should not swim after you eat ice cream?

Indeed, parents persuaded by such a chart might believe that it's causal, and never let their kids eat ice cream near swimming pools or lakes! But luckily for us ice cream lovers, there is an omitted variable lurking in the background. In the summertime, when it is hot people eat more ice cream *and* swim more. More swimming leads to more drowning. Even though people eat more ice cream cones in the summer, eating ice cream doesn't *cause* people to drown.

The **slope** is the change in the value of the variable plotted on the *y*-axis divided by the change in the value of the variable plotted on the *x*-axis.

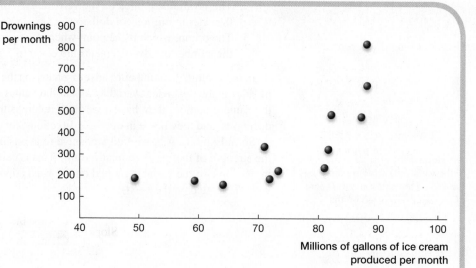

Exhibit 2A.6 Ice Cream Production and Drownings in the United States

We depict the relationship between monthly ice cream production and monthly drownings. Each of the 12 points represents a single month in 2011. Is this relationship causal or is there an omitted variable that is causing these two variables to move together? Hint: the point in the upper right-hand corner of the exhibit is July and the point in the lower left-hand corner of the exhibit is December!

Sources: Centers for Disease Control and Prevention, and Brian W. Gould, University of Wisconsin Dairy Marketing and Risk Management Program.

Just as a heightened shopping season was the omitted variable in the retailer advertisement example, here the omitted variable is heat—it causes us to swim more *and* to eat more ice cream cones. While the former causes more drownings (as we would all expect), the latter has nothing to do with drowning even though there is a positive correlation between the two as shown in Exhibit 2A.6.

Beyond an understanding of how to construct data figures, we hope that this appendix gave you an appreciation for how to interpret visual displays of data. An important lesson is that just because two variables are correlated—and move together in a figure—does not mean that they are causally related. Causality is the gold standard in the social sciences. Without understanding the causal relationship between two variables, we cannot reliably predict how the world will change when the government intervenes to change one of the variables. Experiments help to reveal causal relationships. We learned from the Chicago Heights experiment that incentives can affect student performance.

Appendix Key Terms

pie chart *p. 35*

bar chart *p. 36*

independent variable *p. 36*

dependent variable *p. 36*

time series graph *p. 36*

scatter plot *p. 37*

slope *p. 39*

Appendix Problems

A1. How would you represent the following graphically?

   a. Income inequality in the United States has increased over the past 10 years.

   b. All the workers in the manufacturing sector in a particular country fit into one (and only one) of the following three categories: 31.5 percent are high school dropouts, 63.5 percent have a regular high school diploma, and the rest have a vocational training certificate.

   c. The median income of a household in Alabama was $43,464 in 2012 and the median income of a household in Connecticut was $64,247 in 2012.

A2. Consider the following data that show the quantity of coffee produced in Brazil from 2004 to 2012.

Year	Production (in tons)
2004	2,465,710
2005	2,140,169
2006	2,573,368
2007	2,249,011
2008	2,796,927
2009	2,440,056
2010	2,907,265
2011	2,700,440
2012	3,037,534

   a. Plot the data in a time series graph.

   b. What is the mean quantity of coffee that Brazil produced from 2009 to 2011?

   c. In percentage terms, how much has the 2012 crop increased over the 2009–2011 mean?

A3. Suppose the following table shows the relationship between revenue that the Girl Scouts generate and the number of cookie boxes that they sell.

Number of Cookie Boxes	Revenue ($)
50	200
150	600
250	1000
350	1400
450	1800
550	2200

   a. Present the data in a scatter plot.

   b. Do the two variables have a positive relationship or do they have a negative relationship? Explain.

   c. What is the slope of the line that you get in the scatter plot? What does the slope imply about the price of a box of Girl Scout cookies?

3 Optimization: Doing the Best You Can

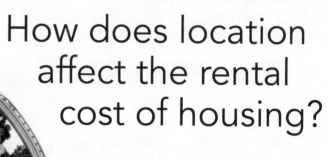

How does location affect the rental cost of housing?

Suppose you have just landed a job near the center of a city and you now need to decide where to live. If you live close to the city center, your round-trip commute will be 15 minutes. If you live in the distant suburbs, your round-trip commute will be 60 minutes. If there are lots of workers like you who work downtown, where will the apartments be relatively less expensive? How will you choose where to live? How should you make the best decision given the trade-offs you face?

In this chapter, we'll dig into the concept of optimization—choosing the best feasible option. You will learn how to optimize by using cost-benefit analysis. And we will apply this knowledge to a single example that we revisit throughout the chapter—choosing an apartment.

CHAPTER OUTLINE

⚙ When an economic agent chooses the best feasible option, she is optimizing.

⚙ *Optimization in levels* calculates the *total* net benefit of different alternatives and then chooses the best alternative.

⚙ *Optimization in differences* calculates the *change* in net benefits when a person switches from one alternative to another, and then uses these *marginal* comparisons to choose the best alternative.

⚙ Optimization in levels and optimization in differences give identical answers.

3.1 Two Kinds of Optimization: A Matter of Focus

In Chapter 1, we described economics as the study of choice. Economists believe that people usually make choices by trying to select the best feasible option, given the available information. In other words, people optimize. Recall that this is the first principle of economics.

> **Economists believe that optimization describes most of the choices that people, households, businesses, and governments make.**

Economists believe that optimization describes most of the choices that people, households, businesses, and governments make. To an economist, seemingly unrelated decisions—for example, where a college student will travel on spring break, which apartment a worker will rent, or what price Apple charges for an iPhone—are all connected by the unifying principle of optimization. Whatever choices people face, economists believe that they are likely to try to choose optimally. Economists don't assume that people *always* successfully optimize, but economists do believe that people try to optimize and usually do a pretty good job with whatever information they have.

In other words, economists believe that people's behavior is *approximated* by optimization. People aren't *perfect* optimizers because optimization is usually not easy, and it is often quite complex. To illustrate the complexity, consider the choice of an apartment. In large cities there are hundreds of thousands of rental apartments. And each apartment has many different characteristics to consider, such as location, views, and neighborhood amenities.

At the heart of this complexity are trade-offs. For example, how do you compare two apartments, one of which has the virtue of lower rent and one of which has the virtue of a shorter commute? How would you determine which apartment is a better choice for you? In this chapter, we are going to see how to optimally evaluate such trade-offs. We will introduce you to the most important optimization tools that economists use.

We have a lot to say about choosing a rental apartment, but we want you to remember that the choice of an apartment is just one illustration of the general concept of optimization.

Optimization in levels calculates the *total* net benefit of different alternatives and then chooses the best alternative.

Optimization in differences calculates the *change* in net benefits when a person switches from one alternative to another and then uses these marginal comparisons to choose the best alternative.

Optimization can be implemented using either of two techniques of cost-benefit analysis. Both techniques emphasize the concept of net benefit—benefit minus cost—which we introduced in Chapter 1.

1. **Optimization in levels** calculates the *total* net benefit of different alternatives, and then chooses the best alternative.
2. **Optimization in differences** calculates the *change* in net benefits when a person switches from one alternative to another and then uses these marginal comparisons to choose the best alternative.

As you'll see in the examples that follow, optimization in levels and optimization in differences should always yield answers in perfect agreement. These techniques are two sides of the same coin.

To get a taste for these two methods, take a peek at the Halloween bag after this paragraph. Think about how much you would enjoy eating the contents of this bag—the bag's benefit to you.

Now think about how much you would enjoy eating the contents of a second bag of candy:

In principle, the bag that offers the greatest total enjoyment is the bag you would choose if you were asked to choose between them. This kind of analysis is an example of optimization in levels. You calculated the benefit of each bag, and then you chose the best bag.

Now consider a second version of *exactly the same decision*. We'll take the same two bags of candy and put them side by side. We'll now reorder the candy bars to highlight the similarities and differences. In this case, all of the bars match except the first bag has a Milky Way and the second bag has a 3 Musketeers. Since all of the candy bars except one are the same, it's natural to focus on this one difference. Does this difference—3 Musketeers replacing Milky Way—increase the value to you of the Halloween Bag? If this one difference increases the value, you should pick the second bag. If this one difference decreases the value, you should pick the first bag.

This is an example of optimization in differences. Optimization in differences analyzes the *change* in net benefits when a person switches from one bag to another and then uses this marginal comparison to choose the best alternative.

We asked you to make the same choice twice—we used the same pair of bags in both choices. The first time you chose, you analyzed each of the Halloween bags in isolation. The second time you chose, you analyzed the difference between the two bags. *This change in focus is all that distinguishes optimization in levels and optimization in differences*. If you choose optimally, this shift in focus shouldn't have changed your final decision, but it might have speeded things along. In many cases, optimization in differences is faster and easier, because you focus on the *key* differences between the options.

Behavioral economics jointly analyzes the economic and psychological factors that explain human behavior.

CHOICE & CONSEQUENCE

Do People Really Optimize?

Economists believe that the framework of optimization approximates how people make most economic choices. But economists don't take optimization for granted. A large body of economic research studies the question: do people really optimize?

Thousands of research papers have been written on this question. This research has broadly concluded that optimization is a good model of economic behavior in most, though not all, situations. One field of economics—**behavioral economics**—identifies the specific situations in which people fail to optimize. Behavioral economists explain these optimization failures by combining economic and psychological theories of human behavior.

Several special situations are associated with behavior that is not optimal. For example, when people have self-control problems—like procrastination, or, far worse, addiction—optimization is not a good description of behavior.

People also tend to fail as optimizers when they are new to a task. For instance, the first time someone plays poker they tend to play poorly—they make rookie mistakes. On the other hand, optimization is a good description of choices when people have lots of experience. For example, as a consumer gains a few years of experience with a new credit card, they become half as likely to miss their monthly payment deadline.

Because people aren't born perfect optimizers, optimization is a useful skill to develop. Economists show people how to be better optimizers—such advice amounts to normative economic analysis.

We hope that you use the concept of optimization in two ways: it is a good description of the behavior of experienced decision makers and it provides an excellent toolbox for improving decision making that is not already optimal.

3.2 Optimization in Levels

Let's explore optimization in levels in more depth. To illustrate ideas, we return to our opening example in which you are an apartment hunter.

Imagine that you have narrowed your choices to four leading candidates—your "short list." Exhibit 3.1 summarizes this short list, including two key pieces of information for each apartment—the monthly rent and the amount of commuting time per month. In Exhibit 3.1, rents fall the farther you are from work. Later in this chapter, we explain why the economic model predicts this relationship between rents and distance from work. We'll also show you empirical evidence that confirms this prediction.

You might wonder about everything that was left out of the summary of information in Exhibit 3.1. What about *other* differences among these apartments, like how long it takes to walk to the neighborhood laundromat or whether there is a park nearby? We also omitted commuting costs other than time, like the direct dollar cost of public transportation or, if you drive yourself, gasoline and tolls. Shouldn't all of these considerations be part of the comparison?

To keep things simple, we will omit other factors for now, even though they *are* important in practice. We omit them to keep the calculations simple and so that the basic economic concepts are easier to see. As you'll discover in the problems at the end of the chapter, once you understand the basic ideas, it is easy to add more details. For now, we will assume that the four apartments—*Very Close, Close, Far,* and *Very Far*— are identical except for the differences in Exhibit 3.1.

Note, too, that we are focusing only on costs in this example—the cost of commuting time and the cost of rent. We are assuming that the benefits of these apartments are the same—for instance, proximity to shopping or public transportation. If the benefits are the same, then cost-benefit analysis becomes simpler. In normal cost-benefit analysis the decision maker finds the alternative with the highest value of *net benefit*, which is benefit minus cost. When the benefits are the same across all the alternatives, cost-benefit analysis simplifies to finding the alternative with the lowest cost. That's what we are going to do next.

Exhibit 3.1 Apartments on Your Short List, Which Differ Only on Commuting Time and Rent and Are Otherwise Identical

Many cities have a single central business district— which is often referred to as the city center—where lots of employers are concentrated.

In most cities, apartments near the city center cost more to rent than otherwise identical apartments that are far away. Why is this so?

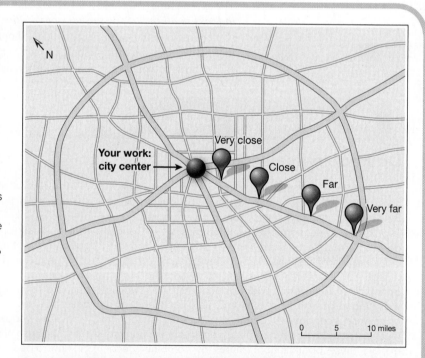

Apartment	Commuting Time (hours per month)	Rent ($ per month)
Very Close	5 hours	$1,180
Close	10 hours	$1,090
Far	15 hours	$1,030
Very Far	20 hours	$1,000

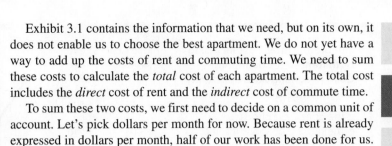

The proximity of local amenities should also go into a complete optimization analysis, because these amenities change the net benefits.

Exhibit 3.1 contains the information that we need, but on its own, it does not enable us to choose the best apartment. We do not yet have a way to add up the costs of rent and commuting time. We need to sum these costs to calculate the *total* cost of each apartment. The total cost includes the *direct* cost of rent and the *indirect* cost of commute time.

To sum these two costs, we first need to decide on a common unit of account. Let's pick dollars per month for now. Because rent is already expressed in dollars per month, half of our work has been done for us. All that remains is to translate the indirect cost—commuting time—into the same unit of measurement.

To do this, we use the concept of opportunity cost, which we introduced in Chapter 1. Let's begin by assuming that the opportunity cost of commuting time is $10/hour. This is the hourly value of the alternative activity that is crowded out when you spend more time commuting. The fact that it is a dollar value doesn't imply that this time would have been spent at work if it weren't spent commuting. An extra hour of time has value to you whatever you would do with that time, including napping, socializing, watching videos, taking longer showers, or working.

If the round-trip commute takes 20 hours per month and the opportunity cost of time is $10/hour, then the dollar cost of that commute is

$$\left(\frac{20 \text{ hours}}{\text{month}}\right)\left(\frac{\$10}{\text{hour}}\right) = \left(\frac{\$200}{\text{month}}\right).$$

The first term on the left is commute time per month, which is expressed in *hours* per month, just as it is in Exhibit 3.1. The term just before the equal sign is the opportunity cost of time, which is expressed as dollars per *hour*. The units in *hours* cancel, leaving a final cost expressed as dollars per month.

Now we are ready to rewrite Exhibit 3.1. Using the calculations that we just illustrated for 20 hours of monthly commuting time, we can calculate costs for a commute of any duration. Exhibit 3.2 reports this commuting cost in dollars per month for all four apartments.

Exhibit 3.2 gives us the answer to our optimization problem. Apartment Far is the best apartment for a consumer with an opportunity cost of time of $10/hour. This apartment has the lowest total cost —$1,180—taking into account both direct rent costs and indirect time costs of commuting.

We can also see this result by plotting the total costs. Exhibit 3.3 plots the total cost of each of the four apartments. It is easy to see that Apartment Far is the best. Economists call the best feasible choice the **optimum**, which you can see labeled on the total cost curve.

The **optimum** is the best feasible choice. In other words, the optimum is the optimal choice.

To sum up our discussion so far, optimization in levels has three steps:

1. Translate all costs and benefits into common units, like dollars per month.
2. Calculate the *total* net benefit of each alternative.
3. Pick the alternative with the highest net benefit.

Exhibit 3.2 Commuting Cost and Rental Cost Expressed in Common Units, Assuming an Opportunity Cost of Time of $10/hour

To optimize, it is necessary to convert all of the costs and benefits into common units. In this example, the common unit is $ per month. The optimum—in bold—is Apartment Far, which has the lowest total cost.

Apartment	Commuting Time (hours per month)	Commuting Cost ($ per month)	Rent ($ per month)	Total Cost: Rent + Commuting ($ per month)
Very Close	5 hours	$50	$1,180	$1,230
Close	10 hours	$100	$1,090	$1,190
Far	**15 hours**	**$150**	**$1,030**	**$1,180**
Very Far	20 hours	$200	$1,000	$1,200

Section 3.2 | Optimization in Levels **47**

Exhibit 3.3 Total Cost Including Both Rent and Commuting Cost, Assuming an Opportunity Cost of Time of $10/hour

If the consumer chooses optimally, he or she will select Apartment Far. This apartment has the lowest total cost, which is the sum of the direct rental cost and the indirect commuting cost (see breakdown in Exhibit 3.2). The commuting cost is calculated by using the consumer's opportunity cost of time, which is $10/hour in this example.

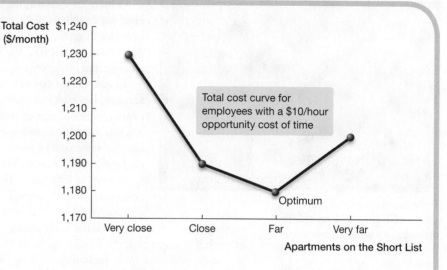

Comparative Statics

Comparative statics is the comparison of economic outcomes before and after some economic variable is changed.

Economic models predict how a person's choices change when something in the environment changes. **Comparative statics** is the comparison of economic outcomes before and after some economic variable is changed. For example, some consumers will choose to drive more expensive cars if their wealth increases. In this example, the car choice is the economic behavior that changes when the variable of consumer wealth changes.

We now return to the example in the previous subsection to conduct a comparative statics analysis. Specifically, we ask what happens when the opportunity cost of time is changed.

Recall that we studied the choice of an apartment assuming that the opportunity cost of time was $10/hour. Let's instead assume that the opportunity cost of time is $15/hour. Why might opportunity cost rise? For example, a freelance worker's opportunity cost of time would rise if their hourly wage rose.

How does this increase in the opportunity cost of time change the predicted behavior? Before we take you through it step-by-step, try to use your intuition. How would a change in the value of time affect the optimal decision of where to live? Should commuters with a higher value of time move closer to where they work or farther away?

To answer this question, we again need to translate the indirect cost—commuting time—into the same units as the direct cost of rent, which is dollars per month. Accordingly, we rewrite Exhibit 3.2, assuming instead a $15/hour opportunity cost of time. Exhibit 3.4 reports this commuting cost in dollars per month for all four apartments.

Exhibit 3.4 provides the answer to our new optimization problem. The best apartment for a consumer with an opportunity cost of time of $15/hour now shifts to Apartment Close

Exhibit 3.4 Commuting Cost and Rental Cost Expressed in Common Units, Assuming an Opportunity Cost of Time of $15/hour

To optimize, it is necessary to convert all of the costs and benefits into common units. In this example, the common unit is $ per month. The optimum—in bold—is Apartment Close, which has the lowest total cost.

Apartment	Commuting Time (hours per month)	Commuting Cost ($ per month)	Rent ($ per month)	Total Cost: Rent + Commuting ($ per month)
Very Close	5 hours	$75	$1,180	$1,255
Close	**10 hours**	**$150**	**$1,090**	**$1,240**
Far	15 hours	$225	$1,030	$1,255
Very Far	20 hours	$300	$1,000	$1,300

from Apartment Far. Apartment Close has the lowest total cost—$1,240—taking into account both direct rent costs and indirect time costs of commuting.

Exhibit 3.5 plots the total cost of each of the four apartments assuming a $15/hour opportunity cost of time. Apartment Close is the best choice—the optimum.

The higher opportunity cost of time caused the optimal choice to change from Apartment Far to Apartment Close. When the opportunity cost of time increases from $10/hour to $15/hour, it becomes more valuable for the commuter to choose an apartment that reduces the amount of time spent commuting. So the optimal choice switches from a relatively inexpensive apartment with a longer commute to a relatively expensive apartment with a shorter commute—Apartment Close.

Exhibit 3.6 takes the two different cost curves from Exhibits 3.3 and 3.5 and plots them in a single figure. The purple line represents the total cost curve for the commuter with an opportunity cost of $10/hour. The orange line represents the total cost curve for the commuter with an opportunity cost of $15/hour. Two key properties are visible in Exhibit 3.6.

1. The $10/hour cost curve lies below the $15/hour cost curve. The $10/curve has lower commuting costs for each apartment, so the total cost, which takes into account both the direct cost of rent and the indirect cost of commuting, is lower for all apartments.

2. The $10/hour curve has a minimum value for Apartment Far, while the $15/hour curve has a minimum value for Apartment Close. In other words, the optimal apartment switches from Apartment Far to Apartment Close when the opportunity cost of time rises from $10/hour to $15/hour.

Exhibit 3.5 Total Cost Including Both Rent and Commuting Cost, Assuming an Opportunity Cost of Time of $15/hour

Given the opportunity cost of $15/hour, the optimal choice is Apartment Close. This apartment has the lowest total cost, which is the sum of the direct rental cost and the indirect commute cost.

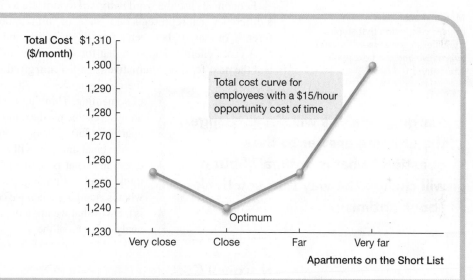

Exhibit 3.6 Total Cost Curves with the Opportunity Cost of Time Equal to $10/hour and $15/hour

As the opportunity cost of time rises from $10/hour to $15/hour, the optimal apartment shifts closer to the city center. Employees with a higher opportunity cost of time should choose the apartment with a shorter commute.

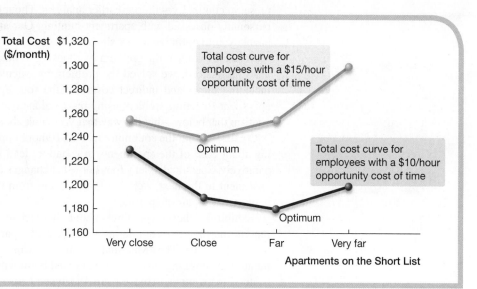

3.3 Optimization in Differences: Marginal Analysis

Until now, we have studied the apartment-hunting problem by calculating the *total* cost of each apartment. As explained above, we call that approach *optimization in levels*. We are now going to discuss an alternative optimization technique: *optimization in differences*. Optimization in differences is often faster to implement than optimization in levels, because optimization in differences focuses only on the way that alternatives differ.

Optimization in differences breaks an optimization problem down by thinking about how costs and benefits *change* as you hypothetically move from one alternative to another. For example, consider two alternative vacations at the same hotel in Miami: a four-day trip versus a five-day trip. Suppose that you are choosing between these two options. If you optimize in levels, you would evaluate the *total* net benefit of a four-day trip and compare it to the *total* net benefit of a five-day trip. Alternatively, you could think about only the *differences* between the two trips. In other words, you could think *only* about the costs and benefits of the *extra* day. An optimizer will take the five-day vacation if the benefit of vacationing for the fifth day exceeds the cost of the fifth day. In choosing between the four- and five-day options, the optimizer doesn't actually need to worry about the first four days, since those four days are shared by both the four-day trip and the five-day trip. The optimizer can focus on the one thing that differentiates the two vacations: the fifth day.

Economists use the word *marginal* to indicate a difference between alternatives, usually a difference that represents one "step" or "unit" more. The fifth day of vacation is the difference, or margin, between a four-day vacation and a five-day vacation.

Marginal analysis is a cost-benefit calculation that studies the difference between a feasible alternative and the next feasible alternative.

A cost-benefit calculation that focuses on the difference between a feasible alternative and the next feasible alternative is called **marginal analysis**. Marginal analysis compares the consequences—costs and benefits—of doing one step more of something. Thinking back to our apartment example, marginal analysis can be used to study the costs and benefits of moving one apartment farther away from the city center.

Marginal analysis will *never* change the ultimate answer to the question "what is optimal?" but it will change the way that you think about optimizing. Marginal analysis forces us to focus on what is changing when we compare alternatives. Marginal analysis is the way that we implement optimization in differences. Marginal analysis is one of the most important concepts in economics.

> **Marginal analysis will *never* change the ultimate answer to the question "what is optimal?" but it will change the way that you think about optimizing.**

Marginal Cost

Let's return to the problem of choosing the best apartment. We go back to this problem to preserve continuity with our earlier analysis. Though it may appear otherwise, we are not personally obsessed with apartment-hunting. Our analysis illustrates techniques that will enable you to optimize in any situation.

When we studied the problem of choosing a rental apartment, we did *not* use marginal analysis. Instead, we solved the problem by calculating and comparing the *total* cost—including direct and indirect costs—of the four apartments. We'll now solve the same apartment-selection problem using marginal analysis. The optimum won't change—we'll confirm that below—but the way that you think about the problem will.

Again consider the commuter with a $10/hour opportunity cost of time. Instead of thinking about each of the apartments in isolation, let's now think about the apartments comparatively. Specifically, let's focus on what changes as we hypothetically "move" from one apartment to the next, stepping farther away from the city center. What is the difference between each pair of apartments?

Exhibit 3.7 helps you think about these changes. The "Commuting Cost" column reports the monthly commuting cost for each apartment assuming a $10/hour opportunity cost of time. The "Marginal Commuting Cost" column reports the value of the extra monthly commuting time that is generated by moving one apartment farther from the city center. For example, to move from *Apartment Close* to *Apartment Far* generates additional

Exhibit 3.7 Relationship Between Levels and Differences (Margins), Assuming a $10/hour Opportunity Cost of Time

We can break the problem down by studying the marginal costs of moving farther from the city center. At what point does it make sense to stop moving farther from the city center?

Apartment	Commuting Cost	Marginal Commuting Cost	Rent Cost	Marginal Rent Cost	Total Cost	Marginal Total Cost
Very Close	$50		$1,180		$1,230	
		$50		−$90		−$40
Close	$100		$1,090		$1,190	
		$50		−$60		−$10
Far	$150		$1,030		$1,180	
		$50		−$30		$20
Very Far	$200		$1,000		$1,200	

Marginal cost is the extra cost generated by moving from one feasible alternative to the next feasible alternative.

commuting costs of $50 per month. In other words, the "Marginal Commuting Cost" column reports the difference between two commuting costs in adjacent positions on the list. In this particular example, the marginal commuting cost is always the same—the commuting cost rises by the same amount with each move farther away from the city center. This won't generally be the case, but we've set it up this way in this problem to keep things simple. In general, **marginal cost** is the extra cost generated by moving from one feasible alternative to the next feasible alternative.

Now turn to the column labeled "Rent Cost," which reports the monthly rent for each apartment. The "Marginal Rent Cost" column reports the change in the rent cost generated by moving from one apartment to the next apartment—one step farther from the city center. For example, to move from *Apartment Very Close* to *Apartment Close* would save you $90 per month, so the marginal rent cost is a negative number, −$90. Likewise, if you moved from *Apartment Close* to *Apartment Far*, you would save an additional $60 per month, so the marginal rent cost is −$60.

Finally, we'd like to know the marginal value of total cost. It turns out that we can calculate the marginal value of total cost in two alternative ways. First, we can add up the marginal commuting cost and the marginal rent cost to obtain the marginal total cost. For example, look at the first row of marginal cost numbers and confirm that $50 + −$90 = −$40. In other words, a move from *Apartment Very Close* to *Apartment Close* raises commuting costs by $50 and changes rent by −$90, producing a combined change of −$40.

Alternatively, we could calculate total cost itself. This is done in the column labeled Total Cost. For instance, for *Apartment Very Close,* the commuting cost is $50 and the rent cost is $1,180, so the total cost is $1,230. For *Apartment Close*, the commuting cost is $100 and the rent cost is $1,090, so the total cost is $1,190. Total cost *falls* by $40 when we move from *Apartment Very Close*, with total cost $1,230, to *Apartment Close*, with total cost $1,190.

Both methods confirm that the marginal total cost is −$40 when moving from *Apartment Very Close* to *Apartment Close*.

Marginal commuting cost + Marginal rent cost = $50 + −$90 = −$40

Total cost of *Close* − Total cost of *Very Close* = $1,190 − $1,230 = −$40

The fact that we calculated −$40 in both cases is no accident. The exact match reflects the fact that it doesn't matter how we decompose costs to calculate marginal total cost. It doesn't matter whether we calculate marginal total cost by summing marginal costs category by category or whether we calculate marginal total cost by subtracting the *total* cost of one apartment from the other. Because the answer is the same, you should calculate marginal total cost whichever way is easier for you.

The last column of Exhibit 3.7—marginal total cost—contains all of the information that we need to optimize. Start at the top of the column and think about how each "move" away from the city center affects the worker. The first move, from *Very Close* to *Close*, has a marginal cost of −$40 per month, so it is cost cutting. That move is worth it.

The second move, from *Close* to *Far*, has a marginal cost of −$10 per month. That move is also cost cutting and consequently it is also worth taking.

The third move, from *Far* to *Very Far*, has a marginal cost of $20 per month. So that move is not worth taking, because it represents an increase in costs.

To sum up, the first two moves paid for themselves and the final move did not. *Very Far* can't be an optimum, since moving from *Far* to *Very Far* made the worker worse off. *Very Close* can't be an optimum, since moving from *Very Close* to *Close* made the worker better off. Finally, *Close* can't be an optimum, since moving from *Close* to *Far* made the worker better off.

We conclude that *Far* is the optimum—the best feasible choice. Moving from *Close to Far* made the worker better off. But moving from *Far* to *Very Far* made the worker worse off. *Far* is the only apartment that satisfies the following property: moving to the apartment makes the worker better off and moving away from the apartment makes the worker worse off. In other words, *Far* has the virtue that it is a better option than its "neighbors."

The optimizer's goal is to make himself as well off as possible. An optimum is the point at which the optimizer cannot do any better. The apartment that is better than all its feasible alternatives is also the apartment that minimizes total costs. This is an example of the **Principle of Optimization at the Margin**, which states that an *optimal* feasible alternative has the property that moving to it makes you better off and moving away from it makes you worse off.

It helps to visualize these ideas. Exhibit 3.8 plots the total cost of each apartment and the marginal cost of moving one apartment at a time farther away from the center of town. For instance, moving from *Very Close* to *Close* lowers total cost by $40. The dashed red line shows a change of −$40 between the total cost of *Very Close* and the total cost of *Close*.

Optimization using marginal analysis will always pick out a single optimal alternative when the total cost curve has the bowl-like shape in Exhibit 3.8. Where the *total* cost (in purple) is falling, marginal cost (in red) will be negative and marginal analysis will recommend moving farther away from the city center, thereby lowering total cost. After total cost bottoms out, marginal cost will afterwards be positive, implying that the renter should move no farther out.

When the total cost curve is *not* bowl-shaped, the analysis gets more complicated, but even in this case, optimization in differences ultimately identifies the same optimum as optimization in levels.

Since optimization in levels and optimization in differences pick out the same optimum, you can use whichever method is easier for the particular problem that you are

The **Principle of Optimization at the Margin** states that an optimal feasible alternative has the property that moving to it makes you better off and moving away from it makes you worse off.

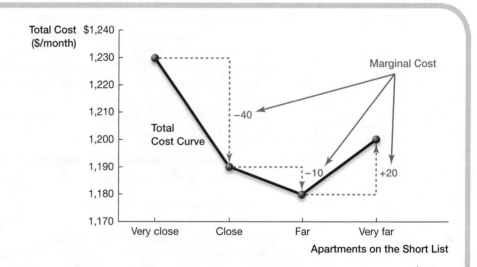

Exhibit 3.8 Total Cost of Each Apartment and the Marginal Cost of Moving Between Apartments, Assuming an Opportunity Cost of $10/hour

The cost-minimizing choice is Apartment Far. We can see this by looking at total cost (in purple) or by looking at marginal cost (in red). Total cost is falling when marginal cost is negative. Total cost is rising when marginal cost is positive. Apartment Far is the only apartment that is better than all of its neighbors. Marginal cost is negative when moving to Apartment Far and marginal cost is positive when moving away from Apartment Far. Thus, Apartment Far is the only apartment that satisfies the Principle of Optimization at the Margin.

analyzing. However, it is important to understand why economists mostly use optimization in differences—in other words, optimization at the margin. Optimization at the margin is simple because you can ignore everything about two alternatives that are being compared except the particular attributes that are different. Marginal analysis reminds you not to analyze information that will turn out to be irrelevant to your decision.

To sum up, optimization in differences has three steps:

1. Translate all costs and benefits into common units, like dollars per month.
2. Calculate the marginal consequences of moving between alternatives.
3. Apply the Principle of Optimization at the Margin by choosing the best alternative with the property that moving to it makes you better off and moving away from it makes you worse off.

Evidence-Based Economics

Q: How does location affect the rental cost of housing?

Throughout this chapter, we've been assuming that rental prices are higher near the city center, holding the quality of the apartment fixed. You may have wondered whether we had our facts right.

People often imagine *dingy* apartments downtown and *nice* houses out in the country. If we want to isolate the effect of location, we need to hold apartment quality constant and vary *only* location.

Economists Beth Wilson and James Frew assembled a database that contains information on many apartments that were available for rent in Portland, Oregon.[1] They used statistical techniques to effectively compare apartments near the city center to similar apartments that were farther away. Such analysis reveals a strong negative relationship between distance and rent, which is plotted in Exhibit 3.9.

Exhibit 3.9 was calculated for apartments that all have the following features—one bedroom, one bathroom, laundry unit in the apartment, covered parking, cable, and air-conditioning—and have none of the following features—a fireplace, access to an exercise room, or access to a pool. The analysis compares the rent of these apartments, holding all of their features constant *except* for the distance to the city center.

Exhibit 3.9 Apartment Rent in Portland, Oregon, Depends on Distance from the City Center

This plot is drawn for apartments that are identical, except for their distance from the city center. The blue line is the approximate location of a ring of highways that encircle most of Portland.

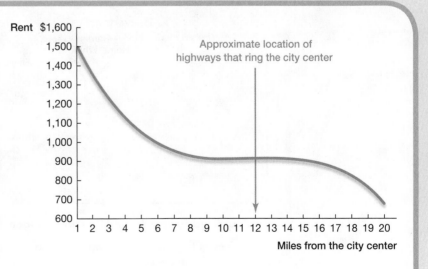

Evidence-Based Economics *(Continued)*

Exhibit 3.9 confirms that proximity to the city center raises rents. The closer you get to the city, the higher the rent goes. For example, at a distance of 6 miles from the city center, the typical rent for an apartment with the specified features is nearly $1,000. For an apartment that is 1 mile from the city center, the rent for the "same" apartment is $1,500.

Exhibit 3.9 also displays a noticeable flattening around 12 miles from the city center. Can you guess why rents stop changing in this region? The answer follows from considerations about the opportunity cost of time and the structure of Portland's highway system. Like most large cities, Portland has a ring of fast highways—a "ring road"—about 12 miles from the center of the city. People who live within a few miles of the ring road have the advantage of being near a highway system that speeds up travel time. Because of the ring roads, commute times change relatively little as you go from 9 miles to 14 miles away from the city center.

Scarcity, Prices, and Incentives

We can now come full circle and return to an important question that we asked previously. *Why* do rental prices fall as you move farther from the city center? What does this have to do with the topic of this chapter: optimization?

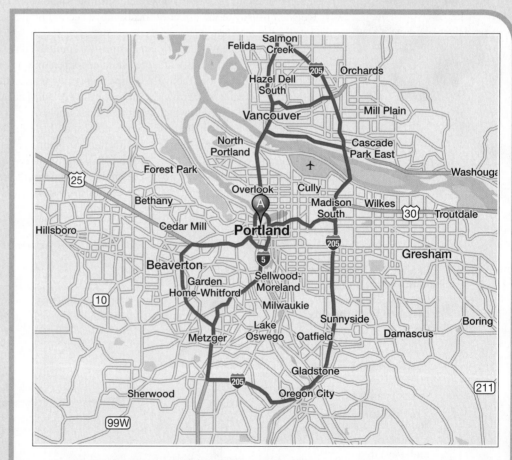

Ring Road System Around Portland, Oregon

Like most large cities, Portland has a ring of fast highways—a "ring road"—about 12 miles from the center of the city.

Mt. Hood rises to the east of Portland and presents a beautiful view to apartment dwellers lucky enough to face that way. But not everyone has such spectacular views. Some apartments are on low floors and some apartments face the less awesome views to the west. Eastern-facing apartments on high floors rent for about 20 percent more than similar apartments that don't have the killer views. To an economist, this price differential is a good way of measuring the dollar value of a scarce resource: a room with a view.

We've shown that many optimizing commuters would love to live in the city center *if* the rental prices were the same downtown as they are in distant neighborhoods. But everyone can't live downtown. Everyone can't have a short commute. There just aren't enough downtown apartments for everyone who would like one. That is an example of economic scarcity—one of the first concepts we studied in Chapter 1.

The market for apartments resolves the question of who gets to have the short commute. Markets allow optimizing landlords and optimizing renters to freely negotiate the rental price of an apartment. In the marketplace, the rental price of apartments is determined by market forces rather than by politicians or regulators. The optimizers with the highest opportunity cost of time push up the rental price of apartments with the shortest commutes.

Market prices—here the rental price of apartments—provide incentives that implicitly allocate economic resources. As the price of downtown apartments rises, only workers with the highest opportunity cost of time will be willing to rent them. Most other workers will choose to move farther away and accept the consequences of a longer commute. That's a trade-off—more time commuting in exchange for a lower monthly rent.

Market prices have the effect of allocating the downtown apartments to the people who are willing to pay the most for them. This allocation mechanism implies that mostly highly paid workers—and others with a high opportunity cost of time—tend to rent the apartments with the best locations.

Some critics of markets complain that markets are unfair—why should the highest-paid workers also get the apartments with the best locations? The defenders of markets respond that people are paying for the privilege of having a good apartment—the apartments with the best locations have higher rents—and the market allocation mechanism guarantees that people who are willing to pay the most for the best apartments get them.

Understanding how the market allocation process works is the subject of our next chapter and many other chapters in this book. As we begin to discuss these issues, we want you to think about how society *should* determine the price of scarce resources, like downtown apartments. Should we have a system that allows optimizing landlords and optimizing renters to negotiate freely to determine rental prices for apartments? What if this produces a system in which the highest-paid workers are the only ones who can afford to live in the most convenient apartments? Is that inequitable? Can you think of a better way to allocate apartments?

Question	Answer	Data	Caveat
How does location affect the rental cost of housing?	In most cities, though not all, the farther you are from the city center, the more rental costs fall (holding apartment quality fixed). For example, in Portland, Oregon, rents fall by 33 percent as you move from the city center to otherwise identical apartments 6 miles out of town.	Rental prices in Portland, Oregon.	Though the analysis uses special statistical techniques to compare similar apartments located at different distances from the city center, it is possible that some important apartment characteristics were not held fixed in the comparison. This would bias the calculations.

Summary

☀ Economists believe that optimization describes, or at least approximates, many of the choices economic agents make. Economists believe that most people optimize most of the time. But economists don't take optimization for granted. Economic research attempts to answer the question: Do people optimize? Using optimization to describe and predict behavior is an example of positive economic analysis.

☀ Optimization also provides an excellent toolbox—especially, cost-benefit analysis and marginal analysis—for improving decision making that is not already optimal. Using optimization to improve decision making is an example of normative economic analysis.

☀ Optimization in levels has three steps: (1) translate all costs and benefits into common units, like dollars per month; (2) calculate the *total* net benefit of each alternative; (3) pick the alternative with the highest net benefit.

☀ Optimization in differences analyzes the change in net benefits when you switch from one alternative to another. The most important example is marginal analysis, a cost-benefit calculation that focuses on the difference between one alternative and the next alternative. Marginal analysis compares the consequences of doing one step more of something. Marginal cost is the extra cost generated by moving from one alternative to the next alternative.

☀ Optimization in differences has three steps: (1) translate all costs and benefits into common units, like dollars per month; (2) calculate the marginal consequences of moving between alternatives; (3) apply the Principle of Optimization at the Margin by choosing the best alternative with the property that moving to it makes you better off and moving away from it makes you worse off.

☀ Optimization in levels and optimization in differences yield answers in agreement. These techniques are two sides of the same coin.

Key Terms

optimization in levels *p. 44*
optimization in differences *p. 44*
behavioral economics *p. 45*

optimum *p. 47*
comparative statics *p. 48*
marginal analysis *p. 50*

marginal cost *p. 51*
Principle of Optimization at the
  Margin *p. 52*

Questions

All questions are available in MyEconLab for practice and instructor assignment.

1. What is meant by optimization? How does optimization in levels differ from optimization in differences?

2. Does the principle of optimization imply that people always make the best choices?

3. What is meant by comparative statics? Explain with an example.

4. Some people choose to live close to the city center; others choose to live away from the city center and take a longer commute to work every day. Does picking a location with a longer commute imply a failure to optimize?

5. Suppose you had information on the sales of similar homes just east and just west of the boundary between two school districts. How could you use those data to estimate the value parents place on the quality of their children's schools?

6. There is a proverb "anything worth doing is worth doing well." Do you think an economist would agree with this proverb?

7. Why do economists mostly use optimization in differences, as opposed to optimization in levels?

8. Explain how the market for apartments allocates the scarce supply of apartments near the city center.

9. Is optimization analysis positive or normative, or both? Explain your answer.

Problems

All problems are available in MyEconLab for practice and instructor assignment.

1. Suppose the government in a certain country wants to reduce urban sprawl. What measures could it take to ensure that people choose to live closer to the central business district? (Urban sprawl refers to the development of residential and commercial areas in the suburbs around the periphery of a city. One of the main problems with urban sprawl is that it leads to increased traffic congestion and air pollution as commuters travel to the city every day.)

2. Suppose you are accepted at all of the three business schools to which you applied. Consider the factors that could matter when it comes to choosing a business school.

    a. How would you go about making an optimal decision about which school to attend?

    b. Suppose you have to give up a job that pays you $40,000 a year to attend business school. How would this affect your calculation of which business school to attend?

3. Determine if the following statements better describe optimization in levels or optimization in differences.

    a. John is attempting to decide on a movie. He determines that the new Batman movie provides him with $5 more of a benefit than the new Spiderman movie.

    b. Marcia finds that the net benefit of flying from Chicago to Honolulu on a non-stop United Airlines flight is $400, and the net benefit for the same trip flying on a one-stop American Airlines flight is $200.

    c. Nikki decided to take the first available parking space as she entered the student lot. She felt that the first available space had a $5 premium compared with all other possible spaces because she did not want to risk being late for her exam.

    d. Reagan determined that the net benefit of taking the combination of two lecture courses and an online lecture course was $100. The same three courses online gave her a net benefit of $80, and all three in a lecture-based format gave her a net benefit of $90.

4. You are taking two courses this semester, biology and chemistry. You have quizzes coming up in both classes. The following table shows your grade on each quiz for different numbers of hours studying for each quiz. (For the purposes of this problem, assume that each hour of study time can't be subdivided.) For instance, the table implies that if you studied one hour on Chemistry and two hours on Biology you would get a 77 on Chemistry and a 74 on Biology.

Hours of Study	Chemistry	Biology
0	70	60
1	77	68
2	82	74
3	85	78

Your goal is to maximize your average grade on the two quizzes. Use the idea of optimization in differences to decide how much time you would spend studying for each quiz if you had only one hour in *total* to prepare for the two exams (in other words, you will study for one hour on one exam and zero hours on the other exam). How would you allocate that single hour of study time across the two subjects? Now repeat the analysis assuming that you have two hours in *total* to prepare for the two exams. How would you allocate those two hours across the two subjects? Finally, repeat the analysis assuming that you have three hours in *total* to prepare for the two exams. How would you allocate those three hours across the two subjects?

5. Your total benefits from consuming different quantities of gas each week are shown in the following table.

Gallons per Week	Total Benefit (dollar equivalent)	Marginal Benefit
0	0	X
1	8	
2	15	
3	21	
4	26	
5	30	
6	33	
7	35	
8	36	

a. Complete the marginal benefit column starting with the step from 0 gallons to 1 gallon per week.

b. The price of gasoline is $4 per gallon. Use the Principle of Optimization at the Margin to find an optimal number of gallons of gas to consume each week.

c. Some people have suggested a tax of $2 per gallon of gasoline as a way to reduce global warming. (Burning fossil fuels such as gasoline releases greenhouse gases, which are a cause of global warming.) Suppose the price of gasoline (including the tax) rises to $6 per gallon. Use the Principle of Optimization at the Margin to find an optimal number of gallons of gasoline given this new tax on gasoline.

6. Scott loves to go to baseball games, especially home games of the Cincinnati Reds. All else equal, he likes to sit close to the field. He also likes to get to the stadium early to watch batting practice. The closer he parks to the stadium the more batting practice he is able to watch (the garages all open simultaneously). Find Scott's optimal seat type and parking garage using the information that follows.

Location/Seat	Price	Scott's Value of View
Diamond Seats	$235	$200
Club Home	$95	$130
Club Seating	$85	$125
Scout Box	$79	$120
Scout	$69	$100

Parking Location	Parking Fee (game night)	Missed Batting Practice	Benefit of Arrival Time
Westin parking garage	$5	60 min	$0
Fountain Square South Garage	$10	50 min	$10
West river parking	$17	25 min	$35
East river parking	$25	10 min	$50
Under stadium parking	$45	0 min	$60

7. Suppose the total benefit and total cost to society of various levels of pollution reduction are as follows:

(1) Pollution Reduction	(2) Total Benefit	(3) Total Cost	(4) Total Net Benefit	(5) Marginal Benefit	(6) Marginal Cost
0	0	0		X	X
1	20	9			
2	38	20			
3	54	33			
4	68	48			
5	80	65			
6	90	84			

a. Complete column (4).

b. Use optimization in levels to show that if the U.S. Environmental Protection Agency (EPA) wants to maximize total net benefit, then it should require 3 units of pollution reduction.

c. Complete columns (5) and (6), starting with the step from 0 to 1 unit of pollution reduction.

d. Show that the Principle of Optimization at the Margin would also tell the EPA to require 3 units of reduction.

8. Assume that your country's income tax structure has the following tax rates: if your income is $30,000 or less you pay no income tax; if your income is above $30,000, you pay 30 percent of the amount above $30,000. And so, for example, someone who earns $60,000 would pay 30% × ($60,000 − $30,000) = $9,000.

Your marginal tax rate is defined as the taxes you pay if you earn one more dollar. Your average tax rate is defined as the total taxes you pay divided by your income. And so, to continue with this example, someone who earns $60,000 would have a marginal tax rate of 30 percent and an average tax rate of $9,000/$60,000 = 15%.

You have three alternatives. You could not work at all, you could work half time, or you could work full time. If you do not work at all, you will earn $0; if you work half-time you will earn $30,000; and if you work full-time, you will earn $60,000. Any time you do not work, you can spend surfing. You love to surf: surfing full-time is worth $50,000 per year to you, surfing half-time is worth $25,000 per year to you, and not surfing at all is worth nothing to you. As you are making your decision about how much to work, should you pay attention to your average tax rate or to your marginal tax rate? Explain your answer carefully.

9. Consider the total cost of traveling from point A to point B. The cost of traveling by car would include the cost of gasoline and the opportunity cost of time; the cost of hopping on a bus would include the bus ticket and the opportunity cost of time. Assume that the bus ticket costs less than the gasoline. Does this imply that using a bus to get to the destination involves lower total costs than getting there by car? What if the bus doesn't take the fastest route from point A to point B?

4 Demand, Supply, and Equilibrium

How much more gasoline would people buy if its price were lower?

During 2013, the retail price of a gallon of gasoline in the United States fluctuated between $3 and $4 per gallon. How much gasoline do you buy now? How much would you buy if the price were lower—say, $1 per gallon? How low would it have to go to tempt you to take lots of road trips? What if the price were $0.04 per gallon, so that gasoline was practically free? Amazingly, that's what Venezuelans paid for gas in 2013, due to an extraordinary government subsidy.

In this chapter, we study how buyers and sellers respond to the changing price of goods and services, and we use the energy market and gasoline as our leading example. How does the price of gas affect the decisions of gas buyers, like households, and gas sellers, like ExxonMobil? How do the decisions of buyers and sellers jointly determine the price of gas when it isn't dictated by government policies?

CHAPTER **OUTLINE**

KEY IDEAS

☀ In a perfectly competitive market, (1) sellers all sell an identical good or service, and (2) any individual buyer or any individual seller isn't powerful enough on his or her own to affect the market price of that good or service.

☀ The demand curve plots the relationship between the market price and the quantity of a good demanded by buyers.

☀ The supply curve plots the relationship between the market price and the quantity of a good supplied by sellers.

☀ The competitive equilibrium price equates the quantity demanded and the quantity supplied.

☀ When prices are not free to fluctuate, markets fail to equate quantity demanded and quantity supplied.

4.1 Markets

Every year over one billion drivers pull into gas stations around the world. These drivers almost never find that gas stations are "sold out." Most of the time, it takes less than 10 minutes to fill the tank and pull back on the road.

The efficiency of this system is amazing. Nobody tells the companies that run the gas stations how many drivers to expect, and nobody tells the drivers where to fill their tanks. No "fill 'er up" tickets are presold by Ticketmaster or Live Nation. But somehow, there is almost always enough gas for every driver who wants to fill the tank. Drivers get the gas they are willing to pay for, and gasoline companies make enough money to pay their employees and send dividends to their shareholders.

This chapter is about how the gasoline market and other markets like it work. A **market** is a group of economic agents who are trading a good or service, and the rules and arrangements for trading. Agricultural and industrial goods like wheat, soybeans, iron, and coal are all traded on markets. A market may have a specific physical location—like Holland's Aalsmeer Flower Auction—or not. For example, the market for gasoline is dispersed—located on every corner you find a gas station. Likewise, Monster.com (a Web-based job market) operates wherever there's a computer and an Internet connection. To an economist, dating Web sites like okcupid.com or christianmingle.com are markets, too.

We focus the discussion on markets in which all exchanges occur voluntarily at flexible prices. This chapter explains how markets use prices to allocate goods and services. Prices act as a selection device that encourages trade between the sellers who can produce goods at low cost and the buyers who place a high value on the goods.

We will illustrate all of this by studying the market for gasoline, which is refined from crude oil, as well as the broader market for energy. You'll see that the price of gasoline is set in a way

A **market** is a group of economic agents who are trading a good or service, and the rules and arrangements for trading.

Prices act as a selection device that encourages trade between the sellers who can produce goods at low cost and the buyers who place a high value on the goods.

This warehouse in Aalsmeer, Holland, covers an area larger than 100 football fields and hosts thousands of daily auctions for wholesale (bulk) flowers.

If all sellers and all buyers face the same price, it is referred to as the **market price.**

In a **perfectly competitive market,** (1) sellers all sell an identical good or service, and (2) any individual buyer or any individual seller isn't powerful enough on his or her own to affect the market price of that good or service.

A **price-taker** is a buyer or seller who accepts the market price—buyers can't bargain for a lower price and sellers can't bargain for a higher price.

When two gas stations are located at the same intersection, their prices tend to be very close, and sometimes are exactly the same.

that implies that gas stations are ready to sell a quantity of gasoline that is equal to the quantity of gasoline that drivers want to buy.

Competitive Markets

Think of a city filled with hundreds of gas stations, each of which has an independent owner. The gas station on your block would lose most of its business if the owner started charging $1 more per gallon than all of the other stations. Likewise, you wouldn't be able to fill your tank if you drove around town offering gas station attendants $1 less per gallon than they were charging their other customers. Gas station attendants usually don't cut special deals with individual customers. Drivers of Cadillacs and Kias pay the same price for a gallon of regular unleaded.

To prove that pleading poverty and haggling for a better gas price won't work, try bargaining for a discount the next time you need to fill your tank. Try this only if you have enough gas to reach the next station.

If all sellers and all buyers face the same price, that price is referred to as the **market price.** In a **perfectly competitive market,** (1) sellers all sell an identical good or service, and (2) any individual buyer or any individual seller isn't powerful enough on his or her own to affect the market price. This implies that buyers and sellers are all **price-takers.** In other words, they accept the market price and can't bargain for a better price.

Very few, if any, markets are perfectly competitive. But economists try to understand such markets anyway. At first this sounds kind of nutty. Why would economists study a thing that rarely exists in the world? The answer is that although few, if any, markets are perfectly competitive, many markets are nearly perfectly competitive. Many gas stations do have nearby competitors—often right across the street— that prevent them from charging more than the market price. There are some gas stations that don't have such nearby competitors—think of an isolated station on a country road—but such examples are the exception. If sellers have nearly identical goods and most market participants face lots of competition, then the perfectly competitive model is a good approximation of how actual markets work.

On the other hand, there are some markets in which large market participants—like Microsoft in the software market—can single-handedly control market prices; we'll come to markets like that in later chapters.

In this chapter, our goal is to understand the properties of markets that have flexible prices and are perfectly competitive (identical goods and market participants who can't influence the market price). Along the way, we'll ask three questions.

1. How do buyers behave?
2. How do sellers behave?
3. How does the behavior of buyers and sellers jointly determine the market price and the quantity of goods transacted?

Each of the next three sections addresses one of these fundamental questions.

4.2 How Do Buyers Behave?

We start by studying the behavior of buyers. We assume that these buyers are price-takers: they treat the market price as a take-it-or-leave-it offer and don't try to haggle to lower the price. We want to study the relationship between the price of a good and the amount of the good that buyers are willing to purchase. At a given price, the amount of the good or service that buyers are willing to purchase is called the **quantity demanded**.

> **Quantity demanded** is the amount of a good that buyers are willing to purchase at a given price.

To illustrate the concept of quantity demanded, think about your own buying behavior. When gas prices rise, do you tend to buy less gas? For example, if gas prices rise, a student who lives off campus might bike to school instead of driving. She might join a carpool or shift to public transportation. If gas prices rise high enough, she might sell her gas guzzler altogether. Even a student who lives on campus might cut back her gasoline consumption. During spring break, she might take the bus from Boston to her parents' home in Washington, D.C., rather than driving her car.

Let's quantify these kinds of adjustments. Take Chloe, a typical consumer who responds to increases in gasoline prices by reducing her purchases of gasoline. Chloe may not be able to adjust her gasoline consumption immediately, but in the long run she will use less gas if the price of gas increases—for instance, by switching to public transportation. The relationship between Chloe's purchases of gasoline and the price of gasoline is summarized in the shaded

From 2005 to 2008, gasoline prices rose by 30 percent and Hummer sales fell by 50 percent. At that time, no other car brand experienced sales declines that were this steep. Hummer demand fell so quickly that General Motors shut down the brand in 2010.

Exhibit 4.1 Chloe's Demand Schedule and Demand Curve for Gasoline

The lower the price of gasoline, the more gasoline that Chloe chooses to buy. In other words, her quantity demanded increases as the price of gasoline decreases. Demand curves are downward-sloping—the height of the curve falls as we move from left to right along the horizontal axis.

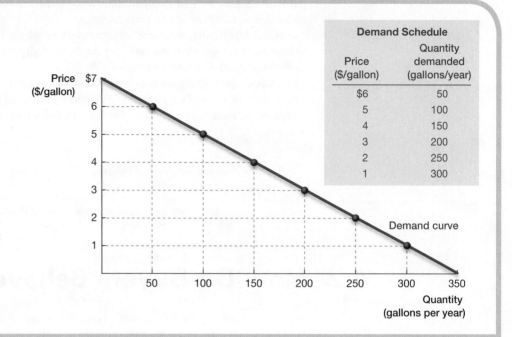

Demand Schedule	
Price ($/gallon)	Quantity demanded (gallons/year)
$6	50
5	100
4	150
3	200
2	250
1	300

A **demand schedule** is a table that reports the quantity demanded at different prices, holding all else equal.

Holding all else equal implies that everything else in the economy is held constant. The Latin phrase *ceteris paribus* means "with other things the same" and is sometimes used in economic writing to mean the same thing as "holding all else equal."

The **demand curve** plots the quantity demanded at different prices. A demand curve plots the demand schedule.

Two variables are **negatively related** if the variables move in the opposite direction.

Law of Demand: In almost all cases, the quantity demanded rises when the price falls (holding all else equal).

box in the upper-right corner of Exhibit 4.1. This table reports the quantity demanded at different prices and it is called a **demand schedule**. Chloe's demand schedule for gasoline tells us how Chloe's gasoline purchases change as the price of gas changes, **holding all else equal**. The phrase "holding all else equal" implies that everything other than the price of gas is held constant or fixed, including income, rent, and highway tolls. The demand schedule reveals that Chloe increases the quantity of gasoline that she purchases as the price of gasoline falls.

Demand Curves

We'll often want to plot a demand schedule. That is what the demand curve does. The **demand curve** plots the relationship between prices and quantity demanded (again, holding all else equal). In Exhibit 4.1, each dot plots a single point from the demand schedule. For example, the leftmost dot represents the point at which the price is $6 per gallon and the quantity demanded is 50 gallons of gasoline per year. Similarly, the rightmost dot represents the point at which the price is $1 per gallon and the quantity demanded is 300 gallons of gasoline per year. Notice that the horizontal axis (the *x*-axis) represents the quantity demanded. The vertical axis (the *y*-axis) represents the price per gallon. Economists always adopt this plotting convention—quantity demanded on the horizontal axis and price on the vertical axis. Economists usually "connect the dots" as we have in Exhibit 4.1, which implies that prices and quantities demanded don't always have to be round numbers.

The demand curve has an important property that we will see many times. The price of gasoline and the quantity demanded are **negatively related**, which means that they move in opposite directions. In other words, when one goes up, the other goes down, and vice versa. In Chloe's case, a gas price of $6/gallon generates a quantity demanded of 50 gallons per year, and a price of $1/gallon generates a much greater quantity demanded of 300 gallons per year. The price of gas and the quantity demanded move in opposite directions.

Almost all goods have demand curves that exhibit this fundamental negative relationship, which economists call the **Law of Demand**: the quantity demanded rises when the price falls (holding all else equal).

In this book all demand curves, demand schedules, and graph labels related to demand are in blue.

Willingness to Pay

Chloe's demand curve can also be used to calculate how much she is willing (and able) to pay for an additional gallon of gasoline. One extra gallon of gasoline is called a marginal gallon. The height of her demand curve at any given quantity is the amount she is willing to pay for that marginal unit of the good. In other words, the height of her demand curve is the value in dollars that Chloe places on that last gallon of gasoline.

For example, Chloe is willing to pay $4 for her 150th gallon of gasoline. In other words, with 149 gallons already at her at her disposal in one year, Chloe's willingness to pay for an additional gallon of gasoline is $4. **Willingness to pay** is the highest price that a buyer is willing to pay for an extra unit of a good.

On the other hand, Chloe is willing to pay only $3 for a marginal gallon of gasoline if she already has 199 gallons (for use that year). Chloe's willingness to pay for an additional gallon is negatively related to the quantity that she already has—this is the quantity on the horizontal axis in Exhibit 4.1. The more gasoline that she already has, the less she is willing to pay for an additional gallon. For most goods and services, this negative relationship applies. The more you have of something—for instance, slices of pizza—the less gain there is from acquiring another unit of the same good.

This is an example of a concept called **diminishing marginal benefit**: as you consume more of a good, your willingness to pay for an additional unit declines. An easy way to remember this concept is to think about donuts. My first donut in the morning is worth a lot to me so I am willing to pay a lot for it. My fourth donut in the same sitting is worth much less to me, so I am willing to pay less for it. In general, the more donuts I eat, the less I am willing to pay for an extra donut.

From Individual Demand Curves to Aggregated Demand Curves

So far we've talked about a single consumer, Chloe. But we can easily extend the ideas that we have discussed to all buyers of gasoline, including consumers and firms.

Think about the worldwide market for energy. Chloe's demand curve implies that she will increase her use of gasoline when the price of gasoline goes down. Other gasoline users will also increase their consumption of gasoline as its price falls.

Though all individual demand curves are downward-sloping, that's about all they have in common. For example, a schoolteacher in Kenya may earn $1,000 per year. For any given price of gasoline, the schoolteacher probably won't consume nearly as much gasoline as a typical worker in the United States (who has about 50 times as much income to spend).

This leaves us with a challenge. How do we account for the gasoline demand of billions of consumers worldwide? All of their demand curves will obey the Law of Demand, but otherwise they won't look alike. To study the behavior of the worldwide energy market, economists need to study the worldwide demand curve for gasoline, which is equivalent to the sum of all the individual demand curves. Economists call this adding-up process the **aggregation** of the individual demand curves.

We'll begin by showing you how to add up the demand of just two individual buyers. We'll first teach you how to do it with demand schedules. Then we'll show you what that implies for plotted demand curves. Remember that these different ways of thinking about demand are equivalent. Each method reinforces the other.

Exhibit 4.2 contains two individual demand schedules and a total demand schedule. To calculate the total quantity demanded at a particular price, simply add up Sue's and Carlos's quantity demanded at that price. For example, at a price of $4 per gallon, Sue has a quantity demanded of 200 gallons per year. At that same price, Carlos has a quantity demanded of 400 gallons per year. So the aggregate level of quantity demanded at a price of $4/gallon is 200 + 400 = 600 gallons per year.

Conceptually, aggregating quantity demanded means fixing the price and adding up the quantities that each buyer demands. It is important to remember that quantities are being added together, not prices. Here's an example to help you remember this point. Consider a bakery selling donuts at $1 each. Suppose that two hungry students walk into the bakery and each wants a donut. The total quantity demanded by the two students would be two donuts at a price of $1 per donut. Remember this tale of two donuts and you'll avoid getting confused when you calculate total demand schedules.

Exhibit 4.2 also contains plotted demand curves. When a demand curve is a straight line, as in this exhibit, the relationship between price and quantity demanded is said to

---

Willingness to pay is the highest price that a buyer is willing to pay for an extra unit of a good.

Diminishing marginal benefit: As you consume more of a good, your willingness to pay for an additional unit declines.

The process of adding up individual behaviors is referred to as **aggregation.**

Exhibit 4.2 Aggregation of Demand Schedules and Demand Curves

Demand schedules are aggregated by summing the quantity demanded at each price on the individual demand schedules. Likewise, demand curves are aggregated by summing the quantity demanded at each price on the individual demand curves.

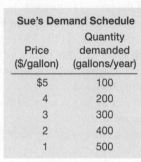

Sue's Demand Schedule	
Price ($/gallon)	Quantity demanded (gallons/year)
$5	100
4	200
3	300
2	400
1	500

Carlos's Demand Schedule	
Price ($/gallon)	Quantity demanded (gallons/year)
$5	200
4	400
3	600
2	800
1	1,000

Total Demand Schedule	
Price ($/gallon)	Quantity demanded (gallons/year)
$5	300
4	600
3	900
2	1,200
1	1,500

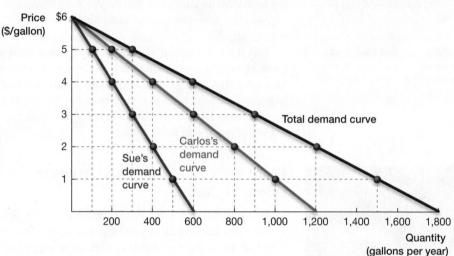

be linear. Economists often illustrate demand curves with straight lines because they are easy to explain and easy to express as equations. On the other hand, real-world demand curves don't tend to be perfectly straight lines, so the linear model is mostly used as an illustrative case.

The plotted demand curves in Exhibit 4.2 can be aggregated the same way that the demand schedules are aggregated. Again, look at the quantities demanded at a single price, say $4/gallon. Sue's demand curve has a quantity demanded of 200 gallons per year. Carlos's demand curve has a quantity demanded of 400 gallons per year. Total quantity demanded at a price of $4 per gallon is the sum of the two individual quantities demanded: 200 + 400 = 600 gallons per year.

Building the Market Demand Curve

Exhibit 4.2 shows you how to add up demand curves for just two buyers. We would like to study the demand of all buyers in a market. Economists refer to this as the **market demand curve**. It is the sum of the individual demand curves of all the potential buyers. The market demand curve plots the relationship between the total quantity demanded and the market price, holding all else equal.

The **market demand curve** is the sum of the individual demand curves of all the potential buyers. It plots the relationship between the total quantity demanded and the market price, holding all else equal.

Over 1 billion economic agents purchase gasoline every year. If we added up the total quantity of gasoline demanded at a particular market price, we could calculate the market demand for gasoline at that price. But economists rarely study the market demand for gasoline. Economists who study energy markets recognize that the gasoline market is very closely tied to all of the other markets for products produced from crude oil. Jet fuel, diesel fuel, and automobile gasoline are all produced from oil. Accordingly, when economists study the market for gasoline, we aggregate to the total market for oil. Exhibit 4.3 reports a rough approximation of the worldwide demand curve for billions of "barrels of oil" (there are 42 gallons per barrel), which is the unit of measurement that is commonly used in this market.

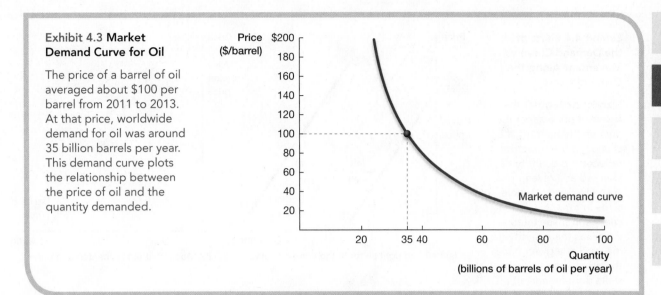

Exhibit 4.3 Market Demand Curve for Oil

The price of a barrel of oil averaged about $100 per barrel from 2011 to 2013. At that price, worldwide demand for oil was around 35 billion barrels per year. This demand curve plots the relationship between the price of oil and the quantity demanded.

Finally, note that the demand curve in Exhibit 4.3 is not a straight line, and therefore looks a bit different from the straight demand curves that you saw earlier. This serves as a reminder that the key property of a demand curve is the negative relationship between price and quantity demanded. Demand curves can exhibit this negative relationship without being straight lines.

Exhibit 4.3 also contains a horizontal dashed line that represents the market price of oil from 2011 to 2013: $100 per barrel. The horizontal price line crosses the demand curve at a point labeled with a dot. At this intersection the buyers' willingness to pay (the height of the demand curve) is equal to the market price of oil. Buyers keep purchasing oil as long as their willingness to pay is greater than or equal to the price of oil. At a market price of $100 per barrel, the demand curve implies that buyers will keep purchasing oil until they reach a quantity demanded of 35 billion barrels of oil per year.

Shifting the Demand Curve

When we introduced the demand curve, we explained that it describes the relationship between price and quantity demanded, holding all else equal. It's now time to more carefully consider the "all else" that is being held fixed.

The demand curve shifts when these five major factors change:

- Tastes and preferences
- Income and wealth
- Availability and prices of related goods
- Number and scale of buyers
- Buyers' beliefs about the future

Changing Tastes and Preferences   A change in tastes or preferences is simply a change in what we personally like, enjoy, or value. For example, your demand for oil products would fall (holding price fixed) if you became convinced that global warming was a significant global problem and it was your ethical duty to use fewer fossil fuels. Because your willingness to buy oil products decreases as a result of your growing environmental worries, your demand curve shifts to the left. We refer to this as a "left" shift in the demand curve because a lower quantity demanded for a given price of oil corresponds to a leftward movement on the horizontal axis. If many people have experiences like this—say an environmental documentary convinces millions of drivers to buy hybrids—then the market demand curve will experience a shift to the left. See Exhibit 4.4 for an example of a left shift in a demand curve.

Naturally, a taste change could also shift a demand curve to the right, corresponding to an increase in the quantity demanded at a given market price. For example, this would happen to your individual demand curve if you started dating someone who lives a few towns away, thereby increasing your transportation needs. Exhibit 4.4 also plots a right shift in a demand curve.

Exhibit 4.4 Shifts of the Demand Curve vs. Movement Along the Demand Curve

Many factors other than a good's price affect the quantity demanded. If a change in these factors reduces the quantity demanded at a given price, then the demand curve shifts left (panel (a)). If a change in these factors increases the quantity demanded at a given price, then the demand curve shifts right (panel (a)). On the other hand, if only the good's own price changes, then the demand curve does not shift and we move along the demand curve (panel (b)).

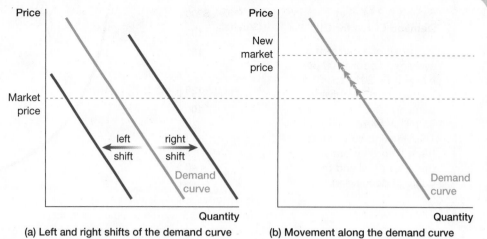

(a) Left and right shifts of the demand curve

(b) Movement along the demand curve

The **demand curve shifts** only when the quantity demanded changes at a given price.

If a good's own price changes and its demand curve hasn't shifted, the own price change produces a **movement along the demand curve.**

This example illustrates two key concepts:

- The **demand curve shifts** only when the quantity demanded changes at a given price. Left and right shifts are illustrated in panel (a) of Exhibit 4.4.
- If a good's own price changes and its demand curve hasn't shifted, the own price change produces a **movement along the demand curve**. Movements along the demand curve are illustrated in panel (b) of Exhibit 4.4.

It is important to master these terms, because they will keep coming up. Use Exhibit 4.4 to confirm that you know the difference between a "shift of the demand curve" and a "movement along the demand curve." It helps to remember that if the quantity demanded changes at a given price, then the demand curve has shifted.

We now continue with a discussion of the key factors, other than tastes and preferences, that shift the demand curve.

Changing Income or Changing Wealth A change in income or a change in wealth affects your ability to pay for goods and services. Imagine that you recently got your first full-time job and went from a student budget to a $40,000 annual salary. You might buy a car and the gas to go with it. You'd probably also start taking more exotic vacations: for instance, flying to Hawaii rather than taking the bus to visit your friends in Hackensack. Your willingness (directly and indirectly) to buy fuel will now be higher, holding the price of fuel fixed, implying that your demand curve shifts to the right. For a **normal good**, an increase in income causes the demand curve to shift to the right (holding the good's price fixed).

For an inferior good, rising income shifts the demand curve to the left. No insult intended to Spam lovers.

On the other hand, consider a good like Spam, which is canned, precooked meat. In the developed world, as people's incomes rise, they are likely to consume fewer canned foods and more fresh foods. If rising income shifts the demand curve for a good to the left (holding the good's price fixed), then the good is called an **inferior good**. This seemingly insulting label is actually only a technical term that describes a relationship between increases in income and leftward shifts in the demand curve.

Changing Availability and Prices of Related Goods A change in the availability and prices of related goods will also influence demand for oil products (holding the price of

For a **normal good,** an increase in income causes the demand curve to shift to the right (holding the good's price fixed).

For an **inferior good,** an increase in income causes the demand curve to shift to the left (holding the good's price fixed).

Two goods are **substitutes** when the fall in the price of one leads to a left shift in the demand curve for the other.

Two goods are **complements** when the fall in the price of one, leads to a right shift in the demand curve for the other.

oil fixed), thereby shifting the demand curve for oil. For example, if a city cuts the price of public transportation, drivers are likely to partially cut back use of their cars. This produces a left shift in the demand curve for gas. Two goods are said to be substitutes when the fall in the price of one leads to a left shift in the demand curve for the other. Public transportation and gas are **substitutes**, because a fall in the price of public transportation leads people to drive their cars less, producing a left shift in the demand curve for gas.

On the other hand, there are some related goods and services that play the opposite role. For example, suppose that a ski resort located 200 miles from where you live decreases its lift ticket prices. The price cut will lead some people to increase their visits to the ski resort, thereby increasing their transportation needs and shifting right their demand curve for gas. Two goods are said to be **complements** when the fall in the price of one good, leads to a right shift in the demand curve for the other good.

Changing Number and Scale of Buyers   When the number of buyers increases, the demand curve shifts right. When the number of buyers decreases, the demand curve shifts left. The scale of the buyers' purchasing behavior also matters. For example, if the mayor of a small town switches all of the town buses from gasoline to battery power, this will have a much smaller impact on worldwide gasoline demand than a switch by the mayor of the world's largest city, Tokyo.

Changing Buyers' Beliefs About the Future   Changing buyers' beliefs about the future also influence the demand curve. Suppose that some people begin losing their jobs during the first months of an economy-wide slowdown. Even if you hadn't lost your job, you might still be worried. You could lose your job at some point in the near future, and anticipating this possibility might lead you to build up a rainy-day fund right now. To do this, you might cut your spending by carpooling or eliminating weekend trips to local ski resorts. Such belt-tightening tends to reduce gas usage and shifts the demand curve for oil to the left.

Summary of Shifts in the Demand Curve and Movements Along the Demand Curve

The demand curve shifts when these factors change:

1. Tastes and preferences
2. Income and wealth
3. Availability and prices of related goods
4. Number and scale of buyers
5. Buyers' beliefs about the future

The *only* reason for a movement along the demand curve:

A change in the price of the good itself

Evidence-Based Economics

Q: How much more gasoline would people buy if its price were lower?

We've explained that the quantity of gasoline demanded falls as the price rises. We're now ready to study empirical evidence that backs this up.

Brazil and Venezuela share a border, and they have similar levels of income per person. Both are also large oil producers—each produced about 3 million barrels per day in 2013. However, they have radically different energy policies. Like most countries, Brazil heavily taxes the sale of gasoline. In contrast, Venezuela aggressively subsidizes the sale of gasoline. To compare their policies, we report the U.S. dollar price of gasoline in 2013, when Brazilian drivers paid $5.58 per gallon and Venezuelan drivers paid only $0.04 per gallon. The Venezuelan government provided enough of a subsidy to make

Evidence-Based Economics *(Continued)*

4.1

4.2

4.3

4.4

4.5

gasoline practically free. The Venezuelan government is a major oil producer and supplies enough gas to meet consumer demand, even when the price was $0.04 per gallon.

The Law of Demand predicts that a lower price should be associated with a higher quantity demanded, all else held equal. In fact, per person gasoline consumption is almost five times higher in Venezuela than in Brazil.

Exhibit 4.5 plots the price of gasoline on the vertical axis (including taxes and subsidies) and the quantity of gasoline demanded on the horizontal axis. As you can see, there is a negative relationship between price and quantity demanded. We've also added Mexico to this figure to give you a sense of how another Latin American country (with similar per person income) compares. Mexico provides a small subsidy on gasoline and consequently falls between the other two countries. The Law of Demand predicts a negative relationship between price and quantity demanded, and the data confirms that prediction.

Exhibit 4.5 The Quantity of Gasoline Demanded (per person) and the Price of Gasoline in Brazil, Mexico, and Venezuela

There is a negative relationship between price and quantity demanded in the gasoline market. Quantity demanded is from the OECD. After-tax, after-subsidy gasoline prices are from AIRINC.

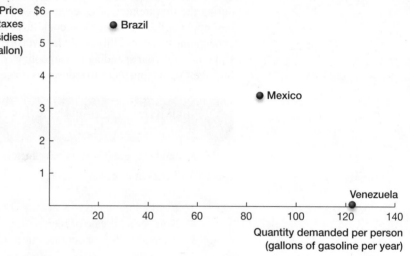

Question	**Answer**	**Data**	**Caveat**
How much more gasoline would people buy if its price were lower?	Venezuelans, who paid only $0.04 per gallon of gas, purchased five times as much per person as Brazilians, who paid $5.58 per gallon.	We compare the quantity of gasoline demanded in Latin American countries with similar levels of income per person and very different gas prices. The variation in gas prices is caused by differences in taxes and subsidies.	Though income levels per person are similar in these countries, the countries have other differences that are not accounted for in this analysis.

4.3 How Do Sellers Behave?

You now understand the behavior of buyers. To understand the complete picture of a market, we also need to study sellers. The interaction of buyers and sellers in a marketplace determines the market price.

We want to analyze the relationship between the price of a good and the amount of the good that sellers are willing to sell or supply. At a given price, the amount of the good or service that sellers are willing to supply is called the **quantity supplied**. Note that in this book, all supply curves, supply schedules, and graph labels relating to supply are in red.

Quantity supplied is the amount of a good or service that sellers are willing to sell at a given price.

To build intuition for the concept of quantity supplied, think about a company like ExxonMobil. As the price of oil goes up, ExxonMobil increases its willingness to supply oil that is relatively expensive for the company to discover and extract. Some oil is in deep-water locations where the ocean depth is 2 miles and the oil is another 8 miles below the seafloor. Such wells are drilled by specialized ships two football fields long, which are staffed by hundreds of workers and equipped with robotic, unmanned submarines. Because of the enormous expense, such wells are only drilled when the price of oil is over $70 per barrel.

Drilling for oil from offshore platforms above the Arctic Circle is even more costly. If a single small iceberg could sink the *Titanic*, imagine the challenge of building and protecting oil rigs in areas where tens of thousands of large icebergs pass each year. Offshore oil wells within the Arctic Circle are only drilled when the price of oil is over $80 per barrel.

Drilling from offshore platforms above the Arctic Circle is not profitable unless the price of oil exceeds $80 per barrel. At the other extreme, oil from the deserts of Saudi Arabia costs less than $20 per barrel to extract.

The higher the price of oil goes, the more drilling locations become profitable for ExxonMobil. Many observers talk about oil and warn that we are running out of it. In fact, companies like ExxonMobil are only running out of cheap oil. There is more oil under the surface of the earth than we are ever going to use. The problem is that much of that oil is very expensive to extract and deliver to the market.

Supply Curves

A **supply schedule** is a table that reports the quantity supplied at different prices, holding all else equal.

ExxonMobil responds to increases in the price of oil by developing new oil fields in ever more challenging locations. The relationship between ExxonMobil's production of oil and the price of oil is summarized in the boxed supply schedule in Exhibit 4.6. A **supply schedule**

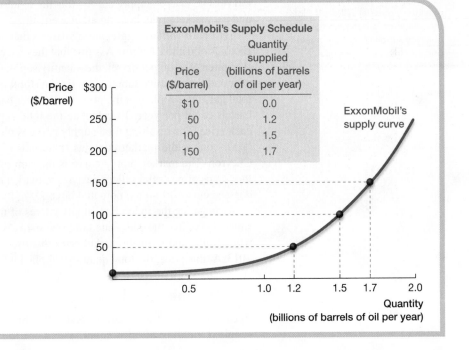

Exhibit 4.6 ExxonMobil's Supply Schedule for Oil and Supply Curve for Oil

The quantity supplied rises with the price of oil, so quantity supplied and price are positively related. Equivalently, we could say that the supply curve is upward-sloping—the height of the curve rises as we move from left to right along the horizontal axis.

ExxonMobil's Supply Schedule

Price ($/barrel)	Quantity supplied (billions of barrels of oil per year)
$10	0.0
50	1.2
100	1.5
150	1.7

The **supply curve** plots the quantity supplied at different prices. A supply curve plots the supply schedule.

Two variables are **positively related** if the variables move in the same direction.

Law of Supply: In almost all cases, the quantity supplied rises when the price rises (holding all else equal).

Willingness to accept is the lowest price that a seller is willing to get paid to sell an extra unit of a good. Willingness to accept is the same as the marginal cost of production.

The **market supply curve** is the sum of the individual supply curves of all the potential sellers. It plots the relationship between the total quantity supplied and the market price, holding all else equal.

is a table that reports the quantity supplied at different prices, holding all else equal. The supply schedule shows that ExxonMobil increases the quantity of oil supplied as the price of oil increases. Exhibit 4.6 also plots ExxonMobil's **supply curve**, which plots the quantity supplied at different prices. In other words, a supply curve plots the supply schedule.

The supply curve in Exhibit 4.6 has a key property. The price of oil and the quantity supplied are **positively related**. By positively related we mean that the variables move in the same direction—when one variable goes up, the other goes up, too. In almost all cases, quantity supplied and price are positively related (holding all else equal), which economists call the **Law of Supply**.

ExxonMobil starts to produce oil when the price exceeds a level of $10 per barrel. An oil price of $50 per barrel generates a quantity supplied of 1.2 billion barrels per year. A higher oil price of $100 per barrel generates a higher quantity supplied of 1.5 billion barrels per year. At the highest price of oil listed in the supply schedule, the quantity supplied rises further to 1.7 billion barrels per year.

Willingness to Accept

If ExxonMobil is optimizing, the firm should be willing to supply one additional barrel of oil if it is paid at least its marginal cost of production. Recall from the chapter on optimization (Chapter 3) that marginal cost is the extra cost generated by producing an additional unit. As long as an oil producer is paid at least its marginal cost per barrel, it should be willing to supply another barrel of oil.

For an optimizing firm, the height of the supply curve is the firm's marginal cost. For example, ExxonMobil's supply curve implies that if the price of oil is $100, then the quantity supplied is 1.5 billion barrels per year. We can turn this around and say it another way—ExxonMobil is willing to accept $100 to produce its 1.5 billionth barrel of oil. That's what the supply curve tells us. Economists call this ExxonMobil's **willingness to accept**, which is the lowest price that a seller is willing to get paid to sell an extra unit of a good. For an optimizing firm, willingness to accept is the same as the marginal cost of production. ExxonMobil is willing to accept $100 for an additional barrel, because $100 is ExxonMobil's marginal cost when it produces its 1.5 billionth barrel in a year.

From the Individual Supply Curve to the Market Supply Curve

When we studied buyers, we summed up their individual demand curves to obtain a market demand curve. We're now ready to do the same thing for the sellers. Adding up quantity supplied works the same way as adding up quantity demanded. We add up quantities at a particular price. We then repeat this at every possible price to plot the **market supply curve**. The market supply curve plots the relationship between the total quantity supplied and the market price, holding all else equal.

Let's start with an aggregation analysis that assumes there are only two oil companies, ExxonMobil and Chevron. Assume that they have the supply schedules listed in Exhibit 4.7. At a price of $100 per barrel, the quantity supplied by Chevron is 1 billion barrels of oil per year and the quantity supplied by ExxonMobil is 1.5 billion barrels of oil per year. So the total quantity supplied at the price of $100 per barrel is 1 billion + 1.5 billion = 2.5 billion barrels of oil per year. To calculate the total supply curve, we repeat this calculation for each price. The resulting total supply curve is plotted in Exhibit 4.7.

Of course, the market contains thousands of oil producers, not just ExxonMobil and Chevron. The market supply curve is the sum of the individual supply curves of all these thousands of potential sellers, just as the market demand curve is the sum of the individual demand curves of all the potential buyers.

Aggregating the individual supply curves of thousands of oil producers yields a market supply curve like the one plotted in Exhibit 4.8. We've included a dashed line at $100/barrel, which is the approximate market price that prevailed in the world oil market from 2011 to 2013. At this price, the total quantity supplied is 35 billion barrels of oil per year.

Shifting the Supply Curve

Recall that the supply curve describes the relationship between price and quantity supplied, holding all else equal. There are four major types of variables that are held

Exhibit 4.7
Aggregation of Supply Schedules and Supply Curves

To calculate the total quantity supplied at a particular price, add up the quantity supplied by each supplier at that price. Repeat this for each price to derive the total supply curve.

Chevron's Supply Schedule		ExxonMobil's Supply Schedule		Total Supply Schedule	
Price ($/barrel)	Quantity supplied (billions of barrels of oil per year)	Price ($/barrel)	Quantity supplied (billions of barrels of oil per year)	Price ($/barrel)	Quantity supplied (billions of barrels of oil per year)
$10	0.0	$10	0.0	$10	0.0
50	0.8	50	1.2	50	2.0
100	1.0	100	1.5	100	2.5
150	1.1	150	1.7	150	2.8

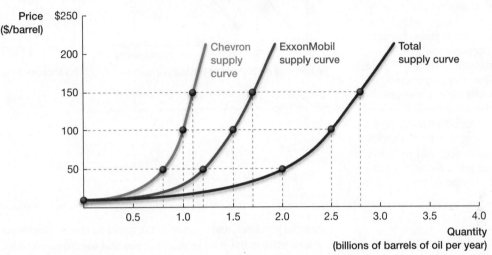

Exhibit 4.8 Market Supply Curve for Oil

The market supply curve is upward-sloping, like the supply curves of the individual sellers.

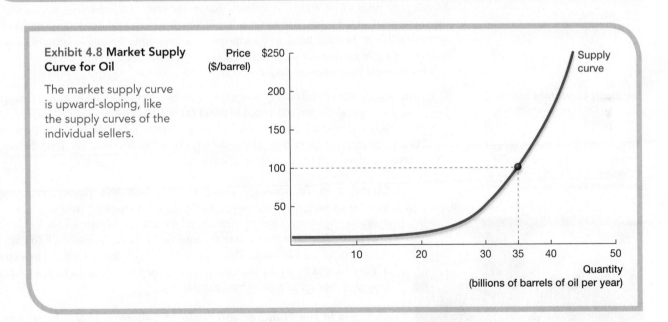

fixed when a supply curve is constructed. The supply curve shifts when these variables change:

- Prices of inputs used to produce the good
- Technology used to produce the good
- Number and scale of sellers
- Sellers' beliefs about the future

Changing Prices of Inputs Used to Produce the Good   Changes in the prices of inputs shift the supply curve. An **input** is a good or service used to produce another good or service. For instance, steel is used to construct oil platforms, to create oil drilling machinery,

An **input** is a good or service used to produce another good or service.

Exhibit 4.9 Shifts of the Supply Curve vs. Movement Along the Supply Curve

Many factors other than a good's price affect the quantity supplied. If a change in these factors decreases the quantity supplied at a given price, then the supply curve shifts left (panel (a)). If a change in these factors increases the quantity supplied at a given price, then the supply curve shifts right (panel (a)). On the other hand, if only the good's own price changes, then the supply curve does not shift and we move along the supply curve (panel (b)).

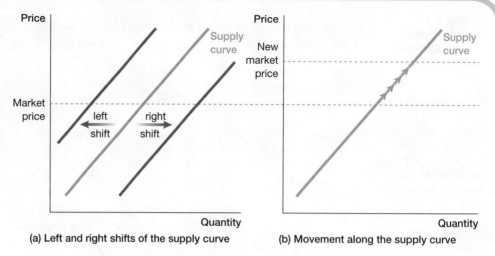

(a) Left and right shifts of the supply curve

(b) Movement along the supply curve

to build pipelines, and to construct oil tankers. Hence, steel is a critical input to oil production. An increase in the price of steel implies that some opportunities to produce oil will no longer be profitable, and therefore optimizing oil producers will choose not to supply as much oil (holding the price of oil fixed). It follows that an increase in the price of steel shifts the supply curve of oil to the left. In other words, holding the price of oil fixed, the quantity of oil supplied falls. On the other hand, a fall in the price of steel shifts the supply curve of oil to the right. Panel (a) of Exhibit 4.9 plots these left and right shifts in the supply curve.

This example illustrates two key concepts:

The **supply curve shifts** only when the quantity supplied changes at a given price.

If a good's own price changes and its supply curve hasn't shifted, the own price change produces a **movement along the supply curve.**

- The **supply curve shifts** only when the quantity supplied changes at a given price. Left and right shifts are illustrated in panel (a) of Exhibit 4.9.
- If a good's own price changes and its supply curve hasn't shifted, the own price change produces a **movement along the supply curve**. Movements along the supply curve are illustrated in panel (b) of Exhibit 4.9.

Changes in Technology Used to Produce the Good Changes in technology also shift the supply curve. In recent years, "fracking" (induced hydraulic fracturing) has revolutionized the energy industry. This technology uses pressurized fluids to create fractures in the underground rock formations that surround a drilled well. The fractures enable oil and natural gas to seep out of the rock and be drawn from the well. Fracking has caused a right shift in the supply curves for petroleum and natural gas.

Changes in the Number and Scale of Sellers Changes in the number of sellers also shift the supply curve. For example, in 2011 Libyan rebels overthrew Muammar Gaddafi, a dictator who had controlled the country for 42 years. Gaddafi loyalists defended his regime and the fighting dragged on for 6 months. During this period, Libya essentially stopped oil production. Before the war, Libyan wells had been producing about 1.5 million barrels per day. This is the scale of Libyan production. During the Libyan civil war, the worldwide supply curve shifted to the left by 1.5 million barrels per day.

A photograph of a Libyan oil refinery burning during the 2011 civil war that overthrew Colonel Muammar Gaddafi. During the war almost all of Libya's oil production was shut down, shifting the world oil supply curve to the left.

Changes in Sellers' Beliefs About the Future Finally, changes in sellers' beliefs about the future shift the supply curve. For example, consider the market for natural gas. Every winter, natural gas usage skyrockets for home heating. This creates a winter spike in

Summary of Shifts in the Supply Curve and Movements Along the Supply Curve

The supply curve shifts when these factors change:

1. Prices of inputs used to produce the good
2. Technology used to produce the good
3. Number and scale of sellers
4. Sellers' beliefs about the future

The *only* reason for a movement along the supply curve:

A change in the price of the good itself

natural gas prices. Expecting such price spikes, natural gas producers store vast quantities during the summer (when prices are low by comparison). In other words, natural gas producers use much of their summer natural gas production to build up stockpiles instead of selling all of the summer production to the public. This implies that natural gas suppliers shift the supply curve to the left in the summer. This is an optimization strategy. By pulling supply off the (low-price) summer market and increasing supply in the (high-price) winter market, natural gas suppliers obtain a higher average price. Summarizing this strategy, natural gas producers adjust their supply throughout the year in response to expectations about how the price of natural gas will move in the future.

4.4 Supply and Demand in Equilibrium

Up to this point, we have provided tools that explain the separate behavior of buyers and sellers. We haven't explained how to put the two sides of the market together. How do buyers and sellers interact? What determines the market price at which they trade? What determines the quantity of goods bought by buyers and sold by sellers? We will use the market demand curve and the market supply curve to answer these questions. We'll continue to study a perfectly competitive market, which we'll refer to from now on as a "competitive market."

Competitive markets converge to the price at which quantity supplied and quantity demanded are the same. To visualize what it means to equate quantity supplied and quantity demanded, we need to plot the demand curve and supply curve on the same figure. Exhibit 4.10 does this.

> **Competitive markets converge to the price at which quantity supplied and quantity demanded are the same.**

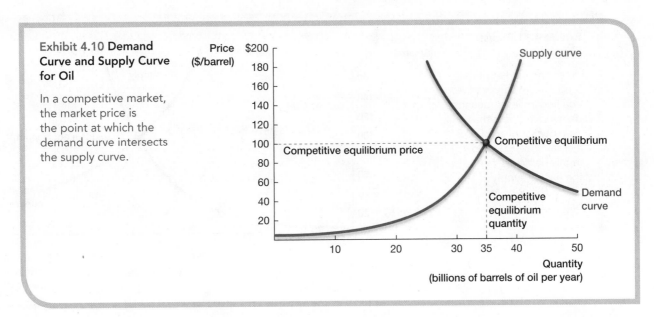

Exhibit 4.10 Demand Curve and Supply Curve for Oil

In a competitive market, the market price is the point at which the demand curve intersects the supply curve.

In Exhibit 4.10, the demand curve (in blue) and the supply curve (in red) for the oil market cross at a price of $100 per barrel and a quantity of 35 billion barrels. Because the demand curve slopes down and the supply curve slopes up, the two curves have only one crossing point. Economists refer to this crossing point as the **competitive equilibrium**. The price at the crossing point is referred to as the **competitive equilibrium price**, which is the price at which quantity supplied and quantity demanded are the same. This is sometimes referred to as the market clearing price, because at this price there is a buyer for every unit that is supplied in the market. The quantity at the crossing point is referred to as the **competitive equilibrium quantity**. This is the quantity that corresponds to the competitive equilibrium price.

> The **competitive equilibrium** is the crossing point of the supply curve and the demand curve.

> The **competitive equilibrium price** equates quantity supplied and quantity demanded.

> The **competitive equilibrium quantity** is the quantity that corresponds to the competitive equilibrium price.

At the competitive equilibrium price, the quantity demanded is equal to the quantity supplied. At any other price, the quantity demanded and the quantity supplied will be unequal. To see this, draw a horizontal line at any other price. Only the horizontal line at the competitive equilibrium price equates quantity demanded and quantity supplied.

Exhibit 4.11 illustrates a case in which the market is not in competitive equilibrium because the market price is above the competitive equilibrium price. The higher price makes selling more desirable and buying less desirable, raising the quantity supplied above its competitive equilibrium level and lowering the quantity demanded below its competitive equilibrium level. When the market price is above the competitive equilibrium price, quantity supplied exceeds quantity demanded, creating **excess supply**. For example, Exhibit 4.11 shows that at a market price of $140 per barrel for oil, the quantity supplied of 38 billion barrels of oil per year exceeds the quantity demanded of 29 billion barrels of oil per year.

> When the market price is above the competitive equilibrium price, quantity supplied exceeds quantity demanded, creating **excess supply**.

If the market stayed in this situation, sellers would pump 38 billion barrels of oil per year, but buyers would purchase only 29 billion of those barrels, leaving the difference—9 billion barrels—unsold each year. This would push down oil prices, as enormous stockpiles of oil started to build up around the world. Because existing oil storage tanks are limited in scale and expensive to build, sellers would start undercutting each other's prices to get rid of the rising inventory of unsold oil. Prices would fall. As a result, the situation in Exhibit 4.11 normally wouldn't last for long. Sellers, who are selling nearly identical barrels of oil, would compete with one another for customers by cutting prices. This would continue until the market price fell back to the competitive equilibrium price. This competitive process plays an important role in pushing the market toward the aptly named competitive equilibrium.

> When the market price is below the competitive equilibrium price, quantity demanded exceeds quantity supplied, creating **excess demand**.

Exhibit 4.12 illustrates the opposite case. When market price is below the competitive equilibrium price, quantity demanded exceeds quantity supplied, creating **excess demand**. In Exhibit 4.12 the quantity demanded of 44 billion barrels of oil per year exceeds the quantity supplied of 30 billion barrels of oil per year. Buyers want 44 billion barrels of oil, but there are only 30 billion barrels available on the market.

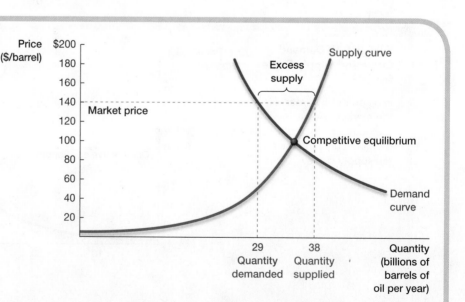

Exhibit 4.11 Excess Supply

When the market price is above the competitive equilibrium level, quantity demanded is less than quantity supplied. This is a case of excess supply. In this particular example, the excess supply is 38 − 29 = 9 billion barrels of oil per year.

Exhibit 4.12 Excess Demand

When the market price is below the competitive equilibrium level, quantity demanded is greater than quantity supplied. This is a case of excess demand. In this case, the excess demand is 44 − 30 = 14 billion barrels of oil per year.

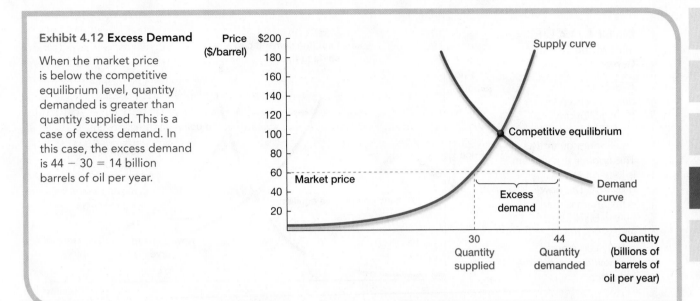

The situation in Exhibit 4.12 also normally won't last long. Buyers who aren't getting the goods they want will compete with one another by offering to pay higher prices to get the limited quantity of oil. This will continue until the market price rises to the competitive equilibrium price of $100 per barrel.

Curve Shifting in Competitive Equilibrium

We are now ready to put this framework into action. We'd like to know how a shock to the world oil market will affect the equilibrium quantity and the equilibrium price of oil.

For example, what would happen if a major oil exporter suddenly stopped production, as Libya did in 2011? This causes a left shift of the supply curve, as illustrated in Exhibit 4.13. Since oil has become more scarce, the price of oil needs to rise from its old level to equate quantity supplied and quantity demanded. The rise in the equilibrium oil price is associated with a movement along the demand curve (which hasn't shifted). Because the demand curve is downward-sloping, a rising price causes a reduction in the quantity demanded. In fact, the outbreak of full-scale fighting in Libya and the consequent shutdown of the Libyan oil fields did correspond with an increase in the world price of oil.

Exhibit 4.13 A Left Shift of the Supply Curve

A left shift in the supply curve raises the equilibrium price and lowers the equilibrium quantity. The original equilibrium is located at the grey dot. The new equilibrium is marked by the black dot, where the original demand curve and the new supply curve intersect.

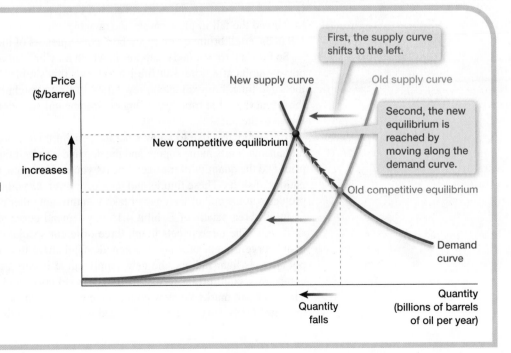

Exhibit 4.14 A Left Shift of the Demand Curve

A left shift in the demand curve lowers the equilibrium price and lowers the equilibrium quantity. The original equilibrium is located at the grey dot. The new equilibrium is marked by the black dot, where the original supply curve and the new demand curve intersect.

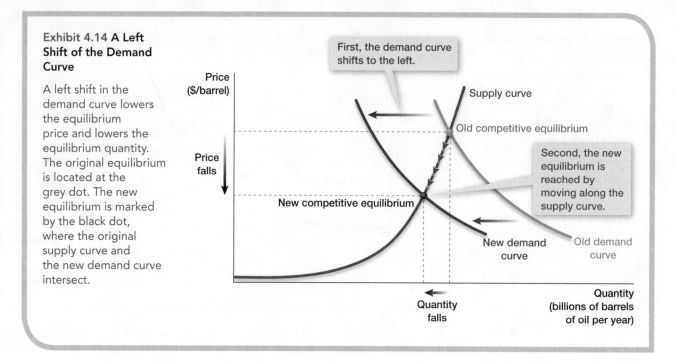

We can also predict the effect of a shift in the demand curve. For example, what would happen if rising environmental concerns led consumers to cut back their carbon footprint by using less oil? This change in consumer tastes shifts left the demand curve for oil, which is plotted in Exhibit 4.14. Oil demand has decreased, so the price of oil needs to fall from its old level to equate quantity supplied and quantity demanded. The decrease in the equilibrium oil price is associated with a movement along the supply curve (which hasn't shifted). Because the supply curve is upward-sloping, a falling price causes a reduction in the quantity supplied.

Using demand and supply curves to study markets enables economists to resolve puzzles. For example, in Exhibit 4.14, the market price of oil drops and people buy less oil! Hearing those two facts might sound perplexing. Shouldn't a drop in the price of oil lead to an increase in oil buying? In Exhibit 4.14, you can see that the drop in the price of oil is caused by a shift of the market demand curve to the left. This left shift causes the price to fall and the fall in price causes the quantity supplied to fall. So the fall in price and the fall in the equilibrium quantity are both consequences of the left shift in the demand curve.

So far we have studied examples in which only one curve—either the demand or supply curve—shifts at a time. But life isn't always this simple. Sometimes both curves shift at the same time. For example, a revolution in Libya might shift the supply curve for oil to the left at the same time that rising environmental consciousness shifts the demand curve for oil to the left.

We would also like to know what happens in mixed cases. Exhibit 4.15 shows how simultaneous shifts in the supply and the demand curves translate into changes in the market price and the quantity of transactions. As you can imagine, there are many possible combinations of shifts. These figures and their captions take you through one group of cases. The problems at the end of the chapter take you through other cases.

In all three panels of Exhibit 4.15 the demand curve shifts left and the supply curve shifts left. The three panels graph three different special cases. We represent the old demand curve in light blue and the new demand curve in dark blue. Likewise, the old supply curve is light red and the new supply curve is dark red. The grey dot marks the old competitive equilibrium, where the old demand curve and the old supply curve intersect. The black dot marks the new competitive equilibrium, where the new demand curve and the new supply curve intersect. The old competitive equilibrium price is P_1 and the new

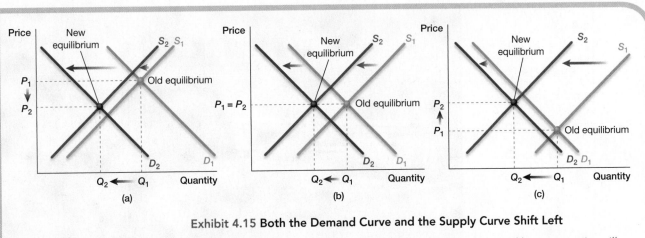

Exhibit 4.15 Both the Demand Curve and the Supply Curve Shift Left

When both supply and demand shift left, the competitive equilibrium quantity will always decrease (Q_2 is always less than Q_1). On the other hand, the competitive equilibrium price may decrease (P_2 less than P_1), stay the same (P_2 equal to P_1), or increase (P_2 greater than P_1).

competitive equilibrium price is P_2. The old competitive equilibrium quantity is Q_1 and the new competitive equilibrium quantity is Q_2.

In all three panels, the equilibrium quantity falls: Q_2 is less than Q_1. However, the equilibrium price responds differently depending on the relative size of the shifts in the demand and supply curves. In the first panel, the left shift in demand dominates and the equilibrium price falls from P_1 to P_2. In the second panel, the equilibrium price stays exactly the same: $P_1 = P_2$. In the third panel, the left shift in supply dominates and the equilibrium price rises from P_1 to P_2. Summing up, when both supply and demand shift left, the competitive equilibrium quantity will always decrease, but the competitive equilibrium price may move in either direction or stay the same.

4.5 What Would Happen If the Government Tried to Dictate the Price of Gasoline?

Our analysis has concluded that competitive markets will end up at the competitive equilibrium—the point where the supply and the demand curves cross. But this can happen only if prices are allowed to respond to market pressures.

However, some markets have prices that are set by laws, regulations, or social norms. Economists are interested in the way that all markets work, even markets that are not allowed to reach a competitive equilibrium. We illustrate these issues by considering markets without a flexible price.

Take another look at Exhibit 4.12. When the market price of gasoline is artificially held below the level of the competitive equilibrium price, the quantity of gasoline demanded exceeds the quantity supplied. Accordingly, many drivers who would like to buy gas at the market price won't be able to do so.

In a situation like this, the allocation of gasoline is determined by something other than who is willing to pay for it. During the U.S. oil crisis of 1973–1974, the U.S. government

At the end of 1973, the U.S. government effectively capped the price of gasoline, creating a situation of excess demand.

effectively capped the price of gasoline, causing quantity demanded to exceed quantity supplied. This is referred to as a price ceiling. Drivers soon realized that there was excess demand at the capped price, leading them to show up early to get whatever gas was available. Lines began to form earlier and earlier in the day.

A New York Times reporter wrote, "Everywhere lines seemed to be the order of the day. In Montclair, N.J., Mrs. Catherine Lee got up at 4:20 one morning and drove to her filling station to be first on line. She had to settle for second place—No. 1 had gotten there at 3:15. Mrs. Lee fluffed up the pillow she had brought, threw two comforters over herself, and slept for three hours until the station opened." Some drivers devised ingenious means of getting around the system. "In Bedford, Massachusetts, a businessman drove his auto into a Hertz car rental lot, ordered a car, received it complete with a full tank of gas, siphoned the gas into his own car, paid Hertz their daily rental fee—no mileage charge, of course—and drove home in his car to enjoy his full tank of gas."[1]

The lines were an optimal response by buyers who understood that there was excess demand. Because quantity demanded exceeded quantity supplied, gas stations frequently ran out of gas. During the peak of the crisis, 20 percent of stations ran out of fuel. Getting in line early—very early—was an optimal way of assuring that you'd be able to fill your own tank.

Some folks didn't like waiting in long lines, particularly when they suspected that the station was going to run out of fuel before they got their turn at the pump. "They're out of their minds, they're turning sick. They'll kill you. They're fighting amongst themselves. They'll shoot you with a gun. They're all sick." Does this sound like a scene from World War Z? It's actually a gas station attendant describing his customers during the gasoline crisis of 1973–1974. An owner of another station put it this way: "It was mayhem. They were fighting in the streets and one customer pulled a knife on another one. And that was *before* we opened."

Economic history is filled with stories of governments that try to fix the price of goods instead of letting the market generate an equilibrium price. Price controls often do not work out well and governments keep forgetting this lesson.

The following Choice & Consequence feature details one more example of a failed effort to fix a price. As you read it, ask yourself how the goods in question could have been allocated differently.

This photograph was taken in 1974. Why don't we see signs like this today?

CHOICE & CONSEQUENCE

The Unintended Consequences of Fixing Market Prices

What would happen if your town announced a first-come, first-served sale of 1,000 Apple laptops for $50 each? Would the residents form an orderly line and patiently wait their turn?

In Henrico County, Virginia such a laptop sale was actually conducted. County residents began lining up at 1:30 A.M. on the day of the sale. When the gates opened at 7 A.M., more than 5,000 people surged into the sale site, pushing and shoving their way to get to the computers. Elderly people were trampled underneath the human tidal wave, and a baby's stroller was crushed. Eventually, about 70 police officers were called in to restore order. Seventeen people were injured and four landed up in the hospital. And after the uproar died down, over 4,000 people were left with nothing to show for all the trouble. Of those that did manage to obtain one of the computers, many later sold them.[2]

The Henrico County computer sale resulted in a situation of excess demand. At the fixed price set by the county, $50 per laptop, the quantity demanded of 5,000 exceeded the quantity supplied of 1,000. Exhibit 4.16 illustrates the fact that there were not enough laptops to go around. The people who got laptops were not necessarily the ones who were willing to pay the most.

Instead, the consumers who got the laptops were the ones who were able and willing to fight their way through the crowd. Even if we assume that the laptops were subsequently resold to other people who valued the laptops more, the stampede itself caused many injuries. A stampede is a bad way to allocate society's resources.

Economists are often asked to provide advice on how to design markets that will work well. Naturally, a flexible price would have made this market work better and it would have raised far more revenue for Henrico County.

Alternatively, the market could have been organized as an auction with bids received by phone or e-mail. The county could have auctioned off the 1,000 laptops to the 1,000 highest local bidders.

Even a random lottery would have worked much better than the stampede. The stampede allocated the laptops to the people who were the strongest and the pushiest and led to numerous injuries. A random lottery would allocate the laptops to the people who get lucky. And these lucky winners would be free to sell their laptop to anyone who valued it more than they did.

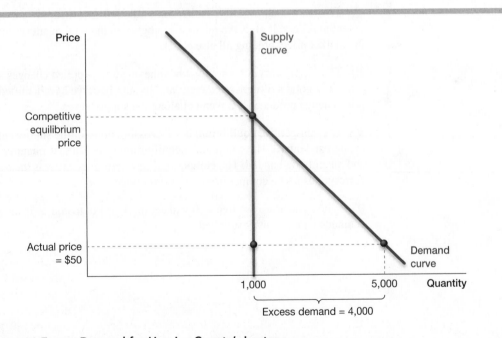

Exhibit 4.16 Excess Demand for Henrico County's Laptops

By fixing the price at $50 per laptop, Henrico County created a situation of excess demand. At this price, the quantity demanded (5,000 laptops) exceeded the quantity supplied (1,000 laptops). To equate the quantity demanded and the quantity supplied, a much higher price was needed: the competitive equilibrium price. The vertical supply curve reflects the fact that the supply of laptops at the $50 sale was fixed at 1,000 units.

Summary

A market is a group of economic agents who are trading a good or service, and the rules and arrangements for trading. In a perfectly competitive market, (1) sellers all sell an identical good or service, and (2) individual buyers or individual sellers aren't powerful enough on their own to affect the market price of that good or service.

Quantity demanded is the amount of a good that buyers are willing to purchase at a given price. A demand schedule is a table that reports the quantity demanded at different prices, holding all else equal. A demand curve plots the demand schedule. The Law of Demand states that in almost all cases, the quantity demanded rises when the price falls (holding all else equal).

The market demand curve is the sum of the individual demand curves of all the potential buyers. It plots the relationship between the total quantity demanded and the market price, holding all else equal.

The demand curve shifts only when the quantity demanded changes at a given price. If a good's own price changes and its demand curve hasn't shifted, the own price change produces a movement along the demand curve.

Quantity supplied is the amount of a good or service that sellers are willing to sell at a given price. A supply schedule is a table that reports the quantity supplied at different prices, holding all else equal. A supply curve plots the supply schedule. The Law of Supply states that in almost all cases, the quantity supplied rises when the price rises (holding all else equal).

The market supply curve is the sum of the individual supply curves of all the potential sellers. It plots the relationship between the total quantity supplied and the market price, holding all else equal.

The supply curve shifts only when the quantity supplied changes at a given price. If a good's own price changes and its supply curve hasn't shifted, the own price change produces a movement along the supply curve.

The competitive equilibrium is the crossing point of the supply curve and the demand curve. The competitive equilibrium price equates quantity supplied and quantity demanded. The competitive equilibrium quantity is the quantity that corresponds to the competitive equilibrium price.

When prices are not free to fluctuate, markets fail to equate quantity demanded and quantity supplied.

Key Terms

market *p. 61*
market price *p. 62*
perfectly competitive market *p. 62*
price-taker *p. 62*
quantity demanded *p. 63*
demand schedule *p. 64*
holding all else equal *p. 64*
demand curve *p. 64*
negatively related *p. 64*
Law of Demand *p. 64*
willingness to pay *p. 65*
diminishing marginal benefit *p. 65*

aggregation *p. 65*
market demand curve *p. 66*
demand curve shifts *p. 68*
movement along the demand curve
  p. 68
normal good *p. 68*
inferior good *p. 68*
substitutes *p. 69*
complements *p. 69*
quantity supplied *p. 71*
supply schedule *p. 71*
supply curve *p. 72*

positively related *p. 72*
Law of Supply *p. 72*
willingness to accept *p. 72*
market supply curve *p. 72*
input *p. 73*
supply curve shifts *p. 74*
movement along the supply curve *p. 74*
competitive equilibrium *p. 76*
competitive equilibrium price *p. 76*
competitive equilibrium quantity *p. 76*
excess supply *p. 76*
excess demand *p. 76*

Questions

All questions are available in MyEconLab *for practice and instructor assignment.*

1. What is meant by holding all else equal? How is this concept used when discussing movements along the demand curve? How is this concept used when discussing movements along the supply curve?

2. What is meant by diminishing marginal benefits? Are you likely to experience diminishing marginal benefits for goods that you like a lot? Are there exceptions to the general rule of diminishing marginal benefits? (*Hint*: Think about batteries that you would use in a flashlight that requires two batteries.) Explain your answer.

3. How is the market demand schedule derived from individual demand schedules? How does the market demand curve differ from an individual demand curve?

4. Explain how the following factors will shift the demand curve for Gillette shaving cream.

   a. The price of a competitor's shaving cream increases.

   b. With an increase in unemployment, the average level of income in the economy falls.

   c. Shaving gels and foams, marketed as being better than shaving creams, are introduced in the market.

5. What does it mean to say that we are running out of "cheap oil"? What does this imply for the price of oil in the future?

6. What does the Law of Supply state? What is the key feature of a typical supply curve?

7. What is the difference between willingness to accept and willingness to pay? For a trade to take place, does the willingness to accept have to be lower, higher, or equal to the willingness to pay?

8. Explain how the following factors will shift the supply curve for sparkling wine.

   a. New irrigation technology increases the output of grapes of a vineyard.

   b. Following an increase in the immigration of unskilled labor, the wages of wine-grape pickers fall.

   c. The government sets a minimum wage for seasonal employment.

9. How do the following affect the equilibrium price in a market?

   a. A leftward shift in demand

   b. A rightward shift in supply

   c. A large rightward shift in demand and a small rightward shift in supply

   d. A large leftward shift in supply and a small leftward shift in demand

10. Why was a fixed price of $50 not the best way of allocating used laptops? Suggest other possible ways of distributing the laptops that would be efficient.

Problems

All problems are available in MyEconLab for practice and instructor assignment.

1. Suppose the following table shows the quantity of laundry detergent that is demanded and supplied at various prices in Country 1.

P ($)	Quantity Demanded (million oz.)	Quantity Supplied (million oz.)
2	65	35
4	60	40
6	55	45
8	50	50
10	45	55
12	40	60
14	35	65

a. Use the data in the table to draw the demand and supply curves in the market for laundry detergent.

b. What is the equilibrium price and quantity in the market?

c. The following tables give the demand and supply schedules for two of its neighboring countries, Country 2 and Country 3. Suppose these three countries decide to form an economic union and integrate their markets. Use the data in the table to plot the market demand and supply curves in the newly formed economic union. What is the equilibrium price and quantity in the market?

Country 2

P ($)	Quantity Demanded (million oz.)	Quantity Supplied (million oz.)
2	35	5
4	30	10
6	25	15
8	20	20
10	15	25
12	10	30
14	5	35

Country 3

P ($)	Quantity Demanded (million oz.)	Quantity Supplied (million oz.)
2	40	10
4	35	15
6	30	20
8	25	25
10	20	30
12	15	35
14	10	40

2. In 1999, the Coca-Cola Company developed a vending machine that would raise the price of Coke in hot weather. Present a supply-and-demand diagram for soft drinks to explain the logic behind this machine.

3. Explain how simultaneous shifts in demand and supply curves could explain these situations:

a. The price of insulin injection kits, used by diabetic patients, increases from $45 to $52, but the equilibrium quantity remains the same.

b. A pest attack on the tomato crop increases the cost of producing ketchup. A mild winter causes cattle herds to be unusually large, causing the price of hamburgers to fall. The equilibrium quantity of ketchup is unchanged.

4. Suppose people who are thinking about buying a home (demanders in the housing market) and current home owners who are thinking about selling their homes (suppliers in the housing market) suddenly believe that home prices are likely to be significantly higher next year than this year.

a. Will this change in expectations cause the demand curve for housing this year to shift to the left or shift to the right? Explain.

b. Will this change in expectations cause the supply curve for housing this year to shift to the left or shift to the right? Explain.

c. Will these shifts in the demand and supply curves lead to an increase or a decrease in the price of housing this year? Use supply and demand curves to explain your answer.

5. Brazil is the world's largest coffee producer. There was a severe drought in Brazil in 2013–14 that damaged Brazil's coffee crop. The price of coffee beans doubled during the first three months of 2014.

a. Draw and discuss a supply and demand diagram to explain the increase in coffee prices.

b. Are coffee and tea substitutes or complements? Explain.

c. What do you think the impact of this drought has been on the equilibrium price and quantity of tea? Draw a supply and demand diagram for the tea market to explain your answer.

6. There is a sharp freeze in Florida that damages the orange harvest and as a result, the price of oranges rises. Will the equilibrium price of orange juice rise, fall, or remain constant? Will the equilibrium quantity of orange juice rise, fall, or remain constant? Present a supply-and-demand curve diagram to explain your answers.

7. An appendectomy is an operation to have your appendix removed. To simplify analysis, assume that everyone has health insurance, so that anybody who needs an

appendectomy will have one. (a) Show that the demand curve for appendectomies is vertical. (b) There is a technological breakthrough that allows surgeons to perform appendectomies at a much lower cost. Will the equilibrium price of appendectomies rise, fall, or remain constant? Will the equilibrium quantity of appendectomies rise, fall, or remain constant? Present a supply-and-demand curve diagram to defend your answers.

8. Land in Sonoma, California, can be used either to grow grapes for pinot noir wine or to grow Gravenstein apples. The demand for pinot noir shifts sharply and permanently to the right. What will be the effect of the rightward shift in demand for pinot noir on the equilibrium price and quantity of Gravenstein apples?

9. Suppose one of your friends offered the following argument:

A rightward shift in demand will cause an increase in price. The increase in price will cause a rightward shift of the supply curve, which will lead to an offsetting decrease in price. Therefore, it is impossible to tell what effect an increase in demand will have on price.

Do you agree with your friend? If not, what is the flaw in your friend's reasoning?

10. The UK government is contemplating introducing a minimum price for alcohol to reduce binge drinking and the consumption of alcohol in general. Suppose the following diagram shows the alcohol market in the UK. The current price of alcohol is 23 pence per unit, and 8 units of alcohol are consumed each week. What happens in the market if the government sets a minimum price of 30 pence per unit of alcohol? Will there be an excess supply or an excess demand for alcohol if the government adopts this policy? Explain.

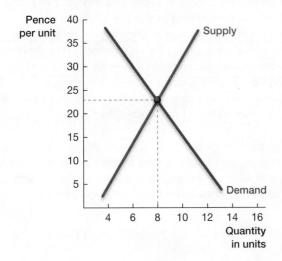

11. Lobsters are plentiful and easy to catch in August but scarce and difficult to catch in November. In addition, vacationers shift the demand for lobsters further to the right in August than in any other month. Compare the equilibrium price and quantity of lobsters in August to the equilibrium price and quantity of lobsters in November. Present and discuss a supply-and-demand diagram to explain your answers.

12. The market price of rice in Thailand is 100 baht. The Thai government offers to buy rice for 140 baht.

   a. How is this likely to affect other buyers in the domestic market for rice?

   b. Present a supply and demand diagram to show how much rice the Thai government will have to purchase under this program.

13. As part of U.S. sugar policy (in 2013), the government offered to buy raw sugar from domestic sugarcane mills at an average price of 18.75 cents per pound. This government offer was made for as much raw sugar as the sugarcane mills produced. Any raw sugar purchased by the government was not sold in the domestic market, as this might have caused raw sugar prices to fall.

   a. Under this policy, what do you think the government's demand curve for sugar looks like?

   b. What impact does this policy likely have on domestic sugar prices? Explain your reasoning with a supply-and-demand diagram.

14. *Note: This problem requires some basic algebra.* The demand for computers is $Q_D = 15 - 2P$, where P is the price of computers. Initially, the supply of computers is $Q_S = P$.

   a. Find the original equilibrium price and quantity.

   b. Suppose the prices of memory chips and motherboards (two important components in computers) rise and as a consequence, the supply curve for computers becomes $Q_S = -3 + P$. Find the new equilibrium price and quantity.

Consumers and Incentives

Would a smoker quit the habit for $100 a month?

At first thought, you might believe that convincing people to quit smoking really has nothing to do with economics. In fact, you might think that smoking isn't even an economic decision. This chapter shows you how economics touches every aspect of our lives by focusing on incentives—rewards or penalties that motivate a person to behave in a particular way. For instance, you may want to earn an "A" in this course to make your parents proud. Or, maybe you want to do well in this course because you think it will help you gain admission to a premier graduate program or land a high-paying job upon graduation. Or maybe you want to succeed just to prove to yourself that you can do it.

Incentives are as numerous as the behaviors they're designed to change. Some are financial in nature, as when a salesperson earns a commission on a sale. Others are moral or ethical in nature, like that impulse to make your parents proud. Others are coercive; if you don't use your hockey stick properly in a game of ice hockey—say you trip your opponent with it—you'll find yourself sitting in the penalty box.

In many ways, you can think of economics as the study of incentives. One of the main tasks of an economist is recognizing these various motives and taking them into account when designing incentive schemes. Economists have been designing incentive schemes for decades—whether to get people back to work after a spell of unemployment, to promote safe sex, or to stimulate charitable contributions—nothing is off-limits to an economist.

So, does a financial incentive like paying people to stop smoking work? We'll find out the answer to that question in this chapter. This chapter also explains why human behavior is often so predictable. In short, the chapter provides you with the economic tools to design incentive schemes to promote your own goals, as well as better understand the world we live in.

CHAPTER OUTLINE

KEY IDEAS

❖ The buyer's problem has three parts; what you like, prices, and your budget.

❖ An optimizing buyer makes decisions at the margin.

❖ An individual's demand curve reflects an ability and willingness to pay for a good or service.

❖ Consumer surplus is the difference between what a buyer is willing to pay for a good and what the buyer actually pays.

❖ Elasticity measures a variable's responsiveness to changes in another variable.

5.1 The Buyer's Problem

The first question that we explore is "How do consumers decide what to buy?" We can frame this question as a problem—the buyer's problem. You might be thinking, "Hey, why is it a problem to spend money? It's not that hard!"

Economists would agree with you. By "buyer's problem" we mean how consumers arrive at a choice as to what to purchase. There are, in fact, three necessary ingredients to the buyer's problem:

1. What you like
2. Prices of goods and services
3. How much money you have to spend

Together, these elements provide the foundations for the demand curves introduced in Chapter 4. In the next chapter, we see the other side of the coin, so to speak—the elements that make up the "seller's problem," which provide the foundation for the supply curves introduced in Chapter 4.

First, as a buyer, you want to buy goods and services that you like, because you prefer to buy what tastes good, sounds good, or looks good. You must also consider prices of the various goods and services that interest you. Prices are important because that extra dollar spent on an iPhone means one less dollar spent on a latte at Starbucks. Alongside prices is a third consideration: how much money you have to spend. We wish our wallets were bottomless, but all of us have limited money to spend, and your budget constraint forces you to make important trade-offs.

> **Simply knowing these three ingredients—what you like, prices, and how much money you have to spend—leads to a set of powerful implications.**

Under certain assumptions, simply knowing these three ingredients—what you like, prices, and how much money you have to spend—leads to a set of powerful implications and rules that govern the buyer's problem. What emerges from this straightforward economic model are answers to simple questions, such as whether to buy a new pair of shoes at Zappos.com or to spend your money on a skateboard. We now look in more detail at these three key ingredients.

What You Like

The benefits that you receive from consuming goods and services is a direct result of your tastes and preferences. If you like the taste of Diet Coke, for example, you will receive benefits from drinking a can. The only assumption that economists make in formulating this part of the buyer's problem is that the consumer attempts to maximize the benefits from consumption. This makes sense. When you buy something, you want to buy what you think will give you the most satisfaction.

As part of the buying decision, consumers must figure out how to make the most of every dollar and, in the process, must consider the trade-offs that they face. For example, the dollar used to help buy a Wii could have helped buy a Kindle or a new laptop instead. These are the opportunities that you forgo when purchasing a Wii.

What do our buying decisions signal about us as consumers? Consider a common situation. Suppose that you decide to take your birthday money to the mall. If you purchase a pair of Lucky jeans for $50, we know that you like Lucky jeans, but what else do we know? In fact, we know that you wouldn't trade your new pair of jeans for a $50 pair of shoes at the mall. Indeed, we know that of all the things that you could have purchased for $50, at the moment you bought the jeans you thought *nothing* in the mall was better to purchase.

Your own tastes and preferences might not seem obvious to you. They might depend on your current mood or change as you grow older. Your buying decisions, however, will reveal a great deal about your tastes and preferences. They will show that from the set of all the things that you are *able* to buy, you most prefer the things that you *choose* to buy.

Prices of Goods and Services

Prices are the most important incentives that economists study. Prices allow us to formally define the relative cost of goods. Say that a pair of jeans has a price of $50 and a sweater has a price of $25. What these prices imply is that the opportunity cost of buying a pair of jeans is two sweaters. So if you purchase a pair of jeans, we know that you like those jeans more than you like two sweaters. In this chapter, we assume that each good has a price that is fixed—a non-negotiable sticker price—and that consumers can buy as much of any good they want at the fixed price if they have sufficient money to pay for it. In this way, our consumer is a price-taker. As we discussed in Chapter 4, this is an assumption typically made to describe perfectly competitive markets.

The rationale behind this assumption is that an individual consumer tends to buy only a tiny fraction of the total amount of a produced good. Because each buyer is only a small part of the market, an individual purchase will not have an effect on the market as a whole. For example, when you go to the mall you might purchase only one of millions of pairs of jeans sold annually, so your decision to buy does not meaningfully affect the price of jeans.

When considering prices, you must take account of not only the price of the good you wish to purchase but the prices of all other goods that are available. The relative prices of goods determine what you give up when you purchase something, so they are important when making the purchase decision.

CHOICE & CONSEQUENCE

Absolutes vs. Percentages

You are planning on purchasing a flat-screen television for your dorm room. After doing some research you find that the local Walmart is selling your preferred brand for $500. The Best Buy located across town is selling the exact same television for $490. Do you drive across town to buy it?

You figure $10 is just not enough of a savings from $500, so you choose to buy from the local Walmart.

Now consider another purchase decision: buying a calculator. In this case, Walmart has your preferred calculator for $20. The BestBuy located across town is selling the exact same calculator for $10. Do you drive across town

to buy it? Makes sense to drive across town, right? You are saving 50 percent!

You have just committed a common decision-making error. When making optimal decisions, you should focus on the *absolute* marginal benefits and marginal costs, not the *proportional* ones. Had you focused on absolute marginal benefits, you would have noticed that these decision problems are identical: in each case you would have saved $10 by driving across town.

If it pays to drive across town to purchase the calculator, it certainly pays to do the same for the flat-screen television. $10 is $10!

How Much Money You Have to Spend

5.1

5.2

5.3

5.4

5.5

A **budget set** is the set of all possible bundles of goods and services that can be purchased with a consumer's income.

The final ingredient of the buyer's problem is what you can buy. The **budget set** is the set of all possible bundles of goods and services that a consumer can purchase with his income. Economists usually describe the budget set in the context of another concept—the *budget constraint*. The budget constraint represents the goods or activities that a consumer can choose that exactly exhausts the entire budget. We will make two assumptions about the budget constraint. First, we'll assume that consumers do not save or borrow. We know, of course, that many consumers do save and borrow, but for now we want to keep our model simple by focusing exclusively on buying decisions. This assumption allows us to focus more sharply on how we can use the budget constraint to learn about important economic concepts. Second, we plot the budget constraint as a smooth line, even though our examples will be using whole units. We do this as a matter of convenience, and it does not affect the analysis.

Let's continue with the example of your birthday money. Assume for your 21st birthday that your parents and grandparents decide to surprise you with a $300 shopping spree. For simplicity, assume that this money is to be spent on *only* two goods—jeans or sweaters. Of course, in reality you could buy any number of other goods, but focusing on two goods draws out the most important insights from the economic model. And, once you understand the two-good case, it is usually straightforward to extend the analysis to more goods. Remember that you have exactly $300 to spend, and the price of jeans is $50 per pair and the price of each sweater is $25. Exhibit 5.1 provides the budget constraint and budget set for your shopping spree problem.

A first aspect of Exhibit 5.1 that might be confusing is the axis labels. Note that the quantity of pairs of jeans and sweaters are plotted on the *x*- and *y*-axes, respectively. In Chapter 4, we focused on demand and supply curves, which have quantity and price on the *x*- and *y*-axes. When plotting the budget constraint, however, the quantity of each good is on the *x*- and *y*-axes. That means the intercepts of the budget constraint represent the maximum quantity of each good that can be purchased if you buy only that good. So, the intercept values are the total dollars available divided by the price of the good measured on that axis. For example, the *x*-intercept is calculated as $300 divided by $50, or 6 pairs of jeans.

A second feature of Exhibit 5.1 is the triangular area. This area represents the budget set—all the possible combinations of goods (often called "bundles" in economics) that you can purchase. The solid blue line represents the budget constraint—the various quantities that you can purchase using all of your birthday money. The budget constraint is a straight line because you face a fixed price for jeans and sweaters that does not change with the number of goods that you buy. What else is the figure telling us?

Exhibit 5.1 The Budget Set and the Budget Constraint for Your Shopping Spree

With $300 to spend on sweaters and jeans, the budget set summarizes the bundles of sweaters and jeans that could be purchased. The budget constraint shows the bundles that exactly exhaust the entire budget. The table shows a few possible bundles on the budget constraint, while the figure plots the quantity of jeans on the *x*-axis and the quantity of sweaters on the *y*-axis.

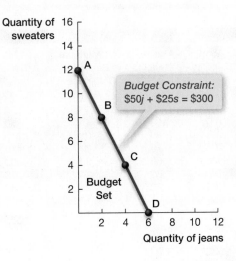

Four Bundles on the Budget Constraint

Bundle	Quantity of Sweaters	Quantity of Jeans
A	12	0
B	8	2
C	4	4
D	0	6

1. We can see that the scarcity principle discussed in Chapter 1 is at work: choosing to buy more sweaters means buying fewer pairs of jeans, and vice-versa. For example, with Bundle B you are buying 2 pairs of jeans and 8 sweaters. Compared to Bundle A you have 2 more pairs of jeans but at the expense of 4 sweaters. If you look at the table accompanying the graph, you can see the trade-offs between the amounts of pairs of jeans and sweaters.

2. Because your budget constraint is a straight line, its slope is constant. This means that your opportunity cost is constant.

We can compute your opportunity cost of buying jeans using a simple formula:

$$\text{Opportunity cost}_{\text{jeans}} = \frac{\text{Loss in sweaters}}{\text{Gain in jeans}}$$

where the loss in sweaters measures the number of sweaters that you must give up for one additional pair of jeans. Remember that the price of jeans is double that of sweaters, so opportunity cost$_{\text{jeans}}$ = 2 sweaters—this represents the opportunity cost of buying one pair of jeans. Another way to compute the opportunity cost of buying jeans is to consider the budget constraint. Because in this case it is a straight line, you can divide the y-intercept (12) by the x-intercept (6) to compute your opportunity cost of buying jeans.

A similar formula provides the opportunity cost of buying sweaters:

$$\text{Opportunity cost}_{\text{sweaters}} = \frac{\text{Loss in jeans}}{\text{Gain in sweaters}}.$$

Opportunity cost$_{\text{sweaters}}$ = ½ pair of jeans. This simply means that for every 2 sweaters that you decide to purchase you have to give up 1 pair of jeans. This follows from the fact that the price of jeans is twice the price of sweaters ($50 versus $25). Again, you can also compute this opportunity cost from the x- and y-axes of the budget constraint (6 divided by 12 = ½ pair of jeans).

5.2 Putting It All Together

Now that we have the three ingredients of the buyer's problem in place, we can begin to construct how we use these elements to optimize, or do the best we can given our preferences, prices, and budget. As an example, consider Exhibit 5.2, which lists all of the ingredients to solve the shopping-spree problem. In Exhibit 5.2 we have assumed that you have certain preferences, as indicated by the marginal benefits derived from each of various quantity levels. Note that in the benefits columns, we do not specify what units of

Exhibit 5.2 Your Buyer's Problem ($300 available)

The total benefits from consuming a given number of sweaters or jeans are presented, as are the marginal benefits from consuming each additional unit. Finally, the marginal benefit per dollar spent is included. The bolded rows are the quantity of sweaters and jeans that maximize total benefits when you have $300 to spend.

Quantity	Sweaters $25			Jeans $50		
	Total Benefits (A)	Marginal Benefits (B)	Marginal Benefits per Dollar Spent = (B) / $25	Total Benefits (C)	Marginal Benefits (D)	Marginal Benefits per Dollar Spent = (D) / $50
0	0			0		
1	100	100	4	160	160	3.2
2	185	85	3.4	310	150	3
3	260	75	3	**410**	**100**	**2**
4	325	65	2.6	490	80	1.6
5	385	60	2.4	520	30	0.6
6	**435**	**50**	**2**	530	10	0.2
7	480	45	1.8	533	3	0.06
8	520	40	1.6	535	2	0.04
9	555	35	1.4	536	1	0.02
10	589	34	1.36	537	1	0.02
11	622	33	1.32	538	1	0.02
12	654.5	32.5	1.3	539	1	0.02

measurement we are working with—for example, dollars or some other measure of value. But it is helpful to use similar units when comparing benefits and costs. For illustrative purposes, therefore, let's assume that the benefits are measured in dollars, because working with common units enables us to combine, and therefore *compare*, costs and benefits using operations like addition and subtraction.

So, how should you spend your $300? The problem calls for an approach based on marginal thinking. Using such an approach, you purchase the available good that yields the highest marginal benefits per dollar spent. As such, you should ask yourself: on which good should my first dollars be spent? Let's see how this approach works:

> **An optimizing buyer makes decisions at the margin.**

(1) The first sweater yields $100 in marginal benefits, whereas the first pair of jeans yields $160 in marginal benefits. Even though the first sweater has a lower marginal benefit than jeans, its price is half that of jeans, so you find that buying the sweater still yields the highest marginal benefits per dollar spent (the sweater yields 4 ($100/$25) in benefits per dollar spent, whereas the jeans yield 3.2 ($160/$50)). So you should purchase the sweater.

(2) Still thinking at the margin, you realize that your next choice should be to buy another sweater: buying the first pair of jeans yields $160 in marginal benefits, whereas buying another sweater yields $85 in marginal benefits. The marginal benefits per dollar spent favor buying the sweater.

(3) If you continue to reason in this way, you will find the quantities at which you optimize your total benefits—buying 6 sweaters and 3 pairs of jeans, exactly exhausting your budget of $300 and yielding $845 in total benefits. This optimal choice, which is bolded in Exhibit 5.2, maximizes your total benefits because there is no other spending pattern that yields a greater level of total benefits.

This solution highlights two important features of the buying problem. First, you should make your purchase decisions based on marginal benefits per dollar spent. Second, in doing so an important conclusion results: when optimizing, the marginal benefit that you gained from the last dollar spent on each good is equal.

This decision rule can be summarized via a simple equation:

$$\frac{MB_s}{P_s} = \frac{MB_j}{P_j},$$

where MB_s is the marginal benefit from sweaters, MB_j is the marginal benefit from jeans, and P_s and P_j are the respective prices of sweaters and jeans.

Economists sometimes call this the "equal bang for your buck" rule. In our shopping-spree example, you received $50 of marginal benefits from buying the sixth sweater and $100 of marginal benefits from buying the third pair of jeans. Therefore, we have:

$$\frac{\$50}{\$25} = \frac{\$100}{\$50}.$$

Why does this rule hold? Because if marginal benefits are not equal, then you can do better—be happier—by shifting consumption toward the good that has higher marginal benefits per dollar spent.

This rule can easily be extended to the case with a large number of goods. It teaches us that in equilibrium, the ratio of marginal benefits to price must be identical across goods. If this is not the case, then you can purchase a different basket of goods and be better off. You will notice that this rule of making decisions at the margin follows directly from the cost-benefit principle discussed in Chapter 1.

At this point, you might be thinking that while the example of sweaters and jeans works, the world might not always fit so neatly together algebraically. For example, there are some goods that are indivisible and have a high price—large-ticket items such as big-screen televisions, automobiles, houses, and yachts—which typically are consumed only infrequently.

This point is valid and very thoughtful. In these instances, buying the first house might provide higher marginal benefits per dollar spent than you gain from consuming other goods, but buying the second house yields fewer marginal benefits per dollar spent than other goods. In cases where goods are not easily divisible and our decision rule cannot be met exactly, the general intuition still holds: you should always spend each additional dollar on the good for which your marginal benefits per dollar spent are the largest.

What factors might change how many jeans and sweaters you purchase in equilibrium? There are two important ones that we now consider: changes in price and changes in income.

Price Changes

Consider what happens to our buyer's problem if the price of sweaters doubles to $50. Jeans and sweaters now have the same price. What must happen to the budget constraint with this change in price? Exhibit 5.3 gives us the answer. If you now buy all sweaters on your shopping spree, you can only buy 6 sweaters, so the *y*-intercept must change to 6. Does the *x*-intercept change? No, because the price of jeans has not changed.

What Exhibit 5.3 shows is that when the price of one good relative to the other good changes, the slope of the budget constraint must also change. Now if you buy an additional sweater you can purchase 1 less pair of jeans, so the opportunity cost$_{\text{sweaters}}$ = 1 pair of jeans. This stands to reason because the prices are now equal.

A *decrease* in the price of either good will cause the budget constraint to pivot outwards. For example, let's return to our original set of prices, but now assume that the price of jeans is cut in half—to $25 per pair. In this case, the budget constraint pivots outward and the *x*-intercept moves to 12. Exhibit 5.4 shows how the budget constraint pivots with a decrease

Exhibit 5.3 An Inward Pivot in the Budget Constraint from a Price Increase

Reproducing the figure in Exhibit 5.1 with an increase in the price of sweaters, we see that the budget constraint pivots inward. (Note that the term "pivot" signifies that one of the intercepts does not change.) This is because the consumer's income can buy fewer units of a good if the price goes up. The slope also changes because the opportunity cost changes when the price of one good changes.

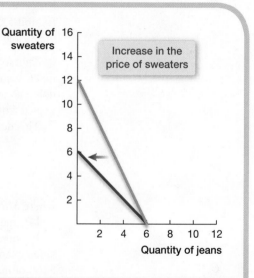

Exhibit 5.4 A Rightward Pivot in the Budget Constraint from a Price Decrease

A decrease in the price of one good causes the budget constraint to pivot outwards. This is because the consumer's income can buy more units of a good if the price goes down. The slope also changes because the opportunity cost changes when the price changes.

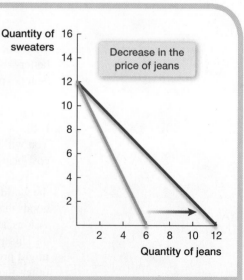

in the price of jeans. Again, the prices are identical after this price change, and therefore the opportunity cost$_{\text{jeans}}$ = 1 sweater.

How do price changes affect the buyer's problem? When a price changes, the opportunity cost changes. This will cause the buyer to change the optimal quantities consumed. Below we show how such price changes influence how many jeans and sweaters you purchase.

Income Changes

Another important factor that influences how many jeans and sweaters you purchase is how much money you have to spend—such cases revolve around changes in an individual's income, or budget. One example is if your shopping-spree gift turned out to be $600 instead of $300. Exhibit 5.5 shows the new budget constraint and how this change in income causes the budget constraint to shift outward. When income is doubled, the y-intercept and x-intercept of the budget constraint also must double because you have twice as much income. You can now buy more.

But the slope of the budget constraint does not change because the relative prices have not changed. Because the relative prices have not changed, the opportunity cost remains the same, too: buying 1 additional pair of jeans still precludes the purchase of 2 sweaters.

In the Evidence-Based Economics discussion and the appendix to this chapter we present examples of how income changes affect how many jeans and sweaters you purchase.

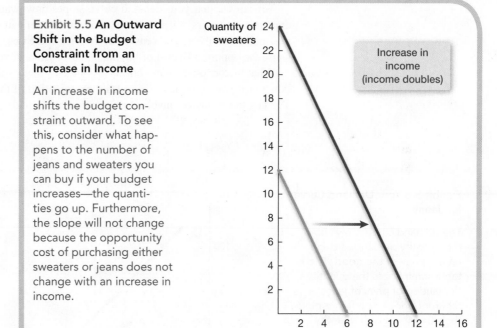

Exhibit 5.5 An Outward Shift in the Budget Constraint from an Increase in Income

An increase in income shifts the budget constraint outward. To see this, consider what happens to the number of jeans and sweaters you can buy if your budget increases—the quantities go up. Furthermore, the slope will not change because the opportunity cost of purchasing either sweaters or jeans does not change with an increase in income.

5.3 From the Buyer's Problem to the Demand Curve

With an understanding of how to spend optimally, we can begin to construct demand curves. Recall from Chapter 4 that willingness to pay is the highest price that a buyer is willing to pay for a unit of a good. Hence, if your willingness to pay for 1 gallon of orange juice is $10.00, it means that's the *highest* price that you are willing to pay for it.

An individual's willingness to pay measured over different quantities of the same good makes up the individual's *demand curve*. As we learned in Chapter 4, the demand curve isolates the contribution that a good's own price makes toward determining the *quantity demanded* in a given time period, keeping everything else the same. We also saw in Chapter 4 that quantity demanded refers to the amount of a good that buyers are willing to purchase at a particular price. A demand curve maps how quantity demanded responds to price changes, holding all else equal. We all have demand curves for many goods—from dinner dates to movies to oranges to cars to the *Twilight* series.

Let's look at a demand curve by continuing with the shopping-spree example. Once the three components of the buyer's problem are understood, we can derive your demand curve. We saw from our marginal analysis above that when the price of jeans is $50, you purchase 3 pairs of jeans. Thus, one point on your demand curve for jeans is price = $50, quantity demanded = 3.

What about if the price of jeans rises to $75? Using marginal analysis similar to what we used above, from Exhibit 5.2 we can compute that you now purchase 2 pairs of jeans. And, when the price of jeans rises to $100, your quantity demanded is 1 pair. Similarly, if the price decreases to $25, then your quantity demanded is 4 pairs of jeans. These combinations represent the demand curve and are displayed in Exhibit 5.6.

We produce Exhibit 5.6 by making optimal decisions based on the buyer's problem. Every point on your demand curve represents a unique price and quantity level. Therefore, the demand curve provides an indication of how many pairs of jeans you would like to buy at each price level. In Exhibit 5.6 we plot the demand curve as smooth, even though you would be unable to buy 3.5 pairs of jeans. We do this merely for convenience. As we move from the individual to the entire market of buyers, the units of quantity demanded will be so large that the demand curve will be smooth.

We can see that your demand curve slopes downward: at a price of $25 your quantity demanded is 4 pairs of jeans, but at a price of $50 per pair your quantity demanded decreases to 3 pairs. It only makes sense that as price increases, quantity demanded decreases because the opportunity cost of buying a pair of jeans increases.

What factors other than your tastes and preferences and the price of jeans might affect how many pairs you buy? Our earlier examination of the buyer's problem provides hints. The key to the answer involves prices of related goods and the budget set. Changes in the

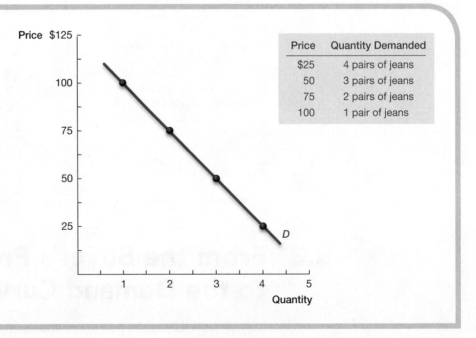

Exhibit 5.6 Your Demand Curve for Jeans

The demand curve shows how the quantity demanded depends on the price of the good. The table summarizes the quantity demanded of pairs of jeans at different prices. The figure plots those numbers with quantity demanded on the x-axis and price on the y-axis.

Price	Quantity Demanded
$25	4 pairs of jeans
50	3 pairs of jeans
75	2 pairs of jeans
100	1 pair of jeans

prices of related goods and the amount of money available both cause the demand curve to shift. In addition, as mentioned in Chapter 4, if your expectations of what is going to happen in the future change, then that also will shift the demand curve.

5.4 Consumer Surplus

Consumer surplus is the difference between what a buyer is willing to pay for a good and what the buyer actually pays.

Consumer surplus is the difference between the willingness to pay and the price paid for the good.

So far we've learned that in an effort to do the best we can, we should recognize the incentives that we face and make decisions based on marginal analysis. That is, we should consider the marginal benefits and marginal costs in our decision making. In markets, the process of optimal decision making by consumers often yields total benefits well above the price that we pay for goods. Economists give these market-created benefits a name— *consumer surplus*. **Consumer surplus** is the difference between the willingness to pay and the price paid for the good.

To illustrate how to calculate consumer surplus, let's continue with the shopping-spree example and consider the purchase of jeans more closely. Exhibit 5.7 provides the relevant points from your demand curve in Exhibit 5.6. Exhibit 5.7 shows that your willingness to pay for the first pair of jeans is $100. Because the market price is $50, you have gained $50 ($100 − $50) in consumer surplus from purchasing this first pair of jeans. Your willingness to pay for the second pair of jeans is $75; thus you gain $25 in consumer surplus from purchasing the second pair of jeans. How much consumer surplus do you gain from the third pair of jeans? The answer is zero, because your willingness to pay ($50) is exactly equal to the price ($50) that you pay for this pair of jeans.

At this point, you might be wondering why your consumer surplus ($75) is considerably lower than the total benefits that you received from buying the three pairs of jeans (from Exhibit 5.2, the total benefits from purchasing three pairs of jeans is $410, and you pay $150 for the jeans, yielding net benefits of $260). This is because the two measures are importantly different: consumer surplus measures the difference between your willingness to pay (the height of your demand curve) and what you actually pay for the good. The total benefits displayed in Exhibit 5.2 provide how much overall *satisfaction* you gain from consuming the good.

Computing consumer surplus for the market as a whole is calculated similarly. As we learned in Chapter 4, we can horizontally sum individual demand curves to obtain a market

Exhibit 5.7 Computing Consumer Surplus

Consumer surplus is the vertical distance between your maximum willingness to pay and the market price, which we represent with blue lines.

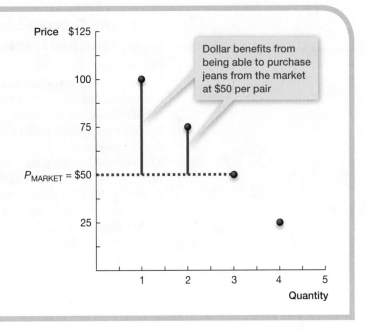

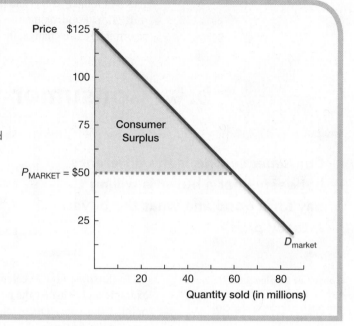

Exhibit 5.8 Market-Wide Consumer Surplus

Here we plot a market demand curve for jeans—notice that the quantity sold has increased considerably. Visually, you can think of the market-wide consumer surplus as the area of the triangle below the market demand curve and above the market price.

demand curve. Assume that upon doing so, we find that the market demand curve for jeans is given by Exhibit 5.8.

In Exhibit 5.8, "consumer surplus" represents the total market consumer surplus. Because the demand curve is linear, the area of the consumer surplus triangle can be computed as the base of the triangle multiplied by the height of the triangle multiplied by ½.

$$\text{Consumer surplus} = \frac{\text{Base of triangle} \times \text{Height of triangle}}{2}$$

$$= \frac{60 \text{ million} \times \$75}{2} = \$2.25 \text{ billion.}$$

Thus, the consumer surplus that all consumers receive from the jeans market is $2.25 billion. We can see from Exhibit 5.8 that this surplus is gained by those customers who actually buy jeans—the set of customers who are willing to pay $50 for jeans. These are customers on the top left portion of the demand curve.

An Empty Feeling: Loss in Consumer Surplus When Price Increases

Policymakers often use consumer surplus to measure the dollar value of consumer gains from a specific market and how those gains change with proposed legislation. How might it be useful in a practical sense? When working in the White House, one of the authors considered various policies to clean up groundwater. One potential solution was that jeans manufacturers would have to stop using certain chemical treatments on their fabrics. Say that the government concluded that if this policy took effect, the treatment chemical prohibition would increase the market price of jeans from $50 to $75. What happens to consumer surplus in the jeans market if everything else stays the same except for this price change? Exhibit 5.9 provides the answer.

Exhibit 5.9 shows the new consumer surplus, shaded in light blue. We find that market consumer surplus is now equal to 40 million × $50/2 = $1 billion. As a consumer, this development gives you an empty feeling, as many price increases do, because you have lost consumer surplus. In this situation, the market has lost $1.25 billion ($2.25 billion − $1 billion) in consumer surplus, which is shaded in orange.

Exhibit 5.9 Market-Wide Consumer Surplus When Prices Change

When price increases, consumer surplus decreases. This graph visually summarizes why—the higher the price, the smaller the difference between the willingness to pay and the market price. Furthermore, the higher the price, the lower the quantity demanded.

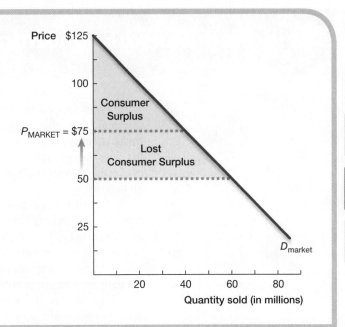

You, personally, have just lost $50 in consumer surplus from jeans market (your surplus is now $25). When determining whether to enact the new prohibition, policymakers compare such losses in consumer surplus to the benefits gained in cleaner groundwater to make a final policy decision (they also consider changes in *producer surplus*, which we discuss in the next chapter).

Evidence-Based Economics

Q: Would a smoker quit the habit for $100 per month?

At the beginning of this chapter, we posed a question concerning whether *a smoker would quit the habit for $100 a month*. Within the economics literature, an approach that is gaining popularity is to *pay* people to quit smoking. The tools of this chapter can help us begin to think about whether such an incentive can work, and why it might work.

In thinking about such a reward, we have learned that the impact of an increase in income leads to changes in the consumer budget constraint and subsequently the demand for goods and services. To see these tools in action, we return to the shopping-spree example. Exhibit 5.5 shows the mechanics behind the effects of an increase in what we have available to spend.

With that foundation laid, we can return to the question of quitting smoking for a month. Given our economic framework, the very same principle that was at work in the shopping-spree problem applies when considering the smoker's problem. By providing $100 for not smoking, we create a trade-off between the current benefits of smoking and the benefits obtained by $100 of increased income. There is also another saving: by not smoking, you save the money otherwise spent on cigarettes or cigars (shifting your budget constraint outward even more). For simplicity, let's assume that is another $100 per month. Thus the comparison that we need to make is whether, at the margin, $200 of additional monthly income provides more benefits than the current benefits you gain from smoking. If they do, then you quit smoking. If they do not, then you continue smoking and miss out on the $200 incentive.

Evidence-Based Economics *(Continued)*

5.1

5.2

5.3

5.4

5.5

As we discussed in the introduction, incentives come in many different forms—not just money. Another complementary approach that is often used to curb smoking is nonfinancial incentives. Such an approach includes advertisements highlighting what smoking does to your teeth and gums, warnings prominently placed on packs of cigarettes, counseling, social pressure, and banning smoking in public places, forcing smokers to go outside.

To explore whether financial and nonfinancial incentives can encourage smokers to quit smoking, researchers have designed randomized experiments. The experiments typically are carried out as follows. The researcher actively recruits smokers who are voluntary participants in a research experiment to help them quit smoking. The researcher then randomly assigns these participants to test and control groups. To measure compliance, biochemical tests are used to confirm that the participants have not smoked during the experimental period. In this way, if you are in the incentive treatment, you receive the financial incentive if the biochemical test reveals that you are smoke-free. If you are found to have smoked, then no financial incentive is rewarded.

One such study enrolled 179 subjects at Philadelphia Veterans Affairs Medical Center in a 10-week program to stop smoking. Subjects were randomly assigned to either a control group that received only the standard program or to a test group that received incentives in addition to the standard program.[1] The standard program comprised informational meetings every 2 weeks where 2 weeks' worth of nicotine patches were distributed to the participants. In addition to the informational meetings and nicotine patches, the participants in the test group received $20 for each meeting attended, and $100 if they were smoke-free 30 days after the program was completed.

The main results of the experiment are displayed in Exhibit 5.10. Exhibit 5.10 measures the percentage of people in the test and control groups who were smoke-free 30 days after the program was completed. The results highlight the power of incentives: 16.3 percent of the incentivized participants were found to have quit smoking. This rate is nearly four times greater than the 4.6 percent quitting rate of the nonincentivized group. This short-term effect of incentives is supported by several other studies, as discussed in an article which surveys this literature.[2]

Equally as important, however, is whether these people remained smoke-free after the incentive program was over. The Philadelphia Veterans Affairs experiment followed up with the experimental subjects 6 months after the program, again using biochemical tests. What do you think the researchers found?

Which would make you quit smoking?

Exhibit 5.10 Experimental Results from Smoking Study

This figure summarizes the results from the smoking study. Each bar depicts the percentage of participants that quit smoking. As you can see, the percentage of smokers that quit in the incentive group is a great deal higher than in the no incentive group.

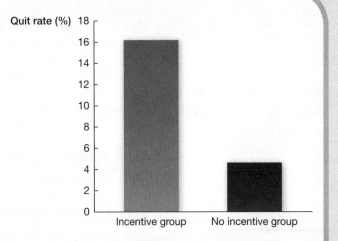

The results are enlightening. The researchers report that the 16.3 percent quit rate observed among the incentivized group had dropped to 6.5 percent. This was only slightly larger than the percentage of quitters in the nonincentivized control group, which remained at 4.6 percent. A clear conclusion is that the financial incentives are quite powerful: when incentives are in place, many people quit smoking because the benefits of quitting ($100 per month plus the money saved from not buying cigarettes) exceed the benefits of smoking. But when the financial incentives end, people tend to return to their old habit of smoking.

Can you think of other behaviors that financial incentives might change? Upon reading this chapter, you will likely not be surprised to learn that economists have. For example, as we learned in the appendix to Chapter 2, economists have used financial incentives to improve student performance. As those data suggest, receiving a financial reward of $50 per month caused high school students to improve their academic performance considerably—their grades and attendance levels improved. In another study, economists have measured the effects of paying students to go to the gym. Again, the results confirm the power of financial incentives—students in the incentivized group were much more frequently in the gym working out than those not receiving financial rewards. With these results in hand, several normative questions arise: should the government use taxpayer dollars to pay people to quit smoking or to go to the gym or to finish high school? We leave this for you to decide.

Question

Would a smoker quit the habit for $100 a month?

Answer

Yes, some will!

Data

Field experimental data.

Caveat

One should take care to understand that after the incentives are removed, many people who quit to earn the cash begin smoking again.

5.5 Demand Elasticities

Elasticity is the measure of sensitivity of one variable to a change in another.

So far, we've learned the nuts and bolts about where the demand curve comes from and whether quantity demanded increases or decreases when price changes. But suppose we want more precise answers as to exactly how responsive quantity demanded is to a change in price. Economic analysis can provide such answers with the concept of *elasticity*. **Elasticity** measures the sensitivity of one economic variable to a change in another. In other words, it tells us how much one variable changes when another changes. More precisely, an elasticity is the ratio of percentage changes in variables.

> **Elasticity measures the sensitivity of one economic variable to a change in another.**

By measuring changes in percentage terms, elasticity goes a step deeper than a simple recognition of the slope relationship of how one variable changes in relation to another. This is an important step because it permits not only a recognition of the direction of change but also the size of change. Elasticities come in many forms, but in this chapter we focus on the most important ones associated with demand curves:

1. The price elasticity of demand
2. The cross-price elasticity of demand
3. The income elasticity of demand

The Price Elasticity of Demand

The **price elasticity of demand** measures the percentage change in quantity demanded of a good due to a percentage change in its price.

We know from the Law of Demand that when the price of a good increases, the quantity demanded generally falls. But what we do not know from this law is *by how much* quantity demanded falls. The **price elasticity of demand** measures the percentage change in quantity demanded of a good resulting from a percentage change in the good's price. Formally, the price elasticity of demand is calculated as

$$\text{Price elasticity of demand}(\varepsilon_\text{D}) = \frac{\text{Percentage change in quantity demanded}}{\text{Percentage change in price}}.$$

To show how to calculate this elasticity, let's consider your demand schedule for jeans in Exhibit 5.6. When the price is $25 per pair you buy 4 pairs, but when the price increases to $50 per pair you buy only 3 pairs. This means that when the price increases by 100 percent (from $25 to $50), your quantity demanded decreases by 25 percent (from 4 to 3 pairs), yielding an elasticity of demand equal to

$$\frac{-25\%}{100\%} = -0.25.$$

Two features of this computation are important. First, because of the Law of Demand, the price elasticity of demand will generally be negative. Because this is the case, economists often drop the minus sign when reporting elasticities (mathematicians denote this as an absolute value), so we would state here that our price elasticity of demand is 0.25. We follow that convention here. As such, higher price elasticities mean that consumers are more responsive to a change in price.

Second, the distinction between whether a good has a price elasticity of demand greater than or less than 1 is of great import. Why? Suppose that you are working at your university bookstore and the manager wants to increase *revenues* from mug sales. Currently your store sells 20 mugs per week for $5 each, yielding revenues of $100 (20 mugs × $5). To increase revenues, your manager's first instinct might be to raise the price of mugs from $5 to $6.

We know from the Law of Demand that this 20 percent price increase will lower the *quantity* of mugs purchased, but we need to understand the elasticity of demand before we can make predictions about how revenues change. Assume that after the price increase, your store sells 12 mugs per week, yielding revenues of $72 (12 mugs × $6). Even though you raised the price of mugs, your revenues decreased. What is happening here?

The price elasticity of demand provides the answer. In this case, when price increased by 20 percent, the percentage change in quantity demanded decreased by 40 percent (8/20).

This means that the price elasticity of demand is 2 (40 percent/20 percent). When the price elasticity of demand is greater than 1, the percentage change in quantity demanded is greater than the percentage change in price. This means that any price increase will lead to lower revenues.

Alternatively, if the price elasticity of demand had been less than 1, the percentage change in quantity demanded would be lower than the percentage change in price. Consider the case where the same 20 percent price increase lowers quantity demanded by only 10 percent. The price elasticity is now 0.5 (10 percent/20 percent). In this case, mug revenues would increase to $108 (18 mugs × $6) if you raised the price from $5 to $6.

Finally, had the price elasticity of demand been exactly equal to 1, a 20 percent price increase lowers quantity demanded by exactly 20 percent. In this situation, any price increase would leave revenues unchanged. In sum, the revenues that your store brings in critically depend on the price elasticity of demand.

Moving Up and Down the Demand Curve

At this point, you might be wondering if the elasticity varies over the demand curve. Let's consider an example to find out.

Economists have found that many people value preserving ecosystems. Exhibit 5.11 uses data from a recent exercise that explored how much people are willing to pay to preserve cut throat trout in Yellowstone National Park. The demand curve is for Jacob, and shows how much he would pay to preserve various quantities of trout (which are measured in 100s on the x-axis). Point A on the demand curve informs us that at a price of $5, Jacob's quantity demanded is to preserve 100 trout; point B tells us that at a price of $1, Jacob's quantity demanded is to preserve 500 trout. What is the price elasticity at these two points?

First, let's calculate the price elasticity beginning at the higher price point on the demand curve, Point A ($P = \$5$, $Q = 100$). Say that price drops to $1, effectively moving along the demand curve until point B. In this case, price decreases by 80 percent ($4/$5) and quantity demanded increases by 400 percent (400/100). Therefore, the price elasticity of demand is equal to 5 (400/80 = 5). So Jacob is very responsive to price changes at point A.

Second, let's calculate the price elasticity of demand beginning at point B ($P = \$1$, $Q = 500$), for a price increase to $5. This moves along the demand curve from point B to point A. Now the price elasticity is 0.20 (the percentage change in quantity demanded is 80 percent, and the percentage change in the good's price is 400 percent).

This analysis reveals three important insights about elasticities. First, elasticity is a much different concept than the slope of the line. Even though the slope is the same over the entire demand curve (because demand is linear), the elasticity varies. This is because the ratio of price to quantity is different along the demand curve. For example, at Point A, the ratio is 5/100 whereas at Point B it is 1/500. As this ratio grows, demand becomes more elastic.

This leads to the second insight: elasticities tend to vary over ranges of the demand curve. You can see this in Exhibit 5.11. On the upper half of a linear demand curve, the elasticity is greater than 1, and on the lower half, the elasticity is less than 1. What this means is that

Exhibit 5.11 Jacob's Demand Curve for Trout Preservation

A linear demand curve for trout preservation is plotted, highlighting the way that price elasticity varies along a linear demand curve. The figure shows that the lower on the demand curve, the more inelastic is demand. At point A demand is elastic, whereas at point B demand is inelastic.

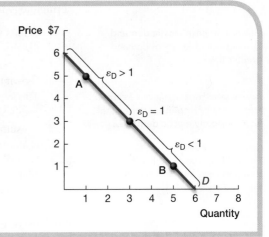

The **arc elasticity** is a method of calculating elasticities that measures at the mid-point of the demand range.

Moving Up and Down the Demand Curve

Arc Elasticities

One thing that you might be puzzled by is the fact that the elasticity is different depending on what you use as the starting and ending points. This is one reason why economists use the approach described in the text for small price changes.

Another measure that economists often calculate is **arc elasticity**. The arc elasticity achieves a stable elasticity regardless of the starting point by using the average price and quantity in the calculation:

$$\text{arc } \varepsilon_D = \frac{(Q_2 - Q_1) / [(Q_2 + Q_1) / 2]}{(P_2 - P_1) / [(P_2 + P_1) / 2]}$$

The upside of this formula for calculating elasticities is that regardless of where you start, the elasticity will be the same if you are examining changes over the same range of the demand curve. This is because the arc elasticity is a method of computing elasticities that measures at the mid-point of the range.

To see this fact, let's return to our example of trout preservation. First, let's calculate the price elasticity of demand beginning at $P = \$5$, $Q = 100$, and explore what happens when price drops to $1. Plugging the numbers into the formula, we have

$$\text{arc } \varepsilon_D = \frac{(500 - 100) / [(500 + 100) / 2]}{(1 - 5) / [(1 + 5) / 2]}$$

which equals 1. If we begin instead at the point $P = \$1$, $Q = 500$, and consider a price increase to $5, we estimate the arc elasticity as

$$\text{arc } \varepsilon_D = \frac{(100 - 500) / [(100 + 500) / 2]}{(5 - 1) / [(5 + 1) / 2]}.$$

Again, this equals 1. With this approach, moving from point A to point B provides an elasticity identical to moving from point B to point A.

When doing economic analysis we recommend that you compute the arc elasticity because this will provide you with a more accurate description of consumer responsiveness.

the elasticity from point A to point B is different from the elasticity from point B to point A. Finally, in the exact middle of a linear demand curve, the elasticity is equal to 1 at that point.

Elasticity Measures

Because of the importance of the price elasticity of demand, economists have developed a terminology to classify goods based on the magnitude of the price elasticity:

Goods that have **elastic demand** have a price elasticity of demand greater than 1.

- Goods with a price elasticity of demand greater than 1 have **elastic demand**. When the price elasticity of demand is greater than 1, the percentage change in quantity demanded is greater than the percentage change in price. Economic research has shown that peanut butter and olive oil tend to have elastic demand.

A very small increase in price causes consumers to stop using goods that have **perfectly elastic demand.**

- Theoretically, demand may be **perfectly elastic**, which means that demand is highly responsive to price changes—the smallest increase in price causes consumers to stop consuming the good altogether. The blue (horizontal) line in panel (a) of Exhibit 5.12 is an example of a perfectly elastic demand curve.

Goods that have **unit elastic demand** have a price elasticity of demand equal to 1.

- Goods with a price elasticity of demand equal to 1 have **unit elastic demand**. For such goods, a 1 percent price change affects quantity demanded by exactly 1 percent. In this case, a price increase does not affect total expenditures on the good. Economists have found that wine has unitary elastic demand. The blue line in panel (b) of Exhibit 5.12 is an example of a unit-elastic demand curve, where elasticity is measured using the arc elasticity.

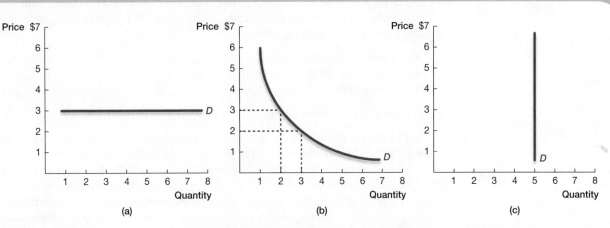

Exhibit 5.12 Examples of Various Demand Curves

From left to right, three demand curves are plotted to visually summarize a perfectly elastic, a unitary, and a perfectly inelastic demand curve. Although we will mainly deal with simple linear demand curves, extreme cases like these can be useful to consider for intuition.

Goods that have **inelastic demand** have a price elasticity of demand less than 1.

- Goods with a price elasticity of demand less than 1 have **inelastic demand**. When the price elasticity of demand is less than 1, the percentage change in quantity demanded is less than the percentage change in price. Research within economics has taught us that goods such as cigarettes and potato chips are not very responsive to price changes and thus have inelastic demand.

Quantity demanded is unaffected by prices of goods with **perfectly inelastic demand.**

- Demand can also be **perfectly inelastic**, which means that quantity demanded is completely unaffected by price. The blue (vertical) line in panel (c) of Exhibit 5.12 is an example of perfectly inelastic demand. The phrase "gotta have it" describes such goods, which include insulin for diabetics.

Determinants of the Price Elasticity of Demand

Exhibit 5.13 lists a handful of elasticity estimates that economists have generated with consumption and price data over the past several decades. One way to think about these numbers is to consider the types of goods that you might purchase when shopping at a supermarket. For example, as you walk in you might see a display of olive oil. Economists have found that olive oil has an elastic demand: a 1 percent increase in the price of olive oil yields a 1.92 percent decrease in quantity demanded of olive oil. This means that consumers are quite sensitive to changes in olive oil prices. You might walk an aisle over and see ketchup, which also is an elastic good, with a price elasticity equal to 1.36. At the end of the next aisle, you might see potato chips, which are an inelastic good because the price elasticity is equal to 0.45. This means that changes in their price cause small changes in quantity demanded: a 1 percent increase in the price of potato chips leads to a 0.45 percent decrease in the quantity demanded of potato chips.

Exhibit 5.13 Examples of Various Price Elasticities

Price elasticities are presented for a number of goods that are commonly consumed. The higher the price elasticity of demand, the more elastic is the demand for that good. For example, demand for shampoo is inelastic, whereas demand for olive oil is elastic.

Good Category	Price Elasticity[3]
Olive Oil	1.92
Peanut Butter	1.73
Ketchup	1.36
Wine	1.00
Laundry Detergent	0.81
Shampoo	0.79
Potato chips	0.45
Cigarettes	0.40

What do you think makes some goods, such as olive oil and ketchup, elastic, whereas others, such as shampoo and potato chips, are inelastic? Economists have pinpointed three primary reasons for elasticity differences:

- Closeness of substitutes
- Budget share spent on the good
- Available time to adjust

Let's look at each of them a little more closely.

(**1**) *Closeness of substitutes*. Say there is a strike among local cheese factory workers and the price of pizza skyrockets. You should ask yourself, "Is there another good, a *substitute good*, available that I like nearly as much as pizza?" If the answer is yes, then you will be more likely to switch to that good—perhaps hamburgers—rather than continue to purchase pizza at the higher price. In this way, the number of available substitutes affects how responsive consumers are to price changes: *as the number of available substitutes grows, the price elasticity of demand increases.*

(**2**) *Budget share spent on the good*. The budget share relates to how important the good is in your consumption bundle. People should give more weight to "important" goods and less weight to unimportant ones. If the good represents a small fraction of your overall purchases—say, a $0.50 key chain that you replace every five years—you likely will not be overly concerned if the local factory workers strike and the price of key chains doubles. It is just not important to your overall budget and so you are not sensitive to price changes, even large ones. Alternatively, if the good represents a large fraction of your budget—say, a house or furniture purchase—then you are likely to be more responsive to price changes. In general, *as you spend more of your budget on a good, the price elasticity of demand increases.*

(**3**) *Available time to adjust.* Time is an important element in that people are more responsive to price changes in the long run than in the short run. When the price of oil jumped to $150 per barrel in the summer of 2008 and a gallon of gasoline nationwide was $4, would a Hummer owner immediately trade it in for a hybrid? Probably not. Would the Hummer owner immediately stop driving and take public transit everywhere? Likely not, but she may have skipped that extra trip to the grocery store or passed on an extra visit to Grandma's house to save on gasoline.

The hummer

As we discussed in Chapter 4, gas prices led some Hummer owners to trade in their gas guzzlers.

The key is that it is difficult to make major changes in the short run, because you are constrained with what can be done over a short period of time. For example, the Hummer owner may have wanted to trade in her Hummer for a hybrid, but there may have been significant switching costs that prevented a reasonable trade. Her options would have been much more flexible in the long run; for example, she could arrange to carpool to work or move to an apartment near where she works. Such instances highlight the fact that *consumers, in general, respond much less to price changes in the short run than in the long run.*

The Cross-Price Elasticity of Demand

Cross-price elasticity of demand measures the percentage change in quantity demanded of a good due to a percentage change in another good's price.

Economists are interested in much more than merely how a good's price affects consumers. Another type of elasticity that economists consider is how quantity demanded for one good changes when the price of a substitute or complement good changes. This is called the **cross-price elasticity of demand** and is a measurement of the percentage change in quantity demanded of a good due to a percentage change in another good's price. Formally, the cross-price elasticity is written as:

$$\text{Cross-price elasticity} = \frac{\text{Percentage change in quantity demanded of good x}}{\text{Percentage change in price of good y}}.$$

This measure provides the elasticity of demand for good x with respect to the price of good y.

If a cross-price elasticity is negative, then the two goods are complements. As discussed in Chapter 4, two goods are complements when the fall in the price of one leads to a right shift in the demand curve for another. For example, if the price of iPods falls, you want more of them, but also your demand for headphones is likely to increase. The size of the cross-price elasticity determines the strength of the positive shift in your demand for headphones.

If a cross-price elasticity is positive, then the two goods are substitutes. Two goods are substitutes when the rise in the price of one leads to a right shift in the demand curve for the other. For example, an iPhone would be a substitute for an iPod—both are music storage devices. Thus, as the price of an iPod increases, instead of spending your money on the iPod, you might buy an iPhone instead.

Exhibit 5.14 summarizes a handful of cross-price elasticities that economists have generated with consumption and price data over the past several decades. A first insight from these examples is that goods such as meat and fish, clothing and entertainment, and whole and low-fat milk are substitutes for one another. At the other end of the spectrum, meat and potatoes and food and entertainment are complements. A second insight from Exhibit 5.14 is the magnitudes of the cross-price elasticities. For example, when considering whole milk and low-fat milk, a cross-price elasticity of 0.5 tells us that a 10 percent increase in the price of whole milk leads to a 5 percent increase in demand for low-fat milk. Economists have found such estimates useful to predict how changes in one part of the economy will influence demand in another. Policymakers use such estimates to gain an understanding of how taxation of one good affects the demand for another.

The Income Elasticity of Demand

The income elasticity of demand measures the percentage change in quantity demanded due to a percentage change in income.

A third type of elasticity measurement has to do with how changes in income affect consumption patterns. The **income elasticity of demand** informs us of the percentage change

Exhibit 5.14 Examples of Various Cross-Price Elasticities

This table of cross-price elasticities for a variety of goods shows that meat and fish are substitutes, whereas food and entertainment are complements.

Goods	Cross-Price Elasticity[4]
Meat and Fish	1.6
Clothing and Entertainment	0.6
Whole Milk and Low-Fat Milk	0.5
Meat and Potatoes	−0.2
Food and Entertainment	−0.7

Exhibit 5.15 Examples of Various Income Elasticities

At the top of the table are luxury goods, such as vacation homes, followed by other normal goods, such as gasoline, and finally by inferior goods, such as rice and public transit.

Goods	Income Elasticity[5]
Foreign Vacation	2.10
Domestic Vacation	1.70
Vacation Home	1.20
Healthcare	1.18
Meats	1.15
Housing	1.00
Fruits and Vegetables	0.61
Gasoline	0.48
Cereal	0.32
Environment	0.25
Electricity	0.23
Rice	−0.44
Public Transit	−0.75

in quantity demanded of a good due to a percentage change in the consumer's income. The income elasticity is calculated as

$$\text{Income elasticity} = \frac{\text{Percentage change in quantity demanded}}{\text{Percentage change in income}}$$

and reveals how a change in income affects the quantity demanded of a good. The sign and magnitude of income elasticities are of particular interest to economists. Goods are usually classified into two categories:

When income rises and consumers buy more of a good, it is a **normal good.**

- **Normal goods**: A good is normal if the quantity demanded is directly related to income; when income rises, consumers buy more of a normal good.

When income rises and consumers buy less of a good, it is an **inferior good.**

- **Inferior goods**: A good is inferior if the quantity demanded is inversely related to income; when income rises, consumers buy less of an inferior good.

Exhibit 5.15 summarizes a handful of income elasticity estimates that economists have generated. These data show that goods such as foreign vacations, healthcare, and electricity

 LETTING THE DATA SPEAK

Should McDonald's Be Interested in Elasticities?

Businesses are interested in the bottom line—profits. But before any profit target can be reached, businesses must bring in revenues. Revenues are simply the amount of money a business brings in from selling its goods and services. For example, a back-of-the-envelope calculation suggests that in 2011, McDonald's sold 15.6 billion hamburgers at a price of about $2.50 each. Therefore, McDonald's brought in $39 billion dollars of revenues through hamburger sales.

How hamburger revenues respond to price and income changes is a question of particular interest to McDonalds. As we discussed in this chapter, the secret to determining how revenues change when prices change is elasticity.

As we showed, when demand is inelastic, an increase in McDonald's hamburger prices will lead to an increase in revenues. On the other hand, when demand is elastic, an increase in the price of burgers will cause a decrease in revenues. This is the case because when demand is inelastic, an increase in price causes a relatively small decrease in quantity demanded, so revenues will increase. When demand is elastic, an increase in price causes a relatively large decrease in quantity demanded—so large that revenues actually decrease.

Because of this interesting property, price elasticities are important to businesses and policymakers. Studies of the elasticity of demand for fast-food restaurants suggest an *industry* elasticity of 0.8.[6]

So why doesn't McDonald's raise the price of its hamburgers? (*Hint*: Think about whether McDonald's faces the industry elasticity. If not, will the elasticity McDonald's faces be greater or less than the industry elasticity? Another consideration is how hamburger prices affect sales of other products at McDonald's.)

We have just learned that other elasticities are important, too. For example, food and entertainment have a negative cross-price elasticity (−0.7), meaning that they are complements.

If McDonald's hamburgers have a similar relationship with entertainment, then when the price of entertainment goes up by 10 percent, McDonald's can expect the demand for its product to decrease by 7 percent—an important insight for pricing and inventory purposes.

Likewise, upon understanding how income changes affect demand for its products, McDonald's can use advertising, pricing, or other means to maintain a healthy bottom line.

are normal goods. At the other end of the spectrum, goods such as rice and public transit are inferior: the more we earn, the less we consume.

Exhibit 5.15 shows that the *magnitude* of the income elasticity for normal goods can vary significantly. For example, if your income increases by 10 percent, your consumption of electricity increases by only 2.3 percent. The same 10 percent change in income, however, leads to a large change in foreign vacations—a 10 percent rise in income is associated with a 21 percent increase in foreign vacation expenditures. Goods with an income elasticity above 1 are called *luxury goods*.

Economists have found income elasticities useful to forecast how income changes will affect the overall economy. These numbers are important for policymakers because they help to inform how proposed rulemakings concerning income taxes might influence consumption of various goods and services.

Summary

☼ As a consumer, you optimize by solving the buyer's problem, which dictates that you make decisions at the margin, recognizing both financial and nonfinancial incentives.

☼ Individual demand curves are derived from the three components of the buyer's problem: what we like, prices, and how much money we have to spend.

☼ Consumer surplus measures the difference between an individual's willingness to pay and what the consumer actually pays for a good or service. Policymakers often use consumer surplus to measure how proposed legislation impacts consumer surplus.

☼ An elasticity measures the sensitivity of one economic variable to a change in another. Important elasticity measures include the price elasticity of demand, the income elasticity of demand, and the cross-price elasticity of demand. Elasticity measurement is especially important for businesses and policymakers who want to understand how consumer behavior changes in response to a price or policy change.

☼ Combining knowledge of the decision making rules that result from the buyer's problem with an understanding of elasticities, we can more reliably understand how we ourselves will respond to incentives, and we are better able to create the proper incentives to change behavior of others in a predictable way.

Key Terms

Questions

All questions are available in MyEconLab *for practice and instructor assignment.*

1. Why are consumers in a competitive market considered to be price-takers?

2. How does a consumer's budget set differ from his budget constraint? For a consumer with a given level of income, will the budget set have more combinations of goods or will the number of combinations be higher for the budget constraint?

3. Consider the following figures where the light blue line is the original budget constraint for a consumer and the dark blue line is the new one. Examine each case and explain what could have caused the change.

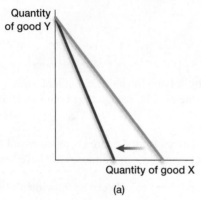

(a)

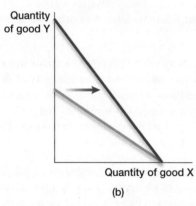

(b)

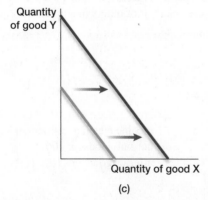

(c)

4. Why is a consumer's satisfaction maximized when marginal benefit from the last dollar she spent on one good is equal to the marginal benefit from the last dollar she spent on another good?

5. What is meant by consumer surplus? How is it calculated?

6. Consider the following supply and demand diagram:

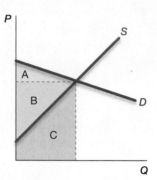

Identify which of the three areas labeled A, B, and C represents consumer surplus in this market.

7. Do all consumers receive the same level of consumer surplus? Explain with an example.

8. Consider a good that you do not like at all, perhaps turnips. Given the market price for turnips, what would be your consumer surplus?

9. Why does a demand curve with a constant slope not have a constant elasticity?

10. What does the price elasticity of demand show? In the market for sweaters, suppose Green's price elasticity of demand is 0.2, Smith's price elasticity is 1.2, and the price elasticity of all the other consumers is greater than 0.2 but less than 1.2. Could the market price elasticity be less than 0.2 or greater than 1.2?

11. How is the price elasticity of demand calculated using the arc elasticity method?

12. How is cross-price elasticity of demand used to determine whether two goods are substitutes or complements?

13. What can income elasticity of demand tell us about the nature of a good?

14. Examine the accuracy of the following statement: "Given that burgers and fries are complementary goods, if the price of fries increases the quantity demand for both goods will fall."

15. If a good is considered to be a luxury good, does it mean that the Law of Demand does not hold?

Problems

All problems are available in MyEconLab for practice and instructor assignment.

1. Tim is working on a school report on the proposed merger between American Airlines and U.S. Airways. He finds that U.S. Airways' annual revenue for 2012 rose by 3.7 percent over the previous year, while the revenue for American Airlines recorded an increase of almost 6 percent. Based on this, he concludes that, in 2012, passenger traffic must have increased more for American Airlines than for U.S. Airways. Is Tim's conclusion correct? Explain your answer.

2. Maya earns $1,000 per month and spends her income on clothing and books. Suppose the price of books is $40 and the price of clothing is $25.

   a. Show Maya's budget constraint in a diagram. Identify the slope and intercepts of this budget constraint.

   b. Suppose the price of books rises to $50, Maya's income remains $1,000, and the price of clothing remains $25. Draw a new diagram that shows Maya's new budget constraint. Identify the slope and intercepts of this budget constraint.

   c. Now suppose the price had remained at $40 but the price of clothing had fallen to $20 and Maya's income had fallen to $800. Draw a new diagram that shows Maya's new budget constraint. Identify the slope and intercepts of this budget constraint.

   d. Compare the budget constraints you drew to answer parts b and c of this question.

3. Suppose the price of X is $40, the price of Y is $50, and a consumer has income of $400.

   a. Draw the budget constraint for this consumer. What is the opportunity cost of buying one unit of good X?

   b. Which of the following combinations of X and Y will be represented by a point on the consumer's budget constraint? Plot the three bundles in your budget constraint diagram.

      i. 10 units of X and 1 unit of Y

      ii. 5 units of X and 4 units of Y

      iii. 1 unit of X and 2 units of Y

4. Akio consumes two goods, books and sweaters. His income is $24, the price of a sweater is $4, and the price of a book is $2.

   a. Suppose Akio's parents give him $8 for his birthday. Draw Akio's budget set.

   b. Now suppose Akio's parents had given him two sweaters for his birthday instead of giving him $8. Akio is a very polite young man and would never return a gift that his parents had given him. Draw Akio's budget set.

   c. Based on your answers to parts a. and b., is it possible that

   Akio would prefer a gift of $8 to a gift of two sweaters?

   He would prefer a gift of two sweaters to a gift of $8?

   He would be indifferent between a gift of $8 and a gift of two sweaters?

5. Hanna has $100 to spend on movies and concerts. Suppose the price of a movie ticket is $10 and the price of a concert ticket is $50.

   a. Create the budget constraint for movie tickets and concert tickets for Hanna.

   b. Show the change in the budget constraint that would occur if the price of concert tickets dropped to $40.

   c. Show the change in the budget constraint that would occur if the price of movie tickets doubled.

   d. Show the change in the budget constraint that would occur if Hanna had $200 rather than $100.

   e. Explain why we are not able to determine where on the budget constraint Hanna would choose to consume.

6. Georgina, an economics student, notices that the price of oil has been increasing steadily. She also observes that the total consumption of oil has actually increased. Georgina concludes that this is an exception to the Law of Demand. Do you agree? Explain your answer carefully.

7. You have decided to spend $40 this month on CDs and movies. The total benefits you receive from different quantities of CDs and movies are shown in the table below. The price of a CD is $10 and the price of a movie is $10.

	CDs			Movies		
	Total Benefit	Marginal Benefit	Marginal Benefit per Dollar	Total Benefit	Marginal Benefit	Marginal Benefit per Dollar
Quantity	(A)	(B)	(C)	(D)	(E)	(F)
0	0	x	x	0	x	x
1	200			140		
2	360			260		
3	500			360		
4	620			440		

   a. Complete columns B, C, E, and F in the table above.

   b. What combination of movies optimizes your total benefit? Explain your reasoning.

   c. Suppose the local movie theater decides to offer a student discount and as a result the price of a movie falls to $5. If the price of CDs remains $10 and you continue to spend $40 on CDs and movies, now what combination of movies optimizes your total benefit? Explain your reasoning.

8. Consider the following demand schedule:

Price	Quantity
$12	5
$10	10
$5	20
$3	30

a. Use the midpoint formula to calculate the elasticity of demand when price rises from

  i. $3 to $5

  ii. $5 to $10

  iii. $10 to $12

b. When price rises from $3 to $5, does expenditure rise, fall, or remain constant? What about when price rises from $5 to $10? When price rises from $10 to $12?

c. Why should you have anticipated your answers to (b) once you had answered part (a)?

9. Early in 2012, Starbucks, a global coffeehouse company, raised the prices of some of its beverages in certain parts of the country, mostly the Northeast and the southern states. While some thought that this was not a good idea, most analysts agreed that the price increase would not adversely affect its revenues. What would have to be true for the analysts' claim (that Starbucks' revenues would not fall) to hold?

10. When Sven graduated from college and got a job, his income rose from $15,000 to $60,000. His consumption habits also changed drastically. Use the following information to determine his arc income elasticity of demand and state whether the good is normal, inferior, or a luxury good. The arc income elasticity uses the midpoint of income and quantity.

a. Ramen noodles—consumption falls from 7 packs a week to zero.

b. Neckties—consumption rises from 1 per year to 11 per year.

c. Burrito at Sven's favorite burrito place—consumption rises from 1 per week to 2 per week.

11. Walmart and Target are both discount retailers. However, during the Great Recession of 2009, Target's same-store sales fell while sales at Walmart actually increased. Examine the following statements and identify the ones that could explain this outcome.

i. Walmart stocks more goods like food and health items than Target.

ii. Target positions itself in the market as a low-cost retailer of home accessories and clothing.

iii. Walmart's annual revenues have, on average, been higher than Target's annual revenues.

iv. Both Target and Walmart attract a lot of price-sensitive customers.

v. The unemployment level in the United States increased substantially during the recession of 2009.

12. During an economic slump such as the 2008 recession, what pricing strategies could a fast-food chain such as McDonald's use to maintain its sales? Use some of the concepts discussed in this chapter in your answer.

13. Nadia consumes two goods, food and clothing. The price of food is $2, the price of clothing is $5, and her income is $1,000. Nadia always spends 40 percent of her income on food regardless of the price of food, the price of clothing, or her income.

a. What is her price elasticity of demand for food?

b. What is her cross-price elasticity of demand for food with respect to the price of clothing?

c. What is her income elasticity of demand for food?

Appendix

Representing Preferences with Indifference Curves: Another Use of the Budget Constraint

Our goal in this chapter was to learn how consumers make choices. Through the lens of the buyer's problem, we learned about the importance of preferences, prices, and the budget constraint. Although we focused mainly on prices and the budget constraint, preferences are also very important. Exhibit 5.2 shows the "benefit" of each pair of jeans and each sweater. Where those preferences come from is too advanced for an introductory book, but in this appendix we touch upon the question of how economists think about preferences and consumer choice.

Returning to the shopping-spree example, recall that you have $300 to spend on sweaters and jeans. Similar to representing the budget constraint, we can show your preferences plotted graphically. To do so, economists commonly use a concept called the **indifference curve**. An indifference curve is the set of bundles that provide an equal level of satisfaction for the consumer. Economists often call this level of satisfaction **utility**, which is simply an abstract measure of satisfaction.

Exhibit 5A.1 uses the data from Exhibit 5.2 and displays two such indifference curves alongside your $300 budget constraint. The intuition of an indifference curve is that regardless of where you are on that curve, you are equally happy, or have the same level of utility. Consider the first indifference curve ($U = U_1$). If we choose point A (6 sweaters and 3 pairs of jeans), we know that it gives you the same level of satisfaction as point B (4 sweaters and 5 pairs of jeans). In fact, from Exhibit 5.2 we know that each bundle gives you $845 in total benefits.

What's convenient about indifference curves is that they summarize every possible bundle of sweaters and jeans for which you are indifferent based on your preferences. When this curve is plotted with the budget constraint, all of the elements of the buyer's problem are summarized. The budget constraint summarizes what you can afford and the indifference curve summarizes what you like. The combination of the two shows the point at which you should choose—or where you maximize your utility, or satisfaction, subject to your budget constraint.

To see this idea graphically, we focus on the budget constraint and the indifference curve in Exhibit 5A.1 where $U = U_1$. Along this indifference curve your utility is constant and along the budget constraint is every bundle of sweaters and jeans that you can afford. The point of tangency of the two, at point A, is the bundle that you can both afford and maximizes your satisfaction. You'll notice that the tangency of the indifference curve in Exhibit 5A.1 and the budget constraint from earlier is at 6 sweaters and 3 jeans, just as we found in our marginal analysis before.

An **indifference curve** is the set of bundles that provide an equal level of satisfaction for the consumer.

Utility in economics is a measure of satisfaction or happiness that comes from consuming a good or service.

Exhibit 5A.1 Introducing Indifference Curves

Plotting the budget line from Exhibit 5.1, this graph introduces two indifference curves, which are derived from the benefit data in Exhibit 5.2. Along each curve, consumers are indifferent—that is, their total benefits are constant. Take $U = U_1$; at points A and B total benefits are equal.

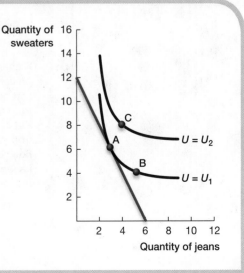

Indifference curves can also help us think about how choices change in response to changes in prices or income. In Exhibit 5A.1 we plot only two indifference curves, but for any given level of utility, there is an indifference curve. As we learned in this chapter, as income increases, the budget constraint shifts to the right; likewise, the budget constraint pivots in response to a price change. Combining an understanding of indifference curves with knowledge of the budget constraint informs us about how consumption changes when income or prices change. We avoid discussing the exact mechanics of this here, but just about every intermediate microeconomics textbook includes a discussion of these building blocks.

Instead, we will briefly discuss one of the most important conceptual issues associated with price changes. Consider if the price of jeans is cut in half: instead of $50 per pair, they are now $25 per pair. You might react in one of two ways: this is super news: "I feel 'wealthier' now so I am going to buy more jeans *and* sweaters." Economists call this an **income effect**, because this change in consumption moves you to a higher indifference curve. A second way in which you might react is to say: "jeans are now relatively cheap compared to sweaters, so I will buy more jeans and fewer sweaters." Economists call this a **substitution effect**, because this change in consumption moves you along a given indifference curve.

So, what do you think is the end result of these two effects? We know that you will certainly buy more jeans—our marginal analysis and demand curve told us that at a price of $25, you will purchase 4 pairs of jeans relative to the 3 pairs you were purchasing when the price was $50. And by the same marginal analysis, we know you will also buy more sweaters (8 instead of 6). However, how we get to this final optimum is a far more subtle point. On the one hand, jeans are relatively more affordable, meaning the substitution effect should increase your quantity demanded of jeans. On the other hand, looking back to Exhibit 5.2, we can see that the marginal benefit of jeans drops off very quickly after the fourth pair, whereas sweaters stay a consistently good deal, meaning the income effect may favor sweaters. It becomes an empirical question.

For our example, we find that with this price change, the number of jeans purchased increases to 4, and the number of sweaters increases to 8. Exhibit 5A.2 shows both effects graphically. Point A is the original optimum from the shopping spree where you buy 6 sweaters and 3 pairs of jeans. When the price of jeans drops to $25, the budget constraint pivots outward. Point C is the new optimum after the price of jeans drops to $25. The price drop causes you to buy 4 pairs of jeans and 8 sweaters. How do you get there? Through a combination of income and substitution effects.

To graphically visualize the two effects we start at point A and ask: in theory, how many sweaters and pairs of jeans would you buy at our original indifference curve ($U_1 = \$845$) with jeans at this new, lower, price? The answer is found at the tangency of our original indifference curve and the dashed budget constraint with the same slope as our new, pivoted-out red budget constraint. This dashed-line curve has a slope of -1 (since the ratio of the price of jeans to the price of sweaters is now $25/$25 = 1) and intersects both the *x*- and *y*-axes at 8.5 units. This tells us that the substitution effect due to cheaper jeans has given us the chance to achieve the same utility as before ($845) while spending less money

An **income effect** is a consumption change that results when a price change moves the consumer to a lower or higher indifference curve.

A **substitution effect** is a consumption change that results when a price change moves the *consumer along a given indifference curve.*

Exhibit 5A.2 Income and Substitution Effects

A change in price has two effects on consumption—an income effect and a substitution effect. If the price of jeans is halved, then the budget line pivots outward from the original blue line to the new red line. Point A is the original optimum and point C is the new optimum.

Exhibit 5A.3 Your Buyer's Problem ($300 available; price of jeans dropped to $25)

As in Exhibit 5.2, each row summarizes the benefits from consuming a given quantity of sweaters or jeans. The total benefits from consuming a given number of sweaters or jeans are presented, as are the marginal benefits from each additional unit. Finally, the marginal benefit per dollar spent is included. Note the significant drop-off in marginal benefits per dollar spent after the fourth pair of jeans.

Quantity	Sweaters $25			Jeans $25		
	Total Benefits (A)	Marginal Benefits (B)	Marginal Benefits per Dollar Spent = (B) / $25	Total Benefits (C)	Marginal Benefits (D)	Marginal Benefits per Dollar Spent = (D) / $25
0	0			0		
1	100	100	4	160	160	6.4
2	185	85	3.4	310	150	6
3	260	75	3	410	100	4
4	325	65	2.6	490	80	3.2
5	385	60	2.4	520	30	1.2
6	435	50	2	530	10	0.4
7	480	45	1.8	533	3	0.12
8	520	40	1.6	535	2	0.08
9	555	35	1.4	536	1	0.04
10	589	34	1.36	537	1	0.04
11	622	33	1.32	538	1	0.04
12	654.5	32.5	1.3	539	1	0.04

($25 × 8.5 = $212.50 < $300), a feat that would be impossible at the former $50 price point for jeans. The new tangency occurs at point S* and it tells us that the substitution effect moves your consumption of jeans from 3 to 4 and your consumption of sweaters from 6 to 4.5 (for convenience, we assume that you can purchase half units).

But stopping there would mean neglecting the $87.50 "extra" you now have to spend—the new lower price of jeans has made you relatively wealthier. Moving from point S* to point C summarizes the income effect of the new lower price. You can see that the income effect has a large impact, moving consumption of sweaters from 4.5 to 8 while keeping consumption of jeans unchanged at 4. For jeans, this might seem like a counter intuitive result—having *more* income left the quantity of jeans that you buy unchanged after the substitution effect. But let's not forget our discussion of marginal analysis and income elasticity.

Consider Exhibit 5A.3, which updates the marginal benefits per dollar spent to account for the decrease in the price of jeans. Notice that when buying the fifth pair of jeans, the marginal benefit per dollar spent is $1.2 ($30/$25), whereas purchasing a fifth sweater has a marginal benefit per dollar spent of $2.4 ($60/25). In fact, after the fourth pair of jeans, you really have little interest in buying more jeans because the marginal benefit of an extra sweater is always higher. What does this suggest about the income elasticity for jeans over this range? Importantly, it shows that whether jeans are a normal good depends on how many pairs of jeans you already own.

Appendix Questions

A1. What is an indifference curve? Can two indifference curves intersect? Explain your answer.

A2. Explain the income and substitution effects of an increase in the price of one good on an individual's consumption choice.

A3. Consider indifference curves for goods X and Y. Suppose we plot the quantity of good Y on the vertical axis and the quantity of good X on the horizontal axis.

a. Why are indifference curves downward-sloping?

b. What is the economic interpretation of the slope of an indifference curve?

c. Following what we learned in the Appendix to this chapter, indifference curves would flatten out as someone consumes more of good X and less of good Y. What are we assuming when we draw indifference curves that become flatter?

Appendix Key Terms

indifference curve *p. 111*
utility *p. 111*

income effect *p. 112*

substitution effect *p. 112*

6 Sellers and Incentives

How would an ethanol subsidy affect ethanol producers?

In every market, there are buyers and sellers. Taco Bell sells tacos, Apple sells iPods, Old Navy sells casual clothing, and Amazon.com sells Kindles. Service markets also feature buyers and sellers: you purchase tune-ups from mechanics, guitar lessons from music instructors, and haircuts from barbers. In the previous chapter, you learned a set of decision rules that led to optimal outcomes for the buyer. In this chapter, you'll learn a set of decision rules that optimize outcomes for the seller.

We begin with the seller's problem, which is nearly identical to the buyer's problem discussed in Chapter 5. In much the same way that consumers choose the optimal bundle of goods and services to maximize their net benefits, sellers choose what to produce and how much to produce to maximize *their* net benefits: profits.

Our discussion in this chapter continues to focus on perfectly competitive markets. We show that like optimizing consumers, optimizing sellers rely on marginal thinking. We will learn that simply knowing market prices and how much it costs a firm to produce a good or a service leads to a set of decision rules that govern the seller's problem. These insights will help you understand and predict how proposed public policies influence behavior and outcomes of firms. They also provide general guidance into how you should run your own business interests should your entrepreneurial spirit inspire you to start up an Internet company, open a Subway sandwich shop, or open an ethanol plant.

CHAPTER **OUTLINE**

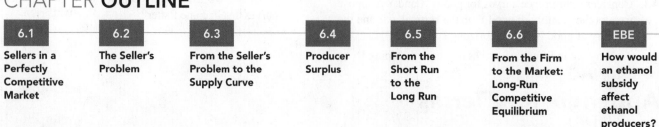

⚙ The seller's problem has three parts: production, costs, and revenues.

⚙ An optimizing seller makes decisions at the margin.

⚙ The supply curve reflects a willingness to sell a good or service at various price levels.

⚙ Producer surplus is the difference between the market price and the marginal cost curve.

⚙ Sellers enter and exit markets based on profit opportunities.

6.1 Sellers in a Perfectly Competitive Market

We will begin our study of how firms make decisions by assuming that they do so in *perfectly competitive markets*. Three conditions characterize perfectly competitive markets:

- No buyer or seller is big enough to influence the market price.
- Sellers in the market produce identical goods.
- There is free entry and exit in the market.

The first two assumptions are important because they ensure that agents in this type of market are price-takers—a term we've already met in Chapters 4 and 5. Just as a consumer is a price-taker by buying as much as she wants at the market price if she has enough money, sellers in perfectly competitive markets are price-takers in that they can sell as much as they want at the market price. The rationale behind this assumption is that an individual seller tends to sell only a tiny fraction of the total amount of a good produced. Because the seller's output is small relative to that of the market, the individual choice of how much to produce isn't going to be important for market outcomes. But the *combined* effect of many sellers' decisions *will* affect the market price.

We can see this through the lens of the decisions of a local farmer. If the farmer decides to rotate crops and grow corn this year rather than soybeans, this choice does not cause price fluctuations throughout the world. However, if every farmer in the world decided to grow corn this year instead of soybeans, the price of corn would decrease dramatically and the price of soybeans would increase.

The third assumption—that firms can enter and exit industries as they please—has important consequences for the market as a whole. One example of a market where sellers can enter and exit as they please is selling on eBay. At any time you can decide to enter the DVD market by auctioning off your DVD collection on eBay. Sellers can pretty much enter and exit freely in many other familiar markets, including lawn care, automobile repair, retail shops, and farming.

6.2 The Seller's Problem

The overarching goal of the seller is to maximize net benefits, or profits. The seller's problem therefore revolves around the question: "How do sellers decide what and how much to produce?" We can frame this question as a problem—the seller's problem—just as when

6.1
6.2
6.3
6.4
6.5
6.6

we looked at the buyer's problem in Chapter 5 and discussed how consumers make buying decisions.

Think of your local pizzeria. The owner first buys ingredients, then creates a masterpiece with dough, sauce, and toppings, after which he takes it to the market. In this analogy, the seller's problem has three main components. First, the seller must know how the inputs combine to make the outputs. For example, how many tomatoes are necessary for just the right sauce? Second, the seller must know how much it costs to produce a pizza. For instance, how much does the brick oven cost, and what about the electricity cost and workers' wages? And, does it matter that new ingredients need to be purchased each time he produces a pizza, while the oven sits ready for use? Finally, the seller must know how much he can sell the pizza for once it is produced. So we can say that the three elements of the seller's problem are:

1. Making the goods
2. The cost of doing business
3. The rewards of doing business

We'll now look at each of these elements in more detail.

Making the Goods: How Inputs Are Turned into Outputs

A **firm** is any business entity that produces and sells goods or services.

Production is the process by which the transformation of inputs to outputs occurs.

A **firm** is a business entity that produces and sells goods or services; it can consist of thousands of people, a few people, or a single person. Every firm faces the decision of how to combine inputs to create outputs. **Production** is the process by which the transformation of inputs (such as labor and machines) to outputs (such as goods and services) occurs. The relationship between the quantity of inputs used and the quantity of outputs produced is called the *production function*.

To begin to understand the production function, let's consider a real-life company in Sun Prairie, Wisconsin: The Wisconsin Cheeseman. The firm is a mail-order gift company that packs and mails food and floral products and ships them all over the world. Let's focus exclusively on one of the services that it provides: packing cheese into cheese boxes. The Cheeseman relies on two main inputs, labor to pack the cheese into boxes—a task that one of the co-authors of this book spent two teenage summers doing—and **physical capital** (equipment and structures). Physical capital is any good, including machines and buildings used for production.

Physical capital is any good, including machines and buildings used for production.

The **short run** is a period of time when only some of a firm's inputs can be varied.

The **long run** is a period of time when all of a firm's inputs can be varied.

A **fixed factor of production** is an input that cannot be changed in the short run.

A **variable factor of production** is an input that can be changed in the short run.

Marginal product is the change in total output associated with using one more unit of input.

Whereas hiring and firing workers can be done in a short period of time, altering physical capital takes a much longer period of time. Economists denote the **short run** as a period of time when only some of a firm's inputs can be varied—for The Cheeseman, labor. Alternatively, the **long run** is defined as a period of time wherein a firm can change any input. This means that physical capital is a **fixed factor of production**—an input that cannot change in the short run—and that labor is a **variable factor of production**—an input that can change in the short run.

Exhibit 6.1 provides information on The Wisconsin Cheeseman's short-run production function. It shows how the output varies with the number of workers employed (we've changed actual numbers because those are proprietary information). Columns 1 and 2 show how The Cheeseman's daily production of cheese boxes varies with the number of employees it hires. The first worker can complete 100 cheese boxes per day. Two workers can pack 207 cheese boxes per day. As such, the **marginal product** of adding the second worker is 107 cheese boxes in a day because this is the amount by which total output changes with the addition of the second worker (207 − 100). So we can define marginal product as the additional amount of output obtained from adding one more unit of input (in this case, workers).

For The Cheeseman, the only way to change production in the short run is to change the number of workers. Exhibit 6.2 provides a graphical summary of the relationship between the number of workers and the number of cheese boxes packed: the short-run production function. Exhibits 6.1 and 6.2 reveal three important characteristics of production for The Cheeseman.

(1) *The marginal product increases with the first few workers.* This feature suggests that, for example, two laborers working together can produce more than the sum of their production in isolation. This might happen because the first two workers *specialize* in a particular

6.1

6.2

6.3

6.4

6.5

6.6

Exhibit 6.1 Production Data for The Wisconsin Cheeseman

The Wisconsin Cheeseman is tasked with choosing how much output to generate per day, and the table summarizes the number of workers the firm will need for any given level of output. The first column is the number of cheese boxes produced per day, the second column is the number of workers employed, and the third column is marginal product: the additional output produced by each additional input (in this case, workers).

Details of Production		
(1) Output Per Day	(2) # Employed	(3) Marginal Product
0	0	
100	1	100
207	2	107
321	3	114
444	4	123
558	5	114
664	6	106
762	7	98
854	8	92
939	9	85
1019	10	80
1092	11	73
1161	12	69
1225	13	64
1284	14	59
1339	15	55
1390	16	51
1438	17	48
.	.	.
.	.	.
.	.	.
1934	38	10
1834	39	−100

Exhibit 6.2 The Short-Run Production Function for The Cheeseman

Plotted here is the number of workers on the x-axis and the number of cheese boxes produced on the y-axis. As the number of workers goes up, the number of cheese boxes that can be produced tends to increase, but notice that the first 10–15 workers lead to much steeper increases in production than the 25th–35th additional worker. Also notice that the last worker actually reduces productivity.

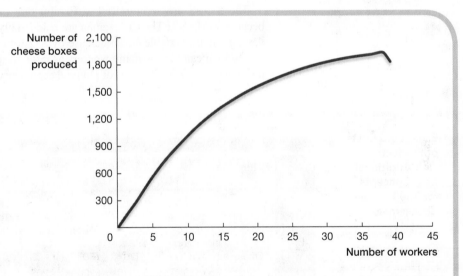

Specialization is the result of workers developing a certain skill set in order to increase total productivity.

portion of the cheese-packing task that they are good at completing. In **specialization**, workers develop specific skill sets so as to increase total productivity. To see specialization in action, during your next visit to Subway, watch how the first worker prepares the bread and places the meats just right. Then watch the second worker prepare the veggies, sprinkle oils, and cut the sandwich. After which, the third worker prepares the final product and tallies the bill. A true assembly line of beauty, something that specialization has created naturally.

(2) *The marginal product eventually decreases with successive additions of workers.* This characteristic means that as more and more workers are added they begin to add less and less to total production. For example, the marginal product of the fourth worker is 123 boxes, whereas it is only 114 boxes for the fifth worker. Economists call this decreasing production pattern the **Law of Diminishing Returns**. This law states that at a certain point of successive increases in inputs, marginal product begins to decrease. This law might apply for a number of reasons. For example, with a set amount of physical capital,

The **Law of Diminishing Returns** states that successive increases in inputs eventually lead to less additional output.

successive increases in labor eventually lead to lower output per worker because there is idle time—workers cannot use the machines as often as they would like.

(3) *Adding too many workers can actually decrease overall production.* This point refers to the fact that adding too many workers can be counterproductive. Indeed, this is exactly the situation with the last worker that The Cheeseman hires: Exhibit 6.1 shows that adding the thirty-ninth worker has a negative marginal product of 100 boxes! You can see this situation vividly in Exhibit 6.2, where the production curve begins to slope downward at that point. Management should send this worker home, dispatch him to a different task, or even have him wash the owner's dog, because he is lowering production of cheese boxes. This might happen because congestion causes workers to get in the way of one another.

The Cost of Doing Business: Introducing Cost Curves

We now look at the second component of the seller's problem: what the firm must pay for its inputs, or the **cost of production**. Similar to the two factors of production discussed above, there is a natural division in the total cost of production:

$$\textbf{Total cost} = \text{Variable cost} + \text{Fixed cost.}$$

This equation has three parts. **Total cost** is the sum of variable and fixed cost. **Variable costs** are those costs associated with variable factors of production. In The Cheeseman's case, these are costs associated with workers and therefore change with the level of production in the short run. In contrast to variable costs, a **fixed cost** is a cost associated with a fixed factor of production, such as structures or equipment, and therefore does not change with production in the short run. Indeed, in the short run, The Wisconsin Cheeseman has to pay for these factors even if it produces nothing because the firm cannot sell its plant and equipment in the short run.

These costs are summarized in Exhibit 6.3. Column 4 shows variable costs (*VC*)—because workers at The Cheeseman are paid a daily wage of $72 ($9 per hour, 8 hours per day), the daily variable costs increase by $72 for each worker hired. We assume that The Cheeseman can hire as many workers as it wants at this wage. The cost of structures and machinery represents the cost of physical capital, and this is computed by management to be

The **cost of production** is what a firm must pay for its inputs.

Total cost is the sum of variable and fixed costs.

A **variable cost** is the cost of variable factors of production, which change along with a firm's output.

A **fixed cost** is the cost of fixed factors of production, which a firm must pay even if it produces zero output.

Exhibit 6.3 Costs of Production with Additional Cost Concepts for The Wisconsin Cheeseman

The Wisconsin Cheeseman produces cheese boxes; this exhibit summarizes the cost of various levels of production. The total cost is the sum of fixed and variable cost. The average total cost is the sum of average fixed and average variable cost. The marginal cost is the change in total cost associated with producing one more unit of output. For convenience the numbers are rounded.

					Cost of Production				
(1)	(2)	(3)	(4)	(5)	(6)	(7)	(8)	(9)	(10)
Output Per Day (Q)	# Employed	Marginal Product = change in (1)	Variable Cost (VC) = $72 × (2)	Fixed Cost (FC)	Total Cost (TC) = (4) + (5)	Average Total Cost (ATC) = (6)/(1)	Average Variable Cost (AVC) = (4)/(1)	Average Fixed Cost (AFC) = (5)/(1)	Marginal Cost (MC) = change in (6)/ change in (1)
0	0		$ 0	$200	$ 200				
100	1	100	$ 72	$200	$ 272	$2.72	$0.72	$2.00	$0.72
207	2	107	$ 144	$200	$ 344	$1.66	$0.70	$0.97	$0.67
321	3	114	$ 216	$200	$ 416	$1.29	$0.67	$0.62	$0.63
444	4	123	$ 288	$200	$ 488	$1.10	$0.65	$0.45	$0.59
558	5	114	$ 360	$200	$ 560	$1.00	$0.65	$0.36	$0.63
664	6	106	$ 432	$200	$ 632	$0.95	$0.65	$0.30	$0.68
762	7	99	$ 504	$200	$ 704	$0.92	$0.66	$0.26	$0.73
854	8	92	$ 576	$200	$ 776	$0.91	$0.67	$0.23	$0.78
939	9	85	$ 648	$200	$ 848	$0.90	$0.69	$0.21	$0.85
1019	10	80	$ 720	$200	$ 920	$0.90	$0.71	$0.20	$0.90
1092	11	73	$ 792	$200	$ 992	$0.91	$0.73	$0.18	$0.99
1161	12	69	$ 864	$200	$1,064	$0.92	$0.74	$0.17	$1.04
1225	13	64	$ 936	$200	$1,136	$0.93	$0.76	$0.16	$1.13
1284	14	59	$1,008	$200	$1,208	$0.94	$0.79	$0.16	$1.22
1339	15	55	$1,080	$200	$1,280	$0.96	$0.81	$0.15	$1.31
1390	16	51	$1,152	$200	$1,352	$0.97	$0.83	$0.14	$1.41
1438	17	48	$1,224	$200	$1,424	$0.99	$0.85	$0.14	$1.50

6.1

6.2

6.3

6.4

6.5

6.6

$200 per day. These are the fixed costs (*FC*) given in column 5 of Exhibit 6.3. These costs are the same no matter how many workers are hired. Thus, fixed costs do not vary in the short-run, but variable costs do. Column 6 shows total cost (*TC*), which is the sum of variable and fixed costs for a particular quantity of output.

We are provided with three more interesting cost concepts if we divide both sides of our total cost equation by output (quantity The Cheeseman produces):

$$\frac{\text{Total cost}}{Q} = \frac{\text{Variable cost}}{Q} + \frac{\text{Fixed cost}}{Q}.$$

Average total cost (ATC) is the total cost divided by the total output.

The term on the left-hand side of this equation is called **average total cost (*ATC*)**, which is total cost divided by total output. Column 7 in Exhibit 6.3 shows the average total cost for The Cheeseman. For example, the ATC for The Wisconsin Cheeseman with an output of 321 units is computed by taking the total cost of $416 and dividing it by the total output of 321, which yields $1.29, as shown in Exhibit 6.3. This means that when it produces 321 units, the average cost per cheese box packed is $1.29.

Average variable cost (AVC) is the total variable cost divided by the total output.

The first term on the right-hand side of this equation is called the **average variable cost (*AVC*)**, which is the total variable cost divided by total output. For The Cheeseman, when it produces 321 units, its AVC is $0.67, which means that it pays its variable factor of production (labor) an average of $0.67 per cheese box packed.

Average fixed cost (AFC) is the total fixed cost divided by the total output.

Finally, **average fixed cost (*AFC*)** is the total fixed cost divided by the total output. For The Cheeseman, when it produces 321 units, its AFC is $0.62, which means that it pays its fixed factor of production (physical capital) an average of $0.62 per cheese box packed. What this all means is that of the $1.29 average total cost when The Cheeseman produces 321 units, $0.67 goes to variable costs (labor) and $0.62 goes to fixed costs (physical capital).

Marginal cost is the change in total cost associated with producing one more unit of output.

Our last cost concept is **marginal cost**, which is presented in column 10 of Exhibit 6.3. Marginal cost (*MC*) is the change in total cost associated with producing one more unit of output. Marginal cost can be written as:

$$\text{Marginal cost} = \frac{\text{Change in total cost}}{\text{Change in output}}.$$

When The Wisconsin Cheeseman produces 321 units, a *MC* of $0.63 means that it costs The Cheeseman $0.63 to produce the 321st cheese box. Exhibit 6.3 also reveals another interesting relationship: marginal cost and marginal product are inversely related to one another. As one increases the other automatically decreases. To see why, consider The Cheeseman's production and cost relationships. When The Cheeseman adds its first few workers (up to 4), the total output goes up and the marginal product also increases, decreasing marginal cost. After too many workers are hired, they find themselves wasting time, waiting to use equipment. This leads to lower marginal product and higher marginal cost.

Using the data from Exhibit 6.3, Exhibit 6.4 shows a graphical representation of the important relationships between costs and quantity produced: the marginal cost curve, average total cost curve, and average variable cost curve for The Cheeseman. Output quantity is plotted on the *x*-axis and costs (in dollars) on the *y*-axis. One interesting feature about these cost curves is that when the marginal cost curve is below the average cost curves (both average total cost and average variable cost), they must be falling or sloping downward, and when the marginal cost curve is above the average cost curves, they must be rising or upward-sloping.

Why? This is by itself the very nature of the definition of marginal cost. To capture this intuition, think of your overall grade point average (GPA) as average total cost and your semester GPA as marginal cost. Say that in your freshman year you earn all B's, a 3.0 GPA. Now let's say that in your sophomore year you earn straight A's, a 4.0 GPA. What will happen to your overall GPA? It will rise; in fact, if you take the exact same number of credits in each of your freshman and sophomore years, your cumulative GPA will now be 3.5. Now what happens to your overall GPA if in your junior year you earn all C's, a GPA of 2.0? It decreases. This is because your new grades are below the average that you established in your first two years.

This also provides the intuition for why *MC* intersects *AVC* and *ATC* at their minimums: when *MC* is below *ATC* and *AVC* they must be falling, and when *MC* is above *ATC* and *AVC* they must be rising, as in Exhibit 6.4. An understanding of these curves leads to powerful implications, as we discuss next.

6.1
6.2
6.3
6.4
6.5
6.6

Exhibit 6.4 Marginal Cost, Average Total Cost, and Average Variable Cost Curves for The Wisconsin Cheeseman

This figure plots several cost measures with the output (or quantity) on the x-axis and the cost (or price) on the y-axis. Each cost measure is plotted across various output levels. Notice that the MC curve intersects the ATC and AVC curves at their respective minimums.

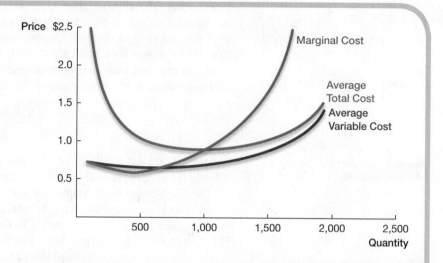

CHOICE & CONSEQUENCE

Average Cost Versus Marginal Cost

Imagine that you are asked to help in a fund-raising effort for your college.[1] You learn that your college has an old call center that it doesn't use. You ask why and the reply is "Well, the cost of making a call is $1, while the cost of mailing a letter is only $0.50." You are shocked: how could each call be that expensive?

After a little prodding, your college admits how the people who prepare their mailings calculated this figure of a dollar per call. They had simply summed the cost of the computer-networked phone-banking system your school had purchased years before and the cost of paying students to make calls and divided by the total

number of calls to obtain the average total cost of a call. Of course, they didn't take into account the fact that the school had already bought the computers and that the *marginal* cost of every call was very, very low—equal only to the amount you would have to pay a caller for a minute of time! If you know that the donation rate over the phone is much higher than the donation rate from mailings, and the marginal cost of sending a letter exceeds that of making a phone call, then after reading this chapter, you will know to immediately advise your college to pick up the phones and start dialing!

The Rewards of Doing Business: Introducing Revenue Curves

We are now ready to look at the third component of the seller's problem: the price at which a firm can sell its goods. A firm makes money from selling goods, and The Wisconsin Cheeseman is no different. The **revenue** of a firm is the amount of money it brings in from the sale of its outputs. Revenue is determined by the price of goods sold times the number of units sold:

Revenue is the amount of money the firm brings in from the sale of its outputs.

$$\text{Total revenue} = \text{Price} \times \text{Quantity sold}.$$

Recall that in perfectly competitive markets, sellers can sell all they want at the market price. Thus, they are price-takers.

But what determines the price of cheese boxes? Chapter 4 can lend insights to this question: the price comes from the intersection of the market demand curve and the market

> **The overarching goal of the seller is to maximize net benefits, or profits.**

supply curve. This is just like any other market equilibrium you learned about in Chapter 4: the intersection of market supply and market demand gives the equilibrium price.

Exhibit 6.5 reveals this intuition. Panel (a) of Exhibit 6.5 shows the market supply and market demand curves. Recall that we can construct the market demand curve as described in Chapters 4 and 5. We can construct the market supply curve in exactly the same manner as the market demand curve—through horizontally summing the individual supply curves. To see how this works, let's assume that in equilibrium, the cheese box packing industry has 10,000 identical firms, which each produce 1,225 cheese boxes per day. Thus, a total of 12,250,000 cheese boxes are packed daily in this market. As shown in panel (b) of Exhibit 6.5, this equilibrium quantity occurs at an equilibrium price of $1.13 per cheese box packed.

At this point, it is important to recognize the difference between the demand curve facing The Cheeseman and the demand curve in a perfectly competitive market. As panel (b) of Exhibit 6.5 reveals, a perfectly competitive firm, such as The Wisconsin Cheeseman, faces a horizontal demand curve, or a demand curve that is perfectly elastic. What this means is that The Cheeseman can pack as many cheese boxes as it desires and be paid the market equilibrium price ($1.13) for every cheese box packed. If The Cheeseman attempts to charge a little bit more than $1.13 per box, it will have no customers because buyers can go to a different packer and pay $1.13 per box. In addition, there is no reason for The Cheeseman to lower its price below $1.13 to attract buyers because it can sell all it wants at $1.13 per box.

Besides showing the demand curve facing The Cheeseman, panel (b) of Exhibit 6.5 shows the *marginal revenue* curve. **Marginal revenue** is the change in total revenue associated with producing one more unit of output. In a perfectly competitive market, marginal revenue is equal to the market price. Therefore, the marginal revenue curve is equivalent to the demand curve facing sellers. Because the price that The Cheeseman faces is $1.13, the marginal revenue is $1.13 for every cheese box packed. We are now in a position to learn about the good stuff—making money!

Marginal revenue is the change in total revenue associated with producing one more unit of output.

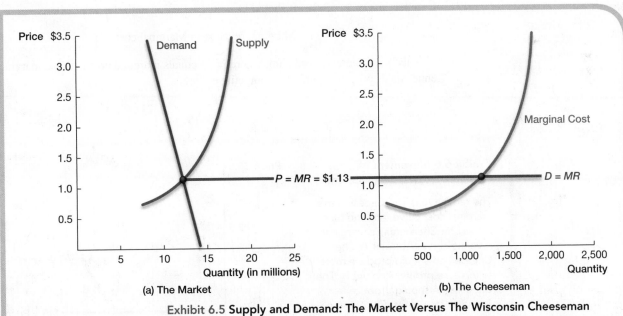

Exhibit 6.5 Supply and Demand: The Market Versus The Wisconsin Cheeseman

Panel (a) summarizes the market supply and market demand curves for cheese boxes. The price determined by the market equilibrium is the price The Cheeseman faces, which is shown in panel (b). We think of that price as representing the demand curve The Cheeseman faces, which is the flat blue line. This demand curve is equal to marginal revenue because it represents the change in revenues from selling one more cheese box.

6.1

6.2   The **profits** of a firm are equal to its revenues minus its costs.

6.3

6.4

6.5

6.6

Putting It All Together: Using the Three Components to Do the Best You Can

Now that we have the three components of the seller's problem in place, we can begin to construct how these three elements are used to maximize the firm's profits. The **profits** of a firm are the difference between total revenues and total costs:

$$\text{Profits} = \text{Total revenues} - \text{Total costs}.$$

For The Wisconsin Cheeseman to determine its profits, there is only one more question to answer: how much to produce? To figure out what quantity maximizes profits, we need to think about a production level and conduct a thought experiment as to how producing a bit more or a bit less affects both revenues and costs. That is, the key behind maximizing profits is to think about the firm's marginal revenues and marginal costs. This is an application of optimizing from Chapter 3.

To see how this works, consider Exhibit 6.6, which recreates panel (b) of Exhibit 6.5. Let's first think about point A in the exhibit. At this point, The Cheeseman hires 9 workers and it produces 939 cheese boxes. At this production level it costs $0.85 to pack the last cheese box, as given by the marginal cost in Exhibit 6.3. We know that The Cheeseman is paid $1.13 for each packed box.

Can The Cheeseman earn higher profits? Yes. If it produces one more cheese box, it increases revenues by $1.13, which is greater than the $0.85 it costs to produce. Profit could be increased by $0.28 just by selling one more cheese box! This provides a general rule: if a firm can produce another unit of output at a marginal cost that is less than the market price (that is, $MC < \text{price}$), it should do so, because it can make a profit on producing that unit.

Consider the other side of the coin: if The Cheeseman was producing at point B—hiring 17 workers and producing 1,438 units. Its marginal cost of producing the last unit is now greater than the market price ($1.50 versus $1.13); thus it loses money by producing that last unit. It therefore shouldn't produce it and should hire fewer workers.

In fact, with this marginal decision making in mind, it's straightforward to see how a firm maximizes its profits. It should expand production until the point where:

$$\text{Marginal revenue} = \text{Marginal cost}.$$

This is the same as producing where price equals marginal cost because marginal revenue equals price in a perfectly competitive market.

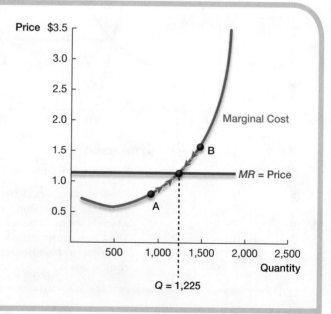

Exhibit 6.6 Movement of Production toward Equilibrium

The red curve is The Cheeseman's marginal cost curve, and the blue line is The Cheeseman's marginal revenue curve. At point A, The Cheeseman should produce more to increase profits. At point B, The Cheeseman should produce less. To maximize profits, Cheeseman produces where marginal cost equals marginal revenue.

6.1

6.2

6.3

6.4

6.5

6.6

How can we compute the level of profits at this point? One aid is to overlay the average total cost curve to Exhibit 6.6, which we do in Exhibit 6.7. Because total revenues = price × Q and total costs = ATC × Q, we can write total profits as:

$$\text{Price} \times Q - ATC \times Q = (\text{Price} - ATC) \times Q.$$

In other words, we can compute total profits by taking the difference between price and average total cost at the point of production and multiplying that difference by the total quantity produced. In the case of producing at $MR = MC$, this provides the shaded area in Exhibit 6.7.

We can compute this area as follows:

$$(P - ATC) \times Q = (\$1.13 - \$0.93) \times 1,225 = \$245.$$

This follows because The Cheeseman is paid $1.13 per box at a production level of 1,225 boxes. At this level of production, the average total cost is $0.93 (see Exhibit 6.3). So, taking the price of $1.13 and subtracting the average total cost of $0.93, we get $0.20, which is per-unit profit. We then multiply this per-unit profit by quantity sold, or 1,225, to find the daily profit figure of $245. This profit level is equal to the base times the height of the shaded rectangle in Exhibit 6.7. Because marginal revenue equals marginal cost ($MR = MC$) at this level of production, we know that this choice optimizes profits and represents the equilibrium for The Cheeseman: once producing at this point, The Cheeseman will not change its production activities unless something else in the market changes.

Profits of only $245 a day might seem trivial, but note that when economists discuss profits we are expressing something much different from what you're used to reading about in the newspapers. For example, when a major corporation reports "record profits," it is reporting what economists call **accounting profits**. Accounting profits are equal to revenues minus explicit costs. Explicit costs are the sorts of line-item expenditures that accountants carefully tally and report, like wages for workers or equipment expenditures. But firms also face implicit costs. For example, the owner of The Wisconsin Cheeseman may have a high opportunity cost of time that he is sacrificing in order to run The Cheeseman (to see where an implicit cost like this would play out in Exhibit 6.3, the cost of the owner's time would be in the Fixed Cost column). Much like the cost of labor and machines, this implicit cost is subtracted away from revenues to produce our conception of profits, **economic profits**. Economic profits are equal to total revenue minus both explicit and implicit costs. As a result, it is still feasible to run a business that is earning small (or even zero) economic profits, as we demonstrate later in this chapter.

Accounting profits are equal to total revenue minus explicit costs.

Economic profits are equal to total revenue minus both explicit and implicit costs.

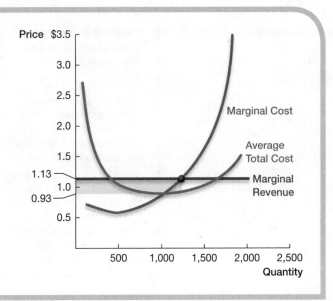

Exhibit 6.7 Visualizing The Wisconsin Cheeseman's Profits with MC, MR, and ATC

Adding The Cheeseman's ATC to Exhibit 6.6 allows us to visualize profits graphically. The shaded box represents The Cheeseman's profits. To see why, remember that profits are the difference between total revenue and total costs. Because MR represents price and ATC represents the cost per unit produced, their difference at the quantity where marginal cost equals marginal revenue multiplied by quantity produced yields total profits: ($1.13 − $0.93) × 1225 = $245.

6.1

6.2

6.3

6.4

6.5

6.6

CHOICE & CONSEQUENCE

Maximizing Total Profit, Not Per-Unit Profit

One common way of thinking is that if you maximize per-unit profit, you will maximize total profit. It only makes sense, right? If the firm is earning $10 per unit, it must be doing better than if it were earning $8 per unit. The flaw in this reasoning is that it only takes half of the optimal solution into consideration. That is, from the total profit equation it only takes (price − ATC) into consideration.

Recall that total profit comprises not only *how much* you sell each unit for in the market but also *how many* units you actually sell. If the $10 per unit is earned with 500 units of sales, then total profits are $5,000. But if the $8 per unit is earned with 1,000 units of sales, then the profit is $8,000—considerably more, even though the per-unit profits are lower.

The data in Exhibit 6.3 show this intuition for The Wisconsin Cheeseman. Because marginal revenue is a horizontal line, the per-unit profit is maximized when the ATC is at its lowest point. This happens to be point A in Exhibit 6.6. But it's not difficult to compute that The Cheeseman's profit at this point is lower than when production is expanded until MR = MC. In fact, at point A daily profit is $215.97. This is much smaller than the daily profit of $245 when profits are optimized. This might seem like a trivial difference, but if you translate these numbers across several plants and over several years, you're talking about big money.

6.3 From the Seller's Problem to the Supply Curve

> **The firm's supply curve relates output to prices.**

The *MR = MC* rule is powerful because, by linking the market price to the marginal cost curve, we can determine in the short run how a competitive firm changes its output when the market price changes. That is, it permits us to describe the firm's supply curve, which relates output to prices. To see why, think about how the market price determines the firm's output choice.

For instance, how would The Cheeseman change its behavior if the price for packing cheese increased to $1.41 per box, as shown in Exhibit 6.8? We would expect The Cheeseman to increase its quantity supplied, but by how much? Using the intuition discussed earlier, we expect The Cheeseman to expand production until *MC = MR₃*, which occurs at 1,390 units.

Exhibit 6.8 Impact of Price Changes on The Wisconsin Cheeseman

If the market price changes, the marginal revenue curve that The Cheeseman faces will also change. Here, when The Cheeseman faces an upward shift of the marginal revenue curve to MR_3, production will increase. On the other hand, if The Cheeseman faces a downward shift of the marginal revenue curve to MR_2, production will decrease.

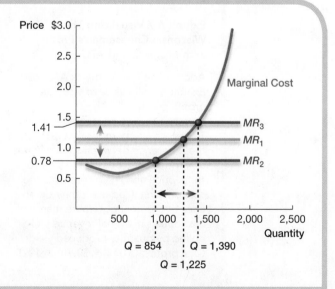

6.1

6.2

6.3

6.4

6.5

6.6

If, however, the market price for cheese boxes decreased to $0.78 per box (also shown in Exhibit 6.8), The Cheeseman would decrease production until $MC = MR_2$, which occurs at 854 units. Importantly, we can trace out The Cheeseman's supply curve by completing this exercise for various price levels.

Price Elasticity of Supply

Price elasticity of supply is the measure of how responsive quantity supplied is to price changes.

When considering how responsive the firm is to price changes, much like the case with demand in Chapter 5, we can use elasticity measures. In this case, the most important measure that economists use is called the **price elasticity of supply**, the measure of how responsive quantity supplied is to price changes is computed as:

$$\text{Price elasticity of supply } (\varepsilon_s) = \frac{\text{Percentage change in quantity supplied}}{\text{Percentage change in price}}.$$

The price elasticity of supply will tend to be positive because as price increases, firms tend to increase their quantity supplied.

Characterizing supply curves is quite similar to the descriptions we used to describe demand curves in Chapter 5. For example, an *elastic supply* means that quantity supplied is quite responsive to price changes: any given percentage change in price leads to a larger percentage change in quantity supplied. Panel (a) in Exhibit 6.9 shows the extreme case: a perfectly elastic supply curve. In this case, even a very small change in price leads to an infinite change in quantity supplied.

Alternatively, an *inelastic supply* means that any given percentage change in price causes a smaller percentage change in quantity supplied. An extreme case is depicted in panel (c) of Exhibit 6.9. Here the supply curve is perfectly inelastic: at every price level the same quantity is supplied. An example of such a case is an oil refinery that is operating at full capacity: even if gasoline prices increase, it cannot increase production in the short run. Similarly, if corn prices suddenly jump in July, it is difficult for Iowan farmers to produce more corn in the short run. They can plant more corn next year, but not this year.

In between these two extremes are typical supply curves—those that are upward-sloping. One example is presented in panel (b) of Exhibit 6.9. In these cases, the steeper the supply curve, the less sensitive quantity supplied is to price changes. Panel (b) of Exhibit 6.9 shows a special type of supply curve, one that is *unit-elastic*. A price increase from $5 to $6 (a 20 percent increase) leads to a 20 percent increase in quantity supplied; likewise, a price decrease from $6 to $5 (a 17 percent decrease) leads to a 17 percent decrease in quantity supplied. For unit-elastic supply curves, the elasticity is equal to 1: a 1 percent change in price leads to a 1 percent change in quantity supplied.

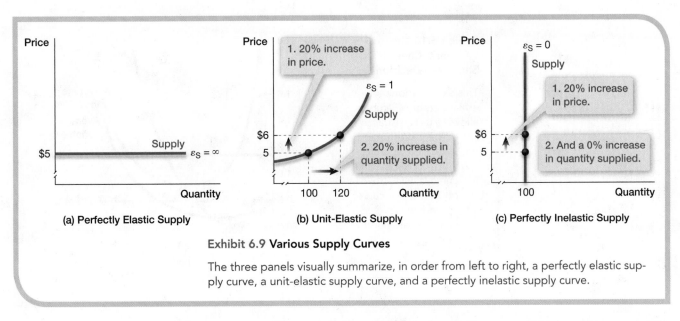

Exhibit 6.9 Various Supply Curves

The three panels visually summarize, in order from left to right, a perfectly elastic supply curve, a unit-elastic supply curve, and a perfectly inelastic supply curve.

6.1

6.2

6.3

6.4

6.5

6.6

Shutdown is a short-run decision to not produce anything during a specific period.

Much like demand elasticities, the size of supply elasticities is determined by several factors. Key determinants include whether the firm has excess inventories—if The Cheeseman has several tons of cheese on hand, it can more easily increase production quantities. Likewise, how long the firm has to respond to price changes is important—the longer the time to respond, the more elastic the supply. Finally, if workers are readily available, then supply will be more elastic because the firm can respond to price increases by quickly hiring workers.

Shutdown

With an understanding of how quantity supplied responds to price changes, we can consider extreme market situations, such as when the firm should **shut down**, or suspend, operations. A shutdown is a short-run decision to not produce anything during a specific time period. Think about the case when the market price drops to $0.59 per cheese box. Now the $MR = MC$ rule directs The Cheeseman to produce at point S in Exhibit 6.10 (444 units). Is this a profit-maximizing point of production?

The answer is no. This is because at this particular price the firm does not even bring in enough money to cover its average variable cost of $0.65 per unit. Why? Note that the price is below average variable cost at this point ($0.59 < $0.65); thus if The Cheeseman continues operations, it is paying the variable input—workers—more to produce cheese boxes than the firm is bringing in per cheese box.

The Cheeseman should shut down because by doing so it would lose only the fixed costs of production ($200) rather than the fixed costs ($200) plus the uncovered variable costs ($0.06 per unit, or 444 × $0.06 = $26.64). This is so because by shutting down the plant, it employs no workers, and hence has zero variable cost.

You might think, "Wait a second! Why shut down and absorb the fixed costs? By producing, The Cheeseman can at least earn some revenues." That is true. The Cheeseman would bring in money by remaining in operation, but for every unit it produces it is paying labor $0.06 more than it is receiving in marginal revenue. The optimization rule that follows is that if revenues do not cover all of the variable costs, then shutdown is optimal in the short run:

The firm should shut down if price is less than *AVC*.

So, should The Cheeseman ever produce in the short run if total costs exceed total revenues? The answer is yes. Consider point C in Exhibit 6.10. This is a point of production where price is greater than average variable cost, but price is less than average total cost. In this case, the price is greater than the average variable cost; thus all of the variable costs are covered by revenues. This is an instance when The Cheeseman should continue operations

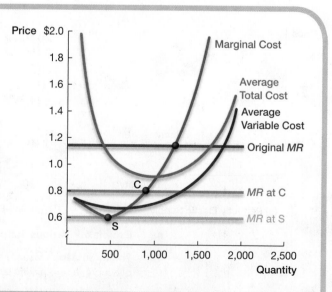

Exhibit 6.10 The Wisconsin Cheeseman's Shutdown Decision

This exhibit shows several different *MR* curves, allowing us to visualize when The Cheeseman produces and when it shuts down. The original *MR* curve is well above the other two *MR* curves introduced, which intersect the *MC* curve at points C and S.

6.1

6.2

6.3

6.4

6.5

6.6

Exhibit 6.11 Short-Run Supply Curve: Portion of the *MC* Above AVC

Here we reproduce Exhibit 6.4, but we've done two things to the original *MC* curve. First, we're now referring to it as the short-run supply curve and second, the portion below the *AVC* curve is cut off because at prices below the minimum *AVC* the firm shuts down.

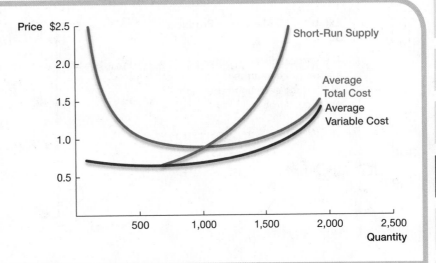

even though it is losing money because besides covering all of the variable costs, it is also covering a fraction of the fixed costs.

You might think that it does not make sense for The Cheeseman to continue production at point C; after all, the firm is losing money! Why not shut down? The key is that we assume fixed costs are **sunk costs**, which are a special type of cost that, once they have been committed, can never be recovered (think of a 5-year building lease—The Cheeseman is by law required to pay rent over the entire 5-year period). That is, The Cheeseman can't retrieve sunk costs in the short run. One of the important things to remember about sunk costs is that once they are committed, *they shouldn't affect current or future production decisions*. The reason for this is simple: these costs are sunk—that is, lost, regardless of what action is chosen next—they can't affect the relative costs and benefits of current and future production decisions. By continuing operations at point C, The Cheeseman is at least covering some of the fixed cost.

These examples lead to construction of the short-run supply curve for The Cheeseman: *it is the portion of its marginal cost curve that lies above average variable cost.* If the market price puts The Cheeseman at a point on its marginal cost curve that lies below the minimum of the average variable cost curve, then the firm should shut down. Otherwise, it should produce. Exhibit 6.11 shows The Cheeseman's short-run supply curve as the marginal cost curve above the average variable cost curve.

Sunk costs are costs that, once committed, can never be recovered and should not affect current and future production decisions.

6.4 Producer Surplus

Similar to the concept of consumer surplus, economists have a means of measuring surplus for sellers. This is called *producer surplus.* **Producer surplus** is computed by taking the difference between the market price and the marginal cost curve.

Thus, graphically, producer surplus is the area above the marginal cost curve and below the equilibrium price line. In this way, it is distinct from economic profits, as we measured in Exhibit 6.7, because economic profits include a consideration of total cost, not just marginal cost.

Let's consider producer surplus for The Cheeseman. Assume that The Cheeseman is facing a market price of $2, as depicted in Exhibit 6.12.

As it turns out, The Cheeseman can produce many units at a marginal cost below the market price. In Exhibit 6.12, we depict this surplus as the pink-shaded region that is below the market price and above The Cheeseman's marginal cost curve. Notice the similarity between this and consumer surplus—whereas a

Producer surplus is the difference between the market price and the marginal cost curve.

> Producer surplus is computed by taking the difference between the market price and the marginal cost curve.

6.1

6.2

6.3

6.4

6.5

6.6

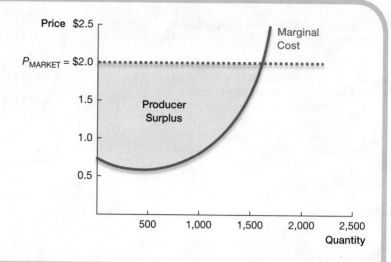

Exhibit 6.12 Measuring Producer Surplus

The vertical distance between the market price and the marginal cost to produce each unit represents producer surplus.

consumer's surplus arises from having a willingness to pay above the market price, a producer's surplus arises from selling units at a price that is above marginal cost.

Similar to consumer surplus, we can add up sellers' producer surplus to obtain the total producer surplus in the market. We do this by measuring the area above the marginal cost curve that is below the equilibrium price line to compute producer surplus for the entire market.

When we have linear supply curves, we can use a mathematical formula to compute the producer surplus. Consider panel (a) of Exhibit 6.13, which shows a supply curve for daily trucking services to ship cheese from Madison, Wisconsin to Milwaukee, Wisconsin. If the equilibrium market price is $100 per trip, then we compute the producer surplus as the base of the triangle multiplied by the height of the triangle multiplied by ½:

Producer surplus = ½ × (Base of triangle × Height of triangle) = ½ × (4 × $80) = $160.

This means that total producer surplus per day is $160 in this market.

There are several ways in which producer surplus can increase or decrease. For example, if there is a shift in the market demand curve that causes a higher equilibrium market price, producer surplus increases because the area above the supply curve and below the equilibrium price line gets larger. This is shown in panel (b) of Exhibit 6.13. Now producer surplus is ½ × (5 × $100) = $250.

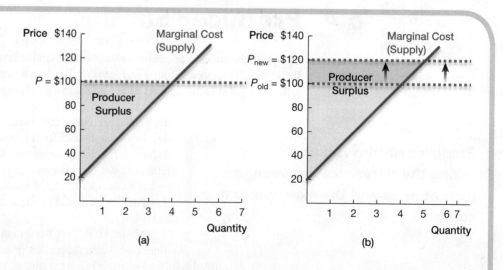

Exhibit 6.13 Producer Surplus for Trucking Services

The two panels show the supply curve for trucking, with dotted red lines representing the *MR* curve faced by the producer. Panel (a) shows that producer surplus is the triangle below *MR* and above the supply (marginal cost) curve. Panel (b) shows what happens to producer surplus when the price increases.

6.5 From the Short Run to the Long Run

6.1

6.2

6.3

6.4

6.5

6.6

Thus far we have only considered The Cheeseman's daily production decision, and in doing so, we've treated the facilities and machinery (or physical capital) that The Cheeseman uses as fixed. But firms often think about more than just each day's production. For example, many businesses issue quarterly or annual reports that discuss the firm's long-term outlook. In this section we move from the daily supply decision to the long run, where The Cheeseman can combine any quantity of labor and physical capital to maximize profits.

What exactly is the long run, though? As we have already noted, the long run is defined as a period of time in which all factors of production are variable. That is, in the long run there are no fixed factors of production because even machines and buildings can be retrofitted, purchased, expanded, or sold. Because of this fact, there are important differences between a firm's short- and long-run supply curves.

These differences can be understood by considering The Cheeseman's production decisions. In the short run, if it wants to change production, it can only do so by hiring more workers or laying off workers. This is because only labor is variable in the short run. In the long run, however, The Cheeseman searches for the optimal combination of workers *and* building size (physical capital). That is, in the long run, The Cheeseman is able to combine workers and physical capital to achieve the minimal *ATC* for each output level. This difference causes the short-run cost curves to be above the long-run cost curve.

To see the relationship between the short- and long-run cost curves, consider short-run *ATC*s for three different plant sizes: one small, one medium, and one large. These are each shown in panel (a) of Exhibit 6.14. Because in the long run The Cheeseman is able to choose the plant size that minimizes costs, its long-run *ATC* lies below the three short-run *ATC*s. One way to think about it is that the average cost rises more in the short run with increased production because The Cheeseman can only hire more labor; in the long run it can hire more labor and purchase more physical capital.

As Exhibit 6.14 shows, the long-run *ATC* curve has a pronounced U-shape. On panel (a) of the U, *ATC* decreases as output increases. Over this range, **economies of scale** exist. For The Wisconsin Cheeseman, we find that economies of scale occur over the daily output range until about 444. Such an effect might occur because as the scale of the plant gets bigger, workers have more opportunities to specialize. When *ATC* does not change with the

Economies of scale occur when ATC falls as the quantity produced increases.

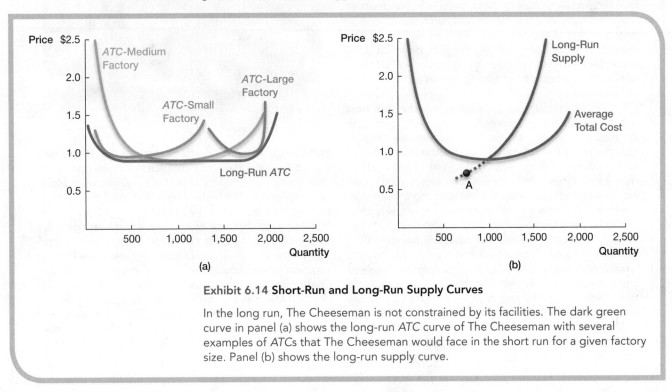

Exhibit 6.14 Short-Run and Long-Run Supply Curves

In the long run, The Cheeseman is not constrained by its facilities. The dark green curve in panel (a) shows the long-run *ATC* curve of The Cheeseman with several examples of *ATC*s that The Cheeseman would face in the short run for a given factory size. Panel (b) shows the long-run supply curve.

6.1

6.2

6.3

6.4

6.5

6.6

Constant returns to scale exist when ATC does not change as the quantity produced changes.

Diseconomies of scale occur when ATC rises as the quantity produced increases.

Exit is a long-run decision to leave the market.

level of output, the plant experiences **constant returns to scale**. This occurs over the output range of 444 to 1,690. **Diseconomies of scale** occur when *ATC* increases as output rises. For The Cheeseman, this occurs at output levels exceeding 1,690. This might happen because management teams begin to get spread too thin or duplication of tasks occurs.

Long-Run Supply Curve

Panel (b) of Exhibit 6.14 shows the long-run supply curve (marginal cost curve) alongside the long-run *ATC* curve. We can use this marginal cost curve to construct The Cheeseman's long-run supply curve in a way similar to how we derived the short-run supply curve from the marginal cost curve.

Consider point A. Should The Cheeseman produce at this price? The answer is no. This is because this price is lower than average total cost, and therefore The Cheeseman is spending more money to produce cheese boxes than it is paid for them. So total revenue is less than total costs, leading to a negative economic profit.

There is really no choice for Cheeseman but to **exit** the industry because it cannot profitably exist at the equilibrium price. Note that exit is a long-run decision to leave the market. We can therefore state a long-run decision rule:

Exit if: Price is less than *ATC* or, likewise, if total revenue is less than total cost.

This reasoning naturally leads to the construction of a long-run supply curve for The Cheeseman that is different from its short-run supply curve: *the long-run supply curve is the portion of its marginal cost curve that lies above average total cost.* This is shown in panel (b) of Exhibit 6.14 with the solid red line depicting the long-run supply curve.

CHOICE & CONSEQUENCE

Visiting a Car Manufacturing Plant

Recently, we visited Chrysler's car manufacturing plant in Sterling Heights, Michigan, where thousands of cars are produced annually by thousands of workers. The assembly plant houses highly skilled workers and plenty of robotics to put together the various pieces to create a final product—combining sheet metal with hundreds of loose parts to make a shiny rimmed automobile.

In one part of the plant, we saw a welded frame (the chassis) moving along a large conveyor belt. The conveyor belt swerved through many teams of workers, who were responsible for adding to this initial baseline component.

One team carefully set the engine in place. The next put in front and rear suspension, a different team later installed the transmission, then another team was responsible for the steering box, and yet another for the brake system. Before the car was painted with three coats of shiny paint, inspectors made sure no defects were apparent. Finally, before leaving the lot, even more inspectors made sure that the brakes, windshield wipers, windows, and other parts were operating up to standard.

What is noteworthy about this process is the *specialization* that occurred. Each worker had a single job: install a specific part, inspect, or paint. Each specific job involved a complex set of tasks that must be precisely completed to provide the quality and quantity necessary to ensure the plant was optimizing profits.

We can imagine that if workers instead were dispatched to build these cars separately, they would not be able to produce one per day in total. But, with specialization, this

plant can produce hundreds of cars per day. In this way, a large assembly plant can produce more cars per worker than a small assembly plant. This is exactly what Henry Ford realized in 1908 when he introduced the world to the first affordable car—the Model T.

Although at the time Ford had many advantages—for example, the success of the Model T arose in part from using Vanadium steel, which put Ford years ahead of its competition—specialization was especially important. Ford's plants and every car plant now reaps economies of scale. Much as for The Wisconsin Cheeseman, economies of scale are achieved when *ATC* declines as output increases. One of the key features in prosperous modern economies is that specialization leads to more production per worker.

The dotted line below *ATC* is the portion of the supply curve that exists in the short run, but not in the long run because it is between the *AVC* and *ATC* curves.

The Cheeseman's total profit in the long run is computed identically to its short-run profit: total revenue minus total cost. Thus, profit equals the difference between price and average total cost multiplied by the quantity sold: $(P - ATC) \times Q$. Accordingly, when computing producer surplus in the long run, we take the difference between market price and the seller's long-run marginal cost curve.

From knowing how to derive the short-run and long-run supply curves, a natural question arises: what factors determine where the firm's supply curve is located on the graph? Because the supply curve is the marginal cost curve above the *AVC* curve (in the short run) or above the *ATC* curve (in the long run), the answer to this question revolves around cost considerations. Similar to the individual demand curve, there are factors that cause the firm's supply curve to shift leftward or rightward. These factors were more fully discussed in Chapter 4, but include input prices (such as labor costs) and technological innovations.

6.1

6.2

6.3

6.4

6.5

6.6

6.6 From the Firm to the Market: Long-Run Competitive Equilibrium

Much like the short-run and long-run analysis for the individual firm, at the industry level there are critical distinctions between the short run and the long run. The primary difference is that even though the number of firms in the industry is fixed in the short run, in the long-run firms can enter or exit the industry in response to changes in profitability because in the long run they have the ability to change both labor *and* physical capital.

> Even though the number of firms in the industry is fixed in the short run, in the long run firms can enter or exit the industry in response to changes in profitability.

Firm Entry

When would a firm decide to enter a market? Steve's Wholesale Cheese (an actual firm in Sun Prairie, Wisconsin located near The Wisconsin Cheeseman) is considering entering the cheese-packing industry, which currently has 10,000 identical firms. Suppose Steve's Wholesale is identical to The Cheeseman and to the other firms. Further, assume that the current market price is above Steve's minimum long-run average total cost, as in point E of Exhibit 6.15.

Should Steve enter? The answer is yes. Notice that because the price is $1.13, which is greater than Steve's average total cost of $0.93, Steve can enter the industry and make a profit of $(P - ATC)$ on each unit produced. In this case, Steve would earn profits given by the area of the shaded rectangle $(P - ATC) \times Q$. Therefore, Steve's Wholesale Cheese should take advantage of this opportunity and enter the cheese-packing business.

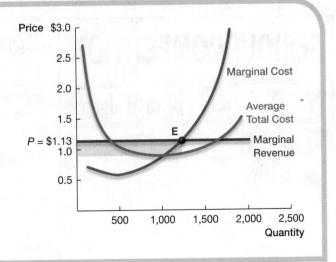

Exhibit 6.15 Steve's Wholesale Cheese Entry Decision

Considering a new firm, Steve's Wholesale (which is identical to The Cheeseman), we see that there are potential profits to earn by entering. We can see this by noting that the area of the shaded box representing economic profits is greater than zero when the market price is at $1.13.

6.1

6.2

6.3

6.4

6.5

6.6

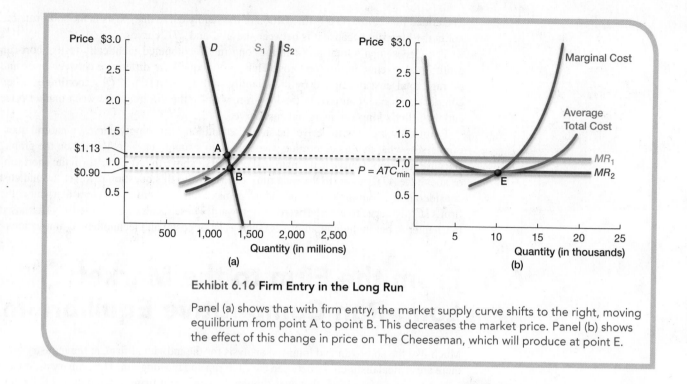

Exhibit 6.16 **Firm Entry in the Long Run**

Panel (a) shows that with firm entry, the market supply curve shifts to the right, moving equilibrium from point A to point B. This decreases the market price. Panel (b) shows the effect of this change in price on The Cheeseman, which will produce at point E.

There is **free entry** into an industry when entry is unfettered by any special legal or technical barriers.

It's not hard to imagine that *many* firms would make this calculation, realize they can be profitable in the industry, and decide to enter. What would happen then? If there is **free entry** into the industry—which means entry is unfettered by any special legal or technical barriers—the entry process continues until the last entrant drives the market price down to the minimum average total cost. Let's walk through why this is the case.

First, think about what entry of new firms does to the market supply curve. Because the market supply curve is the summation of individual firms' supply curves, adding new firms causes the industry to provide higher quantity at any given price. After all, the entrants must be added to the existing industry total. In other words, entry shifts the market supply curve to the right.

This shift will cause the market price to fall. Why? Panel (a) of Exhibit 6.16 provides the intuition. We know that the market price in a perfectly competitive industry is determined by the intersection of the market demand and market supply curves (point A in the exhibit). A shift to the right of the market supply curve from S_1 to S_2 lowers the market price from $1.13 to $0.90 (point B in panel (a) of Exhibit 6.16).

Will another firm decide to enter? No, because the market price drops to the minimum of the average total cost curve (point E in panel (b) of Exhibit 6.16). At this point, the market reaches an equilibrium because no more firms will enter. For this example, Steve entering the market moved the price down to the minimum average total cost of the industry, resulting in zero economic profits. There is now no longer a profit incentive for other suppliers to enter.

If upon entry the new price would have been above the minimum average total cost, then another firm would have entered because there remains an incentive to enter. This would further shift the market supply curve to the right, lowering the market price even more. This would continue until the market price was driven to the minimum average total cost of the industry.

Firm Exit

Now suppose that once we reach that equilibrium, a group of researchers issues a report claiming that touching cheese can give skin irritations to toddlers. This announcement causes the market demand curve for cheese boxes to shift leftward. Assume that this shift of the market demand curve for cheese boxes causes the equilibrium price to change from $0.90 to $0.71, as in panel (a) of Exhibit 6.17, where the price drops

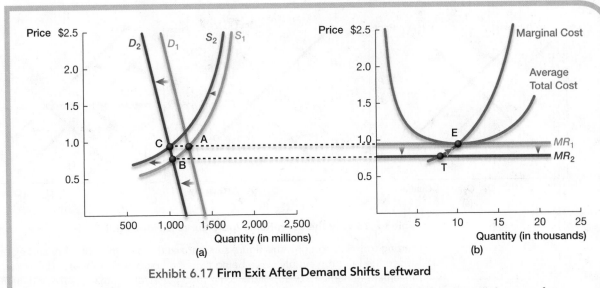

6.1

6.2

6.3

6.4

6.5

6.6

Exhibit 6.17 Firm Exit After Demand Shifts Leftward

Panel (a) shows that if market demand shifts to the left, price will decrease from point A to B. At this new price, firms will exit, which will cause the market supply curve to shift to the left, moving the market equilibrium to point C and putting The Cheeseman at point E in panel (b).

There is **free exit** from an industry when exit is unfettered by any special legal or technical barriers.

from point A to B. The price is now below the minimum average total cost of the firms, as shown in panel (b) of Exhibit 6.17 at point T. This causes firms in the industry to make negative profits. Therefore, if there is **free exit** from the market—in which a firm's exit is unfettered by any special legal or technical barriers—in the long run some cheese packers will close shop and leave the industry. Because we've assumed that all firms are identical, all firms in the market are equally unprofitable and would prefer to exit. You might wonder which firms exit. There are a couple of ways to think about this. One is that there are a lucky few who figure out that they're losing money before the others, and they leave first. The other, probably more realistic, possibility is that there are cost differences across firms, and the highest-cost firms exit first. We examine an example of this in the appendix to this chapter, but for now let's continue with the example of all firms being identical.

This exit from the industry causes the market supply curve to shift leftward, raising the market price from point B to point C in panel (a) of Exhibit 6.17. Just as entry continued until the price was driven down to the minimum average total cost, exit continues until the market price rises to the minimum average total cost. Once this point is reached, we are in a long-run equilibrium. This occurs at point E in panel (b) of Exhibit 6.17.

Notice that regardless of initial demand or supply shifts and accompanying price changes in the market, entry or exit causes the market to reach the minimum of the long-run average total cost curve. That is, the equilibrium quantity in the market might change due to market demand and supply shifts, but the equilibrium price *always* returns to the minimum of the long-run average total cost.

Zero Profits in the Long Run

We can see that free entry and free exit are forces that push the market price in a perfectly competitive industry toward the long-run minimum average total cost. This leads to two important outcomes under our perfectly competitive market assumption.

First, even though the industry's short-run supply curve is upward-sloping for the reasons we discussed above, the industry's *long-run* supply curve is horizontal at the long-run minimum average total cost level. Why? Price always returns to the minimum average total cost, and because average total cost does not change, price always remains the same in the long run. This is because variations in long-run industry output are absorbed by firm entry and exit, causing long-run quantities to change, but not equilibrium prices.

Let's walk through an example to illustrate this intuition. Consider panel (a) in Exhibit 6.18, which shows an initial market demand of D_1 and supply of S. The initial equilibrium quantity is Q_1 and price is P_1, which we know is equal to the minimum average total cost.

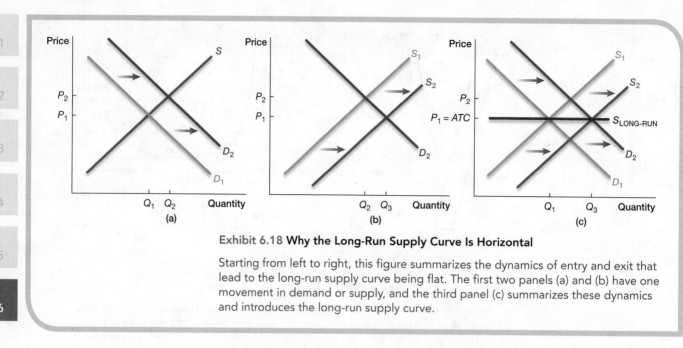

Exhibit 6.18 Why the Long-Run Supply Curve Is Horizontal

Starting from left to right, this figure summarizes the dynamics of entry and exit that lead to the long-run supply curve being flat. The first two panels (a) and (b) have one movement in demand or supply, and the third panel (c) summarizes these dynamics and introduces the long-run supply curve.

Suppose market demand shifts rightward to D_2. While prices might temporarily rise, entry of new firms in the long-run shifts the supply curve to the right, as in panel (b) of Exhibit 6.18. As entry continues, supply eventually reaches S_2 and price falls back to the long-run minimum average total cost, or a price of P_1. If we connect the two long-run equilibria, we have the market's long-run supply curve $S_{LONG-RUN}$, which is horizontal at P_1, shown in panel (c) of Exhibit 6.18.

So, we see that in the long run price equals the minimum of average total cost because of entry and exit. Because there are a number of identical firms standing ready to enter or exit the industry, in the long run as much quantity as necessary can be produced at the minimum average total cost.

The second long-run outcome achieved with free entry and exit is that firms in a perfectly competitive market earn zero economic profits in equilibrium. Economic profits serve an important signal as to whether firms are better off in this industry or some other industry: if economic profits are positive, then entry occurs until economic profits fall to zero. If economic profits are negative, exit occurs until economic profits rise to zero. Free entry and exit forces price to the minimum average total cost, and therefore economic profits are zero in the long-run equilibrium.

An important assumption that we make in this analysis is that firms are identical and can hire inputs (labor and physical capital) at a constant cost (i.e. the industry can hire as many workers as it desires at $72 per day). When firms are not identical in terms of their cost structure, we find results that diverge from this zero economic profit conclusion. In such cases, low-cost firms can earn positive economic profits in long-run equilibrium. We leave this case to be discussed further in the appendix.

Economic Profit versus Accounting Profit

If you're thinking from an entrepreneur's perspective, maybe the zero-profit implication of firm entry and exit makes you despair a little. After all, why even try to start a business if the end result will be profitless? As we discussed earlier, there is one important reason why you shouldn't think this way: economic profits are not the same as accounting profits. As a business owner, when economic profits are zero, it simply means that you cannot earn more money if you take your talents to a different industry—you are being paid at least your opportunity cost of time.

Let's think through the difference between accounting and economic profits with an example. On January 20, 2011, newspaper clippings in Sun Prairie, Wisconsin, read:

Wisconsin Cheeseman Closing. Workers at the Wisconsin Cheeseman Company in Sun Prairie were told Thursday that the company is closing. Wisconsin Cheeseman President and CEO Dave Mack said the company is being restructured. He said 80 mostly full-time employees were put on notice Thursday that they could lose their jobs in two months.

To some, this came as a surprise because they believed that The Wisconsin Cheeseman had been earning a profit. Why would a company earning a profit go out of business, many wondered. The answer lies in the definition of profit—even though The Cheeseman might have been earning positive accounting profits, economic profits might have been negative. For instance, assume that if The Cheeseman were not in its current line of business, its next best use for its management team and physical capital would be to set itself up as a warehouse for fast-food storage for nearby Madison.

In fact, let's go further and assume that The Cheeseman could increase its profits considerably if it decided to shift from the cheese-packing industry to the fast-food storage business. In such a case, accounting profits of cheese packing might indeed be positive, whereas economic profits are negative. This is because the implicit costs of cheese packing—the opportunity cost of management time and plant—must be considered. Much like the cost of labor, this implicit cost is subtracted from revenues to produce the economist's conception of profits.[2]

6.1
6.2
6.3
6.4
6.5
6.6

Evidence-Based Economics

Q: How would an ethanol subsidy affect ethanol producers?

A t the beginning of this chapter, we posed a question concerning whether an ethanol **subsidy** would affect ethanol producers. The ethanol production industry is approximately perfectly competitive, so the tools of this chapter can help us understand this question. Later, in Chapter 10, we discuss taxes and subsidies more fully.

We can begin to shed light on this issue by exploring whether economic profits for the industry increase when subsidies are given. We have learned in this chapter that one sign of positive economic profits is firm entry. Thus, we can ask, how did the number of ethanol plants change when the U.S. government subsidized the ethanol industry? Exhibit 6.19 plots the total number of ethanol plants in orange and the number of new plants under construction/expanding in blue. In 2006, every gallon of ethanol-based fuel was effectively subsidized by $0.51 with a refundable tax credit, and when President Bush announced in his 2006 State of the Union Address that ethanol plants would remain in favor, the number of ethanol plants under construction skyrocketed, as displayed in Exhibit 6.19. In 2009, the subsidy dropped to $0.45 cents per gallon and construction of new firms fell back considerably, to levels observed before 2006 (though the construction rates had been falling from 2007 to 2009).

A **subsidy** is a payment or tax break used as an incentive for an agent to complete an activity.

Exhibit 6.19 Number of Ethanol Plants and the Number of Plants under Construction

We plotted the total number of ethanol plants and number under construction/expanding in this exhibit. Note the vertical dark-blue line. It denotes the day that President Bush promoted ethanol in his State of the Union Address.

Source: http://www.ethanolrfa.org/pages/statistics#C.

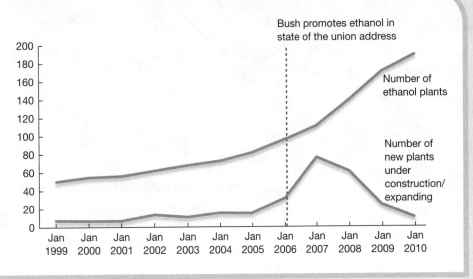

Ultimately, the increase and decrease in ethanol plants in response to subsidies suggests that economic profits were driving entry and exit, but the ethanol industry was affected by *many* factors during this time period, making it difficult to pinpoint if the subsidies themselves caused the number of plant openings to change. For example, prices of corn—an important input to ethanol production—dipped to record lows in 2005. This by itself could lead to expansion of ethanol plants if investors believed corn prices would stay low. And macroeconomic conditions changed dramatically during 2008, so these impacts could influence plant construction and expansion.

One approach to provide further evidence into our question of interest is to construct an artificial market where everything is identical except the presence of the subsidy and then compare it to the market that receives the subsidy. In a lab experiment where students act as potential ethanol producers we did just that.[3]

Put yourself in the shoes of a subject who participated in this laboratory experiment. The experiment was set up to examine cases that included government subsidies for ethanol production and cases where ethanol subsidies were not available. In this experiment, each of 12 producers received the same cost curves and each producer made the entry decision in each of six periods (that is, they made the entry choice six times). If they enter, then their plant capacity is to produce 2 million gallons of ethanol and they are paid the difference between their revenues and their costs as their earnings. Panel (a) of Exhibit 6.20 plots the marginal cost and average total cost curves for sellers in the no-subsidy treatment. The cost curves in the subsidy treatment are shown in panel (b) of Exhibit 6.20. Each firm in the subsidy treatment has a $0.25 lower cost of production for every gallon.

The experimental subjects are told that supply-and-demand conditions dictate that prices will be as displayed in Exhibit 6.21, which shows that if one seller enters the market, then there will be 2 million gallons produced and the price per gallon will be $1.40. In this case, for the subsidized seller, the profits are ($1.40 − $1.00) × 2 million ((*P* − *ATC*) × quantity), or $800,000. For the nonsubsidized seller, the profits are ($1.40 − $1.25) × 2 million ((*P* − *ATC*) × quantity), or $300,000.

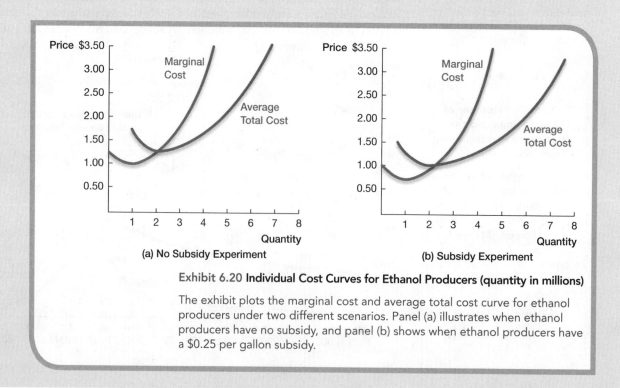

Exhibit 6.20 Individual Cost Curves for Ethanol Producers (quantity in millions)

The exhibit plots the marginal cost and average total cost curve for ethanol producers under two different scenarios. Panel (a) illustrates when ethanol producers have no subsidy, and panel (b) shows when ethanol producers have a $0.25 per gallon subsidy.

6.1

6.2

6.3

6.4

6.5

6.6

Exhibit 6.21 Price and Quantities in Lab Experiment

The table summarizes the price and quantity of ethanol for experimental subjects. The left-hand column shows the price in increments of $0.05. The right-hand column shows the corresponding quantity, in millions of gallons, in the market.

Price per Gallon	Total Number of Gallons on the Market (in millions)
$1.40	2
$1.35	4
$1.30	6
$1.25	8
$1.20	10
$1.15	12
$1.10	14
$1.05	16
$1.00	18
$0.95	20
$0.90	22
$0.85	24

What do you think happened in each round of the no-subsidy and subsidy treatments? How would you choose if you were an experimental participant? Exhibit 6.22 provides a summary of the experimental results. Panel (a) in Exhibit 6.22 shows that in round 1 of the no-subsidy treatment, 11 of the 12 sellers entered the market. Thus, 22 million gallons of ethanol were produced and the equilibrium price was $0.90 per gallon. Therefore, every seller lost $0.35 per gallon ($P - ATC$, or $0.90 - $1.25). These losses caused 3 sellers to drop out of the market for round 2, leaving 8 sellers and a price of $1.05 per gallon. Still, in round 2 sellers are losing money. This cannot continue in equilibrium. Exhibit 6.22 shows that it does not: by the fourth round, the equilibrium number of sellers prevails—4 sellers enter, yielding a market price of $1.25 per gallon. This number continues for the remainder of the experiment. Ethanol prices converged to the point where price equaled the minimum ATC, yielding economic profits of zero for every subject.

Panel (b) of Exhibit 6.22 reveals the data for the subsidy treatment. In this case, too few sellers (5) enter the market in round 1. With only 5 sellers, a price of $1.20

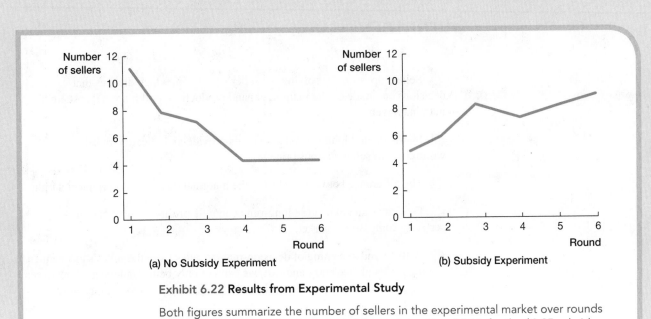

(a) No Subsidy Experiment

(b) Subsidy Experiment

Exhibit 6.22 Results from Experimental Study

Both figures summarize the number of sellers in the experimental market over rounds of trading. Panel (a) is for the no-subsidy condition. Panel (b) is for the $0.25 subsidy.

prevails. This means that every seller earns $0.20 per gallon produced ($P - ATC$, or $1.20 - 1.00). Profits cause other firms to enter, as can be seen in panel (b) of Exhibit 6.22. By the 6th round, the equilibrium number of 9 sellers enters the market, leading to a price of $1 per gallon. Again, price ends up equaling the minimum ATC. In this case, even though there is a subsidy, quantity increases to drive economic profits to zero, just as theory would predict.

This experiment confirms what we would expect from a competitive industry. Entry and exit stabilize to a zero-profit equilibrium in each case. That is, regardless of the presence of a subsidy, economic profits are driven to zero in the long run. As far as our opening question, what we have learned is that producers in perfectly competitive industries are influenced in the short run by subsidies, but firms in a competitive industry—like the ethanol industry—should not pin their hopes on reaping positive economic profits in the long run because entry will drive long-run economic profits to zero.

Question

How would an ethanol subsidy affect ethanol producers?

Answer

It depends if we are considering the short run or the long run. The ethanol producer should understand that long-run economic profits will be zero in equilibrium.

Data

Market data combined with a lab experiment.

Caveat

It might be difficult to generalize results from the lab experiment. Also, during the time period we examined data from the ethanol industry many factors were changing at once, making it difficult to establish cause and effect.

Summary

✸ Sellers optimize by solving the seller's problem, which dictates that decisions are made on the margin: expand production until marginal cost equals marginal revenue.

✸ Short-run and long-run supply curves provide an indication of sellers' willingness to sell at various price levels.

✸ The difference between price and the marginal cost curve is producer surplus.

✸ Free entry and exit cause long-run economic profits to equal zero in a perfectly competitive market.

✸ With an understanding of decision-making rules from the seller's problem and the forces of free entry and exit, we can not only better understand how to run our own business but also better predict how sellers will respond to incentives.

Key Terms

firm *p. 116*
production *p. 116*
physical capital *p. 116*
short run *p. 116*
long run *p. 116*
fixed factor of production *p. 116*
variable factor of production *p. 116*
marginal product *p. 116*
specialization *p. 117*
Law of Diminishing Returns *p. 117*
cost of production *p. 118*
total cost *p. 118*

variable cost *p. 118*
fixed cost *p. 118*
average total cost (*ATC*) *p. 119*
average variable cost (*AVC*) *p. 119*
average fixed cost (*AVC*) *p. 119*
marginal cost *p. 119*
revenue *p. 120*
marginal revenue *p. 121*
profits *p. 122*
accounting profits *p. 123*
economic profits *p. 123*
price elasticity of supply *p. 125*

shutdown *p. 126*
sunk costs *p. 127*
producer surplus *p. 127*
economies of scale *p. 129*
constant returns to scale *p. 130*
diseconomies of scale *p. 130*
exit *p. 130*
free entry *p. 132*
free exit *p. 133*
subsidy *p. 135*

Questions

All questions are available in MyEconLab *for practice and instructor assignment.*

1. Suppose one firm accounts for 55 percent of the global market share for a product, while 147 other firms account for the remaining 45 percent of the market. With such a large number of buyers and sellers, is this market likely to be competitive? Explain your answer.

2. Do you think sellers in a perfectly competitive market can price their goods differently? Explain your answer.

3. How would the introduction of legal or technical barriers to entry affect the long-run equilibrium in a perfectly competitive market?

4. Use a graph to show the relationship between the marginal cost curve and the average total cost curve for a competitive firm. What can you conclude about average total cost when marginal cost is less than average total cost?

5. Why is it that the industry demand curve slopes downward when the demand curves faced by individual firms in perfectly competitive markets are horizontal?

6. How does a firm in a competitive market decide what level of output to produce in order to maximize its profit?

7. Is it possible for accounting profit to be positive but economic profit to be negative? Explain with an example.

8. The following graph shows three supply curves with varying degrees of price elasticity:

Identify the perfectly elastic, perfectly inelastic, and unit-elastic supply curves.

9. Would a profit-maximizing firm continue to operate if the price in the market fell below its average cost of production in the short run?

10. What is meant by producer surplus? How is producer surplus in a competitive market calculated?

11. In each of the following cases, identify whether a competitive firm's producer surplus will increase, decrease, or remain unchanged.

    i. The demand for the product increases.

    ii. The firm's marginal cost of production increases.

    iii. The market price of the product falls.

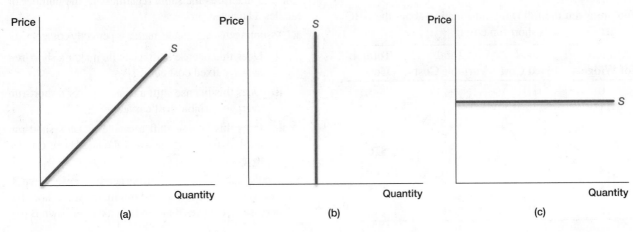

(a)   (b)   (c)

12. The following graph shows the long-run average total cost curve for a perfectly competitive firm:

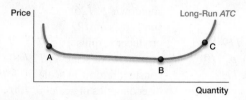

Refer to points A, B, and C on the graph and identify where the firm would experience economies of scale, constant returns to scale, and diseconomies of scale.

13. How does the long-run supply curve differ from the short-run supply curve for a perfectly competitive firm? Explain your answer.

14. If some sellers exit a competitive market, how will this affect equilibrium?

Problems

All problems are available in MyEconLab for practice and instructor assignment.

1. Fixing up old houses requires plumbing and carpentry. Jack (who is a jack of all trades but is a master of none) is a decent carpenter and a decent plumber, but is not particularly good at either. He can fix up two houses in a year if he does all of the carpentry and plumbing himself. His wage is $50,000 per year.

   a. What is Jack's average total cost of fixing up two old houses?

   b. George is an excellent plumber and Harriet is an excellent carpenter. George can do all of the plumbing and Harriet can do all of the carpentry to fix up five houses per year. Each earns a wage of $50,000 per year. If George and Harriet work together and fix up five old houses each year, what is their average cost?

   c. What does this problem tell you about one of the sources of economies of scale?

2. Salmon fishing in Alaska is a seasonal business; May through September is the best time to bait salmon and halibut. Toland Fisheries, a small commercial fishery, recorded its highest ever catch last year. They started this year's fishing season with the same number of workers and equipment. With the new season also starting well, Toland has increased hiring substantially. However, the fishery did not make any additional investment in trawlers and other fishing equipment.

   a. Other things remaining unchanged, what is likely to happen to the marginal product of each new worker in the short run?

   b. Is the outcome likely to be different in the long run? Explain your answer.

3. You are given the following information about the ABC Widget Company's short-run costs:

Quantity of Widgets	Total Fixed Cost	Total Variable Cost	Total Cost
0	$10	–	–
1	–	$1	–
2	–	$3	$13
3	–	$6	$16
4	–	$10	–
5	–	–	$25
6	$10	$21	–

   a. Find the average fixed cost of producing 5 widgets.

   b. Is the marginal cost of the third widget greater than the average total cost of producing 2 widgets? Does the production of the third widget lead to an increase in average total cost or does it decrease average total cost?

   c. Find the average total cost of producing 4 widgets.

   d. Find the marginal cost of producing the sixth widget.

4. Suppose the market for T-shirts in the country of Argonia is perfectly competitive, and the price of a T-shirt is $20. A producer in this market has the following total cost and marginal cost functions:

$$TC(q) = 500 + 0.1q^2,$$
$$MC(q) = 0.2q.$$

   a. What part of the total cost function represents fixed costs?

   b. Write the equation for the firm's average variable cost.

   c. Compute the number of T-shirts the firm will produce to maximize profit.

   d. Compute the average total cost of producing the profit-maximizing quantity of T-shirts.

   e. What is the average variable cost of producing the profit-maximizing quantity of T-shirts? Will the firm continue to operate or will it shut down?

   f. Is the firm making any profit? Does this reinforce your answer to part (e)? Why or why not?

5. Every candle maker in Town A must have a license. The cost of a license is the same regardless of the number of candles a business produces.

   a. Assuming that the candle market is perfectly competitive:

      i. Does this license shift a candle maker's short-run average fixed cost curve?

      ii. Does this license shift a candle maker's short-run average variable cost curve?

      iii. Does this license shift a candle maker's short-run profit maximizing choice of the number of candles to produce?

   b. Candle makers in Town B do not need a license. Town B, however, has passed a new minimum wage law that increases the wages that candle makers in Town B pay their workers. Assuming that the candle market is perfectly competitive:

   i. Does this minimum wage shift a candle maker's short-run average fixed cost curve?

   ii. Does this minimum wage shift a candle maker's short-run average variable cost curve?

   iii. Does this minimum wage shift a candle maker's short-run profit maximizing choice of the number of candles to produce?

6. The following graph shows the cost curves of a perfectly competitive firm.

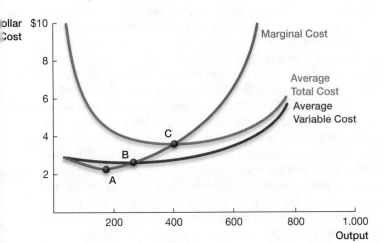

a. If the market price is $6 per unit, what is the approximate quantity of output the firm will produce?

b. At a market price of $6, is the firm's economic profit positive or negative? Explain your answer.

c. Consider the three points, A, B, and C, marked on the graph. At which point will economic profit be zero?

d. Suppose the market demand for this good declines substantially and the price falls to $2 per unit. Should the firm continue to produce or should it shut down? Explain.

e. How would the cost curves change if the total fixed cost of production for this firm increased?

7. You saw in Chapter 5 that economists often use arc elasticity when they calculate the price elasticity of demand. Similarly, they often use arc elasticity when they calculate the elasticity of supply. That is, they use the average of the new and the old quantity when they calculate the percentage change in quantity and the average of the new and the old price when they calculate the percentage change in price. Use the idea of an arc elasticity to calculate the price elasticity of supply in the following examples, then determine if supply is relatively elastic or inelastic, or perfectly elastic or inelastic.

a. When the price of a pen increased from $1.00 to $1.25, the quantity supplied by a firm increased from 200 to 300 pens.

b. When the price of bottled water decreased from $1.25 to $1.20, the quantity supplied by a firm decreased from 1,000 to 980 bottles.

c. Even though the price of an acre of land increased from $6,000 to $10,000, the quantity supplied did not change.

8. Some cities have much stricter zoning laws and regulatory controls than other cities. A recent study found that increases in the demand for housing in cities with strict zoning laws led to large increases in the price of housing. It also claimed that in cities with lax zoning laws, increases in the demand for housing led to much smaller increases in the price of housing. What, in your opinion, could explain these results? (*Hint*: Zoning laws regulate the uses of land in a city.)

9. Crabby Bob's is a seafood restaurant in a beach resort in Delaware. Crabby Bob's earns a profit each month from May through September, suffers losses in October, November, and April but remains open, and remains closed from December through March. Given that the restaurant market in this town is perfectly competitive, how would you explain Crabby Bob's decisions?

10. This problem asks you to think carefully about sunk costs.

a. The International Space Station (ISS) is a habitable satellite that was launched by NASA and space agencies of other countries. In 2009, NASA was considering shutting down the ISS within the next 5 to 6 years. Among those who were opposed to this idea of de-orbiting the ISS was Senator Bill Nelson, who was quoted as saying, "If we've spent a hundred billion dollars, I don't think we want to shut it down in 2015." Identify the flaw in the Senator's reasoning.

b. You are planning to build an apartment building. Your market research department estimates that your revenues will be $9.0 million. Your engineering department estimates the cost will be $6.0 million. You have started construction and spent $ 1.5 million to build the foundation when the recession begins. This causes the market research department to revise its revenue estimates downward to $4.0 million. Should you complete the apartment building?

11. Larry Krovitz is a salesman who works at a used-car showroom in Sydney, Australia. It's the last week of July, but he is yet to meet his sales target for the month. A customer, Harold Kumar, who wants to buy a Ford Fiesta, walks into the showroom. After taking one of the cars for a test drive, Harold decides to buy it. While $11,000 was the least that Larry would have been willing to accept for that car, he quotes a price of $15,000. After some bargaining, the car is sold for $12,000.

a. What is the producer surplus in this case?

b. If Larry bought the car for $8,000, what is his profit?

c. Is producer surplus always equal to profit? Explain your answer.

12. The table shows the long-run total costs of three different firms.

Output	Firm I	Firm II	Firm III
1	$8	$5	$7
2	$14	$12	$12
3	$18	$21	$15
4	$20	$32	$24

a. Do firms I and II experience economies of scale? Or do they experience diseconomies of scale?

b. Minimum efficient scale is the lowest level of output where long-run average cost is minimized. Find firm III's minimum efficient scale.

Appendix

When Firms Have Different Cost Structures

We have thus far considered cases with many identical firms. However, this likely does not represent the makeup of industries that you generally imagine. Some firms have better technologies than others. Some firms have more experienced or savvy entrepreneurs than others. Some might have access to critical inputs, such as natural resources. For example, some farmers might have land more suitable to growing certain crops than others. All of these factors might lead firms to have different costs of production. What do supply curves look like in such industries? How does the equilibrium change?

It is important to note that our main lesson from above remains in this case: *every firm expands production until MC = MR = P, unless shutdown or exit is optimal.* And we continue to construct the market supply curve from the summation of individual firm supply curves. The main difference between the case of identical firms and the case where firms are different is that the equilibrium price in the latter equals the long-run average total cost of the last entrant. This has important implications because in this case some firms earn positive economic profits, even in the long run equilibrium.

To see why this is so, suppose that a new seed is developed that produces a wonderful new fruit. Market demand is enormous for this fruit, which can be grown across pasturelands in the United States. But the best growing conditions are gently rolling plots of land because laborers can more easily pick the fruit. In this case, we are able to rank farmers by their average total cost to produce a bushel of this new fruit based on their land type.

In this scenario, we would expect that farmers with the lowest average total cost would enter the market first and earn the greatest economic profits. After they enter, the next farmers to enter the market have land that is not as well suited for growing the fruit. Therefore, those farmers will have a higher average total cost than the first set of market entrants. If we continue with this thought experiment, we find that the last farmer to enter the market will be the farmer with zero economic profits. This farmer is indifferent between entering the industry at the market price and not entering. Indeed, if the market price were to fall even a little, he would not wish to enter the industry.

To show how this works, consider Exhibit 6A.1. A rightward shift in the market demand curve leads to an increase in price, as panel (a) of Exhibit 6A.1. This increase in price causes firms to enter the industry, thereby shifting the supply curve rightward, as in panel (b) of the exhibit. These new entrants have higher costs than the existing firms, causing the equilibrium price to settle at the point where the last entrant has zero economic profits: price equals the minimum of his long-run average total cost. In this case, an upward-sloping long-run supply curve results, as in panel (b) of the exhibit. With an upward-sloping long-run supply curve, the equilibrium price is above the average total cost for the farmers with the best plots of land (those with the lowest *ATC*). This allows these low-cost farmers to enjoy profits in the long run compared to the case of a horizontal long-run supply curve. This result shows that in equilibrium, economic profits can be positive in the long run if sellers have different costs.

Exhibit 6A.2 recaps the basic results we obtain when we consider the implication of free entry and exit in a competitive market.

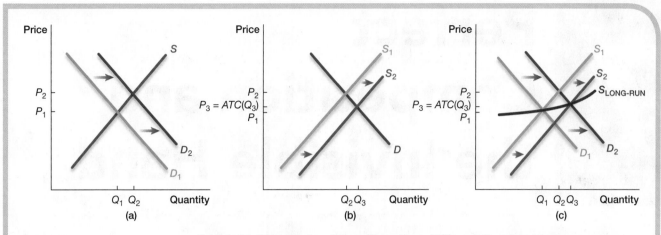

Exhibit 6A.1 Equilibrium When Firms Have Different Cost Structures

Panel (a) shows an increase in industry demand, so demand shifts right (increases) from D_1 to D_2. The resulting increase in price from P_1 to P_2 means that firms are now realizing positive economic profits in this industry ($P > ATC$).

In response to this increase in economic profits, there is entry into the industry, which causes the industry supply to shift right (increase), as shown in panel (b). In response to entry, industry output increases, and the price in the market begins to fall from P_2.

Entry will continue until the marginal firm (the last firm to enter the industry) earns zero economic profits, which occurs at the new price. But, since there is heterogeneity in firm costs, with the lowest cost producers being first in the market, entry subsides before price returns to its initial level, P_1. Note that in panel (b), the final equilibrium price, P_3 is greater than the initial equilibrium price in the market, P_1.

Panel (c) combines the initial increase in market demand with the subsequent market entry to illustrate both the initial equilibrium in the market (P_1, Q_1) and the final market equilibrium (P_3, Q_3). Again, since firms have different cost structures, the zero profit condition holds when the marginal firm faces a price equal to its average total cost. The long-run supply curve for the market is simply the locus of long run market equilibria, and is upward-sloping.

Exhibit 6A.2 Economic Outcomes in Models of Identical and Nonidentical Firms

Short-run and long-run profits and supply curves are summarized for two different types of markets. The first set of rows is for a market with identical firms. The second set of rows is for nonidentical firms.

Profits and Industry Supply in the Short Run and Long Run		
Firm Cost Structures	Short Run	Long Run
All firms have identical cost structures	Positive economic profits possible	All firms earn zero economic profits
	Upward-sloping industry supply curve	Horizontal industry supply curve
Firms' cost structures vary	Positive economic profits possible	All firms except marginal firm earn positive economic profits
	Upward-sloping industry supply curve	Upward-sloping industry supply curve

Perfect Competition and the Invisible Hand

Can markets composed of only self-interested people maximize the overall well-being of society?

In the previous two chapters we provided descriptions of the decision problems facing the main actors in any market: buyers and sellers. We found that when each of them follows certain rules of behavior, each will maximize his or her *own* well-being—a good thing because we all want to improve our lot in life. But when all of these self-interested people are put together in a competitive market, can anything but chaos result?

At first glance it does seem as if pandemonium reigns in many markets—bidding wars on eBay, stockbrokers frantically waving their arms as they try to buy or sell, buyers and sellers haggling over prices at flea markets. Obvious disarray. All of this chaos, it seems, is driven by market participants simply looking out for #1—themselves.

CHAPTER **OUTLINE**

7.1
Perfect Competition and Efficiency

7.2
Extending the Reach of the Invisible Hand: From the Individual to the Firm

7.3
Extending the Reach of the Invisible Hand: Allocation of Resources Across Industries

7.4
Prices Guide the Invisible Hand

7.5
Equity and Efficiency

EBE
Can markets composed of only self-interested people maximize the overall well-being of society?

☀ The invisible hand efficiently allocates goods and services to buyers and sellers.

☀ The invisible hand leads to efficient production *within* an industry.

☀ The invisible hand allocates resources efficiently *across* industries.

☀ Prices direct the invisible hand.

☀ There are trade-offs between making the economic pie as big as possible and dividing the pieces equally.

Adam Smith, the father of economics, viewed the chaos quite differently. He conjectured that self-interest was a necessary ingredient for an economy to function efficiently. This view is put forth most elegantly in his treatise *The Wealth of Nations* (1776):

> It is not from the benevolence of the butcher, the brewer, or the baker, that we expect our dinner, but from their regard to their own interest.[1]

This insight has become known as the power of the "invisible hand." It is a forceful idea in economics because it suggests that when all of the assumptions of a perfectly competitive market are in place, the pursuit of individual self-interest promotes the well-being of society as a whole, almost as if the individual is led by an invisible hand to do so.

In this chapter, we discuss the important implications of the invisible hand. We will show that when we impose the assumptions of perfect competition, the market system creates harmony between the interests of the individual and those of society. We will find that in such cases the free market is almost magical in that it allocates the production and final consumption of goods and services in a perfectly efficient manner. We will learn that the secret to how the market efficiently allocates scarce resources is by allowing prices to direct buyers and sellers—regardless of whether we are discussing traders at the New York Stock Exchange, buyers and sellers in flea markets in Chattanooga, or people frequenting garage sales in Los Angeles. In this way, once we grasp the workings of the invisible hand, we better understand the world around us.

7.1 Perfect Competition and Efficiency

Reservation value is the price at which a trading partner is indifferent between making the trade and not doing so.

To begin, let's consider more carefully the perfectly competitive markets discussed in Chapters 4–6. For simplicity, let's assume that our market is composed of only seven buyers and seven sellers who are price-takers. Each wants to buy or sell a used Apple iPod Nano 5th Generation, in excellent condition. Because the iPods are all in similar condition, we can assume that they are identical. Madeline, Katie, Sean, Dave, Ian, Kim, and Ty are buyers in the market, and each of their **reservation values** (willingness-to-pay values) is contained in Exhibit 7.1. A reservation value is the price at which a person is indifferent between making the trade and not doing so. We learn from Exhibit 7.1 that Madeline is willing to pay $70 for an iPod, Katie $60, on down to Ty, who is willing to pay $10 for an iPod. Together, these data can be combined to form the market demand curve displayed in Exhibit 7.2.

Exhibit 7.1 Reservation Values of Buyers and Sellers in the iPod Market

In the iPod market, we have seven buyers and seven sellers, each with their own reservation values for an iPod. Together, the seven buyers make up the market demand for iPods and the seven sellers comprise the market supply for iPods.

Buyers	Reservation Value ($)	Sellers	Reservation Value ($)
Madeline	70	Tom	10
Katie	60	Mary	20
Sean	50	Jeff	30
Dave	40	Phil	40
Ian	30	Adam	50
Kim	20	Matt	60
Ty	10	Fiona	70

Tom, Mary, Jeff, Phil, Adam, Matt, and Fiona are all sellers in the market, and each of their reservation values (willingness-to-sell values, or marginal costs) is also contained in Exhibit 7.1. From the exhibit, we learn that Tom is willing to sell his iPod for $10, Mary for $20, on up to Fiona, who will sell her iPod for no less than $70. Together, these values can be combined to make up the market supply curve displayed in Exhibit 7.2.

What is the equilibrium price in this case? The equilibrium price is determined by the intersection of the market demand and market supply curves. Exhibit 7.2 shows that this intersection yields a price of $40—which happens to be the price at which Dave is willing to buy an iPod and Phil is willing to sell his iPod.

What is the quantity traded at this equilibrium price of $40? Similar to equilibrium price determination, we compute the equilibrium quantity level by again looking at the intersection of the market demand and market supply curves. On so doing, we find that the equilibrium quantity is four iPods. This follows because four people (Madeline, Katie, Sean, and Dave) are willing to pay *at least* $40 for an iPod, while four sellers (Tom, Mary, Jeff, and Phil) have reservation values less than or equal to $40. In this example, we assume that if a person is indifferent to trading, as Dave and Phil are at $40, they trade.

Social Surplus

An important outcome from buyers and sellers optimizing in perfectly competitive markets is that *social surplus* is maximized. **Social surplus** is the sum of *consumer surplus*

Social surplus is the sum of consumer surplus and producer surplus.

and *producer surplus*, which we studied in Chapters 5 and 6. As we discussed in those two chapters, consumer surplus is the difference between the buyers' reservation values and what the buyers actually pay, and producer surplus is the difference between the price and

Exhibit 7.2 Demand and Supply Curves in the iPod Market

When we plot the demand and supply schedules from Exhibit 7.1, we end up with stepwise curves because each individual only demands or supplies one unit. The curves intersect at the equilibrium price of $40, and at that price, four iPods will be sold, identifying the equilibrium quantity of iPods.

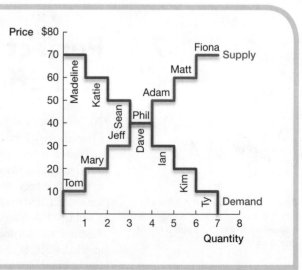

the sellers' reservation values (marginal cost). So, social surplus represents the total value from trade in the market. For social surplus to be maximized, the highest-value buyers are making a purchase and the lowest-cost sellers are selling. In this way, buyers and sellers as distinct groups are doing as well as they possibly can—they're optimizing.

To see why social surplus is maximized at the competitive market equilibrium, look at panels (a), (b), and (c) of Exhibit 7.3, which breaks down Exhibit 7.2 into simpler chunks. Notice that social surplus—the sum of the areas shaded blue and pink—is graphically given in all three panels by the area between the market demand and market supply curves from the origin to the quantity traded. Panel (b) shows the social surplus at the competitive market equilibrium. We compute this surplus by summing the consumer and producer surplus of each market participant. For example, because Madeline is willing to pay $70 for an iPod, but actually pays only $40, her consumer surplus is $30. Likewise, because Tom is willing to sell his iPod for $10, but receives $40, his producer surplus is $30. By performing this computation for each of the people who trade, we learn that the social surplus adds up to $120, composed of $60 in consumer surplus and $60 in producer surplus.

To understand a little better why the competitive equilibrium maximizes social surplus, consider what would happen if we restricted the quantity sold in the market to be below the equilibrium quantity. Say we restrict the number of trades to two: that is, the two highest-value consumers buy from the two lowest-cost sellers. That means Madeline and Katie buy and Tom and Mary sell. Regardless at what price the trade occurs, the result will be as depicted in panel (a) of Exhibit 7.3. In this situation, we find a lower total surplus compared to the competitive market equilibrium outcome: the market now achieves $100 in total surplus (this can be found by taking the difference between the reservation values of Madeline and Katie ($130) and Tom and Mary ($30)). This figure is lower than the $120 of surplus achieved in the competitive equilibrium of panel (b).

What would happen if, instead, we expanded the trading opportunities and enforced trade of five iPods? That is, we have the five highest-value buyers purchasing from the five lowest-cost sellers. Panel (c) of Exhibit 7.3 illustrates this case. With five sellers, we need to go all the way up the supply curve and include Adam, the fifth-lowest-cost seller. Likewise, we need to go all the way down the demand curve to Ian, the fifth-highest-value buyer. We now not only obtain the surplus in the competitive market equilibrium (when four trades are made, as in panel (b) of Exhibit 7.3) but we also obtain the yellow-shaded region in panel (c).

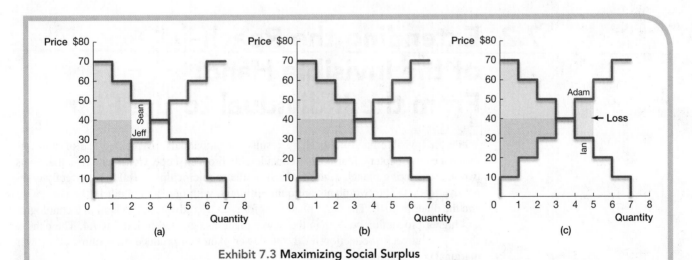

Exhibit 7.3 Maximizing Social Surplus

When a cap of two iPods is imposed, the situation is as depicted in panel (a). Social surplus is not maximized because Sean and Jeff do not make profitable trades. On the flip side, when a minimum of five iPods traded is imposed, as in panel (c), Adam and Ian now trade, even though the cost to the seller (Adam) is higher than the benefit to the buyer (Ian), leaving us worse off compared to the social optimum. Leaving the iPod market to act without outside direction, as in panel (b), generates the maximum amount of social surplus precisely because it does not leave out profitable trades (as in (a)) or force unprofitable trades (as in (c)).

The yellow-shaded region in panel (c) represents losses from forcing a fifth trade. This is because the seller values the fifth item more than the buyer does. The loss in this case is equal to $20: $50 − $30, or Adam's cost minus Ian's benefit. This loss occurs because the marginal benefit of having Ian receive an iPod ($30) is less than the marginal cost of having Adam give up his iPod ($50). Because marginal benefits are lower than marginal costs, our decision rules developed in earlier chapters suggest that this is not an optimal action to take. In this case, total surplus decreases from $120 in the competitive equilibrium to $100 ($120 − $20).

Pareto Efficiency

We now know that the competitive market equilibrium is efficient in the sense that all mutually advantageous trades take place: no more, no less. In this way, there are no unexploited gains to trade. Accordingly, the competitive market equilibrium maximizes social surplus: this is the best that society as a whole can do if it is simply interested in maximizing the total size of the economic pie.

> **The competitive market equilibrium maximizes social surplus: this is the best that society as a whole can do if it is simply interested in maximizing the total size of the economic pie.**

An outcome is **Pareto efficient** if no individual can be made better off without making someone else worse off.

But in many situations we are also interested in who gets what—the allocation of surplus. One natural place to start is to ask: in the competitive market equilibrium, can we make any individual better off without harming someone else? The answer is no. This concept is called *Pareto efficiency*, and is related to social surplus. An outcome is **Pareto efficient** if no individual can be made better off without making someone else worse off. As it turns out, besides maximizing social surplus, the competitive market equilibrium is also Pareto efficient.

So we can say that in a perfectly competitive market, the first distinct function of the equilibrium price is that it efficiently allocates goods and services to buyers and sellers. The theory that purely self-interested individuals, without any specific direction, are led by the invisible hand to maximize the total well-being of society—almost as if they were ordered to do so—represents one of the deepest insights within economics. Later in the chapter, we discuss the empirical evidence (recall that this is knowledge gained through direct observation and measurement) of whether this theoretical prediction has empirical support.

7.2 Extending the Reach of the Invisible Hand: From the Individual to the Firm

While the invisible hand holds sharp results for individuals, by making use of concepts introduced in Chapter 6 it also has a considerably broader scope. Consider a firm that owns two manufacturing plants, each of which produces microchips to sell in a perfectly competitive market. The two plants are quite different, with one being built in the late 1970s and the other in 2010. The older plant therefore has less advanced production technologies and higher production costs than the newer plant, as depicted in Exhibit 7.4. The exhibit shows that at each production level, the newer plant can produce microchips at a lower marginal cost than the older plant.

The firm has historically allowed each plant to operate independently, with both plant managers tasked with maximizing their own plant's profits. If the price of microchips is $10, what quantity of microchips should each of the plant managers choose in order to maximize profits? An application of the seller's decision rule that we learned in Chapter 6 is appropriate: in the short run, if price is greater than average variable cost ($P > AVC$), then each plant should expand production until marginal cost equals price. Let's assume that $P > AVC$.

Therefore, the manager of the older plant will expand production until the marginal cost equals price (or, $MC = P = MR$), because marginal revenue equals price in a perfectly competitive market, as we learned in Chapter 6. This occurs at a quantity level of 20,000, as shown

Exhibit 7.4 Marginal Costs for Two Manufacturing Plants

The old manufacturing plant, with its less productive capital, faces a higher marginal cost to produce than the new plant. Represented graphically, this means that the old manufacturing plant's marginal cost curve (pink) is higher than the new plant's marginal cost curve (red) for any given quantity of production.

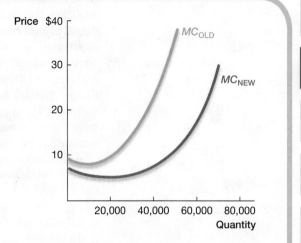

Exhibit 7.5 Optimal Production Quantity at the Old Manufacturing Plant

The old manufacturing plant will maximize profits by producing at the point where the benefit from selling an additional unit ($10) is equal to the cost of producing that additional unit. The old plant achieves this goal at a quantity of 20,000 units. The total costs that the old plant faces are represented by the shaded region. Recall that economic profits = $Q(P - ATC)$ = 20,000($10 - $10) = $0.

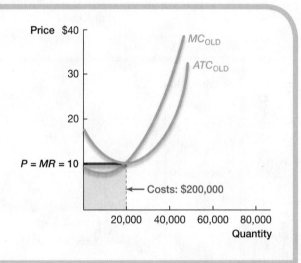

Exhibit 7.6 Optimal Production Quantity at the New Manufacturing Plant

Just as in the case of the old manufacturing plant in Exhibit 7.5, the new plant takes the market price ($10) and produces at the point where marginal cost equals the market price. Given that the new plant faces a lower marginal cost than the old plant, we would expect that at the price of $10, the new plant would have a higher level of production, and this is precisely the case, as the new plant produces 50,000 units. Note also that the new plant is earning economic profits because $P > ATC$. In this case, profits = 50,000($10 - $7.5) = $125,000.

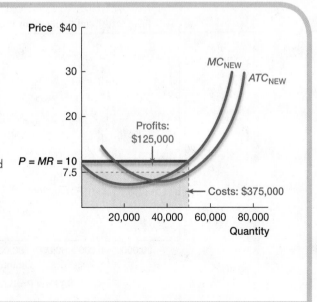

in Exhibit 7.5. The manager of the new plant will make her optimization decision similarly and have her plant produce 50,000 units, as shown in Exhibit 7.6.

The total cost of production can be computed by multiplying the average total cost times the quantity ($ATC \times Q$), as shown in the shaded region under the average total cost (ATC)

curve in Exhibits 7.5 and 7.6. For the old plant, we see that this total cost is $10 \times 20,000 =$ $200,000. For the new plant, we see that total cost is $7.50 \times 50,000 = $375,000. While the old plant is earning zero economic profits (because $P = ATC$), the new plant is earning an economic profit of $50,000(\$10 - \$7.5) = \$125,000$.

At the annual shareholder's meeting, both plant managers report important statistics to the new CEO, including production and cost figures. The CEO is devastated by these figures, stressing that "given the differences in technologies and costs, I am astounded that the older plant is producing at all!" He assumes that it must be due to the "old boys" network, further noting that "we cannot continue to keep old and inefficient plants open just because our friends work there."

As his first edict, the new CEO announces that "it is time to move to the 21st century; we must immediately move all production to the new plant. This new plant will produce the entire 70,000 microchips (20,000 + 50,000) itself because of its better technologies; in this way, we will demonstrate to the world how our firm is moving progressively forward to make our shareholders better off."

The plant managers try to explain to the CEO the errors in his economic reasoning—that he should be thinking on the margin—but the CEO is sure of his intuition on this one. The CEO's directive is enforced and leads to the plants' annual production changes, as shown in Exhibit 7.7. At the enforced levels of production, the total cost of production is given

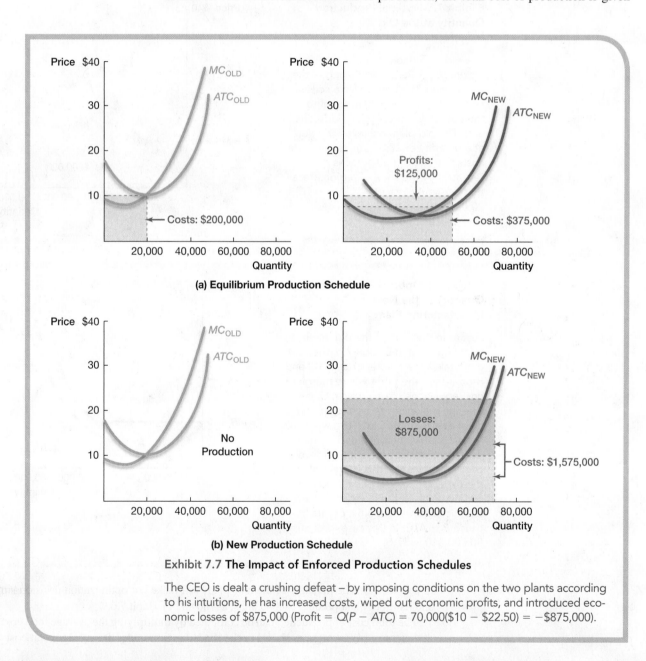

Exhibit 7.7 The Impact of Enforced Production Schedules

The CEO is dealt a crushing defeat – by imposing conditions on the two plants according to his intuitions, he has increased costs, wiped out economic profits, and introduced economic losses of $875,000 (Profit = $Q(P - ATC)$ = 70,000($10 - $22.50) = -$875,000).

by $ATC \times Q$, or the shaded regions under the ATC curves in the exhibit. The CEO has achieved what he desired: the new plant is now producing all 70,000 microchips.

A year passes. At the next annual shareholder's meeting, the new plant manager returns to report statistics once again to the CEO. The manager discloses that market demand and market supply conditions have yielded the same pricing environment as that of last year: $10 per microchip. The CEO views this as great news—he suspects that profits will rise handsomely because of his edict; he envisions people comparing him to Warren Buffet because of his sharp business acumen.

But he is crushed to learn that overall profits are down considerably from last year. Whereas the old production schedule brought $125,000 in economic profits, the new schedule erases those profits and replaces them with economic losses of $875,000 (and we have not even considered the fixed costs of the old plant!) The CEO, almost never at a loss for words, is speechless, only able to mutter words of amazement about how his plan could backfire so drastically. The plant manager, understanding the power of the invisible hand, shows the CEO Exhibit 7.8, which includes marginal costs and the CEO's quantity restrictions. Panel (a) of Exhibit 7.8 shows the older plant's marginal cost curve, and panel (b) shows the newer plant's marginal cost curve.

The plant manager explains that under the CEO's plan, the new plant produced the last microchip at a marginal cost of $30, as shown in panel (b) of the exhibit. This marginal cost is much greater than the $10 that it would have cost the older plant to make its first microchip, as displayed in panel (a) of the exhibit. In this way, if production of that one unit could have been shifted from the new plant to the older plant, overall costs would have been lowered by $20 = $30 − $10, enhancing overall profits by $20!

The CEO wonders just how far one can push this marginal reasoning. The plant manager shows him the arrows in Exhibit 7.8, which indicate that the same logic can be used until the marginal costs are equalized across plants, or at a point where $MC_{OLD} = MC_{NEW}$. The manager stresses that at this point, the overall production costs across the two plants will be minimized because they cannot profitably shift production any further.

In an inspired moment, the CEO notes that these optimal production numbers are exactly the levels reached by the plants a year earlier, before the CEO intervened ($MC_{OLD} = MC_{NEW} =$ Price = $10). He openly wonders how, in the pursuit of their own self-interest, the plant managers could organize production to minimize total costs, in turn optimizing profits for the firm. In his own roundabout way, the CEO has just stumbled across one of the most important insights described by Adam Smith in *The Wealth of Nations*, when noting that the entrepreneur: "intends only his own gain. . ." but he is "led by an invisible hand to promote an end which was no part of his intention."

The moral of the fable? Under the assumptions of a perfectly competitive market, allowing the market to operate freely not only permits each plant manager to maximize his or her own plant's profits by producing where $MR = MC$ but in so doing the plants achieve

Exhibit 7.8 Marginal Cost Curves for the Old Plant and the New Plant

Under the CEO's imposition, the old plant (pink) produces zero, while the new plant (red) produces 70,000 units. The exhibit shows that the CEO could have shifted production from the new plant to the old plant and saved money.

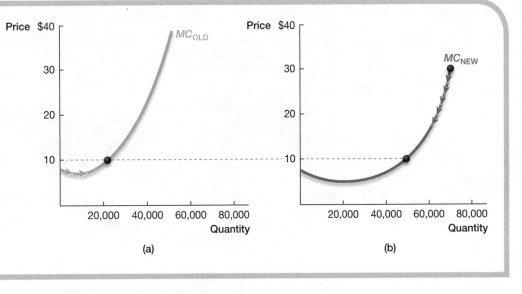

(a)

(b)

Where's his hand?

something that neither plant manager set out to do: minimize total costs of production. This is true because $MC_{OLD} = MC_{NEW}$, which is a necessary condition to minimize total costs across the producers.

Importantly, in so doing the plant managers also maximize the total profits of the two plants combined. In this sense, it is remarkable that market forces dictate that production across the two plants is allocated in a manner that is optimal for the social good: producing goods using the least amount of scarce resources. This is exactly what the CEO aimed to do, but failed. Yet when the competitive market is allowed to operate efficiently, we do not need a central planner (or a CEO) dictating goals for the betterment of society. Plant managers are willing to do that chore on their own, without even knowing it. So we can say that *in a competitive market, the second distinct function of the equilibrium price is that it efficiently allocates the production of goods within an industry.* Why? Because an optimizer expands production until $MC = P$; thus marginal costs are equalized across firms, because all firms face the same market price.

7.3 Extending the Reach of the Invisible Hand: Allocation of Resources Across Industries

We just learned that the invisible hand optimally allocates scarce resources and arranges production patterns *within* an industry. But the economy is much more complicated than two plants in a small town. How can we determine if any specific industry is producing too much or too little? Let's turn to a new example to explore if the invisible hand has power in allocating scarce resources *across* industries. To do so, we need to dig a level deeper into the lessons learned in Chapter 6.

As an illustration, consider a different perfectly competitive market—the delivery of paper products for publishing houses—with identical sellers making positive economic profits in the short run. This market situation is depicted in Exhibit 7.9. As you can see in the exhibit, at a price of $25 per ton, there are economic profits. But with economic profits, what happens?

Chapter 6 taught us that positive economic profits are a powerful force that attracts entrants. Other delivery companies want to enter because they, too, would like to earn economic profits. We illustrate the effect of entry in panels (a) and (b) of Exhibit 7.10. Panel (a) shows that firm entry causes the market supply curve to shift rightward (from S_1 to S_2). This shift causes the equilibrium price to decrease (from $25 to $12) and the equilibrium quantity to increase (from 500 million to 620 million).

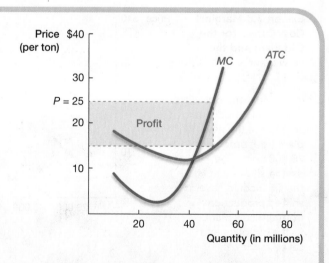

Exhibit 7.9 Economic Profits in the Paper Delivery Business

The paper delivery business faces a market price of $25 per ton. Average total costs are well below $25 at the chosen quantity, generating economic profits (represented by the green rectangle). With free entry into this industry, others will enter the paper delivery business.

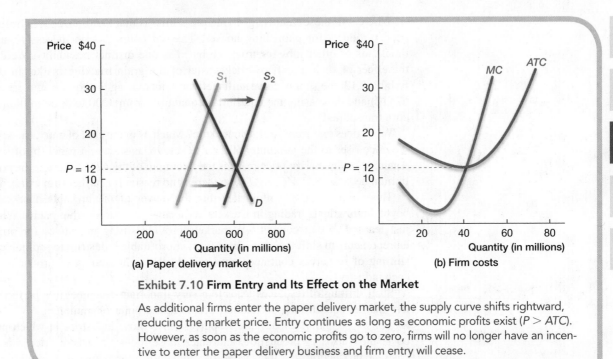

(a) Paper delivery market

(b) Firm costs

Exhibit 7.10 Firm Entry and Its Effect on the Market

As additional firms enter the paper delivery market, the supply curve shifts rightward, reducing the market price. Entry continues as long as economic profits exist ($P > ATC$). However, as soon as the economic profits go to zero, firms will no longer have an incentive to enter the paper delivery business and firm entry will cease.

When does entry stop? As we learned in Chapter 6, entry stops when the market price decreases all the way down to where the marginal cost curve intersects the average total cost curve. In this example, the equilibrium price is $12 per ton, as shown in panel (b) of Exhibit 7.10. This is because at any price higher than $12 per ton, other delivery firms would still like to enter because they can earn positive economic profits. Once price reaches the minimum of the ATC curve, we are in equilibrium because $P = MC = ATC$, which means that there is zero economic profit and therefore no reason for more firms to enter.

This example shows what happens when positive economic profits exist in an industry: resources flow to that industry because of the profits available. This behavior causes resources to flow from less productive uses to more productive uses. That is, businesses seek to improve their profits, and in so doing they move resources into the production of goods and services that society values the highest.

What happens if the equilibrium price lies *below* the ATC curve? Consider a related delivery business: the trucking market in the corn belt, where truckers haul corn from farmers' fields to grain mills for $10 per ton of corn. This market is currently in a situation where price is less than average total cost ($P < ATC$), as depicted in Exhibit 7.11. This means that truckers should exit because they are earning negative economic profits, or losses.

Exhibit 7.11 Economic Losses in the Trucking Market

The trucking market faces a market price of $10 per ton of corn delivered. At this price, average total costs are higher, generating economic losses (represented by the pink rectangle). With free entry and exit, truckers will exit this industry.

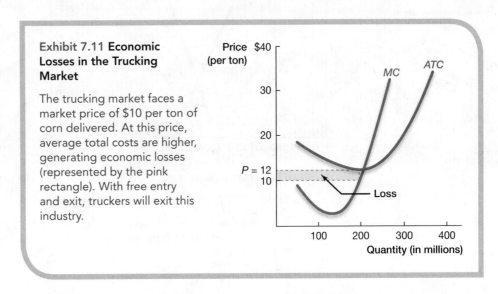

Where will these truckers go? One possibility is that the truckers will begin to deliver paper products for publishing houses. This, of course, is not necessary, as there are thousands of other jobs for truckers, but it is one distinct possibility. We demonstrate the effect of such a shift of truckers out of the grain trucking market in panel (a) of Exhibit 7.12: the supply curve shifts leftward, increasing the equilibrium price (from $10 to $12) and decreasing the equilibrium quantity (from 3200 to 3000 millions of tons of corn transported).

When does exit from hauling corn stop? Much as in the case of entry, truckers exit until the price rises to the minimum of the *ATC* curve, as shown in panel (b) of Exhibit 7.12. Again, once the market price reaches the minimum of the *ATC*, we are at the point of equilibrium because $P = MC = ATC$, so there is no reason for further firm exit.

This simple example illustrates that the power of the invisible hand extends well beyond individuals trading in markets and managers at microchip plants. What we have just learned is that competitive markets provide strong incentives for profit-seeking entrepreneurs to shift their resources from unprofitable industries to profitable ones. This shifting of resources continues until exactly the right amount of production occurs in each industry.

Such shifting of resources leads to a very important outcome: in a perfectly competitive market equilibrium, production occurs at the point of minimum *ATC*, as shown in Exhibits 7.10 and 7.12. Because resources leave those industries in which price cannot cover their costs of production, and enter those industries where price can cover their costs of production, the total value of production is maximized in equilibrium. In this way, the market price is acting as an incentive for sellers to promote the greatest good for society—move scarce resources to their highest possible use—even though sellers are solely attempting to maximize their own profits.

This reasoning leads to a third distinct function of equilibrium prices in a competitive market: *they allocate scarce resources across industries in an optimal manner.* This is because the industry equilibrium is where $P = ATC = MC$, and this happens only at the minimum point of the *ATC* curve. Viewed through this lens, entry and exit of firms is a good sign that the market is working, not a sign that something has run afoul.

Indeed, if we observe no entry and no exit, we should be worried that the free market is not functioning well: the carrot of economic profit and the stick of economic losses might not be serving their allocative purposes in this case.

> **Entry and exit of firms is a good sign that the market is working, not a sign that something has run afoul.**

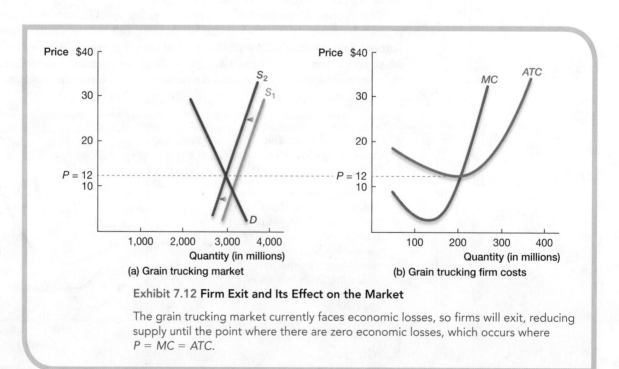

Exhibit 7.12 Firm Exit and Its Effect on the Market

The grain trucking market currently faces economic losses, so firms will exit, reducing supply until the point where there are zero economic losses, which occurs where $P = MC = ATC$.

7.4 Prices Guide the Invisible Hand

The fact that the market can do the world's work without anyone being in charge might strike you as a scientific mystery as fascinating as the great challenges facing humankind today: What is the universe made of? What is the biological basis of consciousness? From the economic vantage point, you might wonder just how far we can crack open the mystery of the invisible hand.

What we know so far is that when the right conditions are in place—and we should stress that these conditions are quite strict—self-interest and the social interest are perfectly aligned. This is what led Adam Smith to comment that when markets are functioning well, those who are promoting their self-interest are also promoting the interests of society more broadly, as if led by an "invisible hand" to do so. This fundamental point teaches us that when markets align self-interest with social interest, we obtain very desirable results.

But what is it that leads agents to act in this manner? The short answer is that the incentive is prices. Market prices act as the most important piece of information, leading the high-value buyers to buy and the low-cost sellers to sell. For example, prices adjust until the quantity demanded of oceanfront property equals the quantity supplied of oceanfront property. Likewise, prices force entrepreneurs to allocate the production of goods efficiently, whether it is across firms in the same industry or across industries in the global economy. The flow of labor and physical capital to sectors with the highest rewards causes the production to be at just the right level in a competitive market equilibrium.

It seems almost unrealistic to believe that prices can be the sole organizer of thousands of markets that are linked in ways that we still do not begin to understand. No one has knowledge of all of the links between timber markets in Canada, corn markets in Iowa, fishing markets on Cape Cod, tea markets in China, and the tourism market in Costa Rica, but the fact that the pricing system can order behavior across such a vast array of markets, individuals, and groups, highlights the power of incentives within the market system.

Nobel Laureate Vernon Smith, a pioneer in the use of laboratory experimentation in economics, had this to say about prices:

> How is it that the pricing system accomplishes the world's work without anyone being in charge. . . . Smash it in the command economy and it rises as a Phoenix with a thousand heads. . . . No law and no police force can stop it, for the police become as large a part of the problem as of the solution. . . . The pricing system . . . is a scientific mystery . . . to understand it is to understand something about how the human species got from hunter-gathering through the agricultural and industrial revolutions to a state of affluence.[2]

We can understand some of the workings of how price guides the invisible hand when considering a stark anecdotal example that one of the authors experienced when he lived in central Florida in the late 1990s. During that time, there was a flurry of hurricane warnings and activity. In each instance, goods such as sheets of plywood to board windows, bottled water and ice, and generators in case of power outages were in strong demand. As you now know, such a surge in demand shifts the demand curve rightward, increasing price.

To illustrate, consider the market for bottled water. What would happen if the demand for bottled water in central Florida suddenly increased? This situation is depicted in Exhibit 7.13. At any given price level, more units are desired under the new demand curve (D_2) than under the old demand curve (D_1).

A **price control** is a government restriction on the price of a good or service.

How would the invisible hand operate in this case? The increase in price would reverberate through the economy, incentivizing water distributors to make special trips to central Florida to fill the increased demand. Indeed, seeing trucks with out-of-state license plates unloading bottled water was a common occurrence during such periods. The invisible hand guided these out-of-state truckers to meet demand by trucking water to Floridian consumers because they could make more profits than they otherwise would have earned in their other activities.

Local officials understandably complained of price gouging during this time. In some cases, officials tried to force price to remain unchanged during times of hurricanes. Government restrictions on the price a firm can charge for a good or service is called a **price control**.

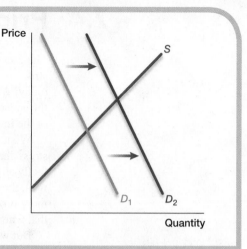

Exhibit 7.13 An Outward Shift of the Demand for Bottled Water

With a hurricane looming, demand for bottled water shifts out from D_1 to D_2. In response, sellers increase their quantity supplied until the market achieves a new equilibrium, where D_2 intersects S.

As we discussed in Chapter 4, if price controls are binding (that is, price is held below the equilibrium price), a shortage results: quantity demanded exceeds quantity supplied, as shown in Exhibit 7.14.

It is interesting to note that during hurricane season when price gouging was especially criticized and sellers were more forcefully told to keep prices low, fewer truckers with out-of-state license plates would arrive with fresh bottled water. This response makes sense within the model of the market system: if prices are not allowed to rise and reward market participants, suppliers' response will not be as swift, if at all. This is because restricting the price to its old level does not give entrepreneurs an incentive to supply their product—in this case, water. If truckers did not service the market before the hurricane under the old prices, why would they now if they were interested solely in maximizing profits? The price control that the officials enforced eliminated the price incentive, ensuring that residents would have *less* drinking water than they otherwise would have had without such price controls.

By artificially limiting quantity, the price control creates another problem: how do we allocate the bottled water that is available (Q_1 in Exhibit 7.14)? Free markets ration goods with prices—anyone who desires a bottle of water at the market price simply pays it and receives the water. The market is efficient because those who are willing to pay the most receive the good. But when price controls are imposed the market is no longer free to operate efficiently. In cases like this, long lines of people waiting to purchase the water is a typical outcome. This is not only frustrating but inefficient, because our time is valuable and the water does not always go to those who value it the most.

Deadweight Loss

Economists call the decrease in social surplus that results from a market distortion a **deadweight loss**. The deadweight loss from a price control can be seen in Exhibit 7.15.

Deadweight loss is the decrease in social surplus from a market distortion.

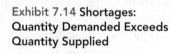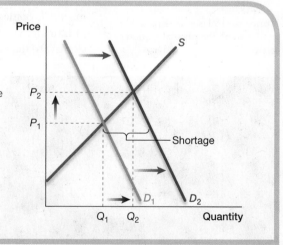

Exhibit 7.14 Shortages: Quantity Demanded Exceeds Quantity Supplied

If we hold the price at the old equilibrium price, suppliers have no extra incentive to meet the increased demand for bottled water, creating a shortage.

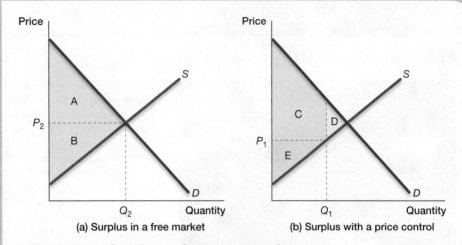

Exhibit 7.15 Deadweight Loss from Price Controls

Panel (a) shows a free market. Equilibrium price (P_2) and quantity (Q_2) leads to consumers receiving triangle A and producers receiving triangle B. Social surplus is maximized. In Panel (b), there is a price control in place: price is restricted to be below the equilibrium price. A deadweight loss equal to area D results. Now consumer surplus is area C and producer surplus is area E. Social surplus has decreased by the deadweight loss because of the price control.

> **The decrease in social surplus that results from a market distortion is a deadweight loss.**

Panel (a) of Exhibit 7.15 shows the social surplus if the market is allowed to operate freely: quantity traded is Q_2 at an equilibrium price of P_2. Consumer surplus is Triangle A and producer surplus is Triangle B. Thus, social surplus is Triangle A + Triangle B.

Panel (b) shows how restricting the price to P_1 affects the market. The price control prevents buyers and sellers from realizing all of the gains to trade. With the price control in place, consumers pay a price of P_1 per bottle of water and they consume Q_1 bottles. Consumer surplus is now area C and producer surplus is triangle E. By keeping price artificially low, the government helps consumers (area C in panel (b) is larger than triangle A in Panel (a)) but hurts producers (the area of triangle B in panel (a) is larger than the area in triangle E in panel (b)). Overall, there is lost surplus because of this imposition. The loss in surplus is triangle D in Panel (b). This area is called the deadweight loss from the price control. It becomes a normative question whether you are comfortable making this trade-off.

In sum, binding price controls have three effects: (1) they lower social surplus, because the number of trades decreases compared to a free market; (2) they redistribute surplus from one side of the market to the other. In the case of a price ceiling, as shown here and discussed in Chapter 4, the surplus is transferred from producers to consumers; and (3) for the people who benefit, there is a reallocation of surplus, which occurs through non-price mechanisms. In our example of price controls, those consumers who are willing to wait the longest, are the most connected, or simply those who are the strongest, receive the good. As a result, some consumers benefit, while others are made worse off.

You will note that this situation is very similar to what occurred in our iPod example above. When we restricted the quantity traded to two iPods, we found a lower total surplus compared to the competitive market equilibrium outcome. Going back to Exhibit 7.3, we can see that the deadweight loss of restricting trade in the iPod example was $20: the surplus of the trade between Sean and Jeff. In Chapter 10 we discuss at much greater length how taxes lead to deadweight loss.

The Command Economy

To understand the difficulty of what the invisible hand accomplishes, it is instructive to consider cases where countries have attempted to place strong controls on the economy, in effect trying to do the job of the invisible hand. One example of the dramatic differences

CHOICE & CONSEQUENCE

FEMA and Walmart After Katrina

In the wake of Hurricane Katrina in the summer of 2005, much of the Gulf Coast had been pummeled by wind and inches upon inches of rain. Water was everywhere, but often undrinkable. Basic provisions we take for granted, like drinking water, weren't easy to come by and the Federal Emergency Management Agency (FEMA) was caught flat-footed.

In response to catastrophic events like a hurricane or an earthquake, the caricature of private industry is that firms will gouge customers. And sometimes this is true, but in response to Katrina, there was one unlikely hero: Walmart. In fact, the Mayor of Kenner, a suburb of New Orleans, had this to say about Walmart's response: ". . . the only lifeline in Kenner was the Walmart stores. We didn't have looting on a mass scale because Walmart showed up with food and water so our people could survive."

Indeed, in the three weeks after Katrina, Walmart shipped almost 2,500 truckloads of supplies to storm-damaged areas. These truckloads reached affected areas

before FEMA, whose troubles responding to the storm were so great that it shipped 30,000 pounds of ice to Maine instead of Mississippi. These stories and more are in Horwitz (2009), which summarizes the divergent responses to Katrina by private industry and FEMA.

How was Walmart so effective in its response? Well, it maintains a hurricane response center of its own that rivals FEMA's, and prior to the storm's landfall it anticipated a need for generators, water, and food, so it effectively diverted supplies to the area. Walmart's emergency response center was in full swing as the storm approached with 50 employees managing the response from headquarters.

This sounds like the sort of response FEMA should have produced; so if that's the job of FEMA, why did Walmart respond so heroically? Simple economics. Walmart understood that there would be an important shift of the demand curve for water, generators, and ice in response to the storm and the textbook response to such shifts is an increase in quantity supplied. Lucky for us, few are better at shipping provisions around the country than Walmart.

Walmart enjoys one other advantage over FEMA. The company knows the market for provisions. Every day, Walmart must consider the demands of its millions of consumers and supply products that maximize its profits. FEMA, on the other hand, faces no such incentives, so when it is suddenly tasked with responding to a devastating storm like Katrina, FEMA will be trying to intuit what people need and by the time they're ready to act, a private firm like Walmart will have already solved the shortage.[3]

that can result is the case of Korea. After World War II in 1945, the Soviet Union and the United States agreed on the surrender and disarming of Japanese troops in Korea. The Soviet Union accepted the surrender of Japanese weaponry north of the 38th parallel, and the United States accepted the surrender south of the 38th parallel. Both countries established governments and market systems sympathetic to their own ideologies, leading to Korea's current division into two political entities: North Korea and South Korea.

The economic system implemented by the Soviet Union in North Korea remains today as one of the few remaining command economies, where a centralized authority determines the goods and services produced. With the aid of the United States, South Korea established a market economy based upon price signals and strong economic incentives. The market economy in South Korea remains vibrant today. This situation is, in effect, a unique natural experiment that permits an exploration of what happens to two similar areas when we impose a command economy in one and a market economy in the other.

Let's look at the two economies a little more closely. One place to start is the market value of final goods and services produced in each country in a given period of time, or what economists call the **gross domestic product** (GDP). Exhibit 7.16 shows the real per capita GDP in North Korea and South Korea from 1950 to 2008. The differences are dramatic. For North Korea, per capita GDP grew from $850 to only $1,133 over this time period. Alternatively, for South Korea, per capita GDP grew from roughly $850 to $18,356. To put these differences into perspective, consider that very poor countries such as the Sudan and Nicaragua have per capita GDP of approximately $1,015, very close to North Korea's level. In fact, today the wealth of Bill Gates exceeds the annual GDP of North Korea.

Gross domestic product (GDP) is the market value of final goods and services produced in a country in a given period of time.

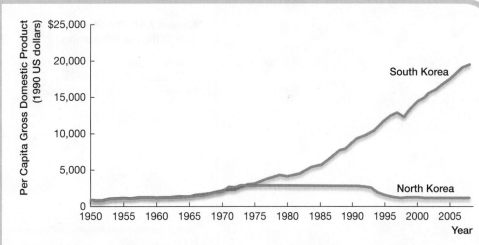

Exhibit 7.16 Per Capita GDP of North Korea and South Korea, 1950–2008

Starting in the mid-1970s, South Korea began pulling away from North Korea in terms of per capita GDP. As of 2008, South Korea has exhibited tremendous growth, whereas North Korea has been stagnant.

Source: Statistics on World Population, GDP and GDP Per Capita, 1–2008 AD (Horizontal file, copyright Angus Maddison). Available at http://www.ggdc.net/maddison/.

Exhibit 7.17 North Korea and South Korea Compared along a Variety of Dimensions

Here, the picture from the previous exhibit is examined more deeply, showing the vibrancy of trade in South Korea and the reliance on agriculture in North Korea.

	South Korea	North Korea
2008 GDP	$1,344 billion	$40 billion
2008 GDP rank	13th	95th
2008 exports value	$355,100 million	$2,062 million
2008 imports value	$313,400 million	$3,574 million
% of GDP Industrial	39.5%	43.1%
% of GDP Services	57.6%	33.6%
% of GDP Agricultural	3%	23.3%

Exhibit 7.17 highlights other differences between North and South Korea measured in recent years. The exhibit shows the dramatic differences in imports, exports, outputs in agricultural and manufacturing areas, and the level of services available. Interestingly, the statistics point to the fact that under a command system, North Korea has had a very difficult time developing beyond an agricultural economy.

Perhaps the most vivid image of the differences between North and South Korea is Exhibit 7.18. This amazing image was made in December of 2000 by a U.S. satellite taking shots of regions of the world at night. In a news briefing on December 23, 2002, Defense Secretary Donald Rumsfield commented: "If you look at a picture from the sky of the Korean Peninsula at night, South Korea is filled with lights and energy and vitality and a booming economy; North Korea is dark." While the most vibrant area is the capital city of South Korea, Seoul, even outside of Seoul several locations within South Korea dwarf the lighted developments of the sharpest blip in North Korea, which occurs in the capital city, Pyongyang.

The Central Planner

Why is it difficult for command economies to operate effectively and experience significant, sustained GDP growth? Let's take an extreme case by putting yourself in the shoes of a central planner. Pretend that you are in charge of the U.S. economy with the goal of maximizing the well-being of your citizens and that you have a command economy, not a free-market economy, on your hands. What would you do? How would you coordinate the millions of individual consumers, businesses, resource suppliers, and sellers? How would

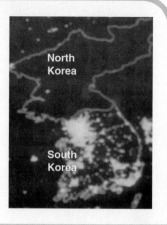

Exhibit 7.18 The Story of Two Different Economies

The night sky paints a stark picture of the economic differences between North and South Korea.

North Korea

South Korea

you make sure that the tractor manufacturing plant in Racine, Wisconsin, had the necessary steel, rubber, glass, and other critical inputs to produce tractors? How many cars should the Chrysler plant in Belvidere, Illinois, produce? Should the last bit of copper from mines in Utah be used to produce electrical wires or pots and pans? What about the natural gas that flows from the fields of Texas; should those cubic meters be used to warm homes in Boston or in Denver? Or should they be used to power the chemical plants in Biloxi, Mississippi?

After considering these queries, you likely have begun to more fully appreciate the linkages between industries. If the silica sand mines do not produce enough silica, glass manufacturing plants will be unable to meet their production goals. This shortage of glass will result in a lower quantity of glass for goods such as lights, mirrors, countertops, LCDs, and windshields for cars. If windshields are not provided to the Chrysler plant in Belvidere, Illinois, in a timely manner, workers will experience significant down time, leading in turn to Chrysler not meeting its production goals. The chain reaction will continue as fewer cars move off the line and fewer cars are shipped via rail and over the road, resulting in the shipping companies not meeting their shipping goals. Automobile dealerships subsequently will receive fewer cars to sell, thereby lowering the number of new cars sold and the commissions of car dealers. This lowering of income will in turn cause car dealers to take fewer vacations to sandy beaches, which sets off its own chain reaction in the tourism industry. And on and on in a great game of dominoes!

> When the interests of economic agents coincide, a **coordination problem** of bringing the agents together to trade arises.

As you can see, the **coordination problem** of bringing agents together to trade is a difficult one for central planners. And after you have solved the coordination problem, you need to think about how to tackle the **incentive problem**: that is, aligning the interests of the agents. In market economies, prices—not central planners—incentivize producers, and the bottom line of profits is what determines success for entrepreneurs.

> When the optimizing actions of two economic agents are not aligned, these agents face an **incentive problem.**

But in planned economies, rewards are based on meeting quantity targets. Consider the plant manager who is dispatched to produce wood boards for backyard decks. If he is told the target is based on weight, he produces only very long, wide, bulky boards, because he wants to maximize weight and is unresponsive to shipping costs or consumer desires. If he is told the target is based on quantity, he produces only very short, narrow, and thin boards. He doesn't much care if they fall apart when a consumer stands on them while barbequing, because the manager is not rewarded for quality. Stories such as these abound from planned economies.

Difficulties like these suggest that the reason for the fall of most planned systems (Cuba and North Korea represent the last bastions of command economies) is that the central planner does not fully understand consumer wants and needs and the production capabilities of every sector of the economy, and it is difficult to incentivize workers if prices are not utilized. Because any individual knows only a small fraction of all that is known collectively, it is impossible to replicate the work of the invisible hand. This truth is captured in Nobel Laureate Friedrich Hayek's words:

> The marvel is that in a case like that of a scarcity of one raw material, without an order being issued, without more than perhaps a handful of people knowing the cause, tens of thousands of people whose identity could not be ascertained by months of investigation, are made to use the material or its products more sparingly; that is, they move in the right direction.[4]

CHOICE & CONSEQUENCE

Command and Control at Kmart

"Attention, Kmart Shoppers! Attention, Kmart Shoppers! Handbag sale on aisle 3, 50% off; handbag sale on aisle 3, 50% off. Get there fast before they are all gone."

If you have ever frequented Kmart, you surely have heard an announcement like this. You likely remember the flashing blue light, and the accompanying flock of shoppers rushing to the celebrated aisle to fight over the swag.

The Blue Light Special began in 1965 in a local Indiana Kmart. The clever store manager made good use of a police car light to draw attention to items that were languishing in the store. Sam Walton, founder of Walmart, has lauded the idea as one of the greatest sales promotion ideas ever.

What few people know is that behind this brilliance is a command system that surely limits its profitability. In the early days of the Blue Light Specials, Kmarts were allowed to choose goods to be discounted, taking advantage of local knowledge and weather-related conditions.

Nowadays, rather than permitting each store to choose the goods to be discounted, all goods sold on Blue Light Specials are dictated from the corporate office in Hoffman Estates, Illinois, months in advance. Moreover, every day exactly the same goods are sold on Blue Light Specials, regardless of whether the store is located in Laramie, Wyoming, or Washington, D.C.

Much as the central planner loses the benefits of observing unfettered market prices when she directs production decisions, Kmart has lost the ability over the

years to take advantage of the decentralized knowledge of its store managers.

Clearly, when a December winter storm hits Laramie, the local Kmart should not be bound to decisions made thousands of miles away the previous July. Local market conditions dictate a different mix of products to be offered.

Likewise, when a torrid summer dry spell hits Washington, D.C. and a rainy spell hits Seattle, Washington, why should the Blue Light Specials at D.C. Kmarts be exactly the same as the Blue Light Specials at Kmarts in Seattle?

It is important to remember that the beauty of the invisible hand does not merely lie in the operation of traditional markets that we frequent. It manifests itself everywhere—within friendships, families, communities, firms, and countries. In the case of Kmart, it would be better if the decision maker was not a central planner but the invisible hand itself, which is an allocation device difficult to replicate.[5]

7.5 Equity and Efficiency

A market economy has features that are remarkable at providing price signals that guide resources in a way that maximizes social surplus and makes the economy efficient. Market forces act to eliminate waste—guiding resources to their correct destination—and provide incentives for all market participants to promote their own interests, which in turn promote the broader interests of society. In this way, maximizing efficiency directs us toward making the societal pie as large as possible.

But it is important to recognize that the standard of maximizing social surplus is just one way to measure the progress of an economy. Another consideration is how the pie is allocated. For example, many citizens might believe that every person should have proper access to food, housing, and basic healthcare. Pushing this notion even further, a social planner might also be concerned with **equity**. Equity is concerned with how the pie is allocated to the various economic agents. To some, equity means an even distribution of goods across society. Several important questions arise concerning equity and efficiency.

Should we help the homeless man on the corner, or assist an unemployed worker? What about starving children in Africa? They have virtually no income, implying that they are excluded from almost every market because their willingness to pay is not high enough to buy many goods. In fact, they cannot afford even the most basic necessities at the market price. Just because the competitive market equilibrium maximizes social surplus, and is efficient, does not mean that the resulting distribution is morally satisfactory.

Equity is concerned with the distribution of resources across society.

"Now that we've hired you we would like to restructure the position."

Several important questions arise concerning equity and efficiency. These are questions within the domain of normative economics, and are often debated by policymakers and economists. In a perfectly competitive equilibrium, we know that Pareto efficiency holds. This means that it is not possible to make a starving African child better off without making someone else worse off. Thus, it is possible that in order to increase the well-being of a starving child, it will be necessary to take a few hundred dollars from other people.

Of course, such redistribution of wealth is important to modern societies, and we'll see in later chapters that governments and private charities intervene in the functions of the market for this very reason. We will find that this kind of intervention presents an important trade-off between efficiency and equity, and that as a society we continually have choices over efficiency and equity. This is one major purpose of taxation. We will learn in later chapters that a host of interesting questions arise when we consider taxation and government's role in the economy.

Evidence-Based Economics

Q: Can markets composed of only self-interested people maximize the overall well-being of society?

The discussion in this chapter may have piqued your interest about the workings of the invisible hand. But, it may have left you longing for more concrete demonstrations of whether the theory is actually descriptive of reality. In particular, you may be thinking that although we conceptually showed various features of the competitive market equilibrium, we never presented any empirical evidence suggesting that any of it is actually true in practice—or at least approximately true.

To do so is difficult, however, because much like the central planner in planned economies, we do not observe market demand and market supply curves, so we cannot test whether prices and quantities are tending toward their equilibrium values. How could we ever go beyond the conceptual arguments of this chapter and show some real empirical evidence that the invisible hand does, in fact, operate as economists believe?

To show how economists have tackled this thorny question, let's narrow it down and put you in the shoes of a trader on the New York Stock Exchange via a small experiment. Say you walk into your economics classroom and find on the desk in front of you a note card that tells you two things: whether you are a buyer or a seller, and your reservation value. That is, for buyers, the value on the card represents the highest price that they will pay (reservation value), and for sellers, the value on the card represents the lowest price that they will accept (again, a reservation value but from the opposite point of view). So, for example, referring back to the scenario at the beginning of this chapter, we would see that Madeline's card would specify "$70: Buyer" and Adam's card would specify "$50: Seller."

You are then informed that if you are a buyer, you can buy one unit per period, and if you are a seller, you can sell one unit per period. There will be 5 periods in the experiment. Your earnings will be determined as follows: for both buyers and sellers, the difference between the trade price and the reservation price will determine market earnings. Thus, for instance, if you are a buyer with a reservation value of $25 and you manage to buy a unit at $20, your market earnings are $5. You might recall that we call this *consumer surplus*. Likewise, if you are a seller with a reservation value of $5 and you manage to sell a unit at $20, then you've earned $15 of producer surplus. After completion of each trade, the exchange price is announced so that all buyers and sellers are made aware of the most recent transaction.

Each market period lasts 10 minutes. During the market period, buyers should raise their hand to make public offers, which the monitor for the experiment will write on the board.

Sellers should do the same. The prices that the buyers submit are called *bid prices* in Wall Street lingo, and the prices that sellers submit are called *ask prices*. The basic idea is that buyers want to buy from the sellers with the lowest ask prices, and sellers want to sell to the buyers with the highest bid prices. Once a sale has been cleared, the bids and asks are removed and a new set of bids and asks can be submitted. This simple arrangement has similarities to how trading actually works on the New York Stock Exchange—bids and asks are yelled out and if they match, a trade is executed.

We are now ready to begin the experiment.

The bell rings to start Trading Period 1, and very quickly, bid prices and ask prices come in. A buyer to your right yells out "Bid $10!" The experimenter writes down this bid on a whiteboard. Other buyers behind you follow suit, raising the $10 bid successfully. At the same time, sellers submit their asks, each narrowly beating the last so they can have the business of the highest buyer. You yell out "buy $20!" and a seller takes your offer. Having a reservation price of $25, you feel good because you just netted $5 in Trading Period 1. You can now rest on your laurels until Trading Period 2 begins.

Double Oral Auction

A **double oral auction** is a market where sellers orally state asks and buyers orally state offers.

This type of experiment has come to be known as a *double oral auction* and was first experimentally studied by Vernon Smith. In a **double oral auction**, both bids and asks are orally stated, just as we have in this experiment. In his study of such auctions, Smith found re-assuring results. He tested many different market variants, varying the elasticity of supply and demand and the numbers of buyers and sellers. In spite of all of these changes, the markets still approached equilibrium price and quantity with great accuracy.

Exhibit 7.19 shows one example. Panel (a) of the exhibit shows the supply and demand curves for participants in Smith's double oral auction experiments with quantity on the

Exhibit 7.19 One Example from Smith's (1962) Experiments

In panel (a), we see the supply and demand curves that describe the double-oral auction market. The intersection of the supply and demand curves identifies the equilibrium price and quantity. Although these equilibrium values are theoretical predictions, they are borne out in the real-life activities of Smith's buyers and sellers, as the equilibrium price approaches the predicted value in panel (b).

Source: Vernon L. Smith, "An Experimental Study of Competitive Market Behavior," *Journal of Political Economy,* 70, no. 2 (1962): 111–135.

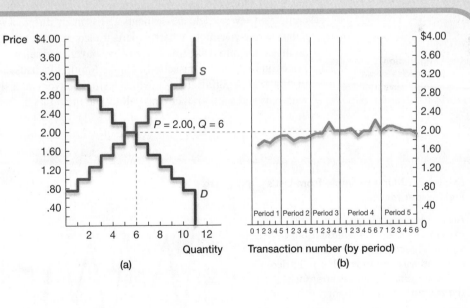

Evidence-Based Economics *(Continued)*

7.1

7.2

7.3

7.4

7.5

x-axis and price on the *y*-axis. The supply and demand curves are just the summation of each buyer's or seller's reservation values, which have been given to them at the beginning of the experiment—just like the example in Exhibit 7.2. Panel (b) of Exhibit 7.19 shows the price of each completed transaction in each period plotted in the order that each transaction occurred. That is, the *x*-axis is the transaction number and the *y*-axis is the price paid, with the horizontal dotted line representing the equilibrium price predicted by the supply and demand curves in panel (a). Initially, the market price is below the market equilibrium, but by the third trading period, the price is very close to the equilibrium prediction.

From the perspective of markets like the New York Stock Exchange, Smith's double oral auction results are a triumph for the incredible workings of the invisible hand. Smith's results show the power of our theory, in that the equilibrium price is very close to where the supply and demand curves intersect. Digging deeper into these and related data, we find that the high-value buyers buy, the low-cost sellers sell, and no one else executes a trade.

You might be thinking that yes, this is a swift example, but it's a far cry from the markets that you typically frequent. That is, how often do you encounter markets that resemble the conditions of a double oral auction? Unless you have worked as a trader on Wall Street, your answer is probably "never." If you consider the sorts of markets in which you have participated, you are probably much more likely to have frequented the local grocery store where prices are on price tags, or even a market where you can haggle with sellers, such as a used-car lot or an open-air market.

Bilateral Negotiations

If we allowed buyers and sellers to mingle with one another and negotiate privately to buy and sell goods, would the results be as promising as what Smith found in his double oral auctions? This is exactly the question that one of the authors (List) addressed, when he completed several field experiments across many different types of open-air markets: from sports card conventions where experts traded sports cards, to Disney World where kids and adults traded pins. Like Smith, List gave buyers and sellers reservation values and recorded prices publicly after transactions. Unlike Smith, List had actual buyers and sellers engaging in **bilateral negotiations**—in which a single buyer and a single seller confront each other with bids and asks—rather than yelling out the offers to the group.

A **bilateral negotiation** is a market mechanism in which a single seller and a single buyer privately negotiate with bids and asks.

Exhibit 7.20 One Example from List's Field Experiments

Although the participants in List's experiment did not have the benefit of a central auctioneer to help announce bids and asks, he found that the prices of the negotiated trades approached the theoretical equilibrium price.

Source: John A. List, "Testing Neoclassical Competitive Theory in Multilateral Decentralized Markets," *Journal of Political Economy,* 112, no. 5 (2004): 1131–56.

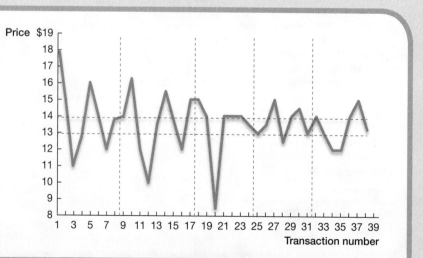

Price $19

Transaction number

Across a myriad of settings—using a range of different trader types, market demand and market supply curves, and different numbers of buyers and sellers—List found a strong tendency for prices to approach the competitive equilibrium. The result even held for young children! One example from List's study is given in Exhibit 7.20. The exhibit shows the price of each transaction on the y-axis, and each transaction is represented sequentially on the x-axis. These data indicate that the market converges to the intersection of supply and demand (which is represented here as a price between the two dotted lines, one at $13 and one at $14).

[**The invisible hand is much stronger than many first assumed.**]

An implication of this research is that even in decentralized real-world markets, prices and quantities converge to where demand meets supply. In fact, even with a small number of buyers and sellers—as few as six of each—List found that price and quantity converged to the intersection of demand and supply. In this way, the invisible hand is much stronger than many first assumed, as these markets often come close to full efficiency: social surplus is nearly maximized in many of the markets. And the question that we posed at the beginning of this chapter—*can markets composed of only self-interested people maximize the overall well-being of society?*—is answered in the affirmative.

Question

Can markets composed of only self-interested people maximize the overall well-being of society?

Answer

Yes.

Data

Lab and field experiments.

Caveat

Experiments explore whether the high-value buyers buy, whether the low-cost sellers sell, and whether the correct number of trades occurs. Data are not gathered across firms in an industry or across industries. Therefore, we only show the first of the three basic results of a perfectly competitive equilibrium.

If you stopped reading this book at this point, you would be a rabid free-market proponent. This is because the beauty of the economic system is unparalleled. Yet, there are important instances that frustrate the workings of the invisible hand. For example, when a firm produces, it might pollute the air or water, causing harm to people. Likewise, if a firm is not a price-taker, but has the power to set prices, the firm might be able to cause a reallocation of resources toward itself and social surplus might not be maximized.

We explore how these, and other, realistic situations frustrate the invisible hand's workings in the coming chapters. Such examples lead us to consider the appropriate mix between free markets and government intervention. We will learn that all successful modern economies have a mix of government and free markets.

Summary

🌟 When the strong assumptions of a perfectly competitive market are in place, markets align the interests of self-interested agents and society as a whole. In this way, the market harmonizes individuals and society so that in their pursuit of individual gain, self-interested people promote the well-being of society as a whole.

🌟 The remarkable tendency of individual self-interest to promote the well-being of society as a whole is all orchestrated by the invisible hand.

🌟 The invisible hand efficiently allocates goods and services to buyers and sellers, leads to efficient production *within* an industry, and allocates resources efficiently *across* industries.

🌟 The invisible hand is guided by prices. Prices incentivize buyers and sellers, who in turn maximize social surplus—the sum of consumer surplus and producer surplus—by simply looking out for themselves.

🌟 We can measure the progress of an economy by measuring social surplus—how big the societal pie is. But we can also measure progress by considering questions of equity—how the pie is distributed across agents.

Key Terms

reservation value *p. 145*
social surplus *p. 146*
Pareto efficient *p. 148*
price control *p. 155*

deadweight loss *p. 156*
gross domestic product *p. 158*
coordination problem *p. 160*
incentive problem *p. 160*

equity *p. 161*
double oral auction *p. 163*
bilateral negotiation *p. 164*

Questions

All questions are available in MyEconLab *for practice and instructor assignment.*

1. All else being equal, does elastic or inelastic demand curve result in higher social surplus? How does elasticity of supply affect social surplus?

2. How do economic profits and losses allocate resources in an economy?

3. How will the invisible hand move corn prices in response to:

   a. a flood that destroys a great deal of the corn crop?

   b. a rise in the price of wheat (a substitute for corn)?

   c. a change in consumer tastes away from corn dogs toward hot dogs?

   d. an increase in the number of demanders in the corn market?

4. Hardware stores charge higher prices for snow shovels after a big snow storm. What role do prices play in the snow shovel market?

5. The market for economics textbooks is in equilibrium. The government decides to relax export restrictions on paper, leading to an increase in the demand for paper. How does social surplus in the market for textbooks change? Why? Present a diagram as part of your explanation.

6. What could explain why South Korea's gross domestic product (GDP) per capita increased so much faster since the 1970s than North Korea's GDP per capita?

7. In a command economy, a planning agency sets prices for various inputs and final goods. In a market economy, supply and demand decide the prices of various goods. In both cases, there is a set of prices operating in the economy. Then why are market economies considered more efficient than planned economies?

8. If your professor decided to give all students the highest grade in the class, would that affect your classmates' incentives to study?

9. Sofia, a political science student, thinks that the government should intervene to revive declining industries like video stores and print newspapers. The government, she

reasons, can resolve the coordination problem of getting the agents in these markets to trade. Do you agree with her? Explain your answer.

10. Are all efficient outcomes also equitable? Explain.

11. Are there real-world markets that resemble double oral auctions? Suppose you had to organize a double oral auction for a good that has perfectly elastic demand. Do you expect prices to approach the competitive equilibrium?

12. Imagine you are a buyer in a double oral auction with a reservation value of $10 and there is a seller asking for $8.

    a. How much will you gain from accepting this offer?

    b. If you are the only buyer, and you know that the lowest ask price is $2, should you accept this offer?

Problems

All problems are available in MyEconLab for practice and instructor assignment.

1. The following diagram shows the market demand and market supply for sweaters. Calculate consumer surplus, producer surplus, and social surplus in this market.

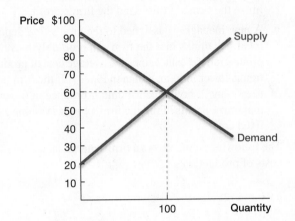

2. Look at Exhibit 7.1 in the chapter that shows the reservation values of the buyers and sellers in the iPod market. Suppose trades are arranged in this market such that everyone can make a trade without losing money. So, Madeline buys from Fiona at a price of $70, Katie buys from Matt at a price of $60, Sean buys from Adam at a price of $50, and so on.

Since everyone who wants an iPod obtains one, and everyone who wants to get rid of their iPod sells it at the price they wanted, is social surplus maximized in the market?

3. There are four consumers willing to pay the following amounts for an electric car:

Consumer 1:	Consumer 2:	Consumer 3:	Consumer 4:
$70,000	$20,000	$80,000	$40,000

There are four firms that can produce electric cars. Each can produce one car at the following costs:

Firm A:	Firm B:	Firm C:	Firm D:
$30,000	$60,000	$40,000	$20,000

Each firm can produce at most one car.

Suppose we wanted to maximize the difference between consumers' willingness to pay for electric cars and the cost of producing those cars; that is, we wanted to maximize social surplus.

    a. How many electric cars should we produce?

    b. Which firms should produce those cars?

    c. Which consumers should purchase those cars?

    d. Find the maximum social surplus in the electric car market.

4. Let us continue with the electric car example from problem 3. Suppose the market for electric cars is competitive.

    a. Show that the equilibrium price in this market is $40,000.

    b. Which firms will produce an electric car if the price is $40,000?

    c. Which consumers will buy an electric car when the price is $40,000?

    d. Calculate consumer surplus, producer surplus, and social surplus when the price is $40,000.

    e. Compare your answers to those for problem 3.

5. The following figure shows the demand and supply of television sets in a city. Since TVs are considered normal goods, demand increases from D_1 to D_2 in response to an increase in consumers' income.

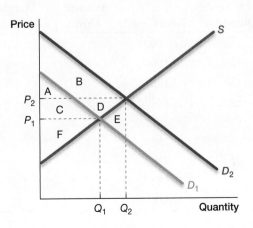

a. Use the figure to complete the table below.

	Before Income Rose	After Income Rose	Change
Consumer Surplus			
Producer Surplus			
Social Surplus			

b. Use your answers to part (a) of this problem to answer the following questions:

   i. Did consumer surplus definitely rise, definitely remain constant, or definitely fall, or is the direction of the change in consumer surplus unclear?

   ii. Did producer surplus definitely rise, definitely remain constant, or definitely fall, or is the direction of the change in producer surplus unclear?

   iii. Did social surplus definitely rise, definitely remain constant, or definitely fall, or is the direction of the change in social surplus unclear?

6. The market for electric drills in a certain country is characterized by a large number of buyers and sellers and every buyer who wants a drill and can afford one has bought one. In other words, the market for drills is in equilibrium.

a. Does this also mean that it is Pareto efficient? Explain your answer.

b. If some of the buyers in this market are now willing to pay more than they did earlier, would your answer change?

c. Compared to the market for cars, the market for vintage buttons has fewer buyers and sellers. Social surplus is likely to be higher in the market for cars than in the vintage button market. Is it then correct to assume that the outcome in the car market is Pareto efficient while in the vintage button market it is not? Explain.

7. The following tables show a small firm's long-run average cost of manufacturing a good at two different plants:

	Plant 1		
Quantity	Total Cost	Average Cost	Marginal Cost
1	50		
2	106		
3	164		
4	224		
5	287		
6	355		
7	430		
8	520		
9	618		

	Plant 2		
Quantity	Total Cost	Average Cost	Marginal Cost
1	20		
2	52		
3	90		
4	130		
5	175		
6	227		
7	285		
8	345		
9	407		

a. Complete the third and fourth columns of each table.

b. Suppose the price of the good is $60. How much should the firm produce in each plant in order to maximize the firm's profit? Find the firm's profit.

c. A new manager is assigned to the production department. He thinks that the firm can profitably move all production to Plant 2 since the average cost of production is lower in Plant 2 than in Plant 1. If the firm only uses Plant 2, how much should it produce in order to maximize profits? Find the firm's profit. Assume zero fixed cost.

8. The following figure shows a firm's marginal and average costs of production:

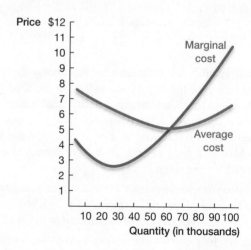

a. The equilibrium price in this market is $5. At this price, does the firm earn economic profits or is it incurring economic losses?

b. From the given information, can you conclude whether the firm is operating in a competitive market? Explain your answer.

c. The price of the good increases to $8. How does this change your answer to parts (a) and (b)?

9. Hospitals in Springfield are profit-maximizing, perfectly competitive firms. Hospitals in Maybury, on the other hand, are run by nonprofit charities that try to minimize the long-run average cost of treating patients. Hospitals in both cities have the same average and marginal cost. Show that hospitals in both cities will be the same size.

10. The equilibrium rent in a town is $500 per month, and the equilibrium number of apartments is 100. The city now passes a rent control law that sets the maximum rent at $400. The diagram below summarizes the supply and demand for apartments in this city.

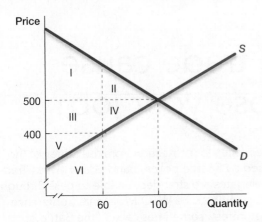

   a. Use the figure to complete the table below.

	Before Rent Control	After Rent Control	Change
Consumer Surplus			
Producer Surplus			
Social Surplus			

   b. Use your answers to part (a) of this problem to answer the following questions:

   i. Did consumer surplus definitely rise, definitely remain constant, or definitely fall, or is the direction of the change in consumer surplus unclear?

   ii. Did producer surplus definitely rise, definitely remain constant, or definitely fall, or is the direction of the change in producer surplus unclear?

   iii. Did social surplus definitely rise, definitely remain constant, or definitely fall, or is the direction of the change in social surplus unclear?

11. According to reports in the Chinese media, commuters in Beijing are facing a somewhat paradoxical situation: they find it difficult to get a cab while hundreds of cabs lie idle during rush hour. The demand for taxis in Beijing has increased as average incomes have risen. Government-determined gasoline prices have also increased. But the government, worried about rising prices for cab rides, has left the cabs' base fare unchanged.

   a. Use supply and demand curves to explain what has happened in the market for cabs in Beijing.

   b. Based on your understanding of how the invisible hand works, what do you think should be done to correct this problem?

12. The following quote is from a section on food shortages in a book on the Soviet economy:

   "Why there is no fish . . . I can't imagine," wrote one indignant citizen to Anastas Mikoyan, head of the Food Ministry, in 1940. "We have seas, and they are still the same as before, but then you could have as much [fish] as you wanted of whatever kind, and now I have even forgotten what it looks like."

   Industries and agriculture in the former Soviet Union were state controlled and the economy's resources were allocated by a central agency, Gosplan. In the passage above, the citizen cannot understand why there is a shortage of fish although the country possesses the same resources that it did before the economy transitioned to central planning. What could explain this outcome?

8 Trade

Will free trade cause you to lose your job?

As protesters cover their faces for protection from the fumes of the fire and tear gas released by Seattle police, hundreds of World Trade Organization (WTO) delegates are stranded, unable to pass through the blockade of 40,000 people at the WTO Ministerial Conference of 1999. This free trade protest, sometimes called "the Battle of Seattle," was not an uncommon event, as its predecessor—the worldwide "Carnival Against Capitalism"—garnered a similar number of demonstrators.

Faced with such passionate opposition to free trade, you may be surprised to learn the major lesson of this chapter: *free trade always benefits both trading partners* and therefore represents the key reason why we observe so much interdependence in the world. If this is true, what has upset these protesters? Are they being irrational? Would a brief course in economics have prevented 40,000 people from blockading the streets of Seattle?

In fact, we will see that there is nothing irrational in the protesters' stance and that they likely will not be comforted by even the best course in economics. This follows from the second lesson of the chapter: *within any trading country, some individuals may be made worse off by trade.* The losses potentially arise from reduced consumer or producer surplus, lost jobs, or lower wages. But importantly, we will learn that the gains from trade reaped by the winners more than compensate for the losses of the losers. The key is to develop policies so that everyone can reap the gains from trade.

CHAPTER OUTLINE

- The production possibilities curve tells us how much we can produce from existing resources and technology.

- The basis for trade is comparative advantage.

- Specialization is based on comparative, not absolute, advantage.

- There are winners and losers within trading states and countries.

- The winners from trade can more than compensate the losers.

- Important arguments against free trade exist.

8.1 The Production Possibilities Curve

Take a look at your tennis shoes. Where were they made? We'd guess in China, the world's largest shoe exporter. Do you own a Wii? It's manufactured in Japan, one of the major exporters of consumer electronics. What about your haircut? We suspect that you did not trim those bangs yourself. Why do so many people and countries rely on others for goods and services? What are the gains to such interdependence?

The underlying motivation for trade, whether it occurs between a barber and a butcher or between the United States and China, relies on one simple principle: *we can all be better off by trading with one another because trade allows total production to be maximized.* To see how, we begin with an example that might hit close to home.

In an effort to make some spare cash, you take on a freelance weekend job creating Web sites and computer programs to run on each Web site. Your first job is to create 240 Web sites and produce 240 specific computer programs to run applications on each Web site. Because each Web site and computer program is unique, you must start from scratch to produce each one. You now have to figure out how to complete these tasks. Taking an economic approach, you recognize that your new job resembles, in a sense, a two-good economy (Web sites and programs), and you want to figure out how much you can accomplish—your production possibilities—in an 8-hour day.

After some experimentation, you gather enough data to create Exhibit 8.1. The exhibit shows output levels for various amounts of time for each of the two tasks. For instance, if

Exhibit 8.1 Your Production Schedule

The exhibit shows how the time you spend maps into the number of Web sites and computer programs. For example, you could spend 6 hours producing Web sites and 2 hours producing computer programs. In this case you would produce 6 Web sites and 4 computer programs.

Hours Spent on Web Sites	Number of Web Sites Produced	Hours Spent on Computer Programs	Number of Computer Programs Produced
8	8	0	0
7	7	1	2
6	6	2	4
5	5	3	6
4	4	4	8
3	3	5	10
2	2	6	12
1	1	7	14
0	0	8	16

you work an entire 8-hour day creating computer programs, you are able to produce 16. Alternatively, if you focus your entire work day on designing Web sites, you can create 8. Spending a little time on each task yields intermediate production levels.

A simple way to plot these data is with a **production possibilities curve (PPC)**, which shows the relationship between the maximum production of one good for a given level of production of another good. Exhibit 8.2 takes the data from Exhibit 8.1 to show your "economy's" *PPC* by indicating the combinations of Web sites and computer programs that you can produce in an 8-hour period. The *PPC* is quite similar to the budget constraint that we discussed in Chapter 5: it tells us how much we can produce from existing resources and technology.

In the exhibit, the *x*-axis represents the number of individual Web sites that you complete, and the *y*-axis represents the number of computer programs that you complete. The exhibit highlights the trade-offs that you make when deciding what to produce. If you committed all of your effort to making Web sites, you could prepare 8 of them per day. Alternatively, if you spent all of your time programming, you could complete 16 computer programs per day. These are the most extreme trade-offs that can be made. As such, they form the endpoints of the *PPC* for your economy, which is represented by the blue line.

But there are choices that you can make between these extremes. When considering a *PPC*, it is useful to remember the following rules:

- Points *on* the *PPC*, such as point B in Exhibit 8.2—6 Web sites produced and 4 computer programs produced—are attainable and efficient.
- Points *inside* the *PPC*, such as point A—4 Web sites produced and 4 computer programs produced—are attainable but inefficient.
- Points *beyond* the *PPC*, like point C—8 Web sites produced and 8 computer programs produced—are unattainable.

Therefore, any point on or below the *PPC* represents possible production levels in an 8-hour day. Production combinations on the *PPC* are both attainable and efficient; that is, they can be achieved, and they make full use of your resources (your time, in this case). Any combination outside the line, like point C, is unattainable. This is because within an 8-hour day you cannot produce this amount of Web sites (8) and programs (8)—it is technically not feasible given your skills and available resources.

Why do we say that any point inside the *PPC* is attainable but not efficient? The reason is that you could produce more with your time. Consider point A. In this case, you could, for example, use your time more efficiently and produce 2 more Web sites (moving rightward

8.1

8.2

8.3

8.4

8.5

I will always choose a lazy person to do a difficult job . . . Because, he will find an easy way to do it. —Bill Gates

A **production possibilities curve (PPC)** shows the relationship between the maximum production of one good for a given level of production of another good.

Exhibit 8.2 The Production Possibilities Curve

The *PPC* is a graphical representation of the production schedule. Much like the budget constraint from Chapter 5, the slope represents the number of computer programs that you forego when you produce an additional Web site. Points on the *PPC* (such as point B and point D) are attainable and efficient, points inside the *PPC* (such as point A) are attainable and inefficient, and points outside the *PPC* (such as point C) are unattainable.

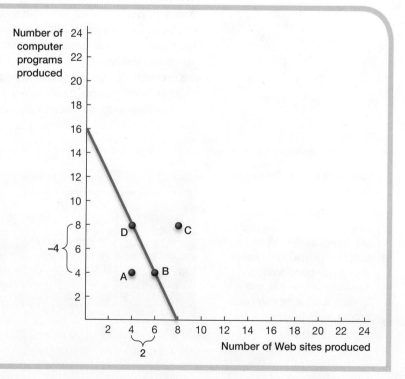

from point A to point B), or 4 more computer programs (moving upward from point A to point D), or a combination of some number of additional Web sites and computer programs (moving up and right from point A to your *PPC*). People and firms are inside their *PPC* when they do not efficiently produce. For example, a car manufacturer, such as Chrysler, might not have the optimal ratio of workers to machines, leading it to produce inside its *PPC*. In general, it is optimal to find a point on the *PPC* where production combinations are both attainable and efficient, such as points B or D of the exhibit.

Calculating Opportunity Cost

Exhibit 8.2 shows that when you produce more Web sites, you produce fewer computer programs. This makes sense—if you are spending your time producing Web sites, then you cannot produce computer programs. This is the opportunity cost, or what you give up to produce one additional Web site. Just like the trade-off you faced in Chapter 5 on your buying spree, you can compute the opportunity cost of Web sites by using a formula:

$$\text{Opportunity cost}_{\text{Web sites}} = \frac{\text{Loss in computer programs}}{\text{Gain in Web sites}}$$

where the loss in computer programs measures the number of computer programs that must be given up for the gain in Web sites. How do we get these numbers?

We get them by taking the absolute value of the slope of the *PPC* in Exhibit 8.2. To find the slope, we take the "rise" between two points on the vertical *y*-axis and divide it by the "run" on the horizontal *x*-axis. The rise is the amount by which computer programs change, and the run is the amount by which Web sites change. In Exhibit 8.2, we see that from point D to point B, the value on the *y*-axis changes from 8 to 4. On the *x*-axis, the value changes from 4 to 6. So, we have

$$\text{Opportunity cost}_{\text{Web sites}} = -\frac{4}{2} = -2$$

The absolute value of −2 is 2. The opportunity cost of creating one more Web site, then, is 2 computer programs. A similar formula provides the opportunity cost of producing computer programs:

$$\text{Opportunity cost}_{\text{Web sites}} = \frac{\text{Loss in Web sites}}{\text{Gain in computer programs}}$$

So we have

$$\text{Opportunity cost}_{\text{programs}} = -\frac{2}{4} = -\frac{1}{2}$$

The absolute value is ½. Thus, the opportunity cost of creating computer programs is ½ a Web site, which means that for every computer program you produce, you give up being able to produce ½ of a Web site (you will notice that the opportunity costs are reciprocals; this is always the case for a linear *PPC*).

Upon making these calculations, you become rather nervous about completing the tasks of your new job while trying to maintain your grades and an active social life—you will need to spend 45 days just to finish the first task! This is because it will take you 15 full days to complete the computer programs (240 = 16 per day for 15 days), and an additional 30 full days to complete the Web sites (240 = 8 per day for 30 days).

Your friend, another economics major, calmly advises you not to worry because she knows a student named Olivia who has taken on a similar freelance job. You do not really understand how this helps you, because anyone saddled with a similarly horrific job would have no time to assist a complete stranger!

Nevertheless, you are desperate, so you approach Olivia. After a discussion, you learn that Olivia faces the same Mount Everest that you do—completing 240 computer programs and 240 Web sites while trying to maintain her grades and an active social life.

But there's an interesting wrinkle to the situation: Olivia has talents different from yours. She is relatively more proficient at Web site production. Exhibit 8.3 overlays Olivia's *PPC* on your *PPC*; you can see that Olivia's opportunity cost is different from your opportunity cost.

Exhibit 8.3 Two Production Possibilities Curves

Olivia's *PPC* is represented together with your *PPC*. While you must sacrifice 2 computer programs to produce an additional Web site, Olivia only needs to sacrifice ½ of a computer program for an additional Web site. Can you trade to lower the number of workdays?

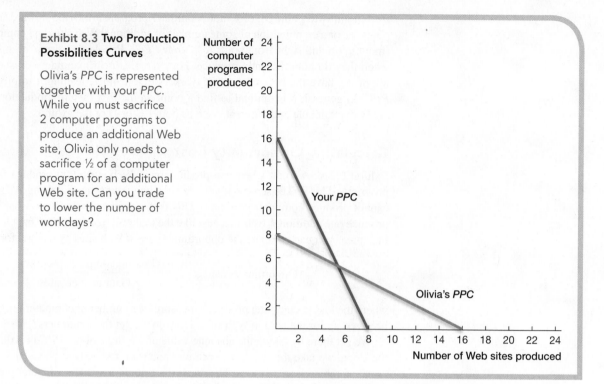

You also realize that Olivia is in exactly the same boat as you—she needs to spend 45 days to complete her first job too (30 days for the computer programs and 15 days for the Web sites).

How can you and Olivia minimize your work time? Should you rely on each other, or go it alone? And if you believe that joining forces is the correct path forward, how should the work be allocated between the two of you?

8.2 The Basis for Trade: Comparative Advantage

Comparative advantage is the ability of an individual, firm, or country to produce a certain good at a lower opportunity cost than other producers.

A first place to start when answering such questions is to recognize the principle of *comparative advantage*, which revolves around the notion of figuring out what you are relatively good at doing. More formally, **comparative advantage** is the ability of an individual, firm, or country to produce a certain good at a lower opportunity cost than other producers. Do you have a comparative advantage at producing either of the goods? What about Olivia—does she have a comparative advantage? The answer to both questions is yes.

The key to determining who has a comparative advantage is to compare individual opportunity costs. You have a comparative advantage in producing computer programs because you forego only ½ of a Web site to produce one computer program. Olivia foregoes 2 Web sites to produce one computer program. Because ½ is less than 2, your opportunity cost of producing computer programs is the lower one in this two-person economy.

Performing similar calculations, we find that Olivia has a comparative advantage in producing Web sites because she foregoes only ½ of a computer program to produce each Web site, whereas you forego 2 computer programs to produce each Web site. The following table summarizes the opportunity cost for Web sites and computer programs:

> **The key to determining who has a comparative advantage is to compare individual opportunity costs.**

	Web Site Opportunity Cost	Computer Program Opportunity Cost
You	2 computer programs	½ Web sites
Olivia	½ computer program	2 Web sites

Specialization

So what does all of this mean? It means that if you *specialize* in producing what you are relatively good at, and Olivia specializes in producing what she is relatively good at, then you will both be better off if you trade. Complete specialization occurs when each individual, firm, or country produces only what it has a comparative advantage in and relies on trade for the other goods and services it needs.

The gains from trade in this case are tremendous, as revealed in Exhibit 8.4. To understand how to construct Exhibit 8.4, consider if both you and Olivia committed all of your time to producing computer programs. 24 computer programs would be produced. Now if we were to take one hour away from computer program writing and allocate it to Web site construction, whose hour (which worker's time) would we switch to Web site production? Since the opportunity cost of Olivia producing a Web site is lower than yours (1/2 a computer program foregone versus 2 computer programs foregone), we would shift an hour from Olivia. If we wanted even more Web sites, we would continue to shift Olivia's hours until she is completely specializing in Web site production (Point T in Exhibit 8.4). If we wanted to produce even more than 16 Web sites, the tradeoff/opportunity cost will now increase to 2 computer programs forgone for each additional Web site because we begin to have you produce Web sites.

A key insight from Exhibit 8.4 is that at point T you and Olivia can produce a daily output of 16 Web sites *and* 16 computer programs. This works because you specialize in what you are good at—writing programs—and Olivia specializes in what she is good at—creating Web sites.

So upon complete specialization, you produce all 480 computer programs and Olivia produces all 480 Web sites. Of these 480 computer programs, you use 240 of them for your freelance job and give the remaining 240 to Olivia. In turn, she gives you 240 Web sites. The mere ability to trade with one another leads both of you to completely specialize, decreasing your work time from 45 days to 30 days!

Absolute Advantage

At this point you might be thinking that the example above is "cooked." The key, you might argue, is that you and Olivia have different talents and, indeed, symmetrical ones at that: your opportunity cost is the inverse of Olivia's opportunity cost. To see that the power of comparative advantage is more general than this simple scenario, let's continue with the example and

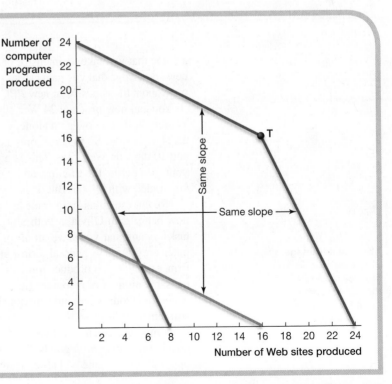

Exhibit 8.4 The Gains from Specialization

With complete specialization, you produce 16 computer programs and Olivia produces 16 Web sites (point T on the graph). The change in the output of both computer programs and Web sites left of point T is determined entirely by the slope of Olivia's *PPC*. Similarly, it is your *PPC* that determines the change in total production to the right of point T.

🌳 **CHOICE & CONSEQUENCE**

An Experiment on Comparative Advantage

Suppose that you walk into an economics lab experiment to make a little money. When you arrive, the experimenters pair you with another student and lets you know that you can produce combinations of keys and locks at the rate specified by the blue line in the chart to the right, and that your partner can do so at the rate specified by the tan line. Your task is to select a production point along your *PPC*. At the same time, your partner makes her choice.

After you have made your selection, your choice will be combined with that of your partner. Every key and lock *pair* entitles each partner to $10. Spare keys and locks are worth nothing.

What key/lock production combination should you choose?

A key consideration is what do you and your partner have a comparative advantage in producing? The production possibilities and opportunity costs are summarized in the table below the chart.

In this type of experiment, many subjects either maximize the pairs that they *alone* can produce or simply choose the largest number they can. For example, subjects like you typically choose 8 keys, and your partner typically maximizes what he or she can produce, choosing 6 keys. In this case, you *both* wind up earning nothing!

Why? Though you can produce more keys than locks, you should choose to make only locks because you have a comparative advantage in producing locks. Likewise, your partner should choose to make only keys. In this way, you each can produce 6, allowing you to walk away with earnings of $60 each. Following your comparative advantage leads you and your partner to coordinate production.

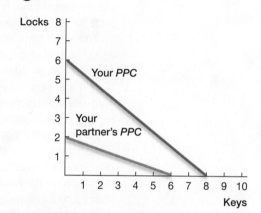

Individual	Production Possibilities	
	Keys	Locks
You	8	6
Experiment Partner	6	2

Individual	Opportunity Costs	
	Opportunity Cost of Keys (locks foregone to gain a key)	Opportunity Cost of Locks (keys foregone to gain a lock)
You	3/4 of a lock	4/3 of a key
Experiment Partner	1/3 of a lock	3 keys

Each individual should specialize in the production of the item in which they have a comparative advantage (e.g., lower opportunity cost), so your experiment partner should specialize in producing keys, producing a total of 6 keys, and you should specialize in producing locks, manufacturing a total of 6 locks.

assume that you take an intensive one-week course on Web site production and design. The new knowledge that you gain causes your Web site productivity to triple, causing your *PPC* to pivot about the *y*-axis. Your new *PPC* is shown in Exhibit 8.5, alongside Olivia's *PPC*.

You can now produce 24 Web sites in one day, as compared with 8 before the training. Therefore, if you now go it alone, you can produce a daily output of 16 computer programs or 24 Web sites. So you will only need to work 25 days—15 days on computer programs and 10 days on Web sites. This is much less than the 45 days when you were working on your own before the training, and it is even less than the 30 days you needed to work when you traded with Olivia. But does it mean that trade cannot help in this case?

No, but the gains from trade are now less obvious. You might be thinking that you are now better than Olivia at both tasks, so why do you need her help? Being better at both tasks means that you have an *absolute advantage* at producing both Web sites and computer programs. In general terms, an **absolute advantage** is the ability of an individual, firm, or country to produce more of a certain good than other competing producers, given the same number of resources (in this case, production in an 8-hour day).

Despite your newfound superior skill, you might be surprised to learn that gains to trade still remain. This is so because even though you can produce more Web sites and computer programs in a given day than Olivia can produce, you do *not* have a comparative advantage in producing *both* goods. With linear *PPCs*, unless two people have exactly the same opportunity cost, one will always have a comparative advantage in producing one good and

Absolute advantage is the ability of an individual, firm, or country to produce more of a certain good than other competing producers, given the same number of resources.

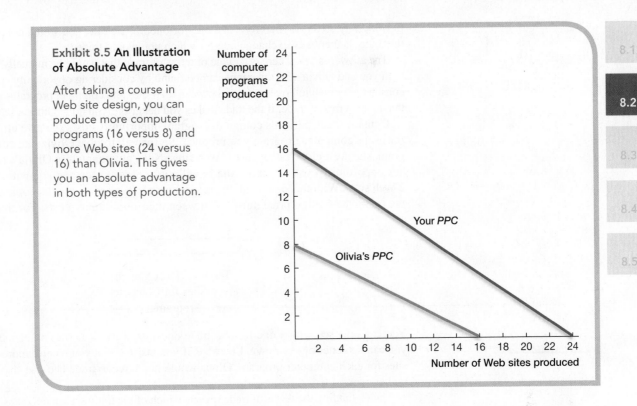

Exhibit 8.5 An Illustration of Absolute Advantage

After taking a course in Web site design, you can produce more computer programs (16 versus 8) and more Web sites (24 versus 16) than Olivia. This gives you an absolute advantage in both types of production.

the other person the other good. Why? Because one person is relatively better at one task than the other, and vice versa.

So what are the gains to specialization and trade in this case? To answer this question, we must first compute who has a comparative advantage in production of each of the goods. The following table summarizes the new opportunity cost:

	Web Site Opportunity Cost	Computer Program Opportunity Cost
You	⅔ computer programs	½ Web sites
Olivia	½ computer programs	2 Web sites

Even though you have taken classes in Web site production, Olivia still has a comparative advantage in producing Web sites. At ½ a computer program, her opportunity cost remains lower than your opportunity cost of producing a Web site, ⅔ computer programs. Likewise, you maintain your comparative advantage in producing computer programs because your opportunity cost is ½ Web sites, whereas Olivia's is 2 Web sites.

Accordingly, we can follow the example above and have each of you completely specialize: you produce 480 programs and Olivia produces 480 Web sites. And you can get the jobs done by both working 30 days.

Does this make sense? How come that even after receiving Web site training, you are no better off? Do you really need Olivia's help? Without her, you need to work only 25 days—15 days on computer programs and 10 days on Web sites. What should you do?

The Price of the Trade

The reason why this example does not lead to a more advantageous outcome for you is because we held the *terms of trade* constant from the first example: 1 Web site for 1 computer program. The **terms of trade** is the negotiated exchange rate of goods for goods. The principle of comparative advantage, while powerful, does not provide an exact terms of trade, but it does provide a range within which trade will occur. In this way, it prescribes how the gains to trade are split between the two parties.

As this example shows, if the exchange rate is 1 computer program for 1 Web site, you are worse off from trade because you are working 30 days, whereas with no trade you need

The **terms of trade** is the negotiated exchange rate of goods for goods.

to work only 25 days. Therefore, at a one-for-one trading rate, you would not participate in the trade. Is there any exchange rate for which you would trade?

The answer is yes. There is a range of terms of trade that would be mutually beneficial to both you and Olivia, and this range can be found by considering opportunity cost. You both consider your own internal trade-off between Web sites and computer programs and compare that to the terms of trade. If the trade makes you better off, you do it. Otherwise you do not.

Consider each person's computer program opportunity cost. You give up ⅓ Web sites for every computer program you produce. So for you to give Olivia one computer program, she must give you at least ⅓ Web sites. Now, put yourself in Olivia's shoes. Given her opportunity cost, the most she is willing to give up for one computer program is 2 Web sites. With those in hand, the rule is straightforward: for both people to engage in the trade, the trading price must lie between their opportunity costs. For this example:

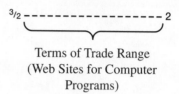

Terms of Trade Range
(Web Sites for Computer
Programs)

You can now see why a one-for-one trade does not work: it is outside of this range and you can do better on your own. Likewise, if you insisted that you receive more than 2 Web sites for each computer program, Olivia would not agree to trade because she is better off on her own.

Understanding the terms of trade reveals which of the trading partners reaps the gains of trade. Prices closer to ⅓ Web sites per program favor Olivia, while prices closer to 2 Web sites per program favor you. Why? This is so because Olivia is producing Web sites, and the fewer she gives up per program, the better off she will be. Likewise, you are producing programs, and the more Web sites you receive in return for each program, the better off you will be. A price right in the middle—1.75 Web sites per program—provides you and Olivia with the same gains from trade.

> **The gains to trade shrink as the trading partners become more alike.**

This example also highlights that the gains to trade shrink as the trading partners become more alike. Before you took the intensive one-week course on Web site production and design, trading with Olivia showed great gains because you were each good at different tasks: you were proficient at writing computer programs and Olivia at producing Web sites. This led to a substantial gain due to trade. As you became more similar to Olivia, the gains to trade shrank.

8.3 Trade Between States

Just as you and Olivia have different talents, individual states in the United States have quite distinct advantages. Consider the undergraduate student living in Minnesota. On any given day, she wakes up to a chilled glass of orange juice, slips on her leather boots, and drives her Chrysler Jeep to class. Just in these three simple tasks, she has taken advantage of goods produced in Florida, California, and Michigan. Although you might not realize it, many of the everyday products you consume are produced in states outside of where you live. Why is that the case?

Think of it this way: Alaska would have a difficult time producing pineapples just as Hawaii would provide a relatively poor environment for growing corn. If trade were not allowed to occur between states—say, by law or because transportation costs were too high (think of life for your great-great grandparents)—some people might lack even the most basic modern necessities. Cotton clothing would be an unknown in the northern states, while technologies that make our life easier, like iPads, would be everywhere in California but might not yet have arrived in the eastern part of the country. Many states would have no access to salmon, while states like New York and Nebraska would be without grapefruit juice. Citizens of Wyoming might still be riding horseback, and people living in many northern states might suffer vitamin C deficiencies.

CHOICE & CONSEQUENCE

Should LeBron James Paint His Own House?

Having won four National Basketball Association MVPs and two championships in the past 5 years, LeBron James is known as the best basketball player on the planet. But his talents extend well beyond dunking a basketball. In fact, with a wingspan of over 7 feet, LeBron is proficient at many tasks.

Think about interior painting. Coupling his wingspan with his 6-foot-8-inch height, LeBron can paint entire interior walls of homes without ever using a ladder! In this way, LeBron is much more efficient than many professional painters—he has an absolute advantage in not only basketball but also painting.

With such talents, does it make sense for him to paint the interior walls of his own house when he wants a color change?

As you've learned, it does not. Everyone (including LeBron) will be better off if LeBron sticks to the task for which he has a comparative advantage—playing basketball—everyone except the opposition, that is.

An **export** is any good that is produced domestically but sold abroad.

An **import** is any good that is produced abroad but sold domestically.

Of course, states do not exist in isolation; just as for you and Olivia, differences in comparative advantage permit trading partners to gain from trade. Producers in every state in the United States ship goods to other states, and every state has citizens who consume goods made in other states. A good that is made in California and shipped to Wisconsin is called an **export** for California and an **import** for Wisconsin. Below we discuss trade between countries. In this case, an export is any good that is produced domestically but sold abroad. An import is any good that is produced abroad but sold domestically. Exports and imports are a useful way to measure trading activity.

Exhibit 8.6 reveals just how important interstate trade is today. The Bureau of Transportation Statistics (BTS) keeps track of all interstate commodity shipments by state of origin and state of destination. In addition, the BTS tracks commodity shipments from U.S. states to other countries. Exhibit 8.6 captures all this information in a way that provides an indication of how vibrant trade is between U.S. states. In the exhibit, for each state, the total value of interstate trade (state to state) is divided by the total value of international trade. This exhibit tells us just how large a role interstate trade plays in the grand scheme of U.S. global trade.

We find that this ratio is the highest in Tennessee, which means that of all the states, Tennessee trades the most with other states compared to its trade with other countries. This is partly because Tennessee sends a lot of agricultural, chemical, and transport products to other states. States such as Arkansas, Oklahoma, Rhode Island, and Wyoming also engage in substantial interstate trade compared to trading with other countries. Overall, the average ratio of interstate to international trade is 7.86 across the United States, meaning that trade between states is almost 8 times more valuable than international trade!

An interesting pattern in Exhibit 8.6 is states with lower ratios of interstate-to-international trade are typically coastal/border states, while states with high ratios of interstate-to-international trade are typically in the interior of the United States. This tendency highlights the importance of transportation costs in determining trade patterns.

Economy-Wide PPC

Trade between you and Olivia revolved around comparative advantage and was shown in your joint *PPC*. Imagine adding together the production possibilities of hundreds of thousands or millions of people—you quickly get a smoothly curved line pointing away from the origin, as in Exhibit 8.7. The exhibit shows a production possibilities curve for apples on the *y*-axis and oranges on the *x*-axis. Point A corresponds to production that is attainable but inefficient. Point B is attainable and efficient. Point C is unattainable with current resources and technology.

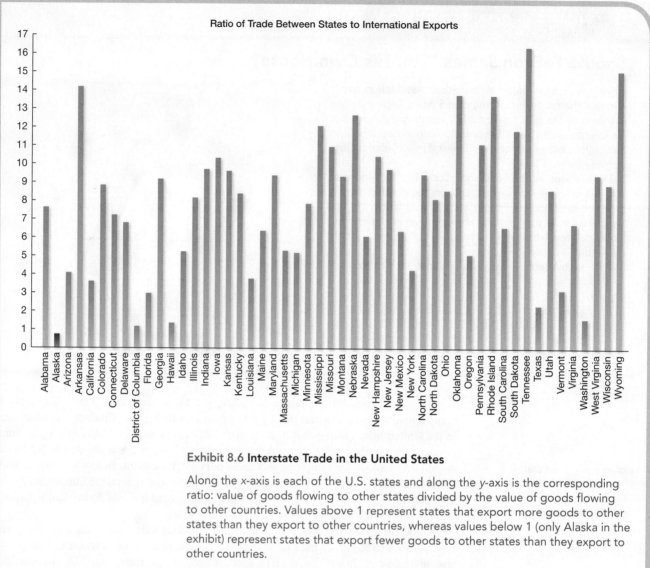

Ratio of Trade Between States to International Exports

Exhibit 8.6 Interstate Trade in the United States

Along the *x*-axis is each of the U.S. states and along the *y*-axis is the corresponding ratio: value of goods flowing to other states divided by the value of goods flowing to other countries. Values above 1 represent states that export more goods to other states than they export to other countries, whereas values below 1 (only Alaska in the exhibit) represent states that export fewer goods to other states than they export to other countries.

Sources: Bureau of Trade Statistics Commodity Flow Survey 2007, U.S. Census Bureau.

Exhibit 8.7 A Production Possibilities Curve

When we encountered *PPCs* before, the opportunity cost of one good in terms of the other was constant—the slope of the *PPC*. However, with a curved *PPC*, we see that whereas going from producing 0 oranges to 1 orange reduces apple production by a small fraction, moving from 6 oranges to 7 oranges reduces apple production by more than 2, demonstrating an increase in opportunity costs.

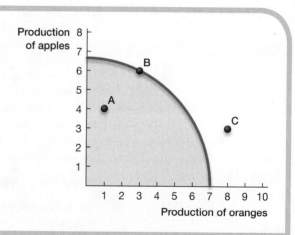

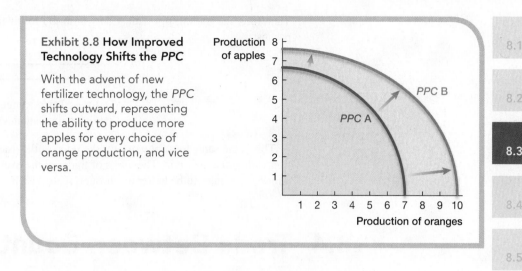

Exhibit 8.8 How Improved Technology Shifts the PPC

With the advent of new fertilizer technology, the *PPC* shifts outward, representing the ability to produce more apples for every choice of orange production, and vice versa.

The curvature represents the general principle of increasing opportunity cost mentioned in Chapter 1. We see increasing opportunity costs in the economy-wide *PPC* because moving to production extremes is difficult, as some inputs are quite well suited for producing apples, whereas other inputs are better suited for producing oranges. Thus, as you move resources increasingly into production of one good, the opportunity cost of doing so increases at an increasing rate.

What determines the location of a state's *PPC*? In the short run, the *PPC* is fixed. But in the long run, resources are not fixed, so increases in natural resources or changes in productivity due to population growth, changes in technology, and increases in worker education shift the *PPC* outward. Among U.S. states, the factors that contribute most to the location of the *PPC* are the natural resources and the stock of man-made resources (technology) available to the state, as well as the education, work habits, and experience of the labor force, the relative abundance of labor and physical capital, and the climate.

Exhibit 8.8 shows an example of how one of these productivity catalysts—improved technology—makes us better off and shifts the *PPC* outward. Suppose that a new fertilizer is invented that increases maximum orange production by 3 units and maximum apple production by 1 unit. These increases will cause the *PPC* shown in Exhibit 8.8 to shift from *PPC* A to *PPC* B, where we can produce more apples and more oranges with our current set of resources.

Comparative Advantage and Specialization Among States

In our earlier example, we learned that the ability to trade allowed you and Olivia to specialize in production of the goods that you were best at producing. As a result, both of you were better off. Exactly the same forces that operate on the individual level to form the basis for trade also operate on the state level.

Consider another example. Suppose that the states of California and Florida are both producers and consumers of apricots and of bananas but that California has a comparative advantage in producing apricots and Florida has a comparative advantage in producing bananas. What do you think should happen?

Similar to you and Olivia, California should focus its production on apricots, whereas Florida should focus on producing bananas. Such comparative advantage represents a basis for trade. In addition, the trading price would be determined by the opportunity costs. For instance, assume that the opportunity costs are as follows:

	Apricots Opportunity Cost	**Bananas Opportunity Cost**
California	⅕ bananas	5 apricots
Florida	8 bananas	⅛ apricots

Therefore, the trading price must be within the following range to be acceptable to both parties:

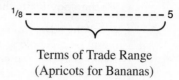

Terms of Trade Range
(Apricots for Bananas)

This is the same logic at work for the price of the trade that we saw in the previous section with you and Olivia. The terms of trade, or the exchange rate of apricots for bananas, allows both states to be better off through specialization and trade.

8.4 Trade Between Countries

We suspect that if you sneak into your grandparents' closet and check the tag on your grandma's 1970 dress, it will say that the dress was manufactured in the United States. Do the same for your grandpa's 1963 suit that he wore for his wedding—perhaps it was made in Chicago or Philadelphia? Conduct the same investigation in your parents' closets and you will find a mix of goods that were much more likely produced abroad. Now take a peek at the tags on your own clothes—they were likely manufactured in another country that might not even have been manufacturing clothes in the 1960s and 1970s.

Such differences in sources for apparel are due to international trade. As Exhibit 8.9 shows, since 1960 the volume of U.S. trade has grown dramatically. In 2010 alone, the value of imported goods into the United States was more than $2,300,000,000,000. That is a whopping 2.3 *trillion* dollars of imported goods annually! This number is over 14 times greater than imports in 1960. Moreover, these increases in trade are not purely due to an increased level of production over time: in 1980, imports were only 5.2 percent of overall U.S. production, whereas now imports are more than 16 percent of overall U.S. production. The world is most definitely becoming more interdependent.

Our exports have also grown dramatically: they are now more than 12 times greater than our level of exports in 1960. Yet, they lag our current level of imports, making the U.S. a **net importer**—that is, a country for which imports are worth more than exports over a given time period. In fact, as Exhibit 8.9 shows, the United States has been a net importer since the mid-1970s. In later chapters, we return to this pattern of trade and discuss whether U.S. citizens should be concerned about the high levels of net importation in recent years.

A **net importer** means that imports are worth more than exports over a given time period.

Exhibit 8.9 U.S. Exports and Imports Since 1960

Here, we plot the total value of U.S. exports and imports from 1960 to 2013 in real dollars. While nearly identical in the earlier years, the gap between U.S. imports and exports becomes apparent in the mid-1970s and continues to expand as imports grow faster than exports.

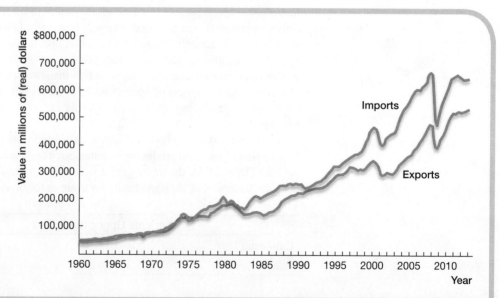

Exhibit 8.10 U.S. Imports and Exports of Crude Oil Since 1960

Contrast the relative difference between the (real) dollar values of total U.S. imports and exports (Exhibit 8.9) and the relative difference in imports and exports of crude oil. This is just one example of the diversity in trade behavior that is missed if we consider only aggregate data.

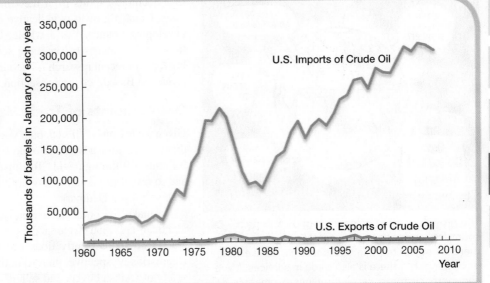

This aggregate trading pattern, however, does not hold true for all types of goods. For example, the United States has historically exported very little crude oil, but it has imported millions of barrels of crude oil monthly. In fact, the level of imports has substantially increased since 1960, as shown in Exhibit 8.10.

So what types of goods are causing this major shift in the balance of imports and exports for the United States that we observe in Exhibit 8.9? As Exhibit 8.11 shows, manufactured goods have played an important role. The exhibit shows that although the United States has continued to increase the number of manufactured goods that it produces, it has been importing more and more from developing nations.

Until recently, most manufactured goods on the world market were produced in advanced economies—the United States, Germany, and the United Kingdom. Recently, however, China has surpassed the United States in manufactured exports, as shown in panel (b) of Exhibit 8.11. The value of manufactured exports of China now far exceeds the value of

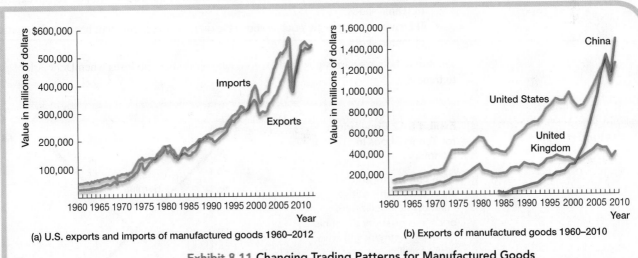

(a) U.S. exports and imports of manufactured goods 1960–2012

(b) Exports of manufactured goods 1960–2010

Exhibit 8.11 Changing Trading Patterns for Manufactured Goods

This exhibit presents a deeper dive into the aggregate U.S. export and import data depicted in Exhibit 8.9 by excluding the contribution of services (consulting, medical care, etc.). Taken together, the panels suggest that a large part of the changing global trading patterns coincides with developing countries, such as China, exporting much more.

Note: Disaggregated tracking of China's manufacturing exports only begins in 1984 as part of a general policy of internal economic liberalization and reform.

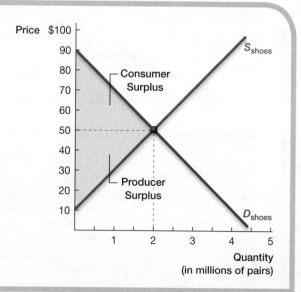

IS THIS TECH SUPPORT?

YES SIR. GOOD MORNING...

WHAT SEEMS TO BE...

THE PROBLEM?

Our Outsourced World

The growth in outsourcing (relying on foreign countries for goods and services) has proven that there is not just trade in traditional goods like cars or clothing, but there is also trade in services. More and more, customer service hotlines are managed overseas, for example.

Free trade is the ability to trade without hindrance or encouragement from the government.

A **world price** is the prevailing price of a good on the world market.

manufactured exports from the United States and other developed nations. China's growth is indicative of the pattern of trade observed for developing countries as a whole. Understanding the determinants of these trade patterns merits more serious consideration and has been a hot topic of recent research for economists. We return to this trend in the Evidence-Based Economics section.

Determinants of Trade Between Countries

Given the lessons of this chapter, you will likely not be surprised to learn that comparative advantage underlies the trading patterns observed in Exhibits 8.9 through 8.11. To illustrate this key idea more succinctly and to reveal its economic underpinnings, let's consider the market for tennis shoes in Denmark.

To make the point most clearly, we assume that tennis shoes are identical and that Denmark is a price-taker. Further, we assume that Denmark currently does not trade with other countries. From Denmark's perspective, therefore, the market for tennis shoes consists solely of Danish buyers and sellers.

As Exhibit 8.12 shows, under these assumptions, the domestic price is given by the intersection of the Danish demand and the Danish supply curves. In this case, the equilibrium price for a pair of tennis shoes is $50, and the equilibrium quantity of tennis shoes is 2 million pairs. As we learned in Chapter 5, consumer surplus is the triangle below the demand curve and above the market price. Likewise, as Chapter 6 showed, producer surplus is the triangle above the supply curve and below the market price.

If the Danish government decides to open its borders to **free trade**, which is the ability to trade without government hindrance or encouragement, will Denmark be an importer or an exporter of tennis shoes? That is, will it *buy* tennis shoes from other countries or will it *sell* tennis shoes to other countries? The answer is not yet clear because we don't know the price of tennis shoes outside of Denmark. We need a **world price** for tennis shoes, that is, the prevailing price of tennis shoes on the world market.

Then, the answer to whether Denmark will import or export comes down to a simple comparison: is the Danish domestic price for tennis shoes above or below the world price for tennis shoes?

- If Denmark's domestic price is below the world price, then it will become an exporter of tennis shoes.
- If Denmark's domestic price is above the world price, then it will become an importer of tennis shoes.

We turn to both scenarios now and explore who wins and who loses when Denmark begins to trade.

Exhibit 8.12 Equilibrium for Tennis Shoes in Denmark

With our assumption of a perfectly competitive market, the equilibrium price and quantity of tennis shoes in Denmark will arise in the familiar way—at the intersection of the domestic supply and demand curves.

Price

$100
90
80
70
60
50
40
30
20
10

S_{shoes}

Consumer Surplus

Producer Surplus

D_{shoes}

1   2   3   4   5

Quantity
(in millions of pairs)

LETTING THE DATA SPEAK

Fair Trade Products

What's Behind the Boom?

In response to the feeling that the growth of free trade has led to the exploitation of developing countries, a new market has opened up for the consumer concerned with a broad variety of production-related issues, including the environment, fair labor practices, or child labor in the developing world. Goods imported from the developing world—so called "fair trade" products—are certified by third-party organizations as fair trade products.

To receive a fair trade label, the production of a good has to meet certain standards. For example, if the producer doesn't allow unionization, uses child or slave labor, or doesn't adhere to the U.N. Charter on Human Rights, then it can't be classified as fair trade.

Consumers can't seem to get enough of fair trade products. Sales growth for fair trade goods has reached double-digit proportions over the past decade. Surprisingly, sales continued to expand even in spite of the 2008 recession, growing 15 percent in 2009.[1]

In spite of the recent surge in demand for fair trade products, not everyone is a fan. Overseeing billions of dollars of production isn't easy, and the capacity for certifying organizations to enforce labor standards sometimes can't keep up with the increasing demand for fair trade products.[2]

Exporting Nations: Winners and Losers

Let's delve a little more deeply into the scenario in which Denmark's domestic price for tennis shoes is below the world price, and it becomes an exporter. We'll assume that the world price for a pair of tennis shoes is $75—well above the equilibrium domestic price of $50. Will Danish suppliers continue to supply Danes with tennis shoes for $50? The answer is no, because they can sell as many pairs of tennis shoes on the world market for a price of $75 and make more money.

As Exhibit 8.13 shows, in this case Danish suppliers will increase their production from 2 million pairs of tennis shoes to 3.25 million pairs and receive the world price of $75 per pair. At that price, Danish consumers no longer demand as many pairs of tennis shoes: the price has gone up, so they decrease their quantity demanded by moving along their demand curve until the price of $75 is reached. This movement stops when the quantity demanded reaches 0.75 million pairs, at a price of $75.

This situation leads to an excess supply of production in Denmark. This excess supply of 2.5 million pairs of tennis shoes (3.25 − 0.75 = 2.50) is subsequently sold on the world market. Because Denmark is a small producer of tennis shoes, this added supply does not change the world price.

So who wins and who loses when Denmark opens its borders to trade and becomes an exporter? A comparison of producer and consumer surplus measures provides the answer. A first consideration is that Danish sellers are clearly better off. They are now selling more tennis shoes, and the price is higher for each pair. The sellers' gain can be computed from the change in producer surplus. In Exhibit 8.13, we see that before trade was allowed, Danish producer surplus was equal to area A. This is the area above the supply curve and below the market price. After permitting trade, the new producer surplus is equal to areas A + B + C. Thus, Danish sellers experience an increased producer surplus of B + C because of trade.

For Danish consumers, though, the story is much different. Without trade, they purchased 2 million pairs of shoes per year at $50 per pair, receiving a consumer surplus of areas B + D in Exhibit 8.13. After opening to trade, they purchase only

Will his shoes be sold domestically or abroad?

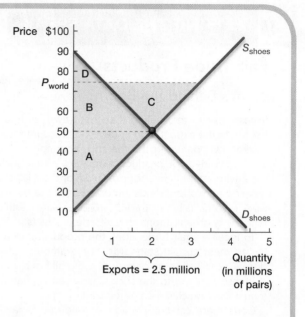

Exhibit 8.13 Winners and Losers in an Exporting Nation

Once Denmark is open to free trade, its suppliers take a market price that is higher than the domestic equilibrium price of $50, increasing their quantity supplied to 3.25 million shoes. However, at this higher price, domestic quantity demanded is reduced, and the surplus shoes are sold to the world market. In this case, producers win by being able to charge a price above $50 per pair, thus capturing areas B and C in addition to A (which they already had prior to free trade). On the other hand, Danish consumers see a reduction in surplus due to the higher price they must pay for tennis shoes, losing area B to producers.

0.75 million pairs of shoes and pay $75 per pair. Now consumer surplus is only area D. Thus, Danish buyers experience a decreased consumer surplus equal to area B because the country opened to trade.

We can therefore draw two conclusions about what happens when a country opens itself to trade and becomes an exporter of goods and services:

1. Sellers win.
2. Buyers lose.

However, we also need to look at the big picture—there are gains to trade for Denmark as a whole. In Exhibit 8.13, area C represents what Danes as a whole gained from opening to trade. In principle, this area highlights that Denmark is better off because of trade and that the winners' gains are greater than the losses of the losers, opening up the possibility that the winners can compensate the losers. If the Danes were so inclined, one way for this to happen is to tax shoe producers and transfer the revenues to shoe consumers (though the situation of winners fully compensating losers rarely happens, as we discuss below).

Importing Nations: Winners and Losers

Now let's consider the flip side. If Denmark's domestic price is above the world price, then it will be an importer of tennis shoes. Let's assume that the world price for a pair of tennis shoes is now $25, well below the equilibrium domestic price of $50. We depict this scenario in Exhibit 8.14, which shows that in this case Danish suppliers will curb their production to 0.75 million pairs of shoes by changing quantity supplied, or sliding down the market supply curve until $25 is reached. At that price, Danish consumers demand 3.25 million pairs of shoes: the price has gone down, so they move along their demand curve until the price of $25 is reached (shown on the rightmost dotted line). This movement stops when the quantity demanded reaches 3.25 million pairs at a price of $25.

These movements lead to excess demand in Denmark. This excess demand of 2.5 million pairs of tennis shoes ($3.25 - 0.75 = 2.50$) is subsequently purchased on the world market, making Denmark an importer of tennis shoes. Because Denmark is a small buyer of tennis shoes, this added demand does not change the world price.

So who wins and who loses when Denmark opens its borders to trade and becomes an importer? Again, a comparison of producer and consumer surplus measures allows us to answer this question. For sellers, producer surplus is lowered because they are now selling fewer pairs of tennis shoes and the price of each pair sold is lower. Their loss can be seen

Exhibit 8.14 Winners and Losers in an Importing Nation

Once Denmark is open to trade, its buyers will only pay the world price, which is lower than the domestic equilibrium price without trade of $50. This decreases quantity supplied to 0.75 million shoes. However, at this lower price, domestic quantity demanded is increased and the excess demand is covered by shoes from the world market. In this case, consumers are better off because they pay a price below $50 per pair, thus capturing areas C and D in addition to B (which they already had prior to trade). On the other hand, producers in Denmark see a reduction in surplus due to the lower price, losing area C to consumers.

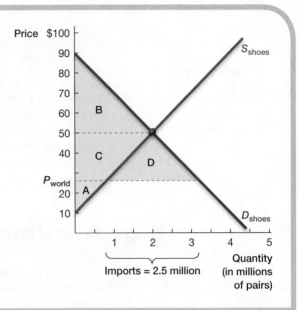

from the decreased level of producer surplus in Exhibit 8.14: before trade, producer surplus was areas A + C; after trade, it is only area A. Thus, Danish sellers experience a decreased producer surplus of area C.

For consumers, the story is the opposite. They are now purchasing more shoes at a lower price, so they must be better off. Exhibit 8.14 shows by how much: before trade, consumer surplus was area B; after trade, it is areas B + C + D. Thus, Danish buyers experience an increased consumer surplus equal to areas C and D because the country opened to trade.

We can therefore draw two conclusions about what happens when a country opens itself to trade and becomes an importer of goods and services:

1. Sellers lose.
2. Buyers win.

And once again, the overall gains to trade for Denmark are positive, represented by area D in Exhibit 8.14. This area highlights the fact that even when countries are net importers, they are net gainers. As a whole, Denmark is much better off, allowing the winners to potentially compensate the losers. Taxing consumers and sending the revenues to shoe producers is one way in which such compensation can take place. (We discuss further the pros and cons of such taxation in Chapter 10.)

Where Do World Prices Come From?

In the cases above when we illustrate the impact that free trade has on Denmark's tennis shoe market, we fix the world price for tennis shoes to make a point about the winners and losers of free trade. But where do world prices for tennis shoes, or any good for that matter, come from? It turns out that our supply and demand framework does a good job of telling us. As countries open up their borders and act upon their comparative advantages, the sum of all these actions lets us talk about a world supply and a world demand for a product. The intersection of these two (world supply curve and world demand curve) determines the world price.

Determinants of a Country's Comparative Advantage

You may now be wondering what determines a country's comparative advantage and whether it can predict trade flows before opening itself to trade. As in our analysis of state-level trading in the United States, the factors that contribute most to comparative advantage at the country level are:

1. Natural resources (to a large degree, beyond the countries' control, unless squandered)
2. Stocks of man-made resources (more controllable; depend on *PPC*)

3. Technology
4. Education, work habits, and experience of the labor force
5. Relative abundance of labor and physical capital
6. Climate

Because of the wide array of these determinants and their changing nature, it is clear that comparative advantage can change over time—just as when you took the computer programming course! A country-level example is Japan's investment in human capital, which helped to nurture skills and technology to generate a winning formula for becoming a leading car manufacturing nation. Likewise, technological advances that permit a more cost-effective means to exploit a country's stock of natural resources can change the nature of comparative advantage.

8.5 Arguments Against Free Trade

We've seen the significant gains associated with free trade between countries, so why would any country ever want to hinder trade? Why were the protestors cited in the opening to this chapter so passionate in their opposition to free trade? Several arguments are typically set forth:

1. National security concerns
2. Fear of the effects of globalization on a nation's culture
3. Environmental and resource concerns
4. Infant industry arguments
5. Potential negative effects on local wages and jobs

We briefly discuss the first four arguments in turn, reserving the fifth argument concerning wages and jobs for our last section on Evidence-Based Economics.

We drive Japanese cars, drink French wine, eat Mexican food, use American computers, buy Canadian lumber and take vacations in Italy. How can you OPPOSE free trade?

National Security Concerns

As we learned in Chapter 7, allowing resources to flow freely has the effect of allocating resources within and across industries efficiently. But that may mean the creation of "banana republics"—nations that specialize in the production of one good. Though this might be efficient economically, it may not be optimal in a defense-oriented world, where national security is an important consideration. A country will not produce just oranges if it fears military attack from other nations. Rather, it will invest in steel production and defense technology and will maintain a variety of agricultural industries to preserve its integrity in times of war. Likewise, even in times of peace, a country might be hesitant to completely specialize because it might find itself too reliant on other countries. For example, because many modern economies depend on oil imports, many cite such reliance as a national security concern.

Fear of Globalization

Globalization is the shift toward more open, integrated economies that participate in foreign trade and investment.

Protectionism often is justified simply as a counter to globalization. **Globalization** is the shift toward more open, integrated economies that participate in foreign trade and investment. Some nations, however, want to maintain their culture's uniqueness and therefore view globalization as a serious concern. That is to say, as the world becomes increasingly interdependent, it also becomes increasingly similar—decades ago China had no McDonald's; now in large cities there is one on every corner. In addition, Starbucks now serves coffee in more than sixty countries—some people fear the loss of their cultural identity through such globalization. Such preferences are an important consideration for leaders around the world.

Environmental and Resource Concerns

Tangible goods such as clothing and food are not the only things traded by countries; abstract goods such as environmental quality may be traded as well. Countries with lax environmental policies allow for relatively more pollution from firms than countries with strong environmental policies. Opponents of free trade often cite these policy differences as creating "pollution havens" in poor countries. These countries, in an effort to promote economic growth and jobs, use lax pollution regulations to attract industry. A similar argument exists for natural resources, such as ivory. The argument is that free trade endangers the stock of animals that provide ivory (for example, elephant, walrus, narwhal) because openness to trade leads to higher demand for ivory, threatening species extinction. In the next chapter, we discuss more broadly how governments protect such resources.

Infant Industry Arguments

Opponents of free trade also cite the "infant industries" argument, in which governments protect their fledgling domestic industries against more advanced competitors. For example, to help Toyota grow, the Japanese government forced General Motors and Ford out of the country in 1939. Generally, infant industry arguments rely on the idea that in industries with economies of scale, or substantial learning by doing, it is important for policymakers to protect local firms early in their development. In addition, starting a company in isolation may deprive it of "technological spillovers" that its competitors, all located near one another, may enjoy—the isolated company will be the last to learn of trade secrets.

Ultimately, the basis of any infant industry argument is that a company is currently too weak to withstand competition from other firms. To survive, the company requires government protection. **Protectionism** is the idea that free trade can be harmful, and government intervention is necessary to control trade.

Protectionism takes many forms, and has been used as a means to block the growing interdependence in the world. We now turn to one such example—*tariffs*.

The Effects of Tariffs

As we discussed in the chapter opener, many individuals worry about their own jobs when trade increases between countries. Historically, one of the most popular forms of government protectionism is to impose **tariffs**, which are taxes levied on goods and services transported across political boundaries. Protectionism via an imposed tariff is not free, however. Indeed, by their very nature, tariffs interfere with equilibrium prices and quantities, artificially reducing social surplus in a country.

To show how, let's reconsider the example of Denmark as an importing nation of tennis shoes. Assume that for infant industry reasons, the Danish government decides to invoke a $15 tariff on every pair of imported tennis shoes to protect Danish suppliers. That is, the government collects $15 from the foreign producer for every pair of tennis shoes that crosses Danish borders. Exhibit 8.15 shows the effect of such a tariff.

Notice that before the tariff is imposed, consumer surplus is given by the sum of the colored regions labeled B, F, E, and G, H, I, and J. This is the area under the demand curve but above the world price line. The pink triangle labeled area A is domestic producer surplus. This is the area above the supply curve but below the world price line.

After Denmark imposes a $15 tariff on shoes, the local market price rises from $25 to $40. The imposition of the tariff reduces consumer surplus to the area above the new price line and below the domestic demand curve—areas B, F, and H. Therefore, the loss in consumer surplus from the tariff is areas E, G, I, and J. Where does this lost surplus go?

Area E goes to producers, so their new surplus is areas A + E. They are better off because they can now sell shoes to the local market at $40 rather than $25. The government is also better off since area I goes to the government. The government receives the number of import goods times the tariff price in revenue. This revenue equals $15 × 1 million = $15 million, or the area of rectangle I.

What about areas G and J? This is the deadweight loss of the tariff. As we discussed in Chapter 7, market distortions often lead to deadweight loss. In this case, the Danish

Does free trade lead to more e-waste going from the United States to developing countries, such as India?

Protectionism is the idea that free trade can be harmful, and government intervention is necessary to control trade.

Tariffs are taxes levied on goods and services transported across political boundaries.

> By their very nature, tariffs interfere with equilibrium prices and quantities, artificially reducing social surplus in a country.

Exhibit 8.15 The Effect of a Tariff

Here we revisit the example of Denmark as an importing country, but now the government of Denmark enacts a tariff. By raising the price using the tariff, the government earns revenues from the tariff (area I), and producer surplus rises by area E. But consumers are worse off (they lose areas E, G, I, and J), and there is a deadweight loss of areas G and J because of the tariff.

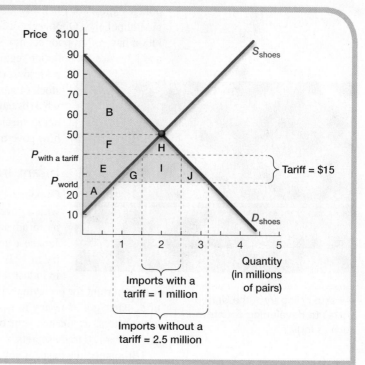

economy loses the two triangles labeled G and J. This is the cost that the Danes pay to protect the tennis shoe industry by imposing a tariff.

From this analysis, we can see one reason why economists in general do not favor such protectionism—it raises prices for consumers and lowers social surplus. This might be one reason why some countries have been moving away from using tariffs. Exhibit 8.16 shows the dutiable imports ratio from 1891 to 2008. This is a measure of the ratio of tariff revenues (duties) collected to the value of dutiable imports. The orange line marks a series of tariff increases, called the Smoot-Hawley tariffs, in the United States during the Great Depression. After the imposition of these peak tariffs, the United States quickly learned about one repercussion of limiting free trade—other countries will respond in kind! Other nations began charging American companies new duties. America consequently reduced its tariffs, likely saving millions of dollars through increased consumer and producer surplus.

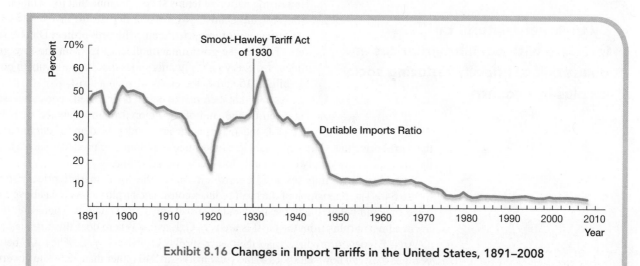

Exhibit 8.16 Changes in Import Tariffs in the United States, 1891–2008

The x-axis is time and the y-axis is the dutiable imports ratio. This is the ratio of tariff revenues (duties) collected to the value of dutiable imports. It is usually reported as a percentage. We see that the 1920s and 1930s saw a dramatic increase in this ratio. Over time, however, the ratio has been steadily decreasing.

Evidence-Based Economics

Q: Will free trade cause you to lose your job?

The **North American Free Trade Agreement (NAFTA)** is an agreement signed by Canada, Mexico, and the United States to create a trilateral trade bloc and reduce trade barriers among the three countries.

Is there a link between opening to trade and a loss in jobs and wages in the importing country? We have learned in this chapter that opening a country to trade may make some individuals worse off: fewer shoes are made in Denmark when the country becomes an importer. Perhaps this depresses wages in Denmark or puts cobblers out of work.

You might be thinking: "Wait a minute! We just learned that whether a country becomes an importer or an exporter doesn't matter; the winners can more than compensate the losers, at least in theory. So, why does it matter if wages fall and jobs are lost? Can't we all still be better off?"

This is a keen insight, and theoretically correct. But in practice, complete compensation of losers from opening an economy to international trade is difficult. First, as we discuss in Chapter 10, the government might not be able to effectively carry out such policies. Second, it is often difficult to pinpoint exactly who the winners are and how much they each gained, and who the losers are and how much they each lost. It is often the case that the losers are spread throughout the economy and sometimes touched in very small ways. Thus, we can conclude that opening an economy up to trade clearly expands the pie, but some people might end up with a smaller piece than they used to have.

In trying to answer the question of whether opening an economy to trade adversely affects jobs and wages, it is instructive to consider the experience of the United States when it began to trade with countries that held a comparative advantage in certain industries. Over the last half-century, new countries that produce textiles and other manufactured goods have emerged (Exhibit 8.11 shows the emergence of China).

We've also seen in this chapter that when a country is a net importer—as is the United States for manufactured goods—domestic consumers gain and domestic producers lose. For example, New England was a key producer of textiles and manufactured goods during the first half of the twentieth century, but with the importation of manufactured goods from abroad, thousands of textile workers lost their jobs. So jobs are lost because of the effects of international trade. Nevertheless, with the expansion of other sectors, such as the high-tech and Internet-based industries, the unemployment rate in New England states has been among the lowest in the United States. This example highlights the fact that people whose skills become obsolete because of the effects of international trade can invest time and resources in more education and training. Upon doing so, they have a good chance to find work. Consistent with this evidence, the data also suggest that many workers displaced because of NAFTA's passage soon found gainful employment.

Even though the U.S. experience suggests that workers have an opportunity to land on their feet, another key empirical question related to lost jobs remains: how important has opening to trade been in affecting wages? Economists have spent a fair amount of time and effort in addressing this question. The typical approach is to draw upon large data sets, which span several years and include information on hundreds of thousands of workers' wages across several different sectors of the economy. These data sets are then examined to determine if wages of workers in exporting- and importing-competing sectors change as an economy opens to trade.

The first wave of economic studies published in the 1990s reports very small, or inconsequential, effects of trade on wages of workers in those parts of the labor force that produce goods competing with those coming in from abroad.[3] These studies suggest that there is no strong evidence from the data to back the major claim of trade critics.

Yet before concluding that wages are not negatively influenced when a country opens to trade and becomes a net importer, Exhibit 8.11 of this chapter points to an important phenomenon that has occurred in recent years. Led by China, which has a comparative advantage in labor with its large workforce, manufacturing imports from developing countries have risen dramatically since 1990. Overall, imports from developing countries have grown from roughly 2.5 percent of U.S. GDP in 1990 to 6 percent of U.S. GDP in 2006. This trend is important because developing countries have a large pool of workers who are paid considerably lower wages than the manufacturing workers of our historical trading partners.

This could mean that in more recent years trade has had a much more important effect on wages in the states than we observed in the past. Scholars are just beginning to address this issue, using more recent data. The evidence gathered thus far does not point to anything conclusive. For example, economist Robert Lawrence reports that using more recent data does not change the overall picture of the studies published in the 1990s—there remains little empirical evidence that trade negatively influences wages.[4] Meanwhile, economist Paul Krugman, the 2008 Nobel Laureate, has argued that the data are far too murky to yield reliable empirical results.[5] In the end, we believe that at this point there is little evidence suggesting that opening to trade leads to lost jobs and lower wages. But, empirical work should continue. Do you have any ideas about how to proceed?

Question	**Answer**	**Data**	**Caveat**
Will free trade cause you to lose your job?	Some workers might lose their jobs, but there is no systemic evidence that shows opening up to trade hurts workers broadly.	Import and export data combined with local wage and job data.	U.S. trading partners have changed over recent years to include countries with a comparative advantage in labor, opening up the possibility that trade with our new partners is actually hurting workers more than previous data suggest.

Summary

✹ People and countries are dependent on each other for goods and services. Although there are potential costs to this interdependency, the gains associated with taking advantage of specialization in the production of goods and services can be considerable.

✹ Specialization and trade, which are driven by comparative advantage, not only allow us to consume beyond our individual PPC but also lead to a wider variety of goods and services.

✹ Whereas comparative advantage revolves around measuring production relative to the opportunity costs that you and the other person incur, absolute advantage relates to production per unit of inputs.

✹ When a country opens up to trade, there are winners and losers. The gains from trade are larger than the losses. One key to avoiding protests about free trade, like the one we saw in Seattle in 1999, is to develop policies so that everyone can reap the gains from trade.

✹ Empirically, it is difficult to find the vast job losses for U.S. workers that such critics cite. There is certainly a displacement of workers due to trade, but many workers soon find other jobs. Likewise, the supposed negative effect of trade on wages is difficult to find in the data. Beyond lost jobs, however, those against free trade often cite national security concerns, loss of cultural identity, environmental and resource concerns, and infant industry arguments.

Key Terms

production possibilities curve (PPC) *p. 172*
comparative advantage *p. 174*
absolute advantage *p. 176*
terms of trade *p. 177*

export *p. 179*
import *p. 179*
net importer *p. 182*
free trade *p. 184*
world price *p. 184*

globalization *p. 188*
protectionism *p. 189*
tariffs *p. 189*
North American Free Trade Agreement (NAFTA) *p. 191*

Questions

All questions are available in MyEconLab for practice and instructor assignment.

1. Consider the figure below. The blue line shows how many units of goods A and B a worker in Taiwan can produce, and the tan line shows the number of units of goods A and B that a worker in Korea can produce. Does this figure indicate anything about either worker having a comparative or absolute advantage in either good?

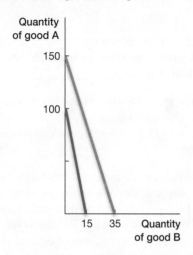

2. Is it true that a country needs to have an absolute advantage in the production of a good in order to benefit from trade in that good? Explain.

3. What is meant by terms of trade? How is it determined?

4. What does a production possibilities curve (*PPC*) show? What is the difference between a *PPC* that is linear and a *PPC* that is curved away from the origin?

5. Explain the impact, if any, of each of the following on the production possibilities curve.

   a. Europe's population fell by 30 to 60 percent following an outbreak of bubonic plague, also known as the Black Death, in the fourteenth century.

   b. In the next 20 years, a sizeable proportion of the U.S. labor force is expected to include many people who are above the age of 65.

   c. Canada recently discovered large reserves of shale gas (shale gas is natural gas that is trapped in fine-grained sedimentary rock).

6. How has the pattern of trade changed in the United States since 1960? What are the types of goods that are causing the shift in the balance of imports and exports in the United States?

7. Many service-sector jobs in the United States have moved to other countries where these jobs are done at a fraction of the cost. The outsourcing of jobs overseas is heavily debated by politicians, policymakers, and economists in the United States. Based on your understanding of trade and the benefits and losses from trade, how do you think outsourcing affects social surplus in the domestic economy?

8. What are the sources of a country's comparative advantage?

9. What are some of the common arguments against free trade?

10. What is the problem with the argument that infant industries need to be protected from foreign competition?

11. If opening an economy up to trade always benefits both trading partners, why is free trade controversial?

12. The mercantilist economic doctrine was widely followed from the sixteenth to the eighteenth centuries in Europe. Mercantilists advocated the use of tariffs to restrict trade, as they believed that countries that export more than they import will increase wealth. What could be the problem with such an economic policy?

13. Since the "winners" from free trade can more than compensate the "losers" why does it matter if wages and employment fall when a country engages in free trade?

Problems

All problems are available in MyEconLab for practice and instructor assignment.

1. Pam and Max run a food truck that serves cupcakes. Before they open, they have 1 hour to make chocolate and vanilla cupcakes. The following table shows how many chocolate and vanilla cupcakes they can each make in 1 hour.

	Pam	Max
Chocolate Cupcakes	16	18
Vanilla Cupcakes	15	25

   a. Does either Pam or Max have an absolute advantage in making either type of cupcake?

   b. Based on comparative advantage, who should make chocolate cupcakes and who should make vanilla cupcakes?

2. A country has two types of workers, skilled and unskilled. Workers can produce either computers or steel. Output per worker is as follows.

	Output per Worker	
	Computers	**Steel**
Unskilled Workers	3	2
Skilled Workers	5	3

Do skilled workers have an absolute advantage in the production of computers? Do unskilled workers have a comparative advantage in the production of steel? Explain your answers carefully.

3. Suppose a country has 100 westerners and 100 easterners. A westerner can produce either 6 units of food or 2 units of national defense; an easterner can produce either 2 units of food or 1 unit of national defense.

   a. Show that easterners have a comparative advantage in the production of defense.

   b. Suppose this country has decided it wants to produce 60 units of defense. Would the country have more food to consume if the westerners produced these 60 units of defense or if the easterners produced this defense?

   c. Why should you have anticipated your answer to part (b) of this question?

   d. Now suppose this country institutes a draft and chooses people for the military randomly. Suppose further that it drafts 20 westerners and 20 easterners (who together will produce 60 units of defense). How much food will the country produce if it chooses to have a military draft?

   e. Compare the cost in terms of foregone food production under a draft to the cost under a volunteer army where the country pays the easterners enough to persuade them to become soldiers.

4. There are 10 workers in Thailand and each can produce either 2 computers or 30 tons of rice. There are 20 workers in the United States and each can produce either 5 computers or 40 tons of rice.

   a. Draw the production possibilities frontier for each country. In each case, identify the intercepts and the slopes of the production possibilities frontier.

   b. What is the opportunity cost of computers in Thailand? What is the opportunity cost of computers in the United States?

   c. Which country has a comparative advantage in the production of computers?

   d. In the absence of trade, if Thailand consumes 150 tons of rice, how many computers can it consume? In the absence of trade, if the United States consumes 50 computers, how many tons of rice can it consume?

   e. Someone now proposes that the United States and Thailand enter into a trade agreement. Under this agreement, the United States will give Thailand 10 computers and Thailand will give the United States 120 tons of rice. If Thailand continues to consume 150 tons of rice, how many computers will it be able to consume under this proposal? If the United States continues to consume 50 computers, how many tons of rice will it be able to consume under this proposal?

   f. Should Thailand accept this proposal? Should the United States accept this proposal?

5. Amanda and Raj are both students working part-time at an insurance company. Amanda can work only 5 hours a day. Her manager informs her that she needs to review 250 documents and process 250 insurance claims in the next 10 days. The following table shows how many documents and claims Amanda can work on in a given number of hours:

Hours Spent on Documents	Documents	Hours Spent on Insurance Claims	Claims
1	10	1	5
2	20	2	10
3	30	3	15
4	40	4	20
5	50	5	25

   a. Create a production possibilities curve for Amanda.

   b. What is the slope of the curve?

   c. What is her opportunity cost of reviewing one document?

6. Refer to Amanda's production possibilities curve in the previous problem. Amanda meets Raj at the water cooler and finds out that Raj also needs to review 250 documents and process 250 insurance claims in the next 10 days. Raj also works 5 hours a day. The following table shows how many documents and claims Raj can work on in a given number of hours.

Hours Spent on Documents	Documents	Hours Spent on Insurance Claims	Claims
1	5	1	10
2	10	2	20
3	15	3	30
4	20	4	40
5	25	5	50

   a. Create a production possibilities curve for Raj.

   b. What is the slope of the curve?

   c. Can both Amanda and Raj benefit from helping each other? If so, what should be their terms of trade?

7. The remote island nations of Nearway and Farway produce fish and coconuts and have recently decided to engage in trade with one another. Use the table to answer the following questions.

	Coconuts		Fish	
	Nearway	Farway	Nearway	Farway
Optimal Production without Trade	200	300	100	200
Specialization: Optimal Production with Trade		600	500	
Traded Goods	250			250
Post-Trade Allocation				
Gains from Trade				

a. Calculate the opportunity costs of producing fish and coconuts in Nearway and Farway, and then determine who has the competitive advantage in the production of each good.

b. Using what you learned in part (a), fill in the blanks in the table.

c. Which nation received the better deal in this trade? Explain using the exchange rate range.

d. Would Nearway and Farway ever trade 60 coconuts for 20 fish? Why or why not?

8. The most widely consumed fruit in the United States is the humble banana. Most of the bananas consumed are imported from Latin America. Ecuador is one of the largest exporters of bananas in the world and is a major supplier of bananas to the United States.

Suppose panel (a) in the following figure shows the market for bananas in the United States and panel (b) shows the market for bananas in Ecuador.

a. Who gains from trade in the United States—sellers or buyers?

b. Who gains from trade in Ecuador—sellers or buyers?

c. As a whole, does the United States or Ecuador benefit from trade?

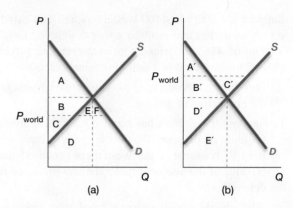

(a)   (b)

9. Suppose your country imports wheat. The price of wheat rises from P_1 to P_2 and your country continues to import wheat. Present and discuss a diagram to answer the following questions: Did imports rise or fall? Did consumer surplus rise or fall? Did producer surplus rise or fall? Did social surplus rise or fall?

10. Suppose your country exports wheat. The price of wheat rises from P_3 to P_4. Present and discuss a diagram to answer the following questions: Did exports rise or fall? Did consumer surplus rise or fall? Did producer surplus rise or fall? Did social surplus rise or fall?

11. Consider the following diagram. The discussion in the text implies that if this country imposes a tariff, social surplus will fall by the sum of area A and area B. Intuitively, why is A part of the deadweight loss from this tariff? Intuitively, why is B part of the deadweight loss from this tariff?

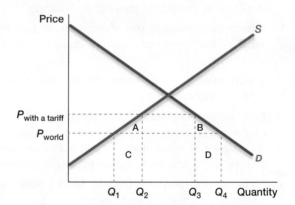

12. Suppose the following figure shows the domestic market for hockey sticks in a certain country. The government has recently imposed tariffs on hockey sticks. While the world price of a hockey stick is $60, the price in this country (with the tariff) is $75.

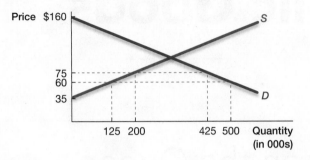

a. How did the quantity of imports change when the government imposed a tariff?

b. How much does the government earn from the tariff?

c. How does the value of consumer surplus change after the tariff is introduced?

d. How does the value of producer surplus change after the tariff is introduced?

e. What is the value of the deadweight loss from the tariff?

f. What is the value of social surplus after the tariff? How will social surplus change if the tariff is eliminated and the price of hockey sticks falls to the world price?

9 Externalities and Public Goods

How can the Queen of England lower her commute time to Wembley Stadium?

Imagine yourself sitting in your economics classroom waiting for the start of class. You are chatting with your neighbors about how free trade might not be so bad after all, and other students are buzzing about the power of the invisible hand as they search for their preferred seats. Your professor strolls in with her usual materials in tow, but something unusual is clutched in her right hand. After setting down her bag, she takes out a match from a matchbox. Confidently, she strikes the match and lights up the cigar in her right hand. One student gasps; another shrieks in delight. Your economics professor is smoking a cigar in class! "Students, welcome to the world of externalities," your professor says boldly.[1]

You might ask yourself, how do externalities fit in with the markets we have studied thus far? In short, they don't. So far in our study of markets, we have focused solely on buyers and sellers, who are the only ones affected by the market transaction. But we know that many times, the actions of one party affect the well-being of countless other parties—like people smoking cigars or factories belching out smoke. In situations like these, the invisible hand may fail to allocate resources efficiently. For instance, many people may suffer from a polluting factory's emissions without ever benefiting from the production that caused the pollution.

CHAPTER OUTLINE

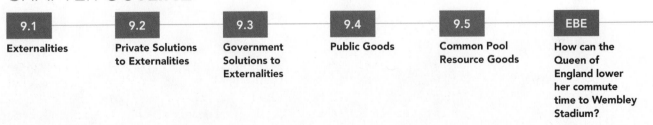

KEY IDEAS

☀ There are important cases in which free markets fail to maximize social surplus.

☀ This chapter discusses three such cases: externalities, public goods, and common pool resources.

☀ One common link between these three examples is that there is a difference between the private benefits and costs and the social benefits and costs.

☀ Government can play a role in improving market outcomes in such cases.

Economists call such examples *externalities*. An *externality* occurs when there is a spillover from one person's actions to a bystander. If left alone, people will generally not account for how their actions affect others—whether positive or negative. For instance, think about automobiles for a minute. They not only contribute to the global warming problem but also create traffic congestion. But have you ever chosen *not* to drive a car because of the extra congestion that your vehicle will cause? Neither have we. And that is the crux of why such externalities are called market failures.

In this chapter, we will see that in the case of externalities, governments can enact policies to push market outcomes toward a greater level of social well-being. For example, one possible policy to alleviate traffic jams is to impose a fee on automobile drivers using particular roads. It's precisely that proposal that we'll examine in our Evidence-Based Economics feature at the end of the chapter, which will help us answer the opening question about lowering the Queen's commute time.

A related example of when the free market fails to arrive at a socially efficient outcome if left alone is in the provision of *public goods* (such as national defense) or in the protection of *common pool resources* (such as an open-access lake). The link between all three of these market failures is that there is a difference between social and private benefits or social and private costs, causing the individual to face different incentives than society faces. Accordingly, much like the case with externalities, we will find that government can play a critical role in providing public goods and protecting common pool resources.

9.1 Externalities

It's morning, and you wake up to an alarm clock buzzing. You roll out of bed, walk to the bathroom, flip on the light, and turn on the shower. Hot water bursts out, and the exhaust fan ensures that the shower area remains fog-free. You have been awake for only 15 minutes on this day, but you already have made use of electricity 4 times—the alarm clock, the bathroom light, the water heater, and the ceiling fan.

Exhibit 9.1 The Market for Electricity

The downward-sloping market demand curve intersects the upward-sloping market supply curve to determine the equilibrium price (P_{market}) and equilibrium quantity (Q_{market}) of electricity.

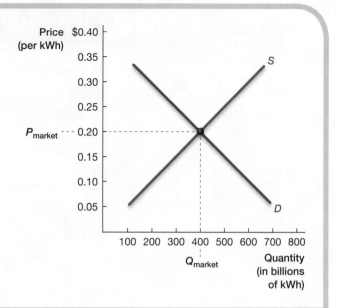

Electricity obviously benefits all of us in many ways, but the power company incurs production costs to provide electricity. As we learned earlier, the market arrives at a price for electricity that reflects both of these factors—marginal benefits and marginal costs. In Exhibit 9.1, we make the assumption that the electricity industry is a perfectly competitive market. The market demand curve in the exhibit shows consumers' willingness and ability to pay for electricity, and the market supply curve reflects producers' marginal costs of generating it. As we learned in Chapter 7, it is at the equilibrium point where these two lines intersect that the invisible hand most efficiently allocates resources: the point at which social surplus is maximized.

But what Exhibit 9.1 does *not* show is that when producing electricity, plants typically emit nasty pollutants, including sulfur dioxide and nitrogen oxides, which can cause lung irritation, bronchitis, and pneumonia. You also cannot see in a graph like this that at high dosage levels, the mercury released from coal-burning power plants has been linked to birth defects. Global warming has also been linked to pollutants emitted from power plants.

In economic terms, the power plant imposes an externality on the public as a by-product of producing electricity. An **externality** occurs when an economic activity has either a spillover cost or a spillover benefit on a bystander. In this case, the plant is imposing a negative externality, because by producing electricity it creates a spillover *cost* that it does not consider when making production decisions. Because the owners of the plant do not have to pay for the costs that the plant imposes on society, they do not take into account the health or discomfort of the citizenry in their production decisions. That is, free markets allocate resources in a way that ignores these negative externalities.

An **externality** occurs when an economic activity has either a spillover cost or a spillover benefit on a bystander.

A "Broken" Invisible Hand: Negative Externalities

Let's return to Exhibit 9.1, where we show the market demand and market supply curves for electricity. We can first ask ourselves, why is this outcome efficient? The answer is that it is efficient because at that point social surplus is maximized: every buyer who is willing and able to pay the equilibrium price for electricity ends up, in fact, consuming electricity. And, because plants expand production until $MC = MR = P$, social surplus is maximized: both consumers and producers do as well as they can in equilibrium.

Many firms pollute when they produce goods for us to consume.

When there are negative externalities present, however, this market outcome is no longer efficient. This is because negative externalities impose an *additional cost on*

Exhibit 9.2 The Socially Optimal Quantity and Price of Electricity

Negative externalities lead to external costs of production that the private firm will not account for when making decisions. The marginal external cost is the vertical distance between supply and marginal social cost (*MSC*). If we take the marginal external cost into account, a higher equilibrium price and a lower equilibrium quantity result.

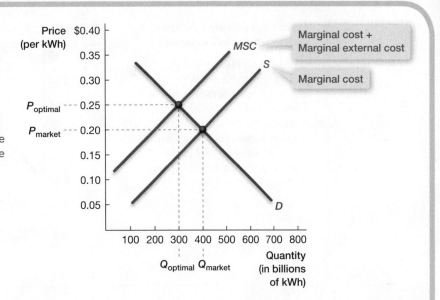

> **Negative externalities impose an additional cost on society that is not explicitly recognized by the buyers and sellers in the market.**

society that is not explicitly recognized by the buyers and sellers in the market. For electricity generation, this additional cost comes from pollution, a by-product of electricity production. In computing the efficient outcome, we must adjust the supply curve to take account of the negative externalities or external costs. That is, as we discussed in Chapter 6, the supply curve is the marginal cost curve for the firm and includes a plant's expenditures for inputs such as labor. The external costs that society bears as a result of the plant's pollution are ignored. However, to arrive at the efficient production level, we need to recognize both the firm's *marginal cost* and the *marginal external costs* of production. Together, they sum to the *marginal social cost* of production.

So what does this mean for the efficient level of output? Exhibit 9.2 shows the answer graphically. Exhibit 9.2 reveals that at each level of production we must include both the marginal cost of the plant to produce plus the marginal external cost of the pollution. This new curve is called the *marginal social cost (MSC)* curve because it includes both the marginal cost of the firm and the marginal external cost imposed on society (*MSC* = marginal cost + marginal external cost). Recall that the original supply curve is the marginal cost curve of the electricity producer—the *MSC* is therefore the marginal cost of the externality plus this marginal cost.

Taking into account the extra costs imposed on society by the plant's pollution, we can see that Q_{optimal} is less than Q_{market} because when a negative externality must be accounted for, a smaller quantity of electricity should be generated since it is now more costly to produce each unit. Thus, in cases where there are negative externalities, markets (if left alone) will produce too much, resulting in too much pollution.

You might wonder just how much this negative externality costs society. We can explore this question graphically by considering Exhibit 9.3. Let's begin with the equilibrium quantity level, Q_{market} = 400 billion kWh (kilowatt hours). In the free market, this is the unit of production that equates marginal willingness to pay with the marginal cost of producing that unit of electricity ($0.20 = $0.20). But with the negative externality, we see that the marginal social cost is $0.30 for the last unit, not $0.20. This means that by producing that last unit, we actually caused social well-being to go down by $0.10 = $0.30 − $0.20 (the marginal social cost from producing the last unit minus the marginal benefit from producing the last unit). This means that if we do not produce that last unit, we will save $0.10. Recall from Chapter 7 that *deadweight loss* is a decrease in social surplus that results from a market distortion. If producing that last unit caused a deadweight loss of $0.10, what is the total deadweight loss associated with the externality?

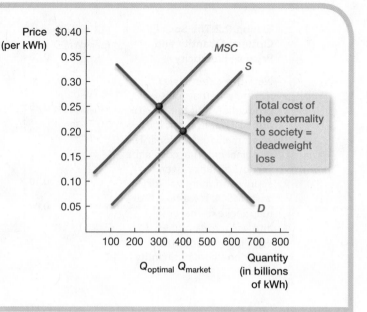

Exhibit 9.3 Deadweight Loss Due to a Negative Externality

In producing the last unit of production a deadweight loss of $0.10 resulted. Doing a similar exercise for all units produced to the right of the social optimal production level ($Q_{optimal}$), we can graphically represent the deadweight loss as the yellow triangle.

Extending the reasoning from the last unit produced to all units produced between $Q_{optimal}$ and Q_{market}, we arrive at the yellow-shaded region in Exhibit 9.3. This is the area between the marginal social cost curve and the market demand curve between units $Q_{optimal}$ and Q_{market}. The triangle represents the sum of the losses for each unit—the difference between the total marginal cost and total marginal benefits to society as a whole. Thus, the yellow-shaded triangle represents the deadweight loss of the negative externality. As a way to check your work, the deadweight loss is usually in the form of a triangle with the arrow pointing in the direction that society would prefer. In the case depicted in Exhibit 9.3, the arrow of the triangle points leftward, meaning society prefers less production than the free market provides.

One important feature of this discussion is that pollution is not driven to zero—that is not the goal. Rather, the optimal solution calls for us to recognize the marginal cost of the pollution externality to society. Upon recognizing the marginal external cost, as in this example, it is often the case that we are left with some pollution. This is for two main reasons: pollutants in moderate dosages are in many cases not very damaging, and it is very costly to produce some goods without releasing any pollution.

A "Broken" Invisible Hand: Positive Externalities

There are important situations that are a mirror image of negative externalities—positive externalities, which occur when an economic activity has a spillover *benefit* that is not considered when people make their own decisions. As with negative externalities, positive externalities are all around us. For instance, a resident of Sarasota who landscapes her property will probably enhance the value of her neighbors' property, even though they had nothing to do with the decision to landscape.

Another important example of a positive externality is educational attainment, which not only helps a student through better employment opportunities and higher wages but also confers significant benefits on others. These benefits can come in many forms, but the ones most often cited are the following:

1. Education often increases civic engagement, thereby contributing to a more informed democratic society.
2. An educated workforce is vital for innovation and adoption of new technologies.
3. An educated citizenry will be less likely to commit crime.

Among economists and policymakers, the positive externality argument is a commonly cited justification for government involvement in education. To show why, let's begin with Exhibit 9.4, which illustrates the market demand and market supply curves for education.

Exhibit 9.4 The Market Equilibrium for Education

As in Exhibit 9.1, we depict a market without externalities. The optimal production is reached where the market demand curve for education intersects the market supply curve for education.

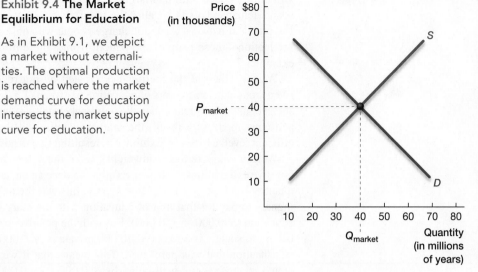

For clarity, let's continue with the assumption that education is a perfectly competitive market. Therefore, Q_{market} is an efficient outcome: with no externalities, the invisible hand is driving the market to an efficient equilibrium.

In the case of positive externalities, however, the invisible hand does not yield socially efficient results. This is because positive externalities create external social *benefits* that are reaped by others. Exhibit 9.5 reveals an example of positive externalities, which can be thought of as the difference between the demand curve (which is marginal benefit) and the *marginal social benefit (MSB) curve*. Therefore, the *MSB* curve is the marginal (private) benefit plus the marginal external benefit: *MSB* = marginal benefit + marginal external benefit.

Consider Exhibit 9.5 more closely. The efficient amount of education from the viewpoint of society is given by $Q_{optimal}$. This is where society's marginal benefit from another unit of education equals the marginal cost of producing that unit of education. But this

> **Positive externalities create external social benefits that are reaped by others.**

Exhibit 9.5 Deadweight Loss of a Positive Externality

Features of an educated populace, such as better informed policy making, mean that private benefits of education will understate total benefits. Graphically, this means that the marginal social benefit curve will be higher than the demand curve for any amount of production. This leads to an underproduction of education, leading to a deadweight loss to society, equal to the yellow triangle.

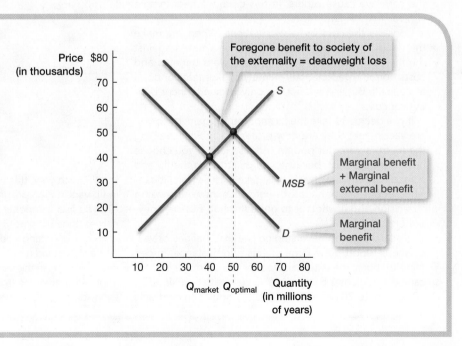

won't be the same as the equilibrium quantity in a free market. The education industry will only produce until its marginal cost equals the *private* demand for education, not the social demand. This is because the industry can only sell its output to education buyers. For practical reasons, it cannot charge people who enjoy the external benefit of education production—those people who benefit from a more informed citizenry or less crime, for example.

We can now see the inefficiency created by not recognizing the positive externality. Even though there are years of education (between Q_{market} and $Q_{optimal}$) from which marginal social benefits are greater than the marginal cost to produce, these years are never produced and consumed. As a result, the market quantity will be too low relative to the socially efficient level, as seen in Exhibit 9.5, resulting in a deadweight loss.

We can compute the deadweight loss in much the same way as we did in the case of negative externalities. Consider Exhibit 9.5 once again, and let's begin with the equilibrium quantity level, Q_{market}. In the free market, this was the unit of production that equated willingness to pay for that unit of education with the marginal cost of producing that unit of education ($40,000 = $40,000). But with the positive externality, we see that the marginal benefit to society is $60,000 ($40,000 private + $20,000 external benefit) for the last unit of education that was purchased. This means that if we would produce that last unit, we would increase social well-being by $20,000 = $60,000 − $40,000 (the marginal social benefit of the last unit − the marginal social cost of the last unit).

In fact, with the higher marginal benefit due to the positive externalities, we see that we should keep producing because the marginal gains to society are greater than the marginal costs to produce. This reasoning continues until we reach point $Q_{optimal}$. The amount of economic benefit that could be gained if we produced the optimal quantity is shown in the yellow-shaded region of the exhibit. This is the area between the marginal social benefit curve and the marginal cost curve between units Q_{market} to $Q_{optimal}$. This area reflects how

CHOICE & CONSEQUENCE

Positive Externalities in Spots You Never Imagined

Externalities are the result of agents trying to do the best they can and ignoring how their actions affect others. In this sense, it would be wrong to think of externalities as "mistakes." Externalities may result from just *not knowing* the harm we cause others. In this case, we might make choices that we later regret.

Consider the case of flu vaccinations. When you make the decision of whether or not to be vaccinated against the flu, you likely consider only the private benefits and costs from the vaccination—namely, the benefits or costs to yourself. But you are not the only person to incur benefits or costs.

If you decide to take the flu shot, others gain: once you are vaccinated, they are now protected against catching the flu from you. But people can also lose if you choose not to get the shot, because you could catch the flu and spread it. Many of us would not take such externalities—whether positive or negative—into account when making a decision about whether to get a flu shot. But they nevertheless exist.

Researchers who have studied the externalities of vaccinations report quite large effects.[2] For instance, in certain situations, the external effect of you getting a flu shot can be as high as 1.5 infections. Given that approximately 10 percent to 20 percent of the U.S. population contracts

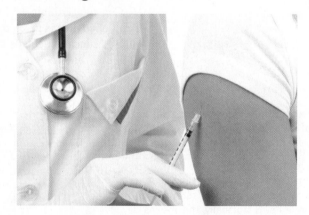

the flu each year, this estimate reveals the potential value in flu vaccination programs.

If you find it important to take account of your own externalities, the next time you are weighing your private benefits and costs of getting a flu vaccination, remember that not getting a shot could result in as many as 1.5 more infections for everyone else. In this sense, by avoiding the needle you have imposed a great externality on the rest of the population—even some of those who have gotten the shot!

much society could increase social surplus if it produced at the efficient level. Again, you will notice that deadweight loss takes the form of a triangle with the arrow pointing in the direction that society would prefer.

Pecuniary Externalities

You might be thinking as you read this chapter that every market action has an externality. For example, if millions of new consumers decide to buy iPods, market demand will shift rightward, increasing price. If you were planning on buying an iPod, these consumers have just imposed a negative externality on you!

This is good intuition. Every market does have this type of externality, at least in the short run. Economists think of this kind of externality as a different animal compared to the externality examples above. The two types of externalities we have just studied have much different implications—they create market inefficiencies.

The example of more people buying a good and thereby causing a negative market impact for others is called a **pecuniary externality**. Pecuniary externalities exist when market transactions affect other people, but only through the market price. This defining attribute of pecuniary externalities—that they act only through prices—is critically important. It means that pecuniary externalities do not create market inefficiencies. Here's why.

Remember that negative and positive externalities lead to "wrong" equilibrium quantities. They do so because they create an external cost or external benefit that is not reflected in the market price. Pecuniary externalities don't create these effects. Precisely because their impact is completely embodied in prices, the market price *correctly* reflects the society-wide impact of market transactions. You could say that pecuniary externalities are necessary for efficient markets because as goods become more or less scarce their price should change. Negative and positive externalities, such as pollution and education, cause market inefficiencies because goods are either over or under produced and consumed.

> A **pecuniary externality** occurs when a market transaction affects other people only through market prices.

9.2 Private Solutions to Externalities

When externalities are present, the market outcome is inefficient. Exhibits 9.3 and 9.5 in the previous section reveal the inefficiencies of not taking externalities into account. Conceptually, the exhibits show the following two important points:

1. When there are negative externalities present, free markets produce and consume too much.
2. When there are positive externalities present, free markets produce and consume too little.

If, in the presence of negative externalities, too much of a good is being produced, and in the presence of positive externalities, too little of a good is being produced, then how does society achieve a more efficient outcome? Several possibilities have emerged—some involve private citizens working it out themselves while others include government intervention. In this section, we consider a number of private solutions.

One fundamental theme unites the multiple solutions to externalities, whether public or private: *internalizing the externality*. When individuals or companies take into account the full costs and benefits of their actions because of some public or private incentive, economists say that they are **internalizing the externality**. When the external effects of their actions are internalized, the general result is that the market equilibrium moves toward higher social well-being.

> When an agent accounts for the full costs and benefits of his actions, he is **internalizing the externality**.

To understand how internalizing the externality works in the area of private solutions, we'll consider the scenario of a power plant that is currently emitting tons of toxins in waterways, and this adversely affects local fishermen. Place yourself in the seat of a city mayor and think about what you would do if the fishermen came clamoring to you for help in curbing the plant's emissions.

Your first thought might be to read the city pollution ordinances to check if there is a law against polluting the waterways. Say that upon doing so, you find that there is no such regulation—the power plant has the right to pollute for free. Thus, in actuality, the power plant has the right to pollute. Amazing!

Your next thought might be to impose laws that establish new regulations on the power plant. This is most people's first instinct because a common misperception is that government is the *only* source of change when, in fact, private organizations have affected change for years. Such private solutions to externality problems usually require parties to negotiate with one another or a social enforcement mechanism to be in place. Let's see how bargaining can work.

Private Solution: Bargaining

To gain a sense of how bargaining can work, we'll continue with the power plant and fishermen example. Say you discover the power plant can eliminate the toxins that it emits by purchasing and installing scrubbers (a technology that cleans water and air before they are released into the ecosystem). But scrubbers are expensive to purchase and maintain. The best cost estimate is that over the next decade, the cost of the necessary scrubbers will be $5 million. However, because the power plant holds the right to pollute by law, it does not have to install expensive equipment.

On the other side of the equation are the fishermen. Their scientists tell them the pollution has gotten to such dangerous levels that there is a chance the entire fishing industry could be shut down within a matter of years. Their analysis further tells them that the power plant is, in fact, the main culprit, emitting tons of toxins into the waterways weekly. The fishermen conclude that if they can convince the power plant to install the scrubbers, they will receive benefits over the next decade of approximately $7 million.

In this case, what is the outcome if the fishermen and power plant do not communicate? Left to itself, the power plant is clearly not interested in spending $5 million on scrubbers because it does not gain from such a purchase. As you can see, this market outcome is not socially efficient because total well-being could be increased. In fact, the amount of money left on the table is $2 million ($7 million − $5 million). You might recall from Chapter 8 that you can think of this as the gains to trade.

So does this mean that pollution will continue at the current rate because the power plant has the legal right to do what it desires? Can economics help solve this impasse? As it turns out, economics *does* play a critical role.

The legal rights do not have to be the deciding factor; a private deal can be struck. How can we be so sure? You know that fishermen are willing to pay up to $7 million to rid the waterways of the power plant's pollution, whereas it costs the power plant only $5 million to abate pollution. Therefore, a deal will be brokered in which the fishermen give an amount of money between $5 million and $7 million to the power plant, and the power plant installs and maintains the scrubbers. What is not clear is where exactly in the $5-million to $7-million price range the deal will be struck (as was observed in Chapter 8 about the range of possible terms of trade).

Now let's consider when the opposite case is at work: upon looking into the local ordinances, say that you had found that there was a law against the power plant polluting the waterways. You would have then informed the power plant that it was out of compliance. If it chose at that point not to shut down, it would then have installed the scrubbers, thereby eliminating the water pollution.

The remarkable bottom line is that regardless of whether the law permits the power plant to pollute or not, the economically efficient outcome is achieved either way—the plant installs and maintains the scrubbers because abating pollution provides the highest social value.

The Coase Theorem

This insight—that negotiation leads to the socially efficient outcome regardless of who has the legal **property right** (ownership of property or resources)—is called the **Coase Theorem**, after the Nobel Laureate economist who proposed it, Ronald Coase. The

A **property right** gives someone ownership of a property or resources.

The **Coase Theorem** states that private bargaining will result in an efficient allocation of resources.

> The end result of the Coase Theorem . . . is that government intervention is not necessary to solve externality problems—private bargaining can do the job.

theorem's implication is powerful: private bargaining will lead to an efficient allocation of resources. This means that the person who values ownership the most will end up owning the property right.

The end result of the Coase Theorem, then, is that government intervention is not necessary to solve externality problems—private bargaining can do the job. Although we reach the efficient outcome regardless of initial property rights, who holds the initial property rights is not irrelevant. This is because the initial property right allocation is an important determinant of the distribution of surplus.

That said, we should be cautious about relying too much on private solutions to externalities for the following reasons:

1. The assumption that the parties involved—those creating the externality and those suffering from it—can negotiate economically is critically important. This means that as long as the *transaction costs* associated with negotiating aren't too high, the efficient economic outcome can be achieved.
2. Whether the property right is clearly defined is important; in many cases, the law is not clear on who holds it.
3. The number of agents on each side of the bargaining table matters. It's easy enough to imagine that bargaining can lead to an efficient solution with a small number of affected people. But it is more difficult to see how such bargaining could work between, say, a power plant and 100,000 affected fishermen.

The Coase Theorem applied to this situation would say that whether the plant has the right to pollute or the 100,000 fishermen have the right to clean water, the end result will be the efficient amount of water quality. If the plant does have the right to pollute, then 100,000 fishermen must coordinate on how to pay the plant to cut back its emissions. If the fishermen have the right to clean water, then the power plant will have to pay them to be able to emit pollution if that is the efficient solution. But as a practical matter, it is difficult for 100,000 fishermen to somehow negotiate their own agreements with a plant about the allowable level of emissions and who gets compensated. In this case, a governmental rule might be the most efficient means to address the externality.

This is because the *transaction costs* associated with bargaining might be too high. Hence, even when property rights are perfectly established, the cost of bargaining itself—the **transaction costs** associated with making an economic exchange—might be too high to permit this sort of arrangement from happening. This transaction cost not only includes direct expenditures, such as legal fees and your time, but also the cost of an awkward situation: it might be difficult to walk next door and bargain with your neighbor about the amount of dog droppings his pet can leave on your front yard. With this in mind, we turn to a second popular private means to address the market failure of externalities: social enforcement mechanisms.

Transaction costs are the costs of making an economic exchange.

Private Solution: Doing the Right Thing

Does the logo to the left look familiar? If you've seen it on your kitchen appliances, your computer, or your windows, you have approved energy-efficient products. The ENERGY STAR program is a joint program introduced in 1992 by the U.S. Environmental Protection Agency (EPA) and the U.S. Department of Energy to promote energy-efficient products. ENERGY STAR is a voluntary labeling program designed to identify and promote energy-efficient products to reduce greenhouse-gas emissions. The first kinds of products to be labeled ENERGY STAR were computers and monitors. The program now includes over 60 product categories, including major appliances, office equipment, lighting, and home electronics. Today, you can hardly miss the stickers when entering a workplace.

The ENERGY STAR program has worked both because there are financial incentives associated with such products (reduced electricity cost and potential tax savings) and because it involves a social

Do you buy Energy Star goods?

enforcement mechanism: it gives us information about "green products" and invokes a moral code that you should "do the right thing" and purchase them. There are no official government regulations that tell people that they have to buy ENERGY STAR products, but the substantial growth in the program since 1992 is a testament to the power of motivating people to try to do their part for the environment. In economic language, the moral code of doing one's part is internalizing externalities.

Once you give it some thought, you realize that social enforcement mechanisms are operating all around us and help us to take account of externalities. For instance, we will learn later in this chapter that private organizations such as the Sierra Club are quite successful at protecting the environment. The charity Smile Train does incredible work with overseas children who have cleft palates. Closer to home, when waiting in line for a ride at *Disney World* or in a supermarket checkout line, we rarely observe people "line jumping." People generally refrain from the practice not because there is a stiff financial penalty for doing so, but because their actions will likely be frowned upon by the people who bear the costs of their rudeness. Such socially imposed costs lead to a reduction in the quantity of line jumping to the net benefit of society. Shame, guilt, and the risk that we will be publicly decried are all effective social enforcement mechanisms. In particular, all of these social controls help to internalize the negative externality imposed on others, leading to less of such behavior.

Although private solutions can prove quite effective, direct government intervention might be necessary when private interventions fail. Such solutions usually take the form of rules that restrict production in some form, taxation, or requiring permits for production. We now consider several examples of government solutions to externalities.

9.3 Government Solutions to Externalities

There are many ways in which markets fail, or at least fall short of the ideal competitive market outcomes described in Exhibits 9.1 and 9.4. Whenever markets fail, policymakers need to consider the following question: can the government bring about a particular outcome more efficiently than the market? We have learned that there are potentially important private solutions to externalities, including bargaining over outcomes and relying on social enforcement mechanisms. Yet these also are apt to fall short in certain situations.

Governments respond to externalities in two main ways:

1. *Command-and-control policies*, in which the government directly regulates the allocation of resources
2. *Market-based policies*, in which the government provides incentives for private organizations to internalize the externality

Let's return to the case of the power plant's release of pollutants. Suppose the plant also emits air pollutants that affect millions of households in neighboring states. In such a case, the costs are dispersed in a manner that makes private negotiations impossible. Put yourself in the shoes of the federal regulator and think about what you would do in this case: a situation in which you are certain that curbing the pollutant emissions from the plant will be beneficial to society. You will find yourself relying on the two major approaches just listed, to which we now turn in more detail.

Government Regulation: Command-and-Control Policies

If you knew that curbing emissions would benefit society, then you realize that $Q_{market} > Q_{optimal}$, and an approach to lower the quantity produced (and thereby pollution) is a step in the right direction. One common approach to solving this problem is by using *command-and-control regulation*. Under **command-and-control regulation**, policymakers either directly restrict the level of production or mandate the use of certain technologies.

Command-and-control regulation either directly restricts the level of production or mandates the use of certain technologies.

Many early environmental regulations, including the landmark clean water and clean air legislation of the 1970s, were command-and-control regulations. In this case, the government required polluters to adopt the best available pollution-reducing technologies. For example, the Clean Water Act stipulated *exactly* the types of technologies that each plant had to install if they were to continue operations. Similar regulations can be found in the various Clean Air Act Amendments. For example, under the 1977 Clean Air Act Amendments, new polluting plants had to install certain abatement technologies.

As you might have guessed, there are many ways to regulate polluters, and the command-and-control technique might not be the most efficient course of regulatory action to curb pollution. For one thing, this type of regulatory action typically provides few incentives for producers to search for more cost-effective ways to reduce pollution itself. This happens because regulators have directed attention to the wrong target—they mandate the technology that the producer must use. This pushes the producer to develop efficient methods to use the mandated technology. Yet, rather than focusing producer efforts on developing cheaper ways to use the mandated technology, the regulator should incentivize producers to find or develop the most cost-effective technologies.

Government Regulation: Market-Based Approaches

A **market-based regulatory approach** internalizes externalities by harnessing the power of market forces.

Given that you are interested in efficient regulation, you decide not to make use of the command-and-control approach and instead turn to a **market-based regulatory approach**. A market-based approach internalizes externalities by harnessing the power of market forces. What does this mean in terms of the power plant scenario? With the market-based approach, the method for reducing pollution is essentially left to the emitter—the power plant itself. Thus, there is a greater incentive to develop new ways to reduce pollution than in the command-and-control approach.

Corrective Taxes and Subsidies

The most prominent market-based approaches to dealing with externalities are *corrective taxes and subsidies*. Let's return to the case of the local power plant. Because its production is creating a negative externality, it is producing too much. So you want the power plant to cut back on production, because doing so moves the quantity produced toward the efficient level. You can do this through taxes on the production from the plant. Such government taxes are called **corrective taxes** or **Pigouvian taxes**, named after economist Arthur Pigou, a pioneer in describing how such taxes would work. A corrective tax is a tax designed to induce agents who produce negative externalities to reduce quantity toward the socially optimal level.

A **Pigouvian tax** or, a **corrective tax,** is a tax designed to induce agents who produce negative externalities to reduce quantity toward the socially optimal level.

Given that you understand there is an externality, what should you do? Your first step is to estimate the marginal external cost. Economists have developed tools to help policymakers calculate such costs, and below in the Letting The Data Speak box we discuss one example. In this case, let's assume that policymakers estimate the marginal external cost as given in Exhibit 9.6. The next step is to levy a corrective tax in this amount to reduce the equilibrium quantity to the social optimum.

That is, you levy a per-unit tax equal to the marginal external cost of the externality—which is \$0.10 per unit, as shown in Exhibit 9.6. Because the level of the tax is equal to the difference between S and MSC, plants' now choose a profit-maximizing output that is equal to $Q_{optimal}$. Looked at in another way, the Pigouvian tax creates a virtual market supply curve that is identical to the MSC curve by having each plant consider the externality when making production choices. They consider the externality because they account for the corrective tax when making their production decisions. Thus, the tax exactly aligns private and society's incentives. In effect, the corrective tax internalizes the pollution externality. This results in the efficient market outcome.

The same reasoning that holds for negative externalities also applies to positive externalities: the government can use **corrective subsidies** or **Pigouvian subsidies** to internalize the externality. A **corrective subsidy** is designed to induce agents who produce positive externalities to increase quantity toward the socially optimal level. In the case of positive externalities, a subsidy is used to correct the externality.

Corrective subsidies or **Pigouvian subsidies** are designed to induce agents who produce positive externalities to increase quantity toward the socially optimal level.

Exhibit 9.6 Effect of a Pigouvian Tax

As the social planner, you understand that you must internalize externalities. One solution is to tax each unit of production by the amount of the negative externality. Such a tax allows the externality to be internalized, resulting in a more efficient outcome.

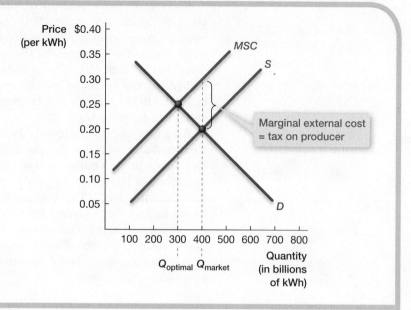

Let's return to the case of education, which is shown in Exhibit 9.7. In this case, what should you do? Much like when there is a negative externality, you need to first estimate the marginal social benefit of education. Upon doing so, the next step is to levy a corrective subsidy in this amount to increase the equilibrium quantity to the social optimum.

That is, you levy a per-unit subsidy equal to the marginal social benefit of the externality—which is $20,000 per year, as shown in Exhibit 9.7. This is the difference between D and MSB. Again, because the level of the subsidy is equal to this difference, individuals now have an incentive to choose the socially efficient level of education, or $Q_{optimal}$. In this manner, the Pigouvian subsidy creates a virtual demand curve that is identical to the MSB curve by having individuals consider the externality when making their education choices. You consider the externality because when deciding whether to obtain more years

LETTING THE DATA SPEAK

How To Value Externalities

A key challenge to policymakers is estimating the external costs or benefits of an activity. For instance, in the case of air pollution from the local power plant, how do policymakers know the costs of lower air quality? One approach is to examine how prices of goods that trade in markets are affected by air quality. This is exactly what economists Kenneth Chay and Michael Greenstone did to evaluate the value of cleaning up of various types of air pollution after the Clean Air Act of 1970.[3] Before 1970, there was little federal regulation of air pollution, and the issue was not high on the agenda of state legislators. As a result, many counties allowed factories to operate without any regulation on their pollution, and in several heavily industrialized counties, pollution had reached very high levels. In particular, in many urban counties, air pollution, as measured by the amount of total suspended particles had reached dangerous levels.

The clean air act established guidelines for what constituted excessively high levels of five particularly dangerous

pollutants, and according to these guidelines, the Environmental Protection Agency and the states would enforce reductions in total suspended particle quantities in counties that were in "non-compliant" status. Following the Act in 1970 and the 1977 amendment that strengthened the implementation of the Act, requiring any increasing emissions coming from new investments to be offset by reductions in emissions from other sources in the same county, there were improvements in air quality (again gauged by total suspended particle measure).

Chay and Greenstone then investigate how housing prices changed in the counties where, because of the Clear Air Act, there was a large improvement in air quality. They find significant improvements in house prices (and no appreciable change in average county incomes). As a result, they estimate that there was approximately $45 billion aggregate increase in housing values because of the Clean Air Act. Policymakers make use of such estimates to help guide their choices of corrective taxes and subsidies.

Exhibit 9.7 Effect of a Pigouvian Subsidy on the Education Market

By introducing Pigouvian subsidies, the government can increase the equilibrium quantity. This subsidy moves us toward a more efficient outcome.

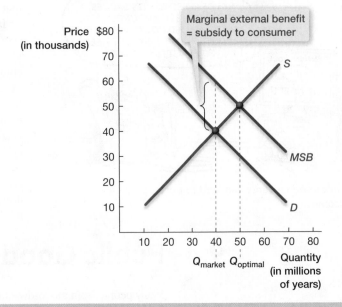

of schooling, you take account of the corrective subsidy. Thus, the subsidy exactly aligns your and society's incentives. In effect, the corrective subsidy internalizes the positive externality. This results in the efficient market outcome.

As you likely know firsthand, such incentives are often put to use in practice. The federal government subsidizes education tremendously, beginning in pre-kindergarten classes and up through the PhD. The creative ways in which such government subsidies are structured range from funding public education to special government college scholarships to highly subsidized school loans. All of this occurs because the government is trying to

LETTING THE DATA SPEAK

Pay As You Throw: Consumers Create Negative Externalities Too!

If you have any roommates, you're probably well aware of a perfect setting for a Pigouvian tax: trash. In particular, you and your roommates probably throw out lots of stuff, and when the trash can gets full, it's often a lot of work to carry the bag of trash out to the dumpster or trash can. Sometimes roommates anticipate this cost and just let the trash in the can pile higher and higher.

Ultimately someone has to take it out, though, and there is often no great mechanism to incentivize this behavior. Cities have a similar problem, but on a much more massive scale. Namely, people buy and throw out tons of stuff and disposing of all that trash isn't free. In an attempt to reduce this waste and the cost it imposes, cities have adopted Pigouvian taxes that have been called "Pay-As-You-Throw." These programs charge people a small price for each bag of trash that they produce. That price, of course, is the cost to the city for disposing of each bag, and in theory, this sort of tax should move people to internalize the cost of their behavior on the city.

Pay-As-You-Throw programs have been run in 4,032 communities in 43 states, covering about 10 percent of the population in the United States, and the overwhelming conclusion is that these programs reduce the amount of trash people throw out. One survey of communities suggested that moving to a Pay-As-You-Throw program reduced household trash by more than a ton per year![4]

This reduction comes in part from a reduction in waste creation but also an increase in recycling. All told, the Pigouvian tax on trash does seem to accomplish what Pigou theorized so long ago—that with a corrective tax, consumer decisions will start to move toward the social optimum.

50% OF RESPONDENTS SAY YES, 40% SAY NO, 35% ARE UNDECIDED, AND 3% ARE HIDING UNDER THE BED ABOUT WHETHER CITIZENS NEED TO BE BETTER IN MATH.

OPINION POLL

An informed citizenry can lead to better political outcomes.

encourage education in an attempt to correct the market failure that occurs when you make your education choices.

In sum, externalities potentially drive a wedge between social benefits and costs and private benefits and costs. This wedge creates a distortion (deadweight loss) if the free market equilibrium quantity levels diverge from the social optimum quantity levels. Corrective taxes and subsidies can cause agents to internalize their externalities. In using such taxes, the government raises tax revenues, but that is not its main goal. Rather, it is attempting to align private and social incentives. To do so, it critically relies on estimates of externalities. A vibrant area of research within economics continues to develop to estimate the costs and benefits of externalities. How would you estimate the dollar value of externalities?

9.4 Public Goods

Many people from the Midwest are familiar with the blare of a tornado siren signaling that a funnel cloud is swirling toward their city. Once the siren sounds, no one can exclude others from hearing it, and one person hearing the siren does not affect the ability of others to hear it. These two properties—that no one can prevent others from consumption and that one person's consumption doesn't prevent another person's consumption—distinguish *public goods*. They are different from the goods we've studied so far—*private goods*—which are traded in markets where buyers and sellers meet and, if they agree on price, ownership is transferred.

To understand the nature of a public good, it is useful to compare and contrast public goods and private goods in more detail. There are two characteristics that differentiate them:

Once a **non-excludable good** is produced, it is not possible to exclude people from using the good.

A **non-rival good** is a good whose consumption by one person does not prevent consumption by others.

A **public good** is both non-rival and non-excludable.

1. Excludability: Private goods are excludable, meaning that people can be kept from consuming them if they have not paid for them. Public goods are **non-excludable**, meaning that once they are produced, it is not possible to exclude people from using them.
2. Rivalry in consumption: Private goods are rival in consumption, meaning that they cannot be consumed by more than one person at a time. Public goods are **non-rival in consumption**, meaning that one person's consumption does not preclude consumption by others.

To summarize, we can say that private goods are excludable and rival in consumption and **public goods** are non-excludable and non-rival in consumption.

We provide Exhibit 9.8 to aid in our thinking about different types of goods in the economy based on their degree of excludability and rivalry. Let's look at the four categories of goods in the exhibit in more detail.

(1) Ordinary private goods, shown in the upper-left corner of Exhibit 9.8, are both highly excludable and highly rival in consumption. Think about a Snickers candy bar that you have just purchased at the book store: once you purchase and eat that specific candy bar, no one else can; you have perfectly excluded others from buying that particular Snickers

Exhibit 9.8 Four Types of Goods

Goods can be classified along two features: excludability and rivalry. Excludability decreases from left to right, whereas rivalry in consumption decreases from top to bottom.

		Excludability	
		High	Low
Rival in Consumption	High	Ordinary Private Goods (clothes, food, furniture)	Common Pool Resource Goods (fish, water, natural forests, food at a picnic)
	Low	Club Goods (cable TV, pay-per-view TV, Wi-Fi, music downloads)	Public Goods (national defense, early warning systems, earth protection programs)

bar. Thus, your consumption has reduced the ability of another person to consume the candy bar; in fact, your consumption has created a one-to-one reduction in Snickers bars available to others. A large fraction of the goods and services that we buy and sell in the market economy have these same properties, and that is why we have implicitly assumed this to be the case when modeling demand and supply in previous chapters.

(2) In the lower-left corner of the exhibit, we find another category of goods—those that are highly excludable but non-rival in consumption. We call such excludable, non-rival goods **club goods**—economists also commonly refer to them as "artificially scarce" goods. For instance, perhaps after you read this chapter, you will turn on the television to watch your favorite cable television show. In so doing, you will not affect the ability of others to watch that same show. Therefore, cable TV is a non-rival good because many people can watch at the same time without disrupting the ability of others to watch. However, individuals can be excluded from watching cable TV if they do not pay for the service. Thus, it is a good that is excludable. Club goods present a bit of a conundrum when sold as a private good. They are non-rival, so the marginal cost of providing one extra unit is small (perhaps even zero), but they tend to require large fixed costs, like wiring cable all around the world for cable TV. If sold at marginal cost, firms would never cover the large fixed costs they bear. Consumers oftentimes have a positive willingness-to-pay for such goods, though. As a result, club goods typically are not sold in perfectly competitive markets.

(3) The upper-right corner shows a category of goods called **common pool resource goods**, which are non-excludable but rival in consumption. For instance, an open-access lake is available to all fishermen, but the fish they catch cannot be caught by another fisherman and are thus rival. Likewise, if you are at a picnic, what happens when the hamburgers run out? You are left with your second choice, a hot dog. We discuss this type of good in further detail later in the chapter.

(4) A much different class of goods appears in the lower-right corner of the exhibit— public goods. Recall that they are goods that are non-rival in consumption and are non-excludable. Consider protecting the earth from climate change. Governments around the world spend billions of dollars annually to curb harmful greenhouse gases. Even if people failed to pay their taxes to support such environmental programs, governments cannot exclude them from enjoying the benefits. That is, while cable television is an excludable good, enjoying earth's comfortable climate is not. National defense and local warning systems are other examples of public goods that we enjoy daily.

Public goods present particular problems for markets to provide because consumers do not see the value proposition in buying them. When purchasing a Nintendo DS, it is clear what you get for your $100. What are you getting if you send in $100 to the U.S. government for national defense? You will be protected by the Defense Department regardless of whether you sent in the cash. And because your $100 makes no appreciable difference between a successful and unsuccessful national defense system, you likely will not send in $100 in the first place. Why send $100 to the U.S. government and receive little in return when you can send the same $100 to Amazon.com and get a Nintendo DS game system?

This example represents a key problem with efficiently providing public goods: we want them, but we aren't willing to pay for them because we can't be excluded from consuming them once they are provided. And the same is true for everyone. Thus, public goods suffer from what economists call a **free-rider problem**, in which a person has no incentive to pay for a good because failure to pay doesn't prevent consumption. Free riders either consume more than their fair share or pay less than their fair share of its cost.

Such cases represent situations in which government intervention can potentially raise social surplus. But how much of the public good should the government provide if it wants to maximize social surplus? Are there other ways to provide it? We turn to these questions now.

Government Provision of Public Goods

What makes public goods different from private goods is precisely their non-rival and non-excludable nature. Their non-excludability represents a distinct opportunity for government to step in and provide them because it can levy taxes for their provision. Standard cost-benefit logic applies to the case of providing public goods: the government should expand production until marginal benefits equal marginal costs. That is, if the marginal benefits exceed the marginal costs of providing the next unit, it should be provided.

A **club good** is non-rival but excludable.

Common pool resource goods are a class of goods that are rival and non-excludable.

A **free-rider problem** occurs when an individual who has no incentive to pay for a good does not pay for that good because nonpayment does not prevent consumption.

CHOICE & CONSEQUENCE

The Free-Rider's Dilemma

Imagine that you and nine other students walk into an economics lab experiment with the hope of earning some cash. The moderator gives each of you ten dollars and explains that you can anonymously, and simultaneously, contribute any portion of it back to a public goods (or group) account. The contributions collected will be doubled and then redistributed equally among you and the nine other students.[5]

For example, if you each contribute half of your endowment, or $5, to the group account, it then contains $50 = 10 × $5. After the doubling, that would mean that $100 is to be split equally between all 10 players. In the end, you walk away with $15: $10 from the group account and the $5 you opted not to put into the group account.

How much of your $10 would you contribute?

It is clear that to maximize the group's take-home earnings, everyone should contribute the full ten dollars to the group fund. This would increase the total money earned in the experiment from $100 to $200, or $20 per person. Why, then, do experiments show that contributions average less than two dollars, with around half of the participants contributing nothing?

For the group, the marginal benefit of contributing outweighs the marginal cost of contributing. But, for the individual that isn't the case. If you give $1 to the group account, then the group as a whole receives $2 (a marginal benefit of $1), but you yourself are only guaranteed 20 cents of that dollar back. That is, by contributing that $1 to the group account you cost yourself 80 cents!

Armed with this knowledge, you can see that you can maximize your take-home earnings by contributing *nothing* to the group account.

Let's walk through a simple illustration. Let's just assume that everyone else contributes everything to the group account. What are your payoffs if you contribute nothing versus if you contribute everything?

Contribute zero payoff:

$$\$10 + \frac{\$90 \times 2}{10} = \$28.$$

Contribute everything payoff:

$$\$0 + \frac{\$100 \times 2}{10} = \$20.$$

As you can see, by free riding and contributing nothing to the public good, you are $8 better off versus when you contribute everything.

Because the same incentives are alive in the real world when it comes to public goods, it is not surprising that many of us are free-riders!

Conceptually, we can calculate the optimal level of public good provision once we know the market demand curve and the marginal costs associated with providing various levels of a public good. To construct the market demand curve, we must first know the individual demand curves. Before doing so, let's revisit how we constructed the market demand curve for private goods.

Recall in that case that we added horizontally. That is, we summed the total quantity demanded of all consumers at a given price to compute the market demand at that price. Exhibit 9.9 provides a summary example of a two-person market. Panel (a) contains your

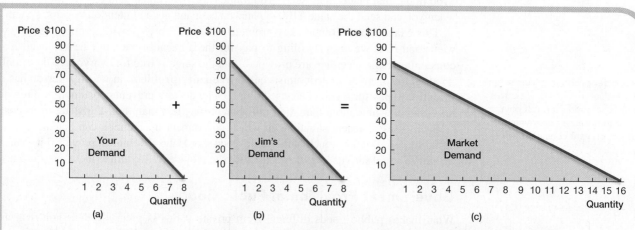

Exhibit 9.9 Constructing a Market Demand Curve for a Private Good

To derive the market demand curve, we find how much quantity you and Jim demand at a given price and then sum horizontally to depict the market demand curve.

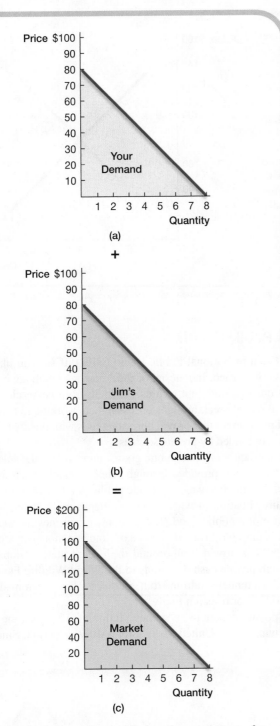

Price $100

80
70
60
50
40
30
20
10

Your
Demand

1 2 3 4 5 6 7 8
Quantity

(a)

+

Price $100

90
80
70
60
50
40
30
20
10

Jim's
Demand

1 2 3 4 5 6 7 8
Quantity

(b)

=

Price $200

180
160
140
120
100
80
60
40
20

Market
Demand

1 2 3 4 5 6 7 8
Quantity

(c)

Exhibit 9.10 Constructing a Market Demand Curve for a Public Good

Public goods need to be valued based on the marginal benefit that a single unit of the good provides to society. For this reason, market demand curves for public goods are added along the vertical axis, producing a total willingness to pay for each unit of the public good.

demand curve for pairs of jeans, and panel (b) contains Jim's demand curve for pairs of jeans. For simplicity, both curves are drawn smoothly even though it would be hard for you to buy 2.5 pairs of jeans. At a price of $50, you demand 3 pairs and Jim demands 3 pairs. This leads to a total market demand of 6 pairs at $50, as depicted in panel (c) of the exhibit. Upon summing all of the quantities demanded horizontally, we are left with the market demand curve in panel (c).

Construction of the market demand curve for public goods follows similar logic. However, the nature of public goods' non-rivalry and non-excludability matters a great deal when moving from the individual to the market demand curve for public goods. Instead of summing horizontally, as is the case for private goods, the market demand for public goods is found by *vertically* summing the individual demand curves. This is necessary because the public good is non-rival, so you and Jim can each consume every unit of the good at the same time. Therefore, to arrive at a market demand curve, we add the individual demand curves vertically because this gives us a measure of the amount of money consumers are willing to pay for each unit of the public good.

Let's put this intuition into action. Assume that we are again talking about you and Jim, but now we are considering the demand for space missions, a public good that potentially leads to new insights that will help all of mankind (by unlocking the mysteries of space, that are non-excludable and non-rival). For comparison purposes, assume that you and Jim have exactly the same demand curve for space missions as you had for jeans, again made smooth for simplicity.

Exhibit 9.10 shows your demand curve for space missions in panel (a), Jim's in panel (b), and the market demand curve for the public good in panel (c). At each level of public good provision, the market demand curve tells us how much the market would be willing to pay for an additional unit of the public good.

As you can see, because you value the first space mission at $70, and Jim also values it at $70, the total marginal benefit for this first space mission trip is $140, as shown in panel (c). This is called the market demand for one unit because it is the total amount of money consumers are willing to pay for the first unit of the public good. Likewise, you value the third space mission at $50, and Jim values it at $50. Therefore, the marginal benefit to society of this third space mission is $100, as shown in panel (c). In other words, prices are summed at each quantity level on the individual demand curves to derive the market demand curve for public goods.

To compute exactly how much of the public good the government should provide, the supply (marginal cost curve) of space missions must be plotted alongside the market demand curve for space missions. We do this in Exhibit 9.11. To compute the equilibrium level of space missions, we follow our decision principles discussed earlier: we should expand the number of space missions until the marginal benefit equals the marginal cost, which occurs at $Q_{optimal}$ in Exhibit 9.11. At this point, total surplus is maximized because all of the gains in the market are reaped. This is because quantity demanded equals quantity supplied, or marginal benefits equal marginal costs. In the next chapter, we explore the different ways in which the government can raise funds to pay for public goods such as space missions.

Exhibit 9.11 The Equilibrium Point for Providing a Public Good

Once the market demand and supply (marginal cost) curves for space missions are set, we can rely on the decision rules that we've learned so far to find the optimal amount of space missions for society. This quantity will be at the intersection of the market demand and market supply curves, where the marginal benefit of the last space mission equals the marginal cost.

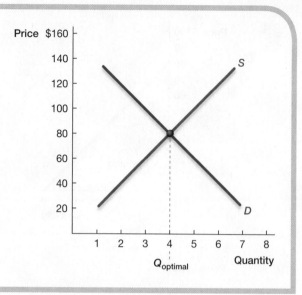

Private Provision of Public Goods

Over breakfast, you might listen to National Public Radio (NPR). If so, you likely have learned about the rain forests of Borneo, Indonesia, or the Amazon, which are being purchased by private organizations as an attempt to preserve them from being clear-cut. Or perhaps you have heard about recent breakthroughs of researchers working to cure cancer. Each of these activities, and many more that provide private goods with positive externalities or provide public goods, are funded by private sources.

Although governments importantly provide public goods, they are not the sole providers. Many public goods are routinely provided through other channels, such as private donations, which are, indeed, an effective way to provide public goods. **Private provision of public goods** refers to any situation in which private citizens make contributions to the production or maintenance of a public good. There are many avenues for such provision, but the most important is through private donations of time and money. For example, through private donations, NPR is provided all around the United States. Globally, rain forests are being saved through private cash donations to the World Wildlife Fund. Cures for ailments ranging from carpal tunnel syndrome to heart disease have been made in part from individuals donating dollars for research funds.

So what is the scope of private donations of money? Exhibit 9.12 shows the tremendous growth in charitable giving in the United States over a 40-year period. Since 1971,

Private provision of public goods takes place when private citizens make contributions to the production or maintenance of a public good.

Exhibit 9.12 Total Giving in the United States Over Time

Over the last 40 years, contributions to charity in the United States have more than doubled, with especially fast growth during the late 1990s.

Source: Giving USA 2012.

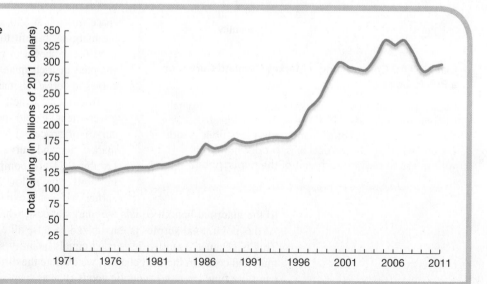

individual contributions to charitable causes have increased from roughly $125 billion annually to approximately $300 billion per year by 2011. Even though the recent giving levels already represent an important fraction of our economy, experts predict that the combination of increased wealth and an aging population will lead to an even higher level of giving in the coming years.

But there is more to the world than just the United States. How does giving in the United States compare to giving rates in other countries around the world? We must be careful when making such comparisons; differences could arise because some countries use taxes to fund more public goods than others. In this case, all else being equal, we should expect low-tax countries to have fewer public goods provided by the government and more public goods provided by charitable giving. Likewise, many people volunteer time to a charitable cause rather than give money. With such considerations in mind, we consider one of the most comparable data sets across countries. In 2010, the polling company Gallup asked people all over the world one simple question: "Have you donated money to a charity in the past month?" Exhibit 9.13 shows that a majority of people answer, "Yes" in developed countries. Even in underdeveloped countries, the proportion of people giving is above 10 percent, suggesting that donations to charity are an important phenomenon all over the world.

You might be thinking that considering the voluntary nature of giving, this form of public good provision might be preferred to governments providing public goods. But we should be careful with this line of reasoning because there might be certain important public goods, such as national defense or local weather alerts, that will be considerably underprovided if left to private sources.

An example can help us understand the danger of leaving public good provision entirely in the hands of the private market. Many scientists believe that species are currently going extinct at a faster rate than at any time in the history of our planet, with the exception of cataclysmic encounters, such as collisions with extraterrestrial objects or massive volcanic eruptions. To deal with this problem, hundreds of conservation groups have been formed with the help of private donations. Which types of species do you think their donors are most likely to help? The answer, interestingly, is that charismatic species and those that most resemble humans, such as panda bears and monkeys, receive the most support. If such funding comes at the expense of funding keystone species—species that play an important role in the ecosystem—it will be dangerous for the vitality of our ecosystem. Of course, the government is not perfect either, and we return to this very issue in the next chapter.

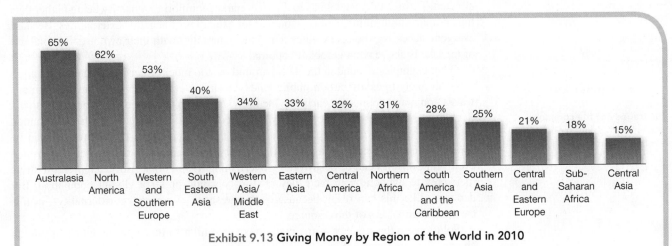

Exhibit 9.13 Giving Money by Region of the World in 2010

Here we depict the percentage of people answering "Yes" to the question "Have you donated money to a charity in the past month?" by world region. For example, 65 percent of people asked in Australasia (Australia, New Zealand, New Guinea, and neighboring islands) answered "Yes."

Which Species Would You Rather Preserve?

Potential donors tend to support charismatic species, such as panda bears, rather than keystone species, such as ochre sea stars, that do not have as much visual appeal.

9.5 Common Pool Resource Goods

Another important class of goods that are related to public goods are common pool resource goods. As summarized in Exhibit 9.8, common pool resource goods are not excludable, so anyone can consume as much of them as they can find—for example, urban parking places, coral reefs, and hamburgers at a student picnic. Unfortunately, common pool resources *are* rival goods, meaning that every Diet Coke that Jack drinks at the student party results in one less Diet Coke for others to drink. This leads to an important negative externality that Jack imposes on all others.

The externality involved with a common pool resource arises because of the combination of open access and depletion through use. When deciding how much to fish in a lake, for example, people using the lake consider only their own private marginal costs of use. But this use depletes the resource for everyone. This is a classic negative externality: individuals use too much of the resource because they do not consider how others are affected. This result is analogous to the free-market equilibrium quantity being higher than the optimal equilibrium quantity in our earlier examples of negative externalities. Because everyone accessing the lake creates this same externality with their own use, the total use of the lake is above what is socially optimal.

Other examples abound in the world around us: too much water is extracted from aquifers, too many trees are cut on public lands, too many communications devices jam airwaves, too many donuts are eaten by one individual from the office donut box, and so on. Such overuse can result in the **tragedy of the commons**, which occurs when a common resource is used too intensely. In some cases, the consequences of this overuse can be severe: instead of preserving a sustainable fishery, for example, complete populations and even whole species can be destroyed by overfishing. It's not that fishermen prefer to drive their prey to extinction; in fact, they obviously would prefer a vibrant population. But depletion like this can result because of the presence of a negative externality—in this case, too many users of the resource.

Solutions to the tragedy of the commons are similar to those discussed earlier in the chapter for some types of externalities. These interventions can be used by governments or other organized public or private regulatory bodies. For example, a Pigouvian tax can be applied to every fish that is taken out of Lake Michigan. Or, because users of common pool resources have incentives to join together to self-regulate use of the resource, it might be possible for people to organize a system that implements a maximum catch in any given year.

The **tragedy of the commons** results when common pool resources are dramatically overused.

CHOICE & CONSEQUENCE

Tragedy of the Commons

In medieval times property rights were poorly defined. Typically, royalty controlled all the property and through arcane mechanisms land was divvied up for use. The fact that the market was not allowed to act led to some bizarre practices, perhaps none as famous to social scientists as the management of feeding livestock.

Livestock were the lifeblood of any community, offering dairy and meat, but this came at a cost, namely, livestock had to be fed, typically by grazing the land. And those who owned livestock were frequently required to feed them in a common patch of land.

This reliance on common land led to perverse incentives. In particular, owners of livestock could purchase an extra goat or cow and reap all the rewards privately. That extra livestock had to graze somewhere, though, and the cost of lost grazing land was born equally by all in the community. Thus, the common grazing area would slowly but surely be overused.

This phenomenon became known as the *tragedy of the commons*, a term popularized by an ecologist, Garrett Hardin, but the example of livestock overgrazing common land comes from a nineteenth-century essay by the early British economist William Forster Lloyd.[6]

What makes the tragedy of the commons so tragic isn't just economic inefficiencies. It's that, at the extreme, the owners of livestock could one day find themselves with nowhere to feed their animals because of overgrazing. The same perverse incentive structure is at work in many real-world situations.

Can you name some? What economic tools can we use to solve the tragedy of the commons?

When feasible, outright privatization of the resource—turning its control over to a single owner—can also work. Ownership eliminates the externality problem because any depletion from use is borne by the owner, who controls access to the resource. It gives the owner incentives to regulate access in a way that maximizes the resource's value to the owner. Because efficient use of the resource creates the biggest "pie" for the owner—that is, maximizes what users are collectively willing to pay to access it—the owner has the incentive to encourage an efficient level of use.

CHOICE & CONSEQUENCE

The Race to Fish

Imagine that you are a fisherman who owns a private pond fully stocked with 100 bluegill fish. Because you own the property rights to the pond, you are the only one who can fish at the pond. Therefore, you can catch as many bluegill as you want. But you know that in the late spring in 70°F water, the female deposits around 40,000 eggs in a shallow nest near the sandy shore. Two to six days later, the eggs hatch and the male guards the young fry during their first days.

Knowing this, how many fish will you catch?

You will likely not decide to catch all of the bluegill, instead leaving many in the pond to restock your supply for the next season.

Now imagine that this pond is a common pool resource—anyone and everyone can fish from it, and one more fish on another angler's line means one less fish on yours. Would you still be careful to leave a lot of fish in the pond for next season?

Both real-world situations and lab experiments conducted by Nobel Laureate Elinor Ostrom have shown us that you probably wouldn't.[7,8] After all, if you decide to leave, say, 50 fish in the pond, who is to stop another fisherman from catching those fish?

This line of thinking may lead everyone to keep fishing until there is absolutely nothing left. As you just learned, this type of situation is referred to as the *tragedy of the commons*; a dilemma in which multiple individuals acting in their own self-interest deplete a shared limited resource when in the long run it isn't in anyone's best interest to do so.

How might the fishermen in our example prevent this from happening?

Evidence-Based Economics

Q: How can the Queen of England lower her commute time to Wembley Stadium?

In the late 1990s, traffic became so congested in central London that travel times dipped below the nineteenth-century average—before the introduction of the car![9] Elected on a reformist platform, London's mayor vowed to make a strong play for fixing London's traffic woes once and for all.

As we learned in this chapter, the basic theory behind externalities is straightforward: if there is a negative externality that you wish to solve, a Pigouvian tax can internalize the externality. In this case, the negative externality is that drivers enter the road without regard to how their presence is affecting others. Thus, a Pigouvian tax can help lesson the congestion problem.

This may sound simple, but translating economic theory to the real world can sometimes be challenging. One problem to be solved in London was how to charge for use of the roads. Simple tollbooths can often create just as many traffic jams as they are tasked to prevent.

Another question to answer was what the size of the tax should be. London settled for a daily flat charge of 5 pounds per day (although this was later increased to 10 pounds per day with hybrid vehicles paying no tax).[10] This fee was called a "congestion charge." Although one might argue that instead of a daily usage tax the government should have charged a mileage-based tax, policymakers decided that for the sake of simplicity, they would charge a daily usage tax. And to avoid creating unnecessary congestion, the daily charge would be enforced with the use of video cameras at roads on the outside of the city. Drivers would have to buy a daily pass at retail outlets, online, or with their cell phones, and drivers caught without having a daily pass were charged heavy fines.

How did it all turn out? Exhibit 9.14 provides some summary details. Comparing traffic patterns the year before the congestion charge was implemented to the year after, total traffic had been reduced by 12 percent, and this gain was mostly due to lower automobile traffic. All in all, economists estimated that the congestion charges had reduced traffic circulating in the city center by 15 percent and traffic entering the zone by 18 percent. Also important in analyzing the benefits of the policy was its impact on the reliability of travel (or the variability of travel time), which improved by an average of 30 percent.

As Exhibit 9.14 shows, the introduction of the congestion tax had an effect of increasing the use of public transportation. As drivers became discouraged from driving into the city because of the congestion charge, they began relying on buses. In addition, more people chose to travel by bicycle. All in all, the program has been a huge success; the Queen of England can now get to Wembley Stadium to watch a Rolling Stones concert in a more timely fashion!

If mayors of American cities would like to achieve similar success, they might wish to take London as an example. But they should be aware of the political landmines

Exhibit 9.14 Results of the Congestion Charge

In comparing total kilometers traveled by different types of vehicles just before and just after congestion pricing, we see that drivers of private vehicles (cars, vans, and trucks) all reduced their use, whereas drivers of taxis, low-emission vehicles (motorcycles and bicycles), and high-occupancy vehicles (buses) all increased their use. Taken together, these trends suggest that London's congestion charge helped to achieve the mayor's goal.

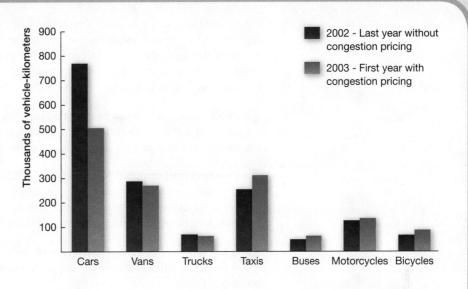

they will face along the way. A similar plan was put forward by New York City Mayor Michael Bloomberg, who proposed to introduce congestion pricing in Manhattan. The plan was greeted with much resistance, as it was blocked by the New York State legislature, and with Mayor Bloomberg's retirement the congestion tax is no longer being considered. In the next chapter, we dive deeper into government taxation, and learn why taxes have their critics.

Question

How can the Queen of England lower her commute time to Wembley Stadium?

Answer

She can convince the mayor of London to enact a tax on automobiles in and around London.

Data

Actual policy enacted in London in the late 1990s and still in place today serves as a model.

Caveat

This is only one of several approaches. Others include private solutions such as social mechanisms and voluntary compliance.

Summary

⚙ The three major examples of when the invisible hand fails are: externalities, public goods, and common pool resources. In each case, free markets typically do not maximize social surplus.

⚙ Externalities come in many shapes and sizes: they can be either positive or negative and occur in consumption or production. The solution to externalities can come through private or public means. The key to each is internalizing the externality; in so doing, we can align private and social incentives so that we can maximize overall well-being.

⚙ Public goods, which can be provided publicly or privately, are non-rival in consumption and are non-excludable. This means that once they are provided no one can be excluded and we can all consume them at the same time.

⚙ Common pool resource goods are not excludable but *are* rival. This leads to an important negative externality that one person imposes on all others: once the bluegill is taken out of the stream no one else can catch it. Therefore, solutions to common pool resource problems mirror solutions to externalities.

⚙ A key link between externalities, public goods, and common pool resources is that there is a difference between the private benefits and costs and the social benefits and costs.

Key Terms

externality *p. 200*
pecuniary externality *p. 205*
internalizing the externality *p. 205*
property right *p. 206*
Coase Theorem *p. 206*
transaction costs *p. 207*
command-and-control regulation *p. 208*

market-based regulatory approach *p. 209*
corrective taxes or Pigouvian taxes *p. 209*
corrective subsidies or Pigouvian subsidies *p. 209*
non-excludable goods *p. 212*

non-rival goods *p. 212*
public goods *p. 212*
club goods *p. 213*
common pool resource goods *p. 213*
free-rider problem *p. 213*
private provision of public goods *p. 216*
tragedy of the commons *p. 218*

Questions

All questions are available in MyEconLab *for practice and instructor assignment.*

1. Why are externalities called market failures? Are pecuniary externalities also an example of market failure?

2. Explain whether the following are examples of externalities.

   a. Alisha did not sleep well because her neighbor was playing loud music.

   b. Rochelle was late for a job interview because her alarm did not go off.

   c. José, who is allergic to pollen, is sick from the flowers that grow in his garden.

3. If the production of a particular good causes a negative externality, would the equilibrium quantity in a competitive market be less than the efficient quantity or would it be greater than the efficient quantity?

4. What does it mean to say that an individual or firm has internalized an externality?

5. What is the Coase Theorem? Under what conditions will the Coase Theorem break down?

6. How does a command-and-control policy differ from a market-based policy?

7. What are Pigouvian taxes and subsidies? How do governments decide when to levy a tax or provide a subsidy?

8. Classify the following goods as private goods, common pool resources, club goods, or public goods.

   a. Health insurance

   b. Radio spectrum

   c. A video on YouTube

   d. A mosquito control program in a city

   e. A library's collection of e-books

9. How do public goods differ from common pool resources? Explain.

10. Why is it difficult for the market to deliver socially efficient quantities of goods like clean air or street lighting?

11. When does the free-rider problem arise?

12. Why is the market demand curve for public goods calculated as a vertical summation of individual demand curves?

13. What is meant by the tragedy of the commons? Use an example to explain your answer.

Problems

All problems are available in MyEconLab for practice and instructor assignment.

1. The European Union banned certain pesticides for two years after studies found links between the use of these insecticides and a decline in the bee population. In particular, research has shown that the use of imidacloprid, clothianidin, and thiamethoxam on flowering crops have adversely affected the honeybee population in North America and Europe.

   a. Consider the private market for these pesticides. Use supply and demand curves to show the equilibrium level of pesticides that will be produced and consumed.

   b. How might the impact of the insecticide on honeybees be modeled as a marginal external cost? Show the deadweight loss from this externality in the graph you drew for the first part of this question.

   c. Is the private market outcome socially efficient?

2. Suppose that you put an invisible tracking device on your computer that will instantly lead police to it if your computer is ever stolen. Does your purchase of the tracking device provide a positive or negative externality for other computer owners? What kind of externality do you provide for other computer owners when you purchase a visible computer lock in order to prevent theft?

3. Caithness Energy, a firm that produces renewable energy, runs a wind farm in Ione, Oregon. The families that live close to this farm have complained to the county planning commission about the high noise levels from the wind turbines. Although the government regulates the amount of noise that is allowed in a town or a city, it is difficult to decide what the appropriate level should be and how it should be measured. Following the complaints, a Caithness representative offered households $5,000 if they agreed not to complain about the noise. Is this consistent with what the Coase Theorem predicts would happen? Explain.

4. Jones and Smith live in the same apartment building. Jones loves to play his opera recordings so loudly that Smith can hear them. Smith hates opera. Jones receives $100 worth of benefits from his music and Smith suffers $60 worth of damages.

   a. From an efficiency perspective, should Jones be allowed to play his opera music?

   b. Suppose the apartment building does not have any rules about noise. Jones and Smith can bargain at zero cost. Will they reach an agreement where Jones gives up his beloved operas?

   c. Now suppose the apartment building passes a rule that says residents are not allowed to play music their neighbors can hear if any of the neighbors object. As before, Jones and Smith can bargain at zero cost. Will Jones be allowed to play his music?

5. In your environmental economics study group, a friend argues that using taxes to control pollution is not efficient because, even with taxes, a positive amount of pollution is still produced. Do you agree?

6. Malaria is spread by mosquitoes. That is, a mosquitoe spreads malaria by biting an infected person and later infusing malaria into a different person. A study by Jeffrey Sachs and others shows a strong correlation between the incidence of malaria in a country and poverty. Malaria is known to exist in poor countries; it has also been found that the incidence of malaria exacerbates poverty. One of the simplest and effective ways of preventing the occurrence of malaria is by using insecticide-treated nets (ITNs).

   a. Consider the private market for ITNs. Use supply and demand curves to show the equilibrium level of nets that will be produced. Is this outcome socially efficient?

   b. In the graph, how would you account for the ITNs' effect on poverty? What happens to the level of output in the market?

   c. How could the government encourage the production of the efficient number of ITNs?

7. Many cities tax or ban plastic grocery bags. The rationale for these taxes and bans is an externalities argument: plastic bags are an eyesore, take up space in landfills, and damage fish, birds, and other wildlife.

   a. In a diagram, show the efficient number of plastic bags and the equilibrium number of plastic bags in the absence of any government policies.

b. Show the efficiency loss from plastic bags in your diagram.

c. Show the tax on plastic bags that would lead to the efficient outcome.

8. The U.S. government recently raised its estimate of the social damage from greenhouse gases such as carbon dioxide. Steel production generates a great deal of carbon dioxide. Present and discuss a diagram to help explain your answers to the following two questions.

a. Will the new higher estimate of social cost imply a higher or lower efficient quantity of steel?

b. Will the new higher estimate of social cost imply a higher or lower level of the Pigouvian tax required to lead to the efficient level of steel?

9. There is a road between the suburbs and downtown. The road is congested at rush hour. If 100 people use the road at rush hour, the trip takes 30 minutes. If the 101st person enters the road, everyone has to slow down and the trip now takes 31 minutes. People value their time at $6 per hour (that is, $0.10 per minute). For simplicity, ignore all of the costs of using the road other than the cost of time.

a. What is the total social cost of 100 people using the road at rush hour?

b. What is the marginal social cost of the 101st person?

c. The governor of this state (who has taken a Principles of Economics course) would like to institute a toll that would equal the costs the last driver who uses the road imposes on the other drivers. How high should the toll be on this road during rush hour?

d. Suppose at noon 50 people are using the road. The road is not congested and the trip takes just 20 minutes. If the 51st driver enters the road, no one has to slow down and the trip continues to take 20 minutes. How high should the toll be at noon?

10. A three-person city is considering a fireworks display. Anne is willing to pay $50 to see the fireworks, Bob is willing to pay $15, and Charlie is willing to pay $15. The cost of the fireworks is $60.

a. In terms of efficiency, should the fireworks display be offered?

b. Will any single citizen provide the display on his or her own?

c. Suppose the town decides to put the matter to a vote. If at least two people vote in favor of the fireworks display, each person will be taxed $20 and the fireworks display will be held. How many people will vote in favor of the display?

11. Three roommates—Tinker, Evers, and Chance—share an apartment. It is really cold outside and they are considering turning up the thermostat in the apartment up by 1, 2, 3, or 4 degrees. They know that each time they raise the temperature in the apartment by one degree their heating bill will rise by $8. Their individual marginal benefits from making it warmer in the apartment are as follows:

	Tinker	Evers	Chance
1 degree	$5	$4	$3
2 degrees	$4	$3	$2
3 degrees	$3	$2	$1
4 degrees	$2	$1	$0

They know that each time they raise the temperature by 1 degree, their heating bill goes up by $8.

a. Find the marginal social benefit from making it 1, 2, 3, or 4 degrees warmer.

b. By how many degrees should they raise the temperature?

12. Rhino poaching is a serious problem in South Africa, where a large proportion of Africa's rhino population is found. The demand for rhino horns, used in traditional Chinese medicine, has increased the prices of rhino horns substantially. This has fueled an illegal market for rhino horns. What economic tools can be used to solve this problem? (*Hint*: Look up Elinor Ostrom's Nobel Lecture "Beyond Markets and States: Polycentric Governance of Complex Economic Systems.")

13. In *Horton Hears a Who* by Dr. Seuss, Horton the Elephant hears voices coming from a speck of dust. He soon learns that the speck is actually a tiny planet where the Whos live. None of the other animals in the jungle can hear the Whos and they threaten to boil the speck in Beezelnut Oil. The only way the Whos can save themselves is by making so much noise that the other animals in the jungle can hear them. Horton and the Mayor of Whoville have trouble convincing all of the Whos to contribute to the noise-making effort. Finally, "a very small shirker named JoJo" joins in and together all of the Whos make enough noise to avoid disaster.

Dr. Seuss (whose real name was Theodor Seuss Geisel) took two economics classes at Dartmouth College while he was an undergraduate. Do you think he did well in those classes?

10

The Government in the Economy: Taxation and Regulation

What is the optimal size of government?

It's early November, and the presidential race is at fever pitch, growing more intense every day. You are beginning to grasp the major issues but are still in need of a bit more information before casting your vote next week. As you eat breakfast, you decide to flip on the TV to learn more about the candidates. You listen to a persuasive argument from the Democratic candidate, who is urging businesses to reduce their carbon emissions. She states that if elected, she will propose new taxes on polluters to address the inherent dangers of climate change: polluters must pay for their pollution! This makes sense to you: why not levy a tax on polluters to more closely align their interests with those of society? She closes by confidently stating that "now is the time to improve our lives, with the helping hand of a government working for you."

Later that day, you return home from economics class and decide to veg out on the couch for a few hours. After this morning's viewing, you are now firmly in the Democratic camp. But when you turn on the TV, this time you see the Republican candidate, who is complaining about the inefficiencies created by taxes and the oversized, incompetent government bureaucracy. New pollution

226

KEY IDEAS

⚙ In the United States, governments (federal, state, and local) tax citizens and corporations to correct market failures and externalities, raise revenues, redistribute funds, and finance operations.

⚙ Through direct regulation and price controls, governments can intervene to influence market outcomes.

⚙ Although government intervention sometimes creates inefficiencies, it often results in improved social well-being.

⚙ Weighing the trade-offs between equity and efficiency is one task of an economist.

⚙ It is up to each individual to decide when and where government intervention makes the most sense.

taxes will harm *all* consumers, he claims. He suggests that corruption has become commonplace in government: even seemingly honest officials are bamboozling the taxpayer. What we need, he says, is less government intrusion in our lives. He ends with a persuasive line: "The beginning of massive government intervention is the end of any great society."

Uh-oh. Now you are torn. The Republican candidate was quite convincing. But so was the Democratic one. Which story is correct? Who should you believe? Do we need more or less government intervention in the economy?

In this chapter we will learn that by its very nature, government intervention can be a double-edged sword. Well-designed regulation can improve societal outcomes, but poorly designed regulation stifles economic efficiency. We'll also look at where the government's money comes from and where it goes, how government intervenes in the economy, and what that intervention costs. Along the way, you will pick up tools that will help you answer the complex question of the optimal role of government in our economy—how much government intervention is necessary? How much is desirable?

10.1 Taxation and Government Spending in the United States

The federal government is the central government established by the U.S. Constitution. It is the largest governing body in the United States, holding jurisdiction over all fifty states. Yet when we refer to "the government," we do not necessarily mean just the federal government. In fact, the federal government collects only about two-thirds of total taxes in the U.S. economy.

There are also state and local governments that impose and collect taxes and spend the revenues they generate. State governments, as the name implies, hold jurisdiction over particular states. Local governments exist at the county and city levels; they, too, collect taxes from, and spend them in, the interest of their respective residents. A single citizen can fall under the jurisdiction of a city government, county government, state government, and federal government simultaneously and thus owe taxes to each.

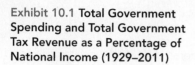

Exhibit 10.1 **Total Government Spending and Total Government Tax Revenue as a Percentage of National Income (1929–2011)**

Total government spending and tax revenues have been increasing over the last several decades. When government spending exceeds tax revenues, the government is running a budget deficit. Conversely, when government tax revenues exceed spending, there is a budget surplus.

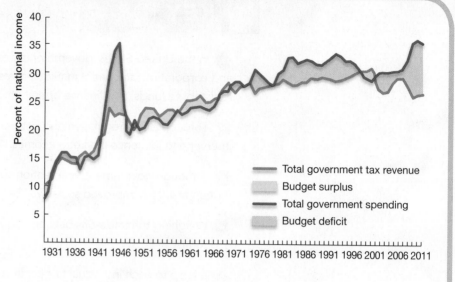

To appreciate the reach of government in the United States, consider Exhibit 10.1, which plots total government spending and tax revenues. This exhibit shows that government spending has grown over time and now accounts for more than 40 percent of U.S. national income. Notice the spike in the mid-1940s, which shows a substantial increase in government spending due to World War II. Tax revenues have also grown in tandem. For example, in 2011, total government tax revenues stood at $2,651.4 billion. It may be hard to believe that such massive tax revenues fall short of spending, but Exhibit 10.1 shows that this is often the case. When government tax revenues fall below spending, the government runs a **budget deficit**. When the converse happens and tax revenues exceed spending, the government is running a **budget surplus**.

A **budget deficit** occurs when tax revenues do not cover government spending.

A **budget surplus** occurs when tax revenues exceed government spending.

Tax revenues, or **receipts**, are the money a government collects through a tax.

A **payroll tax** (also known as **social insurance tax**) is a tax on the wages of workers.

Where Does the Money Come From?

Exhibit 10.2 provides a summary of how the federal government raises revenues. In 2011, for example, the federal government collected over $2,311 billion in **tax revenues,** or **receipts**, which is equivalent to about $15,044 per person in the labor force. These receipts are collected via various types of taxes, as shown in the exhibit.

1. *Individual income taxes* represent the largest portion—roughly 47 percent in 2011.
2. *Payroll taxes* represent about a third of the federal government's receipts. A **payroll tax**, also known as a **social insurance tax**, is a tax on wages that employers are

Exhibit 10.2 **Federal Receipts by Category in 2011**

The largest component of federal government revenues comes from the individual (federal) income tax, followed by social insurance tax receipts. Corporate income tax, excise taxes, and other sources of income make up a much smaller percentage of federal receipts. Components do not sum to 100% due to rounding.

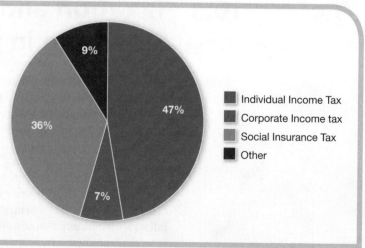

Corporate income taxes are taxes paid by firms to the government from their profits.

Excise taxes are taxes paid when purchasing a specific good.

required to withhold from employees' pay. On your paystub, these are often listed as Federal Insurance Contribution Act taxes, or FICA taxes.

3. *Corporate income tax* provides 7 percent of the overall pie. **Corporate income tax** is generated from taxing profits earned by corporations.

4. *All other taxes* make up the remaining 9 percent. This includes **excise taxes**, which are taxes paid when purchasing specific goods such as alcohol, tobacco, and gasoline.

The sources of revenue for state and local governments are quite different from those of the federal government. Exhibit 10.3 displays the types of taxes levied by these governments and the receipts brought in by each. The pie chart of revenue in the exhibit is split into five pieces.

(1) The largest slice of the pie at 30 percent is the *All Other* category, which encompasses miscellaneous taxes and fees that state and local governments collect. These include, among others, tolls on roads and sales from public transportation tickets, vehicle licenses, and hunting and fishing licenses.

(2) The next biggest portion at 25 percent is *Revenue from the Federal Government*, which are taxes collected at the federal level and then redistributed to the states (often used to redistribute resources toward poorer states with otherwise relatively low tax receipts).

Sales taxes are paid by a buyer, as a percentage of the sale price of an item.

(3) Sales taxes account for the next largest portion at 18 percent. Unless you live in one of the few states that does not have a sales tax, you are likely quite familiar with sales taxes, which are calculated as a percentage of the sale price of an item and are usually collected from a buyer by a seller at the time of sale. The seller then passes the tax on to the proper government agencies. Some items, such as basic necessities, are exempt from sales taxes; these exemptions are determined independently by each state and local government. The value-added tax (VAT) is similar to the sales tax, except that it is imposed at each stage of the production process leading up to the final sale rather than being entirely collected at the time of sale of the final good.

(4) At 17 percent of tax revenues, *property taxes* also constitute a robust slice of the revenues. These are taxes on land and structures on which local governments rely to fund schools, libraries, and public services such as police and fire protection.

(5) Similar to the federal government, forty-three state governments and many local governments collect *individual income taxes*. These amounted to 11 percent of total receipts in 2011. Though the type of tax is the same, each state's rates vary and are generally less than federal individual income tax rates. The seven states that do *not* collect any income taxes are Alaska, Florida, Nevada, South Dakota, Texas, Washington, and Wyoming (in addition, New Hampshire and Tennessee only tax dividend and interest income). Before you plan your next big move, however, keep in mind that these states tend to make up for not taxing income with higher tax rates in other categories or lower provision of public goods.

Exhibit 10.3 State and Local Receipts by Category in 2011

State and local governments receive a much smaller fraction of their tax revenues from individual income taxes than does the federal government. Instead, property taxes, income taxes, and transfers from the federal government account for the bulk of their revenues. Components do not sum to 100% due to rounding.

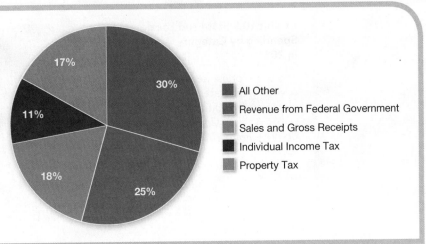

- All Other
- Revenue from Federal Government
- Sales and Gross Receipts
- Individual Income Tax
- Property Tax

Some state and local governments also collect *corporate income taxes,* though this category accounts for a much smaller share of receipts—2.5 percent in 2011.

Why Does the Government Tax and Spend?

There are four main factors underlying government taxation and spending decisions:

- Raising revenues
- Redistributing income via transfer payments
- Financing operations
- Correcting market failures and externalities

Raising Revenues   Most taxation in our economy is intended to raise revenues for the funding of public goods such as national defense, public education, police protection, and infrastructure projects. We saw in Chapter 9 that markets will in general fail to provide optimal amounts of public goods. This failure in turn motivates governments to levy taxes and use the returns for the provision of public goods, which benefit a large number of citizens.

Exhibit 10.4 provides a summary of how federal government revenue is spent and shows that national defense and Social Security comprise the two largest categories of federal spending. The federal government does not spend a large fraction of its budget on education, policing, and infrastructure, which are all included in the "Other" category. But state and local governments do, as we see in Exhibit 10.5.

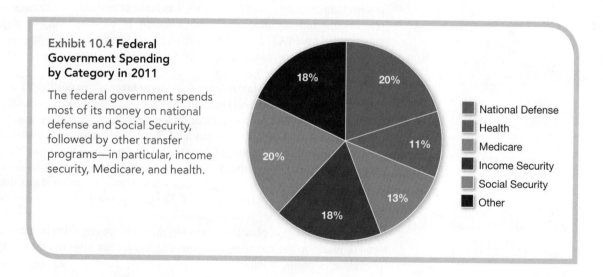

Exhibit 10.4 Federal Government Spending by Category in 2011

The federal government spends most of its money on national defense and Social Security, followed by other transfer programs—in particular, income security, Medicare, and health.

- National Defense
- Health
- Medicare
- Income Security
- Social Security
- Other

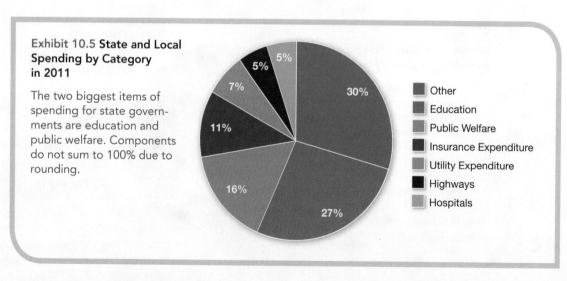

Exhibit 10.5 State and Local Spending by Category in 2011

The two biggest items of spending for state governments are education and public welfare. Components do not sum to 100% due to rounding.

- Other
- Education
- Public Welfare
- Insurance Expenditure
- Utility Expenditure
- Highways
- Hospitals

Exhibit 10.5 indicates that 27 percent of state and local government spending went toward public education, which includes schools from kindergarten all the way up to state universities. Large fractions of these state and local receipts were also spent on highways, one type of infrastructure spending. Policing, together with firefighting, libraries, transportation, parks, and sewage, were included in the "Other" category.

Redistributing Funds The second major objective of government taxation and spending is redistribution. As we discuss in the next chapter, market outcomes can be quite inequitable, with high levels of inequality and poverty coexisting alongside huge fortunes for a few. Governments in all advanced economies in general, and the U.S. government in particular use transfer payments and the tax system to limit the extent of such inequality and the economic hardships that poorer households in the society suffer.

Transfer payments refer to payments from the government to certain individual groups, such as the elderly or the unemployed (which are not made as a payment for the provision of a good or service). In Exhibit 10.4, you can see that after national defense spending, the bulk of federal government spending is made up of payments under the umbrella of Social Security, Medicare, and Health. *Social Security*, also known as the Old-Age, Survivors, and Disability Insurance program, is the largest transfer program and was introduced by President Franklin D. Roosevelt in 1935 to provide economic security to the elderly, disabled, widows, and fatherless children.

Medicare, introduced by President Lyndon Johnson in 1965, provides health insurance to Americans age 65 and above and makes up another large part of federal spending. *Income Security* includes unemployment compensation, Supplemental Security Income, the refundable portion of the Earned Income and Child Tax Credits, food stamps (also known as the Supplemental Nutrition Assistance Program), family support, child nutrition, and foster care. Health comprises such major mandatory programs as Medicaid, the State Children's Health Insurance Program, federal employees' and retirees' health benefits, and healthcare for Medicare-eligible military retirees.

Exhibit 10.5 shows that public welfare also makes up a significant part of state and local budgets. This item consists of transfer payments to persons in need, including direct cash assistance (under the Old Age Assistance and Temporary Assistance for Needy Families programs), vendor payments made to private purveyors for medical care, burials, and other services provided under welfare programs, as well as payments to other governments for welfare purposes.

In addition to transfer payments, governments rely on progressive income taxes to limit inequality and distribute the tax burden more toward the shoulders of the rich.

A **progressive tax system** is one in which tax rates increase with taxable base incomes, so that the rich pay higher tax rates than the less well-to-do. To understand this system more precisely, we need to distinguish between *average* and *marginal tax rates*. The **average tax rate** faced by a household is the total tax paid divided by total income earned. The **marginal tax rate**, on the other hand, refers to how much of the last dollar earned the household pays in taxes. The United States has a progressive federal income tax system in that high-income individuals pay higher average taxes and higher marginal taxes. The "Letting the Data Speak" box illustrates the relationship between marginal and average tax rates in a progressive system, using federal tax information from 2013.

Exhibit 10.7 shows an important consequence of a progressive tax system: the rich earn a high share of the national income but pay even a higher share of total taxes. For example, the richest 1 percent earns 14.9 percent of national income, but also pays 24.2 percent of total federal taxes. People between the 60th and 80th percentiles of the income distribution, on the other hand, pay about the same percentage in taxes as they earn, while those in the bottom 60 percent of the earnings distribution pay less in taxes than their percentage of the national income.

The alternatives to the progressive tax system are the *proportional* and *regressive tax systems*. In a **proportional tax system**, households pay the same percentage of their incomes in taxes regardless of their income level; in other words, the marginal and average tax rates do not vary with income. In a **regressive tax system**, the marginal tax and average tax rates decline with income so that low-income households pay a greater percentage of

Transfer payments occur when the government gives part of its tax revenue to some individual or group.

A **progressive tax system** involves higher tax rates on those earning higher incomes.

The **average tax rate** for a household is given by total taxes paid divided by total income.

The **marginal tax rate** refers to how much of the last dollar earned is paid out in tax.

> "The United States has a progressive federal income tax system in that high-income individuals pay higher average taxes and higher marginal taxes."

In a **proportional tax system**, households pay the same percentage of their incomes in taxes regardless of their income level.

A **regressive tax system** involves lower tax rates on those earning higher incomes.

10.1

10.2

10.3

10.4

10.5

💬 LETTING THE DATA SPEAK

Understanding Federal Income Tax Brackets

Your "tax bracket" corresponds to your marginal tax rate (which is higher than your average tax rate because the federal tax system is progressive). Exhibit 10.6 gives the marginal tax rate single individuals had to pay in 2013.

Using the information provided in this exhibit, you can compute the amount you have to pay in taxes. Suppose that your taxable income (after deductions and exemptions) is equal to $100,000. Then your tax would be calculated as follows:

$$(8,925 - 0) \times 10\% = \$892.50$$

$$+ (36,250 - 8,925) \times 15\% = \$4,098.75$$

$$+ (87,850 - 36,250) \times 25\% = \$12,900$$

$$+ (100,000 - 87,850) \times 28\% = \$3,402$$

Total = $21,293.25

This puts you in the 28 percent tax bracket, because your *marginal tax rate*—the tax rate applied to the last dollar added to your taxable income—is 28 percent. But your *average tax rate* is lower. In particular, it is given by the total amount of taxes you pay, $21,293.25, divided by your total income, $100,000, and is thus $\frac{21,293.25}{100,000} = 21.29\%$.

Exhibit 10.6 Federal Taxes in 2013 for a Single Individual

If your taxable income is between . . .	Your tax bracket is . . .
$0 and $8,925	10%
$8,925 and $36,250	15%
$36,250 and $87,850	25%
$87,850 and $183,250	28%
$183,250 and $398,350	33%
$398,350 and $400,000	35%
$400,000 and above	39.6%

Source: Tax Rate Schedule X, Internal Revenue Code section 1c.

Exhibit 10.7 The Distribution of Income and Federal Taxes in 2010

To interpret the exhibit, match colors across columns. For example, the purple boxes show that those in the 60th to 80th percentiles of income earn 20.4 percent of national income, and pay 17.6 percent of the federal taxes.

Source: Adapted from visualizingeconomics .com.

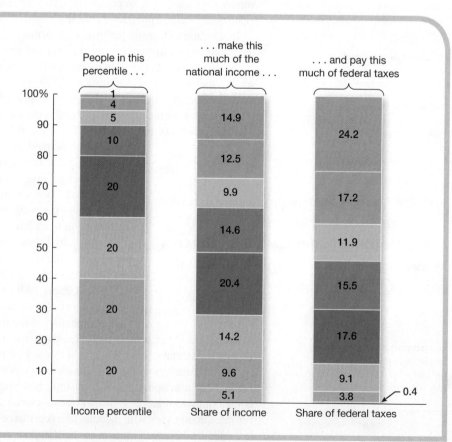

Exhibit 10.8 Three Tax Systems

With a progressive tax system, those earning more, like family C in this exhibit, pay a higher tax rate than the rest (families A and B). In a proportional tax system everybody pays the same tax rate. In a regressive tax system family C pays a lower tax rate than those households earning less (such as families A and B).

Progressive Tax			
	Income	Percentage of Income Paid in Tax	Amount of Tax
Family A	$ 10,000	10%	$ 1,000
Family B	$ 50,000	20%	$10,000
Family C	$100,000	30%	$30,000

Proportional Tax			
	Income	Percentage of Income Paid in Tax	Amount of Tax
Family A	$ 10,000	20%	$ 2,000
Family B	$ 50,000	20%	$10,000
Family C	$100,000	20%	$20,000

Regressive Tax			
	Income	Percentage of Income Paid in Tax	Amount of Tax
Family A	$ 10,000	20%	$2,000
Family B	$ 50,000	4%	$2,000
Family C	$100,000	2%	$2,000

income in taxes than do high-income households. Exhibit 10.8 provides examples of progressive, proportional, and regressive taxes. In the United States, income taxes are progressive, and Social Security and property taxes tend to be regressive.

As a result of transfer programs and progressive taxation, the post-tax income distribution in the United States is more equal than the pre-tax income distribution. We depict this in Exhibit 10.9, which plots the pre-tax and the post-tax income shares of the top (richest) 1 percent and the lowest (poorest) 20 percent of households in the United States. Even though these figures do not include the transfer payments related to healthcare, they already indicate that government redistribution reduces inequality by a significant amount. For example, in 2010 the pre-tax income share of the lowest 20 percent of U.S. households was 5.1 percent, while their post-tax income share was 6.2 percent; the pre-tax income share of the top 1 percent of U.S. households was 14.9 percent, while their post-tax income share was 12.8 percent.

Exhibit 10.9 The Pre- and Post-Tax Income Share of the Top 1 Percent and Bottom 20 Percent (as a Percentage of National Income) from 1979 to 2010

Because of the progressivity of the federal tax system, the post-tax income share of the top 1 percent is less than their pre-tax income share, while the post-tax income share of the bottom 20 percent is more than their pre-tax income share.

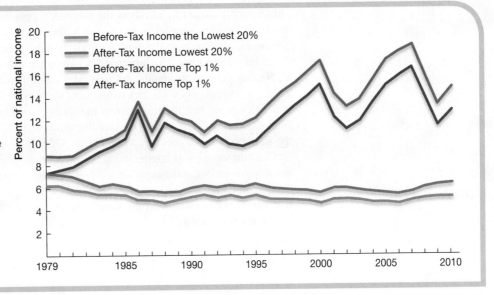

Before-Tax Income the Lowest 20%
After-Tax Income Lowest 20%
Before-Tax Income Top 1%
After-Tax Income Top 1%

Financing Operations Governments also tax to pay for their own operations, including the salaries of presidents, congressmen, and other politicians, and for the sizable bureaucracy in charge of the day-to-day running of government operations and services. Some economists such as William Niskanen[1] argue that politicians and government bureaucrats have a tendency to increase government revenues and their size—independent of the more useful roles of government listed above. Though most economists and social scientists would not agree that this is the major driver of government size, many would agree that certain parts of the government bureaucracy are inefficiently large. We return to this issue later in this chapter.

Correcting Market Failures and Externalities In Chapter 9 we saw how the government sometimes imposes taxes to correct market failures or externalities. Though important in principle, most taxes in practice are not imposed to deal with a specific market failure or externality, but because of one of the other three factors listed above. Because of this, and the fact that we discussed Pigouvian taxes in Chapter 9, we focus on the other three factors in this chapter.

> **"Market outcomes can be quite inequitable, with high levels of inequality and poverty coexisting alongside huge fortunes for a few. Governments use transfer payments and the tax system to limit the extent of such inequality and the economic hardships that poorer households in the society suffer."**

Tax incidence refers to how the burden of taxation is distributed.

Taxation: Tax Incidence and Deadweight Losses

Who bears the *burden of taxes*—meaning, who actually pays the tax?

At first glance, the answer to the question of who bears the tax burden seems obvious: whoever is taxed bears the burden. If a tax is imposed on a consumer, then the consumer bears it. If it's imposed on sellers (producers), they bear it. But we will learn in this section that interestingly enough, things that are not simple: the tax burden can be shared between a buyer and a seller even if it seems to fall on just one of them. The term **tax incidence** refers to how the burden of the tax is distributed across various agents in the economy.

To illustrate, let's consider city government officials in New Orleans, who want to raise money to build a park next to Bourbon Street. Understanding that the local restaurants are doing well, they decide to levy a tax of $2 on every plate of jambalaya being sold per day. Every time a restaurant sells a plate of jambalaya, it must send $2 to the city government. Let's see how this tax on sellers affects market outcomes.

Panel (a) of Exhibit 10.10 shows the market demand and market supply of jambalaya plates and the pre-tax equilibrium, which involves a daily quantity of 4,000 plates of jambalaya being sold at the equilibrium price of $6.50 a plate. Panel (b) in Exhibit 10.10 shows what happens when a tax of $2 per plate is imposed on the sellers. We include a virtual supply curve (S_{tax}) to show the post-tax supply curve. We see that at every quantity level, the post-tax supply curve (S_{tax}) is $2 higher than the old (pre-tax) supply curve S. To understand why, note that with $2 from the sale of every plate going to the government, the sellers are receiving $2 less than the sale price. For example, if the sale takes place at $6.50, they get not this amount but only $4.50. But then, after the tax, at $6.50, they will be willing to supply only what they would have supplied at $4.50 on the original supply curve. Panel (b) shows that the tax reduces the quantity of jambalaya plates purchased per day from 4,000 to 2,500 and raises the equilibrium price to $7.50 a plate. (This means that, after the $2 in tax, a seller now receives $5.50 = $7.50 − $2 and market supply is 2,500 plates.)

Can you see what is happening here? First, there is a gap of $2 between what the consumer pays and what the supplier receives, resulting from the $2 tax on jambalaya plates. Second, not all of this falls on the restaurants: the consumer is paying $1 more per plate—half the $2 tax burden—and the supplier is receiving $1 less per plate (thus also bearing half of the tax burden).

This change in market equilibrium affects consumer and producer surpluses, as shown in panel (b) of exhibit 10.10. Consumer surplus is now given by the blue-shaded area labeled CS, and producer surplus is given by the pink-shaded area PS. The green area represents the portion of revenues that producers pass on to the government. This is the tax revenue, and it is equal to the size of the tax multiplied by the number of plates sold. In this case, with a $2 tax, 2,500 plates are served per day at a price of $7.50 (the intersection point of D and S_{tax}). So, daily tax revenues are given by $2,500 \times \$2 = \$5,000$.

This decomposition in panel (b) also shows that the yellow triangle, which was part of consumer and producer surplus before the tax, is now part of neither. Nor does it accrue to the government as revenue. It therefore represents the *deadweight loss of taxation*. The deadweight loss of taxation is the loss in total surplus—or, put differently, the decline in consumer and producer surpluses not made up by the increase in tax revenues—due to the gap that the tax has created between the price received by sellers and the price paid by consumers. In this example, this gap is exactly equal to the $2 tax. The deadweight loss can be computed easily using the formula for the area of a triangle: ½ base (change in quantity) × height (tax). In our case, this is equal to = ½ × $2 × 1,500 = $1,500.

To understand tax incidence we turn to panel (c) of Exhibit 10.10. Here we see that the government has taken the portion of pre-tax consumer surplus labeled "Incidence on consumers." We calculate this by finding the portion of tax revenue that lies above the pre-tax

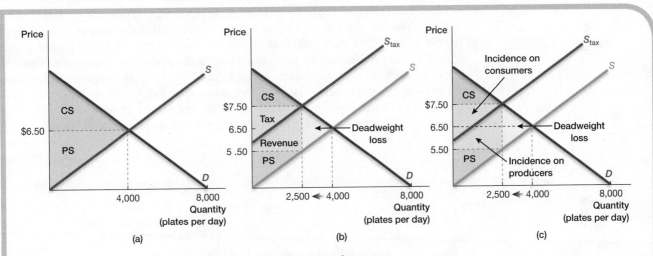

(a) (b) (c)

Exhibit 10.10 A $2 Tax on Producers

In panel (a) the pre-tax equilibrium is 4,000 plates at $6.50 per plate. In this panel, we can also see the consumer surplus (CS), the area underneath the demand curve and above the price of $6.50, shaded blue, and the producer surplus (PS), the area above the supply curve and below the price of $6.50, shaded pink.

In panel (b), we see the implications of a tax of $2 on a plate of jambalaya. Because for every plate of jambalaya they sell, restaurants have to pay $2 to the government, the post-tax supply curve is to the left. The intersection of this post-tax curve and the demand curve gives the post-tax equilibrium, where the price of a plate of jambalaya is now $7.50 and 2,500 plates are consumed. This panel also shows how consumer surplus and producer surplus have shrunk. In between the two, shaded in green, is the tax revenue, given by $2 times 2,500 = $5,000. The yellow triangle represents the deadweight loss of taxation, the loss in total surplus due to the tax.

Panel (c) shows tax incidence. Consumers are now paying $7.50 per plate of jambalaya, $1 more than in the pre-tax equilibrium; and sellers are taking home $5.50 per plate, $1 less than in the pre-tax equilibrium, so that in this example the tax incidence is 50 percent on consumers and 50 percent on sellers.

equilibrium price of $6.50. This portion of tax revenue used to be part of consumer surplus but is no longer part of it. Thus it represents the incidence of taxes on consumers. Similarly, the portion of tax revenue that lies below the pre-tax equilibrium is the incidence of the tax on producers—the portion of tax revenue that is lost producer surplus. This result shows that although the tax is placed on sellers of jambalaya, both buyers and sellers bear its burden. In fact, in the example we have shown in Exhibit 10.10, the incidence on consumers is equivalent to 50 percent of the tax, even though the tax was placed on sellers!

Let's return to the government officials in New Orleans, who now face another challenge. After the tax is in place for only a few months, the local merchants begin to clamor. They are unhappy with paying the $2 tax. In a town hall meeting, the merchants hatch a seemingly clever plan: "Because most of our patrons are from out of town, let's tax *buyers* $2 for every plate of jambalaya that they purchase. This way, they—not us—will pay for our new park." The town officials, anxious to placate the restaurant owners, think this is a great idea. They immediately repeal the tax on restaurants and impose it on consumers. They conclude that since buyers are now responsible for paying the tax, sellers should be much better off. Is this true?

Exhibit 10.11 helps us to answer this question. In panel (a) of the exhibit, we see that the $2 tax on every plate of jambalaya creates a new (virtual) demand curve for jambalaya, labeled D$_{tax}$.

We construct this virtual demand curve by subtracting $2 from the price associated with every quantity on the pre-tax demand curve D. Indeed, now when producers charge $5.50 consumers in addition have to pay a tax of $2 and thus face a total cost of $7.50. We can once again calculate the new equilibrium, the deadweight losses, and tax incidence.

Upon doing so, you will see that the equilibrium quantity is the same as in panel (b) of Exhibit 10.10: 2,500 plates are sold per day (consumers pay $7.50, and suppliers get $5.50 per plate). And here is the important point: the deadweight loss, again represented by the yellow triangle, is also identical—equal to $1,500. Let's again compute tax incidence: the incidence on consumers—the portion of tax revenue that lies above the pre-tax equilibrium price (in this case, $6.50)—is given by the same green rectangle. The incidence on producers—the portion of the tax revenue that lies below the pre-tax equilibrium price—is

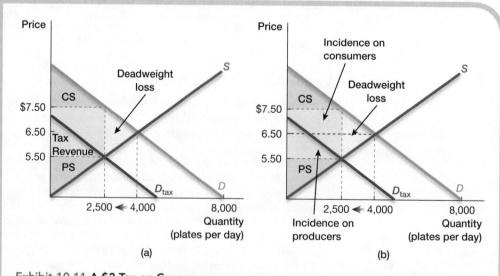

Exhibit 10.11 A $2 Tax on Consumers

When the $2 tax is imposed on consumers, we see that the post-tax equilibrium is the same quality as in the case where the $2 tax rate was imposed on sellers. The sizes of the consumer and producer surpluses, tax revenue, and deadweight loss are also the same as in Exhibit 10.10. Panel (b) shows that, perhaps even more strikingly, 50 percent of the incidence is on consumers and 50 percent is on sellers, just as in Exhibit 10.10. This illustrates a more general phenomenon: in competitive markets, tax incidence, as well as the equilibrium, is independent of whether the tax is imposed on consumers or sellers.

also the same green rectangle. Remarkably, the outcome is identical to the case in which the tax was imposed on producers!

We seem to have stumbled across a conundrum. Notice that the incidence of the tax on producers doesn't change even though under the original tax system jambalaya producers had to pay the government, whereas in the new tax system, consumers have to pay the government. Why doesn't it change? It's because in the first case, when producers of jambalaya were taxed, menu prices rose from $6.50 to $7.50. Thus, consumers paid $7.50 per plate and producers' net revenue was $5.50 ($7.50 − $2 tax) per plate. In the second case, when consumers are directly taxed, the equilibrium menu price decreases to $5.50 because of the consequences of the tax. Thus, again producers receive $5.50 per plate in net revenues, but because of the tax, consumers pay a total of $7.50 for every dish of jambalaya they consume.

We are encountering a general phenomenon here: in competitive markets, tax incidence and equilibrium prices and quantities are independent of whether the tax is imposed on consumers or producers.

> **In competitive markets, tax incidence and equilibrium prices and quantities are independent of whether the tax is imposed on consumers or producers.**

The Effects of Demand and Supply Elasticities on the Tax Burden   The fact that the incidence of the tax is identical for buyers and sellers in the examples above is due to how we drew the market demand and market supply curves. That is, buyers and sellers were equally as sensitive to price changes at the original equilibrium. However, in general, the elasticity of market demand will *not* be identical to the elasticity of market supply.

CHOICE & CONSEQUENCE

The Deadweight Loss Depends on the Tax

Prime Minister Margaret Thatcher and President Ronald Reagan shared views on many taxation policies.

The deadweight losses of taxation imply that for every dollar of tax raised, the cost is greater than a dollar. This is what the economist Arthur Okun called the "leaky bucket"—the government finds that it must pour in more than one gallon of revenue to finance one gallon of services.[2]

But some types of taxes might create fewer leakages than others. *Lump-sum taxes*, which are taxes that require every citizen to pay the same amount, regardless of his or her circumstances, typically create fewer leakages than

taxes on income or transactions. This is because they do not introduce the gap that leads to the deadweight loss of taxation shown in Exhibits 10.10 and 10.11. Imagine that the government imposed a lump-sum tax on all residents of New Orleans rather than the tax on plates of jambalaya; then the equilibrium in the jambalaya market would not be subject to the tax distortions we saw there. With lump-sum taxes, all citizens in an economy would pay the government the same fee—say, $5,000—regardless of their earnings or market demand. Such taxes do not distort behavior and therefore there is no deadweight loss associated with imposition of such taxes. Although such taxes are rare, there are examples in practice. For example, during the third administration of Prime Minister Margaret Thatcher, the government in Great Britain enacted a law in 1989 requiring local authorities to replace their system of local property taxes with a lump-sum head or poll tax. Every adult would now pay the same amount of tax, called the Community Charge, to the local government, with the amount determined by each locality. In practice, these types of taxes are rarely used because they go against one of the major objectives of governments: redistribution.

As we have seen, governments often tax so as to redistribute away from the rich and toward the poor, the disabled, or the elderly. But lump-sum taxes force rich and poor people to pay the same amount—and thus incur a higher tax rate on the poor. They are thus regressive taxes.

Exhibit 10.12 Tax Incidence When Supply Is More Elastic than Demand

Tax incidence falls more on the inelastic part of the market. In panel (a), tax incidence falls equally on consumers and sellers. In panel (b), we keep the demand curve the same, but consider a more elastic (flatter) supply curve. Now tax incidence falls much more on consumers.

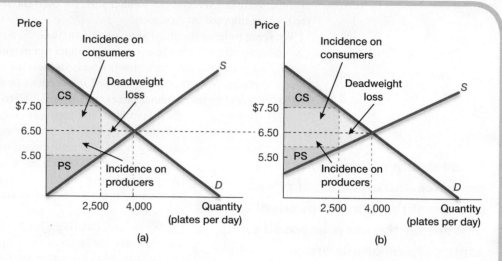

(a)

(b)

Exhibit 10.12 provides an illustrative example. Panel (a) of the exhibit shows the market for jambalaya using the same figures as in the example above. In panel (b) of the exhibit, we make the market supply curve more elastic than the market demand curve. This means that sellers are more responsive to price changes than buyers.

Panel (b) reveals that when the supply curve becomes more elastic, a smaller portion of tax revenue lies below the pre-tax market price. So buyers bear more of the tax burden because the market supply curve is more elastic than the market demand curve.

What would happen if we reverse the situation and make the demand curve more elastic than the supply curve? Exhibit 10.13 provides the answer: now it is the producers who bear more of the burden of the tax.

This leads us to a general rule:

The tax burden falls less heavily on the side of the market that is more elastic—that is, more responsive to price changes. When supply is more elastic than demand, the tax burden falls more heavily on buyers. When demand is more elastic than supply, the tax burden falls more heavily on sellers.

The intuition behind why this is true revolves around what an elasticity measures. Recall that when buyers are more price-elastic, they have more alternatives to turn to. Thus, when the price rises, they can easily switch to purchasing another good. If buyers

Exhibit 10.13 Tax Incidence When Demand Is More Elastic than Supply

Tax incidence falls more on the inelastic part of the market (again). In panel (a), tax incidence falls equally on consumers and sellers. In panel (b), we keep the supply curve the same, but consider a more elastic (flatter) demand curve. Now tax incidence falls more on the sellers.

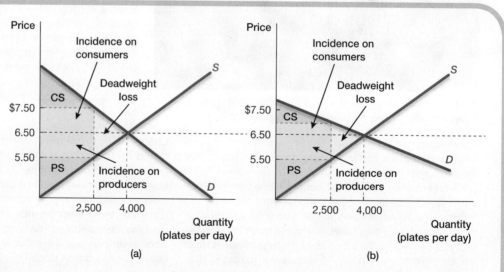

(a)

(b)

are price-inelastic, or not sensitive to price changes, they have few good alternatives. Thus, they must "swallow" the higher price and continue to purchase the taxed good despite the higher price. This means that the more elastic buyer will bear less of the price increase than the less elastic buyer. The same logic applies to the producer side.

There is another impact of elasticities on the tax burden, which can also be seen from Exhibits 10.12 and 10.13: as supply or demand becomes more price-elastic, the deadweight loss of taxation increases. This means that the greater the price elasticity of either supply or demand, the greater the deadweight loss, all things being equal.

10.2 | Regulation

Regulation refers to actions by the federal or local government directed at influencing market outcomes, such as the quantity traded of a good or service, its price, or its quality and safety.

The main tool that governments use to deal with externalities and other market failures is *regulation* (including direct regulation and price controls). **Regulation** refers to actions by the federal or local government directed at influencing market outcomes, such as the quantity traded of a good or service, its price, or safety. This also may involve antitrust activities preventing some firms from exercising excessive monopoly power, as well as activities that are useful for enforcing laws and property rights and resolving disputes to improve the market allocation of resources. We saw in Chapter 9 how the government can use Pigouvian taxes and subsidies to correct externalities. In many instances, however, the government often directly regulates the activity that creates negative externalities. For example, governments typically prevent firms from dumping hazardous waste into rivers rather than simply taxing them. Governments also often use regulation to limit the market power of certain firms, which, by creating a departure from competitive markets, constitutes another major source of market failures, as we discuss in Chapter 12. In this section, we look at direct regulation and price controls as used by the government to affect market outcomes.

Direct Regulation

Direct regulation, or **command-and-control regulation**, refers to direct actions by the government to control the amount of a certain activity.

A common form of government intervention in markets is **direct regulation** (or **command-and-control regulation**, as discussed in Chapter 9 in regards to pollution). Direct regulation, or commandand-control regulation, refers to direct actions by the government to control the amount of a certain activity. Direct regulations affect just about every walk of life, from the safety of foods and drugs to the miles per gallon our automobiles achieve to when we can drop out of school. In many cases, such regulations serve important purposes. For example, consider a prominent regulator of the quality of goods: the Food and Drug Administration (FDA). The FDA represents one of the most complex bureaucracies in the United States, employing 9,000 people and operating on a budget of approximately $2 billion per year. It is not a perfect organization. Far from it—it is often blamed, sometimes deservedly, for being slow to allow new drugs to reach the market as rapidly as they should. Nevertheless, the FDA does play an important role. It makes sure that drugs that are marketed do, in fact, have the functions that they are supposed to have. The FDA is also charged with preventing fly-by-night companies from selling snake oil, so to speak, to unsuspecting consumers.

This type of regulation, aimed at ensuring that complex products meet certain quality and disclosure requirements, would be difficult to leave to the market itself, as it would be costly for each consumer to obtain such information. If each consumer had to individually verify that a drug was safe to take, it would lead to a massive duplication of effort.

Though regulation plays an indispensable role in modern society, it has costs and limitations. Consider a quick thought experiment on quantity regulations. Quantity regulations, which include fishing quotas, zoning restrictions, antismoking laws, and blue laws (laws that restrict liquor sales on Sundays), can be found throughout any market economy. Let's assume now that the government determines that there is a shortage of physicists. In fact, it pronounces that because of the positive externalities that physicists bestow on society we should have 5,000 more of them. It proceeds to use quantity regulation to choose 5,000 people to become physicists, without any market mechanism to guide those choices. Would this approach yield an efficient result?

Likely not. Unlike market forces that guide resources to their best use, this type of command system would probably fail miserably. The reason is that a gifted artist or a dedicated bond trader might be forced into a career solving complicated mathematical equations for which they have no particular talent. As we learned in Chapter 9, a Pigouvian subsidy is a viable alternative because it uses market forces to encourage people at the margin to internalize the externality. If there is an appropriately chosen subsidy to becoming a physicist, then it won't be random people who choose to enter physics, but those who had the talent to become a physicist and yet were previously indifferent between, say, a career as a bond trader and one as a physicist, thus attracting the right people into this profession.

Price Controls: Price Ceilings and Price Floors   As we discussed in Chapter 7, sometimes the government intervenes in a market directly by setting a maximum or minimum price for which goods and services sell. Such intervention to regulate prices is called price controls. Here we examine two types of price controls—price ceilings and price floors.

Price Ceilings   A **price ceiling** is a cap on the price of a market good or service. One important example is rent control—referring to the maximum amount that landlords can charge renters or the maximum amount by which they can increase rent. Rent controls are often introduced partly as a redistributive tool—because renters are typically poorer than landlords and wind up spending a large portion of their incomes on rent.

In the United States, rent controls began during World War I and remain in many cities today, including New York City, San Francisco, Los Angeles, and Washington, D.C. The idea of rent control is noble. However, economic analysis shows that rent control does create important inefficiencies; some of these may help potential renters and others may not. Thus a careful economic analysis is necessary for evaluating the benefits and costs of rent control.

Consider the case of small apartments in San Francisco. In an effort to help renters, let's say that the local government places a price control on apartments in the form of a price ceiling. You can see in Exhibit 10.14 that without rent control, the equilibrium is a rent of $1,200 per month and 4,000 apartments are rented. Now consider a rent control imposing a price ceiling of $750 per month. What are the implications of this regulation?

Exhibit 10.14 helps us answer this question. At $750 per month, shown by the black line, the quantity supplied (Q_S) decreases to 2,500 units. At this lower rent, quantity demanded (Q_D) has increased to 5,500 units. In consequence, there is now a *shortage* of 3,000 apartment units at the price of $750: (5,500 − 2,500 = 3,000). Landlords won't supply as many apartments at the lower rate of $750 as they would at the price of $1,200. For instance, at $750, rather than rent, they might use some apartments as a secondary residence for themselves. At the same time, more renters will want to rent at the lower price, but there won't be

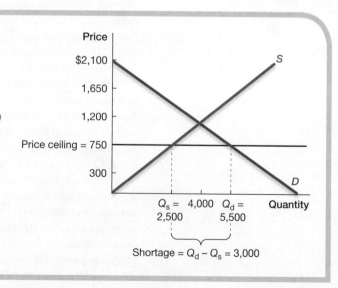

Exhibit 10.14 The Effect of a Price Ceiling

Without rent control, the intersection of the market supply and market demand curves for apartments leads to an equilibrium at the price of $1,200 per month and 4,000 units are rented. A rent control imposing a price ceiling of $750 reduces the rent per unit to $750 but also creates a shortage of 3,000 apartments: at this lower price, the quantity demanded increases to 5,500 units, while landlords, moving down the supply curve, reduce the quantity supplied to 2,500.

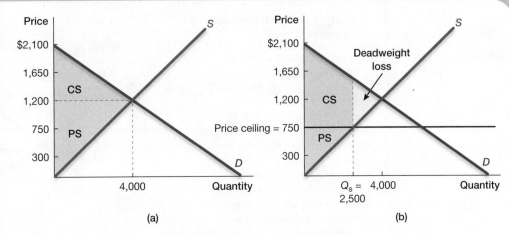

Exhibit 10.15 Consumer and Producer Surplus with Rent Controls

Without rent control, the equilibrium is at a rent of $1,200 per month, and panel (a) shows that the consumer surplus is given by the area shaded blue and the producer surplus by the area shaded pink. Panel (b) depicts the situation after rent control at $750 per month. Producer surplus falls because landlords receive only $750 rent for 2,500 units (this can be seen with a smaller shaded pink triangle). Consumer surplus depends on which ones of the 5,500 potential renters get the 2,500 units on the market at the rent of $750 per month. Panel (b) draws the consumer surplus under the assumption that those with the highest willingness to pay are the first in line for apartments. Even in that best case scenario, the sum of consumer and producer surpluses is less than in panel (a), and the difference is the deadweight loss created by rent control shown as the yellow triangle.

as many apartments available. There is excess demand. What we conclude is that the price ceiling has caused an inefficiently low quantity of apartments to be available.

As we discussed in Chapter 7, this shortage caused by the government-imposed rent control carries a cost—a deadweight loss. Panel (a) of Exhibit 10.15 shows consumer and producer surplus before the government imposes a price ceiling. Panel (b) shows the situation after government-imposed regulation, assuming that among the renters, those with a greater willingness to pay are first in line to get an apartment. Under this assumption, the 2,500 units go to the 2,500 consumers with the highest willingness to pay. The resulting deadweight loss is shown by the yellow triangle in the exhibit.

You might ask yourself: if rent control is so clearly welfare-reducing, why do we have it in practice? One reason is that it does not reduce everybody's welfare. As you can see by comparing panels (a) and (b) in Exhibit 10.15, consumer surplus is higher under the rent control (panel (b)) than without the rent control (panel (a)). In addition, if those renters are also poor and the government wished to redistribute income from more well-to-do landlords toward this group, rent control will have achieved this goal. But of course, some renters are hurt by the rent control: fewer of them are now able to find an apartment. Moreover, rent control may discourage landlords from maintaining apartments since even a poorly maintained apartment will find takers in the market with a shortage of apartments.

When Price Ceilings Have No Bite   Consider what would happen if a large manufacturing plant in Oakland expanded and hired thousands of people from San Francisco. Now many people want to live in Oakland rather than San Francisco. The demand curve for rental units in San Francisco shifts leftward, as shown in Exhibit 10.16. This shift of the demand curve leads to an equilibrium market price of $600 corresponding to the intersection of the new demand curve and the original supply curve. Now the government regulation has no bite because this price is below the price ceiling of $750. As you can see in Exhibit 10.16, the only time price ceilings have an effect on the market is when they are *below* the market clearing price.

Price Floors   Sometimes the government steps in to impose a minimum price on a product or service. The result is a **price floor**, which represents a lower limit on the

A **price floor** is a lower limit on the price of a market good.

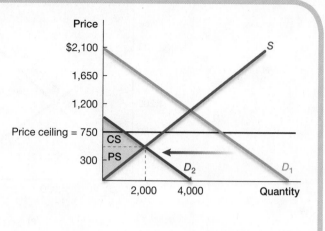

Exhibit 10.16 A Leftward Shift of the Demand Curve

If the demand curve for apartments shifts to the left, so that without rent control the intersection between the market supply and market demand curves would now be at a rent of $600 per month, then the rent control regulation at $750 a month would have no bite because the price ceiling is now above the price that would prevail in the absence of the rent control.

price of the product or service. A prominent example of price floors is that of minimum wage requirements. Minimum wage laws were first enacted in New Zealand in 1894, and now more than 90 percent of all countries have them. In the United States, the federal government has set a minimum wage of $7.25 per hour, meaning that it is the lowest wage an employer may pay a worker (workers receiving tip income can be paid $2.13 per hour). Several states have minimum wage laws prescribing that within their boundaries employers have to pay even more. For example, in the state of Illinois, employers must pay workers at least $8 per hour.

A price floor has similar implications to those of a price ceiling, except that instead of a shortage, a price floor causes a surplus—quantity supplied at a price floor would typically be greater than quantity demanded. Because price floors tend to keep the price artificially high, surplus is shifted from consumers to producers. Thus, a price floor not only has deadweight loss but also reallocates surplus to sellers.

10.3 Government Failures

We have now seen several ways in which governments may intervene in the economic system. Though many of these interventions have well-defined, worthy objectives and some of them are essential for the proper functioning of markets we have seen that they also create a range of inefficiencies that need to be taken into account. Those include deadweight losses of taxation or inefficiencies from price controls or direct regulations. Those who hold that the role of the government in the economy should be minimized emphasize not only these costs but also a broader set of inefficiencies associated with government interventions, sometimes also called **government failures**, which need to be weighed against the market failures that the governments are correcting. In this section, we outline some of these costs.

Government failures refer to inefficiencies caused by a government's interventions.

The Direct Costs of Bureaucracies

Every government program needs bureaucrats and bureaucracies to monitor its implementation. Bureaucrats have to be paid. They are also taken out of the productive sectors of the economy. That is, instead of working at a manufacturing plant or as a manager at Amazon.com, the bureaucrats are engaged in regulation or tax collection. This observation does not suggest that bureaucrats are unproductive at what they do—they implement regulation. However, in the absence of regulation, these workers would have been productive in other jobs, and this lost production represents the opportunity cost of government work.

In this way, the allocation of time and talent of individuals to bureaucracy is an important cost of government. This cost is increased by the fact that bureaucracies sometimes don't function efficiently. Though the various government agencies employ many well-intentioned and efficient individuals, there are long lines, arbitrary decisions, and always a few not-so-helpful employees. These are the kinds of inefficiencies we have come to expect from big bureaucracies. Government intervention in the form of direct regulation may also entail similar costs as firms and their employees work to meet certain government-set objectives rather than creating goods and services.

Corruption

Corruption refers to the misuse of public funds or the distortion of the allocation of resources for personal gain.

Equally as important as the deadweight losses associated with government intervention and the inefficiencies of bureaucracies is the **corruption** that large governments engender. Corruption refers to the misuse of public funds or the distortion of the allocation of resources for personal gain. Consider one example—the billions of dollars that go annually to African governments as foreign aid. In the last 60 years, more than $1 trillion has been transferred from developed countries to Africa, and foreign aid to all countries in 2011 exceeded $130 billion. Much of it comes from governments of developed nations and a significant portion from charities.

But only a small fraction of this money ever reaches its target audience. Economists have estimated that the amount of money that actually reaches its intended destination may be as little as from 5 percent to 15 percent—that means as little as a nickel of every dollar that you send reaches the recipient! Some of the lost aid is eaten up by the inefficiencies of the bureaucracies that operate the foreign aid machine, and even more is appropriated by corrupt politicians and bureaucrats. For example, a recent study found that only 13 percent of education grants reached schools (and most schools received no aid) in Uganda.[3] This type of corruption is extreme, but not unusual.

You might be thinking that corruption is not an issue in developed countries, where there is a good system of checks and balances and watchdog agencies waiting for a public official to misstep are everywhere. The evidence suggests otherwise. For instance, in the United States, corruption is not difficult to find. In 2008, 15 sitting congressmen or senators (and 9 former members of the Senate or the House of Representatives) were under criminal investigation, mostly for inappropriately using public funds or gifts from businesses that constituted conflicts of interest.

If we consider the number of convictions of public officials across states, similar insights are gained. For instance, from 1977 to 1987 there were roughly 800 corruption convictions per year.[4] The most corrupt state, New York, had roughly 50 times more corruption convictions than the average state during that time period. Such corruption levels continue unabated across states today. In 2008, the Department of Justice reported that 1,129 federal, state, and local employees had been convicted on corruption charges. In spite of recent drama, New York is no longer the heavyweight champion of corruption though—Florida actually leads all states in convictions from 1999 to 2008.

All in all, we cannot expect the government to function as seamlessly as the exhibits in this chapter indicate. The government will often make mistakes, the bureaucracy will be inefficient and slow, and politicians can be corrupt, seeking to capture the process of decision making and exploiting it for their own benefit or their own ideological ends. When evaluating government policies, these costs of government have to be considered. How

"Now THAT is a thin line. Let's ignore it."

these costs weigh against the benefits of government determine, to a large degree, whether the government is a night watchman or a central commander of resources.

Underground Economy

You have likely seen lawn care workers, snow shovelers, and babysitters handed cash for their work. Or you may have a waiter friend who makes killer tips but does not report them on his taxes. The *underground economy*, sometimes also referred to as the black market, includes activities, such as those above, where income taxes are not paid, as well as illegal activities, such as drug dealing and prostitution.

In modern economies, black markets cover an array of activities and are generally found in areas where the benefits of such activities are the highest—either because of high tax rates or because the activity is illegal and therefore the good is not provided in the formal market.

One prime example of an underground economy created because of an illegal product was the result of Prohibition in the 1920s. After the United States outlawed alcohol in 1919, smugglers arranged deliveries to speakeasies and private bars. The result was an era of big organized crime—think of Al Capone—and an estimated $500 million in lost tax revenues annually. Such an example illustrates some of the problems that an underground economy generates:

1. When they involve goods and services that have been legally banned, the underground economy undermines the ban.
2. When underground transactions occur in markets for legal goods and services in order to avoid taxes or regulations, they put legitimate businesses at a disadvantage.
3. To compensate for the lost revenue, governments must levy higher taxes.
4. Criminals spend vast resources trying to evade the law (and authorities spend resources to catch criminals), which are not effective uses of society's resources.

10.4 Equity Versus Efficiency

The **equity-efficiency trade-off** refers to the trade-off between ensuring an equitable allocation of resources (equity) and increasing social surplus or total output (efficiency).

It is worth emphasizing that despite all these government failures, government intervention often plays important social roles, such as redistributing resources to ensure a more equitable society. The core issue when governments redistribute resources, fully recognizing that this does entail some inefficiencies, revolves around the **equity-efficiency trade-off**. The equity-efficiency trade-off refers to the trade-off between ensuring an equitable allocation of resources (equity) and increasing social surplus or total output (efficiency). Most would agree that equity and efficiency are the two most important goals for government policy.

Exhibit 10.17 depicts the typical trade-off society faces. What it shows is that the two goals—equity and efficiency—are often, but not always, in conflict. When social inequality is high, above the point marked A in the exhibit, further increases in inequality reduce social surplus: as we move up the vertical axis, further increasing social inequality, we also move down the horizontal axis, reducing social surplus. This could be for several reasons: for example, greater social inequality prevents some people from competing with others on a level playing field or increases conflict in society, creating distortions via this channel. But for levels of social inequality below point A, further declines in inequality also come at the cost of lower social surplus, for example, because of the deadweight losses involved in redistributive taxation. Now as we limit social inequality moving down the vertical axis, we also move down the horizontal axis, reducing social surplus. This trade-off between equity and efficiency represents the nub of the conflict between those who support big government and those who call for smaller government.

> The trade-off between equity and efficiency represents the nub of the conflict between those who support big government and those who call for smaller government.

Where do you want to be along this curve? This is a decision problem that social welfare-maximizing governments have to confront. But economic analysis informs us on how the government can do this best. For instance, economic analysis helps us understand where point A is located, beyond which there is no trade-off between reducing social inequality and reducing social surplus. Below this point, however, the choice crucially depends on value judgments. Some people would prefer to live in a fairly efficient society even if this

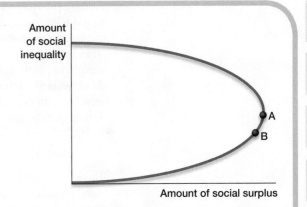

Exhibit 10.17 The Equity–Efficiency Trade-off

The government can often achieve greater social equality but only at the expense of greater inefficiencies, thus introducing a trade-off between equity and efficiency over a certain range. When social inequality is very high, there may be no conflict between equity and efficiency.

comes at the cost of considerable social inequality (corresponding to a point like B). Others would be willing to put up with greater inefficiencies and lower social surplus in order to achieve greater equality (approaching the origin). In a broad sense, the portion of the curve between the origin and point A represents the dividing line between Democrats and Republicans: Presidents Clinton and Obama have emphasized the importance of reducing social inequality, for example, arguing that the rich need to pay more in taxes. Presidents Reagan and George W. Bush, on the other hand, have argued that high tax rates distort decisions and have opted for tax reforms based on efficiency grounds.

The actual fact is that all developed nations seek to achieve some degree of equality in their society. The **welfare state** refers to the set of insurance, regulation, and transfer programs utilized to create a safety net, reduce poverty, and redistribute income from the rich to the poor. In the United States, for example, the welfare state comprises several programs, such as Medicaid and food stamps, which are targeted to the poor. The welfare state is even more expansive in Europe. Despite the deadweight loss associated with such systems, many European nations choose to promote some degree of equality in income.

> The **welfare state** refers to the set of insurance, regulation, and transfer programs operated by the government, including unemployment benefits, pensions, and government-run and financed healthcare.

10.5 Consumer Sovereignty and Paternalism

Beyond promoting equality, some economists have argued that government intervention is necessary because individuals may suffer from decision errors or may find it difficult to evaluate certain choices. For example, many people do not have the finance background necessary to navigate the world of retirement savings account options. In such situations, they can make mistakes that are costly to themselves. Should the government try to prevent them from making such mistakes?

One answer as to whether the government should engage in these types of actions relates to the concept of **consumer sovereignty**. Consumer sovereignty is the view that choices made by a consumer reflect his or her true preferences, and outsiders, including the government, should not interfere with these choices. Some economists argue that we should evaluate all resource allocations according to the preferences of consumers at the time they make a decision. If those preferences are wrong or turn out to be wrong after the fact, so be it.

At the other end of the spectrum is **paternalism**. Paternalism is the view that consumers do not always know what is best for them, and the government should encourage or induce them to change their actions. Many crucial reformers who played important roles in the founding of the welfare state, from William Beveridge in the United Kingdom to Franklin Delano Roosevelt and Lyndon Johnson in the United States, hold this view. This approach gives the government an active hand in helping individuals make the right decisions and in designing choices so that people make the right decisions when they are unlikely to do so by themselves.

The Social Security system in the United States, which forces individuals to save for old age, is born out of paternalism. Laws that ban substance abuse are also motivated, in

> **Consumer sovereignty** is the view that choices made by a consumer reflect his or her true preferences, and outsiders, including the government, should not interfere with these choices.

> **Paternalism** is the view that consumers do not always know what is best for them, and the government should encourage or induce them to change their actions.

part, by paternalism. By contrast, in a world with no externalities, consumer sovereignty would allow individuals to consume as many drugs as possible, even if they are addictive and potentially harmful.

In fact, the big difference between paternalism and consumer sovereignty is again a normative one. How much do we value consumer sovereignty in and of itself? And how much do we want to allow the government to interfere in individual decision making? It's a murky area. Nevertheless, economists find their voices on both sides of the debate. We briefly review both sides now.

The Debate

Those economists toward the paternalistic end of the spectrum would probably say that some mistakes simply result from the fact that individuals are not used to making decisions of a certain type. For example, most people, when first confronted with investing in the stock market may not understand the implications of their decisions. One role of this economics course is to educate you in economic decision making. In the same way, those who want government to take an active role would approve of the government's provision of information so that people can make better decisions. In their view, this is not a violation of consumer sovereignty; in fact, it corresponds to a strengthening of it because better decisions are a result of better information.

Some economists go somewhat further and suggest that the government should also play the role of "nudging" individuals in the right direction. If the government is convinced, for example, that individuals are not saving enough for retirement, or are making investment choices that are too risky, then it can design savings schemes to encourage people to save more or to invest in less risky assets.

The pure consumer sovereignty view would be that the government's business is not to "nudge" people into choices they can make on their own. Economists favoring this view would suggest that any kind of paternalism requires that some group of people (the government, the elite, intellectuals) knows what's good for consumers. Although this may sometimes be true, it generally raises several philosophical and practical problems. How can the government make extremely complicated decisions for us? How can we trust the government to really have our interests in mind? How can we distinguish between differences in opinions and preferences and those cases in which people really are making mistakes?

Beyond these questions, it is important to note that every government intervention is costly and paid for by tax revenues. Thus, every activity relinquished to the government increases the deadweight loss that society faces. In the end, we urge you to be the judge of how acceptable you find government intervention in individual choices. It is a normative question.

Evidence-Based Economics

Q: What is the optimal size of government?

As you have probably concluded by now, this question is difficult to answer, because it will depend on your value judgments. We can probably state with some certainty, however, that a minimal amount of government intervention in the economy is necessary. An economy needs some amount of law and order, some national defense, some regulation, some redistribution, and so on. So, most people would agree that government needs to be in the picture in some way.

But that still leaves a broad range, and you have to use your own value judgments to decide where you want to be in that range. Economics can be helpful in guiding you within this range and in deciding on the types of activities in which government should be involved. Rather than answering the question "Is more government good or bad?" economics is useful in helping us evaluate the costs and benefits of government intervention and in suggesting potential ways of designing better government policies.

Let's consider two specific areas to make our general point about how the tools of economics can help you think about the optimal size of government.

1. As we have shown, a major efficiency loss of taxation is deadweight loss. Thus, the debate on the reach of government should hinge on the effect of its actions: the larger the deadweight loss, the worse the policy, all else equal. In those cases with large deadweight losses, one can make the argument that it is a bad place for the government to intervene.

2. The government typically operates in a slow-moving manner. A significant drag on the economy can result if regulators cannot move swiftly in response to changing market conditions.

We now focus on the first of these and then discuss the second in the box at the end of this section.

A first consideration with this approach is that a heavy reliance on income taxation may result in more deadweight loss than a broader spectrum of taxes (federal sales tax, estate taxes, etc.). This is because deadweight loss is increasing geometrically with the tax rate (i.e., all else equal it is better to have many small tax rates rather than one large one because the large one has a lot of deadweight loss). In this sense, when formulating policies we should always compare the marginal deadweight loss of the last dollar raised from different sources of taxation to the marginal benefit of an additional dollar of tax revenue. For a tax that distorts behavior, the marginal benefit may not be worth the deadweight loss, which suggests the need to decrease this tax.

Let's think about the income tax more carefully and see if it distorts people's decision to work. At the extremes......

In the United States, the bulk of tax revenue is raised from income taxes. At the extremes, economists have a pretty good idea of the impact of income taxes on a worker's decision to supply labor. If there is a 100 percent tax on income, then there is really no reason to work—your take-home pay would always be $0! A tax that large is likely to be labeled absolutely inefficient by economists because the cost to society of no one working would be much larger than the tax revenue generated.

But what if the tax rate was closer to present levels of the marginal federal tax rate (25 percent for someone earning $40,000 a year; see Exhibit 10.6)? If Americans get to keep 75 cents of every dollar that they earn, will everyone stop working or will they just carry on as if there were no tax on their income at all? The elasticity of labor supply gives us an easy number to assess this question. Remember that elasticities are just a percentage change in quantity divided by a percentage change in price. In the case of labor supply, the tax rate changes the price of working—how much you get paid—and the quantity is the number of hours worked.

If the supply of labor is elastic, then the number of hours someone works is very sensitive to the wage rate. Thus, an increase in income taxes will have a large impact on labor supply. This lost work will create a lot of deadweight loss. But if labor supply is inelastic, then a tax increase won't cause a big change in the number of hours a worker supplies, which means that the size of the deadweight loss won't be large.

To estimate the elasticity of labor supply, economists have used data taken from workers' responses to large changes in income tax rates. Early empirical studies found that the Reagan tax cuts of the 1980s led to around a 6 percent increase in the number of hours worked—resulting in a relatively large elasticity estimate.[5] However, when economists used richer data sets to estimate the same elasticity, they found a very small elasticity estimate, ranging between 0 and 0.1.[6]

As research progressed, economists began to focus on the impact of tax rates on a worker's reported taxable income. Initial analysis found very high elasticities of between 1.3 and 1.5,[7] but much of the early research on this topic looked only at the *short-run* response to higher marginal tax rates. However, this can be different from the *long-run*

Evidence-Based Economics *(Continued)*

elasticity, because individuals may respond more strongly to a temporary change in taxes (that is, you may want to work more for a year if taxes are very low during that year, but if taxes are very low permanently you may not end up working as hard). Subsequent research focusing on long-run elasticities in fact yielded much smaller estimates.

In general, these estimates suggest that the labor supply results have been decidedly mixed. This is probably why the two views of labor taxation persist today, and why this topic represents an important area for future research. As soon as the estimates begin to point to a smaller elasticity range, economists will be able to provide more precise estimates of the deadweight loss of income taxation.

But the size of government isn't just a question of how inefficient it is to raise tax revenues. Even if there is very little deadweight loss associated with raising taxes, the sorts of government failures discussed above might also tip the scale against government intervention. Quantitative analysis of such government failures is another active area of current research.

Question

What is the optimal size of government?

Answer

It depends, but the deadweight loss of taxation and other costs of government intervention play a key role.

Data

Various data sources, including measures of the elasticity of labor supply.

Caveat

A range of empirical estimates of labor supply elasticities has surfaced.

 LETTING THE DATA SPEAK

The Efficiency of Government Versus Privately Run Expeditions

A glimpse into the possibility that the government may operate more slowly than private, profit-seeking enterprises is provided by a study comparing the success rates of government-funded expeditions to the North Pole and Northwest Passage versus privately funded voyages.[8] The research, conducted by economist Jonathan Karpoff, found that privately funded expeditions were smaller, cheaper, less likely to lose personnel, less likely to lose their ships, and more likely to achieve their objective. Plus, the difference in outcomes between private and public expeditions was large. For example, publicly funded expeditions had an average of 5.9 deaths versus 0.9 deaths per privately funded expeditions.

Karpoff was able to go a step further and see *why* privately funded expeditions were so much more successful than public expeditions. He found that their chief advantage was an ability to adapt to new technology

quickly. Many publicly funded expeditions were so slow to adapt to new technology that they didn't even supplement their crew's diets with vitamin C, even though knowledge of the relationship between scurvy and vitamin C deficiency had been known for centuries. Privately funded expeditions also developed innovations of their own. Chief among these was their ability to learn from the native population about shelter, clothing systems, and overland travel.

This research provides one example of the nimbleness of private voyages compared to that of public voyages. Although not definitive, it provides an example of how the tools of economics can help you think about the optimal extent of government intervention. How general this result is remains a question, but it does illustrate a common criticism of big government: its slow movement can be a drag on economic efficiency.

Summary

⚙ Government can play an important role in ensuring that markets are competitive, efficient, and equitable.

⚙ Key roles of the government include: taxation to raise funds to provide public goods such as national defense, policing, and infrastructure investments that would not be provided adequately by the market; the use of tax and transfer programs in order to achieve a more equitable distribution of resources in society; and the use of taxes and subsidies as well as regulation to correct market failures.

⚙ The costs of government interventions must be compared carefully with their benefits.

⚙ Economics is most useful not as a value judgment on whether government is good or bad, but in understanding what sorts of activities require government intervention.

Key Terms

budget deficit *p. 228*
budget surplus *p. 228*
tax revenues (or receipts) *p. 228*
payroll tax, or social insurance
   tax *p. 228*
corporate income taxes *p. 229*
excise taxes *p. 229*
sales taxes *p. 229*
transfer payments *p. 231*

progressive tax system *p. 231*
average tax rate *p. 231*
marginal tax rate *p. 231*
proportional tax system *p. 231*
regressive tax system *p. 231*
tax incidence *p. 234*
regulation *p. 239*
direct regulation, or command-and-
   control regulation *p. 239*

price ceiling *p. 240*
price floor *p. 241*
government failures *p. 242*
corruption *p. 243*
equity-efficiency trade-off *p. 244*
welfare state *p. 245*
consumer sovereignty *p. 245*
paternalism *p. 245*

Questions

All questions are available in MyEconLab for practice and instructor assignment.

1. When does a government run a budget surplus?

2. Government spending in the United States has grown over time and now accounts for more than 40 percent of U.S. national income. Does this mean that government has been consistently running a budget deficit?

3. How does the federal government raise revenue. What is the largest source of revenue for the federal government? Do state governments raise revenue from the same sources as the federal government?

4. What are the factors underlying government taxation and spending decisions?

5. How do governments use spending and taxation to reduce inequality and poverty in an economy?

6. What are the different types of tax systems? Give one example of each type of tax.

7. What is meant by tax incidence? Is the entire burden of the tax always borne by those on whom it is imposed?

8. Are lump-sum taxes regressive or progressive? Is the deadweight loss of taxation the same for different types of taxes?

9. What is meant by direct regulation? Give a few examples of direct regulation.

10. What are the costs associated with government intervention in an economic system? Given that there are costs involved with government intervention in an economy, why do governments choose to intervene in markets?

11. What is a black market? What types of goods are likely to be traded in a black market? What problems do black markets pose in an economy?

12. How would you depict the trade-off between equity and efficiency on a graph? How would a government decide where it wants to be on this curve?

13. Explain the terms "paternalism" and consumer "sovereignty."

14. Why are there two different views on the effect of taxation on labor supply in the United States?

Problems

All problems are available in MyEconLab for practice and instructor assignment.

1. The following table gives the 2013 federal income tax rates for a single individual.

Income	Rate
$0 to $8,925	10%
$8,925 to $36,250	15%
$36,250 to $87,850	25%
$87,850 to $183,250	28%
$183,250 to $398,350	33%
$398,350 to $400,000	35%
$400,000 and above	39.60%

   a. Calculate the total tax payable for an individual who earns $250,000 a year.

   b. What is the marginal tax rate?

   c. Calculate the average tax rate.

2. Britain taxed windows from 1696 until 1851. Under the 1747–1757 tax rates, you would pay no tax if your home had 0–9 windows, but if your home had 10–14 windows you would pay a tax of 6 pence per window *for every window in your home.*

   a. In what way is the window tax similar to the U.S. income tax?

   b. In what way is the window tax different from the U.S. income tax?

   c. Do you think from 1747–1757 the number of new homes with 9 or fewer windows increased from the pre-1747 days? Explain.

3. Many people have argued that an income tax should be "marriage neutral," that is, two people should pay the same total tax whether they are married or they are single. Suppose Amanda earns nothing, Ben earns $60,000, and Cathy and Dylan each earn $30,000. They are all single.

   a. Amanda pays no tax because she has no income. If they all live in a country that has a progressive income tax, which will be higher: the tax that Ben pays or the sum of the taxes Cathy and Dylan pay?

   b. Amanda marries Ben and Cathy marries Dylan. This country taxes married couples based on a family's total income. Show that the newlyweds Amanda and Ben will pay the same tax as Cathy and Dylan's family.

   c. Is the income tax in this country marriage neutral?

4. The following graph shows the equilibrium price and quantity in the market for chewing gum in the country Argonia. Suppose the government of Argonia passes a bill to impose a tax of 2 Argonian dollars on the production of chewing gum.

   a. What is the new equilibrium price and quantity?

   b. What is the amount of tax revenue earned by the government?

   c. What is the deadweight loss of this tax?

   d. Which is greater: the loss in consumer surplus or the loss in producer surplus?

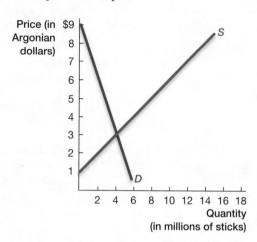

5. The demand and supply schedules in the market for shoes are given in the following table.

Price	Demand	Supply
$1.00	1,000	0
$1.50	900	0
$2.00	800	0
$2.50	700	100
$3.00	600	200
$3.50	500	300
$4.00	400	400
$4.50	300	500
$5.00	200	600

   a. Find the initial equilibrium price and quantity.

   b. Suppose the government imposes a new $1.00/unit tax on the producers of shoes. Find the new equilibrium price and quantity.

   c. Senator Jones has proposed legislation that would change the shoe tax by switching it from the seller to the buyer. If the bill passes, what will be the new equilibrium price and quantity?

   d. Will consumers prefer the original bill, will they prefer the Jones bill, or will they be indifferent between the two bills? Explain.

   e. Will shoe producers prefer the original bill, will they prefer the Jones bill, or will they be indifferent between the two bills? Explain.

6. Suppose the supply and demand curves for a good are linear.

   a. Present and discuss a diagram to show that the deadweight loss from a tax is equal to one-half the product of (1) the tax per unit of the good and (2) the change in the equilibrium quantity of the good as result of the tax.

b. Use your answer to part a to answer the following question. If your goal is to minimize the deadweight loss from a tax, would you tax goods for which demand is elastic or goods for which demand is inelastic, everything else being equal?

7. In the chapter, we focused on the effects of a tax on a good. Now consider a subsidy. In particular, suppose the government pays $2 to the buyers of a good for each unit of the good they purchase. The diagram below shows the demand and supply for this good.

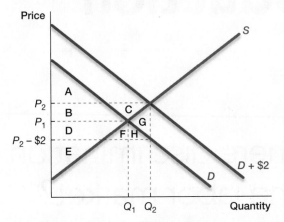

a. Fill in the table to explain how the subsidy affects consumer surplus, producer surplus, tax revenue, and total surplus.

	No Subsidy	$2 Subsidy	Change
Consumer Surplus			
Producer Surplus			
Tax revenue			
Total Surplus			

b. Does this subsidy lead to a deadweight loss?

8. Suppose the supply and demand schedules for cell phones are as follows:

Price	Demand	Supply
$2	10	0
$3	9	0
$4	8	0
$5	7	1
$6	6	2
$7	5	3
$8	4	4
$9	3	5
$10	2	6
$11	1	7
$12	0	8

a. Find the equilibrium price and quantity in the cell phone market.

b. Find consumer surplus, producer surplus, and total surplus in the cell phone market.

c. Suppose the government sets a maximum price (that is, a price ceiling) of $6. How many cell phones are traded in the market at $6?

d. Find consumer surplus, producer surplus, and total surplus now that there is a price ceiling of $6.

e. Find the deadweight loss from the price ceiling.

f. Suppose the government sets a minimum price (that is, a price floor) of $10. How many cell phones are traded in the market at $10?

g. Repeat parts (d) and (e) for this price floor.

9. In an attempt to help the poor, India announced a policy to implement price ceilings on several essential drugs in December 2012. Some industry analysts, however, claimed that this would actually end up hurting the poor more than helping them. Do you think this is a possibility? Explain your answer.

10. Some government agricultural policies involve price controls. Other agricultural policies, however, involve quantity controls.

a. The equilibrium price of wheat is $5 and the equilibrium quantity is 100. Draw a supply and demand diagram that shows the equilibrium in the wheat market.

b. Suppose the government institutes a policy that prohibits wheat farmers from growing more than 80 bushels of wheat in total. How would this policy change the supply curve for wheat?

c. Use your supply and demand diagram to show that the government policy in part b would raise the equilibrium price and lower the equilibrium quantity of wheat.

d. Show that the policy in part (b) will lead to a deadweight loss in the wheat market.

11. New York levies the highest cigarette tax in the country—$5.85 per pack. Other states in the United States impose taxes that are much lower. The state of Virginia levies a tax of 30 cents per pack, which is the second lowest after Missouri. How would this explain the thriving black market for cigarettes in New York?

12. The Internal Revenue Service defines the estate tax as a tax on your right to transfer property at your death. The fair market value of the estate is taken into account when levying the tax. Once the gross value of the tax is computed, certain deductions are allowed to arrive at the value of the taxable estate. What do you think are the equity and efficiency implications of imposing an estate tax?

11 Markets for Factors of Production

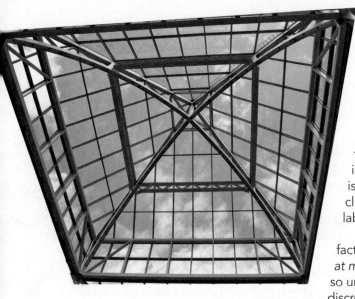

Is there discrimination in the labor market?

As she withdrew her nomination from the 2008 Democratic primary, Senator Hillary Rodham Clinton noted that "although we weren't able to shatter that highest, hardest glass ceiling this time, thanks to you it's got about eighteen thousand cracks in it." The "glass ceiling" that she referred to implies that there is a limit to how far certain individuals—in this case, women—can climb in the workforce. Does a glass ceiling really exist in the U.S. labor market?

As always, data help us answer the question. One interesting fact is that over the past several decades, women have represented *at most 3 percent* of U.S. CEOs. Why do women appear to be so underrepresented in the upper echelons of companies? Is the discrepancy because of discrimination against women? Is it because they tend to take time away from working to raise their children?

The lack of women at the top of companies is only the tip of the iceberg when it comes to differences across people in labor markets. For example, in the past several decades, for every dollar men earned, women earned roughly 80 cents. Similar differences are found when comparing people of different race, age, and even physical attractiveness!

Can economics explain such differences?

CHAPTER **OUTLINE**

☼ The three main factors of production are labor, physical capital, and land.

☼ Firms derive the demand for labor by determining the value of marginal product of labor.

☼ The supply of labor is determined by trading off the marginal benefit from labor given by earnings against the marginal cost, the value of foregone leisure.

☼ Wage inequality can be attributed to differences in human capital, differences in compensating wages, and discrimination in the job market.

☼ In addition to labor, a producer must derive the demand for physical capital and land to achieve its production objectives.

So far, we have focused our attention on goods that we as consumers buy: cell phones, cheese boxes, cakes, and electricity. In this chapter we examine what producers buy: *inputs to produce those goods*. The major inputs that we will consider are labor, machines (physical capital), and land. In so doing, we explore reasons why people earn different wages in the labor market, and why some rise to the top while others remain at mid-level. Our discussion of the labor market will bring us to a general understanding of the determinants of wages. When thinking about how well our model represents the real world, we will return to our opening question.

11.1 The Competitive Labor Market

The market for labor is of particular importance in the economy because it affects all of us. You are directly influenced by the labor market when you are looking for a job or are employed and earning money. In this chapter, instead of firms acting as suppliers, as we have seen so far, firms are the buyers (demanders) of labor. And, individuals, like you, are the suppliers of labor.

The market for labor, then, is composed of suppliers (workers) and demanders (firms). Workers produce goods and services and therefore are known as factors of production—a term we've met before in Chapter 6. Remember that a factor of production is used in the production of other goods.

The markets for factors of production are somewhat different from markets for goods and services that we consume because the demand for factors of production is *derived* from the demand for final goods and services. A firm first makes the decision to produce a good or service and then decides which factors to use to produce that good or service.

Although firms tend to use many factors of production, the main factors that we will focus on are labor, machines (physical capital), and land. For instance, consider the iPad. To produce it, Apple uses labor (in the form of computer hardware and software engineers), physical capital (in the form of machinery to build the good), and land (from Cupertino, California to Chengdu, China to house its various production sites).

In the market for labor, the roles of demander and supplier are reversed: Businesses are buyers (demanders) of labor and individual workers are suppliers.

All firms rely on labor as a major factor of production.

The Demand for Labor

A typical firm in modern economies uses dozens, likely hundreds, of different machines, ranging from computers to lasers to old-fashioned assembly lines. Nevertheless, all firms rely on labor as a major factor of production. Workers operate machines and often perform tasks more efficiently than machines because human beings have judgment skills that machines still lack. In this sense, a firm's desire to achieve its production objectives causes it to demand labor.

Let us return to The Wisconsin Cheeseman, the cheese-packing firm we discussed in Chapter 6. We'll begin by holding fixed the other factors of production that this company uses—physical capital and land—and focus exclusively on labor. That is, we will focus on the short-run decisions facing The Cheeseman. We'll also assume that this company is a price-taker in the product market.

We saw in Chapter 6 that The Wisconsin Cheeseman can increase the production of cheese boxes by employing more people. Exhibit 11.1 shows the relationship between the number of cheese boxes produced and the number of workers employed. The numbers that underlie the figure are shown in Exhibit 11.2. Exhibits 11.1 and 11.2 make clear the Law of Diminishing Returns, which we studied in Chapter 6. Recall that this law states that the marginal productivity of an additional unit of labor eventually decreases as we increase the number of workers.

The **value of marginal product of labor** is the contribution of an additional worker to a firm's revenues.

From Chapter 6, we are familiar with the first three columns in Exhibit 11.2. For example, column (3) gives the marginal product of labor. This informs us of how many more cheese boxes will be produced when The Cheeseman hires another worker. When we multiply this number by the price of cheese boxes, we obtain the **value of marginal product of labor (VMPL)**. The *VMPL* is the contribution of an additional worker to a firm's revenues; it is equal to the marginal product of labor times the price of a cheese box. For mathematical clarity, we assume the price of a cheese box is $2, so column (4) obtains the value of marginal product of labor by multiplying the number in column (3) with 2.

Now assume that The Wisconsin Cheeseman currently employs 14 workers and is considering expanding its workforce. Exhibit 11.2 shows that the value of the marginal product of the 15th worker is $110 per day (additional revenue = *VMPL* = 55 additional boxes of cheese × $2 per box = $110). If The Cheeseman is maximizing its profits, should it hire the 15th worker?

Let's start with a daily wage of $118. Should The Cheeseman expand to the 15th worker? No. We know this because the value of adding the last worker is his *VMPL*—$110 for the 15th worker. It is not profitable to pay a worker $118 who brings in only an additional $110 in revenues.

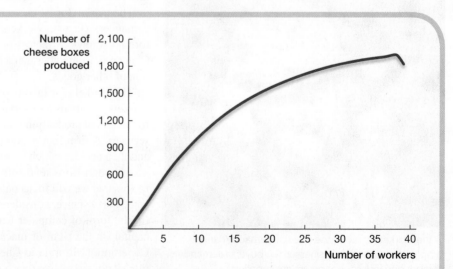

Exhibit 11.1 The Cheeseman's Production Function

The production function describes the number of cheese boxes that The Cheeseman can produce by hiring additional workers. Crucially, eventually each additional worker that The Cheeseman hires has a smaller incremental effect on the number of cheese boxes produced, demonstrating the Law of Diminishing Returns.

Exhibit 11.2 Production Data for The Wisconsin Cheeseman

The Cheeseman is tasked with choosing how much output to generate per day and how many employees to hire to produce that level of output. The table summarizes the number of workers the firm will need for any given level of output and how much value each additional worker adds. Column 1 shows cheese boxes produced per day, column 2 shows number of workers employed, column 3 shows the marginal output produced by each additional worker, and column 4 shows the *VMPL*, which denotes the value of marginal product of labor. This represents the dollar value of this additional output.

(1) Output per Day	(2) Number of Workers Employed	(3) Marginal Product	(4) VMPL = MPL × P = Column (3) × $2
0	0		
100	1	100	$ 200
207	2	107	$ 214
321	3	114	$ 228
444	4	123	$ 246
558	5	114	$ 228
664	6	106	$ 212
762	7	98	$ 196
854	8	92	$ 184
939	9	85	$ 170
1,019	10	80	$ 160
1,092	11	73	$ 146
1,161	12	69	$ 138
1,225	13	64	$ 128
1,284	14	59	$ 118
1,339	15	55	$ 110
1,390	16	51	$ 102
1,438	17	48	$ 96
.	.	.	
.	.	.	
.	.	.	
1,934	38	10	$ 20
1,834	39	−100	$−200

What about at a daily wage of $105? Now the story changes. Hiring the 15th worker increases profits because the daily wage is less than the additional revenue of $110. The implication is that for The Cheeseman to be optimally purchasing labor—not paying more than it's worth—it expands its workforce until the *VMPL* = wage.

This optimizing action enables us to translate the value of marginal product of the firm into its labor demand. Exhibit 11.3 illustrates the labor demand of The Wisconsin Cheeseman, which traces the value of marginal product shown in Exhibit 11.2. The labor demand curve of a firm is downward-sloping because its value of marginal product is decreasing—a consequence of the Law of Diminishing Returns. In Exhibit 11.3, we assume that the market wage rate is $110 per day. At this wage, the optimal number of workers for The Cheeseman to hire is 15, where the demand for labor intersects the market wage.

Two ideas are implicit in this derivation, and it is useful to spell them out. First, The Wisconsin Cheeseman sells its cheese boxes in a competitive market, and therefore from

Exhibit 11.3 Demand for Labor

We can depict the quantity of labor demanded at each wage rate. In orange, we assume that the marginal cost of an additional worker is $110. This allows us to identify the equilibrium quantity of 15 employees, where *VMPL* = wage.

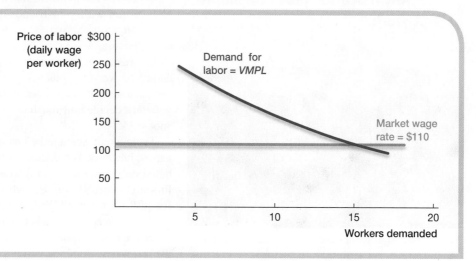

Chapter 6 we know that it can sell as many cheese boxes as it wants at the market price. Second, we assume that the labor market is also competitive, so The Cheeseman can hire as many workers as it wishes at the market wage.

We have now seen two ways in which a firm like The Wisconsin Cheeseman maximizes its profits:

1. In Chapter 6, it chose the total quantity of production in order to maximize profits, and we saw that this led to the condition: expand production until marginal cost = price.

2. In this chapter, we see that the firm maximizes profits by optimally choosing its labor by expanding its workforce until the *marginal product of labor × price = VMPL = wage.*

How do these two conditions relate to each other? Do they conflict? That is, does a competitive firm struggle to optimize the number of employees it hires while simultaneously optimizing its output?

Reassuringly, these two conditions are *identical*: once one is in place, the other follows. To see this, divide both sides of

$$\text{Marginal product of labor} \times \text{Price} = \text{Wage}.$$

by the marginal product of labor (MPL), which leads to

$$\text{Price} = \frac{\text{Wage}}{\text{MPL}}.$$

This is simply the wage divided by the marginal product of labor. Say that an additional worker costs $110 per day and has a marginal product of 55 boxes of cheese. In this case, producing 55 more cheese boxes costs $110. Thus, the marginal cost is $110/55, or $2. This shows that wage/MPL equals marginal cost. Therefore,

$$\text{Marginal cost} = \frac{\text{Wage}}{\text{MPL}} = \text{Price}.$$

This derivation shows that when The Wisconsin Cheeseman expands its workforce until *VMPL = wage*, it is also producing where price = marginal cost.

11.2 The Supply of Labor: Your Labor-Leisure Trade-off

> You must decide how much to work and how much to "play" or simply "not work."

Would you rather work over the summer or master Call of Duty?

When considering whether you should take a summer job at a firm like The Cheeseman, what trade-offs are you facing? On the one hand, you can more easily afford a new laptop if you decide to work, but it comes at an expense—missing out on fun with your friends over the summer. Economists denote nonpaying activities, such as having fun with your friends, as "leisure."

In Chapter 5, we focused on the buyer's problem, in which your choice between various goods and services determined your level of satisfaction. When considering the choice between labor and leisure, you must decide how much to work and how much to "play" or simply "not work."

There would seem to be one major difference between the two scenarios, however. You decide whether or not to buy goods and services based on their prices—an iPad might cost $600, whereas a MacBook Pro might cost $1,200. But what's the price of hanging out with your friends? Isn't it free? Well, just as we learned in Chapter 1 that Facebook isn't free, the same is true for leisure. This is because the "price" of leisure is the *opportunity cost of leisure*, and that opportunity cost is the lost wages from not working.

Exhibit 11.4 Total Days of Labor Supplied per Year for Alice and Tom

Here we can see how the labor-leisure trade-off plays out for Alice and Tom. For example, if the going rate for an 8- hour day is $50, Alice will work 50 days that year, but Tom won't work at all. However, at a daily rate of $125, Alice triples her annual working days to 150 days and Tom works 50 days.

Wage Rate (per 8-hour day)	Alice	Tom
$ 50	50	0
$ 75	100	0
$100	125	50
$125	150	50
$150	175	50
$175	200	50
$200	225	100
$225	250	100
$250	275	150
$275	300	150
$300	350	200
$400	350	300

So, how do you make an optimizing decision when deciding how much to work or hang out with your friends? By now, you likely anticipate the answer: you should set marginal benefits equal to marginal costs. In this case, that means you should consume leisure up to the point where the marginal benefit equals the marginal cost, where the marginal cost is the wage rate. We can write this condition simply as

$$\text{Marginal benefit of leisure} = \text{Wage.}$$

Let's put these observations into action by considering an example. Exhibit 11.4 shows the total days of labor supplied per year for Alice and Tom at the various wage rates. For example, at a wage rate of $100 per day, Alice would work 125 days per year and Tom would work 50 days per year. One first consideration is how the number of days worked changes with increases in the wage rate. Both Alice and Tom work more at higher wage rates. This is intuitive: if the campus bookstore offered you $64 per day (for working 8 hours) you might not accept, but if it raised the hourly wage to $200 per day you might wait in line for a chance to work. Exhibit 11.5 translates Alice's and Tom's labor supply choices in Exhibit 11.4 to individual labor supply curves.

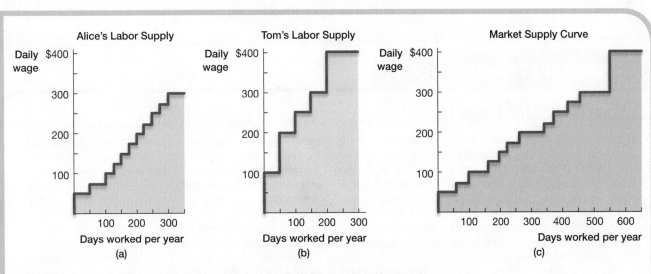

Exhibit 11.5 Individual Labor Supply Curves

Panel (a) depicts Alice's annual work days at each daily wage, and panel (b) does the same for Tom. By summing (horizontally) the hours that Alice and Tom are willing to work at a given daily wage, we construct the labor market supply curve. Thus, at a daily wage of $175, Alice works for 200 days and Tom works for 50 days. Together they work 250 days at a daily wage of $175.

CHOICE & CONSEQUENCE

Producing Web Sites and Computer Programs

You might recall that in Chapter 8, you accepted a free-lance job producing Web sites and computer programs. Let's say that your wage was $10 per hour. If your employer raised your wage to $10,000 per hour, would that lure you to work more hours? For many, the answer may not be completely obvious. On the one hand, you can maintain a nice lifestyle by working very few hours if you are paid $10,000 per hour. On the other hand, the cost of leisure—your foregone wages—just increased by a great deal.

An economic analysis of the problem *does not* imply that along the entire wage range labor supply slopes up when wages go up. Over the wage range that most people think about, it does make sense that on average, people work more for more money, just like Alice and Tom. This is called the *substitution effect*, a term that we

introduced in the Appendix to Chapter 5. The substitution effect implies that when the price of leisure increases, people will substitute into working more (and relaxing less).

However, another term we discussed in Chapter 5 is the *income effect*, which implies that when wages increase, your total income increases and you can afford more expensive things, such as more leisure time. The relative strength of these opposing forces on each individual's decision making determines the slope of his or her labor supply curve.

Economists have explored many situations to determine whether the slope of the labor supply curve is positive or negative. What do you think they found? One example is in the next "Letting the Data Speak."

To construct the *market* supply curve, we need to aggregate the individual labor supply curves. To do this, we *horizontally* sum the individual labor supply curves. Suppose the market consists of only Alice and Tom. In this case, at a daily wage rate of $50, they combine to provide 50 days of work (Alice works 50 days; Tom does not work). At a daily wage rate of $100, they combine to provide 175 days of work (Alice works 125 days; Tom works 50 days). Summing at each wage level produces the market supply curve, which is depicted in panel (c) of Exhibit 11.5.

Labor Market Equilibrium: Supply Meets Demand

Let us now put labor demand and labor supply together and explore the equilibrium implications in the cheese-packing industry. Consider Exhibit 11.6, where we aggregate over several hundred laborers and several dozen firms competing in the labor market for cheese packers. The intersection, as usual, gives the market equilibrium, which determines both

LETTING THE DATA SPEAK

"Get Your Hot Dogs Here!"

One difficulty of measuring the labor supply curve in practice is that many employees do not have perfect flexibility in choosing how many hours to work. For example, many office workers must agree to work 9 to 5, and they may not have a lot of flexibility in deciding their overtime hours. This does not mean that the trade-off between earnings and leisure that we have emphasized is unimportant. But it does mean that estimating labor supply will be difficult.

An interesting study by economist Gerald Oettinger overcomes this difficulty by looking at the labor supply of stadium vendors in a major league baseball stadium during the season.[1] These vendors, who sell hot dogs, beer, cotton candy, lemon ice, peanuts, popcorn, and soda at major-league games, are subcontractors who decide their own working hours. They do not receive a

fixed wage; instead, their effective wage is determined by the demand for products they sell. More people at the games means more sales for the vendors, and people attend games at predictable times—particularly on the weekends and on nice weather days. The advantage of this set-up to test economic theory is that individual vendors are free to set their working hours, thus approximating the situation we have modeled.

Oettinger found that the vendors, who determine whether or not to work on a given day simply by looking at a calendar and the weather forecast, worked 55 percent to 65 percent more often when they expected their earnings to double. In essence, these vendors display the sort of behavior that economic theory would predict. Namely, when presented with a higher potential salary, they work more.

Exhibit 11.6 Labor Market Equilibrium

By putting together what we have learned about diminishing marginal returns to labor and a positive relationship between wages and labor provided, we can now fully describe the labor market with a downward-sloping demand curve and upward-sloping supply curve, the intersection of which determines the equilibrium wage rate and quantity of labor.

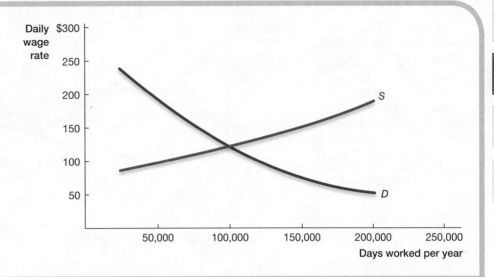

the equilibrium wage rate and the amount of labor supplied and demanded in the market. The market supply and demand curves allow us to further our understanding of how different factors affect the market demand and market supply of labor.

Labor Demand Shifters

There are several key determinants of where the labor demand curve will be situated. Two important factors are:

1. Price of the good that the firm is producing
2. Technology of the firm

Concerning the price of the good that the firm is producing, let's again consider The Wisconsin Cheeseman. Assume that the popularity of cheese increases, which causes a rightward shift in the market demand curve for cheese boxes. This shift increases the equilibrium price of cheese boxes. The higher price increases the *VMPL*—the value of marginal product of laborers who pack cheese. This in turn will cause The Cheeseman and other firms in the industry to demand more workers, leading to a rightward shift of the labor demand curve (to D_2), as shown in Exhibit 11.7. This shift will cause the equilibrium wage and employment level to increase, as shown in the exhibit.

A second factor that shifts the labor demand curve is the technology of the firm. For example, assume that robots take over part of the cheese-packing process, lowering the marginal product of labor. This could happen if the robots were a substitute for labor and leaves workers doing menial tasks that are not as productive as cheese packing. How would that affect the labor demand curve? This would cause the labor demand curve to shift to the left, lowering equilibrium wages and employment levels. This type of technology is denoted as a **labor-saving technology**. It is a type of technology that substitutes for existing labor inputs, reducing the marginal product of labor.

There are also **labor-complementary technologies**, such as the case when an automated process increases cheese packers' productivity. Labor-complementary technologies are those that complement existing labor inputs, increasing the marginal product of labor. Workers can now pack many more boxes because of the technology. Such a change in technology that increases the marginal product of labor shifts the labor demand curve to the right, as shown in Exhibit 11.7.

Labor Supply Shifters

Shifts in labor supply also affect equilibrium wage and employment levels. We discuss three main factors that shift labor supply:

1. Population changes
2. Changes in worker preferences and tastes
3. Opportunity costs

Labor-saving technology is a type of technology that substitutes for existing labor inputs, reducing the marginal product of labor.

Labor-complementary technologies are technologies that complement existing labor inputs, increasing the marginal product of labor.

Exhibit 11.7 A Rightward Shift in the Labor Demand Curve

The labor demand curve shifts rightward if the price of the good that the firm is producing increases. It also shifts rightward if a labor-complementary technology is introduced. Both of these cause the labor demand curve to shift to the right.

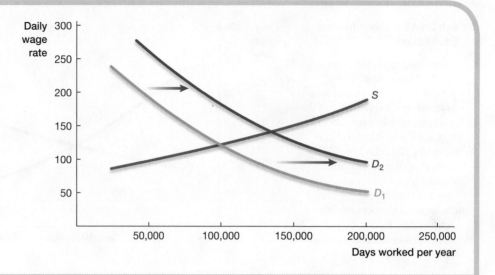

Let's discuss each in turn.

In terms of population changes, the Census Bureau projects that the U.S. population will grow from its current 313 million people to 393 million people by 2050—an increase of roughly 80 million people. This is because of both a greater number of births and immigration. The immigration projections tell an interesting story—the Census Bureau estimates that 60 percent of the population increase will be attributable to immigration. In the simplest scenario, when immigrants move into an area, the supply of workers increases. This increase causes the labor supply curve to shift rightward, as in Exhibit 11.8. Such a shift causes lower wages and higher employment levels.

Changes in preferences and taste also affect the labor supply. In 1975, 46.3 percent of women were working. By 2009, this number had increased to greater than 60 percent. One explanation for this phenomenon is that women might have more of a "taste" for work than they did decades ago. This could have occurred because many women began entering the labor force during the mobilization for World War II and continued to do so, especially over the last three decades. Over time, preferences may have evolved such that women now are both more willing to, and are socially expected to, participate in the labor market than they were before World War II. As more and more women enter the labor market, the labor supply curve shifts rightward, as in Exhibit 11.8. Because women have higher college enrollment rates than men (71.3 percent as compared with 61.3 percent for 2012 high school

Exhibit 11.8 A Shift in the Labor Supply Curve

Through an increase in the labor force population, a shift in tastes, or a reduction in outside opportunities, more workers are willing to work at any given wage rate, shifting the labor supply curve rightward.

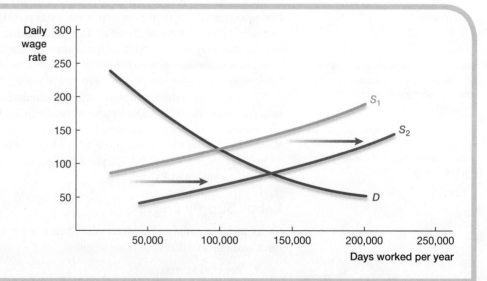

LETTING THE DATA SPEAK

Do Wages Really Go Down if Labor Supply Increases?

To test whether an increase in labor supply leads to lower wages, economist Joshua Angrist turned to the Palestinian occupied territories in the West Bank of the Jordan River and the Gaza Strip.[2] These territories were captured by Israel from Jordan and Egypt in 1967. Though their economies flourished due to the integration with Israel, no institutions of higher education existed in the area for another five years. Accordingly, anyone pursuing a university degree had to leave to do so, and similarly, anyone in these territories with a university degree had earned it elsewhere.

In 1972, to increase employment opportunities for Palestinians in occupied territories, Israel spearheaded the creation of twenty institutions of higher education in the West Bank and the Gaza Strip. As you might expect, these new institutions dramatically and rapidly increased the local supply of workers with a higher education.

Using data gathered from the Territories Labor Force Survey between 1981 and 1991, Angrist found that the average schooling level of men ages 18 to 64 increased from 7.7 years in 1981 to 8.65 years in 1991. The fraction of the labor force with at least 13 years of schooling increased by five percentage points, and the fraction

with less than 12 years of schooling fell by fourteen percentage points. Between 1981 and 1986 alone, over 6,600 students graduated from a university in the West Bank or the Gaza Strip. In this same span of time, wages earned by highly educated workers—those with 13 or more years of schooling—dropped significantly. Before the increase in educated labor supply, highly educated workers earned up to 40 percent more than high school graduates. However, after the increase they earned less than 20 percent more.

Does this prove that an increase in labor supply lowers wages? It is certainly consistent with that notion, but it is important to recognize that there may be other explanations for what we see in the data. For example, neighboring Jordan funded a portion of public-sector employment in the territories, but the growth of its economy slowed around 1982. This likely staunched the flow of resources into the territories, pulling wages and employment down, while strikes, curfews, and civil disorder during the Palestinian uprising could also be partly responsible for the lower earnings of highly educated workers in the Palestinian territories.

graduates according to the Bureau of Labor Statistics), this change in preference might be here to stay because more women will likely want to reap the returns from their education by entering the labor market.

Finally, opportunity costs play a role. For example, if we focus on the labor market for cheese packers, if other job opportunities diminish, the workforce of potential cheese packers grows. More specifically, if the local steel mill shuts down, many workers will be unemployed and looking for work. Some of them will turn to cheese packing, and this increase in the number of workers willing to pack cheese will shift the labor supply curve rightward, as in Exhibit 11.8. This shift, in turn, will lead to lower wages for cheese packers.

When might opportunity costs lead to a lower number of cheese packers? Think of the case where a new Toyota plant opens in the city. Now cheese packers have better job opportunities, and therefore some of them begin working at the new Toyota plant. This will cause the labor supply curve for cheese packers to shift leftward, raising equilibrium wages.

11.3 Wage Inequality

The model of the labor market we developed in the previous section determines a single equilibrium wage for a single industry. In practice, there is considerable inequality in wages and earnings among workers within a given industry and across industries. Exhibit 11.9 shows the distribution of average wages for hourly workers in the United States in 2012.

The exhibit puts workers into one of ten groups. People in the first group represent workers in the lowest 10 percent of earners. People in the tenth group represent the top 10 percent of earners. Groups between these two extremes represent earners from 10 percent to 20 percent (Group 2), 20 percent to 30 percent (Group 3), and so on. What we readily observe from Exhibit 11.9 is that the top-earning workers earn much

Exhibit 11.9 U.S. Hourly Wage Distribution (2012)

If there were no wage inequality, we would expect all the bars to be the same height. However, it is evident from the graph that this is not the case, indicating considerable inequality in wages.

Source: State of Working America, Economic Policy Institute, *Wages Data.* Retrieved January, 2014 from http://www.stateofworkingamerica.org/data/.

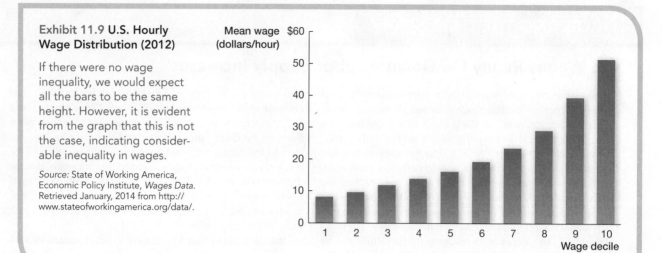

more than other workers. In fact, these workers earn more than 5 times what the lowest-earning workers are paid.

Why do these differences in wages arise? How can we extend our model of labor market equilibrium to incorporate them? We turn to a discussion of three important features of the labor market that may give rise to differences in wages across workers:

1. Differences in human capital
2. Differences in compensating wages
3. The nature and extent of discrimination in the job market

Differences in Human Capital

One explanation for the wage differences observed in Exhibit 11.9 is that people have very different levels of skills and therefore different levels of productivity. Economists refer to each person's stock of skills for producing output or economic value as **human capital**. Differences in human capital result in differences in wages.

One major source of human capital differences is education attainment. You and everyone in your class are working to increase the knowledge that you can use in your working life. Mathematics will help you solve problems and train your reasoning skills, economics will help you to develop an ability to evaluate the consequences of your actions, and English will help you to better express your ideas. All of these skills, and many more, are necessary to produce competitively many goods and services.

Another way to improve your human capital is through experience. The empirical evidence shows that the more time you spend at a particular job, the more productive you will become. This type of productivity increase tends to be either job-specific or industry-specific. Job-specific (or firm-specific) human capital is accrued when a worker learns

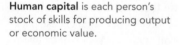

Human capital is each person's stock of skills for producing output or economic value.

Why does Peyton Manning earn more than a physical education teacher?

CHOICE & CONSEQUENCE

Paying for Worker Training

Many union advocates argue that firms should pay for all training sessions. After all, a good training program makes workers better at their job—that is, training makes them more productive.

We must remember that in a competitive market, any worker who has improved basic ("general") skills will also be more productive in general . . . at *any* firm. So, firms will compete for this worker until they push wages up to the value of marginal product of labor. But this means that the worker collects all of the gains from his training (by receiving a higher wage). This means that the firm providing the training does not gain anything from its training expenditure, but the worker does gain from having the general training (he has a higher wage). Therefore, the firm will have no incentive to invest in basic skills training, but the worker himself will have a strong

incentive to do so. Workers are often able to invest in their basic skills on the job by taking a wage cut so as to indirectly "pay" for their training costs (that is, to compensate the firm that is incurring these costs but has nothing to gain from this training).

The same is not true for job-specific training, however. Job-specific training results in gains to a worker's employer (in terms of the worker's productivity), but it does not result in gains to the worker in the labor market. Because the worker will have no market gains from job-specific training, he will not pay for this training. But the firm will gladly pay.

This reasoning suggests that under our economic framework, firms should be willing to pay only for job-specific training. The workers themselves should bear the costs of improving their general skills.

how best to complete a task at her specific job, but that experience does not make her more productive when working for other firms. For example, learning how to operate a unique inventory system gives a worker a skill that translates to more productivity in her firm, but not necessarily to more productivity in other firms.

In contrast, industry-specific training may be accrued when a mechanic learns how to change tires and thus becomes more productive not only in his own firm, but also in competing firms. One often cited factor explaining why men earn more money than women is because women tend to spend more time out of the labor force. Because of this, they are able to accrue less job-specific and industry-specific human capital.

Differences in Compensating Wage Differentials

Just as people achieve different levels of education with their schooling choices, they also choose different types of work. For example, some work is very high risk—construction work, trucking, mining, and military service are all industries with significant mortality rates. For the labor market to be in equilibrium, it must be true that the marginal worker is paid a wage high enough so that he is indifferent between working in his current job and working in his best lower-risk (but lower-wage) alternative.

Compensating wage differentials are wage premiums paid to attract workers to otherwise undesirable occupations.

The wage differences that are used to attract workers to otherwise undesirable occupations are known as **compensating wage differentials**. Wage differentials based on risk and unpleasantness are important factors to consider when examining wage differences across jobs, but there are also reasons why we may see workers in the same job getting paid differently. For instance, the office conditions might be unpleasant, local housing prices and rents might be high, or the local air quality might be low.

We can see some evidence of compensating differentials at work in Exhibit 11.10, which lists average annual salaries taken from the Bureau of Labor Statistics. For example, consider the case of the fast-food cook versus the garbage collector. Both positions have no degree requirements and involve relatively little training, but garbage collectors are paid nearly twice the annual salary of fast-food cooks. Why? Again, it is important to remember that an equilibrium wage makes the marginal person with a particular set of skills indifferent to either job. In this case, it is likely that in order to motivate individuals to wake up early and be willing to handle refuse as their job, they would need more pay than for a life of fast-paced food preparation.

Discrimination in the Job Market

Will workers with the same productivity always receive the same wage for exactly the same job? Will they even be hired for the same job? Not necessarily. A third major factor

Exhibit 11.10 Average Annual Salary in 2013 by Occupation

Here we see occupations with a varying degree of required training and desirability listed with their respective annual salaries.

Source: Bureau of Labor Statistics, U.S. Department of Labor, *Occupational Employment Statistics.* Retrieved January, 2014 from http://www.bls.gov/oes/current/oes_nat.htm.

Occupation	Average Annual Salary
Fast-food cook	$ 18,780
Retail salesperson	$ 25,310
Garbage collector	$ 34,150
Embalmer	$ 43,680
Firefighter	$ 47,850
Explosives worker	$ 49,380
Financial analyst	$ 89,410
Economist	$ 99,480
Nuclear engineer	$107,140
Surgeon	$230,540

CHOICE & CONSEQUENCE

Compensating Wage Differentials

What do you want to be when you grow up? As a child, you probably thought about this question from time to time, and now, as a college student, you may have honed your thinking to exclude certain careers. Among the excluded careers may be those of garbage collector, sewage worker, or truck driver. Given the choice between becoming a truck driver and, say, a teacher, the majority of students would probably opt for a career path devoted to enriching the minds of youths. The job of teacher is well respected, features reasonable hours, and includes summers off. Driving a truck is monotonous, dangerous, and sedentary (one of the authors of this book has realized this firsthand!).

But what if you learned that the average starting salary for a teacher coming out of college was around $33,000 per year, and the average salary for a truck driver was $51,000? Would you be tempted? What if you learned that being a truck driver in Iraq could get you squarely into the six figures? Now would you reconsider?

The economic principle at work here is a compensating wage differential. If a job is relatively more dangerous, dirty, or in some other way undesirable, employers must use incentives to lure potential workers away from easier and cleaner jobs. In considering which careers to pursue, people take into account both wages and the amenities of the job—things like convenient hours, prestige, on-the-job risks, and difficulty. When the amenities make a job more appealing, lower wages may be offered because of the number of other incentives. If the amenities are largely negative, however, employers must offer higher wages to attract qualified laborers, which is why teachers and bank tellers make significantly less money than truck drivers.

How much less? How much would you require in extra compensation to be a truck driver rather than a teacher or bank teller?

in determining wages in the labor market is the nature and extent of discrimination that is present. Economists have pinpointed two major theories for why employers might discriminate: *taste based discrimination* and *statistical discrimination.*

The Nobel Prize-winning economist Gary Becker is famous in part for developing the market implications of **taste-based discrimination**, which occurs when people's preferences cause them to discriminate against a certain group.[3] For example, if an employer is a bigot, he might prefer not to work with certain types of people. Some wage statistics are *consistent* with American employers having a taste for discrimination. For example, among hourly wage workers, non-Hispanic workers make 36 percent more than Hispanic workers in America, on average, as shown in Exhibit 11.11.

It is important to note that wages can be different between groups not only because an employer has a taste for discrimination but also because of other factors, such as human capital—in particular, in the form of education and experience. In fact, Hispanic workers have lower educational attainment, on average, than non-Hispanic workers. This difference in human capital could therefore be the driver of the wage differences observed in Exhibit 11.11.

An interesting additional possibility is that wage differences between workers are driven by hard-to-observe factors. For example, perhaps non-Hispanic workers are better employees because their English skills help them to communicate more effectively with coworkers and customers. Maybe differences in communication abilities alone cause some of the differences observed in Exhibit 11.11. Is it discrimination if employers hire on the basis of that perception (whether true or false)?

Economists call this type of discrimination **statistical discrimination**. It occurs when employers use an observable variable (such as race or gender) to help determine if the person will be a good employee. Thus, it occurs when expectations cause people to discriminate against a certain group.

For instance, if you are in your teens or twenties, why do you think your car insurance costs more than your parents' car insurance? It is because the insurance company uses statistical group averages to determine that people your age get in more accidents than people your parents' age. In this way, even though the variable age by itself is not perfect, it provides an indication of how risky the driver will be. Employers perform similar calculations when deciding on which type of person to hire and use gender, race, age, or any other variable they believe is indicative of who will be a good worker.

An important distinction between taste-based and statistical discrimination is that employers are willing to forego profits when engaging in taste-based discrimination. That is, to cater to their prejudicial preferences, they will not hire or promote a specific type of worker. On the other hand, employers engaging in statistical discrimination are trying to

Taste-based discrimination occurs when people's preferences cause them to discriminate against a certain group.

Statistical discrimination occurs when expectations cause people to discriminate against a certain group.

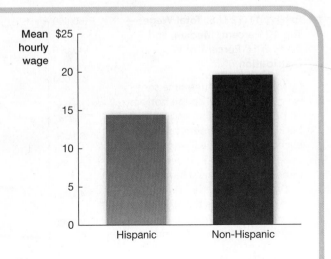

Exhibit 11.11 Mean Hourly Wage of Hispanic and Non-Hispanic Workers (2013)

For hourly wage workers, non-Hispanics earn more than Hispanic workers. It is important to note, however, that there are numerous possible explanations for this difference, only one of which is taste-based discrimination.

Source: Bureau of Labor Statistics, U.S. Department of Labor, *Current Population Survey.* Retrieved January, 2014 at http://www.bls.gov/cps/earnings.htm#demographics.

enhance their profits. We return later to how we might measure the impact of discrimination in the labor market.

Changes in Wage Inequality Over Time

We have just discussed three major reasons for why wages vary across the economy: human capital differences, compensating wage differentials, and discrimination. One outstanding question is how wage differences have changed over time. At first glance, you might think that because discrimination has become less socially acceptable over time—especially since the 1950s and 1960s—wage inequality must have decreased. You might be surprised, however, to see Exhibit 11.12, which plots the wage distribution for the United States from 1967 to 2010. It shows wage trends for people at the bottom, in the middle, and at the top of the wage distribution.

> **The increase in the wage gap since 1967 has been dramatic.**

The exhibit shows that wage inequality since 1967 has increased dramatically. Whereas the top 10 percent of earners have increased their wages by over $50,000 per year, those at the bottom remained effectively flat. A similar story plays out for the median wage earner. This dramatic change in wage inequality over time is likely due to several sources, but economists have pinpointed one factor in particular that has driven a large wedge between high- and low-earning workers: *technological change.*

As we discussed earlier, technology can either be labor saving or labor complementary. It can also be skill saving or skill complementary, more often referred to as *skill biased.* **Skill-biased technological changes** increase the productivity of skilled workers relative to that of unskilled workers. The primary technological change over this time period has been advances in computing power. This change appears to have been broadly skill biased, improving the marginal productivity of skilled workers and causing the demand for their labor and pay to increase.

Skill-biased technological changes increase the productivity of skilled workers relative to that of unskilled workers.

On the flip side, enhanced computing power has also replaced many tasks performed by the unskilled, thereby decreasing the labor demand for such workers and lowering their wages. This effect can be observed throughout the economy: many customer service centers are now automated by voice-recognizing software. In the past, trouble with a telephone bill would not require communication with an automaton. Likewise, cars, pizzas, and even the beds we sleep in are now being made by advanced technologies. Technology has advanced so far and so fast over the past few decades that perhaps before you get your first job, robots behind the counter at the local fast-food franchise may smile and ask, "Would you like fries and Coke with that hamburger?"

Exhibit 11.12 U.S. Total Wages—Top 10 Percent, Median, and Bottom 10 Percent of Wage Distribution

By following the three time series, we can see that while the bottom 10 percent (blue line) and median (red line) wage earners have experienced little to no real wage growth since 1967, the top 10 percent (green line) of earners have seen a 50 percent increase in wages. One explanation is that skill-biased technological change increased top wage earners' marginal product.

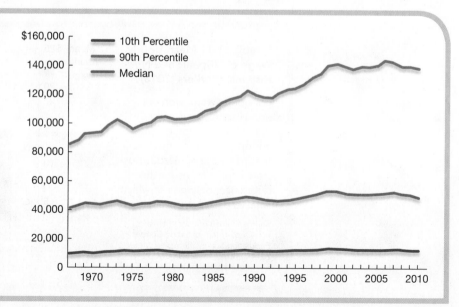

11.4 The Market for Other Factors of Production: Physical Capital and Land

Despite our focus so far on labor as an input to production, there are other factors equally important to the production process. In this section, we discuss the market for physical capital (such as machines) and the market for land.

Recall that the value to a firm of adding each consecutive unit of labor is given by multiplying the output price and the marginal product of labor. We denoted this marginal value as *VMPL* (value of marginal product of labor), and derived the optimal action of the firm to hire labor up until the point where the wage rate = *VMPL*.

A firm's physical capital requires an identical treatment. As we discussed in Chapter 6, physical capital is any good, including machines and buildings, used for production. It may be the belt on an assembly line, the credit card machine at a restaurant, or the forklift at a construction site. Similar to hiring workers, a firm will expand its physical capital until it is not worthwhile to do so. This implies that just as The Wisconsin Cheeseman hired labor until *VMPL* = wage, it will employ physical capital until the **value of the marginal product of physical capital (*VMPK*)**—economists commonly denote physical capital with a K—equals the price of physical capital. The value of marginal product of physical capital is the contribution of an additional unit of physical capital to a firm's revenues.

The **value of marginal product of physical capital** is the contribution of an additional unit of physical capital to a firm's revenues.

Land includes the solid surface of the earth and natural resources.

The same is true for uses of **land**. Land includes the solid surface of the earth where structures are built and natural resources. A firm will continue to purchase and use land—say for building space—until the value of the marginal product of land equals the price of land.

Although the economic framework for deciding how much of the three inputs to use is identical, labor has one major difference from physical capital and land: both physical capital and land can be either rented or owned, whereas labor (of others) cannot be owned. When rented, the firm must pay the *rental price* of physical capital, and to use land it must pay the *rental price* of land. By **rental price**, we mean the price of using a good for a specific period of time. For simplicity, we assume that the firm rents physical capital and land rather than owns them; we treat investment more broadly in Chapter 15.

The **rental price** of a good is the cost of using a good for some specific period of time.

To make this discussion more concrete, let's consider an example of how we can arrive at an equilibrium in the physical capital market. Suppose that a labor-saving technological innovation makes it possible for The Wisconsin Cheeseman to use only one unit of labor—a computer programmer—to produce cheese boxes. Recall that the number of machines on the assembly line determines how many cheese boxes The Cheeseman produces. Exhibit 11.13 represents the production schedule for physical capital, where each unit of physical capital is one machine. Suppose that the equilibrium price of cheese boxes remains at $2. This means that the value of marginal product of physical capital (*VMPK*) = $2 × marginal product of capital per unit (MPK). This relationship is displayed in column 4 of Exhibit 11.13.

In Exhibit 11.14 we plot this schedule. If the market for machines has a rental price of $80 per machine, then we can see that The Cheeseman will use 10 machines in its assembly line, producing 524 cheese boxes per day. This is optimal because the firm has set *VMPK* = market rental rate, thereby maximizing its profits.

We can arrive at equilibrium in the land market using an identical approach. This will determine how much land The Cheeseman demands.

So how does The Cheeseman put all of this together and choose its optimal mix of labor, physical capital, and land? You will not be surprised to learn that The Cheeseman considers marginal benefits and marginal costs when making its choices. In this case, The Cheeseman optimizes by hiring inputs until their marginal cost equals their marginal benefit. In equilibrium, this will lead to the marginal product from the last dollar spent on each input being equalized (this is similar to the "equal bang for your buck" story that we learned about in Chapter 5 and resources being allocated efficiently in Chapter 7).

> **The Cheeseman optimizes by hiring inputs until their marginal cost equals their marginal benefit.**

Exhibit 11.13 Production Schedule for The Wisconsin Cheeseman

As before, The Cheeseman is tasked with choosing how much output to generate per day. The difference now is that The Cheeseman's output is determined by the number of machines it purchases. The table summarizes the number of machines it will need for any given level of output and how much value each additional machine adds. Column 1 shows cheese boxes produced per day, column 2 shows the number of machines used in production, column 3 shows the marginal product of each additional machine, and column 4 shows the dollar value of this additional output (*VMPK*).

(1) Output per Day	(2) Number of Machines	(3) Marginal Product	(4) VMPK = MPK × P = Column (3) × $2
0	0		
50	1	50	$100
104	2	54	$108
161	3	57	$114
227	4	66	$132
294	5	67	$134
346	6	52	$104
396	7	50	$100
442	8	46	$ 92
484	9	42	$ 84
524	10	40	$ 80
561	11	37	$ 74
596	12	35	$ 70
628	13	32	$ 64
658	14	30	$ 60
685	15	27	$ 54
710	6	25	$ 50
734	17	24	$ 48

Exhibit 11.14 Demand for Physical Capital

As with labor, a derived demand market exists for machines. Here we graph the quantity of machines demanded at each price (rental rate). In orange, we assume that the marginal cost of an additional machine is $80. This allows us to identify the equilibrium quantity of 10 machines.

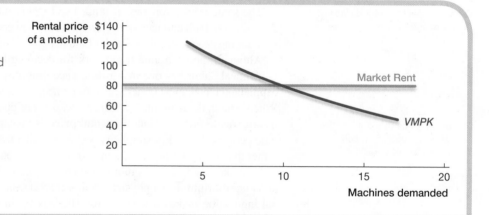

Evidence-Based Economics

Q: Is there discrimination in the labor market?

Have economists found evidence that discrimination might exist in labor markets? The answer is unequivocally yes—studies analyzing several different labor markets have made a case that discrimination against minorities and women exists. The studies are typically split between field experiments and studies that use statistical techniques to analyze existing (naturally occurring) data.

One intriguing example of a field experiment is a study by economists Claudia Goldin and Cecelia Rouse.[4] They use audition notes from a series of auditions among national orchestras to determine whether or not blind auditions—those in which musicians audition behind a screen—help women relatively more than men.

The authors considered three rounds of auditions: preliminary, semifinal, and final. They found that for women who made it to the finals, a blind audition increased their likelihood of winning by 33 percentage points. What this means is that women were much more likely to be chosen for national orchestras when the judges were not aware of their gender. As the authors note, without blind judging, discrimination has limited the employment of female musicians.

A related field experiment focusing on hiring practices within sales, administrative support, clerical, and customer services jobs was conducted by economists Marianne Bertrand and Sendhil Mullainathan.[5] Following a long line of research using similar techniques, the authors focused on testing for discrimination against African Americans in the workforce. They sent nearly 5,000 resumes in response to help-wanted ads in Chicago and Boston, randomly assigning Caucasian-sounding names, such as Emily or Greg, and African-American-sounding names, such as Lakisha or Jamal, to the identical résumé. The outcome they were interested in was whether a given resume generated a callback or an e-mail for an interview.

We would expect that, without discrimination, callbacks would be distributed evenly between African-American-sounding and Caucasian-sounding names. After all, each group had identical resumes. Yet, Bertrand and Mullainathan found that résumés with Caucasian-sounding names had a 9.65 percent chance of receiving a callback, while résumés with African-American-sounding names had only a 6.45 percent chance. This means that those with Caucasian-sounding names were about 50 percent more likely to receive a callback than those with African-American-sounding names.

These two studies provide evidence of discrimination against two different classes of individuals—women in the case of orchestra hiring and people with African-American-sounding names in the case of the sales and clerical jobs.

One aspect that is left on the sidelines in these two studies is the relative wages of people once hired. Economists Kerwin Charles and Jon Guryan tackled this issue by examining a large data set on wages.[6] They used careful statistical techniques in an attempt to account for differences in productivity and human capital as well as differences in compensating wage differentials. Their key result is that taste-based discrimination accounts for as much as one-fourth of the gap in wages between African Americans and Caucasians. This level of discrimination accounts for a total loss in annual earnings for African Americans of thousands of dollars. As you can see, this is real money that is being shuffled because of discrimination. But the good news is that the researchers found that this type of discrimination has lessened over time.

These three studies have only scratched the surface of empirical work that explores the issue of discrimination. Overall, there is a fair amount of evidence suggesting that there is discrimination in labor markets, and in some cases, it is leading to considerable differences in wages across groups of people. What remains difficult to determine is whether such discrimination is taste-based or statistical. Perhaps you can think of research ideas to determine the precise nature of discrimination?[7]

Question

Is there discrimination in the labor market?

Answer

Yes.

Data

Both survey and field experimental data suggest that discrimination is evident in many labor markets.

Caveat

Whether this discrimination is taste-based or statistical is difficult to uncover.

Summary

✹ Producers determine the optimal mix of labor, physical capital, and land when making production decisions. Markets for these factors of production operate in much the same way that markets for final goods and services function: firms expand their use until marginal benefits equal marginal costs.

✹ Determining the demand for labor centers on the concept of the value of marginal product of labor, which is the contribution an additional worker makes to the firm's revenues.

✹ When making decisions on how to spend our time, we face opportunity cost. There is a trade-off between labor, which comprises activities that earn money, and leisure, which is time spent on activities other than earning money. The opportunity cost for one hour of leisure is the income that we would have earned by working for that hour.

✹ Large wage differences exist across people and jobs. The differences stem from three main sources: human capital differences, compensating wage differentials, and discrimination.

✹ As with labor, firms expand their use of physical capital until the value of the marginal product of physical capital equals the price of physical capital, and they likewise use land until the value of the marginal product of land equals the price of land.

Key Terms

value of marginal product of labor (*VMPL*) *p. 254*
labor-saving technology *p. 259*
labor-complementary technologies *p. 259*
human capital *p. 262*

compensating wage differentials *p. 263*
taste-based discrimination *p. 265*
statistical discrimination *p. 265*
skill-biased technological changes *p. 266*

value of marginal product of physical capital (*VMPK*) *p. 267*
land *p. 267*
rental price *p. 267*

Questions

All questions are available in MyEconLab *for practice and instructor assignment.*

1. How do firms estimate the demand for labor?

2. How does the labor-leisure trade-off determine the supply of labor?

3. In a competitive labor market, what is the profit-maximizing number of workers that a firm will hire?

4. We showed above that a profit-maximizing firm will hire the number of workers such that the wage is equal to the value of the marginal product of labor. But, as the text showed in an earlier chapter, a profit-maximizing firm will produce the quantity of output such that price equals marginal cost. Are these two rules inconsistent?

5. How would the following factors affect equilibrium in the market for labor?

   a. An increase in the demand for the product that a firm is producing

   b. The use of a new technology that halves the time that workers will take to produce a good

   c. An increase in the age when people begin to receive Social Security benefits

6. Suppose wages in the market for plumbers increase. Some plumbers start taking on extra plumbing jobs while others cut back on the number of hours they work. What could explain this?

7. How do labor-saving technologies differ from labor-complementary technologies? Give an example of each.

8. Some people think it's unfair that celebrities like Kim Kardashian earn a lot more than people who add so much more value to society, like teachers. What do you think explains this wage differential?

9. In the United States in 2011, there were 104 fatalities per 100,000 workers in the logging industry. This is the second-highest rate after the fisheries industry. Everything else equal, would you expect workers in the logging industry to be paid higher wages than workers with similar levels of education in other industries? Explain.

10. What is the difference between statistical and taste-based discrimination? The owner of a company that manufactures automobile parts states that it will not hire gay or lesbian employees. Is this an example of statistical or taste-based discrimination?

11. What factors could explain why wage inequality in the United States has been increasing over the last several decades?

12. How does the market for inputs like labor differ from the market for goods and services?

13. Suppose an identical tax is levied on capital, labor, and land. Would the tax have the same effect in each of these markets? Explain your answer.

Problems

All problems are available in MyEconLab for practice and instructor assignment.

1. Suppose that, at your firm, the relationship between output produced and the number of workers you hire is as follows:

Labor	Total Product
0	0
1	12
2	23
3	32
4	38
5	42
6	45

  a. Find the marginal product of labor for each worker.

  b. Is the relationship between output and labor consistent with the Law of Diminishing Returns?

  c. Suppose your firm is a perfect competitor in the output market and the labor market. If the price of output is $9 and the wage rate is $27, how many workers should your firm hire?

  d. If the price of output falls to $3 and the wage remains $27, how many workers should your firm hire?

2. For Acme Manufacturing, the marginal product of labor (MP) is $MP = 200 - 4L$. Acme is a perfect competitor, sells its output at a price of $10 per unit, and pays a wage of $200 per worker. Find Acme's profit-maximizing number of workers.

3. Equal pay for work of comparable worth is the idea that certain jobs, though completely different, must have the same pay because they are deemed to be of similar value. For example, an X-ray technician's job may be deemed to be as valuable as a dental assistant's job and therefore, both these jobs should be paid the same salaries. Implementing equal pay for comparable worth has been suggested as a measure that would reduce discrimination and inequality in the job market. Do you agree? What could be the other possible effects of such a policy? Explain your answer.

4. A friend tells you that he thinks that the salesmen who work at Apple stores are paid very low wages, given their productivity. Dividing Apple's revenues by the total number of employees shows that each employee contributed an average of $473,000 in revenues in 2011. But most of Apple's sales staff are paid about $25,000 a year. What is the flaw, if any, in your friend's reasoning?

5. The table shows the average salary for major league baseball players. As you can see, the average salary of $3,440,000 in 2012 is nearly 20 times larger than the average salary in 1970.

Year	Average Salary*
1970	$ 173,397
1980	$ 408,198
1990	$1,035,515
2000	$2,649,988
2010	$3,472,326
2012	$3,440,000

*In constant 2012 dollars.

  a. Explain what economic forces will encourage ball players in 2012 to play an extra year compared to those in 1970.

  b. Are there any economic reasons for ball players to retire earlier than those in 1970?

6. For a long time, your firm has been paying its workers a wage of $20 per hour and your employees have been happy to work 40 hours per week at this wage. Business is suddenly booming and your firm would really like your workers to agree to a 50-hour work week in order to meet this new demand for your product. You are considering two strategies. Under the first, you would raise the wage for all hours worked from $20 per hour to $22 per hour; under the second, you would leave the wage for the first 40 hours per week at $20 but offer $30 per hour for hours worked above 40 hours (that is, you would offer time-and-a-half for overtime). Both strategies have the same cost of $1,100 if a worker chooses to work 50 hours. Which strategy is more likely to lead your employees to agree to a 50-hour work week?

7. One of the common arguments against "sweatshops" in developing countries is that the wages workers are being paid are too low. Commentators often use dollar comparisons to show that, compared to U.S. standards, "sweatshop" workers are paid unfairly low wages. Use what you have read about the supply of labor to examine this argument.

8. The Patient Protection and Affordable Care Act (ACA) requires all employers with at least 50 full-time equivalent workers to offer health insurance to their full-time employees or pay a fine of up to $2,000 per employee (see http://www.hhs.gov/healthcare/rights/index.html for a description of the ACA). Some people have argued that ACA will lower employment. This problem looks at an important issue in this debate.

   a. Suppose the government passes a law that requires firms to offer health insurance to their workers. The cost of the insurance is equal to $1 for each hour an employee works. How will this law affect firms' demand for labor?

   b. Suppose workers consider a dollar of health insurance paid by firms to be the equivalent of $1 in wages. How will this law affect the supply curve of labor?

   c. Consider an industry where the equilibrium wage is $15 per hour and 100 workers are employed. How will this law affect the equilibrium quantity of labor in this labor market? How will it affect the equilibrium wage in this industry?

   d. Now suppose workers consider a dollar of health insurance paid by firms to be worth less than $1 in wages. How will this law affect the equilibrium quantity of labor in this labor market? How will it affect the equilibrium wage in this industry?

9. Denmark has high marginal tax rates and offers its citizens generous unemployment benefits and other welfare payments. While the unemployment rate in Denmark is relatively low, the proportion of people who are not in the labor force is quite high. After accounting for factors like the average age of the population, what else do you think could explain this?

10. In 2010, President Obama said that technological progress kills jobs. Recall that labor-saving technology substitutes for existing labor inputs and reduces the marginal product of labor. Taking the example of an ATM (Automatic Teller Machine), Obama said that the fact that ATMs have replaced tellers pointed to a structural problem in the economy. Is labor-saving technology necessarily a bad thing?

11. Suppose you are the CEO of a firm that manufactures surgical equipment. You have a production plant in Alabama where you employ highly skilled labor. Your firm is considering moving its production facilities from Alabama to Guangzhou in China in an attempt to lower labor costs. When you compare wages in China and in the United States, you notice that the average wage in China is significantly lower than the average American wage. What factors other than wages should you consider when you decide whether or not to move production to China? Explain.

12. According to a 2011 study by the American Association of University Women (AAUW), about 40 percent of full-time faculty nationwide in 2005 were women, yet they made up only 22 percent of faculty in computer and information sciences, 19 percent of mathematics faculty, and 12 percent of engineering faculty (the STEM fields). In 2005, the then president of Harvard University, Lawrence Summers, suggested that differences in math and science aptitude could explain part of this pattern. What reasons other than differences in aptitude could explain why women are underrepresented in the these fields?

12 Monopoly

Can a monopoly ever be good for society?

Neuroscientists have taught us that the mere mention of the word *monopoly* conjures up negative associations deep in the brain that only words such as *death* and *murder* can match. In this chapter, we explore why that is the case, focusing on the economics of monopolies. Throughout the chapter we follow Schering-Plough Corporation, a global pharmaceutical company based in the United States, which introduced the allergy drug Claritin in the early 1980s. During the development process, the U.S. government deemed the drug to be truly original and granted Schering-Plough a *patent*, which gave the company the exclusive right to manufacture and sell Claritin for 20 years.

Put yourself into the shoes of the CEO of Schering-Plough at that point in time. If you were CEO, how would you take advantage of this product exclusivity to optimize profits from your new wonder drug?

Your intuition might suggest that delivering enormous profits will be easy. With so many people in need of allergy medicine and no competitors to worry about,

CHAPTER OUTLINE

KEY IDEAS

- ☀ Monopoly represents an extreme market structure with a single seller.

- ☀ Monopolies arise both naturally and through government protection.

- ☀ Monopolists are price-makers and produce at the point where marginal revenue equals marginal cost.

- ☀ The monopolist maximizes profits by producing a lower quantity and charging a higher price than perfectly competitive sellers. By doing so, deadweight loss results.

- ☀ Efficiency can be established in a monopoly through first-degree price discrimination or government intervention.

you are a *monopolist* and therefore should set very high prices for Claritin, capturing as much consumer surplus from buyers as possible. Knowing that some people might really need Claritin to function from day to day, you might even consider charging as much as $100 or more per tablet!

In this chapter, you will learn about the monopolist's problem—how it is similar to and different from the competitive seller's problem we discussed in Chapter 6. The lesson of this chapter is that a company with market power behaves quite differently from the way that a competitive firm behaves. Compared to competitive firms, monopolists produce less and charge more. They thus make themselves better off, with the potential of earning economic profits in both the short run and the long run. But their gain will come at the cost of making consumers worse off and decreasing social surplus.

All of this has led the public to be quite distrustful of monopolies. For this reason, as we shall see, governments actively monitor and regulate monopolies. However, can a monopoly ever be good for society? We'll attempt to answer that question by the end of the chapter.

12.1 Introducing a New Market Structure

Thus far we have assumed that sellers operate in competitive markets: identical goods are produced by many different sellers and sold at the market-determined price. The firm is simply a passive price-taker, and the invisible hand directs the self-interested pursuits of buyers and sellers to yield socially efficient outcomes. Exhibit 12.1 provides an aerial view of perfect competition, which we studied in Chapters 6 and 7, and the new market structure that we will be studying in this section—monopoly.

Studying perfectly competitive markets provided important insights into how agents interact in markets and how markets equilibrate. But it proves to be a special type of market. A more common market situation is one in which a firm is not simply a price-taker, but a **price-maker**—a seller that sets the price of a good. It has the ability to set the price of

Price-makers are sellers that set the price of a good.

12.1

12.2

12.3

12.4

12.5

12.6

12.7

Exhibit 12.1 Two Market Structures

Many differences exist between perfect competition and monopoly. Each row highlights those differences across various characteristics of the two market structures.

	Perfect Competition	Monopoly
Number of Firms/Sellers/Producers	Many	One
Type of Product/Service Sold	Identical (homogeneous)	Good or service with no close substitutes
Example of Product	Corn grown by various farmers	Patented drugs; tap water
Barriers to Entry	None: free entry and exit	Yes: high
Price-Taker or Price-Maker?	Price-taker; price given by the market	Price-maker—no competitors; no close substitutes
Price	$P = MR = MC$	Set $P > MR = MC$
Demand Curve Facing the Firm	Horizontally sloped; perfectly elastic demand curve	Downward-sloping
Social Surplus	Maximized	Not maximized, but sometimes society benefits from research and development
Equilibrium Long Run Profits	Zero	Potentially greater than zero

Market power relates to the ability of sellers to affect prices.

Monopoly is an industry structure in which only one seller provides a good or service that has no close substitutes.

the good because it has **market power**. Column 2 in Exhibit 12.1 summarizes the most extreme form of market power: a *monopoly*.

A **monopoly** is an industry structure in which only one seller provides a good or service that has no close substitutes. In this way, a monopolist is not concerned with the behavior of other sellers. The price chosen by the monopolist is the one that makes the company the highest profit.

12.2 Sources of Market Power

What does it mean to have market power? Where do we have to look to see firms thrive with limited competition? Perhaps it is a titan of social media like Facebook. Maybe it is an innovative company like Google. In fact, for the monopolist, market power arises because of *barriers to entry*.

Barriers to entry are obstacles that prevent potential competitors from entering the market. As such, they provide the seller protection against competition. Barriers to entry range from complete exclusion of market entrants to prevention of a new firm from entering and competing on an equal footing with an incumbent firm.

There are two types of market power that arise from barriers to entry: **legal market power** and *natural market power*. We now take a look at these two types in more depth.

Barriers to entry provide a seller with protection from potential competitors entering the market.

Legal market power occurs when a firm obtains market power through barriers to entry created not by the firm itself, but by the government.

Legal Market Power

Legal market power occurs when a firm obtains market power through barriers to entry created not by the firm itself, but by the government. These barriers can take the form of *patents* and *copyrights* that are issued to innovative companies. With a **patent**, the government grants an individual or company the sole right to produce and sell a good or service. For example, when Schering-Plough applied to the government for a patent to produce and sell Claritin, the government granted the company the exclusive right to manufacture and sell the drug for 20 years. With a **copyright**, the government grants an individual or company an exclusive right to intellectual property. For example, when Malcolm Gladwell wrote the best-selling book *Blink*, he copyrighted the work.[1] This meant that he was given a government guarantee that no one else could print and sell the book without his permission. In effect, Gladwell was granted monopoly rights in the sale of his book. Copyright protection is different across countries and in many cases extends long after the author's death. For example, in the United States, it extends decades after the author's death.

A **patent** is the privilege granted to an individual or company by the government, which gives him or her the sole right to produce and sell a good.

A **copyright** is an exclusive right granted by the government to the creator of a literary or artistic work.

My that sure is a cute and fuzzy copyright infringing puppy.

Natural market power occurs when a firm obtains market power through barriers to entry created by the firm itself.

12.1

12.2

12.3

12.4

12.5

12.6

12.7

Such exclusivity laws represent a significant benefit for the innovator-turned-monopolist. For instance, monopolists Schering-Plough Corporation and Gladwell can charge higher prices than would occur under perfect competition. As consumers, we are all worse off because we must pay higher prices for these goods, but there are a few silver linings. First, patents and copyrights are only temporary, and eventually the protected goods enter the public domain, and at that point other producers are able to distribute them. Second, blockbuster drugs and best-selling books are difficult and costly to produce, and without the increased incentive for creative activity, the expensive investment to create new prescription drugs or best-selling books might never be made. We return to a discussion of whether patents are indeed helpful in stimulating innovation in the Evidence-Based Economics section at the end of this chapter.

Natural Market Power

A second common source of barriers to entry occurs naturally rather than by design. **Natural market power** occurs when a firm obtains market power through barriers to entry created by the firm itself. Within this category, there are two main sources of monopoly power:

1. The monopolist owns or controls a *key resource* necessary for production.
2. There are *economies of scale* in production over the relevant range of output.

 CHOICE & CONSEQUENCE

Cleaning Up While Cleaning Up

The 1977 Clean Air Act Amendments (CAAA) represent a choice made by the U.S. government to impose strict rules on new factories regarding their emissions of pollution. The amendments mandated that if a new firm wanted to build a plant in an area where there was already a lot of air pollution, the firm must invest in expensive scrubbers and other environmental technologies before commencing production.

Many industry executives applauded the new pollution laws. They were happy because the rules did not apply to the already established plants; they were "grandfathered" under the older, less stringent rules. Thus, existing plants had much lighter requirements as to how much pollution reduction they needed to take on.

We've already learned that many choices yield important market consequences. One unintended consequence (or was it?) of this kind of regulation was that by raising entry costs for new firms, a barrier to entry was created that expanded the market power of existing firms. In some cases, the CAAA impact on market power was ultimately so large that it outweighed the direct costs these firms had to pay to reduce pollution!

Accordingly, firm profits actually increased even as these firms cleaned up the environment. The downside fell on the consumers, of course, because prices rose substantially.

The next time you hear a company arguing for tighter environmental standards that clearly raise industry costs, before praising the CEO for his "greenness," be sure to ask yourself whether such standards might make his firm better off.

12.1

12.2

12.3

12.4

12.5

12.6

12.7

Key resources are materials that are essential for the production of a good or service.

Network externalities occur when a product's value increases as more consumers begin to use it.

Control of Key Resources

Key resources are those materials that are essential for the production of a good or service. The most basic way for a firm to develop market power naturally is to control the entire supply of such resources (assuming that there are no close substitutes). For example, if renters are willing to pay a premium for an apartment with a lake view and there is only one apartment complex on the lake, the owner of that apartment complex has considerable market power. Likewise, by controlling 80 percent of the production from the world's diamond mines, the South African diamond company De Beers famously exercised significant market power in the diamond market throughout the twentieth century. In a similar spirit, Alcoa controls a key manufacturing resource with its ownership of bauxite (aluminum ore) mines.

Another key resource is individual expertise. For example, Sergey Brin and Larry Page are exceptional at search engine design. Thus, Google's power arose from two of its personnel, whose key economic resource is their creative talents.

In much the same way, Web sites that we use daily, such as eBay, Facebook, and Twitter, control a key resource: they attract the largest numbers of consumers. Their value subsequently increases because of network externalities. **Network externalities** occur when a product's value increases as more consumers begin to use it. Because eBay has the largest number of buyers and sellers, it makes sense for sellers to part with their goods on eBay. Similarly, Facebook and Twitter today are synonymous with social networking. Because each now has millions of users, they own a key resource: millions of people log in daily. Accordingly, Facebook is now much more valuable than MySpace because it has more people using it—a fact that attracts even more customers. In this way, network externalities set off a profitable cycle for Facebook.

Economies of Scale

Monopolies also form because it is practical for both producers and consumers. Consider the case of the transmission of electricity. If your town had multiple providers of electricity transmission, there would have to be multiple sets of wires laid throughout town and extraordinary start-up costs would be borne by multiple providers of electricity (and eventually passed on to you, the consumer).

In this case, it is better to have one provider serve the entire town because of the economies of scale that the single provider enjoys. As we discussed in Chapter 6, economies of scale occur when the average total cost per unit of output decreases as total output increases. As your electricity provider increases its transmission, the average total cost per unit of output decreases. The intuition is that if your electricity provider wants to hook up and create electricity for a new subdivision, the initial fixed costs will be high, but as more and more houses are added, costs will be spread over more households. Exhibit 12.2 shows just such a relationship between average total cost, marginal cost, and output. You will note that in this case we have assumed a constant marginal cost. This means that over the entire production range of interest, the marginal cost is

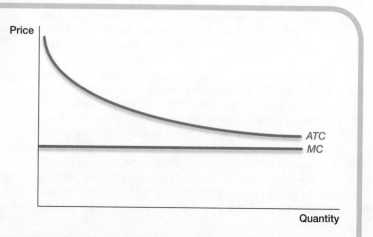

Exhibit 12.2 Average Total Cost and Marginal Cost for a Natural Monopoly

Natural monopolies are characterized by substantial fixed costs and economies of scale. To see this, at a low quantity level the average total cost (*ATC*) is very high, and as quantity increases the *ATC* decreases, approaching marginal cost.

the same. In previous chapters we have dealt with upward-sloping marginal cost curves, but in certain cases a constant marginal cost curve represents a good description of the cost structure of a firm.

For goods and services that have economies of scale over the relevant range of output, it is efficient for a single firm to serve the entire market because it can do so at a lower cost than any larger number of firms could. We denote such cases as *natural monopolies*, because they arise naturally. A **natural monopoly** arises because the economies of scale of a single firm make it efficient to have only one provider of a good or service. Often such firms are the first suppliers in a given market, and the cost advantages they achieve through producing a large number of goods preclude would-be competitors from entering the market. Examples of natural monopolies include providers of clean drinking water, natural gas, and electricity.

You may wonder why Facebook, Twitter, and eBay are not considered natural monopolies. All three exhibit network externalities, and such network effects seem to present barriers to entry, don't they? So why aren't these companies considered natural monopolies? Remember that natural monopolies arise because of economies of scale—the firm's *ATC* curve decreases over the important range of output. But network externalities arise from consumer benefits and have nothing to do with costs and economies of scale. There are some goods that feature both economies of scale and network effects, such as operating system software and telephone networks.

In contrast to monopolies that arise through legal means, natural monopolies emerge when unique cost conditions characterize their industry. Because of these cost conditions, natural monopolists worry less about potential market entrants than monopolies that arise through legal means. As large economic profits attract entrants like bees to honey in legal monopolies such as the pharmaceutical, diamond, and Internet industries, the economic profits in the natural monopoly scenario are not as attractive. This is because potential entrants realize that they cannot achieve the low costs of the natural monopolist because upon entry they likely will "split the market." Such splitting of the market will render much higher costs and lower profits to each seller.

This doesn't mean that industries that are currently monopolized will never evolve to be more competitive. There have been many cases where the market grew sufficiently large so that the natural monopoly evolved into a multiseller market. Throughout the 1990s and early 2000s, Microsoft's Internet Explorer (IE) was the default browser for just about all Web traffic. Estimates put IE's market share at well over 95 percent at its peak. But as the number of households connected to the Internet boomed, new companies entered the market. Even though there are significant economies of scale to developing, coding, testing, and marketing a new browser, the increase in demand has generated opportunities for Mozilla Firefox and Google's Chrome, with IE's market-share dropping to below 70 percent.

Regardless of why a firm enjoys market power—whether legally or naturally—it faces exactly the same decision problem when it comes to production and pricing choices. We turn to that discussion now.

12.3 The Monopolist's Problem

The monopolist's problem shares two important similarities with the perfectly competitive seller's problem we discussed in Chapter 6. First, the monopolist must understand how inputs combine to make outputs. Second, the monopolist must know the costs of production. Accordingly, all of the production and cost concepts we learned earlier apply directly to the monopolist's problem.

We do, however, find one important difference between the perfectly competitive seller's decision problem and the monopolist's decision problem. Recall from Chapter 6 that to maximize profits the perfectly competitive firm expands production until marginal cost (*MC*) equals price (*P*), where price is determined by the intersection of the market demand and market supply curves.

Chapter 6 also showed that marginal revenue equals price for a perfectly competitive firm because the firm faces a perfectly elastic demand curve (a horizontal demand curve),

12.1

12.2

12.3

12.4

12.5

12.6

12.7

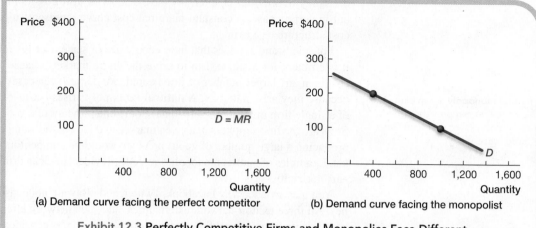

Exhibit 12.3 **Perfectly Competitive Firms and Monopolies Face Different Demand Curves**

Panel (a) shows one of the key results from Chapter 6—that in a perfectly competitive market, the demand curve facing the firm is perfectly elastic. The demand curve faced by the monopolist in panel (b) is the entire market and is therefore downward-sloping. Thus, if the monopolist charges $100, it can sell 1,000 units; and if it increases the price to $200, it sells only 400 units.

as shown in panel (a) of Exhibit 12.3 At the market price, the perfectly competitive firm can sell as many units as it wishes. But if it charges a bit more, it will lose all of its business because consumers can buy an identical good from another seller who is ready to sell at a lower price. Also, if it charges a bit less, it sells the same number of units but does not raise as much revenue, so that would not be profit optimizing. As such, a firm facing a perfectly elastic demand curve is a price-taker.

> **Unlike the perfectly competitive firm, the monopoly can increase price and not lose all of its business.**

This situation represents the major difference between the perfectly competitive firm's decision problem and the monopolist's decision problem. Because the monopolist is the sole market supplier, it faces the market demand curve, which is downward-sloping, as in panel (b) of Exhibit 12.3. Unlike the perfectly competitive firm, the monopolist can increase price and not lose all of its business. In fact, the market demand curve tells us exactly the trade-off the monopolist faces when it changes its price.

Consider panel (b) of Exhibit 12.3 more carefully. If the monopolist chooses a price of $100, it can sell 1,000 units. If the price is increased to $200, then the monopolist can sell only 400 units. Of course, the monopolist prefers to sell a lot of units for a high price—say, 1,000 units at a price of $200. But the downward-sloping market demand curve that monopolies face makes this outcome impossible. A monopoly is powerful, but it cannot sell at a point above the market demand curve. This raises an important consideration: how does a monopolist's total revenue change when it raises or lowers price?

Revenue Curves

To illustrate how total revenue changes with price changes, let's consider the task facing you as the CEO of Schering-Plough Corporation. Your company is ready to go to the market with Claritin, and you want to figure out how you can make the most money possible from the drug. Even though there might be other medicines for allergies, we will assume that the conceptual model of monopoly applies because there are no close substitutes for Claritin.

A first step in this process is to understand how much money you will bring in at various price levels—for now, we assume that you have to charge each customer the same price. Recall that the total revenue of a firm is the amount of money it brings in from the sale of its outputs. Marginal revenue is the change in total revenue associated

12.1

12.2

12.3

12.4

12.5

12.6

12.7

Exhibit 12.4 The Market Demand Curve for Claritin

With patent protection from the government, the demand curve that Schering-Plough faces for its sales of Claritin is the entire market. For example, if Schering-Plough chose a price of $4, then it would be able to sell 400 million units, but the demand curve shows that if it chose a price of $6 or higher, it wouldn't sell any Claritin, despite having a monopoly.

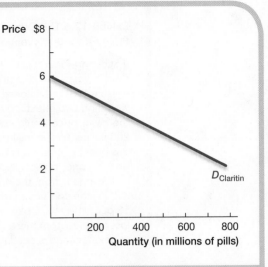

with producing and selling one more unit of output. How do we begin determining total and marginal revenue?

The key is to understand the market demand curve for Claritin. After a thorough market analysis, you determine that a reasonable estimate of the market demand curve is that shown in Exhibit 12.4. The exhibit tells you, for example, that at a price of $5 per pill, you can sell 200 million units of Claritin; and at a price of $3, you can sell 600 million units. This graphical representation reveals the important trade-off between price and quantity sold that the monopolist faces: a higher price yields more revenue per unit sold, but fewer number of units sold.

From this demand curve, you can calculate the total revenue and marginal revenue at each price level, as shown in columns 3 and 4 of Exhibit 12.5. The exhibit also includes fixed costs and marginal costs, which you studied in Chapter 6. You might notice that the fixed costs are relatively large and that the marginal cost is constant over the various output levels. High fixed costs are typical for industries that spend large amounts of money on researching and developing products, such as pharmaceutical companies. In such instances, it is not uncommon for marginal cost to be constant over large ranges of output because mass production of the product leads each additional unit of production to have a constant additional cost per unit.

Exhibit 12.5 Revenues and Costs for Claritin at Different Levels of Output

Revenue and cost data are summarized for Schering-Plough (the data are not actual data). The data show that marginal cost is constant. Although these data are hypothetical, the constant marginal cost of $1 per pill approximates the nature of Schering-Plough's marginal costs (constant everywhere). Marginal revenue is calculated at each point for small changes.

Quantity (in millions)	Price	Total Revenue (in millions)	Marginal Revenue	Total Cost (in millions)	Fixed Cost (in millions)	Marginal Cost	ATC
100	$5.50	$ 550	$ 5	$ 110	$10	$1.00	$1.10
200	$5.00	$1,000	$ 4	$ 210	$10	$1.00	$1.05
300	$4.50	$1,350	$ 3	$ 310	$10	$1.00	$1.033
400	$4.00	$1,600	$ 2	$ 410	$10	$1.00	$1.025
500	$3.50	$1,750	$ 1	$ 510	$10	$1.00	$1.02
600	$3.00	$1,800	$ 0	$ 610	$10	$1.00	$1.017
700	$2.50	$1,750	$−1	$ 710	$10	$1.00	$1.014
800	$2.00	$1,600	$−2	$ 810	$10	$1.00	$1.013
900	$1.50	$1,350	$−3	$ 910	$10	$1.00	$1.011
1000	$1.00	$1,000	$−4	$1,010	$10	$1.00	$1.01
1100	$0.50	$ 550	$−5	$1,110	$10	$1.00	$1.009

12.1

12.2

12.3

12.4

12.5

12.6

12.7

Exhibit 12.6 The Quantity Effect and the Price Effect on Revenues for Claritin

If Schering-Plough set a price of $5 per pill, then it would sell 200 million Claritin pills annually. If it lowered its price to $4 per pill, there would be two effects to total revenue. First, the lower price would lead to more sales (from 200 million to 400 million) and more revenue; this quantity effect is captured by the green box. Second, the lower price would lead to lost revenues from the original consumers: the 200 million consumers who were buying at $5 per pill are now paying only $4 per pill. This lost revenue from these consumers is called the price effect and is captured by the pink box.

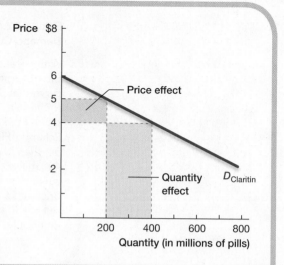

Another important feature that the numbers in Exhibit 12.5 reveal is the relationship between price and total revenue. Let's consider an example. Assume that you lower the price from $5 to $4. In this case, Exhibit 12.5 reveals that you bring in $600 million more in total revenues. This additional $600 million arises from two effects.

First, is a *quantity effect*: the lower price allows you to sell 200 million more units of Claritin. The increase in revenues because of this increased number of sales is shown as the green-shaded region in Exhibit 12.6. Computing the area of the green-shaded region (base times height) yields an increase in revenues of $800 million (200 million multiplied by $4).

But there is a flip side. Those people who were buying at the old price of $5 now only have to pay $4. This loss in revenues is known as the *price effect*; it is shaded pink in Exhibit 12.6. Calculating the area of the pink rectangle, we find that the price effect is equal to $200 million (200 million multiplied by $1). In sum, therefore, the increase in total revenues from the price change is $800 million − $200 million = $600 million. In this case, the price effect is smaller than the quantity effect. As we learned in Chapter 5, this means that demand is elastic over this range of the demand curve.

These observations reveal a more general pattern at work. With price decreases—moving down the demand curve—when the quantity effect dominates the price effect, then total revenue increases. If the price effect dominates the quantity effect, then total revenue falls. Alternatively, if one considers price increases—moving up the demand curve—the nature of these relationships reverses. That is, with price increases, if the quantity effect dominates the price effect, then total revenue decreases. If the price effect dominates the quantity effect, then total revenue increases. The following table summarizes these effects.

	Quantity Effect Dominates	Price Effect Dominates
Price Decreases	Total revenue increases	Total revenue decreases
Price Increases	Total revenue decreases	Total revenue increases

Price, Marginal Revenue, and Total Revenue

We are now in a position to put this intuition into action. To do so, we begin by plotting the entire relationship among price, marginal revenue, and total revenue in Exhibit 12.7. Panel (a) uses the information from Exhibit 12.5 to graph the demand curve and the marginal revenue curve for Claritin. The curves begin at the same point on the price axis because the price of Claritin is the marginal revenue from selling the first unit of Claritin. Thereafter, marginal revenue lies below the demand curve, and as quantity expands the

12.1

12.2

12.3

12.4

12.5

12.6

12.7

Exhibit 12.7 Relationship Among Price, Marginal Revenue, and Total Revenue

Panel (a) combines the demand curve for Claritin from Exhibit 12.4 with the marginal revenue curve faced by Schering-Plough. The marginal revenue curve shows the additional revenue generated for Schering-Plough at each quantity level. When marginal revenue crosses the quantity axis (at 600 million), total revenue decreases with further sales (see panel (b)). This means that total revenue is maximized when the marginal revenue curve crosses the x-axis.

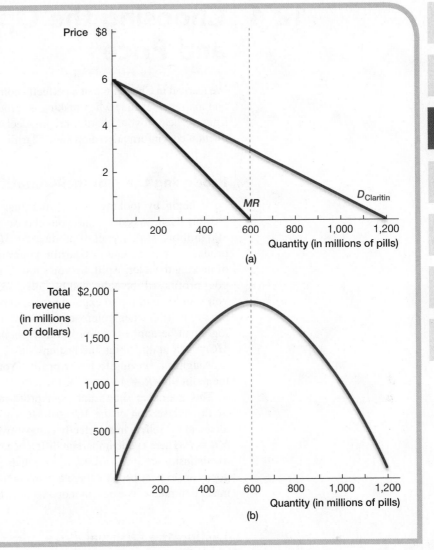

difference between the demand curve and the marginal revenue curve grows larger. This is because for the monopoly to increase its sales, it must lower the price on all goods sold.

In this example, we find that the marginal revenue curve is twice as steep as the demand curve, causing it to reach the quantity axis at 600 million units, whereas the demand curve reaches it at 1.2 billion units. In fact, this will be the case for every linear demand curve because the slope of the marginal revenue curve is twice as large (in absolute value) as the slope of the demand curve.

A second important aspect that Exhibit 12.7 reveals is the relationship between marginal revenue and total revenue. Panel (b) shows the total revenue curve for Claritin, which is hill-shaped. Exhibit 12.7 shows that when total revenue is rising, marginal revenue is positive. This makes sense because if total revenue is increasing, marginal revenue must be positive. Alternatively, when total revenue is falling, marginal revenue is negative. For this reason, total revenue is at its maximum when the marginal revenue curve crosses the *x*-axis (quantity axis)—that is the point where an additional unit of output causes marginal revenue to equal zero.

To perform your job of choosing the optimal price to maximize profits, you can now begin to see how you can eliminate some price levels from consideration. For example, would you ever choose a price of $1.50? No, because at this price, the marginal revenue from the last unit sold is negative, −$3 (see Exhibit 12.5). In other words, you are decreasing total revenues by selling that last unit! From this reasoning, you can see that you would never price below $3, which is the price at which marginal revenue turns negative. To do so would only lower revenues and increase costs.

12.1

12.2

12.3

12.4

12.5

12.6

12.7

12.4 Choosing the Optimal Quantity and Price

We learned in Chapter 6 that a perfectly competitive firm must consider both marginal cost and marginal revenue when making its production decision. A monopolist is no different. Thus, to help in your Claritin pricing decision, columns 5–8 in Exhibit 12.5 include production cost information alongside Claritin revenue information.

Producing the Optimal Quantity

Let's begin by looking just at marginal revenue and marginal cost, as depicted in Exhibit 12.8. Assume that you choose to produce at quantity level Q_L which is 300 million. At this level of production, $MR > MC$, specifically, $\$3 > \$1$. Thus, if you produce one more unit of Claritin, your additional revenue exceeds the additional cost of making the allergy pill. So you should definitely produce one more pill at Q_L because your profits will be enhanced by doing so. With this same reasoning, you can see that you should continue to expand production provided that $MR > MC$. You stop increasing production when you reach the point of $MR = MC$, or at 500 million units. Similar logic can be applied if you initially begin producing at Q_H in Exhibit 12.8. Because $MC > MR$ at this point, the last unit costs more to produce than the additional revenue it brought in, serving to lower profits. You can do better by decreasing production to the point of $MR = MC$.

This reasoning shows that your profit-maximizing level of output produced is given by the intersection of the MR and MC curves. As we learned in Chapter 6, this rule is identical for sellers in a perfectly competitive industry, who produce at the point of $MC = MR = P$. There is one important difference, though: whereas firms in a perfectly competitive industry are *price-takers*, monopolists are *price-makers*—they set the price for their goods or services because there are no competitors. In this sense, after you determine how much to produce, you as a monopolist need to determine where to set Claritin's price.

Setting the Optimal Price

Now that you have figured out the optimal quantity, how do you start to think about where to set the price for Claritin? Your intuition tells you that if millions of people desperately want Claritin, you should set a very high price, whereas if only a few thousand people are vaguely interested in Claritin, you should set a low price. This intuition is spot-on in that

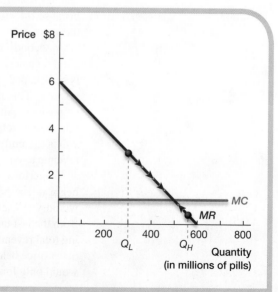

Exhibit 12.8 Marginal Revenue and Marginal Cost for Claritin

If Schering-Plough produces at Q_L, then the 300 millionth pill will earn $3 in additional revenue (marginal revenue) and cost $1 to produce. At this point Schering-Plough should expand production. Why? It will earn more profits! By the same logic, consider Q_H, where Schering-Plough is producing so many units that the marginal cost exceeds the marginal revenue. The last unit of production costs more to produce than it generate in revenue.

One way for you to ease the pain of allergy season is to purchase allergy drugs, such as Claritin.

your pricing decision is, in fact, critically linked to the nature of the market demand curve.

In Exhibit 12.9, we graph the demand curve, the *MR* curve, and the *MC* curve. Once we have found the quantity level where *MR = MC*, your job as the monopolist is to choose the highest possible price that permits you to sell the entire quantity that you have produced. Graphically, you can find this price by using the demand curve.

As shown by the vertical arrow in Exhibit 12.9, you determine Claritin's price by looking at the demand curve to see what price consumers are willing to pay for the quantity you put on the market. Following the arrows in Exhibit 12.9, you see that you maximize your firm's profits by setting a price of $3.50 because this is the highest price that you can charge and still sell the 500 million pills that you have produced (if you search the Web, you might find that Internet prices for a Claritin pill are currently around $0.50 per pill; for illustrative purposes, we chose our equilibrium price to be in the range of observed prices over the lifetime of the Claritin patent).

The following simple flow chart provides the steps to the production and pricing decisions facing the monopolist:

Expand **Q** until **MC = MR**	→	Produce **Q** at that point	→	Trace up to the demand curve	→	Find **P** associated with **Q**

You will likely note that this approach is quite similar to the decision making of our perfectly competitive firm in Chapter 6, but with one major difference: price is set at a level higher than marginal cost for a monopolist, whereas price is equal to marginal cost for a perfectly competitive firm.

In sum, the optimal pricing decision rules are as follows:

Monopolist: Set $P > MR = MC$;   Perfectly competitive firm: $P = MR = MC$.

> **Price is set at a level higher than marginal costs for a monopolist, whereas price is equal to marginal cost for a perfectly competitive firm.**

Note that the marginal decision making concerning the level of production is identical across these two market structures: expand production until $MC = MR$. The major difference arises from the fact that the firm in a competitive industry does not set its price (the market does), whereas the monopolist sets price based on the market demand curve. By inspection of Exhibit 12.9, we can see that the monopolist sets a price that is on the elastic portion of the demand curve (recall from Chapter 5 that the top half of a linear demand curve is elastic).

Exhibit 12.9 Choosing the Profit-Maximizing Price for Claritin

Schering-Plough expands production until *MC = MR*. To determine the price that maximizes profits, it goes directly upward to the demand curve and over to the y-axis (the price axis) to determine the profit-maximizing price. In this case, a price of $3.50 is the profit-maximizing price for Schering-Plough.

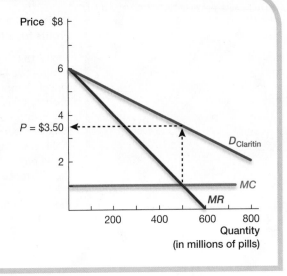

How a Monopolist Calculates Profits

How much will your company earn in economic profits from Claritin if you follow this optimal decision rule? Computing economic profits for a monopoly works exactly the same as computing economic profits for a perfectly competitive firm:

$$\text{Profits} = \text{Total revenue} - \text{Total cost} = (P \times Q) - (ATC \times Q) = (P - ATC) \times Q.$$

Taking the numbers from Exhibit 12.5, we can compute monopoly profits in equilibrium. Exhibit 12.10 graphically depicts the total profits with the green-shaded area. To summarize how we obtain this green-shaded area, we begin by finding the point where $MC = MR$. This gives us the profit-maximizing output of 500 million units. Moving upward from this point to the demand curve, we find the profit-maximizing price of $3.50. At that quantity, subtracting the average total cost of $1.02 from the $3.50 price gives us $2.48 of profits per unit sold. We then multiply this number by 500 million units to obtain total economic profits of $1.24 billion or

$$\$1,240,000,000 = \text{Total revenue} - \text{Total cost} = (\$3.50 - \$1.02) \times 500,000,000.$$

As we discussed earlier, in perfectly competitive markets entry causes long-run economic profits to be zero. With a monopoly, economic profits remain. This is because there is no threat of entry from competitors because of barriers to entry. Therefore, there are no new entrants to increase supply and push price down to eliminate economic profits.

Does a Monopoly Have a Supply Curve?

At this point, you may have found it curious that there has been no mention of monopoly supply curves. After all, Exhibit 12.9 shows the price and quantity combination at which a monopolistic firm will produce by using only the marginal revenue, marginal cost, and demand curves. No supply curve! The reason is simple: monopolists, unlike sellers in competitive markets, do not have a supply curve.

To understand why this is the case, first consider what the supply curve of a competitive market represents. To create a supply curve under perfect competition, it is necessary for firms to be price-*takers*, whose production is based on the *given* market price. Under this assumption, we simply determine the quantity at which the marginal cost of producing the last unit of a good is equal to the market price. Thus, in a competitive market, a supply curve shows all of the price and quantity combinations at which firms will produce.

Monopolists, as price-*makers*, do not vary their production based on market price because *they set the price*; it makes no sense to ask how much of a good a monopolist will produce at a given price. Like sellers in competitive markets, monopolists will produce at

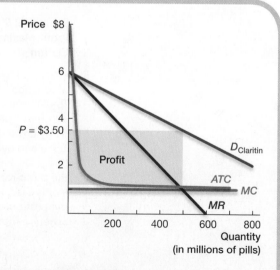

Exhibit 12.10 Computing Profits for a Monopolist

Similar to the perfectly competitive firm, Schering-Plough computes profits as quantity times the difference between price and *ATC* [profits = quantity × (P − ATC)]. In this case, the green rectangle shows profits, which equals the difference between the price of each pill ($3.50) and the *ATC* ($1.02), multiplied by 500 million.

the point where their marginal revenue is equal to their marginal cost. But as you have just learned, marginal revenue is dependent upon the negatively sloped demand curve that the monopolist faces. Because a monopolist's production decision is based on demand, it cannot be depicted as an independent supply curve.

12.1

12.2

12.3

12.4

12.5

12.6

12.7

12.5 The "Broken" Invisible Hand: The Cost of Monopoly

[**A firm that exercises market power causes a reallocation of resources toward itself, thereby sacrificing total surplus.**]

In Chapter 7, we learned that the invisible hand creates harmony between individual and social interests. Such synchronization has the very attractive feature that social surplus is maximized in the competitive equilibrium. The power of the invisible hand is such that even in markets composed of only self-interested people, the overall well-being of society is maximized. One important factor that can "break" the powerful result of the invisible hand is market power. A firm that exercises market power causes a reallocation of resources toward itself, thereby sacrificing social surplus.

One way to think about this is to consider the market for Claritin before and after Schering-Plough's patent expired. In 1981, Schering-Plough was awarded a monopoly, in the form of a patent, on Claritin. Twenty years later, Schering-Plough's monopoly rights expired, and generic prescription drug companies could suddenly enter the market and sell close substitutes, such as Allegra.[2] This entry process drastically changed the market for Claritin in a number of ways.

Panel (a) of Exhibit 12.11 shows the long-run equilibrium of the market after entry by competitive firms when Claritin's patent expired. Firms have a constant marginal cost curve, so $ATC = MC$. You might wonder about fixed costs. Recall that since we are in the long run there are no fixed costs.

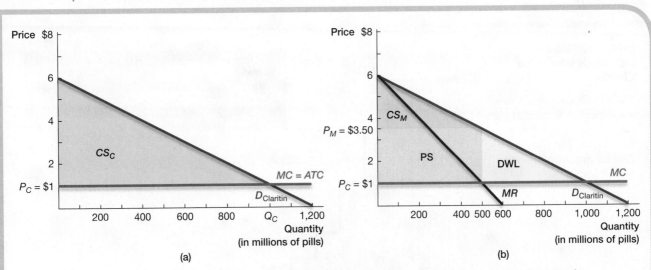

Exhibit 12.11 Surplus Allocations: Perfect Competition Versus Monopoly

Panel (a) shows the consumer surplus from a perfectly competitive market, which is the area under the demand curve and above the market price. Panel (b) shows what happens to consumer surplus when the monopoly maximizes its profits: consumer surplus is substantially reduced, with some of it going to the monopoly, and another large piece that is a deadweight loss (DWL).

The equilibrium price is now dramatically lower—just $1 per pill. This lower price prompts a boom in quantity demanded, all the way to 1 billion pills. Consumer surplus in this perfectly competitive market is depicted by the blue area below the demand curve and above the marginal cost curve. In equilibrium, consumer surplus is $2.5 billion (½ × 1 billion × $5).

To compare outcomes across markets, panel (b) of Exhibit 12.11 presents surplus outcomes *before* Claritin's patent expired. When Schering-Plough's patent was still in effect, consumer surplus was dramatically smaller: $625 million (½ × 500 million × $2.50). Schering-Plough's monopoly power allowed it to capture surplus from consumers. This captured surplus is represented by the pink-shaded box labeled PS.

Schering-Plough's monopolistic pricing didn't just capture surplus from consumers, however. Importantly, social surplus is smaller when Schering-Plough exercises monopoly power. This cost to society is deadweight loss and is represented as the yellow triangle labeled DWL in panel (b). This is surplus that would exist in the competitive equilibrium but is lost when Schering-Plough is a monopolist. The deadweight loss from Claritin's monopolistic pricing is $625 million (½ × 500 million × $2.50).

Does this mean that patents are counterproductive? Not necessarily. Remember that because fixed costs were so high to develop Claritin, the government had to create an incentive to induce companies to spend money on research and development. The incentive that is used with pharmaceutical companies is a temporary patent, and the cost to society of this incentive is the deadweight loss from monopoly while the patent is held. Overall, was the bargain worth it? We'll explore that question in more depth below.

12.6 Restoring Efficiency

Beyond waiting until the Claritin patent expires, are there any other means to restore efficiency in this market? The answer is yes. To illustrate, consider Exhibit 12.12 and its accompanying table, which provides a glimpse of five buyers in the market for Claritin. In this example, Augie is willing to pay $5 per pill, Gary $4, Joyce $3, Dawn $2, and Sandi $1.50. At the monopolist's price of $3.50, only Augie and Gary buy Claritin, even though Joyce, Dawn, and Sandi all have willingness to pay values above marginal cost.

One way to restore social efficiency (that is, maximize social surplus) is to have a social planner choose the monopolist's quantity and price. This "all-knowing" social planner

Exhibit 12.12 Select Individuals Who Value Claritin

The exhibit and table show the maximum price that each buyer would pay for one Claritin pill. The marginal cost for producing remains $1 per unit.

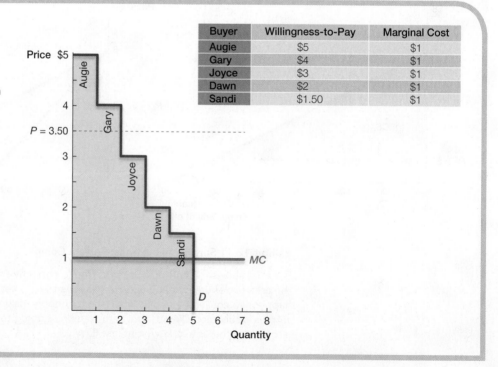

Buyer	Willingness-to-Pay	Marginal Cost
Augie	$5	$1
Gary	$4	$1
Joyce	$3	$1
Dawn	$2	$1
Sandi	$1.50	$1

12.1

12.2

12.3

12.4

12.5

12.6

12.7

would need to know both the monopolist's marginal cost and the buyer's willingness to pay for the Claritin pill. The social planner would want consumers like Joyce, Dawn, and Sandi to buy Claritin because their willingness-to-pay values are all higher than the marginal cost of producing Claritin. If they buy, social surplus increases by the difference between their willingness-to-pay values and the marginal cost of production, or $2 + $1 + $0.50 = $3.50. Indeed, the social planner could choose the same outcome as that which results in the perfectly competitive equilibrium because that outcome maximizes social surplus.

In analyzing how Schering-Plough produces in its monopoly equilibrium, the planner would view the quantity produced as too low. So the social planner would direct Schering-Plough to produce many more Claritin pills than the firm would prefer to produce. This is the reason why monopolies cause a breakdown of the invisible hand results discussed in Chapter 7.

So why doesn't Schering-Plough produce extra Claritin pills and charge a slightly lower price to Joyce, Dawn, and Sandi? The reason is that by so doing, it would then have to charge a slightly lower price to *all* buyers, such as Augie and Gary—a move that would lower profits, as we showed earlier in the chapter in our discussion of optimal profits and the price and quantity effects associated with changing price.

Because the all-knowing social planner is merely a mythical construct, we can ask if there is any practical, realistic way to attempt to reach the maximum level of social surplus achieved in a perfectly competitive market. Is there any recourse beyond having the government step in and direct Schering-Plough how to price? The answer is yes, but we suspect that it is an approach that may make you less than fully comfortable. Let's discuss that now.

Three Degrees of Price Discrimination

Have you ever wondered why some people seem to get all the deals? Maybe you buy a plane ticket home for $500, only to learn that the frequent flyer in the seat next to you paid $350. Likewise, you might get irked if you're standing in a checkout line at Walmart when the man in front of you pulls out a coupon for a free T-shirt—the same shirt you're about to purchase for $15!

In such situations, consumers are often displeased and struck with the perceived unfairness of the transaction. Producers, however, are ecstatic because of their success at *price discrimination*. **Price discrimination** occurs when firms charge different consumers different prices for the same good or service. Provided that buyers who receive low prices cannot simply turn around and sell to buyers who receive high prices (we call this arbitrage), companies might be able to enhance their profits by engaging in price discrimination.

We typically discuss three types of price discrimination:

1. **First-degree**, or **perfect price discrimination**, in which consumers are charged the maximum price they are willing to pay
2. **Second-degree price discrimination**, in which consumers are charged different prices based on characteristics of their purchase, such as the quantity they purchase
3. **Third-degree price discrimination**, in which different groups of consumers are charged different prices based on their own attributes (such as age, gender, location, and so on)

Let's see how first-degree price discrimination works by continuing with the example from Exhibit 12.12. In this scenario, if Schering-Plough knew each individual's willingness to pay, it would charge the five consumers exactly that amount—$5 per pill for Augie, $4 for Gary, $3 for Joyce, $2 for Dawn, and $1.50 for Sandi. By so doing, Schering-Plough can extract all consumer surplus from the buyers.

Extending this logic to the entire market reveals some interesting insights. If you, as the monopolist, are able to perfectly price discriminate, then the outcome would be not only to maximize your own profits but *also* to maximize social surplus. To see why, let's reconsider the monopoly outcome, which is summarized in panel (a) of Exhibit 12.13. Panel (b) of the exhibit shows the monopoly outcome with perfect price discrimination. As panel (b)

Price discrimination occurs when firms charge different consumers different prices for the same good or service.

Perfect price discrimination, also known as **first-degree price discrimination,** occurs when a firm charges each buyer exactly his or her willingness to pay.

Second-degree price discrimination occurs when consumers are charged different prices based on characteristics of their purchase.

Third-degree price discrimination occurs when price varies based on a customer's attributes.

If you as the monopolist are able to perfectly price discriminate, then the outcome would be not only to maximize your own profits but also social surplus.

12.1

12.2

12.3

12.4

12.5

12.6

12.7

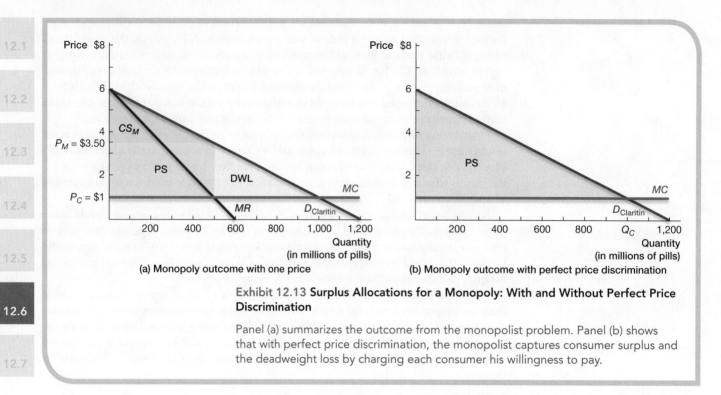

Exhibit 12.13 **Surplus Allocations for a Monopoly: With and Without Perfect Price Discrimination**

Panel (a) summarizes the outcome from the monopolist problem. Panel (b) shows that with perfect price discrimination, the monopolist captures consumer surplus and the deadweight loss by charging each consumer his willingness to pay.

shows, with perfect price discrimination you expand production until the demand curve intersects the marginal cost curve (point Q_C). When doing so, Schering-Plough's producer surplus includes the entire consumer surplus and the deadweight loss because it expands production until $P = MC$, and charges each consumer his willingness to pay.

The exhibit shows that you have been able to dramatically increase Schering-Plough's surplus through perfect price discrimination. Yet, it also shows that in aggregate consumers clearly suffer. Because the monopolist is able to extract every penny each consumer would be willing to pay when it practices first-degree price discrimination, consumer surplus equals zero.

We are now in a position to compare social surplus in the Claritin market before and after first-degree price discrimination. The entire story is found in Exhibit 12.13, which shows with perfect price discrimination, we have completely eliminated the deadweight loss of monopoly. Thus, perfect price discrimination is *socially efficient*: it provides the maximum level of social surplus. This equilibrium is also a Pareto-efficient equilibrium (as we discussed in Chapter 7) because no one can be made better off without making someone else worse off. What might concern you is the extreme inequity in the allocation of surplus—buyers receive no surplus and the seller receives all of it!

In practice, perfect price discrimination is difficult. There are two reasons. First, it is hard to charge every consumer a unique price. Second, it is challenging to know every consumer's willingness to pay. Therefore, other forms of price discrimination are more prevalent in practice. In many of these cases, the monopolist does not know the exact willingness to pay of different consumers but can still improve its profits by charging different prices based on perceived differences in willingness to pay.

We focus next on third-degree price discrimination because it affects all of us daily. Third-degree price discrimination occurs when price varies by customer or location attributes. You might wonder why movie theatres, restaurants, golf courses, and the like charge a lower price to children and senior citizens. Likewise, we have found that sometimes car dealerships base their negotiating practices on the gender or race of the car buyer. These are all attempts to price discriminate based on an observable characteristic that the seller believes is correlated to the consumer's willingness to pay. In such cases, the monopolist segments its customers into groups and maximizes profits by effectively acting like a monopolist in each submarket, setting $MR = MC$ in each.

Following up on our Claritin example, if the willingness-to-pay values for Augie, Gary, Joyce, Dawn, and Sandi were indicative of the population at large, it would be profitable for the firm to segment by gender and charge men a higher price than women. For example, simply moving from charging one price of $3.50 to charging men $4 per pill and women $2 per pill would increase profits significantly. By paying $4 instead of $3.50, Augie and Gary provide $1 more in total profits. And, whereas at a price of $3.50 the three women do not purchase Claritin and therefore add nothing to Schering-Plough's profits, when they are charged $2 they add $2 to profits because both Joyce and Dawn now purchase Claritin.

Both first- and third-degree price discrimination are examples where the monopolist charges different prices to different people based on their perceived differences in willingness to pay. There are important cases, however, when sellers are not able to differentiate between types of consumers. Perhaps they do not have good indicators of how much various consumers are willing to pay. Even in this situation price discrimination can exist. For example, Apple gives discounts if you purchase a large quantity of song downloads from its iTunes music store. Tire salesmen often sell four tires for $200 and one for $75. Bakeries sell a dozen doughnuts for $7, whereas two doughnuts sell for $1.50. Likewise, a standard arrangement between industrial customers and providers is that those who buy in bulk enjoy substantial discounts.

In cases where consumers are charged different prices based on characteristics of their purchase, second-degree price discrimination is said to exist. Beyond the examples above, can you think of situations when you were a consumer and a firm practiced second-degree price discrimination?

 LETTING THE DATA SPEAK

Third-Degree Price Discrimination in Action

Third-degree price discrimination can often rear an ugly head. Consider a recent field experiment that compared people confined to wheelchairs with a group of non-disabled people. The subjects of interest were in need of car repairs. For the disabled, it's a hassle to even leave the house, much less shop around for a few price quotes. This means that there are real search differences between the disabled and non-disabled.

It turns out that the disabled aren't the only ones who know this. Mechanics know it, too, and adjust the prices they charge the disabled accordingly.

We know this because field experiments[3] have been conducted that have randomized whether a disabled or nondisabled person brings a banged up (but still specially equipped for the disabled) car to an auto repair shop. What do the data say?

If it happens that a disabled person is the one who is asking for a price quote, then the price he is charged is 20 percent higher than the price a nondisabled person is charged. You can see this in the accompanying exhibit by just comparing the orange and purple lines above the word Baseline: the disabled are quoted an average price of $600, whereas the nondisabled pay around $500.

You might be thinking that this isn't necessarily price discrimination based on search differences. It might just be that mechanics don't like people in wheelchairs. But the same study tested this idea by also having every person in both groups say the following line when they were getting a quote, "I am getting a few price quotes today."

Turns out that just saying this simple line caused the price quotes that the handicapped were getting to drop

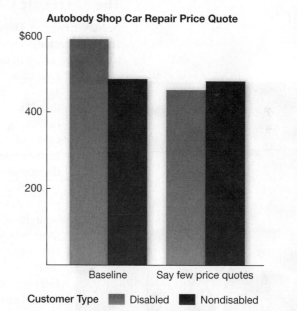

Autobody Shop Car Repair Price Quote

Customer Type ▮ Disabled ▮ Nondisabled

a lot. To see this, just compare the first orange line to the one above "Say few price quotes" in the exhibit.

What about the nondisabled? Their price quotes stayed about the same, suggesting that there was never any doubt in the minds of mechanics that the nondisabled shop around for the best price.

This case represents an example of third-degree price discrimination: body shop mechanics were using the fact that the disabled had a hard time searching so they tended to charge all disabled people a higher price in an effort to enhance their profits.

12.1

12.2

12.3

12.4

12.5

12.6

12.7

12.7 Government Policy Toward Monopoly

Antitrust policy aims to regulate and prevent anticompetitive pricing.

The Department of Justice in the United States, and many similar agencies in other countries, actively attempts to keep various industries in check. One of their main purposes, sometimes referred to as **antitrust policy**, is to prevent anticompetitive pricing, low quantities, and deadweight loss from emerging and dominating markets. Some monopolies, such as natural monopolies, are unavoidable. But, as we learned in this chapter, monopoly pricing is potentially detrimental to society and quite costly for consumers. The goal of antitrust policy is to keep markets open and competitive.

In the United States, antitrust policy started in 1890 with the Sherman Act, even though several states had adopted similar statutes prior to this legislation. This was the era of the so-called "robber barons"—men such as John D. Rockefeller, Andrew Carnegie, and Cornelius Vanderbilt, who had dominated certain industries—who were often accused of using questionable methods and unfair practices. The Sherman Act and the policies of Presidents Theodore Roosevelt and Woodrow Wilson were pitched against such monopolies.

The Sherman Act prohibited any agreements or actions that would put restraints on trade—in essence, prohibiting anything to do with monopolizing markets. Moreover, it made such attempts felonies, punishable not only by large fines but also by prison sentences. These antitrust policies led to the breakup of Standard Oil and introduced greater regulation of other large monopolies, including the dominant banks of the era, which were becoming increasingly powerful. Today, U.S. antitrust policy is still based on the Sherman Act.

The Microsoft Case

In May 1998, the Department of Justice filed a lawsuit under the Sherman Act against arguably the most successful corporation of the 1990s, Microsoft. It claimed that Microsoft was engaging in unfair practices in order to monopolize the market. The crux of the case concerned the fact that Microsoft was bundling its Windows operating system with its Internet Explorer browser. The Department of Justice argued that Microsoft made it effectively impossible for alternative browsers, such as Netscape, to maintain a large market share. As a result, Microsoft was accused of achieving monopoly power through unfair practices. The suit was filed the day Windows 98 was released with Internet Explorer bundled into the operating system.

After a long trial, the ruling ultimately went against Microsoft—both in this case brought by the U.S. Department of Justice and in similar cases brought against it in Europe by the European Commission. At some point, there was even the possibility that Microsoft would be broken into separate companies—one unit for selling the Windows operating system and the other for selling applications software. In the end, Microsoft paid various fines and agreed to change its operating system and marketing practices to make it easier for alternative browsers and other applications to be used with Windows.

The Microsoft case is interesting, not only because it illustrates the power of antitrust laws in the United States but also because it raises questions about what should be considered monopoly power in today's new and dynamic industries. Could Microsoft really develop a monopoly in the same way as Standard Oil did in the oil business? Some believe that the answer is yes, and this reasoning was the one that prevailed in the courts. In fact, some economists believe that the dangers of such monopolization are even stronger today, because many software products are subject to network externalities. Compatibility issues are the main source of such network effects, and they are undoubtedly present in many products.

Bill Gates spent much of his time defending Microsoft in an antitrust case filed by the U.S. Department of Justice in 1998.

A simple example of a network effect is your choice of a DVD player. At some point, both HD DVD and Blu-Ray were viable choices for the next generation of DVDs. Network effects are important in consumer choices—when all of your friends purchase and use Blu-Ray, then HD DVD becomes much less attractive for you because you will be unable to exchange discs with them. Ultimately, if all stores carry mostly Blu-Ray, then it will be difficult for you even to find HD DVD discs. Such network effects were the basis of the claim that in many software-related industries, products that achieve sufficient market share become difficult to compete against and thus develop monopoly power.

Some other economists recognize the importance of network effects but nevertheless believe that software and other IT industries are inherently competitive and cannot be monopolized in the same way that the oil business was a century ago. This group thought that the Department of Justice's case against Microsoft was beyond the scope of the original Sherman Act. They argued that if Microsoft's operating system became too expensive, a new operating system, with greater compatibility with other products, would be supplied at a lower price, because software innovations cannot come to an end. There are always potential competitors watching the industry, and they will seize any opportunity to make a profit as soon as it becomes available. The Microsoft case still remains one of the most debated among economists today.

Price Regulation

In the past, one government solution has been to allow the monopoly to keep its market share but regulate the price it may charge. The notion is that a lower price will expand the purchase opportunities for consumers. This seems like a simple enough solution . . . until it is time to decide on the "fair" price a monopolist may charge. Two pricing options have dominated discussions: setting price equal to marginal cost, and setting price equal to average total cost.

It may seem that the proper choice is obvious: set price equal to marginal cost because, as we know, that is the price at which total surplus is maximized. A price set at marginal cost is called the **efficient** or **socially optimal price**. Unfortunately, the choice is not this simple. As we have learned, in some cases marginal cost is lower than average total cost at every level of quantity (this occurred in our Claritin example). This means that setting price equal to marginal cost will cause the firm's total revenue to be less than the total cost, so the firm will experience an economic loss and will eventually exit the industry if this sort of regulation is imposed.

> An **efficient**, or **socially optimal price** is set at marginal cost.

One solution to this problem is to have the government make up for any losses incurred by the monopolist. Unfortunately, the government must raise this money through taxes, and as we learned in Chapter 10, government taxes lead to a deadweight loss. Another solution is to allow the monopolist to charge a higher price—a price equal to its average total cost. This price level is called a **fair-returns price**. Although the fair-returns price does not maximize surplus—we again have a deadweight loss—it does allow the monopolist to make zero economic profits. This means that the monopolist can stay in business without the government making up for the losses incurred.

> A price set at average total cost is a **fair-returns price**.

Unfortunately, these two forms of regulation have their own efficiency problems. The main one is that there is now a loss of incentive for the firm to minimize costs, because in either case the firm is guaranteed to make zero economic profits. There is also a lack of profit motive to innovate and produce new goods and services because the firm will not reap the economic rewards.

Now that we have considered ways in which government can regulate monopoly, we should consider whether regulating monopoly is the right course of action in the first place. In both cases, there are costs to consumers. With an unregulated monopoly, consumers pay a higher price, quantity is lower than socially optimal, and there is a deadweight loss. With a regulated monopoly, consumers pay a lower price but there is a deadweight loss either as a result of "tax and transfer" to the monopolist or as the result of an inefficient price. Many economists have argued that allowing unregulated monopolies to exist is, in practice, more efficient than price regulation. We turn to some of this evidence now.

12.1

12.2

12.3

12.4

12.5

12.6

12.7

Evidence-Based Economics

Q: Can a monopoly ever be good for society?

Research and development (R&D) is the investment by firms in the creation of products not yet available on the market.

After learning the rather grim details about monopoly pricing and the deadweight loss associated with monopolies, many might wish to turn their backs on monopolies forever. You might think, "What could be worse than greedy monopolists rolling in money at the expense of ripped-off customers?" Indeed, that is what happened when you set the price for Claritin tablets for Schering-Plough.

Perhaps this is why countries such as Canada and India do not permit such extravagant monopoly profits. In Canada, the government controls prices for pharmaceuticals, and India does not afford innovators strong patent protection. Maybe these countries have it right—why not restrict monopolists in some shape or form?

We must keep in mind that it is the ability to make extraordinary profits that serves as an important motivator to many inventors. Firms that are allowed monopoly profits search out every possible avenue for innovative technologies that they can bring to market, whether it is a cure for AIDS or a programming code for a search engine that will make our lives easier. If we lived in a world of perfect competition, firms would have less of a reason to invest in the creation of new products—**research and development (R&D)**—because they would not enjoy the same levels of profit from innovation. Through entry, economic profits would be driven to zero in the long run.

This presents us with a conundrum: if we allow a firm to have monopoly power, we are assuredly not maximizing social surplus because of deadweight loss. But if we do not grant innovators protection, we might not experience a wide variety of goods and services because profits may not be available to spur invention. In the case of Claritin, the issue boils down to whether you want to suffer with more sneezing, itchier eyes, and a runnier nose or pay $3.50 per tablet for Claritin.

The question naturally becomes an empirical one. Just how much more innovation do we have because of patent and copyright protection?

When a company obtains a patent, it receives exclusive rights to produce and sell a good or service. This exclusive right allows the firm to act as a monopolist and to set its own price, which, as we have learned in this chapter, is higher than the equilibrium price in a perfectly competitive market. If what we've read thus far about monopolies is true, then why would the government encourage and even provide the legal framework for such monopolistic behavior?

The answer is innovation.

There's no perfect dataset to address the impact of patent and copyright protection on innovation, but let's discuss several sources to develop an understanding. Our first stop will be the nineteenth-century World's Fairs.

In the nineteenth century, inventors and firms flocked to the World's Fairs. If the only type of fair you've seen is a state fair, then you might not be able to appreciate the scale of a World's Fair. For example, the 1851 World's Fair was held in the largest enclosed space at the time, attracted more than 6 million visitors, and gave space to more than 17,000 inventors from 40 countries. Consider the following: to see every exhibit at the 1876 World's Fair would have required walking more than 22 miles!

What's so exciting to economists about the World's Fair is that at the time, patent laws varied considerably from country to country, and unlike today, it was very difficult to patent an invention outside the country of origin. As a result, data from guides for the nineteenth-century World's Fairs, which had information on the country of the inventor, the industry of the invention, and whether the inventor had patented his or her invention, are a perfect test of the idea that patent laws are necessary for innovation.

An analysis of these data yields a nuanced answer that makes perfect sense: Some industries need patent protection more than others.[4] In particular, inventors from countries without strong patent laws focused their attention on hard-to-duplicate inventions

like scientific instruments and food processing because they could easily hide the production techniques required to keep their invention a secret. On the other hand, inventors from countries with strong patent protection provided the bulk of innovations for manufacturing and other machinery, in part because these innovations are easily reverse-engineered.

What does this mean for us today? First, for innovations that aren't easily kept secret we need patent protection. But on the other hand, not all industries need the same level of protection. For example, pharmaceutical drugs, which are easily copied by competitors that specialize in mass-producing generic drugs, might need a lot more protection than a clothing company that develops a new textile shrouded in secrecy.

However, too much protection isn't a guarantee for more innovation in the long run. In the 1990s, two major efforts were undertaken to decode the human genome. One was an open-source effort, called the Human Genome Project. The other was a private effort by a firm called Celera. As time went on, some pieces of the genome were decoded by the Human Genome Project first and made freely available to everyone. Other pieces were decoded by Celera first, but in those instances Celera used intellectual property law to prevent the Human Genome Project from decoding their sequences.

The difference in subsequent research on parts of the genome sequenced by the Human Genome Project and Celera is overwhelming. On average, 70 percent more scientific work was conducted on Human Genome Project sequences than Celera sequences.[5]

The takeaway is that innovation doesn't just respond to incentives—it also requires inventors to be able to stand on the shoulders of those who came before them. In that vein, the monopoly power enjoyed by patent and copyright holders may both spur and hinder innovation. The optimal policy for granting innovators a monopoly over their invention should balance these costs and benefits.

Analyzing more than 20 years of data on competition and innovation seems to support this contention. In particular, the relationship between the level of competition that firms face and the amount of innovation arising from firms shows that innovation isn't driven by (1) firms that face perfect competition or (2) firms that have an iron-clad monopoly. Rather, those firms in market structures in between—firms that enjoy some monopolistic power but are in industries with plenty of brilliant competitors to mimic and spur innovation—are the best to drive technological advancements.[6]

Question	**Answer**	**Data**	**Caveat**
Can a monopoly ever be good for society?	There is evidence that market power can be an important factor to innovation.	Patent laws and World's Fair inventions, human genome sequencing, patent data, and industry competitiveness.	The data paint the strongest picture for firms that enjoy some monopolistic power but are in industries with plenty of brilliant competitors to mimic and spur innovation.

Summary

⚙ A monopoly is an industry structure in which only one firm provides a good or service that has no close substitutes. Monopolies arise because of barriers to entry, which take two forms: legal and natural. In the legal form, government creates the barrier, as with a patent or copyright. In the natural form, control of key resources or achieving economies of scale in providing such goods as natural gas and electricity can result in a natural monopoly.

⚙ Barriers to entry permit the monopolist to exercise market power in making quantity and pricing decisions. The optimal action of the monopolist is to set Price > Marginal revenue = Marginal cost. This differs from a perfectly competitive industry, where Price = Marginal cost = Marginal revenue.

⚙ In equilibrium, monopoly leads to less quantity and higher prices compared to a perfectly competitive market equilibrium. In this way, because consumers are standing by ready to purchase from the monopolist for a price greater than marginal cost, social surplus is not maximized, leading to a deadweight loss.

⚙ There is an appropriate place for monopolies, and understanding whether a firm is occupying a monopoly status appropriately is a major concern of U.S. lawmakers. Even though there are costs to allowing firms to have monopoly power, the extra profit incentive might translate into better and more productive research and development for new products, medicines, and technologies.

Key Terms

price-makers *p. 275*
market power *p. 276*
monopoly *p. 276*
barriers to entry *p. 276*
legal market power *p. 276*
patent *p. 276*
copyright *p. 276*
natural market power *p. 277*

key resources *p. 278*
network externalities *p. 278*
natural monopoly *p. 279*
price discrimination *p. 289*
perfect, or first-degree price
    discrimination *p. 289*
second-degree price
    discrimination *p. 289*

third-degree price discrimination *p. 289*
antitrust policy *p. 292*
efficient or socially optimal
    price *p. 293*
fair-returns price *p. 293*
research and development (R&D) *p. 294*

Questions

All questions are available in MyEconLab for practice and instructor assignment.

1. What is meant by market power? What are the ways in which a monopoly gains market power?

2. Use a graph to explain the difference between a competitive firm's average total cost curve and the average total cost curve of a natural monopoly.

3. What does it mean to say that a good generates network externalities?

4. Why is national defense better off as a natural monopoly? What other industry or service do you think should be a natural monopoly?

5. How does a natural monopoly differ from a firm that becomes a monopoly due to network effects?

6. People who need life-saving drugs cannot do without them and surely will be willing to pay very high prices for them. So why can't producers of life-saving drugs charge any price that they wish?

7. What is the shape of a monopolist's demand curve and marginal revenue curve?

8. What is the relationship between price, marginal revenue, and total revenue for a monopolist?

9. Both competitive firms and monopolies produce at the level where marginal cost equals marginal revenue. Then, other things remaining the same, why is price lower in a competitive market than in a monopoly?

10. Why does a monopoly firm not have a supply curve?

11. Examine the following statements and identify the type of price discrimination in each case:

    a. A popular club in a city waives its entry fees for women who arrive before 11 p.m.

    b. A combo meal of a burger, a soft drink, and fries at a fast-food outlet costs less than how much it would cost to buy each separately.

    c. A guy selling counterfeit watches on the street states a different price to each person who wants to buy a watch.

12. To restrict a firm's monopoly power, why can't antitrust authorities just set a price floor or a price ceiling in the market?

13. Are there any cases where a monopoly is beneficial to the economy? Explain.

Problems

All problems are available in MyEconLab for practice and instructor assignment.

1. As this chapter explains, a monopoly is an industry structure where only one firm provides a good or service that has no close substitutes. This question explores the last part of this definition further.

    a. At one time Sirius Satellite Radio and XM Satellite Radio were the only two satellite radio providers in the United States. The Department of Justice (DOJ) and the Federal Communications Commission (FCC) approved the merger of the two companies in 2008 even though Sirius-XM would then control 100 percent of the satellite radio market. How do you think the two companies convinced the DOJ and the FCC to allow the merger to proceed?

    b. In 1947, the United States government charged the DuPont Company with a violation of the Sherman Act. The government argued that DuPont was monopolizing the cellophane market. At trial, the government showed that DuPont produced nearly 75 percent of all of the cellophane sold in the United States each year. Nonetheless, the U.S. Supreme Court ruled in favor of DuPont and dismissed the case. How do you think DuPont convinced the Supreme Court that it had not violated the Sherman Act?

2. Critically analyze the following and explain whether you agree or disagree:

    a. Janet knows a lot of people who do not like Marmite®, a yeast extract that is used as a spread on toast. She says that Marmite is so unpopular that Unilever, the company that manufactures Marmite®, cannot possibly have any monopoly power.

    b. Edgar says that a single firm in the wind power industry is unlikely to have a significant degree of monopoly power for an extended period of time. Since the cost of producing an additional unit of wind energy is so low, a large number of firms can enter the market and compete away economic profits.

3. Since many people use the Microsoft Windows operating system, software developers have an incentive to write new programs for Windows, computer manufacturers make new models of their computers that use Windows, and firms that make printers will be certain their printers work well on Windows computers.

    a. Show that Microsoft Windows is an example of a network externality.

    b. Suppose there are 10 people who use personal computers and that the value to each of them from using Windows is as follows:

Number of People Using a Windows Computer	Value to Each Person Who Uses a Windows Computer
1	110
2	120
3	130
4	140
5	150
6	160
7	170
8	180
9	190
10	200

    Suppose for the moment all 10 people are using Windows and so Microsoft is a monopolist in the market for computer operating system. Why would it be difficult for a company to offer a new alternative to Windows? Explain.

4. Textbook publishers hope to maximize profits. Authors, however, face very different incentives. Authors are typically paid royalties, which are a specified percentage of total revenue from the sale of a book. And so, for example, if an author's contract says that she will receive 20 percent of the revenues from the sale of a text and the publisher's total revenues are $100,000, the author's royalties will be $20,000. Who will prefer a higher price for the text, the publisher or the author?

5. You are a monopolist facing the following demand schedule:

Quantity	Price
1	$20
2	$18
3	$16
4	$14

You produce this good at a constant average and marginal cost of $12.

a. Calculate marginal revenue for each level of output.

b. Find the profit-maximizing price and quantity.

c. How much profit will you earn?

6. Consider a monopolist who faces a linear demand curve $P = 24 - Q$, where P is the price the monopolist charges and Q is the quantity consumers purchase. The monopolist's marginal revenue is $MR = 24 - 2Q$ (as the chapter explains, if demand is linear then demand and marginal revenue have the same intercept but marginal revenue has twice the slope). The monopolist produces this good at a constant average and marginal cost of $6.

a. Show that the monopolist's profit-maximizing price is $15.

b. Suppose the government imposes a tax of T dollars per unit on the monopolist, and therefore the monopolist's marginal cost is now $6 + T$. Show that the monopolist will pass along half of the tax to its customers, that is, show that the profit-maximizing price is now $15 + (T/2)$.

7. The following graph shows the demand, marginal revenue, and marginal cost curves in a monopoly market.

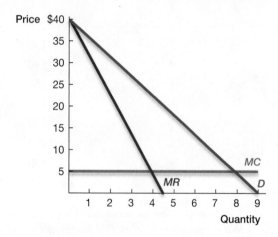

a. Identify the profit-maximizing price and quantity for this monopolist.

b. What is the value of the consumer surplus, producer surplus, and deadweight loss in the market?

c. How would consumer surplus change if this market was competitive?

8. Priceline is a web site that sells flights and hotel bookings based on the price that a consumer states that he or she is willing to pay. So consumers who want to book a flight or a hotel room need to tell Priceline the price they are willing to pay, and the seller lets Priceline know whether it is willing to accept that price.

a. How do sellers make profits by using this form of pricing?

b. In 1999, Priceline attempted to replicate this pricing strategy with groceries and gasoline. Using this pricing strategy with these two goods soon proved unprofitable. What could explain this?

9. Suppose you are a monopolist and you have two customers, Joseph and Monique. Each will buy either zero or one unit of the good you produce. Joseph is willing to pay up to $50 for your product; Monique is willing to pay up to $20. You produce this good at a constant average and marginal cost of $5.

a. If you could not engage in price discrimination, what price would you charge? How much profit would you earn?

b. If you could practice price discrimination, what prices would you charge? How much profit would you earn? For simplicity, assume that if consumers are indifferent between buying and not buying, they will buy.

10. This chapter explains that a firm engaging in second-degree price discrimination charges the same consumer different prices for different units of a good. You are a monopolist with many identical customers. Each will buy either zero, one, or two units of the good you produce. A consumer is willing to pay $50 for the first unit of this good and $20 for the second. You produce this good at a constant average and marginal cost of $5. For simplicity, assume that if a consumer is indifferent between buying and not buying, he will buy.

a. If you could not engage in second-degree price discrimination, what price would you charge? How much profit per customer would you earn?

b. Suppose you offer your customers what seems to be a very generous deal: "Buy one at the regular price of $50, and get 60 percent off on a second." How many units of this good will each customer buy? How much profit per customer will you earn?

11. Imagine that you arrive at an economics experiment with six other people and are told that you will simulate a market. You will be the only seller. The other five people will be assigned a dollar value that they will receive if they buy the good for any amount of money (so if a person's value is $6, he will buy the good for any price less than $6 and will be happy). You are also given the following demand curve and told that it represents the values that the "buyers" are assigned:

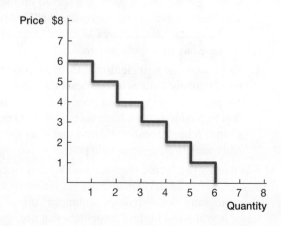

a. If you are told that you can produce as many units as you like at a cost of $2 per unit, what would your marginal cost curve look like? Add the marginal cost curve that you face as the monopolist to the graph.

b. Draw the marginal revenue curve that you face as the monopolist, based on the demand curve given above.

c. What price would you set and what quantity would you produce if you have to post one price at which everyone can purchase the good?

d. Based on the price and quantity you selected in part c, what would consumer surplus be? What would producer surplus be? Is there a deadweight loss?

e. Imagine that you are told that now you can have a discussion with each buyer privately to negotiate a price. Would you still charge everyone the same price? Explain your answer.

f. Calculate the surplus and the deadweight loss for the scenario with perfect price discrimination.

12. The annual demand for a new drug HealthyHeart is shown in the diagram below.

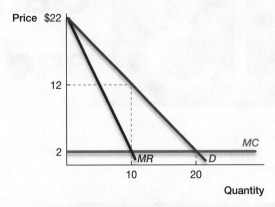

The one-time cost of developing HealthyHeart is $2,000. Once the drug has been developed, the marginal cost of an additional pill is $2.

a. Show that if the government gives the company that develops HealthyHeart a 20-year patent the company will be able recover the $2,000 it spent to develop the drug.

b. Find the total deadweight loss over the 20-year life of the patent.

13 Game Theory and Strategic Play

Is there value in putting yourself into someone else's shoes?

Imagine yourself in the shoes of a person who has just committed armed robbery of a bank—in other words, you are the robber. Say that you have a partner in crime named Josie. You are both caught in the get-away vehicle, but before apprehension you both toss your guns into a storm drain. The police take both of you in to the local precinct and place you in separate interrogation rooms. When the detectives enter your room, they outline a set of three options for you and tell you that they are giving Josie the same three options:

1. If neither of you confesses to having a gun during the crime, you are both looking at jail time of 2 years for the robbery.
2. If one confesses to having a gun, the confessor goes free and the other serves substantial jail time—10 years.
3. If both of you confess to having a gun, then jail terms will be negotiated down to 5 years.

What should you do?

The simple economic framework we have developed thus far is not equipped to handle situations like these where your "payoffs" (satisfaction, profits, etc.) depend on the behavior of others and your behavior affects their payoffs. These situations include, among others, how to allocate scarce resources in partnerships, firms, friendships, and families. You may wonder what economics has to do with friendships and families. Well, as it turns out, a lot.

CHAPTER OUTLINE

KEY IDEAS

* There are important situations when the behavior of others affects your payoffs.

* Game theory is the economic framework that describes our optimal actions in such settings.

* A Nash equilibrium is a situation where none of the players can do better by choosing a different action or strategy.

* Nash equilibria are applicable to a wide variety of problems, including zero-sum games, the tragedy of the commons, and the prisoners' dilemma.

Game theory is the study of strategic interactions.

Game theory is the study of situations in which the payoffs of one agent depend not only on his actions, but also on the actions of others. It emerged as a branch of mathematics that first focused on the analysis of parlor games. For example, when you're playing poker and trying to figure out your opponent's next move, you're using game theory concepts. In 2000, a U.C.L.A. grad student named Chris Ferguson applied game theory concepts at the World Series of Poker, helping him secure prize money of $1.5 million and the championship bracelet (his father taught game theory at U.C.L.A.!). But its use is considerably broader than in parlor games. Economists, political scientists, and sociologists use game theory to analyze a variety of problems, ranging from competition between firms (as we will see in the next chapter), negotiations and bargaining (as we will see in Chapter 17), social cooperation (as we discuss in this chapter and in Chapter 18), voting and other political decisions, and many others.

In this chapter, we present the basic tools of game theory and explain how they are useful for understanding and analyzing many different economic decisions. Such an understanding provides you with an invaluable resource for studying individual interactions that you face daily, and for analyzing topics as varied as international trade negotiations, nuclear arms races, and labor arbitration. We will learn that many times it is, indeed, quite valuable to put yourself into another's shoes.

13.1 Simultaneous Move Games

Let's return to the scene of the crime in the opening anecdote and explore how a game theorist would look at your problem. To begin, it is important to recognize the three key elements of any game:

Strategies comprise a complete plan describing how a player will act.

1. The players
2. The **strategies**
3. The payoffs

Let's first identify these three key elements in this particular game:

Players: You and Josie
Strategies: Confess or hold out
Payoffs: See Exhibit 13.1

A **payoff matrix** represents the payoffs for each action players can take.

A **payoff matrix** represents the payoffs for each action players can take in a game. In the payoff matrix shown in Exhibit 13.1, one player's actions are read across in rows; the other player's actions are read down in columns. The cells where the actions intersect give the payoffs, which for now are assumed to correspond only to the number of years in prison each player

Exhibit 13.1 Payoffs in the Prisoners' Dilemma

The payoff matrix gives each player's payoff from every possible combination of strategies of all players in the game. For example, in the prisoners' dilemma, which has two players, the payoff matrix shows that if you confess and Josie also confesses, you will each serve 5 years in prison. In contrast, if you both hold out, you will each receive 2-year prison sentences.

		Column Player: Josie	
		Confess	Hold Out
Row Player: You	Confess	• You get 5 years • Josie gets 5 years	• You are released • Josie gets 10 years
	Hold Out	• You get 10 years • Josie is released	• You get 2 years • Josie gets 2 years

receives. In particular, more years in jail represent lower payoffs. Game theory can easily include things like loyalty and kindness payoffs, but here we remove those considerations.

The convention in writing payoff matrices is that the first number listed is always the payoff to the Row Player, and to make it even clearer, we have also put this number in red. The second number listed, which is in blue, is always the payoff to the Column Player. So, in this game, if you—the first player—confess and Josie also confesses, you each get 5 years in prison.

The scenario depicted in Exhibit 13.1 is a classic one known as the "prisoners' dilemma." Despite its simplicity, the prisoners' dilemma illustrates several important features common to game theory. It involves interactions among a few players (in this case, two). This game is called a **simultaneous move game** because players select their actions at the same time. In the prisoners' dilemma, this implies that both you and Josie have to pick your action simultaneously without knowing the other person's choice. But it is assumed that you each do know the entire payoff matrix—that is, you each know the payoffs for both players.

When constructing a payoff matrix, it is important to understand that *all* relevant benefits and costs of each action are taken into account. In this example, we assume that the payoffs represent all of the relevant payoffs to this game. Thus, we are assuming that other potentially important features, such as retribution after jail time is served, do not influence the payoffs of this game.

We are now in a position to ask the question game theory equips us to answer: what should you do?

Best Responses and the Prisoners' Dilemma

A first step in figuring out how to play any game is to put yourself in the shoes of the other player. That is, a good way to reason through which action you should choose—confess or hold out—is to think about what every possible action of the other player might be and then what *your* best choice will be for each of them. For example, suppose that Josie decides to confess. In that case, your payoffs when she chooses to hold out are no longer relevant—you should simply focus on the situation when she confesses. So, we can strike the column for Hold Out in Exhibit 13.1. We then end up with the single column shown in Exhibit 13.2.

Exhibit 13.2 makes it clear that in this instance when you hold out and Josie confesses, you will receive 10 years in prison, whereas if you also confess, you will serve 5 years. Therefore, your *best response* when you expect Josie to confess is to confess yourself. A **best response** is simply one player's optimal strategy *taking the other player's strategy as given.*

Suppose, instead, that you expect Josie to hold out. With the same best-response approach as used above, we now strike the column for Confess in Exhibit 13.1. After doing so, we obtain Exhibit 13.3.

Going through the same steps, you see that confessing allows you to walk away with no jail time, whereas holding out puts you in prison for 2 years. Your best response in this case is again to confess. You now understand that no matter what you think Josie will do, you should *always* confess. This means that when you are placed in such a game, you should always choose to confess, regardless of what you think your partner will do.

In **simultaneous move games,** players pick their actions at the same time.

> A first step in figuring out how to play any game is to put yourself in the shoes of the other player.

A strategy of a player is a **best response** to the strategies of the others in the game if, taking the other players' strategy as given, it gives her greater payoffs than any other strategy she has available.

Exhibit 13.2 Prisoners' Dilemma Game with Your Partner Confessing

To determine your best response to a specific strategy by Josie, you first consider the column corresponding to that strategy. In this case, you take the column for Josie corresponding to Confess. You then compare your payoffs under your two strategies, Confess and Hold Out. You can see that when you confess in this case you will get 5 years, whereas if you hold out, you will get 10 years.

		Josie
		Confess
You	Confess	• You get 5 years • Josie gets 5 years
	Hold Out	• You get 10 years • Josie is released

Exhibit 13.3 Prisoners' Dilemma Game with Your Partner Holding Out

To determine your best response to Josie's holding out, you consider the column under Josie's strategy of Hold Out and again compare your payoffs under your two possible strategies. In this case, if you confess you will walk free, and if you hold out you will spend 2 years in prison.

		Josie
		Hold Out
You	Confess	• You are released • Josie gets 10 years
	Hold Out	• You get 2 years • Josie gets 2 years

Dominant Strategies and Dominant Strategy Equilibrium

A **dominant strategy** is one best response to every possible strategy of the other player(s).

When a player has the same best response to every possible strategy of the other player(s), then we say that the player has a **dominant strategy**. In the game of Exhibit 13.1, confessing is a dominant strategy because it is your best response to *any* strategy choice of your partner.

In the prisoners' dilemma game, after doing the same exercise for Josie, you can reason that Josie has a dominant strategy of confessing, too. When a dominant strategy exists for both players, the notion of equilibrium for the game is straightforward. A strategy combination for the players is a **dominant strategy equilibrium** if the relevant strategy for each player is a dominant strategy. In the game above, there is a dominant strategy equilibrium: both players should confess because confessing is a dominant strategy for each player.

A combination of strategies is a **dominant strategy equilibrium** if each strategy is a dominant strategy.

Interestingly, this equilibrium leads to an outcome that is *not* best for both players. Even though both you and Josie would be better off if you both held out, the dominant strategy equilibrium is for both of you to confess! This situation is the heart of the paradox that we have been studying so far—the "prisoners' dilemma." The "dilemma" part arises because by confessing, you and Josie will each spend 5 years in prison. However, if you were both to hold out, you would each spend 2 years in prison. Because less prison time is preferred to more, the (Confess, Confess) strategy combination gives strictly lower payoffs to both players than (Hold Out, Hold Out). Nevertheless, it is not in your (or in Josie's) best interest to hold out, and this leads to the unique dominant strategy equilibrium in which you both confess. Thus the dilemma arises.

Games without Dominant Strategies

The prisoners' dilemma game has a dominant strategy for each player. Yet, there are many games without a dominant strategy. Consider the case wherein you and your friend Gina, both avid surfers, open up a surf shop—Hang Ten in Da Den. Your main competition is a surf shop down the street, La Jolla Surf Shop. One key decision that you must make is

Exhibit 13.4 **The Advertising Game**

In this payoff matrix, the payoffs of the two surf shops depend on whether each decides to advertise or not to advertise. For example, the cell at the top left-hand corner shows that if you both advertise, you will each receive a payoff of $400, while the cell at the bottom right shows that if you both choose not to advertise, you will each receive a payoff of $800.

		La Jolla	
		Advertise	Don't Advertise
Hang Ten	Advertise	• Hang Ten earns $400 • La Jolla earns $400	• Hang Ten earns $700 • La Jolla earns $300
	Don't Advertise	• Hang Ten earns $300 • La Jolla earns $700	• Hang Ten earns $800 • La Jolla earns $800

whether to advertise. In fact, both your shop and La Jolla Surf Shop have similar decisions to make, which we assume are made simultaneously. Upon doing the necessary market research, you construct Exhibit 13.4, which provides the payoffs for this simple game.

A summary of the three key elements in this game are as follows:

Players: Hang Ten in Da Den and the La Jolla Surf Shop
Strategies: To advertise or not to advertise
Payoffs: See Exhibit 13.4

In the exhibit, the two rows correspond to your strategies and the two columns correspond to La Jolla Surf Shop's strategies. The top left cell gives both surf shops' daily profits of $400 if both opt to advertise. In contrast, the lower right cell indicates that if both do not advertise, each shop earns a daily profit of $800. The higher profits from each of you not advertising are explained by the high cost of advertising and its lack of effectiveness: in this market, the main effect of advertising is to steal business from the other shop, not to persuade new customers into the market.

The other two cells (lower left and upper right) show the scenarios in which one of the shops advertises and the other does not. In these cases, whoever is advertising does considerably better than the other shop because the surf shop that advertises steals some consumers from the other shop. For example, if you place ads and La Jolla Surf Shop does not, you earn $700 per day while La Jolla Surf Shop earns only $300 per day.

What should you do? Let's start with considering your best response. Suppose that you expect La Jolla Surf Shop to advertise. How should you best respond? Consider Exhibit 13.5, which excludes the column for Don't Advertise from Exhibit 13.4.

Exhibit 13.5 makes it clear that when La Jolla Surf Shop chooses to advertise, your surf shop will earn $400 if you choose to advertise and will earn $300 if you do not. Therefore, your *best response* is to advertise when you expect that La Jolla Surf Shop will advertise because $400 > $300.

Suppose, instead, that you expect La Jolla Surf Shop to not place advertisements. We now strike the column for Advertise from Exhibit 13.4, and we are left with Exhibit 13.6. Your best response when La Jolla Surf Shop chooses not to advertise is to not advertise yourself. This is because when advertising, your shop earns $700 and when not advertising your shop earns $800, making you prefer not to advertise.

Exhibit 13.5 **When La Jolla Surf Shop Advertises**

To determine your best response to La Jolla choosing to advertise, you take the column under Advertise (corresponding to La Jolla's choice of advertising) and compare your payoffs from advertising to not advertising. In this case, advertising gives you $400, whereas not advertising gives you $300. You should advertise.

		La Jolla Advertise
Hang Ten	Advertise	• Hang Ten earns $400 • La Jolla earns $400
	Don't Advertise	• Hang Ten earns $300 • La Jolla earns $700

Exhibit 13.6 When La Jolla Surf Shop Does Not Advertise

To determine your best response to La Jolla choosing not to advertise, you take the column under Don't Advertise, and compare your payoffs from advertising and not advertising. In this case, advertising gives you $700, whereas not advertising gives you $800. You should not advertise.

	La Jolla Don't Advertise
Hang Ten — Advertise	• Hang Ten earns $700 • La Jolla earns $300
Hang Ten — Don't Advertise	• Hang Ten earns $800 • La Jolla earns $800

Do you have a dominant strategy in this game? No; this is because your optimal strategy depends on what La Jolla Surf Shop chooses. Does La Jolla Surf Shop have a dominant strategy? By similar reasoning, it also does not have a dominant strategy. Thus there is *not* a dominant strategy for your surf shop or for La Jolla Surf Shop. In this case, you remain unsure as to what to do because your optimal choice depends on the choice of La Jolla Surf Shop. This particular game illustrates a key concept in game theory: you don't always have a simple best response (a dominant strategy) that works against all strategies of others, as you do in games with a dominant strategy, such as the prisoners' dilemma game.

Life doesn't always present a game that has a dominant strategy. In the advertising example, what is best for your shop depends on what you expect the La Jolla Surf Shop to do. In such cases, where should we expect to end up in the payoff matrix—does your shop advertise? Does La Jolla Surf Shop advertise? Do both of you advertise? What is the equilibrium of this game?

13.2 Nash Equilibrium

Recall that the notion of equilibrium we used in markets requires that all individuals are simultaneously optimizing given the prices that they face in the market and their income levels. To put this differently, no individual can (unilaterally) change his strategy and be better off (or improve his payoff). This is intuitive: if a player did have a strategy that made him better off, then he would choose that strategy instead of the one he chose.

A Beautiful Mind

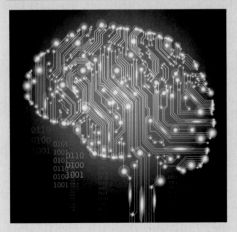

If you are a movie buff, you have surely seen the film based on the life of John Nash—a Hollywood blockbuster called *A Beautiful Mind*. The film was nominated for eight Academy Awards, winning best picture in 2001. The film focuses on Nash's mathematical genius and his struggle with paranoid schizophrenia.

Nash earned a doctorate in mathematics from Princeton in 1950 with a 28-page dissertation on game theory.[1]

Those 28 pages played a central role in developing the foundation of game theory as we know it today. For this reason, the relevant notion of equilibrium in games is referred to as a "Nash equilibrium." Nash was awarded the 1994 Nobel Prize in Economics for this contribution.

13.1

13.2

13.3

13.4

13.5

In equilibrium, no player in a game can change strategy and improve his or her payoff.

A strategy combination is a **Nash equilibrium** if each strategy is a best response to the strategies of others.

This is the essence of the equilibrium concept proposed by John Nash: in equilibrium, no player in a game can change strategy and improve his payoff. Therefore, a combination of strategies is a **Nash equilibrium** if each player chooses a strategy that is a best response to the strategies of others—that is, players are choosing strategies that are mutual best responses. What this means is that no one can change his choice and be better off. Accordingly, the dominant strategy equilibrium that we found in the prisoners' dilemma game is a Nash equilibrium.

This notion of equilibrium depends on two critical factors: (1) that all players understand the game and the payoffs associated with each strategy (so that they will choose what is best for themselves) and (2) that all players understand that *other* players understand the game.

In the context of a Nash equilibrium, we expect that an individual forms correct expectations about the intentions of other players in the game. As we will see when we consider experimental evidence on game theory later in this chapter, experience with a game may be necessary before we can safely assume that people act in the way that we think they are going to act.

Finding a Nash Equilibrium

The key to finding Nash equilibria in simultaneous move games is to follow the logic of finding best responses. Let's return to the advertising decision. Begin by asking yourself: if La Jolla Surf Shop advertises, what should your shop do? As reasoned through above, your best response is to advertise. You then need to ask: once in this cell of the payoff matrix, does either surf shop have a reason to change its strategy?

The answer is no. La Jolla will not change its strategy because if it did, it would earn $300 rather than $400. Likewise, you will not change your strategy because if you did, you also would earn $300 rather than $400. Therefore, both shops choosing to advertise is a Nash equilibrium. That is, once both of you have opted to advertise, neither of you has an incentive to change your behavior.

Suppose instead that La Jolla Surf Shop chooses not to advertise. In this case, what should your shop do? As reasoned through above, your best response is not to advertise. Once in this cell, does either surf shop have a reason to change its strategy?

The answer is again no. La Jolla Surf Shop will not change its strategy because if it did, it would earn $700 rather than $800. Likewise, you will not want to change your strategy because if you did, you would earn $700 rather than $800. Therefore, not advertising is a Nash equilibrium for both surf shops. Once in that cell, neither of you has an incentive to change your strategy. Accordingly, in this particular game we have *two* Nash equilibria:

1. Your shop: advertise; La Jolla Surf Shop: advertise
2. Your shop: don't advertise; La Jolla Surf Shop: don't advertise

To illustrate how to find these two Nash equilibria in a payoff matrix, Exhibit 13.7 revisits the advertising game.

Let's begin by thinking about what would happen if you choose to advertise and La Jolla does not. You will find yourself in the top right cell. Can you do better? Yes. In this case, you would like to change your choice because $800 > $700—thus the red arrow pointing downward from this box (it is red because it refers to you, the Row Player). Likewise, La Jolla would like to change its choice—thus the blue arrow pointing leftward from this box.

You can then use the same reasoning from the bottom left cell. If you are in this cell, both you and La Jolla will again change your behavior: you will opt to advertise because $400 > $300, and La Jolla will not advertise because $800 > $700. This shows that the Nash equilibria are best-response strategies with two arrows pointing in: (Advertise, Advertise) and (Don't Advertise, Don't Advertise). Once two arrows point inward, you can be certain that you have found a Nash equilibrium.

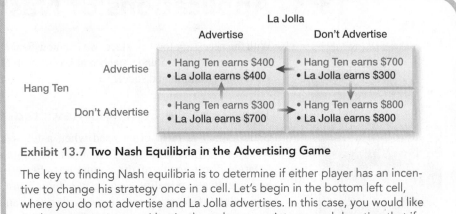

Exhibit 13.7 Two Nash Equilibria in the Advertising Game

The key to finding Nash equilibria is to determine if either player has an incentive to change his strategy once in a cell. Let's begin in the bottom left cell, where you do not advertise and La Jolla advertises. In this case, you would like to change your strategy (that is, the red arrow points upward denoting that if you are in this cell, you would like to change your strategy). La Jolla would also like to move away from this cell (its blue arrow points rightward from this cell). Once you consider every cell using this approach, the arrows are completed, and Nash equilibria occur when both arrows point to a cell. In this example, both strategy combinations (Advertise, Advertise) and (Don't Advertise, Don't Advertise) have the two arrows pointing to them, and are thus Nash equilibria.

It might at first seem odd that there are two Nash equilibria in the advertising game. But a moment's reflection reveals that this is quite natural. It's only worthwhile for you to advertise when La Jolla advertises, and vice-versa. It is, in fact, a common occurrence in game theory to have more than one Nash equilibrium, and in these cases, other factors, such as those we discuss in the box below, may determine which of the two equilibria are played.

 CHOICE & CONSEQUENCE

Work or Surf?

Game theory doesn't just apply to your surf shop's competition with La Jolla Surf shop. You and your partner, Gina, are individually just as affected by each other in the shop.

Consider a simple example of working versus surfing. Suppose that your daily payoffs—with no advertising— are described in the payoff matrix below. You and Gina both receive $400 per day in net benefits if you each work at the surf shop. However, if you shirk your responsibilities and go surfing while Gina works, your shop does not sell as much, but you receive both the benefits from the shop staying open and the benefits from surfing, which sum to $500. If you both go surfing, however, the shop is closed and you both earn only surfing benefits of $200. What should you do?

In this situation, there are two Nash equilibria, as the best-response arrows demonstrate. One is for you to go surfing while Gina tends to the shop. The other is for you to tend to the shop while Gina surfs. When there are multiple Nash equilibria as in this case, which equilibrium will actually be played depends on many factors. For example, if Gina is an assertive character and has always

managed to get what she wants in her prior relations with you, we may expect that you working hard and her surfing might be a natural "focal point" and have a greater likelihood of emerging than the other Nash equilibrium.

The payoff matrix of the work-or-surf game shows your payoffs and Gina's payoffs depending on whether each of you chooses to work or surf. In this game, there are two Nash equilibria: (Surf, Work) indicating that you surf and Gina works, and (Work, Surf), corresponding to you working and Gina surfing.

13.3 Applications of Nash Equilibria

With the necessary tools in place, we can now begin to study some of the ways in which we apply game theory to understand real-world problems. We'll consider two quite different scenarios: pollution and soccer.

Tragedy of the Commons Revisited

Game theory is most often used when a few players make choices that affect each other's payoffs. The same type of reasoning applies even when the number of players is large. The tragedy of the commons—the overuse of common resources resulting in a negative externality—which we studied in Chapter 9, can also be viewed as an application of game theory. In particular, the same reasoning as that in the prisoners' dilemma applies to the tragedy of the commons. When all others pollute the environment, it is a best response for you to do so as well. Unfortunately, it is also the best response to pollute when all others actually go to the trouble of "being green." Therefore, in the tragedy of the commons, just as in the prisoners' dilemma, mutually beneficial behavior may not emerge.

Consider the example of the Gowanus Canal, a canal in the New York City borough of Brooklyn. Pollution has become so bad in the canal that the Environmental Protection Agency placed it on its National Priority List. How could things get this bad in a major city?

Game theory can shed insights into the question. Exhibit 13.8 depicts the weekly profits for two firms on the canal: let's call them Firm 1 and Firm 2. It shows that these profits depend on the firms' pollution choices. Each firm's choices affect each other's profit because if one plant pollutes, it affects the productivity of the other (through both worker productivity as well as processing costs—each firm uses water from the canal for production and dirty water is costly to clean). Unfortunately for the canal, the payoffs also show that, because it is costly to abate pollution, a firm is better off if it pollutes regardless of the other firm's choice.

A summary of the three key elements in this game are as follows:

Players: Firm 1 and Firm 2
Strategies: To pollute or not to pollute
Payoffs: See Exhibit 13.8

As in the prisoners' dilemma game, the dominant strategy equilibrium in Exhibit 13.8 leads to an outcome that is not best for both players—to pollute. Both could have earned $70,000 in weekly profits and be better off if they had both chosen not to pollute. Nevertheless, in the dominant strategy equilibrium, both firms choose to pollute, and both they and society (which suffers from greater pollution) are worse off, creating a tragedy of the commons result.

This simple game structure contains some of the important elements of a crucial situation facing many corporations and individuals today: the pressing issue of not dirtying our

The Gowanus Canal in Brooklyn, one of the most polluted in the United States, shows the tragedy of the commons at work. As game theory would predict, when other firms choose to pollute, it's a best response for your firm to do the same. But everyone is worse off as a result.

Exhibit 13.8 Payoff Matrix for Two Firms

The payoff matrix of the tragedy of the commons game gives Firm 1's and Firm 2's payoffs, depending on whether each decides to pollute or not to pollute.

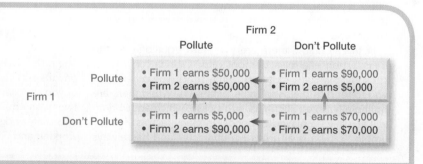

		Firm 2	
		Pollute	**Don't Pollute**
Firm 1	**Pollute**	• Firm 1 earns $50,000 • Firm 2 earns $50,000	• Firm 1 earns $90,000 • Firm 2 earns $5,000
	Don't Pollute	• Firm 1 earns $5,000 • Firm 2 earns $90,000	• Firm 1 earns $70,000 • Firm 2 earns $70,000

planet. And the Nash equilibrium of this game highlights exactly why we end up with dirty water and air, and why government intervention might be necessary.

Zero-Sum Games

Let's move on to something more pleasant—soccer! Suppose that you are the designated penalty kicker for your intramural soccer team. Every time you walk up to the ball, you have an important decision to make: aim for the left of the net or for the right of the net (for simplicity, let's ignore the options of aiming for the middle or shooting high or low). What should you do in such situations?

As in many game-theoretic situations, we can master this question by thinking generally about the incentives of your opponent—the goalie. The goalie will try to anticipate your behavior and will dive to the left or to the right. If he dives to the side where you kick the ball, then he has a pretty good chance of stopping it from going into the net, and if he dives to the opposite side, you are very likely to score.

In a **zero-sum game,** one player's loss is another's gain, so the sum of the payoffs is zero.

In this example, the payoff matrix represents a **zero-sum game**, meaning that because one player's loss is another's gain, the sum of the payoffs is zero. Exhibit 13.9 shows that the outcomes for each strategy in the soccer game in fact constitute a zero-sum game. Let's look at this situation in more detail.

A summary of the three key elements in this game are as follows:

Players: You and the goalie
Strategies: Right or left
Payoffs: See Exhibit 13.9

If you both go left, then the goalie is happy and you are not. Thus, the goalie receives 1 unit of net benefits and you receive −1 unit of net benefits. If you kick right and he dives right, then the same payoff results because he saves the shot: +1 for him and −1 for you. However, if the goalie dives to the opposite side of where you kick the ball, then you score, resulting in a payoff of +1 to you and −1 to the goalie. These cells are in the bottom left and top right of the payoff matrix.

Zero-sum games are quite common in the real world. Whenever we sit down to play poker, our gains are another player's losses. Whenever two companies compete to sell to the same consumers, one company's gain is the other one's loss. Redistribution is also often zero-sum: one person's gain is often another's loss.

Applying our method of finding Nash equilibria, we draw the arrows, as shown in Exhibit 13.9. They show that no Nash equilibrium exists because there is not a cell in the matrix with two arrows pointing in. Therefore, the notion of Nash equilibrium that we have developed so far doesn't make any predictions about the behavior in the penalty kick game.

We're not finished yet, however. In games like this, maybe the best strategy is not to choose any one particular action. For example, what if you randomly choose between kicking left and kicking right and the goalie does too? In that case, you would expect, on average, to be neither the loser with a payoff of −1 nor the winner with a payoff of 1, and thus, on average, you would end up with a payoff of zero.

A **pure strategy** involves always choosing one particular action for a situation.

In fact, choosing randomly has a clear advantage in this game relative to a **pure strategy**, which involves always choosing a single action for a situation. Consider one scenario of a

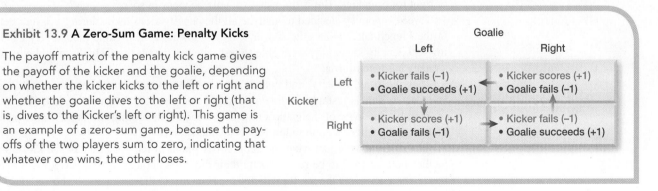

Exhibit 13.9 A Zero-Sum Game: Penalty Kicks

The payoff matrix of the penalty kick game gives the payoff of the kicker and the goalie, depending on whether the kicker kicks to the left or right and whether the goalie dives to the left or right (that is, dives to the Kicker's left or right). This game is an example of a zero-sum game, because the payoffs of the two players sum to zero, indicating that whatever one wins, the other loses.

A **mixed strategy** involves choosing different actions randomly.

pure strategy for yourself: always kick right. If you always kick right, in time goalies will notice and best respond by always diving right. This will result in a certain negative payoff to you of −1. In fact, reasoning this way, we can see that any kind of "predictable" behavior by the kicker can be taken advantage of by the goalie, and vice-versa. If you are the kicker, you should therefore be as unpredictable as possible. Put differently, you should randomize by playing a **mixed strategy**, which involves choosing between different actions randomly (according to some preassigned probabilities). The essence of a mixed strategy is as follows: you should privately flip a fair coin before each penalty kick. When it comes up heads, you kick right; when it comes up tails, you kick left. This strategy represents the basics of the equilibrium in mixed strategies for this game: both the penalty taker and the goalie should randomize with a probability of 50–50 between left and right.

Now that we've seen some real-world applications of game theory, let's analyze how real-world actors play in similar situations and how game theory does in predicting behavior.

13.4 How Do People Actually Play Such Games?

Do people really play Nash equilibrium in practice? What about dominant strategies—are those frequently played? One might think that the answer to these questions should be a simple yes or no. But these questions are difficult to answer—in both the lab and in the real world—for two main reasons.

The first reason is that we often do not know the exact payoffs of individuals playing the game. In constructing the matrix games in the previous sections, we chose the payoffs and assumed that they were correct. In real-world situations, the payoffs are determined by the attitudes and feelings of individuals as well as by their monetary returns.

A second reason why we might not observe what game theory predicts is that it is, in essence, a theory, and models are not literal descriptions of how the world works—they are merely useful abstractions. As such, game theory abstracts from several details. In many situations, one player may be more cunning, wiser, or more experienced than another. For example, of two chess players, the more experienced, more clever player is likely to win. In many matrix games (with two or several players), repetition of the game usually ensures that results come closer to Nash equilibrium. With these caveats in mind, we turn to an example to illustrate how game theory's predictions fare in real-world situations.

Game Theory in Penalty Kicks

Consider again the situation faced by penalty kickers and goalies. As you have already learned, the best move for both sides is to employ a mixed strategy—randomly choose left or right for each kick. But is that what actually happens in soccer games?

Three economists decided to analyze all the penalty kicks taken during a 3-year period in the French and Italian elite soccer leagues in order to test game theory.[2] By examining 459 penalty kicks they were able to test whether the players actually did play mixed-strategy Nash equilibria.

They classified kickers' and goalies' choices into one of three strategies: Left, Right, and Center. This is just a bit more complicated than our Left/Right example earlier in the chapter, but the logic of the game's mixed-strategy Nash equilibrium is the same: penalty kickers and goalies should randomize across the choices.

Amazingly, this is just what the economists found in the actual data. The kickers and goalies both seemed to be randomizing their direction choices almost perfectly. So chalk up a victory for game theory. It predicted the behavior of these players—who certainly had a lot at stake in the games they were playing and therefore had a lot of incentive to optimize their behavior—very well.

A related study found a similar pattern of randomization in serve choices in professional tennis matches (where predictably serving to the right or to the left would enable the other player to return more effectively).[3] Indeed, this research on tennis provides interesting quotes from two tennis greats when it notes: "After a recent match, Venus Williams said she had shown her opponent, Monica Seles, several different types of serves. 'You have to work on that, because it's very easy to become one-dimensional and just serve to your favorite space and the person is just waiting there.' Seles responded, 'She mixed it up very well.'" Game theory at work!

13.5 Extensive-Form Games

An **extensive-form game** is a representation of games that specifies the order of play.

The games that we have discussed so far all revolve around two players choosing an action simultaneously. Suppose that, instead, one player goes first and the other chooses an action only after seeing how the first player chose. This type of situation which specifies the order of play is represented by an **extensive-form game**.

In extensive-form games, the strategies are a little bit richer than in simultaneous games. For instance, in our work-or-surf game, it might be the case that you can decide to go surfing before Gina has a chance to decide. Accordingly, you decide on whether you are going to work or surf and then Gina, after viewing your choice, decides whether she will work or surf. Or Gina might let you know her strategy before you decide on whether to go surfing: "If you go surfing, I will, too."

Recall that strategies are not only the possible actions but are a description of how a player will act given every possible action of the other player. How do we model games with sequential decisions? As a first step, let's contrast extensive-form games and simultaneous move games. Extensive-form games introduce the sense of timing that is missing in simultaneous move games. This sense of timing is relevant for negotiations in which different players make offers to each other over time (sequentially). It is also relevant for many more traditional games—in chess, for example, players do not make simultaneous choices. Rather, they "take turns."

A **game tree** is an extensive-form representation of a game.

So we can say that an extensive-form game specifies the order of play and payoffs that will result from different strategies and uses a **game tree** to represent them. To better understand the difference between extensive-form and simultaneous move games, let's discuss more carefully the work-or-surf decision that you and Gina face. Exhibit 13.10 shows the work-or-surf game tree when you are the first mover.

This game tree has three sets of "nodes." The first, the red node at the far left—represents the first decision maker, in this case, you. This is the spot where you decide whether you will work or go surfing. In essence, your choice is to travel either the green branch—work—or the orange branch—surf.

Backward induction is the procedure of solving an extensive-form game by first considering the last mover's decision.

Gina's decision comes only after she views your decision, represented by one of the two blue nodes labeled "Gina." Whether you place her at the top node (you decided to work) or at the bottom node (you decided to surf), she has the same decision to make: work or surf. The payoffs for each of those decisions are in

Exhibit 13.10 A Game Tree for the Work-or-Surf Game

In the extensive-form game of the work-or-surf game, you first decide whether to work or surf. Then Gina, after observing your choice, decides whether to work or surf. The extensive form is useful in showing the play sequencing. The numbers given at the end are the payoffs to you and Gina. For example, if both you and Gina work, you each earn $400.

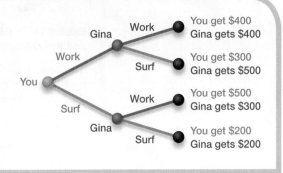

the end of the game tree. These payoffs follow our earlier coloring convention. Given this game form, what should you now do?

Backward Induction

The easiest way of approaching any extensive-form game is to use *backward induction*. **Backward induction** is the procedure of solving an extensive-form game by first considering the last mover's decision. Given the last mover's decision, we then consider the second-to-last mover, and so on. The name derives from the fact that this procedure starts from the end of the game and solves backwards.

To backward-induct, you first consider each decision node at the end of the game. If you work (green branch), then Gina finds herself in the top decision node. Now, Gina has the choices depicted in panel (a) of Exhibit 13.11.

Accordingly, Gina chooses between working, which yields payoffs of (You: $400, Gina: $400), and surfing, which yields payoffs of (You: $300, Gina: $500). In this case, Gina should choose to surf because the net benefits to her are $500, which is $100 higher than the net benefits under the alternative of working ($400). Given that she will choose to surf, your payoff will be $300 if you initially chose to work.

On the other hand, if you choose to surf (orange branch), then Gina finds herself at the bottom decision node, as shown in panel (b) of Exhibit 13.11. Here, she again has the choice between working and surfing. If she works, the payoffs are (You: $500, Gina: $300) and if she surfs, the payoffs are (You: $200, Gina: $200). Thus, if you decide to surf, Gina will choose to go to work because she will earn $100 more in net benefits by working. Given that she will choose to work, your payoff will be $500.

We have now completely described Gina's optimal strategies, which are:

"Choose to work if you surf" and
"Choose to surf if you work."

Why is it important to know Gina's strategies? Because you can now make a decision knowing how Gina will respond to every one of your actions. With this information in hand, you have successfully backward-inducted. Such backward induction allows you to make an informed decision as to whether you should work or surf. So, what should you do?

You know that if you choose to go to work, Gina will surf, netting you a payoff of $300. Alternatively, if you choose to surf, she will work, leaving you with a payoff of $500. The decision now seems straightforward: you should go surfing because you will receive a payoff that is $200 higher than if you go to work.

Recall that when the decisions were made simultaneously, there were two Nash equilibria. Now, with sequential decision making, the backward-induction procedure has delivered a unique equilibrium: you Surf and Gina works.

Backward induction is the procedure of solving an extensive-form game by first considering the last mover's decision in order to deduce the decisions of all previous movers.

(a) Gina's Game Tree If You Decide to Work   (b) Gina's Game Tree If You Decide to Surf

Exhibit 13.11 Gina's Game Trees If You Decide to Work and If You Decide to Surf

Backward induction involves starting at the end of the game and solving it backward. In this case, you look at Gina's decision of whether to work or surf after she has observed whether you have worked or surfed. Panel (a) looks at the case following your choice to work; panel (b) looks at the case following your choice to surf.

First-Mover Advantage, Commitment, and Vengeance

The equilibrium above is much more favorable to you than to Gina: you receive $500, whereas she receives $300. This outcome occurs even though the payoffs to the different actions are the same for you and Gina. We say that the sequential game features a **first-mover advantage** if the first mover earns more benefits than the second mover.

A game has a **first-mover advantage** when the first player to act in a sequential game gets a benefit from doing so.

One particularly relevant form of first-mover advantage is the value of *commitment*. To illustrate the main idea, let's consider an extension of the work-or-surf game.

Using backward induction, we obtained a unique equilibrium in this game: you surf and Gina works, even though she would have been better off if you had chosen to work. If only she could threaten you with punishment, using the following strategy: "If you surf, I will go surfing, too!" But such an action is not credible in the sense that when push comes to shove, Gina will choose not to surf when you go surfing because by so doing she will forego $100 in net benefits. You know that she will choose to work.

Is there any way that Gina can turn the tables on you by taking away the first-mover advantage? In fact, there is. The trick is for her to make a credible commitment. A **commitment** is an action that one cannot turn back on later, even if it is costly. One commitment device would be for her to throw her shop keys into the Pacific Ocean. With no keys, the only way that she can get into the shop is for you to go to work. She has changed the game, making the choice very simple for you. Exhibit 13.12 shows the simple decision tree. Gina has effectively eliminated the possibilities that you surf and she works.

Commitment refers to the ability to choose and stick with an action that might later be costly.

Now what should you do? It is clear that both outcomes when you work ($400 and $300) are better than when you surf ($200). So, given that Gina has credibly committed to not working without you, the way that you maximize your payoff is to go to work. Gina will then choose to surf, securing a payoff for herself of $500, effectively taking advantage of her credible commitment of tossing her shop keys in the ocean. As demonstrated in Exhibit 13.12, such a credible threat leads to a unique equilibrium that is much more advantageous to Gina.

Several modes of behavior may be understood in light of this example. Suppose, for example, that you can consciously or subconsciously (truthfully, or perhaps just for show) establish a reputation as somebody who bears a grudge and who would seek revenge against misdeeds even though this is potentially costly for you (because of the conflicts and fights that such revenge will induce). If you can (in the eyes of others) commit to punishing bullies, you likely won't be bullied. This reasoning also suggests that perhaps vengeance or a reputation for revenge-seeking behavior might have some game-theoretic reasoning.

Now with this understanding of how sequential games work, let us turn to the value of putting yourself into someone's shoes—this time, the shoes of another individual who will respond to your actions.

Exhibit 13.12 An Extensive-Form Game with a Credible Commitment

A commitment is an action that one cannot take back. Commitments, which come before other actions, can change who has the advantage. If Gina throws her keys into the ocean before you decide whether to work or surf, she will have credibly committed to not working, and this will force you to work instead.

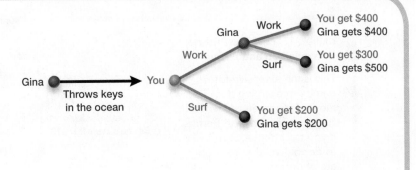

Evidence-Based Economics

Q: Is there value in putting yourself into someone else's shoes?

Bernie Madoff, possibly under arrest.

Abraham Lincoln once said, "When I am getting ready to reason with a man, I spend one-third of my time thinking about myself and what I am going to say, and two-thirds about him and what he is going to say." President Lincoln keenly understood that it was necessary to put himself into the other man's shoes before discussions started. Anticipating the demands and strategies of his opponents made Lincoln one of the United States' most celebrated presidents. He thought deeply about the high-stakes sequential games he had to win to steer the United States through the Civil War.

One way of investigating more systematically the question we pose in this section is to conduct lab experiments using trust games. One variant of the trust game is shown in Exhibit 13.13. There are two players, you and Bernie. You are the first mover and must decide whether or not to trust Bernie. The associated payoffs to this game are as follows: (1) If you choose not to trust Bernie, then both you and Bernie receive a payoff of $10. (2) If you choose to trust Bernie, then Bernie must choose to either defect or cooperate. If he defects, then you receive nothing and Bernie receives $30. If Bernie cooperates, then both of you receive $15.

How will you play this game?

Assuming that Exhibit 13.13 contains all of the relevant payoffs, then you should use backward induction to solve this game. If you put yourself into Bernie's shoes, you would defect if given the chance. This is because by defecting, Bernie earns $30, which is greater than his cooperation earnings of $15. So you should choose not to trust Bernie because you now know that if you did trust him, he would choose to defect, because $30 is greater than $15. So the equilibrium of this game is for you not to trust Bernie. This is a bad outcome in the sense that it is not socially efficient: instead of earning a total of $30, you and Bernie only earn $20 ($10 each) because you do not trust Bernie. In this way, the trust game is a sequential prisoners' dilemma game.

You will notice that many situations in the real world look like this game. Every time you trust a stranger, or even a friend, there is a risk that person will disappoint you. When you call a plumber to repair your leaking faucet, there is a risk that he will take your money but do a shoddy job and the faucet will start leaking again in a few weeks. When you enter a car lot hoping to find a good deal on a used sports car, you face the same risk—what if the car is a lemon?

If the equilibrium is as characterized in Exhibit 13.13, the world would be a sad and dysfunctional place. What factors could cause the equilibrium in Exhibit 13.13 to be different? One important factor is reputational concerns: if the game is played several

Exhibit 13.13 A Trust Game Between You and Bernie

This is the extensive-form game representing trust. You move first and decide whether to trust or not to trust Bernie. If you trust Bernie, then he has to decide whether to cooperate or defect.

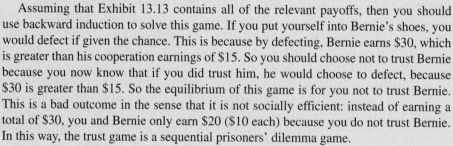

times, the players might attempt to develop a reputation. For example, you visit the same coffee shop, bakery, butcher shop, and dry cleaner, and you often hang out with the same friends. In all of these cases, you and the other agents you are interacting with can develop a reputation for trustworthiness and not misbehaving, and this reputation can then help you achieve better payoffs.

In Exhibit 13.13, even though it makes sense for you not to trust Bernie in a one-shot game, if you were to play, say 100 times, it might make sense for you to trust Bernie and for Bernie to play nicely, because you can both be better off if you receive $15 every round of play rather than $10 each. This long-run strategy might shed light on the kinds of interactions we observe constantly in the real world—for example, why businesspeople trust one another, or friends and families share trust.

How can we shed light on such a game in the real world and compare behavior in one shot versus repeated games? One approach is to run a field experiment, which is what one of the authors of this book (John List) did at several sports card trading shows.[4] At these shows, dealers—think Comic Book Guy from *The Simpsons*—set up booths to buy and sell sports cards. Just like many goods we purchase sports cards have uncertain quality. Not every Derek Jeter rookie card is the same, and just as an experienced mechanic can inspect a car and determine its quality, an elaborate grading system understood by licensed experts is used to determine the quality of trading cards. This quality then determines the value of the card.

John List recruited buyers to approach sellers and purchase baseball cards from sellers who promised to deliver a "Mint" card. (In the baseball card market, there are various degrees of "Mint," determined by grading services or authenticators.) The sellers in the experiment were either local dealers, who frequented the card shows often and therefore had a reputation to uphold, or nonlocal dealers, who lived in another city and therefore rarely frequented the local card shows. Accordingly, they had little reputation at stake. After each transaction, the buyers secretly turned the goods over to List so that he could have the true grade ascertained by a licensed expert.

It is reasonable to believe that local dealers have more of a reputational concern than nonlocal dealers, but there might also be other important differences between them. For example, local dealers might just care more about local customers. To make sure that his findings were not driven by these other differences, List organized a second field experiment in which he had buyers purchase sporting event ticket stubs (stubs of the tickets that permit you entry into a sporting event) at two different points in time. In the first instance, there was no professional grading service to evaluate the quality of the stubs. Directly before the second time period, a grading service had emerged to evaluate ticket stubs. Again, after each transaction, the buyers secretly turned their goods over to List so that he could have the true grade ascertained by a licensed expert. If local dealers were just different or cared about their customers, we should see similar behavior in the two different time instances. If, on the other hand, they were motivated by reputational concerns, they should be much more likely to sell high-quality ticket stubs after introduction of the grading service.

Exhibit 13.14 summarizes the results of the experiments. In the first experiment, among the set of nonlocal sellers, fewer than 10 percent of the cards were at the level promised by the dealer (the leftmost bar in Exhibit 13.14). But at the same time, those sellers who *did* have reputational concerns provided nearly 50 percent of cards at the promised quality level. This is evidence consistent with the importance of reputation.

In the second field experiment, List found that before the third-party quality verification service was introduced, the local dealers had no qualms about selling lemons. In fact, they were not much better than the nonlocal dealers in the first experiment! The second two columns in Exhibit 13.14 show that only 18 percent of the ticket stubs purchased before the introduction of the quality service were at or above the quality level promised by the seller. After the introduction of the service, though, quality levels shot back up.

Evidence-Based Economics *(Continued)*

13.1

13.2

13.3

13.4

13.5

Exhibit 13.14 Percent of Sales at or above Promised Quality Level by Dealer Type

This exhibit shows the percent of cards sold at or above the quality level promised at the trading shows. With verification, nonlocal salespeople of cards only deliver at or above the quality they promise in 10 percent of the transactions. The corresponding number is much higher for local salespeople, presumably because they have reputational concerns. They deliver at or above the quality they promise in nearly 50 percent of the transactions. The exhibit also shows the importance of quality verification: local salesman deliver on their promises considerably, more often when verification is possible.

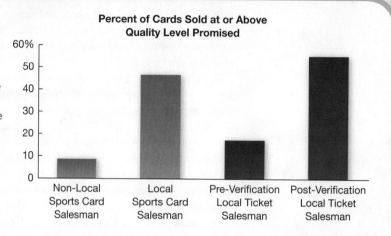

Percent of Cards Sold at or Above Quality Level Promised

These experiments thus show that reputational concerns are quite important. In particular, these reputational concerns made local sellers much more likely to deliver cards at the quality level they promised.

In terms of the trust game between you and Bernie, these results show that if Bernie does not have reputational concerns, he will often defect rather than cooperate, leaving you with the short end of the stick. On the other hand, he is much more likely to cooperate when he does have reputational concerns.

In this case, game theory does a good job in predicting behavior. In games when the second mover has little incentive, it is important for the first mover to backward-induct before making his or her move. Such backward induction can save a lot of money. On the other hand, this example illustrates that you need to understand the incentives of each player when constructing the relevant payoffs. If reputational concerns are important, and you know that to be true, your behavior is much different (and payoffs much higher) than when the second mover is not trustworthy.

Question

Is there value in putting yourself into someone else's shoes?

Answer

In many economic situations, there is great value.

Data

Field experiments on Trust.

Caveat

Many features can influence how people behave and the experiment focuses on a few of those reasons for cooperation.

There Is More to Life than Money

The data from the sports card market show that some sellers deliver high quality even when they have no reputational concerns or there is no financial incentive to do so. Such behavior is in line with people tipping at restaurants to which they never plan to return, anonymous donors giving to private charities, and some firms installing costly pollution abatement equipment voluntarily.

One reason for such deviations from Nash predictions is the presence of *social preferences*, meaning that the individual's benefits are defined not only by his or her own payoffs but also by the payoffs of others. Social preferences play an important role in many economic interactions, and we discuss them in greater detail in Chapter 18.

Summary

⚙️ Game theory provides us with the tools to examine situations when payoffs are intertwined. Whether decisions are made simultaneously or sequentially, game theory is all about being able to see the world through the eyes of your opponent and understand the opponent's incentives.

⚙️ The key concepts of game theory are best responses and Nash equilibrium. A best response is one agent's optimal strategy (action) taking the other player's strategy as given. When the same strategy is a best response against any possible strategies of the other players, then it is a dominant strategy. In most games, players do not possess such a dominant strategy, making their best responses depend on the strategy choices of other players.

⚙️ A Nash equilibrium arises if each player chooses a strategy that is a best response to the strategies of other players. Put differently, a Nash equilibrium is a combination of strategies that are mutual best responses.

⚙️ The concept of Nash equilibrium enables us to make predictions about behavior in a range of situations, including those that can be modeled as the prisoners' dilemma, the tragedy of the commons, and zero-sum games. It also helps us understand why trustworthy behavior is more likely to emerge when players have reputational concerns.

Key Terms

game theory *p. 301*
strategies *p. 301*
payoff matrix *p. 301*
simultaneous move games *p. 302*
best response *p. 302*
dominant strategy *p. 303*

dominant strategy equilibrium *p. 303*
Nash equilibrium *p. 306*
zero-sum game *p. 309*
pure strategy *p. 309*
mixed strategy *p. 310*
extensive-form game *p. 311*

game tree *p. 311*
backward induction *p. 312*
first-mover advantage *p. 313*
commitment *p. 313*

Questions

All questions are available in MyEconLab *for practice and instructor assignment.*

1. What is a dominant strategy equilibrium?

2. Is a player's best response in a game the same as his dominant strategy? Explain.

3. What is meant by the prisoners' dilemma? Do the players in the prisoners' dilemma game have a dominant strategy?

4. What is a Nash equilibrium? How is a Nash equilibrium different from a dominant strategy equilibrium?

5. How can the tragedy of the commons be modeled as a prisoners' dilemma game?

6. What is a zero-sum game? Can you think of any zero-sum games in real life?

7. What is the difference between a pure strategy and a mixed strategy?

8. Suppose that a player has a dominant strategy. Would she choose to play a mixed strategy (such as playing two strategies each with probability 50-50)? Why or why not?

9. Although there are many examples of game theory in the real world, how well do you think specifics like payoff matrices, Nash equilibria, and dominant strategies translate to reality?

10. When can backward induction be used to arrive at the equilibrium for a game?

11. What is meant by the first-mover advantage? How does commitment matter in a game with a first-mover advantage?

    a. Some games have a first-mover advantage and other games do not. Suppose you were playing rock-paper-scissors as an extensive-form game. First you choose rock, or paper, or scissors, and then your opponent makes a choice. Is there a first-mover advantage in this game?

    b. Two firms are thinking of entering a new market. If only one of them enters, it will make high profits. If two firms enter, then both will suffer losses. Suppose that the game is played sequentially, with firm 1 deciding first. Does this firm have a first-mover advantage?

12. The trust game shown in Exhibit 13.13 is a sequential prisoners' dilemma. This means that it is likely that the outcome of the game is not socially efficient. What factors could cause this equilibrium to be different in real life?

13. Economic agents (for example, consumers or firms) often do things that at first glance seem to be inconsistent with their self-interest. People tip at restaurants when they are on vacation even if they have no intention of returning to the same place. Firms, sometimes, install costly pollution abatement equipment voluntarily. How can these deviations from Nash predictions be explained?

Problems

All problems are available in MyEconLab *for practice and instructor assignment.*

1. Suppose there are cable TV companies in your city, Astounding Cable and Broadcast Cable. They both must decide to on a high advertising budget, a moderate advertising budget, or a low advertising budget. They will make their decisions simultaneously. Their payoffs are as follows:

Astounding/ Broadcast	High	Medium	Low
High	Astounding earns $2 million	Astounding earns $5 million	Astounding earns $4 million
	Broadcast earns $5 million	Broadcast earns $7 million	Broadcast earns $9 million
Medium	Astounding earns $6 million	Astounding earns $8 million	Astounding earns $5 million
	Broadcast earns $4 million	Broadcast earns $6 million	Broadcast earns $2 million

Low	Astounding earns $1 million	Astounding earns $0 million	Astounding earns $3 million
	Broadcast earns $2 million	Broadcast earns $5 million	Broadcast earns $3 million

   a. Does Astounding have a dominant strategy? If so, what is it?

   b. Does Broadcast have a dominant strategy? If so, what is it?

   c. Is there a dominant strategy equilibrium? If so, what is it?

   d. Are there any Nash equilibria in this game? If so, what are they?

2. Suppose Russia is deciding to Invade or Not Invade its neighbor Ukraine. The U.S. has to decide to be Tough or Make Concessions. They will make their decisions simultaneously. Their payoffs are as follows:

U.S./Russia	Not Invade	Invade
Tough	U.S. gets 5	U.S. gets 7
	Russia gets 4	Russia gets 3
Make Concessions	U.S. gets 3	U.S. gets 1
	Russia gets 5	Russia gets 9

a. What is U.S.'s best response when Russia chooses *Not Invade*?

b. What is U.S.'s best response when Russia chooses *Invade*?

c. What is Russia's best response when U.S. chooses *Tough*?

d. What is Russia's best response when U.S. chooses *Make Concessions*?

e. What is the Nash equilibrium of this game?

3. In the movie *Princess Bride*, the hero disguised as the pirate Westley is engaged in a game of wits with the villain Vizzini. Westley puts poison in either his own glass of wine or in Vizzini's glass. Vizzini will choose to drink from his own glass or from Westley's; Westley drinks from the glass Vizzini does not choose. (You should think of this as a game where players move simultaneously since Vizzini does not see which glass Westley has chosen).

a. Construct the payoff matrix for this game. Assume drinking the poison and dying gives a payoff of -10 and staying alive has a payoff of 10.

b. Does Vizzini have a dominant strategy? Does Westley have a dominant strategy?

c. Does this game have a Nash equilibrium where players use pure strategies?

d. Now suppose that Westley has another strategy which is not to put poison in any of the glasses, and this will give him a utility of *a* regardless of Vizzini's choice of strategy. For what values of *a* does Westley have a dominant strategy?

4. Suppose that auctions have never been conducted online and eBay is contemplating entering the market for online auctions. Another company, Yahoo! Auctions, also wants to enter this market. If eBay enters the market but Yahoo! Auctions does not, then eBay earns enormous profits and Yahoo! Auctions earns 0. Similarly, if Yahoo! Auctions enters the market but eBay does not, then Yahoo! Auctions earns enormous profits and eBay earns 0. If both enter the market, then each suffers losses. If neither enters, each earns 0.

a. Construct the payoff matrix for eBay and Yahoo! Auctions indicating the strategies they may choose.

b. Find the Nash equilibrium for this game.

5. As this chapter explains, the movie *A Beautiful Mind* is a biography of John Nash. There is a scene in the movie where the John Nash character (played by Russell Crowe) is at a bar with several friends and has the insight that becomes what we now call a Nash equilibrium. Here is a game that summarizes what happened in that scene. Several women enter the bar; one of the women is very beautiful. All of the men would prefer to dance with the beautiful woman. They know that if one man asks the beautiful woman to dance that she will accept, but that if two of the men ask her to dance, she will refuse to dance with either of them. The John Nash character argues that none of the men should ask the beautiful woman to dance but should instead ask the other women. Do you think the director of this movie has studied game theory?

6. Suppose two friends, Rick and Susan, want to go to a movie. The movie tickets cost $10 each. They decide to play a game of Morra to decide who will pay for the tickets. In this game, they hold out one or two fingers simultaneously. Susan wins if the fingers they both hold out add up to an odd number, and Rick wins if they add up to an even number. Susan pays $20 to Rick if she loses and receives $20 from Rick if she wins.

a. Construct the payoff matrix for the game. Is this a zero-sum game? Why or why not?

b. Is there a pure strategy Nash equilibrium in this game? Explain your answer.

7. Use a matrix to model a two-player game of rock-paper-scissors with a payoff of 1 if you win, -1 if you lose, and 0 if you tie.

a. Draw the payoff matrix for this game.

b. Is there an equilibrium in this game where players use pure strategies?

c. Why should you use a mixed strategy to play this game?

8. Two gas stations, A and B, are locked in a price war. Each player has the option of raising its price (R) or continuing to charge the low price (C). They will choose strategies simultaneously. If both choose C, they will both suffer a loss of $100. If one chooses R and the other chooses C, (i) the one that chooses R loses many of its customers and earns $0, and (ii) the one that chooses C wins many new customers and earns $1,000. If they both choose R the price war ends and they each earn $500.

a. Draw the payoff matrix for this game.

b. Does either player have a dominant strategy? Explain.

c. How many Nash equilibria does this game have? Defend your answer carefully.

9. Consider a game with two players, 1 and 2. They play the extensive-form game summarized in the game tree below:

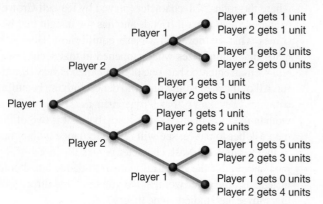

Player 1 gets 1 unit
Player 2 gets 1 unit

Player 1 gets 2 units
Player 2 gets 0 units

Player 1 gets 1 unit
Player 2 gets 5 units

Player 1 gets 1 unit
Player 2 gets 2 units

Player 1 gets 5 units
Player 2 gets 3 units

Player 1 gets 0 units
Player 2 gets 4 units

a. Suppose Player 1 is choosing between the green and red for his second move. Which will he choose if:

   i. Green, Green has been played.

   ii. Red, Red has been played.

b. Suppose Player 2 is choosing between green and red, knowing the information above. Which will he choose if:

   i. Green has been played.

   ii. Red has been played.

c. Finally, suppose Player 1 is choosing between green and red in the first move. Given the information above, which will he choose?

d. Now describe the path that gives an equilibrium in this extensive game.

10. Jones TV and Smith TV are the only two stores in your town that sell flat-panel TV sets. First, Jones will choose whether to charge high prices or low prices. Smith will see Jones's decision and then choose high or low prices. If they both choose High, each earns $10,000. If they both choose Low, each earns $8,000. If one chooses High and the other chooses Low, the one that chose High earns $6,000 and the one that chose Low earns $14,000.

a. Draw the game tree. Use backward induction to solve this game.

b. Suppose Smith goes to Jones and promises to choose High if Jones chooses High. Is this a credible promise?

c. Now suppose Jones starts a new policy that says it will always match or beat Smith's price. It advertises the new policy heavily and so must choose Low if Smith chooses Low. So the game now has the following structure. First, Jones chooses High or Low. Second, Smith chooses High or Low. Third, if Jones has chosen High and Smith has chosen Low, Jones meets Smith's price and chooses Low. Draw the game tree. Use backward induction to solve this game.

11. Two teams played a game called Thai 21 on an episode of the television show *Survivor*. Call the teams Green and Red. The game begins with 21 flags. The teams take turns. When it is a team's turn, it can remove one, two, or three flags. The team that removes the last flag wins. Green goes first. Who should win this game, Green or Red?

12. Pat's and Geno's are two rival cheesesteak restaurants in Philadelphia, Pennsylvania, that are located across the street from each other. Since they serve almost the same food, they are fiercely competitive. With the weather in Philly improving, sales at both firms are expected to increase in the next few months. Suppose both firms are now considering expanding their menu to include cheesecake and other desserts to boost sales further. The payoffs are in the table below:

a. Suppose Geno's and Pat's make their decisions simultaneously. What is the Nash equilibrium in this game?

b. Now suppose that Pat's will decide whether or not to introduce desserts and then Geno's will decide. Draw the game tree for this extensive-form game.

c. Use backward induction to determine how the extensive-form version of this game will be played.

| | | *Pat's* | |
		Introduce Desserts	Don't Introduce Desserts
Geno's	Introduce desserts	Pat's profits will increase by $60,000 Geno's profits will increase by $60,000	Pat's profits will increase by $10,000 Geno's sales will increase by $80,000
	Don't introduce desserts	Pat's profits will increase by $80,000 Geno's profits will increase by $10,000	Pat's profits will increase by $20,000 Geno's profits will increase by $20,000

14

Oligopoly and Monopolistic Competition

How many firms are necessary to make a market competitive?

As an economist working at the Council of Economic Advisers, one of this book's authors worked with the Antitrust Division of the Department of Justice (DOJ) to examine whether the dominance of a few large producers of off-road engines increased market prices. This very question arises for many important industries that touch our lives daily. Consider Apple, and whether its pricing of e-books or its dominance of the digital music market with iTunes might be considered anticompetitive.

A first thought that you might have is that because there are only a few competitors to Apple on the digital music front—mainly Google Play and Amazon.com's MP3 store—the industry must not be very competitive.

Does simply counting the number of firms in an industry tell us whether the market is competitive? If so, then how many firms do we need to make a market competitive?

So far, we've studied two extreme market structures: perfect competition, which features many firms, and monopoly, in which a single firm supplies the entire market. As useful as these models are, they do not provide the necessary tools to help you answer the question of how many

CHAPTER **OUTLINE**

14.1
Two More Market Structures

14.2
Oligopoly

14.3
Monopolistic Competition

14.4
The "Broken" Invisible Hand

14.5
Summing Up: Four Market Structures

EBE
How many firms are necessary to make a market competitive?

322

firms are necessary to make a market competitive. For this task, you need more realistic models of market structure, which lie somewhere *between* perfect competition and monopoly.

In this chapter, we study the two market structures that do, in fact, fall between the two extremes of perfect competition and monopoly: oligopoly and monopolistic competition. An important point of difference between these two market structures and the two extreme market types studied so far is that we must now consider interaction between firms. In so doing, we learn about the nature of competition and how prices are set within such industries. If you read novels, go to the movies, drink Pepsi or Coke, wear designer clothing, or just like to play around on your Mac that you purchased at BestBuy, you are already familiar with products in oligopolistic and monopolistically competitive industries.

This chapter will help you understand the economics underlying these industries. We will learn that in some instances, even markets with only two firms yield competitive outcomes. In other cases, prices that more closely approximate monopoly prices can result when only a few firms serve a market. By the end of the chapter, you will have acquired the economic tools to help you understand just how many firms it takes to make a market competitive. And, you'll learn that much more than just the number of firms determines market prices and producer profits.

14.1 Two More Market Structures

Every day you buy goods and services, such as books and music, from firms that do not naturally fit within the perfectly competitive or monopoly models. You might be thinking, how do Starbucks and Dunkin' Donuts fit in? First, they are price-makers, so they do not fall into the perfectly competitive category. Second, they do not have a monopoly since they compete fiercely with other sellers of coffee and food products.

Coffee and tasty foods are typical examples of **differentiated products**, which are goods that are similar but are not perfect substitutes. They contrast with **homogeneous products**, which are those goods that are identical and are therefore perfect substitutes. Soybeans grown by different farmers are perfect substitutes; books produced by different authors are not.

Industries differ not only in whether or not their products are differentiated or homogeneous but also in the number of sellers present in the industry. Some industries will have

Differentiated products refer to goods that are similar but are not perfect substitutes.

Homogeneous products refer to goods that are identical, and so are perfect substitutes.

Exhibit 14.1
Characteristics of Four Market Structures

Between the two extremes of perfect competition and monopoly, there are oligopoly and monopolistic competition. In oligopoly, there are only a few firms competing, and this could be in the context of either homogeneous or differentiated products. In monopolistic competition, many firms sell differentiated products, and each enjoys some degree of market power.

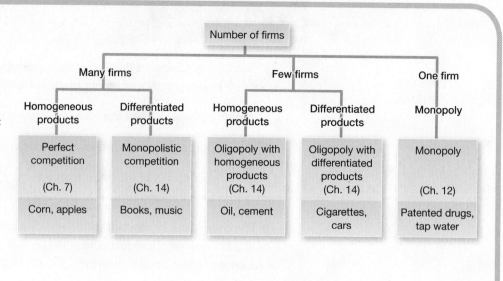

a few sellers, like the airline industry or cable TV carriers in your area. Other industries will have many sellers, like the book or music industries. A useful classification of market structures must therefore distinguish industries along two dimensions:

1. The number of firms supplying a given product
2. The degree of product differentiation

These distinctions lead us to introduce two more market structures, which we present in Exhibit 14.1.

Our first new market structure is **oligopoly**, which refers to a situation in which there are only a few suppliers of a product. As Exhibit 14.1 shows, oligopolies can feature either homogeneous or differentiated products. Because in oligopoly there are only a few firms, each firm's profits and profit-maximizing choices depend on other firms' actions.

Our second new market structure is **monopolistic competition**. That might sound like an oxymoron—how can a monopoly be competitive? The name reflects the basic tension between market power and competitive forces that exists in this market type. All firms in a monopolistically competitive industry face a downward-sloping demand curve, so they have market power and choose their own price like monopolists. These characteristics account for the first part of the name. What's *competitive* about such markets is that there are no restrictions on entry—any number of firms can enter the industry at any time. This means that firms in a monopolistically competitive industry, despite having pricing power, make zero economic profits in the long run. As Exhibit 14.1 shows, similar to a perfectly competitive industry, *monopolistic competition* features many competing firms, but unlike perfect competition, the sellers produce and sell differentiated products.

As we proceed through the chapter, you may want to refer back to Exhibit 14.1, which outlines the similarities and differences between the four types of market structures. We begin with oligopoly.

Oligopoly is the market structure that applies when there are few firms competing.

Monopolistic competition is the market structure that applies when there are many competing firms and products are differentiated.

14.2 Oligopoly

Oligopoly is a word that might strike you as rather strange. It stems from Greek origins: *oligoi* meaning "a few" and *polein* meaning "to sell." Put them together and you have a term referring to a market structure in which there are only a few suppliers of a product. You encounter oligopolies everywhere. As you push your cart down the soap aisle at the local supermarket, you may notice several different brands of bar soap—for instance,

Ivory, Camay, Irish Spring, Caress, Dove, Lifebuoy, and Lever 2000. But if you look more closely, you will see that there are only a few suppliers—among them, Procter and Gamble, Colgate Palmolive, and Lever Brothers.

Oligopolies are tricky to analyze because all sorts of market outcomes can happen, depending on the circumstances. For instance, only three companies—Seagate, Western Digital, and Hitachi—control almost three-quarters of the market for computer hard drives, but they ruthlessly cut prices on one another, and their rivalry has driven prices very close to marginal cost. At the same time, luxury goods makers like Louis Vuitton, Chanel, and Gucci seldom get into price wars.

If you refer back to Exhibit 14.1, you will see that oligopolies can be usefully divided into two categories: those that sell homogeneous goods (for example, hard drives or oil) and those that sell differentiated goods (for example, cigarettes or soda). In this chapter, we discuss two models to help us understand oligopoly:

1. Oligopoly model with homogeneous (identical) products.
2. Oligopoly model with differentiated products.

The first model, oligopoly with identical products, is similar to the monopoly model, but one key difference is that the oligopolist must recognize the behavior of its competitors, whereas the monopolist does not. The second model, oligopoly with differentiated products, is linked to the monopolistic competition market structure with one major exception: entry is impeded in the oligopoly, whereas there is free entry in the monopolistically competitive market.

The Oligopolist's Problem

The oligopolist's problem shares important similarities with the two market types discussed in previous chapters—perfect competition and monopoly. And several of the concepts we have learned, such as those relating to production and cost, apply directly to the oligopolist's problem. From there, the oligopolist's problem can be described as having two unique features:

1. Due to cost advantages associated with the economies of scale of oligopoly or other barriers to entry, entry and exit will not necessarily push the market to zero economic profits in the long run (as is the case with perfect competition and monopolistic competition).
2. Because of relatively few competitors, there is an important interaction between the few sellers that do occupy the market.

Oligopoly Model with Homogeneous Products

Duopoly refers to a two-firm industry.

One of the simplest cases of oligopoly is an industry with only two competing firms—a **duopoly**. Suppose that these two firms compete against one another by setting prices. Consumers observe these prices and then choose from which firm to buy. Such a model is commonly called *Bertrand competition*, after the famous French mathematician Joseph Louis François Bertrand, who first studied the interactions among competing firms that set prices.

To begin, let's suppose that the industry of interest is landscaping and that there are currently two landscaping firms in the city: your company, Dogwood, and a competitor, Rose Petal. You both provide lawn mowing and shrubbery trimming services. In addition, because the local labor market conditions affect you both equally, you have the same marginal cost, which is $30 per landscape job (and you can perform as many jobs as you can get at this marginal cost). We'll make one further assumption: consumers view your services as identical to Rose Petal's services. This means that you and Rose Petal are selling perfect substitutes.

With only two companies, it sounds like a pretty serious oligopoly, right? We would likely expect both firms to have a lot of market power and therefore be able to charge a high price.

To understand how this market works, we first turn to the demand side. Customers in this market have a simple demand rule: they hire landscaping services from the company that sells at the lower price. If both landscapers charge the same price, the consumer flips a coin to determine which firm to choose. The simple demand rule means, in effect, that the landscaper charging the lower price will get all of the demand. If both companies charge the same price, each company will get half of the demand.

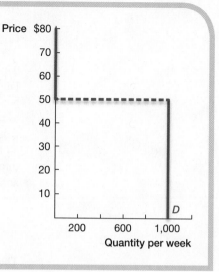

Exhibit 14.2 Market Demand Curve for an Oligopoly with Homogeneous Products

The exhibit depicts the market demand curve for landscape jobs, which are assumed to be homogeneous. The market has a total demand of 1,000 landscaping jobs per week, provided that the price is $50 or below. At any price above $50, the market demand is zero.

The final element you need to know to make your pricing decision is the market demand. For simplicity, let's say that the market has a total demand of 1,000 landscaping jobs per week, provided that the price is $50 or below. At any price above $50, the market demand is zero (because at high prices people do their own yard work). Exhibit 14.2 presents the market demand curve for this situation.

What is directly relevant for a firm's profit-maximizing decisions is not the market demand curve but its **residual demand curve**, which is the demand that is not met by other firms. This residual demand curve depends on the prices charged by all firms in the market. We can derive your residual demand curve in this case from the market demand curve as a function of your price P_{DW} and Rose Petal's price P_{RP}. In particular, in this example it is given as

> 1,000, if your price is less than Rose Petal's, or $P_{DW} < P_{RP}$;
> 1,000/2, if your price is equal to Rose Petal's, or $P_{DW} = P_{RP}$;
> 0, if your price is more than Rose Petal's, or $P_{DW} > P_{RP}$.

Contrasted with the market demand curve, which depends on the "market price"—the minimum of the prices charged in the market—the residual demand curve depends on the prices charged by both you and Rose Petal.

The **residual demand curve** is the demand that is not met by other firms and depends on the prices of all firms in the industry.

Doing the Best You Can: How Should You Price to Maximize Profits?

The task facing you is now clear-cut: you should choose the price that maximizes your profits, realizing that you will sell according to the demand structure above. How should you start? A first consideration is determining costs. Recall that the marginal cost is assumed to be $30 per job for both you and Rose Petal.

A second consideration is to understand how your behavior affects Rose Petal's behavior. Let's start with some simple strategies. Say that you begin by charging a price of $50 and Rose Petal charges $45. What happens in this case? Because your price is higher than Rose Petal's price, Rose Petal will reap all of the business, and will earn $15 above its marginal cost on each of the 1,000 landscaping jobs ($15 = $45 − $30).

Is this a Nash equilibrium? Remember from Chapter 13 that a Nash equilibrium occurs when each player chooses a strategy that is a best response to the strategies of others. Upon some reflection, you can see that this is not a Nash equilibrium, because given Rose Petal's price, you can do better.

How? The answer is to charge a price slightly below $45; in that way, you undercut Rose Petal's price. For example, if you charge a price of $44, you effectively steal the entire market from Rose Petal and now your company earns profits—in fact, you earn $14 more than your marginal cost on every job ($14 = $44 − $30). We depict this situation in Exhibit 14.3.

Exhibit 14.3 Dueling Duopolies and a Pricing Response

In a duopoly with homogeneous products, the best response of a firm that has a higher price is to undercut its rival as long as its rival's price is above marginal cost (denoted $MC = \$30$ in the exhibit). So in this exhibit, when your price is $P_{DW} = \$50$ and that of Rose Petal is $P_{RP} = \$45$, you can increase your profits by cutting your price from $50 to $P'_{DW} = \$44$ (which will increase your sales from 0 to 1,000).

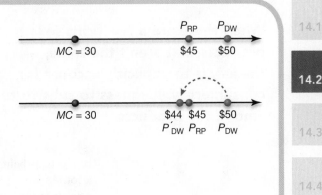

How does Rose Petal now view the situation? Because the price is above marginal cost $MC = \$30$, Rose Petal views this situation in the same manner that you viewed the top portion of Exhibit 14.3. So this is not a Nash equilibrium—given your pricing behavior, Rose Petal can do better. To do so, it can undercut *you*, and charge $43 per landscaping job. This pricing move permits Rose Petal to capture all of the market back from you. And it is now earning $13 above its marginal cost for every completed job.

When does all of this price-cutting end? In other words, what is the Nash equilibrium? Seeing this example through to the end, you will realize that the price-cutting goes on until we reach the unique Nash equilibrium: both firms charge a price equal to marginal cost, or $30 per landscaping job. That is, $P_{DW} = P_{RP} = MC = \$30$ is the unique Nash equilibrium. In this equilibrium, each of the two companies ends up supplying half of the market, and because both are selling at marginal cost, they both earn zero economic profits.

To convince yourself that this is a Nash equilibrium you should ask: are there any other strategies that these two firms could use to make an economic profit? If not, then both firms are playing their best responses, and we have found a Nash equilibrium. The key observation is that, starting from $P_{DW} = P_{RP} = MC$, neither firm can increase its profits. If you try to charge a bit more, you sell nothing. If you cut price further, you will not cover your marginal cost ($P_{DW} < MC = \$30$), so this is not a good strategy either, because you will actually lose money on every landscaping job. Both your firm and Rose Petal would obviously like to make an economic profit, but if either of you raises your price above marginal cost by just a penny, the other will receive all of the business. So the outcome isn't the most preferable outcome for you or Rose Petal, but neither of you can do better by unilaterally changing your price. This is the definition of a Nash equilibrium. (That this is the unique Nash equilibrium also follows from the argument in the previous paragraph, showing that no other combination of prices can be a Nash equilibrium.)

So there is a surprising conclusion to the model of an oligopoly with homogeneous products: in this model, firms engage in quite tough competition in trying to gain market share. In fact, the market outcome is the same as it would be in a perfectly competitive industry: price equals marginal cost in equilibrium. This competitiveness comes from the fact that any one firm can steal all of the market from the other by dropping price slightly. The strong undercutting incentive leads both firms to lower their prices to marginal cost.

This model shares similarities with the prisoners' dilemma game that we discussed in Chapter 13. Even though both you and Rose Petal would be better off if you both chose a high price, the unique equilibrium is for each of you to choose a low price.

Oligopoly Model with Differentiated Products

So far in our discussion of oligopoly models, we have assumed that sellers are engaged in competition to sell homogeneous products. Often, however, a more realistic description of an industry is a set of firms that make *similar but not homogeneous* products. A Boeing airliner is not the same as an Airbus, video game consoles from Microsoft, Nintendo, and Sony are not the same, and a flight on American Airlines

When there are a few firms selling products that aren't the same, the key is to explicitly account for consumers' willingness to substitute among the products.

is not the same as a flight on Southwest, even though these products are all in the same industry. Economists refer to a market in which multiple varieties of a common product type are available as a *differentiated product market*. When there are a few firms selling products that aren't the same, the key is to explicitly account for consumers' willingness to substitute among the products.

Therefore, this is not the "all-or-nothing" demand a firm faces with different prices for homogeneous products. With differentiated products, we assume that consumers view the firms' products as being somewhat distinct. As we'll see, this differentiation helps the seller a lot. As we just learned, when products are homogeneous, the incentive to undercut price is so intense that firms drive the market price down to marginal cost, thereby earning zero economic profits. But that won't happen here, as we'll see in the following example.

To illustrate, let's consider the soft drink industry, where there are two major players: Coca Cola and Pepsi. Because many consumers view the two companies' products as similar, if either firm cuts its prices, it will gain market share from the other. But in this case the firms' products aren't *exact* substitutes (that is, they are not homogeneous goods), so the price-cutting company won't take the entire market just because it prices a bit lower than the other firm. Some people are still going to prefer its competitor's product, even at a higher price.

This means that the demand curve facing each firm includes a consideration of the competitor's price. For example, if Coke raises its price, Pepsi sells more soda. Likewise, Coke will sell more when Pepsi raises its price. The responses of each company's quantity demanded to price changes reflect consumers' willingness to substitute across the two products. But this substitution is of limited magnitude; a firm can't take over the whole market with a 1¢ price cut, as in the homogeneous products case discussed earlier in the chapter.

So, how should Pepsi and Coke determine their prices? Let us highlight the main intuition here. Much like any firm that we have studied thus far, the idea is to set marginal revenue equal to marginal cost. In this case, each firm must put itself in the other's shoes to recognize how its prices will affect the prices of its competitor. For example, Pepsi executives must estimate the demand for Pepsi given *every* possible price for Coke. They can then construct their optimal price for *every* possible price of Coke. They must also estimate what price Coke is likely to set.

Coke makes the same calculations in order to figure out *its* best response to changes in Pepsi's prices. Note that the equilibrium is determined by actions of both Pepsi and Coke. The relevant concept that got us to this point is once again Nash equilibrium, which means that both firms set their prices as best responses to each other.

We have seen that with homogeneous products, two firms competing head-to-head are sufficient to bring the price down to marginal cost. This is no longer true with differentiated products. In fact, in an oligopoly with differentiated products, firms typically

Coke vs. Pepsi, an example of oligopoly with differentiated products.

make positive economic profits, and some oligopolies persist in the long run with positive profits because of barriers to entry (for example, established brands often act as barriers to entry).

But what happens if there is a third firm supplying soda to the market? In that case, the market would continue to be an oligopoly, but now with three firms. In oligopoly with differentiated products, price will typically be lower with three firms competing compared to two firms competing (this contrasts with oligopoly with homogeneous products where, as we just saw, price is equal to marginal cost even with two firms). As the number of firms in an oligopolistic market increases further, prices tend to decline toward marginal cost. If enough entry occurs, it could cause the market to turn into a monopolistically competitive structure. In that case, we have to turn to the monopolistically competitive model, which we present later in this chapter, to understand what would happen.

LETTING THE DATA SPEAK

Airline Price Wars

Airlines have always been known for their rather cutthroat brand of competition. In this business, competition is fierce. When a new, low-price competitor called Southwest Airlines entered the industry and shook it up, economists sat back and watched the price wars begin.

In fact, economists Austan Goolsbee and Chad Syverson have found in their research that price wars began well before Southwest entered the market.[1] These economists studied the three quarters after Southwest announced that it would create flights but before it actually started selling tickets (so, for example, after Southwest announced it would serve Dallas-to-Chicago flights but before it began to sell Dallas-to-Chicago tickets). They found that prices were 24 percent lower in this three-quarter time period—before actual entry could be suspected as a contributing factor.

Why would airlines respond to a competitor before the competitor is actually competing? One reason may be that airlines attempt to "capture" as many consumers as possible. For example, by selling special frequent-flyer deals and luring new customers into a long-term relationship, airlines may be able to compete with new entrants like Southwest. Before Southwest entered the market, it

was not worthwhile for airlines to offer such deals, but faced with new competition, the airlines might have decided that enticing new customer loyalty was worth it.

Another reason why prices might have fallen before Southwest entered the market is because the long-term value of the market had decreased, making collusion less profitable. We discuss economic elements of collusion next.

Collusion: One Way to Keep Prices High

When the government opened bidding for the Federal Communications Commission's Spectrum Licenses, which allowed cellular phone companies to compete for a specified frequency band to provide wireless communication services in a particular market, several puzzling bids were put forth. US West, for some reason, kept submitting bids that ended in the numbers 378, while other companies chose round figures. What is the logic behind this puzzling behavior?

> **It's not in the interest of one company to collude if the other *is* colluding.**

The fact of the matter is that US West was in tight competition for a frequency band in Rochester, Minnesota, block 378 (a zone of airspace). By submitting bids that ended in 378, US West was signaling its intentions to competitors—in many cases, it was signaling that competitors should "stand down" and stop bidding on this frequency band.

The standard oligopoly models discussed so far cannot explain such puzzling behavior. In order to get at the motivations behind the behavior, we must consider a model of *collusion*. **Collusion** occurs when rival firms conspire among themselves to set prices or to control production quantities rather than let the free market determine them.

Collusion occurs when firms conspire to set the quantity they produce or the prices they charge.

To see how collusion works, let's return to your firm and Rose Petal—duopolists in the landscaping business. In the Bertrand model discussed above, we found that the Nash equilibrium resulted in zero economic profits. One way around this zero-profits "problem" is to engage in collusion over prices. Imagine that over coffee you and the CEO of Rose Petal decide to collude by setting your prices jointly rather than independently.

How should you set prices jointly? One model of how an oligopoly might behave is for all the firms to coordinate and collectively act as a monopolist would act and then split the monopoly profits among themselves. This type of oligopoly structure makes sense on one level, with regard to the total profits of the industry as a whole. We know that absent price discrimination, monopoly profits are the highest profits that can be obtained from a given market. Therefore, jointly acting together to earn monopoly profits is the best an industry can do in profit terms.

That means that both your firm and Rose Petal can collude and set prices at $50 per landscaping job. At this price, the market demand is 1,000 jobs, and if both firms have the same price, half of the consumers will go to each firm; therefore both firms will make considerable economic profits. Accordingly, collusion is much more profitable for both of you than competition.

So, should we expect prices in a duopoly to always reach monopoly levels when the two firms can communicate and set prices jointly? There are two main reasons why we might be skeptical. First, even when firms agree on collusion, they have an incentive to disregard their agreements and engage in secret price-cutting to capture more of the profits for themselves. Thus, although collusion is a great deal for oligopolists, it is difficult to sustain. Second, as we discuss later in this section, such price-fixing is illegal. The potential punishment for engaging in such actions has a strong discouraging effect.

The Breakdown of Collusive Agreements Although collusion sounds easy in principle—let's both set a high price and make a lot of money—in practice, it has proven difficult. The logic behind its difficulty lies in game theory: each company has the incentive to cheat on the collusive agreement. Even if both sellers have agreed to collude, they would rather cheat on that agreement than keep their word.

Let's reconsider the landscaping game to see this reasoning. Consider the situation in which the oligopolists are considering cheating on a collusive agreement. For example, let us assume that you and Rose Petal have agreed to set a high price—$50 per job. You each must decide whether to stick with $50 per job or cut the price, which defines a simple game. In fact, the situation is similar to the prisoners' dilemma game we studied in Chapter 13. Your dominant strategy is to cheat on that agreement and secretly cut your price a little bit, say to $49.50 per job. Faced with a price of $49.50 from you and $50 from Rose Petal for this homogeneous service, all consumers will be attracted by your lower price. Therefore, you can take over the entire market with a slight price cut, nearly doubling your economic profits.

Much like confessing in the prisoners' dilemma game in Chapter 13, cheating in this game is a dominant strategy for both you and Rose Petal. This means that the only equilibrium is for you and Rose Petal to continue to cheat until you set price at marginal cost.

When Collusion Can Work Is it possible to sustain collusion if firms recognize that they will be playing this game over and over rather than just once? The answer is yes. There are two important considerations that determine how successful a collusive arrangement is:

1. Detection and punishment of cheaters.
2. The long-term value of the market.

If another player can cheat without being detected—such as giving customers a secret price discount—then it is difficult to maintain collusive agreements on keeping prices high. Sellers simply give secret price discounts because it is their dominant strategy to do so.

Suppose a cheater has been detected. How might he or she be punished? Consider one long-term strategy that you might want to adopt if you are playing the game with Rose Petal: I will keep my price at $50 per job provided that you also keep your price at $50 per job; if you ever cut your price, then I will cut my price to a very low level, say $30, forever. This type of strategy provides incentives for both firms to keep their prices at $50: if you both keep your price at that level, you will both enjoy extraordinary profits. But should Rose Petal cut its price, as soon as you find out about it, you price at marginal cost, or $30 per job forever, thus denying Rose Petal the high profits that it would have enjoyed with the collusive agreement. This type of punishment strategy is called a **grim strategy**.

A second consideration that is important to whether colluders will cheat is the long-term value of the market. The key is how you both trade off today's profits against tomorrow's profits. A colluder who values future monopoly profits more than current cheating profits will abide by the collusive agreement. In this view, impatient firms, for example those in danger of bankruptcy and therefore in desperate need of profits today, are more likely to cheat on the collusive agreement. In addition, if the government bans a product, then firms selling that product will know that on the last day of legal sales, no individual firm has an

A **grim strategy** is a plan by one player to price a good at marginal cost forever if the other cheats on their agreement.

LETTING THE DATA SPEAK

To Cheat or Not to Cheat: That Is the Question

Up to this point, we have discussed models in which sellers set prices. In another type of oligopoly model, sellers compete on quantities rather than prices. This type of model is called *Cournot competition*, after Antoine Augustin Cournot, a French philosopher and mathematician, who modeled duopolies focusing on quantity choices, rather than on price competition.

Perhaps the most famous group that chooses to collude by choosing quantities is OPEC. OPEC (Organization of the Petroleum Exporting Countries) is an oil **cartel** that coordinates the policies of several major oil-producing countries. Maybe you've grumbled about OPEC as you fork over $80 to fill up the gas tank for your trek home for the summer holiday. Yet for all of the concerns, OPEC even has a problem keeping the price of its good—oil—high.

This problem arises from the natural instability of collusive arrangements we have just learned: each country can increase its profits by pumping more oil, but if they all do so they will depress prices, reducing everybody's profits.

OPEC meets monthly to decide on production quotas for each member. Frequently, however, the members choose not to abide by the agreement and subsequently overpump oil. And by "frequently," we mean "pretty much all the time." Take a look at Exhibit 14.4, which shows OPEC's production quota agreements and its actual production from 2001 to November 2007. The blue

line shows OPEC's stated production ceiling. The red line records the actual total production of the cartel. It's obvious that OPEC's member nations can't stick to their agreements. In fact, in only 10 of the 83 months shown is actual production at or below the agreed-upon quota. The data say a lot about each member's temptation to cheat on the agreement.

A **cartel** is a formal organization of producers who agree on anticompetitive actions.

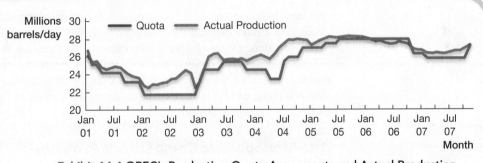

Exhibit 14.4 OPEC's Production Quota Agreements and Actual Production, 2001–2007

The blue line shows the total quota for OPEC members according to their cartel agreements and the red line shows the actual production. Each country has an incentive to increase its production above the quota, with reasoning similar to that of the prisoners' dilemma game. As a consequence, actual production pretty much always exceeds the quota.

incentive to continue playing a cooperative strategy, so all firms cut prices on the last day. This type of incentive might have been at work when airlines began cutting prices long before Southwest entered the market (see the Letting the Data Speak feature on airline price wars earlier in the chapter).

CHOICE & CONSEQUENCE

Collusion in Practice

"The competitor is our friend, the customer is our enemy."

This was the credo in the market for lysine—an additive for animal feed—during the mid-1990s, when Archer Daniels Midland (ADM) colluded with a number of Asian and European agricultural companies to inflate the price of lysine. This might seem like pretty small stuff, but ADM is an enormous corporation. It has its hand in nearly every dish you eat. Lysine is big business.

As hard as collusion is to prove, it might be harder to actually execute. As discussed above, the biggest problem is actually being able to trust your co-conspirators. Most economic models of collusion tend to rely on punishment. If one party reneges on its promise to sell a small quantity at a higher price, then presumably that party will have to be punished in order for collusion to stand any chance of working.

ADM and its co-conspirators weren't able to punish each other, mostly because without a proper audit study it was impossible to know who was cutting prices.

In fact, on one tape capturing a meeting where prices were fixed, an executive suggests that an accounting firm be called in to actually run an audit—"Never mind the legal consequences," the exec states.

No, punishment wasn't the mechanism at work here. Instead, it seems that ADM and its confederates utilized the power of social norms. One tape captures an executive saying to his competitors, "I want to be closer to you than I am to any customers. They're not my friends. You're my friends."

Every company involved tried to establish its credibility in this social manner, often by posturing that its competitor was its friend and its customer its enemy. This mantra is repeatedly caught on secretly recorded tapes. To a certain extent, it's surprising that such a simple mechanism was so effective. The zaniness of the entire arrangement was played up for comedic effect in the movie *The Informant*, which focused on the FBI investigation into ADM.

Even if it makes for humorous fodder now, this zaniness was still profitable. Some estimates are ADM and its co-conspirators extracted millions of dollars from consumers. But they eventually paid. ADM was hit by a record fine by the Department of Justice.

14.3 Monopolistic Competition

We now return to the final major market structure, monopolistic competition. You will recall that a monopolistically competitive market features many firms offering differentiated products. Once we give it some thought, we can see that goods from this type of market structure touch our lives daily: our morning coffee, the clothes we put on every morning, the bike we ride to school, our choice of restaurants for lunch, the movie we watch at night, and the novel we take to bed are all examples of goods supplied by monopolistically competitive industries.

The Monopolistic Competitor's Problem

The monopolistic competitor's problem shares important similarities with the problems of the perfect competitor in Chapters 6 and 7 and the monopolist in Chapter 12. Most importantly, in the short run the mechanics of monopolistic competition are identical to the monopolist's problem, whereas in the long run the equilibrium mirrors perfect competition.

To see these insights in action, let's assume that you have just accepted a part-time job at Dairy Queen, where your job responsibilities include providing advice on pricing. Exhibit 14.5 provides the daily residual demand curve for Dairy Queen ice cream cones—this is the residual demand curve because it gives the demand that is not met by other producers and thus left to be satisfied by Dairy Queen. Because Dairy Queen sells ice cream that is different from the several other ice cream shops in the city, the demand curve it faces is downward-sloping, as in Exhibit 14.5. Thus, much like a monopolist, a monopolistically competitive firm can increase price and not lose all of its business. In fact, the demand curve it faces tells us exactly the trade-off Dairy Queen faces when it changes its price. The marginal revenue curve, as depicted in Exhibit 14.5, is similar in shape to the monopolist's marginal revenue curve.

Exhibit 14.5 Dairy Queen's Demand Curve and Marginal Revenue Curve

The (residual) demand curve facing a monopolistically competitive firm is downward-sloping much like the demand curve facing the monopolist. As a result, the marginal revenue curve is below the demand curve, again just like the marginal revenue curve facing a monopolist.

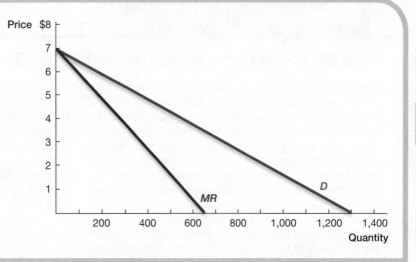

Doing the Best You Can: How a Monopolistic Competitor Maximizes Profits

How should you advise Dairy Queen to maximize its profits? You may not be surprised to learn that the decision rule to maximize profits is *identical* to that for the monopolist:

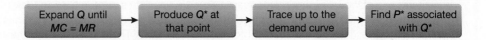

Expand **Q** until **MC = MR** → Produce **Q*** at that point → Trace up to the demand curve → Find **P*** associated with **Q***

Exhibit 14.6 shows how this works in practice. It depicts the demand curve, the marginal revenue curve, and the marginal cost curve for Dairy Queen. As a monopolistic competitor, Dairy Queen must figure out the quantity and price that maximizes its profits. The optimal quantity is found by setting marginal revenue equal to marginal cost, that is, $MC = MR$. To determine price, you trace up to the residual demand curve to see what price consumers are willing to pay for the quantity that you put on the market. Exhibit 14.6 reveals that Dairy Queen can maximize its profits by producing a quantity level of 520 ice cream cones and charging a price of $4.00.

The optimal decision rules are therefore:

Monopolist and Monopolistic Competitor: Set $P > MR = MC$.
Perfect Competitor: $P = MR = MC$.

Exhibit 14.6 Optimal Pricing Strategy for a Monopolistic Competitor

The solution to the monopolistic competitor's problem is identical to the profit-maximizing choice of a monopolist: find where $MC = MR$; drop straight down to find quantity; go straight up to the demand curve; and go left to the y-axis to find the profit-maximizing price.

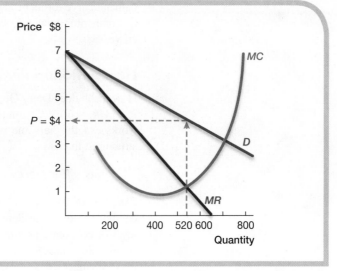

Why Do Some Firms Advertise and Some Don't?

One way in which firms can differentiate their products from those of other firms is to advertise. The right kind of advertising can lead to higher prices and higher profits for the monopolistically competitive firm.

In perfectly competitive markets such as the corn and wheat markets, there is *no* incentive for firms to advertise because they can already sell all the goods that they want at the market price. But a monopolistically competitive firm *does* have an incentive to advertise in order to increase the demand for its product.

Let's look at an example: many winemakers often advertise the superiority of their wines. One example is Kendall-Jackson. If its advertising is successful, consumers believe that Kendall-Jackson wines are superior to other wines. They are then willing to pay a premium for the Kendall-Jackson wines and are less willing to substitute away from such wines—even if the Kendall-Jackson wines are more expensive but very similar to those of other winemakers. In this instance, Kendall-Jackson increases its economic profits at the expense of the consumer. It is this aspect of advertising—the taking advantage of the consumer—that constitutes one of the major arguments against advertising.

Furthermore, critics of advertising claim that advertisements rarely give the public valuable information about the product. Instead, they present misleading situations that convince people that they need a product when they really don't, or that a product is far superior to that of its competitors when it really isn't.

In the past, the government has barred certain industries from advertising. A 1984 article in the *American Economic Review* by John Kwoka concluded that such bans on advertising in the field of optometric services actually *increased* the price for the services by 20 percent.[2]

Initially, this finding may seem counter intuitive—wouldn't optometrists, who were banned from advertising and thus did not have to shell out advertising dollars, be able to charge a lower price? Well, the answer is yes, but because consumers found it difficult to obtain information about the optometry market without any ads to look at, optometrists faced lower competition and could get away with charging higher prices.

Furthermore, advertising can give consumers a signal as to the quality of the service. For example, optometry is a business that relies heavily on repeat customers. Accordingly, an optometrist needs repeat patients in order to afford advertising. Because of this, only those optometrists who believe their patients will be satisfied enough to return after the initial visit will pay for advertising, and thus consumers can look to advertisements to give them an indication of optometrist quality.

These reasons, and the empirical evidence that shows a decrease in price when advertising is allowed, has led the government to repeal many of the advertising bans that had been put in place and allow firms to advertise their business as they see fit.

This summary of the optimal decision rules highlights the fact that the decision concerning the relationship between marginal revenue and marginal cost, which determines the level of production, is identical across the three market structures of perfect competition, monopoly, and monopolistic competition: expand production until $MC = MR$. The major difference arises with the firm in a perfectly competitive industry: it faces a perfectly elastic demand curve for its product, which leads to $P = MR$. For the monopolist and monopolistic competitor, however, we have $P > MR$ because they face a downward-sloping demand curve.

How a Monopolistic Competitor Calculates Profits

How much does Dairy Queen earn per day if it follows the optimal decision rule of setting $P > MR = MC$? Computing economic profits for the monopolistically competitive firm works exactly the same way as computing economic profits for the other three market structures, that is,

$$\text{Profits} = \text{Total revenue} - \text{Total cost} = (P \times Q) - (ATC \times Q) = (P - ATC) \times Q.$$

Panel (a) of Exhibit 14.7 reveals the intuition of this calculation by superimposing the cost curves over the demand and marginal revenue curves. The exhibit shows that the level of economic profits is calculated as the area of the green-shaded rectangle, which equals 520 cones $\times$ ($4 - $2) = $1,040. Because average total cost is below the profit-maximizing price ($P > ATC$) at this quantity level, the firm is making positive economic profits.

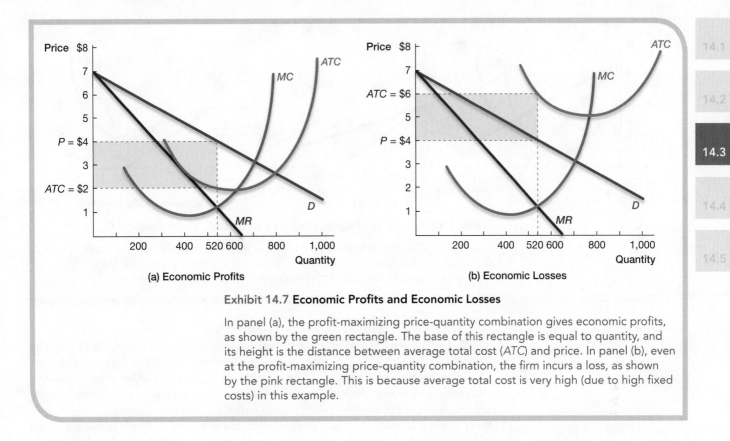

Exhibit 14.7 Economic Profits and Economic Losses

In panel (a), the profit-maximizing price-quantity combination gives economic profits, as shown by the green rectangle. The base of this rectangle is equal to quantity, and its height is the distance between average total cost (*ATC*) and price. In panel (b), even at the profit-maximizing price-quantity combination, the firm incurs a loss, as shown by the pink rectangle. This is because average total cost is very high (due to high fixed costs) in this example.

Similar to sellers in all market structures, economic profits are not *ensured* for the seller in a monopolistically competitive industry. Consider panel (b) of Exhibit 14.7, which is an example of Dairy Queen losing money. That is, because price is less than average total cost, there are losses for Dairy Queen. The level of losses is equal to the pink-shaded rectangle: Total revenue − Total cost = $(P − ATC) \times Q$, which is $520 \times (\$4 − \$6) = -\$1,040$.

Could the situation in panel (b) of Exhibit 14.7 be a short-run equilibrium for Dairy Queen? To answer this question, we consider the decision rule of whether to shut down or continue production in the short run. The decision rule that Dairy Queen should follow, when facing negative economic profits in the short run, is exactly the same as that followed by sellers in the other three market structures that we have studied:

> **What's *competitive* about monopolistically competitive industries is that there are no restrictions on entry—any number of firms can enter the industry at any time.**

1. If total revenues cover variable costs, then continue to produce in the short run.
2. If total revenues do not cover variable costs, then shutdown is optimal, as you will lose less money by shutting down and paying fixed costs than you would by operating.

You might be wondering what happens in the long run. We now turn to a discussion of long-run equilibrium in a monopolistically competitive industry.

Long-Run Equilibrium in a Monopolistically Competitive Industry

So far, the analysis has been identical to the decision problem facing a monopolist. When we consider what happens in the long run for a monopolistically competitive industry, however, the analysis changes starkly—as noted above, from one that looks like the monopolist's problem to one that looks like the perfect competitor's problem. Recall that what's *competitive* about monopolistically competitive industries is that there are no restrictions on entry and exit—firms can freely enter and exit the industry at any time. What does this mean about the economic profits in the long run for firms in a monopolistically competitive industry?

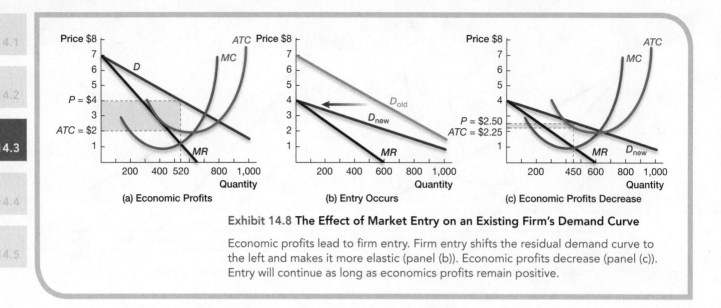

Exhibit 14.8 The Effect of Market Entry on an Existing Firm's Demand Curve

Economic profits lead to firm entry. Firm entry shifts the residual demand curve to the left and makes it more elastic (panel (b)). Economic profits decrease (panel (c)). Entry will continue as long as economics profits remain positive.

Let's first discuss the case of positive economic profits in the short run, which is shown in panel (a) of Exhibit 14.7. Is this a long-run equilibrium? No. The reason is that with positive economic profits, sellers will be attracted to this market. *The key to understanding what happens in monopolistically competitive markets is to recognize what happens to the demand curves of the market's existing firm(s) when another firm enters.*

We know that when there are more substitutes for a good, a firm's residual demand curve shifts to the left and becomes more elastic (less steep). The leftward shift implies that at a given price, the quantity demanded will now be less than what it was before the shift. The more elastic demand curve leads to a lower markup over marginal cost (recall the analysis of monopoly pricing in Chapter 12). To illustrate these ideas, consider the case of Baskin-Robbins deciding to open a store down the street from Dairy Queen. Now there are more substitution possibilities for consumers. Entry of another seller means that Dairy Queen has a residual demand curve that is flatter than what it previously faced. And because demand is being split across more firms, not only is the residual demand curve Dairy Queen faces flatter but it has also shifted to the left.

Exhibit 14.8 shows how the residual demand curve for Dairy Queen changes because of this market entry. Panel (a) of the exhibit repeats panel (a) of Exhibit 14.7 and shows Dairy Queen's profit-maximizing quantity and price that we discussed earlier. Panel (b) shows the new demand curve juxtaposed against the old demand curve. Notice how the new demand curve, D_{New}, is both flatter than, and to the left of, D_{Old}. The marginal revenue curve shifts accordingly.

Even after entry, though, Dairy Queen should continue to act as if it is a monopolist over its residual demand curve. Thus, its maximization problem remains the same: choose quantity where $MR = MC$, and set price using the residual demand curve. In this case, panel (c) of Exhibit 14.8 shows that Dairy Queen produces 450 ice cream cones per day. Dairy Queen's profit-maximizing price is now $2.50, and it earns profits equal to the green-shaded area in panel (c).

As the exhibit shows, it is still the case that Dairy Queen is earning economic profits. We should therefore expect more firms to enter. Each firm that enters will further shift leftward Dairy Queen's residual demand curve as well as make it more elastic.

When does entry stop? Similar to a perfectly competitive industry, entry stops when there are no longer economic profits. This point is shown in Exhibit 14.9. At the long-run equilibrium, Dairy Queen sells 400 cones per day at a price of $2 per cone. Why is Dairy Queen's economic profit zero in equilibrium? Because at this point price equals average total cost; thus, profits are zero since profits = $(P - ATC) \times Q = (\$2 - \$2) \times 400 = 0$. Dairy Queen is just covering its costs of operations (variable and fixed) at this point.

Although the end result of entry is identical to the equilibrium in a perfectly competitive industry—zero economic profits—the mechanics are quite different. Recall that in a perfectly competitive industry, market changes operate through *shifts* in the market supply

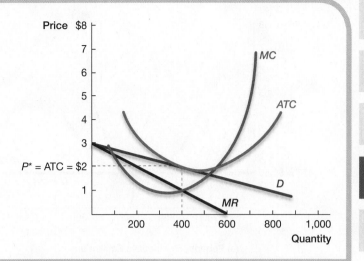

Exhibit 14.9 Zero Profits in Long-Run Equilibrium

The long-run equilibrium in a monopolistically competitive industry is obtained when entry (or exit) stops at the point where the profit-maximizing price is equal to average total cost, yielding zero economic profits.

curve (see Exhibit 6.16 in Chapter 6). In monopolistic competition, market changes occur because the *residual demand curve becomes flatter and shifts leftward with entry.*

Because entry pushes economic profits to zero in the long run, monopolistically competitive firms have an incentive to continually try to distinguish themselves from rivals—in this way, such markets are perpetually in motion. For example, we are barraged by many different advertisements, commercials, and brand names, as well as a never-ending series of modest product innovations. Just consider how Taco Bell continually produces a "new" product from a different assortment of meats, beans, and cheeses. Or how Microsoft continually develops new features for Word and Excel. These "upgraded," "improved," and "new" products are all in the spirit of the ongoing pursuit of the firm to distance itself and its products from potential entrants. In some cases, these attempts at diversification might increase production costs, which also contributes to why, in long-run equilibrium, these firms earn zero economic profit.

Similar market dynamics would have occurred had we started with economic losses (panel (b) of Exhibit 14.7), where price was less than average total cost. In a market with free entry and exit, this situation would have induced Dairy Queen, or other ice cream shops, to exit the ice cream business. This is because, just as in a monopoly, oligopoly, or perfectly competitive market, losses in an industry cause existing sellers to seek greener pastures in the long run. Firm exit will cause the demand curve facing existing individual sellers to shift rightward and steepen (become less elastic).

14.4 The "Broken" Invisible Hand

As we learned in Chapter 12, one important factor that can "break" the powerful result of the invisible hand is market power. Compared to a competitive market, monopolists will be able to charge a price greater than marginal cost, thereby reducing sales and thus total surplus (consumer plus producer surplus). We learned earlier in this chapter that this is also the case with oligopoly with differentiated products. In both market structures, firms have market power and are able to charge prices greater than marginal cost, reducing total surplus.

What about monopolistic competition? With free entry and exit, economic profits in the long-run equilibrium equal zero: in good times sellers enter until all profits are exhausted, and in bad times sellers exit until all losses are extinguished. Such a feature is an important determinant of whether the invisible hand can operate to ensure that selfish agents are maximizing the social well-being. So, does that mean that the invisible hand operates effectively in the monopolistically competitive case? That is, is total surplus maximized under monopolistic competition? The answer is no.

Exhibit 14.10 shows the intuition behind why total surplus is not maximized in a monopolistically competitive market. The key difference between the perfectly competitive industry and monopolistic competition is that the latter restricts quantity to keep price higher.

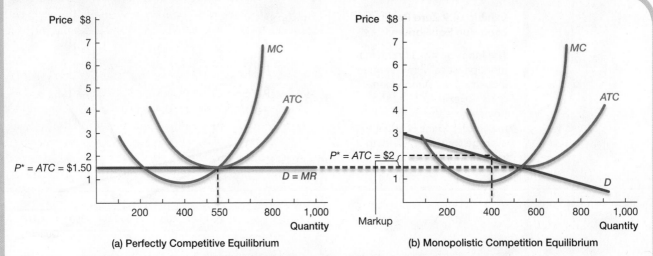

Exhibit 14.10 Equilibria for a Perfectly Competitive Market and a Monopolistically Competitive Market

A perfectly competitive industry produces where average total cost is minimized, which results in a price equaling marginal cost. There is deadweight loss in a monopolistically competitive industry because production occurs at less than the efficient scale—no firm can grow large enough to reach the minimum of its *ATC* curve and price is above marginal cost (denoted as "Markup" in the exhibit).

> **The key difference between the perfectly competitive industry and monopolistic competition is that the latter restricts quantity to keep price higher.**

Panel (a) of Exhibit 14.10 depicts the equilibrium for the perfectly competitive industry, in which all firms are producing at the minimum of their average total cost curves. Thus, firms in a perfectly competitive market produce goods using the least amount of resources. This is an important implication of the invisible hand.

But as panel (b) of Exhibit 14.10 shows, the same does not happen under monopolistic competition. The fact that monopolistic competitors each have a downward-sloping demand curve causes them to act differently than a perfectly competitive seller. First, they produce at a level that is below the efficient scale of production (the minimum of the *ATC* curve). Second, they mark up price above its marginal cost. Both of these features are shown in panel (b) of Exhibit 14.10. The markup causes some buyers who are ready, willing, and able to purchase the good at a price at or above marginal cost to be out of the market. Because of this fact, there is deadweight loss, as the monopolistic competitor produces too little compared to the socially efficient production level. The monopolistic competitor does not engage in this extra production because it would then need to cut the price it charges other customers for its goods, resulting in lower economic profits.

Regulating Market Power

So, should the government step in and regulate oligopolistic and monopolistically competitive markets? There is no straightforward answer to this question. In some cases, the answer is definitely yes. But in some others, the costs of regulation may exceed the benefits.

A clear case in which government regulation is warranted is successful collusion. As we have seen, oligopolists may be tempted to enter into collusive agreements to increase their profits at the expense of consumers. One of the main roles of antitrust policy in most countries, particularly in the United States, is to prevent these types of collusive agreements.

Another strategy oligopolists use to increase their market power is to *merge* with their competitors. Mergers refer to a situation in which two companies form a single company. Starting from an oligopoly with two firms, the merger will lead to a monopoly and thus to greater market power. The cornerstones of U.S. antitrust policy, the Sherman Antitrust

Act of 1890 and the Clayton Act of 1914, are concerned with the regulation of mergers. In particular, the Department of Justice (DOJ) reviews merger cases and decides whether the main objective is to increase market power or whether there are important efficiency gains from such a merger.

One of the main approaches the DOJ adopts in its analysis of mergers is to calculate how *concentrated* an industry is. An industry is deemed concentrated when a few firms account for a large fraction of total sales in that industry. Crucially, what the DOJ looks at, and what economic theory suggests to be important, isn't the number of active firms in the market, but how *concentrated* the market is (meaning whether the distribution of sales in the market concentrates in the hands of a few firms). When a merger stands to increase concentration significantly, the DOJ is less likely to allow the merger.

The **Herfindahl-Hirschman Index** is a measure of market concentration to estimate the degree of competition within an industry.

One of the tools that the DOJ uses to guide its enforcement of the Sherman Act is the **Herfindahl-Hirschman Index** (HHI). The HHI is a measure of market concentration, which is calculated by squaring the market share of each firm competing in the market and then summing the resulting numbers (squaring is done because it gives larger firms greater weight). For example, if there are two firms in an industry and one firm accounts for 75 percent of the sales and the other 25 percent, the HHI is equal to $75^2 + 25^2 = 6{,}250$. The higher the HHI, the more concentrated the industry. The HHI approaches zero when a market consists of a large number of firms of relatively equal size.

Even though the HHI doesn't tell us everything about an industry, it can inform our understanding of industries. For example, take the following three industries: household laundry equipment, motor vehicles, and computers. Which do you think has the highest HHI? The lowest? Estimates from the Department of Commerce suggest that household laundry equipment is the most concentrated, with an HHI of 2,855. Motor vehicles are next with an HHI of 2,676, and computers are the least concentrated with an HHI of 680. A general rule of thumb is that markets in which the HHI is less than 1,000 are considered not concentrated, those between 1,000 and 1,800 are considered to be moderately concentrated, and those in which the HHI is in excess of 1,800 are considered to be concentrated. One should not just rely on concentration to decide how competitive an industry is. Recall, for example, the lawn-mowing oligopoly discussed earlier. There, the degree of concentration was high, but Bertrand competition ensured that price was equal to marginal cost.

There are also limits to how effectively the government can use regulation to reduce market power, particularly in monopolistically competitive markets with many producers. Imagine if the government had to regulate prices for every product sold in monopolistically competitive industries. And imagine further that it would set the number and type of entrants for each product line. This type of intervention would border on a command economy, and there are many difficulties with that approach, as we discussed in Chapter 7.

All in all, economists favor regulation for monopolies and for highly concentrated oligopolies, but are generally comfortable with permitting the more limited market power of monopolistically competitive firms, even though this still reduces total surplus to the economy. Yet, with this lost surplus comes a market structure that provides a variety of products, which is a good feature of monopolistic competition.

14.5 Summing Up: Four Market Structures

We now have studied the four major market types. In Chapters 4–7, we focused on perfect competition. In Chapter 12, we studied monopolists. Between the two extreme market structures—perfect competition and monopoly—are monopolistic competition and oligopoly. Exhibit 14.11 provides a summary of the four market structures across several dimensions.

As we just learned, monopolistic competition and oligopoly share many features with monopolies, including the ability to set prices. The primary difference across these three market structures is the number of competitors, or the number of sellers. A monopoly has only one seller. But monopolistic competition and oligopoly are market structures with more than one seller, and because of this fact, they have to concern themselves with the actions of other firms.

Exhibit 14.11 Four Market Structures

The four market structures are summarized with each row highlighting the number of firms in that market, the degree of product differentiation, barriers to entry, pricing behavior, residual demand curve, social surplus and long-run profits of each market structure.

	Perfect Competition	Monopolistic Competition	Oligopoly	Monopoly
Number of Firms/Sellers/Producers	Many	Many	A few	One
Type of Product/Service Sold	Identical (homogeneous)	Slightly differentiated	Identical or differentiated	Single, undifferentiated product or service
Example of Product	Corn grown by various farmers	Books; CDs	Oil (identical); cars (differentiated)	Patented drugs; tap water
Barriers to Entry	None: free entry and exit	None; free entry and exit	Yes	Yes: high
Price-Taker or Price-Maker?	Price-taker; price given by the market	Price-maker (with a recognition of other sellers)	Price-maker (with a strong recognition of other sellers)	Price-maker—no competitors; no perfect substitutes
Price	$P = MR = MC$	Set $P > MR = MC$	Set $P > MR = MC$ or $P = MR = MC$ depending on type of competition and product differentiation.	Set $P > MR = MC$
Residual Demand Curve	Horizontally sloped; perfectly elastic demand curve	Downward-sloping: slightly differentiated products are available	Downward-sloping	Downward—sloping
Social Surplus	Maximized	Not maximized But society might benefit from product diversity	Not maximized	Not maximized But sometimes society benefits from research and development
Long-run Profits	Zero	Zero	Zero or more than zero	More than zero

Evidence-Based Economics

Q: How many firms are necessary to make a market competitive?

How can we know if there are enough firms in a market to make it competitive? In Chapter 6, we learned that the market is perfectly competitive if there are many firms—so many that each can take the market price of the good that it is supplying as given. But we also learned in the present chapter that just two firms can be sufficient for the market price to be equal to the marginal cost. So how do we answer this question?

Two economists, Timothy Bresnahan and Peter Reiss, came up with a unique angle to obtain an answer.[3] They reasoned that if a market is already effectively competitive, the addition of one more firm should not change prices. Take another look at Exhibit 14.8, which shows that when existing firms have market power, the entry of one more firm will make the market "more competitive" and *will* reduce prices. In contrast, recall that in a perfectly competitive market, both consumers and producers are price-takers, and neither can influence the market price. In a perfectly competitive market, if the size of the market increases, there will be entry of new firms to meet the additional demand, but this will not reduce prices (in fact, new firms, just like existing firms, will be operating at the minimum point of their average total cost curve; recall Exhibits 7.5 and 7.6 in Chapter 7). In summary, when firms have significant market

	Number of Tire Dealers in the Market				
	One	Two	Three	Four	Five
Price	54.9	55.7	54.4	51.6	52.0
Tire Mileage Rating	44.5	47.0	47.7	45.4	43.8

Exhibit 14.12 Tire Prices and Tire Quality in Selected U.S. Towns

Prices with four or five dealers are virtually the same. With three dealers, prices are higher, but this mostly reflects the higher tire mileage rating in these markets. Overall, there is relatively little variation in prices in markets with three, four, or five dealers, suggesting that competition between three or four dealers is sufficient for the tire market to be effectively competitive.

power, further entry reduces prices, while in a competitive market, further entry should leave prices unchanged.

Bresnahan and Reiss examined the prices of tires to find out when further entry leads to no further price decreases. Their investigation thus answers our question of when the market becomes effectively competitive. They obtained information on prices and the number of tire dealers across different towns in the western United States. To approximate markets, they limited the sample to 157 small towns that had at least an 80-mile round-trip to the next large city (if there was a large city nearby, the prices in a particular small town would be less relevant, because the residents of the small town could buy their tires in the nearby large city).

Exhibit 14.12 shows the average tire prices in different towns classified according to whether the towns had one, two, three, four, or five tire dealers. One major reason why there were different numbers of tire dealers in different towns was because the population varied across towns. As the quality of tires could vary within the sample, the second row of the exhibit shows the average tire mileage rating, which is a measure of average tire quality. It is important to know the quality of a product because otherwise we might observe distinct prices not due to differences in market power, but simply due to differences in quality.

Exhibit 14.12 shows a remarkable pattern. There is practically no difference in prices between markets with four and five tire dealers. In fact, Bresnahan and Reiss show that the price difference between markets with three and four dealers is mostly due to the differences in the tire mileage ratings; that is, the average quality of tires appears to be higher in towns with three dealers. Once this difference in tire quality is accounted for, there is no evidence that prices are different between markets with three or four dealers. In sum, the evidence from the Bresnahan and Reiss study suggests that three or four firms are sufficient for the tire market to be (effectively) competitive.

At this point, you may be wondering if towns with different numbers of tire dealers were systematically different along other dimensions. If so, the comparison of prices across towns could be contaminated by such differences. One way of dealing with this problem is to investigate the same question with a laboratory experiment, where such confounding differences will not arise.

Two economists, Martin Dufwenberg and Uri Gneezy, did just that.[4] They designed an experiment in which a number of sellers each chose a bid (selling price) between 2 and 100. Whichever seller made the lowest bid (set the lowest price) kept the dollar amount equal to his or her bid. You may notice the similarity between this experiment and the oligopoly model with homogeneous products. When there are two sellers, this is exactly identical to the duopoly model we studied. Our analysis in that case suggested that each seller should engage in cutthroat competition and bid "2."

Evidence-Based Economics *(Continued)*

You might also reason, though, that in a duopoly you are playing against just one other seller, and you may try to go for a higher bid and take home more money if you happen to have the lower bid. Dufwenberg and Gneezy, in fact, found that in a duopoly, average bids were just below 50, so the experiment does not mirror the theory. However, when the number of sellers increased to four, the sellers acted much more competitively. In fact, with four sellers, the average winning bid at the end of ten rounds of play was close to two! Thus, in the lab too, it appears that *four competitors are sufficient to drive the equilibrium toward the competitive outcome.* As economic theory predicts, prices depend on the fierceness of competition, and the empirical research suggests that the number of competitors does not have to be very large to bring prices very close to the competitive level. Interestingly, this research shows that even in markets with a large HHI, intense competition can be observed.

Although this empirical evidence suggests that four is an important number, we should take great care not to overgeneralize this point. It might be the case that in other industries or in other cities (or in other experiments), it takes many more or fewer firms to generate a competitive market. In the end, economic theory and empirical insights can inform us of general principles, such as when and where to expect anticompetitive pricing, and when to suspect that it is having an important influence. But statements on the actual existence, or effectiveness, of anticompetitive arrangements are quite difficult to make without actually investigating the industry itself.

Question	Answer	Data	Caveat
How many firms are necessary to make a market competitive?	In many industries and in the lab, approximately three or four.	Data on tire prices across various cities combined with data from lab experiments.	Other market specifics beyond the number of sellers also affect the nature of competition. As such, we are unsure how far we can generalize the received results.

Summary

✸ Oligopoly and monopolistic competition are two market structures that lie between the market extremes of perfect competition and monopoly. Firms in these market structures must consider the behavior of competitors, whereas neither a monopolist nor firms in a perfectly competitive industry need do so.

✸ There's no single model of oligopoly that is applicable to every situation. The equilibrium outcome will depend on the unique features of the market—whether the goods are homogeneous or differentiated, how many firms are in the industry, and whether collusion is sustainable. Nevertheless, there are some important general lessons from the study of oligopoly. Economic profits of firms will be higher when goods are differentiated, when there are fewer firms in the industry (unless the goods are in fact homogeneous), and when collusion is sustainable.

✸ In the short run, behavior of the monopolistic competitor and the monopolist are identical: Set Price > Marginal Revenue = Marginal Cost. In the long run, entry and exit cause the equilibrium in a monopolistically competitive industry—zero economic profits—to be identical to equilibrium in perfect competition.

✸ Economics provides a useful set of tools to begin a discussion of whether a market is competitive, but there is no one factor—such as the number of firms—that wholly dictates the nature of competition within a specific industry.

Key Terms

Questions

All questions are available in MyEconLab for practice and instructor assignment.

1. How are the products sold by a monopolistically competitive firm different from the products sold in a perfectly competitive market?

2. How is a monopolistically competitive market similar to a perfectly competitive market? Do monopolistically competitive markets and monopolies share any common features?

3. Both monopolies and monopolistically competitive firms set marginal revenue equal to marginal cost to maximize profit. Given the same cost curves, would you expect prices to be higher in a monopoly or a monopolistically competitive market?

4. Will a monopolistically competitive firm continue to operate in the short run despite earning negative economic profit? Explain your answer.

5. Monopolistically competitive firms earn zero economic profit in the long run as do perfectly competitive firms. Does this mean that total surplus is maximized in a monopolistically competitive market?

6. What happens in a monopolistically competitive market with the entry of new firms?

7. Consider a noncollusive duopoly model with both firms supplying bottled drinking water. The firms choose prices simultaneously. The marginal cost for each firm is $1.50. The market demand is shown by the figure given below.

   a. Find the residual demand curves for each of the firms.

   b. What pricing strategy by each firm would be a Nash equilibrium in this model?

   c. Find the Nash equilibrium when the two firms can collude effectively.

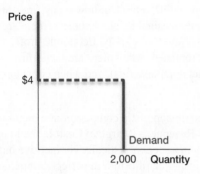

8. In the model of an oligopoly with identical (homogeneous) products, what is the price likely to be?

9. How do oligopolistic firms that sell differentiated products determine their prices?

10. Suppose there are four firms in a market and each of them sells differentiated products. Does it make sense for these firms to engage in a price war? Why or why not?

11. When is a collusive agreement between two firms likely to break down?

12. Suppose the refrigerator industry has an HHI of 2,500 while the aluminum industry's HHI is 6,850. Is this information sufficient to conclude that the aluminum market is more concentrated than the market for refrigerators? Explain your answer.

13. Decide whether each of the following statements is true or false for each of three different types of markets: perfect competition, monopoly, and monopolistic competition.

   a. Firms equate price and marginal cost.

   b. Firms equate marginal revenue and marginal cost.

   c. Firms earn economic profits in the long run.

   d. Firms produce the quantity that minimizes long-run average cost.

   e. New firms are free to enter this industry.

Problems

All problems are available in MyEconLab *for practice and instructor assignment.*

1. Acme is currently the only grocery store in town. Bi-Rite is thinking of entering this market. They will play the following game. First, Bi-Rite will decide whether or not to enter. If it does not enter, then the game ends, Acme earns a payoff of 50, and Bi-Rite earns a payoff of 0. If Bi-Rite does enter, then Acme has to decide to fight by slashing its prices or to accommodate. If Acme decides to fight, then Acme and Bi-Rite each earn 10; if Acme accommodates, then each earns 20.

   a. Draw the game tree for this game.

   b. Use backward induction to figure out how this game will be played.

2. With the growth of the Internet, there are many online retailers and many buyers who shop online.

   a. Why, given the growth of the Internet, would you expect to find that different firms would charge very similar prices for the same good?

   b. Despite the logic of the first part of this question, several recent studies have found that different online retailers often charge quite different prices. How might you explain this result?

3. The diagram below shows the short-run demand curve (*D*), marginal revenue curve (*MR*), average total cost curve (*ATC*), and marginal cost curve (*MC*) for a firm in a monopolistically competitive market.

   a. What level of output should this firm produce?

   b. What price should this firm charge?

   c. Will this firm earn a profit or will it earn a loss?

   d. Would you expect entry or would you expect exit in this industry?

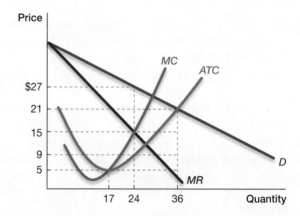

4. Most of your friends prefer drinking Budweiser, Miller, or Coors beer. Budweiser is manufactured by Anheuser-Busch, while Miller and Coors are manufactured by MillerCoors. Based on this information, you conclude that the beer market is oligopolistic. Assuming each of the following statements is true, examine whether each one will independently support or weaken your conclusion.

   i. Anheuser-Busch and MillerCoors are two of the many firms that operate in this market.

   ii. Both MillerCoors and Anheuser-Busch increased the prices of beer when demand had actually fallen in 2009.

   iii. Consumers are unlikely to switch between different brands of beer; most beer consumers are highly brand loyal.

   iv. The fixed cost of setting up a brewery is relatively high.

5. John Maynard Keynes (a famous British economist) said "In the long run we are all dead." An important message in this chapter is, to paraphrase Keynes, "In the long run, all profits in a monopolistically competitive market are dead." Why do firms in a monopolistically competitive industry earn zero profits in the long run? Why might those same firms earn profits in the short run? Why does a monopolist earn profits in both the long run and the short run?

6. Tobacco companies have often argued that they advertise to attract more people who already smoke and not to persuade more people to begin smoking. Suppose there were just two cigarette manufacturers, Jones and Smith. Each can either advertise or not advertise. If neither advertises, they each capture 50 percent of the market and each earns $10 million. If they both advertise, they again split the market evenly, but each spends $2 million on ads and so each earns just $8 million (remember, advertising is not supposed to encourage more people to smoke). If one company advertises but the other does not, then the company that advertises attracts many of its rival's customers. As a result, the company that advertises earns $12 million and the company that does not earns just $6 million.

   a. Show that advertising is a dominant strategy.

   b. Suppose the government proposes a ban on cigarette ads. Should the two cigarette companies favor the ban or should they oppose the ban if advertising did not persuade some people to become smokers?

7. Bombay Fast Food and 2 Bros. Pizza are pizza parlors that are located a few feet away from each other on a street in New York.

   a. Both firms sell pizza slices at a price of $1 each. Given this price, suppose the demand for pizza slices on that street is equal to 10,000 slices per week. What would the market demand curve for these two firms look like?

   b. At one point, both firms were selling a slice of pizza for just 75 cents, which is the marginal cost of a slice of pizza. How would you explain this situation using the prisoners' dilemma?

   c. Suppose that both firms together decide to increase the price to $1. Would this be considered collusion? If you knew that both these firms accounted for a negligible portion of the pizza market in New York, would that affect your answer?

8. Major league baseball teams have imposed what is commonly called the "luxury tax" on themselves. A team is subject to the tax if its payroll exceeds a specified level. The annual threshold for the luxury tax is $189 million for 2014–16. A team that exceeds the threshold must pay 17.5% to 50% of the amount by which its payroll is above the threshold, where the "tax rate" depends on the number of years the team is over. This question looks at why teams might subject themselves to this tax.

   a. Suppose there are two major league baseball teams, Team 1 and Team 2. They will both choose to offer either high salaries to players or low salaries. They will make their decisions simultaneously. If both choose low each will earn $0; if both choose high each will earn $400. If one chooses high and the other chooses low, the team that chooses high will attract the best players and will earn $600, but the team that chooses low will earn just $300. Show that high is a dominant strategy but that both teams would be better off if both chose low.

   b. Under a 1922 Supreme Court decision, major league baseball is not subject to many antitrust laws. Suppose these two teams agree to a "luxury tax." Under this luxury tax, a team that chooses high must pay a tax of $250. Find the new equilibrium in this game.

   c. Some people might argue that the luxury tax in baseball is not ans important determinant of major league salaries. As evidence, they show that team payrolls rarely exceed the threshold level and so teams rarely pay the tax. What does you answer to this question suggest about logic of this claim?

9. Telesource and Belair are two of the largest firms in the wireless carrier market in a certain country. Both these firms account for more than 80 percent of the market.

   a. Given that both firms differentiate their products, how is a Nash equilibrium achieved in this market?

   b. Suppose both Telesource and Belair decide to collude and set the same price. Their payoffs from cheating and colluding are given in the matrix below. What is the Nash equilibrium in this game?

		Telesource	
		Collude	Cheat
Belair	Collude	Belair earns $12 million	Belair earns $2 million
		Telesource earns $12 million	Telesource earns $15 million
	Cheat	Belair earns $15 million	Belair earns $10 million
		Telesource earns $2 million	Telesource earns $10 million

10. Suppose the world demand schedule for oil is as follows:

Price per Barrel	Quantity Demanded
$50	40
$75	30
$125	20

There are two oil-producing countries, A and B. Each will produce either 10 or 20 barrels of oil. To keep things simple, assume they can produce this oil at zero cost.

a. There are four possible outcomes: A produces 10 or 20 and B produces 10 or 20. Find each country's profit for each of these four possibilities.

b. Suppose these countries choose the quantity of oil to produce simultaneously and without consulting with one another. Show that each country will produce 20 barrels of oil and each will earn a profit of $1,000.

c. The oil ministers realize they can do better if they collude and agree that each will produce 10. How much profit will each country earn if each produces 10 instead of 20?

d. Will country A have an incentive to cheat and produce 20 instead of 10? Will country B have an incentive to cheat and produce 20 instead of 10?

11. Suppose that the four largest maple syrup manufacturers decide to collude, and based on demand conditions every year, they decide the quantity of maple syrup that will be supplied to maintain a certain market price.

a. Is this an example of a Cournot oligopoly or a Bertrand oligopoly?

b. Under what conditions would this cartel succeed?

c. How likely are firms to cheat if the cartel decided to fix prices only once as opposed to fixing prices every year?

12. Suppose there are five firms in an industry. Their sales (that is, total revenue) are as follows:

- Firm 1: $90 million
- Firm 2: $50 million
- Firm 3: $36 million
- Firm 4: $14 million
- Firm 5: $10 million

Compute the Herfindahl-Hirschman Index (HHI) for this industry.

Sell your books at
sellbackyourBook.com!

Go to sellbackyourBook.com
and get an instant price
quote. We even pay the
shipping - see what your old
books are worth today!

00000519105

00000519105

15 Trade-offs Involving Time and Risk

Do people exhibit a preference for immediate gratification?

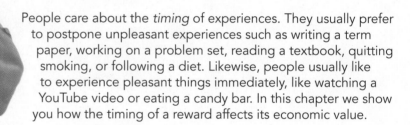

People care about the *timing* of experiences. They usually prefer to postpone unpleasant experiences such as writing a term paper, working on a problem set, reading a textbook, quitting smoking, or following a diet. Likewise, people usually like to experience pleasant things immediately, like watching a YouTube video or eating a candy bar. In this chapter we show you how the timing of a reward affects its economic value.

CHAPTER **OUTLINE**

KEY IDEAS

☀ Interest is the payment received for temporarily giving up the use of money.

☀ Economists have developed tools to calculate the present value of payments received at different points in the future.

☀ Economists have developed tools to calculate the value of risky payments.

15.1 Modeling Time and Risk

Most decisions have costs and benefits that occur at different times. Consider going to college. Lots of college costs come now—hard work, foregone wages (opportunity cost), and tuition payments. On the other hand, many of the economic benefits from a college education come later in life, especially higher wages. If someone is going to make an optimal choice about whether or not to get a college degree, they'll need to somehow put all of the costs and benefits into comparable units and add them up.

Other activities are also associated with up-front costs and delayed benefits: for instance, exercising, dieting, and saving. To analyze choices like these, we need to understand how to predict and value the delayed benefits. Is it optimal to invest a dollar today, so that I can consume the dollar and all of the interest I've earned on it when I retire decades later?

This chapter also discusses how risk affects economic value. To an economist, risk is not a four-letter word—risky options are not necessarily bad options. Risk just means that some of the costs and benefits are not fixed in advance. For example, when you marry someone, you recognize that the success of the marriage is not completely predictable. A person's income, health, and even tastes can change. During a wedding ceremony couples acknowledge some of these risks when they vow "to have and to hold from this day forward; for better, for worse, for richer, for poorer, in sickness and in health."

In general, almost all investments have risky returns. How will the stock market perform? How will housing prices change? Will the degree that you are earning in college turn out to be valuable, or will employers look for different skills in the future? In this chapter, we use economic analysis to evaluate these risks.

The tools that economists use to value delayed rewards have much in common with the tools that we use to value risky rewards. In both cases, economists *weight* rewards. When economists value rewards that will be experienced in the future, we multiply the reward by a positive factor that is *less than 1* to capture the idea that future rewards are worth less than current rewards. When a reward might not occur, economists incorporate this risk by multiplying the reward by the positive probability (again, less than 1) that the reward will occur. This chapter explains how these time- and risk-weighting factors are determined and shows you how to use them.

Even good choices involve risk.

15.2 The Time Value of Money

Financial markets enable people to transfer money through time. For example, to move money into the future, depositors "lend" money to a bank now and then withdraw it, with interest, at a future date.

Economists call such a change an *intertemporal transformation*. "Inter" means between—for instance, when you travel between countries you are travelling internationally. "Temporal" refers to time. *Intertemporal transformations* move resources between time periods.

Future Value and the Compounding of Interest

The key variable that summarizes an intertemporal transformation of money is the interest payment. Let's consider a simple example. Imagine that you deposit $100 in a bank account. The amount of an original investment—in this case $100—is referred to as **principal**. How much money will you have in the account after 1 year, assuming that the account pays an annual **interest** rate of r? The bank account contains your principal of $100 plus interest of $r \times \$100$.

Principal is the amount of an original investment.

Interest is the payment received for temporarily giving up the use of money.

For example, if the interest rate is 5 percent, then the interest rate will be

$$r = 5\% = \frac{5}{100} = 0.05.$$

For a 5 percent interest rate and a $100 deposit, the 1-year interest payment would be $0.05 \times \$100 = \$5$. The total value of the account at the end of a year can then be written:

$$\$100 + (r \times \$100) = (1 + r) \times \$100.$$

The sum of principal and interest is referred to as **future value**.

This is the sum of the principal and the interest and it is referred to as the **future value** after 1 year of accumulation.

Suppose that you decide to leave all of your money—principal plus interest—on deposit at the end of the first year. Your account balance at the beginning of Year 2 is $(1 + r) \times \$100$. Let's call this "Balance." During Year 2 you will receive interest on the balance from the end of Year 1, or interest of $(r) \times$ (Balance). At the end of Year 2 your account will contain the amount that you had in the account at the end of Year 1, which is what we called Balance, plus the interest that you received in Year 2,

$$\text{(Balance)} + (r) \times \text{(Balance)} = (1 + r) \times \text{(Balance)}.$$

Since the Balance from the end of Year 1 was $(1 + r) \times \$100$, the amount at the end of Year 2 is

$$(1 + r) \times \text{Balance} = (1 + r) \times (1 + r) \times \$100 = (1 + r)^2 \times \$100.$$

Do you notice a pattern? If you left your money at the bank for *1* year, you would get this much back at the end of Year 1:

$$(1 + r) \times \$100.$$

If you left your money at the bank for *2* years, you would get this much back at the end of Year 2:

$$(1 + r)^2 \times \$100.$$

For each extra year that you leave your money at the bank, you can multiply your final balance by an additional factor of $(1 + r)$. Consequently, if you leave your money with the bank for T years, you would get this much back at the end of year T:

The **compound interest equation** or **future value equation** calculates the future value of an investment with interest rate r that leaves all interest payments in the account until the final withdrawal in year T.

$$\text{Future value} = (1 + r)^T \times \text{(Principal)} \qquad \textit{Compound Interest Equation}$$

This is called the **compound interest equation** or the **future value equation**. In this equation, r is the interest rate and T is the number of years that the investment lasts. To derive the compound interest equation we assume that none of your interest payments are

How to do it: The compound interest equation includes the expression $(1 + r)^T$. Use the financial calculator available on MyEconLab to evaluate this expression for any interest rate r, and any time horizon T. Most hand-held calculators also have an exponent function that multiplies a number by itself T times.

being withdrawn along the way. Accordingly, you earn interest on *past* interest payments, because all of the earlier interest payments remain in the account until the final withdrawal in year T. To capture the idea of earning interest on interest, economists say that the interest is *compounding*.

The compound interest equation has some remarkable properties. Notice that the equation has an exponential term, $(1 + r)^T$, with exponent T. This implies that the balance of your account grows multiplicatively each year. In other words, each year the account increases by the multiplicative factor $(1 + r)$.

Such compound growth is very powerful, which is convenient if you are trying to save for college tuition, build up a large nest egg for retirement, or prepare for any number of future financial goals. To see the power of compound growth, it helps to think about a few examples. Suppose you put $1 into an account at age 20, and let the money compound (without touching it) until you retire at age 70. In this example, the duration of the investment is $70 - 20 = 50$ years, so $T = 50$. We want to know how much money you'll have in this account at the end of that 50-year period.

Let's begin by considering a very special case in which $r = 0.00$. When the interest rate is exactly 0, your final balance will be:

$$(1 + r)^T \times \$1 = (1 + 0.00)^{50} \times \$1 = 1^{50} \times \$1 = \$1.$$

Because $1^{50} = 1$, you emerge with $1 at the end of your 50-year wait. You've earned no interest and your final withdrawal, $1, is exactly equal to your principal, $1.

Let's now consider some other interest rates. Here's where things get funky. Exhibit 15.1 plots the function $(1 + r)^T$ for a range of interest rates. The figure shows the value of your balance as your age ranges from 20 to 70. Specifically, we consider $r = 2\%$, $r = 4\%$, $r = 6\%$, $r = 8\%$, and $r = 10\%$. Now something extraordinary happens. If the interest rate is 2 percent, your $1 of principal grows to $2.69. In other words, your money nearly triples over 50 years. That's not bad.

But what if the interest rate is 10 percent? Then your deposit grows to $117.39. That's not a typo. Your $1 deposit grows **117** *times* as large over 50 years. Since the future value is $(1 + r)^T \times$ (Principal), the growth factor is the same whether the original principal is $1 or $1,000. So a $1,000 original deposit would grow to about $117,390. Compound growth can be very powerful. Saving when you are young—and letting the interest compound—reaps enormous benefits when you are old.

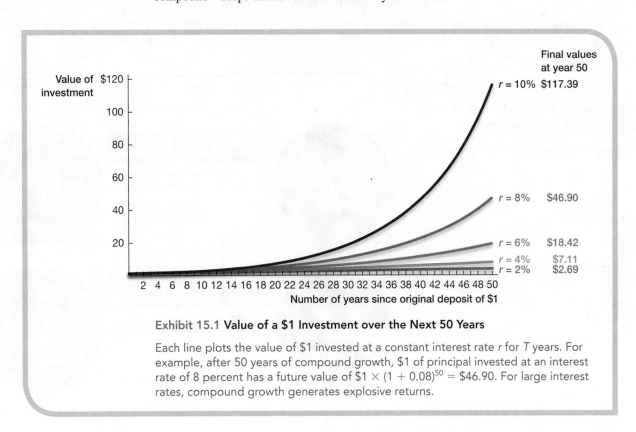

Exhibit 15.1 Value of a $1 Investment over the Next 50 Years

Each line plots the value of $1 invested at a constant interest rate r for T years. For example, after 50 years of compound growth, $1 of principal invested at an interest rate of 8 percent has a future value of $\$1 \times (1 + 0.08)^{50} = \$46.90$. For large interest rates, compound growth generates explosive returns.

Saving money when young reaps returns when old. Most working households should save 10 to 20 percent of their pre-tax income.

> **Borrowing enables you to spend future income today.**

Let's again consider the case of $1 of principal and split the $117.39 final account value into (1) principal and (2) interest. When the bank pays you at the end of 50 years, $1 is repayment of principal, so the remaining $116.39 is the payment of interest. In this case, the interest payment greatly exceeds the repayment of principal. Recall that the interest payment is what the bank pays you over and above your principal, for the privilege of using your money.

Borrowing Versus Lending

Interest payments come in two basic categories, depending on whether you are a lender or a borrower. We have already discussed the interest that you *receive* from a bank as a depositor. On the other hand, you make interest payments to the bank if you borrow money from the bank—for instance, by carrying debt on your bank-issued credit card or by obtaining a home mortgage from the bank.

Making a deposit effectively transfers spending from the present to the future. You deposit money now and you withdraw it (with interest) in the future. When you borrow from the bank you generate the opposite direction of time travel. If you anticipate having money in the future, but you want to spend it *now*, you borrow. Accordingly, borrowing enables you to spend future income today. Exhibit 15.2 summarizes visually how lending and borrowing affect the timing of your spending.

Interest on a deposit and interest on a loan work the same way. With a deposit, you receive

$$(1 + r)^T \times (\text{Principal amount})$$

when you withdraw the money, with interest, in T years. With a loan, you pay

$$(1 + r)^T \times (\text{Loan amount})$$

when you pay back the loan, with interest, in T years (assuming, in this example, that no periodic interest payments are made along the way). Note that both expressions have the same multiplicative factor, $(1 + r)^T$. Consequently, we can use the plots in Exhibit 15.1 to

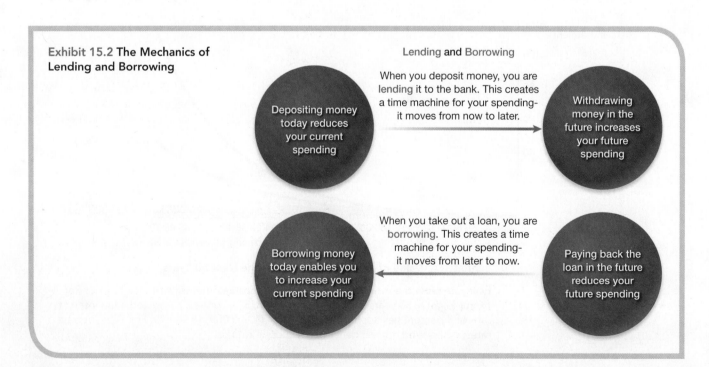

Exhibit 15.2 The Mechanics of Lending and Borrowing

Lending and Borrowing

When you deposit money, you are lending it to the bank. This creates a time machine for your spending—it moves from now to later.

Depositing money today reduces your current spending

Withdrawing money in the future increases your future spending

When you take out a loan, you are borrowing. This creates a time machine for your spending—it moves from later to now.

Borrowing money today enables you to increase your current spending

Paying back the loan in the future reduces your future spending

calculate the payments associated with compounding deposits *or* compounding loans. The mathematical equations are exactly the same in both cases.

There is one difference, however, between loans and deposits that we should highlight. Typical interest rates on loans tend to be higher than typical interest rates paid on investments. For example, it is not uncommon to borrow at 15 percent interest or even 20 percent interest on a credit card. Such high interest rates can produce enormous repayments. By way of illustration, consider a 50-year loan of $1,000 at a 15 percent interest rate. Suppose that no payments were made until year 50, so the loan was compounding for 50 years. For this scenario, the amount due after 50 years would be:

$$(1 + 0.15)^{50} \times \$1,000 = \$1,083,657.44.$$

That's over *1 million dollars due* after 50 years of compound interest!

In practice, such enormous repayments almost never occur on a $1,000 loan. No bank would let you wait 50 years to repay your credit card debt. The bank anticipates that a borrower with 1 million dollars due is more likely to declare bankruptcy than to repay. So the banks don't wait 50 years to get their money back. They'll require interest payments along the way.

Consequently, when thinking about loans it is helpful to consider time horizons that are much shorter than 50 years. A 1 year, $1,000 loan at a 15 percent rate of interest will cost the borrower $150 in interest.

Present Value and Discounting

Suppose someone asked you to lend them money to help fund the construction of a strip mall.

"You lend me $10,000, and I will repay you $20,000 in 20 years."

Assume that you have good reasons to trust this person and you can rely on him to repay your money with certainty. So you are confident that this is a risk-free loan. Even with that confidence, it's still not clear if you should take him up on his offer.

In such a situation, an economist would ask you what alternative use you could make of your $10,000. (To keep things simple, we'll focus on alternative uses that are also risk-free.) In other words, an economist thinks about opportunity cost. What is the next best investment that you could make with your $10,000 of principal?

Suppose that you have another risk-free investment option that will pay 5 percent interest. So you face a choice. Do you participate in the strip mall project, or do you take the alternative project with the 5 percent return?

To compare these projects, you could ask, "If I have access to an investment with a 5 percent return, how much money would I need today to produce $20,000 20 years from now?" We can express this question as a mathematical equation that is similar to the equations that we have already been studying in this chapter:

$$(1 + 0.05)^{20} \times \$x = \$20,000.$$

In this equation, $\$x$ is the amount of money that you would need right now to generate $20,000 in 20 years, assuming that you have access to an investment that will provide an annual return of 5 percent. To solve for x, we just divide both sides by $(1 + 0.05)^{20}$ to find

$$x = \frac{\$20,000}{(1.05)^{20}} = \$7,538.$$

In this case, $x = \$7,538$. You could take $7,538 right now, invest it in a project that has a 5 percent return, and it will deliver $20,000 in 20 years. Consequently, $20,000 in 20 years is worth $7,538 to you right now.

The variable x is the *present value* of $20,000 in 20 years, or in this case, the *present value* of the strip mall project. The **present value** of a future payment is the amount of money that would need to be invested *today* to produce that future payment. Economists say that the present value is the *discounted* value of the future payment. Economists invoke discounting because of the form that the present value equation takes.

The **present value** of a future payment is the amount of money that would need to be invested today to produce that future payment. In other words, the present value is the discounted value of the future payment.

$$\text{Present value} = \frac{\text{Payment } T \text{ periods from now}}{(1 + r)^T} \qquad \textit{Present Value Equation}$$

Discounting brings back money to the present (present value) and involves division; compounding takes present money into the future (future value) and involves multiplication.

Note that (1 + interest rate) is greater than 1, so multiplying it by itself T times yields an expression $(1 + r)^T$ that is also greater than 1. Therefore, in the present value equation the future payment—the payment T periods from now—is divided by a denominator that is greater than 1. In other words, the future payment is *discounted* to calculate the present value.

It is useful to remember that discounting brings back money to the present (present value) and involves division, whereas compounding takes present money into the future (future value) and involves multiplication.

It is helpful to write the present value equation in a slightly different form.

$$\text{Present value} = \left[\frac{1}{(1 + r)^T}\right] \times (\text{Payment } T \text{ periods from now}).$$

This version of the equation is mathematically identical to the previous version, but this second version emphasizes that we are multiplying the future payment by a factor that is less than 1. That factor is the ratio in the square brackets.

One can see that the strip mall project is a bad deal the instant you calculate that its present value is only $7,538. You don't need an economist to tell you that you should not pay $10,000—which is the present cost of buying into the strip mall project—for something that is only worth $7,538. Economists say that this project has a negative *net present value*, because the up-front cost of $10,000 exceeds $7,538, which is the discounted value of the delayed benefits. The **net present value** of a project is the present value of the benefits minus the present value of the costs.

The **net present value** of a project is the present value of the benefits minus the present value of the costs.

$$(\text{Present value of the benefits}) - (\text{Present value of the costs}) = \text{Net present value}.$$

For our example, the net present value is

$$\$7,538 - \$10,000 = -\$2,462.$$

A positive net present value represents a "go" decision for a project; a negative net present value represents a "no-go."

The present value concepts are useful tools, because many economic opportunities generate complex streams of future payments. We can now collapse all of those future payments to a single number—the net present value of the project.

To further illustrate the concept of net present value, consider another investment opportunity. Pay $10,000 today. In return, you'll receive two future payments: $10,000 in 10 years and $10,000 in 15 years. Is this a good deal? Once again, we can use the present value equation to answer this question. We'll use a 5 percent rate of interest.

First, let's calculate the present value of $10,000 in 10 years.

$$\text{Present value of } \$10,000 \text{ in 10 years} = \frac{\$10,000}{(1.05)^{10}} = \$6,139.$$

Then, let's calculate the present value of $10,000 in 15 years.

$$\text{Present value of } \$10,000 \text{ in 15 years} = \frac{\$10,000}{(1.05)^{15}} = \$4,810.$$

These two present values sum up to

$$\$6,139 + \$4,810 = \$10,949.$$

So this project is a good deal. You pay $10,000 today for a project with a present value of $10,949. In other words, the net present value of the project is positive:

$$(\text{Present value of the benefits}) - (\text{Present value of the costs}) = \text{Net present value}$$
$$\$10,949 - \$10,000 = +\$949.$$

Net present value is one of the most important tools in economics and is universally used by businesses and governments to decide which projects to implement. In the exercises at the end of this chapter, you'll get more practice applying this concept.

15.3 Time Preferences

We just showed you how to discount future monetary payments to calculate a present value. We can also discount other future activities. For example, people discount future pleasures—like massages or donuts—when these goods are compared to other pleasures that are available right now.

To illustrate this idea, suppose you were asked to choose between a 60-minute massage in a year or a 50-minute massage right now. Which one would you take? Most people prefer the shorter, earlier massage. This reflects an important principle: people want pleasurable events to occur sooner rather than later. We will now show you how economic models reflect this preference for earlier rewards.

Time Discounting

Utility in economics is a measure of satisfaction or happiness that comes from consuming a good or service.

Suppose there is some future activity that will generate pleasure or some other form of well-being. Suppose that this benefit is not money—for instance, the pleasure of getting a massage. Economists refer to general well-being as **utility**. To make future utility comparable to current utility, we need to multiply the future utility by a factor that is less than 1. In general, this won't be exactly the *same* factor that we use with monetary payments. However, both the factors that multiplicatively discount future monetary payments and the factors that multiplicatively discount future utility are less than 1. Stuff that comes in the future is worth less than stuff that comes right now.

Utils are individual units of utility.

To make these ideas concrete, suppose that an hour-long massage generates 60 units of utility—one **util** for every minute the massage lasts. A util is a single unit of utility. Suppose that people discount utility that will occur one year from now by multiplying those future utils by ½. A multiplicative weight (between 0 and 1) is called a **discount weight**—a discount weight multiplies delayed utils to translate them into current utils. Using a discount weight of ½, we can determine whether a person prefers 50 current utils (from a 50-minute massage) or 60 utils in a year (from a 60-minute massage). In this example, the 60 future utils have a discounted value of:

A **discount weight** multiplies delayed utils to translate them into current utils.

$$\left(\frac{1}{2}\right)(60 \text{ utils in a year}) = 30 \text{ current utils.}$$

We now have the answer. If a person discounts delayed utils with a weight of 1/2, then she prefers 50 utils right now to 60 utils in a year's time. In present value, the 60 delayed utils are only worth 30 utils now. Discount weights enable us to compare delayed utils and immediate utils, helping us identify the preferred option. Once we know your discount weight for a particular time horizon—the psychological value that you place on a delayed util—we can predict the intertemporal trade-offs that you will make.

Here's another example that illustrates these ideas. Suppose you are considering whether or not to eat a hot fudge sundae. Assume that the sundae offers immediate pleasures of 6 utils and delayed costs of 8 utils. The delayed costs would include things like reduced health and fitness.

First, let's imagine that you did not discount the future, so that your discount weight on future utils is 1. Then you would skip the hot fudge sundae, since the costs exceed the benefits.

$$\text{Benefit} - \text{Cost} = \text{Net benefits}$$
$$6 - 8 = -2.$$

Since the net benefit is negative, you decide not to eat the sundae.

Suppose instead that you *do* discount the future. Then, it's not obvious what you would do. For example, if your discount weight were ½, then

$$\text{(Immediate benefit)} - \text{(Discounted value of delayed cost)} = 6 - \left(\tfrac{1}{2}\right)8 = +2.$$

This calculation implies that you would eat the sundae, since the net benefit is positive.

Now suppose that you care a bit more about the future. Suppose that you discount the future with a weight of ⅞. In other words, we are now assuming that a util in the future is worth ⅞ as much as a util today. Then,

$$\text{(Immediate benefit)} - \text{(Discounted value of delayed cost)} = 6 - \left(\tfrac{7}{8}\right)8 = -1.$$

With a discount weight of ⅞, the delayed discounted cost is $(⅞)8 = 7$. This is high enough to *exceed* the immediate benefit of eating the sundae, which is 6. Since $7 > 6$, you decide to forego the sundae.

These examples illustrate an important general principle. The greater your discount weight—in other words, the more highly you weight things that happen in the future—the more your current decisions are driven by the future consequences of those decisions.

Preference Reversals

Let's now enrich our sundae example by thinking about the way that you discount over several days. Suppose that you discount in the following special way. You place full weight on the present and half weight on *all* future days.

	Today	Tomorrow	The Day After Tomorrow
Weight:	1	$\tfrac{1}{2}$	$\tfrac{1}{2}$

This is a slightly odd pattern of weights. It implies that you psychologically draw a sharp distinction between now and all later periods. To you, what really matters is whether a reward comes now (today) or later. Note that the weight you put on tomorrow is the same as the weight you put on the day after tomorrow. For you, all of the future days are roughly alike. It is today that is special. We call this type of preference pattern *present bias*.

Let's again think about your preferences for eating ice cream. Today, you are happy to eat the ice cream, because the immediate benefit exceeds the discounted value of the delayed cost:

$$\text{(Immediate benefit)} - \text{(Discounted value of delayed cost)} = 6 - \left(\tfrac{1}{2}\right)8 = +2.$$

Suppose however, that the ice cream parlor is unexpectedly closed today. Your friend asks you if you'd like to come back tomorrow. What is your answer?

From today's perspective, both tomorrow and the day after tomorrow have the same weight of 1/2. From *today's* perspective, the value of eating ice cream tomorrow is:

$$\text{(Discounted value of delayed benefit)} - \text{(Discounted value of delayed cost)}$$
$$= \left(\tfrac{1}{2}\right)6 - \left(\tfrac{1}{2}\right)8 = -1.$$

Because the discounted net benefit is *negative*, you decide not to eat ice cream tomorrow.

This preference pattern is an example of a *preference reversal*. You decided that you wanted to eat ice cream today. But you also decided that you do *not* want to eat ice cream tomorrow. Of course, this is not entirely consistent. Once the sun rises tomorrow morning, it will once again be like today and you'll once again want to eat ice cream. If you are always planning to stop eating ice cream tomorrow, when will your diet actually begin?

CHOICE & CONSEQUENCE

Failing to Anticipate Preference Reversals

There is nothing necessarily irrational about a preference reversal such as those that we have discussed. However, it is not rational to mispredict those preference changes. For example, if you join an expensive gym expecting to exercise twice a week for the next year but you never actually exercise, that's a forecasting error. Your forecast is irrational if you keep mistakenly believing that you are going to start exercising in the near future. At some point, you need to admit to yourself that you are not going to use the gym so you can then cancel your membership.

Rational people will correctly anticipate their own future behavior. For example, if you are never going to exercise, then you should not pay for a gym membership in the first place. Or maybe you should find a way to force yourself to exercise—perhaps by making a commitment to meet a friend at the gym. To make optimal choices, we need to correctly anticipate our own future behavior. Basing your forecast on your current preference for future behavior is not necessarily rational. You need to base your forecast on the preferences that you will hold when the moment to act actually arrives. It's easy to *intend* to write your term paper tomorrow. It's easy to *intend* to exercise tomorrow. It's easy to *intend* to eat healthfully tomorrow. Do your good intentions match your actions?

Preference reversals arise from discount weights like the ones described above. Specifically, those discount weights imply that today gets much more weight than tomorrow, but tomorrow and the day after tomorrow receive the same (or nearly the same) weight. There are also discount weights that do *not* generate preference reversals.

Most economists do not have a view on what discount weights you *should* have. Instead, we believe that discount weights reflect your tastes. If you sharply devalue things that occur in the future, you have low future discount weights. If you care about the future as much as the present, you have future discount weights that are close to 1. Economists are interested in measuring people's discount weights. Knowing how consumers discount the future helps economists predict people's choices and design public policies that suit people's preferences for intertemporal trade-offs.

Evidence-Based Economics

Q: Do people exhibit a preference for immediate gratification?

Lucky you. You have just been approached by a market tester taking orders for *free* snacks. Here is the list of options: apple, banana, potato chips, Mars bar, Snickers bar, or *borrelnoten*. (You happen to be Dutch, so you know that borrelnoten is a popular salty snack in the Netherlands.)

Order the snack you want today and the market tester will return in a *week* to bring you whatever you chose. Which free snack would you select now to eat next week? Pause for a moment and think about it before continuing.

One week later, the market tester returns and tells you that what you chose a week ago does not matter after all. Instead, you can choose whatever you want from the original list of snacks regardless of what you previously ordered. Do you think you would pick the same snack that you chose a week ago? Or would you switch? If you switched, how do you think your choice might change now that you are going to immediately eat whatever you choose?

When Dutch workers were asked to order a snack one week in advance, 74 percent asked for a healthy snack: bananas or apples.[1] However, when the researchers came back one week later and offered the same subjects the choice of a snack for immediate

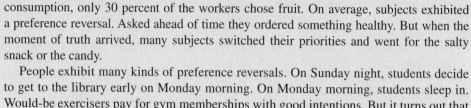

Why do we resolve to eat healthfully before we go to dinner and then change our minds when the dessert cart arrives?

consumption, only 30 percent of the workers chose fruit. On average, subjects exhibited a preference reversal. Asked ahead of time they ordered something healthy. But when the moment of truth arrived, many subjects switched their priorities and went for the salty snack or the candy.

People exhibit many kinds of preference reversals. On Sunday night, students decide to get to the library early on Monday morning. On Monday morning, students sleep in. Would-be exercisers pay for gym memberships with good intentions. But it turns out that it's never the right time to exercise, and visits fall short of expectations. Dieters have good intentions about what they will eat later in the day. But when the dessert cart arrives, the diet is postponed until the next day. People choose hard work, exercise, and healthy snacks for their *future* selves. But they want immediate gratification for the present. This leads to a pattern of preference reversals, as patient plans for the future are often overturned when the future arrives.

Question	**Answer**	**Data**	**Caveat**
Do people exhibit a preference for immediate gratification?	When picking a snack a week in advance, people choose relatively healthy foods, like an apple. When picking a snack for *immediate* consumption, people choose relatively unhealthy foods, like a chocolate bar.	A field experiment involving 200 Dutch workers between the ages of 20 and 40. The experiment was conducted by Daniel Read and Barbara Van Leeuwen.	Did people learn something meaningful during the intervening week that made them change their minds? Or did they really experience preference reversals?

15.4 Probability and Risk

We've completed our discussion of how time affects the value of economic goods and services. We now turn to our other major topic in this chapter: risk.

To an economist, **risk** exists when outcomes are not known with certainty in advance. Risk can even exist if all of the outcomes are "good" outcomes. For example, if you are a contestant on a game show and you will win either $500 or $5,000 (and have no chance of going home empty-handed), it is still the case that your outcome is risky. If something is risky, then it is said to have a component that is **random**.

Risk exists when an outcome is not known with certainty in advance. If something is risky, then it is said to have a component that is **random**.

Roulette Wheels and Probabilities

To understand risk, it is useful to start by thinking about a roulette wheel. In an American casino, a roulette wheel has 38 equal-sized pockets. The person in charge of a roulette wheel is called the croupier. The croupier spins a small white ball around the outer circumference of the roulette wheel. The ball eventually slows down and falls into the center of

An American roulette wheel has 38 pockets. The croupier spins the ball along the circumference of the roulette wheel.

the wheel. The ball bounces around the center of the wheel, eventually coming to rest in one of the 38 pockets.

If a roulette wheel is not rigged by the casino—there are laws against that— there is a 1-in-38 chance that the ball will land in any particular pocket. Without getting too philosophical, let's analyze what this statement means and how we can use roulette wheels to understand most of what you need to know about risk.

To make our discussion easier, imagine a different, hypothetical roulette wheel with 100 pockets, labeled from 1 to 100. Suppose we spun our new wheel once. What is the chance that you will win if you bet on the number 79 (and no other number)? The answer is 1 in 100.

$$\text{Likelihood of winning if you bet on a single number} = \frac{1}{100} = 0.01 = 1\%.$$

Suppose instead that you bet on *both* the numbers 79 and 16? What is the chance you will win in this scenario? There are now two ways to win—either by spinning 79 or 16. So the likelihood of winning is 2 in 100.

$$\text{Likelihood of winning if you bet on two numbers} = \frac{2}{100} = 0.02 = 2\%.$$

You can see the pattern here. Now suppose that you have bets on the following 10 different numbers: 11, 22, 33, 44, 55, 66, 77, 88, 99, and 100. What is the chance of winning? You have 10 ways to win, and there are 100 possible outcomes. So the likelihood of winning is 10 in 100.

$$\text{Likelihood of winning if you bet on ten numbers} = \frac{10}{100} = 0.1 = 10\%.$$

A **probability** is the frequency with which something occurs.

A **probability** is the frequency with which something occurs. In the world of our imaginary roulette wheel, the probability of a specific number coming up is 1 in 100, which we can write as a ratio: 1/100, or 1 percent. Think of the ratio as the frequency of the event occurring.

The probability that one of N particular numbers comes up is just $N/100$. Here are two examples. First, because there are 50 even numbers from 1 to 100 ($N = 50$), the probability of spinning an even number is 50/100, which is 0.5, or 50 percent. Second, the probability of spinning a number less than or equal to 60 is 60/100, which is 0.6, or 60 percent.

Independence and the Gambler's Fallacy

Fair roulette wheels have a special property. The outcome of one spin of the wheel will not help you predict the outcome of the next spin. This lack of connection between spins is called *independence*. When two random outcomes are **independent**, knowing about one outcome does not help you predict the other outcome.

When two random outcomes are **independent**, knowing about one outcome does not help you predict the other outcome.

At first glance, this independence property seems like a natural feature of roulette wheels. After all, if the outcome of the next spin were partly predictable, that might give gamblers an advantage over the house. But the idea that one spin does not predict the next pushes you to accept some interesting consequences.

Suppose you are playing at our imaginary wheel and that you have been betting on the number 64 every time. Suppose that 64 comes up 3 times in a row. Wow. That was good luck! You might be tempted to say that the table is "hot." Or that the number 64 is "hot." Maybe you are on a streak? Alternatively, you might decide to reach the *opposite* conclusion. Maybe you should bet on a different number now that 64 has come up 3 times in a row? It would be shocking if 64 came up again!

These are all tempting conclusions, but they are all wrong. If you are betting on 64 with each spin, the *likelihood of winning on the next spin is always 1 in 100*. This is true whether or not 64 came up on the last spin. This is true even if 64 came up 10 times in a row on the last ten spins. Whatever the past history of spins, the likelihood that 64 will come up on the next spin is always 1 in 100.

15.1

15.2

15.3

15.4

15.5

Many gamblers don't understand the independence property. Some gamblers believe in streaks: if they got lucky on the last spin, they mistakenly believe that they have a higher chance of winning on the next spin. This mistake is called the *hot hand fallacy*. Other gamblers believe that the roulette wheel somehow evens out from one spin to the next: "If the ball landed on the number 64 in the last spin, the chance of 64 coming up on the next spin is *less* than 1 in 100." This last mistake—believing the wheel somehow tends to avoid repeats—is called the *gambler's fallacy*.

You simply need to remember that roulette wheels don't have memory. What happened on the last spin has no bearing on the next spin. In the language of statistics, the spins are *independent* of one another. *Failing* to appreciate independence is a good way to get drawn into gambling. If you mistakenly believe that the last spin somehow helps you predict the next spin, then you might mistakenly believe that you know how to "beat" the casino. Of course, you'll have it backwards, because the more you play roulette, the more money you should expect to lose. We'll calculate how much you'll lose a little bit later in this chapter.

Expected Value

Expected value is the sum of all possible outcomes or values, each weighted by its probability of occurring.

Now that you've had an introduction to probabilities, we can put these ideas to work. We are going to calculate an **expected value**, which is the sum of all possible outcomes or values, each weighted by its probability of occurring. To explain what this means, it is easiest to work through an example.

Let's return to the imaginary roulette wheel. Suppose that you have the following agreement with the house. *"If the ball ends up on the number 64 you win $100. If the ball ends up on 15 you lose $200. If the ball ends up on any other number, nothing happens."* How much will you win on average? In other words, how much would you win on average if you played this bet many times?

We can calculate this average payoff by multiplying the probability of each possible outcome by the dollars associated with each outcome. Here's how:

$$(\text{Probability of "64"}) \times (\$100) + (\text{Probability of "15"}) \times (-\$200)$$
$$+ (\text{Probability of all other numbers}) \times (\$0)$$
$$= \frac{1}{100}(\$100) + \frac{1}{100}(-\$200) + \frac{98}{100}(\$0)$$
$$= \$1 - \$2 + \$0$$
$$= -\$1.$$

The probabilities are 1/100 for the outcome of winning $100 (spinning a "64"), 1/100 for the outcome of losing $200 (spinning a "15"), and 98/100 for the outcome that "nothing happens" (spinning any number other than "64" and "15"). The dollar outcomes are weighted by their associated probabilities. The average payoff, which is called the *expected value* of this bet, is −$1.

Now consider a different bet. *"If the wheel ends up with a number on or below 50, you win $200. If the wheel ends up with a number on or above 51, you lose $100."* What is the expected value of this bet?

Since there are 50 numbers on the imaginary roulette wheel on or below 50, the probability of winning $200 is 50/100, or 50 percent. Because there are 50 numbers on the imaginary roulette wheel on or above 51, the probability of losing $100 is 50/100, or 50 percent. Therefore, the expected value of this gamble is $50:

$$(\text{Probability of winning } \$200) \times (\$200) + (\text{Probability of losing } \$100) \times (-\$100)$$
$$= \frac{50}{100}(\$200) + \frac{50}{100}(-\$100)$$
$$= \$100 - \$50$$
$$= \$50.$$

CHOICE & CONSEQUENCE

Is Gambling Worthwhile?

We've explained that roulette tables don't have memory. They don't have patterns; they don't have streaks; they don't avoid repeats. Because there are no patterns that gamblers can exploit, gamblers can't beat the casino in a game of roulette. Let's calculate how much gamblers lose when they play roulette.

We'll keep our imaginary 100-pocket roulette wheel, but we'll set things up to roughly mimic the odds that gamblers have at a real American roulette table. Assume that the rules work the following way. If the wheel spins any number from 1 through 47, you win x dollars. If the wheel spins on any number from 48 through 100, you lose x dollars. What is your expected winning from playing this game (with "bet" x)?

$$\text{Expected winning} = \frac{47}{100}(\$x) + \frac{53}{100}(-\$x)$$

$$= \$x \left[\frac{47}{100} - \frac{53}{100} \right]$$

$$= \$x \times \frac{-6}{100}$$

$$= -6\% \text{ of } \$x.$$

On *average*, you will lose 6 percent of the amount you bet. Of course, this doesn't mean that you will actually lose this exact amount on each outing to the roulette table. Some nights you'll lose more and some nights you'll lose less, depending on your luck on that visit to the casino. On *average*, you'll lose 6 percent of the money you bet.

You now know the expected cost of playing roulette.[2] If you bet $100 per spin of the wheel, then you should expect to lose $6 on average per spin. If the wheel spins 40 times in an hour, and you bet on each spin, you should expect to lose 40 × $6 = $240 per hour.

Economists are not interested in scolding people about gambling. If gambling is fun for you, most of us won't try to talk you out of the casino. But we do want you to understand the costs of gambling so you can make an informed decision. Economists and statisticians can't help rolling their eyes when people say that they have a system that enables them to break even at the roulette table. The actual expected financial cost is about 6 percent of each bet that you make. It's up to you to decide whether gambling is entertaining enough to justify this implied price.

Extended Warranties

Almost all of the risk that we face is outside of casinos. We can use the imaginary roulette wheel to study these kinds of "gambles" too. We'll illustrate the general applicability of these tools by using them to study the economic costs and benefits of an extended warranty.

Assume that you are buying a $300 TV from BestBuy. The TV automatically comes with a 1-year warranty. Suppose that you can extend that warranty so that it covers years two and three. Suppose further that the extended warranty costs $75. This is the typical cost of an extended warranty on a $300 TV. Is the extended warranty a good deal?

Let's calculate the net present value of the extended warranty. To do this, we'll need to estimate the frequency with which TVs break down. Suppose that each year, the probability of a breakdown is about $\frac{10}{100} = 10$ percent. In other words, each year the chance of a breakdown is equivalent to the chance of spinning a number from 1 through 10 on our imaginary 100-pocket roulette wheel. (This is the actual frequency of breakdowns for the least reliable brands.)

If you have an extended warranty, what do you get in the event of a breakdown? Your out-of-date TV is repaired or replaced. But an out-of-date TV is not as valuable as it was when you originally bought it. During its second year of use, you can replace the original $300 TV with an equally good TV by spending only $250. During its third year of use, you can replace the original TV with an equally good TV by spending only $200. As technology improves, you can replace your old TV with less expensive, more recently built models. To sum up, your TV is worth only $250 in year two and only $200 in year three.

The cost of the extended warranty is paid now. But the benefit of getting a potential replacement TV is realized in year two or year three. We need to discount those delayed benefits. Let's assume that you are buying the TV and the extended warranty on credit, and your interest rate on your credit card is 10 percent.

Now we have all the information that we need to calculate the net present value of buying the extended warranty. Here is the formula:

$$\frac{10}{100} \times \frac{\$250}{(1 + 0.10)^2} + \frac{10}{100} \times \frac{\$200}{(1 + 0.10)^3} - \$75 = \$20.66 + \$15.03 - \$75$$

$$= -\$39.31.$$

Let's interpret the individual terms in the equation above. The first term, $\frac{10}{100} \times \frac{\$250}{(1 + 0.10)^2}$, is the value of having the extended warranty during the second year of ownership. The TV breaks with a probability of $\frac{10}{100} = 10$ percent. If it breaks, you get a replacement, which is worth $250. To calculate the present value of this replacement, we divide by $(1 + r)^2 = (1 + 0.10)^2$, where the exponent of 2 reflects the assumption that the payment is received two years from today.

The second term, $\frac{10}{100} \times \frac{\$200}{(1 + 0.10)^3}$, is the value of having the extended warranty during the third year of ownership. Once again, the TV breaks in the third year with a probability of $\frac{10}{100} = 10$ percent. If it breaks, the replacement is worth $200. To calculate the present value of this replacement, we divide by $(1 + r)^3 = (1 + 0.10)^3$, where the exponent of 3 reflects the assumption that the payment is received three years from today.

The third term, $-\$75$, is the cost of the extended warranty, which is paid at the moment that you purchase the TV. Because it is a cash outflow from you to BestBuy, it is negative.

The net present value is negative and large. As you can see above, the extended warranty provides expected benefits with present value of

$$\$20.66 + \$15.03 = \$35.69,$$

but the extended warranty costs $75. So the net present value of the extended warranty is $35.69 - $75 = -$39.31. Extended warranties are a bad deal for most consumers, unless you are psychologically highly averse to the prospect of a broken TV and the financial cost of replacing it.

Moreover, our analysis ignored some additional reasons to avoid extended warranties, including the potential to misplace the warranty and time-consuming logistics: "Please call again later. Call volume to our warranty center is heavier than anticipated."

15.5 Risk Preferences

Empirical evidence reveals that many people actually *are* extremely averse to the chance of a small financial loss and are therefore willing to buy expensive insurance to reduce the risk of such losses (like the extended warranty that we just discussed). Consequently, stores like BestBuy aggressively market extended warranties, and these extended warranties are the source of most of BestBuy's accounting profits. BestBuy doesn't make an accounting profit when it sells a television set *without* an extended warranty.

A high level of aversion to small financial losses is referred to as *loss aversion*. **Loss aversion** is the idea that people psychologically weight a loss much more heavily than they psychologically weight a gain. When researchers empirically study this difference in weights, the researchers usually find that losses are weighted *twice* as heavily as gains. This degree of loss aversion implies that a person would be indifferent between $0 for sure or a coin

Loss aversion is the idea that people psychologically weight a loss more heavily than they psychologically weight a gain.

toss with the following two outcomes: heads is a gain of $200 and tails is a loss of $100. With loss aversion, the psychological value of this coin toss is

$$\frac{50}{100} \times (\$200) + \frac{50}{100} \times 2 \times (-\$100) = \$0.$$

Note that only the *loss* is weighted by the special factor of **2**, which reflects the impact of loss aversion.

Economists are of two minds about loss aversion. Some believe that loss aversion is a bias that students should be taught to overcome. Other economists believe that loss aversion is a legitimate preference that should be respected and encouraged to express itself in economic life. Daniel Kahneman and Amos Tversky first showed that loss aversion is a common behavior, though they didn't take a position on whether loss aversion is a bias or a legitimate preference.[3] Their work led to a Nobel Prize that was awarded to Kahneman. Tversky died at a young age and the Nobel is not given posthumously.

Loss aversion is one important example of a risk preference. In general, economists distinguish three categories of risk preferences: *risk aversion*, *risk seeking*, and *risk neutrality*. To understand these concepts, consider a person choosing between two investments with the *same* expected rate of return but one investment has a fixed return and the other investment has a risky return. When people are **risk averse**, they prefer the investment with the fixed return. When people are **risk seeking**, they prefer the investment with the risky return. When people are **risk neutral**, they don't care about the level of risk and are therefore indifferent between the two investments. Thousands of empirical studies have shown that people are risk averse in most situations.

> Consider a person choosing between two investments with the same expected rate of return but one investment has a fixed return and the other investment has a risky return. When people are **risk averse**, they prefer the investment with the fixed return. When people are **risk seeking**, they prefer the investment with the risky return. When people are **risk neutral**, they don't care about the level of risk and are therefore indifferent between the two investments.

Summary

- Most decisions have benefits and costs that occur at different times. To optimize, economic agents need to translate all of the benefits and costs into a single time period so they can be compared.

- Interest is the payment received for temporarily giving up the use of money.

- The present value of a future payment is the amount of money that would need to be invested today to produce that future payment. The net present value of a project is the present value of the benefits minus the present value of the costs.

- Utility is a measure of satisfaction or well-being. Utils are individual units of utility. A discount weight multiplies delayed utils to translate them into current utils.

- Risk means that some of the costs and benefits are not fixed in advance.

- A probability is the frequency with which something occurs. For example, a probability of 0.12 means that the event will happen 12 percent of the time on average, or 12 times (on average) out of every 100 attempts. An expected value is a probability-weighted value.

- Loss aversion is the property that people psychologically weight a loss much more heavily than they psychologically weight a gain.

- If two investments have the same expected return, but one investment has a fixed return and the other investment has a risky return, people with risk aversion prefer the investment with the fixed return.

Key Terms

principal *p. 350*
interest *p. 350*
future value *p. 350*
compound interest equation or future
  value equation *p. 350*
present value *p. 353*
net present value *p. 354*

utility *p. 355*
util *p. 355*
discount weight *p. 355*
risk *p. 358*
random *p. 358*
probability *p. 359*
independent *p. 359*

expected value *p. 360*
loss aversion *p. 362*
risk averse *p. 363*
risk seeking *p. 363*
risk neutral *p. 363*

Questions

All questions are available in MyEconLab *for practice and instructor assignment.*

1. Is $1,000 received today worth as much as $1,000 received one year from now? Explain your answer.

2. How is the present value of a future payment calculated?

3. How is net present value used to decide whether a project should be undertaken or not?

4. The greater your discount weight, the more your current decisions are driven by the future consequences of those decisions. Do you agree? Explain.

5. What is meant by present bias?

6. What is meant by a preference reversal?

7. When is an outcome risky?

8. How is the probability of an event defined?

9. When are outcomes said to be independent? What is meant by the gambler's fallacy?

10. What is meant by expected value? How is it calculated?

11. Why might it make sense to avoid paying for extended warranties on televisions and small home appliances?

Problems

All problems are available in MyEconLab *for practice and instructor assignment.*

1. What is the future value of $1 (i) after 18 years if the interest rate is 4 percent, (ii) after 12 years if the interest rate is 6 percent, (iii) after 9 years if the interest rate is 8 percent, and (iv) after 6 years if the interest rate is 12 percent?

2. When you were born, your parents deposited $10,000 in the bank. The bank offered a fixed interest rate of 4 percent. On your eighteenth birthday, your parents decide to withdraw the money that they deposited to pay for your college tuition. How much money can they expect to withdraw? Assume that interest is compounded annually.

3. Suppose you won the Powerball lottery on January 1, 2015. You can choose to receive the entire amount of $400 million either as a lump sum on January 1, 2015 or you can receive four equal annual payments of $102 million paid on January 1 in 2015, 2016, 2017 and 2018. Assume that your lottery winnings are not taxed.

   a. Which option has a higher present value? Assume the interest rate is 2 percent.

   b. Instead suppose that the interest rate is 1 percent. Would your answer to part (a) change?

4. You are considering purchasing a new piece of equipment for your factory. The equipment will cost $3,000 and can be used

for three years. If you purchase it, the machine will generate earnings of $1,100 one year from now, $1,210 two years from now, and $1,331 three years from now. After that, the machine will generate no more earnings and have no resale value.

   a. What is the net present value of this investment if the interest rate is 8 percent? 10 percent? 12 percent?

   b. What is the highest interest rate at which you would be willing to buy this equipment?

5. Stafford loans are student loans that the federal government provides to graduate and undergraduate students to fund their education. Since Stafford loans can be extended up to 30 years, the Congressional Budget Office (CBO) calculates the cost of these loans by discounting the future cash flows from the loan using the interest rate on the 30-year Treasury bond. The risk of default on the 30-year Treasury bond is extremely low. In contrast, over the life of a Stafford loan, on average about 20% of the amount due is never repaid. What do you think are the implications of using the yield on the 30-year bond to calculate the cost of student loans?

6. Suppose a smoker wants to quit smoking. The utility that he gets from smoking a cigarette now is 6 utils, but, in the long run, that cigarette will generate undiscounted

health problems of 10 utils (e.g., an elevated risk of lung cancer). Use the concept of discounting to explain why impatient smokers may not quit smoking even though the undiscounted net utility of smoking is negative.

7. This chapter talked about the idea of independent events.

   a. Suppose you draw a card from a standard deck of cards, *you put that card back in the deck*, and draw a second card. Are the events "Draw a diamond the first time" and "Draw a diamond the second time" independent events?

   b. Suppose you draw a card from a standard deck of cards, *you do not put that card back in the deck,* and draw a second card. Are the events "Draw a diamond the first time" and "Draw a diamond the second time" independent events?

8. Many basketball players and fans believe in the "hot hand." That is, they believe that a player is more likely to make a shot if that player has made several shots in a row. What does the hot hand hypothesis have to do with the idea of independent events? How might you test the hot hand hypothesis?

9. You are considering playing a card game. The rules of the game are such that you pick a card from a standard deck of 52 cards and if the card is a diamond, you win $30. The catch is, you have to pay the dealer a fee of $10 to play this game. What is the expected value of this gamble? [Hint: In a standard deck of cards, ¼ of the cards are diamonds.]

10. Your house is worth $400,000 and you have $300,000 in a savings account. There is a 1 percent chance of a fire in your house. If the fire occurs, there will be $300,000 in damage.

    a. Suppose you do not have fire insurance. If the fire occurs, you will have to pay $300,000 to repair your house. What is the expected value of your wealth (including both the value of your home and your savings account) at the end of the year?

    b. We will say that an insurance policy is fair insurance if the premium for the policy equals the expected value of the claims the insurance company will have

to pay. An insurance company offers you a fire insurance policy. If a fire occurs, it will pay to repair your home. The premium for the policy is $3,000. Has the insurance company offered you fair insurance?

   c. If you are risk averse, would you buy this insurance policy? Defend your answer.

11. In 2004, Ashley Revell sold all of his possessions and gambled his entire wealth of $136,000 on one spin of a roulette wheel. He bet on "Red." If the ball landed on red, he would double his money and have $272,000; if it did not land on red, he would be penniless.

    a. Suppose Revell placed his bet in a casino in Europe. In Europe, a roulette wheel has 18 black slots, 18 red slots, and one green slot ("0"). What is the expected value of his wealth if he makes this bet?

    b. Revell actually placed his bet in a casino in the United States. In the United States, a roulette wheel has 18 black slots, 18 red slots, and two green slots ("0" and "00"). What is the expected value of his wealth if he makes this bet?

    c. Suppose Revell could have somehow found a casino that has a roulette wheel with 18 black slots, 18 red slots, and no green slots. What is the expected value of his wealth if he makes this bet? Would Revell have made this bet at this casino if he were risk neutral? Would he have made this bet at this casino if he were risk averse?

12. Smith will earn a profit of $200 next year if an oil pipeline is built in Nebraska or $60 if the oil pipeline is not built. Jones will earn $20 if the pipeline is built or $120 if the pipeline is not built. The probability that the pipeline is built is 0.25 and the probability it is not built is 0.75.

    a. Find the expected value of Smith's profit and the expected value of Jones's profit.

    b. Smith and Jones are considering forming a partnership and dividing the total profits evenly. Find the expected value of each person's profits.

    c. What is the benefit to Smith and Jones of forming a partnership? [Hint: how has the risk of their payoffs changed?]

16 The Economics of Information

Why do new cars lose considerable value the minute they are driven off the lot?

You're ready to drive your shiny new Kia Optima off the dealer's lot. You've saved carefully for the down payment, and now it's yours. Your older, shoot-from-the-hip brother—your consultant in all things car-related—is with you as you take the turn out of the lot.

"Well," he observes, "your car just went down in value."

"What do you mean?" you ask, a bit indignantly.

"If you sold this car tomorrow to someone, it would go for far less than you just paid."

"No way."

"Any future buyer is going to worry about lemons."

"But this isn't a lemon!"

"The buyer won't know that. So the price will have to adjust."

Leave it to your brother to look at the glass-half-empty situation. But he has actually touched upon an important economic concept called *asymmetric*

CHAPTER OUTLINE

- In many markets buyers and sellers have different information, which can lead to market inefficiencies.

- Asymmetry in information is either due to hidden characteristics or hidden actions.

- In cases with hidden characteristics, agents can use their private information to decide whether to participate in a transaction or a market, causing adverse selection.

- In cases with hidden actions, an agent can take an action that adversely affects another agent, causing moral hazard.

- There are both private and government solutions to reduce the effects of adverse selection and moral hazard.

information, which means that one party has superior information to another party. How does such a situation fit into the models that we have presented thus far? The answer is not very well, because so far we have only considered cases where information is symmetric—that is, buyers and sellers have exactly the same information about the goods and services up for sale. For example, as discussed in our treatment of supply and demand in a perfectly competitive market in Chapters 4–7.

In this chapter, we'll learn about situations in which an agent on one side of the market has an informational advantage over an agent on the other side. For example, used car salesmen know more about their cars than buyers do, you know more about your health than health insurance companies do, and investment banks know more about their financial risk than regulators do. Such "asymmetry" has important implications for economic decision making. We also discuss the interesting market and government solutions that have arisen to solve the negative effects of asymmetric information, and see how thinking about information asymmetries can help answer our opening question.

16.1 Asymmetric Information

In a market with **asymmetric information,** the information available to sellers and buyers differs.

There are **hidden characteristics** if one side observes something about the good being transacted that is both relevant for and not observed by the other party.

There are **hidden actions** if one side takes actions that are relevant for, but not observed by, the other party.

Upon some reflection, you will find that life presents many interactions in which one party to a transaction has different information from the other—information that the other party cares about. We refer to such discrepancies in knowledge between buyers and sellers as **asymmetric information.** We also say that the party with information that the other party to the transaction does not possess has *private information*.

We can distinguish two kinds of asymmetric information: first, **hidden characteristics**, in which one party in a transaction observes some characteristics of the good or service that the other doesn't observe; second, **hidden actions**, in which one party in a transaction takes actions that are relevant for, but not observed by, the other party. For instance, potential customers might not know about the hidden rust patches on a secondhand car that the car salesman knows only too well—thus creating hidden characteristics. Or factory workers

> **If information gaps are large enough, it is possible in theory for a market to *completely shut down* even if everyone could benefit from trade.**

may try to hide the fact that they are taking an extra 10 minutes on their lunch break from their employer—an example of hidden actions.

Both types of asymmetric information can have profound impacts on markets—impacts that are, from a social standpoint, quite negative. If the information gaps are large enough, it is possible in theory for a market to *completely shut down* even if everyone could benefit from trade! Interestingly, the people who suffer from such market failure include not only those with an informational disadvantage but also those with the extra information. We'll explain why shortly. Given the large gains from exchange that asymmetric information can destroy, it's not surprising that many institutions have arisen to mitigate its effects. Before we get to those institutions, though, let's look in more depth first at transactions with hidden characteristics and then at transactions with hidden actions.

Hidden Characteristics: Adverse Selection in the Used Car Market

Suppose that instead of buying a brand-new car, as in our opening chapter scenario, you decide to buy a used car. You begin your search by going online and scanning the local newspaper ads. You find a few nice-sounding vehicles in your price range, including a Ford Fusion and a Toyota Prius. But you end up focusing on a Dodge Smart Car, advertised for $5,000. Yet, a few doubts begin to creep into your mind: why is this person selling such a neat car for only $5,000? Does he expect it to break down? Did it already have problems? Does it look clean because it was just fished out of the local pond? You can't answer these questions; only the owner has information on the extent of his own car's problems, so you're justifiably afraid you might be stuck with a product of low quality—in this case, a lemon.

Suspicious of such private sellers, you decide to try a used car lot. There you find slightly higher prices for similar cars than you found online. You see a car you like, but once again, uncertainty enters your mind: where did the dealer get this car? Was it repossessed from an owner who never had the oil changed? Maybe the fresh coat of paint is hiding fire damage. Will the dealer honor his warranty claim? As with the private sellers, the dealer knows much of this information. But such private information is valuable, so there is an incentive for the dealer to withhold important facts about the car. Have you ever heard of a seller admitting that the odometer has been rolled back? Well, the National Highway Traffic Safety Administration determined that more than 450,000 vehicles sold each year have odometers that are rolled back.

How does such information asymmetry affect the market? To illustrate, let's say that you decide to purchase the Dodge Smart Car offered by a private seller. To understand how information asymmetry plays out, we first need to make some simplifying assumptions. Let's *first* assume that there are two kinds of cars available: high-quality cars ("peaches") and low-quality cars ("lemons"). Let's further suppose that to you, these cars look exactly the same, but you know that half of them are lemons and half are peaches. Only the seller actually knows whether he has a lemon or a peach. Because lemons constantly break down and need repairs often, they are worth zero to you and to the seller. On the other hand, the peaches are sturdy, reliable vehicles that both you and the seller value. Suppose for example that the value of such a peach to you is $5,000 and to the seller is $4,000—the fact that the value to you is greater than that to the seller means that there are gains from trade in this case.

What if this market is the same as those standard markets we've studied so far? In that case, we would have a separate price for lemons and a separate price for peaches. Lemons would be priced at $0, and peaches would sell somewhere between $4,000 and $5,000, depending on the number of sellers and buyers in the market. Thus, only peaches would be traded, and there would be gains to trade because buyers would value the cars more than sellers (in fact, the gains from a trade would be $1,000: $5,000 − $4,000). In this way, at least one of you would be better off because of the trade, and if the price is *between* $4,000 and $5,000, then both of you would be better off. For example, if you buy the car at $4,500, you and the dealer are both $500 better off.

So, the outcome when quality is fully observable to everyone is that people in the market are at least as well off after the transaction as before. This is how well-functioning markets work—they raise the welfare of their participants.

But now let's think about what would happen under asymmetric information, where the seller knows if his car is a peach or a lemon but you do not. All that you know is that half of the used cars you are looking at are peaches and half are lemons. You thus recognize that the probability of any particular car being a peach is 50 percent, and vice-versa. Suppose also that you are *risk neutral*. You will recall from Chapter 15 that this means you will evaluate risky choices with their expected value. For example, suppose a coin is flipped, and if it ends up heads you win $10, and if it ends up tails you lose $10. If you are risk neutral, then this gamble is worth zero to you (or writing it mathematically, $\frac{1}{2} \times (10) + \frac{1}{2} \times (-10) = 0$).

Knowing this, what is the most that you would now be willing to pay for the car? Because you value peaches at $5,000 and lemons at $0, and a car has a 50 percent chance of being either, as a risk-neutral buyer you will evaluate the expected value of buying a car of unknown quality as $\frac{1}{2} \times (5,000) + \frac{1}{2} \times (0) = \$2,500$. This means that if you pay more than $2,500, you will be making a bad choice since your expected value is $2,500.

Now let's think about the seller, who values peaches at $4,000 and lemons at $0. Would the seller give you a peach for $2,500? No, because he values peaches at $4,000. Instead, at $2,500, only owners of lemons will be offering their cars. Thus, if you are willing to pay $2,500 for a used car, the only car you will ever get from a private seller in this market is a lemon. Because sellers have private information on the car, you can now see what happens in this market: *the best you can do is to buy a lemon!* Knowing this, you are not willing to buy any used car that is actually offered for sale. In this case, asymmetric information causes the entire market to shut down even when there are substantial gains to trade!

The phenomenon illustrated here is a specific form of asymmetric information problem known as adverse selection. **Adverse selection** occurs when one agent in a transaction knows about a hidden characteristic of a good and decides whether to participate in the transaction on the basis of this (private) information. In our example, sellers of lemons gain from entering the market. But the limiting case discussed above shows that it is in theory possible for the market to completely shut down even if everyone could benefit from trade. Ironically, in this case, even the people who have superior information may be harmed.

In a market with **adverse selection,** one agent in a transaction knows about a hidden characteristic of a good and decides whether to participate in the transaction on the basis of this information.

Hidden Characteristics: Adverse Selection in the Health Insurance Market

Adverse selection in the used car market arises because sellers have private information. But there are also prominent adverse selection examples in which *buyers* have private information. One such instance occurs in health insurance markets, where the term *adverse selection* was originally introduced.

As we learned in Chapter 15, risk-averse individuals would benefit from having insurance against major risks. Without health insurance even a routine hospital visit in the United States might cost an individual several thousand dollars, and major surgeries and hospital stays can bankrupt all but the wealthiest of families. It is therefore natural that individuals and families should seek insurance against such risks. Since the passage of the Affordable Care Act or so-called Obamacare, in 2010, they are in fact mandated to do so, and we will see why such mandates may actually make sense.

In theory, the health insurance market works just like other insurance markets. Individuals sign up for a health plan and pay monthly premiums. In return, the health insurance company covers a large fraction of the costs for most doctor visits and hospital stays and procedures.

The problem of adverse selection again complicates things. In the used car market, adverse selection results from the fact that sellers know the quality of their car, while buyers do not. In health insurance markets, there is a similar asymmetry, but instead buyers of insurance have superior information because they have a better idea about their health than insurance companies.

Once this asymmetry is in place, the wheels of adverse selection are in motion. To illustrate its effects in health insurance markets, let's assume that there are two types of individuals, high risk and low risk. High-risk individuals are less healthy and are more likely to need expensive treatment in the near future. Clearly, health insurance programs will attract a disproportionate number of high-risk individuals. But these are exactly the individuals that health insurance companies do not want to attract, because they are more often in need of expensive care.

Similar to the market for used cars, the adverse selection problem in the health insurance market can create major inefficiencies. One possibility is similar to the extreme outcome that we witnessed in the used car market: in the same way that bad cars drove out good ones, high-risk individuals can drive out low-risk individuals in the health insurance market.

How does this work? Health insurance companies might start charging higher premiums because they expect to attract many high-risk individuals, but then these higher premiums might discourage low-risk individuals from seeking health insurance. This causes even higher premiums. The cycle, sometimes called the "death spiral," continues, and in theory, can unravel all the way to its logical conclusion of insurance companies charging such high premiums that no one ends up insured!

Market Solutions to Adverse Selection: Signaling

Are markets helpless against adverse selection? Not entirely. In practice, there are ways of dealing with it. One prominent solution for used cars is third-party certification markets, such as CARFAX, to ensure that the used car is not a lemon. More generally, we observe Educational Testing Services (ETS) offering SAT tests for college applicants, U.S. News & World Report ranking universities, Underwriters Laboratories certifying consumer and industrial products, Moody's reporting corporate bond ratings, and accounting companies auditing financial reports for public corporations.

Such market-based solutions can help move markets plagued by adverse selection toward efficient operation. Another mechanism that has arisen to combat the adverse selection problem is that of warranties. *Warranties*, which we first encountered in Chapter 15, are guarantees of quality issued directly by either the manufacturer or the seller. For example, when you buy a big-screen television, the manufacturer often provides a 1-year warranty on parts and services. For cars, manufacturers typically provide a 3-year, or 36,000 mile, warranty on the major parts, such as the engine and transmission.

Signaling refers to an action that an individual with private information takes in order to convince others about his information.

A warranty is an example of **signaling**, in which an individual with private information takes action—sends a signal—to convince someone without the information that he or his products are high quality. How can a warranty be effective in signaling a high-quality good? The idea is that warranties are particularly expensive for low-quality products because these tend to break down more often. But then, because low-quality producers will shy away from offering warranties, the very fact that a seller offers a warranty suggests that he or she is likely to be selling a high-quality product. If it were costless for sellers to provide warranties, then the signal would not be informative. But because warranties are potentially very expensive, low-quality goods are less likely to have warranties. In the Evidence-Based Economics section we discuss the value of automobile certification in the used car market.

Signaling does not just take place on the seller side of the market. Buyers, too, engage in signaling. For example, how can you, as a buyer of health insurance, send a signal of your quality (health)? One way is to show proof of annual physicals and overall good health prospects in the long run—exercising, not smoking, and not taking a lot of risks. Similarly, in the car insurance market, you signal that you are a safe driver by getting good grades in school and passing your driver competency tests.

Aaa	smallest degree of risk
Aa	very low credit risk
A	low credit risk
Baa	moderate credit risk
Ba	questionable credit quality
B	generally poor credit quality
Caa	extremely poor credit quality
Ca	highly speculative
C	potential recovery values are low

Market-based solutions can help limit adverse selection. Third-party certification mechanisms such as Moody's ratings for corporate bonds, warranties for various products, and SAT tests for college applicants help—to a degree—to balance information asymmetries.

CHOICE & CONSEQUENCE

Are You Sending a Signal Right Now?

Why do more educated workers earn more than less educated workers? We learned in Chapter 11 that workers are paid the value of their marginal product. Thus one reason why people are paid differently is because they have different productivities. Yet, in many jobs it is difficult to determine individual productivity. For example, in a consulting firm, no two people manage the same client, so it's difficult to say that any one individual did well handling a given case—there isn't a proper comparison available. This is different from the scenario we considered in Chapters 6 and 11, where each Cheeseman worker packaged a definite number of cheese boxes and the production of one worker could be directly compared to the production of another worker.

Nobel Prize-winning economist Michael Spence suggested an alternative explanation for why more educated workers earn more than less educated ones.[1] Spence developed the theory of signaling, whereby in markets with asymmetric information and adverse selection, individuals could choose costly signals in order to reveal their private information. Education might be such a signal. With a college degree, you might be telling the world, and in particular potential employers, that you have been successfully admitted to a selective college program and that you have the capacity to perform well in a variety of courses.

Such signaling is similar to Toshiba providing a warranty for its plasma TVs, or Ford guaranteeing its car engines for 3 years or 36,000 miles. The key to why signaling can work in the case of obtaining a college degree is that the signal is sufficiently scarce (not everybody has such a degree) and it is more costly to obtain for lower-ability students than for higher-ability students—for example, because lower-ability students have to spend more time and effort to succeed in their studies. These features imply that by acquiring your degree, you are sending a strong signal to your employers that you are a high-ability candidate.

Evidence-Based Economics

Q: Why do new cars lose considerable value the minute they are driven off the lot?

So is the popular wisdom true that the value of a new car will plunge the instant it is driven off the lot? Are there any data to back up that claim?

Exhibit 16.1 provides several illustrative examples showing that this claim is indeed true. The numbers in the exhibit show the price gap in 2010 between 2009 unused year-old cars and 2009 used year-old cars (both certified used cars and noncertified used cars).

What the numbers show is a 20 percent to 40 percent price difference between new and used cars. Could these percentage differences be due entirely to a year of wear-and-tear? Perhaps it's because people don't like driving a car that someone else drove before them? Nobel Prize-winning economist George Akerlof's classic article on the economics of information, published in 1970, starts with the observation that the low price of used cars does not seem entirely justified by wear-and-tear or by the fact that people don't like driving cars that others have previously owned.[2]

Akerlof proposed an explanation based on asymmetric information. You will recall that this explanation rests on the observation that cars sold by their owners might be so

Exhibit 16.1 Price Ranges of New and Used Cars

Used cars sell for about 20 to 40 percent less than new cars of the same model year, particularly when they are not certified by dealers.

Vehicle	Price Ranges in 2010
2009 Toyota Prius (new)	$22–24,000
2009 Toyota Prius (dealer certified)	$19–22,000
2009 Toyota Prius (used)	$16–20,000
2009 Honda Civic (new)	$20–24,000
2009 Honda Civic (dealer certified)	$16–21,000
2009 Honda Civic (used)	$12–16,000
2009 Ford Fusion (new)	$19–26,000
2009 Ford Fusion (dealer certified)	$16–20,000
2009 Ford Fusion (used)	$14–18,000
2009 Ford Edge (new)	$25–33,000
2009 Ford Edge (dealer certified)	$24–31,000
2009 Ford Edge (used)	$21–24,000

cheap because people are worried about getting a lemon. This explanation is supported by the data in Exhibit 16.1 that show consumers pay a premium for transacting with dealers instead of with private parties. Even though you probably shouldn't trust used car salesmen fully either, dealer-certified cars come with warranties and dealers have a reputation to protect, thus reducing the extent of the adverse selection problem and convincing buyers to pay higher prices for such dealer-certified vehicles.

Such evidence suggests the presence of a lemons market, because dealer certification is one way in which customers ensure they aren't getting a lemon. If buyers want to go to private sellers, they take on an increased risk of getting a lemon. There are lots of other differences between private sellers and dealers, however. To find a market for lemons, we would need proof that the used cars sold actually *were* lemons. One way of getting such proof is to study the maintenance records of cars sold and not sold in the private used car market.

The U.S. Census Bureau Truck Inventory Use Survey of 1977 allowed economists Michael Pratt and George Hoffer[3] to look at the maintenance records of a random sampling of pickup trucks purchased new and used. They found considerable differences between those cars kept by their original owners and those cars that people bought used. They concluded that there is evidence of lemons actually reaching the market.

Similar evidence has emerged suggesting that lemons might be clogging the used car market in the Basle City region of Switzerland. Economists Winand Emons and George Sheldon[4] analyzed the vehicle-safety inspection records of all cars in that region. They found that the probability of having a major defect was higher among those cars sold privately, supporting the idea of adverse selection in the used car market. Notably, they found exactly the opposite trend in cars sold by dealers who provided certification for used cars, thus supporting the hypothesis that market mechanisms emerge to combat a lemons problem.

Question

Why do new cars lose considerable value the minute they are driven off the lot?

Answer

Adverse selection considerably influences the private car market.

Data

U.S. Census Bureau Truck Inventory and Use Survey, 1977.

Caveat

There is some evidence of a lemons market, but the question remains controversial.

CHOICE & CONSEQUENCE

A Tale of a Tail

Although the exact importance of signaling in the labor market is controversial, an interesting example of signaling comes from a very unusual corner: the tail of the peacock.[5] Peacocks have famously ornate plumage, often referred to as their tail, which has yard-long feathers and brilliant, iridescent blue-green colors. This tail puzzled evolutionary biologists for a long time. The tail is costly to grow and what's more, it makes the peacock less mobile and an easier prey for predators. Natural selection should have eliminated it.

The reason why it has not been eliminated is that peahens seem to have a preference for mating with peacocks with such ostentatious tails. This fact by itself could explain the evolution of the tail. But is it just an accident that peahens prefer to mate with peacocks with such showy tails? Some biologists argue that it is not an accident at all. The tail is a signal. Only peacocks with good genes can develop such brightly colored plumage. Thus the plumage is a costly way of signaling good genes. It is

a valuable signal, precisely because it is costly and it cannot be easily copied by peacocks with less good genes. The debate about the exact origins of the peacock's tail in biology is by no means settled. But it shows the possibility of signaling in nature and animal behavior.

16.2 Hidden Actions: Markets with Moral Hazard

We have explored the first type of asymmetric information in which there are hidden characteristics observable by one party in a transaction and not the other. We now look at a second type of asymmetric information in which there are hidden actions taken by one party in a transaction that are relevant for but not observed by the other party. When hidden actions on the part of one agent influence another agent's payoffs, we also say that there is **moral hazard**.

Moral hazard is another term for actions that are taken by one party but are relevant for and not observed by the other party in the transaction.

The notion of moral hazard is usually associated with risk and insurance markets but reaches far beyond. The basic idea is that people tend to take more risks if they don't have to bear the costs of their behaviors. So, for example, an insured driver doesn't bear the full marginal cost he imposes on the insurance company when driving more miles or more aggressively. In particular, he does not receive an insurance penalty for aggressive driving, such as "fishtailing" on snow-covered roads or "tailgating" another car on the highway. Both actions are associated with an increased probability of being in an accident, in which case the insurance company will usually have to pay. If drivers had to pay for damages, they would drive more safely, but with insurance they have less of an incentive to avoid actions that raise the likelihood of being in an accident.

> **People tend to take more risks if they don't have to bear the costs of their behaviors.**

Likewise, once insured, home owners near water do not have full incentives to protect themselves from the adverse effects of floods. Some have argued that the National Flood Insurance Program administered by the U.S. government encourages home owners to build—and sometimes *rebuild*—too close to water. As you might guess, knowing that one's beach house will be fully covered by insurance in case of a storm surge doesn't do much to discourage building in a vulnerable location. In effect, the insurance subsidizes risky behavior.

Moral Hazard on Your Bike

At the root of the moral hazard argument is that people who have insurance behave more recklessly. But, do they really? Think of something close to home: wearing a helmet when you're pedaling away on your bike. This is a form of insurance. In case of an accident, you don't have to suffer the full consequences, so you are "insured" against major head damage.

Interestingly, the evidence shows that bicyclists wearing helmets have significantly fewer head injuries *but significantly more non-head injuries* than bicyclists not wearing helmets.[6] This result suggests that they were, in fact, taking extra risks that they would have avoided without helmets. Of course, even with such riskier behavior, helmets protect you against severe injuries, and we definitely recommend that you wear them!

Also of note is the possibility that bicycle helmets change not only risk-taking by bicyclists but might also be affecting the behavior of automobile drivers. At least, that's the evidence from an enterprising psychologist from England who rode his bike around fitted with sensors that could tell how close he was to the road's edge and how close a car was when it passed him.[7] He found that when he wore a helmet, drivers left him much less room.

This evidence definitely does not suggest that you should leave your helmet at home. Just as football players are constantly told to hit only with their shoulder pads, bicyclists should be aware of the risks they might unwittingly take when they strap on a helmet.

Moral hazard extends well beyond insurance markets. Employee theft represents perhaps the clearest example of moral hazard in the workplace. Experts estimate that employee theft costs American business hundreds of billions of dollars annually and is increasing at alarming rates—some say by 15 percent per year. This is an example of a hidden action because if the employees are good at stealing, they do so in a way that the employer cannot detect.

Under moral hazard the uninformed party can sometimes design a contract to incentivize the party with private information. Economists refer to such relationships as a **principal–agent relationship**. The party with the hidden action (thus with the private information) is the *agent*. The uninformed party, who can design a contract before the agent chooses his action, is the *principal*. This contract determines the agent's payoff (for example, wage or salary when the principal is an employer and the agent a worker) as a function of his success or failure or other indicators of his performance. The principal tries to structure the contract so as to provide appropriate incentives to the agent (for example, so as to incentivize the worker to work hard).

> **The party with the hidden action (thus with the private information) is the *agent*. The uninformed party, who can design a contract before the agent chooses his action, is the *principal*.**

In a **principal–agent relationship**, the principal designs a contract specifying the payments to the agent as a function of his or her performance, and the agent takes an action that influences performance and thus the payoff of the principal.

Market Solutions to Moral Hazard in the Labor Market: Efficiency Wages

In a principal–agent relationship, the principal's problem is to create clever plans to mitigate moral hazard. Whether it is a car insurance company trying to induce safer driving habits or an employer trying to stop employee theft, such incentive schemes are everywhere. For their part, economists have spent decades studying such incentive schemes.

THE DETROIT JOURNAL LAST EDITION

HENRY FORD GIVES $10,000,000 IN 1914 PROFITS TO HIS EMPLOYEES

HOUSES SWEPT INTO ATLANTIC BY STORM; CREW OF 32 DROWNS

DOUBLES PAY OF 25,000 IN AUTO WORKS

NATION-WIDE STRIKE IS BEING DISCUSSED BY LABOR LEADERS

Was Henry Ford kindhearted or simply a shrewd businessman?

An early example of one such clever innovation in the labor market can be found at Ford Motor Company. Led by Henry Ford, it was one of the most important corporations in the United States in the early twentieth century.[8] In 1914, Henry Ford did something that at first appeared strange, even paradoxical, in the context of our competitive labor market models. He increased the daily minimum wage of Ford employees from $2.34 to $5.00.

Why would a profit-maximizing employer increase his employees' pay above competitive levels? One possibility is that Ford might have been acting altruistically, out of some type of social responsibility. However, Ford's own account puts the motivation for the five-dollar day as follows: "There was no charity in any way involved. . . . We wanted to pay these wages so that the business would be on a lasting foundation. We were building for the future."

Ford's strategy is consistent with profit maximization in a world of asymmetric information. In fact, what Ford did was an example of paying what economists call *efficiency wages*. **Efficiency wages** refer to wages above the lowest pay workers will accept; employers use the higher wage to increase productivity (people work harder to avoid losing their high-paying jobs). Ford appears to have had such an objective, as he later noted: "The payment of five dollars a day for an eight-hour day was one of the finest cost-cutting moves we ever made."

How could moral hazard be a problem in a Ford factory? Imagine yourself on the assembly line 100 years ago. Your chore is to check for defective parts. Such work is quite monotonous, as is evident by the high turnover and absenteeism rates that Ford was facing before 1914. But there is only a small chance that if you exert low effort, you will be detected by your line manager, thus making your effort choice a hidden action. With a limited scope for being held accountable for mistakes and careless work, many would be tempted not to work hard.

Here is where the problem of asymmetric information arises. The manager at Ford can't tell exactly how many parts an employee checks, just as the manager at a movie theater can't tell if his employee has swept under all of the seats or only a few between showings. On the job, moral hazard refers to shirking from responsibilities.

The basic idea behind Ford's solution to the moral hazard problem is that a worker's effort rises when her wages increase. There are several potential reasons for this relationship.

1. Higher-paid workers might wish to work harder because a higher-paying job is more valuable to them, and the risk of not succeeding in this job—and thus having to quit or be fired—becomes potentially more costly.

2. Higher wages might encourage workers to stay longer in the company, reducing turnover, which is costly to the employer because of the additional recruitment and training that it necessitates. Moreover, the longer employment relationships that result with low turnover might increase worker productivity through experience effects. Higher wages might thus increase profits via both channels.

3. Higher pay might motivate the worker psychologically. For example, workers who perceive generosity from their employers might perceive this as a "gift" and reciprocate by working harder at their jobs—a phenomenon sometimes dubbed *gift exchange* in the economics literature.

Market Solutions to Moral Hazard in the Insurance Market: "Putting Your Skin in the Game"

Just as with adverse selection, many market mechanisms have arisen to reduce moral hazard. One of the key approaches is to align the principal and agent's incentives. Within insurance markets, that means aligning policyholders' incentives with those of the insurer. A typical technique to achieve this goal is to make certain that the insured individuals have some "skin in the game" and will have to share the costs that their actions impose on their insurer. There are several ways to accomplish such an alignment of payoffs between policyholders and insurers.

LETTING THE DATA SPEAK

Designing Incentives for Teachers

Suppose that you are the school superintendent in your school district and you want to improve K–12 education. You are told that a major problem is that the teachers do not work hard enough to invest in the children. They should be given stronger incentives. Your deputy, who has completed the first part of a course on the economics of information, suggests that this can be achieved by making teachers' pay a function of the test score improvements of pupils. The higher the test score improvement of the students, the greater the compensation of the teachers. Would you go ahead with such a plan?

As part of a field experiment in the Chicago Heights school district, Roland Fryer, Steve Levitt, John List and Sally Sadoff implemented precisely such a plan.[9]

At the beginning of the school year, certain teachers were informed that they could participate in a pay-for-performance bonus program based on how their students improved on standardized tests. The program used an end-of-year test to measure the students' improvement relative to the beginning of the year and then awarded the bonus based on those scores. Teachers could earn as much as $8,000 if their students improved, an increase of more than 15 percent of their annual salary. Other teachers were held as the control group to make sure that any differences in test score improvement were due to the incentive program.

On the face of it, providing incentives to teachers sounds like a good idea. Moral hazard is endemic in all service occupations, and teaching is no exception. In the study, the researchers did find that the merit pay worked: students in classrooms with an incentive teacher did much better than those students who had teachers with no financial incentive. Importantly, the researchers were careful to proctor the tests and have them graded independently, just in case the incentives in this program caused unscrupulous behavior among teachers.

But there is also a dark side to incentivizing teachers. A different study by economists Steve Levitt and Brian Jacob used data from actual standardized tests administered to third through eighth graders in the Chicago Public Schools (CPS) system.[10] These test scores were being used to identify schools for closures and repurposing. The intriguing, but also very disturbing, result Jacob and Levitt discovered was endemic teacher cheating in response to these incentives. Focusing on hard-to-believe strings of answers in a student's test as well as looking at the similarity of certain answer strings across students in a particular classroom or school (all telltale signs of teachers giving the answers to students), they found that teacher cheating increased significantly in response to incentives. The lesson is that hidden actions in many real-world situations such as teaching are multifaceted. Incentives should be designed carefully, taking all dimensions of hidden actions into account, or else they might lead to improvements in some dimensions but also significant deterioration in others.

1. *Deductibles* form the portion of claims that policyholders must pay for out of their own pockets. A person with a $500 deductible on his auto insurance, for example, who causes an accident leading to $5,000 of damage, will only obtain $4,500 from the insurer. By imposing some of the costs of claims directly on policyholders, the insurer gives them an incentive to take actions that reduce the likelihood of claims.

2. *Co-payments* work similarly. These are payments (most commonly applied in health insurance markets) that the policyholder makes whenever filing a claim. The $5 or $10 fee you pay for each prescription you obtain through a prescription drug plan, for example, is a common type of co-payment.

3. In *coinsurance*, the responsibility for paying claims is split between the insurer and the policyholder on a set schedule. Many health insurance policies, for instance, pay 80 percent of costs. The policyholder remains responsible for the other 20 percent.

The purpose of each of these three devices is to give policyholders some incentive to reduce the size or likelihood of their claims. These and other practices reduce the impact of moral hazard on insurance markets. But it's important to remember that even when its effects are dampened by these devices, moral hazard can still create inefficiencies and affect the structure of the markets in which it is a factor.

Evidence-Based Economics

Q: Why is private health insurance so expensive?

Health insurance is a first-order issue for society but a difficult one for economists. Competition can spur innovation, lower prices, and in general, increase efficiency. Yet when it comes to health insurance, the case for competition is murky. As described earlier in the chapter, if insurance companies have no way of figuring out the health status of each person interested in an insurance policy, then there is no guarantee that competition will lead to a vibrant health insurance industry. This leads to potential gains from government intervention, such as the Obamacare program we discussed earlier.

In the mid-1990s, a small-scale test of this problem occurred at Harvard University. For ages, Harvard had offered its employees many different insurance plans and had subsidized all of the plans at high levels. For example, the change in premium from the cheapest healthcare option to the most expensive was over $600, but employees only had to pay an extra $300 to get all of that extra coverage because Harvard was subsidizing their health premiums. Then in 1995, as healthcare prices were skyrocketing, Harvard decided to have employees actually pay the extra cost of their expensive healthcare plans. It instituted a program whereby all plans were subsidized at the same base level and consumers had to pay all the extra costs for their more expensive plans. What resulted was that prices went up for every plan, but they went up the most for the most expensive plans.

For some employees, this new plan went into effect in 1995. For others, it went into effect in 1996. Using this difference, economists David Cutler and Sarah Reber were able to test the influence of asymmetric information on the introduction of increased price competition and how beneficial competition would be for the provision of healthcare.[11]

They found that there was a significant increase in adverse selection with the introduction of increased price competition: healthy people decided it wasn't worth it to pay the extra price for the fancy healthcare plans, which increased the percentage of unhealthy people in the most expensive plans. This adverse selection increased the price of the most expensive plans. The authors estimated that the cost of this adverse selection was quite substantial, equivalent to about 2–4 percent of baseline healthcare spending at Harvard—meaning that the cost of greater adverse selection to Harvard staff, on average, was as if the baseline care plans were 2–4 percent more expensive.

So asymmetric information can cause private insurance to have a steeper price tag than it would have otherwise. Can government intervention help? We turn to this next.

Question

Why is private health insurance so expensive?

Answer

The Harvard experiment shows evidence of adverse selection—healthier patients opt out of expensive healthcare coverage.

Data

Harvard University employee healthcare choices.

Caveat

The results are from a single change in the prices of health insurance plans affecting employees at a single university.

16.3 Government Policy in a World of Asymmetric Information

Even when private solutions to adverse selection and moral hazard are effective, there might remain gains to government intervention. To see why, let's consider the case of healthcare. We know that unhealthy people are more likely to require medical care and are therefore more likely to purchase insurance. This adverse selection problem drives up insurance companies' costs, leading to higher prices. If prices increase so much that the marginal consumer decides to opt out of health insurance, the problem is exacerbated until only the sickest consumers are insured at high prices or the market collapses.

The data are broadly consistent with such death spirals, leading to the unraveling of insurance coverage in the United States before the implementation of Obamacare (Affordable Care Act (ACA)). For example, in the spring of 2010, more than 8 million of the 46 million uninsured were between the ages of 18 and 24, and approximately 16.5 million were between the ages of 18 and 34. These younger workers presumably have better health than the average American (who is 36.7 years old) and can be considered as relatively low risk. As they decide not to get health insurance, the average risk of those seeking insurance increases, which necessitates higher premiums and encourages yet more low-risk individuals to drop out of the market. This sort of death spiral in the health insurance market due to adverse selection was in fact one of the motivations for Obamacare, which, by making health insurance mandatory, intended to prevent such unraveling.

The underlying problem is one of hidden characteristics: people who purchase health insurance have more information about their likely medical costs than insurers. An important implication of these hidden characteristics is that even when everyone wants insurance, and will pay more for insurance than the health costs they expect to incur, the market will not necessarily provide insurance to everyone. Accordingly, there is a role for government to step in and potentially improve market outcomes.

The ACA made health insurance mandatory, potentially preventing the market from completely unraveling. The mandate works as a tax: by 2016, individuals who do not have health insurance will pay about $60 per month. The act was signed into law by President Obama in March of 2010.

The goal of the ACA was to increase health insurance coverage for Americans by increasing quality and decreasing the price. Price could potentially decrease because the ACA forces healthier people to buy insurance, lessening the adverse selection problem.

Did this actually work in practice?

Although it is too early to tell if the ACA worked as anticipated, there is a blueprint that economists have empirically examined to explore a similar question. The ACA is very similar to the Massachusetts universal healthcare reform of 2006, in that the Massachusetts plan also included an *individual mandate*. Three economists, Amitabh Chandra, Jonathan Gruber, and Robin McKnight, tested whether the mandate alleviated the adverse selection problem in the Massachusetts health insurance market.[12] By comparing the number of healthy and unhealthy enrollees just before and after the mandate, they found that the rate of healthy enrollees nearly tripled while the rate of unhealthy enrollees only doubled. The finding that the rate of enrollment rose among healthier people suggests that the Massachusetts mandate helped to reduce the adverse selection problem.

The next step is to explore how health insurance prices were influenced. This research is ongoing, but consistent with economic theory, the empirical work has shown that there has been a decrease in the average price of premiums statewide due to the Massachusetts reform.

In March of 2010 president Obama singned into law the ACA.

Government Intervention and Moral Hazard

Can government intervention alleviate problems of moral hazard? The answer is yes, and such interventions are all around us. Let's continue with our healthcare example. Upon introducing the ACA or the Massachusetts reform, a number of potential problems arise. For example, moral hazard could lead to citizens taking less care of their health than when they did not have insurance. With excellent insurance coverage in place, individuals might be more likely to engage in risky activities such as smoking or might engage in fewer preventative activities such as health checkups and screenings.

How can the government intervene to mitigate such moral hazard? One option is to introduce taxes to curb risky behaviors or introduce subsidies to promote healthy choices. As we have already seen, another option is to introduce deductibles and co-payments, similar to what private providers do today.

Of course, government intervention because of asymmetric information goes well beyond healthcare. For example, states mandate car insurance and design incentives to encourage safe driving habits.

> The government can improve equity, but often at the cost of reduced efficiency.

While in theory these solutions make a lot of sense, in practice, as we learned in Chapter 10, the government faces real challenges. First, the market solutions we have discussed prevent the wholesale collapse of the market (which we saw is a possibility in the case of lemons). Second, even in those cases where there are improvements to be made, similar problems of asymmetric information that limit private trade can prevent effective government action. After all, the government cannot observe hidden characteristics or hidden actions either.

In many cases, the problems are the costs created by government policies intended to create a more equitable distribution of income and resources in the presence of asymmetric information. These problems are at the root of the famous trade-off between equity and efficiency, which we discussed in Chapter 10: the government can improve equity, but often at the cost of reduced efficiency.

The Equity-Efficiency Trade-off

Economists understand that some amount of unemployment has always existed in market economies and is largely unavoidable. It takes time for workers to find jobs suited to their skills and interests. But when workers are unemployed, they receive no labor income and their families suffer. Most advanced market economies strive to achieve greater equity by providing unemployment benefits in order to reduce such fluctuations in worker incomes. But, unemployment benefits also create costs because of moral hazard.

Moral hazard is present in the problem facing unemployed workers because how hard a worker is trying to find a job or what possibilities he is turning down is private information. It would be difficult to design an unemployment benefit system that stipulates that generous unemployment benefits will be available to workers who are "trying hard to get jobs." Generous unemployment benefits imply weaker incentives to look for work and the possibility of a longer duration of unemployment.

The presence of moral hazard in the behavior of unemployed workers introduces an unavoidable trade-off in the design of unemployment benefits: greater equity and insurance for unemployed workers and their families come at the cost of reducing worker effort to find new jobs. Naturally, this trade-off does not mean that unemployment benefits are unnecessary or undesirable, but it might imply that unemployment benefits should not be so generous as to remove all incentives to search for new jobs. For example, providing workers with unemployment benefits that are equal to the wage that they would earn if working would definitely be a bad idea.

Crime and Punishment as a Principal–Agent Problem

Problems of asymmetric information are relevant not only when governments engage in redistribution as in the unemployment benefit case but also when they try to enforce law

Moral Hazard Among Job Seekers

The role of moral hazard in the job-seeking behavior of unemployed workers is illustrated by several studies. In the United States, unemployed workers spend an average of just 41 minutes per weekday looking for a job. This number increases to more than 60 minutes per weekday in the week before their unemployment benefits expire (in most states, unemployment benefits expire after 6 months of unemployment).

This evidence suggests that in the presence of unemployment insurance, unemployed workers do not exert as much effort in seeking a new job as they would have done without the insurance.[13] Consistent with this perspective, European workers, who typically receive more generous unemployment benefits than workers in the United States, appear to spend less time looking for a new job.

The job-finding behavior of unemployed workers also confirms that they are more eager to find jobs right before their benefits expire. In Austria, for example, a typical unemployed worker is estimated to be 2.4 times more likely to exit unemployment in the week right before benefits expire than in other weeks.[14]

According to studies, unemployed workers don't exert as much effort in finding a job as they would have without insurance.

and order. Nobel Prize-winning economists Gary Becker and George Stigler suggested that the problem of how to monitor and punish crime should be thought of as a principal–agent problem, with society acting as the principal and a citizen subject to regulations as the agent.

Government rules are everywhere. All states enforce laws, uphold property rights, and prevent crimes. If they didn't, society would have to suffer through the detrimental actions of quite a few bad apples. At the other extreme, if a state wanted to prevent all crime, it would need to have an unmanageably large police force. Somewhere in between, each type of government finds its optimal level of crime and punishment.

Becker and Stigler suggested that crime could be thought of as a principal–agent relationship under moral hazard because the actions of the agent, whether he or she has broken the law or committed a crime, are not perfectly observable by the principal, in this case the state (or the government).[15] Viewed through this perspective, crime prevention is a problem in the design of incentives. Becker and Stigler then suggested that, to a first approximation, incentives will be shaped by expected punishment, defined as the product of two terms as follows:

Expected punishment = Probability of detection × Punishment if detected.

Thus either the probability of detection needs to be sufficiently high, or punishment, if detected, has to be severe enough to reach the level of expected punishment necessary to prevent a crime.

Becker noted that although ensuring a high probability of detection is costly for society, increasing the punishment if detected is not so costly. The optimal "penal code" should have a relatively small probability of detection and thus a small police force, but it should impose a heavy punishment against those who are detected. This is a powerful framework for thinking about the design of laws and their enforcement. It potentially explains why many small crimes go unpunished but how society might still successfully create sufficient deterrence against other, more serious crimes.

Summary

☀ Many real-world markets are characterized by asymmetric information because there are important informational disparities between buyers and sellers.

☀ One type of asymmetric information is driven by hidden characteristics, meaning that certain characteristics are hidden from either sellers or buyers. Hidden characteristics lead to adverse selection when agents can use their private information to decide whether to participate in a transaction.

☀ Another type of asymmetric information is due to hidden actions, which arise when one party to a transaction can take actions, not observed by the other party, affecting everyone's payoffs. Hidden actions lead to moral hazard problems.

☀ Although the market has developed means to deal with information asymmetries, such as warranties, deductibles, certification, and efficiency wages, in many situations these may be insufficient, and government intervention may be useful to limit the inefficiencies that asymmetric information creates.

Key Terms

asymmetric information *p. 367*
hidden characteristics *p. 367*
hidden actions *p. 367*

adverse selection *p. 369*
signaling *p. 370*
moral hazard *p. 373*

principal–agent relationship *p. 374*
efficiency wages *p. 375*

Questions

All questions are available in MyEconLab *for practice and instructor assignment.*

1. What is asymmetric information? What are the two kinds of asymmetric information?

2. Explain why "bad cars drive out the good ones" in the market for used cars.

3. Why does adverse selection occur in the health insurance market?

4. How do third-party certifications and warranties solve the adverse selection problem in the used car market? Explain your answer.

5. Explain the following terms:
   a. Principal–agent relationship
   b. Moral hazard

6. When do firms pay efficiency wages? What is the relationship between moral hazard and efficiency wages?

7. Does the presence of asymmetric information necessarily imply that governments should intervene in a market?

8. How might unemployment benefits create a moral hazard problem?

9. Explain the potential costs of high-powered incentives by considering the case of providing incentives to police officers. Would it be a good idea to pay higher wages to police officers if they make more arrests?

10. How can crime and punishment be modeled as a principal–agent problem? What does the model suggest about crime prevention?

Problems

All problems are available in MyEconLab for practice and instructor assignment.

1. When a major league baseball player's contract has expired, he can either sign a new contract with his current team or become a free agent and sign a contract to play with a different team. If adverse selection is a problem in the market for major league ball players, who do you think are more likely to be injured the season after they sign a new contract: players who re-sign with their current team or players who sign with a new team? Explain.

2. There are fifty low-risk people in a town and fifty high-risk people. A low-risk person has an average of $1,000 in medical expenses each year and is willing to pay $1,200 for medical insurance (this person is risk averse). A high-risk person has an average of $2,000 in medical expenses each year and is willing to pay $2,400 for medical insurance. Insurance companies are unable to tell who is high-risk and who is low-risk.

   a. Show that an insurance company would lose money if it offered medical insurance at a price of $1,600.

   b. Show that if the insurance company offered medical insurance at a price of $2,200, low-risk people would not be insured. Calculate total surplus if the price is $2,200.

   c. Now suppose the government in this town passes a law that requires everyone to purchase medical insurance and sets the price of insurance at $1,600. Calculate total surplus under this law.

   d. The 2010 Patient Protection and Affordable Care Act (commonly called the Affordable Care Act, or "Obamacare") includes an individual mandate that requires everyone to have health insurance. Does this question suggest that there is an efficiency argument in favor of the individual mandate? Defend your answer carefully.

3. This chapter explains that signaling refers to an action that an individual with private information takes in order to convince others about his information. Screening also involves private information but is somewhat different from signaling. Screening refers to an action taken by an *uninformed* person to learn about someone else's private information. So, for example, you are engaged in screening if you have a mechanic inspect a used car you are considering buying.

   The biblical story of King Solomon is in 1 Kings 3: 16–28 (see also http://en.wikipedia.org/wiki/Judgment_of_Solomon). Two young women who both had an infant son came to Solomon for a judgment. One of the women claimed that the other, after accidentally smothering her own son while sleeping, had exchanged the two children to make it appear that the living child was hers. The other woman denied this, and so both women claimed to be the mother of the living son and said that the dead boy belonged to the other. Show that King Solomon understood screening very well.

4. All used cars are lemons or peaches. Owners know whether or not their car is a lemon, but buyers do not, that is, the quality of a car is private information. There are many more buyers than sellers. Buyers value a peach at $4,000 and a lemon at $200; owners value a peach at $3,000 and a lemon at $100. Owners can have their cars inspected for $100. If they do have their car inspected, they will receive a certificate that shows whether the car is a lemon or a peach. Show that owners of peaches will have their cars inspected and will sell those cars for $4,000. Show also that the owners of lemons will not obtain a certificate and will sell their cars for $200.

5. Suppose some workers are capable and others are extraordinary. Firms are willing to pay capable workers a salary of $12,000 and extraordinary workers a salary of $15,000. Workers know if they are capable or extraordinary but firms do not, that is, ability is private information. It would cost capable persons $6,000 to earn a college degree, but it would cost extraordinary persons just $2,000 to earn a college degree since they can finish their education much faster. Show that in equilibrium in this labor market (i) extraordinary people go to college but capable people do not, and (ii) firms pay college graduates $15,000 and high school graduates $12,000.

6. Grade inflation is widespread; college students receive higher grades on tests and exams today for work that would have received lower grades in the past. One recent study found that 41 percent of students had grade point averages of A-minus or higher in 2009, compared to just 7 percent in 1969. In other words, grades improve while actual learning does not. Employers often use grades and college degrees as signals in the job market, where there is asymmetric information. What effect would grade inflation have on the effectiveness of college degrees and grades as signals?

7. The U.S. government, like many governments throughout the world, bailed out large financial institutions that were thought to be "too big to fail" during the 2008 financial crisis. Some critics of the bailouts argued that these policies created a moral hazard problem: banks would undertake too many risky projects if they knew that the government would bail them out if the project failed. This question explores this moral hazard problem.

   a. Suppose a bank has the opportunity to invest in a risky project. If the project is successful, the bank will earn $80; if it is unsuccessful, the bank will lose $100. The probability that the project will be successful is 0.5. What is the expected value of investing in this project? If the bank is risk neutral, will the bank make this investment?

b. Now suppose the government has a policy that helps banks that are suffering losses. Under this policy, the government will give a bank 30 percent of the bank's losses if a project is unsuccessful. Thus, if the project in this problem is unsuccessful, the government will give the bank 0.30 × $100, or $30. What is the expected value of investing in this project? If the bank is risk neutral, will the bank make this investment?

8. Steven Levitt and Chad Syverson compared instances of home sales in which real estate agents are hired by others to sell a home to instances in which an agent sells his or her own home. They found that homes owned by real estate agents sold for 3.7 percent more than other houses and stayed on the market 9.5 days longer, everything else being equal. How could moral hazard explain these results?

9. Sumo wrestling tournaments typically have 66 wrestlers. Each wrestles 15 matches. A wrestler who has a winning record (eight wins or more) is guaranteed to rise in the official rankings; a wrestler with a losing record falls in the rankings. Suppose the last match of a tournament is between Wrestler A, who has won eight matches so far, and Wrestler B, who has won seven. If moral hazard is a serious problem in sumo wrestling, who do you think is more likely to win this match?

10. Janet Yellen, the chair of the Federal Reserve, is married to the Nobel Prize-winning economist George A. Akerlof. When they hired babysitters in the 1980s, they decided to pay wages that were higher than the going wage for babysitters. If they could get a babysitter at a lower wage, what could explain why they decided to pay more?

11. The government wants to reduce white-collar crime.

   a. Suppose for the moment innocent people are never wrongly convicted of a crime. Explain why the Becker model of crime and punishment suggests that we increase the fines people pay if they are convicted instead of hiring more people to investigate white-collar crime.

   b. Now suppose that mistakes happen and innocent people are sometimes convicted of white-collar crime. Why in this case might we want to hire more investigators instead of raising fines? What role does equity or fairness play in this case?

17 Auctions and Bargaining

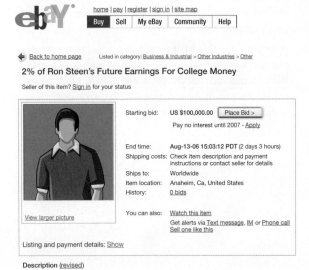

How should you bid in an eBay auction?

As you strain to understand Kepler's First Law for your astronomy test tomorrow, you can't resist peeking at your most recent eBay struggle. Some guy named "MrBigTime" repeatedly tops your bids for a fourth-generation Apple iPod Touch. The auction ends at midnight tonight, and you contemplate your best strategy going forward—bid aggressively now or place a winning bid at the last possible moment (a ploy known as "sniping")? You just cannot get your mind back to astronomy. This auction is much too exciting—there's no time to worry about heavenly bodies now.

Anyone who has bid in an auction can relate. Heart thumping, palms sweating, auctions seem to bring out the animal spirits. Perhaps this is why they have become a normal way of life for millions of people around the globe who wish to buy, sell, or trade. In the United States alone, more than 20 percent of adults participate in online auctions. And they buy and sell all sorts of things. In 2006, a college student posted 2 percent of his future earnings for sale on eBay in exchange for the highest investment in his college education.

Up until now, we have treated you, the consumer, as a price-taker who purchases what best suits your preferences at the market price (assuming you can afford the item). In no way are you able to affect the price you pay—you are just one of many consumers. In reality, there are many situations where you do have some influence over the price that you pay for goods. On eBay, for example, the high bidder wins the item and pays an amount equal to her bid. In markets

CHAPTER OUTLINE

where buyers and sellers engage in active bargaining over prices, such as for cars, houses, and many home appliances, you are an active participant in setting prices by negotiating directly with the seller.

In this chapter, we explore the economics behind situations where you, the consumer, can affect the price you pay. Once again, optimization will be a key component: you will do the best you can within these new economic settings. We discuss how you should optimize in such settings—whether you should adopt a bid-sniping strategy on eBay, for example, or whether you should walk away from a car deal. We also examine how these same bargaining principles affect your everyday life, perhaps in ways that you would have never even imagined. This pursuit will take us into marriage markets and will help us answer a second question: *Who determines how the household spends its money?*

Can you at least wait until your aunt leaves before you auction her gift?

17.1 Auctions

An **auction** is a market process in which potential buyers bid on a good and the highest bidder receives the good.

An **auction** is a market process in which potential buyers bid on a good and the highest bidder receives the good. Auctions have a long and storied past. From the slave auctions in ancient Egypt to the marriage auctions for brides in Asia Minor to the Praetorian Guard auctioning off the Roman Empire in A.D. 193, auctions have been used to allocate goods and services for centuries. While auctions have served an important purpose throughout history and are now used to sell almost anything one can imagine—vintage wines, foreclosed homes, pollution permits, baseball cards, and even future streams of people's incomes, as shown in the photograph at the beginning of this chapter—economists have only recently come to an understanding of the various auction formats we find in markets today.

Why are some goods auctioned at the highest bid price instead of being sold at posted prices like products at Walmart or Home Depot? Put simply, some goods don't have well-established prices, making auctions a particularly useful method of selling that encourages *price discovery*. For example, when you are thinking of selling a painting given to you by your grandparents that might be of interest to only a handful of buyers, auctioning it off might be a good way of discovering what the appropriate price will be and finding the right sort of buyers. In general, it is common for goods that are unique, with relatively few buyers, to be auctioned. For other goods that are interchangeable and have both many sellers and many buyers, price discovery isn't so much

Some goods don't have well-established prices, making auctions a particularly useful method of selling that encourages *price discovery*.

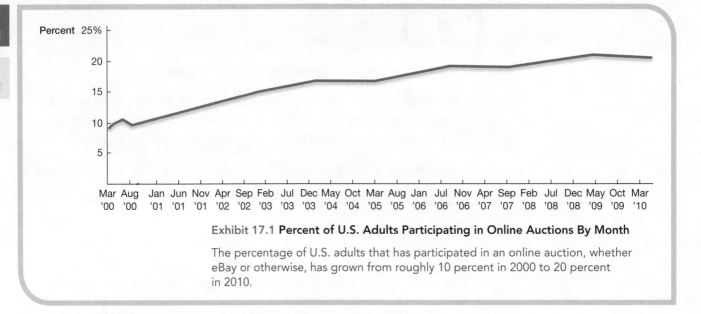

Exhibit 17.1 **Percent of U.S. Adults Participating in Online Auctions By Month**

The percentage of U.S. adults that has participated in an online auction, whether eBay or otherwise, has grown from roughly 10 percent in 2000 to 20 percent in 2010.

of an issue. Accordingly, goods such as cans of tuna and peaches typically sell at grocery stores with posted prices.

However, with the advent of the Internet, auctions have moved beyond the selling of exotic goods with a small number of buyers. It is now easy to find "ordinary" goods such as books, golf balls, iPods, and notebooks—goods for which price discovery isn't the main consideration—for sale in auctions every day. For sellers, Internet auctions represent a quick way to sell items. No one has quite been able to come up with any single reason as to why auctions have become so popular for consumers (although their popularity may have reached its peak[1]). One factor is that auctions can be fun. Many buyers might get a thrill of competing for the Apple iPod Touch on eBay, with the possibility of getting a really good deal, rather than walking into the Apple store and paying the posted price.

These attractive features have led to tremendous growth in participation in online auctions, as shown in Exhibit 17.1. Just over the last decade, the percent of U.S. adults who participate in online auctions has roughly doubled, increasing from 10 percent to more than 20 percent. And what is sold generates billions of dollars: today more than $300 billion is sold annually in auctions.

In this section, we focus on several common auction formats. Across these formats, we will keep an eye on how people bid, what prices they pay, and what revenues sellers receive. You will find that auction analysis helps us understand the formation of markets and is an excellent application of game theory, which we presented in Chapter 13.

Let's begin with some simplifying assumptions. We'll assume that bidders each have their own *private* valuation of a good—in other words, their own willingness to pay that is unknown to other bidders and to the seller. Let's also assume, for simplicity, that an auction has five bidders who are interested in bidding on a pair of Oakland Raiders National Football League (NFL) football tickets.

They have willingness-to-pay values as given in Exhibit 17.2. Of the five bidders, Ashley has the highest willingness to pay for the Raiders tickets: $250. This means that the maximum that Ashley will pay for the tickets is $250. The person with the lowest valuation is Eli. He is willing to pay $50 for the tickets. Billy, Carol, and Dalton all have values in between those of Ashley and Eli. Given these values, we'll now see how our bidders fare in different types of auctions. But before doing so you might ask: why doesn't the seller just charge Ashley $250 for the Raiders tickets? The answer is that the seller doesn't know Ashley's willingness to pay (her private valuation), and the auction is useful partly because the seller doesn't need to know this information (and this is, of course, related to the price discovery role of auctions).

You can even get Raiders tickets in an auction.

Bidder	Value
Ashley:	$250
Billy:	$200
Carol:	$150
Dalton:	$100
Eli:	$ 50

Exhibit 17.2 Bidder Valuations for Raiders Tickets

The five bidders to the right all have their own independent and private values for the Oakland Raider tickets. These values represent the maximum amount they would be willing to pay for a pair of tickets.

Types of Auctions

There are many kinds of auctions. For our purposes, auctions can be usefully split along two features:

1. How people place their bids
2. How price is determined

People typically place their bids by either *open outcry* or *sealed bid*.

An **open outcry auction** is an auction where bids are public and bidders compete actively against one another. A **sealed bid auction** is one in which bidders place their bids privately so that no other bidder knows the bid of another participant. The second feature that distinguishes auctions is how price is determined. In some cases, people pay what they actually bid. In others, another bidder's bid—usually the next highest bid—determines the price. These two distinctions—how bids are made and the way in which price is determined—lead to four major auction types:

1. Open outcry English auctions
2. Open outcry Dutch auctions
3. Sealed bid first-price auctions
4. Sealed bid second-price auctions

In all four cases, we will develop some economic intuition to guide optimal bidding strategies—intuition that will involve a bit of game theory.

An **open outcry auction** is an auction in which bids are public.

A **sealed bid auction** is an auction in which bids are private so that no bidder knows the bid of any other participant.

An **English auction** is an open-outcry auction in which the price increases until there is only one standing bid. That bidder wins the item and pays his bid.

Open-Outcry English Auctions

The *English auction* is probably the auction most familiar to you. This is the "going, going, gone" kind of auction used at establishments like Sotheby's when it sells expensive paintings and antiques, and what you may have witnessed first-hand at estate auctions. An English auction consists of an auctioneer and several bidders. The auctioneer begins the bidding process by announcing a low starting bid. From this point on, bidders bid directly against each other, and each bid must improve upon the last. When no bidder is willing to bid any higher, the bidder with the highest bid pays her bid and wins the good. In sum, an **English auction** is an open-outcry auction in which the price increases until there is only one standing bid. That bidder wins the item and pays the bid.

You might recognize this format as having features similar to many online auctions, such as eBay: bids are shown publicly, and price increases until the end of the auction (an "ascending" price determination), when the high bidder wins and pays his bid. More generally, English auctions are commonly used to sell real estate, foreclosed homes, cars, and antiques and are popular to raise money for charity.

The chance of getting a really good deal makes auctions attractive to buyers and fun!

Optimizing in an English Auction What should your optimal strategy be in an English auction? To answer this question, put yourself in Ashley's shoes as we auction off the pair of Raiders tickets. Say that

I don't have a soul anymore but I do have some nice collectable mugs.

Today you never know what you will find at auction!

All in all, this empirical evidence suggests that it's probably best to spend your time studying astronomy, not sniping!

the auctioneer begins at a price of $25 and asks who would like to bid. Looking at the values in Exhibit 17.2, we see that Ashley, as well as the other four bidders, will bid at this price because each of them has a value for the tickets exceeding $25. Therefore, Ashley should bid at this price. She does so because as a bidder in this type of auction, she is willing to bid *up to* her value for the object, but no more, because she will have to pay her bid if she wins.

Next consider Eli. With the same reasoning as above, he should *not* be willing to bid more than $50 for the Raiders tickets. Therefore, when bidding reaches $50, Eli will no longer bid. This is because if he bids above $50 and wins, he will lose consumer surplus because he only values the tickets at $50. It just doesn't make sense for Eli to bid any amount greater than $50, and he should drop out at $50.

Let's continue with the bidding process. What happens when the price reaches $100? Dalton, who should not bid more than $100, now drops out. What about when the bids reach $150? Now Carol stops bidding. This process continues until we reach $200. Let's say that Ashley bids $200 for the Raiders tickets. Does Billy bid? No, because he would have to bid higher than $200. He values the tickets *at* $200, so he will not bid any higher. Ashley therefore wins the Raiders tickets and pays $200, netting herself $50 in consumer surplus ($250 − $200).

What we just observed is a general result in an English auction: it is a dominant strategy to bid until the price is above your value for the item. In Chapter 13, we noted that a dominant strategy is a strategy that gives you the highest payoffs, regardless of the other players' actions. Thus, the dominant strategy equilibrium, and also therefore the Nash equilibrium in the English auction, is for everyone to bid in this manner.

In equilibrium, the winner will be the highest-value bidder, and she will pay a price equal to the second-highest value (or slightly more if the second-highest bidder bids his

LETTING THE DATA SPEAK

To Snipe or Not to Snipe?

If you've participated in auctions on eBay and Amazon.com, you may have noticed that their rules differ slightly: eBay auctions end at a prespecified time, but Amazon.com auctions end when 10 minutes have gone by without a bid. This small difference leads to bidders placing lots of last-minute bids on eBay auctions—a practice known as *sniping*. Both Web sites offer the option of entering a maximum bid and letting a proxy bidding service automatically place bids in minimum increments until the maximum bid is reached, but many eBayers still snipe at the last minute.

So just how many more snipe bids do bidders on eBay make? Nobel Prize-winning economist Alvin Roth and Axel Ockenfels found that 20 percent of individuals place their final bids in the last 60 minutes of an eBay auction compared to 7 percent of Amazon users.[2] They also discovered that in their sample, at least 40 percent of eBay auctions had last bids placed in the 5 minutes prior to close, with 12 percent in the last 10 seconds!

Do you think that it makes sense to wait until the last minute or second to bid?

Research by economists Sean Gray and David Reiley provides some insights.[3] They explored the benefits of eBay sniping with a field experiment. The two economists ran an experiment in which they themselves placed bids on pairs of identical items (such as DVD movies and die-cast Hot Wheels cars), placing their maximum bid on one item of the pair days before the auction's end and placing the same bid on the other item just 10 seconds before the auction's end time. Results from 70 pairs of objects show no statistically significant benefit to sniping, as final prices for the items were approximately the same.

All in all, this empirical evidence suggests that it's probably best to spend your time studying astronomy, not sniping! This evidence provides some insight into how you should bid in eBay auctions, the topic of our chapter-opening question.

value exactly—for this example, if Billy had bid $200, then Ashley would have won with a bid of $200.01). So in auctioning off the Raiders tickets at an English auction, the seller should expect to receive approximately $200 in revenues for the tickets.

Open-Outcry Dutch Auctions

How much would you pay?

A **Dutch auction** is an open-outcry auction in which the price decreases until a bidder stops the auction. The bidder who stops the auction wins the item and pays his bid.

In the seventeenth century, tulip mania hit the Netherlands. In what many consider to be the first documented economic bubble, it was widely noted that *single* tulip bulbs were selling for more than 10 times the annual income of daily laborers. At the height of the mania, 12 acres of land traded for a single bulb. As we might expect, the speculative bubble fostered many creative ways in which tulips were exchanged. Perhaps the most interesting was the *Dutch auction*.

The **Dutch auction** is also an outcry auction. But one big difference from the English auction is that in a Dutch auction the auctioneer begins the bidding at an offer price far *above* any bidder's value and lowers price in increments until one of the bidders accepts the offer. That is, the auction continues in a descending order of values until someone announces that he is willing to buy at a given price. The first person who accepts at a given price wins the auction and pays that price. In this way, the Dutch auction is an open-outcry *descending* price auction, whereas the English auction is an open-outcry *ascending* price auction.

The Dutch auction is probably not very familiar to you, but it continues to be used in modern economies. Beyond the tulip auctions in Amsterdam that still thrive today, Dutch auctions are used by the Department of the Treasury in the United States to sell securities. Even private firms use Dutch auctions: when Google first offered its stock to the public it made use of a variation on the Dutch auction: OpenIPO. Likewise, many other firms have also used Dutch auctions to repurchase stock shares in their companies.

Optimizing in a Dutch Auction To consider your optimal strategy in a Dutch auction, let's return to our ticket auction. Let's say that the auctioneer begins the bidding at a price of $500. Would anyone accept that price? Scanning the individual values in Exhibit 17.2, we see that none of the five bidders will purchase at this price. The closest is Ashley, but because she is only willing to pay $250, she will not bid at a price of $500. If she did, she would lose $250 in surplus ($500 − $250). So, because no one buys at $500, after a certain period of time the auctioneer lowers his price to $490 . . . then to $480 . . . then to $470, and so on.

When will the auction end? Who will win and what will he or she pay?

Deciding how to bid in a Dutch auction is a bit more difficult than in the English auction, where you simply bid until the price reaches your maximum willingness to pay. To see this, let's consider Ashley's decision when the price in the Dutch auction reaches $250.

Should she announce that she would like to purchase at this price? If she does, then she will win the tickets, but will pay $250. This price will yield zero consumer surplus for her ($0 = $250 − $250). Alternatively, she could "let it ride" and not buy at this price. In this case, she runs the risk of not winning. Crucially, she does not know the values of the other four bidders or how they will bid, so the trade-off facing her is a purchase with zero consumer surplus now versus a *chance* of a higher surplus. Let's assume she lets the auction continue.

When no one buys at $250, the auctioneer lowers the price to $240. Now Ashley has another decision. She can accept the $240 price and gain $10 in consumer surplus ($250 − $240) with certainty, or she can wait until a lower price is announced with the downside risk of someone else buying before her, which will lead to zero consumer surplus for her. What should she do now?

At this point, we need further assumptions to provide guidance to Ashley on her optimal bidding strategy. As you might have guessed, one crucial assumption concerns risk preferences. Recall from Chapter 15 that we refer to people who are neither risk averse nor risk seeking as *risk neutral*. Consider the following bet: a coin is flipped, and if it ends up heads you win $10, and if it ends up tails you lose $10. A risk seeker gladly accepts this bet, a risk averter declines, and a risk-neutral person is indifferent. Risk neutrality is a convenient benchmark for small and moderate stakes, and here we will assume that bidders are risk neutral.

So given risk neutrality, when should Ashley jump in with her bid? The higher her bid, the lower her surplus, but also the higher the likelihood that she'll be the first bidder and win the Raiders tickets. Given that underlying all of Ashley's decision making is her private value, we can see that in such an auction, the higher her valuation, the more she should bid. Another factor should also influence her bidding: the number of bidders competing against her in the auction. If she's only one of two people in the auction, she can take more chances and let the price decrease substantially. But if she is competing with several others, then the chances are that somebody else will jump in before her unless she bids aggressively.

A simple strategy for Ashley to optimize in this case is to multiply her willingness to pay ($250) by the number of competitors (4) divided by the total number of bidders in the auction (5). (Under some assumptions, this strategy can be derived as a Nash equilibrium, but we do not need to get into these derivations).

Since her willingness to pay is $250, and there are four other bidders (five bidders in total), this rule implies that Ashley's optimal action is to announce "buy" when the price reaches $250 \times 4/5 = $200. It turns out that this type of strategy is a Nash equilibrium for all bidders, meaning that it is a best response for Ashley to do this when others are also using the same strategy (bid 4/5 times their own valuation). As a result, in this Nash equilibrium we expect Eli, for example, to announce "buy" when the price reaches $40 ($50 \times 4/5).

In general, as the number of bidders gets really low—say, just two bidders—you bid much less aggressively, which of course makes sense. According to the rule in the previous paragraph, Ashley should bid $250 \times 1/2 = $125 with two bidders.

In contrast, when the competition intensifies—say, the number of bidders goes to 100—you bid much closer to your individual value. With the above rule, for example, Ashley will bid at $250 \times 99/100 = $247.50 with 100 bidders.

If everyone follows this optimizing rule, then in the Dutch auction the bidder with the highest value will win the auction and will pay $200. This is because Ashley is the first to announce "buy," and she will do so at $200. She will therefore receive $50 in consumer surplus. And the seller of the Raiders tickets receives $200 in revenues.

Interestingly, this is identical to what the seller received in the English auction. Note, however, that there is no general rule that the actual payments will be identical between the two auctions. For example, if we changed Billy's valuation in Exhibit 17.2 to $210, then in the Dutch auction Ashley would win again and pay $200 (Billy's strategy would now be to bid $210 \times 4/5 = $168, but again Ashley will clinch the good at $200 before this happens). However, in the English auction, Billy would raise his bid until the price reached $210, and thus Ashley would now end up paying more, $210 instead of $200.

But, what *is* remarkable is that two features are identical in the English and the Dutch auction: first, Ashley, who has the highest valuation, wins in both auction types. Second, although the actual revenues generated by the two auctions can be different depending on the exact valuations of the bidders, it turns out that the *expected revenues* are the same. Think of it this way: if we ran several auctions with many different goods and many different bidders with varying valuations in each auction, on average the revenues that we should expect to raise using each auction type are identical. That is, in theory, the English and Dutch auctions should raise the same amount of money. We will see next that this is actually a much more general phenomenon.

Sealed Bid: First-Price Auction

The two types of auctions we've discussed thus far—English and Dutch auctions—are known as open-outcry auctions in that they are public in nature. Auctions have also arisen in which bidders are allowed to make bids privately. These are known as *sealed bid auctions*. In sealed bid auctions, all bids are made privately so that each bidder knows only her own bid. That is, bidders in this type of auction submit their bids simultaneously without knowing the bids of the other auction participants. One example of a popular type of sealed

Sealed bid first-price auction is an auction in which bidders privately submit bids at the same time. The highest bidder wins the item and pays an amount equal to her bid.

bid auction is called a **sealed bid first-price auction**. In a sealed bid first-price auction all bidders write down their bids privately on cards and hand them to the auctioneer. The winner is the person who has submitted the highest bid; this person wins the item and pays a price equal to her bid.

Optimizing in a Sealed Bid First-Price Auction Let's now return to the auction for the Raiders tickets (again with the values given in Exhibit 17.2). How should Ashley bid in this type of auction? She will not bid more than $250, because she would lose consumer surplus if she were to win with a bid above $250—for example, if she bids $275 and wins, she would realize a $25 loss because the price she pays ($275) is $25 higher than her value for the tickets. So is $250 her optimal bid? That will certainly give her the best chance of winning. But, even if she does win, she'll receive zero consumer surplus because she is paying her maximum willingness to pay. So should she perhaps think about bidding a bit lower? If so, how much lower?

Notice that the trade-off here is exactly the same one Ashley faced in the Dutch auction: a lower bid is less likely to win, but she receives more consumer surplus if she does win. So you may not be surprised to learn that the optimal bidding strategy in a sealed bid first-price auction is the same as that of the Dutch auction.

Therefore, Ashley's optimizing strategy is to submit a bid of $200, or 4/5 of her willingness to pay ($250). The other bidders should use similar strategies when submitting their bids. For example, Eli should submit a bid of $40 ($40 = $50 × 4/5). The equilibrium in the sealed bid first-price auction is for everyone to bid in this manner. Provided everyone does so, no one benefits from changing her bid.

Thus, the seller of the Raiders tickets again receives $200 in revenues, and Ashley receives $50 in consumer surplus.

Sealed Bid: Second-Price Auction

Collectible markets represent one of the most vibrant venues where auctions flourish. Whether antiques, baseball cards, comic books, pins, or Star Wars memorabilia, avid collectors around the globe have hundreds of opportunities daily to bid in auctions to bolster their collections. The market for stamps represents perhaps the oldest and most robust collectors market. Today, at any given time, eBay has thousands of active stamp auctions. But, the number of auctions was not always that large. The hobby of stamp collecting began in earnest in the 1850s. The first 100 stamp auctions took place from 1870 to 1882, most of them in New York City. In the 1890s, such auctions became common, with over 2,000 auctions held worldwide by 1900.

These auctions were typically run using English auction rules. However, many individuals from outside of town wished to bid in the auctions. Accommodations were soon made to such individuals who wished to bid without having to travel to the auction in person. For example, an 1878 stamp auction catalogue reads that "out-of-town collectors may have equal facilities for purchasing with city collectors, bids may be sent to the auctioneers . . . who will . . . represent their bids the same as though they were personally present, and without charge." In those cases where all city bid offerings were lower than the highest mailed-in bid, the highest mail bidder won and paid the *second-highest bid*. The **sealed bid second-price auction** was born!

A **sealed bid second-price auction** is an auction in which bidders privately submit bids at the same time. The highest bidder wins the item and pays an amount equal to the second-highest bid.

Modern sealed bid second-price auctions share many similarities to the 1878 stamp auction. For instance, much like sealed bid first-price auctions, all bidders write down their bids privately and hand them to the auctioneer. The winner is the person who has submitted the highest bid. The major difference between the first- and second-price auctions arises when it comes time to pay for the good. In sealed bid second-price auctions, the highest bidder pays a price equal to the *second*-highest bid. Why this seemingly arbitrary rule?

Optimizing in a Sealed Bid Second-Price Auction To discover the logic behind this type of auction, we consider our optimal bidding strategy in a sealed bid second-price auction for the Raiders tickets. A key consideration is that if you win in this type of auction, you do not pay your bid but rather pay the second-highest bid. This situation is much different from the other three auction formats discussed above, in which you always pay your bid. In particular, the main reason why Ashley did not bid $250 in the first-price auction was because to do so guaranteed her zero consumer surplus.

Should Ashley now bid more than $250 because that will increase her chances of winning? This might make sense because she will only have to pay the second-highest bid. Or maybe she should bid less than $250.

You might be surprised to learn that in this auction, it is a *dominant strategy* to bid exactly your willingness to pay for the item. Let's see why bidding $250 is a dominant strategy for Ashley in this case. We'll do this in two steps: first, we'll see why Ashley should not overbid (that is, why she shouldn't bid more than $250), and then we'll see why she should not bid lower than $250.

Why shouldn't Ashley bid more than $250?

Suppose that, between Billy, Carol, Dalton, and Eli, Billy has the highest bid at $200. Suppose also that Ashley bids $100 more than her value, that is, $350 instead of her true value of $250. In this case, Ashley wins and pays $200 (the second-highest bid). But you will also recognize that in this case, Ashley would have done just as well by bidding her true value of $250: she would have won and once again paid $200. In fact, this will be the case whenever the second-highest bid in the auction is below $250: a $250 bid from Ashley does just as well as a bid above $250.

But next consider the case in which Billy bids $300. Now, bidding $350, Ashley again wins the auction, but she will have to pay the second-highest bid, which is Billy's $300. Uh oh! Ashley now has won the tickets but has to pay $300 for them, which is $50 more than her valuation of $250. Not a good deal. If, instead, she had just bid her true valuation, $250, she would have let Billy win, which is preferable from Ashley's viewpoint given Billy's bid.

This reasoning shows that both Ashley and Billy are better off bidding their valuations, because by overbidding they risk ending up with the tickets at a price that leads to negative consumer surplus.

This is a general result: *any time you bid above your value in a sealed bid second-price auction, you expose yourself to losses at no gain.* There is no gain because if you win when you do not want to win, you will pay too much. Alternatively, if when bidding your value you win the auction, bidding above your true value has no gain.

What about bidding below your value? We turn to this next.

Why shouldn't Ashley bid less than $250?

Let's start by assuming that Ashley bids $100 below her value—a bid of $150 instead of her valuation of $250—but that the highest bid from the others comes from Billy, with a bid of $200. In this case, Billy wins the auction and pays the second-highest bid ($150). Ashley should have won the auction because she has the highest value. In fact, if she had bid her value of $250, she would have won and paid the second-highest bid, $200, and secured a surplus of $50 for herself. So by underbidding, she has just lost out on $50 in surplus. It is clear that bidding below her value hurt her in this case.

What if all the other bids were much lower? For example, suppose that the highest bid from the others is $100. Is Ashley then better off bidding lower than her value in this case? No. Now, Ashley wins and pays the second-highest bid ($100). Note that Ashley would have done just as well by bidding her value of $250: she would have won and paid $100 either way. So in this case, bidding below her value would have had no benefit for Ashley. This, too, is a general result: *any time you bid below your value in a second-price auction, you gain nothing and you risk not getting the good even though it is selling below your valuation.*

These two examples highlight a general economic principle: in a sealed bid second-price auction, a person should bid his value. This is a dominant strategy—you cannot do better by using any other strategy. Since bidding their values is a dominant strategy for all players in the second-price auction, this also means that bidding their values is a Nash equilibrium (and also a dominant strategy equilibrium).

This leads to a somewhat surprising set of insights. In all four auctions the winner is the bidder with the highest valuation. Moreover, all four auctions have the same expected revenue. So, in all of these cases, Ashley wins the tickets and pays $200, and the seller receives $200 in revenues and Ashley receives $50 in consumer surplus.

The Revenue Equivalence Theorem

Exhibit 17.3 summarizes the four major auction formats from the perspectives of bidders and sellers (for the valuations given in Exhibit 17.2). It highlights that in all four

> **The four major auction types will, in expectation, raise the same amount of money for the auctioneer.**

cases, the bidder with the highest value (Ashley) wins, and also, given the valuations in Exhibit 17.2, she pays $200 for the tickets. Though, as already noted, it is not necessarily the case that each auction format will always generate exactly the same revenue, the result is that they will generate the same *expected revenue*. This is in fact the essence of a general result known as the **revenue equivalence theorem**: the four major auction types will, in expectation, raise the same amount of money for the auctioneer.

The **revenue equivalence theorem** states that under certain assumptions the four auction types are expected to raise the same revenues.

William Vickrey, a Nobel Prize-winning economist, was the first to point out that different auction formats yielded identical expected revenue outcomes under certain assumptions.[4] Applying game theory to the study of auctions, Vickrey went even further to develop the following insights, which our discussion so far illustrates:

1. Bidders should view Dutch auctions and sealed bid first-price auctions in the same way: that is, a bidder in the Dutch auction should wait until the price falls to the exact amount she would have bid if she had been participating in a sealed bid first-price auction. This is why our bidding strategy for these two auction types is identical. In this sense, your strategy is the same whether you are bidding in a Dutch or a sealed bid first-price auction.

2. In both the English auction and the sealed bid second-price auction, dominant strategies are at work. For the English auction, it is a dominant strategy to bid up until the price reaches your maximum willingness to pay for the good. As a result, the highest-value bidder wins the auction and pays a price equal to the second-highest bid (which is the second-highest bidder's value). Your strategy as a bidder in a sealed bid second-price auction is similar: you have a dominant strategy to bid your value. If everyone follows his dominant strategy, the highest bidder will pay a price equal to the second-highest bid (which is the second-highest bidder's value).

You might be thinking: this is all well and good in theory, but what actually happens in practice when all of the assumptions of the theory are not guaranteed to hold? We turn to that question next.

Agent	English Auction	Dutch Auction	First-Price Sealed Bid Auction	Second-Price Sealed Bid Auction
Bidder	Bidder with highest value wins (Ashley at $200)	Bidder with highest value wins (Ashley at $200)	Bidder with highest value wins (Ashley at $200)	Bidder with highest value wins (Ashley at $200)
Seller	Seller receives $200	Seller receives $200	Seller receives $200	Seller receives $200

Exhibit 17.3 **Summary of Revenue Determination in the Four Auction Types**

Here, we summarize the results of our four auction types. We also see that all four auctions generate a revenue of $200. Though the exact revenue generated by these auction types could differ, the revenue equivalence theorem guarantees that all four auctions lead to the same expected revenue.

Evidence-Based Economics

Q: How should you bid in an eBay auction?

Empirical tests of auction theory have been conducted primarily through the use of laboratory experiments. These experiments mainly test for the revenue equivalence we described above of the four auction formats—that is, they are conducted to answer the question, "Do all four auction forms yield the same revenue for the auctioneer?" These experiments also test whether individual bidders follow the strategies that we have just discussed.

In a creative study, economist David Reiley ran auctions on the Internet to test whether real-world bidding behavior follows the predictions of auction theory.[5] To do so, Reiley purchased over $2,000 of Magic cards—a collectible card game—and resold them via the four auction formats on the Internet. His basic procedure was to auction two copies of the same card in two different auction formats in order to make direct comparisons of the revenue earned in each one.

For example, he purchased two Chandra (one of the two chief wizards) playing cards, and auctioned one in a Dutch auction and the other in a sealed bid first-price auction. Likewise, he purchased two Jace (the other chief wizard) cards, and auctioned one in an English auction and one in a sealed bid second-price auction. This approach ensured that when he compared revenues and bids across the two auction formats—say, the Dutch auction and the sealed bid first-price auction—his goods were identical, thus permitting a clean test of auction theory.

A first test of consistency with the revenue equivalence theorem is that, for a given playing card (Chandra), the average revenue raised in a Dutch auction (which proxies for expected revenue to which the revenue equivalence theorem applies) should be the same as the average revenue raised in a sealed bid first-price auction. Recall that in our discussion, these two auction types encouraged the same bidding strategy (depending on the number of competing bidders) and led to the same expected revenue. Alternatively, this would mean that the *difference* between the amount of revenue that a Chandra earns in a Dutch auction and the revenue that same card earns in a sealed bid first-price auction should be zero. Reiley tested the above equivalence with matched pairs of identical cards.

In Reiley's experiment, it turns out that on average across all of his auctions, the difference in revenue is greater than zero. He found that he could expect to earn $0.32 more selling the card through a Dutch auction than through a sealed bid first-price auction. Given that the cards sold for roughly $4.50 on average, this difference is noteworthy.

Similarly, Reiley used matched pairs of identical Magic cards to see if revenue from an English auction was equivalent to revenue from a sealed bid second-price auction. Here, he found that there were not significant differences between bidding in an English auction and a sealed bid second-price auction, consistent with the revenue equivalence theorem.

Thus, in the case of these Magic card auction experiments, our bidding theory holds up pretty well in the outcomes for the English and sealed bid second-price auctions, but it is a little off on the comparison between the Dutch and sealed bid first-price auctions. Before advancing a win or loss for auction theory, much more work is necessary. Even as you read this passage, the debate rages on concerning how well auction theory predicts behavior in the field.

Why do you think the Dutch auction raises more money than the sealed bid first-price auction? Maybe you can think of clever ways to test auction theory using Internet auctions?

Question

How should you bid in an eBay auction? Do bidders behave this way?

Answer

Our theory detailed above provides insights on how to bid; the evidence is mixed on whether bidders behave this way.

Data

Field experiment on eBay using Magic trading cards.

Caveat

The field is evolving, with both experimental data and naturally occurring data lending insights into how well auction theory explains real behavior.

17.2 Bargaining

So far in this chapter, we have focused on markets where buyers compete with one another to buy a good. Sellers are passive in the sense that once they choose the auction format, they sit back and watch people fight it out. A different form of exchange is bilateral bargaining (or bilateral negotiation, as we discussed in Chapter 7). Bilateral bargaining is a form of exchange that has one seller actively negotiating with one buyer over the terms of trade. If you have ever used the "best offer" option on eBay, you are experienced at bilateral bargaining. Or if you have visited a flea market, you know something about bilateral bargaining—the exhilaration of a bustling marketplace where merchants offer their goods and services to shoppers looking for the thrill of the "deal." If you are a skilled bargainer, you know this thrill very well—the feeling of haggling and winding up with a great price.

Bilateral bargaining has constituted the foundation of markets for centuries—from Athen's Agora to Rome's Forum to the medieval fairs and markets in England to the 1,000-year-old *souk* in Morocco. Today, there are substantial bazaars and flea markets that litter the landscape of developed and developing countries alike. Although it is difficult to provide an economic estimate of the importance of such markets, the National Flea Market Association reports that the number of flea markets in the United States and the recorded gross sales have grown substantially over the past several years, with more than 2 million licensed vendors and more than $30 billion in sales annually. This is surely a vast underestimate, however, because a nontrivial portion of the transactions are carried out by nonlicensed vendors via nontaxed sales. More broadly, such markets are of great importance, especially in developing countries where the institution represents an integral part of the allocation of goods and services in the formal market.

What Determines Bargaining Outcomes?

You might wonder in bargaining situations who has the upper hand—why, for example, do some sellers always seem to get great prices, while in other cases, buyers seem to get the better deals.

Bargaining power describes the relative power an individual has in negotiations with another individual.

As you might have guessed, much of it comes down to the benefits and costs inherent in the potential exchange. In bargaining terms, the most important element that determines final outcomes is called **bargaining power**. Two principles—the cost of failing to come to an agreement and the influence of one partner on the other—are generally used to describe the bargaining power of each partner engaged in bargaining. For instance, if your influence over the other agent increases, then your bargaining power increases. But, if your cost of not coming to an agreement increases, then your bargaining power goes down.

Let's put this intuition to work with an example. Say that for months you have been desperately trying to find a part-time job. The local economy continues to sputter, so no one near campus is hiring. But, suddenly a job is posted that fits your desires perfectly. The firm—Caribou Coffee—advertises that it needs just one person. But when you arrive to apply, you find yourself in a line of 500 people who are also interested in the position.

After the initial screening, you find yourself in a final pool of ten applicants. Management interviews you again and finds you to be an attractive candidate, but you know that chances are the other nine are equally qualified. Near the end of the interview, they ask you what wage would be needed for you to accept the job. How should you respond?

You should begin by asking yourself who has the bargaining power in this situation. First, you realize that you have little influence over Caribou Coffee—it can hire any of the other nine applicants, who seemingly are equally qualified and are thus perfect substitutes for you. Second, the cost to you of not coming to an agreement is quite high—you have been trying to find a job for months, and finally the perfect fit is here. But Caribou has a very low cost of not coming to an agreement with you because there are several applicants seeking this job.

You have now decided that you have little bargaining power in this case. This means that Caribou Coffee can offer the minimum wage and little in the way of employee benefits should it be so inclined. So, because it seems that you are at Caribou's mercy, you conclude that you should let them know that your compensation demands are minimal.

What could change in this example that would give you more bargaining power? Let's assume that a new Walmart locates in your town, bringing hundreds of jobs to the local community. Now bargaining power has changed since your outside options have improved. Thanks to the presence of a new potential employer, you are less inclined to settle for a low wage package from Caribou, and when asked what wage you will need, you are thus likely to be bolder because it is no longer as costly for you to fail to come to an agreement with Caribou: there's a real possibility that you can obtain a similar job at Walmart. You also have more influence over Caribou because now the number of other workers competing for that job decreases because Walmart will employ many people in the local community.

> **Bargaining power relates to "who holds the chips." The person who has . . . a lower cost of not coming to an agreement and . . . a greater influence over the other person . . . holds the chips.**

As you can see, bargaining power relates to "who holds the chips" or who has the power in the negotiations. The person who has, first, a lower cost of not coming to an agreement and, second, a greater influence over the other person, has the bargaining power and "holds the chips." In turn, bargaining power helps to determine whether, and at what terms, the parties transact.

Bargaining in Action: The Ultimatum Game

How can we go about testing whether economic models can predict what will happen in bargaining situations? If a person with no bargaining power meets a person with much greater bargaining power, will the result be as predicted: the person with no bargaining power gets nothing? One way to test this conjecture is to use a laboratory experiment.

As a college student, you may already have been recruited by a mass e-mail from your school's economics or psychology department, asking you to participate in a laboratory experiment. It might have even been for the game that we now examine—the Ultimatum Game.

Exhibit 17.4 The Ultimatum Game

The game begins with the Proposer's decision. The Proposer can offer any amount from $0 to $10, which we represent as a smooth curve between $0 and $10 in the exhibit. Once the Proposer makes a decision ($x in the exhibit), that decision is conveyed to the Responder as the Proposer's offer. Now, the Responder decides whether to accept the offer (pocketing $x and leaving the Proposer with $10 − x) or to reject the offer (leaving both players with $0).

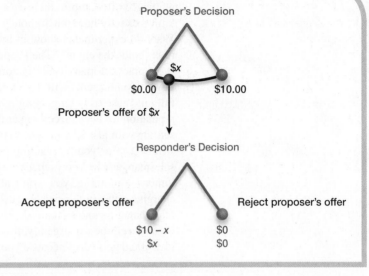

In this game, half of the subjects (Proposers) are given some amount of money—say, $10—and they are paired with a person (Responder) who receives nothing. The game consists of two decisions, one to be made by those playing the role of Proposers and the other by those playing the role of Responders. Each proposer chooses how much of their $10 to offer the Responder. Each Responder then decides whether to accept or reject the offer. An acceptance leads to the proposed allocation taking place, and a rejection leads to both players walking away with zero. Exhibit 17.4 displays the game.

If you were a Proposer, how much would you choose to offer?

We can make use of game theory to find an answer. As explained in Chapter 13, this is an extensive-form game and you can use backward induction to determine how you should play. That is, you can work backwards from the Responder's optimal actions to find out how you should play.

So let's start at the last nodes of the game tree in Exhibit 17.4 and consider the second mover, the Responder. Suppose she receives an offer of 10 cents. If she says no, she'll get 0 and if she says yes she'll receive the 10 cents. Assuming that she prefers more money to less, it will be in her best interest to accept the offer. You'll see that this reasoning applies to any positive offer, so any amount the Proposer chooses to offer, the Responder is likely to accept. By backward induction, you understand that the Responder will accept any positive offer and arrive at the conclusion that your optimal offer is the lowest possible amount— say, one penny. Thus the equilibrium in the Ultimatum Game takes a simple form: the Proposer offers the lowest amount possible to the Responder, and the Responder accepts that offer. As we discussed in Chapter 13, this game has therefore a first-mover advantage.

This equilibrium might strike you as a bad deal for the Responder. As the Responder, you have no bargaining power; the Proposer has all of the chips. But the arrangement still doesn't seem quite right to you—if it only costs you a penny to reject the offer of the Proposer, why not reject it because the proposed split is not fair?

In fact, experimental evidence suggests that such low offers are often rejected. Indeed, Proposers seem to sense that their low offers won't fly, so they rarely offer the paltry figure of just one penny. Instead, their optimal offer is determined by how much they fear a rejection (and ultimately winding up with nothing).

So is this outcome a rejection of the bargaining model? No. It just tells us that something else beyond money—such as fairness—is also important to people. We return to a discussion of fairness and other social preferences in Chapter 18.

More important to the bargaining model are two observations from the vast experimental data. First, Proposers, who have more bargaining power than Responders in the Ultimatum Game, because they hold a first-mover advantage, usually end up with more than half ($5) of the $10 when bargains are struck (when Responders accept their offer). In games executed all over the world, Proposers in general end up with $6 or so, providing evidence that the person with the greater bargaining power does walk away with more of the spoils.

Second, information can importantly determine which player "holds the chips" in bargaining. For example, there is a variant of the Ultimatum Game in which the Proposer knows exactly how much money there is to split, and the Responder does not know this. What do experiments show in these cases where the Proposer has more information and thus "holds the chips"? The Proposer's gains are much closer to the entire $10.

In practice, many other factors other than being the first mover determine bargaining power. Some agents will have a reputation for being a tough bargainer, and this will naturally increase their bargaining power. For example, if you know that the Responder has a reputation for never accepting anything less than $8, you may just give up and offer her $8, settling with just $2 yourself. In other situations, how badly you need the good in question will determine your bargaining power. For instance, if you are bargaining with a used-car salesman, and he knows that you need the car immediately for a cross-country trip starting tomorrow morning, you won't have much bargaining power. He can then get away with charging you a high price because he knows that your demand is price-inelastic. If, on the other hand, he knows that you have already searched and found other good deals and you do not need the car urgently, this will increase your bargaining power and induce him to give you a good deal because you are price-elastic.

Bargaining and the Coase Theorem

Another interesting application of bargaining ties us back to lessons from a previous chapter. You may recall the Coase Theorem from Chapter 9. This theorem states that with certain assumptions in place, two agents can always bargain to reach the efficient outcome.

Where might this theorem apply? In addition to the situations we considered in Chapter 9 (which arose to solve the problem of externalities), the Coase Theorem has particular relevance in the field of law. Divorce law is one such area.

In some countries and U.S. states such as Mississippi and Tenessee, divorce is illegal without the consent of both partners in a marriage (unless there are grounds for "fault divorces"); in others, such as California and Virginia, people have the right to get a divorce whether their partner likes it or not. We'll term the first case "need two to divorce" and the second case "need only one to divorce." Now consider the question: within a state, should a change from "need two to divorce" to "need one to divorce"—in effect, making getting a divorce easier—increase divorce rates?

The Coase Theorem implies that the answer should be no. To see why, imagine a marriage in which one partner (Adam) wants a divorce and the other (Barb) does not. Of course, happiness in marriage cannot just be measured in money. But we can attach a monetary value to the strength of Adam and Barb's feelings, and the happiness they will get from marriage, by considering how much they would sacrifice in order to obtain a divorce (Adam's case) and avoid a divorce (Barb's case). Suppose this is $5,000 for Adam and $10,000 for Barb.

Let's first consider the case where Adam and Barb reside in a state with the less stringent "need one to divorce" laws. Here, only one person is required to initiate the divorce, and hence the one partner wanting the divorce (Adam) is legally decisive and holds the marriage rights.

Therefore, the distribution of bargaining power under these laws favors Adam. But, recall that Barb values the marriage more than Adam values the divorce. So according to the Coase Theorem, we should expect that Barb will pay Adam to prevent a divorce from taking place. More specifically, Barb will prevent Adam from initiating a divorce by paying some amount between $5,000 (Adam's value of getting a divorce) and $10,000 (Barb's maximum value for staying married). Of course, in reality, this payment may not take the form of actual money changing hands. It may be that Adam does fewer household chores or dictates how the money the couple has in the bank is spent. The important thing is that the marriage can be saved by certain transfers from Barb to Adam. And notably, with such a deal, both Adam and Barb are better off—Adam receives a transfer that is above the $5,000 value of divorce, and Barb keeps the marriage alive for less than $10,000.

What about in a "need two to divorce" state? The answer is no divorce once again. In this case, Barb is legally decisive and holds the marriage rights and thus has more bargaining power. As it stands, Adam's

Economics extends everywhere, even to divorce.

Exhibit 17.5 The Coase Theorem in Action

Provided the assumptions of the Coase Theorem hold and Barb values marriage more than Adam values divorce, no divorce will take place under either set of divorce laws.

Case	Outcome
Divorce requires consent of both partners	The partner who values divorce at $5,000 (Adam) is not willing to pay the partner who values marriage at $10,000 (Barb) enough to buy divorce. Result: No divorce.
Divorce requires consent of one partner	The partner who values marriage at $10,000 (Barb) pays the partner who does not (Adam) an amount above $5,000 and below $10,000. Result: No divorce.

value from divorce is low relative to Barb's value from marriage. To arrange a divorce, Adam would need to compensate Barb (to get Barb to agree) with more than $10,000 (for example, offering alimony). Given that Adam only values the divorce at $5,000, the divorce will never take place in this case either. Thus, we see that no matter whose side the law falls on, the decision to get a divorce does not change. Importantly, note that while the identity of the legally decisive partner changes depending on the law, it is always the economically advantaged partner—meaning the partner who values marriage or divorce more—that determines the final outcome, giving a deeper insight behind what it means, in bargaining, to "hold the chips." Note also that at no point did it matter how much larger Barb's value is than Adam's—this example works just the same if we replace $10,000 with $5,001.

But there is an important implication of the divorce laws: because they determine the distribution of bargaining power, they have an impact on how the gains from the efficient outcome are divided. In one case Adam receives transfers from Barb to keep the marriage alive, in the other case he doesn't. So the Coase Theorem in general implies that whether a particular relationship remains active and agreement is reached doesn't depend on who has the rights to make the decision in the first place, but the distribution of the gains from this relationship depends very much on the initial allocation of rights.

Exhibit 17.5 summarizes our discussion and shows that an efficient outcome arises no matter how lawyers and judges decide to construct divorce rights.

Try the opposite case for yourself, imagining that the happy partner values the marriage only at $5,000, while the unhappy partner values divorce at $10,000. You will again find that the divorce rate is identical—in this case, they will get divorced under both laws! Do you think that the data conform to these predictions?

Evidence-Based Economics

Q: Who determines how the household spends its money?

Do you ever wonder how your life will unfold after college? Perhaps you will find a high-paying job, marry, and have three kids. Maybe, instead, you will have three kids with a spouse who has a high-paying job. Perhaps these two cases seem identical—you might be saying to yourself, "Who cares about who makes the money, as long as we have it?" Such thinking implicitly assumes what economists call a **unitary model**: a dollar in the pocket of one spouse is the same as a dollar in the pocket of the other. In consumption terms, this means that the family maximizes its happiness under a budget constraint that pools all of its income, wealth, and time.

Is this model a correct depiction of reality? For example, in a unitary model, if the husband in a household won $500 playing the lottery, the household would buy all of the same goods and services as it would if the wife had instead won the lottery.

A **unitary model** of the household assumes that a family maximizes their happiness under a budget constraint that pools all of their income, wealth, and time.

If we instead think of the household decisions as determined by a bargaining game, how will things change? Recall the two important features underlying bargaining power—the cost of failing to come to an agreement and the influence of one partner on another. In terms of the first feature, a low-income husband may have a great deal to lose if his high-income wife decides to divorce him—an outcome that may occur if the couple fails to agree on how to spend their earnings. However, if the husband receives an unexpected windfall of income, he may suddenly find his bargaining power increase significantly. Consequently, we would expect that after the windfall gain of the husband, spending in this household would be more aligned with the husband's preferences.

Economists have studied the bargaining power hypothesis by examining data from a unique natural experiment in the United Kingdom (UK).[6] In the late 1970s, the UK changed the form of its universal child benefit program. Before the change, men in the household received the child benefit dollars. After the change, receipt of the benefit income shifted from fathers to mothers in two-parent families.

What do you think they found happened after the change? The authors compared household spending before and after the tax law change and found that after the change there was a dramatic shift toward increased expenditures on women's and children's clothing relative to men's clothing. These expenditure items are commonly known to be driven by women's preferences. So when bargaining power shifted, so did the consumption patterns of the household.

A related study finds similar but much more consequential patterns. Economist Nancy Qian studied how mortality and education patterns changed when prices for tea and orchards changed in China.[7] The changes in the rigid central planning institutions that started being reformed after the death of Chairman Mao brought a significant increase in the price of tea, which is generally produced by women in China. These changes also altered the price of orchard products, which generally rely on male labor. These changes provided Qian with information that she could use to test the role of bargaining power.

Interestingly, depending on which commodity had a significant price change in the local area, children in the households under study had quite different outcomes. For example, Qian found that an increase in the value of tea improved female survival rates—meaning that female children were much more likely to live longer after the price of tea increased. Moreover, price increases in tea influenced educational attainment of both boys and girls by about 0.2 years (in many countries women value their kid's education more highly than men value their kids' education). Alternatively, increasing male income (through increases in the value of orchard products) by the same amount actually *decreased* educational attainment of girls and had no effect on the educational attainment of boys. The likely explanation is that women care much more about the health and education of their children than their husbands do, and when they earn more, they are able to spend more to improve these outcomes.

Both of these studies provide empirical evidence of the power of the bargaining model. The lesson here is that you should always be aware of bargaining power, even in situations where you least expect it to matter—as in the household buying decision!

Question	**Answer**	**Data**	**Caveat**
Who determines how the household spends its money?	The person who has the greatest bargaining power; one important determinant of bargaining power is who earns the most money.	Natural experiments in England and China that make use of changes in the relative income of husbands and wives.	Other factors are important, and the relative weighting of each is an open empirical question.

Sex Ratios Change Bargaining Power Too

Above we discussed how female bargaining power can arise from additional income and favorable price changes. Another potential channel for increasing female bargaining power is the sex ratio—the ratio of men to women in a population. The intuition is that as the sex ratio rises, women become relatively more scarce and therefore will have greater bargaining power.

In order to establish this relationship empirically, John List and two colleagues surveyed households in China with high and low shares of ethnic minorities.[8]

Sex ratios vary across ethnicities in China because the one-child policy, which restricted families to a single child, did not apply as strictly to China's ethnic minorities. The one-child policy, when it applies, creates a more distorted sex ratio. For this reason, holding all else equal, it is likely that the sex ratio in areas with low shares of ethnic minorities is higher than areas with high shares of ethnic minorities.

Upon identifying these areas, List and colleagues randomly surveyed households with a three-part survey. First,

all members were asked to record their subjective opinion of their importance in the household. The second component asked about who handles household finances (an objective measure of bargaining power). Lastly, they had each person participate in an experiment wherein they split money between the household and a charity in China. For this last component, each person received 100 yuan to make a decision (in private). Then, the exercise was repeated, but as a collective decision of the household.

Their results suggest that in areas where sex ratios are higher, female bargaining power is stronger in that women report more decision-making power, are more likely to handle household finances, and are more likely to have the collective allocation choice match their private choice. This evidence complements the data from the labor markets we have discussed and shows the importance of using economics to understand what happens in the household.

Summary

✹ In many cases the interaction of buyers and sellers has a role in determining the price of the item being traded. For this reason, studying auctions and bilateral bargaining expands our understanding of how resources are allocated.

✹ There are four common auctions: English, Dutch, and sealed bid first- and second-price auctions. Though these auctions work very differently and optimizing behaviors vary considerably across them, under certain assumptions the outcomes they yield have some remarkable similarities. In particular, with all of these auction formats, the buyer with the highest valuation wins the item being auctioned, and the expected revenue of the seller is the same.

✹ Bargaining power of an individual—who "holds the chips" in bargaining—is critical in determining whether, and at what price, the trade will take place.

✹ In situations where the Coase Theorem applies, the distribution of bargaining power will not affect whether the efficient outcome is reached, but will determine how the gains from this outcome are divided.

Key Terms

auction *p. 385*
open outcry auction *p. 387*
sealed bid auction *p. 387*
English auction *p. 387*

Dutch auction *p. 389*
sealed bid first-price auction *p. 391*
sealed bid second-price auction *p. 391*
revenue equivalence theorem *p. 393*

bargaining power *p. 396*
unitary model *p. 399*

Questions

All questions are available in MyEconLab *for practice and instructor assignment.*

1. How do auctions help in price discovery?

2. What is the difference between an open outcry auction and a sealed bid auction?

3. What is an English auction?

4. What is the dominant strategy for a bidder in an English auction?

5. What is meant by sniping in an auction? Does it make sense to snipe to win an auction?

6. What is a Dutch auction?

7. What is meant by risk neutrality?

8. Suppose a bet is placed on the outcome of the flip of a coin—if the coin comes up heads, you get $25 and if it turns up tails, you lose $25. If you accepted this bet, does it imply that you are risk averse, risk neutral, or risk loving?

9. What are the similarities between an English auction and a Dutch auction?

10. What does the revenue equivalence theorem state?

11. What is meant by bargaining power? What are the two factors that determine an individual's bargaining power?

12. How does the Ultimatum Game work? What does experimental evidence show about the outcome of the Ultimatum Game?

13. Explain why in situations where the Coase Theorem applies, bargaining power does not influence whether the efficient outcome is reached, but affects the distribution of gains.

Problems

All problems are available in MyEconLab *for practice and instructor assignment.*

1. An escalation clause in a real estate contract specifies what a prospective buyer will offer for a home if the seller receives multiple offers. An escalation clause typically includes three elements:

   • The buyer's initial offer

   • How much that offer will rise above any other competitive bid

   • The maximum amount the buyer will offer in case of multiple offers

   So, for example, an escalation clause might state that a buyer is offering $200,000 for a home and that the buyer will bid $1,000 more than other offers up to a maximum of $250,000.

   Suppose you are willing to pay up to $300,000 for a house that is for sale. You decide to include an escalation clause in the contract. What is the maximum amount you should specify in the contract that you will pay if the seller receives multiple offers?

2. The following table shows five bidders' willingness to pay for a piece of art that is being auctioned by an auction house.

Bidder	Willingness to Pay
John	$10,000
James	$20,000
Tim	$30,000
Ryan	$35,000
Alex	$40,000

   a. Assuming that this is an English auction, what is each player's optimal bidding strategy?

   b. Assume that this is a descending Dutch auction and all bidders are risk neutral. The bidding starts at $50,000 and it falls by $1 every minute. Each bidder knows his or her own valuation but does not know the other valuations. What is each player's optimal bidding strategy?

3. The original Filene's Basement in Boston had a unique pricing system. Every article in the store was marked with a tag showing the price and the date the article was first put on sale. Twelve days later, if it had not been sold, the price was reduced by 25 percent. Six selling days later, it was cut by 50 percent, and after an additional six days, it was offered at 75 percent off the original price. After six more days, it was given to charity if it had not been sold.

   a. Was the Filene plan similar to any of the auctions we studied in this chapter?

   b. Suppose you are interested in a coat you have seen in a store that uses the same pricing system as Filene's Basement. ("The Basement" closed its doors in 2011.) The initial price is $200. You are willing to pay as much as $150. Could it be optimal to buy the coat when the price is reduced to $150? Could it be optimal to wait six days and try to buy the coat when the price is reduced to $100? Could it be optimal to wait 12 days and try to buy the coat when the price is reduced to $50?

4. A town wants to build a new bridge. Construction firms will submit sealed bids. The town will award the contract to the firm that submits the lowest bid and will pay the firm the amount of the second lowest bid, that is, the town will conduct a second-price procurement auction. So, for example, if Firm A bids $8 million, Firm B bids $9 million, and Firm C bids $10 million, then the city will award the contract to Firm A (it submitted the lowest bid) and pay Firm A $9 million (the amount of the second-lowest bid). Suppose your firm is willing to build the bridge for a minimum of $9 million.

   a. Show that bidding $9 million is a better strategy than bidding some amount below $9 million—say, $7 million.

   b. Show that bidding $9 million is a better strategy than bidding some amount above $9 million—say, $11 million.

5. U.S. Treasury notes are sold at a discount. A buyer, for example, might offer $950 for a $1,000 note that will become due in two years because (as Chapter 15 explains) money received in the future is not as valuable as money received now. In September 1992, the U.S. Treasury began selling two-year and five-year Treasury notes using a uniform-price auction, in which all winning bidders pay the same price. Before September 1992, the Treasury used a discriminatory-price

auction to sell securities. The following simple example illustrates the difference between the two types of auctions. Bidders A and B each submit a sealed bid for two-year Treasury notes of $1,000. Bidder A bids $950; Bidder B bids $925. Suppose the Treasury accepts both bids. In a uniform-price auction A and B both pay $925; in a discriminatory-price auction A would pay $950 and B would pay $925. Suppose you are willing to pay up to $950 for two-year Treasury bills.

a. Show that a uniform-price auction is similar to a second price sealed bid auction.

b. Should you bid $950 if the Treasury is using a discriminatory-price auction?

c. Should you bid $950 if the Treasury is using a uniform-price auction?

6. Consider the auction for a dollar where there are two bidders. Each bidder can bid 5 cents or multiples of 5 cents each time. The dollar will go to the bidder with the highest bid, but the second-highest bidder will also have to pay his bid to the auctioneer. The auction ends when neither player wants to make a higher bid or the bidding reaches $2, whichever occurs first. Explain how one of the bidders could pay more than one dollar for a one-dollar bid. Can you find the Nash equilibrium in this game?

7. The owners' and the players' union are negotiating over a contract for the upcoming hockey season. In October, the owners will make an offer to the union. If they reach an agreement, they will share $50 of revenues. So, for example, if the owners offer the players $10 in October and the players accept, then the players receive $10 and the owners keep the remaining $40. If the players reject the offer, then they go on strike and negotiations resume in November. In November, the players will make an offer to the owners. If they reach an agreement, they will share just $20 of revenues (revenues have fallen because of the strike). So, for example, if the players offer the owners $10 in November and the owners accept, then the owners receive $10 and the players keep the remaining $10. If the owners reject the November offer, then the strike continues for the rest of the season and the players and the owners both receive zero.

a. What would you expect to happen in November if there is a strike in October? (Hint: think about the ultimatum game.)

b. Use backwards induction to find what would happen in October. For simplicity, assume that if someone is indifferent between accepting or rejecting an offer, they will accept the offer.

8. Suppose Mom gives her 10-year-old son $100 on Christmas. She asks him to share this amount with his younger sister. He can offer her any amount between $0 and $100, but if she refuses to accept what he has offered, both of them will get nothing.

a. What is this type of game called?

b. What set of strategies will lead to a Nash equilibrium in this game?

9. The Johnson Steel Company generates water pollution when it makes steel. It could eliminate this pollution at a cost of $700. The Smith family lives downstream. It suffers $1,000 of damages from the water pollution Johnson creates. Assume that transactions costs are zero.

a. Suppose first that the law says Johnson has the right to pollute. Show that if Johnson and the Smith family negotiate, Johnson will eliminate the pollution.

b. Now suppose the law is changed so that the Smith family has the right to enjoy clean water. Show that Johnson will eliminate the pollution even if Johnson and the Smith family can negotiate. Is the Smith family better off now than in part (a)?

10. Ronald Coase used the example of a farmer and railroad tracks to explain bargaining. Sparks from trains running on tracks near farmland would set off fires in the fields. To avoid this, railroad companies would either have to stop running trains on tracks along fields or incur a cost in fixing a spark arrester along these tracks. Farmers could avoid the cost of fires by leaving land near railroads empty. Suppose that the cost of preventing a fire was equal to $20,000 for a railroad company and not having a fire in the field was worth $10,000 for a farmer. Consider the case where the law stipulated that railroads could not throw sparks along fields. What would be the outcome?

11. Space heaters are dangerous. The U.S. Consumer Product Safety Commission estimates that more than 25,000 residential fires every year are associated with the use of space heaters, resulting in more than 300 deaths. This question asks you to think about the Coase Theorem and the assignment of liability from these accidents. Suppose a company could produce a space heater that is perfectly safe for $225 or a standard space heater for $200. Suppose further that a consumer who buys a space heater will receive $275 of benefits. If he buys a traditional space heater, he will incur (on average) $60 of damages but he will not incur damages if he purchases a safe model.

a. Show that efficiency requires the firm to produce safe space heaters.

b. Suppose the law says that firms are not liable for the damages associated with space heater accidents. Show that the firm will sell only safe space heaters.

c. Now suppose Congress passes a law that says firms are liable for the damages from space heaters, and so on average a firm that sells a standard space heater will have to pay $60 in damages. Show that the firm will produce safe space heaters.

12. This chapter illustrates how the Coase Theorem can be applied to explain the outcome of a divorce in two different systems. In both cases, where the unhappy partner values the divorce at $5,000 and the happy partner values the marriage at $10,000, the equilibrium is "no divorce." Now assume that the situation is reversed: the happy partner, who does not want a divorce, places a lower value on the marriage ($5,000); the unhappy partner, who wants a divorce, values the divorce at a higher value ($10,000). Applying the same concept, analyze the outcome of the marriage under two scenarios: "right not to divorce" and "right to divorce."

Do people care about fairness?

If you have made it this far in the book, you might be feeling a bit uneasy. You might have come to the grave conclusion that the mythical *homo economicus*—the economic man serving as the backbone of the discipline of economics—is essentially a species with which you are unfamiliar. He is self-absorbed in the pursuit of material wealth and unswerving in his drive to satisfy his own needs before the needs of others. As an employer, he hires at the lowest wage possible; as a seller, he charges whatever the market will bear; and as a producer, he pursues profits even at the cost of imposing negative externalities (for example, pollution) on other citizens.

In spite of its obvious simplicities, this economic paradigm has served us well in providing a coherent framework through which to model human behavior. But in the past few decades, some economists have considered an alternative—an economic agent who does not always make decisions solely to promote his own wealth. In fact, this more "human" economic agent cares about others and the fairness of his actions.

As we have stressed throughout this book, economics does not tell us what people *should* value. Rather, it provides us with tools to help us understand how they should behave once we know what they value. In this chapter, we focus on a variant of *homo economicus* who acts more selflessly and who is influenced

CHAPTER **OUTLINE**

- Many people have preferences that go beyond material wealth.

- Charity, fairness, trust, revenge, and conforming to those around us represent a few examples.

- Economic tools can be used to understand when such factors will play an important role.

- Economists have found that such behaviors are important when their opportunity cost is low.

Some economists have considered . . . an economic agent who does not always make decisions solely to promote his own wealth. This more "human" economic agent cares about others and the fairness of his actions.

by his surroundings. In doing so, we will discuss the economics of charity, fairness, trust, and revenge. This will allow us to answer the chapter-opening question on whether people care about fairness. We also consider the importance of peers in shaping the decisions that we make daily. We will find that peer effects are all around us: affecting our waistlines, our finances, and how hard we work at our jobs. In all of these cases economic tools provide us with a deeper understanding of when we should expect such considerations to have importance—the key is the opportunity cost of such actions.

18.1 The Economics of Charity and Fairness

In Chapter 5 we learned about three necessary ingredients to the buyer's problem:

1. What you want.
2. Prices.
3. How much money you have to spend.

Together, these elements provide the foundations for demand curves. Even though we have exclusively focused on tangible goods in our discussions thus far—sweaters, jeans, DVDs, iPads, and the like—the economic model is flexible enough to describe your demand for intangibles such as charity and fairness. Just like your preferences, budget constraint and market price determine whether you purchase an iPad; they also determine your charitable contributions and how much "fairness" you demand in resource allocations. We turn now to a consideration of each.

The Economics of Charity

As a child, you were most likely taught to help those in need. If your brother falls down, help him up. If a friend is in trouble, lend her a hand. If a stranger needs directions, do the best you can to help. As an adult, you are now better able to help others. For example, you can serve soup at the local food pantry or you can donate money to help save the rain forests. As we discussed in Chapter 9, such activities have become very important in modern economies.

Exhibit 18.1 provides a summary of self-reported volunteerism around the globe. What we observe overall is a tremendous amount of volunteering in these thirty-six sampled

Volunteers contribute their time to charities such as the Salvation Army, while others contribute by giving money to charitable causes.

countries. For example, over 50 percent of the Norwegian adult population volunteers some time to at least one charitable cause annually. Citizens in many other countries give their time, too: in the United Kingdom, 30 percent of people give their time. In Sweden, Uganda, and the United States, more than 1 in 5 people volunteer their time to charitable causes every year. Beyond helping others, one motivation for volunteerism is because it makes us feel good (think of that warm, fuzzy feeling you get when helping those in need). Thus, even though the opportunity cost of our time might be quite high, we give our time to help others.

Another important way in which people help charitable causes is to give money. As we have already learned in Chapter 9, although governments are major providers of public goods, they are not the sole providers. Indeed, many public goods are routinely supplied through other channels. For example, through private donations, National Public Radio can be aired all around the United States. Rain forests by the dozens can be saved as a result of private cash donations to the World Wildlife Fund. And cures for ailments ranging from carpal tunnel syndrome to heart disease have resulted in part from charitable gifts.

So what is the scope of private donations of money? As we learned in Chapter 9, individual contributions to charitable causes have increased to more than 2 percent of U.S.

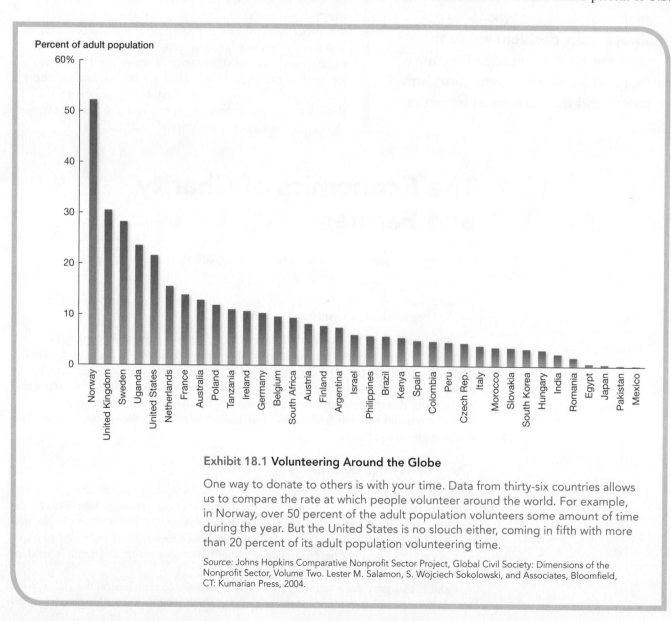

Exhibit 18.1 Volunteering Around the Globe

One way to donate to others is with your time. Data from thirty-six countries allows us to compare the rate at which people volunteer around the world. For example, in Norway, over 50 percent of the adult population volunteers some amount of time during the year. But the United States is no slouch either, coming in fifth with more than 20 percent of its adult population volunteering time.

Source: Johns Hopkins Comparative Nonprofit Sector Project, Global Civil Society: Dimensions of the Nonprofit Sector, Volume Two. Lester M. Salamon, S. Wojciech Sokolowski, and Associates, Bloomfield, CT: Kumarian Press, 2004.

406   **Chapter 18** | Social Economics

Exhibit 18.2 U.S. Household Giving in 2011 by Recipient Status

As is typical in the United States, in 2011 the majority of charitable contributions were to religious causes. Education and environmental causes are also a high priority for U.S. donors.

Source: Giving USA 2012.

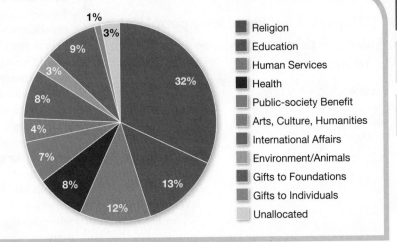

- Religion
- Education
- Human Services
- Health
- Public-society Benefit
- Arts, Culture, Humanities
- International Affairs
- Environment/Animals
- Gifts to Foundations
- Gifts to Individuals
- Unallocated

GDP. To put this number into perspective, consider that Greece's most recent GDP—the value of all of the goods and services produced by the Greek economy—is less than this amount, about $286 billion!

You might wonder where all of this money goes. Exhibit 18.2 provides a glimpse from 2011, which represents a typical year. The majority of contributions—32 percent—by U.S. households went to religious causes. But most people who contribute do so to more than one cause. These remaining gifts are commonly directed to educational purposes, healthcare/medical research, the poor, and combined purposes, as can be seen in Exhibit 18.2. Every so often, major events happen that lead to an outpouring of gifts above and beyond the typical flows documented in Exhibit 18.2. For example, when Hurricane Katrina struck the United States in 2005, monetary donations broke records that were previously set by the 9/11 relief efforts.

 LETTING THE DATA SPEAK

Do People Donate Less When It's Costlier to Give?

The act of giving, just like apples and shoes, can be viewed as an economic good. And similar to other economic goods, as economists, we like to ask the question: if the price increases, does the quantity demanded decrease? And, if so, by how much? This gives us a price elasticity of demand (as we discussed in Chapter 5).

But how do you increase the price of charitable giving?

One way is by reducing its current tax-advantaged status. In the United States, individuals as well as corporations pay taxes on their incomes. However, any of this income that is donated to charities is tax-deductible. For example, imagine that you face a tax rate of 30 percent. Now let's say that you decide to send your favorite charity $100. How much does it really cost? Since you can account for charitable contributions when you pay taxes, your gift of $100 is equal to $70 in after-tax income (that is, if you decided not to give the $100 to charity you would have pocketed $70: $100 (earnings) − $30 (taxes)).

Now let's assume that your tax rate drops to 15 percent; what do you think happens?

Note that the opportunity cost of that charitable gift has changed: your gift of $100 is now equivalent to $85 in after-tax income (that is, if you decided not to give the $100 to charity you would have pocketed $85: $100 (earnings) − $15 (taxes)). So, the price of giving the $100 has just increased from $70 to $85. How do you think such a change affects individuals?

Economist Charles Clotfelter asked this very question in his analysis of the effect of the Tax Reform Act of 1986 on the amount of charitable contributions from U.S. taxpayers.[1] The Tax Act of 1986 reduced the highest tax rate faced by individuals in the United States, producing the very situation that we describe above for the highest earners.

And the result?

Clotfelter found that one group was quite sensitive to this tax change: individuals in the highest income brackets reduced their contributions to charity considerably. In essence, they responded as our model of an optimizer predicts they should: as the price of charity increases, quantity demanded (amount given to charity) decreases.

18.1

18.2

18.3

Only after we know why people give can we provide the proper incentives to promote giving.

Pure altruism is a motivation solely to help others.

Impure altruism is a motivation solely to help oneself feel good.

Why Do People Give to Charity?　An active area of research has developed within economics to explore possible answers to the question: why do people give to charity? Only after we know why people give can we provide the proper incentives to promote giving, should we wish to do so. Economists view the reasons for giving as falling into two broad categories: to help others and to help oneself.

We will denote the first category as **pure altruism**, which is a motivation solely to help others. This is not unlike the conventional notion of altruism, which typically entails a concern for the well-being of others. It is "pure" in the sense that when people give time or money to a charity, they do so solely to help someone or some cause. For example, if you or your parents gave money or time to Hurricane Sandy victims, it might have been because you were simply trying to help people in need. Likewise, if you march for cancer awareness, it might be because you want to help others who could be stricken with the disease.

An alternative reason why people might give to charity is to help *themselves* in an indirect way. Because this type of giving is considered to be driven by a selfish motive, economists refer to it as **impure altruism**. Impure altruism is a motivation based solely to make oneself feel good and means that we give not necessarily to help another person ("out of the goodness of our hearts"), but because there's some private return to our giving (or, similarly, a private cost to not giving). People can be influenced to make charitable gifts by many factors, such as social pressure, guilt, or a desire to earn prestige, friendship, or respect. This doesn't mean that impure altruism is a bad thing; if the deed gets done, then so be it. But as with anything in life, it is good to understand the true motivations behind the action. For charities, this is particularly important because policymakers interested in engineering greater gifts of time and money need to know the exact motivations driving such behavior.

LETTING THE DATA SPEAK

Why Do People Give to Charity?

Imagine you come home to find a flyer on your door that says, "Fundraisers from a children's hospital will be visiting this address between 10 and 11 a.m. tomorrow morning to ask for contributions." Would you change your schedule to make sure to be home between 10 and 11 a.m.? Would you change your schedule to make sure *not* to be at home? What factors would play into your decision?

One aspect of *impure altruism* is social pressure: you give to a charity not because you want to help others, but because of the social pressure applied to you by others. By asking themselves, "Do people give because they *like to give*, or do people give because they *dislike not giving*?" John List together with Stefano DellaVigna and Ulrike Malmendier set out to test the power of *pure altruism* and social pressure in a door-to-door field experiment.[2]

Their goal was to determine how much money was given because of pure altruism and how much because of social pressure. Their hypothesis was that some people give to charities not because they care about the charity, but because they are asked to do so by a person, and they care about what others think of them.

Solicitors were dispatched to the suburbs of Chicago to ask for money for a children's hospital. Sometimes, however, the experimenters put flyers on doors to warn households that solicitors would be coming at a specific time the next day.

In theory, if people dislike being asked for money, then they will try to avoid answering the door during the time specified for charitable solicitations. The result?

Although fewer people answered the door when they knew a solicitor was coming, those who did answer the door gave more to the charity, on average, than their unwarned counterparts. This finding suggests that some people give to charity because of social pressure and avoid interaction with a solicitor when possible. It also suggests that people who do answer the door are quite generous.

In terms of the split between social pressure and pure altruism, the authors found that nearly 75 percent of the giving was due to social pressure. Can you think of other ways to test what drives giving to charity?

The Economics of Fairness

Throughout this text we have studied the behavior of economic agents. Whether dealing with individuals, households, or firms, there was no scope for fairness, or any other social preference, to play a role. A good's price was determined by the intersection of the market supply and market demand curves. Similarly, wages of workers were given by the intersection of labor demand and labor supply.

Even though we know intuitively that social preferences, such as fairness, altruism, and revenge, can play roles in our decision making, for simplicity we ignored them to focus on other important issues. We turn now to a consideration of how such preferences might lead us to revise our economic model.

Fairness on Television? You may have heard of the TV game show *Friend or Foe?* The show, which was hosted by MTV diva Kennedy, premiered on June 3, 2002 and lasted two seasons. The game show worked as follows. After two-person teams were formed, each team was separated into "isolation chambers," where trivia rounds were played. The two-person teams worked together to answer the questions in order to build a "trust fund." A team's "trust fund" could range from $200 to $22,200.

After the trivia portion of the show was complete, the winnings were to be divided beween the players. The division depended on both players' choices. There were three possible outcomes:

1. "Friend-Friend"—If both players chose "Friend," the total trivia winnings were divided equally between them.
2. "Friend-Foe"—If only one player chose "Friend" and the other chose "Foe," the person who chose Foe received the entire amount, leaving the player who chose Friend with nothing.
3. "Foe-Foe"—If both players chose "Foe," then they each walked away with nothing.

Exhibit 18.3 provides the payoff outcomes for one of the games, where we assume that you are playing with another player named Joe for $16,400.

A summary of the three key elements in this game are as follows:

Players: You and Joe
Strategies: Friend or Foe
Payoffs: See Exhibit 18.3

What should you do? If you are only interested in money, your best strategy is to always play "Foe." This is because this choice never leads to lower payoffs than playing "Friend."

How do you think people actually played this game on TV?[3] (For some excellent footage of people in action playing this prisoners' dilemma, we invite you to visit http://www.youtube.com/watch?v=7OQQ-T42Fko.) Overall, the choices were exactly split—of the 234 players examined, 50 percent chose "Friend" and 50 percent chose "Foe." Thus, even though choosing "Foe" is the best action if you want to make as much money as possible, only half of the participants do so.

Exhibit 18.3 *Friend or Foe* TV Game Show: A Variant of the Prisoners' Dilemma

By representing the *Friend or Foe* game in matrix form, we can easily compare your and Joe's payoffs and strategies to figure out the predicted outcome. If you and Joe both choose "Friend," you each earn $8,200. But the incentive to play "Foe" is high —potentially doubling your earnings unless you both play "Foe."

	Joe: Friend	Joe: Foe
You: Friend	• You get $8,200 • Joe gets $8,200	• You get $0 • Joe gets $16,400
You: Foe	• You get $16,400 • Joe gets $0	• You get $0 • Joe gets $0

18.1

Fairness is the willingness of individuals to sacrifice their own well-being to either improve upon the well-being of others or to punish those who they perceive as behaving unkindly.

18.2

18.3

Although there are several reasons for why this might be the case, one of them is that people have preferences for fairness. That is, they think it's unfair to take all of the money that they have just earned in a partnership. Specifically, we can define **fairness** as the willingness of individuals to sacrifice their own well-being to either improve upon the well-being of others or to punish those who they perceive as behaving unkindly.

How would we revise the payoffs in Exhibit 18.3 to account for such preferences? When players have fairness preferences, the total payoffs need to reflect both the monetary payoff and considerations of fairness. For example, maybe you believe that Joe has fairness preferences, too, and when playing this game you view the payoffs in Exhibit 18.4 as applicable.

Now when making your choice you consider not only the monetary payoff but also the "fairness penalty" contained in the payoff matrix, which you incur when you play "Foe" (that is you incur the fairness penalty when you play in an "unfair" manner, choosing "Foe" and reducing the payoff of the other player). Suppose that this "fairness penalty" is $5,000. Note that as a player, you are simply guessing the magnitude of this number. If you make these assumptions, then you simply insert a $5,000 fairness penalty in the matrix and optimize with the new numbers. Inserting $5,000 as the penalty for choosing "Foe" in Exhibit 18.4 yields Exhibit 18.5, which shows the new payoffs when such penalties are used.

Fairness in the Lab?   Although fairness preferences might certainly be at work driving the *Friend or Foe?* decisions, there are other factors at work as well. For example, it is possible that contestants recognize that they are playing in front of millions of people who are scrutinizing their every move—employers, spouses, parents, and even their own kids. For these sorts of reasons, economists have turned to laboratory experiments to measure fairness preferences. One such game that is commonly employed is the Ultimatum Game, which is a one-shot bargaining situation between two players. Exhibit 18.6 displays the game, which was previously discussed in Chapter 17.

In the Ultimatum Game, a Proposer is given an amount of money to split between himself and a Responder. Say that this amount is $10. The Responder is told how the pot has

Exhibit 18.4 *Friend or Foe* TV Game Show with Fairness Preferences

Unlike Exhibit 18.4, there is now an additional penalty imposed on whoever chooses to play "Foe." Depending on the size of this fairness penalty, the unsatisfying prediction of ("Foe, Foe") from Exhibit 18.4 might change to a more socially efficient outcome.

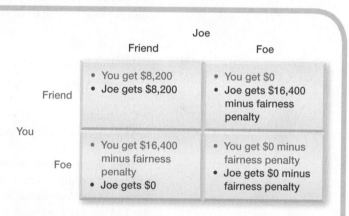

Exhibit 18.5 *Friend or Foe* TV Game Show with a $5,000 Fairness Penalty

Here, the fairness penalty is set at $5,000 and included in the payoffs of the matrix. Once this has been done, we are back to our standard game theory analysis—all of the new "fairness" concerns are already reflected in the payoffs. With such a fairness penalty, if you and Joe find yourselves playing ("Friend, Foe"), neither of you has any reason to change your action, and the same is true if you play ("Foe, Friend").

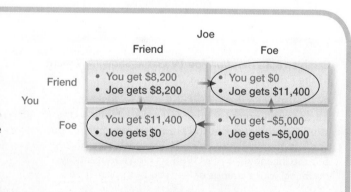

Exhibit 18.6 The Ultimatum Game

The Ultimatum Game begins with the Proposer's decision. The Proposer can offer anywhere between $0 and $10, which we represent as a smooth curve between $0 and $10 in the exhibit. Once the Proposer makes a decision ($x in the exhibit), that decision is conveyed to the Responder as the Proposer's offer. Now, the Responder decides whether to accept the offer (pocketing $x and leaving the Proposer with $10 − x) or to reject the offer (leaving both players with $0). The red numbers at the bottom give the Proposer's payoff and blue numbers are for the Responder.

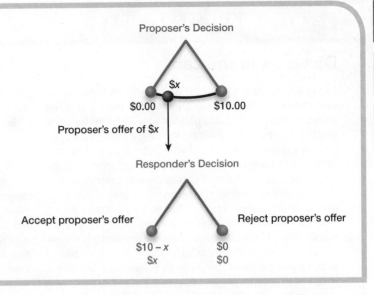

Proposer's Decision

$x

$0.00 $10.00

Proposer's offer of $x

Responder's Decision

Accept proposer's offer   Reject proposer's offer

$10 − x $0
$x $0

Is that an ultimatum?

been split and then decides whether or not to accept the Proposer's decision. Say that the proposed split is $9 for the Proposer and $1 for the Responder. If the Responder accepts this allocation, the Proposer and Responder are paid their proposed shares—in this example, $9 to the Proposer, $1 to the Responder. But if the Responder rejects, both the Proposer and the Responder receive nothing.

As a quick refresher, let's revisit what game theory tells us about the predicted outcome of the Ultimatum Game. If both players are only concerned with their own well-being, we can use the payoffs in Exhibit 18.6 and backward induct to determine how they will play the game. Assuming that the Responder prefers more money to less, we have already shown in Chapter 17 that the Responder accepts any positive offer, meaning that the Proposer will offer the lowest positive amount—in this case, 1 cent.

Even though game theory has stark predictions in this case, we typically do not find this result in laboratory experiments. In fact, a majority of Proposers offer amounts between 25 percent and 50 percent of the original pot, with few offers below 5 percent. Furthermore, Responders frequently reject offers below 20 percent. Why does this happen?

Fairness is a prominent explanation for describing how people play the Ultimatum Game. Recall that people can view a selfish behavior as unfair and may wish to punish it. In this game, Responders are willing to reject unfair offers which typically has a small cost for them because an unfair offer gives them very little of the pot. You should remind yourself that this is not at odds with economics per se: recall that economics does not tell us what people should value. For example, economics does not prescribe that people should or should not value fairness any more than it says that people should or should not value fast cars, a clean environment, or even freckles on coworkers' faces. What economics *does* predict is that, similar to how people should give more to charity when the opportunity cost of doing so is lower, a person valuing fairness should demand more of it at lower prices and less of it at higher prices, holding all else equal—something we are going to discuss in greater detail next.

As such, Responders shouldn't always be willing to punish unfairness. Sacrificing one's well-being to punish an offer of a 90–10 split when the pot is only $10 is understandably easier to do than when the pot is $5,000 (the difference between a punishment price of $1 and $500). Thus, we may expect that as the opportunity cost of exercising fairness concerns increases, the likelihood that an individual will exercise them decreases. Even in the context of fairness preferences, reasoning through the problem with economics can take us quite far. We return to this idea in the Evidence-Based Economics section.

 **LETTING THE DATA SPEAK**

Dictators in the Lab

Say you have volunteered for an economics experiment. Upon entering the lab, you are told that you have been paired with an anonymous partner who is in another room and that the two of you will be splitting a pot of cash. The person assigned the role of *Allocator* decides how the money is to be divided, and the other, called the *Recipient*, must accept whatever choice the Allocator makes.

You have been randomly assigned the role of Allocator and must choose how much of $10 to give to the Recipient and how much of it to keep for yourself. In effect, you are the Dictator. The lab assistants assure you that your identity will remain anonymous to the person you're paired with, so you can be as selfish or as generous as you want. How would you, as the Dictator, split the $10?

Typically, in the Dictator Game, a little more than half of Allocators send the Recipient some of the money, with the average share being about 20 percent of the original pie. Odds are that you won't decide to split the $10 evenly with the Recipient.

But how would your choice change if, instead of being in separate rooms, you and the Recipient were sitting face to face? What if, instead of allocating shares to an anonymous person, the two of you knew one another?

Lab experiments such as these have shown us that the degree of social distance between not only the participants but also between participants and experimenter has an effect on the Allocators' choices. One such experiment found that when no one (including even the experimenters) would ever know the Allocators' choices, more than 60 percent of people kept the entire pot.[4] However, when the Allocator and Recipient were instructed simply to look at each other in silence for a few seconds before the Allocator made his or her choice, approximately 70 percent divided the money evenly.

 # Evidence-Based Economics

Q: Do people care about fairness?

The Ultimatum Game provides a direct situation in which the Proposer sets a "take-it-or-leave-it price" and the Responder has to make a decision on accepting or rejecting. There are many economic decisions that we have discussed that share this quality: a monopolist setting a price, an oligopolist proposing a collusive agreement, or more generally, any bargaining situation that has a take-it-or-leave-it element.

One of the most robust findings in experimental economics is that many Responders in ultimatum games reject unfair offers, leaving themselves and their bargaining partner with a zero payoff. However, in and of itself, this outcome is not at odds with economic theory. What we know less about is whether people care about fairness when the price of being fair considerably increases. Economics makes a clear prediction in this case: people should demand greater fairness when the "price" of fairness is lower, meaning that they can punish unfair behavior at a lower opportunity cost.

Let's trace some history of the economics of fairness. Since the early 1980s, the Ultimatum Game has been one of the most popular experiments in laboratory economics. It has been played hundreds of times by your typical college student and even by natives of the Peruvian Amazon. Dozens of people have had their brains scanned while playing this game. By and large, what the research has found is that Proposers in the game typically offer about 40 percent of the money they are endowed with and Responders reject about 16 percent of the offers. Small offers are much more likely to be rejected than large offers.

Rejecting a positive offer in the Ultimatum Game involves a monetary cost, and whether behavior changes when this cost increases is a question of economic import. The main economic prediction in this setting is this: Responders will be willing to reject unequal offers when the cost of doing so is low but will find it hard to reject such offers when the stakes are large. Many of us might be willing to reject an offer of 1 percent of 10 dollars, yet how many of us would reject 1 percent of 10 million dollars?

Some economists have recently tested this prediction. They traveled to poor villages in Northeast India to run the Ultimatum Game.[5] By using subjects from poor villages, they could use large stakes at an affordable rate. Within these villages, they executed ultimatum games that varied the stakes by a factor of 1,000, permitting them to explore the game over different pot sizes of 20, 200, 2,000 and 20,000 rupees. These amounts corresponded, at the time, to $0.41, $4.10, $41, and $410, respectively. What this means to the people taking part in the experiment becomes clearer when we put it into context: the average daily income in these villages at the time was 100 rupees ($2.05).

The results from the game are summarized in Exhibit 18.7. Panel (a) of Exhibit 18.7 shows the offer proportions across the four stakes levels, in other words, the different percentages offered for various pies. What we find is that for lower stakes, the offer proportions are higher than for the larger stakes conditions. It seems that Proposers recognize that Responders will have a difficult time rejecting an unfair offer in the high-stakes (20,000) treatment, as the average offer is only a little more than 10 percent of the pie. So what do you think happens to these low proposals in the high-stakes treatment? Do they get rejected?

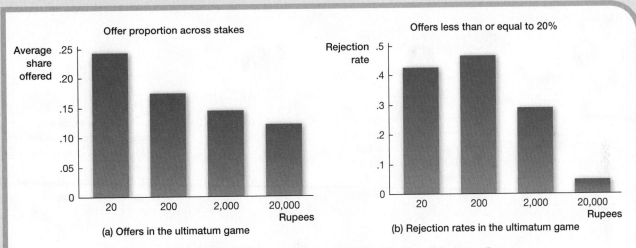

(a) Offers in the ultimatum game

(b) Rejection rates in the ultimatum game

Exhibit 18.7 Offers and Rejection Rates in the Ultimatum Game

The first pattern of data that emerges is that as the size of the pie increases (from 20 rupees to 20,000 rupees), the share of the pie that the Proposer offers to the Responder decreases. This finding alone suggests that stakes matter, but without the data on rejection rates, we have only part of the story.

The exhibit shows the average proportion of the stakes offered to the Responder. Bars represent our four stake treatments of 20, 200, 2,000, and 20,000 rupees to be shared in the Ultimatum Game.

When the authors focus on only the offers that are 20 percent of the total pie or less, we see the conclusive evidence for the importance of the stakes of the game. Whereas over 40 percent of low offers were rejected at the lower stakes, less than 5 percent of such offers are rejected when the total pie is 20,000 rupees. This also explains why Proposers thought they could make lower offers with higher stakes. This evidence shows that fairness, just like any other economic good, responds to price.

Panel (b) of Exhibit 18.7, which shows rejection rates for offers less than or equal to 20 percent of the pie, provides the answer. In short, even though people rejected small offers when the stakes were small, very few people rejected them when the stakes were large. Panel (b) of Exhibit 18.7 shows that even when Proposers made very low offers, once the stakes became large, almost no one rejected the offer. In the 20,000 rupees treatment, for example, only 1 of the 24 offers at or below 20 percent was rejected. That's a very small rejection rate considering that the average offer in that treatment group was just a little bit more than 10 percent of the pot. And this is much smaller than the 40 percent to 50 percent rejection rate observed in the lower-stakes treatments.

> **People do value fairness, but will go only so far when enforcing it.**

This experiment highlights the power of economics in that it shows that people do value fairness but will go only so far when enforcing it. When the cost is low, people vigorously punish unfair offers. But they aren't as willing to punish if it is really expensive to do so. If it costs them too much, they will let their fairness preferences take a backseat. This result is comforting for economists in that it shows that even issues such as fairness have a place in our economic framework: the power of economic reasoning extends well beyond production and consumption of goods and services such as cars, bicycles, iPhones, and haircuts.

Question	**Answer**	**Data**	**Caveat**
Do people care about fairness?	Yes, many people will pay a small price to punish others who are not being fair. But fairness considerations become less important as the cost of being fair increases.	Experimental data from the field in India.	This is one study in a remote part of the world and the stakes must be increased sufficiently to find that fairness considerations become less important as the cost of being fair increases.

18.2 The Economics of Trust and Revenge

> **Trust is a key component in most economic transactions.**

When we step back and think about it, trust is a key component in most economic transactions. This point was stressed by Nobel Prize-winning economist Kenneth Arrow, who wrote "virtually every commercial transaction has within itself an element of trust . . . it can be plausibly argued that much of the economic backwardness in the world can be explained by the lack of mutual confidence."[6] Of course, if someone takes advantage of your trust, you might consider exacting one of mankind's oldest acts: revenge. In this section we discuss the economics of trust and revenge.

The Economics of Trust

18.1

18.2

18.3

Trust and trustworthiness are everywhere in life. You trust that the meal that you ate the last time you dined out was processed, stored, and prepared in the safest manner possible. Likewise, when confiding in a friend, you rely on her trustworthiness to hold your deepest secrets. Economists have come to recognize that most economic transactions require trust and trustworthiness because it is rarely the case that all dimensions of a transaction can be contractually specified and enforced. For instance, it is difficult for Ford Motor Company to monitor the every move of line workers in a factory; workers need to be trusted not to commit sabotage or steal from the plant. Likewise, parties to a commercial transaction must have some degree of trust that each will fulfill the contract agreed upon. Otherwise, all of their time would be spent in court. You might recall from Chapter 16 that these are moral hazard considerations.

Economists have recently begun to study the nature and extent of trust and trustworthiness of people. One popular approach is to use laboratory experiments and observe people in "trust games." One variant of the trust game is shown in Exhibit 18.8. In this game, there are two players, Jen and Gary, who have never met and make their decisions anonymously. Jen is the first mover and must decide whether to trust Gary. Thus, Jen can either trust Gary or not trust Gary. If she does not trust Gary, then both she and Gary receive a payoff of $10. If she chooses to trust Gary, then Gary chooses either to defect or cooperate. If he defects, then Jen receives nothing and Gary receives $30. If Gary cooperates, then both he and Jen receive $15.

If you were in Jen's shoes, how would you decide? Likewise, if you were in Gary's shoes, and Jen trusted you, how would you respond?

Assuming that Exhibit 18.8 contains all of the relevant payoffs, then you should use backward induction, as we learned in Chapter 13, to solve this game. Put in Gary's shoes, you would defect if given the chance because by so doing you earn $30, which is greater than your cooperation earnings of $15. Put in Jen's shoes, you should recognize that Gary's defection will probably occur because of the larger payoff ($30 is greater than $15) coming his way. Thus, you should choose not to trust Gary.

The equilibrium of this game is therefore for Jen not to trust Gary. But this is a bad outcome in the sense that it is not socially efficient: instead of earning a total of $30 between them, they only earn $20 ($10 each) because Jen does not trust Gary. You will notice that many situations in the real world look like this game. Every time you trust a stranger, or even a friend, there is a risk that they will disappoint you. When you call a plumber to repair your leaking faucet, there is a risk that he will take your money but do a shoddy job and the faucet will start leaking again the next day. If the equilibrium was as depicted in Exhibit 18.8, the world would be a sad and quite dysfunctional place.

What factors could cause the equilibrium to be different? One important factor is that Gary might have a preference for being trustworthy. In the same way that there could be a

Is this an economic calculation?

Exhibit 18.8 A Trust Game Between Jen and Gary

In the Trust Game, Jen is the first mover and has to decide whether to trust Gary and let Gary have the final say, or not to trust Gary and settle the game in the first move. Given that Gary, if selfish, will defect, Jen would maximize her earnings by settling the game in her move and never giving Gary a chance. Unfortunately, both players are worse off in this case relative to the case where Jen trusts Gary and he cooperates with her.

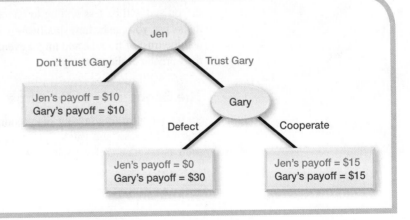

Exhibit 18.9 A Trust Game Between Jen and Gary with a $20 Guilt Penalty

As with Exhibit 18.5, even when we include social preferences in the payoffs, the game can be analyzed using our standard toolkit. In this case, Gary experiences a guilt penalty of $20 for betraying Jen's trust in the first move. This guilt penalty is high enough that Gary will instead cooperate to maximize his earnings. Knowing this, Jen will trust Gary, leading to the outcome (Trust Gary, Cooperate).

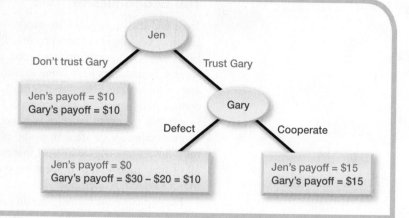

Jen

Don't trust Gary | Trust Gary

Jen's payoff = $10
Gary's payoff = $10

Gary

Defect | Cooperate

Jen's payoff = $0
Gary's payoff = $30 − $20 = $10

Jen's payoff = $15
Gary's payoff = $15

penalty for not being fair, as in *Friend or Foe*, there could be a penalty for Gary if he were to be untrustworthy. Let's say that the penalty is that he would feel terrible when he acts in such a manner.

Exhibit 18.9 shows what the game between Jen and Gary would look like when Gary has a penalty equivalent to $20 for choosing defection. Because of this penalty, his benefits from defection are now $10 rather than $30. Studying Exhibit 18.9, we see that Gary will now prefer to cooperate rather than defect. Recognizing such an outcome, Jen will now prefer to trust Gary rather than not trust him. Thus, simply allowing trustworthiness to be part of the equation could considerably change the incentives facing the agents and move them to a more socially efficient equilibrium.

Another factor that can move the players from the original "bad" equilibrium is if the game stretches out to a "long run"—that is, if the game is played several times over. Even though in a one-shot game with the original payoffs it makes sense for Jen to not trust Gary, if they were to play many times, it might make sense for Jen to trust Gary, because they can both be better off if they each receive $15 every time they play rather than $10. This is exactly the same reasoning that we saw in Chapter 14, supporting collusion as a long-run arrangement between oligopolists.

Let's be a little more explicit about why this is the case. From Exhibit 18.8, in such a repeated relationship, if Jen and Gary cooperate, each will get $15 every time they play the game. Now let's say that Gary defects. In this case, he receives $30 once, but from then on, Jen will choose not to trust Gary, leaving each player with $10 every time they play. So by defecting, Gary will increase his current payoff, but this will be at the cost of reducing his future payoff. Taking this into account, both players might find it in their interest to cooperate as a long-run strategy. In this way, the incentive of future cooperation can effectively discourage defection.

This long-run strategy might shed light on the kinds of interactions we constantly observe in the real world—for example, why friends and families share trust. Similar ideas can apply to society at large if we think of people as playing a "game of life." If you behave badly by stealing a classmate's lecture notes, then your friends might develop a negative opinion of you and will be less willing to cooperate with you in the future. By casting yourself as dishonest, you can be hurt significantly in the future. You might lose future job opportunities and the trust of friends, and might even find that people seek to punish your past actions in their private dealings with you.

The Economics of Revenge

So far, we have focused our discussion primarily on "nice" features of human behavior: charity, fairness, and trust. But, there are preferences that can be distinctly "not nice," such as revenge. Yet we will find that the ability to exact revenge can actually serve a useful purpose. Consider an example from medieval Europe. To promote social order, the communes in the tenth century kept the peace through the threat of revenge: in other words, an "eye for an eye" policy was in place. Even though exacting revenge by punishing people for antisocial behaviors was costly, it was theorized to be efficient because it reduced misbehavior by townspeople.

It is not difficult to find examples of the economics of revenge in modern economies: corporal punishment, public lashings, and other severe means to address misbehavior are to be found everywhere around the globe. But is this to promote social order? And do individuals punish this antisocial behavior of others even when it is costly to them? For example, say you witness a hit-and-run accident: do you take the time to call in the license plate number to the police and go to the precinct and carefully fill out a police report? On a much different level, do you yell at someone for cutting in line knowing that you run the risk of being labeled "aggressive" or "tacky" by others?

We can study the economics of revenge more formally by extending the Trust Game example. Imagine that after Gary decides whether to cooperate or defect, Jen can impose a fine of $20 on Gary. But imposing the fine will cost Jen $10. How does adding such a revenge option change the equilibrium of the Trust Game?

Exhibit 18.10 shows the effect. At the end of the game tree, we have allowed different payoffs for Jen. In the first case, she's not vengeful, so she suffers when she imposes a fine on Gary (she's lost $10 and thus receives a payoff of −$10). In the second case, she is vengeful and she actually derives satisfaction from imposing the fine on Gary (because she's getting revenge on him for not returning her trust). Assuming that this satisfaction is worth $20 for her, her total payoff is $20 + (−$10) = $10.

If Jen is not vengeful and Gary knows this fact, then Gary knows that she will not impose the penalty. So he continues to defect if given the option. But, if Jen *is* vengeful, then Gary knows that if he defects, Jen will happily punish him. Knowing this, Gary must reconsider his strategy: defection doesn't look so good anymore. In particular, in this case Gary realizes that Jen will impose the fine and now chooses to cooperate.

Therefore, we have identified another path to a good equilibrium: the threat of revenge. Jen's ability to exact revenge convinces Gary to act in the interests of the collective. This is very similar to the effect of credible commitments that we discussed in Chapter 13.

Exhibit 18.10 A Trust Game Between Jen and Gary with a Punishment Option

In a setting closer to reality, Jen would see Gary's defection and be able to punish Gary. Here, we model that by giving Jen the first and final say on the outcome of the game. If Jen isn't vengeful, the game ends just as in Exhibit 18.9—knowing that Gary will defect, Jen ends the game in the first move and doesn't trust Gary. However, if Jen is vengeful, then Gary, when it's his turn to decide, will cooperate, preferring $15 to the inevitable $10 he gets if he defects against a vengeful Jen.

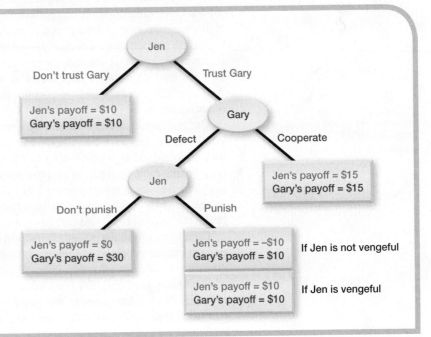

CHOICE & CONSEQUENCE

Does Revenge Have an Evolutionary Logic?

The role that supported long-run trust in the repeated trust game between Jen and Gary was "cooperate until your partner turns on you, and then turn on him." If both players use this strategy, they likely will not have to face the pain of betrayal—the threat of retaliation is too high to make defection worthwhile. Many people, businesses, and even countries have built trusting relationships from the expectation that uncooperative behavior would lead to revenge. In fact, such thinking may have an evolutionary root.

Biologists and anthropologists currently are locked in a heated debate over the power of *group selection*.

Several scholars, such as Robert Boyd, Peter Richardson, Elliott Sober, and David Sloan Wilson, are working to show that although selection may favor the selfish individuals, groups that have built trusting, cooperative relationships should outlast groups composed entirely of selfish individuals.[7] Individual selection implies that the strongest *person* will survive to pass on his genes, while group selection implies that the strongest *groups* will survive to pass on their genes. A general rule of thumb in this research is that "selfishness beats altruism within groups, but altruistic groups beat selfish groups."[8] How could we test whether this is at work in markets?

18.3 How Others Influence Our Decisions

Throughout this book we have referred at various times to our preferences. What factors shape whether we're fair-minded, whether we give in to social pressure, whether we really enjoy the feeling of knowing we did the right thing, or whether we take satisfaction from exacting revenge? Are these factors different from those determining whether we prefer chocolate or vanilla ice cream?

Where Do Our Preferences Come From?

Our preferences are in part determined by biological and chemical processes (e.g., children prefer sweet flavors). In many applications, we can take them as "given" in our economic model. Other dimensions of our preferences, however, are determined and affected by socialization, access to information, and indoctrination.

We are not born with a preference for watching TV or playing video games. These are preferences that we acquire. Such preferences are a function of the society in which we live. We learn to pattern our behavior in ways considered appropriate to that of society. And, the influence of society, especially through friends and family, is an important part of socialization.

Indoctrination is the process by which agents imbue society with their ideology or opinion.

Our preferences are also shaped by a more unsavory force: **indoctrination**. Indoctrination is the process by which agents imbue society with their ideology or opinion. Part of this indoctrination is benign—it's just the process of providing information. For example, antismoking campaigns pay to advertise widely because they believe these ads cause people not to smoke. These groups successfully cultivate a cultural norm against smoking. Most of us prefer not to smoke because we have been provided with information about the negative health effects of smoking and partly because we know that our society frowns upon smoking.

Far different from the potentially helpful spread of information is the power of organizations to change people's preferences through indoctrination. The dangerous temptation of governments and powerful individuals to influence citizens with ideologies or opinions has plagued many countries. For instance, today many North Korean citizens believe that an economy that is ruled centrally is preferred to an economy guided by market forces. As we learned in Chapter 7, this is clearly not the case in theory or practice.

The Economics of Peer Effects

In Chapter 12 we discussed how others influence our lives through *network externalities*. For example, because many of your friends use Twitter, you might feel compelled to get a

LETTING THE DATA SPEAK

Is Economics Bad for You?

Perhaps you will not be surprised to learn that at least three separate laboratory experiments have shown that economics majors cooperate less than students from other disciplines.[9] Whether in a prisoners' dilemma experiment or a dictator game, a student of economics tends to exhibit behavior more in line with the selfish *homo economicus* than with a more cooperative economic man.

Is this a form of indoctrination? Could it be that economics makes people less social and more selfish?

We should note that there are at least two other explanations for these results. First, it might be the case that the economics discipline attracts students who are more "selfish" than the average student. That is, the selection of students who enter the economics major is different from those who enter other majors—those who enter economics are more attracted to dollars. This makes sense because economics majors tend to do quite well in terms of earnings after graduation.

Equally as plausible might be the case that economics majors have misunderstood economic science as prescribing the "correct" behavior in such games. As you now know, as far as economists are concerned, as long as you are making the best choice for yourself given the information you have, you're acting rationally. This doesn't necessarily mean that you maximize your income or that you act selfishly.

But a common misconception is that economics tells us that we *should be* completely selfish—promoting our own earnings at the expense of others. In this way of thinking, economics students are always figuring out the equilibrium in monetary payoffs, to the exclusion of other social preferences.

Perhaps you know the ultimate answer to this question through your interactions with economics majors. We, as economics professors, would like to learn the truth!

Our friends and acquaintances are a major force in shaping both our preferences and the choices we make in life.

Twitter account as well. Likewise, you might go to eBay first if you are interested in buying or selling in an auction because eBay has many buyers and sellers. Equally as important is the influence of others beyond these network externalities. Every day we see people, listen to them, and converse about the correct course of action. What jeans should I wear when I go out tonight? What is the next hot stock? What kind of shoes should I buy?

For better or worse, our social surroundings affect the decisions that we make daily. No one person or group decided that flare-leg jeans would be cool in the 1960s, acid-wash would be cool in the 1980s, and Kim Kardashian's frayed hemline jeans would be "in" right now. But the trends are there.

Our friends and acquaintances are a major force in shaping both our preferences and the choices we make in life. Economists call the influence of the decisions of others on our own choices **peer effects**. People tend to gather information from those around them and use this information to decide on their own behavior. Both the characteristics of our peers—their talents and skills—and their choices affect our lives.

Peer effects are the influence of the decisions of others on our own choices.

A few examples will help to illustrate the power of peers and also reveal why it is challenging to identify peer effects convincingly in the data. The first is a study by economists Oriana Bandiera and Imran Rasul, who noticed interesting peer effects when studying farmers and their adoption of sunflower seed farming in Mozambique.[10] They examined how social ties in the community influenced the adoption of new technology to raise sunflower seeds. They found that those who adopted to sunflower seeds knew a significantly greater number of other people who had switched to farming sunflower seeds than those who chose not to adopt. Intuitively, this outcome makes sense.

Imagine that you are a farmer presented with the option of farming a new crop. You'd be more likely to adopt it if you knew that several people had already done so rather than just one or two people. Why does such a relationship exist between the adoption decision of peers and an individual's decision? One possibility is that each farmer is learning from his or her peers whether sunflower seeds have high productivity: the more your peers adopt, the more likely you are to be convinced that

Peer effects are everywhere.

Peer effects are everywhere.

this is a good idea. Another possibility is that the adoption decisions of peers create social pressure: you might not want to be the only one who hasn't adopted. Yet another possibility is that neighboring farmers' lands are of similar quality and type, and if you are in an area where sunflower seeds are likely to increase yields significantly, then both you and your peers will be more likely to adopt.

In a study that is closer to home, economist Bruce Sacerdote sought to study peer effects in college dorms.[11] He uncovered what he called the "freshman roommate effect." Exploring a natural experiment in which nearly 1,600 Dartmouth college freshmen were randomly assigned a roommate, Sacerdote examined the effects that roommates had on one another. Among other results, he reported that roommates had a significant effect on each other's GPA! It seems that having a roommate who studies all the time helps you to study more yourself. If you are unhappy about your GPA, however, don't go hunting down your roommate just yet, as Sacerdote and other scholars have found that many other important factors influence your GPA, too.

Though clever, Sacerdote's study is also open to alternative interpretations. Imagine that your roommate has no effect on you but your room happens to be next to a busy train station with frequent service in the middle of the night. Both you and your roommate will get no sleep as trains whiz around you. At semester's end both you and your roommate may have low GPAs, but this is not because one of you has influenced the other, but because both of you have been subject to a "common shock"—in this case, train noise keeping you awake all night.

Following the Crowd: Herding

Crowds tend together for a purpose: whether at school, a concert, or a roadside accident, people tend to flock to one another. In these cases, there is usually something specific that attracts attention. However, people can flock together without good reason. In economics, **herding** occurs when individuals conform to the decisions of others.

In general, there are two reasons why individuals might decide to herd. The first might simply be that they are afraid of being wrong—for this reason, they might not value their own instincts highly. Another is the assumption that if many people are making the same decision, they must be doing so for a reason. You might have heard the adage at amusement parks: if there is a long line, jump in it because something good is at the end. Herding creates an informational equilibrium in which people trust the wisdom of others and ignore their own information.

For example, imagine that you are walking down a street and decide that you will stop to eat lunch. You look around for a diner and see two across the street from one another. Both diners are empty. Knowing nothing about them, you randomly choose Big Al's Diner over Kelly's Diner. In doing so, you might have cost Kelly's more than just your own patronage. Let's see why.

Five minutes later, another hungry person walks by looking for somewhere to eat. He, too, sees Kelly's and Big Al's. Perhaps he has heard from some of his friends that Kelly's has good food. But he also sees that Big Al's has a customer (you) and that Kelly's is empty. He takes this information as a signal of quality—Big Al's must be better because it has more customers than Kelly's, and perhaps that customer, you, went to Big Al's because of some valuable information. So he ignores his private information (what he had heard from his friends) and follows you to Big Al's. As more and more people come looking for a diner, they, too, follow this reasoning and follow the herd. So Kelly's sits empty, while Big Al's is full.

This phenomenon is known as an **information cascade**, which occurs when people make choices based on the decisions of others rather than on their own private information—the second customer ignoring the information from friends to follow you to Big Al's. It might seem reasonable to do this, because other people often make decisions based on some relevant information. The results of an information cascade, however, can be significant. For example, some

Herding is a behavior of individuals who conform to the decisions of others.

An **information cascade** occurs when people make the same decisions as others, ignoring their own private information.

Excuse me. Can you direct us to the nearest sea cliff?

LETTING THE DATA SPEAK

Your Peers Affect Your Waistline

The most commonly studied example of peer effects is in the classroom—how peers in your classroom affect you in economically important ways. One group of economists has taken the study of peer effects into a quite different direction. Scott Carrell, Mark Hoekstra, and James West used the random assignment of peer groups in the U.S. Air Force Academy (USAFA) to consider how peer effects impact fitness. Do you think poor fitness or obesity are linked to peer effects? The answer may surprise you.

Carrell, Hoekstra, and West studied the impact of peers on physical ability by using high school and college physical fitness results for students in the USAFA.[12] The USAFA is somewhat unique in that college students are randomly assigned to groups (squadrons) with approximately 30 other students, and these groups spend the majority of their time together. Further, the physical fitness of students at the USAFA is motivated through common training monitored relatively closely through a Physical Education Average score. The score combines a number of different physical activities and certain physical fitness requirements.

We show one of the main results from the research in Exhibit 18.11. The horizontal axis of the figure shows the proportion of students in the 30-student USAFA groups who were in the lowest quintile (20 percent of least physically fit freshman) for a high school measure of fitness involving various activities such as pull-ups and push-ups. The vertical axis records the probability of failing the USAFA fitness requirement. The curves on the graph represent high school fitness. These curves show a stark result: the probability of a student failing the fitness exam increases as the number of unfit students around him increases. Similar to our discussion of the Dartmouth roommate study, this result could be explained by several factors, including some "common shocks" that influence all of the members of a squadron. Nevertheless, it is strongly suggestive that the physical fitness of people around you is correlated with your own health!

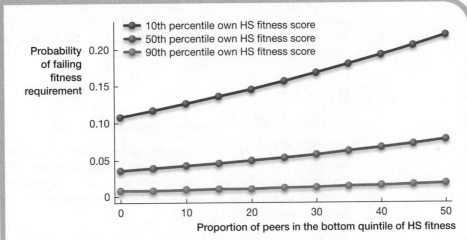

Exhibit 18.11 **The Effects of Peers on Health**

Starting with the green curve, we can see that individuals who were in the 90th percentile of high school fitness seem to be unaffected by their peers in terms of probability of failing the USAFA fitness test. However, as we move toward individuals closer to average (red line) and below average (blue line) fitness in high school, the pattern emerges that the probability of failing the USAFA fitness test increases as the average fitness of your peer group drops (moving left to right along the x-axis).

economists view information cascades as an important reason behind significant asset price increases and subsequent corrections. For instance, people rush to buy the next big thing in the stock market, and the share price rises abnormally high. The subsequent correction lowers the share price, leading to considerable losses for those who got in late.

Another place where information cascades potentially play an important role is in job interviews. An employer might look at a candidate's resume and see that he has been

Are You an Internet Explorer?

Of all the complaints about the Internet, one you will never hear is that there is a shortage of people expressing their opinions. Between the blogosphere, Twitter, and Facebook, if you have an opinion, you can get it onto the Internet (whether or not anyone reads it is a whole different question . . .).

With all of these opinions floating around, most people have little trouble finding the blogs and comments of like-minded individuals; psychologists call this phenomenon *confirmation bias*. Confirmation bias predicts that people only read articles that reaffirm their own beliefs, thus entrenching them further in their own prejudices.

Not all agree, however. A study of the 2004 election concludes that Internet users may be some of the most balanced media consumers.[13] Internet articles, especially blogs, are often formatted to present critiques of others' arguments and then provide the link to the original commentary. This fingertip access to both sides of an argument makes reading contradictory opinions much easier, not to mention cheaper, than subscribing to both The *New York Times* and The *Wall Street Journal*.

unemployed for some time. Even if the interview goes well and the candidate seems well suited for the job, the employer might weigh the information that the candidate has so far been unsuccessful in finding work as a signal that everyone else thinks this worker is unqualified. The employer could then think that he is missing something important in his evaluation of the worker and might ignore his own positive signals in favor of the information contained in the candidate's unemployment history. He won't offer the interviewee a job, and neither will the next employer, or the next . . . this information cascade prolongs the unfortunate interviewee's joblessness.

Summary

☀ There is nothing in economics that dictates agents only value material wealth. Introspection suggests that we value many things beyond wealth, including charity, fairness, trust, revenge, and how others perceive us. Our economic tools provide us with an understanding of when such considerations have importance.

☀ Economists have also explored how predictions within economics change when we consider an agent who acts "more human." Our economic reasoning remains intact when we add such considerations. In this way, predictions from the standard economic model are quite robust and help us to study features of our economy—fairness, revenge, charity, trust, peer effects—that were not previously well understood.

☀ Taken together, these factors help us to understand the world around us and how economics can be extended to every corner of our economy.

Key Terms

pure altruism *p. 408*
impure altruism *p. 408*
fairness *p. 410*

indoctrination *p. 418*
peer effects *p. 419*
herding *p. 420*

information cascade *p. 420*

Questions

All questions are available in MyEconLab for practice and instructor assignment.

1. How does the standard model of *homo economicus* differ from the *homo economicus* that is studied in behavioral and social economics?

2. Suppose the act of giving is viewed as an economic good. How can the price of charitable donations be measured? Does the quantity demanded decrease as the price of giving increases?

3. Is it correct to say that people give to charity only out of selflessness and concern for the well-being of others? Explain your answer.

4. Refer to the experiment in the chapter on soliciting donations for a children's hospital. Experimenters put flyers on doors saying that solicitors would be coming to their house at a particular time. Fewer people opened the door when they knew that a solicitor would be coming, but those who did gave more money, on average, than others who did not know. What can you infer about pure and impure altruism from the results of this experiment?

5. In the context of this chapter, what is meant by having a preference for fairness?

6. In the Friend or Foe game, Foe is a (weakly) dominant strategy for both players. What can explain why, in roughly 50 percent of decisions, players chose Friend and split the sum of money with the other player?

7. Why do lab experiments show a different outcome for the Ultimatum Game compared to the outcome predicted by game theory?

8. In the Dictator Game, the Allocator decides how a certain sum of money is to be divided, and the recipient must accept whatever choice the allocator makes. How does the outcome of the game differ when the Allocator remains anonymous to the Recipient and when the Allocator faces the Recipient?

9. Consider a trust game between two players. Suppose the players care only about their own payoffs. The payoffs are such that, in equilibrium, the players do not trust each other, leading to a socially inefficient equilibrium. How could the game be changed so that in equilibrium the players do trust one another?

10. How does indoctrination affect our preferences? Explain with an example.

11. What does it mean to say that a good exhibits network externalities? Can you think of a good that you use because it has network externalities?

12. What does herding mean? Why do individuals decide to herd?

13. What is an information cascade? Explain with examples.

Problems

All problems are available in MyEconLab for practice and instructor assignment.

1. Under the tax law in 2012, you could claim all of your charitable contributions as a deduction on your federal income tax (if you decided to itemize your deductions), and the top marginal tax rate was 35 percent.

   a. What is the cost of a $100 charitable contribution under 2012 tax law for someone who itemizes and who is in the top tax bracket?

   b. The top marginal tax rate was raised to 39.6 percent in 2013. How would this change affect the cost of a $100 charitable contribution for someone who is in the top tax bracket?

   c. One proposed change to the 2012 law would have left the top tax rate at 35 percent but would have placed a cap on itemized deductions of $25,000. Mr. Smith is in the top tax bracket and has $25,000 of deductions for property taxes and interest on a mortgage. How would this change affect Mr. Smith's cost of a $100 charitable contribution?

2. The organ donation policy in the United States is based on altruism. It is illegal to buy or sell human organs, so patients who need transplants will have to wait until they find an appropriate donor. In Iran, however, donors are compensated in cash for organs. The United States has a long waiting list for organs while there are hardly any such shortages in Iran. What does this tell you about altruism?

3. There are five people in a village. Each has $10. The village is prone to flooding. Flooding is reduced if people contribute to flood control efforts. In particular, each person in the village receives $0.50 of benefits when someone contributes $1 to flood control (flood control is a public good). So suppose, for example, each person contributes $4 to flood control. Total contributions will equal $5 \times \$4 = \$20$, each person will be left with $\$10 - \$4 = \$6$ to purchase goods such as food and clothing, and each person will receive $0.5 \times \$20 = \$10$ in benefits from flood control. Everyone in the village makes their decision about contributions without talking to anyone else in the village.

   a. Suppose people care only about their consumption of goods and their benefits from flood control. Show that contributing $0 is a dominant strategy.

   b. Now suppose that each person cares about the total consumption of goods in the village and everyone's benefits from flood control. Show that everyone in the village will contribute their entire $10 to flood control.

4. Suppose a limited number of tickets to a popular football game had to be rationed among the public. There are three ways of doing this:

i. Auction: The tickets will go to the highest bidder.

ii. Lottery: A certain number of lucky people will get the tickets.

iii. Queues: The tickets will be sold on a first-come, first-serve basis.

a. Which method would yield the most efficient outcome? Rank the three methods in decreasing order of their efficiency.

b. Which method is most likely to be considered "fair"? Rank the three methods in decreasing order of their perceived fairness.

c. Is the most efficient method also the most fair? What can you infer from this?

5. Assume that a charity hired you to improve their results on donations. You decide to mail letters asking for donations. You use three different types of letters:

Letter A: Control—standard letter asking for money.

Letter B: "Once and Done"—standard letter but with a statement at the front noting that: "Make one gift now and we'll never ask for another donation again!"

Letter C: Soft "Once and Done"—an upfront statement of: "It only takes one gift to save a child's life forever."

The results are as follows:

Letter B ("Once and Done") raises much more money than Letter A (Control): In most cases, at least double.

Letter C (Soft "Once and Done") raises more money than Letter A.

Letter B raises about 50% more money than Letter C.

Of the concepts we have discussed in the chapter—social pressure, altruism, and herding—which do you think is most responsible for the success of treatment B?

6. In Mario Puzo's The *Godfather*, Michael Corleone (played by Al Pacino in the movie version of the book) would like to meet with Virgil "The Turk" Sollozzo. Michael was concerned that if he meets with Sollozzo, Sollozzo will kill him. We can think of their problem as a game. First, Michael decides whether or not to meet. If they do not meet, suppose Sollozzo and the Corleones each get a payoff of zero. If they do agree to meet then Sollozzo will decide whether or not to kill Michael. If he decides to kill him, then Sollozzo gets a payoff of 20 and the Corleones get a payoff of −10; if he does not kill him then each gets a payoff of 10.

a. Draw the game tree.

b. Use backward induction to show that Michael will not agree to meet.

c. The Bocchicchio family had a well-deserved reputation for ruthlessness. They had a simple code of vengeance; if you were responsible for the death of a member of their family, they would kill a member of yours, regardless of the cost to them. Suppose that when Michael meets with Sollozzo, he also hires a member of the Bocchicchio family to go to Michael's house. There, the "hostage" will be guarded by Michael's men. If Michael does not return safely, Michael's men will kill the hostage. The Bocchicchio family, seeking revenge, will blame Sollozzo for the death, since he made the promise that Michael will not be harmed, and will eventually kill Sollozzo. If Michael and Sollozzo are both killed, the Corleone family and Sollozzo each gets a payoff of −10. Use backward induction to determine how this game will be played.

7. In the 1950s, sociologists coined the term "homophily"— love of the same—to explain our tendency to associate with people who are like us. Why does homophily make it difficult to estimate peer group effects empirically? How do the studies by Sacerdote and by Carrell, Hoekstra, and West discussed in this chapter avoid the homophily problem?

8. A group of social scientists were working on the Obama campaign in the 2012 presidential election. In order to persuade their supporters to vote, they focused on telling potential voters that most of the people in their neighborhood were planning to vote. The traditional campaign approach involved telling voters that most of their neighbors did not vote and that not voting was a missed opportunity to help their country. Why do you think the Obama team felt that their new approach would work better than the old one?

9. Maya and Paul want to watch a movie. There are two movies available: a comedy and an action film. Maya loves comedies, whereas Paul enjoys action films.

a. As separate individuals, which movie will Maya choose? Which one will Paul choose? Why?

b. If Maya and Paul are on a date, what factors (other than the movie genre) would affect their choices? If Maya decides to watch the comedy, which movie should Paul choose to get the highest payoff?

c. Suppose a group of people just came out of the movie theater gushing about how great the comedy was and another group complaining that the action film was really bad. What movie should Maya and Paul choose? How is this herd behavior? How can it lead to an information cascade?

10. A randomized experiment was conducted to see how others' opinions affect a user's ratings online. Whenever a comment was added on a certain social news site, researchers gave it an up vote, down vote, or no vote. The researchers conducting the experiment noted that comments that were given an up vote were more likely to get another up vote as compared to the comments that were given other ratings. What do you think could explain this?

11. Three psychologists performed the following experiment. They had groups of people ranging in size from just one person to as many as fifteen people stand on a street corner and stare up into the sky. They then observed how many passersby stopped and also looked up at the sky. They found that with only one person looking up, very few passersby stopped. If five people were staring up into the sky, then more passersby stopped, but most still ignored them. Finally, with fifteen people looking up, they found that 45 percent of passersby stopped and also stared up into the sky. How could you use the idea of an information cascade to explain this result?

12. There was a sharp increase in the number of the long-term unemployed following the recession that began in December 2007. Rand Ghayad did the following study to better understand long-term unemployment. He sent out 3,600 fake resumes in response to 600 job openings. He varied the length of time his fake applicants had been out of work, how often they had switched jobs, and their work experience. He found that the longer the "applicants" were out of work, the less likely they were to be offered an interview. How could you use the idea of an information cascade to explain the results of this study?

The Wealth of Nations: Defining and Measuring Macroeconomic Aggregates

In the United States, what is the total market value of annual economic production?

Beginning with this chapter we focus on the economy as a whole. Economists refer to the *total* activity in an economy as *aggregate* economic activity. *Macroeconomics* is the study of *aggregate* economic activity.

The field of macroeconomics has been completely transformed in the last century. Before World War I, no country even had a system for measuring aggregate economic activity. Back then, economists had to guess what was happening by looking at small pieces of the bigger picture. They studied things like the tonnage of steel that

CHAPTER **OUTLINE**

KEY IDEAS

☀ Macroeconomics is the study of aggregate economic activity.

☀ National income accounting is a framework for calculating gross domestic product (GDP), which is a measure of aggregate economic output.

☀ GDP can be measured in three different ways, and in principle these three methods should all yield the same answer: Production = Expenditure = Income.

☀ GDP has limitations as a measure of economic activity and as a measure of economic well-being.

☀ Economists use price indexes to measure the rate of inflation and to distinguish nominal GDP from real GDP (which holds prices fixed).

was manufactured or the volume of freight that was shipped on rail lines. These indicators were used to make educated guesses about aggregate economic activity. If freight shipments were booming, it probably meant that the aggregate economy was booming too, but nobody could be certain.

Today, we no longer have to guess what is happening in the economy. Modern economies have a sophisticated system that measures the level of aggregate activity. Careful measurement has made it possible to study the aggregate economy and to design policies that improve its performance.

In this chapter, we set the stage by answering a foundational question: How does it all add up? How do we calculate the total market value of aggregate economic production?

19.1 Macroeconomic Questions

Until now we've been studying microeconomics: how individuals, households, firms, and governments make choices, and how those choices affect the allocation of resources, the well-being of other agents, and the prices of specific goods and services. Now it's time to turn to macroeconomics. Recall from Chapter 1 that macroeconomics is the study of economic aggregates and economy-wide phenomena, like the annual growth rate of a country's total economic output, or the annual percentage increase in the total cost of living. Macro, which is shorthand for macroeconomics, is our new topic.

Macroeconomic analysis explains past patterns in aggregate economic activity and tries to predict future changes. For example, macroeconomists are interested in the enormous differences in income across countries and the creation of policies that would enable the countries with lower income to catch up.

Income per capita is income per person. This is calculated by dividing a nation's aggregate income by the number of people in the country.

Income per capita—in other words, income per person—in the United States is more than twice the level in Portugal, seven times the level in China, and over one-hundred times the level in Zimbabwe. How do we measure these cross-country differences? What causes them? How long will they persist?

China has been catching up to the United States very quickly. China's economy has been growing four times as fast as the U.S. economy for over 30 years. Will China eventually match the level of U.S. income per capita? Will China surpass the United States? Or, will something else happen? For example, Japan experienced a long-run slowdown in economic growth starting around 1990, when its income per capita was about to overtake that of the

Zimbabwe has spectacular natural resources like Victoria Falls but has not succeeded in developing a healthy economy or a robust tourism industry. Today, most of the visitors to the Falls stay on the Zambian side of the border.

Recessions are periods (lasting at least two quarters) in which aggregate economic output falls.

A worker is officially **unemployed** if he or she does not have a job, has actively looked for work in the prior four weeks, and is currently available for work.

The **unemployment rate** is the fraction of the labor force that is unemployed.

United States. Over two decades later, the United States is still ahead. Why do growth rates slow down as income per capita rises?

What can be done to improve living conditions in impoverished nations like Zimbabwe? Annual income per capita in Zimbabwe was $369 per year in 2010, barely enough for survival. Figuring out how to make low-income countries grow faster is a question of enormous importance for human well-being. Malnutrition and lack of health-care cause tens of millions of annual deaths worldwide. If low-income countries could raise their annual growth by five percentage points, economists estimate that 50 million lives would be saved over the next 20 years.

To understand how to achieve long-run economic prosperity, we need to understand how different government policies augment or undermine economic growth. Corruption and confusion can lead policymakers down the wrong path. What are the bad policies, and will we avoid them in the future?

Macroeconomists also study the year-to-year, or "short-run," fluctuations in economic activity. Why does economic growth sometimes stall, or turn negative? We call an economic downturn lasting at least two quarters a **recession** (a quarter is one-fourth of a year).

During recessions the *unemployment rate*, one of the most important macroeconomic variables, rises. A person is officially **unemployed** if three conditions are satisfied: he or she (1) does not have a job, (2) has actively looked for work in the prior four weeks, and (3) is currently available for work. Fluctuations in the **unemployment rate**—the fraction of the labor force that is unemployed—are covered in detail in Chapter 23.

To see an example of economic fluctuations, consider the period from 2007 to 2009, when the U.S. economy shrank by 4.3 percent and the unemployment rate rose from 5 percent to 10 percent. At the same time, the world experienced a series of financial crises, including stock market crashes, collapsing housing prices, mortgage defaults, and bank failures. Why did these events occur, and what should governments have done to reduce their severity? What caused worldwide stock markets to lose over half their value in a year's time? Why did so many major banks suddenly become insolvent?

Though the financial crisis of 2007–2009 was calamitous, it does not hold a candle to the Great Depression, which stretched from 1929 to 1939. From 1929 to 1933, production fell by nearly 30 percent and the unemployment rate rose from 3 percent to 25 percent of the labor force. In July 1932, the U.S. stock market reached the bottom

During the peak of the Great Depression 25 percent of the U.S. workforce didn't have a job. Some towns put up signs discouraging job seekers from looking for employment in the area.

of an 87 percent roller-coaster plunge from its peak in September, 1929. Are there policies that will enable us to avoid such disasters in the future? Or are we only able to respond after the fact? Could the 2007–2009 financial crisis have turned into another Great Depression?

These are all important questions. To answer them, we need some special tools and new models. The first thing that we must do is measure the thing we are studying: a country's aggregate economy. This is a seemingly impossible task. How can we measure the total activity of millions of economic agents? A hundred years ago, nobody knew how to do this. Fortunately, economic science has progressed. Today, we have a framework called the **national income accounts**, which we use to measure the entire economy. In the United States, the formal name for this system of national accounts is the **National Income and Product Accounts (NIPA)**. Once we understand how the national income accounts works, we will be ready to start answering the interesting and important questions posed above.

> **National income accounts** measure the level of aggregate economic activity in a country.

> The **National Income and Product Accounts (NIPA)** is the system of national income accounts that is used by the U.S. government.

19.2 National Income Accounts: Production = Expenditure = Income

To measure aggregate economic activity, we will need to take both quantities and prices into account. Let's start by considering the hypothetical nation of Fordica. Fordica is a small country with only one employer, the Ford Motor Company, hereafter Ford, which produces 5 million cars each year. We'll assume that Fordica has 200,000 citizens who happen to be the workers in Ford's factories and also the owners of Ford's stock. We'll look at three different ways of thinking about Fordica's economy—a production approach, an expenditure approach, and an income approach.

Production

As economists, we want to measure the total market value of annual production in the nation of Fordica. To keep things simple, we'll assume that Ford only needs its own machines and the labor of Fordica's citizens to build cars. We won't worry right now about other inputs like steel and plastic. In fact, we'll momentarily assume that these other inputs don't exist.

To determine the market value of production in Fordica, we multiply the quantity of cars produced by the market price of each car. For example, if the market price of a Ford is $30,000, then Fordica has total annual production of:

$$(5 \text{ million cars}) \times (\$30,000/\text{car}) = \$150 \text{ billion.}$$

By multiplying production quantities and market prices, we have a measure that reflects the market value of the goods produced in the economy during a particular period of time—in this example, one year. So the economy of Fordica produces goods with a market value of $150 billion per year.

> **Gross domestic product (GDP)** is the market value of the final goods and services produced within the borders of a country during a particular period of time.

Economists call this measure of aggregate economic activity **gross domestic product,** or **GDP**. We define GDP as the market value of the final goods and services produced within the borders of a country during a particular period of time. GDP is always associated with a particular period of time, usually either a year or a quarter. For example, "GDP in 2015" is the market value of the final goods and services produced during the year 2015. "GDP in Q1:2015" is the market value of the final goods and services produced during the first quarter of the year 2015. When talking about aggregate economic activity, the first quarter begins in January (January–March). The second quarter begins in April (April–June). The third quarter begins in July (July–September). The fourth quarter begins in October (October–December).

The definition of GDP includes the word *final*, which signifies that we are interested in valuing the end product in a chain of production. Components that are put together to make a final product—for instance, a car engine is a

The real-life Ford Motor Company employs about 200,000 workers worldwide. It manufactures 5–6 million cars per year, generating annual sales of $150 billion.

component of a car—don't get counted separately because that would imply double-counting. The engine is implicitly counted when we value the final good, which is the complete car.

GDP is a measure of production, not a measure of sales to consumers. So something that is produced is counted in GDP even if it is not sold to a customer. For example, Ford will increase its inventory of (unsold) cars if it manufactures a car in 2015 but doesn't sell it in 2015. Production that goes into inventories counts as part of GDP.

Expenditure

There's a *second* way to think about the level of aggregate activity in the economy of Fordica. This second method yields exactly the same answer as the previous production-based method. Households and firms, some of whom reside in Fordica and some of whom reside in foreign countries, are going to buy all of the cars produced in this economy. If we add up all of these car purchases, we will find that the total expenditure on Fordica's output is exactly $150 billion (again).

You might object by asking, "What if some of the goods don't get sold?" Economists reply that those unsold goods are *owned* by a firm and those goods are therefore counted as part of the firm's inventory. In the accounting system that we are describing here, that inventory is coded as having been "purchased" by the firm. Including both household car expenditures and firm inventory car expenditures, total expenditures sum to $150 billion.

Income

Let's pause for a moment and ask why we are focusing on the goods and services that are produced by Fordica and purchased from producers in Fordica. We could instead have focused on what households and firms located in Fordica earned—in other words, their income. Isn't that really what matters? Let's consider that alternative approach, which happens to be the *third* way to think about the level of aggregate activity.

We've already calculated that Ford generates $150 billion of revenue. It pays $X to its workers, and it keeps ($150 billion − $X) for its owners. So the total income of all the workers and all of the owners in the nation of Fordica is

$$\$X + (\$150 \text{ billion} - \$X) = \$150 \text{ billion}.$$

Note that this is the identical amount—$150 billion—that we determined the economy *produced* in our earlier calculations. It is also the value of expenditures on goods and services produced in Fordica.

The fact that we keep coming up with the amount $150 billion is not a coincidence. Because of the way we've set up the system of national income accounts, every dollar of revenue must either go to some worker or be retained by the firm. So the total value of revenue *must* equal the total value of income received by workers and owners. This necessary equivalence is referred to as an *identity*. Two variables are related by an **identity** when the two variables are defined in a way that makes them mathematically identical. The equivalence of the value of production, the value of expenditure, and the value of income may not be apparent at first glance, but the three concepts have been defined so that they are necessarily identical.

You can now understand the following aggregate accounting identity:

$$\text{Production} = \text{Expenditure} = \text{Income}.$$

This identity is the key conceptual point of this chapter and the foundation on which most macroeconomic analysis is built. Now let's delve more deeply into the system of national income accounts.

Two variables are related by an **identity** when the two variables are defined in a way that makes them mathematically identical.

> **Production = Expenditure = Income,** is the key conceptual point of this chapter and the foundation on which most macroeconomic analysis is built.

Circular Flows

19.1

19.2

19.3

19.4

Factors of production are the
inputs to the production process.

Factors of production are the inputs to the production process. Factors of production come in two key forms: *capital* and *labor*. We'll have more to say about capital below, but for now it is helpful to simplify analysis by thinking of capital as physical capital—for instance, land, factories, and machines. Both physical capital and labor are "owned" by households. Households own most of the physical capital in the economy, either directly or indirectly, because firms are owned by shareholders and most shareholders are households.

To understand how the three parts of the national income accounts—production, expenditure, and income—relate to one another, we need to think about the connections between households and firms. Firms, like the aircraft manufacturer Boeing, demand physical capital and labor and supply goods and services, like airplanes. Households demand goods and services, like air travel, and supply physical capital and labor.

We can explain the connections between households and firms with a circular flow diagram of the type displayed in Exhibit 19.1. This diagram highlights four kinds of economic flows that connect households and firms. It includes the three kinds of flows that we discussed in the Fordica example (Production = Expenditure = Income) and adds a fourth category, Factors of Production.

1. Production
2. Expenditure
3. Income
4. Factors of Production

Exhibit 19.1 is admittedly a simplification of the economy because it leaves out important institutions like governments, markets, banks, and foreign countries. But the circular flow diagram provides a useful way of understanding the basic structure of a modern economy.

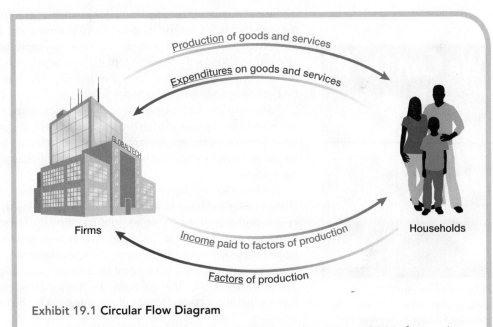

Exhibit 19.1 Circular Flow Diagram

Economists have designed national income accounts that measure GDP in four equivalent ways: production, expenditure, income, and factors of production. The circular flow diagram provides a visual way of remembering the relationships among these four equivalent systems. Firms on the left produce goods and services (<u>Production</u>). Households on the right pay to buy those goods and services (<u>Expenditure</u>). Firms pay households to use households' physical capital and labor (<u>Income</u>). Physical capital and labor are factors of production, which are put to use by firms (<u>Factors</u>). The national income accounting system is set up so that all four sets of flows are equal in market value.

Production and expenditure. A Ford Mustang is produced by Ford (production) and it is purchased by Ford's customers (expenditure).

The circular flow diagram presents two main decision makers—firms and households—and it shows the four types of flows that we listed a moment ago.

Production represents the goods and services that are produced by firms. These goods and services are ultimately sold to households. We therefore draw an arrow from the firm sector to the household sector when talking about production. For example, a Ford Mustang starts life on the factory floor and ends up in someone's garage.

Expenditure represents the payments for goods and services. These payments are made by households to firms. So we draw an arrow from the household sector to the firm sector when talking about expenditure. Continuing our earlier example, the household pays Ford $30,000 for a Mustang. Note that production and expenditure both involve goods and services, so these two flows are grouped together. They jointly represent the market for goods and services.

Income represents the payments that are made from firms to households to compensate the households for the use of their physical capital and labor (in other words, the use of the households' factors of production). These payments include things like wages, salaries, interest, and dividends. We therefore draw an arrow from the firm sector to the household sector when talking about income. For instance, the average labor compensation received by Ford's employees is $65,000 per year.

Factors of production represent the productive resources that are owned by households and used by firms in the production process. Because factors of production—both labor and physical capital—are directly or indirectly owned by households, we draw an arrow from the household sector to the firm sector when talking about factors of production.

The remarkable thing about these four types of transactions or "flows" is that they must all be *exactly* the same in market value. That's where the system of national income accounts comes in. If we do the accounting correctly, the market value of expenditure *must* equal the market value of production. Likewise, the market value of expenditure *must* equal the market value of income of the households in the economy. In the same way, the market value of income *must* equal the market value of the factors of production—labor and physical capital—that are receiving those income payments. These relationships are just mathematical consequences of the ways that we define the system of national income accounts.

Although the circular flow diagram contains four sets of flows with identical market values, in the discussion that follows we return to our earlier three-part system of national income accounts: Production = Expenditures = Income. In practice, these are the three parts of the national income accounts that government statisticians actually measure.

National Income Accounts: Production

We now revisit each of the methods for calculating national income and dig a little deeper. First, let's consider production-based national income accounts. Production-based accounts sum up the market value that is added by each domestic firm in the production process. More formally, production-based accounts measure each firm's **value added,**

A factor of production and a source of income. This famous image of a factory worker appeared in a poster designed to boost worker morale during World War II.

Production-based accounting measures each firm's **value added,** which is the firm's sales revenue minus the firm's purchases of intermediate products from other firms.

which is the firm's sales revenue minus the firm's purchases of intermediate products from other firms.

For example, consider the Dell computer company. Two decades ago, Dell assembled almost all of its computers in the United States. These days, Dell buys almost all of its computers from foreign manufacturers. When a customer orders a Dell computer, Dell instructs a foreign producer—usually one in Asia, Mexico, or Ireland—to assemble the computer. Dell then imports the machine from the foreign factory and sends the machine to its U.S. customer. The laptop that Dell purchases from a foreign producer is an intermediate product in Dell's production.

Dell has also shifted its business strategy on the retail side. Dell now markets some, though by no means all, of its computers through other companies. For example, you can buy a Dell computer at BestBuy, Staples, or Walmart.

Exhibit 19.2 puts all of these pieces together. As the exhibit shows, consumers buy about $50 billion worth of Dell computers in the United States each year. About $15 billion of sales of Dell computers comes from customers who buy at third-party retailers, like Walmart. About $35 billion of sales comes from customers who buy directly from Dell.

Retailers like Walmart pay Dell about two-thirds of the revenue that Walmart receives from the sale of Dell's computers. So Dell receives $10 billion from third-party retailers and another $35 billion from direct-sale customers: $45 billion in total. Dell pays its foreign suppliers $30 billion for assembling Dell computers. That leaves Dell with $15 billion in net revenue from its U.S. operations. Out of that revenue, Dell pays its domestic costs, such as employee wages and construction costs for building warehouses.

Let's determine what value Dell (including its domestic employees) has added to the production process. That amount will be Dell's contribution to U.S. gross domestic product (GDP). The answer is $15 billion, which is a lot less than the $50 billion that U.S. consumers spent on Dell computers. We came to $15 billion by taking the revenue that Dell itself

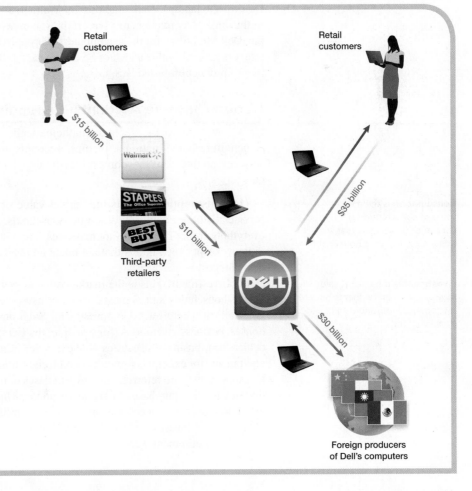

Exhibit 19.2 Dell's Value Added

U.S. consumers spend $50 billion annually on Dell computers, but Dell's value added to U.S. GDP is only $15 billion. Dell receives revenue of $45 billion from third-party retailers ($10 billion) and from direct sales to retail customers ($35 billion). Dell pays its suppliers (foreign producers) $30 billion. The difference, $45 billion − $30 billion = $15 billion, is the value added of Dell and its employees.

Retail customers

Retail customers

$15 billion

Walmart

STAPLES
The Office Superstore

BEST BUY

Third-party retailers

$10 billion

$35 billion

DELL

$30 billion

Foreign producers of Dell's computers

received, $45 billion, and subtracting Dell's payments of $30 billion to foreign suppliers for intermediate goods.

Total sales of Dell computers to retail customers:

$15 billion through other retailers + $35 billion in direct sales = $50 billion.

Revenue received by Dell:

$10 billion from third-party retailers + $35 billion from direct sales = $45 billion.

Revenue received by Dell minus purchases of intermediate products = Dell's value added:

$45 billion received by Dell − $30 billion paid for intermediate products = $15 billion.

We could go on to ask what else would get counted as U.S. GDP in this chain of economic activity (even if it isn't counted as part of Dell's contribution). The foreign factories don't count toward U.S. GDP. The production of the foreign laptop factories is part of a foreign country's GDP because the factories are within the boundaries of those foreign countries.

The production-based accounting system implies that importing some good from abroad and selling it to a U.S. consumer at the exact same import price doesn't add value. However, importing something for $1 and reselling it for $1.50 is a source of production—$0.50 of value added to be precise. Dell's ability to mark up its price relative to the import cost comes from a combination of marketing, corporate reputation, customer convenience, and bundled services like access to call centers.

Likewise, Walmart's ability to sell Dell's computers is another source of U.S. value added. Walmart isn't making anything in a factory, but its ability to buy goods at wholesale prices and sell those goods at higher retail prices reflects its value added and consequently its contribution to GDP. Walmart's value added is not the revenue that Walmart receives from its customers. Walmart's value added is the difference between the revenue that Walmart receives when it sells Dell's computers and the amount that Walmart pays Dell for the laptops. Dell's laptops are Walmart's intermediate goods. In our example, all of the third-party retailers receive $15 billion in revenue from selling Dell's computers and pay Dell $10 billion for those computers. Through this chain of transactions, the third-party retailers generate value added of $5 billion ($15 billion − $10 billion), which is counted as part of production-based U.S. GDP.

National Income Accounts: Expenditure

Let's now turn to the second, mathematically equivalent, way of measuring GDP. Expenditure-based national income accounts measure the purchases of goods and services produced in the domestic economy. These purchases can be assigned to five categories.

(1) Consumption. This is the market value of consumption goods and consumption services that are bought by domestic households. Such consumption expenditures cover everything from Frisbees to foot massages. This category includes all consumption expenditures except expenditures that are made on residential construction (which is part of the next category).

(2) Investment. This is the market value of new physical capital that is bought by domestic households and domestic firms. This is technically called *private investment* but is usually just referred to as investment. Such new physical capital includes residential houses, business inventories (for example, the Camaro waiting to be bought at a Chevrolet dealership), business structures (for example, office towers and factories), and business equipment (for example, computers and freight trains). When macroeconomists talk about investment, they are referring only to purchases of *new physical capital* and *not* to financial investments like purchases of stocks or bonds. This difference in usage generates lots of confusion, because noneconomists are more familiar with the everyday financial meaning of "making an investment" (for instance, buying a mutual fund or contributing money to an Individual Retirement Account), which is not what macroeconomists have in mind. In the

Consumption is the market value of consumption goods and consumption services that are bought by domestic households.

Investment is the market value of new physical capital that is bought by domestic households and domestic firms.

language of macroeconomics, investment is only the purchase of new physical capital, like a new supertanker or a new factory or a new house.

Government expenditure is the market value of government purchases of goods and services.

(3) Government expenditure. This is the market value of government purchases of goods and services. Tanks and bridges are two examples of government expenditure. For the purposes of the national income accounts, government expenditure *excludes* transfer payments (for example, Social Security payments to retirees) and also *excludes* interest paid on government debt. These categories are omitted because they represent payments to other agents in the economy who will use those payments to buy goods and services. To avoid double-counting, these government payments to other agents are not counted as government expenditure on goods and services.

Exports are the market value of all domestically produced goods and services that are purchased by households, firms, and governments in foreign countries.

(4) Exports. This is the market value of all domestically produced goods and services that are sold to households, firms, and governments in *foreign* countries.

These first four categories are nonoverlapping. In other words, there is no double-counting. Each purchase appears in only one of the four categories above.

Imports are the market value of all foreign-produced goods and services that are sold to domestic households, domestic firms, and the domestic government.

(5) Imports. This is the market value of all foreign-produced goods and services that are sold to domestic households, domestic firms, and the domestic government. Note that imports are already part of consumption expenditures, investment expenditures, and government expenditures. Hence, imports overlap with the first three categories in our list. We'll explain why this overlap is useful in a moment.

We are now ready to use these five categories to calculate gross domestic product (GDP). Let Y represent the total market value of goods and services that are produced in the domestic economy, which is GDP. We'll use C to represent consumption: household expenditures on consumption of goods and services, including expenditure on consumption of goods and services produced domestically and abroad. Variable I will represent investment: expenditures on investment goods by private agents (excluding the government), including investment goods produced domestically and abroad. We'll let G represent goverment expenditure: government purchases of goods and services, including goods and services produced domestically and abroad.

We need to adjust for the fact that exports (goods produced in the United States, which are sold to households, firms, and governments in foreign countries) count as part of U.S. GDP. On the other hand, imports (domestic expenditures on goods and services produced abroad) don't count as part of U.S. GDP.

> The GDP equation says that the market value of domestic production is equal to the total expenditure of domestic economic agents ($C + I + G$), plus the expenditure of foreign agents on exports (X) minus the value of domestic expenditure that was imported (M).

Let X represent exports: the value of goods and services produced in the domestic economy and purchased by economic agents in foreign countries. Let M represent imports: the value of goods and services produced in foreign countries and purchased by economic agents in the domestic economy. Finally, note that exports minus imports, or $X - M$, is the trade balance. When X is greater than M, exports are greater than imports, so the country runs a trade surplus. When X is less than M, exports are less than imports, so the country runs a trade deficit.

We can now calculate the total value of expenditures on goods and services produced in the domestic economy:

$$Y = C + I + G + X - M \quad \text{(National Income Accounting Identity)}.$$

The **national income accounting identity**, $Y = C + I + G + X - M$, decomposes GDP into consumption + investment + government expenditure + exports − imports.

The GDP equation says that the market value of domestic production is equal to the *total* expenditure of domestic economic agents, $C + I + G$, plus the expenditure of foreign agents on exports, X, minus the value of domestic expenditure that was imported, M. We subtract imports because expenditure on foreign production is included in the terms C, I, and G. To *remove* this expenditure on foreign production, we subtract imports, M.

This identity, which decomposes GDP into ($C + I + G + X - M$), is so important that we give it a name: the **national income accounting identity**. We'll use it many times in our study of the macroeconomy.

Evidence-Based Economics

Q: In the United States, what is the total market value of annual economic production?

Government statisticians measure gross domestic product, the total market value of economic output. In the United States, this work is conducted by the Bureau of Economic Analysis in the Department of Commerce. In 2013, the Bureau of Economic Analysis reported that U.S. GDP was $16.8 trillion. That year, the U.S. population was 316.4 million people. So GDP per person—in other words, GDP *per capita*—was about $53,100.

It is also valuable to study the components of GDP using the national income accounting identity that we just discussed. Exhibit 19.3 reports this data for the United States in 2013. We can observe several important properties. First, the overwhelming share of GDP is represented by household consumption. In 2013, consumption represented 69 percent of GDP. Government expenditure comes in far behind, with only 19 percent of GDP. Investment follows next with 16 percent. Exports account for 14 percent of GDP and imports account for 16 percent of GDP. Notice that imports appear in Exhibit 19.3 with a negative sign, reminding you that when calculating GDP, imports are subtracted out after we add up all of the other components. Confirm that the items in Exhibit 19.3 add up to GDP (with a bit of rounding error).

The fraction of GDP in each category—these are called GDP shares—has been relatively constant over the past 80 years. Exhibit 19.4 reports the GDP shares from 1929 to 2013. In other words, Exhibit 19.4 reports the ratio of each expenditure category to GDP. The sum of these shares, minus the import share, must sum to one. Exhibit 19.4 shows that consumption has consistently represented about two-thirds of economic activity.

Government expenditures have consistently hovered around 20 percent of economic activity, with two exceptions. First, at the very beginning of the sample period, government expenditures accounted for only 10 percent of GDP. Large governments did not become the norm in the modern world until after World War II.

Second, government expenditures temporarily absorbed a particularly large share of GDP during World War II. The high point was nearly 50 percent of GDP. It is natural

MyEconLab Real-time data

	Trillions of Dollars	Share of GDP
Gross domestic product	16.8	100.0%
Consumption	11.5	68.5%
+ Investment	2.7	15.9%
+ Government expenditure	3.1	18.6%
+ Exports	2.3	13.5%
− Imports	−2.8	−16.4%

Exhibit 19.3 U.S. 2013 GDP and GDP Shares (Expenditure-based Accounting)

U.S. gross domestic product in 2013 was $16.8 trillion. Each component of GDP is expressed as a percentage of GDP, or a GDP "share" (component/GDP). Rounding causes the components to fail to sum to total GDP. Rounding also causes small discrepancies between the column in dollars and the column in shares.

Source: Bureau of Economic Analysis, National Income and Product Accounts.

Exhibit 19.4 U.S. GDP Shares (1929–2013)

GDP shares have been relatively constant over time, with the exception of World War II.

Source: Bureau of Economic Analysis, National Income and Product Accounts.

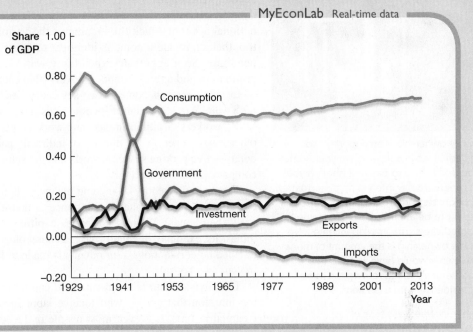

that during major wars the government accounts for a much larger share of a country's economic output because a war effort is run almost exclusively by the government. The rise in government activity during World War II is mirrored by a fall in consumption and a fall in (private) investment.

There is one final property that is important to note in Exhibit 19.4: the export and import shares have both been getting larger in absolute value over the past 80 years. Transportation technology has made it less expensive to ship goods anywhere in the world. Information technology has also made it easier for residents of one country to provide services to residents of other countries (think of call centers in India). Falling transportation and telecommunication costs have fueled an ongoing rise in trade, as optimizers look beyond their national borders to buy the goods and services that they want. Rising exports show up as a rising share of exports. Because imports appear as a negative number in the GDP identity, rising imports show up as a movement in the import share further below zero.

Question

In the United States, what is the total market value of annual economic production?

Answer

In 2013, the Bureau of Economic Analysis reported that U.S. GDP was $16.8 trillion, or $53,100 per capita.[1]

Data

National Income and Product Accounts compiled by the Bureau of Economic Analysis.

Caveat

National income accounts omit many types of economic production, an issue that we discuss later in this chapter.

Home ownership is an important source of capital income. If you own your home, you don't need to pay rent (though you may need to pay interest on a mortgage). Economists consider the "nonpayment" of rent to be a form of capital income to homeowners. The implied income from home ownership is the amount of money the owner would have needed to spend had he or she been renting the same kind of residence from a landlord.

Labor income is any form of payment that compensates people for their work.

Capital income is any form of payment that derives from owning physical or financial capital.

National Income Accounting: Income

So far, we've taken a detailed look at the economy by studying GDP as a production concept—that was the discussion of value added—and then by studying GDP as an expenditure concept—that was the discussion of the national income accounting identity, $Y = C + I + G + X - M$. As we explained at the start of the chapter, we can also study GDP as an income concept. Recall that income-based national accounts track the income of the various agents in the economy. Recall, too, that aggregate income is identical to aggregate production and aggregate expenditure. So if aggregate expenditure was $16.8 trillion in 2013, then aggregate production and aggregate income were also each $16.8 trillion in 2013.

Income payments come in two key categories. First, there is *income paid for people's work*. We call this **labor income**. This category includes familiar items like wages, salary, workers' health insurance, and workers' pension benefits. It also includes every other way that people are directly or indirectly paid for their labor, including signing bonuses, free parking spaces at work, and the value to the CEO of being able to use the company jet on weekends.

The second category of income payments is income (or benefits) realized by the owners of physical capital (for instance, a house) or financial capital (for instance, stocks and bonds). We refer to this as **capital income**. This category includes many things: for example, dividends paid to shareholders, interest paid to lenders, earnings retained by corporations, rent payments made to landlords, and the benefits of living in your own house!

This division into labor income and capital income may encourage the misleading intuition that people who receive labor income are different from those who receive capital income. However, most people in the economy receive both. For example, a 50-year-old worker with a job, a house, and a retirement savings account will receive labor income from her job, capital income from her house (the implicit value of having a roof over her head), and capital income from her retirement savings account (dividends).

It is also important to remember that firms are owned by households. Firms can't own themselves. When a firm earns income, it is the owners of the firm who are the ultimate

---

 LETTING THE DATA SPEAK

Saving vs. Investment

Economists use the national income accounting identities to study saving and investment. To derive an equation for saving, start with GDP, which is equivalent to national income, and subtract the things that households and the government consume. In other words, subtract consumption expenditures and government expenditure. We then find that

$$\text{Saving} = Y - C - G$$
$$= (C + I + G + X - M) - C - G$$
$$= I + X - M.$$

To get from the first equation to the second equation, we replaced Y with its components from the national income accounting identity: $C + I + G + X - M$. The final equation in our derivation can be written out in words:

$$\text{Saving} = \text{Investment} + \text{Exports} - \text{Imports}.$$

In most countries, exports and imports are relatively close in magnitude. In that case, exports minus imports will be close to zero, enabling us to further simplify our expression:

$$\text{Saving} = \text{Investment}.$$

This simplified expression is just an approximation, since exports and imports are never exactly the same when a

country trades with other countries. However, this equation will be *exactly* true for a closed economy, which is an economy that does not trade with other countries. In a closed economy, exports and imports are both equal to zero.

Let's now take the last equation and divide both sides by GDP. You'll then see that the saving rate (saving divided by GDP) is equal to the investment rate (investment divided by GDP):

$$\frac{\text{Saving}}{\text{GDP}} = \frac{\text{Investment}}{\text{GDP}}.$$

Using U.S. data from 1929 to 2013, we can compare the saving rate and the investment rate, year-by-year. Exhibit 19.5 graphs a scatter plot of these two ratios. Each point plots a single year of data: the saving rate for that year is on the horizontal axis and the investment rate is on the vertical axis. As you can see, the saving rate and the investment rate move together very closely and the cloud of data points stays relatively close to the 45 degree line (which is plotted in red).

Exhibit 19.5 implies that saving is roughly equal to investment. We'll use this fact in the next chapter when we start to discuss the determinants of economic growth, including investment in physical capital.

Exhibit 19.5 The Relationship Between the Saving Rate and the Investment Rate (1929–2013)

Each point plots a single year of data: the saving rate for that year is on the horizontal axis and the investment rate for that year is on the vertical axis. The scatter plot implies that the saving rate and the investment rate tend to move together from year to year. The points stay close to the 45 degree line (which is plotted in red). The green circle represents the last year of data in the scatter plot, 2013.

Source: Bureau of Economic Analysis, National Income and Product Accounts.

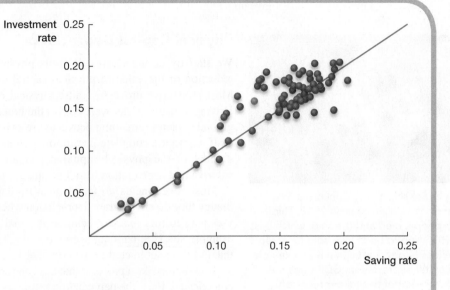

beneficiaries. Most large firms have shares that are traded on the stock market. In this case, the firm is owned by hundreds of millions of shareholders around the globe. The beneficiaries of capital income are these shareholders.

Finally, it is interesting to ask what fraction of income payments are labor payments and what fraction of income payments are capital payments. In the United States and other developed economies, nearly two-thirds of income payments goes to labor and one-third goes to capital.

19.3 What Isn't Measured by GDP?

Before leaving our homes in the morning, many of us go to the Web to look up the current weather conditions. Some weather Web sites report a single temperature and a simple picture.

This weather report leaves a lot of details out. Humidity, haze, wind speed, and hundreds of other factors all contribute to the actual conditions that we experience as we walk to work or sprint for the train. Nevertheless, commuters are grateful for a simple summary that tells them most of what they need to know about the local weather.

Likewise, GDP and national income accounting is a useful system for taking the temperature of the economy. It's not perfect, and it necessarily leaves out a lot of details. Nevertheless, GDP does a good job of telling us much of what we need to know about the level, fluctuations, and long-run trends in economic activity. With this tool in hand, we are ready to try to measure and predict the behavior of the entire economy.

But it's important to discuss what GDP leaves out, so we know what GDP can and can't do. GDP has many quirks that limit its value as a measure of societal well-being or even of overall economic activity.

Economists are a bold breed. Measuring the production of an entire economy can't be done exactly right, but we do it *anyway*. Sticking our collective heads in the sand and waiting

This is a simplified, but useful summary of the weather. Likewise, GDP is a simplified, but useful summary of the economy.

for the perfect system of measurement to be invented is not a satisfactory alternative. We believe that it's much better to have an imperfect measure than to throw up our hands and give up.

Physical Capital Depreciation

We start by noting that GDP omits physical capital depreciation, which is the reduction of the value of physical capital due to obsolescence or wear and tear. Most productive processes cause physical capital to lose some value over time. Driving a tractor trailer wears down the brakes and the tires. Pumping oil from the ground depletes remaining petroleum reserves.

The cruise ship *Costa Concordia* hit a reef off the Italian coast in 2012. Thirty-two people died and the ship, which cost $600 million to build, was sold for scrap. The loss of physical capital is an example of capital depreciation. GDP does not take account of capital depreciation.

If we want a complete picture of economic production, we might want to take account of the physical capital depreciation that accompanies production and *subtract* that depreciation from the value of total production.

Most governments *do* try to measure depreciation in their national accounts, though they do *not* subtract depreciation when calculating GDP. Depreciation analyses tend to find that depreciation is equal to about 10–15 percent of GDP. For example, the U.S. national accounts estimate that depreciation is large enough so that *if* it were subtracted, it would offset 13 percent of GDP.

This sounds like a problem that has been solved, but the situation is actually more complicated. First, the depreciation estimates in the national accounts are more like sophisticated guess work—"guesstimates"—than something that we know how to measure precisely. Second, the depreciation estimates don't even attempt to cover lots of hard-to-analyze categories like oil reserve depreciation. Third, thinking about physical capital depreciation raises many related questions. For example, changes in our health are also left out of the GDP calculations completely. Some productive processes make workers less healthy—for example, backbreaking work in a coal mine or exposure to toxic chemicals in a manufacturing process. If we take account of physical capital depreciation, should we also try to calculate depreciation of health and *human capital* (a concept that we will return to in the next chapter)?

In sum, trying to measure depreciation is a complicated conceptual issue and the standard measure of GDP does not account for any type of depreciation.

Home Production

GDP also stumbles when it comes to home production, which is not included anywhere in the national income accounts. If you grow your own flowers (without buying seeds or shovels from a plant store), the bouquet you create is not measured in GDP, but if you buy domestically grown flowers from the local florist, every dollar is included in GDP. If you knit your own wool cap using wool from the sheep that you keep on your farm, nothing shows up in GDP, but if you knit a cap from the same wool and sell it to your neighbor, every dollar counts in GDP. Sometimes the accounting rules are laughable. For example, GDP goes down if you marry your gardener.

All economists agree that excluding home production is a flaw in the GDP accounts, but we do not yet have a way to measure home production. There is no market transaction, market price, or measurable quantity that accompanies home production. What is the market value of a home-cooked meal? Families have been debating that philosophical question for a long time.

If we were only talking about a home-cooked meatloaf here and there, this omission would not be a big deal. But a large fraction of economic activity takes place in the home. Most families maintain their own homes by personally dusting, vacuuming, mopping, and polishing them. People often mow their own grass, rake their own leaves, and weed their own flower beds. Most families eat most of their meals at home.

Finally, there is the very important category of childcare, which is illustrated by the following example. Suppose there are two parents in *different* households, Avery and Micah. Suppose that they each have kids. If Avery and Micah stay home to care for their *own* kids, there is no market transaction and the childcare is not recorded in GDP. On the other hand, if Avery takes care of Micah's kids and is paid a salary of $40,000, and Micah takes care of Avery's kids and receives a salary of $40,000, then annual GDP rises by the sum, $80,000. Note that the children are being cared for regardless of whether this

Should childcare be measured in GDP, even when it is not a market-based activity?

care is measured by GDP. When each parent cares for his or her own kids, childcare is produced without a market transaction and childcare is omitted from GDP. When each parent takes care of the *other* family's kids, childcare generates a market transaction and GDP is $80,000 higher.

There are two reasons why economists lose sleep worrying about all of this. First, a large fraction of the adult population does stay at home to work. We know from surveys of time use that people who are not officially employed are doing a lot more than watching reruns of *Breaking Bad*. Second, even people with formal jobs are engaged in some home production. If you hold down a day job, it is likely that you also do some cleaning or cooking or childcare when you get home from work.

Let's quantify these effects. In the United States, where the total population was 316.4 million in 2013, there were approximately 144 million working-age adults with formal jobs and another 52 million working-age adults without formal jobs.

Many of the people without formal jobs are engaged in a considerable amount of home production, including food preparation, household maintenance, and childcare. Suppose that the working-age adults without formal jobs have an average annual home production of $20,000 per person. That number averages over people with different amounts of home production. Some people who aren't in the formal labor force care for newborn triplets and others watch YouTube all day.

In addition, suppose that the people *with* formal jobs outside the home also do home production of $10,000 per year.

Adding up all of these different sources of home production we get annual home production in the United States of $2.5 trillion:

$$(52 \text{ million people}) \times (\$20,000/\text{person})$$
$$+ (144 \text{ million people}) \times (\$10,000/\text{person}) = \$2.5 \text{ trillion.}$$

In an economy with $16.8 trillion of market-based production, $2.5 trillion represents nearly 15 percent of additional economic production that has been overlooked in the GDP calculation. Many other estimates of home production are even higher.

The Underground Economy

The *underground economy*—transactions that are intentionally hidden from government statisticians—represents another hole in the GDP accounts. This includes the plumber who asks to be paid in cash and the taxicab driver who negotiates a lower rate if you would just agree to let him turn off the meter. Plumbing and cab driving are perfectly legal, but some workers hide income to avoid paying taxes. Earnings from legal professions may also be hidden for other reasons, for instance, an acrimonious divorce or the lack of a work visa.

The underground economy also includes markets in illegal professions. Drug dealing and prostitution top the list (though some communities have legalized some of these activities). Illegal drug sales alone are estimated to be equal in magnitude to 1 percent of GDP. For the U.S. economy, that is equivalent to the value of *all* agricultural production.

In developed economies with excellent law enforcement systems—think of countries like Switzerland, Japan, Hong Kong, and the United States—transactions in the underground economy add up to about 10 percent of GDP. In developing countries, the fraction of underground economic activity is generally much higher. For example, in Mexico, the underground economy is estimated to be half of measured GDP.

Some countries, including Ireland, Italy, and the United Kingdom have recently started to include underground economic activity, including illicit drug purchases and prostitution, in their GDP calculations.

Negative Externalities

Negative externalities occur when an economic activity has a spillover cost that does not affect those directly engaged in the activity. Positive externalities occur when an economic activity has a spillover benefit that does not affect those directly engaged in the activity. Externalities—both negative and positive—are usually omitted from the GDP calculations. Consider a coal-powered electrical plant generating power for thousands of

The societal cost of pollution is not subtracted from GDP.

homes and simultaneously belching out a continuous stream of toxic airborne pollutants. GDP counts the electricity produced, but fails to subtract the cost of the pollution.

Sometimes negative externalities even get counted as *positive* contributors to economic output. For example, property crimes, like theft, lead people to purchase locks and other security devices. In some cases, property owners hire guards to safeguard their possessions. All of this preventive activity counts as positive contributions to GDP.

Gross Domestic Product vs. Gross National Product

As we've already explained, GDP is the market value of everything produced within the borders of a country during a particular period of time. So GDP includes both the production of a country's residents and the production of visitors. For example, if a U.S. worker spends two months working in Singapore, her production will be counted in the GDP of Singapore and omitted from U.S. GDP. Likewise, if a Japanese auto company—like Honda —opens a plant in Alabama, the value added of this plant will be counted in U.S. GDP and not in Japanese GDP. This would be the case even if the plant were operated entirely by robots and didn't have one U.S. employee. The plant is operating within the borders of the United States, so its value added is counted in U.S. GDP.

At first glance, you might wonder if cross-border activities amount to much. In fact, there are large amounts of such activity. For example, about 70 percent of the "Japanese" cars that are sold in the United States are now manufactured at plants in Canada, Mexico, and the United States.

Gross national product (GNP) is the market value of production generated by the factors of production—both capital and labor—possessed or owned by the residents of a particular nation.

With facts like this in mind, economists have constructed a measure of aggregate economic activity that includes only the output of factors of production owned by residents of a particular country: **gross national product (GNP)**. U.S. GNP includes the production of a worker who normally resides in the United States, even if the production occurred when the worker was temporarily working abroad. For example, if a U.S. professor gives a summer course at the National University of Singapore, her two-month salary, which was paid by the National University of Singapore, would be included in U.S. GNP and excluded from Singapore's GNP.

Likewise, U.S. GNP would exclude the value added of machines owned by a Japanese car manufacturer, even if those machines operate in Alabama. On the other hand, U.S. GNP would include the value added of U.S. workers who are employed in a Japanese auto plant in Alabama. U.S. GNP is carefully constructed to count only the value added of factors of production possessed or owned by U.S. residents, no matter where those factors of production operate in the world.

GNP is therefore a measure of national production, where the word *national* signifies the factors of production—like capital and labor—possessed or owned by the residents of a particular nation. To calculate GNP, begin with GDP and first add in the production of U.S.-owned factors of production that operate within the borders of foreign countries. Then subtract the production of foreign-owned factors of production that operate within the borders of the United States.

Gross national product = (Gross domestic product)
  + (Production of U.S.-owned capital and labor within the borders of foreign countries)
  − (Production of foreign-owned capital and labor within U.S. borders).

Plugging in the actual (rounded) numbers for 2013, we find that U.S. GNP ($17.1 trillion) is higher than U.S. GDP ($16.8 trillion). Specifically, the market value of production of U.S. capital and labor within the borders of foreign countries ($0.8 trillion) exceeds the market value of production of foreign capital and labor within U.S. borders ($0.6 trillion). In 2013, U.S. GNP was 1.5 percent larger than U.S. GDP.

For a few countries, GNP and GDP diverge much more substantially. For example, Kuwait—a wealthy oil exporter in the Persian Gulf—owns a very large portfolio of foreign assets, and residents of foreign countries own comparatively few assets inside Kuwait. The income from Kuwait's foreign assets is counted in Kuwait's GNP but excluded from Kuwait's GDP. Accordingly Kuwait's GNP is substantially larger—generally about

10 percent larger—than its GDP. However, Kuwait's situation is uncommon. For most countries, GNP and GDP are nearly the same.

Leisure

Leisure is another sore spot in the GDP system. The GDP accounts give an economy no credit for producing leisure. However, most people would agree that leisure is a key ingredient in human well-being. For example, in time-use surveys, people report that they are happiest when they are socializing.[2] Likewise, people report that they are the least happy when they are at work or commuting to and from work. When you think about GDP comparisons across countries, you need to remember that different countries are working at different levels of intensity. Of course, the goal in life is *not* to maximize your income by working every moment that you can. If that were our goal, nobody would ever retire or take a vacation. A more reasonable goal is to maximize human well-being—this is another example of optimization. GDP tells us how many material goods are being produced by an economy, but it does not tell us whether all of those material achievements are being used to optimize human happiness.

Does GDP Buy Happiness?

Despite the omission of leisure, GDP per capita is often used as a summary measure of the well-being of a society. We would like to know whether GDP per capita is *actually* a good predictor of human happiness. Social scientists do not have a foolproof way of measuring happiness, but we do have a crude way of gauging whether a person is satisfied with life: ask them. It's not an ideal method—for instance, people may not tell the truth: "I'm fine, how are you?"—but it's a start. When survey researchers ask about happiness in millions of interviews around the world, some remarkable patterns appear in the data.

GDP per capita turns out to be an excellent predictor of life satisfaction. Exhibit 19.6 displays a positive relationship between GDP per capita and self-reports of life satisfaction in a large sample of countries. The countries with higher levels of GDP per capita report higher levels of life satisfaction. The exhibit plots GDP per capita on the horizontal axis and average life satisfaction on the vertical axis. Life satisfaction was measured with a 10-point scale. Each circle represents a different country, and the size of the circle reflects the size of the population in that country. The large circle on the right is the United States. The two large circles on the left are India and China.

> GDP per capita turns out to be an excellent predictor of life satisfaction.

Exhibit 19.6 GDP per Capita and Life Satisfaction

A strong positive relationship is visible when we compare GDP per capita to mean life satisfaction (measured on a 10-point scale) in a large sample of countries.

Source: Angus Deaton, "Income, Health and Wellbeing Around the World: Evidence from the Gallup World Poll," *Journal of Economic Perspectives* 22, no. 2 (2008): 53–72.

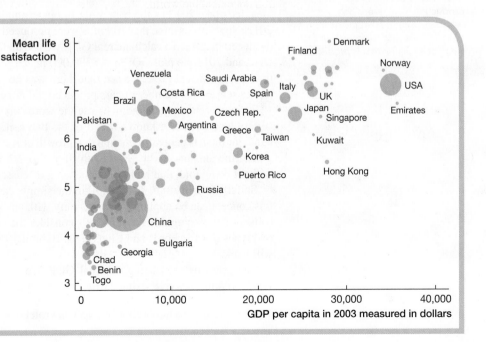

The same relationship also shows up within each country. In other words, when economists study household-level data on income and life satisfaction, we find that low-income households within a country report substantially lower life satisfaction than higher-income households within the same country.[3]

19.4 Real vs. Nominal

GDP is particularly useful as a tool for determining how the overall economy is growing. To implement this growth analysis, we would like to separate the increase in the value of GDP that is due to overall price increases (in other words, inflation, a concept we will define below) from the increase in the value of GDP that is due to increases in the quantity and quality of goods and services.

For example, suppose the country of Fordica makes 10 cars in 2012 and 10 identical cars in 2013. Here we'll make the simplifying assumption that the quality of the cars hasn't changed over time. Economists have sophisticated tools for handling improvements in quality, but we'll sidestep those issues to keep the analysis as simple as possible. Holding quality fixed, assume that the price of each car rises from $30,000 to $40,000 from 2012 to 2013. In this case, GDP in 2012 would be (10 cars × $30,000/car) = $300,000 and GDP in 2013 would be (10 cars × $40,000/car) = $400,000. At first glance, the economy has grown by 33 percent, or

$$\frac{(\text{GDP in 2013}) - (\text{GDP in 2012})}{\text{GDP in 2012}} = \frac{(\$400,000) - (\$300,000)}{\$300,000} = \frac{1}{3} = 0.33 = 33\%.$$

But the actual number of cars produced hasn't grown at all. It's still 10 cars. If we counted the *number* of cars, rather than their market value, the growth rate of the economy from 2012 to 2013 would have been 0 percent. We don't want to pat ourselves on the back because prices have gone up (holding car quality fixed as we are in this example).

Naturally, we would like to separate the growth that is due simply to price increases from the growth that is due to increases in the production of goods and services. To do this, we contrast the concepts of *nominal GDP* and *real GDP*. Nominal GDP is the standard GDP measurement that we've been discussing throughout this chapter. **Nominal GDP** is the total market value of production, using *current* prices to determine value per unit produced.

Real GDP is based on the same idea as nominal GDP—summing up the market value of the quantities of final goods and services—but real GDP uses prices from a base year that may be different from the year that the quantities were produced. To illustrate this idea, let's take 2012 as the base year. In our example, the price of a Ford was $30,000 in 2012. Now let's assume that 10 Fords were produced in 2012 and 10 (identical) Fords were produced in 2013. To calculate real GDP, we use the 2012 prices to value the output in *both* 2012 and 2013. So real GDP was $300,000 in 2012 and was still $300,000 in 2013. Using the concept of real GDP, we see that there was no growth between 2012 and 2013. That makes sense—the number of cars produced did not change.

To increase clarity, economists use the words *nominal* or *real* in their analysis to make certain that the reader knows which of the two concepts is being discussed. On the other hand, journalists generally assume that growth of *real* GDP is the only game in town. When a headline announces, "U.S. Growth Slows to 2.2%," the readers are assumed to know, without being told, that real growth is being discussed.

So far we have studied real GDP in the simple case of a one-good economy. Naturally, this concept can be applied to an economy with any number of goods and services. To get some practice using this concept, let's consider the case of an economy that manufactures two types of cars: Fords and Chevrolets. Exhibit 19.7 reports the raw data with which we will work.

Let's start by calculating nominal GDP. We simply add up the total market value of goods sold in each year, using current prices. In 2012, nominal GDP is

(10 Fords) × ($30,000/Ford) + (5 Chevrolets) × ($20,000/Chevrolet) = $400,000.

Nominal GDP is the total value of production (final goods and services), using current market prices to determine the value of each unit that is produced.

Real GDP is the total value of production (final goods and services), using market prices from a specific base year to determine the value of each unit that is produced.

In 2013, nominal GDP is

(10 Fords) × ($40,000/Ford) + (20 Chevrolets) × ($25,000/Chevrolet) = $900,000.

Check these totals against the values in the column of Exhibit 19.7 labeled Nominal GDP.

To calculate real GDP, we will use 2012 as the base year. That means that we keep using 2012 prices in the calculation of *both* 2012 and 2013 real GDP. This doesn't rock the boat for 2012. Real GDP for 2012 is calculated with 2012 quantities and 2012 prices (exactly matching our calculation of nominal GDP in 2012):

(10 Fords) × ($30,000/Ford) + (5 Chevrolets) × ($20,000/Chevrolet) = $400,000.

The boat rocking comes when we calculate real GDP in 2013, using 2012 as the base year. Now we need to use quantities from 2013 and prices from 2012. In 2013, real GDP is

(10 Fords) × ($30,000/Ford) + (20 Chevrolets) × ($20,000/Chevrolet) = $700,000.

By holding prices constant—using prices from a single base year, 2012—we are able to make meaningful comparisons across years. Economists say that such analysis uses *constant dollars*. In this case, the constant dollars are based on prices from 2012. To make the base year clear to their audience, economists say that the analysis uses "constant 2012 dollars."

Now that you understand how to calculate real GDP, we are able to talk about the growth rate of real GDP, which is usually referred to as **real GDP growth**. For example, the formula for real GDP growth in 2013 is given by

Real GDP growth is the growth rate of real GDP.

$$\text{Real GDP growth in 2013} = \frac{(\text{Real GDP in 2013}) - (\text{Real GDP in 2012})}{\text{Real GDP in 2012}}.$$

By focusing on real GDP growth—which holds prices fixed across time—we compare the total value of real output in 2012 ($400,000 in our example) and the total value of real output in 2013 ($700,000 in our example). In this example, real GDP has grown by 75 percent:

$$\frac{(\$700,000 - \$400,000)}{\$400,000} = \frac{3}{4} = 0.75 = 75\%.$$

The concept of real GDP growth lets us focus on the thing that we care the most about—how much the economy is producing at different points in time—without letting price movements muddy up the comparison.

Finally, don't let this teaching example mislead you. Unfortunately, *actual* growth rates for real GDP are much lower than they are in our illustration. Since 1929, when reliable national income accounts were first created, real GDP growth in the United States has averaged 3.3 percent per year. Even rapidly growing developing countries achieve average real GDP

	Ford		Chevrolet			
	Quantity	Price	Quantity	Price	Nominal GDP	Real GDP using 2012 Base Prices
2012	10	$ 30,000	5	$ 20,000	$ 400,000	$ 400,000
2013	10	$ 40,000	20	$ 25,000	$ 900,000	$ 700,000

Exhibit 19.7 Quantities (Q) and Prices (P) in an Economy with Two Goods

The yellow box contains Ford's quantities and prices in years 2012 and 2013. The orange box contains Chevrolet's quantities and prices. Nominal GDP is the total value of production using prices and quantities from the same year. Real GDP in 2012 using 2012 prices is the same as nominal GDP in 2012. Real GDP in 2013 using 2012 prices is the total value of quantities in 2013 using prices from 2012.

The **GDP deflator** is 100 times the ratio of nominal GDP to real GDP in the same year. It is a measure of how prices of goods and services produced in a country have risen since the base year.

growth of only 5 percent to 10 percent per year. We'll analyze long-run real GDP growth in Chapter 21, and we'll study short-run fluctuations in real GDP growth in Chapter 26.

The GDP Deflator

We can also use real GDP to study the level of prices in the overall economy. Specifically, if we divide nominal GDP by real GDP in the same year and multiply the resulting ratio by 100, we end up with a measure of how much prices of goods and services produced in a country have risen since the base year. This ratio is called the **GDP deflator**:

$$\text{GDP deflator} = \frac{\text{Nominal GDP}}{\text{Real GDP}} \times 100.$$

To understand why this ratio is a measure of rising prices, it helps to write out the formula. Consider again the example in Exhibit 19.7, in which we treat 2012 as the base year for calculations of real GDP. To get our feet wet, let's first evaluate the GDP deflator for 2012. We've written out the expressions for nominal GDP and real GDP below, putting the quantities in blue and the prices in red. Using the data in Exhibit 19.7, you can confirm the numbers in the formula below:

$$\text{GDP deflator (2012)} = \frac{\text{Nominal GDP (2012)}}{\text{Real GDP (2012)}} \times 100$$

$$= \frac{\text{Cost of buying everything produced domestically in 2012 using 2012 prices}}{\text{Cost of buying everything produced domestically in 2012 using base-year prices}} \times 100$$

$$= \frac{10 \times 30{,}000 + 5 \times 20{,}000}{10 \times 30{,}000 + 5 \times 20{,}000} \times 100$$

$$= 100.$$

This first calculation reminds us that in the base year (2012 in this example), nominal GDP matches real GDP. Consequently, in the base year, the GDP deflator is exactly equal to 100.

Now let's consider 2013, the year after the base year. Once again, you can use the data in Exhibit 19.7 to confirm the numbers in the equation below:

$$\text{GDP deflator (2013)} = \frac{\text{Nominal GDP (2013)}}{\text{Real GDP (2013)}} \times 100$$

$$= \frac{\text{Cost of buying everything produced domestically in 2013 using 2013 prices}}{\text{Cost of buying everything produced domestically in 2013 using base-year prices}} \times 100$$

$$= \frac{10 \times 40{,}000 + 20 \times 25{,}000}{10 \times 30{,}000 + 20 \times 20{,}000} \times 100$$

$$= \frac{900{,}000}{700{,}000} \times 100$$

$$= 128.6.$$

In the formula for the 2013 GDP deflator, the numerator and the denominator have exactly the same quantities (in blue): 10 Fords and 20 Chevys. These are the quantities that are sold in 2013. The only things that change between the numerator and the denominator are the prices (in red). The numerator (top) has the 2013 prices, which are used to calculate nominal GDP in 2013. The denominator (bottom) has the 2012 prices that are used to calculate real GDP for 2013—recall that the 2012 prices are the base-year prices.

The numerator shows what it would cost to purchase everything that the economy produced in 2013 using 2013 prices. The denominator shows what it would cost to purchase everything that the economy produced in 2013 using 2012 prices. The GDP deflator is the ratio that reflects the rising cost of buying everything produced in 2013, holding the goods and services produced in 2013 fixed, but changing the prices from the 2013 prices (in the numerator) to the 2012 prices (in the denominator).

The 2013 GDP deflator is telling us how the 2013 prices (in red in the numerator) compare with the 2012 prices (in red in the denominator), holding the quantities fixed in the numerator and the denominator. You can think of the (blue) quantities as weights. The higher the 2013 quantity, the more weight that good or service gets in determining the overall ratio. This makes sense. Goods or services with large quantities *should* get more weight when we form an overall measure of the price level.

Economists study the percentage change in the GDP deflator from year to year. For example, the percentage change in the GDP deflator in 2013 is given by

Percentage change in GDP deflator in 2013

$$= \frac{(\text{GDP deflator in 2013}) - (\text{GDP deflator in 2012})}{\text{GDP deflator in 2012}}.$$

The percentage change in the GDP deflator is a measure of the percentage change in the overall level of prices. In our illustrative example, the GDP deflator was 100 in 2012, and it was 128.6 in 2013. So an economist concludes that prices have risen 28.6 percent:

$$\frac{(128.6 - 100)}{100} = \frac{28.6}{100} = 0.286 = 28.6\%.$$

Note that this overall rate of price inflation is between the rate of price inflation for Fords ($30,000 to $40,000, or a 33 percent increase) and the rate of price inflation for Chevrolets ($20,000 to $25,000, or a 25 percent increase). The relative weights of Ford and Chevy prices is determined by their quantity weights.

Exhibit 19.8 plots the value of the *actual* U.S. GDP deflator from 1929 to 2013, using 2009 as the base year. Because 2009 is the base year, the GDP deflator is exactly 100 in

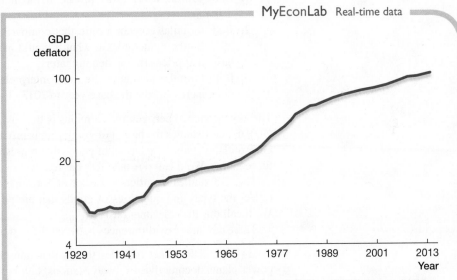

MyEconLab Real-time data

Exhibit 19.8 The Value of the GDP Deflator from 1929 to 2013, Using 2009 as the Base Year

Because 2009 is the base year, the GDP deflator is exactly 100 in 2009. Notice that the GDP deflator is less than 100 before 2009 and greater than 100 after 2009. The deflator is an indicator of the overall level of prices in the economy. In an economy with rising prices, the deflator rises over time. The only period of sharp declines in the GDP deflator was the period from 1929 to 1933, which was the Great Depression. The series is plotted on a scale with constant proportionality, implying that changes of equal size on the printed page represent equal proportional movements. For example, going from the level of 4 to 20 (a multiple of 5) has the same step size on the printed page as going from the level of 20 to 100 (another multiple of 5).

Source: Bureau of Economic Analysis, National Income and Product Accounts.

2009. The GDP deflator is less than 100 before 2009 and greater than 100 after 2009. From 1929 to 2013 the GDP deflator increased on average 2.9 percent per year, which is a measure of how quickly prices rose on average during this period.

There are many different ways to measure overall movements in prices, which causes some degree of confusion. In fact, the general public is largely unaware of the GDP deflator and its usefulness as a tool for measuring price movements. The most well-known price measure is the Consumer Price Index, which we come to next.

The Consumer Price Index

As you now know, the GDP deflator is the ratio

$$\text{GDP deflator (2013)} = \frac{\text{Nominal GDP (2013)}}{\text{Real GDP (2013)}} \times 100$$

$$= \frac{\text{Cost of buying everything produced domestically in 2013 using 2013 prices}}{\text{Cost of buying everything produced domestically in 2013 using base-year prices}} \times 100.$$

For example, if the base year were 2009, then the prices that are used in the denominator are the prices that existed in the economy in 2009.

The Bureau of Labor Statistics calculates a related formula called the **Consumer Price Index (CPI)**. As you can see, the CPI looks almost identical to the formula for the GDP deflator:

The **Consumer Price Index (CPI)** is 100 times the ratio of the cost of buying a basket of consumer goods using 2013 prices divided by the cost of buying the same basket of consumer goods using base-year prices.

$$\text{CPI (2013)} = \frac{\text{Cost of buying a particular basket of consumer goods using 2013 prices}}{\text{Cost of buying a particular basket of consumer goods using base-year prices}} \times 100.$$

As you can see, the GDP deflator and CPI formulas are nearly indistinguishable:

1. Both formulas use 2013 prices in the numerator and base-year prices in the denominator.
2. Both formulas contain a ratio that compares what it would cost to buy "stuff" in 2013 (in the numerator) to what it would have cost to buy "the same stuff" using base-year prices (in the denominator).
3. Both formulas also have the same interpretation: a higher ratio implies a greater price increase from the base year to 2013.

The key difference between the formulas is the basket of goods that is being bought. The GDP deflator studies the basket of goods that is produced domestically. In other words, the GDP deflator studies the basket of goods that represents the total production of the domestic economy. We'll call this the GDP basket.

The CPI studies a particular basket of consumer goods. This basket is constructed to reflect the types and quantities of goods that are purchased by a typical U.S. household. We'll call this the consumer basket.

There are three key differences between the two baskets:

(1) The GDP basket includes things that households don't purchase, like coal-fired power plants, locomotives, subway stations, city buses, aircraft carriers, and nuclear submarines. Consumers use services provided by governments and firms that purchase these items, but no consumer purchases them directly, so they appear in the GDP basket (in the year they are purchased) but not in the consumer basket.

(2) The consumer basket includes things that households purchase but are not counted in GDP. For example, GDP only counts *domestic* production, so it does not count imports, such as a laptop manufactured abroad. A Chinese laptop that is purchased by a U.S. consumer does not get counted in the U.S. GDP basket but would get counted in the U.S. consumer basket.

(3) Even if a product is included in both the GDP basket and the consumer basket, it is likely to have a different weight in the two baskets. For example, housing-related expenditures are in both the GDP basket and the consumer basket, but housing has a larger role in the consumer basket. Housing—including the cost of shelter, utility bills, and household furnishings—represents over 40 percent of the consumer basket, but these items jointly represent less than 20 percent of the GDP basket.

With all of these differences, it's natural to wonder whether the GDP deflator and CPI tell very different stories about the evolution of prices in the overall economy. In fact, in practice it almost makes no difference, as we demonstrate next.

Inflation

The rate of increase in prices is the **inflation rate**. It is calculated as the year-over-year percentage increase in a price index.

The rate of increase in prices is the **inflation rate**. It is calculated as the year-over-year percentage increase in a price index. For example, to calculate the overall U.S. inflation rate in 2013, we use the following formula, with either the GDP deflator or the CPI as the "price index":

$$\text{Inflation rate in 2013} = \frac{(\text{Price Index in 2013}) - (\text{Price Index in 2012})}{\text{Price Index in 2012}}.$$

It turns out that the choice of the price index doesn't have a large impact on the resulting rate of inflation. Exhibit 19.9 plots the historical rate of inflation calculated with either the GDP deflator (blue) or the CPI (dashed red line). As you can see, the two inflation series move very closely together.

This similarity may partially explain why there are relatively few news stories about the GDP deflator. The GDP deflator doesn't have much to add once we know the CPI. Moreover, CPI is released on a monthly basis, so it is more timely than the GDP deflator, which is released quarterly. Finally, CPI describes inflation that matters the most for households. In this sense, CPI has more personal relevance for the typical consumer.

Adjusting Nominal Variables

You can't make meaningful comparisons across time without adjusting nominal variables. For example, William Howard Taft was paid $75,000 per year for his service as president. He was inaugurated in 1909. In 2013, the U.S. president was paid $400,000. So who was paid more?

When we ask that question, we don't mean "Who received more dollars?" We really mean "Whose salary was worth more?" or, in the language of economics, "Who had more buying power?" There has been a lot of inflation between 1909 and 2013, so a dollar paid out in 1909 bought much more than a dollar in 2013. To compare Taft's salary to a modern presidential salary, we need to translate Taft's salary into current dollars.

There's a formula that enables us to do this:

$$\text{Value in 2013 dollars} = \frac{\text{Price index in 2013}}{\text{Price index in 1909}} \times \text{Value in 1909 dollars}.$$

MyEconLab Real-time data

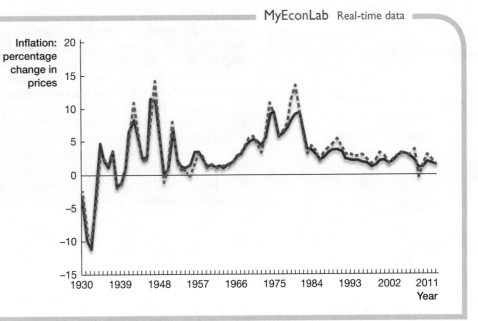

Exhibit 19.9 The Annual U.S. Inflation Rate from 1930 to 2013

The annual percentage change in the GDP deflator from 1930 to 2013 is plotted in blue; it is one measure of inflation. The exhibit also plots the annual percentage change in the Consumer Price Index over the same period (dashed red line). This is another measure of inflation. The two measures have a very similar historical pattern.

Source: Bureau of Economic Analysis, National Income and Product Accounts; and U.S. Bureau of Labor Statistics.

The ratio on the right-hand-side of this equation tells us how much prices have risen, enabling us to transform value expressed in 1909 dollars into value expressed in 2013 dollars. We can fill in these numbers using the 2013 CPI and an historical estimate of what the CPI was in 1909 (official government CPI calculations do not start until 1913).

$$\text{Value in 2013 dollars} = \frac{\text{Price index in 2013}}{\text{Price index in 1909}} \times \text{Value in 1909 dollars}$$

$$= \frac{233}{9} \times \$75,000$$

$$= \$1.9 \text{ million.}$$

The ratio of price indices tells you that, on average, prices rose by a factor of 233/9 = 25.89 over this time period, so having $1 in 1909 is equivalent to having $25.89 in 2013. Scaling Taft's annual salary of $75,000 in 1909 by this ratio of price levels implies that his 1909 salary has equivalent purchasing power to $1.9 million in 2014. Taft's salary was worth more than 4 times Barak Obama's presidential salary.

We can use this simple formula to express any historical price (or value) in dollars for a more recent year (say, 2013). We generally have a good intuition for what 2013 dollars can buy, and we generally have a poor intuition for a dollar's buying power in 1909. Therefore, this type of transformation can come in very handy. We'll use it many times throughout this textbook.

Summary

⚙ Macroeconomics is the study of economic aggregates and the economy as a whole. An aggregate is a total. Macroeconomics studies total economic activity.

⚙ Gross domestic product (GDP) is the market value of the final goods and services produced within the borders of a country during a particular period of time (for instance, a year). GDP is defined in three equivalent ways: Production = Expenditure = Income. The circular flow diagram explains these identities and adds a fourth identical way of measuring economic activity: factors of production.

⚙ Like a short weather report—"92 degrees and partly cloudy"—GDP is just a summary measure of economic activity and economic well-being. GDP leaves many details out, including depreciation, home production, the underground economy, externalities, leisure, and cross-border movements of capital and labor. Nevertheless, residents of countries with relatively high levels of GDP per capita report relatively high levels of life satisfaction.

⚙ Economists distinguish nominal values and real values. Real GDP measures the market value of economic production holding prices fixed at a particular base year. The GDP deflator is a measure of the overall level of prices in the economy. The Consumer Price Index (CPI) is another measure of the overall level of prices. Both the GDP deflator and the CPI can be used to measure the overall rate at which prices are rising: the inflation rate.

Key Terms

income per capita *p. 427*
recession *p. 428*
unemployed *p. 428*
unemployment rate *p. 428*
national income accounts *p. 429*
National Income and Product Accounts
  (NIPA) *p. 429*
gross domestic product (GDP) *p. 442*
identity *p. 430*

factors of production *p. 431*
value added *p. 432*
consumption *p. 434*
investment *p. 434*
government expenditure *p. 435*
exports *p. 435*
imports *p. 435*
national income accounting
  identity *p. 435*

labor income *p. 435*
capital income *p. 438*
gross national product (GNP) *p. 442*
nominal GDP *p. 444*
real GDP *p. 444*
real GDP growth *p. 445*
GDP deflator *p. 446*
Consumer Price Index (CPI) *p. 448*
inflation rate *p. 449*

Questions

All questions are available in MyEconLab *for practice and instructor assignment.*

1. Find and list three recent stories in the media that would typically be studied in macroeconomics. (Cite the date and source of the stories you choose.) Discuss why they would fall within the subject matter of *macroeconomics*.

2. How is gross domestic product defined?

3. What is an accounting identity? Explain the accounting identity Production = Expenditure = Income.

4. Use the circular flow diagram to show how expenditure, production, and income relate to one another.

5. How is production-based accounting used to estimate GDP? Discuss the role of value-added.

6. How is GDP calculated using expenditure-based accounting?

7. Which category of expenditure accounts for the highest share of GDP in the United States?

8. How is the level of economic activity calculated using the income method?

9. If the level of aggregate expenditure was $16.8 trillion in 2013, what was the level of aggregate income? Explain your answer.

10. What is meant by capital depreciation?

11. Explain three important factors that GDP leaves out.

12. You decide to cook your own meal rather than eat in a restaurant. How will this affect GDP?

13. When would a country's gross domestic product exceed its gross national product?

14. Nobel laureate Simon Kuznets, who did significant work on national income accounts in the 1930s, said that the welfare of a nation can scarcely be inferred from a measurement of national income. Would you agree with him? Why or why not?

15. Why is it essential to differentiate between real and nominal growth rates of GDP?

16. What are the key differences between the Consumer Price Index (CPI) and the GDP deflator?

17. How is the Consumer Price Index similar to the GDP deflator?

Problems

All problems are available in MyEconLab *for practice and instructor assignment.*

1. Which of the following would be considered a final good in the calculation of U.S. GDP? Explain your answers.

   a. Processors manufactured in California for Apple's new range of laptops (that will be sold in the US).

   b. Foot massages at spas in California

   c. Defense equipment purchased by the federal government

2. By how much would GDP change as a result of each of the following changes. Briefly explain your answers.

   a. A parent switches from buying pre-made ham and cheese sandwiches for a family dinner, which would have cost $20, to buying the raw ingredients, which cost only $6, and making the same ham and cheese sandwiches at home.

   b. On the rebound again, a famous rock star marries her butler, whom she formerly paid $50,000 a year. After they are married, her husband continues to wait on her as before, and she continues to support him as before—but as a husband rather than as an employee, that is, not with a regular salary.

3. Suppose that there are only two small countries in the world: Ascot, with a population of 30,000 people, and Delwich, with a population of 20,000 people. Ascot's GDP is equal to $150 million while Delwich's GDP is $250 million. Delwich's GNP has been estimated to be equal to $280 million. Use this information to calculate Ascot's GNP, the GDP per capita in Ascot, and the GNP per capita in Delwich.

4. The following table gives data for a small country, Magnolia:

Component	Expenditure (in thousands)
Social Security payments	$250
Depreciation	$ 47
Private investment	$630
Exports	$260
Imports	$300
Salaries earned by foreigners working in Magnolia	$160
Household consumption	$850
Purchases of raw materials	$270
Government purchases	$900
Capital income	$290
Salaries earned by Magnolian residents working abroad	$350

a. Use the data to calculate GDP for this economy using the expenditure method.

b. Calculate the value of Magnolia's GNP. Does Magnolia's GDP differ from its GNP? Why?

5. In 2013, the value of the Consumer Price Index (CPI) in a certain country, Polonia, was 230 index points and median (nominal) household income was $31,200. In 1950, the CPI was 51 index points and median (nominal) household income was $9,500.

a. Calculate median real household income in 1950 and in 2013, using 2013 as the base year.

b. In which year was life satisfaction likely to be higher? Explain your answer.

6. Most products we buy go through a lengthy series of intermediate steps before they are available for us to purchase. For this problem, say we are tracing the stages, and the associated transaction values, involved in the production of a hypothetical loaf of bread:

Farmer sells wheat to miller	$0.50
Miller grinds wheat into flour, and sells to baker	$1.00
Baker bakes the loaf, and sells to a grocery wholesaler	$2.00
Wholesaler sells loaf to various chain retail outlets	$2.50
Retailer sells loaf to public	$3.25

a. Which expenditure category of GDP increased as a result of the production and sale of the loaf?

b. Calculate the addition to GDP contributed by this loaf, using all three methods covered in the text: expenditure-based accounting, income-based accounting, and production-based accounting.

7. The country of Sylvania produces and consumes only three goods: Red Bull, pizza, and T-shirts. The quantity produced and price of each good in 2011 and 2012 are given in the following table:

	2011		2012	
	Quantity	Price	Quantity	Price
T-Shirts	100	$25	110	$25
Red Bull (cans)	500	$1	500	$1.50
Pizza (slices)	1000	$2	900	$4

a. Calculate nominal GDP for 2011 and 2012.

b. Using 2011 as the base year, calculate real GDP for 2011 and 2012.

c. Based on your answer from part b, by what percentage did real GDP grow between 2011 and 2012?

d. Now, calculate real GDP for 2011 and 2012 using 2012 as the base year.

e. Based on your answer from part d, by what percentage did real GDP grow between 2011 and 2012?

f. Using 2011 as the base year, what was the GDP deflator in 2011 and 2012?

g. Based on your answer from part f, by what percentage did prices change between 2011 and 2012?

8. A typical resident of the country of Collegia consumes a simple basket of goods consisting of life's essentials: soda, pizza, and Advil. A year's basket contains 1,000 sodas, 100 pizzas, and 50 bottles of Advil. The price of these goods in each of the past 8 years is given in the following table:

	Soda	Pizza	Advil
2005	$1.00	$ 8.00	$10.00
2006	$1.50	$ 8.00	$10.00
2007	$1.50	$ 8.50	$11.00
2008	$2.00	$ 8.50	$11.50
2009	$2.50	$ 9.00	$11.00
2010	$2.50	$ 9.00	$10.00
2011	$2.00	$10.00	$12.00
2012	$3.00	$10.00	$13.00

Using 2008 as the base year,

a. calculate the CPI for each year.

b. calculate the rate of inflation for each year from the previous year, starting with 2006.

9. Social Security payments in the United States are currently linked to the Consumer Price Index for Urban Wage Earners and Clerical Workers (CPI-W). This means that as the CPI-W shows an increase in the price level, Social Security payments will also increase, keeping the real value of the payment constant. The following table shows the weighting given to the different components in the CPI-W consumption basket.

Item	Weight
Food and beverages	15.948
Housing	39.867
Apparel	3.623
Transportation	18.991
Medical care	5.767
Recreation	5.528
Education and communication	6.766
Other goods and services	3.510
Total	**100.000**

It has been suggested that using the CPI-W to adjust Social Security payments understates inflation for seniors. Do you agree? Why might this be the case?

10. Recall the method of calculating real GDP detailed in the chapter. As you may already have noticed, this method has a problem: in calculating aggregate output, this method weights the output of the various goods and services by their relative prices in the base year.

Say, for example, a textbook cost $100 in the base year, and a laptop cost $2,000. This means that the laptop would have 20 times the weight of a book in calculating aggregate output.

But, what happens when relative prices change? As you know, the prices of most high-tech items, including laptops, have generally been decreasing over time. Suppose the price of a laptop declined from $2,000 to $1,000 in the period from the base year to the current year. Now a laptop costs only 10 times as much as the book. So, using base-year relative prices would overweight laptops in calculating real GDP in the current year.

In response to this problem, in 1996 the BEA switched to what is called a *chain-weighted* method of calculating real GDP. Say the base year is 2008. To calculate the growth rate of real GDP between 2008 and 2009, for example, the BEA calculates real GDP for 2008 using 2008 as the base, and then real GDP for 2008 using 2009 as the base. Then, the Bureau calculates real GDP for 2009 using 2009 as the base, and real GDP for 2009 using 2008 as the base. For each base, the growth rate is then calculated as:

$$\frac{2009\ \text{GDP}_{(2008\ Base)} - 2008\ \text{GDP}_{(2008\ Base)}}{2008\ \text{GDP}_{(2008\ Base)}},$$

$$\frac{2009\ \text{GDP}_{(2009\ Base)} - 2008\ \text{GDP}_{(2009\ Base)}}{2008\ \text{GDP}_{(2009\ Base)}}.$$

So, they end up with two different growth rates, which are then averaged. Given this averaged growth rate, and the level of GDP in 2008 at 2008 prices, the Bureau then calculates real GDP for 2009 as 1 plus the average growth rate previously calculated, times 2008 output in 2008

dollars. The growth rate between 2009 and 2010 is then calculated similarly.

Suppose that laptops, economics textbooks, and energy drinks are the only three goods produced in the United States. The following table gives the quantity of each produced (in millions) and their price in the years from 2011 to 2013:

	P Laptops	Q Laptops	P Texts	Q Texts	P Eng. Drnk	Q Eng. Drnk
2011	1500	7	100	7	2	25
2012	1200	9	110	9	4	30
2013	1000	9	120	10	4	35

a. Calculate nominal GDP and real GDP (using 2011 as the base year) for each year.

b. Calculate real GDP for 2012 and 2013 using the chain-weighted method outlined above.

11. On May 22, 2013, *Forbes* magazine reported that Bill Gates had overtaken Mexican businessman Carlos Slim as the "richest man in the world." Gates's fortune on that date was estimated at $70 billion, whereas Slim's was a mere $69.86 billion. (http://www.forbes.com/sites/erincarlyle/2013/05/22/bill-gates-is-worlds-richest-bumps-slim/)

But, does this make Gates the richest American who ever lived?

John D. Rockefeller, the founder of Standard Oil, is usually credited with this distinction. At the time of his death in 1937, the founder of the Standard Oil empire had an estimated net worth of $1.4 billion.

a. Go to the BLS CPI site at http://data.bls.gov/cgi-bin/surveymost?cu. Under "Consumer Price Index-All Urban Consumers," select "US All Items, 1982–84 = 100" and click the "Retrieve data" button at the bottom of the page. Adjust the years to retrieve data from 1937 through 2013.

Use the data under the "Annual" column to calculate Gates's 2013 net worth measured in 1937 dollars. You should find that Gates's wealth does have more buying power than Rockefeller's wealth.

b. Some analysts say that Rockefeller's net worth was economically equivalent to $250 billion today. However, this figure is arrived at in a particular way. First, his net worth in 1937 is calculated as a *percentage* of total U.S. GDP in 1937. That percentage is then multiplied by the current level of GDP to arrive at the equivalent figure in current dollars. See if you can approximate the $250 billion figure. You can find the relevant GDP figures at http://research.stlouisfed.org/fred2/data/GDPA.txt.

c. What are the pros and cons of the two different methods—reviewed in the previous parts of this question—of adjusting Rockefeller's net worth to make it comparable to the wealth of business leaders today?

20 Aggregate Incomes

Why is the average American so much richer than the average Indian?

We live in a world of great disparities. Standards of living, educational opportunities, health services, and infrastructure differ tremendously across countries. Poverty is endemic in many parts of the world, particularly in sub-Saharan Africa, South Asia, and parts of South America, while most people in the United States, Canada, Western Europe, and a few other fairly rich countries live in relative comfort, even abundance. These differences are so great that if you travel around the globe, you will be struck by the contrast of how different living conditions are in some parts of the world from those back home. The realization that there are such great disparities may have been one of the factors that sparked your interest in economics in the first place. They are also the reason why many people from all over the world emigrate to richer countries, where standards of living are higher.

CHAPTER **OUTLINE**

⚙ There are very large differences across countries in income or GDP per capita.

⚙ We can compare income differences across countries using GDP per capita at current exchange rates or adjusted for purchasing power parity differences.

⚙ The aggregate production function links a country's GDP to its capital stock, its total efficiency units of labor, and its technology.

⚙ Cross-country differences in GDP per capita partly result from differences in physical capital per worker and the human capital of workers, but differences in technology and the efficiency of production are even more important.

Macroeconomics provides a useful conceptual framework for studying these issues and explains why such disparities exist. In this and the next two chapters, we study questions related to economic inequalities across countries and economic growth (sometimes called "long-run macroeconomics") before turning to the study of economic fluctuations (sometimes called "short-run macroeconomics") in the subsequent five chapters. In particular, in this chapter, we explain how we can measure differences in standards of living across countries and why such disparities exist. In the next chapter, we turn to the study of economic growth, that is, how and why an economy grows and becomes more prosperous over time. In our last chapter in this series, Chapter 22, we discuss the fundamental factors that keep poor countries poor.

20.1 Inequality Around the World

Before we can understand the variation of income across the world, our first step is to define our measurements. How do we quantify the differences in standards of living and economic conditions across countries? Income per capita is one robust measure.

Measuring Differences in Income per Capita

We learned in the last chapter how to measure aggregate income or GDP. We can do so by approaching it from the production side, from the expenditure side, or from the income side. From the national income accounting identity, all three give exactly the same answer: gross domestic product, or GDP for short. Dividing GDP by the total population in the country gives us **income per capita** (per person) or **GDP per capita**.

Income per capita or **GDP per capita** is GDP divided by total population.

We use the two terms interchangeably in this textbook because they represent the same number. (Often we use income per capita when we wish to emphasize that the number is the average income of the citizens of a country and GDP per capita when we wish to emphasize that the number is what the economy produces per person.)

More formally, we have:

$$\text{Income per capita} = \text{GDP per capita} = \frac{\text{GDP}}{\text{Total population}}.$$

For example, the United States in 2010 had GDP equal to about $14.45 trillion. With a total population of approximately 310 million, income per capita was approximately $46,613.

How does this compare to the income per capita of other countries? Let us look to a neighboring country: Mexico. Income in Mexico is, of course, not calculated in U.S. dollars but in pesos. Thus with a similar computation, we find income per capita in Mexico in the same year, 2010, to be approximately 116,036 pesos. This number is not directly comparable to the $46,613 for the United States because it is expressed in different units. But we can convert it to the same units by using the exchange rate. For example, on January 1, 2010 one U.S. dollar was worth 12.9 pesos, or one peso was worth 1/12.9 = 0.078 dollars. Using this ratio, we can convert the average income in Mexico into dollars as follows (where p.c. stands for "per capita"):

$$\text{Mexican income p.c. in } \$ = \text{Mexican income p.c. in pesos} \times \$/\text{peso exchange rate}$$
$$= 116,036 \times 0.078$$
$$= \$9,051$$

So the average Mexican had an income per capita of approximately $9,051. This number would be useful if you wanted to think about how much an individual with the average Mexican income per capita, all of which was earned in Mexico, would be able to consume in the United States.

Using this exchange-rate-based measure, we can compute income per capita in every country for which we have data on GDP and population. For example, in 2010, income per capita in Sweden was $50,549 and in Switzerland it was $69,167. While income per capita in Sweden and Switzerland is similar to that in the United States, large disparities emerge when we compare the United States to several other countries. For example, we have already seen that the U.S. income per capita is about 5 times that of Mexico. It is also 30 times greater than income per capita in India, 43 times greater than income per capita in Senegal, and approximately 155 times greater than income per capita in Ethiopia.

Exchange rates allow us to compare GDP across countries using the same units, but we favor a tool that provides even better comparisons of income per capita across countries: purchasing power parity (PPP). Exchange rates convert currencies into the same units but fail to account for the fact that the *prices* of many goods and services will differ across countries. For example, some things—like phone calls—are cheaper in the United States than in Mexico because better technology is available in the United States and because there is a telecommunications monopoly in Mexico, keeping prices relatively high. But other goods—like guacamole and haircuts—are cheaper in Mexico, often because labor and other inputs are cheaper.

We saw in the previous chapter how to adjust economic variables like GDP to correct for changes in prices over time (which led to the notion of *real GDP*). We should make a similar adjustment when comparing GDP between countries. But the exchange rate between dollars and pesos doesn't do this. To see why, recall that the exchange rate between the peso and the dollar was 12.9 on January 1, 2010. If instead we had used the exchange rate on January 1, 2009, which was 13.8 pesos per dollar, the average income in Mexico would have been $8,408 rather than $9,051. But this fluctuation has little to do with changes in prices households face in Mexico or the United States. Rather, it is just a consequence of converting Mexican income into dollars using the current exchange rate, which (as we will see in Chapter 29) fluctuates for a variety of reasons unrelated to differences in the cost of living.

Purchasing power parity provides a better way to convert GDP in domestic currencies into common units. The idea here is very similar to the adjustment we developed for converting nominal GDP into real GDP in the previous chapter. Specifically, the **purchasing power parity (PPP)** constructs the cost of a representative bundle of commodities in each country and adjusts GDP so that a dollar in each country can purchase this representative bundle. The resulting measure is a country's GDP in PPP-adjusted U.S. dollars. For example, this representative bundle cost $1 in the United States and 8.64 pesos in Mexico in 2010. On this basis, the PPP factor between U.S. dollars and pesos is $1 for 8.64 pesos or 1 peso for 0.116 = 1/8.64 U.S. dollars.

Using this procedure, income per capita in Mexico in PPP would be:

$$\text{Mexican income p.c. in PPP } \$ = \text{Mexican income p.c. in pesos} \times \$/\text{peso PPP}$$
$$= 116,036 \times 0.116$$
$$= \$13,460$$

Comparing this result for Mexico with the $9,051 obtained using the peso/$ exchange rate, we see that there is often a significant difference between exchange-rate-based measures and PPP-based measures of income per capita, with the gap between the United States

The **purchasing power parity (PPP)** constructs the cost of a representative bundle of commodities in each country and uses these relative costs for comparing income across countries.

LETTING THE DATA SPEAK

The Big Mac Index

In 1986, *The Economist* magazine proposed the Big Mac index as an alternative measure of exchange rates. This index would simply be the ratio of prices of a Big Mac in two countries. There were already McDonald's restaurants in many countries in 1986, so the price of a Big Mac could be computed for a large number of countries, giving an alternative measure of the exchange rate between any two of them. Though proposed tongue-in-cheek, the Big Mac index caught on and is now commonly used. In fact, there is a good reason for this. The Big Mac index is a simple example of a purchasing power parity adjustment. Its shortcoming is that instead of a representative bundle of diverse goods, this index only compares a bundle consisting of a single good, the Big Mac, which is only a small fraction of people's consumption. Thus, its price will not reflect true cost-of-living differences across countries.

economy and poorer economies generally being smaller when we use PPP-based measures. This pattern reflects the lower cost of living in countries with lower income per capita—that is, the fact that exchange-rate-based measures of GDP ignore the fact that many commodities are cheaper in poorer countries.

Inequality in Income per Capita

There are still very large disparities across countries when we use PPP-based measures. Exhibit 20.1 shows a graph of PPP-adjusted income per capita across countries in 2010 (expressed in terms of 2005 constant dollars, where the notion of constant dollars was defined in the previous chapter). Note that there are 19 countries with less than $1,000 per capita, including the Democratic Republic of Congo, Ethiopia, Liberia, Madagascar, and Togo, and another 23 with incomes of between $1,000 and $2,000, including Afghanistan, Haiti, Kenya, Tajikistan, Uganda, and Zambia. These measures contrast sharply with those of the United States ($41,365), France ($31,299), and Germany ($34,089) in the same year.

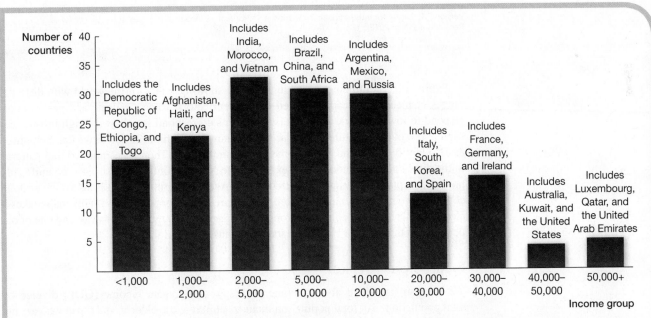

Exhibit 20.1 Income per Capita Around the World in 2010 (PPP-adjusted 2005 Constant Dollars)

There are wide disparities in income per capita across countries. Nineteen countries had income per capita less than $1,000 in 2010 (in PPP-adjusted 2005 constant dollars) while only a few countries had income per capita above $40,000.

Source: Data from Penn World Table; Alan Heston, Robert Summers and Bettina Aten, Penn World Table Version 7.1, Center for International Comparisons of Production, Income and Prices at the University of Pennsylvania (Nov 2012).

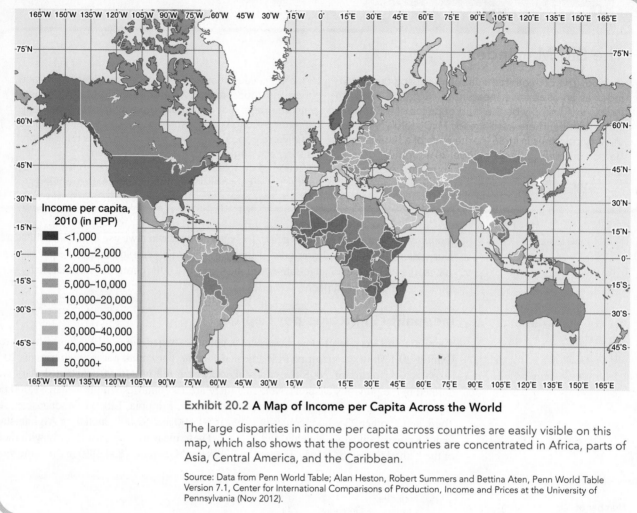

Exhibit 20.2 A Map of Income per Capita Across the World

The large disparities in income per capita across countries are easily visible on this map, which also shows that the poorest countries are concentrated in Africa, parts of Asia, Central America, and the Caribbean.

Source: Data from Penn World Table; Alan Heston, Robert Summers and Bettina Aten, Penn World Table Version 7.1, Center for International Comparisons of Production, Income and Prices at the University of Pennsylvania (Nov 2012).

Exhibit 20.2 complements Exhibit 20.1 by showing a map of the world with different ranges of income per capita shaded in different colors. Reds, oranges, and yellows correspond to lower income per capita, and greens correspond to relatively high income per capita. The overall picture is similar to that shown in Exhibit 20.1, yet we can now more easily identify where the rich and the poor countries are. There are some striking patterns to the differences in incomes. For example, the African continent appears to be uniformly poorer, except for a few spots. Much of South Asia and Latin America is also quite poor. In contrast, North America and Western Europe are relatively prosperous. This map makes it clear that there are indeed major economic disparities throughout the world, and one of our purposes in this chapter is to understand the causes behind them.

Income per Worker

We have so far talked about income per capita—aggregate income (GDP) divided by total population. But total population includes children, the elderly, and those who are not employed, who do not take part in production (though in many less developed economies, child labor is quite common). This raises the possibility that part of the variation in income per capita across countries might be due to differences in what fraction of the population works. Therefore, a natural alternative that avoids this problem is to focus on **income (or GDP) per worker**, defined as GDP divided by "workers," meaning those in employment. That is:

Income (or GDP) per worker is defined as GDP divided by the number of people in employment.

$$\text{Income per worker} = \frac{\text{GDP}}{\text{Number of people in employment}}.$$

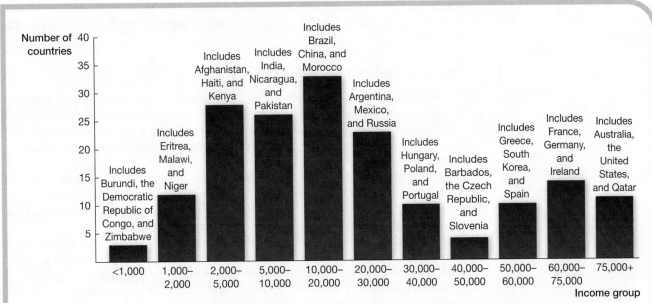

Exhibit 20.3 Income per Worker Across Countries in 2010 (PPP-adjusted 2005 Constant Dollars)

The distribution of countries by income per worker looks similar to the distribution by income per capita shown in Exhibit 20.1. One visible difference is that it is shifted to the right compared to Exhibit 20.1, because every country has higher income per worker (GDP divided by the number of people in employment) than income per capita (GDP divided by total population).

Source: Data from Penn World Table; Alan Heston, Robert Summers and Bettina Aten, Penn World Table Version 7.1, Center for International Comparisons of Production, Income and Prices at the University of Pennsylvania (Nov 2012).

This measure gives us a better picture of how much each worker produces on average by excluding those who do not work.

Exhibit 20.3 is similar to Exhibit 20.1, but uses (PPP-adjusted) income per worker. If there were large differences in the ratio of workers to the total population, this exhibit would look very different from Exhibit 20.1. A direct comparison shows that the overall patterns are very similar, though naturally income per worker is higher for every country than income per capita because the denominator is always smaller for income per worker. For example, PPP-adjusted income per capita in 2010 (in 2005 constant dollars) for Mexico is $11,939 (we saw that this was equal to 13,460 in *current* dollars), whereas PPP-adjusted income per worker for Mexico in 2010 (again in 2005 constant dollars) is $27,625. For India, the two corresponding numbers are $3,477 and $9,010. As a reflection of this, the group of countries with the highest income per worker now corresponds to $75,000+ instead of $50,000+ as in Exhibit 20.1.

Productivity

The main reason why income per capita or income per worker varies across countries is because productivity varies across countries. **Productivity** here refers to the value of goods and services that a worker generates for each hour of work. From our discussion of the national income accounting identity in Chapter 19, you will recall that the value of goods and services produced in a country, GDP, is equal to the total income in that country. Thus productivity also measures income per hour of work. Income per worker and productivity are very closely related and thus vary across countries for the same reasons. (The only reason why the two concepts differ is that the total number of hours of work per worker may also vary across countries, but in practice, this variation is small.)

It is useful to focus on productivity differences across countries because it emphasizes that to understand the huge differences in

Productivity refers to the value of goods and services that a worker generates for each hour of work.

> To understand the huge differences in income per capita across countries, we have to look at the production side.

income per capita across countries, we have to look at the production side. In particular, we need to study the factors that make labor much more productive in some countries than in others.

Incomes and the Standard of Living

A natural question is whether income per capita or income per worker is the quantity we should focus on. The answer depends on what we are trying to measure. Income per worker is particularly informative when we would like to understand why some economies are more productive than others, because it focuses directly on differences in GDP relative to those in employment.

Another reason why we care about disparities in income across countries is that we would like to measure differences in the standards of living across countries. For this purpose, income per capita is a natural first step because the conditions of the whole population, including children and the elderly, are conveyed by this measure.

However, there is much that is left out of income per capita, as you have already seen in the previous chapter. Even though, again as shown in the previous chapter, income per capita is a fairly good predictor of average life satisfaction in a country, we cannot capture the diverse dimensions of well-being and the standards of living of an entire population by looking at a single number. For example, income can vary widely within countries as well as across them. In the United States, the coasts are richer than the middle of the country. In Mexico,

People living at the poverty level.

The **one dollar a day per person poverty line** is a measure of absolute poverty used by economists and other social scientists to compare the extent of poverty across countries.

there are great differences between the north and the south. High income inequality in general prevents measures of average income (like GDP per capita) from giving a complete picture of how comfortably most people in a country actually live. Finally, as already mentioned in the previous chapter, people do not just care about income and consumption, but also about factors such as pollution, the quality of healthcare, and public safety. Variations in these factors across countries are not captured by income per capita numbers (as you learned at the end of the last chapter).

All of this implies that we should refrain from making sweeping generalizations about the welfare of a country's citizens based on its income per capita alone. Nevertheless, there is quite a bit we can learn from income per capita about the standards of living. In the previous chapter, we saw the relationship between income per capita and average life satisfaction. In addition, one of the things we care about when discussing a particular country is whether there are many people living in extreme poverty. Researchers at the World Bank have come up with the notion of *absolute poverty*, corresponding to living on less than $1.08 per day in 1993—a measure commonly referred to as the **one dollar a day per person poverty line**. This measure has now been updated to $1.25 per person per day (in 2005 U.S. dollars), though it is still sometimes referred to as one dollar a day. For most of us, it is difficult to imagine how anybody could survive on such a tiny sum, but more than 1.4 billion

CHOICE & CONSEQUENCE

Dangers of Just Focusing on Income per Capita

A common error in comparing standards of living across countries is to focus only on income per capita, without thinking about its composition. This error is most clearly illustrated by looking at the situation in South Africa. Until 1994, South Africa was ruled by a minority white population under a repressive system of racial segregation known as *apartheid*—a word meaning "separateness." The apartheid regime prevented blacks from political participation and regulated their economic activities. It also created a

variety of repressive arrangements intended to keep the wages of black workers low. According to the economic historian Charles Feinstein, the result was that although the South African economy became more prosperous as a whole during much of the twentieth century, the incomes of its black citizens did not increase during this entire period.[1] So if we were to look at just income per capita in South Africa, it would not inform us about the very low incomes and poor living conditions of most of its black citizens.

Exhibit 20.4 The Relationship Between Poverty and Income per Capita in 2010 (PPP-adjusted 2005 Constant Dollars)

Absolute poverty, measured here by the fraction of the population living on less than $1.25 per day, is higher among countries with lower income per capita. In the exhibit, when you focus on countries with income per capita above $10,000, this relationship disappears because relatively few people in these relatively prosperous countries actually live on less than $1.25 per day.

Source: Data from the Penn World Table and World Bank DataBank; Alan Heston, Robert Summers and Bettina Aten, Penn World Table Version 7.1, Center for International Comparisons of Production, Income and Prices at the University of Pennsylvania (Nov 2012).

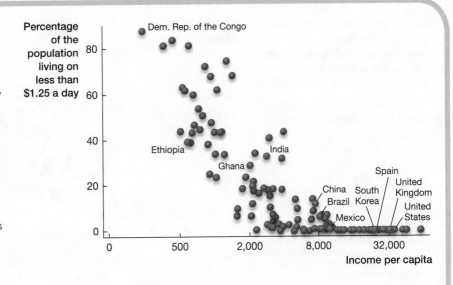

people in 2005 did in fact try to make do with less than $1.25 per day. Exhibit 20.4 shows a scatter plot with the fraction of a nation's population living in poverty (according to this definition) on the *y*-axis and its income per capita on the *x*-axis. The exhibit shows a strong association, indicating that income per capita gives us a fairly good idea of which countries have populations suffering from extreme poverty.

Note that in this and similar exhibits, the horizontal axis is stretched, so that a 10 percent change in income per capita represents the *same* absolute distance on the horizontal scale, whether we're starting from a lower level, like $500, or a higher level, like $8,000. For example, at the point labeled $500, a 10 percent increase takes the same horizontal distance as a 10 percent increase at the point labeled $8,000. This is the same strategy we used for the vertical axis in Exhibit 19.8 in the previous chapter, and why this is an informative way of representing variables such as income or GDP per capita will become clearer when we discuss economic growth in the next chapter.

Another reason why we care about income per capita is that poverty often brings poor health. One way to measure the health of a nation is by looking at the average life expectancy at birth. Exhibit 20.5 shows a scatter plot with life expectancy on the *y*-axis and income per capita on the *x*-axis, and again there is a strong association, indicating that this non-income-based measure of the standard of living also correlates strongly with income per capita.

Exhibit 20.5 The Relationship Between Life Expectancy at Birth and Income per Capita in 2010 (PPP-adjusted 2005 Constant Dollars)

This exhibit shows that people in countries with higher income per capita also have higher life expectancy at birth, meaning that on average, people in richer countries tend to live longer lives.

Source: Data from the Penn World Table and World Bank DataBank; Alan Heston, Robert Summers and Bettina Aten, Penn World Table Version 7.1, Center for International Comparisons of Production, Income and Prices at the University of Pennsylvania (Nov 2012).

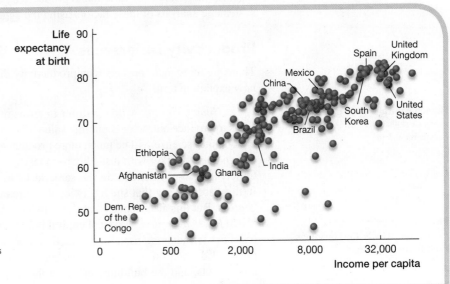

Exhibit 20.6 The Relationship Between the Human Development Index and Income per Capita in 2010 (PPP-adjusted 2005 Constant Dollars)

The Human Development Index combines information on income per capita, life expectancy, average years of schooling for those above age 25, and the enrollment of children in school. This exhibit shows that countries with higher income per capita tend to have higher levels of this index.

Source: Data from Penn World Table (Alan Heston, Robert Summers, and Bettina Aten, Penn World Table Version 7.1) and United Nations Development Programme.

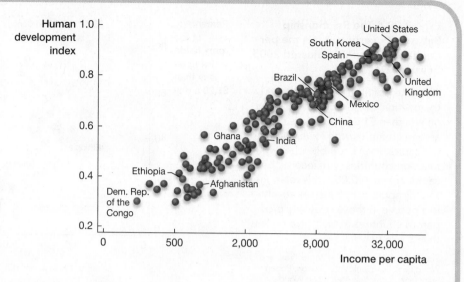

There are also several other factors we should take into account when measuring the standards of living across countries. One alternative is the United Nations' Human Development Index, which combines income per capita, life expectancy, and measures of education to more holistically measure the standard of living. Exhibit 20.6 presents a scatter plot with the Human Development Index on the *y*-axis and income per capita on the *x*-axis. It shows that there is once again a strong association between income per capita and this measure.

Overall, the relationship between income per capita and several measures of the standard of living, including poverty, life expectancy, and the Human Development Index, suggests a simple strategy: first focus on income per capita and then look in greater detail at issues related to health, education, poverty, and inequality within and across countries. This is the strategy we adopt here.

20.2 Productivity and the Aggregate Production Function

As we noted above, to understand differences in income per capita or income per worker across countries, we need to understand differences in productivity. To do so, we first outline the main sources of variation in productivity across countries. Then, we turn to a more systematic analysis of these factors using the aggregate production function.

Productivity Differences

There are three main reasons why productivity differs across countries, each of which we now explain in turn.

Human capital is each person's stock of skills to produce output or economic value.

(1) *Human capital:* Workers differ in terms of **human capital**, which is their stock of skills to produce output or economic value. For example, a worker with a university degree in computer science will be much more productive in computer programming or Web page design than a worker with just a high school degree. Suppose, for example, that in one day the computer scientist can do the same tasks as two workers with high school degrees. In this case, we say that she has twice the human capital as the workers with high school degrees. But this also implies that she is twice as *productive*.

Physical capital is any good, including machines and buildings, used for production.

(2) *Physical capital:* **Physical capital** is any good, including machines (equipment) and buildings (structures), used for production. For example, in agriculture, aggregate production will depend on agricultural machinery, the equipment used for transporting inputs and outputs, and the buildings in which the output is stored. Though these inputs are all

The **physical capital stock** of an economy is the value of equipment, structures and other non-labor inputs used in production.

An economy with better **technology** uses its labor and capital more efficiently and achieves higher productivity.

different, we can aggregate them into a single measure and obtain the **physical capital stock** of the economy using their dollar value. Workers will be more productive when the economy has a bigger physical capital stock, enabling each worker to work with more (or better) equipment and structures.

(3) *Technology:* An economy with better **technology** uses its labor and capital more efficiently and thus achieves higher productivity. We will see below that an economy can have better technology either because it uses superior knowledge in production (for example, new manufacturing techniques not available to other economies) or because it organizes production more efficiently.

The Aggregate Production Function

Human capital, physical capital, and technology each play a part in determining how productive workers in an economy are. The aggregate production function is our tool for understanding how these three ingredients all come together to generate GDP in an economy.

> Human capital, physical capital, and technology each play a part in determining how productive workers in an economy are.

In the previous chapter, we saw how we can aggregate tens of thousands of commodities into a single measure of GDP. For our analysis here, we can go one step further. Once we have made the simplification of aggregating everything into GDP, we can just think of GDP as if it were a single commodity. Even though this simplification ignores the *composition* of GDP, it allows us to more clearly look at what determines the *level* of GDP, which is our main purpose in this chapter.

The advantage of looking at GDP in this way is that once we start thinking of the world in terms of a single commodity, we can study the aggregate production function of the economy, which describes the relationship between GDP and its various inputs. This is similar to how we study the relationship between the output of a single firm and the inputs that it uses. For example, if we wanted to understand how much corn a farm produces, we would first specify the relationship between total corn production and its key inputs, for example, the number of workers on the farm and the equipment that the farm uses.

A key concept in our study of the aggregate production function is *factors of production*. You will recall from the previous chapter that factors of production are the inputs to the production process—goods or services purchased in the market for producing other goods, in this case for producing GDP. To understand a nation's output, we will look at a production function that describes how the factors of production are combined to produce GDP. But differently from the case in which we study a single firm, our focus is not specific commodities, such as T-shirts or iPhones, but all of GDP, and we therefore refer to this function as the **aggregate production function**.

The aggregate production function is useful for understanding not only how GDP is determined but also why productivity varies across countries.

An **aggregate production function** describes the relationship between the aggregate GDP of a nation and its factors of production.

Labor

The first and most important factor of production is labor. A nation can increase output by employing more workers. For example, more workers can be deployed for tilling the soil and harvesting corn.

Remember, though, that not all workers are the same. Some will have greater human capital than others and will be able to produce more output or economic value (and this is the reason why, as we have seen, human capital is a major determinant of productivity). Such differences in workers' human capital make looking at the total number of workers in an economy a poor indicator of how much the economy can produce. Instead, we need to know the total efficiency units of labor. **Total efficiency units of labor** is defined as the product of the total number of workers and the average human capital (efficiency) of (employed individuals) workers. For example, suppose a computer science graduate can perform the same job as two high school graduates. Then, it would be natural to give twice the weight to her labor than that of high school graduates. Now applying the same idea more broadly, we can compute the total efficiency units of labor, denoted by H, as the

Total efficiency units of labor is the product of the total number of workers in the economy and the average human capital of each worker.

product of the total number of workers in the economy, L, and the average efficiency or human capital of workers, h. Thus, we write:

$$H = L \times h.$$

This equation implies that the total efficiency units of labor in the economy can be increased either if more workers take part in the production process (for example, because employment increases) or if each worker becomes more productive. Acquiring more skills through formal schooling is one way for a worker to increase productivity.

Physical Capital and Land

The second major factor of production is physical capital, typically denoted by K (corresponding to the first letter of "Kapital," the German spelling of capital). When an economy has more physical capital, or equivalently, a greater physical capital *stock*, its workers can work with more and better equipment and structures, and thus the economy will produce more GDP.

A third factor of production is land. For example, if we think of an economy in the eighteenth century, land and other natural resources would be the key factors of production. Yet other factors of production include natural resources and the entrepreneurial talent of the economy (the skills and capabilities of its entrepreneurs and businesspeople). To simplify the discussion, we focus only on physical capital and labor (specifically, total efficiency units of labor). When we do so, the value of land and natural resources can be included in the physical capital stock (the same way that the value of buildings is). We will return to the role of entrepreneurial talent in the context of our discussion of technology below.

Representing the Aggregate Production Function

Let us represent the aggregate production function as follows:

$$Y = A \times F(K,H).$$

When we read an expression like the one above aloud, we say, "Y is a function of K and H." We read our notation as follows:

1. Y stands for GDP.
2. K is the physical capital stock of the nation.
3. H is the efficiency units of labor that the economy uses in production.
4. The function F signifies that there is a relationship between physical capital, labor, and GDP. In particular, GDP is generated through a combination of physical capital and the efficiency units of labor.
5. A is an index of technology. A higher A implies that the economy produces more GDP with the same level of physical capital stock and total efficiency units of labor. We discuss the role of technology in greater detail below.

As we have already emphasized, this aggregate production function is similar to the production function of an individual firm for producing a specific type of commodity. In particular:

(1) Just like the production function of a specific firm, the aggregate production function will show that GDP is increasing in both physical capital and labor—put differently, more is better. Holding labor constant, if we have a greater physical capital stock, we will be able to produce more GDP. Holding physical capital constant, if we have more labor, we will also be able to produce more GDP.

(2) The aggregate production function is also subject to the Law of Diminishing Marginal Product (which is related to our discussion of diminishing marginal benefit in Chapter 4). The **Law of Diminishing Marginal Product** states that the marginal contribution of a factor of production to GDP diminishes when we increase the quantity used of that factor of production (holding all other factors of production constant). We can illustrate the aggregate production function graphically by holding the total efficiency units of labor constant, as in Exhibit 20.7, or by holding the physical capital stock constant, as in Exhibit 20.8. Let's start with Exhibit 20.7.

The **Law of Diminishing Marginal Product** states that the marginal contribution of a factor of production to GDP diminishes when we increase the quantity used of that factor of production (holding all others constant).

Exhibit 20.7 The Aggregate Production Function with Physical Capital Stock on the Horizontal Axis (with the Total Efficiency Units of Labor Held Constant)

Holding the total efficiency units of labor constant, the aggregate production function shows the relationship between the physical capital stock and GDP in the economy. As the physical capital stock increases, so does GDP. But the relationship becomes less and less steep as the physical capital stock of the economy increases because of the Law of Diminishing Marginal Product. For the same one-unit increase in the physical capital stock, the increase in GDP is greater at point A (with lower physical capital stock) than at point B (with greater physical capital stock).

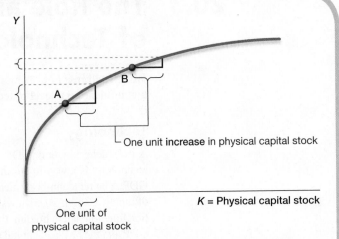

This exhibit shows both the increasing relationship between physical capital and output, and the Law of Diminishing Marginal Product. In particular, the marginal contribution of an additional unit of physical capital to output—how much output increases as a result of a unit increase in the physical capital stock—is decreasing in the total physical capital stock. We see this by comparing the increase in output for a unit increase in physical capital stock at two different points of the aggregate production function in Exhibit 20.7. Consider a unit increase close to the origin (point A). When there is less physical capital in the economy, the corresponding increase in output is large. When we have the same unit increase farther to the right, corresponding to more physical capital (point B), the resulting increase in output is smaller, as shown by the smaller vertical increase at B than at A. This visual difference captures the Law of Diminishing Marginal Product.

Exhibit 20.7 holds the efficiency units of labor, H, constant and looks at the relationship between the physical capital stock and GDP. Exhibit 20.8 does the opposite, holding the physical capital stock, K, constant and looking at the relationship between the efficiency units of labor of the economy and GDP. This relationship also satisfies the Law of Diminishing Marginal Product.

Exhibit 20.8 The Aggregate Production Function with the Efficiency Units of Labor on the Horizontal Axis (with Physical Capital Stock Held Constant)

Holding the physical capital stock constant, the aggregate production function shows the relationship between the total efficiency units of labor and GDP. Once again, as the total efficiency units of labor increase, so does GDP, but consistent with the Law of Diminishing Marginal Product, the relationship becomes less and less steep as the total efficiency units of labor increase.

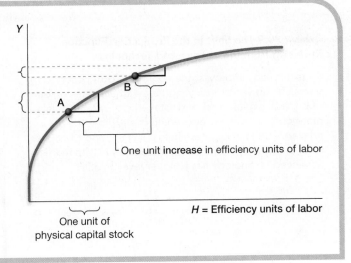

20.3 The Role and Determinants of Technology

We now discuss how technology affects the aggregate production function and the factors that influence the level of technology of an economy.

Technology

A third determinant of GDP is technology. The aggregate production function specifies that technology is a way of summarizing the relationship between the factors of production and GDP. A better technology means that the economy can generate more output from the same set of inputs. Exhibit 20.9 shows the implications of better technology for the aggregate production function: again holding the efficiency units of labor, H, constant, the relationship between GDP and the physical capital stock shifts left. Therefore, for every level of the efficiency units of labor, a better technology implies that the economy will produce more GDP.

Our study of the aggregate production function thus clarifies why productivity depends on human capital, physical capital, and technology. Holding the total number of workers constant, greater human capital, a larger stock of physical capital, and better technology will all increase GDP. Because the total number of workers (and hours of work per worker) is constant, this also corresponds to an increase in productivity.

Dimensions of Technology

Technology, as we have defined it, is rather broad, and in fact has two very distinct components. The first is *knowledge*. Today, we know how to produce many new goods, such as smart phones and tablets, which were not available previously. In addition, this knowledge also enables us to perform certain tasks more efficiently. For example, when you use a computer for writing an essay or doing computations for a class, you are making use of the computing power, which comes from the knowledge that society has acquired and has applied to its production process. Part of this knowledge is in the human capital of the workers: workers today can perform a range of tasks more productively than their grandparents could. But an important part of this knowledge is embodied in the physical capital stock of firms: the computers that firms are using are part of the physical capital stock of the economy.

Nevertheless, there is also a sense in which technology is different from the physical capital stock of the economy. Your great-grandparents, however much they may have wished to pay for a computer, would not have been able to do so, because computers were not yet commercially sold. Your grandparents would have had to pay an enormous price for a computer with fewer capabilities than the one you are using now, and it would have likely been a

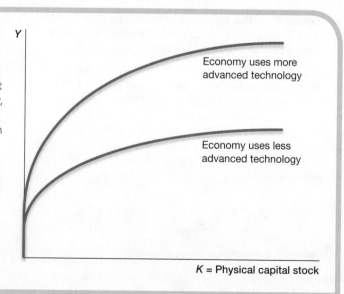

Exhibit 20.9 The Shift in the Production Function Resulting from More Advanced Technology

As technology improves, the aggregate production function shifts upwards, indicating that with the same amount of physical capital stock and total efficiency units of labor, more output can be produced. In this exhibit, the total efficiency units of labor are held constant, and for a given level of physical capital stock, the economy with more advanced technology has a higher level of GDP.

Economy uses more advanced technology

Economy uses less advanced technology

K = Physical capital stock

💬 LETTING THE DATA SPEAK

Moore's Law

A long-term trend of rather remarkable regularity in the development of computer microprocessors has been observed since 1965. It's dubbed Moore's Law after Intel cofounder Gordon Moore, who predicted in that year that the number of transistors on a chip would double approximately every 2 years.[2] The number of transistors is a key determinant of how fast a computer processor is. So roughly speaking, Moore's Law implies that computer processor power should double approximately every 2 years. So far, this seems to have been borne out by developments in computer technology, as illustrated in Exhibit 20.10. Several other measures of technological advances in computing have also behaved according to Moore's Law. For example, the number of pixels in digital cameras and RAM storage capacity have also doubled every 2 years or so, while power consumption of computer nodes and hard disc storage costs appear to have been halved approximately every 2 years.

Naturally, there is nothing predetermined about the relationship between time and progress in technology that would make this into an actual "law." This progress results from the investments of several companies in new computer technologies, which are in turn driven by the profitability of these investments. It also relies on government support for university and private research and on the ability of the United States and other advanced and developing nations to attract increasing numbers of young, talented students into science, engineering, and related fields. Things can change in the future, halting this rapid progress in technology. Fewer college students could choose to major in science and engineering in the future, or governments could decide to limit or even stop their support for private or university research, weakening incentives for further technological advances. Moreover, even without a major cutback in funding or a change in the profitability of research in this area, the rate of advance may slow down from its current breakneck pace. Nevertheless, the relationship so far has been very accurate and, assuming it continues in the years to come, the implications for lives are enormous.

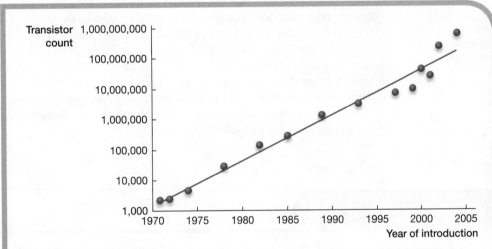

Exhibit 20.10 Moore's Law

Gordon Moore predicted in 1965 that the speed of computer processors would improve steadily. This has turned out to be a very accurate prediction, with the number of transistors packed in a computer chip doubling approximately every 2 years. This remarkable trend, which has come to be known as Moore's Law, now symbolizes the sustained technological improvements of our era.

Source: Intel, "Moore's Law: Raising the Bar," *Backgrounder* (2005), available at: http://www.bandwidthco.com/whitepapers/hardware/cpu/moore/Moores%20Law%20-%20Raising%20the%20Bar.pdf.

Research and development (R&D) refers to the activities directed at improving scientific knowledge, generating new innovations, or implementing existing knowledge in production in order to improve the technology of a firm or an economy.

giant machine rather than the small notebooks that many of you are using. Thus advances in technology—in this specific instance, in computer technology—directly increase the number of tasks we can perform and the speed at which we can accomplish them.

Advances in technology sometimes happen by chance, but more often, they result from the purposeful, optimizing decisions of economic agents. For example, society achieves such advances with **research and development (R&D)**, which involves a wide range of activities like research on new scientific ideas in universities and private labs, research directed at finding

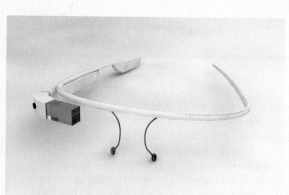

> **Advances in technology sometimes happen by chance, but more often, they result from the purposeful, optimizing decisions of economic agents.**

Efficiency of production refers to the ability of an economy to produce the maximal amount of output from a given amount of factors of production and knowledge.

new ways of applying science to production on the factory floor, and development activities geared at commercializing existing knowledge and products. R&D is a major activity in the United States economy. Almost 1.41 million people worked as researchers in 2007 (the most recent year for which this information is available), and $430 billion—2.77 percent of total GDP—was spent on research and development. Of this amount, about $270 billion was spent by businesses, while the remaining portion was spent by the U.S. government, universities, and other institutions.

Economists often use the term *technology* more broadly than to describe advances in our knowledge about production processes. To see this, imagine two economies. In one, the allocation of resources is determined by the market, and in the other, resources are allocated randomly across individuals and firms. As a specific example, say that both of these economies have two types of workers, economics professors and basketball players, and two types of tasks, teaching and basketball.

The first economy relies on the market for allocating workers to tasks. Basketball players who are better at basketball than teaching will play basketball, and economics professors will do the teaching. In the second, allocation takes place randomly. Suppose that economics professors are assigned to do the basketball playing and the basketball players do the teaching. There are no differences in the knowledge available for production between the two economies, and both have the same human capital. But the first economy will be much more successful (especially in basketball), and will produce more output (more and better basketball and perhaps even better teaching).

What is the difference between the two economies? This difference has to do with the **efficiency of production**—the ability of society to produce the maximal amount of output at a given cost or for given levels of the factors of production and knowledge. When the economy is able to increase the efficiency of production, there will be a shift in the aggregate production function similar to that shown in Exhibit 20.9. We therefore include efficiency of production as part of our definition of technology because it captures the differences in how much output an economy can generate with given amounts of inputs.

The importance of technology for GDP is the reason why we include A and represented the aggregate production function as:

$$A \times F(K,H).$$

LETTING THE DATA SPEAK

Efficiency of Production and Productivity at the Company Level

Economist James Schmitz Jr. studied the experience of the iron ore industries in the United States and Canada in the face of competition from Brazilian producers.[3] His findings provide a particularly clear illustration of how changes in the organization of firms can lead to improvements in the efficiency of production—or "technology"—and thus increase productivity significantly.

Schmitz documents that productivity—for example, measured as output of iron ore per hour—was constant since at least 1970 in the Canadian and the U.S. iron ore industries when they faced little foreign competition. In the early 1980s, however, Brazilian producers entered the U.S. market and started to deliver iron ore to Chicago and other central markets. Schmitz shows that in the course of the next decade, productivity in the U.S. and Canadian iron ore industries, which had been flat for a long time, doubled. He shows that this was not

due to more intensive use of capital or materials, nor was it driven by the use of new production techniques. Rather, it resulted from a significant reorganization of production.

Iron ore production plants were heavily unionized—a fact that, according to Schmitz, prevented the plants from efficiently allocating labor across different tasks. For example, despite industry studies suggesting that there was an excess number of repair workers for a large variety of equipment, union contracts did not permit reduction in repair staff. Following the increase in competition, these work rules were changed, enabling a more productive use of labor. Schmitz provides a variety of additional evidence showing that these and other changes in work rules allowed a more flexible allocation of labor across tasks and therefore better utilization of equipment, resulting in the dramatic increase in productivity.

Greater A corresponds to better technology and increases GDP for given levels of efficiency units of labor and physical capital stock, which shifts the aggregate production function left, as shown in Exhibit 20.9. But note that A is *not* a factor of production. Although it designates the technology available to the economy, it does not correspond to an input that the producer can purchase in the marketplace.

Entrepreneurship

A particularly important reason why efficiency of production and productivity might differ across economies relates to entrepreneurship. As we discuss in greater detail in Chapter 22, various factors might influence whether the individuals with a comparative advantage for entrepreneurship become entrepreneurs. When they fail to do so, the efficiency of production of an economy is lower—in the same way as the mismatch between basketball players and economics teachers, though perhaps more importantly.

LETTING THE DATA SPEAK

Monopoly and GDP

When Mexico entered the North American Free Trade Agreement, NAFTA, with the United States in 1994, many economists predicted that Mexico's economy would grow rapidly. But in the first 15 years after signing NAFTA, Mexico's growth was much less than most analysts expected. Monopolies and barriers against the entry of new companies are just some of the reasons why the country has not achieved more significant growth.

Consider the telecommunications sector in Mexico, which was for a long time operated as a state monopoly. It subsequently was privatized, but turned into a private monopoly under the ownership of Carlos Slim, who has now become one of the richest people in the world. In contrast, the telecommunications sector in the United States is very competitive, with many firms competing in both wireless and broadband. The Mexican telecommunications sector not only charges higher prices than other countries but also invests less than other comparable countries, as shown in Exhibit 20.11.

Removing monopolies and entry barriers that prevent the efficient allocation of resources is one important way of increasing GDP.

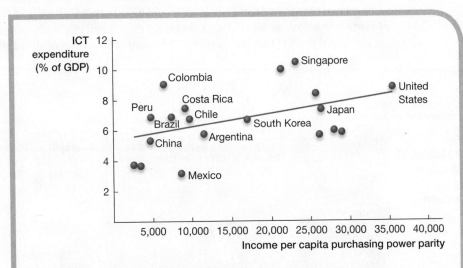

Exhibit 20.11 Underinvestment in Information and Communication Technology in Mexico Relative to Countries with Comparable Income

Monopolies and barriers against the entry of new companies often discourage investment and slow down technological progress. For example, Mexico, where the telecommunications sector is monopolized, invests in information and communication technology less than other countries with similar income per capita.

Source: World Bank DataBank.

Evidence-Based Economics

Q: Why is the average American so much richer than the average Indian?

To understand the variation in productivity and income per worker between the United States and India (and other countries), it is useful to focus on three factors: human capital, physical capital, and technology. To see the relative importance of any one of these factors in explaining differences in income (GDP) per worker across countries, we can compare a country's actual income per worker with what *would be* if the country had access to the same human capital, physical capital stock, or technology of another country. This is exactly what we do in Exhibit 20.12, specifically with technology.

Using data on education attainment (a key aspect of human capital) and employment, we calculate the efficiency units of labor. Column 3 records the average years of schooling per worker of each country. It shows that most countries have significantly lower levels of average schooling than the United States.

Then, using data on investment over several decades, we calculate the physical capital stock for each country. Column 4 shows the ratio of the physical capital stock per worker of each country relative to the physical capital stock per worker in the United States. Most countries have a significantly lower physical capital stock per worker than the United States (but there are also countries like Norway, not shown in the exhibit, that have higher levels than the United States).

Using estimates of the shape of the aggregate production function (we provide details of this estimation in the appendix to this chapter), we can then see how the efficiency units of labor and physical capital stock are translated into income per worker. Comparing these contributions of human capital and physical capital with *actual* income per worker (recorded in column 2 of Exhibit 20.12), we can then infer how much of a contribution technology makes to income per worker. Specifically, any GDP that cannot be accounted for by physical capital and labor, we assume to be accounted for by technology.

Given the estimates of the aggregate production function, we can now compute what the income level of all of these countries would have been if they had had access to exactly the same technology as the United States (using their actual efficiency units of labor and physical capital stock). This information is recorded in column 5 of the exhibit. The difference

Exhibit 20.12 The Contribution of Human Capital, Physical Capital, and Technology to Differences in Income per Worker

Source: Data from Penn World Table (Alan Heston, Robert Summers, and Bettina Aten, Penn World Table Version 7.1).

Country (1)	Income per Worker in 2010 (2)	Average Years of Schooling (3)	% of U.S. Physical Capital Stock per Worker in 2010 (4)	Income per Worker If Technology Were at U.S. Level (5)
United States	82,359	13.1	100.0	SAME
United Kingdom	67,025	9.8	65.8	61,548
South Korea	54,315	11.8	87.7	74,496
Spain	54,539	10.4	83.9	68,684
Mexico	27,625	9.1	33.5	47,725
Brazil	15,975	7.5	16.9	35,045
China	12,961	8.2	14.9	34,881
India	9,010	5.1	8.9	24,071
Ghana	4,928	7.1	4.2	21,502
Afghanistan	3,980	4.2	3.7	16,818
Dem. Rep. of the Congo	628	3.5	0.8	9,625

between actual incomes and these hypothetical numbers illustrates the contribution of technology.

The exhibit reveals some powerful facts. Consistent with the patterns we have already seen in Exhibits 20.1–20.3, income per worker in the United States is about 9 times that in India (82,359/9,010 ≃ 9). We also see that Indians have average years of schooling of 5.1 compared to 13.1 in the United States and that the physical capital stock per worker in India is about 9 percent of that of the United States.

So how much would a typical Indian worker produce with this amount of human capital and physical capital if he, hypothetically, had access to the U.S. level of technology?

Column 5 shows that the answer is $24,071. This implies that the hypothetical income per Indian worker if India's technology were at the U.S. level is nearly 3 times as much as its current income per worker: 24,071/9,010 ≃ 2.7, suggesting a sizable impact of technology differences. If, in addition, India also increased its human capital and physical capital per worker to U.S. levels, it would increase its income per worker to the U.S. level. (This is by construction: if India has the same level of human capital and physical capital per worker, and the same technology as the U.S., it would have the same income per worker as the U.S.). In the Indian case this would correspond to an increase by another 3½ times (82,359/24,071 ≃ 3.5).

Recall, however, that the technology differences that appear so important (roughly as important as total efficiency units of labor and physical capital combined) are not just differences in the knowledge available to the economy and to firms for production. They also reflect differences in the efficiency of production, as our example of economics professors and basketball players illustrated, and if there is any mismeasurement in factors of production, this will appear as technology differences. For example, in practice, human capital across countries differs not only because of average years of schooling but also because of major differences in the quality of schooling. If rich countries have a systematically higher quality of schooling, our methodology can lead to exaggerated technology differences.

Question

Why is the average American so much richer than the average Indian?

Answer

Differences in total efficiency units of labor and physical capital are important. If India had access to the same technology as the United States (including differences in the efficiency of production), its income (or GDP) per worker would be $24,071 instead of $9,010, almost 3 times as high. Increasing India's total efficiency units of labor and physical capital to U.S. levels would increase its income per worker by another 3½ times.

Data

Cross-country data on PPP-adjusted income per worker, schooling, and investment.

Caveat

Technology differences include differences in the efficiency of production and may also reflect mismeasurement.

Summary

✦ Income per capita, defined as aggregate income or gross domestic product (GDP) divided by total population, varies greatly across countries, with some nations such as the United States and Norway having more than 40 times the income per capita of some other nations such as Afghanistan, Niger, and the Democratic Republic of Congo.

✦ Income (or GDP) per capita across countries can be compared using exchange-rate-based measures, which rely on current exchange rates, or purchasing power parity-based measures, which compare estimates of the cost of the representative bundle of commodities in each country. The latter tends to be more reliable as it more appropriately captures differences in relative prices across countries, and is not subject to fluctuations resulting from changes in exchange rates. Though income per capita omits a wealth of other important information about a country (health, schooling, inequality, and poverty), it provides a good summary of prosperity and is typically correlated with higher life expectancy, greater schooling, and lower poverty.

✦ The aggregate production function links the GDP of a nation to its total efficiency units of labor, physical capital stock, technology, and efficiency of production. Greater efficiency units of labor and physical capital, as well as better technology and efficiency of production, increase GDP.

✦ Though the total efficiency units of labor and physical capital stock matter a great deal for GDP, the most important determinant of cross-country differences in income (or GDP) per worker appears to be differences in technology and the efficiency of production.

Key Terms

income per capita or GDP per capita
  p. 455
purchasing power parity (PPP) *p. 456*
income (or GDP) per worker *p. 458*
productivity *p. 459*
one dollar a day per person poverty
  line *p. 460*

human capital *p. 462*
physical capital *p. 462*
physical capital stock *p. 463*
technology *p. 463*
aggregate production function *p. 463*
total efficiency units of labor *p. 463*

Law of Diminishing Marginal Product
  p. 464
research and development (R&D)
  p. 467
efficiency of production *p. 468*

Questions

All questions are available in MyEconLab for practice and instructor assignment.

1. Suppose you are comparing the income per capita in the United States and Ghana. You first convert the values into U.S. dollars using the current exchange rate between the U.S. dollar and the Ghanaian cedi. You also convert both values to U.S. dollars using the purchasing power parity-adjusted exchange rate. Which measure is likely to give you a more accurate picture of the living standards in both countries? Explain your answer.

2. What are the disadvantages of using Big Macs to measure purchasing power parity?

3. Suppose that country A has higher income per capita than country B. Explain why this does not imply that most citizens of country A have higher income than most citizens of country B. Try to construct an example in which both countries have 10 citizens to demonstrate this point.

4. Is income per capita more relevant in understanding differences in international living standards than income per worker?

5. What is the correlation between income per capita and welfare measures like absolute poverty and life expectancy? What does this suggest about income per capita as a measure of welfare?

6. What does the Human Development Index measure? What is the correlation between this index and income per capita in a country?

7. What is productivity? Why does it vary across countries?

8. What are the two components of technology?

9. What are factors of production? What does the aggregate production function describe?

10. What are the total efficiency units of labor? What is the relationship between this concept and human capital?

11. Use the following diagram to explain the relationship between a country's physical capital stock and GDP.

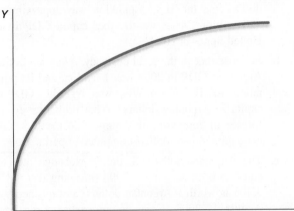

12. Explain the difference between the terms "physical capital" and "human capital."

13. Explain what distinguishes physical capital from natural resources.

14. How do increases in technology affect the aggregate production function?

15. What does Moore's Law state? Is Moore's Law borne out by historical data?

16. Why is the average American so much richer than the average Indian?

17. What policies can be used to raise GDP in a country?

Problems

All problems are available in MyEconLab for practice and instructor assignment. Problems marked 🌐 update with real-time data.

1. You read a newspaper report that compares wages paid to employees at Starbucks in India and in the United Kingdom. At the time, 1 pound was equal to 87 rupees. The report says that Starbucks baristas in India are paid a mere 56 pence an hour, which is lower than the cheapest coffee that Starbucks sells in the United Kingdom. A friend of yours who read the report is appalled by this information and thinks that Starbucks ought to raise its salaries substantially in India. Is your friend necessarily correct? Explain your answer.

🌐 2. The following table lists 2012 GDP per capita for four countries. The data are given in the national currencies of the countries. It also lists the price of a Big Mac burger in local currency in each country in 2012.

	2012 GDP per Capita	2012 Big Mac Price
Norway (krone)	579,162	41 krone
Poland (zloty)	41,398	9.1 zloty
Turkey (Turkish lira)	19,580	6.6 Turkish lira
United Kingdom (British pound)	24,740	2.49 pounds

Source for GDP: UNECE Statistical Database, compiled from national and international (CIS, EUROSTAT, IMF, OECD) official sources.

Source for Big Mac Prices: http://bigmacindex.org/2012-big-mac-index.html

The price of a Big Mac in the United States in 2012 was $4.20.

Using the Big Mac burger as a representative commodity common to the countries, calculate the purchasing power parity (PPP)-adjustment factor for each country, and then the PPP level of per capita GDP in each country.

3. Let us use what we have learned in the first part of the chapter to compare living standards in the United States and a hypothetical country, Argonia, in 2008.

   a. The U.S. GDP in 2008 was approximately 14 trillion dollars and the U.S. population was approximately 300 million. What was the per capita GDP in the United States in 2008?

   b. Suppose that in the local currency, Argonian dollars, Argonia's GDP in 2008 was 1 trillion, and its population was 10 million. What was Argonia's GDP per capita in Argonian dollars? What problems do you foresee in comparing this number to the U.S. GDP per capita in U.S. dollars computed in part a?

   c. The Argonian dollar/U.S. dollar exchange rate was equal to 6 on January 1, 2008 (meaning that 1 U.S. dollar is worth 6 Argonian dollars) and reached 9 on August 1, 2008. Compute an exchange-rate-based measure of the GDP per capita in Argonia in U.S. dollars on these two dates. Do you think the change in Argonia's exchange-rate-based measure of GDP per capita between these two dates reflects a true change in living standards?

   d. McDonald's has a thriving business in Argonia and sold a Big Mac for 7 Argonian dollars in 2008, while at the same time, a Big Mac sold for $3.50 in the United States. Using this information, provide an alternative estimate of GDP per capita in Argonia. Would you trust this estimate better than the one based on exchange rates? Why or why not?

4. Suppose you are given the following information for the country Lusitania:

	2011
Population; total in Lusitania	190 million
Employment	80 million
Gross Domestic Product (GDP)	2,476 billion U.S. dollars

   a. What is the income per capita in Lusitania?

   b. What is the income per worker in Lusitania?

The following table gives you the same information for the country Arctica.

	2011
Population; total in Arctica	80 million
Employment	40 million
Gross Domestic Product (GDP)	3,600 billion U.S. dollars

   c. What is the income per capita in Arctica?

   d. What is the income per worker in Arctica?

   e. Based on the given information, would Arctica be considered more productive than Lusitania? Explain your answer.

   f. How would you use the information given in both these tables to compare living standards in Lusitania and Arctica?

5. Suppose that the GDP in current dollars for Polonia is higher than Ruritania's GDP. However, using purchasing power parity-adjusted dollars, Ruritania's GDP is higher than Polonia's GDP. Based on this information, what would you conclude about living standards in Polonia and Ruritania?

6. In 2011, China revised its poverty line upward to 2,300 yuan per year, or 6.3 yuan per day. At the prevailing exchange rate, this was equal to a little less than a single U.S. dollar. Some commentators felt that China's poverty line fell short of the World Bank's poverty line of $1.25 per day, in 2005 purchasing power parity (PPP) U.S. dollars. Would you agree? What other information would you need to evaluate this claim?

7. In this question, we will use what you learned in the second part of the chapter to compare the performance of an economy in two different time periods, as its physical capital stock and efficiency units of labor change.

   a. Suppose that from period 1 to period 2, the unemployment rate in the economy increases. Everything else remains unchanged. What happens to the total efficiency units of labor? Express your results formally as an inequality, using the formula for total efficiency units of labor presented in the chapter (in particular, recall that total efficiency units of labor in two periods can be written as $H_1 = L_1 \times h_1$ and $H_2 = L_2 \times h_2$; where L is the total number of employed workers).

   b. What are the consequences of this increase in unemployment for GDP? Express your results formally as an inequality, using the aggregate production function presented in the chapter.

   c. What are the consequences for GDP per capita and GDP per worker?

   d. Suppose that there is a technological advance from period 1 to period 2 but, at the same time, a decrease in physical capital stock. Can you say whether GDP will increase or decrease? Why or why not?

8. The following table shows the change in GDP in Lithasia with changes in efficiency units of human capital.

GDP (in Millions of Dollars)	Stock of Physical Capital (Units)	Efficiency Units of Labor
100	15,000	16,000
150	15,000	20,000
180	15,000	24,000
200	15,000	28,000
210	15,000	32,000

a. Comment on the rate of change in GDP as the economy uses more efficiency units of labor.

b. How would the aggregate production function of this economy look if GDP is measured along the vertical axis and efficiency units of labor on the horizontal axis?

c. What explains the shape of this aggregate production function?

Links: http://www.worldbank.org/depweb/english/beyond/global/chapter15.html; http://data.worldbank.org/indicator/NY.GNP.PCAP.PP.CD; http://www.worldbank.org/depweb/english/beyond/global/chapter2.html

9. The old Soviet Union devoted enormous resources exclusively to increasing its physical capital stock, and yet eventually the increase in the country's GDP came to an end. Based on the discussion in the chapter, explain why this was inevitable.

10. Draw a graph showing the aggregate production function, assuming diminishing marginal returns to physical capital. Label the axes.

11. Redraw your graph from Problem 10. Now show what would happen if there is a technological advance. Make sure to label the axes once again, and indicate clearly the direction of any changes to your graph.

12. First Japan, then Korea, and now China have managed to grow very rapidly without devoting many resources to research and development (R&D). Given the importance noted in the text of technological advance as an engine of growth, this seems to be a contradiction.

Explain how rapid growth in these countries (and others as well) could have been achieved without a substantial R&D commitment on their part.

13. Give an algebraic and an intuitive explanation of the concept of "efficiency of production." Why is efficiency of production so important to GDP?

Appendix

The Mathematics of Aggregate Production Functions

How did we compute, in Exhibit 20.12, what the average income per worker in India would have been if India had access to the U.S. level of technology?

We worked with the aggregate production function $Y = A \times F(K,H)$ using the following form, which is often estimated as an empirical approximation to data:

$$Y = A \times F(K,H) = A \times K^{1/3} \times H^{2/3}.$$

It is referred to as a Cobb-Douglas function and has several attractive features.[4] For one, the coefficients to which K and H are raised to add up to 1 ($\frac{1}{3} + \frac{2}{3} = 1$). This ensures that the production function exhibits *constant returns to scale*: that is, increasing K and H by 1 percent would lead to a 1 percent increase in Y. Moreover, this functional form is consistent with the empirical fact that, roughly speaking, about two-thirds of national income goes to labor and one-third to physical capital.

Let us now divide both sides of the above equation by the total number of workers in the economy, L, to obtain:

$$Y \times \frac{1}{L} = A \times K^{1/3} \times H^{2/3} \times \frac{1}{L}.$$

This can be rewritten as:

$$y = \frac{Y}{L} = A \times K^{1/3} \times H^{2/3} \times \frac{1}{L^{1/3} \times L^{2/3}},$$

where y is income per worker, or GDP divided by the number of workers in the economy. The last term simply rewrites $1/L$ differently to derive the next equation.

Now rearranging the previous equation, we obtain

$$y = A \times \left(\frac{K}{L}\right)^{1/3} \times \left(\frac{H}{L}\right)^{2/3}.$$

Finally, recalling that $H = L \times h$, this can be rewritten as

$$y = A \times \left(\frac{K}{L}\right)^{1/3} \times h^{2/3}.$$

Stated differently:

GDP per worker = Technology $\times$ *(Capital per worker)*$^{1/3}$ $\times$ *(Human capital per worker)*$^{2/3}$.

This derivation also shows why there is a very tight relationship between cross-country differences in GDP per worker and cross-country differences in productivity. For simplicity, assuming that each worker works the same number of hours in every country, the left-hand side of this equation is also GDP per hour worked and thus the productivity of a country. The equation therefore demonstrates that productivity is determined by the three ingredients we have emphasized in the text: technology, physical capital, and human capital.

We next use data on GDP per worker together with data on the physical capital stock (K), or physical capital per worker, and data on human capital per worker (h). Data on GDP are available from various sources (with original information coming from national income accounts). These sources also provide information on investment, which we can use to compute physical capital stocks. Finally, we can compute human capital differences across nations from differences in average years of schooling. In particular, we know how much more a worker with one more year of schooling earns. We can use this information to create an index, h—on the basis of differences in average years of schooling—that captures differences in human capital across nations. For example, say college graduate workers will typically have 16 years of schooling and earn twice as much as workers with 6 years of schooling. Then if we set $h = 1$ for a country with 6 years of schooling on average, we would have $h = 2$ for a country with 16 years of schooling on average.

Now let us start by computing the technology for the United States, denoted by A_{US} Using the previous equation, we arrive at:

$$A_{\text{US}} = \frac{y_{\text{US}}}{\left(\dfrac{K_{\text{US}}}{L_{\text{US}}}\right)^{1/3} \times h_{\text{US}}^{2/3}}.$$

As we have seen, the U.S. GDP per worker is given by

$$y_{\text{US}} = A_{\text{US}} \times \left(\frac{K_{\text{US}}}{L_{\text{US}}}\right)^{1/3} \times h_{\text{US}}^{2/3}.$$

The expression above is obtained simply by rearranging this.

In the same fashion, we can find the contribution of technology to the GDP of India, which is A_{INDIA}:

$$A_{\text{INDIA}} = \frac{y_{\text{INDIA}}}{\left(\dfrac{K_{\text{INDIA}}}{L_{\text{INDIA}}}\right)^{1/3} \times h_{\text{INDIA}}^{2/3}}.$$

We can then ask how the GDP of India would be different if instead of A_{INDIA} we used A_{US} in the preceding expression. We can calculate the hypothetical GDP per worker of India in the situation in which India has the same technology term, A_{US}, as the United States:

$$y_{\text{INDIA WITH US TECHNOLOGY}} = A_{\text{US}} \times \left(\frac{K_{\text{INDIA}}}{L_{\text{INDIA}}}\right)^{1/3} \times h_{\text{INDIA}}^{2/3}.$$

Using our estimates of $A_{\text{US}}, K_{\text{INDIA}}, L_{\text{INDIA}}, h_{\text{INDIA}}$, for example, we can compute the hypothetical GDP per worker of India, if India were able to use American technology, as $24,071. In the same way, we can plug in the U.S. technology terms into the aggregate production function of any country, which enables us to do the rest of the computations in Exhibit 20.12.

21 Economic Growth

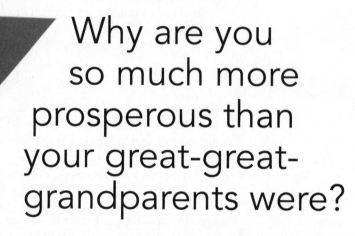

Why are you so much more prosperous than your great-great-grandparents were?

The United States was not always as prosperous as it is today. Its (real) GDP per capita today is about 25 times what it was in 1820. At that time, only a small fraction of the population lived in cities; most people worked in agriculture. People could not even imagine, let alone have access to, many of the goods, services, and technologies that we take for granted, including radio, television, indoor plumbing, shopping malls, cars, planes, or even trains.

The United States and several other countries have vastly increased their GDP (income) per capita over the last 200 years, developing new goods, services, and technologies. We call this process *economic growth*. The key questions we address in this chapter are how and why the United States and several other countries have managed to achieve such notable economic growth over the past two centuries.

CHAPTER **OUTLINE**

KEY IDEAS

☀ Economic growth measures how much (real) GDP per capita grows over time.

☀ Today's high levels of GDP per capita in many nations are a result of rapid economic growth over the last two centuries.

☀ Sustained economic growth relies on technological progress.

☀ There are sizable differences in the historical growth rates of different economies, which are largely responsible for their differences in the levels of GDP per capita.

☀ Economic growth is a powerful tool for poverty reduction.

21.1 The Power of Economic Growth

We saw in Chapter 20 how aggregate incomes (GDP) are determined. We can now start using these ideas to understand why several countries, including the United States, have managed to become so much richer over the past 200 years and in the process, gain a new perspective on the differences across countries that we documented in the previous chapter. Throughout this chapter, by GDP we refer to *real* GDP which uses market prices from a specific base year (in this chapter generally 2005) to express the value of production in the economy, as we discussed in Chapter 19.

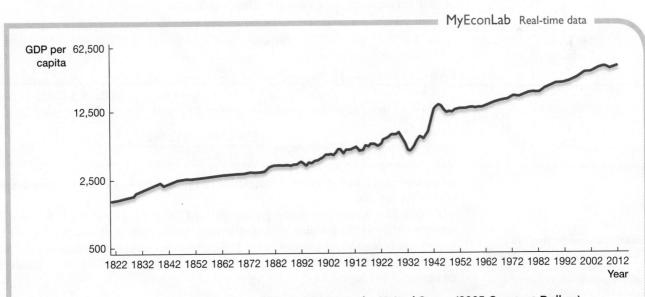

MyEconLab Real-time data

Exhibit 21.1 GDP per Capita in the United States (2005 Constant Dollars)

The growth of GDP per capita in the United States has been relatively steady and sustained, except during the Great Depression and its aftermath. Note that the vertical axis has a proportional scale so that the vertical distance between 500 and 2,500 is the same as that between 2,500 and 12,500.

Source: Data from Maddison Project (1820–1959) and World Bank DataBank: World Development Indicators (1960–2012); J. Bolt and J. L. van Zanden, The First Update of the Maddison Project; Re-Estimating Growth Before 1820. Maddison Project Working Paper 4 (2013).

A First Look at U.S. Growth

As a first step, Exhibit 21.1 depicts GDP per capita in the United States over the past 200 years. In Chapter 20, we adjusted incomes in terms of the cost of a given basket of commodities in order to compare them meaningfully across countries. Similarly, we saw in Chapter 19 how to make a similar adjustment for inflation to obtain *real GDP* (or real income), which can be meaningfully compared over time. Recall that this involves adjusting GDP or incomes according to a base-year dollar value, which we call *constant dollars*. This is what we do in this chapter also. Exhibit 21.1, for example, plots the level of GDP per capita in the United States in 2005 constant dollars, so the income for the year 1967, for example, is expressed as what it would be equal to in year 2005 dollars.

Exhibit 21.1 clearly illustrates the *economic growth* in the U.S. economy between 1820 and 2012. **Economic growth**, or simply **growth**, refers to the increase in GDP per capita of an economy. The exhibit shows this type of economic growth and a marked increase in GDP per capita in the U.S. economy over the last 200 years, though the increase is not entirely steady and there are some jagged movements, corresponding to economic fluctuations. One of these stands out: the Great Depression, which started in 1929 and recorded a major contraction in U.S. GDP per capita. Despite its importance and its impact on the lives of millions, the Great Depression was a temporary event—sustained and steady growth of GDP per capita characterizes the U.S. economy both before and after it. In this chapter, we focus on such longer-run movements, returning to economic fluctuations like the Great Depression in subsequent chapters.

As a result of the continued economic growth depicted in Exhibit 21.1, U.S. GDP per capita and standards of living are much higher today than they were in 1820. For example, GDP per capita has increased from $1,858 in 1820 to $13,056 in 1950 and to $45,336 in 2012 (all numbers in 2005 constant dollars). (Notice that the vertical axis of this exhibit has a proportional scale, similar to those we have used in several exhibits in Chapters 19 and 20, and ensures that the distance between $500 and $2,500 is the same as that between $2,500 and $12,500. We explain why this is a good way of presenting the data shortly.)

Let us first specify the measurement of growth in a little more detail. A **growth rate** is defined as the change in a quantity—here, GDP per capita—between two dates, relative to the baseline (beginning of period) quantity. Let's choose two dates, say t and $t + 1$, and denote GDP per capita in these two dates by y_t and y_{t+1}, respectively. Then the growth rate of GDP per capita between these two dates is defined as

$$\text{Growth}_{t,t+1} = \frac{y_{t+1} - y_t}{y_t}.$$

Let us focus on annual differences, so that, for example, t and $t + 1$ correspond to the years 2005 and 2006, respectively. The U.S. economy had GDP per capita of $42,482 in 2005 and $43,215 in 2006, so the growth rate between 2005 and 2006 can be computed as

$$\text{Growth}_{2005,2006} = \frac{\$43,215 - \$42,482}{\$42,482} = 0.017$$

(or equivalently, $0.017 \times 100 = 1.7\%$). Using this formula, we can compute growth rates of GDP for any country.

Exhibit 21.2 depicts the annual growth rate of GDP per capita of the U.S. economy between 1950 and 2012, which is computed using this formula. It shows that the average growth rate is positive, at approximately 2.03 percent, but economic fluctuations are also visible here, including the one starting in 2008, the "Great Recession" which we discuss in greater detail in Chapter 26.

Exponential Growth

Central to our discussion of economic growth is the idea of **exponential growth**, which refers to the process by which a quantity grows at an approximately constant growth rate. This results because the increase in the value of a variable ($y_{t+1} - y_t$ in terms of the above equation) is proportional to its current value (y_t in terms of the above equation). As we will next see, exponential growth results because new growth builds on past growth and its

Economic growth, or **growth,** is the increase in GDP per capita of an economy.

The **growth rate** is the change in a quantity, for example, GDP per capita, between two dates, relative to the baseline (beginning of period) quantity.

Exponential growth refers to a situation in which the growth process can be described by an approximately constant growth rate of a variable such as GDP or GDP per capita.

[**Exponential growth results because new growth builds on past growth and its effects compound.**]

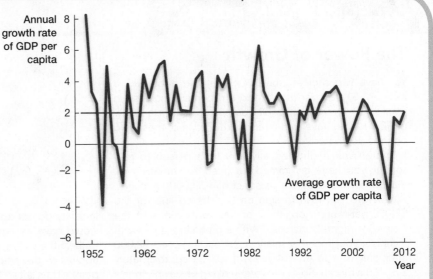

Exhibit 21.2 The Annual Growth Rate of GDP per Capita in the United States Between 1950 and 2012 (2005 Constant Dollars)

The (annual) growth rate of GDP per capita shows the short-run fluctuations around the average growth rate.

Source: Data from Penn World Table (1950–1959) and World Bank DataBank: World Development Indicators (1960–2012); Alan Heston, Robert Summers and Bettina Aten, Penn World Table Version 7.1, Center for International Comparisons of Production, Income and Prices at the University of Pennsylvania (Nov 2012).

effects compound. This implies that relatively modest differences in growth rates translate into large differences in the level of a quantity after many years of growing.

The exponential nature of economic growth is one of the major reasons why there are such large differences in GDP per capita across countries like the ones we saw in the previous chapter.

To understand both exponential growth and its implications, consider a simple example, where a variable Y_t starts out with the value 1 in the year 2000 and has a constant growth rate of 5 percent (0.05) in subsequent years. What will be the value of this variable in the year 2015? A first guess might be obtained by adding the increment of $1 \times 0.05 = 0.05$ to the base value 15 times (once for every year between 2000 and 2015). This would give us an increase of $15 \times 0.05 = 0.75$, thus producing the value $Y_{2015} = 1.75$.

But this is not a correct depiction of how growth takes place because the power of compounding has to be factored in. Let's see why this is so by starting with 2001. With a growth rate of 5 percent, we will have $Y_{2001} = 1.05$. What about in 2002? The key here is that the additional 5 percent growth between 2001 and 2002 will start from 1.05—not from the initial level of 1.00. Hence, we will have $Y_{2002} = 1.05 \times 1.05 = 1.1025$. Similarly, $Y_{2003} = 1.1025 \times 1.05 = 1.1576$, and by continuing like this, we obtain $Y_{2015} = 2.0789$.

The reason why this number is greater than the naive guess of 1.75 is because of compounding, the root cause of exponential growth. Exponential growth results because current growth builds on past growth. For example, to obtain Y_{2003} we started from the level at 2002, $Y_{2002} = 1.1025$, and built on it, so the incremental growth between 2002 and 2003 was more than 0.05.

One implication of exponential growth is that to depict variables that have exponential growth (approximately constant growth rates), it is much more convenient to use an axis with a proportional scale, like the vertical axis in Exhibit 21.1. This is intuitive: a 10 percent growth rate starting from a base of 1,000 will take us to 1,100, but if we had started with 100,000, it would have taken us to 110,000. The increment is very different in two cases (100 vs. 10,000), but it is the same as a *proportion* of the base value—10 percent. As a result, it is more instructive to show this change on a proportional scale where the 10 percent growth corresponds to the same distance on the vertical axis regardless of whether we start from a base of 1,000 or 100,000. Exhibit 21.3, on the other hand, shows how Exhibit 21.1 would look if we were to use the usual nonproportional scale. You can see that this exhibit creates a misleading impression that GDP per capita in the United States was accelerating, whereas with a proportional scale in Exhibit 21.1, we can clearly distinguish the approximately constant rate of growth of U.S. GDP per capita.

To see the power of exponential growth on economic growth, consider two countries with the same level of GDP per capita in 1810, say $1,000 (in 2005 constant U.S. dollars). Furthermore, suppose that growth is exponential and, in particular, that GDP per capita in one of these countries grows at 2 percent per year while in the other one it grows at just 1 percent. At first glance, this difference seems small. And it is true that such a difference in growth will have only small implications over one or two years.

CHOICE & CONSEQUENCE

The Power of Growth

You have two choices. You can either start a job with a salary of $1,000 per month and a 6 percent increase in your salary every month. Or you can start with a salary of $2,000, but never get a raise. Which one of these two options do you prefer?

The answer might naturally vary from person to person. If you have an immediate need for money, you may be attracted by the prospect of a $2,000 paycheck. But before you rush to sign on the dotted line for the $2,000-per-month job, think of the implications of the 6 percent monthly increase. With a 6 percent-per-month increase, your monthly salary will already exceed $2,000 after only a year. After 4 years, it will be approximately $16,400 a month. So if you were thinking of staying in this job for more than a year, starting with a lower salary might be a much better idea.

The first option is attractive, at least for those of you intending to stay with it for a while, precisely because of exponential growth. The 6-percent-per-month increases

in salary do not apply to the base salary (if they did, this would have increased your salary by $60 every month). Rather, they compound, meaning that each 6 percent applies to the amount that has accumulated up to that point. Thus after 1 month, your salary will be $1,060. After 2 months, it is $1,060 × 1.06 = $1,123.60. After 3 months, it is $1,123.60 × 1.06 = $1,191.02, and so on. We will next see that exponential growth plays the same role in countries' growth trajectories as in your potential income in these two hypothetical jobs.

MyEconLab Real-time data

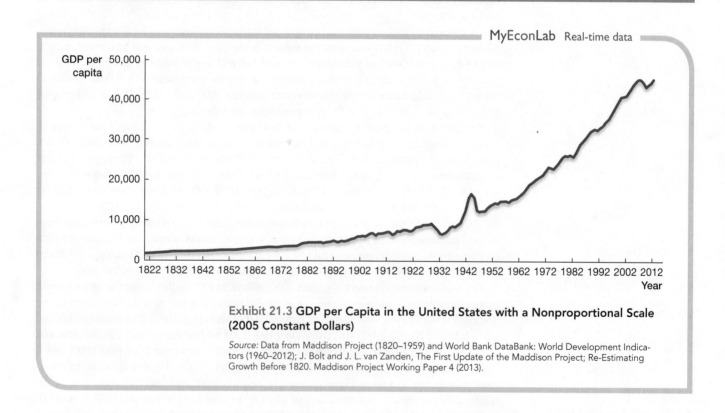

Exhibit 21.3 GDP per Capita in the United States with a Nonproportional Scale (2005 Constant Dollars)

Source: Data from Maddison Project (1820–1959) and World Bank DataBank: World Development Indicators (1960–2012); J. Bolt and J. L. van Zanden, The First Update of the Maddison Project; Re-Estimating Growth Before 1820. Maddison Project Working Paper 4 (2013).

But the implications of this difference 200 years later will be quite impressive. The country growing at 1 percent per year will achieve GDP per capita of approximately $7,316 in 2010. In contrast, because of the exponential nature of growth, the country growing at 2 percent per year over the same period will reach a GDP per capita of $52,485. Thus, there will be a more than sevenfold difference between these two countries resulting from "just" a 1 percent difference in growth rates.

If instead of 1 percent growth per year, the second country had no growth (that is, 0 percent growth rate), then it would remain at the same level of GDP per capita, $1,000, in 2010.

The gap between the two countries, in this case, would be a truly striking fifty-two-fold! This example again illustrates the power of exponential growth—or, in this case, the lack thereof.

Patterns of Growth

Exponential growth is largely responsible for how the large differences in GDP per capita that we observe today (and discussed in the previous chapter) emerged over time. The nations that are relatively rich today have grown steadily over the past 200 years, whereas those that are poor have failed to do so.

To see these effects of economic growth on economies in the real world, we now turn to Exhibit 21.4, which shows the patterns of growth in GDP per capita across a number of countries between 1960 and 2010 (in PPP-adjusted 2005 constant dollars, where PPP again stands for "purchasing power parity"). The third column of the exhibit summarizes growth between 1960 and 2010. Instead of showing the growth rate between these two dates using the formula we described above, this column provides the *implied* annual growth rate, which shows how much on average each country needed to grow each year to reach the 2010 level starting with the 1960 number. (Exactly how this number is computed is explained in the appendix to this chapter.)

What do these comparisons tell us? For one thing, we see that GDP per capita has increased significantly in the United States, the United Kingdom, and France; the growth rates in the last column confirm this. For example, both the United States and the United Kingdom show an average annual growth rate of about 2 percent between 1960 and 2010.

The exhibit also tells us that there has been an even greater increase in GDP per capita and correspondingly higher growth rates for Singapore, Spain, South Korea, Botswana, and China. All five of these countries were significantly poorer than the United States in 1960, but they closed some or almost all the gap with the United States by 2010. Such

success is reflected in the higher growth rates for these countries. For example, the average annual growth rates of GDP per capita in Botswana, South Korea, and Singapore during this period were above 5 percent, and China's was 4.72 percent.

The exhibit also shows other countries that have *not* closed the gap between themselves and richer countries, or have done so only to a limited extent. These nations include Mexico, Brazil, and India, which show similar or only slightly higher growth rates than the United States. Guatemala, Kenya, Ghana, Rwanda, and Haiti had even lower growth rates than the United States over this time period and thus have become relatively poorer. In fact, we see from the data in this exhibit that GDP per capita in Kenya has essentially been stagnant over this almost 50-year period, and GDP per capita in Haiti has declined at the rate of 0.14 percent a year. As a result, Haiti was much poorer at the end of 2010 than it was in 1960. Things have only gotten worse for Haiti since its devastating earthquake in 2010, which not only killed over 200,000 Haitians but also destroyed the country's already crumbling infrastructure.

How has GDP per capita evolved in these countries relative to the United States? Exhibit 21.5 illustrates this by taking some of the countries from Exhibit 21.4 and plotting their levels of GDP per capita divided by GDP per capita in the United States, all in PPP-adjusted 2005 constant dollars.

The overall patterns are consistent with those shown in Exhibit 21.4, but the growth of these economies over time also reveals some interesting facts. For example, GDP per capita in the United Kingdom has remained at about 70 to 80 percent of the GDP per capita of the United States since the 1950s. Spain and South Korea showed early spurts of rapid growth, even though they started with very different income levels at the beginning of the period. By the 1980s, both countries had closed much of the gap between

Exhibit 21.4 GDP per Capita and Growth in Selected Countries (PPP-adjusted 2005 Constant Dollars)

GDP per capita in 2010 is determined both by GDP per capita in 1960 and the average annual growth rate of GDP per capita in between these two years. We see how Botswana is much richer than Kenya and Ghana today, even though Botswana started out poorer, because Botswana grew on average at 5.47 percent while the average annual growth was only 0.40 percent for Kenya and 0.98 percent for Ghana. For the same reasons, today South Korea is richer than Brazil and Singapore is richer than Spain.

Source: Data from Penn World Table; Alan Heston, Robert Summers, and Bettina Aten, Penn World Table Version 7.1, Center for International Comparisons of Production, Income and Prices at the University of Pennsylvania (Nov 2012).

	GDP per Capita		Implied (Average) Annual Growth (%)
	1960	2010	
United States	15,398	41,365	2.00
United Kingdom	11,204	34,268	2.26
France	10,212	31,299	2.27
Spain	6,316	27,332	2.97
Mexico	4,914	11,939	1.79
Singapore	4,383	55,862	5.22
Guatemala	2,930	6,091	1.47
Brazil	2,483	8,324	2.45
South Korea	1,656	26,609	5.71
Haiti	1,513	1,410	−0.14
Ghana	1,286	2,094	0.98
Kenya	1,020	1,247	0.40
China	772	7,746	4.72
Rwanda	760	1,025	0.60
India	720	3,477	3.20
Dem. Rep. of the Congo	696	241	−2.10
Botswana	674	9,675	5.47

MyEconLab Real-time data

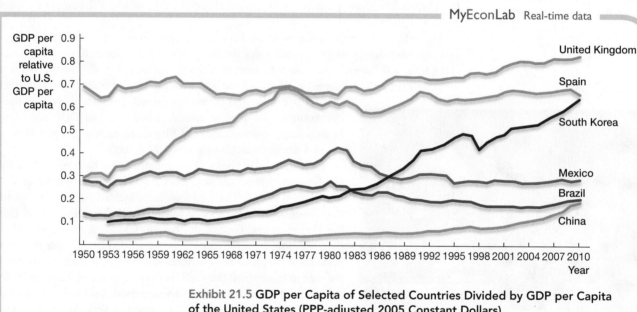

Exhibit 21.5 GDP per Capita of Selected Countries Divided by GDP per Capita of the United States (PPP-adjusted 2005 Constant Dollars)

Plotting the evolution of GDP per capita in selected countries relative to GDP per capita in the United States shows how countries such as South Korea and China have been catching up with the United States relatively steadily, while Mexico and Brazil have not.

Source: Data from Penn World Table; Alan Heston, Robert Summers, and Bettina Aten, Penn World Table Version 7.1, Center for International Comparisons of Production, Income and Prices at the University of Pennsylvania (Nov 2012).

themselves and the United States, though they both also show periods of relative decline. Brazil also experienced relatively rapid growth in the 1950s and 1960s, closing some of the gap with the United States. But around 1980, this process went into reverse, and by 2010, GDP per capita in Brazil was about 20 percent of the GDP per capita of the United States—not much above where it started, in relative terms, in the 1950s. Finally, although there was a huge gap between the United States and China during the communist dictatorship of Mao Tse-tung (Mao Zedong), this gap started narrowing rapidly following Mao's death in 1976 and the opening of the Chinese economy in 1978.

LETTING THE DATA SPEAK

Levels versus Growth

Is China now poorer relative to the United States than it was in 1980? We saw in Exhibit 21.5 how Chinese GDP per capita relative to that of the United States has increased greatly over the past 30 years. Yet now consider Exhibit 21.6, which plots GDP per capita in China and the United States since 1950. This picture creates the impression that the gap between the United States and China is opening up and that China is becoming relatively poorer. This is not the case, however. In fact, trying to decide whether China is becoming poorer or richer compared to the United States from a figure such as Exhibit 21.6 is an example of a common error: comparing *levels* of variables exhibiting exponential growth. You will have noticed that precisely to avoid this type of fallacy, in Exhibit 21.5 we do not simply plot the GDP per capita levels of different countries; rather, we look at these levels divided by GDP per capita in the United States. By doing so, we directly examine the ratio between GDP in the given country and in the United States.

To see the advantage of this procedure, consider two hypothetical countries. Say that the first one is twice as rich as the second and has GDP per capita of $20,000, while the second has GDP per capita of $10,000. Now suppose that they both grow by 10 percent. The first country will then have GDP per capita of $22,000 and the second one will have GDP per capita of $11,000. The ratio between the two has not changed, but the absolute gap in incomes has increased by $1,000. Thus, comparing levels of GDP is not enlightening when there is exponential growth. In the presence of exponential growth, when relative GDP remains stable, absolute gaps will increase. For this reason, looking at ratios is the right thing to do in Exhibit 21.5. It is an oft-repeated error to compare levels of variables exhibiting exponential growth such as GDP or investment rather than ratios.

MyEconLab Real-time data

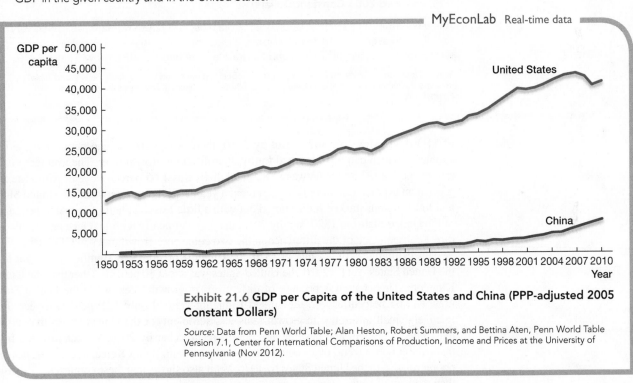

Exhibit 21.6 GDP per Capita of the United States and China (PPP-adjusted 2005 Constant Dollars)

Source: Data from Penn World Table; Alan Heston, Robert Summers, and Bettina Aten, Penn World Table Version 7.1, Center for International Comparisons of Production, Income and Prices at the University of Pennsylvania (Nov 2012).

To convey a more complete picture of growth patterns over the last 50 years, Exhibit 21.7 shows a graph of the growth rates of all countries for which we have data between 1960 and 2010. It shows that there is a wide range of growth rates. Some countries, such as Haiti and the Democratic Republic of Congo, have grown at negative rates during this period, while others, such as South Korea and Singapore, have achieved very high growth rates.

Using historical data, we can compare growth across countries even further back in time than 1960. To show these growth patterns in a simple way, Exhibit 21.8 lists levels of GDP per capita for several countries (in PPP-adjusted 1990 constant dollars) in 1820, 1870, 1920, 1970, and 2010 and their annual growth rates between 1820 and 2010 and between 1920 and 2010.

We see that income levels are not all that different across countries in 1820. For example, the United States was only about twice as rich as Mexico (U.S. GDP per capita

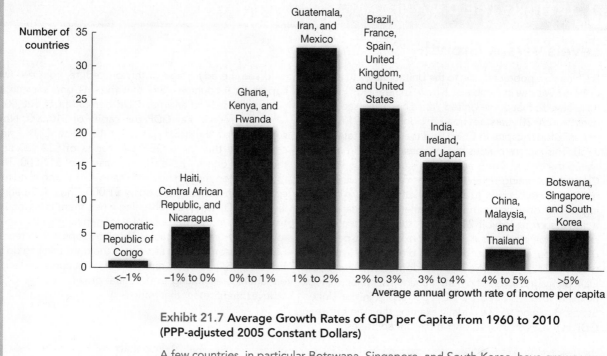

Exhibit 21.7 Average Growth Rates of GDP per Capita from 1960 to 2010 (PPP-adjusted 2005 Constant Dollars)

A few countries, in particular Botswana, Singapore, and South Korea, have grown very rapidly, with average growth rates above 5 percent, while others, such as Haiti, the Democratic Republic of Congo, and Nicaragua have had negative growth since 1960.

Source: Data from Penn World Table; Alan Heston, Robert Summers, and Bettina Aten, Penn World Table Version 7.1, Center for International Comparisons of Production, Income and Prices at the University of Pennsylvania (Nov 2012).

of $1,361 vs. Mexico's $627). But by 2010, there was a sizable gap between these two countries, which can be accounted for by their different growth rates. The average growth rate of the United States between 1820 and 2010 was 1.65 percent a year, while Mexico grew at an average rate of only 1.33 percent a year. The contrast between the United States and India is even starker. India started out with a little less than half of the GDP per capita of the United States in 1820. But by 2010, the gap was nearly tenfold. Once again, this is a direct consequence of the difference in the two countries' growth rates in GDP per capita.

This exhibit also shows that in 1820, the United Kingdom was significantly richer than the United States. Yet by 2010, the United States was about 30 percent richer than the United Kingdom. This change is because of differences in growth rates: while the United States grew at 1.65 percent a year, the United Kingdom grew at only 1.29 percent a year. This relatively small difference in growth rates was sufficient for the United States to overtake the United Kingdom and become about 30 percent richer by 2010. We can also see from this exhibit how several other countries, including Spain, South Korea, and China, became poorer relative to the United States by 1970. Yet it also shows that these countries grew faster than the United States over the past 40 years, closing the gap that had opened up previously.

Catch-up growth refers to a growth process whereby relatively poorer nations increase their incomes by taking advantage of knowledge and technologies already invented in other, technologically more advanced countries.

Part of this growth is what we call **catch-up growth**, meaning that these nations are catching up with the income and technology leader of the world, in this case the United States. Countries undergoing catch-up growth do so mostly by benefiting from available technologies, but also by increasing their saving, efficiency units of labor, and efficiency of production. Catch-up growth is very important in practice, though as the examples of slow growth and stagnation in Exhibit 21.8 demonstrate, it is far from automatic. In the next chapter, we discuss in greater detail why many countries have failed to take advantage of this type of catch-up growth.

Sustained growth refers to a growth process where GDP per capita grows at a positive and relatively steady rate for long periods of time.

Finally, Exhibit 21.8 drives home yet another important idea. The United States and several other countries—for example, the United Kingdom, France, and Spain—demonstrate **sustained growth** between 1820 and 2010 in the sense that there is a positive and relatively steady growth rate in every 50-year period, and the growth rate for the entire period is significantly positive for these countries. Our next task is to understand how this type of sustained growth emerges and what factors determine the growth rate of an economy.

Exhibit 21.8 GDP per Capita since 1820 in Selected Countries (PPP-adjusted 2005 Constant Dollars)

Countries had fairly similar levels of GDP per capita in 1820. Since then, differences in GDP per capita have grown because some countries, such as the United States and the United Kingdom, have grown steadily, while others have not.

Sources: Data from Maddison Project and Bureau of Economic Analysis, National Income and Product Accounts Table 1.1.9; J. Bolt and J. L. van Zanden, The First Update of the Maddison Project; Re-Estimating Growth Before 1820. Maddison Project Working Paper 4 (2013).

	1820	1870	1920	1970	2010	Average Growth (1820–2010)	Average Growth (1920–2010)
UK	2,854	4,390	6,259	14,817	32,722	1.29%	1.85%
U.S.	1,873	3,365	7,641	20,684	41,961	1.65%	1.91%
France	1,562	2,582	4,441	15,702	29,556	1.56%	2.13%
Spain	1,387	1,661	2,996	8,696	23,116	1.49%	2.30%
Brazil	940	981	1,325	4,207	9,467	1.22%	2.21%
Mexico	863	896	2,509	5,945	10,619	1.33%	1.62%
China	826	729	760	1,071	11,054	1.37%	3.02%
India	734	734	874	1,195	4,640	0.98%	1.87%
Morocco	592	775	977	2,224	5,542	1.18%	1.95%
South Korea	461	464	839	2,982	29,865	2.22%	4.05%
Ghana	–	604	1,075	1,960	2,645	–	1.01%
Haiti	–	–	–	1,265	944	–	–
Kenya	–	–	–	1,259	1,570	–	–

21.2 How Does a Nation's Economy Grow?

The aggregate production function, which we studied in the previous chapter, gives us a first answer to this question. Recall that the aggregate production function, $Y = A \times F(K, H)$, links GDP to the two factors of production, the physical capital (K) and total efficiency units of labor (H). The aggregate production function also depends on the level of technology (A), which captures the knowledge available to the economy and the efficiency of production. When A changes, the aggregate production function shifts.

A nation can increase its GDP by increasing its stock of physical capital, K; by increasing the total efficiency units of labor, H (for example, by increasing the human capital of workers); and by improving its technology, A. In this section, we look more closely at these three areas.

Let us consider the physical capital stock, K, which represents the value of all of the equipment (for example, machines, cars, planes, and computers) and structures (like buildings) of the economy. The physical capital stock (and therefore GDP) can be increased by investment, a process also known as *physical capital accumulation.*

You will recall from Chapter 19 that the national income accounting identity implies that $Y = C + I + G + X - M$, where C is consumption (household expenditures on consumption of goods and services), I is investment (expenditures on investment goods by private agents), G is government purchases of goods and services, X is exports, and M is imports. Recall that in a closed economy, there are no exports or imports, and if we also ignore the government (as we have done here), then we have $G = X = M = 0$. Therefore, the national income accounting identity implies

$$Y = C + I.$$

In other words, GDP is equal to the sum of aggregate consumption and investment. This also implies that investment comes directly from aggregate saving. This is because in our closed economy without government spending, all income will be either consumed or saved, so GDP is also equal to aggregate consumption plus aggregate saving or, in other words, $Y = C + S$. Thus

$$I = S.$$

Interpreted differently, this relationship says that all the resources households decide to save will be allocated to firms that will use them for investment (for example, by banks that will take money deposited by households and lend it to firms for investment). Consequently, a nation with a high saving rate will accumulate physical capital rapidly—that is, increase its physical capital stock rapidly—and, by the aggregate production function, increase its GDP. Thus to determine whether and how rapidly an economy will increase its physical capital stock, we need to understand the saving decisions of households, which we turn to next.

Optimization: The Choice Between Saving and Consumption

Consider the U.S. economy in 2008, when its GDP (aggregate income) stood at 14.44 trillion dollars. Naturally, not all of this output was consumed. Firms and the government invested some portion of it in the physical capital stock of the nation—for example, in new machines, roads, and bridges. But the resources for this investment come from the savings of households. For example, in a closed economy without the government, we have just seen that $I = S$.

Thus to understand how the GDP of a nation is divided between consumption and investment, we need to study the preferences of consumers, who decide how much of their income will be allocated to savings. This involves studying how households trade off consumption today versus consumption tomorrow, because saving is a way of allocating some of today's resources for consumption tomorrow (or more generally, consumption in the future). This is yet another example of optimization on the part of individuals and households. Each household typically faces different priorities and needs that influence its decisions to consume its income today versus save it for tomorrow. For example, those preparing to send their children to college may save more today.

As with all optimization problems, such choices are affected by prices. In this case, the relevant price is the *interest rate*, which determines the rate of return that households expect on their savings. (How the interest rate is determined will be discussed in detail in Chapter 24.) Higher interest rates typically encourage more saving. In addition, expectations of future income growth and perhaps taxes will have an impact on the saving decision. For instance, households that expect rapid income growth in the future may have less reason to save to finance future consumption (because future income growth will enable them to do this) or even to save "for a rainy day" (against potential future hardships). Conversely, if they expect high taxes in the future, households may save more in order to be able to pay these taxes without reducing future consumption.

The **saving rate** designates the fraction of income that is saved.

These trade-offs determine the **saving rate** of the economy, which corresponds to the fraction of income that is saved. (In practice, in addition to households, firms and the government also save, and we include these in the total saving of the economy.) We can compute the saving rate by dividing total saving by GDP (aggregate income). For example, in 2013, the level of total saving in the U.S. economy was $2.18 trillion, while GDP was $16.80 trillion (both in current dollars). Then the saving rate is

$$\text{Saving rate} = \frac{\text{Total saving}}{\text{GDP}} = \frac{\$2.18 \text{ trillion}}{\$16.80 \text{ trillion}} = 12.98\%.$$

What Brings Sustained Growth?

Can physical capital accumulation by itself generate sustained growth—where GDP per capita grows at a positive and relatively steady rate for an extended period of time? The answer to this question is "no" for a simple reason: *the diminishing marginal product of physical capital.*

Let's look a little more closely at this reasoning. As Exhibit 20.7 from the previous chapter shows, because of the diminishing marginal product of physical capital, more and more physical capital will translate into smaller and smaller increases in GDP. This precludes the possibility of sustained growth by just accumulating more and more physical capital.

What about steadily raising the efficiency units of labor in the economy? Can't the efficiency units of labor be raised just by increasing the number of workers in the economy? Can't we raise GDP steadily by increasing human capital?

First consider increasing the workforce—the number of people taking part in the production process. Holding all other factors of production and technology constant, every additional worker will increase GDP by less and less because of *diminishing marginal product*

CHOICE & CONSEQUENCE

Is Increasing the Saving Rate Always a Good Idea?

Suppose that you control the saving rate in a country and your objective is to improve the standard of living of the citizens of this country. Is it always a good idea to increase the saving rate? We have seen that greater saving increases the physical capital stock of the economy and consequently raises GDP. But this doesn't mean that increasing saving is always good for society. Imagine the extreme case where as the supreme ruler of a country, you are able to encourage saving so much that every dollar earned in the country is saved. This will indeed increase GDP. But it will not improve the standard of living of the citizens because it will require them to consume little or nothing. In the extreme case where the saving rate reaches 100 percent, consumption drops to zero. This implies that there must exist an optimal level of saving for a society, where saving above this level would make the society worse off because it would significantly reduce consumption.

of labor (or diminishing marginal product of total efficiency units of labor). Therefore, we cannot guarantee a steady increase in GDP per capita by just increasing the workforce either.

Note that we can also increase the efficiency units of labor for a given workforce by increasing the human capital of workers—for example, by raising their educational attainment or skill level. Although such changes will indeed increase GDP, they will, by themselves, not achieve *sustained* growth. Because each individual has a finite life, there is a limit to how many years of schooling he or she can obtain, and, of course, more and more schooling would also imply fewer and fewer years in the workforce where an individual actively takes part in production. Thus, achieving greater and greater levels of efficiency units by continuously increasing the years of schooling of the workforce does not appear feasible.

"But hold on," you might say. "What about continuously upgrading the quality of education? Wouldn't that work toward increasing the efficiency units of labor?" Not really. Empirically, the extent to which such improvements can ensure steady growth also appears to be limited, as we will see in greater detail in the Evidence-Based Economics section of this chapter. Therefore, even though investments in education and skills do play a major role in increasing GDP per capita, we cannot achieve sustained growth of about 1.5–2 percent a year just by continuously increasing the educational achievement of the workforce.

These considerations imply that in order to achieve sustained growth, we need something else. And that something else is *technology*—particularly advances in the technical knowledge used in production.

Knowledge, Technological Change, and Growth

You will recall that Moore's Law, which we first encountered in the previous chapter (Exhibit 20.10), claims that the number of transistors on memory microchips will double every 2 years, thereby increasing the computational power of computers. This trend has been true for at least the last 50 years and probably for longer. For example, around 1900, before microprocessors and extra mechanical devices, it was prohibitively expensive to make anything but the most trivial calculations. By 1950, with the technologies associated with the vacuum tube, society had access to the technology to make one relevant computation per second at a cost of $1,000 (in today's dollars). By the 1970s, with the advent of the transistor, we could make up to 100 calculations per second for $1,000. And by the late 1990s, with the widespread use of integrated circuits, almost 10 million calculations per second could be performed for the same cost. Moore's Law is an example of *technological change*.

Technological change is the process of new technologies and new goods and services being invented, introduced, and used in the economy, enabling the economy to achieve a

Technological change is the process of new technologies and new goods and services being invented, introduced, and used in the economy, enabling the economy to achieve a higher level of GDP for given levels of physical capital stock and total efficiency units of labor.

higher level of GDP for given levels of its factors of production, physical capital stock, and total efficiency units of labor.

Consider another example of technological change—the reduction in the cost of light over the past 200 years—as shown in Exhibit 21.9.[1] Obtaining lighting, both for firms and households, has become much cheaper over the past two centuries because of the invention of the lightbulb and ongoing improvements in the quality of lightbulbs, lighting technology, and the transmission of energy.

Technological change, as it turns out, is exponential. In particular, using the same definition of exponential growth from earlier in this chapter, this means that improvements in technology take place at an approximately constant rate—rather than by constant increments. There is a simple reason for this exponential nature of technological change. As we have seen, growth in GDP per capita is exponential because growth compounds—that is, it takes place on the basis of the current level of GDP whose increase is already a result of past growth. There is a similar logic to technological change. New innovations and technologies build on the knowledge stock resulting from past innovations—building on the shoulders of giants, so to speak. This ensures that innovations improve our productive capacity in GDP not by a constant amount but by a constant *proportional* amount. So if we improve technology starting with a technology level that produces a GDP per capita of $1,000, then innovations that enable us to be more productive by a certain amount—say 10 percent—will raise GDP per capita from $1,000 to $1,100. But if we instead start with a technology level that produces $100,000 of GDP per capita, similar innovations bringing a 10 percent improvement will take us to $110,000.

The exponential nature of technological change illustrated by these two examples is also responsible for the fact that improvements in technology need not necessarily run into diminishing marginal product (whereas, as we have seen, increases in the use of factors of production run into diminishing marginal product). For this reason, improvements in technology appear to be the most plausible engine of sustained growth.

> **New innovations and technologies build on the knowledge stock resulting from past innovations— building on the shoulders of giants, so to speak.**

By now, you will have realized that there is a nice symmetry between our treatment of cross-country differences in GDP per capita in the previous chapter and of over-time differences, corresponding to growth, in this chapter. In both, the physical capital stock and efficiency units of labor play important roles, but they are insufficient to explain the major differences. Both across countries and over time, technology instead plays the central role.

Exhibit 21.9 The Real Price of Light over Time

The source of sustained growth is technological progress, which continuously increases the amount that an economy can produce. Here we see one reflection of this technological progress, showing how improvements in lighting technology, the quality of lightbulbs, and transmission of energy have reduced the cost of lighting over time.

Source: William D. Nordhaus, "Do Real-Output and Real-Wage Measures Capture Reality? The History of Light Suggests Not," Cowles Foundation Discussion Papers 1078, Cowles Foundation for Research in Economics (1994).

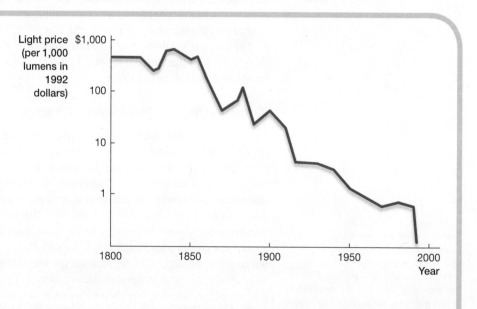

Evidence-Based Economics

Q: Why are you so much more prosperous than your great-great-grandparents were?

The theoretical discussion in the previous section supports the central role of technology in explaining sustained growth. We will now see that empirical evidence also bolsters the conclusion that technology plays a key role.

To evaluate the sources of U.S. economic growth, we follow the same strategy as in the previous chapter. There, we used the aggregate production function and estimates of the physical capital stock and the efficiency units of labor across different countries to evaluate their contributions to cross-country differences in GDP. The only major difference here is that higher-quality U.S. data enable us to conduct the analysis for GDP per hour worked rather than GDP per worker, thus allowing us to measure the labor input more accurately. We start the analysis in 1950.

Exhibit 21.10 records average GDP per hour worked (in 2005 constant dollars), the average value of the physical capital stock per hour worked, and the most important component of the human capital of workers—the average years of schooling—for 10-year periods starting in 1950. (To remove the short-term effects of the last recession from our calculations on long-term growth, the last period is 2000–2007.) The exhibit shows the steady increase in GDP per hour worked, physical capital stock per hour worked, and educational attainment in the United States between 1950 and 2007.

We then use a methodology similar to that in the previous chapter to compute the contribution of physical capital, human capital (efficiency units of labor), and technology to the growth of GDP in the United States. The results are recorded in columns 4, 5, and 6 of the exhibit (in percentages). Column 7 then gives the annual growth rate of GDP per hour worked, which is the sum of the contributions of physical capital, human capital, and technology.

This exhibit highlights the central role that technology has played in U.S. growth. Let's examine the 1960s, shown in the second row. The 0.17 percent recorded as the contribution of human capital indicates that if the human capital of U.S. workers had remained constant in the 1960s, then the growth rate of GDP per hour worked in the 1960s would have been lower by 0.17 percent (3.09 percent instead of 3.26 percent). In

Time Period	GDP per Hour Worked (2005 Constant Dollars)	Physical Capital Stock per Hour Worked (2005 Constant Dollars)	Average Years of Schooling	Growth (%) Resulting from Physical Capital (*K*)	Growth (%) Resulting from Human Capital (*H*)	Growth (%) Resulting from Technology (*A*)	*Annual Growth Rate of GDP per Hour Worked*
	(1)	(2)	(3)	(4)	(5)	(6)	(7)
1950–1959	8.30	102,548	9.38	0.89	0.28	2.37	3.54%
1960–1969	11.50	119,593	10.16	0.89	0.17	2.20	3.26
1970–1979	14.96	128,591	11.15	0.88	0.01	1.22	2.11
1980–1989	17.46	137,637	12.07	0.86	0.30	0.45	1.61
1990–1999	20.95	144,354	12.77	0.84	0.36	0.87	2.07
2000–2007	27.06	158,755	13.22	0.99	0.19	1.29	2.47

Exhibit 21.10 Contribution of Technology, Physical Capital, and Human Capital to the Growth of GDP per Hour Worked in the United States between 1950 and 2007.
Column 6 is computed by subtracting columns 4 and 5 from column 7.

Sources: Data from Bureau of Labor Statistics, Bureau of Economic Analysis, and United States Census Bureau.

Evidence-Based Economics *(Continued)*

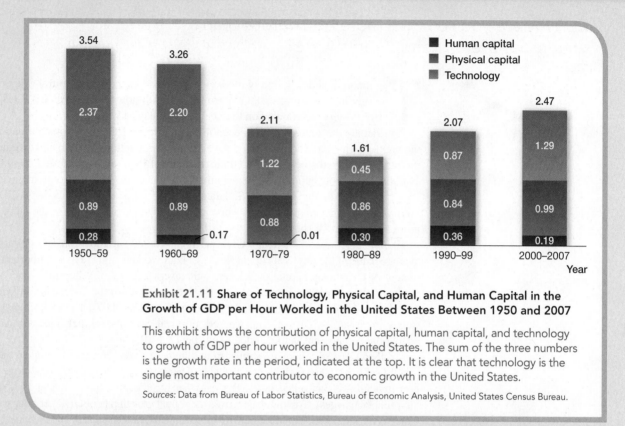

Exhibit 21.11 Share of Technology, Physical Capital, and Human Capital in the Growth of GDP per Hour Worked in the United States Between 1950 and 2007

This exhibit shows the contribution of physical capital, human capital, and technology to growth of GDP per hour worked in the United States. The sum of the three numbers is the growth rate in the period, indicated at the top. It is clear that technology is the single most important contributor to economic growth in the United States.

Sources: Data from Bureau of Labor Statistics, Bureau of Economic Analysis, United States Census Bureau.

contrast, if technology had stayed constant, the annual growth rate of GDP per hour worked would have been lower by 2.20 percent. The other rows of the exhibit paint a similar picture. Mirroring our findings on the role of technology in accounting for cross-country differences in the previous chapter, technology accounts for the bulk of growth in U.S. GDP per hour worked in most periods.

Exhibit 21.11 presents the same information as the last four columns of Exhibit 21.10 in a bar chart, more clearly showing the decomposition of growth between the two factors of production and technology. It also highlights the central role of technology. The total height of each bar is the annual growth of GDP per hour worked during the corresponding period, while the orange part of the bar shows the contribution of technology. It shows that, except between 1980 and 1989, technology was the most important contributor to U.S. growth.

The contribution of technology was somewhat lower during the 1970s and 1980s, which were decades of relatively low growth in GDP per hour worked, while the stock of physical capital in the economy continued to increase—partly because there was considerable investment in information technology capital during these decades.

An important caveat to the conclusions supported by Exhibits 21.10 and 21.11 is worth noting. As pointed out in the previous chapter and in Exhibit 21.10, the contribution of technology is obtained as the fraction of growth in GDP not explained by physical capital and human capital. This implies that if we understate the contribution of physical capital or human capital to GDP growth, which could happen, for example, because we do not fully take into account the improved quality of our physical capital stock, then the contribution of technology may be somewhat exaggerated.

❓	Ⓐ	🔬	⚙️
Question	**Answer**	**Data**	**Caveat**
Why are you so much more prosperous than your great-great-grandparents were?	It is mostly due to better technology, though greater physical capital and greater human capital of workers have also contributed.	Estimates of GDP per hour worked, physical capital stock per hour worked, average educational attainment, and average professional experience of the workforce in the United States between 1950 and 2007.	If we understate the contribution of physical capital or human capital to GDP, the contribution of technology may be somewhat exaggerated.

21.3 The History of Growth and Technology

Exhibit 21.8 depicted economic development in several countries since 1820. This 200-year period is sometimes referred to as "modern times." But what about before then? Did patterns of growth before the nineteenth century look similar to those we have documented so far in this chapter? If not, what changed?

Growth Before Modern Times

Humanity had, of course, a long history before the nineteenth century, during which there were several major achievements in science, technology, and the arts. But from an economic point of view, the period before 1800 is distinguished by one thing: a lack of sustained growth. Looking back at Exhibits 21.1 and 21.2, we see that the U.S. economy has had some downturns and one big setback during the Great Depression, but on the whole, it has experienced relatively steady economic growth in GDP per capita.

Though the world before 1800 was certainly not stagnant, it did not experience the type of sustained growth we see in Exhibit 21.1. There were a few notable periods of economic growth and even technological improvements, some of which continued for as long as a century or even more. The periods that are most well known are those in ancient Greece, ancient Rome, and Venice. During the heydays of these civilizations, standards of living improved and economic activity increased significantly. But this growth didn't last. Ancient Rome may have grown, although relatively slowly, for over 300 years, but its growth ultimately came to an end. The situation was similar in Venice.

Even though there was some economic growth during all of these eras, *sustained* economic growth was rare or even absent. There is a simple way to see why growth in these ancient civilizations could not have been sustained. The World Bank's definition of absolute poverty as living off the equivalent of $1.25 per day, which we discussed in the previous chapter, is not an entirely arbitrary one. An individual needs to consume a certain amount of calories in order to live, and, of course, people need shelter and clothing. Though estimates vary, it is practically impossible for a country to have income (GDP) per capita

21.1

21.2

21.3

21.4

The **subsistence level** is the minimum level of income per person that is generally necessary for the individual to obtain enough calories, shelter, and clothing to survive.

of much less than $500 or so per year, because this would imply that a large fraction of the population would be living on much less than $500 per person. We call this level of income per capita below which an individual cannot easily survive the **subsistence level** (even if there isn't one unique subsistence level that applies in every environment). The general idea is simple: regardless of the exact level, there exists a minimum level of income per person that is necessary for individual survival and subsistence. When income falls below this level, much of the population will starve.

Of course, there were no national income and product accounts 10,000 years ago, 1,000 years ago, or even 200 years ago. All the same, we know that income per capita in all places in which there were human civilizations could not have been much less than $500 per capita in today's dollars. Moreover, we know from Exhibit 21.8 that at the beginning of the nineteenth century, incomes in much of the world were not much higher than $500 per capita. In the United States, for example, income per capita was about $1,361, and in Western Europe, it was only a little higher. Therefore, there cannot have been much sustained growth before 1800.

There are two reasons for this lack of sustained growth before modern times. The first—the more important one—is related to the major factor that explains sustained growth: technology. Before 1800, though there were some important technological breakthroughs, the pace of technological change was much slower, almost stagnant compared to what came thereafter. Second, whatever improvements in aggregate incomes (GDP) were realized did not typically translate into increases in income per capita. This last point was the basis of the theory of Thomas Malthus, which is sometimes referred to as the Malthusian model. We next discuss the Malthusian model and how the world broke out of it.

Malthusian Limits to Growth

Fertility refers to the number of children per adult or per woman of childbearing age.

Thomas Malthus had a particularly dismal view of the workings of the economy. This was partly because, writing in 1798, he had not seen a period of steady growth like the one Europe experienced in the nineteenth century.[2] Malthus thought that **fertility**—defined as the number of children per adult or per woman of childbearing age—would adjust so that income always would remain close to a subsistence level, a number like the $500 a year we mentioned earlier. In Malthus's theory, couples have more children when the standard of living is above the subsistence level. Then, assuming that aggregate income (GDP) could not grow faster than the population, Malthus concluded that increasing population would push income per capita down toward—and possibly below—the subsistence level. This fall in income per capita in turn would trigger famines or wars that would kill a large fraction of the population. With a given level of aggregate income, a lower population would then cause income per capita to increase again. So in a pattern sometimes referred to as the **Malthusian cycle**, increased aggregate income would raise income per capita above subsistence, fueling population growth, which in turn would put pressure on resources and reduce income per capita back to its initial level or sometimes even below it. This pattern subsequently "corrects" the increase in population through reduced fertility and higher mortality, often due to famines.

The **Malthusian cycle** refers to the preindustrial pattern in which increases in aggregate income lead to an expanding population, which in turn reduces income per capita and puts downward pressure on population.

Dismal though it may be, the Malthusian model seems to be a good representation of how the world actually was before 1800.

The **demographic transition** refers to the decline in fertility and number of children per family that many societies undergo as they transition from agriculture to industry.

Around the same time or shortly thereafter, fertility declined. This process, which has both economic and social causes, is referred to as the **demographic transition**. Economists typically emphasize the importance of the transition from agriculture and rural areas toward industry and cities as a major cause of the demographic transition. Urban families did not need to rely on child labor for help in the field in the same way that rural families did, and the increasing costs of rearing children, particularly when they had to stay in school longer rather than work in the fields, created incentives for smaller families.

Many historians and economists view the demographic transition as a central ingredient to modern growth, because it enabled the economies that experienced reduced fertility to break away from the Malthusian cycle. Until the demographic transition in the nineteenth century, there were recurrent Malthusian cycles. After this date, there was relatively sustained growth in income per capita in many economies, particularly in the Western world.

The Industrial Revolution

But the demographic transition by itself would not have been sufficient to kick-start growth. If all that happened was that fertility declined and stabilized around a lower number, there would not necessarily have been any qualitative changes in the patterns of GDP growth per capita. Instead, sustained growth was due to another major change that occurred around the same time: the *Industrial Revolution*, which opened the way for more steady and rapid technological changes that underpinned modern economic growth.

Contrary to its name, the **Industrial Revolution** was a gradual process rather than a short period of rapid disruption. It is the term coined to designate the arrival of many new machines and methods of production in Britain, starting in textile manufacturing and thereafter spreading into other sectors. The Industrial Revolution is important both as an event in itself (because it was the first time technology and scientific methods were used in production in such a coordinated manner) and also as the starting point of the wave of industrialization that spread to many other countries around the world. We have already seen that the countries that are rich today are those that have managed to achieve steady growth rates over the past 200 years. Those are also the ones that have managed to benefit from the technologies brought about by the Industrial Revolution.

Although clearly new technologies and new knowledge were created before, innovation and the application of new technologies to the production of goods and services became more systematic and pervasive during and in the aftermath of the Industrial Revolution. The available evidence thus suggests that changes in technology that are the root cause of the sustained growth we observe today started with the Industrial Revolution at the end of the eighteenth century in Britain.

Industrial Revolution is the term used for describing the series of innovations and their implementation in the production process that started to take place at the end of the eighteenth century in Britain.

Growth and Technology Since the Industrial Revolution

Many of the technologies that we take for granted today—from railroads to automobiles and airplanes; from radio and TV to telecommunication technologies, computers, the Internet, and social networking; from electricity to almost all of the technologies used on the factory floor to produce the goods we use in our everyday life; from almost all of the drugs that save hundreds of millions of lives every year around the world to basic sanitation including indoor plumbing—have been invented and made available to us over the last 250 years. Such advances are the result of the exponential growth in our knowledge and technology since the Industrial Revolution. An important foundation of this growth has been research and development (R&D) activity, which firms, universities, and governments undertake in order to improve this knowledge base. The United States today spends 365 billion dollars, or 2.79 percent of its GDP, on R&D every year. This number is even higher in some other countries—for example, 4.66 percent in Israel, 3.00 percent in Switzerland, and 3.70 percent in Sweden. To a large extent, our high standards of living today are the return on this R&D investment.

21.4 Growth, Inequality, and Poverty

> **The fact that an economy is growing does not necessarily imply that all citizens are benefiting equally from that growth.**

The fact that an economy is growing does not necessarily imply that all citizens are benefiting equally from that growth. In fact, in recent decades, rapid growth in the U.S. economy has gone hand-in-hand with increases in inequality. There are almost always some households and individuals with significantly higher-than-average incomes and some with significantly lower-than-average incomes. In fact, economic growth is sometimes associated with increasing inequality because only some workers and businesses benefit from the new technologies that are driving this growth.

Growth and Inequality

There are several reasons why a society might care about inequality. Some may wish to live in a society that does not have great disparities in the living standards of its citizens.

LETTING THE DATA SPEAK

Income Inequality in the United States

Exhibit 21.12 shows a simple measure of inequality in the United States: the share of total U.S. income accruing to the richest 10 percent (the other 90 percent of Americans earned less than individuals in this top decile, and their aggregate earnings correspond to the remaining fraction). The data, compiled by economists Thomas Piketty and Emmanuel Saez, show that until 1940, the top 10 percent earned about 45 to 50 percent of total income.[3] This proportion then declined to about 35 percent, corresponding to a significant decline in income inequality. It then remained there until the late 1970s. Starting in the late 1970s, however, inequality

started increasing, and by the end of the 1990s, the share of the top 10 percent is again up to about 50 percent. Piketty and Saez also show another interesting pattern. Before the 1970s, much of the earnings of the very rich came from capital income—that is, income from sources other than wages and salaries, like dividends, accrued wealth, income from ownership, and so on. But over the last 30 years, the contribution of wages to the income of the very rich has changed dramatically, rising to 60 percent in 2000 (though it subsequently fell to 38 percent in 2007). More and more, even the rich have to work.

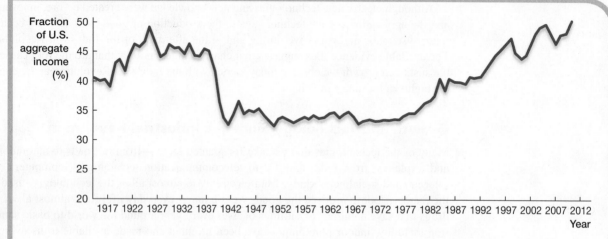

Exhibit 21.12 Fraction of U.S. Aggregate Income Accruing to the Top 10 Percent of Earners

Though growth in the United States has been relatively steady and sustained, the distribution of gains from that growth has changed considerably over time. At the beginning of the twentieth century, the richest Americans—the top 10 percent of earners—captured almost 50 percent of total income. The distribution of income became more equal in the 1940s and remained so until the mid-1970s. Inequality then started increasing again, with the share of the top 10 percent of earners in total income reaching 50 percent once again today.

Source: Data available at: http://elsa.berkeley.edu/~saez/TabFig2012prel.xls.

We may feel that greater inequality leads to more social polarization or even to a greater incidence of crime in society.

So far, we have focused on income (GDP) per capita as the main measure of the productivity and living standards of a nation. But average income per capita of a nation at a particular point in time is not the same as the income of all individuals in that nation. As we already noted in Chapter 20, this distinction cautions us against focusing just on income per capita without taking into account the distribution of income in a given society.

While it is certainly justifiable to care about inequality in and of itself, one reason why many policymakers and citizens are concerned about it is because it is associated with poverty. Poverty, particularly of the extreme sort captured by the $1.25 per day measure of the

CHOICE & CONSEQUENCE

Inequality versus Poverty

Consider a society consisting of just two types of people: rich and poor. Suppose also that half of the population is rich and the other half is poor. Now consider two scenarios. In Scenario 1, the rich have $50,000 each, while the poor have $1,000 each. In Scenario 2, the rich have $5,000, while the poor have $500. Which society would you like to live in?

The answer to this question will naturally depend on several factors. Different people will evaluate inequality and poverty differently. Suppose first that you only care about average income and not at all about equity. Then the comparison is straightforward. You will easily compute that average income in Scenario 1 is $25,500, while it is only $2,750 in Scenario 2. The first scenario clearly dominates.

Suppose, on the other hand, that you only care about equity. One way of thinking about this is to just focus on a measure of inequality and nothing else. In that case, you will see that Scenario 1 has greater inequality because

the ratio of rich-to-poor incomes is 50. In contrast, in Scenario 2, the same ratio is only 10. So if you care only about inequality and nothing else, you may be tempted to say that Scenario 2 is preferable.

There is a fallacy here, however. Most of us would care about inequality because we associate it with poverty and low living standards for part of the population. Yet Scenario 1, despite having greater inequality, also has much less poverty. In Scenario 1, the poor individuals have $1,000 each, whereas in Scenario 2, each poor individual has only $500, regardless of that economy's greater equality. Therefore, even if we strongly care about the welfare of others and the level of poverty in society, just focusing on inequality would be an error. In fact, in this case, Scenario 1 has both greater average income and lower poverty. If, instead of noticing this, we just focused on inequality, presuming that a more equal allocation would also have lower poverty, we would have made an error in judgment.

World Bank, leads to serious economic, health, and social problems. High infant mortality, child malnourishment, lack of access to education, and the inability to take part in several major economic activities are just some of the problems typically associated with extreme levels of poverty. However, it is important to distinguish between inequality and poverty, as we do in the above Choice & Consequence box.

Growth and Poverty

What is the relationship between growth and poverty? We saw in the previous chapter how countries with higher levels of income (GDP) per capita have fewer people living in poverty, as measured by the $1.25 per day measure of the World Bank. Exhibit 21.13

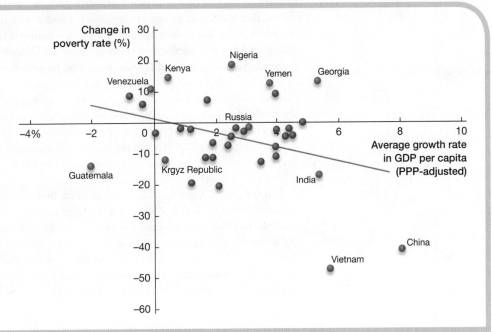

Exhibit 21.13 The Relationship Between Growth and Change in Poverty in the Early 1990s and the Early Twenty-first Century

Economic growth tends to reduce poverty, though the relationship is noisy and less than perfect. Red dots correspond to countries identified by name.

Source: Data from Penn World Table and World Bank DataBank: World Development Indicators; Alan Heston, Robert Summers, and Bettina Aten, Penn World Table Version 7.1, Center for International Comparisons of Production, Income and Prices at the University of Pennsylvania (Nov 2012).

complements this picture by showing that, on average, growth of income per capita is associated with a decline in poverty. For each country in the data, the vertical axis shows the percentage rise or decline in poverty between 1993 and the late 2000s (depending on data availability), while the horizontal axis shows the average growth between the same dates.

Those in the lower-right quadrant are the countries that have experienced positive growth and declines in poverty and include China, India, and Vietnam, among others. Venezuela in the upper-left quadrant is one of only three countries that has a negative growth rate and has also experienced an increase in poverty. The exhibit also includes the line that best fits these points. Although there are some countries where growth and poverty have both increased (such as Yemen, Nigeria, and Georgia), on the whole there is a negative association between growth over the recent decades and the fraction of the population living in poverty. Yet the exhibit also shows that there is quite a bit of dispersion around that best-fit line.

Even though this association does not prove that growth in income per capita is the direct *cause* of declining poverty, it is the type of evidence that bolsters many economists' belief that economic growth is one of the most effective ways of reducing poverty. Nevertheless, it is important to remember that there is no guarantee that economic growth will automatically reduce poverty (as the cases of Georgia, Nigeria, and Yemen in the exhibit show). It will do so only if it is not associated with a significant rise in inequality.

How Can We Reduce Poverty?

Many different policies have been pursued in order to reduce international poverty, and, for reasons that we discuss in greater detail in the next chapter, many have failed. Thus it is quite likely that there are no silver-bullet policies for reducing poverty around the world.

Nevertheless, economic analysis suggests several potentially useful approaches. One solution, which we explore further in Chapter 28, is international trade, which can be beneficial to all countries that take part in it. Although international trade does create losers as well as winners, the overall benefit from international trade is generally positive and significant. This is particularly so for many poor countries that have natural resources and produce agricultural goods that could be exported to the European Union or the United States but are blocked by high tariffs and prohibitive quotas. Reducing tariffs and quotas that wealthy nations impose on poor countries would be one way of creating gains in GDP and perhaps even growth for these nations. In fact, trade might have even further benefits. If international trade also brings with it more interaction with wealthy nations, such cross-country contact might facilitate the transfer of technology.

Another important aspect of improving standards of living around the world is to continue improving the knowledge and technology available in the world economy. The United States spends a sizable fraction of its GDP on R&D, and a significant fraction of its workforce works in science and engineering. The improvements that result from these efforts in the United States and in countries such as Canada, the United Kingdom, France, and Germany improve not only the standards of living in these nations but also those all around the world. For example, improvements in communications technology that originated in the United States and Western Europe now enable cell phones to be used globally, which has helped improve the lives and the business opportunities of billions of people elsewhere. Before wireless communication became available, people in many countries had to rely on wireline telephones for communication.

But wireline telephone industry was often under state control or a private monopoly, and as a consequence, it was very expensive and not widely available. The advances in wireless technology have partly broken the hold of these monopolies on consumers. As the technology improves, wireless telecommunication can be used for better healthcare delivery, and it is already being used as an important part of business deals, starting with improving communication between firms. Similarly, innovations in pharmaceuticals allow lives to be saved around the world, not just in the United States or Germany or France.

LETTING THE DATA SPEAK

Life Expectancy and Innovation

Life expectancy around the world was much lower 70 years ago than it is today.[4] In 1940, child and infant mortality rates were so high and adult diseases, such as pneumonia and tuberculosis, were so deadly (and without any cure) that life expectancy at birth in many nations stood at less than 40 years. For example, the life expectancy at birth of an average Indian was an incredibly low 30 years. In Venezuela, it was 33; in Indonesia, 34; in Brazil, 36. Life expectancy at birth in many Western nations was also low but still considerably higher than the corresponding numbers in the poorer nations. Consider that life expectancy at birth in the United States was 64 years.

In the course of the next three or four decades, this picture changed dramatically. As we saw in the previous chapter, while the gap in life expectancy between rich and poor nations still remains today, health conditions have improved significantly all over the world, particularly before the spread of the AIDS epidemic in sub-Saharan Africa starting in the 1980s. Life expectancy at birth in India in 1999 was 60 years. This was twice as large as the same number in 1940. It was also 50 percent higher than life expectancy at birth in Britain in 1820 (40 years), which had approximately the same GDP per capita as India in 1999. How did this tremendous improvement in health conditions in poor nations take place?

The answer lies in scientific breakthroughs and innovations that took place in the United States and Western Europe throughout the twentieth century. First, there was a wave of global drug innovation, most importantly the development of antibiotics, which produced many products that were highly effective against major killers in developing countries. Penicillin, which provided an effective treatment against a range of bacterial infections, became widely available by the early 1950s. Also important during the same period was the development of new vaccines, including ones against yellow fever and smallpox.

The second major factor was the discovery of DDT (Dichlorodiphenyl trichloroethylene). Although eventually the excess use of DDT as an agricultural pesticide would turn out to be an environmental hazard, its initial use in disease control was revolutionary. DDT allowed a breakthrough in attempts to control one of the major killers of children in relatively poor parts of the world—malaria. Finally, with the establishment and help of the World Health Organization (WHO), simple but effective medical and public health practices, such as oral rehydration and boiling water to prevent cholera, spread to poorer countries.

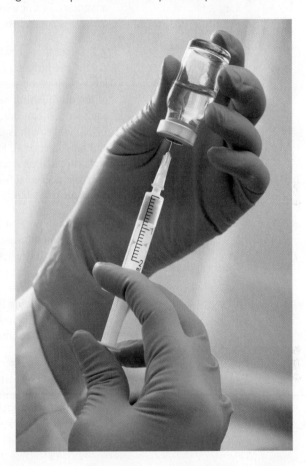

Therefore, although not directly useful for closing the gap between wealthy nations and the rest of the world, continuing with the innovative agenda in the United States and Europe is an important weapon in the fight against international poverty.

In this and the previous chapter, we have focused on how physical capital, human capital, and technology determine the potential for economic growth and cross-country differences in GDP per capita. We have seen how an economy—rich or poor—can grow by investing more in physical capital, upgrading the human capital of its workforce, and improving its technology and efficiency of production. The natural question then is why many countries in the world do not pursue such improvements but remain poor or submit to low growth instead. This is the topic of our next chapter.

Summary

✺ Many countries, including the United States, have experienced rapid economic growth over the last 200 years, increasing their GDP per capita several times over. For example, current U.S. GDP per capita is about 25 times U.S. GDP per capita in 1820. In addition, U.S. growth has been relatively sustained, meaning that GDP per capita has grown relatively steadily, with the exception of the Great Depression and the decade following it.

✺ Economic growth can sometimes take place rapidly due to catch-up growth, whereby relatively poorer nations increase their GDP per capita by taking advantage of knowledge and technologies already invented in other, more advanced countries.

✺ Economic growth results from an economy increasing its physical capital, raising the human capital of its workers (so that it has greater efficiency units of labor for a given size of the workforce), and improving its technology. Because of the diminishing marginal product of physical capital and limits to how much each worker can invest in his or her human capital before joining the workforce, sustained growth is generally impossible to achieve just by building up physical and human capital. Rather, the most plausible driver of sustained growth is technological progress. Empirical evidence also suggests that technological progress accounts for the bulk of the increase in GDP per capita (or per hour worked) in the United States.

✺ Though the last 200 years have been characterized by sustained economic growth in many parts of the world, the preceding centuries did not experience steady growth. Instead, most economies during these times experienced Malthusian cycles: increases in GDP-fueled population growth, which reduced the standard of living and subsequently acted as a check on further population growth by reducing fertility and survival. The world broke out of the Malthusian cycle through the Industrial Revolution, which started a process of rapid technological progress, underpinning the sustained growth of the last two centuries.

✺ Economic growth has the capacity to significantly reduce poverty, provided that such growth is not associated with much greater inequality.

Key Terms

economic growth or growth p. 480
growth rate p. 480
exponential growth p. 480
catch-up growth p. 486

sustained growth p. 486
saving rate p. 488
technological change p. 489
subsistence level p. 494

fertility p. 494
Malthusian cycle p. 494
demographic transition p. 494
Industrial Revolution p. 495

Questions

All questions are available in MyEconLab *for practice and instructor assignment.*

1. What is meant by economic growth? How has the U.S. economy grown over the past 200 years?

2. What are catch-up growth and sustained growth? Explain with examples.

3. According to the aggregate production function, how does GDP increase?

4. The chapter emphasizes the importance of saving in economic growth.

   a. How is the saving rate in an economy defined?

   b. What factors help households decide whether to consume or save their income?

   c. How do household saving decisions impact investment in the economy?

5. Holding all else equal, will increasing the efficiency units of labor lead to sustained growth? Why or why not?

6. What explains economic growth in the United States over the past few decades?

7. Why was there no sustained economic growth before modern times, that is, before 1800?

8. What did Malthus predict about economic growth? Did his predictions come true? Why or why not?

9. How did the Industrial Revolution affect economic growth?

10. Does an increase in GDP per capita of a nation imply that all its citizens have become richer? Explain.

11. Based on your understanding of the chapter, how can poverty best be reduced?

12. What factors explain the dramatic increases in life expectancy that we saw in most countries in the twentieth century?

Problems

All problems are available in MyEconLab *for practice and instructor assignment.*

1. (Note: All figures in this problem are given in constant, 1990 dollars.)

   In 1950, GDP per capita in Germany was only $4,281. GDP per capita in Argentina that same year was $4,987. So, in 1950 Argentina was actually "richer" in per capita terms than Germany.

   By 1992, however, GDP per capita in Germany was $19,351, whereas GDP per capita in Argentina was only $7,616.

   a. By what total percentage did per capita GDP in each country increase between 1950 and 1992?

   b. Explain how a country that has a lower GDP per capita than another country in some year can end up with a larger GDP per capita in later years.

2. Currently, some of the fastest-growing countries in the world remain desperately poor. For example, of the top five fastest-growing economies in 2013, three—South Sudan, Sierra Leone, and Turkmenistan—had real per capita GDP that are 144th, 155th, and 95th in the world, respectively. (*Source:* CIA Factbook estimates for 2013, PPP basis.)

   This seems like something of a contradiction. Using the equations for growth given in the chapter, explain why a country that has a very low per capita GDP can also have a very high growth rate.

3. The following table lists GDP per capita from 1970 to 2010 for South Korea and the United States. As you can see, both grew substantially over that 40-year period.

Year	South Korea GDP per Capita	U.S. GDP per Capita
1970	317	5247
1980	1778	12598
1990	6642	23955
2000	11948	36467
2010	22151	48358

[Data from the World Bank, *World Development Indicators*]

   a. Plot the five data points for each country on a graph using a nonproportional scale, as in Exhibit 21.3 in the chapter. Connect the points to create a line graph.

   b. Plot the five data points for each country on a graph using a proportional scale, that is, a scale where equal distances represent equal *percentage* changes. Connect the points to create a line graph.

   c. Interpret the differences you see in the two graphs.

4. China's economy is one of the fastest-growing economies in the world. Growth in China is primarily driven by investment and exports. You are discussing the sustainability of China's growth model with your friend. He says that according to the aggregate production function, all China needs to do to ensure sustainable economic growth is to continue to increase its physical capital stock. Do you agree? Explain.

5. The graph below shows an index of world GDP per capita from 1000 BC to the year 2000.

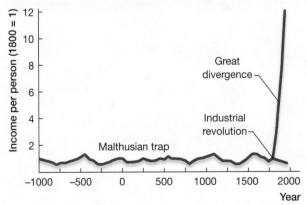

Source: Jeff Speakes, "Economic History of the World," Center for Economic Research and Forecasting, California Lutheran University

   As you can see, over most of that period, global economic growth was virtually nonexistent. While there were periods that experienced some increase in per capita income, sustained growth begins only in the mid-18th century, and explodes after that—by the year 2000, income per capita is 12 times what it had been 250 years before.

Explain what accounts for such a dramatic change in economic growth beginning in the18th century.

6. Economists have long debated the causes of the slowdown in productivity (GDP per hour worked) in the United States during the 1970s and 1980s. This slowdown can be clearly seen in Exhibits 21.10 and 21.11.

   a. Based on the data in Exhibit 21.10, is it physical capital, human capital, or technology that is most responsible for the overall decline in the annual growth rate of GDP per hour worked in these two decades? Explain your answer with reference to the exhibit.

   b. An interesting study of the slowdown has been done by Yale economist William Nordhaus, which is summarized at http://www.nber.org/digest/jun05/w10950 .html. What are the two main conclusions that Nordhaus reaches concerning the 1970s slowdown? Which industries were most affected by the slowdown, and why?

7. The concept of diminishing returns to a factor of production applies not only to physical capital but to labor as well. Use the concept of diminishing returns to labor to explain and illustrate why there was no sustained growth in living standards prior to the Industrial Revolution. Draw a graph to illustrate the relationship between population and GDP, where population is measured on the horizontal axis. Explain how your graph changes after the Industrial Revolution.

8. In 1968, Paul Ehrlich, a Stanford University professor, claimed that overpopulation would lead to famines and starvation in the 1970s and 1980s. In his book *The Population Bomb*, he said that unless population growth was curbed, millions around the world would die. However, as we now know, this did not happen. What do you think was the flaw in Ehrlich's argument?

9. The Letting the Data Speak box on levels versus growth points out how one important index of health—life expectancy—has changed in various countries over time.

   To see a dramatic animation of the data mentioned in the box, go to http://www.gapminder.org/videos/200-years-that-changed-the-world-bbc,/#.U8aTaJRdXTo. Hans Rosling is an expert in global health and is known for his creative presentation of statistics. Watch the brief video, and answer the following questions.

   a. What was the upper limit on life expectancy in almost all countries in 1810? Which two countries were slightly better off?

   b. Which countries failed to improve much in life expectancy and income as a result of the Industrial Revolution?

   c. As of 1948, had disparities in life expectancy and income between countries narrowed or widened? Which were some of the countries that had not made much improvement in either measure by 1948?

   d. As of 2009, what was the general situation regarding the distribution of countries in terms of health and income? What countries still lagged behind?

   e. Based on the video, how can country averages disguise the wide variation in living standards *within* a country? Give an example from the video.

10. Suppose that a 10 percent increase in the physical capital stock increases GDP by 10 percent. Now consider an additional 10 percent increase in the physical capital stock. Will this increase GDP by less than 10 percent, 10 percent, or more than 10 percent? Explain.

11. Challenge Problem: Refer to Exhibit 21.4. If the United States, Mexico, China, Rwanda, and Haiti continue to grow at the rates given in the exhibit, how many years (starting from 2010) would it take each to catch up to the United States in terms of per capita GDP?

Appendix
The Solow Growth Model

The main tool that economists use for formally studying how GDP is determined is the *Solow model*, named after the economist Robert Solow.[5] In this appendix, we present the Solow model to show how it can be used to study the process of economic growth in greater detail. We have placed this material in the appendix rather than in the main body of the chapter because it can be skipped without interfering with the other key ideas in this chapter and elsewhere in the book.

The Three Building Blocks of the Solow Model

The Solow model consists of three building blocks. The first one is the aggregate production function, which we saw in the previous chapter. Recall that the aggregate production function, $Y = A \times F(K,H)$, links GDP to physical capital (K), total efficiency units of labor (H), and the level of technology (A). Technology includes the knowledge available to the economy and the efficiency of production and is a shifter of the aggregate production function.

The second building block is an equation for physical capital accumulation. Most of the equipment and structures making up the physical capital stock of an economy are durable. When you purchase a computer, you will be using it for several years; many household durables are typically used for much longer. Structures—buildings, roads, and bridges—last even longer. But the durability of physical capital is not infinite. Physical capital is subject to *depreciation*, meaning that any equipment or structure goes through "wear and tear" and ultimately becomes obsolete. For example, when you buy a truck and use it for a year, it will have more miles and its brakes may be worn out. As a result of this wear and tear, some of its value will have been lost, and you will get quite a bit less if you try to sell it than you paid last year. Depreciation erodes the value of physical capital, but it can be slowed or reversed by continual investment and upkeep. In the case of your truck, you could also invest in it by having the brakes, oil, or tires changed. This type of investment counterbalances depreciation and increases the value of the truck.

The same is true for the physical capital stock of the economy, as captured by the following physical capital accumulation equation:

$$K_{\text{now}} = K_{\text{last year}} - K_{\text{depreciated}} + I$$

or

$$K_{\text{now}} = K_{\text{last year}} - (\text{Depreciation rate} \times K_{\text{last year}}) + I$$

or

$$K_{\text{now}} = (1 - d) \times K_{\text{last year}} + I.$$

K_{now} is the physical capital stock this year. This directly depends on the physical capital stock last year, $K_{\text{last year}}$, specifically the fraction $1 - d$ of that physical capital stock that doesn't depreciate between the two dates. The remaining $dK_{\text{last year}}$ is the equivalent of the decline in the value of your truck. In the meantime, the firms in the economy undertake investments and purchase new machines to increase the physical capital stock of the economy, in the same way that you may have invested in new gadgets or maintenance to increase the value of your truck. In the above equation, this is represented by the investment amount I.

This equation is not only useful for the Solow growth model, but in fact is one of the key equations that economists use to compute the actual value of physical capital stock in practice, such as in national income accounts.

The third building block of the Solow model is saving by households. Recall from our discussion in the body of this chapter that investment is determined by household saving behavior. Then investment in the economy will be

$$I = s \times Y,$$

where, as you will recall, Y denotes GDP, s is the saving rate, and I is aggregate investment. Now, using the first building block, the aggregate production function, we can write

$$I = s \times Y = s \times A \times F(K, H).$$

This relationship is drawn in Exhibit 21A.1. The red curve represents the aggregate production function, or more specifically the relationship between GDP and the physical capital stock for given levels of efficiency units of labor and technology. This shows the same shape as Exhibit 20.7 from the previous chapter. The green curve shows the relationship between the level of investment and the physical capital stock given the saving rate of households, s. It is simply given by a downward shift of the aggregate production function—because it represents GDP times the saving rate, s. By definition, therefore, the distance between the green curve and the horizontal axis at a given level of physical capital stock corresponds to aggregate saving or investment, as shown in the exhibit. Because the red curve represents GDP in the economy, as shown in the exhibit, the distance between the red and green curves represents consumption (since $Y = C + I$).

Steady-State Equilibrium in the Solow Model

A natural situation for us to study is one in which the physical capital stock last year and physical capital stock now are equal:

$$K_{now} = K_{last\ year} = K.$$

A **steady-state equilibrium** is an economic equilibrium in which the physical capital stock remains constant over time.

We will refer to such a situation as a **steady-state equilibrium**, which is similar to our usual notion of equilibrium with supply being equal to demand but also requires that the physical capital stock is the same between the two dates.

This equation, combined with the physical capital accumulation equation above, immediately implies that, in order for the physical capital stock to be unchanged between years, we need to have investment equal a fraction d of the physical capital stock, written as follows:

$$I = d \times K.$$

Exhibit 21A.1 Aggregate Income and Aggregate Saving

The aggregate production function shows how much GDP can be produced from a given amount of physical capital stock, total efficiency units of labor, and technology. In the exhibit, this is the length of the line between the aggregate production function and the horizontal axis. This aggregate income is in turn divided between consumption and saving (we are ignoring government spending). Saving is also equal to investment in the aggregate.

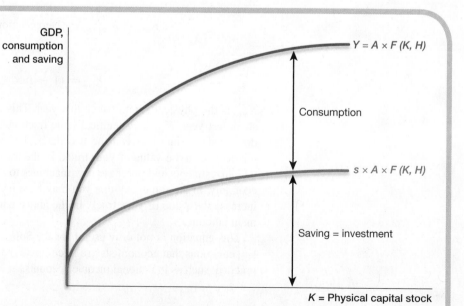

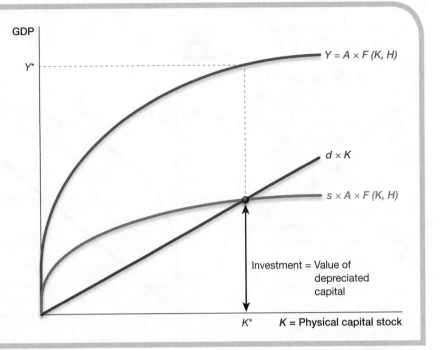

Exhibit 21A.2 Steady-State Equilibrium in the Solow Model

The steady-state equilibrium in the Solow model is given as the point of intersection of the curve denoting total saving in the economy (as a function of the physical capital stock) and the line designating the amount of investment necessary to replenish depreciated physical capital. In the exhibit, the steady-state equilibrium corresponds to the physical capital stock of K* and GDP of Y*

(To see how to derive this, note that in a steady state, the physical capital accumulation equation becomes $K = (1 - d) \times K + I$, and solving this for I gives the desired equation).

In other words, for the physical capital stock of the economy to remain constant over time, the amount of investment must equal the depreciated value of the physical capital stock, which is the depreciation rate of the economy, d, times the physical capital stock, K. Returning to our example above, the value of your truck will remain constant only if the new investment you put in is equal exactly to the depreciation—the reduction in the value of the truck due to wear and tear.

We now put the different ingredients of the Solow model together to determine the steady-state equilibrium. This can be done in Exhibit 21A.2 by also plotting the line representing the value of depreciated physical capital, $d \times K$. The steady-state equilibrium is given by the intersection between this blue line and the green curve (which represents the investment level implied by the saving decisions of households). This follows simply because at this point of intersection, new investment—$I = s \times A \times F(K,H)$—is equal to the value of depreciated physical capital—$d \times K$.

This exhibit shows that there is a unique point where the blue straight line intersects the green curve representing investment. This intersection is the steady-state equilibrium of the Solow model. It gives the steady-state equilibrium level of physical capital stock on the horizontal axis, marked $K*$, and the steady-state equilibrium GDP level on the vertical axis, $Y*$. The exhibit also shows the level of investment (saving) and the value of depreciated physical capital, which equal each other by definition in a steady-state equilibrium, as well as the level of consumption in this equilibrium.

Once we have the steady-state equilibrium of the Solow model, we can use it to study the determinants of GDP.

Determinants of GDP

Exhibit 21A.2 makes it clear that one of the key determinants of GDP is the saving rate, as we discussed in the text. The impact of a higher saving rate on the steady-state physical capital stock and GDP can be seen in Exhibit 21A.3, where we drop the curve for the aggregate production function, $A \times F(K,H)$, and simply show the investment level given by $I = s \times A \times F(K,H)$.

In this exhibit, we compare two economies that have access to the same aggregate production function and have the same population and same efficiency units of labor, but have different saving rates. The economy with the higher saving rate, $s' > s$, is depicted with the dark green curve, while the one with the lower saving rate, s, is shown with the

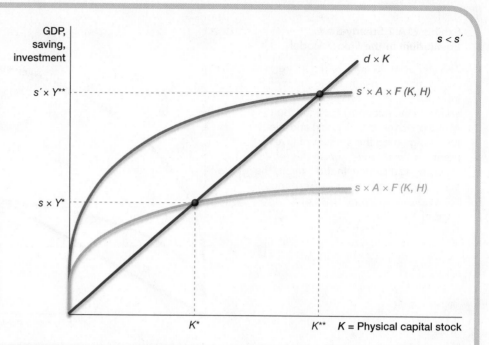

Exhibit 21A.3 The Impact of the Saving Rate on the Steady-State Equilibrium

An increase in the saving rate rotates up the curve denoting total saving in the economy and increases the steady-state equilibrium physical capital stock and GDP level. In the exhibit, the physical capital stock increases from K^* to K^{**} and GDP from Y^* to Y^{**}. (Hence, the level of saving and investment, shown on the vertical axis, increases from $s \times Y^*$ to $s' \times Y^{**}$.

light green curve. (By assumption, both economies have the same rate of depreciation, so the same line represents the value of depreciation). The exhibit shows that the economy with the higher saving rate will have a steady-state equilibrium to the right and above the original one. This corresponds to a greater physical capital stock and hence to greater GDP. Because population is kept constant in this exercise, this also translates into greater GDP per capita.

Both better technology and better human capital of workers also imply that the same amount of physical capital will translate to greater GDP. If the economy has workers that have better human capital, this will increase its efficiency units of labor, H, and given the increasing relationship between efficiency units of labor and GDP shown in Exhibit 20.8 in the previous chapter, we will have greater GDP for a given level of physical capital stock. Therefore, in terms of the relationship between GDP and the physical capital stock, greater human capital of workers implies a shift of the aggregate production function. As a result, aggregate saving shifts to the curve drawn in dark green in Exhibit 21A.4, and the steady-state equilibrium will again be to the right and above the original one, as shown in the exhibit. This implies that higher human capital leads to both higher steady-state equilibrium physical capital stock and higher GDP for the country. Because there has not been any change in the population (or working-age population), the higher GDP again translates into higher GDP per capita.

Exactly the same analysis applies to technology. Recall that better technology corresponds to higher A in terms of our aggregate production function. It can be the result of better knowledge being used in production or of greater efficiency of production. In either case, it will lead to a shift in the aggregate production function that is identical to that in Exhibit 21A.3 (except that it is now the total efficiency units of labor, not the saving rate, that is changing). Consequently, the implications are also identical. There will be a higher steady-state equilibrium level of physical capital stock and a greater steady-state equilibrium level of GDP. Because population is again constant, this will imply greater GDP per capita.

Dynamic Equilibrium in the Solow Model

The Solow model is not only useful for understanding the determinants of steady-state equilibrium but is also the main vehicle that economists use for thinking about economic growth.

As the qualifier "steady-state" hints, we can also imagine an equilibrium that is not a steady-state equilibrium. Such an equilibrium, often referred to as a **dynamic equilibrium**, traces out the behavior of the economy over time. As such, a dynamic equilibrium doesn't correspond to a single point, but to a *path* (of physical capital stock and GDP levels) that will be realized over time.

A **dynamic equilibrium** traces out the behavior of the economy over time.

Exhibit 21A.4 Change in the Steady-State Equilibrium Resulting from an Increase in the Human Capital of Workers

When the human capital of workers increases, so does the total efficiency units of labor. This implies that the economy can produce more with the same physical capital stock and technology, so the curve for the aggregate production function shifts up. This leads to a new steady-state equilibrium with higher physical capital stock and GDP. In particular, the physical capital stock increases from K^* to K^{**} and GDP from Y^* to Y^{**}.

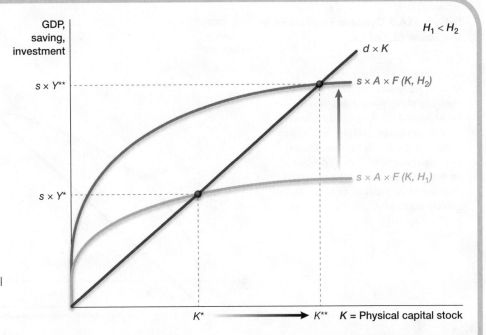

To understand this notion, let us look at Exhibit 21A.5, which is the same as Exhibit 21A.2 except without the curve for $A \times F(K,H)$. The steady-state equilibrium again occurs at the point where the blue straight line intersects the curve representing the investment level; thus K^* is the physical capital stock and Y^* is GDP in this steady-state equilibrium.

Now imagine that, starting from K^*, suddenly some of the physical capital in this economy is destroyed, for example, because of war. As a result, the physical capital stock of the economy is now represented by $K_0 < K^*$. Suppose also that nothing else changes; in particular, the aggregate production function, the saving rate, the efficiency units of labor, and technology all remain the same. At this point, even though just one variable has changed, we are no longer in a steady-state equilibrium because physical capital is no longer being replenished precisely at the rate at which it is depreciating.

What will the level of production in the economy be now? Because the physical capital stock is now equal to K_0 but the efficiency units of labor have not changed, GDP will continue to be given by the aggregate production function at Y_0 (and corresponds to the point marked as $s \times Y_0$ on the vertical axis in Exhibit 21A.5). However, this exhibit also makes it clear that at this new point (K_0, Y_0), the economy is above the straight line. Recall that, along this straight line, investment is just equal to the amount of depreciated physical capital. Above it, investment does not just make up for depreciated physical capital, but exceeds it. Recall now the physical capital accumulation equation, which tells us that $K_{\text{now}} = K_{\text{last year}} - K_{\text{depreciated}} + I$. This equation implies that, as investment exceeds depreciated physical capital, we have $I > K_{\text{depreciated}}$, and thus the physical capital stock will increase. Put differently, there will be a dynamic equilibrium path that takes us back toward the steady-state equilibrium at K^*. The dynamic equilibrium path is shown in Exhibit 21A.5 by the green arrows. It starts at (K_0, Y_0) and traces out the path of the economy toward (K^*, Y^*). This highlights both the fact that a dynamic equilibrium corresponds to a path showing the behavior of the economy over time and also the key result that such a dynamic equilibrium will take the economy back toward the steady-state equilibrium (K^*, Y^*).

Sources of Growth in the Solow Model

We can now use the Solow model to return to the discussion of sustained growth in the text. First, Exhibit 21A.6 demonstrates that increases in the saving rate and physical capital accumulation cannot be the source of sustained growth. It shows that, with given levels of total efficiency units of labor and technology, there is a maximum amount of

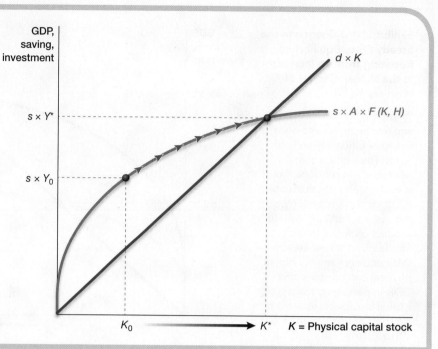

Exhibit 21A.5 Dynamic Equilibrium in the Solow Model

Suppose the economy starts with a physical capital stock of $K_0 < K^*$, that is, with a physical capital stock less than the steady-state equilibrium. What happens? The exhibit shows that at this point, saving and investment are greater than the amount of physical capital that depreciates, so the physical capital stock increases. This dynamic process takes us to the steady-state physical capital stock of K^*.

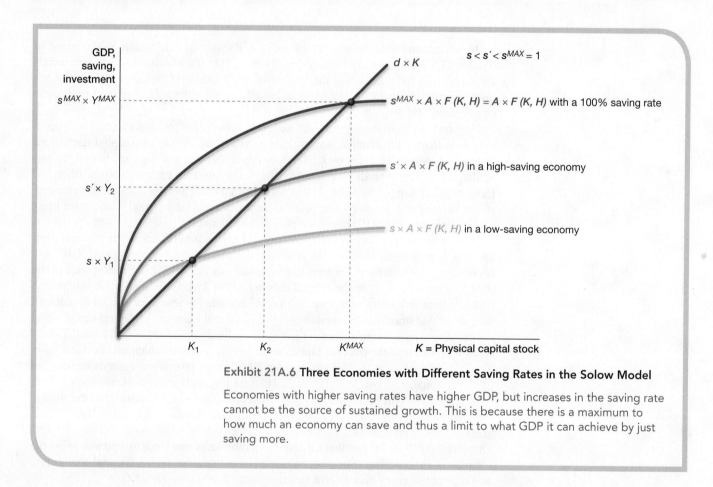

Exhibit 21A.6 Three Economies with Different Saving Rates in the Solow Model

Economies with higher saving rates have higher GDP, but increases in the saving rate cannot be the source of sustained growth. This is because there is a maximum to how much an economy can save and thus a limit to what GDP it can achieve by just saving more.

GDP that an economy can achieve by increasing saving, since we can never go above a saving rate of 100 percent. This determines the level of GDP, Y^{MAX}, beyond which the economy cannot expand with a given aggregate production function and total efficiency units of labor.

The presence of such a maximal level of GDP, Y^{MAX}, implies that sustained growth is not possible by just increasing saving. To see this, note that if an economy grows at a constant

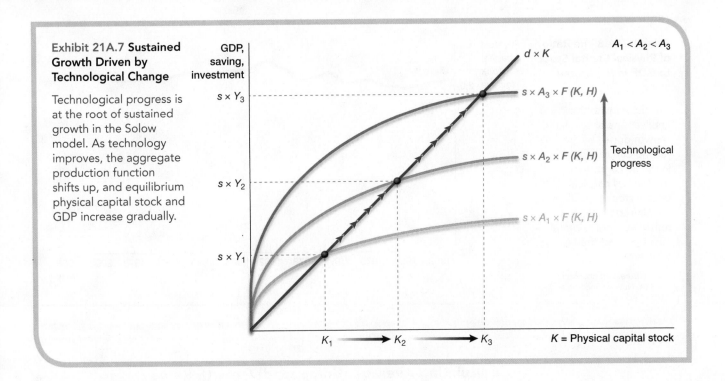

Exhibit 21A.7 Sustained Growth Driven by Technological Change

Technological progress is at the root of sustained growth in the Solow model. As technology improves, the aggregate production function shifts up, and equilibrium physical capital stock and GDP increase gradually.

rate, such as 2 percent per year, it will eventually reach and exceed any fixed level of GDP, such as Y^{MAX}. This is consistent with historical evidence. Over the past 200 years, countries have not achieved steady growth by simply increasing their saving rates. Overall, this discussion and Exhibit 21A.6 show that *increases in the saving rate can increase GDP, but they cannot generate sustained growth.*

To show how technological improvements can lead to sustained growth in the Solow model, Exhibit 21A.7 revisits our by-now familiar figure for the determination of the steady-state equilibrium. It shows that as technology improves, the aggregate production function (and consequently the investment curve) shifts up. This raises the equilibrium levels of physical capital stock and GDP.

Notably, these improvements take place along the straight line of the steady state as shown in the exhibit. Recall that the straight line is given by the equation $d \times K$ and does not shift as a result of technological improvements.

At each point of intersection, we have $s \times Y = d \times K$. Rewriting this gives $K/Y = s/d$, which thus implies that throughout there is a constant ratio of the physical capital stock to GDP. Therefore, the implication of the Solow model for sustained growth is that the *ratio of the physical capital stock to GDP should be constant as the economy grows.*

Exhibit 21A.8 plots the historical evolution of the value of the physical capital stock to GDP in the U.S. economy. The ratio of the physical capital stock to GDP is roughly constant over the last 50 years, with a value of about 2. This pattern is consistent with the implication of the Solow model based on sustained growth driven by technological improvements, which, as we just saw, also implies a constant ratio of physical capital stock to GDP as the economy grows.

What about catch-up growth? In contrast to sustained growth, catch-up growth can result both from the accumulation of physical capital and human capital and from technological change. The nature of catch-up growth can be illustrated by the dynamic equilibrium path of an economy starting with a level of physical capital stock such as K_0 below its steady-state equilibrium K^*, as depicted in Exhibit 21A.5. This dynamic equilibrium path represents the growth trajectory of an economy that is temporarily below its steady-state equilibrium or improves its technology and thus raises its steady-state equilibrium level of physical capital stock and GDP. This exhibit thus shows that, typically, such an economy will rapidly grow toward its steady-state equilibrium. Such rapid growth is a hallmark of the catch-up process as shown by the experiences of several countries depicted in Exhibits 21.4, 21.5, and 21.8.

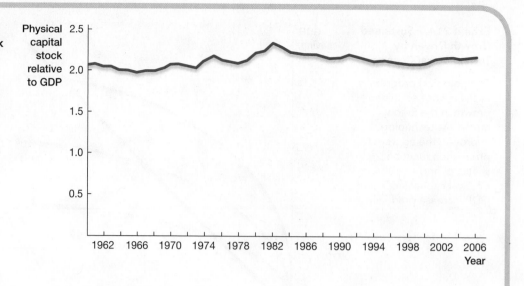

Exhibit 21A.8 The Ratio of Physical Capital Stock to GDP in the United States

Consistent with the implications of sustained growth driven by technological progress in the Solow model, the ratio of physical capital stock to GDP in the United States has remained approximately constant over the last 50 years.

Source: Bureau of Economic Analysis, National Income and Product Accounts.

Calculating Average (Compound) Growth Rates

Now let's discuss how to calculate average growth rates by returning to Exhibit 21.4. Consider the United States. Its GDP per capita was $15,398 in 1960 and $41,365 in 2010 (in PPP-adjusted 2005 constant dollars). We can now compute the 50-year growth rate (between 1960 and 2010) as 168.64 percent, using the formula provided in the text. In particular, this number is obtained as

$$\frac{41{,}365 - 15{,}398}{15{,}398} = 1.6864,$$

corresponding to 168.64 percent growth.

One way of computing the average growth rate is to use the arithmetic average and divide this number by 50 to obtain the average annual growth rate. This would give an annual growth rate of 3.4 percent. The number in Exhibit 21.4 is different—2.00 percent. How is this number obtained, and why is it different?

The answer to this question is related to the importance of the exponential nature of growth, which we discussed earlier in the chapter. Suppose that an economy grows at the rate of $g = 0.034$ (that is, 3.4 percent) every year for 50 years. How much will its GDP per capita have gone up at the end of the 50 years? To compute this, we have to note that after one year its GDP per capita will have increased by $1 + g$. From the second to the third year, it will increase by another $1 + g$, so between the first and third years, it will have gone up by $(1 + g)^2$. Continuing with this reasoning, at the end of 50 years, its GDP per capita will have increased by $(1 + g)^{50}$. If we take $g = 0.034$, we find that its GDP per capita will be 5.32 times higher at the end of the 50 years, which is considerably greater than the numbers for the United States. Instead, these numbers imply that at the end of the 50 years, U.S. GDP per capita was about 2.6864 times higher. (This number can be obtained simply as $41{,}365/15{,}398 = 2.6864$, that is, GDP per capita in 2010 divided by GDP per capita in 1960, or you can note that it is $1 + 1.6864$, where 168.64 percent was the growth rate of the U.S. economy between 1960 and 2010.)

By dividing the total growth between 1960 and 2010 by 50, we have ignored the cumulative effects of growth and overestimated the annual growth rate that would lead to the observed increase in GDP per capita.

This discussion also indicates that a more sophisticated way of computing the average annual growth rate is by using the geometric average. In this case, we would calculate the growth rate as

$$(1 + g)^{50} = 2.6864.$$

We can then use this equation to arrive at the correct average annual growth rate, g. (More technically, we would invert this equation and compute $g = 2.6864^{1/50} - 1$.) This approximately gives the (average) annual growth rate as $g = 0.020$, as recorded in the exhibit. In most cases, using either the arithmetic or the geometric average to compute average growth rates gives similar answers, provided that we are looking at short periods. The reason why there is a sizable difference in this case is because we are considering a long period of time.

Appendix Key Terms

steady-state equilibrium *p.* 504   dynamic equilibrium *p.* 506

Appendix Problems

All problems are available in MyEconLab *for practice and instructor assignment.*
Problems marked 🌐 *update with real-time data.*

A1. Use a diagram to represent the Solow growth model using the aggregate production function and the relationship between the physical capital stock and aggregate saving.

   a. Which point in the figure represents the steady-state equilibrium? Why?

   b. Use the diagram to show the impact of an increase in human capital on GDP.

A2. In the 1980s, the saving rate in Japan was extremely high. Gross savings as a percentage of GDP ranged between 30 and 32%. Can such a high saving rate lead to sustained economic growth? Use the Solow model to explain your answer.

   Data source: http://data.worldbank.org/indicator/NY.GNS .ICTR.ZS/countries/JP?page=5&display=default

🌐 **A3.** India's GDP per capita increased from $310 in 1991 to $1,489 in 2012.

   Data source: http://data.worldbank.org/indicator/NY.GDP .PCAP.CD

   a. Calculate the arithmetic average annual rate of growth of the Indian economy during this period using the arithmetic average.

   b. Calculate the geometric average annual growth rate of India during this period. How does the number you find differ from the number given in Exhibit 21.3? Speculate on what accounts for any difference.

A4. The appendix details the important distinction between arithmetic and geometric averages in determining growth rates.

   a. Using the procedure outlined in the Appendix for *geometric* average growth rates (in the section titled "Calculating Average (Compound) Growth Rates," see if you can reproduce the "Implied (average) annual growth" figures given in the last column of Exhibit 21.4 for the following countries: France, Singapore, Botswana, India and Kenya.

   b. Using the procedure outlined in the Appendix for finding *arithmetic* average growth rates, calculate the arithmetic average growth rate for the five countries. Compare these with the rates you obtained in part a. Does the arithmetic average understate or overstate the actual growth rate? Explain.

22

Why Isn't the Whole World Developed?

Are tropical and semitropical areas condemned to poverty by their geographies?

If you look back at the map of GDP per capita of the world shown in Exhibit 20.2 in Chapter 20, you will notice a striking regularity: many of the poorest nations are close to the equator in the tropical and semitropical areas of the world. Conversely, countries in the temperate areas away from the equator are much more prosperous. The Democratic Republic of Congo, for example, is cut in the middle by the equator. In 2010, its GDP per capita adjusted for purchasing power was $241 (in 2005 constant dollars). Move up along the map all the way to the sixtieth parallel, and you will find Finland. In that same year, its GDP per capita was $32,989 (in 2005 constant dollars). You can do the same exercise for almost all countries around the equator. Move up the line of longitude to find the corresponding countries at the fortieth, fiftieth, or sixtieth parallels, and almost always you will see that the ones further away from the equator are considerably richer than the ones nearest it. This pattern has led many social scientists to conjecture that there is something particularly pernicious about the economic and

CHAPTER OUTLINE

⚙ Proximate causes of prosperity link prosperity and poverty of nations to the levels of inputs, while fundamental causes look for reasons why there are such differences in the levels of inputs.

⚙ The geography, culture, and institutions hypotheses advance different fundamental causes of prosperity.

⚙ Inclusive and extractive economic institutions affect economic development.

⚙ Creative destruction is integral to economic growth through technological change.

⚙ Reversal of fortune evidence provides support for the institutions hypothesis.

social conditions in the areas around the equator. Many have gone so far as to assert that tropical and semitropical areas condemn a nation to poverty.

Can this be true? Can geography determine a nation's prosperity? By the end of this chapter, we provide some answers to this intriguing question. We'll also have developed a much better understanding of why the whole world isn't developed, and why there are wide disparities in GDP per capita across countries.

22.1 Proximate Versus Fundamental Causes of Prosperity

In Chapter 20, we documented the huge differences in GDP per capita and living standards across countries. You may recall the huge gap in GDP per capita between the United States and the Democratic Republic of Congo, Ghana, or Haiti. In that chapter, we emphasized how these gaps can be explained in terms of cross-country differences in physical capital, human capital, and technology.

Yet an explanation based on these causes alone immediately begs the question of why some countries have accumulated more physical capital, invested more in human capital, and developed and adopted better technologies than other countries. After all, if investing in physical and human capital and adopting cutting-edge technologies can lead to major improvements in GDP, wouldn't all countries in the world wish to do so? Why isn't the whole world as developed as the United States or West European nations?

These deeper questions make us realize that differences in physical capital, human capital, and technology are only *proximate causes* of economic performance. We call them **proximate causes of prosperity** because they link high levels of prosperity to high levels of the inputs to production, but without providing an explanation for why the levels of those inputs are high.

To get at the reasons why some countries are either unable or unwilling to invest in different amounts of physical capital, human capital, and technology, we have to dig deeper. Causation can be complex, as we discussed in Chapter 2. We sometimes have to see what lies beneath the surface to understand the true causes of an observed phenomenon. We refer to these underlying factors as the **fundamental causes of prosperity**, which are defined as those causes that are at the root of the differences in the proximate causes of prosperity. The relationship between the fundamental and the proximate causes of prosperity is shown in Exhibit 22.1.

Proximate causes of prosperity are high levels of factors such as human capital, physical capital, and technology that result in a high level of GDP per capita.

Fundamental causes of prosperity are factors that are at the root of the differences in the proximate causes of prosperity.

Exhibit 22.1 Fundamental and Proximate Causes of Prosperity

Societies become prosperous when they have abundant human and physical capital and use advanced technology efficiently in production. But these are proximate causes because they are in turn shaped by other, deeper factors. Fundamental causes, such as geographic, cultural, and institutional factors, have an impact on prosperity by affecting proximate causes such as investment in human capital, physical capital, and technology.

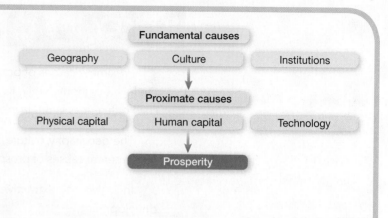

To see the distinction between proximate and fundamental causes more clearly, it is useful to consider an analogy. Say you are experiencing some symptoms of flu—sore throat, fever, and headache—that might motivate you to take drugs, such as throat decongestants or aspirin. In this example, the proximate cause of why you take these drugs is that you have a sore throat, a high fever, and a headache. But the fundamental cause—the reason why you have the symptoms in the first place—is that you have the flu. The flu thus induces both the symptoms and your response of taking drugs. Similarly, if a country underinvests in human capital, physical capital, and/or technology, we should ask why. Both proximate and fundamental causes have to be considered for a complete understanding of why some nations are prosperous and others aren't.

Although there are many different theories about the fundamental causes of poverty and prosperity—theories about why poorer nations around the world have worse technologies and do not invest in physical and human capital as much as rich ones—it is useful to classify them into three categories: theories of geography, culture, and institutions. We next describe these hypotheses and then discuss whether they are consistent with empirical evidence.

Geography

The **geography hypothesis** claims that differences in geography, climate, and ecology are ultimately responsible for the major differences in prosperity observed across the world.

One approach, which we will refer to as the **geography hypothesis**, claims that differences in geography, climate, and ecology ultimately determine the large differences in prosperity across the world. According to this hypothesis, some countries have highly unfavorable geographical, climactic, or ecological circumstances that are outside of their control. Some are situated in areas where much of the soil may be inhospitable for agriculture, daytime temperatures are very high, or a lack of navigable rivers makes transport prohibitively costly. These conditions, some argue, make it impossible or unlikely for such countries to accumulate or effectively use the factors of production.

Many leading thinkers throughout the ages have advocated the geography hypothesis. One of its great proponents was the famous French philosopher Montesquieu, who argued that climate was a key determinant of work effort and thus prosperity.[1] He wrote:

> The heat of the climate can be so excessive that the body there will be absolutely without strength. So, prostration will pass even to the spirit; no curiosity, no noble enterprise, no generous sentiment; inclinations will all be passive there; laziness there will be happiness. . . . People are . . . more vigorous in cold climates. The inhabitants of warm countries are, like old men, timorous; the people in cold countries are, like young men, brave.

Another major proponent of this view was Alfred Marshall, who was the first economist to write a book (just like ours) aimed at making the principles of economics accessible to a broad population of students.[2] He stated:

> Vigor depends partly on race qualities: but these, so far as they can be explained at all, seem to be chiefly due to climate.

These views emphasizing the effect of climate on work effort and vigor are outdated (and sometimes tinged with racist overtones). But other versions of the geography hypothesis are still popular. Today, many believe that geographic characteristics determine the technology available to a society, especially in agriculture. The economist Jeffrey Sachs has been a strong proponent of this view in his academic writings.[3] Using it as the basis of his influential policy recommendations to the United Nations and the World Health Organization, Sachs, for example, argues:

> By the start of the era of modern economic growth, if not much earlier, temperate-zone technologies were more productive than tropical-zone technologies. . . .

If geography is the major fundamental cause of prosperity (or its absence), then the poor nations of the world have little reason to expect much improvement in living standards.

Jeffrey Sachs and others also argue that many parts of the world, particularly sub-Saharan Africa, are disadvantaged economically because infectious diseases, such as malaria and dengue fever, spread there more easily. When it is serious and widespread, an illness can indeed destroy a large amount of a country's human capital.

If geography is the major fundamental cause of prosperity (or its absence), then the poor nations of the world have little reason to expect much improvement in living standards. They are permanently disadvantaged, and we should not expect them to catch up with the rest of the world and become economically developed anytime soon—or so the thinking goes.

Not all variations of the geography hypothesis are equally pessimistic. In some, large-scale investments in transport technology or disease eradication may partially redress these geographic disadvantages.

Culture

The **culture hypothesis** claims that different values and cultural beliefs fundamentally cause the differences in prosperity around the world.

Another potential fundamental cause of differences in economic performance has to do with cultural differences. According to the **culture hypothesis**, different societies respond differently to incentives because of specific shared experiences, religious teachings, the strength of family ties, or unspoken social norms. Culture is viewed as a key determinant of the values, preferences, and beliefs of individuals and societies and, the argument goes, these differences play a key role in shaping economic performance. For example, some societies may have values that encourage investment, hard work, and the adoption of new technologies, while others may nurture superstition and suspicion of new technologies and discourage hard work.

The most famous link between culture and economic development was proposed by the German sociologist Max Weber, who argued that the origins of industrialization in Western Europe could be traced to Protestantism.[4] In his view, the Protestant worldview was crucial to the development of a market economy and economic growth because it encouraged hard work and saving (and thus investment).

Another common version of the culture hypothesis contrasts the Anglo-Saxon culture of the United States and the United Kingdom, which is viewed as conducive to investment and the adoption of technology, with the supposedly less dynamic and more closed-minded Iberian culture of peoples with Spanish and Portuguese origins. Many social scientists have attempted to explain the contrast between North and South America in these terms.

Almost 20 years ago, the Harvard political scientist Samuel Huntington coined the term "clash of civilizations" to capture what he thought would be the defining conflict of the twenty-first century—the conflict between the West and Islam.[5] More broadly, Huntington has supported the view that culture plays a central role in shaping prosperity. For example, his explanation for why South Korea grew rapidly in the twentieth century and Ghana did not summarizes his overall approach:[6]

> Culture had to be a large part of the explanation. South Koreans valued thrift, investment, hard work, education, organization, and discipline. Ghanaians had different values.

Of course, a society's culture is not immutable: cultures change, though they do so slowly.

Institutions

Institutions are the formal and informal rules governing the organization of a society, including its laws and regulations.

A third potential fundamental cause for the differences in prosperity involves **institutions**, the formal and informal rules governing the organization of a society, including its laws and regulations. For example, economic historian Douglass North, who was awarded the Nobel

Prize in economics largely because of his work emphasizing the importance of institutions in the historical development process, offers the following definition of institutions:[7]

> Institutions are the rules of the game in a society or, more formally, are the humanly devised constraints that shape human interaction.

This definition captures three important elements that define institutions:

1. They are determined by individuals as members of a society.
2. They place constraints on behavior.
3. They shape behavior by determining incentives.

First, institutions are "humanly devised." In contrast to geography, which is largely outside of human control, and culture, which changes very slowly, institutions are determined by man-made factors. That is, institutions do not just appear out of thin air, but develop due to the choices members of a society make over how to organize their interactions.

Second, institutions place constraints on individual behavior. On the positive side, institutions constrain the ability of an individual to steal from others or to walk away from debts that he has built up. On the negative side, they might prevent people from entering into occupations or opening new businesses. Such constraints need not be absolute. Individuals around the world break laws and skirt regulations every day. For example, Apple did not own a license to sell iPads in Taiwan in 2010, so selling the device was illegal. Through online auctions, however, people were able to purchase iPad *cases* for more than $1,000, which happened to include a "free" iPad.[8]

Policies, regulations, and laws that punish or reward certain types of behavior will naturally have an effect on behavior. Though some citizens can circumvent a law that bans, for example, the adoption of certain technologies, such a law still discourages their adoption.

This observation leads us to the third important element in North's definition—institutions affect incentives. The constraints that institutions place on individuals—whether formal constraints such as banning certain activities or informal ones discouraging certain types of behavior through customs and social norms—shape human interaction and affect incentives. In some sense, institutions, much more than the other candidate fundamental causes, are about the importance of incentives.

The **institutions hypothesis** maintains that the differences in the way that humans have chosen to organize their societies—differences that shape the incentives that individuals and businesses in the society face—are at the root of the differences in their relative prosperity. For example, when markets allocate individuals to the occupations in which their productivity is highest, laws and regulations encourage firms to invest in physical capital and technology and the educational system enables and encourages people to invest in their human capital, the economy will generate higher GDP and achieve greater prosperity than when its institutions fail to do so.

To sum up, the institutions hypothesis relies on the following chain of reasoning:

1. Different societies typically have different institutions.
2. These different institutions create different types of incentives.
3. The incentives help determine the degree to which societies accumulate the factors of production and adopt new technology.

The idea that the prosperity of a society depends on its institutions is not a new one. It goes back at least to Adam Smith, the father of economics, who, in *The Wealth of Nations*, emphasized the importance of markets in generating prosperity through the workings of the invisible hand and warned how constraints on markets—for example, in the form of restrictions on trade—could destroy such prosperity.[9]

A Natural Experiment of History

The Korean peninsula is divided in two by the thirty-eighth parallel. To the south is the Republic of Korea, also known as South Korea. We saw in Chapter 21 how South Korea has had one of the fastest-growing economies in the last 60 years and has by now achieved living standards comparable to many countries in Europe.

To the north of the thirty-eighth parallel there is another Korea: the Democratic People's Republic of Korea, or simply North Korea. Living standards in North Korea are similar to those in a sub-Saharan African country. The best estimate suggests that in 2010 GDP per capita (in PPP-adjusted 2005 constant dollars) was $1,612 in the North, making its

The **institutions hypothesis** claims that differences in institutions—that is, in the way societies have organized themselves and shaped the incentives of individuals and businesses—are at the root of the differences in prosperity across the world.

inhabitants worse off than the citizens of Sudan or Yemen. In contrast, in that same year GDP per capita (in PPP-adjusted 2005 constant dollars) in the South was $26,609. What explains these large differences? Could it be geography? Culture? Highly unlikely. The North and South share the same geography, essentially the same climate, the same access to the ocean, and the same disease environments. There are also no noticeable differences between their cultures, certainly not before 1947 when the country was split into two. Korea was at that point an unusually homogeneous country, both ethnically and culturally. If we were to believe that geography or culture were important factors in determining South Korea's economic development after 1947, we would then expect a similar process of economic development in North Korea. Nothing of the sort happened.

In fact, the great disparities between the two nations did not exist before World War II when the two parts of Korea were united. They emerged only when the two were separated and adopted very different institutions.

The separation of Korea into two halves was not something to which its citizens willingly agreed. It was an outcome of a geopolitical deal between the Soviet Union and the United States, who agreed at the end of World War II that the thirty-eighth parallel would be the dividing line for their spheres of influence in Korea and set up different governments in the North and the South.

These governments adopted very different ways of organizing their economies. In North Korea, Kim Il-Sung, a leader of anti-Japanese communist partisans during World War II, established himself as dictator. With the help of the Soviet Union, Kim Il-Sung introduced a rigid form of communism, the *Juche* system. Resources in North Korea were allocated through central planning, private property was outlawed, and markets were banned. Freedoms were curtailed not only in the marketplace but also in every sphere of North Koreans' lives—except for those that happened to be part of the very small ruling elite around Kim Il-Sung. This cronyism persisted under his son Kim Jong-Il, who ruled until his death in 2011, and continues today under Kim Il-Sung's grandson, Kim Jong-Un.

In the South, institutions were shaped by the Harvard- and Princeton-educated, staunchly anti-communist Syngman Rhee, with significant support from the United States. Though Rhee and his successor, General Park Chung-hee, were autocrats, they supported a market-based economy, providing incentives to businesses for investment and industrialization and investing in the education of South Koreans. South Korea did eventually become democratic in the 1990s and further liberalized its economy.

If institutions are a major determinant of economic prosperity, then the sharply divergent institutions of the two Koreas should have led to divergent economic fortunes. And that's exactly what happened. Exhibit 22.2 shows how GDP per capita in North and

> **If institutions are a major determinant of economic prosperity, then the sharply divergent institutions of the two Koreas should have led to divergent economic fortunes. And that's exactly what happened.**

Exhibit 22.2 GDP per Capita in North and South Korea (in PPP-adjusted 2005 Constant Dollars)

The economic fortunes of North and South Korea, starting from parity in the 1940s when they were united, have diverged sharply. South Korea, with institutions mostly based on a market economy, has reached a high level of GDP per capita. In contrast, North Korea, under a communist dictatorship, has failed to grow and has less than 1/16th of the level of the GDP per capita of the South.

Source: Data from Maddison Project (1820–2010); J. Bolt and J. L. van Zanden, "The First Update of the Maddison Project; Re-Estimating Growth Before 1820." Maddison Project Working Paper 4 (2013).

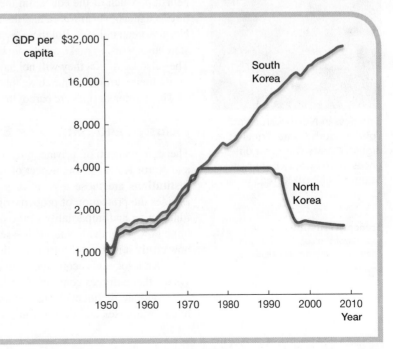

South Korea has sharply diverged over the last 60 years to arrive at the great disparities that we observe today.

The Korean case depicts what we often call a natural experiment or an experiment of history. A country was split in half by a military outcome. The two newly formed, culturally identical, and geographically similar countries proceeded to develop very different institutions. While the South remained a market economy, the North adopted a very rigid form of communist rule with little room for markets, private property, or entrepreneurship. The reason this episode approximates a natural experiment is that while institutions were changing in this radical way, geography and culture remained largely unchanged. It was the changes in institutions that led to massive changes in economic prosperity, as shown in Exhibit 22.2. The Korean example thus provides strong support for the institutions hypothesis (but it does not provide direct evidence against geography and culture because these were held fixed in this comparison).

22.2 Institutions and Economic Development

Teenagers in South Korea grow up just like us. Many obtain a good education, and face incentives that encourage them to exert effort and excel in their chosen vocation. South Korea is a market economy. South Korean teenagers know that, if successful, one day they can enjoy the fruits of their investments and efforts. They can buy computers, clothes, cars, houses, and healthcare. They can start businesses and bequeath their property to their offspring.

This is in large part because the South has well-enforced **private property rights**, meaning that its citizens can hold property like businesses, houses, cars, and many other things without fearing that the government or anyone else will arbitrarily take it away. Just as in the United States, if you own a business in South Korea, you know that the income it generates is yours, other than the taxes you pay, which are often used to provide public goods and services valued by the citizens of the country. Your property is well protected because the state upholds law and order, and if you write business contracts, the courts enforce them. It is possible for entrepreneurs to borrow money from banks and financial markets, for foreign companies to enter into partnerships with South Korean firms, and for individuals to obtain mortgages to buy houses.

Teenagers in North Korea face vastly different lives from those in the South. They grow up in poverty, without high-quality education to prepare them for skilled work or entrepreneurship. Much of the education they receive at school is pure propaganda about foreign threats against North Korea and the benevolent leadership of their supreme leader and the North Korean military. But these teenagers know that they will not be able to own property, start businesses, or make much money because there is no private property in North Korea. They also know that they will not have access to markets where they can deploy their skills or use their earnings to purchase the goods that they need and desire.

These different rules are part of the institutions under which North and South Koreans live.

Inclusive and Extractive Economic Institutions

The enforcement of private property rights, which differs so sharply between South and North Korea, is one aspect of what we refer to as economic institutions. **Economic institutions** are those aspects of a society's rules that concern economic transactions. Besides the protection of property rights, economic institutions include such things as the functioning and impartiality of the judicial system, the financial arrangements that determine how individuals and businesses can borrow money, and the regulations that shape how costly it is to enter into a new line of business or a new occupation.

When a society's economic institutions provide secure property rights, set up a judicial system that enforces contracts and upholds the law, allow private parties to sign contracts for economic or financial transactions, maintain relatively open and free entry into different businesses and occupations, and enable people to acquire the education and skills

Private property rights mean that individuals can own businesses and assets and their ownership is secure.

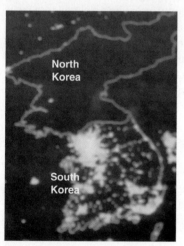

Darkness in North Korea and light in South Korea: lights at night illustrate the huge differences in prosperity between South and North Korea.

Economic institutions are the aspects of the society's rules that concern economic transactions.

Inclusive economic institutions protect private property, uphold law and order, allow and enforce private contracts, and allow free entry into new lines of business and occupations.

Extractive economic institutions do not protect private property rights, do not uphold contracts, and interfere with the workings of markets. They also erect significant entry barriers into businesses and occupations.

Political institutions are the aspects of the society's rules that concern the allocation of political power and the constraints on the exercise of political power.

to take part in such businesses and occupations, we say that they are **inclusive economic institutions**. The economic institutions in South Korea approximate these types of inclusive economic institutions. They are inclusive in the sense that they encourage the participation of the great majority of the population in economic activities in a way that best makes use of their talents and skills.

As we have seen, inclusive economic institutions do *not* describe the situation in North Korea. Economic institutions to the north of the thirty-eighth parallel fail to enforce property rights or contracts, erect prohibitive entry barriers, and all but destroy the workings of the markets. We refer to such arrangements as **extractive economic institutions**. This terminology stems from the fact that such institutions are often shaped by those who control political power to *extract resources from the rest of the society*. Extractive economic institutions are not just associated with communist North Korea. Societies ruled by monarchs, dictators, and juntas as well as several that hold elections for their parliaments and presidents have had, and still have, extractive economic institutions. In fact, most societies throughout history have had economic institutions that are closer to the extreme extractive economic institutions of North Korea than to the ideal of inclusive economic institutions we have defined here.

Examples of market economics that have extractive economic institutions include former Soviet republics, such as Azerbaijan, Turkmenistan and Uzbekistan, Myanmar, and Pakistan in Asia, Argentina, Guatemala, and Peru in Latin America, and the Democratic Republic of Congo, Egypt, and Kenya in Africa. Even if the specific forms of these institutions differ from the extreme form of central planning in North Korea, they share the fact that they fail to enforce property rights and instead privilege a few at the expense of the many.

Extractive economic institutions do not exist in a vacuum. It is no accident that North Korea is a repressive dictatorship. Without the political elite's tight control of the state, North Korea would not be able to maintain a system that condemns tens of millions to poverty. This meshing of political and economic power underscores the important role of **political institutions**, which determine who holds political power and what types of constraints exist on the exercise of that power. Extractive economic institutions tend to be supported by certain types of political institutions, which concentrate political power in the hands of the political elite and put little constraint on how political power can be used. Similarly, inclusive economic institutions tend to coexist with different types of political institutions, which tend to distribute political power more equally in society so that no single individual or group is able to use that political power for its own benefit at the expense of the rest of society.

Heck. I thought you were kidding. I guess you really do want democracy.

How Economic Institutions Affect Economic Outcomes

The contrast between South Korea and North Korea, and between Austria and Czechoslovakia discussed in the next Letting the Data Speak box, illustrates a general principle: *inclusive economic institutions foster economic activity, productivity growth, and economic prosperity, while extractive economic institutions generally fail to do so.*[10] Property rights are central to this principle because only those who have secure property rights will be willing to invest and increase productivity. A farmer who expects his output to be expropriated—meaning stolen, taken away, or entirely taxed away—will have little incentive to work, let alone any incentive to undertake investments and innovations. Extractive economic institutions distort incentives in exactly this fashion. Farmers, traders, businessmen, and workers will be discouraged from investing and producing when they have no property rights. On top of that, firms will not be able to form the trust-based relationships that are necessary to productively do business when private contracts are worth little more than the paper they are written on or when some contractual agreements are banned outright. Finally, because they erect market entry barriers rather

Divergence and Convergence in Eastern Europe

Between 1948 and 1989, citizens of Central and Eastern European countries, just like those of North Korea, lived under a communist dictatorship. Large, state-owned enterprises were the norm in these economies. These firms did not compete in the market but instead worked toward arbitrary targets set by Communist Party officials (which they almost always failed to meet). As a consequence, shortages of food and consumer goods were common. In a market economy, companies that fail to motivate workers, produce goods of reasonable quality, or meet their production targets are ultimately driven out of the market. But state-owned enterprises under communism did not have to worry about competition or about being driven out of the market, because there was no competition, and it was the state that set prices and footed the bill if these enterprises lost money.

In 1948, Austria and Czechoslovakia, two neighbors in central Europe, each had GDP per capita of about $4,000. But in Czechoslovakia, farms were subsequently taken forcibly from their owners and collectivized, a command economy was established, and political freedoms that existed before World War II were abolished. In Austria, a market system, along with economic institutions much more inclusive than those in communist Eastern Europe, flourished. The consequences were similar to what we have seen in the case of North and South Korea. Not surprisingly, Czechoslovakia kept falling behind its neighbor, Austria, for 40 years.

The two countries, which had very similar histories, geographies, and cultures, had achieved vastly different levels of prosperity by 1989 when the communist regime finally collapsed. Those Central and Eastern European societies that had been under communist rule transitioned to democracy and a market economy, became more inclusive, and started to grow rapidly as the share of the private sector in the economy increased from 5 percent to 80 percent. Exhibit 22.3 shows the divergence between Austria and Czechoslovakia during the communist period and the convergence that started after Czechoslovakia transitioned to a market economy in the 1990s.

Exhibit 22.3 GDP per Capita in Austria and the Neighboring Czechoslovakia since 1948 (in PPP-adjusted 2005 Constant Dollars)

Starting from approximately the same level of GDP per capita, the economies of Czechoslovakia and Austria diverged after 1948 while subject to different economic and political institutions. Following the collapse of communism and subsequent transition to a market economy, first Czechoslovakia, and subsequently the newly formed nations of Czech Republic and Slovakia after its dissolution in 1993, started growing rapidly and closing the gap with Austria.

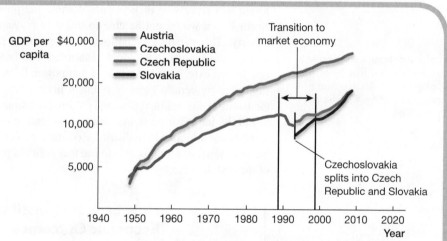

Source: Data from Maddison Project (1820–2010); J. Bolt and J. L. van Zanden, "The First Update of the Maddison Project; Re-Estimating Growth Before 1820." Maddison Project Working Paper 4 (2013).

than create an environment that would encourage entry, extractive economic institutions tend to support inefficient firms and prevent entrepreneurs with new ideas from entering into the right lines of business and workers from working in occupations to which their skills are best suited.

Exhibit 22.4 is helpful for illustrating why extractive economic institutions discourage economic activity. There, in a hypothetical economy, we rank potential entrepreneurs in descending order according to the return they will make if they enter and start a business.

Exhibit 22.4 How Extractive Economic Institutions Reduce the Number of Entrepreneurs

Panel (a): The return-to-entrepreneurship curve shows the number of entrepreneurs with at least the return indicated on the vertical axis. It is obtained by ranking potential entrepreneurs from higher to lower return to entrepreneurship. The opportunity cost schedule indicates the value to a potential entrepreneur of her best alternate activity. The intersection of the two curves gives the equilibrium number of entrepreneurs. For example, in panel (a), all potential entrepreneurs with return greater than or equal to $50,000 choose entrepreneurship.

Panel (b): Extractive economic institutions shift the return-to-entrepreneurship curve to the left, as shown in panel (b). Two reasons this shift might occur are the following: first, weak property rights prevent entrepreneurs from capturing their full returns, and second, with a lack of legal backup, entrepreneurs cannot easily form reliable contracts with business partners, which can reduce profitability by making supplies more expensive and revenues more precarious.

Panel (c): Extractive economic institutions also shift the opportunity cost schedule upward because they erect entry barriers that make entry into entrepreneurship more expensive. Panel (c) shows the overall impact of extractive economic institutions on the equilibrium number of entrepreneurs resulting from a leftward shift of the return-to-entrepreneurship schedule and an upward shift of the opportunity cost schedule.

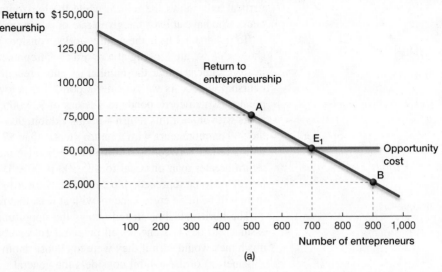

(a)

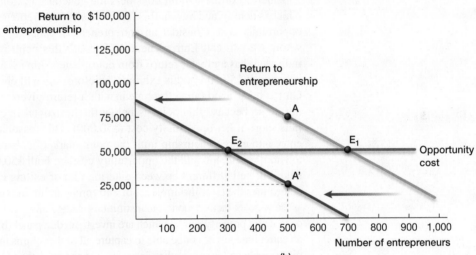

(b)

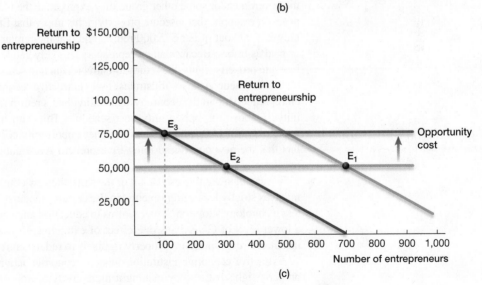

(c)

The return-to-entrepreneurship curve in the exhibit (shown in blue) plots these returns. The vertical axis shows the return, while the horizontal axis depicts the number of entrepreneurs who have at least the given rate of return (or higher).

To understand how the figure works, consider point A in panel (a). The vertical axis shows that we are looking at a return to entrepreneurship of $75,000. The horizontal axis, in turn, indicates that the number of entrepreneurs with at least this return to entrepreneurship is 500. As we consider a point with a lower return to entrepreneurship, such as point B, which corresponds to a return of $25,000, naturally there will be more entrepreneurs with at least this return—in this exhibit, 900 of them. This is because, in addition to the 500 entrepreneurs with a return greater than $75,000, there are also 400 entrepreneurs with a return between $25,000 and $75,000, so the total number of entrepreneurs with a return greater than or equal to $25,000 is 900. This reasoning immediately implies that the return-to-entrepreneurship curve is downward-sloping—as we consider a lower return, there will be more entrepreneurs with at least that return.

The horizontal line in red shows the opportunity cost of entrepreneurship, which is assumed to be the same for all potential entrepreneurs. This could be, for example, how much they would earn if they were to choose another occupation.

Panel (a) of the exhibit considers the general question of entry into entrepreneurship, which is determined by whether one's returns to entrepreneurship are above or below one's opportunity cost. Consider an entrepreneur in panel (a) with a return given by point A, whom we will call Entrepreneur A. Because this point is above the horizontal line, this individual has a greater return from entrepreneurship ($75,000) than her opportunity cost, which is at $50,000 in this exhibit. Therefore, she will choose to become an entrepreneur. On the other hand, an entrepreneur with a return given by point B (Entrepreneur B) will not do so because this point is below the horizontal line, and thus the return ($25,000) falls short of her opportunity cost ($50,000). This reasoning establishes that there will be entry into entrepreneurship until the point marked E_1 is reached. At this point, the return to entrepreneurship and the opportunity cost are both $50,000, so any additional entrepreneur will be indifferent between entering into or exiting entrepreneurship. Thus, point E_1 determines the equilibrium level of entrepreneurship in our economy.

How do extractive economic institutions change this picture? First consider the implications of insecure property rights, which are investigated in panel (b). Under insecure property rights, an entrepreneur will not be able to capture all of the returns that he or she creates; for example, the government or some other group may expropriate the returns of his or her enterprise. Suppose, for example, that insecure property rights imply that Entrepreneur A will be able to keep only $25,000 out of her $75,000 return, and that the remaining $50,000 will be expropriated or paid as bribes. Because all entrepreneurs similarly can keep less of what they make under insecure property rights, the return-to-entrepreneurship schedule will shift to the left.

Entrepreneur A also illustrates how extractive economic institutions affect overall entrepreneurship in the economy. This individual's return to entrepreneurship, $75,000, was initially above the opportunity cost schedule. But with insecure property rights, she can make only $25,000, which is less than her opportunity cost of $50,000, as indicated by the fact that the new point describing Entrepreneur A's situation, point A', now lies below the opportunity cost line.

We can then see that as a result of the shift, the new equilibrium will be at point E_2, which involves strictly less entrepreneurship. Less entrepreneurship implies less business creation, less technology adoption, lower returns to education and capital accumulation, and therefore a lower level of GDP. Thus one effect of extractive economic institutions, working in this instance through insecure property rights, is to reduce entrepreneurship and GDP.

Extractive economic institutions distort economic activity not only by creating insecure property rights but also by making it more costly or impossible to write contracts with suppliers, to borrow money, or to use the courts to uphold business arrangements. For example, say that an entrepreneur would make $75,000 if she could engage the right supplies for her business. But without courts to uphold her contracts, she cannot make the deals necessary for obtaining supplies, and this lack of legal backup will reduce her returns from entrepreneurship by $50,000. These effects will also shift the return-to-entrepreneurship schedule to the left, as shown in panel (b), with the same result of depressing entrepreneurship and GDP in the economy.

Finally, extractive economic institutions can create entry barriers, preventing otherwise profitable businesses from being founded, and may also encourage entrepreneurs to engage in other, nonproductive activities rather than entrepreneurship (for example, joining the underground economy). These factors thus increase the opportunity cost of entrepreneurship, as shown in panel (c) of the exhibit. Using the same numerical example as in panel (b), we can see that without entry barriers, entrepreneurs who can generate returns greater than $50,000 will open businesses (see the light red line on the graph). But if each entrepreneur also has to get a license that costs $25,000, only entrepreneurs who have returns greater than $75,000 will find it profitable to enter (see the dark red line on the graph, now shifted upward). We interpret this additional $25,000 as shifting the opportunity cost upward because it is a cost that entrepreneurs have to pay before they enter, therefore making their second-best alternative more attractive by $25,000. Thus panel (c) of the exhibit simultaneously shows two possible implications of extractive economic institutions:

1. By creating insecure property rights and limiting legal backup, they make entrepreneurship less profitable and shift the return-to-entrepreneurship schedule to the left.
2. By erecting entry barriers, they make entry more costly and shift the opportunity cost schedule upward.

The resulting equilibrium, shown at E_3, now corresponds to even less entrepreneurship. As before, an economy at point E_3, with less entrepreneurship, will have lower prosperity than point E_1 because—as more potential entrepreneurs are discouraged—investment, business creation, and technological development are held back, and the economy generates a lower level of GDP.

The Logic of Extractive Economic Institutions

Exhibit 22.4 shows how extractive economic institutions tend to reduce entrepreneurship and economic activity, thus adversely affecting economic outcomes. It clarifies how there may be large differences in prosperity between two otherwise similar societies that differ in terms of their institutions—one having inclusive economic institutions similar to those in South Korea, and the other one having extractive economic institutions as in North Korea.

But why would a society adopt extractive economic institutions in the first place, particularly as they seem to lead to relative poverty and a lack of economic development? It might seem obvious that everyone should have an interest in creating the type of economic institutions that will bring prosperity. Wouldn't every citizen, every politician, and even a predatory dictator want to make their countries as wealthy as they could?

Unfortunately for the citizens of many countries in the world, the answer is no. To understand why, we turn to a concept first proposed by the famous Austrian economist Joseph Schumpeter.[11] Schumpeter emphasized the notion of *creative destruction* as a central element of technological change. **Creative destruction** refers to the process in which new technologies replace old ones, new businesses replace old ones, and new skills make old ones redundant. The process of creative destruction implies that technological change, which, as we saw in Chapter 21, is the main driver of economic growth, also creates economic losers as it replaces otherwise profitable firms or technologies with new ones. Because creative destruction is an inseparable part of the process of technological change and economic growth, there will be firms and individuals that will lose as a result of this process and will be opposed to it, and this opposition to technological change can provide support for the continuation of extractive economic institutions.

Extending Schumpeter's ideas, we can also introduce the notion of **political creative destruction**, which refers to the process in which economic growth destabilizes existing regimes and reduces the political power of rulers. This might be because new technologies will also bring new actors on the scene who will make political demands, or because new economic activities may fall outside of the control of existing rulers. If the process of economic growth is also associated with political creative destruction, then we would expect that the politically powerful who fear losing their privileged positions will be opposed to this process.

In the context of North Korea, for example, the communist elites are powerful and enjoy a privileged position. The current leader, Kim Jong-Un, and his cronies could open up the

Creative destruction refers to the process in which new technologies replace old ones, new businesses replace existing businesses, and new skills make old ones redundant.

Political creative destruction refers to the process in which economic growth destabilizes existing regimes and reduces the political power of rulers.

economy, let markets work, allow citizens to open businesses and import technologies, and start strengthening their ties with South Korea and the West. All these initiatives would kick-start economic growth and lift millions of North Koreans out of poverty. But this process would also allow new leaders to emerge—and perhaps also discredit the old leadership that has kept the country in poverty for so long. Because Kim and his allies put their own interests ahead of those of ordinary North Koreans, they prefer to maintain the status quo rather than reform economic institutions to enhance economic growth.

In fact, fear of creative destruction and political creative destruction makes many rulers, not just communist dictators, explicitly ban the adoption of new technologies and block the process of economic development.

> **Fear of creative destruction and political creative destruction makes many rulers . . . explicitly ban the adoption of new technologies and block the process of economic development.**

Inclusive Economic Institutions and the Industrial Revolution

We saw in Chapter 21 how the process of technological change gathered speed during the Industrial Revolution in Britain, which first involved a series of major innovations in textiles that then spread to other areas—for instance, resulting in the famous advances in the steam engine, which laid the foundation of modern production as well as the railroad.

LETTING THE DATA SPEAK

Blocking the Railways

A key technology fueling the process of economic growth during the nineteenth century was the railroad. Rapid railway construction reduced transport costs and permitted greater and cheaper trade within and between countries. By 1860, Britain had laid 9,073 miles of railways, Germany 6,890 miles, and the United States 30,626 miles.

While many countries were investing in railways rapidly, two of the most powerful empires in continental Europe—Russia and Austria-Hungary—did not. Russia started doing so only after its bitter defeat in the Crimean war in 1856. Even in the early twentieth century, the number of railway journeys per inhabitant per year was 21.9 in Britain, but only 1.7 in Central and Eastern Europe.

Why did Russia and Austria-Hungary not invest in railways?

The answer is related to political creative destruction. The monarchs in both countries feared that railways and the accompanying process of industrialization would undermine their power and destabilize their regimes. For example, Francis I, who ruled Austria-Hungary in the early nineteenth century, and his right-hand man, Klemens von Metternich, were opposed to industrialization and railways. When the English philanthropist Robert Owen tried to convince the government of Austria-Hungary that some social reforms were necessary to improve the living standards of the citizens, one of Metternich's assistants, Frederick Gentz, replied:

> We do not desire at all that the great masses shall become well off and independent. . . . How could we otherwise rule over them?

This attitude is likely what made Francis I and Metternich oppose railway construction because it would make their subjects more difficult to rule.

This was also the view of Nikolai I, who ruled the Russian Empire between 1825 and 1855. He thought that the railways were the harbinger of worker unrest, industrial demands, and instability, so he opposed them. Austria-Hungary and Russia thus blocked technology adoption and economic development because they feared the political instability that they would bring.

The blocking of productive technologies is not something that just happened in history. The Internet is one of the most important technologies of today and offers a huge amount of information to individuals and firms, as well as a platform for the expression of ideas and media. But according to the organization Reporters Without Borders, Bahrain, Belarus, Myanmar, Cuba, Iran, North Korea, Saudi Arabia, Syria, Turkmenistan, and Uzbekistan seriously curtail the use of the Internet or suppress online expression. As was the case with Russia and Austria-Hungary in the nineteenth century, oftentimes these policies are related to political creative destruction: limiting the content that can be accessed online is a strategy to control dissent and maintain political power.

Economic historians have long debated why the Industrial Revolution took place in Britain rather than in France or some other European nation or in China, and why it started in the second half of the eighteenth century instead of some other time in history.

A complex social and economic process such as the Industrial Revolution seldom has a single cause. Economic historians have come up with scores of explanations for why it occurred. Despite this variety, though, many of these explanations either depend on Britain's relatively inclusive economic institutions or simply take them as given. This is because it would be next to impossible to imagine how the Industrial Revolution could have taken place in Britain without such inclusive economic institutions.[12] The defining characteristic of the Industrial Revolution was that new technologies were being developed and implemented by businessmen for profit. Without secure property rights, these businessmen would not have been encouraged to seek and undertake such innovations. The innovations were profitable, in turn, because Britain already had a well-developed market system, and those who could adopt new technologies to improve quality and reduce costs in textiles and other areas could reach a larger market and make sizable profits.

Britain also had a patent system that allowed the inventors of new technologies to protect their property rights not only in tangible assets but also in ideas. In fact, the protection of new ideas and innovations, just like the protection of other economic assets, was a major impetus to innovation and technological change in Britain.

Britain, in contrast to many other countries in the eighteenth century, also allowed relatively free entry into different lines of business. Although different interests tried to block entry of competitors and were sometimes successful in this endeavor (as when woolen manufacturers temporarily convinced Parliament to ban cotton imports), these entry barriers were often short-lived. By international standards, Britain gradually created a much more level playing field for its potential businesspeople. These institutional features of British society were the key prerequisites for the Industrial Revolution.

Notably, British economic institutions were also supported by the appropriate political institutions. The development of these economic institutions was preceded by major political reforms, in particular the Glorious Revolution of 1688, which introduced a constitutional monarchy and considerable constraints on the political powers of the monarch. The political institutions enshrined in the Glorious Revolution and further developed in the subsequent century were the bulwarks upon which the inclusive economic institutions that underpinned the Industrial Revolution were built.

Evidence-Based Economics

Q: Are tropical and semitropical areas condemned to poverty by their geographies?

How do we determine whether tropical geographic conditions condemn a nation to poverty? We cannot do this by varying a nation's geography and seeing whether this affects its long-run economic development because, by definition, geographic conditions are largely immutable.

To gauge the importance of geographic factors in differences in prosperity and poverty, we can look at whether countries with the same geographic conditions have significantly changed their relative prosperity as their institutions have changed. We have already seen one example of the profound effect of institutions on prosperity in this chapter: North Korea and South Korea. In this section, we answer our opening question by looking at another interesting historical episode.

Europeans came to dominate much of the world starting in the late fifteenth century after they went around the southern end of Africa to reach the Indian Ocean and they discovered the New World. These events led to the process of colonization, in which European nations built new colonies around the world and came to conquer many

Evidence-Based Economics *(Continued)*

Are the more than one billion poor people in tropical and semitropical parts of the world condemned to poverty by the climate and geography of the countries they live in?

existing empires and states. Many of the non-European parts of the world were under their command at one point or another during the 500 years between the end of the fifteenth century and the middle of the twentieth century.

Europeans set up very different institutions in various parts of the world. We in the United States live in a former European colony, and the strength of our institutions today has a lot to do with the fact that Europeans set up a very different system in North America than in other colonies. Political participation quickly became relatively broad in North America and, equally importantly, production came to be supported by fairly inclusive economic institutions. Small agricultural holders were the main producers in the early stages of the American colonies. Though many Europeans first came to North America as indentured servants who were obliged to supply their labor at a very low wage to those who brought them to the new continent, they soon largely acquired economic and political rights and became citizens with relatively secure property rights.

The situation could not have been more different in other colonies. Like North America, Barbados and Jamaica were British colonies. But the British did not set up inclusive economic institutions in these islands. Rather, they developed as clear exemplars of extractive economic institutions: they were plantation economies, with a small minority dominating a majority brought over as slaves from Africa. Slaves had no political rights and essentially no economic rights. They were forced to work for very long hours. Their situation was so terrible that many of them died from the onerous work and the unsanitary conditions in which they were kept. These people could not effectively defend their interests because under the law of the land, the plantation owners controlled all of the power and all of the guns.

These types of extractive economic institutions were not just confined to the Caribbean islands, where the majority of the population consisted of imported slaves. The living conditions of the native population areas that now correspond to Mexico, Guatemala, Peru, and Bolivia were only a little better. The descendants of the Mayas, Incas, and Aztecs were stripped of all rights (not that they had many before the Europeans arrived) and were forced to work in mines and on agricultural estates for low wages and under violent threats. These people also did not have any political representation, and their property rights were far from secure.

In sum, Europeans set up widely different economic institutions. In some places, they were inclusive; in others, highly extractive. Given this variation in institutions, we can try to evaluate whether it is the institutions that matter or whether some parts of the world are condemned to poverty by their geography. In particular, we can achieve this by examining how relative prosperity has changed after European colonization in different areas that were part of the European empire.

But there is a problem. How do we measure the GDP per capita and prosperity of places 500 years ago? Today, we can use the national income accounts, as we saw in Chapter 19. But the inhabitants of the Caribbean islands or the Aztecs and the Incas, let alone the Native Americans occupying the North American plains, did not have national income accounts.

Fortunately, we can use measurements of urbanization (the fraction of the population living in urban centers with 5,000 or more inhabitants) as a fairly good proxy for measuring the prosperity of a nation. This is because only countries that can generate sufficient agricultural surplus and develop a transportation and trading network to bring this surplus to cities can support a large urban population. Much historical evidence documents a causal relationship between urbanization and prosperity. Even in the late twentieth century, when many nations around the world had long been industrialized, there was still a very strong association between GDP per capita and urbanization.

Exhibit 22.5 The Relationship Between Urbanization and GDP per Capita in 2010

This exhibit shows the relationship between urbanization (as measured by the fraction of the population living in urban centers with more than 5,000 inhabitants) and GDP per capita (in PPP-adjusted 2005 constant dollars) in 2010 together with the best-fit line. It suggests that even today, urbanization is a good proxy for prosperity.

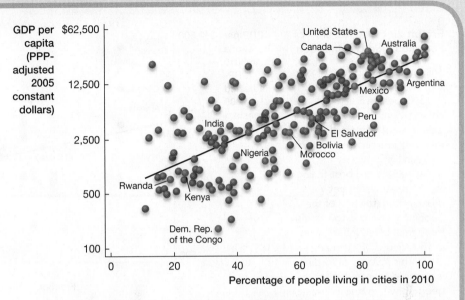

Sources: Data from Penn World Table (2010) and World Bank DataBank: World Development Indicators (2010). Alan Heston, Robert Summers and Bettina Aten, Penn World Table Version 7.1, Center for International Comparisons of Production, Income and Prices at the University of Pennsylvania (Nov 2012).

Exhibit 22.5 shows this relationship in 2010. On the vertical axis, we have GDP per capita (in PPP-adjusted 2005 constant dollars) and on the horizontal axis, we have the fraction of the population living in urban centers with 5,000 or more inhabitants. The exhibit shows that even today there is a fairly strong positive association between urbanization and GDP per capita.

Exhibit 22.6 shows the relationship between urbanization in 1500, estimated from various historical sources, and GDP per capita today. The remarkable thing that the exhibit reveals is what we call "the reversal of fortune," as shown by the best-fit line in this figure. This reversal differs from the pattern of persistent prosperity that we are generally used to seeing around the world. As we saw in Chapter 21, most of the countries that are rich today are those that were rich 50 years ago or even 100 years ago. Thus, holding all else equal, we expect to see the persistence of relative prosperity over time. We would therefore expect areas that were highly urbanized centuries ago to still be the ones that are relatively prosperous today, even if some of their advantage may have been eroded.

But Exhibit 22.6 shows something very different. The areas that were relatively more urbanized in 1500, and thus relatively more prosperous, today are generally poorer. In 1500, places like Mexico, Peru, North Africa, and India were relatively more prosperous than the parts of North America that were later to become the United States and Canada, Australia, New Zealand, and Argentina, which were sparsely populated and scarcely urbanized. Today, the picture has changed. There is a sharp reversal.

Admittedly, Exhibit 22.6 uses a limited sample that excludes sub-Saharan African countries, for which we do not have urbanization data in 1500. But we can extend the sample by using another proxy. The same reasoning that led to the use of urbanization rates as a proxy for prosperity also suggests that we can use population density as a proxy. Only areas with sufficient agricultural surplus, a developed trading and transport structure, and sufficiently healthy living conditions can support a high population density. We therefore adopt this approach in Exhibit 22.7 to include data from places like sub-Saharan Africa. Even with this larger sample, the reversal of fortune persists: areas that were relatively more prosperous as measured by their population density in 1500 are today relatively less prosperous.

Exhibit 22.6 The Reversal of Fortune Using Urbanization

The former European colonies that were more prosperous in 1500, before European colonization, as proxied by their level of urbanization, are relatively less prosperous today. This can be shown by the negatively sloped best-fit line for the relationship between urbanization (fraction of the population living in towns with more than 5,000 inhabitants) in 1500 and GDP per capita in 2010. This reversal of fortune is strong evidence against the geography hypothesis because the relative prosperity of these nations has changed greatly while potential geographic determinants of prosperity haven't.

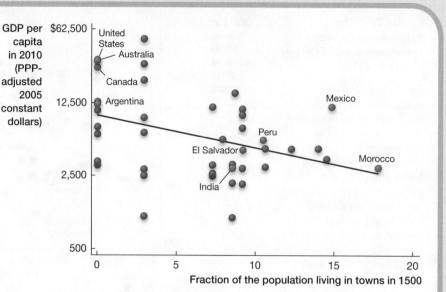

Sources: Data from Penn World Table (2010) and Acemoglu, Johnson, and Robinson (2002). Alan Heston, Robert Summers and Bettina Aten, Penn World Table Version 7.1, Center for International Comparisons of Production, Income and Prices at the University of Pennsylvania (Nov 2012); and Daron Acemoglu, Simon Johnson, and James A. Robinson, "Reversal of Fortune: Geography and Institutions in the Making of the Modern World Income Distribution," *Quarterly Journal of Economics* 117, no. 4 (2002): 1231–1294.

Exhibit 22.7 The Reversal of Fortune Using Population Density

There is also a strong negative relationship between population density in 1500, another potential proxy for prosperity before European colonization, and prosperity today. Colonized areas that were capable of supporting larger populations (per acre of arable land) in 1500 are less prosperous today. This pattern is another piece of evidence against the geography hypothesis and is consistent with the role of institutions in shaping prosperity. That is, the reversal in the relative rankings of countries by prosperity since 1500 is largely a result of the fact that Europeans set up more extractive economic institutions in colonies that had greater population densities.

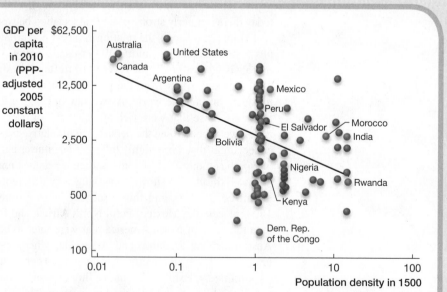

Sources: Data from Penn World Table (2010) and Acemoglu, Johnson, and Robinson (2002). Alan Heston, Robert Summers and Bettina Aten, Penn World Table Version 7.1, Center for International Comparisons of Production, Income and Prices at the University of Pennsylvania (Nov 2012); and Daron Acemoglu, Simon Johnson, and James A. Robinson, "Reversal of Fortune: Geography and Institutions in the Making of the Modern World Income Distribution," *Quarterly Journal of Economics* 117, no. 4 (2002): 1231–1294.

Understanding the Reversal of Fortune

How do we explain this reversal of fortune? One possibility could have been to appeal to geography. In fact, if we had found that places such as Mexico, India, and sub-Saharan Africa were much poorer than North America and Australia 500 years ago, it may have been plausible to think that these differences were due to geography. It could have been argued that agriculture was more productive in the temperate soils of North America and Australia than in the semitropical soils of Peru or India, and these differences were the reason why North America and Australia were richer than South America and South Asia.

But the pattern in the data shows the opposite. Five hundred years ago, many parts of South America, South Asia, North Africa, and sub-Saharan Africa were more developed than North America, Australia, and New Zealand, but today they are much poorer. Thus a geographic explanation cannot account for the patterns that we are seeing in Exhibits 22.6 and 22.7. Geographic conditions are fixed. Therefore, if the geographic conditions of Peru, India, the Caribbean, and African nations condemn them to low agricultural productivity and poverty, we should see that same poverty in 1500 as well as today. But the fact that these places were relatively more prosperous back then suggests that we must look to what actually changed between 1500 and today to understand the root of their reversal of fortune. And what changed was not these countries' geography but their institutions after European colonization.

To be fair, one could come up with more sophisticated geographical hypotheses that could account for such a reversal. For example, we could argue that geography has a time-varying effect. Perhaps the geographic characteristics that were conducive to economic growth in 1500 have become a burden.

Although this supposition is, in theory, possible, it is not plausible in practice. Today, most countries' wealth is generated by industry, trade, and services. And these are precisely the kind of economic activities that depend less on climate and more on institutions. Diseases matter today, but we are much better at controlling them, and many semitropical areas have been able to eradicate deadly diseases such as malaria. Thus, if anything, geographic handicaps such as poor soil quality, a worse disease environment, and more adverse transport conditions should have mattered much more 500 years ago than today. To the extent that sub-Saharan Africa and the tropical parts of Asia and Latin America have adverse geographic conditions, these should have disadvantaged them 500 years ago, not today. If such a sophisticated geography hypothesis were correct, today we should see them having a comparative advantage in industry and trade (the very opposite of what we see, where these poor nations are still largely agricultural).

These observations lead us to conclude that geographic characteristics are *not* the main reason why tropical and semitropical parts of the world are today much poorer than North America and Australia.

Instead, we can view the reversal of fortune as the consequence of an institutional reversal in the sense that *Europeans established more extractive economic institutions in places that were previously more developed and set up more inclusive economic institutions in places that were previously less developed.* This pattern resulted from a simple logic. European colonialism was driven by a profit motive, and in places where Europeans encountered relatively developed civilizations, it was profitable for them to set up extractive economic institutions to funnel gold, silver, and agricultural surplus to their countries and to themselves. Most importantly, they were able to use the labor in these relatively densely populated areas to achieve their objectives, often taking over the existing institutions of the empires they dominated and setting up their own extractive economic institutions.

In contrast, in areas where they did not encounter such developed civilizations and the land was sparsely settled, such as North America, Europeans themselves went in to colonize and develop institutions under which they themselves would live. They had the incentives and the ability to structure these institutions in a more inclusive fashion. As a result, the lands of the former Aztec and Inca empires—Mexico, Peru, and their surroundings—ended

Evidence-Based Economics *(Continued)*

up with extractive economic institutions, while Europeans who settled in the lands that were later to become the United States and Canada ended up with more inclusive economic institutions. This institutional reversal then led to the reversal of prosperity. Areas under inclusive economic institutions rapidly developed, particularly in the nineteenth century when they could readily adopt the new technologies of industry, while those under extractive economic institutions stagnated and grew much less rapidly.

We can now suggest an answer to the question posed in the title of this chapter: *Why isn't the whole world developed?* The answer is that inclusive economic institutions are at the root of the wealth of nations because when market participants are not harassed by excessive regulations or paralyzed by uncertainty about the future that extractive economic institutions create, they will work, invest, innovate, and create a vibrant economy where opportunities for success feed on each other. While luck does inevitably play some role in the fate of individuals even in countries with inclusive economic institutions, an uncorrupt justice system that protects life and property and an environment where risk taking and experimentation are not frowned upon are the pillars that provide economic and social incentives that enrich individuals and nations.

> **Inclusive economic institutions are at the root of the wealth of nations.**

Question

Are tropical and semitropical areas condemned to poverty by their geographies?

Answer

No. Many of these countries were relatively more prosperous 500 years ago than countries further from the equator that have become prosperous today. This reversal of fortune is not a reflection of changing geographic features but of different institutional structures (extractive versus inclusive) being imposed during European colonization.

Data

Urbanization rates and data on population density in the 1500s and data on GDP per capita and urbanization rates in 2010.

Caveat

The evidence presented here does not deny that geographic factors could play a role in economic development. Rather, it suggests that these are not the main cause of the poverty of tropical and semitropical areas today.

22.3 Is Foreign Aid the Solution to World Poverty?

In the chapter on economic growth, we discussed certain policies that can help poor countries grow. But what about foreign aid?

Many in the Western world think that, if at all feasible, we should take steps toward improving the lives of the hundreds of millions of people who live in poverty. This conviction has led to a substantial effort over the past 60 years to provide foreign aid—in fact "development aid"—to poor nations. Development aid, given by charitable organizations, the World Bank, and the United Nations, or sometimes by bilateral deals between countries, is meant to alleviate or even fundamentally eradicate poverty around the world.

A solution to world poverty? Angelina Jolie is one of many Hollywood celebrities devoting their time and money to humanitarian efforts aimed at alleviating poverty. Are these efforts likely to eradicate poverty?

Many in the international community—for example, high-level officials of the World Bank and the United Nations and several journalists and commentators—have much hope pinned on development aid. But has this type of foreign aid been effective in reducing poverty around the world?

You might at first be surprised, but economists' overall verdict is that foreign aid has been on the whole ineffective in alleviating poverty. For example, over the past 50 years, hundreds of billions of dollars have been given to Africa as development aid, but as we have seen, African nations are still much poorer than the United States or Western Europe. Why is that the case?

Though surprising at first, once we use economics to understand how foreign aid might work and recognize the difficulties faced, this conclusion turns out to be quite reasonable for three reasons. First, we know from our analysis so far that GDP per capita can be increased and economic growth can be triggered if the levels of a country's physical capital, human capital, and/or technology can be increased significantly. Although generous from the viewpoint of the donor nations, the amount of foreign aid given to even the poorest countries is not large enough to lead to a sizable increase in physical capital or to significantly increase the educational attainment of the countries' population. It also generally does not have an impact on technology or the efficiency of production. In view of this, the fact that foreign aid hasn't made significant progress in increasing GDP per capita among the poorest nations in the world shouldn't be too surprising.

Second, in practice, much of foreign aid does not even get invested in new technology or education. Problems related to corruption and political economy imply that money given to governments or other organizations in poor countries is often captured

---

 CHOICE & CONSEQUENCE

Foreign Aid and Corruption

In the 1990s, the government of Uganda spent a fifth of its budget on primary education. A sizable fraction of this money was provided by the international community as developmental aid.

When policymakers and academics evaluate the effectiveness of spending, they generally ask whether initial objectives were met and whether the benefits of a project exceeded its costs. But in the case of foreign and governmental aid, the money often does not even reach its intended target, precluding the chance to even try to use the money effectively. A survey by economists Ritva Reinikka and Jakob Svensson has revealed that only 13 percent of schools in Uganda actually received the grants to which they were entitled in the period studied.[13]

The study found that a large portion of the money intended for schools was stolen by local officials. Interestingly, the schools located in the richer regions typically received more money than the schools located in the poorer areas. This disparity appears to be partly due to the fact that schools in richer areas have more resources to start with and better connections. So they may have been able to secure more of the money that was intended for them. Very little of the intended resources for students

in the poorest regions actually reached their destination. This type of corruption and siphoning off of government resources and aid money is unfortunately all too common and poses a formidable obstacle to the effective distribution of foreign aid in many countries. As in the Ugandan case, it may often also contribute to greater inequality of resources across regions and schools within a country.

and distributed to corrupt officials. Studies indicate that only about 15 percent of any money given to foreign aid actually reaches its destination, and often it does so in a rather distorted manner.

There is also a third, and a more fundamental, reason for why foreign aid has a limited impact in alleviating poverty. If the root of poverty is the extractive economic institutions of many countries around the world, then foreign aid working within the framework of these same institutions will not fix the fundamental causes. In fact, in some instances, foreign aid funneled to dictators sitting atop of these extractive economic institutions might strengthen or enrich them, as suggested by the Choice & Consequence box on the previous page.

All of the evidence on the costs and limits of foreign aid doesn't mean that foreign aid is bad or useless. Often, foreign aid is a transfer to some of the poorest people in the world and helps alleviate their hardships, albeit temporarily, and as such serves a useful, even if limited, role. Still, we must also devote our energy to developing policies that address the fundamental causes of prosperity—like institutions—if we wish to enduringly improve living conditions in the world's impoverished countries.

Summary

☀ Physical capital, human capital, and technology are proximate causes of prosperity in the sense that, though they determine whether a nation is prosperous or not, they are themselves determined by other, deeper factors. Put differently, if we want to understand why some nations are poor, we have to ask why they do not sufficiently invest in physical capital or human capital and why they do not adopt the best technologies and organize their production efficiently.

☀ The fundamental causes of prosperity include factors that potentially influence the physical and human capital investment and technology choices of nations and, via this channel, shape their prosperity.

☀ Three leading fundamental causes of prosperity are geography, culture, and institutions. According to the geography hypothesis, geographic aspects such as climate, topography, or disease environment determine whether or not a nation can be prosperous. According to the culture hypothesis, it is the cultural values of the country's people that powerfully determine its potential for prosperity. According to the institutions hypothesis, it is the institutions, in particular the formal and informal rules governing the organization of society and economic interactions therein, that are central to prosperity.

☀ Inclusive economic institutions are those that provide secure property rights, and a judicial system that allows and facilitates private contracting and financial transactions and maintain relatively open and free entry into different businesses and occupations. Extractive economic institutions, by contrast, create insecure property rights, a partial judicial system, and entry barriers that protect the businesses and incomes of a small segment of society at the expense of the rest. According to the institutions hypothesis, inclusive economic institutions tend to generate prosperity, while extractive economic institutions do not.

☀ Though the inequalities in GDP per capita around the world have multiple causes, the evidence from the economic experiences of former European colonies suggests that institutional factors, and not geography, are central to explaining these disparities. In fact, the major patterns—for example, the reversal of fortune, whereby areas that were relatively prosperous became relatively less prosperous after European colonization—cannot be explained by geographic factors.

☀ Foreign aid can be useful to temporarily alleviate extreme poverty or manage crises but is unlikely to be a solution to low economic development in many parts of the world. This is because aid largely fails to address the institutional roots of poverty.

Key Terms

Questions

All questions are available in MyEconLab *for practice and instructor assignment.*

1. How are the proximate causes of prosperity different from the fundamental causes of prosperity?

2. What does the geography hypothesis state?

3. According to the geography hypothesis, what could be done in order to improve incomes in poor countries?

4. What does the culture hypothesis state?

5. In the context of this chapter, what is meant by an institution? What are the three important elements that define institutions?

6. How does the institutions hypothesis explain the difference in prosperity among nations?

7. What does it mean to say that private property rights are well-enforced in an economy? How does it foster economic development?

8. How do inclusive economic institutions differ from extractive economic institutions?

9. What does the return-to-entrepreneurship curve show? What is meant by the opportunity cost of entrepreneurship?

10. How does the existence of extractive institutions discourage entrepreneurship in an economy?

11. Suppose a country has well-enforced private property rights for entrepreneurs, but a large fraction of the population does not have access to education and thus cannot become entrepreneurs. Moreover, their productivity as workers is low. Would you say that this country has inclusive economic institutions? Is it likely to achieve a high level of economic development?

12. What is meant by political creative destruction? How would this concept explain the existence of extractive institutions?

13. Parts of the world that were relatively more prosperous 500 years ago have experienced a reversal of fortune and are relatively poorer today. What factors could explain this?

Problems

All problems are available in MyEconLab *for practice and instructor assignment.*

1. The chapter discusses Max Weber's argument that the origins of industrialization in Western Europe could be traced to Protestantism. According to Weber, the Protestant work ethic was crucial to the development of a market economy and economic growth. Weber, however, also claimed that religions like Confucianism in China and Hinduism in India were not conducive to the development of capitalism. Given that India and China are now among the fastest-growing economies in the world, how effective do you think the culture hypothesis is in explaining economic development?

2. After the Second World War, Germany was divided into two parts, East Germany and West Germany. East Germany was controlled by the former Soviet Union, while West Germany was controlled by the other Allied governments: the United States, the United Kingdom, and France. The war had destroyed most of Germany's economy. The Soviet Union as well as the Allied occupation forces sought to rebuild the economies of their respective parts. Before the fall of the Berlin Wall reunited East and West Germany in 1990, West Germany's economy grew at an annual average growth rate of 4.4 percent, which was about 3 times higher than East Germany's rate. Draw the parallel between the natural experiment discussed in the chapter and the case of East and West Germany. Based on the information given in the question and your own research, why do you think two otherwise similar areas had such divergent growth rates?

3. Suppose the country of Burondo is one of the poorest countries in the world. Its economy is heavily reliant on income from the export of oil. There are only two oil-extracting companies in Burondo. Both are owned by the government. A large part of the earnings from oil exports goes toward financing the president's lifestyle and entourage. Burondo has not had a single democratic election ever since it gained independence 50 years ago. Although Burondo is said to have abundant oil resources, only a small proportion is extracted every year because the extraction process is so inefficient. Transporting goods in and out of the country is costly, as Burondo is surrounded by lofty mountain

ranges. School enrollment in this country is very low and as a result, most of the adult population is illiterate. Life expectancy is also quite low. Agriculture is collectivized in Burondo and so food shortages are common in the country.

Using the information given, distinguish between the fundamental and proximate causes of prosperity (or its absence) in Burondo.

4. Look at the following map of Nogales, a twin city that is divided by the U.S. border.

One part of Nogales lies in the United States, in Arizona, and the other part lies in Sonora, Mexico. Life in Nogales, Mexico is very different from life in Nogales, Arizona. The average income in Nogales, Mexico is about one-third the average income in Nogales, Arizona. Education levels, life expectancy, and health conditions are better in Nogales, Arizona than in Nogales, Mexico. Unlike Nogales in Arizona, Nogales in Mexico has only recently adopted political reforms, bringing it closer to functioning as a democracy. Crime rates are also lower in Nogales, Arizona than in Nogales, Mexico. Since both cities are located so close to each other, they share similar geographical conditions and climate. The inhabitants of both cities also share a common ancestry and enjoy the same types of food and music.

Based on this information and your own research, what factors do you think can explain why Nogales, Arizona is so much more prosperous than Nogales, Mexico?

5. Zimbabwe, formerly known as Rhodesia, was a British colony for around ninety years. It became independent in 1980. The prime minister of newly formed Zimbabwe, Robert Mugabe, implemented a forced land redistribution policy, in which commercial farms were confiscated from white farmers. Mugabe also proceeded to confiscate shares in companies owned by whites. In the following years, agricultural production in the country fell sharply. Zimbabwe, the country that used to be called the breadbasket of Africa, is now seeing food shortages in certain parts of the country.

a. Would Zimbabwe be considered to have extractive or inclusive institutions? Explain your answer.

b. Why would a government undertake policies that would adversely affect the lives of its citizens? Explain your answer with reference to the Zimbabwean situation.

6. The chapter points out how important entrepreneurship is to economic growth, and discusses the factors that foster or exhibit the activities of entrepreneurs.

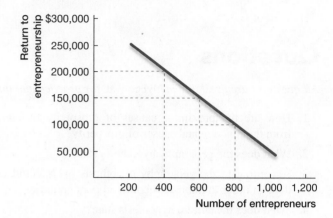

a. The above graph shows the return-to-entrepreneurship curve in a certain country. If the opportunity cost of entrepreneurship in this country is $150,000, find the equilibrium level of entrepreneurship in the economy.

b. Suppose the government of this country decided to expropriate the assets of private firms. Expropriation here means that the government is either taking away the assets of private firms or forcing their owners to sell at low prices. What do you think will happen to the equilibrium level of entrepreneurship in the economy? Use the graph to explain your answer.

c. Suppose the government reduces the fee that needs to be paid to obtain a trade license in this country. Other things remaining the same, how will this policy affect entrepreneurship? Use your graph from part a to explain your answer.

7. Using a graph like the one in the chapter showing returns to entrepreneurship and the opportunity cost of entrepreneurship, illustrate how each of the following historical events shifted one (or both) of the curves.

a. Between 1959 and 1963, the Cuban government passed a series of laws called the Agrarian Reform Laws. These laws expropriated any landholdings above a certain size and turned them over to peasants and cooperatives.

b. From independence in 1947 until the 1990s, there was in place in India that came to be known as the "Paper Raj." The term referred to a series of rules and regulations that put strict controls on business, and forced business owners to navigate a bureaucratic labyrinth in order to start and run their companies. For example, one entrepreneur complained that simply to import a computer, he had to make 50 trips to New Delhi to get the necessary permits. Starting in the 1990s, many of these restrictions were abolished. A series of reforms made it much easier for firms to conduct business. (Based on the series *Commanding Heights*, PBS, 2002.)

c. In 2007 and 2008, the Venezuelan dictator Hugo Chavez nationalized many large firms in several key sectors of the country's economy, including telecommunications, electric utilities, steel, and banking. Subsequently, taxes on banking and other activities were also raised significantly.

8. Suppose the return and cost of entrepreneurship curves are described by the following equations (with numbers measured in the thousands):

$$R = 250,000 - 50,000N,$$
$$C = 50,000 + 150,000N,$$

where

R = returns to entrepreneurship,

C = cost of entrepreneurship,

N = number of entrepreneurs.

a. Based on the equations given, how does the cost of entrepreneurship curve differ (in overall shape) from the one drawn in the chapter? Explain how this difference might arise.

b. Find the equilibrium number of entrepreneurs in this economy and the equilibrium returns to entrepreneurship.

c. The government enacts a license fee of $50,000 to file the paperwork necessary to start a firm. What is now the equilibrium number of entrepreneurs and the equilibrium returns to entrepreneurship?

9. Jointly published by the *Wall Street Journal* and The Heritage Foundation, "The Freedom Index" gives an annual ranking of most of the countries of the world based on their level of economic freedom. Factors considered in the rankings include the status of property rights, the extent of corruption, and the ease of starting and running a business. The index can be found at http://www.heritage.org/index/.

a. Go to http://www.heritage.org/index/ranking and find three countries in each of the freedom categories ("Free," "Mostly Free," etc.). Click on the country name in the table for each country you select, and read about the rationale for their ranking. Provide a summary for the nations you selected.

b. Now go to http://www.heritage.org/index/explore?view=by-variables. Note the per capita GDP of the three countries you selected in each category, and calculate the average of the three you selected in each category.

What pattern do you notice? What preliminary conclusions can you draw concerning the relationship between economic freedom and economic development? Which of the three hypotheses mentioned in the chapter do your results tend to support? Explain.

c. Sub-Saharan Africa is known to be one of the poorest regions of the world. Go to the "Interactive Freedom Heat Map" at http://www.heritage.org/index/heatmap. Into which freedom categories do the majority of countries of the region fall? Which two countries are the exceptions to the overall pattern?

10. Initial phases of the growth process are often accompanied by increasing income inequality within a country. Using the concepts developed in the chapter, explain why this might be the case.

11. Which of the three hypotheses developed in the chapter would be most likely to view foreign aid as essential for economic development? Explain.

12. In his book *The Elusive Quest for Growth*, development economist William Easterly discusses the relationship between foreign aid and investment in poor countries. He posits that to establish the effectiveness of aid in promoting investment, two tests should be passed: First, there should be a positive statistical association between aid and investment; second, aid should pass into investment 1 for 1, that is, a 1 percent (of GDP) increase in aid should result in a 1 percent (of GDP) increase in investment. Using a dataset of 88 countries from 1965 to 1995, he finds that only 17 of 88 countries pass the first test, and of them, only 6 pass the second.

Based on the information in the chapter, and perhaps your own reading, explain why foreign aid designed to spur investment usually does not work.

23 Employment and Unemployment

What happens to employment and unemployment if local employers go out of business?

Economic shocks frequently hit local communities. A weak car market causes Ford to shutter an assembly plant. A weak regional economy causes a big-box-retailer—like JCPenney, Kmart, or Sears—to shut one of its megastores. Falling coal prices cause a mining company to mothball an open-pit coal mine. Competition from new suppliers causes a clothing company to close a textile factory. Do the workers who lose these jobs quickly find new ones? Do the local labor markets quickly bounce back? Or do these communities experience persistent unemployment?

In this chapter, we study the determinants of employment and unemployment, and investigate how various economic shocks affect the labor market equilibrium.

CHAPTER **OUTLINE**

23.1 Measuring Employment and Unemployment

After 17 months of unsuccessful job applications, one unemployed worker wrote in a letter to the *New York Times* that "nothing stops the omnipresent feeling of loneliness, worthlessness and desperation."[1] For most people, enduring a long period of unemployment takes a terrible toll on their well-being. Long-term unemployment generates three simultaneous traumas: a loss of income, a loss of skills, and a loss of perceived self-worth.

> **Because of its enormous economic and social costs, politicians and policymakers try to limit the amount of unemployment in an economy.**

Because of its enormous economic and social costs, policymakers try to limit the amount of unemployment in an economy. To do so, they must have a way of measuring and tracking unemployment over time. Unfortunately, just measuring unemployment is challenging. For example, it seems reasonable that a 30-year-old without a job who is actively looking for work should count as unemployed. But should we also count another 30-year-old who has lost a job but has decided *not* to look for work? What about full-time college students or stay-at-home parents: people who are busy and work hard but don't receive a paycheck for their labor?

Economists have agreed on a standard, though nevertheless controversial, way of defining employment and unemployment. In the United States, this standard is set by the Bureau of Labor Statistics (BLS) in the Department of Labor, which tracks the official employment statistics for the U.S. economy. We describe the BLS definition here.

Classifying Potential Workers

To determine who is employed and unemployed, we start by identifying the population of workers whose employment behavior we want to measure. This group includes everyone in the general population with three exceptions: children under 16 years of age, people on active duty in the military, and institutionalized people, like those in nursing homes or jail. The BLS calls the remaining population the *civilian non-institutional population ages 16 and over*. For simplicity, we'll refer to them as **potential workers**. In January 2014, the United States had 246.9 million potential workers.

Potential workers includes everyone in the general population with three exceptions: children under 16 years of age, people on active duty in the military, and institutionalized people, like those in nursing homes or jail.

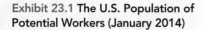

Exhibit 23.1 The U.S. Population of Potential Workers (January 2014)

The population of potential workers is 246.9 million people—otherwise known as the civilian non-institutional population ages 16 and over. Potential workers can be divided into three subgroups: employed workers (145.2 million), unemployed workers (10.2 million), and those not in the labor force (91.5 million). The labor force is the combination of the employed and unemployed workers (155.5 million with rounding).

Source: U.S. Bureau of Labor Statistics.

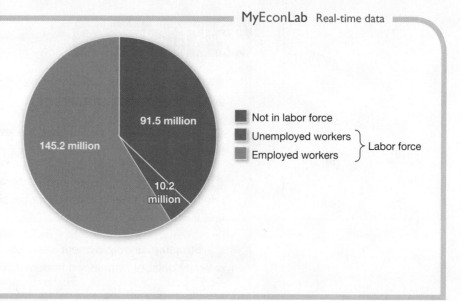

Within the population of potential workers, people are classified into one of three categories: "employed," "unemployed," or "not in the labor force." Those holding full-time or part-time *paid* jobs are officially classified as **employed**. In other words, as long as a person works for pay at least part-time, she is classified as employed. Using the official definition, in January 2014, there were 145.2 million employed workers in the United States.

> A person holding a full-time or part-time paid job is **employed.**

Potential workers are classified as **unemployed** if they do not have a paid job, have actively looked for work in the prior four weeks, and are currently available for work. This definition of unemployment makes it easy to classify the workers we had trouble considering above. Laid-off workers will only be considered unemployed if they are actively looking for a new job. Similarly, students and parents who don't have a paid job and aren't looking for one will not count as unemployed. In January 2014, there were 10.2 million unemployed workers in the United States.

> A worker is **unemployed** if she does not have a job, has actively looked for work in the prior four weeks, and is currently available for work.

The **labor force** is the sum of all employed and unemployed workers:

$$\text{Labor force} = \text{Employed} + \text{Unemployed}.$$

> The **labor force** is the sum of all employed and unemployed workers.

Finally, all potential workers who don't fit the criteria for being employed or unemployed are classified as "not in the labor force." People in this category include the stay-at-home parents and students as well as disabled workers, retirees, and any other potential workers who don't have a paid job and aren't looking for one. In January 2014, 91.5 million potential workers were not in the labor force. Exhibit 23.1 depicts the relationship between potential workers, employed workers, unemployed workers, and those not in the labor force.

Calculating the Unemployment Rate

Using these classifications, economists calculate a number of statistics to describe the labor market. The **unemployment rate** is defined as the percentage of the labor force that is unemployed:

> The **unemployment rate** is the percentage of the labor force that is unemployed.

$$\text{Unemployment rate} = 100\% \times \frac{\text{Unemployed}}{\text{Labor force}}$$

$$= 100\% \times \frac{\text{Unemployed}}{\text{Employed} + \text{Unemployed}}$$

Similarly, the **labor force participation rate** is defined as the percentage of potential workers that are in the labor force:

> The **labor force participation rate** is the percentage of potential workers that are in the labor force.

$$\text{Labor force participation rate} = 100\% \times \frac{\text{Labor force}}{\text{Potential workers}}$$

Using these equations and our numbers from before, we can calculate what the labor force, unemployment rate, and labor force participation rate were in January 2014. The components are rounded, which explains why the first sum doesn't match exactly.

$$\text{Labor force} = \text{Employed} + \text{Unemployed} = 145.2 \text{ million} + 10.2 \text{ million}$$
$$= 155.5 \text{ million}.$$

$$\text{Unemployment rate} = 100\% \times \frac{\text{Unemployed}}{\text{Labor force}} = 100\% \times \frac{10.2 \text{ million}}{155.5 \text{ million}} = 6.6\%.$$

$$\text{Labor force participation rate} = 100\% \times \frac{\text{Labor force}}{\text{Potential workers}} = 100\% \times \frac{155.5 \text{ million}}{246.9 \text{ million}}$$
$$= 63.0\%.$$

While these calculations reflect the main way that economists measure unemployment, it's important to note that they are just summaries and therefore leave out many important details. In particular, the way we officially count unemployed workers omits two important categories of workers who are frustrated by the lack of jobs: discouraged workers and underemployed workers.

Discouraged workers are potential workers who would like to have a job but have given up looking for one. Because they are not actively looking for work, these workers are not included in the unemployment rate as we defined it above. Instead, discouraged workers will be counted as out of the labor force. There were 837,000 discouraged workers in the United States in January 2014, representing 0.5 percent of the labor force.

Similarly, we count all paid workers as employed, even if they would like to work more hours. Many workers in difficult economic circumstances would like to work more hours to support themselves and their families but don't have the option to do so. Although such workers are *underemployed*, they are not included in the official unemployment statistic. There were 7.3 million underemployed workers in the United States in January 2014, representing 4.7 percent of the labor force.

Trends in the Unemployment Rate

As the overall economy fluctuates, so does the unemployment rate. When the overall economy suffers a *recession*—a period in which GDP falls—the unemployment rate tends to rise. During typical U.S. recessions the unemployment rate reaches a level between 6 percent and 9 percent. When the economy is healthy and expanding, the unemployment rate tends to fall to around 5 percent.

Severe recessions produce the largest increases in the unemployment rate. For example, in early 2007—before the start of the recession later that year—the U.S. unemployment rate hovered around 4.5 percent. The 2007–2009 recession led to a sharp rise in the unemployment rate and a peak rate of 10.0 percent in October 2009. During the Great Depression of the 1930s—the most severe contraction of the U.S. economy in the twentieth century—the unemployment rate reached 25 percent.

Exhibit 23.2 shows the evolution of the monthly unemployment rate in the U.S. economy since 1948. The unemployment rate is relatively high during and following recessions—the shaded areas on the exhibit correspond to recessions. For example, the unemployment rate was high following the oil price shocks in the mid-1970s and then again during the recession of 1981–1982. Since World War II, the peak in unemployment, 10.8 percent, occurred during the 1981–1982 recession. This peak is even higher than the 10.0 percent peak during the severe 2007–2009 recession.

It is also noteworthy that the unemployment rate is never close to zero. Since 1948, the U.S. unemployment rate has gone below 3 percent during only one period in the early 1950s. Even during the economic boom in the 1990s, the unemployment rate reached a low of only around 4 percent. Later in this chapter, we'll explain why some amount of unemployment—usually around 4 percent or 5 percent—is a necessary attribute of a well-functioning modern economy, while an unemployment rate of 10 percent is a national crisis that policymakers actively try to avoid.

Some amount of unemployment— usually around 4 percent or 5 percent—is a necessary attribute of a well-functioning modern economy.

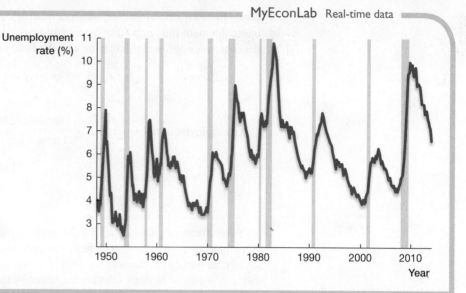

Exhibit 23.2 The U.S. Unemployment Rate from 1948 to 2014

This exhibit shows the evolution of the U.S. unemployment rate from January 1948 to January 2014 (monthly data). Shaded bars are recessions. Note that the unemployment rate increases during recessions.

Source: U.S. Bureau of Labor Statistics and FRED.

MyEconLab Real-time data

Who Is Unemployed?

The prevalence of unemployment varies widely across different segments of the labor force. One of the most noticeable disparities is that unemployment is much higher among those with low levels of education. Exhibit 23.3 shows, for example, that the unemployment rate among those in the labor force with less than a high school diploma was 11.0 percent in 2013. For people in the labor force with a college degree, the unemployment rate was only 3.7 percent.

There are many factors that explain why more educated workers tend to have lower rates of unemployment. The principle of optimization provides part of the answer. When people lose a job, they tend to spend some of their time looking for a new job and some of their time engaged in production at home. There are many "home production" activities, like cleaning out the attic or painting the house, and most of them do not require high levels of formal education. People with higher levels of education aren't necessarily more skillful in these home production activities.

However, more educated workers tend to earn higher wages than less educated workers when working *outside* the home (and this is a consequence of the fact that there is greater demand for their labor because of their additional human capital, as we have seen in Chapter 20). More educated workers therefore have a higher *opportunity cost of time.* An unemployed cab driver might be indifferent between driving a cab and staying home for a few weeks to paint his house. An unemployed engineer might be just as good at house painting as the taxi driver, but the engineer would be much better off getting back to

MyEconLab Real-time data

Exhibit 23.3 Unemployment Rates for Different Educational Groups

Unemployment rates fall as educational attainment rises. The unemployment rates are calculated for all civilian, non-institutional U.S. adults ages 25 and over. The unemployment rates in this exhibit are for 2013.

Source: U.S. Bureau of Labor Statistics.

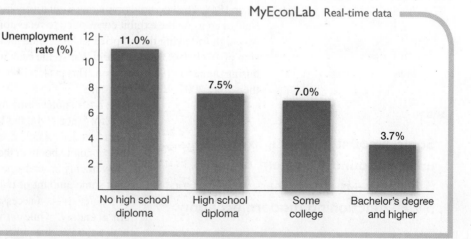

work designing robotic assembly lines, earning a relatively high income, and using some of that income to hire someone *else* to paint her house. Higher wages make the cost of unemployment higher for workers with more education. Similarly, unemployment is often much lower among middle-aged workers, who tend to have more experience and skills—and therefore higher wages—than younger workers.

23.2 Equilibrium in the Labor Market

To study how employment and unemployment are determined, we first need to understand how the labor market works. Like any other market, supply and demand play the key roles. We develop the demand curve for labor and the supply curve for labor separately and then put them together to describe the labor market equilibrium.

The Demand for Labor

When we first studied demand curves in Chapter 4, we discussed households demanding goods and services. Now that we are studying the *labor market*, the role of households flips. In the labor market, households supply labor and firms demand labor. Firms are now on the demand side because they need to hire workers for production.

Optimizing firms try to maximize profits, so they demand the quantity of labor that produces the greatest feasible *profit* (defined as revenues minus costs). How does a firm determine the profit-maximizing quantity of labor? By comparing the revenue that a worker produces with the cost of employing that worker.

To see how this works, consider a barbershop. If the barbershop has only one barber, let's assume that he'll almost always be busy cutting hair and that he'll generate revenue of $25 per hour. Let's also assume that the market wage for barbers is $15 per hour. So the barbershop earns $10 per hour by employing this first barber: $25 − $15 = $10 per hour. If the shop adds a second barber, the barbershop will sell more haircuts, but from time to time, there won't be enough customers to keep both barbers busy. So the addition of the second barber does not double sales at the barbershop. Suppose instead that the second barber increases sales by only $20 per hour. Because the market wage for barbers is $15 per hour, employing the additional barber will still increase profits by $20 − $15 = $5 per hour. So an optimizing barbershop will also hire the second barber.

Now consider what will happen if the barbershop adds a third barber. The third barber will increase sales a bit more, but will do so by even less than the addition of the second barber because it will rarely be the case that the shop has enough customers to simultaneously keep all three barbers busy. Suppose that this third barber increases sales by only $10 per hour. Because the market wage is $15 per hour, hiring this third barber will actually *lower* the profits of the barbershop ($10 − $15 = −$5), so the shop will refrain from hiring a third barber. Thus, the barbershop optimizes—in other words, maximizes its profits—by employing only two barbers.

The barbershop scenario demonstrates two important facts about labor demand. First, as we have also seen in Chapters 20 and 21, firms typically experience *diminishing marginal product* of labor. Recall that the marginal product is the amount of output that one additional worker produces. Diminishing marginal product of labor means that each additional worker creates less marginal output than the workers who were hired before. For example, additional barbers will increase the haircuts that the barbershop offfers, but each additional barber won't be as productive as the last one because there won't be enough customers to keep them all busy. Economists call the market value of a worker's marginal product the *value of the marginal product of labor*. In the barbershop, the first barber creates $25 of additional revenue, the second $20, and the third only $10. Because the value of the marginal product of each additional barber is diminishing, hiring more barbers increases the *total* revenue of a firm by less and less.

Even if a customer just walked in the door, the marginal product of the second and third barbers is still zero.

Exhibit 23.4 The Value of the Marginal Product of Labor Is the Labor Demand Curve

Because the marginal product of labor diminishes as the quantity of labor increases, the curve that plots the value of the marginal product of labor is downward-sloping. Profit maximization implies that the firm should hire workers up to the point where the market wage is equal to the value of the marginal product of labor. The value of the marginal product of labor schedule is also the labor demand curve.

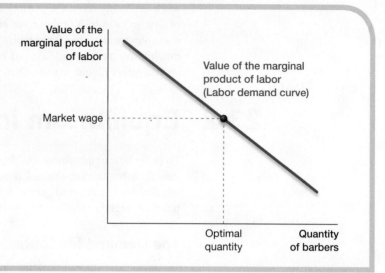

The second important fact illustrated by the barbershop example is that a firm hires workers until it cannot increase profits by hiring an additional worker. The firm keeps hiring as long as the revenue that an additional worker brings in for the firm—the value of the marginal product of labor—is at least as great as the cost of employing that worker, which is the *market wage*. To see why this is the case, consider Exhibit 23.4, which plots the value of the marginal product of labor against the number of workers employed. Because the value of the marginal product decreases as the number of workers employed increases, the curve is downward-sloping.

If the firm employs fewer workers than the optimal quantity shown in Exhibit 23.4, then it can increase profits by hiring more workers, because the revenue those workers bring in (the value of their marginal product) is greater than the cost of employing them (the market wage). Similarly, if the firm employs more workers than the optimal quantity, the firm can increase profits by laying off workers, because the revenue those workers bring in is less than the market wage, the cost of employing them.

Therefore, *the profit-maximizing firm will hire the amount of labor that makes the value of the marginal product of labor equal to the market wage.* As we change the market wage, the quantity of labor demanded moves *along* the curve depicting the value of the marginal product—the firm adjusts the number of workers it employs to make the value of the marginal product equal to the wage. Thus, the downward-sloping curve in Exhibit 23.4—the value of the marginal product of labor—is also the **labor demand curve**, because it shows how the quantity of labor demanded varies with the wage.

Shifts in the Labor Demand Curve

The labor demand curve depicts the relationship between the quantity of labor demanded and the wage. A *movement along the labor demand* curve occurs when the wage changes and no other economic variables change other than the quantity of labor demanded. On the other hand, there are many factors that cause the entire labor demand curve to shift to the left or right—as depicted in Exhibit 23.5.

Any change that affects the schedule relating the quantity of labor and the value of the marginal product of labor will shift the labor demand curve. We discuss four shifters in this section:

- **Changing output prices:** When the price of haircuts goes down, the value of the marginal product of barbers also declines. This implies that the firm would like to hire fewer barbers at any given wage, shifting the labor demand curve to the left.
- **Changing demand for the output good or service:** When the demand for haircuts declines, this will impact the value of the marginal product of barbers even if it does not directly change the price of haircuts. Falling demand for haircuts lowers the number of customers coming to the barbershop, leading each barber to spend more time waiting idly rather than cutting hair. Such declines in demand for output will shift the labor demand curve to the left.

The **labor demand curve** depicts the relationship between the quantity of labor demanded and the wage. The value of the marginal product of labor is also the labor demand curve, because they both show how the quantity of labor demanded varies with the wage.

Exhibit 23.5 Downward-Sloping Labor Demand Curve

The labor demand curve, which shows the relationship between the quantity of labor demanded and the wage, is downward-sloping. The exhibit depicts left and right shifts in the labor demand curve. The labor demand curve shifts when the quantity of labor demanded changes at a given value of the wage.

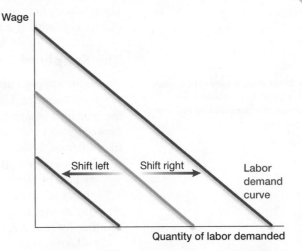

- **Changing technology:** When the value of the marginal product of labor increases, the labor demand curve shifts to the right. For example, technology that was developed in the late nineteenth century first enabled hair stylists to straighten or curl hair: "perms." The ability to offer perms increased the marginal product of hair stylists and shifted the demand curve for hair stylists to the right. Technological progress and increases in productivity typically shift the labor demand curve to the right, but in rare cases the opposite can happen. For example, machines sometimes substitute for labor and shift the labor demand curve to the left. We discuss one such example later in the chapter.
- **Changing input prices:** Businesses use labor and *other* factors of production, like machines and tools, to produce goods and services. When the cost of these other factors goes down, businesses purchase more of those other factors. This usually increases the marginal product of labor, shifting the labor demand curve to the right. For example, mechanical hair clippers enable barbers to cut hair more quickly. If a barbershop acquires more hair clippers (because the cost of hair clippers falls), the barbers will increase the number of customers that they can serve per hour.

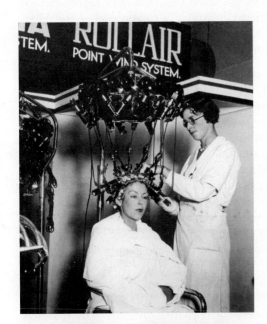

Technological innovation in the hair business. The technology for permanent waves—now called perms—was first developed in the nineteenth century and has continuously advanced since then.

Until now, we've illustrated most ideas with the labor demand curve of a single barbershop or hair stylist. To study the level of employment and unemployment in the *total* economy, we need to derive the labor demand curve of the entire economy. To derive this economy-wide, or "aggregate," labor demand curve, we proceed in two steps. First, we derive the labor demand curve for each industry. For example, this is done by adding together the labor demand curves of every barbershop. If there were 100,000 barbershops in the economy, and each hired two barbers when the wage for barbers is $15 per hour, then the total quantity of labor demanded at that wage would be 200,000 barbers. To derive the rest of the labor demand curve for this industry, we repeat this summation at every wage.

Once we have derived the labor demand curve of each industry, we can sum these industry labor demand curves to obtain the aggregate labor demand curve. In principle, we will also need to account for spillover effects among the different industries and also between workers and firms. For example, expansion in one industry might create additional demand for the products of another industry. In addition, changing the overall level of wages and employment will affect workers' demand for the products of firms. When more workers are employed, they have more income to buy the products that other workers produce. We return to these issues in Chapter 26.

Notice that we are simplifying our model by treating the economy as if it contains a *single* aggregate labor demand curve. In practice, workers have different skills and receive different wages. Nevertheless, the simplifying assumption enables us to generate key insights about how the overall economy functions without having to specify how different segments of the labor market function, even if it also means that we are omitting some interesting details about the performance of these segments.

The Supply of Labor

The **labor supply curve** represents the relationship between the quantity of labor supplied and the wage.

The **labor supply curve** represents the relationship between the quantity of labor supplied and the wage. Like the labor demand curve, the labor supply curve is derived from the principles of optimization. In this case, workers optimally allocate their limited time between paid work, leisure, and other activities, which might include home production like childcare, home maintenance, cooking, or cleaning. When market wages are higher, it makes sense for workers to spend more time working outside the home. For instance, if you are paid by the hour and your employer is running overtime shifts, you can get paid 1.5 times your normal hourly wage in those special shifts. For many workers this is a tempting arrangement, leading them to work more outside the home and accordingly have less time for chores at home or for leisure.

This kind of reasoning implies that as the wage increases, the quantity of labor supplied rises. Accordingly, the labor supply curve is upward-sloping, as shown in Exhibit 23.6.

Shifts in the Labor Supply Curve

As we have noted, the labor supply curve is the relationship between the quantity of labor supplied and the wage. A *movement along the labor* supply curve occurs when the wage changes and no other economic variables change (other than the quantity of labor supplied).

On the other hand, there are many factors that cause the entire labor supply curve to shift to the left or right (both shifts are depicted in Exhibit 23.6). *Any change that affects the entire schedule relating the quantity of labor supplied and the wage will shift the labor supply curve.* We discuss three potential changes here:

- **Changing tastes:** Changing tastes or social norms affect people's willingness to take a paid job. For example, before World War II, married women working for pay outside the home were frowned upon. However, during World War II, most governments encouraged women to work in armaments factories as an act of patriotism. Factory work during the war was one early step in a worldwide shift toward acceptance of female labor force participation. As a result of this shift in social norms, female labor force participation in the United States rose from 25 percent in 1940 to almost 60 percent in the 1990s, corresponding to a large rightward shift in the labor supply curve.
- **Changing opportunity cost of time:** Devices like vacuum cleaners, dishwashers, laundry machines, and lawnmowers lower the opportunity cost of working outside the home by freeing up time that was previously needed for home production. This encourages people to shift more time out of home production into paid employment,

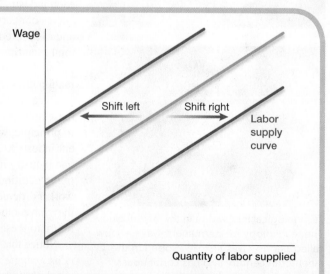

Exhibit 23.6 Upward-Sloping Labor Supply Curve

The labor supply curve, which shows the relationship between the quantity of labor supplied and the wage rate, is upward-sloping. As the wage rises (holding all else equal), people's willingness to work rises. The exhibit also depicts left and right shifts in the labor supply curve. The labor supply curve shifts when the quantity of labor supplied changes at a given value of the wage.

generating a rightward shift in the labor supply curve. This sort of technology-induced change in the opportunity cost of time has also been a factor contributing to the rise in female labor force participation.

- **Changes in population:** Increases in the size of the population, corresponding to increases in the number of potential workers in the economy, also shift the labor supply curve to the right. One factor increasing population is immigration. For example, each year, the United States experiences a net immigration inflow of roughly 1 million people, implying that the population grows one-third of 1 percent per year due to immigration. This inflow shifts the domestic U.S. labor supply curve to the right.

As with the labor demand curve, the labor supply curve of the entire economy (the "aggregate" labor supply curve) can be derived by summing over the labor supply of each potential worker in the economy.

Equilibrium in a Competitive Labor Market

Recall from Chapter 1 that we define an *equilibrium* as a situation in which nobody would benefit by changing his or her own behavior. Moreover, recall from Chapter 4 that a *competitive equilibrium* is given by the intersection of the supply and demand curves. Equilibrium in a competitive labor market works the same way. In particular, the equilibrium in a competitive labor market is given by the point of intersection between the labor supply and labor demand curves, as shown in Exhibit 23.7. At the competitive equilibrium wage, w^*, the quantity of labor supplied is equal to the quantity of labor demanded. At a wage above w^*, the quantity of labor supplied would exceed the quantity of labor demanded and push the wage down. At a wage below w^*, the quantity of labor demanded would exceed the quantity of labor supplied and push the wage up. Thus w^* is the unique wage that equates the quantity of labor supplied and the quantity of labor demanded. This *equilibrium quantity of labor*, shown by L^* in Exhibit 23.7, is also referred to as *equilibrium employment*.

We refer to the competitive equilibrium wage as the **market-clearing wage**. At this wage, every worker that wants a job can find one: the quantity of labor demanded matches the quantity of labor supplied.

We refer to the competitive equilibrium wage as the **market-clearing wage**. The label market-clearing should remind you that every worker that wants a job can (eventually) find one: the wage has adjusted so that the quantity of labor demanded matches the quantity of labor supplied. This distinguishes the market-clearing wage from the wage that results from wage rigidities, which prevents the wage from adjusting to equate the quantity of labor demanded and the quantity of labor supplied. As we'll see later in this chapter, such rigidities will generate unemployment.

We will use the labor market equilibrium depicted in Exhibit 23.7 to model the *overall* level of employment in an economy. As mentioned above, we are simplifying our analysis by focusing on a single type of labor. But the labor market equilibrium shown in Exhibit 23.7 can be readily applied to study equilibrium in a specific segment of the market

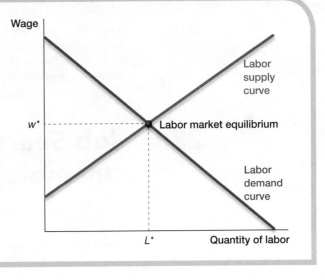

Exhibit 23.7 Equilibrium in the Labor Market

The upward-sloping labor supply curve and the downward-sloping labor demand curve intersect at the market-clearing wage, w^*, and the quantity of labor L^*. At the market-clearing wage, the quantity of labor supplied is equal to the quantity of labor demanded.

or in a local labor market as well. For example, we could consider the supply of and demand for workers with computer programming skills (or doctors or gardeners, etc.) and derive the equilibrium wage and employment level in that specific labor market.

It is useful to note that the labor market depicted in Exhibit 23.7 is what is sometimes referred to as a *frictionless* labor market. In a frictionless market, firms can instantly hire and fire workers, both workers and firms have complete information about each other, and the wage adjusts instantly to clear the market (setting the quantity of labor supplied equal to the quantity of labor demanded). We will see next why departures from this frictionless labor market are often useful for understanding real-world labor markets and unemployment.

23.3 Why Is There Unemployment?

At the market-clearing wage w^* in Exhibit 23.7, the labor supply and labor demand curves intersect. Accordingly, the quantity of labor demanded equals the quantity of labor supplied—every worker who wants to work at wage w^* has a job. There are people who are not working—represented by the segment of the labor supply curve that lies *above* the market-clearing wage. The people on this part of the labor supply curve are only willing to work for wages *above* the market-clearing wage w^*.

In the economy depicted in Exhibit 23.7, there are employed workers and workers who are not employed because they are unwilling to work at the market-clearing wage w^*. In a competitive equilibrium, there should be no workers looking for work (they are either employed or unwilling to work at the market-clearing wage). This implies that in a competitive equilibrium there shouldn't be people who are not employed and looking for work. But then, how would we explain the fact that there were 10.2 million *officially* unemployed Americans in January 2014, who are thus counted as not employed and looking for work?

A first possibility is that the official unemployment statistics are probably counting *some* workers who are only willing to work for a wage above the market-clearing wage w^*. Because unemployment survey questions do not specify that the workers should be looking for work at the *current prevailing market wage*, some people might be counted as unemployed even though they are looking only for jobs that pay more than the current prevailing market wage.

However, the available evidence suggests that most unemployed workers *would* be willing to work at the prevailing market wage but are unable to find employers that are willing to hire them at this wage.[2] Thus, we must find another way to explain why 10.2 million Americans couldn't find a job in January 2014.

When economic models do not predict what we observe in the world, we must ask ourselves whether the assumptions we made in our model are correct. In our model of the labor market, we made an assumption that might not actually hold.

We assumed that workers and firms have full information about the job market. For instance, we assumed that they know what the equilibrium wage is, what qualifications employers are looking for, and where the jobs are. This means that workers can instantly find the right job for themselves whenever it is available and no open job will be left unfilled. On the other hand, when firms and workers lack important information about the labor market, workers cannot always be matched to open jobs, and this mismatch will cause unemployment.

We next discuss this type of unemployment, which we call frictional unemployment. We then turn to two other economic factors that explain why unemployment exists and also why it varies over time.

23.4 Job Search and Frictional Unemployment

In the economy described by Exhibit 23.7, any worker wishing to be employed at the market-clearing wage w^* can do so. Up until this point, our analysis of the labor market assumes that the labor market is frictionless, which implies that the worker can *instantly* find an employer that is willing to hire her. Yet if you've ever looked for a job, you've probably

> **Because each person has specific capabilities, experience, and job preferences, finding the right match between an unemployed person and a firm usually takes time.**

discovered that finding the right job is not simple and might take a lot of legwork. It might be simple to find a summer job at McDonald's, but it's hard to land a job that is a good fit for your particular skills and capabilities.

To find the right job, you need to determine which firms are hiring and try to learn how pay, benefits, and other job characteristics vary among them. You have to line up references and send out résumés. It also helps to network with family and friends to find some acquaintance of an acquaintance who happens to work where you are applying. You need to set up interviews and survive them. Finally, you wait for the people who conduct those interviews to finish interviewing the other leading candidates. In most cases, someone else gets chosen and then you start all over again.

Job search refers to the activities that workers undertake to find appropriate jobs.

Economists refer to job-hunting activities as **job search**. Because each person has specific capabilities, experience, and job preferences, finding the right match between an unemployed person and a firm usually takes time.

Search frictions arise both because of the time-consuming logistics of finding, applying, and interviewing for jobs and because firms and workers have imperfect information about each other and the state of the economy. Imagine a Detroit autoworker who loses his \$40/hour job during the 2007–2009 recession. Shortly afterward, he hears about job offers in the service sector for \$20/hour. Instead of pursuing those jobs, he keeps looking for higher-paying jobs in the auto industry. Only after months of unsuccessful searching in the auto sector, does he have enough information to conclude that his best options are the \$20/hour jobs in the service sector. Examples like this illustrate that gathering information and searching for the right job takes time.

Frictional unemployment refers to unemployment that arises because workers have imperfect information about available jobs and need to engage in a time-consuming process of job search.

Unemployment resulting from imperfect information about available jobs and from the time-consuming process of job search is **frictional unemployment**.

Though it might at first seem strange, you can think about the dating market in the same way that you think about the job market. It takes a long time to find a person who is a good match as a romantic partner. In this sense, people who are not in a relationship, but looking for one, are romantically unemployed. We don't expect single people to find a new romantic partner overnight and we shouldn't expect unemployed workers to instantly find a job either.

23.5 Wage Rigidity and Structural Unemployment

> **Holding the market wage above the market-clearing wage causes some workers who would like to work at the market wage to be unemployed.**

Frictional unemployment resulting from job search activities is a normal and necessary feature of every labor market. However, unemployment also arises because wages are sometimes above the market-clearing level w^*, meaning that the quantity of labor supplied is greater than the quantity of labor demanded. When wages are held fixed above the competitive equilibrium level that clears the labor market, this is referred to as **wage rigidity**. **Structural unemployment** arises when the quantity of labor supplied persistently exceeds the quantity of labor demanded. Wage

Wage rigidity refers to the condition in which the market wage is held above the competitive equilibrium level that would clear the labor market.

rigidity is a key factor in leading to such a persistent gap. Wage rigidity can occur for many reasons, which we discuss next but the economic effects are all the same: holding the market wage above the market-clearing wage causes some workers who would like to work at the market wage to be unemployed. To illustrate how wage rigidity impacts the labor market, we start with minimum wage laws because it is easy to understand their effect using the supply and demand framework. However, other causes of wage rigidity are much more important in the U.S. labor market and we study those in turn.

Structural unemployment arises when the quantity of labor supplied persistently exceeds the quantity of labor demanded.

Minimum Wage Laws

In most countries, legislation specifies a minimum level for the hourly wage. Such legislated wage floors, often called *minimum wage laws*, can prevent the market wage from

CHOICE & CONSEQUENCE

The Luddites

Does technology cause unemployment? In a Phillips electronics factory in China, hundreds of employees work on an assembly line that manufactures electric shavers. Meanwhile, in the Netherlands, the same shavers are assembled by an army of 128 robotic arms. With video cameras for eyes and computer-calibrated hydraulics, these robots tirelessly go about their work. Robot-filled factories raise the possibility that technology can reduce a firm's demand for labor. Throughout history, workers have complained about technological innovation that reduces employment.

The most famous episode began in 1811, when gangs of British textile workers started burning down factories and smashing newly invented mechanized looms. The rioters also targeted inventors and mill owners, burning down their homes and in one instance conducting an assassination. These so-called Luddites—named after the worker Ned Ludd, who was reputed to have smashed textile machines several decades earlier—opposed the mechanization of production. The riots became so frequent and so destructive that the British army was called in to restore order. Dozens of rioters were hanged and the movement faded in 1813. Ultimately, the Luddites could not stop the mechanization of textile manufacturing.

Were new machines really destroying the livelihoods of the textile workers in 1811? The likely answer is yes. The new machines enabled workers to complete tasks in minutes that had previously taken hours. Consequently, the mills needed to employ fewer workers. Many skilled artisans lost their jobs and their families suffered. So the Luddites were not mistaken in believing that the machines were putting some of them out of work.

Technological progress *can* destroy jobs in a single industry such as textiles. However, historical evidence shows that technological progress does not produce unemployment in a country as a *whole*. Technological progress increases productivity and incomes in the overall

A drawing of workers smashing a mechanized loom in Britain during the period of the Luddite riots (1811–1813).

economy, and higher incomes lead to higher demand for goods and thus higher demand for labor. As a result, workers who lose jobs in one industry will be able to find jobs in others, although for many of them this might take time and some of them, like the Luddites, will end up with lower wages in their new jobs.

Today, the term *Luddite* is synonymous with opposition to new technology. The British textile workers of 1811 were unlucky. They were victims of technological progress. For most people, however, ongoing technological progress improves their lives by raising their productivity and lowering the cost of the goods and services they buy.

---

falling to the market-clearing wage that equates the quantity of labor supplied with the quantity of labor demanded. In the United States, the federal government chooses a national minimum wage and state legislatures can choose even higher minimum wages for in-state jobs. In January 2014, for example, the federal minimum wage was $7.25, while the highest state minimum wage was $9.32, which applied in Washington State.

Minimum wages might prevent the quantity of labor supplied from equaling the quantity of labor demanded, as depicted in Exhibit 23.8. In this exhibit, the minimum wage is labeled with a line beneath it to signify that the minimum wage is a wage floor: $\underline{w}$. In Exhibit 23.8, the minimum wage, $\underline{w}$, is above the market-clearing wage, w^*. At the minimum wage, $\underline{w}$, the quantity of labor demanded by employers is less than the quantity of labor supplied by workers. Consequently, some workers—represented by the gap between the quantity supplied and the quantity demanded at $\underline{w}$—aren't able to find jobs. These unemployed workers are willing to work at the going wage, $\underline{w}$, and would even be willing to work at wages lower than $\underline{w}$. The minimum wage legislation prevents employers from

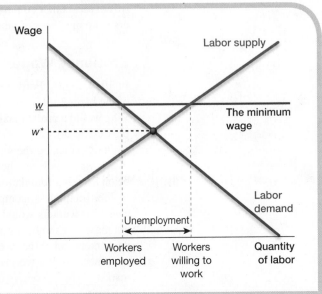

Exhibit 23.8 Labor Supply and Labor Demand in a Market with a Minimum Wage

When the minimum wage (<u>w</u>) is above the market-clearing wage (w*), the quantity of labor supplied exceeds the quantity of labor demanded, creating unemployment (quantity of labor supplied minus quantity of labor demanded).

hiring these workers at wages that would equalize the quantity of labor supplied and the quantity of labor demanded.

Minimum wage laws are an example of a policy that creates winners and losers. The winners are the workers who get jobs at wages above the wage that equates quantity supplied and quantity demanded. The losers are the firms that have to pay the higher wage and the unemployed who would like to work but can't find a job at the prevailing wage, <u>w</u>. The costs and benefits of the minimum wage are actively debated, with economists divided on the question of whether the United States should raise its minimum wage.

The minimum wage produces structural unemployment, but it cannot be the only cause of unemployment. For example, in January 2014, there were 1.6 million college graduates who were unemployed. The median hourly wage for a college graduate was $29.85 per hour in 2013, four times the level of the minimum wage. Because almost all college graduates are paid far more than the minimum wage, it is not the minimum wage that prevents the labor market for college graduates from clearing.

In the overall workforce, including all education levels, 1.0 percent of workers are paid the minimum wage. Accordingly, the impact of the minimum wage on the labor market is modest. The minimum wage does prevent the market for some types of low-skilled workers from clearing but has little impact on the general labor market.

Labor Unions and Collective Bargaining

Another source of wage rigidity is **collective bargaining**, which refers to the contract negotiations that take place between firms and labor unions. A labor union is an organization of workers that advocates for better working conditions, pay, and benefits for its members. Unions use the threat of going on strike—a mass work stoppage—as a bargaining chip in these negotiations. Collective bargaining often leads to equilibrium wages and benefits that are greater than what workers would have received under the market-clearing wage. Collective bargaining has the same effect on unemployment as minimum wage laws that we saw in Exhibit 23.8. By keeping the equilibrium wage above the market-clearing wage, unions cause the quantity of labor supplied to be greater than the quantity of labor demanded, thus creating structural unemployment. Through such collective bargaining, unions benefit their members but make it difficult for non-members to find work.

However, just like the minimum wage, collective bargaining is unlikely to be the most important factor causing wage rigidity in the U.S. labor market because union membership is relatively low in the United States. For example, in 2011, 10.6 percent of employed workers in the United States were members of labor unions. Unions play a more important

In October 2010, striking teachers, postal workers, and transport workers protested the French government's proposal to raise the retirement age from 60 to 62.

Collective bargaining refers to contract negotiations between firms and labor unions.

role in most other countries. For example, in Italy, in 2011, 35.2 percent of employed workers were members of labor unions.

Efficiency Wages and Unemployment

In 1914, Henry Ford, founder of the Ford Motor Company, seemed to go bonkers. Out of the blue, Ford increased the daily wage of most of his employees from $2.34 to $5.00. Why would a profit-maximizing employer double his employees' pay without any external pressure to do so?

Ford explained the wage of $5 per day as an act of *self*-interest. There was "no charity in any way involved," he said. "We wanted to pay these wages so that the business would be on a lasting foundation. We were building for the future."

In a frictionless, competitive labor market, paying an above-market wage (or above the wage that workers would accept) would not be optimal for a firm—in other words, it would not maximize the firm's profits. In such a "perfect" market, the firm knows everything about its workers and observes everything that they do at work. In this idealized environment, there is no need to pay workers more than the market wage to obtain their labor. But in actual markets, where workers can shirk (slack off) on the job, paying *more* than the going wage can have benefits for the firm. Ford's wage premium is an example of what economists call **efficiency wages**. By paying wages above the wage that workers were willing to accept (and in fact above the market wage), Ford was able to increase the productivity and profitability of his company.

Efficiency wages increase productivity and firm profitability for a number of reasons. First, efficiency wages reduce worker turnover. Working on an assembly line is monotonous, causing a relatively high level of turnover. Recruiting and training new workers is costly to the company. If workers are paid more than the prevailing market wage by their employer, they are more motivated to keep their job because they would face lower wages if they needed to find a job elsewhere. Second, the fear of losing a high-paying job motivates employees to work harder than they otherwise would, increasing their hourly output. Third, there is the possibility that employees would be grateful for an above-market wage, leading them to reciprocate this apparent generosity by working harder—another boost to their hourly output. Finally, efficiency wages also improve the quality of the pool of workers who apply for a job in the first place.

If efficiency wages increase productivity, employers like Henry Ford might find it profitable to pay a higher wage than the market-clearing wage. Like minimum wage laws and collective bargaining, this results in a form of wage rigidity. As before, this will cause the quantity of labor supplied to be greater than the quantity of labor demanded, leading to structural unemployment, just as we saw in Exhibit 23.8. One difference is worth noting, however. The minimum wage and collective bargaining force employers to pay a wage above the market-clearing wage level, whereas with efficiency wages, the equilibrium wage is above the market-clearing level because profit-maximizing firms voluntarily prefer to pay such wages.

Downward Wage Rigidity and Unemployment Fluctuations

Another type of wage rigidity results from the fact that workers are highly averse to reductions in their wage, resulting in what economists call **downward wage rigidity**. Cuts in the wage hurt worker morale and lower productivity. As a result, most firms would rather fire workers than cut their wages. Typically, only firms on the brink of bankruptcy attempt to talk their workers into accepting wage reductions.

Downward wage rigidity, like the other forms of wage rigidity we have studied so far, causes wages to remain above the market-clearing level and causes structural unemployment. To see this, consider the following scenario, depicted in Exhibit 23.9. Assume that the labor market begins in a competitive equilibrium with no unemployment (at the point labeled E_1). Next, imagine that the labor demand curve shifts to the left because the economy slows down (we'll have much more to say about why the economy fluctuates in Chapter 26).

Efficiency wages are above the wage that workers would accept, where the extra pay increases worker productivity and improves the profitability of the firm.

Downward wage rigidity arises when workers resist a cut in their wage.

Exhibit 23.9 Shifts in Labor Demand Affect Equilibrium in the Labor Market

With flexible wages, a shift to the left in the demand for labor reduces the equilibrium wage and employment (the economy moves from point E_1 to point F). With a downward rigid wage, the same leftward shift has a larger impact on employment (the economy moves from point E_1 to point E_2). Employment now falls all the way to L_2 instead of L_F, because none of the impact of the leftward shift in the labor demand curve is absorbed by the wage, which remains at its original (rigid) level. Moreover, downward wage rigidity causes unemployment: because the wage does not change, the quantity of labor supplied remains the same, but the quantity of labor demanded falls to L_2. The gap between the quantity of labor supplied and the quantity of labor demanded (at the rigid wage) corresponds to unemployment.

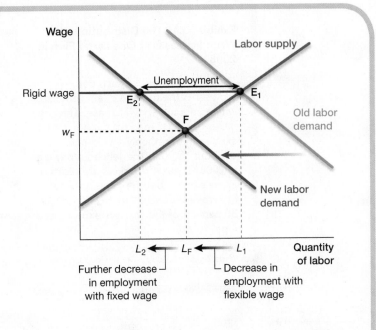

When the wage is flexible, the leftward shift in labor demand moves the market to a new equilibrium (point F) in which the equilibrium wage is w_F as shown in Exhibit 23.9, and the quantity of labor demanded falls to L_F. The exhibit also shows that at this new equilibrium, the quantity of labor supplied is equal to the quantity of labor demanded and so unemployment is still equal to zero.

However, when the wage is rigid, it won't fall to its market-clearing level and will instead stay at its initial level, marked in Exhibit 23.9. This downward wage rigidity causes the quantity of labor supplied, which is still at L_1, to be greater than the quantity of labor demanded, which has now fallen to L_2, thus leading to (structural) unemployment, as shown in Exhibit 23.9.

As we will see in more detail in Chapter 26, the downward wage rigidity depicted in Exhibit 23.9 is one of the causes of unemployment fluctuations. Recessions are periods of leftward (adverse) shifts in labor demand. This, combined with downward wage rigidity, increases the rate of unemployment.

The effect of downward wage rigidity can be seen in Exhibit 23.10, which shows the wage growth of workers in a large company for 2008, right in the middle of the 2007–2009 recession.[3] Each bar shows the fraction of workers whose wage grew by the percentage depicted on the horizontal axis. We see a large bulge in the distribution at zero, meaning that wages were frozen instead of being cut. Wage cuts were so infrequent (only 46 out of 15,000 employees) that they are not even visible on the graph. Although the extent of downward wage rigidity does vary from company to company and industry to industry, this type of rigidity is overall quite pervasive throughout labor markets and can have a significant effect on unemployment, especially during recessions, as we will see in greater detail in Chapter 26.

The Natural Rate of Unemployment and Cyclical Unemployment

As we noted earlier, the U.S. economy always has some unemployment. In addition, the unemployment rate fluctuates considerably as shown in Exhibit 23.2. To distinguish the "normal" rate of unemployment from fluctuations around that normal rate, economists use the concept of the *natural rate of unemployment*. The **natural rate of unemployment** is the rate around which the actual rate of unemployment fluctuates. In practice, the natural rate of unemployment is calculated by averaging the unemployment rate over an extended

The **natural rate of unemployment** is the rate around which the actual rate of unemployment fluctuates.

Exhibit 23.10 The Distribution of Wage Increases at One Large Firm in 2008

The vertical height of each bar represents the fraction of all workers with a particular pay increase. The pay increase can be read off the horizontal axis. At this firm, only 46 workers out of about 15,000 experienced a pay cut in 2008. These 46 workers are plotted in the exhibit, but the bars to the left of zero are too small to be seen. Over 50 percent of the workers experienced a pay freeze.

Source: Nathan Hipsman, "Downward Nominal Wage Rigidity: A Double-Density Model," Harvard University Working Paper (2012).

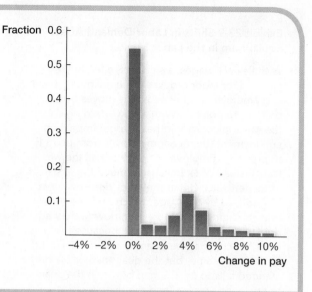

Cyclical unemployment is the deviation of the actual unemployment rate from the natural rate of unemployment.

time period. For example, in Spain, the unemployment rate has averaged 16.1 percent from 1977 to 2013. In the United States, the unemployment rate has averaged 6.5 percent over the same period.

Cyclical unemployment is defined as the deviation of the unemployment rate from its natural rate. Cyclical unemployment usually rises in recessions (when the labor demand curve shifts to the left) and falls in economic booms (when the labor demand curve shifts to the right). Chapter 26 discusses the relationship between unemployment and economic fluctuations in depth.

In 2013, the Spanish unemployment rate was 26.1 percent, implying that cyclical unemployment was 10.0 percent (using the natural rate of 16.1 percent). In 2013, the U.S. unemployment rate was 7.4 percent, implying that cyclical unemployment was 0.9 percent (using the natural rate of 6.5 percent).

The natural rate of unemployment includes frictional unemployment, which is a necessary part of any well-functioning labor market. But the natural rate of unemployment also includes long-term structural unemployment, which is generally considered to be economically inefficient. Accordingly, the natural rate of unemployment should not be confused with the rate of unemployment that is socially optimal or desirable—so some might say there is nothing "natural" about it. To see this, consider an economy that is subject to a significant level of downward wage rigidity. As Exhibit 23.9 shows, this economy will have a relatively high level of structural unemployment and this will increase the long-term average rate of unemployment. This is not a desirable state of affairs, because many potential workers who could have been gainfully employed are out of work and are unable to use their labor productively. This example illustrates that the long-term average rate of unemployment—the natural rate of unemployment—includes some inefficient sources of unemployment.

Just as the natural rate of unemployment has both frictional and structural components, so does cyclical unemployment. During recessions, fewer firms try to hire new workers, and this increases the difficulty that workers face in locating a suitable job, raising frictional unemployment. In addition, as Exhibit 23.9 shows, in the presence of downward wage rigidity, the leftward shift of the labor demand curve during a recession leads to a rise in structural unemployment as the rigid wage remains above the market-clearing wage.

Evidence-Based Economics

Q: What happens to employment and unemployment if local employers go out of business?

From 1990 to 2007, the unemployment rate in Pittsburgh fell by 1.8 percentage points. Pittsburgh had both good and bad economic news during this period, but one particularly lucky factor is that economic activity in Pittsburgh was concentrated in industries that were not highly exposed to Chinese imports. Pittsburgh specialized in industries such as paper, print, and metal products that had "low exposure" to competition from Chinese imports, meaning that across the entire U.S. economy these sectors experienced relatively slow growth of Chinese imports.

The experience of the Raleigh-Durham area in North Carolina, shown in a map of Eastern United States together with the Pittsburgh area in Exhibit 23.11, was very different between 1990 and 2007. In the Raleigh-Durham area, unemployment *increased* by 1.9 percentage points. In addition, many workers in this area are now out of the labor force because they have stopped looking for jobs entirely. One factor contributing to Raleigh-Durham's weakening labor market was its specialization in industries such as textiles and apparel, electrical products, and computers that have "high exposure" to competition from Chinese imports.

By comparing *hundreds* of regions with different levels of exposure to Chinese imports (of which Pittsburgh and Raleigh-Durham are just two examples), economists David Autor, David Dorn, and Gordon Hanson were able to identify leftward shifts in labor demand caused by high exposure to Chinese imports, similar to the shift in Exhibit 23.9.[4] Their analysis shows that high-exposure communities experienced sharper declines in manufacturing employment than low-exposure communities. The rate of unemployment also rose more in the areas with high exposure than those with low exposure.

The study confirms the model of labor market analysis depicted in Exhibit 23.9, in which a leftward shift in the labor demand curve, combined with downward wage

Exhibit 23.11 A Tale of Two Cities

Pittsburgh and Raleigh-Durham have had very different changes in their local unemployment rate between 1990 and 2007. Pittsburgh saw its unemployment rate decline from 7.3 percent to 5.5 percent, while Raleigh-Durham experienced an increase in its unemployment rate from 4.0 percent to 5.9 percent. This difference arose at least partially because Raleigh-Durham has high exposure to Chinese imports, meaning that it specialized in manufacturing industries, which experienced relatively rapid growth in competition from Chinese imports. In contrast, Pittsburgh has low exposure to Chinese imports.

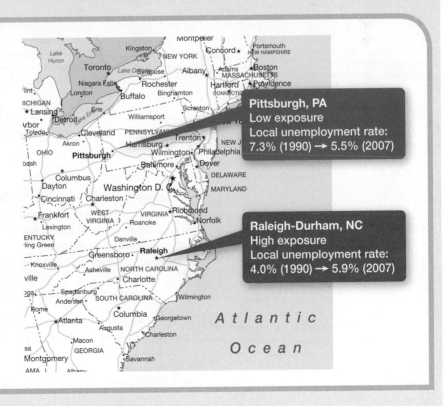

Pittsburgh, PA
Low exposure
Local unemployment rate:
7.3% (1990) → 5.5% (2007)

Raleigh-Durham, NC
High exposure
Local unemployment rate:
4.0% (1990) → 5.9% (2007)

rigidity, reduces the number of jobs and increases the rate of unemployment. Consistent with the model's predictions about wage rigidity, the authors found no decline in manufacturing wages despite the leftward shifts in labor demand. It is therefore likely that some of the higher unemployment in high-exposure areas was due to wage rigidity, as in Exhibit 23.9. However, the authors also find a significant decline in non-manufacturing wages in high-exposure areas, confirming that wage rigidity only applies to a worker's existing job and does not carry over to the new jobs that unemployed workers find. Laid-off manufacturing workers are offered lower wages when they search for new jobs, and they are willing to accept those lower wages to find work.

This analysis might lead you to conclude that the United States should ban Chinese imports to increase U.S. employment, but doing so would generate far more problems than it would solve. Chinese imports are beneficial to most U.S. households, which enjoy the lower prices of the imported goods. Nevertheless, it is true that some domestic workers lose their jobs due to international trade, and much of the debate about trade revolves around the personal and economic dislocation caused by these job losses and the policies that can be used to mitigate these costs. We return to these important issues in Chapters 28 and 29, where we provide a full discussion of the effects of international trade.

Question	**Answer**	**Data**	**Caveat**
What happens to employment and unemployment if local employers go out of business?	Communities with a high level of exposure to competition from Chinese imports between 1990 and 2007 experienced an increase in the local rate of unemployment relative to communities with a low level of exposure to competition from Chinese imports.	Community-level data on employment, unemployment, and industry composition. National U.S. data on industry-by-industry growth in Chinese imports. The study covers the period from 1990 to 2007.	Many factors other than competition from Chinese firms contribute to movements in unemployment rates.

Summary

✹ Potential workers are defined as the civilian non-institutional population ages 16 and older. Those holding a paid full-time or part-time job are classified as employed, while those without a paid job who have actively looked for work in the prior 4 weeks and are currently available for work are unemployed. Potential workers who are employed and unemployed make up the labor force, while the rest of the potential workers are classified as out of the labor force. The unemployment rate is the percentage of the labor force that is unemployed.

✹ The unemployment rate fluctuates significantly over time. It is higher during and in the immediate aftermath of recessions.

✹ Different demographic groups have different unemployment rates. For example, more educated workers tend to have lower unemployment rates.

✸ Employment is determined by labor demand and labor supply. The labor demand curve is downward-sloping because of the diminishing marginal product of labor and profit maximization by firms. The labor supply curve, on the other hand, tends to be upward-sloping because higher wages generally encourage workers to supply more hours to the labor market.

✸ The competitive labor market equilibrium is given by the intersection of the labor demand and labor supply curves. The competitive equilibrium wage is also called the market-clearing wage.

✸ In a competitive labor market equilibrium in which all workers know the market-clearing wage, there will be no unemployment because every worker willing to work at the market-clearing wage can find a job. Workers who are not willing to work at the market-clearing wage will stop searching and will therefore not be counted as unemployed.

✸ Frictional unemployment exists because workers need to learn about the condition of the labor market and search for a job that suits them. Even in a healthy labor market, there will always be some unemployed workers in the process of changing jobs, or finding a new job after losing their previous one, or finding their first job after entry into the labor market. Structural unemployment results when the market wage is above the market-clearing level, causing the quantity of labor supplied to be greater than the quantity of labor demanded. This is often referred to as wage rigidity and can result from institutional features of the labor market like minimum wage legislation or collective bargaining. More importantly, it can result from efficiency wages or from downward wage rigidity.

✸ Efficiency wages arise when employers pay wages higher than the market-clearing wage to increase worker productivity. Downward wage rigidity arises because of the unwillingness of workers to accept wage cuts and prevents wages from immediately falling in response to a leftward shift of the labor demand curve.

✸ The most important cause of unemployment fluctuations is a shifting labor demand curve. When wages are flexible, a shift to the left of the labor demand curve reduces both employment and wages but does not increase unemployment because the labor market clears. When wages are rigid, the same leftward shift creates a larger decline in employment because the wage does not decline and unemployment increases.

✸ The natural rate of unemployment is the long-term average rate of unemployment. Cyclical unemployment is the difference between the current rate of unemployment and the natural rate of unemployment. Cyclical unemployment is positive in recessions and negative in economic booms.

Key Terms

Questions

All questions are available in MyEconLab for practice and instructor assignment.

1. Unemployment statistics are measured and released by the Bureau of Labor Statistics (BLS), a division of the U.S. Department of Labor.

   a. When does the Bureau of Labor Statistics (BLS) officially classify a person as being employed? When are potential workers classified as being unemployed?

   b. What do the following terms mean and how are they calculated?

      i. The unemployment rate

      ii. The labor force participation rate

2. Explain whether each of these individuals will be counted as a part of the labor force.

   a. Jane is working full-time toward a Ph.D. in philosophy but volunteers at nursing homes during her spare weekends.

   b. Kristen left her full-time job as a journalist to spend more time with her kids and now makes some income working part-time for a children's magazine.

   c. In the past four weeks, Harry did not respond to a call from a firm seeking to interview him for a job opening. But he recently applied for another job that he feels will better suit his qualifications.

3. Consider Exhibit 23.2. What were the two highest rates of unemployment since 1948? When did they occur?

4. What could explain why unemployment is lower among workers with a relatively higher level of education?

5. What is the value of the marginal product of labor? Explain how it is computed with an example.

6. List two factors that can cause a shift in the labor demand curve. Explain why a change in each factor can lead to a shift of the curve.

7. Why does the labor supply curve slope upward and what can cause the labor supply curve to shift?

8. Should a country with a healthy economy have a zero unemployment rate?

9. What is meant by job search? How does it lead to frictional unemployment?

10. What is the difference between frictional and structural unemployment?

11. Sometimes new technology in production reduces the time that a worker takes to complete a task. Technological innovations can also completely replace a factory worker. Does this mean that technological progress will lead to large-scale unemployment? Explain your answer.

12. What is wage rigidity? List and explain two factors that can increase wage rigidity in the labor market.

Problems

All problems are available in MyEconLab for practice and instructor assignment.
Problems marked 🌐 update with real-time data.

🌐 1. The following table shows the annual averages of the employment level, unemployment level, and the labor force participation rate in the United States in the years from 2001 to 2011. Use the given data to complete the table and answer the following questions. (*Note*: Adult population is for individuals 16 years and over, not in the military, and not institutionalized. All rates are in percent.)

Year	Number Unemployed (in thousands)	Number Employed (in thousands)	Labor Force Participation Rate	Employment Rate	Unemployment Rate	Labor Force	Adult Population
2001	6,830,000	136,939,000	66.8%				
2002	8,375,000	136,481,000	66.6%				
2003	8,770,000	137,729,000	66.2%				
2004	8,140,000	139,240,000	66.0%				
2005	7,579,000	141,710,000	66.0%				
2006	6,991,000	144,418,000	66.2%				
2007	7,073,000	146,050,000	66.0%				
2008	8,951,000	145,370,000	66.0%				
2009	14,301,000	139,888,000	65.4%				
2010	14,815,000	139,070,000	64.7%				
2011	13,743,000	139,873,000	64.1%				

Note: Annual averages based on data from the Bureau of Labor Statistics (Series: LNS12000000, LNS11300000, LNS13000000).

a. In which year did the economy witness the sharpest change in the unemployment rate? What could possibly explain this?

b. Use the data on the size of the labor force and potential workers to compute the percentage of adults out of the labor force for the year 2002. Verify that your calculation is equal to one minus the labor force participation rate.

c. What are the general trends that you observe in the data?

2. In April 2012, The Bazanian Daily, a leading newspaper in the country of Bazania, carried a report titled "20,000 jobs added in the last quarter; unemployment rate shoots up from 5 percent to 6.7 percent." How could the unemployment rate in Bazania increase even when new jobs were created?

3. In macroeconomics, a "leading indicator" is defined as a measurable economic variable that changes prior to when the economy as a whole starts to follow a given trend. Conversely, a "lagging indicator" is a measurable variable that only changes in the latter phases of an overall trend in the economy—or even afterwards.

   Study Exhibit 23.2 carefully. Would you describe unemployment as a leading or lagging indicator of an economic downturn? Explain.

4. Suppose Die Cast Aluminum Co. is a subcontractor for the auto industry and makes specialized auto parts. There is a bracket it manufactures that it sells for $1.50. The following table shows the number of brackets that can be produced from a given number of labor hours. Assume that the company cannot hire labor for a fraction of an hour.

Hrs. Labor	Q
0	0
1	50
2	90
3	120
4	140
5	150
6	155
7	157

a. Find the marginal product (in brackets), and the value of the marginal product (in dollars), of each hour of labor.

b. If the wage paid to workers in Die Cast's plant is $25/hour, how many hours of labor should the firm employ? How many hours will be employed if the wage increases to $35/hour? Explain.

c. How many hours will be employed if the wage is $35/hour, but the price of a bracket declines to $1?

5. In a recent study for the National Bureau of Economic Research (NBER), four researchers looked at the effect of generous unemployment benefits on the local unemployment rate. They compared the unemployment situation in adjoining counties, which happened to lie in two different states with different laws regarding the amount and duration of unemployment benefits.

   The authors of the study found that the unemployment rate "rises dramatically in the border counties belonging to the states that expanded unemployment benefit duration" during the Great Recession. Why might this be so? (Based on Hagedorn, Karahan, et al., "Unemployment Benefits and Unemployment in the Great Recession: The Role of Macro Effects." NBER working paper 19499, October 2013.)

6. Every month, statistics on employment and unemployment are compiled by the Bureau of Labor Statistics.

   a. The unemployed worker whose frustration was discussed at the beginning of section 23.1 had been unemployed for 17 months. Go to www.bls.gov and consult Table A-12. Find the average (mean) duration of unemployment (seasonally adjusted) in the most recent month. Based on what you find, is 17 months higher or lower than average?

   b. List some possible reasons for the quoted worker's unemployment that would make his joblessness qualify as frictional unemployment. List reasons that would fall in the category of structural unemployment.

7. Suppose the equilibrium wage in the market for food service workers is $11 per hour. The government then establishes a minimum wage at $9 per hour. What will be the effect of the minimum wage on the market for labor in the food service industry? Explain.

8. The following graph shows the demand for and supply of labor in a market with a minimum wage set at $8 per hour. Use the graph to answer the following questions.

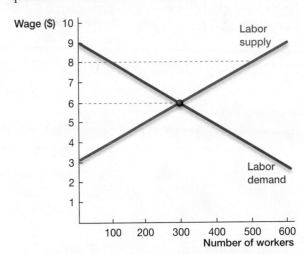

a. How many workers will be unemployed due to the minimum wage? What kind of unemployment is this?

b. What would happen to the quantity of labor demanded and supplied if the minimum wage were less than $6?

c. Who are the winners and the losers when the minimum wage is $8?

d. In the United States, does minimum wage legislation have a significant impact on unemployment in the overall labor force? Why or why not?

9. In response to high unemployment, the Spanish government enacted a series of labor market reforms in 2012. Among other measures, the government reduced severance pay and the influence of unions in setting wages and hours of work. What could be the rationale behind using these measures to boost employment?

10. According to salary.com, the average salary for a software engineer level III (a higher-level position in software design and implementation) in the Silicon Valley area of California is $108,244. However, Google pays its level III software engineers an average salary of $124,258. Explain why Google would pay a salary higher than the equilibrium salary for equivalent positions in the same area.

11. The following figure shows the demand and supply curves in the market for workers in Starbucks coffee shops (called "baristas"). The hourly wage in this market has been fixed at $6 and cannot be changed.

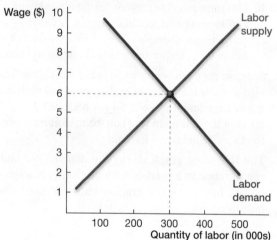

a. Suppose that, due to concerns about the high number of calories in many Starbucks drinks, the demand for Starbucks products declines. Use a graph to explain what will happen to employment in the market for baristas.

b. Now suppose the wage is flexible. How would your answer to part (a) change?

12. The period from 2007 to 2009 was a time of economic contraction that some called the "Great Recession." During periods of recession, most firms experience a decline in demand for their product. All other things being equal, macroeconomic theory predicts that the wage of most workers should decline in recessionary periods. However, this was not the case in the 2007–2009 recession, or during many other economic downturns throughout recent history.

Based on the discussion in the chapter, explain why this might be so, and what the implications are for unemployment.

24 Credit Markets

How often do banks fail?

Financial service companies, such as banks, insurance companies, and investment companies, want you to believe that they are rock-solid. They try to convey that message with stone pillars and marble lobbies. Sometimes they choose names that imply indestructibility, like Northern Rock, Blackrock, and Blackstone. Prudential, a leading insurance company, nicknamed itself "The Rock" and adopted the Rock of Gibraltar, a mountain fortress, as its corporate symbol. Those are encouraging words, but are financial institutions really impregnable?

CHAPTER OUTLINE

☀ The credit market matches borrowers (the source of credit demand) and savers (the source of credit supply).

☀ The credit market equilibrium determines the real interest rate.

☀ Banks and other financial intermediaries have three key functions: identifying profitable lending opportunities; using short-run deposits to make long-run investments; and managing the amount and distribution of risk.

☀ Banks become insolvent when the value of their liabilities exceeds the value of their assets.

24.1 What Is the Credit Market?

You've got your first business idea and you can't think about much else. You are going to be the founder and CEO (chief executive officer) of your own company. OK. Catch your breath. And get down to work. Most new businesses fail within 5 years, and you are going to do everything that you can to avoid becoming one of those casualties.

You want to create a taxi and limo company that uses only vehicles that are 100 percent battery powered, just the sort of thing you reckon would appeal to your fellow New Yorkers. You call your new firm BatteryPark. Everyone you know loves the idea and promises to use your start-up if you manage to get it off the ground. You've even been able to convince numerous local companies to sign up for your service for their employees and clients.

Now you need to raise money to buy or rent the necessary equipment and buildings: licenses, electric vehicles, battery-charging systems, a reservation office with computers, and a few garages spread around the city so that your taxis can easily get a fresh battery when they run out of juice. You also need to hire staff, train them, and advertise. You figure you need about $500,000 to start your business and quickly reach an efficient scale of operation. That's not a trivial amount by any stretch of the imagination, but you think it's worth taking the risk, considering what you expect to make from your new business.

But how will you raise $500,000? You certainly don't have it in your checking account, and neither do any of your friends. You think of asking your parents and grandparents, but then you imagine how you would feel if your business went south and a family member lost his or her life savings. So what's the solution?

Borrowers and the Demand for Loans

The good news is that you are not alone in your quest for funds. Every year, hundreds of thousands of entrepreneurs in the United States and millions around the world borrow money to start new businesses. Many, many more businesses that are already in operation also borrow funds to expand their existing operations or simply to pay their bills.

Consumers, too, borrow to purchase big-ticket items like automobiles and houses. Some households borrow to sustain their quality of life during a temporary period of unemployment. Many people borrow to put themselves or their children through college. Almost everyone who pursues graduate studies in business, law, or medicine borrows to pay some of their bills. We refer to economic agents who borrow funds—including entrepreneurs, home buyers, and medical students—as **debtors**. And the funds that they borrow are referred to as **credit**.

Debtors, or borrowers, are economic agents who borrow funds.

Credit refers to the loans that the debtor receives.

Most businesses and individuals obtain credit from banks, but the credit market is much broader than banks. It includes several non-bank institutions, as well as the market for commercial debt, where well-established, large businesses obtain large loans.

Of course, borrowed money is not lent for free. You need to pay *interest*. The original amount of borrowed money is referred to as principal. The **interest rate** is the additional payment, above and beyond the repayment of principal, that a borrower needs to make on a *one-dollar* loan (at the end of one year). We can also say that the interest rate is the annual cost of a one-dollar loan.

The **interest rate** (also referred to as the **nominal interest rate**), i, is the annual cost of a one-dollar loan, so $i \times L$ is the annual cost of an $L loan.

Let's now scale up that one-dollar loan into an $L loan. The total interest payment a borrower needs to make for an $L loan is the loan amount multiplied by the interest rate. Put differently, if you borrow $L with a one-year loan at an annual interest rate of i, at the end of one year you pay back the L dollars of principal *plus* $i \times L$ dollars in interest. To distinguish it from the real interest rate, which we define next, we'll also refer to the interest rate, i, as the **nominal interest rate**.

Let's now return to your blockbuster business idea. You have enough confidence in your plans that you would be willing to pay a 10 percent interest rate to get your loan. That means you would be willing to make an annual interest payment of $50,000 to get a $500,000 loan ($500,000 × 0.10 = $50,000). In fact, you are so confident that you would take the loan even if you had to pay 20 percent interest.

But what if the interest rate were 50 percent? An interest payment of $250,000 per year on a $500,000 loan is a bit steep. At that interest rate, there won't be much profit left for you. Perhaps you should scale back your plans and take a smaller loan. Instead of hiring a large team of 20 employees, you might want to start with just a few coworkers.

And what if the interest rate were 100 percent? Principal plus interest one year later would then be $500,000 + $500,000 = $1,000,000 on a $500,000 loan. That is, you would need to pay back twice as much as you borrowed. If so, it might make sense for you to forget about this new idea altogether. It's hard to imagine that any business could make money if it had to finance itself this way.

In reality, most businesses do not need to pay 50 percent or 100 percent interest rates on loans. We present such cases to explain why a rise in the interest rate causes a fall in the quantity of credit demanded. As the interest rate goes up, fewer firms and individuals are willing to pay the high price to acquire credit.

Real and Nominal Interest Rates

The real interest rate is given by the nominal interest rate minus the inflation rate.

The *real* annual price of your loan isn't simply given by the *nominal interest rate* you pay, for example the 10 percent, 20 percent, 50 percent, or 100 percent we have just mentioned. Instead, it is given by the **real interest rate**, r. The real interest rate is the nominal interest rate minus inflation. The inflation rate measures how much less valuable one dollar becomes because of the increase in the overall price level.

The relationship between the nominal and real interest rate is very similar to the relationship between nominal and real GDP growth, which we studied in Chapter 19. To turn nominal GDP growth into real GDP growth, we need to subtract the inflation rate from nominal GDP growth. Similar logic applies to the relationship between the nominal and the real interest rate:

$$\text{Real interest rate} = \text{Nominal interest rate} - \text{Inflation rate.}$$

Or using symbols,

$$r = i - \pi,$$

Optimizing economic agents will use the real interest rate, r, when thinking about the economic cost of a loan.

where r is the real interest rate, i is the nominal interest rate, and π denotes the rate of inflation. Economists call this the Fisher equation, naming it after Irving Fisher (1867–1947) whose research emphasized the distinction between the nominal and real interest rates.[1] Here is an example of the Fisher equation in action. If the nominal interest rate is 5 percent and the inflation rate is 2 percent, then the real interest rate is

$$3\% = 5\% - 2\%.$$

Why will optimizing economic agents use the real interest rate, r, when thinking about the economic cost of a loan? If you borrow one dollar for a year, you will need to pay back $(1 + i)$ dollars in a year. Inflation implies that each dollar that you borrowed (and spent) at the beginning of the year has the same purchasing power as $(1 + \pi)$ dollars a year later because the inflation rate is π. It would be misleading to compare a dollar paid back at the end of the year to a dollar with more purchasing power borrowed at the beginning of the year. Optimizers recognize that they should compare what they pay back at the end of the year to what they borrowed at the beginning of the year, adjusting the dollars they borrowed for a year's worth of inflation. In essence, the relevant *real* price of the loan is the difference between what the borrower pays back $(1 + i)$ and the inflation-adjusted value of the dollar he or she originally borrowed, $(1 + \pi)$:

$$(1 + i) - (1 + \pi) = i - \pi.$$

Recall that the real interest rate is $i - \pi$, which appears on the right-hand side of the last equation. We have shown that the real interest rate is equal to the difference between what the borrower pays back and the inflation-adjusted value of the dollar he or she originally borrowed. The real interest rate is the real (inflation-adjusted) cost of a \$1 loan. (In the next chapter we will return to this equation and discuss the role of inflationary expectation in thinking about the real interest rate.)

The Credit Demand Curve

The **credit demand curve** is the schedule that reports the relationship between the quantity of credit demanded and the real interest rate.

Because it is the real interest rate, r, that matters for business and individual decisions, the demand for credit will also be a function of this real interest rate. The **credit demand curve** is the schedule that reports the relationship between the quantity of credit demanded and the real interest rate.

Exhibit 24.1 plots the credit demand curve, with the quantity of credit demanded on the horizontal axis and the real interest rate on the vertical axis. The credit demand curve slopes downward because the higher the real interest rate, the lower the quantity of credit demanded. As BatteryPark's demand for credit illustrates, the higher the interest rate a firm pays to borrow money, the lower the borrower's profit. So, fewer borrowers will be willing to obtain a loan at a higher interest rate. This is conceptually the same as other demand curves: when the price of any good—like carrots or caviar—goes up, consumers tend to buy less of it. Credit works the same way, where the real "price" of credit is the real interest rate. The steepness of the credit demand curve tells us about the sensitivity of the relationship between the real interest rate and the quantity of credit demanded.

1. When the credit demand curve is relatively steep, the quantity of credit demanded doesn't change that much in response to variation in the real interest rate.
2. When the credit demand curve is relatively flat, the quantity of credit demanded is relatively sensitive to variation in the real interest rate.

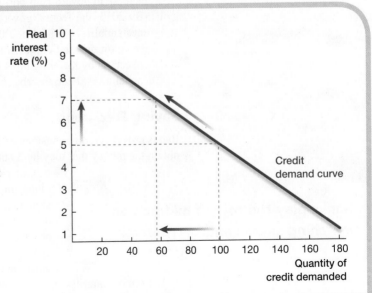

Exhibit 24.1 The Credit Demand Curve

The quantity of credit demanded is plotted on the horizontal axis and the real interest rate is plotted on the vertical axis. As the real interest rate rises, the quantity of credit demanded falls. This is a movement along the credit demand curve.

Having emphasized that the *real* interest rate is the price that appears on the vertical axis of Exhibit 24.1—you can think of it as the price of borrowing money—it is important to remember that almost all loans are made at a *nominal* interest rate. For example, banks quote a nominal interest rate when you apply for a mortgage. Businesses also borrow at a nominal interest rate when they take out a loan. However, what is relevant for the decisions of an optimizer is the implied real interest rate. The real interest rate will play a central role in macroeconomic analysis in the next several chapters, especially the real interest rate for long-term borrowing (like 30-year mortgages or 10-year corporate loans). For now, we focus on the relationship between the real interest rate and the demand for credit. We return to the nominal interest rate and its relationship to the real interest rate in the next chapter. When using the credit demand curve it is important to draw a very careful distinction between *movements along* the credit demand curve, as in Exhibit 24.1, and *shifts* of the credit demand curve. You have already encountered this distinction when we first introduced it in Chapter 4, and it still applies here. Exhibit 24.2 illustrates shifting demand curves. Many factors cause the demand curve to shift:

- **Changes in perceived business opportunities for firms.** Businesses borrow to fund their expansions. For example, if an airline like United Airlines notices that more and more travelers are trying to buy plane tickets, then United's demand for airplanes will increase. United will then have to borrow money to buy or lease more planes, so its credit demand curve will shift to the right. If other businesses are experiencing similar trends and increasing their demand for credit at a given real interest rate, then the market (or aggregate) credit demand curve will shift to the right.
- **Changes in household preferences or expectations.** Households borrow for many reasons: buying a home, a car, that gargantuan flat-screen TV, or paying college tuition bills. If household preferences change so that they would like to consume more of these goods and services, they will tend to borrow more. Likewise, they'll be more willing to borrow when they grow more optimistic about the future, for example, because they expect that they'll be in a good position to pay back those loans later. Such changes in household preferences or expectations shift the market credit demand curve to the right. Likewise, if households become more pessimistic about the future, then they will cut their desired borrowing at each interest rate, shifting the market credit demand curve to the left.
- **Changes in government policy.** Government borrowing in the credit market can swing violently from year to year. For example, in 2007 the U.S. federal government ran a deficit of $0.4 trillion, which implies that it borrowed $0.4 trillion on the credit market. As the 2007–2009 recession deepened, household and business income fell; this situation in turn reduced tax revenues collected by the government. At the same time, government spending rose both to help out struggling families and to stimulate the contracting economy. By 2009, the government deficit was $1.5 trillion. Holding all else equal, an increase in government borrowing shifts the market credit demand curve to the right. (By 2013, the federal government deficit had shrunk to $0.8 trillion, representing a substantial reversal from 2009.) Finally, the government's tax policies can also shift the credit demand curve. Sometimes the government stimulates investment in physical capital by lowering taxes on profits or explicitly introducing subsidies for physical capital investment, thereby shifting the market credit demand curve to the right.

Saving Decisions

Banks provide credit to businesses and households that wish to borrow. But where do banks obtain the money that they lend out?

Other economic agents with excess cash have deposited their money in the bank. In this sense, banks play the role of middlemen, matching savers and borrowers. Banks aren't the only middlemen in the market for credit. Many different kinds of institutions—we provide a partial list later in this chapter—play the critical role of linking people with savings to people or firms who want to use those savings.

Banks play the role of middlemen, matching savers and borrowers.

Let's momentarily ignore the institutions that serve as the middlemen and focus on the depositors—in other words, the savers—who are the initial source of the funds that

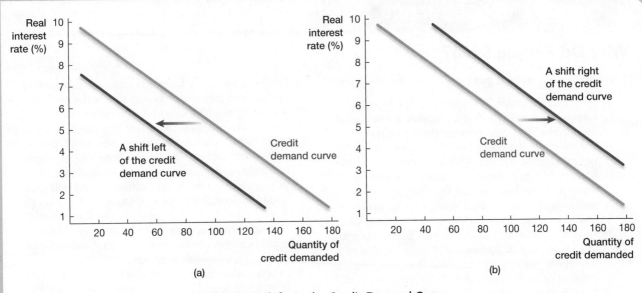

Exhibit 24.2 Shifts in the Credit Demand Curve

Changes in perceived business opportunities for firms, changes in household preferences or expectations, and changes in government policy may decrease the quantity of credit demanded for a fixed level of the real interest rate, shifting the credit demand curve to the left (panel (a)). When they increase the quantity of credit demanded for a fixed level of the real interest rate, the credit demand curve shifts to the right (panel (b)).

Buried treasure earns no interest. Savings accounts do.

borrowers will ultimately receive. Savers have money that they are willing to lend out because they prefer to spend it in the future rather than today. Of course, they could keep their money under a mattress or bury it under a palm tree on a deserted island. But buried treasure doesn't pay interest.

The Credit Supply Curve

People and firms with saved money obtain interest by lending the money to a bank or some other financial institution. In some cases, this "lending" takes the form of depositing the money at the bank in return for interest on a savings account. How much money are the savers willing to lend in this way? To answer this question, we need to understand the optimizing behavior of savers.

Saving results from a natural trade-off: people can spend their income on consumption today or can save it for consumption in the future. Because saving requires giving something up—current consumption—people will only save if they get something worthwhile in return. The real interest rate is the compensation that people receive for saving their money because a dollar saved today has $1 + r$ dollars of purchasing power in a year, where r is the real interest rate. Put differently, the real interest rate is the opportunity cost of current consumption—what you are giving up in terms of future purchasing power. Consequently, a higher real interest rate increases the opportunity cost of current consumption and encourages a higher level of saving.

On the other hand, a higher real interest rate might actually *lower* the saving rate. For example, if the real interest rate is relatively high, savings put aside when a person is young will grow relatively quickly, enabling a young worker to save *less* while still achieving a long-run goal of accumulating a retirement nest egg of a certain targeted size. Note, though, in most situations this negative effect on saving is thought to be weaker than the (positive) opportunity cost effect discussed above. In other words, for most people, a higher real interest rate induces a higher saving rate.

CHOICE & CONSEQUENCE

Why Do People Save?

There are five key reasons that people save for the future.

1. First and foremost, people save for retirement. When you retire, you'll only receive a fraction of the income that you received during working life. For example, the Social Security program pays the typical U.S. household a bit less than half of the household's preretirement income. If you don't want your consumption to fall sharply when you retire, you'll need to save some of your preretirement income. Most advisers recommend that working households in the United States contribute 10 percent to 20 percent of their income to a retirement savings account—for instance a 401(k) account or an IRA (Individual Retirement Account).

2. People save "for their kids," for example, for their weddings or their future educational investments like college and postgraduate school. A small fraction of parents also leave significant amounts of money to their kids in their wills. (Such gifts are called *bequests.*)

3. People save to pay for predictable large expenses, like a home purchase, *durable goods* (for instance, a washing machine or a car), and vacations.

4. People save so they can invest in a personal business. Small businesses sometimes can't obtain loans from banks. The bank's loan officer might not believe in your latest, greatest business idea. (If you were a bank's loan officer, would you give a loan to a recent college graduate with a plan to open a new taxi and limo service like BatteryPark?) In cases where outside funding can't be obtained, small business owners must use their own savings to fund their breakthrough ideas.

5. People save for a "rainy day." Your roof might spring a leak and require an expensive repair. You might lose your job. You might have a large medical expense that is not covered by insurance. In situations like these, you'll need a fund that you can lean on to get through hard times.

The **credit supply curve** is the schedule that reports the relationship between the quantity of credit supplied and the real interest rate.

This leads us to conclude that the **credit supply curve**, which is the schedule that reports the relationship between the quantity of credit supplied and the real interest rate, is upward-sloping. Specifically, a higher real interest rate encourages more saving, increasing the amount of funds that banks can lend and thereby increasing the quantity of credit supplied. Exhibit 24.3 plots the credit supply curve.

As before, it's important to carefully distinguish between movements along the credit supply curve, as in Exhibit 24.3, and shifts of the credit supply curve, as in Exhibit 24.4. Movements along the supply curve correspond to savers' response to changes *only* in the

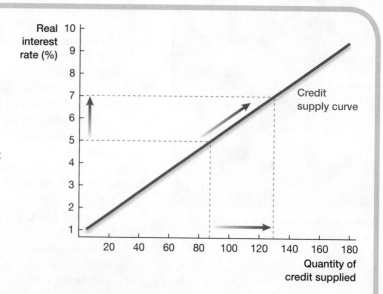

Exhibit 24.3 The Credit Supply Curve

The quantity of credit supplied is plotted on the horizontal axis and the real interest rate is plotted on the vertical axis. As the real interest rate rises, the quantity of credit supplied increases. This is a movement along the credit supply curve.

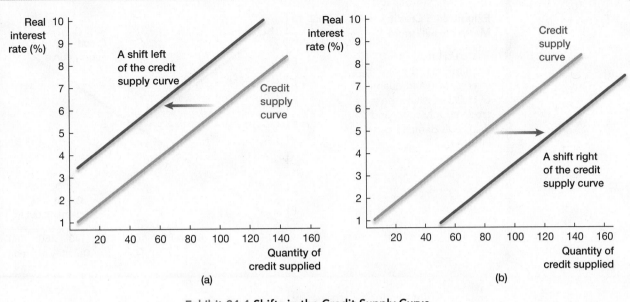

Exhibit 24.4 Shifts in the Credit Supply Curve

Changes in the saving motives of households or firms may decrease the quantity of credit supplied for a fixed level of the real interest rate, shifting the credit supply curve to the left (panel (a)). When households and firms increase the quantity of credit supplied for a fixed level of the real interest rate, the credit supply curve shifts to the right (panel (b)).

real interest rate. Shifts in the credit supply curve are driven by changes in the saving motives of optimizing economic agents, holding fixed the real interest rate.

- **Changes in the saving motives of households.** As discussed above, households save for many reasons—like retirement—but these motives change over time, shifting the credit supply curve. For example, if households start to predict economic hard times ahead, they will save more because they want to build up a store of wealth to be better prepared. This shifts the credit supply curve to the right. Likewise, demographic trends can change the savings behavior of households. For example, as households approach the age of retirement their saving rate tends to rise.
- **Changes in the saving motives of firms.** A firm has positive earnings if its expenses—including the cost of paying employees—are less than the firm's revenue. Some firms pass such earnings back to their stockholders—for example, by paying shareholder dividends. But some firms retain these earnings, depositing them in the firm's bank account and saving them for future investment. The magnitude of such *retained earnings* shifts over time. When firms are nervous about their ability to fund their business activities in the future, they tend to hold on to more retained earnings instead of paying them out as dividends. This shifts the credit supply curve to the right, another form of saving for a rainy day.

Equilibrium in the Credit Market

Exhibit 24.5 plots *both* the credit supply curve and the credit demand curve. This completes our picture of the **credit market**, where borrowers obtain funds from savers. It is sometimes referred to as the *loanable funds market*.

The **credit market** is where borrowers obtain funds from savers.

We've simplified the credit market by assuming that different borrowers all have identical risks of defaulting on their loan. In other words, all borrowers have the same risk of not repaying their loan. This simplification implies that there will be a single equilibrium real interest rate in the credit market. (In actual markets, borrowers with different risks of defaulting face different real interest rates to compensate lenders for these differential default risks.)

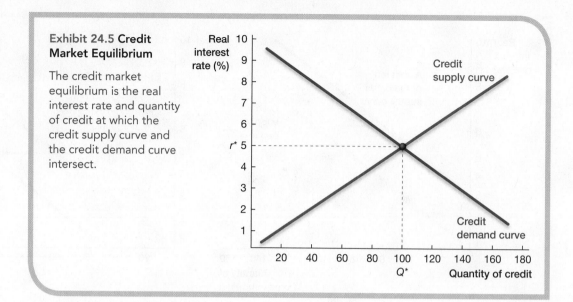

Exhibit 24.5 Credit Market Equilibrium

The credit market equilibrium is the real interest rate and quantity of credit at which the credit supply curve and the credit demand curve intersect.

Like other markets represented by a supply curve and a demand curve, the equilibrium in the credit market is the point at which the curves intersect. This intersection determines both the total quantity of credit in the market (Q^*) and the equilibrium real interest rate (r^*). At the equilibrium real interest rate, the quantity of credit demanded is equal to the quantity of credit supplied. A real interest rate above this level would lead to an excess supply of credit, which would typically put downward pressure on the real interest rate. A real interest rate below the equilibrium level would lead to an excess demand for credit, creating upward pressure on the real interest rate.

To see this in action, consider how a shift in the credit demand curve affects the credit market equilibrium, as shown in Exhibit 24.6. For example, assume that the government introduces a tax credit for business investment expenditures so that every dollar a firm invests by building plants or purchasing equipment reduces the taxes that it owes by 30 cents. Such a tax credit reduces the cost of investment to firms and thus raises the net benefit—benefits minus costs—of investment. As a consequence, an optimizing firm's willingness to borrow in the credit market (to fund investment in plants and equipment) will increase. Consequently, the credit demand curve shifts to the right. The new equilibrium point has a higher real interest rate (r^{**}) and a greater quantity of credit supplied and demanded (Q^{**}).

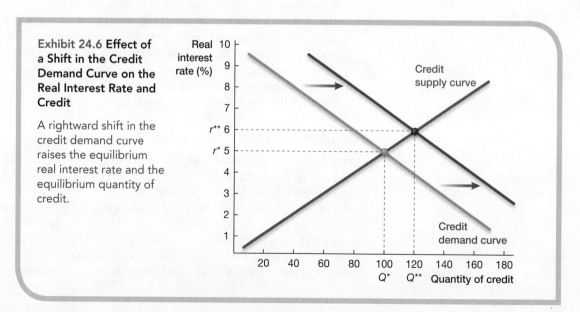

Exhibit 24.6 Effect of a Shift in the Credit Demand Curve on the Real Interest Rate and Credit

A rightward shift in the credit demand curve raises the equilibrium real interest rate and the equilibrium quantity of credit.

> By enabling savers to lend their excess money to borrowers, the credit market improves the allocation of resources in the economy.

Credit Markets and the Efficient Allocation of Resources

Credit markets play an extremely valuable social role. By enabling savers to lend their excess money to borrowers, the credit market improves the allocation of resources in the economy.

There is a simple way of seeing this. Suppose there was no credit market and you had $1,000 you wanted to save for next year. What could you do with it? You could put it in a safe box in your house—"putting the money under your mattress"—in which case you would just have $1,000 next year. With no inflation, you will have received a real interest rate of zero. If there is inflation, say 5 percent, then the real interest rate you will have received is much worse, -5 percent, because inflation eroded 5 percent of the purchasing power of your money.

We can also work through these examples by using the Fisher equation, which gives the formula for the real interest rate: $r = i - \pi$. If you receive no nominal interest (so $i = 0$), then the real interest rate is $r = 0 - \pi$. When the inflation rate is zero (so $\pi = 0$ percent), the real interest rate is $r = 0 - 0 = 0$ percent. When the inflation rate is 5 percent (so $\pi = 5$ percent), then the real interest rate is $r = 0 - 5 = -5$ percent.

You might do better than a 0 percent nominal interest rate by lending your money to your uncle who has some business venture in mind. But unless your uncle happens to be a good businessman, this choice might be worse than the mattress option.

Unknown to you, there could be several borrowers (possibly more reliable than your uncle!) who need that $1,000 for their investment. Without credit markets, they would also suffer because many of them would not be able to raise the necessary funds.

The valuable social role of credit markets is to match savers like you with borrowers. When credit markets work, you will get a reasonable return on your $1,000 saving (typically an average real return of 1 percent to 5 percent depending on how much risk you take), and worthy potential borrowers will be able to raise the funds they need.

24.2 Banks and Financial Intermediation: Putting Supply and Demand Together

Banks and other financial institutions are the economic agents connecting supply and demand in the credit market. Think of it this way: when you deposit your money in a bank account, you do not know who will ultimately use it. The bank pools all of its deposits and uses this pool of money to make many different kinds of loans: credit card loans to households; mortgages to home buyers; small loans to entrepreneurs; and large loans to established companies like General Electric, Nike, and Ford. Banks even make loans to other banks that need cash.

Running a bank is a complicated operation, and, so far, we've taken it all for granted. When we talked about the market for credit in the last section, we assumed that the lenders and borrowers could easily find each other. But in real life, matching lenders and borrowers is complex. Banks are the organizations that provide the bridge from lenders to borrowers, and because of this role, they are called *financial intermediaries*. Broadly speaking, **financial intermediaries** channel funds from suppliers of financial capital, like savers, to users of financial capital, like borrowers.

Financial intermediaries channel funds from suppliers of financial capital to users of financial capital.

Financial capital comes in many different forms, including credit (which is also referred to as debt) and equity. When a saver turns her savings into *credit*, she loans her savings to another party in exchange for the promise of repayment of her loan with interest. When a saver turns her savings into *equity*, she uses her savings to become a shareholder in a company, which means that she has obtained an ownership share and a claim on the future profits of the company. These profits are paid out as dividends to the company's shareholders.

Securities are financial contracts. For example, securities may allocate ownership rights of a company (stocks), or promise payments to lenders (bonds).

Banks Are Only One of Many Types of Financial Intermediaries

Many different types of financial institutions act as financial intermediaries, channeling funds from suppliers of financial capital—in other words, savers—to users of financial capital. In addition to banks, financial intermediaries include, but are not limited to, asset management companies, hedge funds, private equity funds, venture capital funds, bank-like businesses that comprise the "shadow banking system," and even pawnshops and shops that give payday loans.

Asset management companies, like Blackrock, Fidelity, and Vanguard, enable investors to use their savings to buy financial **securities** like *stocks* and *bonds*. When you buy a company's stock, you are buying a share of ownership in that company. When you buy a bond, you are effectively lending money to the company that issued the bond. These stock and bond investments are often made through mutual funds, which are large, diversified pools of securities. The value of all mutual funds in the United States in 2012 was approximately $13 trillion.

Hedge funds are investment pools gathered from a small number of very wealthy individuals or institutions, like university endowments. Hedge funds tend to follow risky, nontraditional investment strategies, like buying large tracts of land that can be used to grow timber, or buying stock in companies that are in financial trouble and have recently experienced large drops in their stock value. Hedge funds charge fees that are much higher than those of mutual funds. The value of all hedge funds in the United States in 2012 was approximately $2 trillion.

Private equity funds are investment pools that also typically involve a small number of wealthy investors. Private equity funds hold securities that are not publicly traded, so you can't buy them on a stock exchange. For instance, private equity funds might buy a company that is privately owned, like a family business. Alternatively, they might take a publicly traded company private by buying all of the shares in the company. The value of all private equity funds in the United States in 2012 was approximately $3 trillion.

Venture capital funds are a particular kind of private equity fund. They invest in new companies that are usually just starting up and therefore have no track record. For instance, in 1999, two venture capital funds—Kleiner-Perkins and Sequoia Capital—invested $25 million in a start-up company with a funny name—Google—founded the previous year. That single investment is now worth over $25 billion, implying a 1,000-to-1 return on every dollar invested. However, venture capital is a highly risky type of financial intermediation, and the typical venture capital firm didn't make any money in the decade after the tech bubble burst in 2000. The value of all venture capital funds in the United States in 2012 was about $200 billion.

The *shadow banking system* is comprised of thousands of institutions that are not officially banks because they don't take deposits, but nevertheless act like banks in the sense that they raise money and then make loans with those funds. Lehman Brothers, whose bankruptcy fueled the 2008 financial crisis, was one example of a shadow bank. Instead of taking common deposits, Lehman would take loans from large investors like insurance companies and use them to trade stocks and bonds, to make loans to businesses, and to create new financial products that they could sell to other institutions and wealthy investors.

Assets and Liabilities on the Balance Sheet of a Bank

To understand what banks do, it helps to first look at a bank's balance sheet, which summarizes both its *assets* and its *liabilities*. Assets include the investments the bank has made, government securities the bank holds, and the money the bank is owed by borrowers, including households and firms that have taken loans from the bank. The bank's liabilities include claims that depositors and other lenders have against the bank. For example, when a household deposits $10,000 at a bank, that deposit is a liability for the bank—money that the bank owes to the depositor.

Accountants call this statement of assets and liabilities a *balance* sheet because it is set up so that the assets and liabilities are balanced one for one. Think of the words *own* and *owe* to clarify the balance sheet—the balance sheet states what the bank owns (assets) and what it owes (liabilities).

Exhibit 24.7 summarizes some key features of the balance sheet of Citibank at the end of 2013, following the convention of listing assets in the left-hand column and liabilities in the right-hand column. The right-hand column also lists stockholders' equity, which is defined as total assets minus total liabilities and represents the value of the owners' (stockholders') stake in the company. Let's look in a bit more detail at the key categories that make up the assets and liabilities of the balance sheet.

Assets   Citibank's assets are simplified by being divided into three categories: reserves, cash and cash equivalents, and long-term investments.

Official **bank reserves** consist of vault cash and deposits at the Federal Reserve Bank.

1. **Bank reserves** include vault cash (dollars and coins held by Citibank in its own vault) and its holdings on deposit at the Federal Reserve Bank, often called the Fed, which is a special bank that is an agency of the government and is used to regulate the entire monetary system. We have much, much more to say about the Fed in the next chapter. In Exhibit 24.7, Citibank's reserves account for $294 billion of Citibank's total assets.

2. *Cash equivalents* are riskless, liquid assets that Citibank can immediately access, like deposits with other banks. An asset is riskless if its value doesn't change from day to day. An asset is liquid if it can quickly and easily be converted into cash, with little or no loss in value. In Exhibit 24.7, cash equivalents account for $192 billion of Citibank's total assets.

3. *Long-term investments* mostly comprise loans to households and firms but also include things like the value of the real estate that the bank uses for its operations, such as its bank branches and corporate headquarters. Long-term investments account for $1,398 billion of Citibank's total assets.

Liabilities and Stockholders' Equity   In Exhibit 24.7, Citibank's liabilities and stockholders' equity are divided into four categories: demand deposits, short-term borrowing, long-term debt, and stockholders' equity.

Demand deposits are funds that depositors can access on demand by withdrawing money from the bank, writing checks, or using their debit cards.

1. **Demand deposits** are funds "loaned" to the bank by depositors. Most depositors don't think of this as a loan to a bank, but rather as a deposit to a checking account. These deposits are referred to as *demand deposits* because the depositor can access the funds on demand—meaning, at any time—by withdrawing the money from an ATM or bank teller, writing a check, or using a debit card to make a store purchase. Even though demand deposits are "cash in the bank," so to speak, they are liabilities from the perspective of Citibank, because it owes this money to its depositors. Citibank owes depositors $938 billion in demand deposits. We look at these more closely in the next section.

Exhibit 24.7 Citibank's Balance Sheet, June 2013 (billions of dollars)

Citibank's balance sheet from June 2013 summarizes the assets that the bank owns, as well as the claims that depositors and other financial intermediaries have against the bank—the bank's liabilities. Stockholders' equity is defined as the difference between total assets and total liabilities, so liabilities plus stockholders' equity is exactly equal to the value of total assets.

Source: Citigroup Inc., 2013 Second Quarter Form 10-Q.

Assets		Liabilities and stockholders' equity	
Reserves	294	Demand Deposits	938
Cash equivalents	192	Short-term borrowing	527
Long-term investments	1,398	Long-term debt	221
		Total Liabilities	**1,686**
		Stockholders' equity	198
Total assets	**1,884**	**Total Liabilities + Stockholders' equity**	**1,884**

2. *Short-term borrowing* comprises short-term loans that Citibank has obtained from other financial institutions. All of these loans need to be repaid in the next year, and many of these loans are overnight loans that Citibank needs to repay the next day! Usually, such overnight loans are rolled over from one day to the next, meaning that Citibank repays its overnight loans and then instantly arranges new overnight loans with the same lenders. Unfortunately, heavy reliance on short-term debt generates some fragility in the banking system. If lenders suddenly start to worry that Citibank will have difficulty paying back short-term debt, Citibank might have trouble borrowing new funds and would therefore lack the funds it needs to conduct its day-to-day operations. Despite these risks, Citibank funds its operations by borrowing $527 billion of such short-term debt.

3. *Long-term debt* is defined as debt that is due to be repaid in a year or more. Citibank has $221 billion in long-term debt, representing 13 percent of its liabilities. This proportion contrasts sharply with the asset side of the balance sheet, where nearly 75 percent of the assets are long-term. The difference between long-term debt and long-term assets introduces a source of risk for the bank—a topic that we explore later in this chapter.

4. **Stockholders' equity** is defined as the difference between the bank's total assets and total liabilities.

Stockholders' equity is the difference between a bank's total assets and total liabilities.

$$\text{Stockholders' equity} = \text{Total assets} - \text{Total liabilities.}$$

This difference is equal to the estimated value of the company, or what the total value of Citibank's shares should be worth if the accountants got everything right.

We can rearrange the identity for stockholders' equity to find that

$$\text{Total assets} = \text{Total liabilities} + \text{Stockholders' equity.}$$

Looking at this equation, you can see that the two sides (left and right) of the balance sheet match up. Given the way in which accountants define stockholders' equity, the liability side of the balance sheet and the asset side of the balance sheet are always perfectly balanced.

24.3 What Banks Do

We can use the bank's balance sheet to identify three interrelated functions that banks perform as financial intermediaries.

1. Banks identify profitable lending opportunities.
2. Banks transform short-term liabilities, like deposits, into long-term investments in a process called *maturity transformation*.
3. Banks manage risk by using diversification strategies and also by transferring risk from depositors to the bank's stockholders and, in some cases, to the U.S. government.

We discuss each of these three functions in turn.

Identifying Profitable Lending Opportunities

One of the main roles of banks is to find creditworthy borrowers and channel savings of depositors to them. Thus, banks bring together the two sides of the credit market. Banks are in a good position to do this because, given their willingness to lend, they attract a large number of would-be borrowers and choose the more creditworthy among them. Banks employ armies of investment specialists and loan officers trained in identifying the best loan applications.

Maturity Transformation

Recall from Exhibit 24.7 that 87 percent of Citibank's liabilities, which are shown on the right-hand side of its balance sheet, are short-term (made up of demand deposits and short-term borrowing), while nearly 75 percent of its assets, shown on the left-hand side, are long-term investments. Citibank has transformed its short-term liabilities into long-term assets.

Maturity refers to the time until debt must be repaid.

Maturity is the time until debt must be repaid. Demand deposits have a 0-year maturity, because the depositor can take back her money at any time. In contrast, when banks lend to borrowers, such loans usually have a maturity ranging from several years up to 30 years. The transfer of short-term liabilities like demand deposits into long-term investments is called **maturity transformation**.

Maturity transformation is the process by which banks take short-maturity liabilities and invest in long-maturity assets (long-term investments).

Maturity transformation is what enables society to undertake significant long-term investments. But it also implies that banks wind up with a mismatch between the short-term maturities of their deposits and the long-term maturities of their loans. This maturity mismatch could get them into trouble if lots of depositors were to simultaneously ask to make withdrawals. Banks can't simply recall their long-term loans if their short-term depositors want their money back. To ensure that they can fulfill demands for withdrawals, banks do not lend out all of their deposits. They hold back some fraction of the deposit pool as *reserves* or some other form of cash-like security.

Banks have a large number of depositors, and typically only a tiny fraction of depositors demand their funds on any given day. Banks are also able to exploit the fact that withdrawals of existing deposits and inflows of new deposits are roughly offsetting on most days. Banks therefore usually need only a small pool of reserves to meet the net withdrawals of deposits. This enables them to commit most of their demand deposits to long-term investments.

Management of Risk

A bank promises that depositors will never lose a penny. This is a striking promise, since the bank makes risky loans with the depositors' savings. For example, banks often invest in *mortgages*—loans to households to purchase houses—which are risky. About 12 percent of the mortgages held by banks at the beginning of the 2007–2009 financial crisis ended up late on payments or in default.

Banks manage risk in two ways. First, they hold a *diversified* portfolio: a typical bank invests not only in mortgages but in a diverse set of assets, including business loans, loans to other financial institutions, and government debt. A diversified portfolio is useful because all the diverse assets of the bank are unlikely to underperform at the same time.

But diversification by itself isn't sufficient to manage risks because sometimes a large fraction of even a diverse set of assets may underperform. Most types of assets lost value during the 2007–2009 financial crisis. But even then, depositors remain safe, because of banks' second strategy of risk management: shifting risk to stockholders, and ultimately, during severe financial crises, to the U.S. government.

To understand how risk is transferred, consider what happens to a simplified bank balance sheet after its long-term investments lose 10 percent of their value. To keep things simple, we analyze a bank with exactly $11 billion in assets, which is allocated to $1 billion in *reserves and cash equivalents* and $10 billion in *long-term investments*.

Panel (a) of Exhibit 24.8 reports an original balance sheet, while panel (b) of Exhibit 24.8 reports a new balance sheet with two changes. First, the value of long-term assets has

Exhibit 24.8 Illustrative Balance Sheet

In panel (a), the bank has $11 billion in assets and stockholders' equity of $2 billion. In panel (b), a $1 billion reduction in the value of the bank's assets reduces stockholders' equity to $1 billion, as stockholders' equity is defined as total assets minus total liabilities.

Panel (a) Before Investment Loss (Billions of Dollars)			
Assets		**Liabilities and stockholders' equity**	
Reserves & cash equivalents	1	Demand deposits	9
Long-term investments	10		
		Total liabilities	**9**
		Stockholders' equity	2
Total assets	**11**	**Total liabilities + stockholders' equity**	**11**

Panel (b) After $1 Investment Loss (Billions of Dollars)			
Assets		**Liabilities and stockholders' equity**	
Reserves & cash equivalents	1	Demand deposits	9
Long-term investments	10 − 1 = 9		
		Total liabilities	**9**
		Stockholders' equity	2 − 1 = 1
Total assets	**11 − 1 = 10**	**Total liabilities + stockholders' equity**	**11 − 1 = 10**

decreased by 10 percent, or $1 billion. Second, the value of stockholders' equity has been reduced by $1 billion. Recall that stockholders' equity is defined as the difference between the value of assets and liabilities. Since the value of the demand deposits has not changed—these are contractual promises from the bank to its depositors—but the value of the assets has declined by $1 billion, the value of stockholders' equity must also fall by $1 billion.

This example illustrates that stockholders bear all of the risk that the bank faces, *as long as stockholders' equity is greater than zero*. In other words, as long as the bank's assets exceed its liabilities, every change in the value of the assets is absorbed one-for-one by stockholders.

When the value of the bank's assets falls below the value of its liabilities, stockholders' equity goes to zero. Now the bank owes more than it owns. At about that moment, the government shuts down the bank. The government bank regulator—the Federal Deposit Insurance Corporation (FDIC)—steps in and takes control of the bank. The FDIC will either (1) shut down the bank's operations and make payouts to depositors or (2) transfer the bank to new ownership.

In the payout scenario, the FDIC takes over the assets of the bank and makes full payouts to all individuals with deposits at that bank up to a cap of $250,000; deposits up to $250,000 are "FDIC-insured." The FDIC may also make payouts for deposits in excess of $250,000 if sufficient funds are available. However, most other creditors and all of the stockholders of the bank will be wiped out, meaning that they will receive nothing.

More often, however, the FDIC does not pay out to depositors, but instead arranges for a speedy takeover by a healthy bank. Bank takeovers usually protect *all* deposits—even those greater than $250,000—but in most cases, the stockholders are still wiped out. The next business day the bank opens for business as usual, though it might have a different name on the front door. If the failed bank's depositors aren't paying attention, they may miss the fact that anything has happened at all.

These maneuvers don't always come cheap. In most cases, the failed bank has liabilities, principally demand deposits, that exceed the value of its assets. In technical terms, the failed bank is **insolvent**, meaning that the value of its assets is less than the value of its liabilities. On the other hand, the healthy bank that is taking over the failed bank is **solvent**, meaning that the value of its assets is greater than the value of its liabilities. The healthy bank needs some financial inducement to take over the operations of the failed bank. The FDIC has to provide this sweetener.

Bank failures during the financial crisis of 2007–2009 cost the FDIC over $100 billion. And the buck doesn't stop there. Depositors at *all* U.S. banks implicitly pay for these bank failures because the FDIC raises its funds by charging all banks deposit insurance premiums. *All* bank depositors, not just those at failed banks, end up indirectly paying to clean up the mess left in the wake of a bank failure.

Bank Runs

Though socially useful, the maturity and the risk transformation roles played by banks also create some risks. Most importantly, maturity transformation causes many of the bank's assets to become *illiquid*—that is, by turning short-term liabilities into long-term, illiquid assets, the bank effectively locks up money that it might need to give back to depositors or other creditors on short notice.

During a banking panic, a substantial fraction of depositors may try to withdraw their deposits at the same time. If the bank has mostly long-term, illiquid assets, the bank may have a hard time coming up with the cash that it will need to pay out those withdrawals. As word gets out that the bank's cash is running low, more depositors will try to make withdrawals in the hope that they can get what little cash remains.

In this way a banking panic can be self-fulfilling—it feeds on itself. An unusually large amount of withdrawals reduces the bank's cash, and this cash shortage begets even *more* withdrawals as depositors race to withdraw their deposits before the bank runs out of cash. Even if a bank was healthy before the panic, it might no longer be healthy after losing many of its depositors and being forced to sell its illiquid assets in "fire sales" where the bank doesn't get a good price for the assets because it doesn't have enough time to find the buyers who are willing to pay the highest price. The expanding panic and rising flood of withdrawals is called a **bank run**.

Bank runs have various economic costs. Most importantly, a run forces a bank to liquidate its long-term, illiquid assets prematurely. This sometimes involves abandonment

Seal of the U.S. Federal Deposit Insurance Corporation. The FDIC was founded in 1933. Today, it insures deposits at over 7,000 banks in the United States.

A bank becomes **insolvent** when the value of the bank's assets is less than the value of its liabilities.

A bank is **solvent** when the value of the bank's assets is greater than the value of its liabilities.

A banking panic can be self-fulfilling—it feeds on itself.

A **bank run** occurs when a bank experiences an extraordinarily large volume of withdrawals driven by a concern that the bank will run out of liquid assets with which to pay withdrawals.

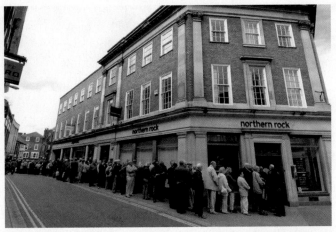

Northern Rock, a U.K. bank that specialized in mortgage lending, found it increasingly difficult to raise funds in late 2007. This triggered the first U.K. bank run in 150 years. A few months later, Northern Rock failed and was taken over by the U.K. government.

or inefficient liquidation of long-term investments in physical capital such as construction projects. In addition, since banks are key participants in the credit market, bank runs also disrupt the smooth working of the credit market.

Bank runs occurred in different forms during the most recent financial crisis, although some of the bank runs were hard for the public to see. The most visible bank run occurred in 2007 at Northern Rock, a U.K. bank that specialized in mortgage lending. Northern Rock's depositors were worried that the bank was insolvent, so they started to withdraw their deposits from the bank. These withdrawals snowballed into the first U.K. bank run in 150 years. Northern Rock desperately tried to find a stronger bank that would buy it out and instill confidence in its depositors. No such sale could be arranged, and Northern Rock was subsequently taken over by the U.K. government.

Bank Regulation and Bank Solvency

If bank runs were a frequent occurrence, the banking system would be quite unstable. Fortunately, bank runs like the one on Northern Rock—with tens of thousands of jittery depositors rushing to withdraw their money—have been relatively rare since the 1930s because of deposit insurance. If a bank fails for any reason, depositors' balances are protected up to some cap. All deposits at or below the cap are paid out in full by the relevant (government) insurance agency (the FDIC in the United States).

Deposit insurance didn't stop the bank run at Northern Rock, since the caps were relatively low in 2007 in the U.K. and many depositors had balances above the cap. Even depositors with fully insured accounts also withdrew their money, as they were afraid that the failure of Northern Rock would temporarily prevent them from accessing their money.

But households aren't the only economic agents depositing money at banks. Firms like Nike and Microsoft also hold bank accounts. Moreover, a bank might borrow money from other banks. When large firms and the general banking community lose confidence in a weak bank, an institutional bank run may ensue, in which firms and banks withdraw their deposits (and short-term loans) from the weak bank. FDIC insurance won't prevent institutional bank runs because institutions make deposits and short-term loans that are far too large to be fully insured by the FDIC. Institutional bank runs occurred frequently during the 2007–2009 financial crisis. However, because it is impossible to take a photograph of an institutional bank run, it is hard to know exactly when one of them is occurring.

We do know that the collapse of the investment bank Lehman Brothers in 2008 was preceded by an institutional bank run. Investment banks specialize in helping firms and governments make large financial transactions, especially for clients that need to raise financial capital to make investments. Investment banks are not FDIC-insured and do not take any deposits the way your neighborhood bank does. Instead, *all* of the liabilities on an investment bank's balance sheet are loans from other institutions, including other banks.

Many of the largest institutions that lent money to Lehman Brothers decided to stop making such short-term loans in the two weeks before Lehman went bankrupt. In other words, Lehman experienced an institutional bank run just before it failed. We now know that Lehman was insolvent at this time—its liabilities exceeded its assets. No wonder smart banks were unwilling to extend new loans to Lehman in the weeks before Lehman's bankruptcy.

Naturally, banks are very eager to avoid such financial meltdowns. They have many strategies at their disposal, though some of these strategies work better than others. As always, prevention is the ideal cure. The ultimate source of strength is to have lots of stockholders' equity, implying that a bank has assets that far exceed the value of its liabilities. When a bank owns far more than it owes, it is said to be well capitalized. In this case, the public should have no doubt about a bank's solvency, which reduces the likelihood of a bank run.

If a bank is running short of reserves, it can stop making new loans and it can sell its long-term investments. However, these efforts can backfire, because they may actually reveal that a bank is in trouble and can intensify the panic that may already have begun. In addition, if a bank stops lending, it reduces its ability to act as a financial intermediary and reduces its earnings at exactly the time when it needs those earnings the most.

Evidence-Based Economics

Q: How often do banks fail?

Banks work very hard to create the impression that they are bedrock institutions. But they haven't proved to be as solid as advertised. In the United States alone, nearly 20,000 banks have failed since 1900. However, most of those failures occurred *before* the establishment of the FDIC in 1933, which created deposit insurance and also enforced strict nationwide bank regulations. Nevertheless, even *since* the FDIC was established, more than 3,000 banks have failed.

Bank failures appear to be a regular feature of modern market economies. The U.S. economy has still observed four major waves of bank failures since the beginning of the twentieth century. The first wave of these bank failures occurred from 1919 to 1928—the decade before the Great Depression—when almost 6,000 banks failed, or 20 percent of all banks in the United States. These failures were concentrated among rural banks that issued mortgages to farms with land values that subsequently fell.

The second wave hit during the Great Depression (1929–1939), when more than 9,000 banks failed. This wave of bank failures was far more severe than the failures of the 1920s. For example, in 1933 *alone*, more than 25 percent of all U.S. banks failed. All told, nearly 50 percent of all U.S. banks failed during the Great Depression.

The third wave occurred during the savings and loan crisis in the 1980s and early 1990s. Savings and loan associations are one type of regional bank. During the savings and loan crisis nearly 3,000 banks failed, comprising about 15 percent of all U.S. banks. The crisis was caused by a boom-to-bust cycle of rising and then falling agricultural and oil prices. During the period of rising prices, the banks made risky investments in local farms and businesses. When agricultural and oil prices turned around, those investments were decimated.

The fourth wave of failures resulted from the 2007–2009 financial crisis. By year-end 2012, there were over 460 bank failures, representing less than 5 percent of all U.S. banks. At first glance, this may seem to be relatively small when compared with the earlier waves. But the 2007–2009 wave included the failure of Washington Mutual in 2008, with more than $300 billion in assets. The largest previous bank failure was Continental Illinois, which collapsed in 1984 with $40 billion in assets, which is equal to $90 billion in 2008 dollars.

Even more importantly, the 2007–2009 financial crisis coincided with the collapse of several (nonbank) financial institutions, like Lehman Brothers. As described earlier, investment banks like Lehman are not regular banks since they don't take deposits and their lenders are not

MyEconLab   Real-time data

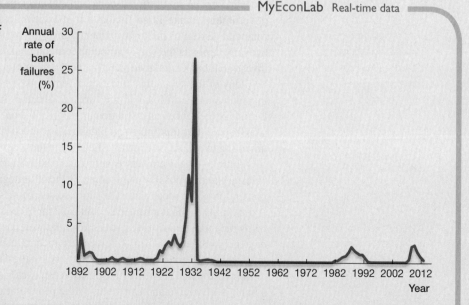

Exhibit 24.9 Annual Rate of Bank Failures in the United States (1892–2013)

The number of annual bank failures in the United States divided by the number of banks in operation.

Sources: Federal Reserve Bank of St. Louis, Federal Reserve System, Federal Reserve Board of Governors, and Federal Deposit Insurance Corporation.

insured by the FDIC. Lehman had $600 billion of loans from other financial institutions, so its balance sheet was nearly twice as large as that of Washington Mutual.

Exhibit 24.9 plots the annual number of bank failures in the United States divided by the total number of banks in operation during that year. Although this measure is not perfect—recall that Washington Mutual counts the same as any other bank, large or small—the data do provide some useful guidance about the pattern of historical bank failures.

Two key facts jump out. First, the Great Depression remains the most severe financial crisis in U.S. history (see the huge peak for 1933 in Exhibit 24.9). Second, after the FDIC regulatory and insurance system was created in 1933, the rate of bank failures plummeted. Note that the FDIC not only insures deposits but also acts as a stringent regulator. Deposit insurance reduces the likelihood of bank runs. Regulation reduces the likelihood that banks take irresponsible risks with their depositors' money. At least so far, the FDIC era has been relatively placid in comparison to the financial mayhem that preceded it.

Question	Answer	Data	Caveat
How often do banks fail?	Although there have been long periods of calm, four waves of bank failures have occurred in the United States since 1900, generating around 20,000 total failures.	Historical banking data from the Federal Reserve and the FDIC.	In some ways, counting bank failures can be misleading, because the failure of one large national bank can be more destructive than the failure of hundreds of small regional banks.

 CHOICE & CONSEQUENCE

Too Big to Fail

Many economists worry that extremely large banks have become too powerful. If a bank is large enough, the government will think twice before letting the bank fail, as this failure will reverberate through the economy. If one bank fails, then all of the banks that are owed money by the failed bank will suffer losses. And the dominoes might keep falling, as one bank after another fails and the ripples of financial losses keep spreading through other banks. In theory, the failure of one megabank could bring down the whole financial system.

Regulators call such large financial institutions *systemically important financial institutions* (SIFIs) and agonize about the consequences of the failure of a SIFI. The government faces a devilish problem: if a SIFI is in trouble, even if this is due to the SIFI's own irresponsible decisions, how could a responsible government *not* bail the SIFI out? For instance, the government could lend the bank some funds (at a low interest rate) thereby enabling the bank to keep operating and avoiding the cataclysmic economy-wide consequences of the bank's failure.

Because the SIFI is "too big to fail"—meaning that the government is afraid of letting the megabank fail and will

rescue it if it gets into trouble—the SIFI might knowingly choose to take irresponsible risks. If things *do* go badly, the bank will still be OK, since the government will be forced to offer a bailout. It's the "heads I win, tails you lose" situation, with the winner being the bank's shareholders and the loser being taxpayers, who indirectly bear the losses when the government sends the financial cavalry in to save the day.

To avoid problems like this, bank regulators have adopted two strategies. First, they now require large banks to explain how they could be wound down in an orderly way if they were to become insolvent. These procedures are referred to as "living wills," and they spell out how the bank would sell its assets and pay off its creditors in the event that it needed to end its business operations. Such living wills are designed to make it more credible and easier for a government to shut down a failing bank, including a failing SIFI.

Second, regulators are now requiring banks to take on less risk and hold more stockholders' equity, reducing the likelihood that a large bank will get into trouble in the first place. We return to these issues in the next chapter.

Asset Price Fluctuations and Bank Failures

After hearing about the waves of failures that sometimes engulf the banking industry, you might be wondering how these waves originate. Why do so many banks go belly up at the same time?

Banks fail when they invest in long-term assets that subsequently fall in price. Since different banks tend to invest in the same types of long-term assets, banks' fortunes often rise and fall together. Even a small percentage decline in the value of a bank's long-term assets can wipe out all of a bank's stockholders' equity, causing the bank to become insolvent.

Large changes in asset values are common in economic history. For example, in the late 1920s, stock prices and land prices skyrocketed, only to plummet subsequently during the Great Depression. Likewise, the savings and loan crisis of the late 1980s was caused by a fall in asset values. One of the contributing factors was a roller-coaster ride in the prices of natural resources, particularly oil. From 1972 to 1980, the price of crude oil rose from about $20/barrel to $100/barrel (in 2010 constant dollars) and then fell back, ending up in 1986 where it started in 1972 (using constant dollars). When oil prices peaked in 1980, most forecasters predicted steep ongoing increases in oil prices. Consequently, the subsequent fall in oil prices was unanticipated, devastating the oil-producing regions in the United States, particularly towns in Texas, Louisiana, and Oklahoma. Local businesses lost value, and over ten thousand of them went bankrupt. In turn, the slowdown in regional economies decimated housing prices.

The most recent financial crisis (2007–2009) was also associated with falling asset prices. The real value of U.S. stocks halved and the real value of residential real estate fell by over a third.

Why do asset prices fluctuate so much? The most established theory of stock prices links them to *fundamentals*— rational forecasts of the future earnings prospects of companies and the future value of interest rates. This theory, often referred to as *the theory of efficient markets* and associated with Nobel prize-winning economist Eugene Fama, asserts that stock market prices are based exclusively on *fundamentals* and are entirely rationally determined.[2] It implies that all movements in stock prices reflect rational appraisals of new information, not a tendency for investors to let their emotions get in the way. In the efficient markets' view, large fluctuations in asset prices are episodes in which important new information became available to investors, who then use this information to rationally update their beliefs about the future profitability of firms traded on the stock exchange.

An alternative view, gaining more traction over the last three decades and developed by another Nobel prize-winning economist, Robert Shiller, links asset price fluctuations to *asset bubbles*.[3] Bubbles occur when asset prices depart from fundamentals. Some economists believe that substantial asset price bubbles arise on occasion, partly driven by psychological factors and biases, particularly during specific episodes such as extended economic and stock market booms. If bubbles can be identified while they are occurring, then subsequent market crashes would be partially predictable.

Whatever the source of crashes in asset prices, most economists agree that banking regulation plays a useful role in helping the banking sector survive these episodes. Regulators around the world are now drafting new rules that will require banks to have more stockholders' equity—more assets relative to their liabilities—thereby increasing their ability to survive sharp declines in the value of the assets on their balance sheets. The chapters that follow contain extensive discussions about macroeconomic fluctuations—like recessions—and the many different policies that governments use to reduce the severity of these events.

Summary

✺ Credit is essential for the efficient allocation of resources in the economy; for example, credit allows firms to borrow for investment or households to borrow to purchase a house.

✺ The relevant price in the credit market is the real interest rate rather than the nominal interest rate. The real interest rate adjusts the price of borrowing or lending for the effects of inflation, thus reflecting the economic trade-off between the present and the future that borrowers and savers face.

✺ Firms, households, and governments use the credit market for borrowing. The credit demand curve summarizes the relationship between the quantity of credit demanded by borrowers and the real interest rate. The credit demand curve results from optimizing behavior of these borrowers.

✴ The credit supply curve summarizes the relationship between the quantity of credit supplied and the real interest rate and also results from optimizing behavior, this time of savers. They trade off consumption today for consumption in the future, taking into account the reward for delaying consumption—the real interest rate.

✴ The intersection of the credit demand curve and the credit supply curve is the credit market equilibrium. At the equilibrium real interest rate, the quantity of credit demanded is equal to the quantity of credit supplied.

✴ Saving and borrowing in the credit market are intermediated by banks and other financial intermediaries. Banks play three key roles in the economy. First, they find creditworthy borrowers and channel savings of depositors to them. Second, they transform the maturity structure in the economy by collecting money from savers in the form of short-term demand deposits and investing that money in long-term projects. Third, they manage risk by holding a diversified portfolio and by transferring risk from depositors to stockholders and, in economic crises, to the government.

✴ Governments provide deposit insurance that reduces the likelihood of bank runs, and governments intervene to save failing banks in order to avert widespread crises. The U.S. economy has experienced four major waves of bank failures since 1900.

Key Terms

debtors *p. 561*
credit *p. 561*
interest rate or nominal interest rate
  p. 562
real interest rate *p. 562*
credit demand curve *p. 563*

credit supply curve *p. 566*
credit market *p. 567*
financial intermediaries *p. 569*
securities *p. 570*
bank reserves *p. 571*
demand deposits *p. 571*

stockholders' equity *p. 572*
maturity *p. 572*
maturity transformation *p. 573*
insolvent *p. 574*
solvent *p. 574*
bank run *p. 574*

Questions

All questions are available in MyEconLab *for practice and instructor assignment.*

1. What is the difference between nominal and real interest rates?

2. Firms, households, and governments use the credit market for borrowing. The credit demand curve shows the relationship between the quantity of credit demanded and the real interest rate.

   a. Why does the credit demand curve slope downward?

   b. What can cause a shift in the credit demand curve?

3. What factors explain why people save for the future?

4. Households and firms with savings lend money to banks and other financial institutions. The credit supply curve shows the relationship between the quantity of credit supplied and the real interest rate.

   a. Why does the credit supply curve slope upward?

   b. What can cause a shift in the credit supply curve?

5. What are the key categories on a bank's balance sheet? Illustrate using a table.

6. What is the shadow banking system?

7. What functions do banks perform as financial intermediaries in the economy?

8. What is maturity transformation?

9. What is stockholders' equity? Who bears the risk that a bank faces when stockholders' equity is greater than zero?

10. What is a bank run?

11. What is deposit insurance? Is deposit insurance successful in preventing bank runs?

12. As the Choice and Consequence box on "Too Big to Fail" notes, bank regulators worry about the prospect of the failure of large financial institutions, dubbed "systemically important financial institutions" (SIFIs).

a. How would the failure of a SIFI affect the economy?

b. What steps do bank regulators take to prevent SIFIs from failing or to minimize the effect of such failures?

13. Banks fail when they invest in long-term assets that subsequently fall in price. What are the two views on why asset prices fluctuate so much that they lead to financial crises and bank failures?

Problems

All problems are available in MyEconLab *for practice and instructor assignment.*

1. Optimizing economic agents use the real interest rate when thinking about the economic costs and returns of a loan.

a. Recently, the average rate paid by banks on savings accounts was 0.45%. However, at the same time, inflation was around 1.5%. What was the average saver's real rate of interest on his or her savings?

b. Banks expect that the rate of inflation in the coming year will be 3%. They want a real return of 5%. What nominal rate should they charge borrowers? Explain using the Fisher equation.

2. The 1970s was a period of high inflation in many industrialized countries, including the United States.

a. Due to the increase in the rate of inflation, lenders, including credit card companies, revised their nominal interest rates upward. How is the rate of inflation related to the nominal interest rate that credit card companies charge? Why would lenders need to increase the nominal interest rate when the inflation rate increases?

b. Usury laws place an upper limit on the nominal rate of interest that lenders can charge on their loans. In the 1970s, in order to avoid usury laws, some credit card companies moved to states where there were no ceilings on interest rates. Why would credit card companies move to states without usury laws during a period of high inflation like the 1970s?

3. Imagine two economies—Nervosa and Chillaxia. In Nervosa, consumers and businesses are very apprehensive about higher interest rates. As soon as the real rate of interest increases, they cut back substantially on their borrowing. In Chillaxia, on the other hand, both households and firms have a much more relaxed response to higher rates. Even when the real interest rate increases, people tend not to curtail their borrowing very much.

Assume the credit supply curve is identical in both countries.

In which country would the equilibrium real interest rate change more in response to a large increase in the national government's deficit? Explain with reference to a well-labeled graph.

4. In August, 1979, the annual rate of inflation in the U.S. was nearly 12%, and the U.S. short-term nominal interest rate was nearly 10%. Over the next 35 years, both the rate of inflation and short-term nominal interest rate tended to fall. By August 2014, the rate of inflation was about 2% and the short-term nominal interest rate was close to 0%. How has the *real* short-term interest rate changed from 1979 to 2014? Why do the inflation rate and the nominal interest rate tend to move together over the long-run?

5. Explain how the equilibrium real interest rate and the equilibrium quantity of credit would change in each of the following scenarios, and illustrate your answer with a well-labeled graph of the credit market.

a. As the real estate market recovers from the 2007–2009 financial crisis, households begin to buy more houses and condominiums, and apply for more mortgages to enable those purchases.

b. Congress agrees to a reduction in the federal deficit, which results in a significant decrease in the amount of government borrowing.

c. Households begin to fear that the recovery from the 2007–2009 recession will not last, and become more pessimistic about the economy.

d. Businesses become more optimistic about the future of the economy, and decide to distribute more of their earnings as dividends to their shareholders.

6. Develop a bank balance sheet with assets and liabilities (or series of balance sheets) showing the changes resulting from each of the following events:

a. A customer deposits $500 in cash into her checking account

b. A bank makes a student loan of $2,500

c. A bank is robbed of $5,000

d. A customer makes a loan payment of $1,000; $800 of the payment represents interest on the balance of the loan, and $200 represents repayment of part of the principal of the loan

e. A million dollar real estate loan that the bank had made previously unexpectedly defaults (becoming a worthless investment for the bank)

7. Banks that practice *narrow banking* match the maturity of their investments with the term of the deposits that they collect from the public. In other words, narrow banks take short-maturity deposits and invest in assets that carry a low level of risk and are also of short-term maturity, like short-term government debt.

   a. Suppose that all FDIC-insured banks decide to adopt narrow banking. How would narrow banking reduce the level of risk in the banking system?

   b. If narrow banking reduces systemic risk, why do banks still practice maturity transformation?

8. If you have studied microeconomics, you may recall a concept called "moral hazard." Moral hazard occurs when an economic agent is incentivized to take risks because some (or all) of the losses that might result will be borne by other economic agents.

   Discuss how federal deposit insurance, administered by the FDIC as described in the chapter, might lead to moral hazard.

9. Recall from the chapter that banks in the United States hold a fraction of their checking deposits as reserves, either as vault cash or as deposits with the Federal Reserve (where they earn very little interest). Regulations require them to hold a certain percentage (currently 10 percent) of their checking deposits as reserves. However, banks are free to hold additional reserves if they choose. The latter are called *excess reserves*. Ordinarily, banks held very few excess reserves. However, starting in the financial crisis of 2007–2009, the amount of excess reserves held by banks went from virtually zero to over 1.8 trillion dollars.

   a. Explain why banks would be expected to try to minimize the amount of excess reserves that they hold.

   b. Based on what you learned about banking in the chapter, explain why you think that the crisis prompted banks to dramatically expand the amount of excess reserves they held.

10. Lehman Brothers Holdings Inc., an investment bank, experienced a bank run in 2008. There was also a run on Northern Rock, a commercial bank, in 2007.

    a. What were the similarities between these two bank runs? How were they different?

    b. Lehman Brothers was not insured by the Federal Deposit Insurance Corporation (FDIC) but deposits at Northern Rock were insured by the U.K. government. What could explain why there was still a bank run at Northern Rock?

11. The "Choice and Consequence" box on "Asset Price Fluctuations and Bank Failures" discusses the relationship between the prices of things like oil and real estate, and the solvency of lending institutions like banks.

    Consider the following two scenarios. Supply the missing entries, and answer the questions that follow.

    Assume that Securitas Bank is a large bank in the country of Hyponatremia. The bank's *only* assets and liabilities at the beginning of the year are given in the following balance sheet:

Securitas Bank Balance Sheet

Assets		Liabilities	
Reserves and Cash Equivalents	$20 Billion	Demand Deposits	$200 Billion
Long-term Investments	$330 Billion	Borrowing from Other Banks	$50 Billion
Total Assets	?	**Stockholders' Equity**	?

Philopericulum Bank is another large bank whose only assets and liabilities are summarized in their balance sheet:

Philopericulum Bank Balance Sheet

Assets		Liabilities	
Reserves and Cash Equivalents	$10 Billion	Demand Deposits	$450 Billion
Long-term Investments	$650 Billion	Borrowing from Other Banks	$200 Billion
Total Assets	?	**Stockholders' Equity**	?

Assume now that due to an economic downturn, the value of each bank's long-term investments declines by 10%. Show the resulting situation on each bank's balance sheet. How would you describe the resulting situation for each bank? Relate your answer to the discussion in the chapter of the concept of "Too Big to Fail."

12. The sharpest one-day percentage decline in the Dow Jones Industrial Average (DJIA) took place on October 19, 1987. The DJIA fell 23% on this one day. Foreign exchange markets and other asset markets also exhibit large fluctuations on a daily basis. Based on the information given in this chapter, discuss some factors that could explain why asset prices fluctuate.

25 The Monetary System

What caused the German hyperinflation of 1922–1923?

During a hyperinflation, a country's price level doubles within 3 years. In 1923, the inflation rate in Germany blew past this threshold. At one point, prices were doubling *every three to four days*. At that pace, prices doubled about 8 times in one month. For example, a single egg cost about 1 million German marks on October 1, 1923, and it cost about 256 million marks 30 days later:

8 Doublings: 2, 4, 8, 16, 32, 64, 128, 256

During the entire period of German hyperinflation, prices rose by a factor of roughly 500 *billion*. German currency lost so much value that a briefcase or, in some cases, a wheelbarrow was needed to carry enough paper currency to buy a day's groceries. Paper currency with low denominations had so little value that it was used to make toys, such as the kite on the left.

You might guess that there is something unique about Germany that caused this mass hysteria. But hyperinflations have occurred in many countries over the last century, including Austria, Argentina, Brazil, Chile, China, Hungary, Greece, Poland, and Zimbabwe, to name a few. In this chapter, we examine why hyperinflations occur and explain how they can be avoided. Using these insights, most countries *have* avoided hyperinflations since the end of World War II. Nevertheless, not all policymakers have learned these lessons. For example, since 2011, Belarus, Iran, and Venezuela have suffered from debilitating hyperinflations.

CHAPTER OUTLINE

KEY IDEAS

⚙ Money has three key roles: serving as a medium of exchange, a store of value, and a unit of account.

⚙ The quantity theory of money describes the relationship between the money supply, velocity, prices, and real GDP.

⚙ The quantity theory of money predicts that the inflation rate will equal the growth rate of the money supply minus the growth rate of real GDP.

⚙ The Federal Reserve, the U.S. central bank, has a dual mandate—low inflation and maximum employment.

⚙ The Federal Reserve holds the reserves of private banks.

⚙ The Federal Reserve's management of private bank reserves enables the Fed to do three things: (1) set a key short-term interest rate; (2) influence the money supply and the inflation rate; and (3) influence long-term real interest rates.

25.1 Money

Money is the asset that people use to make and receive payments when buying and selling goods and services.

The world economy is a phenomenally complex social system. Every year, global GDP totals about $80 trillion of goods and services. **Money** is the asset that people use to conduct these transactions. We can't understand how the world economy works without first understanding how money lubricates the system.

To introduce the role of money, consider a student majoring in English who works part-time in a bookstore; she exchanges her labor for money. Assume she uses her bookstore wages to buy something she wants, say, an iPhone. In this example, money greases the wheels of the exchange: she will give up 20 hours of time in the bookstore to *eventually* obtain an iPhone. Without money, the English major would have a hard time directly trading her labor for an iPhone. It is far more efficient for Apple to take her money than her labor in exchange for the iPhone.

> **"Money simultaneously serves three functions in a modern economy. It is a *medium of exchange*. It is a *store of value*. It is a measure of relative value, or a *unit of account*."**

The Functions of Money

Money simultaneously serves three functions in a modern economy:

1. It is a *medium of exchange*.
2. It is a *store of value*.
3. It is a measure of relative value, or a *unit of account*.

A **medium of exchange** is an asset that can be traded for goods and services.

A **store of value** is an asset that enables people to transfer purchasing power into the future.

A **medium of exchange** is something that can be exchanged in return for goods and services, thereby facilitating trade. For example, when you hand the cashier $10 for a pepperoni pizza, you are using money—in this case currency—as a medium of exchange. The use of money allows for a convenient, universally acceptable way of buying and selling goods and services.

Money serves as a better medium of exchange when it is also a **store of value**—it enables people to transfer purchasing power into the future. We expect that the $10 bill we receive on Tuesday will be accepted as a form of payment on Wednesday, or even a decade

A **unit of account** is a universal yardstick that is used for expressing the worth (price) of different goods and services.

from now. If pizzeria owners didn't trust that the $10 bill would be accepted in the future, they would not accept the $10 bill today.

Money also provides the yardstick for describing prices. What does it cost to buy a pair of jeans? In principle, we could report the price in units of eggs. For example, one pair of jeans might be equal in value to 200 eggs. Alternatively, we could report all prices in units of bananas: one pair of jeans might be worth 100 bananas. But shopping would be difficult if every store used a different yardstick for reporting prices. Life would be easier with a single yardstick for measuring value—a unit of account. Modern economies use money as the **unit of account**—a universal yardstick that expresses the price of different goods and services. We measure the cost of a good by the number of dollars it takes to buy that good, not by the equivalent value in bananas.

Economic transactions are much easier to conduct when there is a medium of exchange, a store of value, and a universal unit of account. Money performs all of these critical tasks simultaneously.

One Benjamin (Franklin)

Fiat money refers to something that is used as legal tender by government decree and is not backed by a physical commodity, like gold or silver.

Types of Money

Paper money was invented around 1,000 AD in China, but *other* forms of money have existed throughout human history. Before the adoption of paper money, people used money that was valuable in and of itself. The most well-known examples are silver and gold, though goats, chickens, and horses were also sometimes used.

Modern societies have switched to using **fiat money**—something that is used as legal tender by government decree and is not backed by a physical commodity, like gold or silver. For example, paper money is valuable only because other people will accept it as money. We don't accumulate Benjamins because we like the fine portrait of Benjamin Franklin on the $100 bill. Rather, $100 bills are useful for exchange, for storing value, and for keeping accounts because we *trust that paper currency will be used for these purposes in the future.*

In theory, any object in limited supply could play the role of fiat money, like used ticket stubs from major league baseball games or cobblestones taken from Peter's Square in the Vatican. But if we used things like ticket stubs or cobblestones for money, there would be a far greater risk of somebody counterfeiting them. This problem is partially resolved by having the government create fiat money that is difficult and illegal to counterfeit (and easy to carry around).

The Money Supply

How much money do you have available to purchase goods and services today? For many people, the answer would be much more than the amount of cash they have in their pocket. Suppose you had $10 of currency in your wallet and a $1,000 balance in your checking account. The minute you pull out your checkbook, the money available to you for purchases jumps from $10 to $1,010. And why stop there? You could increase the balance in your checking account by electronically transferring funds from your savings account.

Money

Hundreds of years ago

Today

CHOICE & CONSEQUENCE

Non-Convertible Currencies in U.S. History

In 1861, at the beginning of the Civil War, the U.S. government paid its soldiers with paper currency that was convertible into gold. However, in 1862 the government ran short of gold and switched to fiat currency, which is not convertible.

You can see the difference in the following pair of images. The top image is paper currency issued in 1861, which is convertible into gold. It was called a Demand Note, because the note could be exchanged for gold "On Demand"—look for those words in the center of the note. The lower image is currency issued in 1862, which could not be exchanged into gold and omits the phrase "On Demand."

When the introduction of fiat money was debated in 1862, the idea was highly controversial. Many politicians believed that money would work only if it were backed by gold or silver. However, once it was issued, the 1862 fiat money quickly gained acceptance and did not generate hyperinflation. Convertibility wasn't reintroduced until 1879.

The Civil War was just one of many periods in which fiat money has been used in the United States. The American colonies temporarily used fiat money during the Revolutionary War. The United States temporarily adopted fiat

A small number of firms now accept payments in bitcoin.

money during the War of 1812. Following each of these episodes, convertibility was eventually reinstated.

Convertibility was gradually eliminated in the twentieth century, and the last vestiges of convertibility were dropped in 1971. Since then, the system of fiat currency has performed well: the buying power of paper currency has been far less volatile than the buying power of gold. Very few economists believe that the United States should return to a "gold standard"—a system in which paper currency is convertible into gold.

In fact, new *non-convertible* electronic currencies are now being introduced by private organizations. Because these new currencies are not endorsed by the government, they are not fiat currencies, and their future success is anyone's guess. These electronic *cryptocurrencies* are protected with computer codes (cryptogaphy) that make theft of the currency difficult, though not impossible. The use of computer codes also hides the identities of the agents who use the currencies. The most famous, and the first, cryptocurrency, is bitcoin.

Cryptocurrencies have had a controversial start. The electronic exchanges on which cryptocurrencies are traded have frequently been used for illegal transactions, such as the sale of cocaine. Moreover, several exchanges have been hacked by rogue computer programmers, resulting in electronic thefts. For example, the bitcoin exchange Mt. Gox declared bankruptcy after $477 million was stolen. Finally, the cryptocurrencies have had volatile valuations, because the public's demand for these new currencies waxes and wanes. For example, during 2013 the value of a bitcoin rose from $13 per bitcoin at the start of the year to a peak of $1,163 per bitcoin on November 30, before falling to $732 by year-end.

Examples of a demand note (top figure), which was convertible into gold, and fiat currency (bottom figure), which was not.

The money supply adds together currency in circulation, checking accounts, savings accounts, travelers' checks, and money market accounts. This is sometimes referred to as M2.

When economists talk about money, we include most forms of assets that can be immediately drawn on to purchase goods and services. With this concept in mind, we define the **money supply** as currency in circulation, checking accounts, savings accounts, and most other types of bank accounts. You'll often hear this definition of money supply referred to as M2. Using this definition, the money supply is overwhelmingly comprised of different types of bank accounts.

There are several different definitions of money supply, which go by the related names M1, M2, and M3. To avoid unnecessarily complicating our discussion, we focus on M2.

Exhibit 25.1 plots the evolution of currency in circulation (which does not include currency in bank vaults) and money supply (M2) from 1959 to 2014. To highlight some

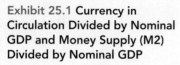

Exhibit 25.1 Currency in Circulation Divided by Nominal GDP and Money Supply (M2) Divided by Nominal GDP

Two ratios: (1) currency divided by nominal GDP and (2) money supply (M2) divided by nominal GDP. "Currency" is currency in circulation, which does not include currency in bank vaults. Money supply (M2) is the sum of currency in circulation, checking accounts, savings accounts, travelers' checks, and money market accounts. The exhibit implies that currency in circulation accounts for about 11 percent of the money supply.

Sources: Data from Board of Governors of the Federal Reserve (money supply and currency in circulation) and Bureau of Economic Analysis, National Income and Product Accounts (GDP). Data is quarterly and covers the period from quarter 1 of 1959 to quarter 1 of 2014, or 1959Q1 to 2014Q1.

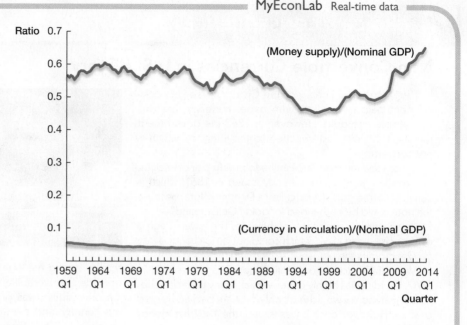

important relationships, we divide everything by the level of nominal GDP. You can see that the ratios have starkly different values. In 2014, there are only about 7 cents of currency in circulation for every dollar of annual GDP. However, there are about 65 cents of total money supply for every dollar of GDP. Hence, the total money supply is about 9 times the magnitude of currency in circulation. This is not surprising once we remember how little cash we carry around compared with the balances in our bank accounts. Moreover, very few of our important financial transactions are conducted with currency. In developed countries, only drug dealers buy a house or a car with a suitcase full of cash. Indeed, even smaller transactions, like paying the rent each month, are rarely conducted with currency.

We can also use Exhibit 25.1 to think about time trends in these ratios. The (Currency in Circulation)/GDP ratio and the (Money Supply)/GDP ratio show no clear long-run time trends, though they do bounce around and they have been rising in recent years.

25.2 Money, Prices, and GDP

We are now ready to study the relationship between money supply, prices, and nominal GDP. Along the way, we will use the fact that the ratio of Money/(Nominal GDP) is relatively stable over the long run.

Nominal GDP, Real GDP, and Inflation

Let's start with a few definitions that we first introduced in Chapter 19. Nominal GDP is the total value of production (final goods and services), using prices from the same year the output was produced. Real GDP is the total value of production (final goods and services), using fixed prices taken from a particular base year, which may or may not be the year the output was produced. Finally, the inflation rate is the growth rate of the overall price level in the economy.

To illustrate these concepts, consider an illustrative economy that only produces soccer balls. Assume that in 2013, this economy produced 10 soccer balls at a market price of $50 per ball, for total sales of $500. In 2014, total sales rise to $550. Therefore, nominal

GDP has risen by $50 = $550 − $500. What has caused the $50 increase? Here are two possibilities:

1. The price of soccer balls is still $50 per ball, and the number of soccer balls produced has risen to 11 balls.
2. The price of soccer balls has risen to $55 per ball, and the number of soccer balls produced has stayed fixed at 10.

Under either Scenario 1 or 2, nominal GDP is $550, 10 percent more than it was the year before.

In Scenario 1 the price hasn't changed, but the number of soccer balls produced has risen from 10 to 11 balls. In this case, we say that inflation is zero and real GDP has grown by 10 percent. For example, using 2013 as the base year for prices, we can see that real GDP rose from 10 × $50 = $500 to 11 × $50 = $550, which is a 10 percent increase.

In Scenario 2 the price has risen from $50 to $55 per ball, but the number of soccer balls produced has stayed fixed at 10 balls in each year. In this case, we say that inflation is 10 percent and real GDP is flat. Using 2013 as the base year for prices, we can see that real GDP held steady at 10 × $50 = $500. In both years, the number of balls produced was 10.

This example illustrates a basic property of nominal GDP. Increases in nominal GDP could arise because of an increase in the price level, an increase in the level of real GDP, or a combination of the two. In fact, we can express the growth rate of nominal GDP as the sum of the growth rate in prices (the inflation rate) and the growth rate in real GDP.

$$\text{Growth rate of nominal GDP} = \text{Growth rate of prices} + \text{Growth rate of real GDP}$$
$$= \text{Inflation rate} + \text{Growth rate of real GDP}.$$

We will now use this basic relationship to derive a theory that describes the connection between the growth rate of the money supply, the inflation rate, and the growth rate of real GDP.

The Quantity Theory of Money

We begin by discussing the relationship between the money supply and nominal GDP. Recall the data from Exhibit 25.1. There we showed that over the long run, the ratio of money supply to nominal GDP is approximately constant.

$$\frac{\text{Money Supply}}{\text{Nominal GDP}} = \text{Constant}.$$

The **quantity theory of money** assumes a constant ratio of money supply to nominal GDP.

The **quantity theory of money** assumes that this ratio is *exactly* constant. In general, that is not the case, as Exhibit 25.1 clearly shows. So in this sense the quantity theory of money is wrong, but it is an *approximation* of how the economy behaves over a few decades, which economists loosely refer to as the *long run*. Look again at Exhibit 25.1, and you will see that although the ratio of money supply to nominal GDP does change over time, it has also been approximately stable over the long run. (The ratio of nominal GDP divided by money supply is referred to as the *velocity* of money— this is the inverse of the ratio plotted in Exhibit 25.1. The concept of the velocity of money does not play a role in our book, but you may encounter it in other courses.)

If the ratio of two variables is constant, then the numerator and the denominator have the same rate of growth. For example, if money supply grows by 10 percent, then nominal GDP also needs to grow by 10 percent to keep the ratio of money supply divided by nominal GDP constant.

So the quantity theory of money implies that the growth rate of money supply and the growth rate of nominal GDP will be the same.

$$\text{Growth rate of money supply} = \text{Growth rate of nominal GDP}.$$

"The quantity theory of money implies that inflation is equal to the gap between the growth rate of the money supply and the growth rate of real GDP."

Using this relationship, we can return to our equation decomposing the growth rate of nominal GDP into (1) the inflation rate and (2) the growth rate of real GDP. Substituting the *inflation rate plus the growth rate of real GDP* for the *growth rate of nominal GDP*, we find that:

$$\text{Growth rate of money supply} = \text{Inflation rate} + \text{Growth rate of real GDP}.$$

We can rearrange this equation to put inflation on the left-hand side. Then we find that

$$\text{Inflation rate} = \text{Growth rate of money supply} - \text{Growth rate of real GDP}.$$

This result is a direct implication of the quantity theory of money. This equation implies that inflation is equal to the gap between the growth rate of the money supply and the growth rate of real GDP. When this gap widens, the inflation rate increases. This equation makes clear predictions that we can test with economic data.

25.3 Inflation

Recall from Chapter 19 that the inflation rate refers to the rate of increase of a price index. Of course, price movements need not always be positive. If a price level decreases, we call the rate by which it decreases **deflation**. For example, if the inflation rate is negative 1 percent, we say that the deflation rate is 1 percent. Rising price indexes have been much more common than falling prices since World War II, though the United States during the Great Depression and Japan during the last two decades both experienced periods of persistent deflation.

The **deflation** rate is the rate of decrease of a price index.

What Causes Inflation?

As we have just seen, the quantity theory of money implies that inflation occurs when the growth rate of money supply exceeds the growth rate in real GDP. This is the implication of the last equation that we derived.

Exhibit 25.2 illustrates this relationship with data from 110 countries over the period 1960–1990. As you can see, the inflation rate (on the vertical axis), is closely related to the growth rate of money supply minus the growth rate of real GDP (this difference is on the horizontal axis). All of these variables are annualized in this exhibit, which means that they are expressed as a rate of increase per year. The quantity theory of money predicts that inflation should rise one-for-one with the growth rate of money supply minus the growth rate of real GDP. That is approximately what you see in Exhibit 25.2: most of the data is close to the 45-degree line, which has a slope of 1. This empirically confirms a key long-run prediction generated by the quantity theory of money.

You might have noticed that some of the countries plotted in Exhibit 25.2 had very high average inflation rates from 1960 to 1990. In the case of Argentina, the most extreme point in Exhibit 25.2, inflation averaged 80 percent per year from 1960 to 1990. Argentina experienced this high average inflation rate during this 30-year period because prices rose extraordinarily quickly in the 1980s, pulling up the three-decade average. At some points in the 1980s, prices rose more than 50 percent *per month*.

Recall from the chapter opener that during a *hyperinflation*, a country's price level doubles within 3 years. Hyperinflationary episodes are always related to extremely rapid growth of the money supply. In almost all cases, such extreme monetary growth is brought about by large government budget deficits. If a government's tax revenues fall short of its expenditures, then it meets its obligations by borrowing from the public and/or printing currency to buy goods and services. When a government prints currency and uses it to make purchases, this increases currency in circulation and thereby increases the money supply. This is also how German policymakers generated the great German hyperinflation of 1922–1923.

The Consequences of Inflation

If relative prices are all that matters for optimization decisions—for instance, the price of a gallon of milk *relative* to a worker's hourly wage—then moderate inflation might not pose a problem. In principle, inflation scales up grocery prices *and* wages, so a worker's ability to buy goods and services is unaffected by economy-wide inflation. Increasing all prices by 5 percent and simultaneously increasing a worker's wage by 5 percent does not change any of the relative prices or the worker's buying power. If inflation simply raised all prices and all wages by the inflation rate, then inflation might not be a big deal.

However, all prices and all wages do not always move in sync (at least not in the short run). An increase in the inflation rate generates windfall losses to some and windfall

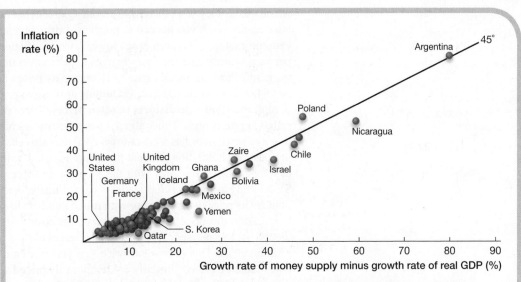

Exhibit 25.2 Testing the Long-Run Prediction of the Quantity Theory of Money

This figure empirically evaluates the long-run predictions of the quantity theory of money, using data from 1960 to 1990 for 110 countries. The vertical axis plots the annualized inflation rate for each country. The horizontal axis plots the annualized growth rate of money supply minus the annualized growth rate of real GDP. Each country is represented by a single point in the figure. We have also plotted the 45-degree line which starts at the origin and has a slope of one, and represents the relationship predicted by the quantity theory of money.

Source: George T. McCandless and Warren E. Weber, "Some Monetary Facts," *Federal Reserve Bank of Minneapolis Quarterly Review* 19, no. 3 (1995): 2–11.

gains to others. Imagine that you have negotiated a 3-year nominal wage contract with your employer. If the inflation rate unexpectedly rises during this 3-year contract, you will be harmed by the unexpected inflation (unless your employer agrees to rewrite the contract). In this example, though you and the other employees of the firm lose out, the shareholders of the firm benefit from the unexpected inflation, because the extra inflation lowers the real (inflation-adjusted) value of the wages that the firm pays its workers.

Next consider a retiree receiving a pension that is not indexed to inflation (in other words, the pension payments do not automatically rise with the overall level of prices). A rise in inflation makes the retiree worse off because the buying power of the pension declines. Here too, there is a winner on the other side of the relationship: the shareholders of the firm that is paying the pension. The real (inflation-adjusted) costs of the pension payments have gone down.

As yet another example, imagine that you have a mortgage at a fixed rate of interest. In other words, you borrowed money from a bank to buy your home and you are repaying that loan back at a fixed (predetermined) interest rate. If the inflation rate rises, your *real* interest rate falls, lowering the real cost of your mortgage. In this case, the consumer is the winner and the bank's shareholders are the losers.

When contracts for wages, pensions, or mortgage payments are *not* indexed to inflation, an increase in inflation hurts some economic agents and helps others.

In these three examples, inflation generates specific winners and losers but no clear *overall* impact on society. However, some consequences of inflation are *generally* socially negative or socially positive. We now turn to those cases.

The Social Costs of Inflation

We first discuss three of the most important reasons that inflation is socially costly.

1. **A high inflation rate creates logistical costs.** In an environment of high inflation, firms need to frequently change their prices. Recall that during the worst months of the German 1923 hyperinflation, prices were doubling every three to four days,

which means they were increasing about 1 percent per hour. Imagine trying to run a business in which you needed to post new prices several times each day! That's an extreme example, but even much lower rates of inflation—for instance, 20 percent per year—necessitate multiple changes to prices over the course of the year. Economists refer to a business's cost of changing its prices as "menu costs," using as a metaphor the new menus that restaurants print when prices change.

2. **A high inflation rate distorts relative prices.** Prices do not stay in sync when the inflation rate is high. Think about a newspaper that charges $1 per paper. Imagine that this newspaper has a cross-town rival that also charges $1 per paper. During a period of high inflation, the real (inflation-adjusted) price of these newspapers falls as long as the papers stick with the $1 price. In other words, the buying power of $1 is falling as the *overall* price level rises. Finally, one of the newspapers acts and doubles its price to $2 (sticking with round numbers to simplify newsstand transactions). After this price change, one newspaper costs *twice* as much as the other, even though the two newspapers pay the same wages to their reporters and have the same printing costs. This newsstand price gap generates a distortion. Two newspapers that should be priced similarly are temporarily priced very differently. During this time, both newspapers might be unprofitable. The lower-priced newspaper isn't charging enough to make money (because its labor and printing costs are rising with the overall price level). The higher-priced newspaper is rapidly losing readers, because its price is twice that of its competitor. Eventually, the lower-priced newspaper will also raise its price to $2, but this might take a few months—complex organizations generally don't make big changes overnight. This is an example of the many ways that inflation causes relative prices to fall out of sync, which reduces the efficiency of economic activity.

3. **Inflation sometimes leads to counterproductive policies like price controls.** Inflation generates voter anger, and politicians sometimes respond by advancing economically destructive schemes, especially price controls. In most of these cases—like the gasoline price controls of the 1970s, which were discussed in Chapter 4—the policy cure is worse than the disease. Price controls cause problems like long lines and supply disruptions. In addition, price controls are partially undone when some of those consumers who are lucky enough to obtain the good at the official capped price resell it at a higher price in the underground economy. Hence, price controls create an inefficient incentive for consumers who don't want to consume the good to buy it anyway, just so they can resell it to someone else at a higher price.

The Social Benefits of Inflation

On the other hand, inflation does generate some social benefits. We mention two here.

1. **Government revenue is generated when the government prints currency.** While printing and spending an *enormous* amount of new currency leads to a hyperinflation, printing/spending a *modest* amount of new currency can be a socially beneficial source of revenue for a government. However, this additional government revenue is a double-edged sword. The citizens gain because their government has more money to spend, but the citizens also lose because the resulting inflation reduces the real value of the currency that the citizens already hold. However, if the amount of money creation is low enough, the net social benefit is positive.

Government revenue obtained from printing currency is called **seignorage.**

The government revenue obtained from printing currency is called **seignorage.** This is not a major source of revenue for most governments, though it is relatively important in the United States because there are many people around the globe—especially traders in the underground economy—who hold vast quantities of U.S. currency. Demand for U.S. currency also derives from entirely legal sources, like people in other countries with an unstable local currency who want a stable store of value. Seignorage generates roughly $30 billion of implicit revenue for the U.S. government each year.

The fact that a government can raise revenue by printing currency makes seignorage a candidate for abuse, and this is the reason why, as we noted above, some governments running large budget deficits often rapidly expand the money supply and cause inflation—as Zimbabwe, Iran, and Venezuela have done recently.

Printing a lot of currency has short-term appeal for a government, but in the long run the strategy of printing currency to pay a government's bills often gets out of hand and leads to devastating episodes of hyperinflation.

2. **Inflation can *sometimes* stimulate economic activity.** Assume that a worker's nominal wage is fixed in the short run. This could result from an annual labor agreement or because nominal wages are above their competitive equilibrium level and downwardly rigid (as we discussed in Chapter 23). Because nominal wages are fixed, the higher the rate of inflation, the more the inflation-adjusted wage falls. The inflation-adjusted wage is the wage divided by the overall price index—for instance, the consumer price index (CPI). We refer to this inflation-adjusted wage as the **real wage**. A fall in the real wage increases a firm's willingness to employ workers. Another way to think about this is that a rise in the overall price level shifts the firm's labor demand curve to the right, since the firm can now sell its goods at a higher price. A rightward shift in the labor demand curve, increases employment and GDP.

Inflation also lowers the real interest rate. Recall from Chapter 24 that the real interest rate is the nominal interest rate minus the inflation rate. If the inflation rate rises and nominal interest rates don't respond one-for-one, then the real interest rate falls. Since the real interest rate is the inflation-adjusted cost of borrowing, a fall in the real interest rate stimulates borrowing that funds consumption and investment. An increase in consumption and investment (holding all else equal), increases GDP.

Modest inflation therefore stimulates the economy in the short-run, by cutting real wages (stimulating employment) and cutting real interest rates (stimulating consumption and investment). We explore these channels in more detail in Chapter 27.

The **real wage** is the nominal wage divided by a price index, like the consumer price index (CPI).

In 2010, Zimbabwe was experiencing hyperinflation. For example, it cost 100 billion Zimbabwe dollars to buy lunch.

Evidence-Based Economics

Q: What caused the German hyperinflation of 1922–1923?

At the end of World War I, the Allies imposed heavy financial penalties on the defeated Central Powers, particularly Germany. German reparation payments were specified in the Treaty of Versailles, which was signed in 1919. Postwar Germany, which is referred to as the Weimar Republic, did not make the required payments and France retaliated by occupying the Ruhr, a small German industrial region, in January of 1923. To protest the French occupation, German workers in the Ruhr went on strike. This crippled the German economy along with the finances of the German government. As the economic situation deteriorated, the German government was able to meet only 8 percent of its financing needs with tax collection. The rest was paid by borrowing from the public and printing paper money.

Exhibit 25.3 plots the explosive growth of German currency in circulation during this episode. As implied by the quantity theory of money, the rapid increase in the German money supply (without a simultaneous increase in real GDP) prompted a surge in inflation. Though it is impossible to completely rule out all other explanations, economists believe that the German hyperinflation would not have occurred if the government had reduced its expenditures, borrowed more from the public, or defaulted on its debt so it could avoid printing so much currency to pay its bills.

The collapse of the German economy partially set the stage for the ascent of the Nazi party. On November 8, 1923, coinciding with the height of the hyperinflation, 3,000 members of the Nazi party attempted to conduct a regional coup in Munich. This

Evidence-Based Economics *(Continued)*

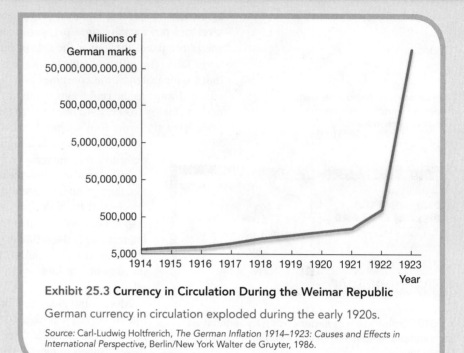

Exhibit 25.3 Currency in Circulation During the Weimar Republic

German currency in circulation exploded during the early 1920s.

Source: Carl-Ludwig Holtfrerich, *The German Inflation 1914–1923: Causes and Effects in International Perspective,* Berlin/New York Walter de Gruyter, 1986.

A plaque commemorating the 1922–1923 German hyperinflation. The inscription reports the price, in German marks, of three basic goods on November 1, 1923: "1 pound of bread, 3 billion; 1 pound of meat, 36 billion; 1 glass of beer, 4 billion." On November, 15, 1923, a new currency, the Rentenmark, replaced the old mark at an exchange rate of 1 new mark for 1 trillion old marks.

coup attempt, which came to be known as the Beer Hall Putsch, ended with Adolf Hitler's arrest and 8-month imprisonment. While in jail, Hitler wrote his autobiography, *Mein Kampf,* or *My Struggle,* which became a rallying point for the Nazi party.

Tragically, Germany's economic nightmare continued 6 years after the 1922–1923 hyperinflation ended. In 1929, the Great Depression enveloped the country and with it came a deep deflation and devastating unemployment. Germany had now experienced three economic catastrophes in little more than a decade: the loss of World War I in 1918 (along with subsequent reparations), hyperinflation in 1922–1923, and depression/deflation in 1929. The Great Depression completed the process of economic impoverishment, catapulting the heretofore unpopular Nazis into power. By 1933, Hitler was chancellor of Germany.

Question

What caused the German hyperinflation of 1922–1923?

Answer

The German government could not make reparation payments to the Allies after World War I. As the German economy struggled, the government started to print more and more currency to pay its bills.

Data

Historical money supply data, specifically currency in circulation.

Caveat

Though the German money supply and the German price level rose together in 1922 and 1923, correlation does not always imply causation. Nevertheless, in this case a large body of other supportive evidence implies that the relationship is likely to be causal.

25.4 The Federal Reserve

In each country, the monetary system is run by a central bank. We now introduce the basic operations of the central bank. We will continue this discussion in Chapter 27, when we describe how central banks counteract recessions and other economic fluctuations. In the current chapter, we introduce the most important tools at the disposal of central banks, and describe the "plumbing" of the monetary system.

The Central Bank and the Objectives of Monetary Policy

The **central bank** is the government institution that monitors financial institutions, controls certain key interest rates, and indirectly controls the money supply. These activities are jointly described as **monetary policy**, and central banks are occasionally referred to as the *monetary authority*.

In the United States, the central bank is called the **Federal Reserve Bank**, or simply, the **Fed**. Note that the Fed is *not* the federal government, but rather an independent regulatory agency/bank that operates almost completely autonomously from the rest of the federal government. Exhibit 25.4 shows the locations of the twelve regional Federal Reserve Banks and the Federal Reserve's Board of Governors, which is located in Washington D.C. The Fed's most important policy decisions are made by the Federal Open Market Committee, comprising the presidents of the twelve regional Federal Reserve banks (five of whom vote on a rotating basis) and the seven members of the Board of Governors.

Monetary policy is multifaceted, both in terms of its goals and its policy tools. At the broadest level, the Fed uses monetary policy to pursue two key goals or objectives: (1) low and predictable levels of inflation and (2) maximum (sustainable) levels of employment. These two goals are referred to as the Fed's *dual mandate*.

The goal of low and predictable inflation is sometimes described as "price stability," but this phrase is slightly confusing, since the Fed and almost all other central banks actually interpret "price stability" to mean around 2 percent annual inflation. The term *inflation targeting* refers to the policy of attempting to obtain a specific low level of inflation over the long run. Most central banks have adopted some form of official or unofficial inflation targeting.

> The **central bank** is the government institution that monitors financial institutions, controls certain key interest rates, and indirectly controls the money supply. These activities constitute **monetary policy**.

> The **Federal Reserve Bank**, or the **Fed**, is the name of the central bank in the United States.

> **"The Fed uses monetary policy to pursue two key goals or objectives: (1) low and predictable levels of inflation and (2) maximum (sustainable) levels of employment. These two goals are referred to as the Fed's *dual mandate*."**

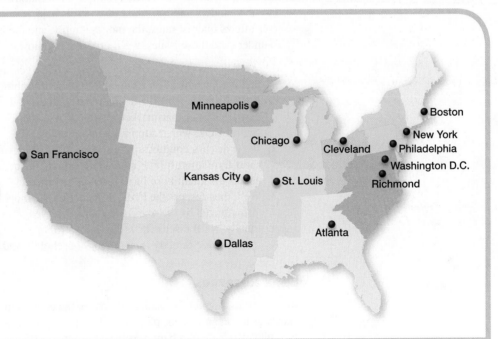

Exhibit 25.4 Geographic Boundaries of the Federal Reserve Districts

The Federal Reserve System was founded in 1913. To avoid political concentration of the central bank's power, the Fed was divided into twelve regional Federal Reserve Banks (color-coded above) and the Board of Governors in Washington D.C. (Alaska and Hawaii are served by the San Francisco district. Puerto Rico is served by the New York district.)

The Board of Governors of the Federal Reserve System is nominated by the President and confirmed by the Senate. In 2014, the Senate confirmed Janet Yellen's nomination as chair of the Board of Governors.

For the European countries that use the euro—the euro-area countries—the European Central Bank (ECB) plays the role of the Fed. But the ECB places greater emphasis on the goal of low and predictable inflation and less emphasis on the goal of maximum employment, partly because of Germany's terrible experience with hyperinflation in the 1920s coupled with its influence on decision making at the ECB.

What Does the Central Bank Do?

The central bank is closely involved in the day-to-day operations of private banks. This involvement takes many forms. First, the central bank is a key regulator of private banks, particularly the largest private banks. The central bank audits the financial statements, or "books," of large private banks, pressing each bank to accurately report the value of assets and liabilities on its balance sheet. The central bank will object if it notices that a private bank is holding a portfolio of assets that is too risky. The central bank also monitors the amount of shareholders' equity in private banks, trying to ensure that it is large enough to absorb possible future losses in the value of the private bank's assets. Such "stress tests" have become an even more important role of central banks since the 2007–2009 financial crisis.

The central bank also oversees interbank payment systems. When one bank transfers money to another—for example, when a depositor writes a check and the recipient of that check deposits the proceeds at a different bank—the central bank processes this transaction. So if a customer at JPMorgan Chase writes a $100 check to a customer at Citibank, then the Fed will clear this check by transferring $100 from JPMorgan Chase to Citibank. In this way, the Fed acts as a *bank for banks*.

The Fed also holds the reserves of private banks (with the exception of vault cash). The management of bank reserves is one of the most important and complex roles that the Fed plays, and this is the focus of the rest of this chapter. As we will see, the Fed's management of bank reserves enables the Fed to do three things:

1. influence short-term interest rates, especially the federal funds rate,
2. influence the money supply and the inflation rate,
3. influence long-term real interest rates.

You may be wondering how employment also comes into this picture. After all, maximizing sustainable employment is one of the two parts of the Fed's dual mandate. Interest rates affect households' and firms' willingness to borrow. *Lowering* interest rates stimulates borrowing, which stimulates spending, thereby shifting the labor demand curve to the right and raising employment. On the other hand, *raising* interest rates discourages borrowing, which reduces spending, thereby shifting the labor demand curve to the left and lowering employment. We'll return to these labor market outcomes in Chapter 27. For now, our task is to understand how the Fed controls bank reserves and why the quantity of bank reserves affects interest rates, the money supply, and the inflation rate.

To understand these issues, we'll proceed as follows:

1. We'll discuss the role of bank reserves in the economy, revisiting some of the issues that we introduced in Chapter 24 when describing the operation of private banks. Bank reserves are traded in a market, and we'll explain the roles of the different participants in that market: private banks, which demand bank reserves, and the central bank, which supplies bank reserves.
2. We'll discuss equilibrium in the market for bank reserves, which pins down a key short-term interest rate (at this interest rate the quantity of bank reserves demanded equals the quantity of bank reserves supplied).
3. We'll then discuss the Fed's influence on the money supply and inflation, which are also affected by the market for bank reserves.
4. Finally, we'll discuss how the short-term interest rate influences long-term interest rates that are directly relevant for households' and firms' investment decisions.

Bank Reserves

As defined in Chapter 24, bank reserves are the combination of deposits that a private bank makes at the central bank plus cash that the private bank holds in its vault—referred to as vault cash. Note that bank reserves are *not* part of M2, which is the money supply that households and (non-bank) firms can use to buy goods and services, but as we will see below, bank reserves can affect the money supply. The quantity of bank reserves plays the key role in the operation of the monetary system. Let's look at how private banks choose the quantity of reserves to hold and how they obtain extra reserves when necessary.

During their regular operations, private banks need to find funds to meet their daily needs. Bank reserves provide this source of funding.

On any given day, a private bank may have more account holders making withdrawals than new deposits coming in. For example, a large corporate account holder at a private bank might pay its employees at the end of the month by withdrawing funds from its corporate bank account. Or a large corporate depositor might withdraw $1 billion of funds from the private bank so the corporation can use those funds for an acquisition of another company.

The private bank may also need funds to make new loans, such as issuing mortgages to home buyers, or making a large commercial loan to a firm building a new plant. Finally, the private bank may need funds to repay other banks from which it has borrowed money in the past.

All of these scenarios imply that the private bank will need **liquidity**, meaning that it will need funds that can be used *immediately* to conduct transactions. We say that a private bank has enough liquidity if it has sufficient funds to conduct its day-to-day business and to meet its regulatory *reserve requirements*. Reserve requirements are set by the central bank. In the United States today, the reserve requirement is 10 percent of a private bank's demand deposits, such as checking accounts and other accounts that can be withdrawn by depositors with no notice ("on demand"). Summing up, the private bank must hold reserves (as vault cash or on deposit at the Fed) that equal 10 percent of the private bank's demand deposits. Reserves in excess of this regulatory minimum are referred to as *excess reserves*.

When a private bank needs funds—liquidity—to conduct transactions, its first line of defense is the reserves that it holds as vault cash or as deposits at the central bank. If the bank has ample reserves, it will use some of these to meet its daily funding needs. However, in some cases, the bank won't have enough reserves to conduct its business. If a bank cannot find a way to raise additional funds at very short notice, it may not be able to make new loans or, in a dire case, it may not be able to pay depositors who wish to withdraw their funds.

Fortunately, banks have a way of obtaining additional liquidity. They can borrow funds from other banks. If some banks face large net withdrawals, then other banks are probably experiencing large net deposits. It is possible that all banks suddenly face large net withdrawals, but most of the time the need for liquidity is not an aggregate phenomenon but specific to a limited set of banks.

To illustrate this point, think about the case of a large employer, like General Electric (GE), on payroll day. GE has 300,000 employees, earning an average salary of about $7,000 per month. To keep things simple, let's assume that GE keeps all of its cash at one bank, pays its employees once per month, and makes all these employee payments electronically. On payroll day, GE's bank account shrinks by 300,000 × 7,000 = $2.1 billion, and the bank accounts of GE's employees swell by $2.1 billion. If GE and its employees all have their accounts at the same bank, this common bank will experience no net withdrawals. Withdrawals and deposits will be offsetting.

But if the accounts are at different banks, which is a more realistic approximation, then GE's bank will receive a net withdrawal of $2.1 billion and the employees' banks will receive net deposits of $2.1 billion. At this moment, GE's bank may be short of reserves, and the employees' banks will be swimming in excess reserves. GE's bank would like to borrow some reserves to address the shortage, and the employees' banks would like to lend out their excess reserves.

Enter the **federal funds market**. This is where banks borrow and lend reserves to one another. In this market banks typically make one-day (24-hour) loans, so the federal funds market is referred to as an overnight market. The loan is typically made in the morning and is repaid the next morning. The term *federal funds* refers to the fact that these are loans of bank reserves held at the Federal Reserve Bank. The interest rate in this market is referred to as the **federal funds rate**.

An overnight loan might sound strange, but large banks are so efficient at making interbank loans that they are happy to make these loans for 24 hours (or less!). *You* wouldn't want a 24-hour mortgage because it would kill you to re-sign all of that paperwork *every* morning for

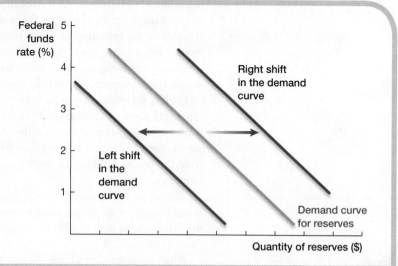

Exhibit 25.5 The Demand Curve in the Federal Funds Market

The (net) demand curve for reserves is downward-sloping: a higher federal funds rate increases the cost of holding reserves and reduces the quantity of reserves demanded by optimizing banks. Conversely, a lower federal funds rate increases the quantity of reserves demanded by banks. Movements in the federal funds rate, holding all else equal, correspond to movements along the demand curve. Shifts of the entire demand curve arise because of economic expansion or contraction, a changing deposit base, or changing liquidity needs.

30 years. However, large banks make billions of dollars of loans to one another each morning in the blink of an eye. Every morning, the banks assess their liquidity needs for the coming business day and borrow or lend accordingly. The following morning, the cycle repeats itself.

The Demand Side of the Federal Funds Market

Exhibit 25.5 graphs the demand curve for reserves. To be precise, these are reserves held on deposit by private banks at the Federal Reserve Bank (so we are not including vault cash held in private banks). The federal funds rate is plotted on the vertical axis, and the quantity of reserves is plotted on the horizontal axis. It is important to emphasize that the demand curve for reserves plots the *total* quantity of reserves held by private banks (*not* just the borrowed reserves). So if one bank has $10 billion in reserves and loans $1 billion of reserves to another bank, the net quantity of reserves demanded is:

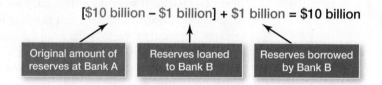

[$10 billion – $1 billion] + $1 billion = $10 billion

To avoid double-counting, the $1 billion of loaned reserves is only counted as reserves for the borrowing bank. In this example, the total quantity of reserves held by private banks is $10 billion.

The demand curve relates the total quantity of reserves demanded by private banks for each level of the federal funds rate. The demand curve slopes down because optimizing banks choose to hold more reserves as the cost of holding those reserves—the interest rate that they pay to borrow reserves—falls. Reserves are a safety net for the banks, and they prefer to have a bigger safety net if the cost of that safety net falls.

Hence, a lower interest rate increases the quantity of reserves demanded. Changes in the federal funds rate (holding all else equal) generate movements along the demand curve for reserves.

On the other hand, if some factor *other* than the federal funds rate changes, the entire demand curve shifts. A shift in the demand curve for reserves corresponds to a change in the quantity of reserves demanded at a given federal funds rate. There are five key reasons for such shifts in the demand curve for reserves, and the last two of these reasons are under the direct control of the Fed:

- **Economic expansion or contraction:** In a booming economy, private banks need to obtain liquidity so they can make new loans to their customers—for instance, a manufacturing firm that wishes to expand production by building a new factory. Reserves provide liquidity that can be used to fund these loans. Therefore, an expansion in private banks' loan originations produces a shift to the right in the demand curve for reserves. Likewise, a contraction in private banks' loan originations produces a shift to the left in the demand curve for reserves.

- **Changing liquidity needs:** If banks expect a flood of withdrawals—for instance, a bank run—this also increases the demand for reserves. Paying out depositors requires liquidity, which is exactly what reserves provide. Hence, an anticipated flood of withdrawals shifts the demand curve for reserves to the right.

- **Changing deposit base:** The demand for reserves is proportional to the total value of bank account balances. Recall that the reserve requirement compels each bank in the United States to hold 10 percent of its customers' bank accounts in either vault cash or in reserves held on deposit at the Fed. So an expansion in the quantity of bank account balances produces a shift to the right in the demand curve for reserves. Conversely, the demand curve for reserves shifts to the left as a consequence of a contraction in bank account balances.

- **Changing reserve requirement:** The Fed has the authority to change the 10 percent reserve requirement. Though it rarely uses this authority, the Fed could raise the reserve requirement, thereby shifting the demand curve for reserves to the right. Likewise, the Fed could lower the reserve requirement, thereby shifting the demand curve for reserves to the left.

- **Changing interest rate paid by the Fed for having reserves on deposit at the Fed:** The Fed pays a modest interest rate when private banks deposit money at the Fed—in other words, when private banks hold reserves at the Fed. In 2014, the interest rate paid by the Fed to private banks with reserves on deposit at the Fed was ¼ of one percentage point. When the Fed raises this interest rate, reserves become more beneficial to private banks, shifting the demand curve for reserves to the right. When the Fed lowers this interest rate, reserves become less valuable, shifting the demand curve for reserves to the left.

Exhibit 25.5 plots right and left shifts of the demand curve.

The Supply Side of the Federal Funds Market and Equilibrium in the Federal Funds Market

We're now ready to talk about the supply side of the federal funds market. To understand the day-to-day operations of the Fed, it is useful to model the supply curve of reserves as a vertical line that is set every morning by the Fed. However, from day to day, the Fed may move this vertical supply curve to the right or to the left—as we will see below. Exhibit 25.6 starts with the simple case in which the vertical supply curve does not respond to right or left shifts in the demand curve.

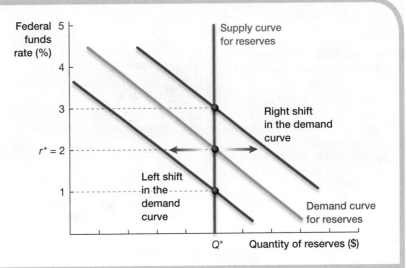

Exhibit 25.6 Equilibrium in the Federal Funds Market

Because the Fed fixes the supply of reserves each day, we represent the supply curve of reserves as a vertical line. The intersection of the downward-sloping demand curve and the supply curve gives the equilibrium in the federal funds market. Assuming that the Fed does not shift the supply curve in response to movements in the demand curve, a shift to the left in the demand curve lowers the federal funds rate, and a shift to the right in the demand curve raises the federal funds rate.

The point where the supply and demand curves cross in the federal funds market is the **federal funds market equilibrium**.

If the Fed wishes to increase the level of reserves that private banks hold, it offers to buy government bonds from the private banks, and in return it gives the private banks more electronic reserves. If the Fed wishes to decrease the level of reserves, it offers to sell government bonds to the private banks and in return the private banks give back some of their reserves. By buying or selling government bonds, the Fed shifts the vertical supply curve in the federal funds market and thereby controls the level of reserves. These transactions are referred to as **open market operations**.

The point where the supply and demand curves cross in the federal funds market is the **federal funds market equilibrium**. Here, the equilibrium quantity of reserves demanded is equal to the equilibrium quantity of reserves supplied by the Fed. The equilibrium federal funds rate is the point at which the demand curve of private banks crosses the vertical supply curve of reserves set by the Fed.

In practice, each dollar of reserves (held at the Fed) is an electronic IOU issued by the Fed to a private bank. Private banks sell the Fed assets in exchange for these reserves. In most cases, the assets that the Fed buys are government bonds, principally bonds issued directly by the federal government or entities sponsored by the federal government, like the Federal National Mortgage Association (informally called Fannie Mae), which provides funding to the mortgage market.

If the Fed wishes to increase the level of reserves that private banks hold, it buys government bonds from the private banks, and in return it gives the private banks more electronic reserves. If the Fed wishes to decrease the level of reserves, it sells government bonds to the private banks and in return the private banks give back some of their reserves. By buying or selling government bonds, the Fed shifts the vertical supply curve in the federal funds market and thereby controls the level of reserves (at the Fed) held by private banks. These transactions are referred to as **open market operations**, and they are the Fed's most important monetary policy tool. The transactions associated with open market operations are illustrated in Exhibit 25.7, and discussed again in Chapter 27.

The Fed chooses between two alternative strategies when it implements monetary policy. First, consider again the case in Exhibit 25.6. In this case, the Fed holds reserves fixed, even when the demand curve shifts. When this strategy is adopted, shifts in the demand curve translate into changes in the federal funds rate.

The Federal Reserve's second strategy is to find the level of reserves that achieves a particular level of the federal funds rate. Exhibit 25.8 shows how to find the level of reserves that generates a particular federal funds rate (2 percent in the exhibit). In this case, the Fed first chooses the federal funds rate and then finds that point on the demand curve that corresponds to that federal funds rate. The Fed makes available the exact level of reserves associated with that point on the demand curve. Using a strategy like this, the Fed can hold the federal funds rate at a particular fixed value, even as the demand curve shifts from day to day. When the demand curve shifts to the right, the Fed increases the supply of reserves to keep the federal funds rate from rising. When the demand curve shifts to the left, the Fed reduces the supply of reserves to keep the federal funds rate from falling.

Over the last 30 years, the Fed has gradually shifted towards this second strategy rather than the first strategy depicted in Exhibit 25.6. In particular, starting in 1995, the Federal Open Market Committee began making regular statements about the level (or range) of the federal funds rate that it was targeting.

Exhibit 25.7 Open Market Operation That Lowers the Federal Funds Rate

An open market operation is an exchange between the central bank and private banks. In the example depicted in Exhibit 25.7, the Fed gives a private bank $1 billion in IOUs, which take the form of reserves held on deposit at the Fed. In exchange, the Fed receives $1 billion in bonds from Bank of America.

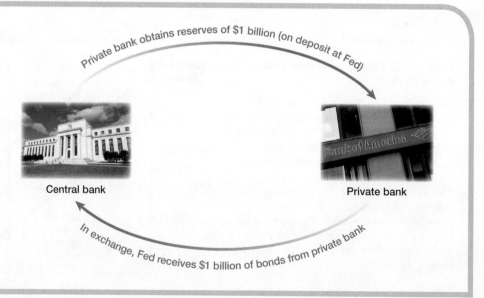

Private bank obtains reserves of $1 billion (on deposit at Fed)

Central bank

Private bank

In exchange, Fed receives $1 billion of bonds from private bank

Exhibit 25.8 Picking Reserves to Keep the Federal Funds Rate Fixed

In response to shifts in the demand curve for reserves, the Fed can adjust the level of reserves to hold the federal funds rate constant. If the blue demand curve for reserves shifts to the right (from D to D_R), the Fed will need to shift the supply curve of reserves to the right by exactly the amount that will make the intersection between the new supply curve and the new demand curve remain at the same federal funds rate (S shifts to S_R). If the demand curve for reserves shifts to the left (from D to D_L), the Fed will need to shift the supply curve of reserves to the left (from S to S_L).

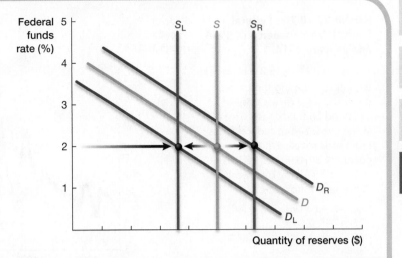

Exhibit 25.8 shows how the Fed can maintain a constant federal funds rate even when the demand curve for reserves shifts. On almost all days since the late 1980s, that is exactly what the Fed has done. But from time to time, the Fed decides to change the federal funds rate in an effort to nudge the economy. As we explain in Chapter 27, raising interest rates will cause economic growth to slow down, whereas lowering interest rates will cause economic growth to speed up. We have a lot to say later in the book about why the Fed raises and lowers interest rates, but for now let's discuss how the Fed makes this happen.

Exhibit 25.9 illustrates how the Fed can raise the federal funds rate by shifting the supply curve for reserves to the left. As we have seen, the Fed can shift the supply curve to the left by selling government bonds to private banks, allowing the private banks to pay for these bonds with their reserves, and thereby lowering the quantity of reserves that private banks hold at the Fed. The shift in the supply curve leads to a new equilibrium with a higher "price" for reserves—a higher equilibrium federal funds rate.

Likewise, Exhibit 25.9 also illustrates how the Fed can lower the federal funds rate by shifting the supply curve for reserves to the right. The Fed can shift the supply curve to the right by buying government bonds from private banks and giving the private banks

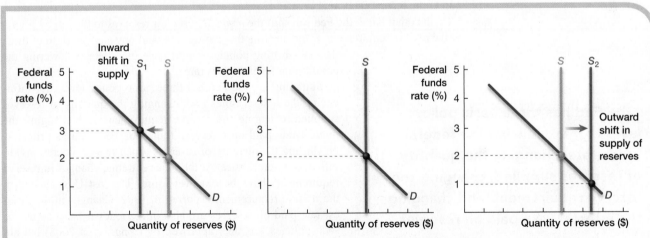

Exhibit 25.9 Shifts in the Federal Funds Rate Induced by a Shift in the Supply of Reserves

The Fed can raise the federal funds rate by shifting the supply curve for reserves to the left. This shift leads to a new equilibrium with a higher equilibrium federal funds rate. Likewise, the Fed can lower the federal funds rate by shifting the supply curve for reserves to the right. This shift leads to a new equilibrium with a lower equilibrium federal funds rate.

Exhibit 25.10 The Federal Funds Rate Between July 1954 and January 2014

The federal funds rate has varied a great deal during the postwar period. During recessions—indicated by the shaded areas in the exhibit—the federal funds rate tends to fall. When the economy is weak, the Fed stimulates the economy by lowering the federal funds rate.

Source: Board of Governors of the Federal Reserve System.

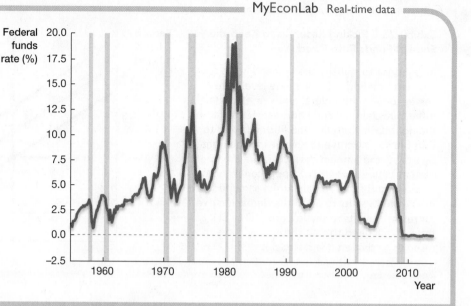

additional reserves in return for these bonds. The shift in the supply curve leads to a new equilibrium with a lower "price" for reserves—a lower equilibrium federal funds rate.

Exhibit 25.10 provides historical perspective on the behavior of the federal funds rate. It depicts fluctuations in the federal funds rate between July 1954 and January 2014. The exhibit shows that the federal funds rate can increase sharply. This volatility arises both from shifts in the supply curve of reserves (as shown in Exhibit 25.9), and from shifts in the demand curve for reserves (as shown in Exhibit 25.6).

Summary of the Fed's Control of the Federal Funds Rate Drawing together what we've discussed so far, the Fed can influence the federal funds rate either by shifting the quantity of reserves supplied (with open market operations) *or* by shifting the demand curve for reserves. Recall that the Fed can shift the *demand curve* for reserves to the right by raising the reserve requirement (which was 10 percent of demand deposits in June 2014) or by increasing the interest rate paid on reserves (which was ¼ of one percentage point in June 2014). Both of these demand-shifting policies would have the effect of increasing the equilibrium federal funds rate.

On the other hand, the Fed can shift the *demand curve* for reserves to the left by lowering the reserve requirement or by lowering the interest rate paid on reserves. Both of these demand-shifting policies would have the effect of lowering the equilibrium federal funds rate.

Summing up, the Fed has three basic policy levers for influencing the federal funds rate: changing the quantity of reserves supplied, changing the reserve requirement, and changing the interest rate paid on reserves. Today the Fed focuses primarily on shifting the quantity of reserves (open market operations) to influence interest rates. At the other extreme, changes in reserve requirements have become very rare. The last U.S. change in the reserve requirement occurred in 1992. Changes in the interest rate paid on reserves are also infrequent (in fact, the use of such policies was only approved by Congress in 2008) but are expected to become more commonplace in the years ahead.

> "The Fed has three basic policy levers for influencing the federal funds rate: changing the quantity of reserves supplied, changing the reserve requirement, and changing the interest rate paid on reserves."

The Fed's Influence on the Money Supply and the Inflation Rate

We've now completed our discussion of the determination of the federal funds rate—a key short-term interest rate. This was the first of *three* consequences of the Fed's management of bank reserves. We're now ready to turn to the second category: the Fed's influence on the money supply and on the inflation rate.

CHOICE & CONSEQUENCE

Obtaining Reserves Outside the Federal Funds Market

During normal times, the federal funds market operates without a hitch. Banks that need extra reserves borrow them, and banks that have excess reserves lend them out. But during extraordinary times, such as during a financial panic, the federal funds market can break down because banks with excess reserves don't know whom they can trust. They don't know which banks are solvent—those that are able to pay back their lenders—and which banks are not. Accordingly, the banks with excess reserves may be unwilling to lend these reserves out.

In such a crisis, the banks that need reserves may not be able to obtain them. Fortunately, the Fed can step in and provide reserves to the banks that need them. The Fed does this by allowing banks to borrow reserves at the "discount window." Because loans from the discount window have a higher interest rate than loans obtained on the federal funds market, the discount window is usually a private bank's *last resort* for borrowing reserves. Sometimes the Fed is referred to as the "lender of last resort." When all else fails, a bank can go directly to the Fed for a loan of reserves.

In fact, the Fed cannot directly control either the money supply or the inflation rate. Some people mistakenly think that the Fed controls the money supply because the Fed controls the quantity of bank reserves. But bank reserves are actually *not* part of the money supply. Instead, the money supply includes deposits by households and firms at private banks and currency in circulation.

Though the Fed doesn't directly control the money supply or inflation, the Fed does try to influence these important macroeconomic variables. Since inflation is part of the Fed's dual mandate (along with employment) and the money supply is not, the Fed cares a great deal about inflation and only indirectly cares about the money supply. Accordingly, if the annual inflation rate is close to the Fed's target of 2 percent, the Fed won't worry about short-run variation in the growth rate of the money supply.

In the long run, the inflation rate is *approximately* equal to the growth rate of the money supply minus the growth rate of real GDP as we saw in our empirical analysis of the quantity theory of money. Because of this relationship, the Fed will try to slow down the rate of money supply growth if the inflation rate starts to rise above the Fed's inflation target.

Note that the money supply increases when banks make new loans. Consider a home buyer who takes out a $200,000 mortgage from Citibank. The person who is selling the home receives these funds from the buyer and deposits them at her bank, which may or may not be Citibank. This deposit increases the money supply by $200,000. Hence, the origination of this new mortgage increases the money supply by $200,000. Accordingly, the origination of many new loans causes the money supply to grow rapidly. When the Fed attempts to slow down the growth of the money supply, it does this by slowing down the growth of loans from private banks to households and firms.

As we explain in the next subsection, the federal funds rate influences the long-term interest rates that affect the quantity of new loans demanded by households and firms. By raising the federal funds rate, the Fed raises the interest rate that households and firms face, thereby lowering the quantity of loans demanded and lowering the growth rate of the money supply.

Summary of the Fed's Influence on the Money Supply and the Inflation Rate

The Fed raises the federal funds rate with three tools. First, the Fed can reduce the quantity of bank reserves by using open market operations. Second, the Fed can increase the reserve requirement. Third, the Fed can increase the interest rate that it pays on reserves. All of these policies will increase the federal funds rate and the interest rates that households and firms face for borrowing. Consequently, a higher federal funds rate reduces the rate of loan growth to households and firms, reducing the rate at which the money supply grows, and reducing the rate of inflation. Likewise, a lower federal funds rate increases the rate of loan growth to households and firms, increasing the rate at which the money supply grows, and increasing the rate of inflation.

The Relationship Between the Federal Funds Rate and the Long-Term Real Interest Rate

We've now completed our discussion of the first *two* consequences of the Fed's management of bank reserves. We're ready to turn to the third, and final, category. By intervening in the market for bank reserves, the Fed influences both the federal funds rate and *the long-term real interest rate*. Recall that the real interest rate is defined as the real price of a loan, or, in other words, the price of a loan adjusted for inflation. It is defined as

$$\text{Real interest rate} = \text{Nominal interest rate} - \text{Inflation rate.}$$

Consider a firm that borrows $100 for a year at a nominal interest rate of 5 percent in an economy with a 2 percent inflation rate. One year later, the firm pays back $100 × (1 + 0.05) = $105 dollars, but inflation has chipped away at the buying power of this money. If the inflation rate is 2 percent, $105 in the payback year has buying power of only $105/(1 + 0.02), or about $103 in the year the loan was issued. This is just $3 more than the original loan amount. So the *real* cost to the borrower is only $3 of buying power, which is 3 percent of the original $100 loan. In general, the real cost of a loan is the nominal interest rate *minus* the inflation rate. In the current example, the real interest rate can be calculated as 5% − 2% = 3%.

Investment depends on the **long-term real interest rate**, which is the *long-term* nominal interest rate minus the *long-term* inflation rate. When we talk about the long-term, we are referring to horizons that are at least 10 years away. The long-term real interest rate is relevant for the economy because many investments require funding for at least a decade. A home loan lasts 30 years. A major corporate research and development project—like the development of the double-decker, "superjumbo" Airbus A380—can take 20 years between the initial conceptualization and the roll-out of the finished product.

In contrast, the federal funds rate is a *short-term* nominal interest rate. So there is a mismatch between the short-term interest rate that the Fed essentially controls and the long-term real interest rates that matter for most investment decisions. To understand the potential impact of the federal funds rate on the long-term real interest rate, it is also useful to think about the real interest rate that is *anticipated* when the loan is made. This is potentially different from the real interest rate that is *realized* over the life of the loan. It is therefore useful to distinguish between a *realized real interest rate* and an *expected real interest rate*.

The **realized real interest rate** is defined as:

$$\text{Realized real interest rate} = \text{Nominal interest rate} - \text{Realized inflation rate.}$$

For example, if a borrower takes out a loan on December 31, 2010 and repays the loan on December 31, 2020, the realized real interest rate would be the nominal interest rate that the borrower agreed to on December 31, 2010, minus the actual realized inflation rate between December 31, 2010 and December 31, 2020. Note that realized inflation is the inflation that actually occurred over a particular period of time. When the loan is first issued, the borrower doesn't yet know what the *realized* inflation rate will be. So the borrower won't be able to calculate the realized real interest rate until the loan ends on December 31, 2020.

But we do have beliefs, or expectations, about the inflation rate between now and then. We can use those expectations to motivate a closely related concept called the **expected real interest rate**:

$$\text{Expected real interest rate} = \text{Nominal interest rate} - \text{Expected inflation rate.}$$

When making loans, optimizing borrowers and lenders consider the *expected* real interest rate; they do not yet know what the realized inflation rate will be. Because the expected real interest rate plays the key role in people's decisions, its components matter, including *inflation expectations*. Economic agents' **inflation expectations** are their beliefs about future inflation rates.

The **long-term real interest rate** is the long-term nominal interest rate minus the long-term inflation rate.

Development of the A380 was started in 1988. The first aircraft was sold in 2008. Twenty-year research and development projects are **not** funded by 365 × 20 = 7,300 overnight loans.

The **realized real interest rate** is the nominal interest rate minus the realized rate of inflation.

The **expected real interest rate** is the nominal interest rate minus the expected rate of inflation.

Economic agents' **inflation expectations** are their beliefs about future inflation rates.

CHOICE & CONSEQUENCE

Two Models of Inflation Expectations

How do people actually form inflation expectations? Some economists believe that people's inflation expectations are determined by the level of inflation in the recent past. For example, "my forecast of the inflation rate next year is the inflation rate that was realized last year." Such *adaptive expectations* are a backward-looking form of inflation expectations. Such backward-looking inflation expectations are plausible, because it is natural to believe that the future will mirror your recent past experiences.

But believing that what will happen in the future is the same as what happened in the recent past is not maximally rational. Many economists believe that people are more sophisticated than the adaptive expectations theory assumes. These critics of the adaptive expectations

model typically endorse the model of *rational expectations*, which assumes that people have inflation expectations that incorporate all of the information that is available when the inflation expectations are being formed and use that information in the most sophisticated way possible. If agents have rational expectations, they are masterful forecasters who make the best possible forecast using a sophisticated understanding of the workings of the economy.

Critics of the rational expectations model complain that it overestimates the degree of human rationality. For decades, economists have debated which of these models—or yet another model of people's belief formation—best describes the actual inflation expectations of consumers and workers. The jury is still out.

We are now ready to ask how a change in the federal funds rate affects the long-term expected real interest rate. Although there is no universally accepted answer, most economists agree that changing the federal funds rate also tends to change—in the same direction—the long-term expected real interest rate.

A fall in the federal funds rate implies that private banks are able to borrow reserves in the federal funds market at a lower interest rate. Because the private banks, own borrowing costs are falling, they start to offer loans at lower interest rates too. This implies that the supply of credit from private banks shifts to the right.

> "Although there is no universally accepted answer, most economists agree that changing the federal funds rate also tends to change—in the same direction—the long-term expected real interest rate."

Moreover, the long-term nominal interest rate falls because a long-term loan is effectively made up of many short-term loans. You can think of a 10-year loan as ten 1-year loans lined up one after the other—like a freight train made up of box cars that are linked together. When the federal funds rate goes down, the first 1-year loan becomes less expensive for the private bank to make. In addition, a change in the federal funds rate is usually not reversed for at least several years, so several of the 1-year loans that are linked together in the first few years of the 10-year loan package are affected. Think of the nominal interest rate for the long-term loan as the average of these ten 1-year loans. Since several of the 1-year loans are affected by a change in the federal funds rate, the long-term nominal rate moves in the same direction.

Ten-year loan

To make this concrete, suppose that the Federal Reserve lowers the federal funds rate from 4 percent to 3 percent, and that this decrease is going to last for 2 years, at which point the federal funds rate will revert to its old level. Then, the 10-year nominal interest rate, which can be thought of as the average of ten 1-year loans, will fall from 4 percent to 3.8 percent. To see why, let's take the average of ten 1-year loans, where the first two loans are made at 3 percent and the last eight loans are made at 4 percent:

$$\frac{3\% + 3\% + 4\% + 4\% + 4\% + 4\% + 4\% + 4\% + 4\% + 4\%}{10} = 3.8\%.$$

To complete our analysis, we now need to determine how changes in the long-term *nominal* interest rate—which we just analyzed—affect the long-term expected *real* interest

Exhibit 25.11 Effect of Open Market Operation on the Long-Term Expected Real Interest Rate

An increase in bank reserves at the Fed lowers the federal funds rate, which in turn lowers the long-term nominal interest rate. With constant inflation expectations, the long-term expected real interest rate falls by as much as the long-term nominal interest rate.

Starting point
Federal funds rate: 4%
Long-term nominal interest rate: 4%
Long-term inflation expectations: 2%
Long-term expected real interest rate: 4% − 2% = 2%

Open market operation increases bank reserves

CAUSES

Federal funds rate to fall from 4% to 3%

CAUSES

Long-term nominal interest rate to fall from 4% to 3.8%

(Assume that inflation expectations don't change)

Ending point
Federal funds rate: 3%
Long-term nominal interest rate: 3.8%
Long-term inflation expectations: 2%
Long-term expected real interest rate: 3.8% − 2% = 1.8%

rate. This requires that we study the effect of monetary policy on both the long-term nominal interest rate and the long-term expected inflation rate.

First, imagine what would happen if inflation expectations don't change in response to a fall in the federal funds rate. If inflation expectations don't change, and nominal interest rates fall, then the expected real interest rate falls. Hence, a fall in the federal funds rate lowers the long-term nominal interest rate and lowers the expected long-term real interest rate.

Exhibit 25.11 summarizes these linkages and provides a numerical example. The exhibit begins with an increase in the reserves held at the central bank. This change results from open market operations conducted by the Fed. Specifically, the Fed buys bonds from banks and gives the banks reserves in exchange for the bonds. The rightward shift in the supply of reserves lowers the federal funds rate—in this example, from 4 percent to 3 percent. This in turn lowers the long-term nominal interest rate from 4 percent to 3.8 percent. If the long-term expected inflation rate remains at 2 percent, then the long-term expected real interest rate falls from $4 - 2 = 2$ percent (before the open market operation) to $3.8 - 2 = 1.8$ percent (after the open market operation).

If inflation expectations do change, the analysis gets more complicated, but even in this case, the long-term expected real interest rate often falls in response to a reduction in the federal funds rate.

Summary of the Fed's Influence on Long-term Expected Real Interest Rates   The long-term real interest rate is the long-term nominal interest rate minus the long-term expected inflation rate. When the Fed influences short-term interest rates, such as the federal funds rate, this affects the long-term nominal interest rate. A long-term loan is like a combination of short-term loans. You can think of a 10-year loan as ten 1-year loans lined up one after the other. When the federal funds rate goes down, the interest rate for the first 1-year loan goes down. In addition, a change in the federal funds rate is usually not reversed for several years, so several of the 1-year loans in the 10-year loan package are affected. In most cases, when the Fed lowers the federal funds rate this has little impact on long-term inflationary expectations. Summing this up, the long-term real interest rate tends to fall when the federal funds rate falls because the long-term nominal interest rate falls and inflation expectations tend to stay roughly the same.

This completes our overview of the Fed's activities. We've discussed the Fed's core activities, but we've left some important details out. We'll fill in the rest of the picture in the next two chapters. The current chapter introduced the concept of money and the fundamental "plumbing" of the Fed's operations, especially the Fed's influence over the federal funds market. In the next two chapters, you'll see how the Fed trades off competing policy goals and how the Fed actually conducted policy during and after the financial crisis and recession of 2007–2009.

Summary

✸ Money plays a vital role in our lives. It makes a range of economic transactions possible, simultaneously serving as (1) a medium of exchange that can be traded for goods and services, (2) a store of value that enables us to save and transfer purchasing power into the future, (3) a common unit of account that expresses the price of different goods and services.

✸ The money supply is the quantity of money that individuals can immediately use in transactions. The money supply is defined as the sum of currency in circulation (which excludes currency in bank vaults) and the balances of most bank accounts at private banks. This measure of the money supply is referred to as M2. This measure of the money supply excludes all forms of bank reserves.

✸ The quantity theory of money links the money supply to nominal GDP, which is the value of total output in the economy measured at current prices. The quantity theory of money implies that the long-term inflation rate equals the long-run growth rate of the money supply minus the long-run growth rate of real GDP.

✸ At a fixed growth rate in real GDP, faster growth of the money supply leads to inflation and, in extreme cases, to hyperinflation. Inflationary growth in the money supply generates social costs, which include "menu costs" that firms incur as they make frequent price changes, distortions in relative prices, and price controls. Moderate growth in the money supply, which produces moderate inflation, also generates certain benefits for society, including seignorage and temporarily lower real wages and real interest rates, which stimulate growth of real GDP.

✸ Central banks, such as the Federal Reserve Bank (the Fed) in the United States, attempt to keep inflation at a low and stable level and also try to maximize the sustainable level of employment.

✸ The Fed holds the reserves of private banks (with the exception of vault cash). The management of these private bank reserves is one of the most important roles that the Fed plays. The Fed's management of private bank reserves enables it to do three things: (1) set the federal funds rate, a short-term interest rate; (2) influence the money supply and the inflation rate; and (3) influence long-term real interest rates.

✸ The Fed has many policy levers that enable it to influence the market for bank reserves and, by implication, the federal funds rate, including shifting the quantity of reserves supplied (which is referred to as open market operations), changing the reserve requirement, and changing the interest rate paid on reserves.

Key Terms

Money *p. 583*
Medium of exchange *p. 583*
Store of value *p. 583*
Unit of account *p. 584*
Fiat money *p. 584*
Money supply *p. 585*
Quantity theory of money *p. 587*
Deflation *p. 588*

Seignorage *p. 590*
Real wage *p. 591*
Central bank *p. 593*
Monetary policy *p. 593*
Federal Reserve Bank, or the Fed *p. 593*
Liquidity *p. 595*
Federal funds market *p. 595*
Federal funds rate *p. 595*

Federal funds market equilibrium *p. 598*
Open market operations *p. 598*
Long-term real interest rate *p. 602*
Realized real interest rate *p. 602*
Expected real interest rate *p. 602*
Inflation expectations *p. 602*

Questions

All questions are available in MyEconLab for practice and instructor assignment.

1. List and explain the three functions of money in a modern economy.

2. How does fiat money differ from commodities like gold and silver that were used as money?

3. How is the M2 money supply defined?

4. Recall the discussion in the chapter about the "quantity theory of money."
   a. Explain the quantity theory of money.
   b. Explain how predictions of the quantity theory of money are borne out by historical data.

5. What is the difference between inflation, deflation, and hyperinflation?

6. What is the most common cause of hyperinflation?

7. What are the costs associated with inflation?

8. Does inflation have any benefits? Explain.

9. What is the federal funds rate? What are the factors that would shift the demand curve for reserves?

10. What is an open market operation? Why does the Federal Reserve conduct open market operations?

11. Why is the Federal Reserve referred to as the "lender of last resort"?

12. How does the Federal Reserve influence the long-term real interest rate?

13. What are the two models that are used to describe inflationary expectations?

Problems

All problems are available in MyEconLab for practice and instructor assignment.
Problems marked 🌐 update with real-time data.

1. Barter is a method of exchange whereby goods or services are traded directly for other goods or services without the use of money or any other medium of exchange.

   a. Suppose you need to get your house painted. You register with a barter Web site and want to offer your car cleaning services to someone who will paint your house in return. What are the problems you are likely to encounter?

   b. Some barter Web sites allow the use of "barter dollars." The registration fee that you pay to a barter Web site gets converted into barter dollars that can be exchanged with other users to buy goods and services. Would the use of barter dollars resolve the problems you listed in part (a)? Explain.

2. Money makes a variety of economic transactions possible. In the following three situations, determine whether money is involved in the transaction.

   a. In prison camps during World War II, and in some prisons today, cigarettes circulate among prisoners. For example, an iPod might cost two cartons of cigarettes, whereas a magazine might cost only two cigarettes. Discuss whether cigarettes are fulfilling all three functions of money in this case.

   b. Over the last 50 years, credit cards have become an increasingly popular way for people to purchase goods and services. Are credit cards money? Explain your reasoning.

   c. Almost every day, many people sign their names to little pieces of paper called checks, which are then accepted in exchange for goods and services. Do these checks constitute money? Why or why not?

3. Yap is a small island in the Pacific Ocean with a total land area of 39 square miles. In the 1900s, there were only three commodities that were traded on this isolated island—fish, coconuts, and sea cucumber. However, the monetary system in Yap was highly sophisticated. The currency that was used on Yap was called "Fei." Fei were large wheels of stone with a hole in the center. These stone wheels were not quarried in Yap but were brought to the island from elsewhere. The value of each wheel as currency depended on its size, which ranged from 1 foot in diameter to 12 feet. Each time a transaction had to be settled in Fei, the ownership of each stone wheel was transferred to the seller, even if the wheel was not physically moved to the seller's house. Explain how Fei fulfilled or failed to fulfill the three functions of money.

4. Bitcoins are defined as a "peer-to-peer decentralized digital currency." The supply of bitcoins is not controlled by the government or any other central agency. The value of each bitcoin is determined on the basis of supply and demand and is defined in terms of dollars. New bitcoins can be generated through a process called "mining." However, new bitcoins will not be created once there are a total of 21 million bitcoins in existence. Some commentators feel that bitcoins can eventually replace most of the major currencies in the world. Would you agree? Explain your answer.

5. Imagine that the chairperson of the Federal Reserve announced that, as of the following day, all currency in circulation in the United States would be worth 10 times its face denomination. For example, a $10 bill would be worth $100; a $100 bill would be worth $1,000, etc. Furthermore, the balances in all checking and savings accounts are to be multiplied by 10. So, if you have $500 in your checking account, as of the following day your balance would be $5,000, etc.

   Would you actually be 10 times better off on the day the announcement took effect? Why or why not?

6. The following four exercises ask you to retrieve and work with macroeconomic data from the FRED Web site of the Federal Reserve Bank of St. Louis.

   a. Go to http://research.stlouisfed.org/fred2/data/GDP .txt. Find the figure for nominal GDP for the latest quarter. (Q1 is January, February, and March; Q2 is April, May, June, etc.) The figure for a given quarter will be listed under the first day of the month beginning the quarter. For example, data for Q1 of 2013 will be listed as of 2013-01-01; for Q2, 2013-04-01; Q3, 2013-07-01; Q4, 2013-10-01.

   b. Go to the following Web page from the Federal Reserve FRED database: http://research.stlouisfed.org/ fred2/data/M2SL.txt. What is the most recent figure for the M2 money stock?

   c. Calculate the average M2 figure for the same quarter you found for GDP in part (a). (Data for a given month is listed under the first day of that month; for example, the data for June of 2013 will be listed under 2013-06-01.)

   d. Divide your answer from part (c) by your answer from part (a), and compare it with the ratios given in Exhibit 25.2. Is it higher, lower, or in line with the data summarized in the graph?

7. According to the BBC, inflation in the country of Zimbabwe reached an annualized rate of 231,000,000 percent in October of 2008. Prices got so high that in January of 2009, the country's central bank—the Reserve Bank of Zimbabwe—introduced a $100 trillion bill.

   (*Sources*: http://news.bbc.co.uk/2/hi/africa/7660569 .stm; http://news.bbc.co.uk/2/hi/africa/7832601.stm.)

   Read the summary of Zimbabwe's experience with hyperinflation in Wikipedia (http://en.wikipedia.org/wiki/ Hyperinflation_in_Zimbabwe). How does the history of hyperinflation in the country illustrate the points made in the chapter regarding the root causes, costs, and benefits of inflation? What were some of the adaptations that citizens of the country used to cope with the situation?

8. The following table shows the cost of producing dollar notes of various denominations. As you can see in the table, it costs only 12.7 cents to produce a $100 bill. Suppose the government decided that it will print new notes to fund its fiscal deficit as well as all its ongoing expenditure. What would be the effects of such a policy?

Note	Cost of Production
$1 and $2	5.4 cents per note
$5	9.8 cents per note
$10 notes	9.0 cents per note
$20 and $50	9.8 cents per note
$100	12.7 cents per note

9. Assume there is an increase in the demand for reserves—in other words, the demand curve for reserves shifts to the right. Suppose also that the Fed did not change the quantity of reserves supplied.

   a. Using a graph of the demand and supply of reserves, show the effect of this increase on the equilibrium federal funds rate and the equilibrium quantity of reserves.

   b. Given your results from part (a), if the Fed wants to restore the federal funds rate to its pre-expansion level, what kind of open market operation would it need to undertake? Show the result of the operation on your graph from part (a).

10. From 2001 to 2006, Japan's central bank, the Bank of Japan (BOJ), engaged in a monetary policy program called quantitative easing. The BOJ increased the value of the excess reserves that commercial banks held with the central bank by selling assets to these commercial banks. Use a graph to show how this policy is likely to have affected the overnight call rate. The overnight call rate in Japan is similar to the federal funds rate in the United States.

11. As the U.S. economy recovered from the recession of 2007–2009, it was widely anticipated that the Fed would raise the federal funds rate.

   Suppose the current federal funds rate is 1 percent, and that this rate is expected to prevail for one more year. Then, the expectation is that the Fed will raise the federal funds rate by 1 percent each year for 4 years, reaching 5 percent in year five and then maintaining the federal funds rate at that level for another 5 years.

   What will be the 10-year nominal interest rate as a result of these expectations? Explain and show your work.

12. The chapter discusses different models of how people form their expectations regarding inflation. Consider the following two investors, who are trying to forecast what inflation will be for next year. Sean reasons as follows: "Inflation was 2.5 percent last year. Therefore, I think it is likely to be 2.5 percent this year." Carlos, on the other hand, thinks this way: "The economy has recovered from recession sufficiently that inflationary pressures are likely to build. Likewise, a weaker dollar means that imports are going to be more expensive. I don't think the Fed will risk slowing the recovery and raising unemployment by raising interest rates to fight inflation. So, in light of all these factors, I expect inflation to increase to 5 percent next year." Using the terminology mentioned in the chapter, explain how you would best describe how each investor is forming his expectations of inflation. Which description better fits your own forecasts of inflation?

What caused the recession of 2007–2009?

The U.S. economy, like any other, experiences economic fluctuations—in other words, the growth rate fluctuates from year to year. Between 1982 and 2007, the U.S. economy tended to grow quickly and experienced only two mild recessions, achieving average growth in real gross domestic product (GDP) of 3.4 percent per year. But starting at the end of 2007, the economy began a deep contraction. The fall in economic activity caused significant hardship for hundreds of millions of households worldwide. In the United States alone, the number of unemployed workers rose by 7.4 million. Many families also lost a large chunk of their life savings; U.S. housing prices fell by a third and stock prices halved. The recession that started in December 2007 lasted until June 2009, when the economy started growing again.

What caused the recession of 2007–2009? In this chapter, we examine the various factors that contributed to this economic and financial free fall. But first we will explore the characteristics of economic fluctuations in general and possible causes for them. In the process, we will develop a model that can help us better understand the short-run causes and consequences of fluctuations in economic activity.

CHAPTER **OUTLINE**

KEY IDEAS

- Recessions are periods (lasting at least two quarters) in which real GDP falls.

- Economic fluctuations have three key features: co-movement, limited predictability, and persistence.

- Economic fluctuations occur because of technology shocks, changing sentiments, and monetary/financial factors.

- Economic shocks are amplified by downward wage rigidity and multipliers.

- Economic booms are periods of expansion of GDP, associated with increasing employment and declining unemployment.

- Three key factors contributed to the 2007–2009 recession: a collapsing housing bubble, a fall in household wealth, and a financial crisis.

26.1 Economic Fluctuations and Business Cycles

> **Growth, even for the most developed economies, is never completely steady.**

Short-run changes in the growth of GDP are referred to as **economic fluctuations** or **business cycles**.

Modern market economies have demonstrated a remarkable ability to generate long-run growth. As we saw in Chapter 21, the U.S. economy grew substantially over the last 100 years. But growth, even for the most developed economies, is never completely steady. Instead, there are periods of good times and bad, of ups and downs. These fluctuations tend to be hard to predict. We refer to short-run changes in the growth rate of real GDP as **economic fluctuations** or **business cycles**.

Exhibit 26.1 plots the level of real GDP (in blue) in the United States from 1929 to 2013, using 2009 as the base year for prices. Recall that real dollars hold the overall price level fixed, implying that the effects of inflation are removed from plots of *real* variables. The plot of real GDP starts in 1929 because that is when high-quality data were first available.

The exhibit also plots a trend line (in red), which represents the level of real GDP that the economy would attain if we could wave a wand and magically maintain a steady rate of growth, thereby avoiding fluctuations. The trend line in Exhibit 26.1 is derived by drawing a path that grows smoothly over time. Such a fluctuation-free economy is not actually feasible—economic fluctuations are a fact of life. Government policies can only reduce the severity—not the very existence—of fluctuations.

In Exhibit 26.1, two major deviations from trend are apparent: the Great Depression (lasting throughout the 1930s) and the period of U.S. participation in World War II (1941–1945). During the Great Depression, the U.S. economy fell far below trend GDP. Conversely, during World War II, the U.S. economy surged ahead of trend GDP.

Exhibit 26.2 provides an alternative way of looking at the same data by plotting the percent deviation between real GDP and its trend. This corresponds to the percentage difference between the blue and red lines in Exhibit 26.1. Looking at Exhibit 26.2, we can again easily

Exhibit 26.1 Real U.S. GDP and a Trend Line (1929–2013; billions of 2009 constant dollars)

The exhibit plots real GDP (in blue) and a red trend line, which represents the level of real GDP that the economy would attain if we could smooth out the year-to-year fluctuations. The trend line is derived by drawing a path that grows smoothly over time. The figure uses a proportional scale for the vertical axis.

Source: Bureau of Economic Analysis, National Income and Product Accounts (GDP). The trend line is calculated by the authors.

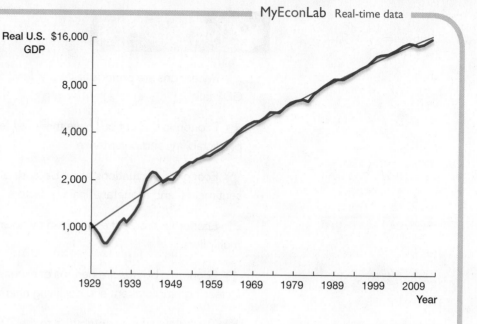

Exhibit 26.2 Percent Deviation Between U.S. Real GDP and Its Trend Line (1929–2013)

Here we show the percent deviation between U.S. real GDP and a trend line for U.S. real GDP (the trend line is plotted in Exhibit 26.1). The percent deviation is calculated as $100 \times$ (Real GDP − Trend)/Trend.

Source: Bureau of Economic Analysis, National Income and Product Accounts (real GDP). The trend line is calculated by the authors.

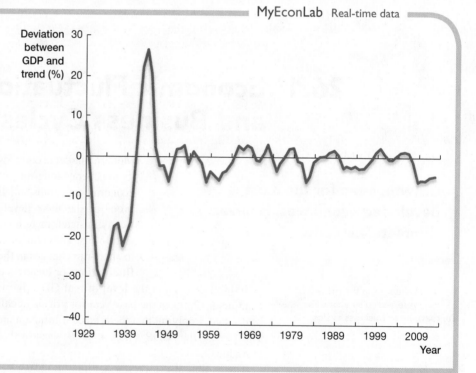

see two big events standing apart from the rest: the Great Depression and World War II. The most recent recession (2007–2009) is visible at the end of the plot. Even in 2013, 4 years after the end of the recession, real GDP remains well below its trend level.

In addition to comparing economic activity to its trend as we did in Exhibit 26.1, economists focus on fluctuations in the annual growth rate of GDP. They refer to periods of positive growth in GDP as *expansions* or *booms* and to episodes of negative GDP growth as *downturns*, *contractions*, or *recessions*.

As we have seen in Chapter 19, recessions are periods (lasting at least two quarters) in which real GDP falls. Of course, we also care about periods of economic growth. **Economic expansions** are the periods between recessions. Accordingly, an economic expansion begins at the end of one recession and continues until the start of the next recession. During the last century, the average economic expansion has been about 4 times as long as the average recession.

Economic expansions are the periods between recessions. Accordingly, an economic expansion begins at the end of one recession and continues until the start of the next recession.

Exhibit 26.3 U.S. Recessions from 1929 to 2013

Since 1929, a recession has occurred about once every 6 years and each recession has on average lasted about 1 year. The recession trough is the low point for real GDP during a recession, corresponding to the end of the recession. In most recessions, the decline in real GDP from peak to trough is less than 3 percent, though in the Great Depression of 1929–1933, the U.S. economy did experience a 26.3 percent drop in real GDP from peak to trough.

Sources: National Bureau of Economic Research (recession dating) and Bureau of Economic Analysis, National Income and Product Accounts (real GDP).

Starting Month	Ending Month	Duration (Months)	Decline in Real GDP from Peak to Trough
August 1929	March 1933	43	26.3%
May 1937	June 1938	13	3.3%
February 1945	October 1945	8	12.7%[1]
November 1948	October 1949	11	1.5%
July 1953	May 1954	10	1.9%
August 1957	April 1958	8	3.0%
April 1960	February 1961	10	0.3%
December 1969	November 1970	11	0.2%
November 1973	March 1975	16	3.1%
January 1980	July 1980	6	2.2%
July 1981	November 1982	16	2.5%
July 1990	March 1991	8	1.3%
March 2001	November 2001	8	0.3%
December 2007	June 2009	18	4.3%

Exhibit 26.3 reports the dates of the 14 U.S. recessions that have occurred since 1929 and the decline in real GDP from peak to trough in each recession. The peak is the high point of real GDP, just before a recession begins. The trough is the low point of real GDP during the recession, which corresponds to the end of the recession. Since 1929, a recession has occurred about once every 6 years, and the average recession length has been about 1 year.

Patterns of Economic Fluctuations

Economic fluctuations have three key properties:

1. Co-movement of many aggregate macroeconomic variables
2. Limited predictability of fluctuations
3. Persistence in the rate of economic growth

We now look at each of these properties in turn.

Co-Movement Many aggregate macroeconomic variables grow or contract together during economic booms and recessions. Economists refer to this pattern as *co-movement*. Exhibit 26.4 illustrates co-movement, focusing on two key variables: consumption and investment both adjusted for inflation, which are referred to as real consumption and real investment. The horizontal axis plots the growth rate of real consumption in a single year, and the vertical axis plots the growth rate of real investment in the same year. Each plotted point is a single year of historical data, so you can read the growth rates for real consumption and real investment by tracing a point to both horizontal (real consumption) and vertical (real investment) axes.

The exhibit shows that points tend to cluster around an upward-sloping line. This means that consumption and investment co-move. When consumption growth is high, investment growth tends to be high as well. When consumption growth is low (or negative), investment growth tends to be low (or negative). In other words, consumption and investment tend to either grow together or shrink together.

Note also that investment is more volatile than consumption. The vertical axis ranges from −100 percent to +150 percent, while the horizontal axis ranges only from −10 percent to +15 percent. The substantial variation in investment growth occurs because firms often drastically cut investment in response to a weakening economy and then raise it rapidly when the economy is booming. However, it is optimal for households to try to *smooth* consumption over time. For example, unless you actually run out of money, you wouldn't want to postpone replacing your smashed smartphone until the economy recovers from a recession.

Employment and GDP also move together with consumption and investment, and unemployment moves negatively with GDP. This implies, for example, that during

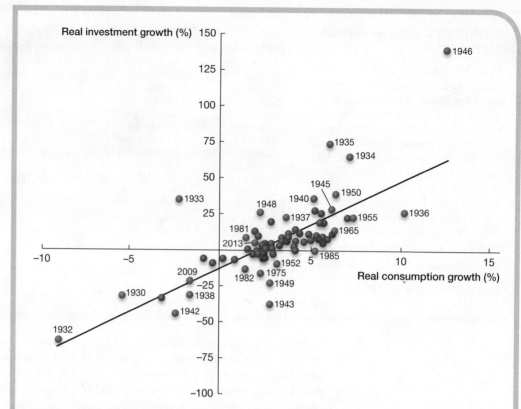

Exhibit 26.4 Real Consumption Growth Versus Real Investment Growth (1929–2013)

The horizontal axis plots the growth rate of real consumption in a single year, and the vertical axis plots the growth rate of real investment in the same year. Each plotted point corresponds to a single year of historical data, so you can read the growth rates for real consumption and real investment by tracing a point to both horizontal (real consumption) and vertical (real investment) axes. For example, on the right-hand side of the exhibit, there is a point marked 1950. That year, real consumption grew about 6 percent (read this off the horizontal axis), and real investment grew about 39 percent (read this off the vertical axis). When consumption growth is relatively high, investment growth also tends to be relatively high. On the left-hand side of the exhibit, there is a point marked 2009. That year, real consumption grew about −2 percent (horizontal axis), and real investment grew about −22 percent (vertical axis). When consumption growth is relatively low, investment growth also tends to be relatively low. Economists say that consumption and investment tend to move together—they exhibit co-movement.

Source: Bureau of Economic Analysis, National Income and Product Accounts.

contractions real consumption, real investment, employment, and real GDP all fall, while unemployment rises.

Limited Predictability The second important feature of economic fluctuations is that of *limited predictability*. If you look back at Exhibit 26.3, showing the duration of recessions in the U.S. economy since 1929, you can see that recessions have been as short as 6 months and as long as 43 months. The 2007–2009 recession was 18 months long. Economic expansions also have highly variable lengths. Since 1929, the shortest expansion was 1 year and the longest was 10 years.

Because recessions and expansions have such variable lengths, it is clear that they do not follow a repetitive, easily predictable cycle. In fact, even with the tools of modern economics, it is impossible to predict far in advance when a recession or an expansion will end. We call this property "limited predictability" rather than "no predictability," because by using sophisticated statistical techniques we can achieve a *small* degree of predictive power. Given the current state of economic science, we are usually able to accurately predict the end of a recession a month or two before the actual end. But it is practically impossible to forecast the end of a recession at the time the recession begins. Moreover, it is also impossible to forecast when an expansion will end. Limited predictability is important to acknowledge because many early theories of business cycles assumed that economic fluctuations had a pendulum-like structure with systematic swings in economic growth. Such predictability is very far from the truth.

Persistence in the Rate of Growth   The third noteworthy regularity of economic fluctuations is that of *persistence*. Even though recessions begin and end at somewhat unpredictable times, economic growth is not random. When the economy is growing, it will probably keep growing the following quarter. Likewise, when the economy is contracting—in other words, when growth is negative—the economy will probably keep contracting the following quarter. So if the economy is in a recession this quarter, our best bet is that it will still be in a recession next quarter as well. Thus there is some amount of persistence in the rate of economic growth.

The Great Depression

We've noted that one event stands out like no other in the history of economic fluctuations. This is the **Great Depression**, which is far and away the most severe U.S. economic contraction since modern methods for measuring GDP were developed about 100 years ago. Although there is no consensus on the definition, the term **depression** is typically used to describe a prolonged recession with an unemployment rate of 20 percent or more. Although the U.S. economy has experienced dozens of recessions, only the 1929 contraction qualifies as a depression. For example, unemployment during the 2007–2009 recession peaked at 10.0 percent, less than half the level of peak unemployment during the Great Depression.

The Great Depression started in 1929, coinciding with a crash in the U.S. stock market. From 1929 to 1933, the crisis deepened as stock markets around the world continued to fall. At its bottom in 1933, the U.S. stock market was about 80 percent below its peak 4 years earlier. Millions of U.S. farmers and homeowners went bankrupt. Real GDP fell 26.3 percent below its 1929 level, and unemployment eventually rose from 3 percent in 1929 to 25 percent in 1933. From 1929 to 1933, the number of banks in the United States fell from 23,679 to 14,207. This decline was driven by failing banks that either went out of business altogether or were acquired by stronger competitors. Similar events occurred in almost all developed countries around the world, though the U.S. contraction was among the most severe.

The Great Depression illustrates the three key properties of economic fluctuations that we just discussed. First, it featured strong co-movement in economic aggregates. Panel (a) of Exhibit 26.5 illustrates this co-movement by plotting real GDP, real consumption, and real investment from 1929 to 1939. The three series started to fall in 1929 and bottomed out in 1932 and 1933. Unemployment moved in lockstep in the opposite direction: starting at 3 percent in 1929 and peaking at 25 percent in 1933. The unemployment rate is plotted in panel (b) of Exhibit 26.5. Finally, the financial markets reflected these movements, also co-moving with real GDP. The Dow Jones Industrial Average, an important stock index, fluctuated with the level of economic activity—see panel (c) of Exhibit 26.5.

The Great Depression also featured limited predictability—or in this case, *no* predictability. In fact, it came as a complete surprise to most economists, policymakers, and business leaders.[2] The preeminent economic forecaster of the late 1920s was Irving Fisher, a Yale professor and newspaper columnist, who repeatedly wrote about the strength of the economy and the low likelihood of adverse economic events. Indeed, one week before the stock market's Great Crash of October 24, 1929, Fisher stated that "stock prices have reached what looks like a permanently high plateau." Even after the initial October stock market crash, and after the broader economy had started to contract, Fisher maintained his optimism. On May 19, 1930, Fisher wrote, "It seems manifest that

An impoverished farm worker and three of her children, photographed in California during the Great Depression.

The **Great Depression** refers to the severe contraction that started in 1929, reaching a low point for real GDP in 1933. The period of below-trend real GDP did not end until the buildup to World War II in the late 1930s.

Although there is no consensus on the definition, the term **depression** is typically used to describe a prolonged recession with an unemployment rate of 20 percent or more.

> The Great Depression . . . came as a complete surprise to most economists, policymakers, and business leaders.

Exhibit 26.5 (a) The Great Depression started in 1929 and real GDP bottomed out in 1933—the trough. During the contraction and the long recovery, real GDP, real consumption, and real investment moved together, as this exhibit demonstrates.

Source: Bureau of Economic Analysis, National Income and Product Accounts.

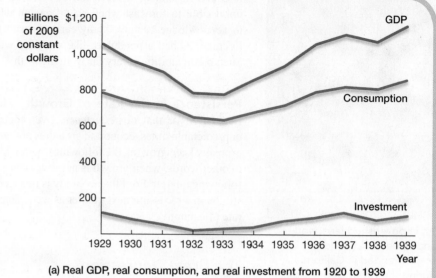

(a) Real GDP, real consumption, and real investment from 1920 to 1939

(b) The unemployment rate tracks fluctuations in GDP but moves in the opposite direction. Unemployment tends to rise when GDP falls. During the Great Depression, unemployment rose from 3 percent in 1929 to a peak of 25 percent in 1933.

Source: U.S. Census Bureau, Historical Statistics of the United States, Colonial Times to 1970, U.S. Department of Commerce, no. 93 (1975).

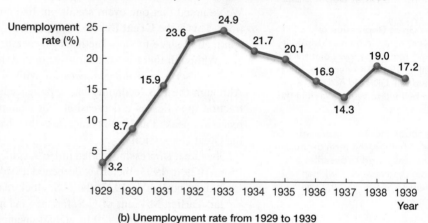

(b) Unemployment rate from 1929 to 1939

(c) Stock prices also tend to move with other measures of economic activity. The Dow Jones Industrial Average is an index that averages together the stock prices of thirty of the most important companies based in the United States.

Source: Global Financial Data.

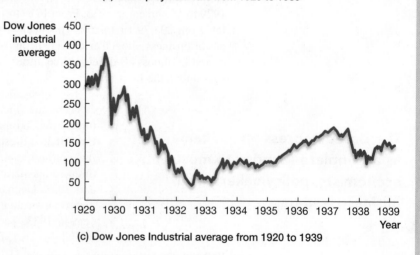

(c) Dow Jones Industrial average from 1920 to 1939

thus far the difference between the present comparatively mild business recession and the severe depression of 1920–1921 is like that between a thunder-shower and a tornado." Unfortunately, unfolding events would soon prove him completely wrong. The contraction of 1920–1921 turned out to be minor when compared to the much deeper contraction that started in 1929.

Fisher's misplaced optimism was common. No leading economic or business forecaster foresaw the Great Depression. Consider this: on January 18, 1930, a group of eminent forecasters at Harvard wrote, "There are indications that the severest phase of the recession is over." In truth, the Great Depression had barely begun.

Finally, the Great Depression featured the third property of economic fluctuations—a great deal of persistence. The period of negative growth in real GDP lasted for 4 years, starting in 1929 and ending in 1933.

26.2 Macroeconomic Equilibrium and Economic Fluctuations

Why are there economic fluctuations? Given the importance of economic fluctuations and the voluminous amount of research on the topic, you might think that we would have a convincing answer—one on which we could all agree. Alas, that is not the case. In fact, there probably isn't another topic that incites as much passionate disagreement among economists. Although this disagreement, often aired in newspaper editorials and blogs, is real, it masks the fact that economists have built up a significant body of shared knowledge about the nature of economic fluctuations. This knowledge forms the basis of the model of economic fluctuations that we will now describe.

Labor Demand and Fluctuations

We begin our analysis by returning to a discussion of the labor market. Recall from Chapter 23 that the intersection of the labor demand and labor supply curves determines the labor market equilibrium. Here we start with a labor market with flexible wages and then show how downward wage rigidity amplifies the impact of labor demand shifts—and thus amplifies the magnitude of economic fluctuations.

Summary of Shifts in the Labor Demand Curve

In Chapter 23, we discussed the most important sources of shifts in the labor demand curve:

1. **Changing output prices:** When the price of the output good goes down, the value of the marginal product of labor also declines. This implies that the firm would like to hire fewer workers at any given wage, shifting the labor demand curve to the left. (When the price of the product the firm produces rises, the value of the marginal product of labor goes up, shifting the labor demand curve to the right.)

2. **Changing output demand:** When the demand for the product the firm produces declines, its price and thus its value of the marginal product of labor goes down, shifting the labor demand curve to the left. (When the demand for the product the firm produces rises, the value of the marginal product of labor goes up, shifting the labor demand curve to the right.) In addition to the factors emphasized in Chapter 23, an expansion in credit (and a decline in the interest rate) can also lead to an increase in output demand, as we have seen in Chapter 24.

3. **Changing technology and productivity:** When the marginal product of labor falls, the labor demand curve shifts to the left. (When the marginal product of labor rises, the labor demand curve shifts to the right.)

4. **Changing input prices:** Businesses use labor and other factors of production, like physical capital and energy, to produce goods and services. When the cost of these other factors goes up, firms purchase less of them. This usually decreases the marginal product of labor, shifting the labor demand curve to the left. (When the cost of these other factors goes down, firms purchase more of them, shifting the labor demand curve to the right.) A change in the credit market equilibrium can also influence labor demand by affecting the firm's cost of financing the acquisition of physical capital.

Panel (a) of Exhibit 26.6, which focuses on the case of flexible wages, reminds you of this relationship by graphing labor demand and labor supply curves and their intersection. Also recall that labor demand reflects profit maximization by firms, and labor supply reflects how households optimally trade off labor and leisure.

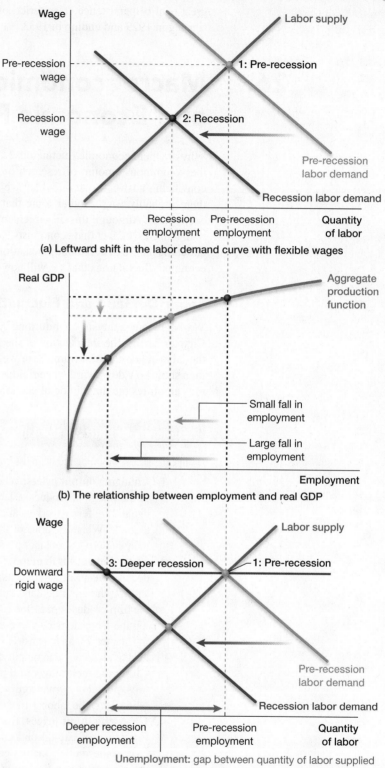

Exhibit 26.6 A shift to the left of the labor demand curve leads to a fall in equilibrium employment and a fall in the wage (point "2: Recession"). This example assumes that wages are flexible and consequently fall as a result of the leftward shift in the labor demand curve.

(a) Leftward shift in the labor demand curve with flexible wages

The decline in employment from the pre-recession equilibrium (point 1) to a recession moves the economy along the aggregate production function relating employment to real GDP, causing a decline in real GDP. The decline in employment is smaller when wages are flexible (point 2, which appears in panel (a)) than when wages are downward rigid (point 3, which appears in panel (c)). Consequently, the fall in real GDP is also smaller when wages are flexible than when wages are downward rigid.

(b) The relationship between employment and real GDP

When wages are downward rigid, a shift to the left of the labor demand curve leads to a sharp fall in equilibrium employment. In the new equilibrium (point "3: Deeper recession"), there are many workers (denoted by the green line) who would like to work at the market wage but can't find a job. These workers are officially classified as unemployed because they would like to work at the market wage but can't find a job.

(c) Leftward shift in the labor demand curve with downward rigid wages

The labor market equilibrium, which corresponds to the wage and employment levels given by the intersection of the labor supply and labor demand curves, is the key building block we will use to construct a model of economic fluctuations. Employment fluctuations correspond to changes in this labor market equilibrium, and real GDP and employment fluctuations are linked. Panel (a) of Exhibit 26.6 illustrates these linkages by depicting a leftward shift in the labor demand curve, which reduces the equilibrium quantity of labor employed. Before a recession begins, the original equilibrium is given by the point labeled "1: Pre-recession." After an economic shock has shifted the labor demand curve to the left, the new equilibrium, which features a lower wage and a lower quantity of labor demanded, is at the point labeled "2: Recession."

Panel (b) of Exhibit 26.6 depicts the aggregate production function, which we discussed in Chapter 20. Holding physical capital and technology constant, this curve shows the relationship between employment and GDP (we are holding human capital per worker constant here, so the efficiency units of labor are proportional to employment). We can see in the panel that as employment declines (due to the leftward shift in the demand curve), so does real GDP (because there is less labor producing goods and services). Accordingly, employment and real GDP rise and fall together, which is another illustration of co-movement among economic aggregates.

In practice, the fall in real GDP might exceed what we show in panel (b) of the exhibit because the decline in employment generates other types of economic adjustment. Laying off a worker also makes the physical capital that the worker was previously using—plant and equipment—less productive, leading firms to shutter plants and mothball equipment. The rate of utilization of physical capital is called *capacity utilization*, and recessions are usually accompanied by a reduction in capacity utilization. For example, during the depths of the 2007–2009 recession, capacity utilization in the United States fell to 67 percent from a normal rate of 80 percent, further depressing real GDP.

When firms shed their workers, utilization of physical capital also falls.

As we discussed in Chapter 23, when wages are downward rigid, the impact of a shift in labor demand is amplified. This is shown in panel (c) of Exhibit 26.6. In the case of downward wage rigidity, firms are unable or unwilling to cut wages because of contractual restrictions or because of morale problems that would result from falling wages. As a result, firms end up laying off more workers than they would have if wages were downward flexible. With downward rigid wages, a leftward shift in the labor demand curve causes employment to fall by even more than it does in the flexible wage

> **When wages are downward rigid, the impact of shifts in labor demand is amplified.**

case. Accordingly, with downward rigid wages there is an even deeper recession and a bigger movement along the aggregate production function than in the flexible wage case (panel (b)).

Downward rigid wages are one source of *unemployment*. At the market wage, which is the downward rigid wage, the number of workers who are willing to work exceeds the number of jobs that firms are willing to fill. The number of unemployed workers in this deeper recession—in other words, workers who would like to work at the market wage but can't find a job—is represented by the green bar at the bottom of panel (c).

Although shifts in the *supply* of labor can also cause fluctuations in employment and unemployment, the most important source of fluctuations are shifts in the *demand* for labor. To understand the nature of short-run macroeconomic equilibrium, we need to know why the demand for labor fluctuates.

Sources of Fluctuations

Economists have tried to identify the forces that affect the demand curve for labor. These forces cause recessions and other aggregate economic fluctuations.

In Chapter 23 we provide one breakdown of the factors that shift the labor demand curve: (1) changes in the output price for a firm's products, (2) changes in the demand for a firm's products, (3) changes in productivity or technology, or (4) changes in the costs of a firm's inputs.

We now offer a different breakdown, by discussing three schools of thought within the economics profession. Each school has a different story to tell about the sources of aggregate economic fluctuations.

1. *Real business cycle theory*: emphasizes changing productivity and technology
2. *Keynesian theory*: emphasizes changing expectations about the future
3. *Financial and monetary theories*: emphasize changes in prices and interest rates

Unemployment and the Growth Rate of Real GDP: Okun's Law

Exhibit 26.6 emphasizes that employment and real GDP are tightly connected through the aggregate production function. This linkage is related to an equation called **Okun's Law**, which is named after economist Arthur Okun, who first noticed in the early 1960s that there is a close connection between falling unemployment and the growth rate of real GDP.[3] Employment tends to increase and the unemployment rate tends to decline when the growth rate of real GDP is high.

In particular, let g represent the annual growth rate of real GDP, in percentage points. Then Okun's Law says that:

$$\text{(Year-to-year change in the rate of unemployment)}$$
$$= -\frac{1}{2} \times (g - 3\%).$$

This equation implies that the unemployment rate holds steady when the growth rate of real GDP is 3 percent. The equation also implies that the unemployment rate falls when g is above 3 percent; and the unemployment rate rises when g is below 3 percent. In other words, the unemployment rate falls when real economic growth is relatively high; and the unemployment rate rises when real economic growth is relatively low. Okun's Law is plotted as a black line in Exhibit 26.7. Although the data don't line up perfectly with the equation, Okun's Law is roughly consistent with the data.

Though the overall relationship between changes in the rate of unemployment and the growth rate of real GDP is clear in the data, these two variables do not *always* move together. Sometimes, a fall in the unemployment rate is delayed by a year or more *after* the growth rate of real

Okun's Law says that the year-to-year change in the rate of unemployment is equal to $-\frac{1}{2} \times (g - 3\%)$, where g represents the annual growth rate of real GDP, in percentage points.

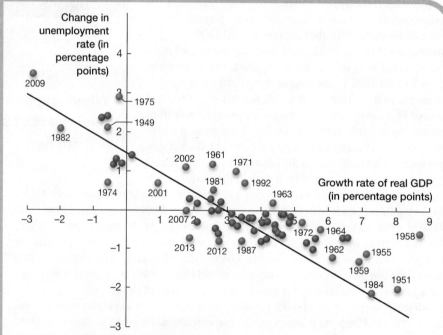

Exhibit 26.7 The Relationship Between the Change in the Rate of Unemployment and the Growth Rate of Real GDP

This exhibit depicts Okun's Law, which shows the relationship between the change in the rate of unemployment and the growth rate of real GDP (g). Okun's Law (the black line) implies that the year-to-year change in the rate of unemployment is

$$-\frac{1}{2} \times (g - 3\%).$$

In other words, unemployment remains constant when the growth rate of real GDP is 3 percent, unemployment declines when the growth rate of real GDP is above 3 percent, and unemployment increases when the growth rate of real GDP is below 3 percent. The exhibit plots annual data from 1948 to 2013.

Sources: Bureau of Labor Statistics (unemployment rate) and Bureau of Economic Analysis, National Income and Product Accounts (real GDP).

GDP picks up at the end of a recession. This delay occurs for several reasons, but the most important one is *labor hoarding*. Because recruiting workers and training them is costly, firms may not want to lay off qualified workers during a temporary slowdown. During a recession some firms will reduce the hours of their workers or even pay those workers to come to jobs at which little gets done, rather than laying the workers off. When the economic recovery comes and these firms increase production, they will not initially need to hire new workers because they can start to ramp up production by fully utilizing the workers they hoarded during the contraction.

Each of these three schools of thought draws upon one or more of the four categories of shifts in the labor demand curve from Chapter 23. Most economists studying business cycles believe each school of thought has generated many key insights, and economists generally don't believe that any one school has all of the answers. The model that we use to describe economic fluctuations expresses the ideas of all of these different schools in a single general framework.

1. Technology Shocks: Explanations from Real Business Cycle Theory In Chapters 20 and 21, we showed that technology differences across firms and workers in different countries help explain differences in cross-country income and growth. Accordingly, one might look for technological reasons to explain economic fluctuations within a given country. For example, imagine that research and development (R&D) leads firms to invent more valuable products (e.g., smartphones replacing traditional cellular phones). This will increase the value of the marginal product of labor, inducing firms to expand their operations, most likely leading them to increase their demand for labor. Firms will also likely seek to increase their productive capacity, raising the level of investment in the economy. These changes will lead to higher household income for three reasons: (1) employment increases, (2) wages rise, and (3) rising corporate earnings make the corporations' stockholders wealthier. For all of these reasons, households will raise their consumption. Thus certain types of technological improvements can lead to increases in labor demand and increases in aggregate economic activity, including investment and consumption.

A version of this view appears in the work of classical economists, most notably, that of Arthur Cecil Pigou.[4] It was revived and extended in the 1980s in what came to be known as **real business cycle theory**—a school of thought that emphasizes the role of technology in causing economic fluctuations.[5]

> **Real business cycle theory** is the school of thought that emphasizes the role of changes in technology in causing economic fluctuations.

But although we know from Chapters 20 and 21 that the rate of technological progress is at the root of long-run variation in economic growth and technological breakthroughs could cause a rapid *increase* in a particular industry's output, purely technological theories have difficulty explaining recessions in which real GDP falls. "Technological regress," in which the technological capabilities of an economy deteriorate, seems an unlikely explanation for recessions. It is unlikely, for example, that a negative technology shock caused the Great Depression.

Nevertheless, the rate of technological progress is believed to play a key role in *long-term* variation in economic growth. As we saw in Chapter 21, countries that consistently develop new technologies, or import cutting-edge technologies from other countries, will attain high rates of growth. So technological progress is a very important determinant of long-term fluctuations in growth—for instance, over several decades—even though it is not the main force driving recessions.

Proponents of real business cycle theory tend to also emphasize the importance of changing input prices—especially the price of oil. We can think of an increase in the price of oil as a decrease in the productivity of firms that use oil. Because almost all firms use oil in one form or another—oil products are a key source of energy—changes in the price of oil function like technology changes. As oil price changes can be abrupt, including large increases in the price of oil, this factor does help to explain recessions.

2. Sentiments and Multipliers: Explanations from John Maynard Keynes
Many modern analyses of economic fluctuations build on the insights of the British economist John Maynard Keynes (1883–1946), who was an academic, stock market trader, and a frequent advisor to the British government. (In case you want to talk about him over dinner in your dining hall, Keynes is pronounced "cains.")

Animal spirits are psychological factors that lead to changes in the mood of consumers or businesses, thereby affecting consumption, investment, and GDP.

Sentiments include changes in expectations about future economic activity, changes in uncertainty facing firms and households, and fluctuations in animal spirits. Changes in sentiments lead to changes in household consumption and firm investment.

Keynes was 46 years old at the start of the Great Depression. As the Depression took hold, Keynes began to develop new theories that attempted to explain its causes. This work culminated in his groundbreaking book *The General Theory of Employment, Interest and Money*.[6] His ideas also had novel implications for government policy. Keynes was highly controversial during his time and remains so today, though few would deny his enormous influence on modern macroeconomics.

Keynes believed in a phenomenon that he dubbed **animal spirits**, which represent psychological factors that lead to changes in the mood of consumers and businesses, thereby affecting consumption, investment, and GDP. In Keynes's view, the animal spirits in an economy could fluctuate sharply even as the underlying fundamental features of the economy changed relatively little. For example, a period of heightened optimism could give way to a period of deep pessimism even though the economic fundamentals—technology, physical capital, and human capital—hadn't changed much at all.

Animal spirits are in fact one example of a broader phenomenon: changing **sentiments**, which include changes in expectations and changes in the (actual or perceived) uncertainty facing firms and households. Changes in sentiments lead to changes in household consumption and firm investment.

For example, consider what happens when firms expect future demand for their products to be low. Such pessimism will have a direct effect on labor demand. When United Airlines becomes pessimistic about future demand for air travel, it cuts back its hiring of flight attendants and pilots. It also cuts back its orders for new planes. This reduces demand for planes at manufacturers like Boeing. Consequently, labor demand both at United Airlines and Boeing shifts to the left.

Consider the effects of this pessimism on GDP. Let's begin by analyzing the fall in investment that occurs when United Airlines cuts back its orders for new planes. Recall the national income accounting identity from Chapter 19:

$$Y = C + I + G + X - M.$$

The change in the behavior of United Airlines causes a decline in investment in the economy (I) and thus also in GDP (Y). But this decline could be at least partially offset by an increase in consumption (C), government expenditure (G), or the difference between exports and imports ($X - M$). With completely *offsetting* movements in C, G, or $X - M$, it is possible for GDP, Y, to remain unchanged despite a sharp decline in investment. For example, if I falls by $5 billion, C could rise by $5 billion, offsetting the reduction in I.

When firms are turning pessimistic and cutting back employment and investment, however, households are unlikely to increase their consumption. In fact, households face a heightened risk of losing their jobs because of the fall in investment. Accordingly, in most instances, consumption moves in the same direction as investment (consistent with our discussion of co-movement above).

The implications for employment were displayed in Exhibit 26.6. Particularly when there is downward wage rigidity, a change in labor demand will have a large effect on employment. Hence, a fall in investment will tend to produce a leftward shift in firms' labor demand curves, reducing employment and ultimately reducing GDP.

The implications of households becoming more pessimistic are similar: they will cut their current spending to build up their "rainy-day" savings and thereby prepare for economic problems ahead. This translates into a decline in the current demand for the products of many firms, shifting the labor demand curve of those firms to the left.

This discussion hints at another major element of Keynes's theory: the possibility that a modest shock could hit the economy and generate a cascade of follow-on effects that ultimately cause a much larger contraction. For example, an increase in pessimism among airline executives will have a series of immediate effects—for instance, lower hiring at United Airlines—that might cascade into a series of follow-on effects—lower hiring at aircraft manufacturers, like Boeing. The cascade keeps building as the ripples spread to more and more interconnected firms, which each start to cut back hiring and shift their own labor demand curves to the left. The pessimism might also spread to households, which, sensing fewer opportunities in the labor market, start to reduce their demand for goods and services. The economic mechanisms that cause an initial shock to be amplified by follow-on effects are called **multipliers**.

To illustrate the potential power of multipliers, imagine that a stock market decline causes a drop in consumer confidence and reduces households' willingness to spend. Such an event

Multipliers refer to economic mechanisms that amplify the initial impact of a shock.

will cause many other dominos to fall. Firms will cut back production and lay off employees. Those newly unemployed workers will be unable to buy goods and services, leading firms that previously sold goods to these consumers to scale back production even more. According to Keynes, such a cycle could have calamitous effects as each round of layoffs further damages the economy, setting off another wave of layoffs. Such cascades of effects will amplify—or multiply—the impact of the initial shock whether the initial shock is negative or positive news. Hence a bit of good economic news can also produce a cascade of positive effects as consumers increase their demand for goods and services and firms respond by shifting the labor demand curve to the right, all of which multiplies the impact of the initial news. Keynes's theory of multipliers plays an important role in many modern economic models.

It is also useful to note that the workings of multipliers involve an element of a **self-fulfilling prophecy**, since the expectation of an event, such as a leftward shift in labor demand in the future, induces actions that lead to the realization of that event, that is, firms cutting their employment now. This is because sentiments can be powerful catalysts of economic change. For example, when a large number of economic actors become pessimistic about the future state of the economy, their resulting actions can indeed reduce the level of future economic activity, partially or even fully justifying their pessimistic beliefs. Consumers might stop buying goods and services. Firms might stop investing in plants and equipment. Labor demand will then shift to the left, reducing employment and raising unemployment. This notion of a self-fulfilling prophecy also highlights that a change in expectations driven by animal spirits might turn out to be "rational"; when households and firms become pessimistic about the economy, the economy will contract as a result of people's pessimistic behavior. So the pessimism ends up justifying itself!

3. Monetary and Financial Factors: Explanations from Milton Friedman

Monetary factors are yet another force that drives business cycles. As we saw in the last chapter, money supply affects nominal GDP. Typically, a fall in nominal GDP, driven by a sharp decline in the money supply, will not only affect the aggregate price level but also real GDP. In this case, changes in the money supply will also drive business cycles. The major proponent of this view has been one of the few macroeconomists to rival Keynes in terms of genius and influence—Milton Friedman.[7]

To understand how monetary factors drive fluctuations in real GDP, consider a scenario in which contractionary monetary policy causes the money supply (M2) to fall sharply.

The fall in the money supply will cause the price level to fall, as predicted by the quantity theory of money (Chapter 25). A fall in the price level reduces employment because of *downward wage rigidity*. To understand why, note that a drop in the aggregate price level implies that firms have cut their output prices reducing their value of marginal product of labor. Consequently, each firm demands a lower quantity of labor at a given wage. In other words, a fall in output prices shifts the labor demand curve to the left. If wages were to fall as much as output prices, then firms would employ as many workers as they had employed before the fall in output prices. However, with a downward rigid wage (recall Chapter 23), wages won't fall and optimizing firms will instead cut back the number of employed workers.

In addition, as we saw in Chapter 25 contractionary monetary policy causes the real interest rate to rise. Recall from Chapter 24 that the real interest rate is the price that a firm pays for another one of its inputs—physical capital. A rise in the real interest rate will therefore make production more costly. Because physical capital is needed by labor, the rising cost of physical capital leads firms to hire less labor, implying a leftward shift in the demand for labor.

Disruptions in the operation of the credit market also cause economic fluctuations. In Chapter 24 we saw how the supply and demand for credit determine the equilibrium interest rate and the amount of credit in the economy. Disruptions in the credit market—for instance, bank failures or other types of financial crises—will reduce the amount of investment and consumption, thereby lowering real GDP and employment. Hence, a leftward shift in the supply of credit will shift firms' labor demand curves to the left.

Multipliers and Economic Fluctuations

Multipliers, which we discussed in the context of changes in sentiment, can amplify the effects of any economic shock, regardless of whether the shock arises from changes in technology, sentiment, or financial markets. Exhibit 26.8 illustrates a simple feedback loop that arises in a contracting economy with multipliers. A shock to consumption causes firms

A **self-fulfilling prophecy** is a situation in which the expectations of an event (such as a left shift in labor demand in the future) induce actions that lead to that event.

Exhibit 26.8 Multipliers in a Contracting Economy

Start the feedback loop at any point in the circle. For example, a shock to consumption causes the firms that produce consumption goods to reduce labor demand, shifting the labor demand curve to the left. The leftward shift in labor demand leads to layoffs, which in turn reduces household income and further reduces household consumption. The cycle continues in the same way, increasing the depth of the economic contraction with each loop around the circle. In this way, the impact of an initial shock is multiplied.

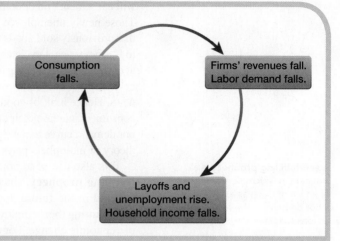

> Multipliers . . . can amplify the effects of any economic shock, regardless of whether the shock arises from changes in technology, sentiment, or financial markets.

to reduce labor demand, shifting the labor demand curve to the left. The leftward shift in labor demand leads to layoffs, reducing household income and further reducing household consumption. The cycle continues in this way, increasing the depth of the economic contraction with each loop around the circle.

The effects of multipliers on wages and employment are graphed in Exhibit 26.9 for the case of flexible wages. Labor supply is shown as the red curve and labor demand as blue. The economy begins at the equilibrium labeled "1: Pre-recession." A shock causes the labor demand curve to shift to the left. The economy is now at a new temporary equilibrium, at the point labeled "2: After shock." We refer to this point as a temporary equilibrium because it does not factor in multiplier effects. In particular, the first wave of layoffs leads unemployed workers to cut back their demand for goods and services, leading the businesses that provide those goods and services to further reduce their labor demand—another leftward shift in the labor demand curve. This moves the economy to the full-blown recession equilibrium labeled "3: Trough." A trough is the low point of real GDP in a recession. This exhibit plots two shifts in the labor demand curve:

a. The initial shock to labor demand (the first shift to the left).

b. A second leftward shift of labor demand due to the layoffs resulting from the *initial* shock. This second shift to the left takes into account multiplier effects.

Exhibit 26.9 Multipliers in an Economy with Flexible Wages

The economy begins at the equilibrium labeled "1: Pre-recession." A shock causes labor demand to shift to the left. The economy is now at a new temporary equilibrium, "2: After shock," which does not include multiplier effects. The layoffs lead to additional reductions in labor demand—more leftward shifts of the labor demand curve—moving the economy to the full-blown recession equilibrium "3: Trough." A trough is the low point of GDP in a recession.

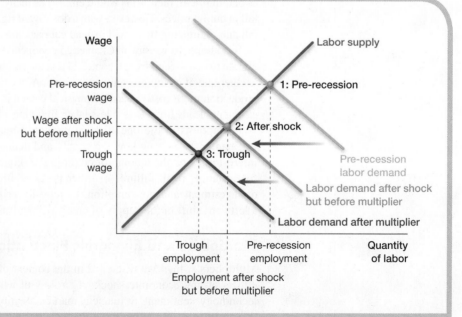

Exhibit 26.10 Additional Multipliers

Start the multiplier loop at any point in the circle. For example, a shock that lowers consumption causes the firms that manufacture consumption goods to reduce labor demand, shifting the labor demand curve to the left. The weak economy leads to layoffs, declining asset prices, mortgage defaults, household bankruptcies, firm bankruptcies, and declining financial intermediation (as banks struggle to survive and some banks fail). All of this in turn reduces consumption and investment. The cycle continues, increasing the depth of the economic contraction with each loop around the circle.

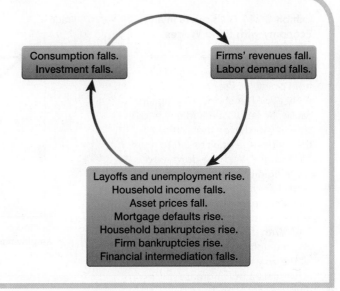

In principle, there could be many more leftward shifts in labor demand, each driven by the last round of layoffs. In practice, economies eventually stabilize and the downward spiral stops. For instance, new businesses replace old firms that have gone bankrupt. If a firm does not have enough demand to remain profitable, the physical and human capital that was employed at that firm will eventually be reallocated to other firms, especially firms in other types of business. The entry of these new firms causes labor demand to stop shifting to the left and eventually start shifting back to the right.

The multiplier loop depicted in Exhibit 26.8 leaves out many of the mechanisms that are important in a modern economy. Exhibit 26.10 adds some of these mechanisms, providing a more complete picture of the factors that multiply the impact of an initial negative shock. These mechanisms include declines in asset prices, such as the value of stocks, bonds, and housing; rising rates of mortgage defaults, which weaken banks' balance sheets; rising rates of household bankruptcies, generating defaults on numerous types of consumer credit including credit card loans; rising rates of firm bankruptcies, causing their lenders to absorb large losses; and falling levels of financial intermediation as banks become unwilling or unable to extend new loans, even to their existing customers. All of these mechanisms create additional multiplier effects and drive down the level of consumption and investment, further depressing labor demand. Falling labor demand leads to additional declines in employment and GDP, further weakening the economy and generating additional rounds of multiplier effects.

Equilibrium in the Short Run, with Multipliers and Downward Wage Rigidity

A more complete picture of recessionary shocks can be seen by combining downward wage rigidity and multipliers. Both of these ingredients amplify the impact of shifts in labor demand on employment. Here is how a shock plays out:

a. An initial shock shifts the labor demand curve to the left.

b. Downward wage rigidity leads firms to adjust to the initial shock by sharply cutting employment rather than reducing both employment and wages by a modest amount.

c. Multipliers cause the labor demand curve to shift leftward even more.

These three factors are illustrated in Exhibit 26.11. Before any shocks, the economy is at the equilibrium labeled "1: Pre-recession." The initial shock causes the economy to move to the new temporary equilibrium labeled "2: After shock." Because we are assuming that the wage is downward rigid, only employment adjusts. When the multipliers kick in, the labor demand curve shifts left again and the economy ends up at the equilibrium labeled "3: Trough." Both the downward wage rigidity and the multipliers have amplified the contractionary impact of the initial recessionary shock. *Without* downward wage rigidity and multipliers, the initial leftward shift of the labor demand curve would have moved the economy to the equilibrium

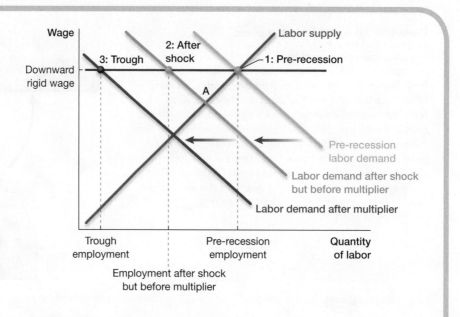

Exhibit 26.11 Multipliers in an Economy with Rigid Wages

A leftward shift in the labor demand curve takes the economy from point "1: Pre-recession" to point "2: After shock." Multipliers cause the labor demand curve to shift leftward even more, moving the rigid-wage equilibrium to point "3: Trough." Without downward wage rigidity and multipliers, the initial leftward shift of the labor demand curve would have moved the economy to the equilibrium labeled "A." With downward wage rigidity and multipliers, the economy moves all the way to "3: Trough," which represents a much greater fall in employment than Point A.

labeled "A." *With* downward wage rigidity and multipliers, the economy moves all the way to "3: Trough," which features a much greater fall in employment than point A.

Equilibrium in the Medium Run: Partial Recovery and Full Recovery

There are many forces—some market-driven and some policy-driven—that tend to reverse the effects of a recession in the course of a few years. We refer to this 2- to 3-year time horizon as the *medium run* to distinguish it from the short run, which corresponds to a few quarters, and the long run, which corresponds to periods of a decade or more. In our discussion, we divide the recovery mechanisms into two categories.

  i. The labor demand curve shifts back to the right due to market forces.
  ii. The labor demand curve shifts back to the right due to expansionary government policies.

Let's now explore each of these in more detail.

  i. *The labor demand curve shifts back to the right due to market forces.* This rebound occurs for many reasons, and here are the most important ones:
  • Labor demand partially recovers (shifts to the right) when excess inventory has been sold off. For example, after an excessive economic boom in housing construction there will be little need for the construction of more new homes, causing the labor demand curve for construction workers to shift to the left. However, the inventory of unsold homes will eventually be sold off, and at that point construction of new homes will start up again, shifting the labor demand curve back to the right. This effect applies to any business that holds an inventory of unsold goods, like car or computer manufacturers. Inventories won't last forever. When they run out, the firm usually increases production. A rightward shift in the labor demand curve is plotted in Exhibit 26.12.
  • Labor demand partially recovers (shifts to the right) when technological advances encourage firms to expand their activities. For example, after the 2007–2009 recession, new drilling technologies enabled energy companies to profitably extract natural gas and oil from oil-shale geological deposits. This led to a rapid expansion in the U.S. energy industry, including drilling activity, pipeline construction, and the growth of industries that have a comparative advantage in regions with ample energy resources.
  • Labor demand partially recovers (shifts to the right) as the banking system—and the rest of the system of financial intermediation—recuperates and businesses are again

Exhibit 26.12 Partial Recovery Due to a Partial Rightward Shift in the Labor Demand Curve

With downward rigid wages, a leftward shift in labor demand to "Labor demand at trough" takes the economy from point "1: Pre-recession" to point "2: Trough." A partial recovery in the labor demand curve takes the economy from point "2: Trough" to point "3: Partial recovery." The economy does not reach the competitive equilibrium (point B) because the wage is downward rigid.

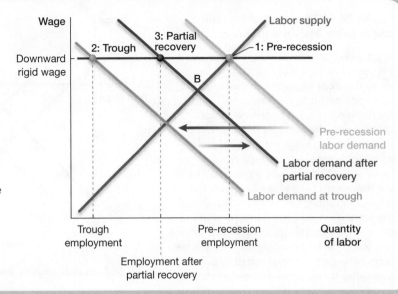

able to use credit to finance their activities. During the 2007–2009 financial crisis, many small firms had a hard time obtaining loans from their banks. When the banks that survived the crisis returned to health, they became more willing to lend to businesses, enabling those businesses to expand their operations and hire more workers. The availability of credit shifted the borrowers' labor demand curve to the right.

ii. *The labor demand curve shifts back to the right due to expansionary government policies.* The next chapter focuses exclusively on these issues. For now, we summarize the key policy levers:

- The central bank can use *monetary policy* to shift labor demand to the right. Lowering interest rates stimulates both firm investment and household consumption.
- Labor demand also shifts to the right as overall *inflation* raises firms' output prices. A rise in output price makes production, and thus increasing employment, more profitable at a given wage. This shifts the labor demand curve to the right. In panel (a) of Exhibit 26.13, we see the implications of this inflation-driven rightward shift of the labor demand curve. With wages pinned down by the downward wage rigidity, the rightward shift of the labor demand curve causes a movement from point A to point B, which corresponds to a partial recovery in employment.

At this point, you might rightly wonder about the labor supply curve. Shouldn't inflation also impact labor supply? As inflation increases output prices, a given wage will buy a smaller consumption bundle. For example, if all prices were to double, a worker who supplied the same hours of work at the same wage would be able to consume only half of what she did before. As a result of inflation, this worker—and, with the same reasoning, all workers—will be willing to supply fewer hours to the market at a given wage. The resulting leftward shift of the labor supply curve is also shown in panel (a) of Exhibit 26.13. The important point, however, is that *as long as we stay at the downward rigid wage*, this shift of labor supply has no impact, and employment is simply given by the intersection of the labor demand curve and the horizontal line representing the downward rigid wage. This brings us to the important conclusion that when wages are pinned down by downward wage rigidity, inflation-driven shifts of the labor demand curve will increase employment.

This analysis also tells us when shifts of the labor supply curve will actually start to matter. If the shifts in question were large enough, which would result from high levels of inflation, then the wage will no longer be pinned down by downward wage rigidity. Rather, the market clearing wage would rise above the downward rigid wage, as shown in panel (b) of Exhibit 26.13. In this case, the equilibrium wage has risen above the downward rigid wage. Once such an

Exhibit 26.13 The Effect of Inflation on the Labor Market Equilibrium

In panel (a), a downward rigid wage (represented by the horizontal line) prevents the labor market from clearing. The "original labor demand curve" and the "original labor supply curve" cross at the point labeled C. At this point, the market clearing wage is below the downward rigid wage. Accordingly, the original labor market equilibrium is point A, where the downward rigid wage intersects the original labor demand curve. Inflation shifts the labor demand curve to the right (firms can sell their output goods at higher prices) and shifts the labor supply curve to the left (a given wage has less purchasing power). Even after these shifts, the market-clearing wage (labeled D) is still below the downward rigid wage. Accordingly, the post-inflation labor market equilibrium is point B, where the downward rigid wage intersects the labor demand curve after inflation.

In panel (b), the original labor market equilibrium is point A, so the downward rigid wage is above the original market-clearing wage (labeled point C). Inflation causes the labor demand curve to shift to the right and the labor supply curve to shift to the left. Now these inflation-induced shifts are large enough to move the market-clearing wage above the downward rigid wage. The final labor market equilibrium is point E. Wages have now risen above the downward rigid wage.

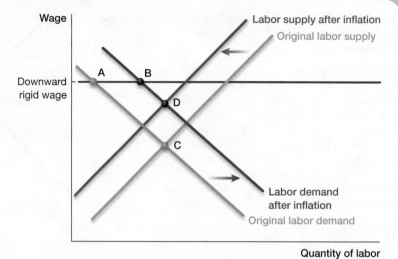

(a) Even after inflation, the market clearing wage remains below the downward rigid wage.

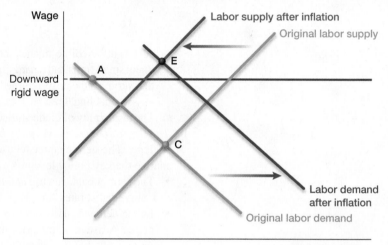

(b) With enough inflation, the market clearing wage rises above the downward rigid wage.

equilibrium wage is reached, further increases in inflation will shift the labor demand and labor supply curves by *equal* amounts, increasing wages but leaving employment unchanged.

• The government also uses *fiscal policy* (government spending and taxes) to shift the labor demand curve to the right. Increasing government spending increases the demand for the products that firms produce, shifting the labor demand curve to the right. Decreasing taxes gives firms and consumers more after-tax income, thereby increasing their purchasing power and increasing demand for the products that firms produce, shifting the labor demand curve to the right.

Exhibit 26.14 puts all of these market-based and policy-driven effects together to illustrate a complete cycle of contraction and recovery. Initially, the economy is at point "1." The combination of downward rigid wages and multipliers creates a rapid contraction in labor demand, which moves the economy to point "2." This is the trough of employment. The labor demand curve then starts to shift back toward its pre-recession level due to both market mechanisms and government intervention. Inflation plays two roles, shifting the labor demand curve to the right and the labor supply curve to the left. At the beginning of the recovery, the equilibrium remains at the rigid wage and the economy shifts from point "2" to point "3."

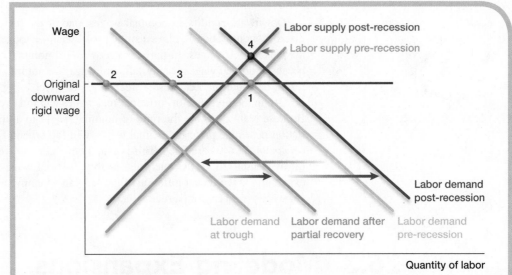

Exhibit 26.14 Full Recovery

The labor demand curve begins at "Labor demand pre-recession" and then shifts to the left: "Labor demand at trough." Because the wage is downward rigid, it does not fall and the economy transitions from point "1" to point "2." As the labor demand curve shifts back to the right ("Labor demand after partial recovery"), the level of employment partially rebounds to point "3." At this point, the downward rigid wage is still preventing the labor market from clearing. Eventually, the combination of rightward shifts in labor demand and leftward (inflation-driven) shifts in labor supply lead the economy to point "4." At this point, downward wage rigidity is no longer a constraint because the market-clearing wage is above the downward rigid wage.

Eventually, the combination of rightward shifts in labor demand and leftward shifts in labor supply lead the economy to point "4." At this point, downward wage rigidity is no longer a constraint because the market-clearing wage is above the downward rigid wage.

In this particular example, the economy returns to its original level of employment. This won't be the case if the original level of employment was generated by an unsustainable economic boom.

Exhibit 26.14 also shows that the post-recession wage is above the pre-recession wage. This results from the accumulation of price inflation during and after the recession. This inflation has lifted both output prices and wages.

Nominal Wages versus Real Wages

Actual wages are also called **nominal wages,** which distinguishes them from wages adjusted for inflation, or **real wages**. To calculate real wages, economists divide nominal wages by a measure of overall prices, for example the Consumer Price Index (CPI).

In this chapter (as in Chapter 23), we've conducted the analysis using the actual wages that workers are paid. Actual wages are also called **nominal wages**, which distinguishes them from wages adjusted for inflation, or **real wages**. The distinction between nominal and real wages is similar to the distinction between nominal and real GDP. To calculate real wages, we divide nominal wages by a measure of overall prices. Real wages can be interpreted as the (price-level-adjusted) buying power of nominal wages.

The entire analysis of labor demand and labor supply can be equivalently carried out using real wages. The change in variables wouldn't change the conclusions, but it would highlight different elements of the story. If we focus on real wages, we emphasize that firms base their hiring decisions on the ratio of how much they pay their workers (nominal wages) and how much they charge their customers (their output prices). It would also emphasize, as we have noted above, that in their labor supply decisions, workers care about the buying power of their wages—in other words, the real consumption bundles that they can afford with their wages.

Downward rigidity in nominal wages, one of the factors that amplifies negative macroeconomic shocks, plays a similar role when we look at the labor market through the lens of real wages. In particular, downward nominal wage rigidity implies that, because nominal wages cannot fall, real wages do not immediately adjust either. As a result, the labor market does not reach the market-clearing real wage.

But in the presence of inflation, real wages can fall even if nominal wages don't. Because real wages are the ratio of nominal wages to a price index, and because inflation raises the price index, real wages will fall when (1) the price index rises and (2) *nominal* wages are fixed. This is exactly the scenario we have highlighted in panel (a) of Exhibit 26.13. As such, the analysis of real wages provides another way of explaining how modest inflation might help an economy with downward rigid *nominal* wages recover from a recession.

26.3 Modeling Expansions

We have so far focused on recessions. The framework we presented can also be used for studying economic booms. Returning to the same example we used earlier, suppose that now United Airlines becomes optimistic about the demand for its products. This will shift its labor demand curve to the right. When many firms become optimistic about their future demand, the aggregate labor demand curve will shift to the right, as shown in Exhibit 26.15.

One important difference from our analysis of leftward shifts is that there is no issue of rigid wages in this case because, as we emphasized in Chapter 23, workers are often unwilling to accept cuts in their wages, but this has no equivalent for increases in their wages. This implies that there is downward, but not upward, wage rigidity. For this reason, in Exhibit 26.15, following the rightward shift in the labor demand curve, employment changes along a labor supply curve (and not along a horizontal line as in, for example, Exhibit 26.11).

Though the impact of the rightward shift in the labor demand curve is not exacerbated by wage rigidities, multiplier effects will continue to be present, amplifying the initial shift. For example, as United increases its purchases of airplanes and other inputs, this will cause the firms that supply United to shift their labor demand curves to the right. Increases in labor demand will tend to raise household income, causing households to start consuming more, triggering another round of multiplier effects. As a result of these multiplier effects, there is a further shift in the labor demand curve, as shown in Exhibit 26.15.

Exhibit 26.15 Rightward Shift in the Labor Demand Curve

Starting from a normally functioning economy, a positive economic shock will lead to a boom. First, the direct impact of the positive economic shock shifts the labor demand curve to the right. This impact is amplified by multipliers. Because wages are flexible upward, all of the adjustment to the shifts in the labor demand curve takes place along the labor supply curve.

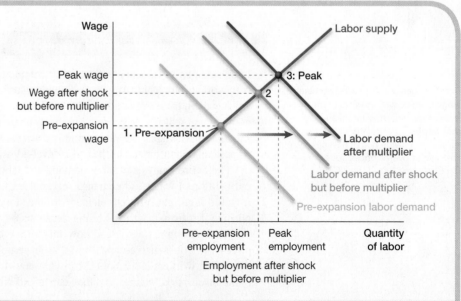

Economic booms also have a dark side. If before the beginning of the boom the economy is close to full employment and full capacity utilization (meaning that the unemployment rate is low and firms are employing most of their capacity), there will be relatively little room for the economy to grow. If so, the optimism or other factors that might have originally triggered the boom are likely to get reversed at some point. But such a reversal involves precisely the sort of leftward shift in labor demand we have analyzed in this chapter. These leftward shifts tend to create negative multiplier effects and might take the economy into a recession rather than gently back to its pre-boom level.

This dark side of economic booms raises some of the most difficult challenges for policymakers. Prudent policymaking would involve attempting to control the economic booms in order to limit the potential negative effects when the boom is ultimately reversed. However, the increase in employment and the fall in unemployment accompanying economic booms increase the popularity of policymakers, encouraging them to let economic booms continue or even to fan their flames (especially during election years).

Evidence-Based Economics

What caused the recession of 2007–2009?

The causes of the recession of 2007–2009 can be likened to chains of dominos, with one negative shock setting off another in a sequence of events that cascaded throughout the American and global economies. Three key factors appear to have played the central roles in the crisis: (1) a fall in housing prices, which caused a collapse in new construction; (2) a sharp drop in consumption; and (3) spiraling mortgage defaults that caused many bank failures, leading the entire financial system to freeze up.

Let's first zoom out to take an aerial snapshot:

1. During the pre-recession years of 2000–2006, a run-up in housing prices caused a boom in housing construction, which produced a large stock of newly constructed homes. When housing prices fell sharply from 2006 to 2009, homebuilders rapidly reduced their rate of new construction because they already held a large inventory of new homes and the falling prices made new construction unprofitable. Consequently, their labor demand curves shifted sharply to the left.

2. The decline in housing prices in turn reduced many consumers' wealth and curtailed their ability to borrow more against their homes—a scenario that in turn sharply reduced consumption. The firms that produce the goods and services that consumers buy were suddenly faced with a substantial drop in demand for their products. Accordingly, they cut back production and their labor demand curves shifted to the left.

3. The decline in housing values led to millions of mortgage defaults (for reasons we explain below). These mortgages, which were held on the balance sheets of many large banks, pushed those banks to the brink—and in some cases over the brink—of solvency. As banks failed, or cut their lending activity to increase their reserves and strengthen their balance sheets, credit to the private sector fell, causing borrowing firms to cut their production and shifting their labor demand curves to the left. The decline in credit to households reduced their consumption and triggered another round of adverse demand shifts.

This was the big picture. We now zoom in on each of these economic events and look at the data.

Housing and Construction: A Burst Bubble

Many economists characterize the rapid rise of housing prices between the late 1990s and 2006 as a *bubble*, meaning that the significant increase in asset prices (in this case housing assets) did not reflect the true long-run value of the asset. Exhibit 26.16 plots a

Exhibit 26.16 Index of Real Home Prices in Ten Major U.S. Cities (January 1987–December 2013)

Real U.S. home prices started rising precipitously in the late 1990s, with real prices more than doubling in a single decade: 1996 to 2006. Prices then fell sharply from 2006 to 2009.

Source: S&P/Case-Shiller home price index and Bureau of Labor Statistics (Consumer Price Index).

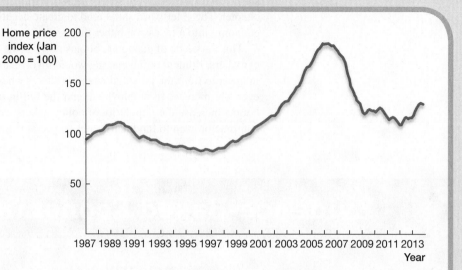

Exhibit 26.17 Real Investment in Residential Construction (1987 q1–2013 q4; Normalized to 100 in 2009)

The flow of real investment in residential construction nearly doubled from 1995 to 2005, peaking just before housing prices peaked. Residential construction then fell sharply, falling well below its level from 1995. As the excess inventory of newly built homes was sold off, home building slowly picked up again after 2011.

Source: Bureau of Economic Analysis, National Income and Product Accounts.

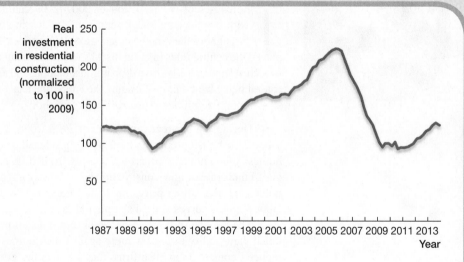

monthly index of housing prices adjusted for inflation in ten major U.S. cities from 1987 to 2013. Notice that the index rose sharply from 100 in January 2000 to 190 in May 2006. Then everything fell apart—the index collapsed to a value of 120 by April 2009 and continued falling a bit more after that. The bubble in housing prices had burst.

Falling housing prices had a devastating effect on the home construction industry. Exhibit 26.17 plots the real value of investments in residential real estate. Note how real investment in new home construction started falling after peaking in the third quarter of 2005. The exhibit shows that when the dust had settled in 2009, the rate of home construction had fallen by nearly 60 percent.

Then the other shoe dropped. As the home construction industry shrank, employment in the industry also plummeted. At its peak in April 2006, there were 3.5 million jobs in the residential construction industry. By 2010, the number of jobs had fallen to 2 million, a 43 percent decline. Related industries also got hit as all real estate prices fell, including commercial real estate, like office buildings and malls. For example, the non-residential construction industry fell from employment of 4.4 million in early 2008—at the start of the recession—to 3.4 million in 2010.

Putting all of the pieces together, the sharp drop in real estate prices caused a large leftward shift in the labor demand curve for construction jobs, which then led to a sharp drop in employment in the construction industry. The key step—a leftward shift in the labor demand curve—was plotted in Exhibit 26.6. Panel (a) of that exhibit plots the flexible wage case. Panel (c) plots the case of downward wage rigidity, which features an even larger fall in employment.

The decline in economic activity in the construction industry also led to multiplier effects. Many construction workers lost their incomes, and many businesses that served those workers—home supply stores like Home Depot—saw demand for their products plummet. Falling home construction and home sales also lowered demand for home appliances—like washing machines and refrigerators. These multiplier effects magnified the effects of the fall in home prices, shifting the aggregate labor demand curve further leftward and deepening the fall in aggregate employment.

Cuts in Consumption

The housing price declines were also associated with large reductions in overall household consumption—the second key factor in the 2007–2009 recession.

During the early 2000s, many households had increased their consumption by using funds that they had borrowed from banks. In most cases, this borrowing took the form of mortgages—for instance, taking out a second mortgage in addition to a first mortgage. "Cash-out" refinancings were also popular—when interest rates fell, homeowners with an existing mortgage would lower their interest rate and increase the size of their mortgage, taking the difference as a cash payout. At the peak of the housing bubble, consumers used second mortgages and "cash-out" refinancing to extract $400 billion of wealth per year from their homes. Even consumers who did not take our more mortgage debt tended to increase their real consumption during the run-up in housing prices from 2000 to 2006, because home price rises increase wealth and consumers' perceptions of what they can afford to consume.

That wealthy feeling started to vanish in 2007. By March 2009, U.S. households had lost about $15 trillion in net worth—both the housing market and the stock market had crashed. Most households cut back their consumption, causing aggregate real consumption to decline by 2.7 percent from the start of the recession in the fourth quarter of 2007 to the end of the recession in the second quarter of 2009. This decline translated into a significantly lower demand for the products of firms, creating another multiplier effect that shifted the labor demand curve further to the left.

Spiraling Mortgage Defaults and Bank Failures

Falling house prices also led mortgage delinquencies to skyrocket: many borrowers stopped making their required mortgage payments. For example, suppose that a family had bought a $300,000 home with almost no down payment in 2006. If we assume that the home's value followed the ten-city index, this home would have fallen to a value of $200,000 by 2009. However, the mortgage debt would not have been affected by the fall in the home value, leaving the borrower owing nearly $300,000 (very little of the initial mortgage would have been paid off within the first 3 years of home ownership). Consequently, the family would find itself with a debt of almost $300,000 on a house worth only $200,000. Owing more on your home than it is worth is referred to as being "upside down" or "underwater." If a household with an underwater mortgage sells their home, they don't receive enough money

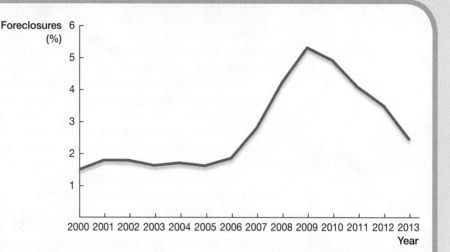

Exhibit 26.18 Percentage of U.S. Home Mortgages That Began Foreclosure Proceedings (2000 to 2013)

This exhibit plots the annual rate of foreclosure filings in the United States. A 2 percent rate of foreclosure filing implies that 2 percent of the homes with a mortgage started foreclosure proceedings in that year.

Source: Mortgage Bankers' Association National Delinquency Survey.

to repay the mortgage. In many U.S. states, households in this situation have a strong incentive to default on their mortgages—that is, stop making their mortgage payments and walk away. This incentive is further strengthened when households face economic hardship (for example, because of unemployment or other negative labor income shocks).

And that is exactly what millions of households did, either because they didn't have a job and couldn't afford to pay their mortgage, or because they recognized that it wasn't optimal to keep paying interest on a mortgage that vastly exceeded the value of the home. Previously, when home prices were rising, foreclosure rates stayed around 1.7 percent per year. In other words, 1.7 percent of U.S. homes with a mortgage entered foreclosure each year. Exhibit 26.18 shows that the foreclosure rate rose to 5.4 percent during the financial crisis. To appreciate the significance of that foreclosure rate, consider that there are approximately 75 million owner-occupied homes in the United States and about two-thirds, or 50 million, have a mortgage. So a foreclosure rate of 5.4 percent translates into almost 3 million foreclosed homes per year at the peak of the crisis. In total, about 10 million foreclosures took place from 2007 to 2012.

Home foreclosures were terrible news not only for homeowners but also for banks. Consider that when a bank seizes a home that is worth $200,000, on which the outstanding mortgage is $300,000, the bank has no way of recouping its money. At best, it can sell the house for $200,000, realizing a $100,000 loss on its $300,000 loan. In practice, the foreclosure sale yields a price significantly *below* $200,000. With so many homes being sold simultaneously, and with no homeowner to put flowers in window pots, mow lawns, or keep vandals from trashing the empty houses or ripping out copper pipes, it's easy to end up selling the house for far less than $200,000.

Consequently, banks suffered enormous losses on their portfolios of mortgages. In 2005, during the run-up in home prices, banks recorded losses in their real estate portfolios equal to only 0.2 percent of the value of their real estate loans. In 2009, banks booked real estate losses that were 40 times greater —8 percent of the total value of their real estate loans.

Many banks could not withstand the extent of the hit they took on their mortgage holdings. Among the 5,000 banks regulated by the FDIC, about 400 failed from 2007 to 2011.

But the biggest story of the 2007–2009 recession was the failure of Lehman Brothers, a bank that was *not* regulated by the FDIC. Lehman did not originate home mortgages of its own, but it did originate commercial mortgages (for businesses) and it did buy mortgages that other banks had issued. As those mortgages lost value in 2008, Lehman Brothers lost huge sums and perhaps more importantly also lost the confidence of its business partners.

Within a two-week period in September of 2008, many of Lehman's biggest institutional trading partners and lenders stopped doing business with the bank. Each new defection bred more uncertainty and a widening loss of confidence in Lehman's future. Lehman experienced an institutional bank run, a special kind of bank run that we discussed in Chapter 24. The bank customers running for the exits were large financial institutions like other large banks and hedge funds. Soon, no institutions would lend money to Lehman, and at that point Lehman was both illiquid and insolvent.

The failure of Lehman Brothers initiated a financial panic that suddenly threatened the prosperity of the world economy. Other major bank crises followed in Iceland, the United Kingdom, Greece, Ireland, Portugal, Switzerland, France, Germany, the Netherlands, Spain, Italy, and Cyprus. Suddenly, many countries teetered on the precipice of another depression.

As financial markets fell, the banking sector cut back on loans to businesses because failed banks obviously couldn't make loans. Even the surviving banks were hesitant to make loans, afraid that these new loans—to households and businesses—would soon end up in default. The retrenchment of the financial sector created yet another multiplier effect, which reduced consumption and investment and shifted the labor demand curve further to the left.

Question

What caused the recession of 2007–2009?

Answer

Real housing prices rose 90 percent from 2000 to 2006 and then fell almost completely back to their 2000 level. Falling house prices led to a collapse in the home building industry, to a sharp decline in real consumption, and to a jump in mortgage defaults. Approximately 10 million U.S. home foreclosures occurred from 2007 through 2012. The defaulting mortgages caused 400 bank failures, including the spectacular failure of the investment bank Lehman Brothers.

Data

Historical data on housing prices (Case/Shiller housing price index), residential investment (NIPA), foreclosure rates (Mortgage Bankers Association), and bank balance sheets (FDIC and Lehman Brothers).

Caveat

Many other factors also contributed to the financial crisis and it is not yet clear what the most important factors were.

Summary

⚙ All economies experience economic fluctuations—in other words, the growth rate fluctuates from year to year. During recessions, real GDP contracts and unemployment increases. On rare occasions a recession turns into a depression, like the Great Depression which started in 1929. From 1929 to 1933 real GDP declined by 26 percent, and the rate of unemployment rose from 3 percent to 25 percent.

⚙ Economic fluctuations display three key properties:

1. Co-movement: consumption, investment, GDP, and employment generally fall and rise together. Unemployment moves in the opposite direction.
2. Limited predictability: economic fluctuations are not pendulum-like with regular up and down cycles. It is difficult to predict in advance when an economy will enter a recession and when a recession will end.
3. Persistence: when the economy is growing, it will probably keep growing the following quarter. Likewise, when the economy is contracting—when growth is negative—the economy will probably keep contracting the following quarter.

⚙ Many factors explain fluctuations in economic activity, most notably:

1. Technology shocks (the theory of real business cycles): changes in firms' productivity translate into shifts in the demand curve for labor, causing fluctuations in employment and real GDP. When the labor demand curve shifts to the left, employment and real GDP fall. When the labor demand curve shifts to the right, employment and real GDP rise.
2. Keynesian factors:
   - Changes in sentiments, including changes in expectations, uncertainty, and animal spirits, influence firm and household behavior. If a firm becomes pessimistic, the demand curve for labor shifts to the left. If a firm's customers become pessimistic, they reduce their purchases, decreasing demand for the firm's products and shifting the firm's labor demand curve to the left.
   - An initial shift in the labor demand curve creates a cascading chain of events, multiplying or amplifying the impact of the initial shock. For example, when firms lay off workers in response to a shock, the laid-off workers cut their own consumption, reducing the demand for the products of other firms and leading to shifts in the labor demand curves of the other firms. Financial factors create additional multiplier effects. Defaults, bankruptcies, and declines in asset prices lead banks to scale back their lending to firms and households, generating another round of adverse shifts in the labor demand curve.
3. Monetary and financial factors: a fall in the price level is contractionary because firms face downward wage rigidities—that is, they are either unable or unwilling to cut wages. Employment declines by more than it would have with flexible wages. In addition, monetary contractions cause the real interest rate to rise, reducing investment. Finally, financial crises reduce the credit available to firms and households. All of these channels will shift the labor demand curve to the left, reducing employment and real GDP.

☀ Multiplier effects help us understand the sharp recession of 2007–2009. Between the late 1990s and 2006, the U.S. housing market experienced a bubble. This bubble burst in 2006 and real housing prices fell by approximately 40 percent. The construction industry, which had been booming until then, began a sharp contraction. Falling housing prices, and by implication falling wealth, led households to cut their consumption. Firms, seeing the demand for their products decline, reduced their labor demand, starting a spiral of layoffs and further reductions in household consumption. The collapse in housing prices also led to mortgage defaults and foreclosures. The defaults and foreclosures generated huge losses for many banks, which either failed or sharply cut lending, further worsening the recession.

☀ Economic booms tend to increase employment and reduce unemployment as the labor demand curve of the economy shifts to the right and the multiplier effects increase employment further. However, economic booms also have a dark side because when they reverse, the economy can sink into a recession. For this reason, some policymakers try to control and dampen economic booms, though other factors might push policymakers and politicians to fan the flames of economic booms rather than follow a prudent course of action.

Key Terms

economic fluctuations or business cycles *p. 609*
economic expansions *p. 610*
Great Depression *p. 613*
depression *p. 613*

Okun's Law *p. 618*
real business cycle theory *p. 619*
animal spirits *p. 620*
sentiments *p. 620*
multipliers *p. 620*

self-fulfilling prophecy *p. 621*
nominal wages *p. 627*
real wages *p. 627*

Questions

All questions are available in MyEconLab *for practice and instructor assignment.*

1. What are economic fluctuations? What is the difference between an economic expansion and a recession?

2. What does it mean to say that an economic fluctuation involves the co-movement of many aggregate macroeconomic variables? Name four variables that exhibit co-movement during an economic expansion.

3. The duration of an economic fluctuation is completely unpredictable. Explain whether this statement is true or false.

4. Does the Great Depression illustrate the three characteristics of economic fluctuations? Explain your answer.

5. How do wage flexibility and downward wage rigidity affect the extent of unemployment in the economy when the demand for labor shifts to the left?

6. How does real business cycle theory explain economic fluctuations?

7. How did John Maynard Keynes use the concepts of animal spirits and sentiments to explain economic fluctuations?

8. The concept of multipliers was one of the key elements of John Maynard Keynes's theory of fluctuations. What is a multiplier? Explain with an example.

9. How can contractionary monetary policy lead to an economy-wide recession?

10. What are two important mechanisms that reverse the effects of a recession in a modern economy?

11. How can the 2007–2009 recession be explained?

12. Between 2000 and 2006, housing prices in the United States increased by about 90 percent. As detailed in the chapter, this increase abruptly reversed.

   a. Why is the rise in housing prices between the late 1990s and 2006 characterized as a bubble by some economists?

   b. How did the fall in housing prices cause the financial system in the United States to freeze up?

Problems

*All problems are available in MyEconLab for practice and instructor assignment.
Problems marked 🌐 update with real-time data.*

1. Consider the data in Exhibit 26.3.

   a. List the recessions since 1929 by duration, with the longest recession first and the shortest last.

   b. List the recessions since 1929 according to decline in real GDP from peak to trough, with the greatest decline first and the smallest decline last. Note which recessions are first and second on your list from part (a) and first and third on your list from part (b). Can you think of a reason why the fall in real GDP at the end of World War II (1945; second recession on your list from part (b)) was so deep even though that recession was very short?

🌐 2. Go to http://research.stlouisfed.org/fred2/series/UNRATE, which shows the U.S. unemployment rate since 1948. Every recession during this period is shown by the gray bars on the graph.

   a. Does the behavior of the unemployment rate illustrate the principle of co-movement discussed in the chapter? Why or why not?

   b. Economic variables are sometimes divided into "leading indicators" and "lagging indicators." Leading indicators are variables that start to change before an economic expansion or contraction. Lagging indicators change only when an expansion or contraction is well underway. Based on the graph of the unemployment rate, is unemployment a leading or lagging indicator of recessions? Explain.

3. The Conference Board publishes data on Business Cycle Indicators (BCI). The Composite Index of Leading Economic Indicators is one of the three components of the BCI. Changes in leading economic indicators usually precede changes in GDP. Some of the variables tracked by the index are listed below.

   i. The average weekly hours worked by manufacturing workers

   ii. The average number of initial applications for unemployment insurance

   iii. The amount of new orders for capital goods unrelated to defense

   iv. The number of new building permits for residential buildings

   v. The S&P 500 stock index

   vi. Consumer sentiment

   Consider each variable and explain whether it is likely to be positively or negatively correlated with real GDP.

4. Suppose that the mythical country Moricana has a downward rigid wage. Moricana is in a recession; capacity utilization in the economy is at an all-time low, and surveys show that firms do not expect economic conditions to improve in the coming year.

   a. Firms in the country are cutting back on capital spending and investment. Use a graph to show how this would affect the labor demand curve (ignore the effects of multipliers).

   b. How would the economy move along the aggregate production function curve?

   c. Is unemployment in Moricana likely to be classified as voluntary or involuntary? Explain your answer.

5. Assuming flexible wages, in which case would the change in total employment be greater during a recession:

   Scenario 1: Workers do not increase their labor supply very much in response to an increase in the wage;

   or

   Scenario 2: Workers increase their labor supply substantially in response to an increase in the wage. Explain your answer fully with a graph.

6. Assume that labor supply and labor demand are described by the following equations:

   $$\text{Labor Supply:} \qquad L^S = 5 \times w.$$
   $$\text{Labor Demand:} \qquad L^D = 110 - 0.5 \times w.$$

   where w = wage expressed in dollars per hour, and L^S and L^D are expressed in millions of workers.

   a. Find the equilibrium wage and the equilibrium level of employment.

   b. Assume that there is a shock to the economy, such that the labor demand curve is now described by the equation:

   $$L^D = 55 - 0.5 \times w.$$

   If wages are flexible, what will be the new equilibrium wage and level of employment? Show your work.

   c. Now assume that wages are rigid at the level you found in part (a). What will employment be at this wage? How many workers will be unemployed?

7. In 1973, the major oil-producing nations of the world declared an oil embargo. The price of oil, a key source of energy, increased. In many countries, this led to a fall in real GDP and employment. Which of the three business cycle theories explained in the chapter—real business cycle theory, Keynesian theory, and monetary theory—would best fit this explanation of the 1973 recession?

8. The Internet boom of the 1990s has changed all of our lives and transformed the way business is conducted. During the late 1990s, the economy was described as the "best of all possible worlds" with quite high employment (and low unemployment). Explain this phenomenon using the real business cycle approach.

9. An old saying goes: "Nothing succeeds like success." Explain how this could relate to Keynes's animal spirits view of economic fluctuations.

10. Use a detailed graph to show the effect of a negative shock on the labor demand curve in an economy. Assume that wages in the economy are rigid and cannot fall in the short run. Compare the point of trough employment on the graph with the point of trough employment if wages were flexible.

11. In the early 1980s, the unemployment rate in the United States rose above 10 percent. The United States was in a severe recession. Both fiscal and monetary policies were used to stimulate the economy. Government spending increased by 18.9 percent, while the Federal Reserve cut interest rates by nearly 11 percentage points. How would these policies affect the labor demand curve? Assuming wages are rigid, use a graph to explain your answer. Be sure to show the pre-recession equilibrium, the situation at the trough of the recession, and the effect of the government policies.

12. The Evidence-Based Economics feature in the chapter identifies three key factors that caused the recession of 2007–2009.

   a. How would Keynes's concept of animal spirits explain the creation of a housing bubble?

   b. What does the national income identity show? Explain how the recession of 2007–2009 affected the consumption and investment components of the national income identity.

13. Some economists stress the role of monetary policy in the period leading up to the recession of 2007–2009. Between 2001 and 2003, the Federal Reserve lowered the target Fed Funds rate from 6.5 percent to 1 percent and kept it there through much of 2004. This resulted in a substantial decline in real interest rates throughout the economy, including mortgage rates.

   Based on the chapter's discussion of monetary and financial factors, explain how the Federal Reserve's policies could have contributed to the economic "bubble" of the pre-recession years of 2000–2006.

27 Countercyclical Macroeconomic Policy

How much does government expenditure stimulate GDP?

You are a key presidential adviser on economic policy: the chairperson of the Council of Economic Advisers (CEA). The CEA consists of three economists who advise the president and help formulate the administration's economic policy. These experts prepare the annual *Economic Report of the President*.

Unfortunately, you happen to be in office during a severe economic downturn. The president asks you, "What would happen if the government increased spending?" How would more government expenditure—for instance, repairing highways, hiring teachers, or building schools—support an economic recovery?

This chapter studies the many ways that policymakers try to smooth out fluctuations in GDP, stimulating the economy during contractions and stepping on the brakes during periods of excessively rapid economic expansion.

CHAPTER OUTLINE

* Countercyclical policies attempt to reduce the intensity of economic fluctuations and smooth the growth rates of employment, GDP, and prices.

* Countercyclical monetary policy reduces economic fluctuations by manipulating bank reserves and interest rates.

* Expansionary monetary policy increases bank reserves and decreases interest rates. Contractionary monetary policy decreases bank reserves and increases interest rates.

* Countercyclical fiscal policy reduces fluctuations by manipulating government expenditures and taxes.

* Expansionary fiscal policy increases government expenditure and decreases taxes. Contractionary fiscal policy decreases government expenditure and increases taxes.

27.1 The Role of Countercyclical Policies in Economic Fluctuations

Countercyclical policies attempt to reduce the intensity of economic fluctuations and smooth the growth rates of employment, GDP, and prices.

In Chapter 26, we discussed the reasons why economic growth fluctuates. In this chapter, we focus on the government and the Fed's efforts to reduce those fluctuations by using what are called *countercyclical policies*. **Countercyclical policies** attempt to reduce the intensity of economic fluctuations and smooth the growth rates of employment, GDP, and prices. (In this chapter, whenever we discuss GDP, we are referring to *real* GDP.)

During a recession, *expansionary policy* aims to reduce the severity of the downturn by shifting labor demand to the right and "expanding" economic activity (GDP). Similarly, *contractionary policy* is sometimes used to slow down the economy when it grows too fast or "overheats."

Countercyclical policies come in two main categories:

Countercyclical monetary policy, which is conducted by the central bank (in the United States, the Fed), attempts to reduce economic fluctuations by manipulating bank reserves and interest rates.

Countercyclical fiscal policy, which is passed by the legislative branch and signed into law by the executive branch, aims to reduce economic fluctuations by manipulating government expenditures and taxes.

1. **Countercyclical monetary policy**, which is conducted by the central bank (in the United States, the Fed), attempts to reduce economic fluctuations by manipulating bank reserves and interest rates.
2. **Countercyclical fiscal policy**, which is passed by the legislative branch and signed into law by the executive branch, aims to reduce economic fluctuations by manipulating government expenditures and taxes.

Though countercyclical monetary and fiscal policies work in different ways and are effective in different circumstances, they also share some common features. Countercyclical monetary and fiscal policies both work by shifting the labor demand curve. During a recession, monetary and fiscal policies are used to stimulate the economy by shifting the labor demand curve to the right. During a runaway boom, monetary and fiscal policies are used to slow the economy by shifting the labor demand curve to the left.

Countercyclical monetary and fiscal policies both work by shifting the labor demand curve.

We plot the case of a recession in panel (a) of Exhibit 27.1 where we first study a labor market with flexible wages. Starting from a pre-recession equilibrium (point 1: Pre-recession), a shock shifts the labor demand curve to the left, reducing employment

Exhibit 27.1 The Effect of Countercyclical Policy on the Labor Market Panel

(a) Flexible Wage Case
During a recession, the labor demand curve has shifted to the left and the equilibrium is at the point labeled 2: Trough. Countercyclical policy can partially reverse this situation by shifting the labor demand curve back to the right. With flexible wages, the equilibrium transitions from 2: Trough to 3: Partial recovery. The rightward shift in the labor demand curve translates into an increase in wages and an increase in employment (represented by the green arrow).

(b) Rigid Wage Case
During a recession, the labor demand curve has shifted to the left and the equilibrium is at the point labeled 2: Trough. Countercyclical policy can partially reverse this low-employment equilibrium by pursuing an expansionary policy that will shift the labor demand curve back to the right. With downward rigid wages, the equilibrium transitions from 2: Trough to 3: Partial recovery. Compare the gains in employment (in green) in the "flexible wage" and "rigid wage" panels of Exhibit 27.1. With downward rigid wages the gains in employment are greater, since downward wage rigidity implies that the rightward shift in the labor demand curve translates one-for-one into employment gains.

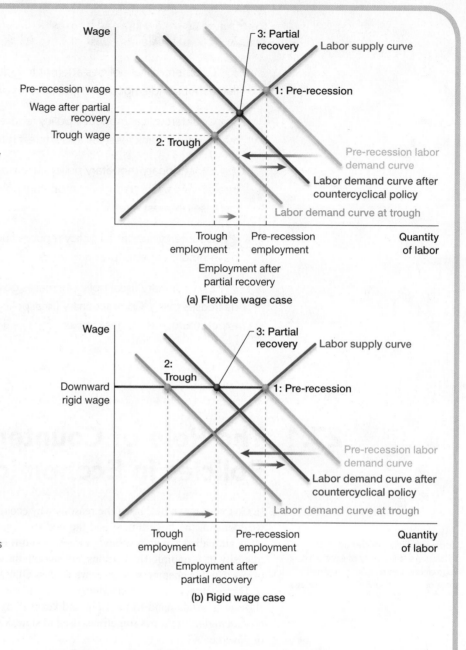

and GDP. This takes us to the point marked 2: Trough, where employment and wages are lower. Successful expansionary policy shields the economy from the full impact of the recession by shifting the labor demand curve back to the right, taking the economy to the point labeled 3: Partial recovery.

As in Chapter 26, when wages are downward rigid, the recession has more severe employment consequences. In panel (b) of Exhibit 27.1, the labor demand curve at trough is exactly the same as it was in panel (a). But the drop in employment—from 1: Pre-recession to 2: Trough—is now larger than it was in panel (a). This is because none of the leftward shift of the labor demand curve can be absorbed by a fall in wages.

Downward-rigid wages also imply that countercyclical policy is relatively more effective. We can see this in panel (b) of Exhibit 27.1, where the same countercyclical shift in the labor demand curve increases employment more than it did in panel (a). The full force of the expansionary policy impacts employment, because there is no wage response in this case. This can be seen by comparing the lengths of the green arrows shown underneath the horizontal axis, representing the employment effects of countercyclical policies in the flexible and rigid wage cases.

Just as expansionary policy reduces the severity of a recession, policymakers sometimes use contractionary policy that reduces economic growth during a boom. Why would policymakers ever intentionally adopt a policy that has the effect of *reducing* GDP growth and *reducing* the level of employment? In many situations, the negative effects on GDP and employment are a by-product of another policy goal. For example, when inflation is consistently above the Fed's target, the Fed will raise interest rates to suppress borrowing, thereby slowing growth of the money supply and reducing the rate of inflation. The rise in interest rates will shift the labor demand curve to the left, causing employment to fall as a by-product of the Fed's efforts to reduce inflation.

In other cases, countercyclical policy may be directly targeting economic expansion. Recall from Chapter 26 that factors such as excessively optimistic sentiments about the economy can result in an *unsustainable economic expansion*. Left alone, such expansions may eventually lead to a severe downturn because optimistic sentiments can implode suddenly and severely (due to multiplier effects). In some cases, contractionary policy attempts to reduce the risks of an *extreme* contraction by trying to cool off the economy *before* it overheats. Such cooling off is achieved by putting gradual leftward pressure on the labor demand curve. Contractionary policy is sometimes referred to as "leaning against the wind."

27.2 Countercyclical Monetary Policy

We now discuss countercyclical policies in detail. We first focus on countercyclical monetary policy, which, as we explained in Chapter 25, is conducted by the Fed.

Expansionary monetary policy increases the quantity of bank reserves and lowers interest rates.

The Fed responds to economic contractions by adopting **expansionary monetary policy**, which increases the quantity of bank reserves and lowers interest rates. Let's begin by getting a big-picture view of the impact of such policies.

The Fed influences short-term interest rates, especially the *federal funds rate*. Recall that the federal funds rate is the interest rate that banks use to make loans to one another, using reserves on deposit at the Federal Reserve Bank.

When the Fed wants to stimulate the economy, it lowers short-term interest rates. This, in turn, usually causes long-term interest rates to fall. Recall from Chapter 25 that the long-term interest rate is related to the long-term average of short-term interest rates.

A fall in long-term interest rates encourages households to buy more durable goods, like cars, because a lower interest rate implies a lower cost of a car loan. To satisfy an increase in household demand for durable goods, firms try to hire more workers, shifting the labor demand curve to the right. Likewise, a fall in long-term interest rates causes firms to engage in more investment in plants and equipment, like building a new factory, because a lower interest rate implies a lower cost of a commercial loan that will fund the construction project. Firms need workers to build and operate these new factories, shifting the labor demand curve to the right. In many different ways, expansionary monetary policy shifts firms' labor demand curve to the right and increases the level of employment, as we saw in Exhibit 27.1. Exhibit 27.2 provides a bird's-eye view of this process.

Exhibit 27.2 Expansionary Monetary Policy

These are the core ingredients of expansionary monetary policy. The first half of this chapter explores the various ways in which the Fed implements the top (red) box in this exhibit.

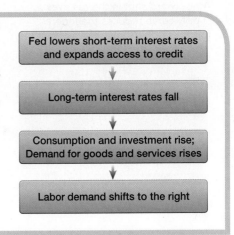

Fed lowers short-term interest rates and expands access to credit

↓

Long-term interest rates fall

↓

Consumption and investment rise; Demand for goods and services rises

↓

Labor demand shifts to the right

To better understand monetary policy we need to discuss *how* the Fed lowers short-term interest rates and expands access to credit. In essence, we need to fill in the details of the red box in Exhibit 27.2. The Fed's most powerful tool in this process is its control of bank reserves and the federal funds rate, which we review next.

Controlling the Federal Funds Rate

The primary tool of monetary policy is the Fed's control of the federal funds rate. By changing the supply of bank reserves available to private banks, which is called open market operations, the Fed influences the federal funds rate. As explained in Chapter 25, in an open market operation, the Fed transacts with private banks to increase or reduce bank reserves held at the Fed. These transactions influence the federal funds rate.

For instance, by increasing the supply of bank reserves available to private banks, the Fed decreases the federal funds rate. This mechanism is shown in Exhibit 27.3. You can see in this exhibit that a shift to the right of the supply of reserves held at the Fed drives down the federal funds rate (which is the price that a bank pays to borrow another dollar of reserves).

It helps to describe how open market operations work with a concrete example. Suppose that the Fed wants to raise bank reserves held on deposit at the Fed by $1 billion. To bring this about, the Fed finds a bank—let's say Citibank—that is willing to sell the Fed $1 billion worth of bonds in exchange for $1 billion in bank reserves on deposit at the Fed. The Fed doesn't use paper currency in this transaction. Instead, the Fed creates the $1 billion in bank reserves with the stroke of a computer key. Poof! The Fed has issued an IOU to the private bank. The IOU takes the form of $1 billion of reserves that the private bank holds on deposit at the Fed.

Following these open market operations, Citibank now has $1 billion *more* in bank reserves on deposit at the Fed and owns $1 billion *less* in bonds: those are the bonds that Citibank sold the Fed in this transaction. On the assets side of its balance sheet, Citibank has an extra $1 billion in bank reserves that it received in exchange for the $1 billion in bonds that are now owned by the Fed and appear on the Fed's balance sheet. *Total* assets at Citibank are unchanged, though the *composition* of assets has tilted away from bonds and toward bank reserves. Exhibit 27.4 illustrates this change on Citibank's balance sheet, showing how reserves on the assets side of its balance sheet increase from $100 billion to $101 billion.

The Fed's balance sheet has also changed. The Fed's assets now include $1 billion more in bonds—this amount represents the bonds that the Fed bought from Citibank. The Fed's liabilities also show a corresponding increase. In particular, the Fed's liabilities now include $1 billion more in the form of reserves—these are the reserves that the Fed electronically created and then exchanged with Citibank. Exhibit 27.5 illustrates this change on

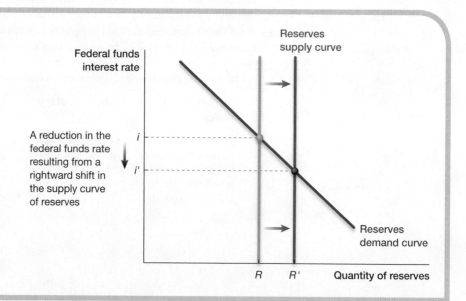

Exhibit 27.3 The Federal Funds Market

A rightward shift in the reserves supply curve reduces the federal funds rate.

	Assets		Liabilities and shareholder's equity	
Before:	Reserves:	$100 billion	Deposits and other liabilities:	$800 billion
	Bonds and other investments:	$900 billion	Shareholder's equity:	$200 billion
	Total assets:	$1000 billion	Liabilities + shareholder's equity:	$1000 billion

	Assets		Liabilities and shareholder's equity	
After:	Reserves:	$101 billion	Deposits and other liabilities:	$800 billion
	Bonds and other investments:	$899 billion	Shareholder's equity:	$200 billion
	Total assets:	$1000 billion	Liabilities + shareholder's equity:	$1000 billion

Exhibit 27.4 Balance Sheet of Citibank Before and After $1 Billion Bond Sale to the Fed

The Fed engages in an open market operation with Citibank. The Fed buys $1 billion in bonds in exchange for $1 billion in reserves that are credited to Citibank. This changes nothing on the liabilities and shareholder's equity side of Citibank's balance sheet. On the assets side, total assets don't change, but the composition of assets does (changes on the assets side are shown in blue). After the trade, Citibank has another $1 billion in reserves on deposit at the Fed and $1 billion less in bonds.

	Assets		Liabilities and shareholders' equity	
Before:	Treasury bonds:	$1000 billion	Reserves:	$1000 billion
	Other bonds:	$1000 billion	Currency:	$1000 billion
	Total assets:	$2000 billion	Total liabilities:	$2000 billion

	Assets		Liabilities and shareholders' equity	
After:	Treasury bonds:	$1001 billion	Reserves:	$1001 billion
	Other bonds:	$1000 billion	Currency:	$1000 billion
	Total assets:	$2001 billion	Total liabilities:	$2001 billion

Exhibit 27.5 Balance Sheet of the Fed Before and After $1 Billion Bond Purchase from Citibank

This exhibit shows the changes in the Fed's balance sheet following its open market operation with Citibank. In return for the $1 billion in bonds, the Fed gives Citibank $1 billion in reserves on deposit at the Fed. On the liabilities and shareholder's equity side of the Fed's balance sheet, the Fed now has another $1 billion of IOUs in the form of reserves, held by Citibank (changes on the liabilities side are shown in red). On the assets side, the Fed has another $1 billion in bonds received from Citibank (changes on the assets side are shown in blue).

the Fed's balance sheet. Note that reserves held at the Fed are an *asset* to Citibank—which can draw on the reserves—and a *liability* to the Fed—which is on the hook to pay out the reserves if asked to do so.

Most of the time, the stock of reserves—including both banks' vault cash and the reserves that banks hold at the Fed—fluctuates between $40 billion and $80 billion. During and after the 2007–2009 recession, however, the Fed *drastically* expanded the quantity of reserves banks held on deposit at the Fed.

Exhibit 27.6 plots this expansion. In August 2008, reserves totaled about $40 billion. You have to squint to see them, because they are hovering close to the horizontal axis. This quantity of reserves was enough to cover banks' reserve requirements, with little left to spare. In other

Exhibit 27.6 Total Reserves on Deposit at the Federal Reserve Bank (Monthly Data from January 1959 through December 2013)

Here we see total reserves of private banks held on deposit at the Fed. Before 2008, reserves fluctuated between $40 billion and $80 billion, which was roughly the minimum amount of reserves that were required to be held—10 percent of demand deposits at large banks. In 2008, in response to the financial crisis, the Fed drastically increased the amount of reserves held at the Fed, causing total reserves to rise to $2.5 trillion by December 2013. This expansion was designed to drive down interest rates, thereby stimulating GDP.

Source: Board of Governors of the Federal Reserve System.

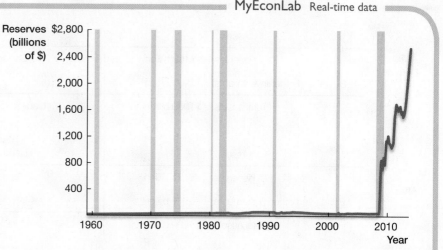

words, the quantity of reserves was roughly equal to the amount of reserves that banks were required to hold—for large banks, 10 percent of the demand deposits of their customers.

Over the next 5 years, the quantity of reserves exploded, exceeding $2.5 trillion. This vast expansion in reserves did not reflect an increase in required reserves, but rather an expansion of reserves far, far above the quantity that was required to be held. Reserves above and beyond the regulatory minimum are referred to as *excess reserves*. The Fed expanded reserves to push the federal funds rate close to 0 and to also lower long-term real interest rates. (Recall how Exhibit 27.3 showed us that a rightward shift in the supply of reserves drives down the federal funds rate.) And this reduction in interest rates is exactly what this policy achieved. In early 2007, before the 2007–2009 recession, the federal funds rate was 5.25 percent. By early 2009, it was only 0.1 percent. The federal funds rate has been kept near 0 from 2009 up to the present day (this textbook went to press in September 2014). Most forecasters expect that the Fed will reverse its policy and start to slowly raise the federal funds rate beginning in 2015.

Other Tools of the Fed

The Fed uses many tools to manipulate interest rates and affect the demand for goods, services, and labor. Like traditional open market operations, which we just discussed, most of these additional tools also work through the Fed's supply of bank reserves. We list these other tools here, many of which will be familiar from Chapter 25.

1. **Changing the reserve requirement.** For large private banks, the current level of required reserves is 10 percent of their customers' demand deposits. The Fed can decrease the quantity of required reserves, which shifts private banks' demand curve for reserves to the left and decreases the federal funds rate. (Likewise, the Fed can increase the quantity of required reserves, which shifts the demand curve for reserves to the right and increases the federal funds rate.)

2. **Changing the interest rate paid on reserves deposited at the Fed.** The Fed currently pays an interest rate of 0.25 percent on reserves deposited at the Fed. The Fed can change this interest rate. A decrease in the interest rate paid on reserves shifts the demand curve for reserves to the left and decreases the federal funds rate. (An increase in the interest rate paid on reserves shifts the demand curve for reserves to the right and increases the federal funds rate.)

3. **Lending from the discount window.** The Fed can lend bank reserves through its *discount window*. For private banks, the discount window is an alternative to the federal funds market as a source of reserves. Lending from the discount window occurs most frequently during financial crises, when private banks are afraid to lend to one another in the federal funds market because they can't be sure that they will be paid back.

4. **Quantitative easing.** The Fed can also change the way that it conducts open market operations. Rather than buying short-term Treasury bonds, which is the usual way that the Fed increases bank reserves in an open market operation, the Fed can buy *long-term* bonds instead. Purchasing long-term bonds in an open market operation pushes up the price on the long-term bonds and thereby drives down long-term interest rates. The interest rate is the (fixed) coupon that the bond pays divided by the price of the bond, so a higher bond price implies a lower interest rate. Quantitative easing occurs when the central bank creates a large quantity of bank reserves to buy long-term bonds, simultaneously increasing the quantity of bank reserves and pushing down the interest rate on long-term bonds. Quantitative easing played a key role in the huge run-up in bank reserves that occurred from 2008 to 2014.

Central banks occasionally invent even more ways of increasing the supply of credit during financial crises by creating specialized lending channels that increase lending in the credit market and thus indirectly stimulate the demand for goods, services, and labor.

For example, immediately after the investment bank Lehman Brothers went bankrupt in September 2008, an even larger financial firm—the American International Group (AIG)—also suffered a cataclysmic liquidity crisis. AIG desperately needed cash because it had to make billions of dollars of immediate payments to hundreds of other financial firms, including many of the largest banks in the United States, Europe, and Asia. AIG was having trouble raising funds because investors feared that AIG was about to declare bankruptcy. The failure of AIG would have triggered a domino effect that could have crippled the global financial system. If AIG declared bankruptcy, any institutions that were owed money by AIG would not immediately receive the funds they were counting on, and some of these *other* firms would be unable to meet their own financial commitments, creating ripples that might cause hundreds of interconnected financial institutions to fail.

The Fed joined forces with the U.S. Treasury Department to prop up AIG by extending AIG loans, credit lines, and other guarantees for a total of nearly $200 billion. AIG eventually recovered, and the Fed and Treasury got back their money. AIG's original shareholders were almost completely wiped out, but AIG was able to pay off its debts to other financial institutions, averting an even worse global financial meltdown.

> **The effectiveness of monetary policy depends on expectations about interest rates and inflation.**

We've now discussed the key tools that the Fed uses in its conduct of countercyclical monetary policy. However, we haven't completed the picture yet. There are several important factors that influence the way the Fed uses these tools. We turn to these issues in the next three subsections.

Expectations, Inflation, and Monetary Policy

The effectiveness of monetary policy depends on expectations about interest rates and inflation. Recall that the federal funds rate, which the Fed directly controls, is the annualized interest rate on overnight loans between banks. In contrast, the interest rate that is relevant for consumers' and firms' investment decisions—for instance, the real mortgage interest rate—is the long-term expected real interest rate:

$$\text{Long-term expected real interest rate} = \text{Long-term nominal interest rate} \\ - \text{Long-term expected inflation rate}.$$

For the Fed to lower the long-term real interest rate, it has to either lower the long-term nominal interest rate or raise long-term expectations of the inflation rate (or both). To do this, the Fed can communicate that it will maintain an expansionary monetary policy, holding down the federal funds rate and propping up the inflation rate, for a long period of time.

LETTING THE DATA SPEAK

Managing Expectations

The Fed's desire to influence long-term expectations is apparent in its monthly policy statements. In the fall of 2010, the economy was slowly recovering from the 2007–2009 recession and consequently the Fed wanted to maintain a low long-term expected real interest rate. In its September 2010 policy announcement, the Federal Open Market Committee—the committee that conducts the Fed's open market operations—wrote that the federal funds rate would be held between 0 and 0.25 percent for "an extended period."

In its December 2012 announcement, the Fed announced an even clearer policy rule, by linking changes in the federal funds rate to future changes in the unemployment rate and the inflation rate:

"The committee decided to keep the target range for the federal funds rate at 0 to 1/4 percent and currently anticipates that this exceptionally low range for the federal funds rate will be appropriate at least as long as

• the unemployment rate remains above 6.5 percent,

• inflation between one and two years ahead is projected to be no more than a half percentage point above the Committee's 2 percent longer-run goal,

• and longer-term inflation expectations continue to be well anchored."

(Federal Open Market Committee, 12/2012)

In this statement, the Fed announced a specific policy rule, which increased the public's ability to forecast future interest rates. In essence, the Fed announced that it planned to keep the federal funds rate close to 0 percent as long as the unemployment rate remained above 6.5 percent and inflation remained close to the Fed's 2 percent target. At the time that this announcement was made, the unemployment rate was 7.7 percent and forecasters anticipated that it would take years for the unemployment rate to fall to the 6.5 percent threshold that the Fed set for itself. As this book goes to press (September, 2014), the unemployment rate has fallen below the 6.5 threshold, and the Fed is now actively talking about raising the federal funds rate during the next year.

William McChesney Martin, Jr., a teetotaler in his personal life, was the chairman of the Fed from 1951 to 1970. He described the Fed's role this way: "I'm the fellow who takes away the punch bowl just when the party is getting good."

Contractionary monetary policy slows down growth in bank reserves, raises interest rates, reduces borrowing, slows down growth in the money supply, and reduces the rate of inflation.

If households and firms believe that the federal funds rate will remain low for several years, then the long-term nominal interest rate will also be low. Intuitively, you can think of the 10-year nominal interest rate as being close to the market's expectations of the average interest rate for overnight loans over the next 10 years. If the Fed promises to keep the federal funds rate low for the next decade, then the 10-year (long-term) nominal interest rate will also be low.

A similar analysis applies to long-term expectations of inflation. To many people, inflation is a four-letter word. But as we already mentioned in Chapter 25, the impact of inflationary expectations on the long-term expected real interest rate also implies that the Fed might wish to create expectations of inflation—if it can. In particular, it might promise to conduct expansionary monetary policy for several years. If the market believes this promise, then inflationary expectations will rise, which will lower the long-term expected real interest rate if the nominal interest rate doesn't rise one-for-one with inflation.

Contractionary Monetary Policy: Control of Inflation

Recall from Chapter 25 that stabilizing inflation is one of the Fed's two mandates. The Fed would like the inflation rate to hover around 2 percent per year, neither deviating far above or far below this target.

Expansionary monetary policy can put this inflation target at risk. In normal circumstances, increasing the quantity of bank reserves enables banks to make more loans. Those loans circulate through the economy and return to the banking system as deposits. Rising bank deposits increase the amount of money in the economy, since the stock of money includes customers' bank deposits. The quantity theory of money, which we studied in Chapter 25, implies that over the long run, the inflation rate will equal the growth rate of M2 minus the growth rate of real GDP. Excessively rapid growth in M2 therefore creates a risk of high levels of inflation. We summarize these linkages in Exhibit 27.7. Countercyclical policy is useful for controlling inflation. In particular, when inflation threatens to rise substantially and persistently above the Fed's target of 2 percent, the Fed uses **contractionary monetary policy**, which slows down growth in bank reserves, raises interest rates, reduces borrowing, slows down growth in the money supply, and reduces the rate of inflation.

Contractionary monetary policy is like expansionary monetary policy, but now the Fed runs everything in reverse. The Fed will *shrink* bank reserves—or slow their growth—to

Exhibit 27.7 The Path from Reserves to Inflation

Increasing the quantity of bank reserves deposited at the Fed usually leads banks to make more loans. Those loans circulate through the economy and return to the banking system as deposits. Rising bank deposits enable banks to make even more loans. The resulting total increase in deposits generates an increase in the stock of money (for instance, M2). If the stock of money grows faster than real GDP, the aggregate price level will rise, generating inflation. This only poses a problem when inflation persistently rises above the Fed's 2 percent target.

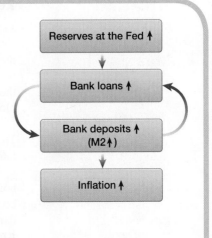

Reserves at the Fed ↑

Bank loans ↑

Bank deposits ↑ (M2 ↑)

Inflation ↑

[**The Fed (plays) a countercyclical role, leaning against the prevailing economic winds.**]

raise the federal funds rate. It might also attempt to change expectations about future monetary policy, leading households and businesses to anticipate more contractionary policies in the future.

In essence, the Fed can run the engine of monetary policy either forward or backwards. During a recession, the Fed employs expansionary monetary policies to partially offset the economic contraction. During a boom, particularly one that is inflationary, the Fed employs contractionary monetary policy to reduce a rising rate of inflation. In both cases, of course, the Fed is playing a countercyclical role, leaning against the prevailing economic winds.

Though it might sound simple to run the engine of monetary policy backwards, controlling inflation is not always easy. Once prices begin rising quickly—for instance, an inflation rate of 5 percent or more—the public starts to expect a high inflation rate in the future and the central bank has a hard time regaining its reputation as an inflation fighter. Such a loss in reputation occurred during the 1970s—a decade of high and rising U.S. inflation caused in part by expansionary monetary policy. By the end of the 1970s, the Fed's reputation as a careful steward of the monetary system was shattered. In 1979, the U.S. public expected that inflation would remain at a high level for the foreseeable future. This is when a new Fed chairman, Paul Volcker, stepped in with a sharply contractionary monetary policy. To cut inflation, he drastically slowed the growth rate of the stock of money, which raised the federal funds rate to 20 percent. This was the beginning of the 1981 recession that turned out to be one of the most severe U.S. recessions since World War II. Volcker's recession generated a peak unemployment rate of 10.8 percent, even greater than the 10 percent peak during the 2007–2009 recession. Volcker believed that the benefits of lowering the rate of inflation offset the costs of this deep recession. Volcker managed to reclaim the Fed's credibility for fighting inflation, and ever since, the Fed has retained its reputation for being serious about controlling the level of inflation.

With historical episodes like this in mind, central banks work hard to protect their reputation for keeping inflation at a low level—around 2 percent per year. Even the slightest hint that inflation is getting out of control might lead a central bank to end a policy of monetary expansion.

Paul Volcker sharply reduced the growth rate of the money stock in the early 1980s to reclaim the Fed's reputation as an inflation fighter. His actions raised interest rates and started a major recession. Despite national protests against his policies, he stayed the course, and he is now viewed as one of the greatest Fed chairmen. This is one central banker you shouldn't mess with. (He also had the odd quirk of testifying before the Senate while puffing on cigars.[1])

Zero Lower Bound

Japan has experienced four recessions and a very low level of overall growth in real GDP since the early 1990s. Many observers refer to the 1990s and 2000s as "lost decades" for the Japanese economy. In response to these economic conditions, Japan's central bank has responded by increasing the supply of bank reserves, thereby lowering Japan's version of the federal funds rate—the interest rate for interbank loans—nearly to zero. Exhibit 27.8 plots this interbank interest rate.

When an interest rate hits zero, economists say that it has "hit the zero lower bound." This language implies that zero is a barrier—or a boundary line—that nominal interest rates can't cross.

To understand the zero lower bound, it is helpful to explain how bizarre a negative nominal interest rate would be if it arose. A *negative* interest rate would imply that a borrower would eventually repay *less* money than he borrowed. For example, suppose that you go to the bank to borrow $100 million for one year at a *negative* interest rate of 1 percent. Assuming that you can store this money—for example, under a very big mattress or in a safe deposit box—then borrowing at a −1 percent interest rate would present a great profit opportunity for you. You borrow $100 million. You store it for a year and then repay your loan by giving the bank $99 million back and pocketing the remaining $1 million!

Of course, lending money at a negative interest rate is a bad deal for banks; they would rather keep the money in their own vaults than lend it to you. At least then they would have $100 million at the end of the year rather than just the $99 million they would get from you.

CHOICE & CONSEQUENCE

Policy Mistakes

On occasion, policymakers fail to recognize what is happening in the economy. Sometimes they mistakenly adopt policies that increase the magnitude of economic fluctuations instead of policies that smooth things out.

Some economists believe that the severity of the 2007–2009 financial crisis and recession was in part caused by unduly expansionary monetary policy from 2002 to 2005. During this period, the Fed, under Chairman Alan Greenspan, lowered the federal funds rate to 1 percent, even though the economy was growing and the housing market was gripped by what we now realize was an unsustainable speculative bubble. Alan Greenspan's unwillingness to increase the federal funds rate was in part caused by his belief at the time that unsustainable speculative bubbles are extremely rare. After the collapse in housing prices, Greenspan publicly revised his views on the frequency of asset bubbles.

Asset bubbles—like the home price bubble that peaked in 2006—do occur from time to time and are often followed by recessions. In other words, asset bubbles increase, or amplify, economic fluctuations. The Fed's expansionary policies of 2002–2005 greased the wheels of the housing bubble and therefore played a partial role in causing the recession that followed. Sometimes central banks administer the wrong monetary medicine.

Central banks have studied this policy failure and many are now attempting to identify asset bubbles as

they are forming. Some central banks, including the Bank of England, are also implementing policies that are designed to suppress asset price bubbles before they grow destructively large.[2]

Exhibit 27.8 Japan's Interbank Lending Rate from 1987 to 2013

The Japanese central bank has kept the interest rate on interbank loans near zero since 1995. The interbank lending rate is analogous to the federal funds rate in the United States. (Shaded periods are Japanese recessions.)

Source: Board of Governors of the Federal Reserve System.

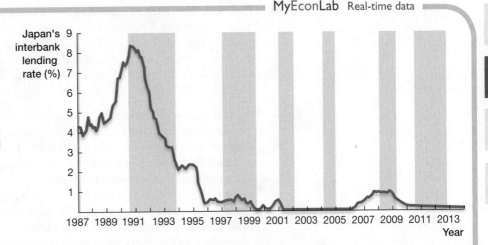

These arguments explain why banks generally won't lend money at an interest rate that is below zero. Banks will hold onto their money rather than make loans at negative interest rates. It therefore follows that central banks can't push nominal interest rates below zero. And that is the zero lower bound.

The zero lower bound is a problem for monetary policy when the rate of inflation is low or negative, which has also been the case in Japan since the early 1990s. Remember that households and firms make investment decisions based on the expected real interest rate. When the nominal interest rate is stuck at or just above 0 and the inflation rate is negative (also called *deflation*), the real interest rate will be positive. For example, a nominal interest rate of 0 and an expected inflation rate of −1 percent jointly imply an expected real interest rate of

$$\text{Nominal interest rate} - \text{Expected inflation rate} = 0\% - (-1\%) = 1\%.$$

If the inflation rate keeps falling (further below zero), the real interest rate will rise, squelching investment and shifting the labor demand curve to the left.

When the economy is in recession or growing only slowly, the central bank usually wants to lower the real interest rate to stimulate economic growth. But what does it do when nominal interest rates can't be lowered any further because they are already at the zero lower bound? As we discussed earlier, the central bank tries to influence expectations of *future* nominal interest rates and *future* inflation. By promising to keep nominal interest rates low for many years and promising to keep inflation at 2 percent in the long run, the central bank attempts to influence the long-term expected real rate of interest, even if the current federal funds rate is at zero and can't be lowered any further.

Policy Trade-offs

We hope you have concluded that the job of a central banker is not easy. Monetary policymakers face many conflicting considerations. For example, the Fed would like to stimulate the economy during a recession, but the Fed does not want to risk runaway inflation. How should the Fed make this trade-off?

Many central banks set the federal funds rate in a way that is approximately described by this formula, also called a *Taylor rule* after economist John Taylor who first suggested it[3]:

Federal funds rate = Long-run federal funds rate target + 1.5(Inflation rate − Inflation rate target) + 0.5(Output gap in percentage points).

This equation relates the federal funds rate to its long-run target (about 3.5 percent), the inflation rate, the inflation target (2 percent), and the output gap in percentage points. The *output gap*, which was first discussed in Chapter 19, is the difference between GDP and trend GDP divided by trend GDP:

$$\text{Output gap} = \frac{\text{GDP} - \text{Trend GDP}}{\text{Trend GDP}}.$$

An output gap of -0.05 is expressed in percentage points as -5 percent—in other words, the economy is 5 percent below trend. Recall from Chapter 19 that trend GDP is a smoothed version of actual GDP. You often will see the output gap expressed with trend GDP replaced by *potential GDP*, which represents the level of GDP that would be attained if the labor force and the capital stock were fully employed in production.

It is useful to spell out the two parts of the Taylor rule:

1. It says that the Fed raises the federal funds rate as the inflation rate rises. A greater inflation rate leads the Fed to raise the federal funds rate, thereby reducing the degree of stimulus. Specifically, the formula says that every percentage point increase in the inflation rate (for a given inflation target) will translate into a 1.5 percentage point increase in the federal funds rate.
2. The Taylor rule also says that the Fed sets a higher federal funds rate the higher the output gap. A larger output gap—in other words, a stronger economy—leads the Fed to raise the federal funds rate, thereby reducing the degree of stimulus. The formula says that every percentage point increase in the output gap will translate into a half percentage point increase in the federal funds rate.

To see the Taylor rule in action, consider the state of affairs in early 2014. Inflation was running at about 1.5 percent, and the economy was about 5 percent below its trend GDP level. Plugging these numbers into the Taylor rule (and assuming a 3.5% long-run federal funds rate target and 2% inflation rate target), the recommended level of the federal funds rate was:

$$\text{Federal funds rate} = 3.5\% + 1.5(1.5\% - 2\%) + 0.5(-5\%) = 0.25\%.$$

Hence, the Taylor rule predicted a federal funds rate of only 0.25 percent, far below its long-run target of 3.5 percent. In fact, the actual federal funds rate in early 2014 was 0.1 percent, not far from the level predicted by the Taylor rule.

The Taylor "rule" is really just a rule of thumb. Monetary policy is as much an art as a science—policymakers need to use their intuition and wisdom, not just a simple formula. However, the Taylor rule is a good starting point for their deliberations and a rough-and-ready summary of the trade-offs that central banks have made in the past.

27.3 Countercyclical Fiscal Policy

Countercyclical monetary policy, which is conducted by the central bank and aims to reduce economic fluctuations by manipulating interest rates, has been our focus so far. Countercyclical fiscal policy is the *other* major category of countercyclical policy. Countercyclical fiscal policy, which is passed by the legislative branch and signed into law by the executive branch, reduces economic fluctuations by manipulating government expenditures and taxes.

Expansionary fiscal policy uses higher government expenditure and lower taxes to increase the growth rate of real GDP. Like expansionary monetary policy, expansionary fiscal policy shifts the labor demand curve to the right, as Exhibit 27.1 showed. **Contractionary fiscal policy** uses lower government expenditure and higher taxes to reduce the growth rate of real GDP. Just like contractionary monetary policy, contractionary fiscal policy shifts the labor demand curve to the left.

We now discuss the reasons that macroeconomists view fiscal policy as a useful tool for offsetting macroeconomic fluctuations. We'll also explain some of its limitations.

Expansionary fiscal policy uses higher government expenditure and lower taxes to increase the growth rate of real GDP.

Contractionary fiscal policy uses lower government expenditure and higher taxes to reduce the growth rate of real GDP.

Fiscal Policy Over the Business Cycle: Automatic and Discretionary Components

Fiscal policy can be divided into automatic and discretionary components.

1. *Automatic countercyclical components* are aspects of fiscal policy that automatically partially offset economic fluctuations. These automatic countercyclical components do not require deliberate action on the part of the government. For example, tax collection falls automatically during a recession because unemployed workers don't owe income tax. Moreover, during a recession, government expenditure automatically *increases*, because government transfer payments rise, including

unemployment insurance and food stamps (otherwise known as the Supplemental Nutrition Assistance Program or SNAP). The less households earn, the more government transfers they receive.

These automatic countercyclical fiscal mechanisms are often referred to as **automatic stabilizers** because they stimulate the economy during economic contractions. Such transfers help households cope with economic hardship and are widely believed to stimulate GDP by enabling millions of households to spend more during recessions.

2. *Discretionary countercyclical components* are those aspects of the government's fiscal policy that policymakers deliberately enact in response to economic fluctuations. In most cases, these new policies introduce a package of specific expenditure increases or temporary tax cuts to reduce economic hardship and stimulate GDP. For example, during the recession of 2007–2009 the U.S. Congress passed the Economic Stimulus Act of 2008—signed by President George W. Bush in February 2008—and the American Recovery and Reinvestment Act of 2009—signed by President Barack Obama in February 2009. The first package contained $152 billion in tax cuts, which were received by households in the spring of 2008. The second package cost $787 billion, with a third of the funding supporting new tax cuts and two-thirds of the funding supporting new government expenditure. The new spending was spread out over several years.

We illustrate the behavior of fiscal policy (combining both the automatic and discretionary components) during the 2007–2009 recession in Exhibit 27.9. The rising budget deficit—government revenue minus government expenditure—provides a summary measure of fiscal policy, because the deficit reflects rising expenditures and falling tax collection. In the fourth quarter of 2007, which was the start of the recession, the budget deficit was $416 billion (all numbers are in constant 2009 dollars). By the end of the recession in the second quarter of 2009, the budget deficit had risen to $1,603 billion. Persistent weakness in the labor market coupled with lags in spending from the 2009 American Recovery and Reinvestment Act caused the deficit to remain high following the end of the recession.

Such deficits have consequences. When the government borrows money to pay its bills, future taxpayers are implicitly responsible for paying back the government's debts.

> **Automatic stabilizers** are components of the government budget that automatically adjust to smooth out economic fluctuations.

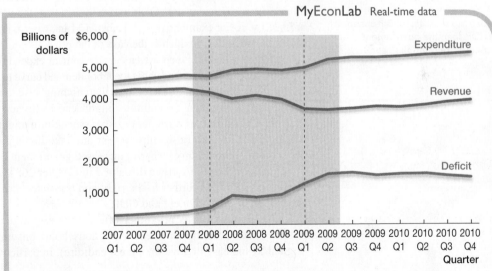

MyEconLab Real-time data

Exhibit 27.9 U.S. Government Accounts from 2007 to 2010 Combining Federal, State, and Local Governments (Constant 2009 Dollars)

During the 2007–2009 recession (December 2007 to June 2009, which corresponds to the shaded area), fiscal policy was implemented in two major pieces of legislation. The first act was passed in February 2008 and was principally focused on tax cuts that were paid out in the spring of 2008 (the second quarter of 2008). The second act was passed in February 2009 and included both tax cuts and spending increases. Vertical lines identify the quarter that each piece of legislation was passed.

Sources: Bureau of Economic Analysis, National Income and Product Accounts; and National Bureau of Economic Research.

> **The basic idea behind fiscal policy is that higher government expenditure and lower taxation play a useful role in recessions by increasing spending by households, firms, and governments.**

Ultimately, the government will have to pay what it owes. Roughly speaking, the 2007–2009 recession generated $2 trillion of *automatic* fiscal adjustments and $1 trillion of *discretionary* fiscal adjustments, implying that future taxpayers will be on the hook for approximately $3 trillion of new government debt. But all of this debt was accumulated for a reason—to conduct countercyclical fiscal policy. The basic idea behind fiscal policy is that higher government expenditure and lower taxation play a useful role in recessions by increasing spending by households, firms, and governments. This increased spending translates into demand for firms' products, which in turn increases demand for labor, shifting labor demand to the right. To the extent that some of this money goes to state and local governments, it enables them to avoid laying off state and local employees.

The remainder of the chapter explains why more government expenditure and lower taxation increases GDP. We first look at expenditure-based fiscal policy and then at taxation-based fiscal policy.

Analysis of Expenditure-Based Fiscal Policy

Let's begin with the national income accounting identity.

$$Y = C + I + G + X - M.$$

Here, Y is GDP, C is consumption, I is investment, G is government expenditure, X is exports, M is imports, and thus $X - M$ is net exports. To start the analysis of fiscal policy, assume (for the moment) that changing government expenditure does not change any of the other terms on the right-hand side of the equation. Then a $1 increase in government expenditure would cause a $1 increase in GDP, Y:

$$[Y + 1] = C + I + [G + 1] + X - M.$$

If a $1 change in government expenditure causes an m change in GDP, then the **government expenditure multiplier** is m.

If we take the change in GDP (Y) and divide it by the change in government expenditure (G), we have what is known as the **government expenditure multiplier**. If government expenditure rises by $1 and causes GDP to rise by m, then the government expenditure multiplier is $m/$1 = m$. For example, if $m = 1$, then a $1 increase in government expenditure generates a $1 increase in GDP (which is the case in the previous equation). In terms of our analysis of Exhibit 27.1, if $m = 1$, then increased government expenditure of $1 raises the demand for firms' goods and services and shifts the labor demand curve to the right, increasing GDP by $1.

Let's now revisit the assumption that nothing else on the right-hand side changes. Additional government expenditure might lead to higher levels of household consumption. For example, the government's extra expenditure might encourage additional business activity, which would raise employment and take-home pay and thereby increase household consumption. In this scenario, increased government expenditure levels are creating a multiplier effect of the sort we discussed in Chapter 26. The multiplier effect shifts firms' labor demand curves further to the right and translates into a larger impact of government expenditure on employment and GDP.

We can illustrate this multiplier effect with the national income accounting identity. Assume that the multiplier effect raises household consumption by $1 (in addition to the original $1 increase in government expenditure). In particular:

$$[Y + 2] = [C + 1] + I + [G + 1] + X - M.$$

In this scenario Y rises by $2—remember that the left- and right-hand sides of this equation must be equal. In this case, the government expenditure multiplier would be $2/$1 = 2$. This means that GDP rises by $2 for every $1 increase in government expenditure.

Advocates of expenditure-based fiscal policy tend to believe that the government expenditure multiplier lies between 1 and 2.

Crowding Out In addition to its useful role of combatting recessions as part of countercyclical fiscal policy, there is also a negative side to government expenditure. Rising government expenditures leads to more government borrowing, and such borrowing can soak up resources that would otherwise have been used by households and firms. Some economists believe that rising government expenditure "crowds out" private economic activity like consumption and investment. **Crowding out** occurs when rising government expenditure partially or even fully displaces expenditures by households and firms. In Exhibit 27.1, crowding out results in a smaller effect of countercyclical policy—in other words, crowding out implies that the labor demand curve shifts to the right less than it otherwise would.

For example, suppose that an extra $1 of government expenditure forces the government to borrow an extra $1 to pay its bills, leading $1 of private savings to switch from funding private investment to purchasing government debt. The switch occurs because the government is willing to pay whatever interest rate it takes to borrow funds, whereas private businesses tend to be more responsive to interest rate changes. As the government borrows to pay its bills, the interest rate in the credit market rises, causing a reallocation of savings from private borrowers—like households and firms—to the government. If private investment becomes too expensive for consumers and firms, it might fall by $1 when the government increases its spending by $1. In effect, the private investment is "crowded out" by the government borrowing. In this scenario, countercyclical government expenditure will *not* shift the firms' labor demand curve to the right because the expansionary effect of the additional government expenditure is offset by the contractionary effect of the fall in private investment. Consequently, GDP does not increase, because the $1 increase in government expenditure crowds out $1 of private investment:

$$Y = C + [I - 1] + [G + 1] + X - M.$$

In this case, the government expenditure multiplier is $[-\$1 + \$1]/\$1 = 0$. Critics of fiscal policy emphasize the importance of crowding out and believe that the government expenditure multiplier is well below 1 and might even be close to 0.

At this point you are probably wondering which scenario is "right." Unfortunately, we are not completely sure. Economists hold a wide range of positions on this question, and everyone in this debate has some data that partially support his or her position. Taking into account *both* multipliers and crowding out, the government expenditure multiplier probably lies between 0 and 1.5, depending on the state of the economy.

If the economy is already running at full steam, it is likely that additional government expenditure will substantially crowd out other kinds of economic activity. For example, if all factories are already operating at full capacity, there may be little the government can do in the short run to increase GDP. Consequently, many economists believe that the government expenditure multiplier is close to zero when the economy is already booming. But that's not particularly relevant to the fiscal policy debate because economists don't recommend expansionary fiscal policy when the economy is already growing rapidly.

The interesting question is what we should expect the government expenditure multiplier to be when the economy is contracting. For example, envision an economy suffering from an extreme contraction, and further assume that monetary policy has been rendered less effective because interest rates have already been lowered to zero and can't be lowered any further—the scenario in which monetary policy has hit the zero lower bound.

This was the situation of the U.S. economy in the aftermath of the 2007–2009 recession. In a situation like this there will be substantial slack in productive resources, like factories running below capacity and significant numbers of unemployed workers. Accordingly, additional government expenditure might only weakly crowd out private consumption and investment. Additional government expenditures can then encourage the utilization of some of the idle capacity and unemployed workers. For instance, President Barack Obama's administration assumed a government-expenditure multiplier of 1.57 when developing the American Recovery and Reinvestment Act of 2009.[4] This number was close to, though slightly above, the estimates of other forecasters at that time.

Most economists endorse some additional government expenditures during a deep recession, but there is substantial debate on this issue. Critics of expansionary government expenditure believe that crowding out is strong even during recessions. Accordingly, the appropriate scale of countercyclical government expenditure remains an open policy question.

We'll now show you how to use the government expenditure multiplier to predict the impact of expenditure-based countercyclical policy. We'll assume that the economy is in a deep recession and that the multiplier is 1.5, approximately the top of its range. The American Recovery and Reinvestment Act of 2009 contained about $500 billion of new spending, but this new spending was spread out over many years. Only $120 billion occurred in 2009, implying an impact of

$$1.5 \times \$120 \text{ billion} = \$180 \text{ billion.}$$

Since GDP was approximately $14 trillion in 2009, a $180 billion increase in GDP amounted to an increase of about

$$\frac{\$180 \text{ billion}}{\$14 \text{ trillion}} = 1.3\%.$$

That might not seem like much, but 1.3 percentage points of extra growth does make a difference when talking about the growth rate of the entire U.S. economy. For example, in 2009 real GDP fell by 2.8 percent. A multiplier of 1.5 implies that the economy would have fallen by 4.1 percent without the impact of the new government expenditures in the American Recovery and Reinvestment Act of 2009.

Analysis of Taxation-Based Fiscal Policy

So far, we've been discussing the use of government expenditure to partially offset an economic contraction. Expansionary fiscal policy can also be implemented by cutting taxes. Let's therefore switch gears and assume that the government gives households a $1 tax cut. To illustrate ideas, let's start with the extreme assumption that consumers spend every penny of the tax cut, raising consumption (C) by $1, but nothing else changes on the right-hand side of the national income accounting identity. Then GDP would rise by $1 and the **government taxation multiplier** would be $1/$1 = 1:

If a $1 reduction in taxation causes an $m increase in GDP, then the **government taxation multiplier** is m.

$$[Y + 1] = [C + 1] + I + G + X - M.$$

But a $1 tax cut need not increase GDP by $1. If it increases it by $m, the government taxation multiplier would be $m/$1 = m.

For instance, there are many reasons why a $1 tax cut might have an impact that is even greater than $1. The rise in consumption might have multiplier effects, causing a domino effect of rising consumption, rising firm revenues, rising firm hiring, rising household income, and yet more consumption. In addition, a cut in the income tax might lead workers to supply more labor because their *after-tax* wages will have risen (though this effect is estimated to be small in magnitude). In Exhibit 27.1, this would shift the labor supply curve to the right. With these kinds of mechanisms in mind, suppose that a $1 decrease in taxation leads to a $2 increase in households' incomes and a $2 increase in consumption. Suppose that nothing else changes on the right-hand side of the accounting identity. In this case, GDP (Y) would rise by $2, so the government taxation multiplier would be $2/$1 = 2.

$$[Y + 2] = [C + 2] + I + G + X - M.$$

On the other hand, tax cuts might generate crowding out of the sort that we described before. As consumers try to spend more, resources that would have previously gone to investment might now be redirected to consumption. For instance, a car company might shift from manufacturing rental cars (an investment for Hertz and Avis) toward manufacturing cars that households buy:

$$[Y + 1] = [C + 2] + [I - 1] + G + X - M.$$

Likewise, as consumers try to spend more, the extra goods might be provided by an increase in imports, lowering net exports. If imports rise by $1, then net exports will fall by $1, so the national income accounting identity becomes:

$$[Y + 1] = [C + 2] + I + G + X - [M + 1].$$

If crowding-out effects are large, the government taxation multiplier will be significantly reduced. In the last two examples that we have discussed, the government taxation multiplier would be [$2 − $1]/$1 = 1.

Critics of using tax policy to manage short-run economic contractions point out that optimizing consumers might not actually spend much of their tax cut right away. In other words, critics worry that consumption might not rise very much as a result of a tax cut. Why might households hold back on spending their tax cuts? There are at least two reasons.

1. If consumption offers diminishing returns—a fifth slice of pizza might not taste as good as the fourth slice—consumers might try to smooth their consumption by

spreading the "extra" spending over the long term rather than consuming the proceeds of a tax cut all at once.

2. Consumers might recognize that the government will have to raise taxes in the future to pay for the current tax cut. Because of this anticipated future tax hike, they may decide that a current tax cut should be saved so that they will be in a position to pay these higher taxes in the future.

The tendency to save the tax cut will be particularly pronounced among wealthy consumers who don't have an urgent reason to consume the tax cut right away. In summary, if some consumers save some or even all of a tax cut, cutting taxes will have only a small effect on consumption, and the government taxation multiplier will be small.

Economists believe that the government taxation multiplier is between 0 and 2. The administration of President Barack Obama assumed a government-taxation multiplier of 0.99 when developing the American Recovery and Reinvestment Act of 2009.[5] The act created total tax cuts of about $300 billion, but only $65 billion of those cuts took effect in 2009. Assuming a government-taxation multiplier of 1, these tax cuts raised 2009 GDP by about $65 billion, representing about 0.5 percent of GDP in 2009.

We can therefore calculate the total impact of the American Recovery and Reinvestment Act of 2009, *if* the government's estimates of multipliers were correct. Expenditures raised GDP by 1.3 percent (see calculations above) and tax cuts raised GDP by 0.5 percent. Hence, the act raised 2009 GDP by

$$1.3\% + 0.5\% = 1.8\%.$$

Actual growth in real GDP was −2.8 percent from 2008 to 2009. If the act raised GDP by 1.8 percent, then *without* the act, growth in real GDP would have been

$$-2.8\% - 1.8\% = -4.6\%.$$

Viewed this way, the act had a considerable impact on GDP growth.

Fiscal Policies that Directly Target the Labor Market

There are a few specific fiscal policies that are directly targeted at the labor market. For example, in the midst of recessions, when many workers have lost their jobs and are unemployed, governments enact policies to lessen the terrible personal toll of joblessness. In the United States, the government extends eligibility for unemployment insurance from 26 to 52 weeks and, in some severe downturns, even to 99 weeks.

More generous eligibility rules have complex effects on the labor market. Lengthening eligibility reduces the hardships that unemployed workers suffer and gives them more time to find a job that is a good fit for their skills, but lengthened eligibility also partially reduces the incentive for unemployed workers to find new jobs. This shifts the labor supply curve to the left, which, holding all else equal, reduces employment.

However, by increasing the incomes of unemployed workers, lengthened eligibility supports household spending and thus limits the negative multiplier effects that result from falling employment. Hence, lengthened eligibility increases household consumption and this effect shifts the labor demand curve to the right.

Adding up the different considerations, the extension of unemployment benefits probably is good policy, but this is due to the suffering that it alleviates and not its effect on GDP. Because of the multiple effects with opposing implications for employment, lengthening eligibility is likely to have only a limited effect on total employment or GDP.

During recessions another type of fiscal policy reduces unemployment by subsidizing wages and thereby encouraging job creation. Such subsidies might be justified when unemployment remains high for a long period of time—for instance, this was the case during the Great Depression. Wage subsidies might also be justified when traditional monetary and fiscal policy have only limited success in combating unemployment. The last three U.S. recessions have been followed by "jobless recoveries," meaning that the rate of employment growth after these three recessions, although positive, has been lower than after earlier recessions.

We show the effect of a subsidy on labor demand and job creation in Exhibit 27.10. With a $1 subsidy received by employers, a wage of $10 per hour would cost employers only $9 per hour. So the subsidy shifts the labor demand curve right by just enough to create a $1 *vertical* gap between the old and new labor demand curves (drop a vertical line from one

Exhibit 27.10 The Impact of a $1 Wage Subsidy

If the government introduces a $1 per hour wage subsidy that is paid to firms, the labor demand curve shifts rightward by enough so that the new labor demand curve and the original labor demand curve are separated by a vertical distance of exactly $1. If a firm was willing to hire a worker at a wage of $w per hour without the subsidy, the firm is willing to hire the worker at a wage of $(w + 1) per hour with the subsidy. At the new equilibrium, employment is higher and the wage has risen to w*. Notice that the increase from the original equilibrium wage, w, to the new equilibrium wage, w*, is less than $1. This is because the rise in employment causes a fall in the (unsubsidized) value of the marginal product of labor (point A).

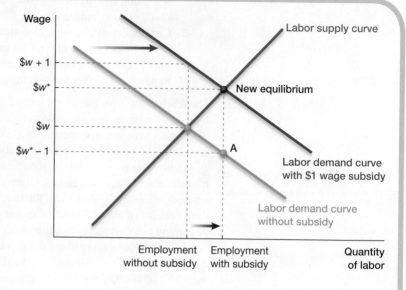

curve to the other to see the $1 gap). An employer who is willing to pay $9 for a worker without the subsidy is willing to pay $10 for that worker once the $1 government subsidy is in effect. Wage subsidies have been used commonly by European governments since the 1990s when their economies were also beset by jobless recoveries.

Policy Waste and Policy Lags

> Though the government typically funds socially valuable projects as part of countercyclical fiscal policy, government waste is often a problem.

Though the government typically funds socially valuable projects as part of countercyclical fiscal policy, government waste is often a problem. The government frequently funds *pork barrel spending*, which is the (derogatory) name given to inefficient public spending that politicians value because it increases their popularity with their constituents. For example, a senator has an incentive to obtain federal funding for an infrastructure project in his or her home state, even if the project is expensive and unnecessary, such as a bridge to nowhere. Since the home state residents only pay approximately 1/50th of the cost of the project (through their federal taxes) but get most of the benefits, they are happy to see it built, and the project improves the senator's in-state popularity. In this sense, the senator is personally optimizing when obtaining federal funding for almost any in-state project, even those with total social costs that exceed their total social benefits.

The efficiency of public expenditures further deteriorates when hundreds of billions of dollars of new government expenditures need to be spent quickly. The urgency makes it harder to identify and efficiently implement the projects that are socially beneficial. In addition, many of the projects with the highest social return have been funded already, raising the chance that a new project won't be socially desirable. Finally, politics and special interests sometimes get in the way, increasing the chances that wasteful projects with negative social value get funded.

Another important determinant of the effectiveness of expenditure-based policies is the lag in implementation. Most spending projects are slow out of the starting gate. It takes a long time to build a bridge, a highway, or a school. Plans have to be drawn up. The local community has to be consulted. The relevant zoning boards need to mull over the proposals, request changes, and then evaluate the amended plans. Environmental impact studies have to be conducted. Contractors have to be hired. And only then, construction begins.

For example, when the most recent recession officially ended in June 2009, practically none of the $230 billion in infrastructure spending legislated in the American Recovery and Reinvestment Act of (February) 2009 had yet been spent. In June 2010—almost a full year after the recession was over—only a *quarter* of the infrastructure budget had been

The "Bridge to Nowhere" was a $398 million project to build a road to Gravina Island, Alaska, which has 50 residents and is served by a ferry. After generating a national protest over pork barrel spending, the bridge was cancelled.

spent. Many of the largest infrastructure projects hadn't spent a penny one full year after the end of the recession. Lags like these raise the concern that by the time many of the projects are implemented, the economy might already be past the point where these projects would have been most useful.

In contrast, taxation-based fiscal policy can sometimes advance more quickly, for example because it doesn't take the Treasury Department long to mail every household a check. Taxation-based policies also have the advantage that the additional spending is done by households themselves so that the money is spent on goods and services that they value. (Government expenditure also *ultimately* puts money in households' pockets, but in the process it may lead to the implementation of projects of negative social value.)

Despite these concerns, expenditure-based policies are still a very useful part of countercyclical strategies. Several expenditure-based policies are not plagued by waste and lags. For example, most economists endorse federal transfers that enable state and local governments to reduce layoffs of teachers, firefighters, and police during recessions. Such countercyclical transfers from the federal government to the states are particularly useful because many states have balanced-budget rules that prevent them from borrowing during a recession. Without federal transfers, states would be forced to lay off many public employees, reducing public services and deepening the recession.

Likewise, most economists endorse infrastructure projects—like repairs to bridges and highways—that have already passed rigorous cost-benefit analysis. Such projects are said to be "shovel ready."

Evidence-Based Economics

Q: How much does government expenditure stimulate GDP?

On December 7, 1941, bombers from six Japanese aircraft carriers attacked the U.S. Pacific fleet. The bombers destroyed or damaged 8 battleships, numerous other ships, and 188 aircraft. The attack on Pearl Harbor catapulted the United States into World War II.

The attack also initiated an enormous increase in war-related spending, including the rebuilding and expansion of the Pacific fleet. A few months *before* the attack, when the United States was not yet a combatant, analysts forecast that preparations for a possible war would cost the United States about $100 billion (1941 dollars). Immediately after the attack, estimates for war-related spending rose to $200 billion. The economic magnitude of these numbers is revealed by comparing this war spending to 1941 GDP, which was $129.4 billion.

Though terrible, wars and the expenditures they trigger can be used to identify the economic effects of government expenditure, as economist Valerie Ramey has shown.[6] She studied 63 years of news articles to identify foreign events that caused a change in U.S. government expenditure. Ramey's data includes many war-related events—like the attack on Pearl Harbor—as well as other events like the surprise launch in 1957 of the Soviet satellite *Sputnik*, the first Earth-orbiting satellite, that sparked the space race between the United States and the Soviet Union. Ramey estimated that the launch of *Sputnik* led to an expansion of $10.3 billion (1957 dollars) in the U.S. government's space program.

27.1

27.2

27.3

27.4

On December 7, 1941, Japanese bombers attacked Pearl Harbor, catapulting the United States into World War II and drastically raising the expected level of future government expenditure.

The 1957 launch of *Sputnik*, the first Earth-orbiting satellite, kicked off a space race between the United States and the Soviet Union.

Surprising foreign events that change government expenditure present us with a natural experiment—recall the discussion of natural experiments in Chapter 2. In Ramey's study, a foreign shock causes the government to spend more for reasons unrelated to the state of the economy. She then compared the growth of GDP after these large random spending shocks to the growth of GDP in periods that did not experience such shocks.

Using such comparisons, Ramey estimated a government expenditure multiplier between 0.6 and 1.2. In other words, when the government raises expenditure by $1 (because of a surprising foreign event), GDP increases by an amount between $0.60 and $1.2. The range of possible values is large because we don't have enough historical data to pin down a more precise answer.

Question

How much does government expenditure stimulate GDP?

Answer

In this study, the government expenditure multiplier is estimated to lie between 0.6 and 1.2.

Data

National income and product account data from the United States (1939–2008) and historical news coverage in *Business Week*, the *New York Times*, and the *Washington Post*.

Caveat

Ramey's analysis measures the government expenditure multiplier that arises from expenditures that are mostly war-related. The analysis might underestimate the government expenditure multiplier during periods of economic slack, like recessions.

27.4 Policies That Blur the Line Between Fiscal and Monetary Policy

Some countercyclical policies represent a mix of fiscal and monetary effects. For example, some government expenditures are intended to affect the supply of credit.

The 2008 Troubled Asset Relief Program (TARP) is an example of such a mixed policy. At the peak of the 2007–2009 financial crisis, the U.S. Congress passed emergency legislation authorizing the Treasury Department to spend $700 billion to stabilize the financial system. The Treasury Department is a government agency that resides in the executive branch and therefore is *not* part of the Fed. Nevertheless, the TARP legislation was developed jointly by Fed and Treasury officials and the legislation required that the Fed chairman be consulted during TARP's implementation.

Of the $700 billion in TARP funds, $115 billion was used to increase the capital of the eight largest U.S. banks, which were all *forced* to participate. In essence, the banks were required to issue new shares that the government bought. Some of the banks didn't like this plan, since the government became a partial owner. In addition, all eight banks were obligated to limit the compensation of their senior executives. An additional $135 billion was used to increase the capital of smaller banks that applied for TARP support.

These bank capital infusions—totaling $250 billion—gave the participating banks breathing room, and the financial system as a whole stabilized. The financial system came back from the brink of a devastating financial contagion in which banks were falling like dominos, each failure instigating other failures as banks couldn't repay their debts to one another. TARP funding is now viewed as a successful policy, though there remain questions about whether it played a causal role in rescuing the economy or simply appeared to be successful because of coincidental timing.

The bank capital infusions ended up costing the government little, since the government was repaid after the crisis had passed. In fact, the government made a small profit from its TARP investments in the banks. However, there were many government programs other than TARP that benefited banks, so banks were net recipients of government support.

You might be wondering about the $450 billion of TARP funding that was not used to buy bank shares. Dozens of other programs were funded by TARP, including investments in the bankrupt car companies General Motors and Chrysler and the nearly bankrupt insurance company AIG. When the dust settled, the government was able to recoup most of its investment, and the government's support prevented these important companies from shutting down their operations at the peak of the crisis. Such shutdowns would have aggravated the crisis, leading to an even deeper recession.

We do not know what would have happened without TARP and the other countercyclical fiscal and monetary policies that were adopted during the financial crisis. It would be convenient if we could set up numerous *identical* economies to study macroeconomic policy interventions, just like a laboratory scientist would do. In one economy, we would include TARP. In another otherwise identical economy, we would not. We could then see which economy had better performance. Because economists can't run experiments like that, we are stuck with making judgments based on less than perfect data and models of economic behavior. Though most economists think that TARP was a success, it is impossible to be sure.

Summary

⚙ Countercyclical policies attempt to reduce the intensity of economic fluctuations and smooth the growth rates of employment, GDP, and prices.

⚙ Countercyclical monetary policy, which is conducted by the central bank (in the United States, the Fed), attempts to reduce economic fluctuations by manipulating bank reserves and interest rates.

⚙ Open market operations refer to the Fed's transactions with private banks to increase or reduce bank reserves held on deposit at the Fed. Open market operations influence the federal funds rate—an increase in the supply of bank reserves lowers the federal funds rate, holding all else equal.

⚙ Expansionary monetary policy increases the quantity of bank reserves and lowers interest rates, shifting the labor demand curve to the right and increasing the growth rate of GDP.

⚙ Contractionary monetary policy slows down the growth in bank reserves and increases interest rates, shifting the labor demand curve to the left and reducing the growth rate of GDP. Contractionary monetary policy is used when inflation is rising above the Fed's long-run target of 2 percent or when the economy is growing excessively quickly.

⚙ Countercyclical fiscal policy, which is passed by the legislative branch and signed into law by the executive branch, reduces economic fluctuations by manipulating government expenditures and taxes.

⚙ Countercyclical fiscal policies might be automatic or discretionary. Automatic stabilizers are components of the government budget, like taxes owed, that automatically adjust to smooth out economic fluctuations.

⚙ Expansionary fiscal policy uses higher government expenditure and lower taxes to increase GDP, shifting the labor demand curve to the right. Crowding out occurs when rising government expenditure partially (or even fully) displaces expenditures by households and firms.

⚙ Contractionary fiscal policy uses lower government expenditure and higher taxes to reduce GDP, shifting the labor demand curve to the left.

⚙ Some policies, like the 2008 Troubled Asset Relief Program (TARP), blur the line between monetary policy and fiscal policy.

Key Terms

countercyclical policies *p. 639*
countercyclical monetary policy *p. 639*
countercyclical fiscal policy *p. 639*
expansionary monetary policy *p. 641*

contractionary monetary policy *p. 646*
expansionary fiscal policy *p. 650*
contractionary fiscal policy *p. 650*
automatic stabilizers *p. 651*

government expenditure multiplier *p. 652*
crowding out *p. 653*
government taxation multiplier *p. 654*

Questions

1. What are the similarities and the differences between monetary and fiscal policies?

2. How do expansionary policies differ from contractionary policies?

3. Briefly explain how expansionary monetary policy shifts the labor demand curve to the right.

4. What is quantitative easing? Why do central banks undertake quantitative easing programs?

5. Other than open market operations and quantitative easing, what tools does the Federal Reserve use to manipulate interest rates in the economy?

6. Does the effectiveness of monetary policy depend on inflation expectations? Explain.

7. Briefly explain how an increase in the quantity of reserves that commercial banks hold at the Federal Reserve could lead to inflation.

8. How does the zero lower bound on interest rates affect the working of monetary policy?

9. When nominal interest rates have hit the zero lower bound, can central banks use interest rates to stimulate the economy? Explain.

10. What does the Taylor rule state?

11. According to the Taylor rule, when should the Federal Reserve lower or raise the federal funds rate?

12. What are the automatic and discretionary components of fiscal policy?

13. How can expansionary expenditure-based fiscal policy lead to crowding out in the economy?

14. What could explain why a decrease in taxes could lead to a less-than-proportionate increase in output?

15. Why is the Troubled Asset Relief Program (TARP) considered an example of a countercyclical policy that represents a mix of fiscal and monetary effects?

Problems

1. The former chairman of the Federal Reserve, Alan Greenspan, used the term "irrational exuberance" in 1996 to describe the high levels of optimism among stock market investors at the time. Stock market indexes such as the S&P Composite Price Index were at an all-time high. Some commentators believed that the Fed should intervene to slow the expansion of the economy. Why would central banks want to clamp down when the economy is growing? What policies could the government and the central bank use to achieve the goal of slowing down the economic expansion?

2. The following figures show the Federal Reserve's balance sheet as well as the balance sheet of a commercial bank, BHZ Bank. Suppose the Federal Reserve wants to lower bank reserves by $1 billion. Assuming that BHZ Bank is willing to transact with the Federal Reserve, show how the Fed's as well as BHZ's balance sheet will change.

The Federal Reserve			
Assets		**Liabilities and Shareholders' Equity**	
Treasury Bonds	$1,500 billion	Reserves	$1,500 billion
Other bonds	$500 billion	Currency	$500 billion
Total assets	**$2,000 billion**	**Total liabilities**	**$2,000 billion**

BHZ Bank			
Assets		**Liabilities and Shareholders' Equity**	
Reserves	$200 billion	Deposits and other liabilities	$700 billion
Bonds and other investments	$800 billion	Shareholders' equity	$300 billion
Total assets	**$1,000 billion**	**Liabilities + shareholders' equity**	**$1,000 billion**

3. Suppose the Fed wants to raise the federal funds rate. Explain the available mechanisms that the Fed can use to achieve this goal. In your answer, use a graph of the money market to show how the Fed's action translates into a higher interest rate.

4. You and a friend are debating the merits of using monetary policy during a severe recession. Your friend says that the central bank needs to lower interest rates all the way down to zero. According to him, zero nominal interest rates will boost lending and investment; consumers and firms will surely borrow and spend when interest rates are zero. Would you agree with his reasoning? How does the level of inflation affect your answer? Explain your conclusions.

5. In the following graph, the dashed line shows what the federal funds rate should have been according to the Taylor rule against the actual federal funds rate. At a symposium of central bankers in 2007, John Taylor, after whom the Taylor rule is named, suggested that if the Fed had been following the Taylor rule, the federal funds rate would have been increasing in 2002 and not falling.

   What is likely to happen if the Fed reduces the federal funds rate when it actually should be increasing it?

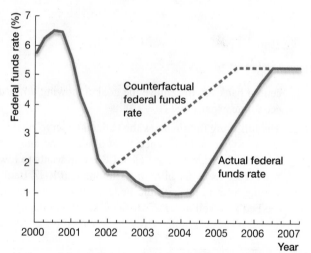

Source: Taylor, John B., "Housing and Monetary Policy" September 2007, http://web.stanford.edu/~johntayl/HousingandMonetaryPolicy--Taylor--JacksonHole2007.pdf

6. The following graph shows actual and projected estimates of potential GDP and GDP. Potential GDP is also a measure of trend GDP. When is the output gap, defined as the percent difference between GDP and potential GDP, negative? According to the Taylor rule, how should a negative output gap affect the federal funds interest rate?

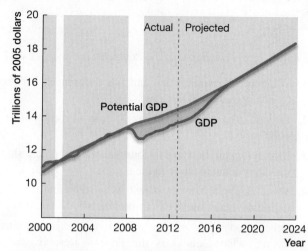

Sources: Congressional Budget Office; Department of Commerce, Bureau of Economic Analysis.

7. Two economists estimate the government expenditure multiplier and come up with different results. One estimates the multiplier at 0.75, while the other comes up with an estimate of 1.25.

   a. What do these different estimates imply about the consequences of government expenditure?

   b. If the current value of GDP is $13.28 trillion and the government is planning to increase spending by $800 billion, what is the percentage increase in GDP for each of the two estimates for the multiplier? Assume the increase in spending occurs all in one year.

8. In 2005, $320 million of the federal government's budget was allocated toward building a "bridge to nowhere" in Alaska that connected two small towns. In 2006, $500,000 was allocated toward a teapot museum in North Carolina, $1 million toward a water-free urinal initiative in Michigan, and $4.5 million toward a museum and park at an abandoned mine in Maine. These projects were requested by specific legislators in order to boost their popularity in their constituencies.

   a. What is this type of expenditure called?

   b. Since government spending increases employment by shifting the labor demand curve to the right, is it always a good idea for the government to increase expenditure? Explain your answer.

9. Milton Friedman, the renowned monetary economist, gave the following analogy about the Fed: "Imagine your house is being heated by a heater. The heater is controlled by a thermostat. The way it's set up, when the house gets a little too warm, the thermostat turns off the heater; if it gets too cold, the thermostat turns the heater back on. If everything

works as planned, the room temperature in the house should roughly be the targeted temperature all the time.

Now suppose the thermostat is not in the same room as the heater. In fact, it's in the last room that is affected by the heater. Say, the attic. And the radiators through which the heater works are really old, and it takes them at least twenty minutes to react. Then, instead of making the temperature more stable, the thermostat would make the temperature swing wildly. For example, if the house is cold, then the thermostat will turn the heater on. But it will turn the heater off only when the attic is warm. By then, the entire house will be scorching hot. When it turns the heater off, it will not turn it back on until the attic is cooler. By then, the house will be freezing."

(In this analogy, the thermostat is the Fed; the house is the entire economy.)

a. What do you think Milton Friedman was trying to say about monetary policy? (*Hint*: You do not need to draw any graphs for this question.)

b. As in the thermostat analogy, what might be some possible unintended consequences of monetary policy? Might there be a similar effect for fiscal policy? If yes, how does it differ from monetary policy?

10. Based on the information in the chapter, discuss the ways in which the 2008 Troubled Asset Relief Program (TARP) had some of the characteristics of monetary policy, and some of the characteristics of fiscal policy.

11. *Challenge Problem.* The chapter mentions that an open market operation by the Fed can increase or decrease the quantity of deposits in banks and therefore the money supply. (See, for example, Exhibit 27.8.)

The expansion in the money supply from a Fed open market operation is given by the following equation (under the simplifying assumption that households don't hold cash so the money supply is equal to demand deposits):

$$\text{Change in money supply} = (\text{Change in reserves}) \times \frac{1}{RR + ER},$$

where RR = the percentage of deposits that banks are required to keep as reserves (expressed as a decimal), and

ER = the percentage of deposits that banks voluntarily hold as excess reserves (expressed as a decimal).

$1/(RR + ER)$ is called the "money multiplier."

Suppose the Fed decides to sell \$14 billion in Treasury bonds. Assume that the reserve requirement is 8 percent and banks hold 4 percent in excess reserves, so $RR = 0.08$ and $ER = 0.04$.

What is the total increase or decrease in the money supply that would result from the Fed's action? Explain your answer and show your calculations. Verify that the quantity of new deposits (which is the change in the money supply in this example) is backed up by an adequate quantity of new reserves:

$(RR + ER) \times (\text{Change in deposits}) = (\text{Change in reserves})$.

12. *Challenge Problem.* Assume that the public in the small country of Sylvania does not hold any cash. Commercial banks, however, hold 5 percent of their checking deposits as excess reserves, regardless of the interest rate. In the questions that follow, use the "money multiplier" equation from Problem 11.

a. Consider the balance sheet of one of several identical banks:

Assets	Liabilities & Net Worth
Reserves \$400	Checking Deposits \$2,000
Loans \$1,600	Net Worth \$0

What is the required reserve ratio in the country of Sylvania?

b. If the total money stock (supply) is \$100,000, find the total amount of reserves held in the banking system. Show your work.

c. The Sylvania Central Bank decides that it wants to cut the money stock in half. It is considering an open market operation. How many dollars' worth of bonds should the Central Bank buy or sell? Assume that excess reserves are 5 percent and the required reserve ratio is what you found in part (a). Show your work.

28 Macroeconomics and International Trade

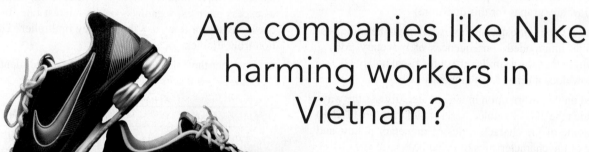

Are companies like Nike harming workers in Vietnam?

Consumers love sneakers. Nike alone sells approximately $15 billion of them each year. Nike conducts much of its production in places like Vietnam, using subcontractors that employ workers with little education who are paid around $4–$5 per day. Some subcontractors even employ children, although it is illegal to do so and Nike officially bans such practices. Employees in many of these factories put in 60-hour work weeks with working conditions that do not come close to meeting U.S. and European safety standards. Critics denounce such sweatshops and student groups have occasionally advocated boycotts of Nike products. Prodded by these protestors, Nike has tried to clean up its act. Even though the Nike subcontractors still pay very little, the factories have become much safer over the past 20 years.

This situation is just the tip of the iceberg of low wages and poor working conditions throughout parts of the interconnected global economy. U.S. consumers are some of the beneficiaries of this trade. Are consumers to blame for buying sneakers manufactured in sweatshops?

CHAPTER OUTLINE

KEY IDEAS

☀ International trade enables countries to focus on activities in which they have a comparative advantage.

☀ The current account includes international flows from exports, imports, factor payments, and transfers.

☀ If a country runs a current account deficit, it pays for this by giving its trading partners financial IOUs. If a country runs a current account surplus, it receives financial IOUs from its trading partners.

☀ The world has become more globalized over the past several decades.

28.1 Why and How We Trade

Trade, both within and between countries, enhances our quality of life by increasing the efficiency of production. In modern economies, goods and services are produced by individuals who specialize in their production. For example, your professor spent years mastering economics. Similarly, the engineers who work for Apple have extensive training in their particular line of work.

An Apple engineer can't produce insightful economics research or teach an economics course. Likewise, an economics professor can't design a miniaturized circuit board and a high throughput factory to manufacture it. In a market system, people choose occupations that suit their talents and interests. Then they develop specialized skills in their chosen industry and trade with others. Trade exploits **gains from specialization**, which are the economic gains that society obtains by having some workers specialize in specific productive activities.

Specialization won't work without trade. Economics professors can't eat economic ideas or live in them. Economists teach, and then get paid with money, and then use the money to buy food and shelter. Apple engineers love the iPhone, but they can't sleep on it or drive it to work. Engineers get paid so they can buy what they want.

Without opportunities for trade, life is bleak. If your economics professor were stranded on an island, he or she would have no students to teach and no policymakers to advise. The professor would have little or no way to put economic knowledge to use. Despite all of that knowledge, day-to-day life would resemble that of a Stone Age hunter-gatherer.

Gains from specialization are the economic gains that society can obtain by having some individuals, regions, or countries specialize in the production of certain goods and services.

> **Without opportunities for trade, life is bleak.**

An economy without trade wasn't great for this castaway.

Absolute Advantage and Comparative Advantage

To gain a deeper understanding of how trade works, consider the late Steve Jobs, the visionary chief executive officer (CEO) of Apple. Jobs was famous for being a great marketer and a brilliant designer.

Because of his knowledge of and love for Apple products, Jobs was a much better salesperson than most of Apple's employees. To illustrate this point, let's assume that Jobs could sell twice as many computers (per time period) compared to the typical Apple storeclerk. In this sense, Jobs had an *absolute advantage* at selling

Exhibit 28.1 Productivity in Sales and Design

	Steve Jobs	Chuck Chores
Sales	2,000 sales/year	1,000 sales/year
Design	1,000 design ideas/year	1 design idea/year

A producer has an **absolute advantage** in producing a good or service if the producer can produce more units per hour than other producers.

computers. A producer has an **absolute advantage** in producing a good or service if the producer can produce more units per hour than other producers.

Of course, selling computers isn't the only skill that Jobs had. As CEO, he *designed* revolutionary new products. Relative to a typical salesclerk, Jobs was a superstar designer. Let's assume that if Jobs allocated his time to design, he would generate 1,000 design ideas per year. If a typical salesclerk worked on design, he would generate only one design idea per year.

Let's give the typical Apple salesclerk a name: Chuck Chores. Exhibit 28.1 reports the estimated productivity of Jobs in the first column of data and the estimated productivity of Chores in the final column.

By looking across the rows of Exhibit 28.1, we see that Jobs has an absolute advantage in both tasks: Jobs was capable of producing twice as many sales per year (relative to Chores) and Jobs was capable of producing 1,000 times as many useful design ideas per year (relative to Chores). Which task should Apple have asked him to do?

To answer this question, let's calculate the opportunity cost *per unit of production* or, more precisely, the opportunity cost of a design idea in terms of forgone sales. This calculation will answer the following question: how many sales are given up to produce a design idea? A worker has a *comparative advantage* in design when the opportunity cost of the worker's design idea is lower than the opportunity cost of other workers' design ideas. More generally, a worker has a **comparative advantage** in producing a good (or service) when he has a lower opportunity cost per unit produced compared to other producers.

A producer has a **comparative advantage** in producing a good (or service) when the producer has a lower opportunity cost per unit produced compared to other producers.

Exhibit 28.1 implies that Steve Jobs forgoes 2,000 sales for every 1,000 design ideas that he generates, or 2,000/1,000 = 2 forgone sales per design idea. On the other hand, Chuck Chores forgoes 1,000 sales for every design idea that he generates.

With that calculation in mind, we can determine how production should be optimally organized. Apple can produce design ideas by allocating Jobs to design, with an opportunity cost of 2 forgone sales per design idea. Or Apple can produce design ideas from Chores with an opportunity cost of 1,000 forgone sales per design idea. Since Jobs has a lower opportunity cost for *each* design idea (2 forgone sales for Jobs versus 1,000 forgone sales for Chores), Jobs has a *comparative advantage in design ideas*. Hence, Apple should allocate Jobs to work on design and Chores to work on sales (as long as it needs both types of activities).

You can verify that the same conclusion would have been reached if we calculated the opportunity cost of a sale in terms of forgone design ideas. Using Exhibit 28.1, we find that Jobs forgoes 1,000 design ideas for every 2,000 sales. Because 1,000/2,000 = ½, Jobs has an opportunity cost of ½ forgone design idea per sale. Chores forgoes 1 design idea for every 1,000 sales, so Chores has an opportunity cost of 1/1,000 forgone design idea per sale. Because Chores has the lower opportunity cost per sale, he should be the one doing sales and Jobs should work on design.

Comparative advantage is the idea that *opportunity cost, not absolute advantage, should be used to determine which producer is assigned to which task.* Just relying on absolute advantage would not have been sufficient for Apple to determine whether Jobs should work in design or in sales: Jobs has an absolute advantage in working as a salesclerk *and* he has an absolute advantage in working as a designer.

Until now, we have assumed that the work allocation decision is being made by Apple. Although such decisions are sometimes made by corporations, in practice they are often the result of choices that individuals make for themselves. Jobs himself decided to found Apple and work as a designer, while many individuals such as Chores apply to become salesclerks, not designers. Why is this?

The career choices that individuals make are also a consequence of comparative advantage, but, in this case, the key economic signals are market prices. In fact, one of the powerful implications of comparative advantage is that market prices will induce individuals to choose occupations and activities that line up with their comparative advantage.

To see this, suppose that Jobs and Chores sell their skills in a competitive labor market in which their wages are equal to their (personal) contribution to value added (recall from Chapter 19 that value added is defined as a firm's sales revenue minus the firm's purchases of intermediate products from other firms). To simplify the analysis, suppose that the economy consists *only* of workers like Jobs and Chores and that the economy needs both design and sales functions to be performed. We will now see that equilibrium prices must be such that workers with productivity similar to Jobs will choose to work in design and those with productivity similar to Chores will choose to work in sales.

Let's start by assuming that the prices in this economy are such that the value added from each computer sale is $50 and the value added from each design idea is also $50. If you multiply output in Exhibit 28.1 by value added per task, you'll generate the results in panel (a) of Exhibit 28.2. These numbers imply that both Jobs and Chores will maximize their own wages if they work in sales: $100,000 for Jobs in sales versus $50,000 for Jobs in design; $50,000 for Chores in sales versus $50 for Chores in design. Hence, workers like Jobs and workers like Chores will both work in sales. But this cannot be a market equilibrium because the economy needs both functions—design and sales—to be performed. If everyone is working in sales, there will be no design ideas in this economy, pushing the value added from design much higher than $50 (there would be a shortage of design, raising the relative wages of designers).

What happens if market prices for design become much higher so that value added from each design idea now shoots up to $100,000 (holding fixed value added from sales at $50)? The resulting wages are shown in panel (b) of Exhibit 28.2. Now we have a situation in which both Jobs and Chores have higher wages in design, thus all workers in this economy will now choose design careers. But this also cannot be a market equilibrium. Now there will be no sales in the economy and a lot of design ideas. Yet again the economy needs both functions to be performed, and this will push the relative wages of salespeople higher.

You have probably already guessed that equilibrium prices will need to settle somewhere between these two extremes. Equilibrium prices should induce some people to do design and some others to do sales. Take another combination of values: $50 of value added per sale and $5,000 of value added per design idea. The resulting wages are shown in panel (c) of Exhibit 28.2. At these wages, it is clear that Chores will choose to work in sales while Jobs focuses on design. Indeed, at these wages Jobs would be greatly misallocating his time if he worked as a salesclerk.

The key insight is that market prices will adjust so that individuals choose occupations consistent with their comparative advantages. This is the sense in which trade in the market supports and reinforces comparative advantage. In fact, without such trade we could not realize the gains from comparative advantage. For example, it is trade that allowed Steve Jobs to hire other people to work as salesclerks in Apple stores, enabling him to focus on his comparative advantage: designing the next beautiful gizmo that everyone wants to have.

At this point, you might be curious about whether one could have picked a value added for each sale and a value added for each design that would make Jobs choose sales while Chores would prefer to do design. Comparative advantage implies that the answer is no.

Exhibit 28.2 Wages in Sales and Design

(a) With Value Added of $50 from Sales and $50 from Design		Steve Jobs	Chuck Chores
	Sales	$100,000/year	$50,000/year
	Design	$50,000/year	$50/year

(b) With Value Added of $50 from Sales and $100,000 from Design		Steve Jobs	Chuck Chores
	Sales	$100,000/year	$50,000/year
	Design	$100,000,000/year	$100,000/year

(c) With Value Added of $50 from Sales and $5,000 from Design		Steve Jobs	Chuck Chores
	Sales	$100,000/year	$50,000/year
	Design	$5,000,000/year	$5,000/year

Steve Jobs, Apple's most productive salesclerk.

If their different opportunity costs lead Jobs and Chores to choose different tasks, comparative advantage always implies it will be Jobs who earns more in design than in sales, and Chores who earns more in sales than in design.

Comparative Advantage and International Trade

To illustrate how *international* trade exploits comparative advantage—much like the division of labor between Steve Jobs and Chuck Chores—consider a particular Apple product, the iPod. In some sense, the iPod is a U.S. product—designed by engineers in the United States by a company headquartered in the United States. However, it is not actually manufactured in the United States. Each iPod is composed of hundreds of parts, most of which are manufactured and assembled outside the United States.

Let's consider some of the key components. The iPod has a hard drive where the songs and videos and photos are stored. This is produced in Japan. It also has a memory card, which is produced in Korea. The central processing unit, on the other hand, is produced in the United States. Specialization explains this proliferation of locations. For example, the Japanese company Toshiba specializes in hard drive manufacturing and has become a world leader in the production of tiny hard drives with very low failure rates. Gains from specialization are realized by delegating production of two of these three key parts to manufacturers outside the United States. Finally, all of the components are combined into the final product on a Chinese assembly line.[1]

Comparative advantage in international trade explains why Chinese workers assemble iPods, even though U.S. workers have an absolute advantage in assembly. Let's begin by considering the hourly productivity of U.S. and Chinese workers in different tasks. For the moment, we'll assume that in terms of their productivity, the U.S. workers are all identical to one another and the Chinese workers are also all identical to one another—a simplifying assumption that we'll revisit later in the chapter.

The first row of Exhibit 28.3 shows that a U.S. worker would assemble 20,000 iPods per year, which is 15,000 more than a Chinese worker would assemble. The difference between U.S. and Chinese workers in their productivity arises for a variety of reasons. Workers in the United States currently have relatively more education and thus greater *human capital* (recall from Chapter 20 that human capital is each person's stock of ability to produce output or economic value). This greater human capital makes U.S. workers more productive in a range of tasks. In addition, U.S. workers currently have access to more physical capital per worker and better technology—for instance, robotic assembly lines—than their Chinese counterparts.

Consider another task, which we refer to as research and development, or R&D. We assume that U.S. workers generate 10 R&D innovations per year. We assume that Chinese workers, who currently don't have as much education as U.S. workers, would be much less effective at this, and we assume that their productivity in R&D is 1 innovation per year.

Looking across the rows in Exhibit 28.3, we see that U.S. workers have an absolute advantage in both assembly and R&D. Considering only absolute advantage, it's tempting to guess that both assembly and R&D should be performed in the United States. But this is the wrong conclusion for the same reason that Steve Jobs shouldn't have been working as a salesclerk.

To determine the optimal allocation across industries, we again need to use the concepts of opportunity cost and comparative advantage. We can verify that U.S. workers have a comparative advantage in R&D. Their productivity in assembly relative to R&D is 20,000/10 = 2,000/1. In other words, U.S. workers forgo the assembly of 2,000 iPods for every R&D innovation they generate. Chinese workers' productivity in assembly relative to R&D is 5,000/1. Chinese workers forgo the assembly of 5,000 iPods for

Exhibit 28.3 **Productivity in Assembly and R&D (Research and Development)**		**U.S. Worker**	**Chinese Worker**
	Assembly	20,000 iPods/year	5,000 iPods/year
	Research and Development	10 innovations/year	1 innovation/year

Exhibit 28.4 Wages in Assembly and R&D		U.S. Worker	Chinese Worker
	Assembly	$30,000/year	$7,500/year
	Research and Development	$50,000/year	$5,000/year

every R&D innovation they generate. The U.S. workers thus have a lower opportunity cost per R&D innovation (2,000 forgone iPod assemblies) compared to Chinese workers (5,000 forgone iPod assemblies). This implies that U.S. workers have a comparative advantage in R&D and should focus on R&D, while Chinese workers should (currently) specialize in assembly.

To further illustrate the allocation of tasks between U.S. and Chinese workers, suppose that workers in both economies are paid the value added they generate and that the value added from each iPod assembly is $1.50 and the value added from each R&D innovation is $5,000. If you multiply output in Exhibit 28.3 by value added per task, you'll generate the results in Exhibit 28.4, which describes annual wages of U.S. and Chinese workers in assembly and R&D.

iPod assembly line in China.

Looking at Exhibit 28.4, you can see that the U.S. worker will choose to specialize in R&D and the Chinese worker will specialize in assembly. In fact, for the same reasons that we highlighted in our discussion of the allocation problem of Steve Jobs and Chuck Chores, value added and market prices cannot be such that both U.S. and Chinese workers all have greater value added in assembly or such that they all have greater value added in R&D, because otherwise the world economy would not generate *both* iPod assemblies and R&D ideas. Given the current pattern of comparative advantage (in R&D for U.S. workers and in iPod assembly for Chinese workers), if these workers are choosing different tasks, then it must be the case that it is the U.S. workers who are specializing in R&D and the Chinese workers who are working in assembly.

As in our earlier example, trade is essential to achieve an efficient allocation of resources. If there were no international trade, then U.S. workers would end up spending less time on R&D and more time on assembly, lowering the value of their total output.

Efficiency and Winners and Losers from Trade

By exploiting comparative advantage, international trade increases overall economic efficiency. For example, if Apple could not assemble iPods in foreign countries, it would have to do so in the United States, and the cost of making an iPod would rise. As a result, iPods would likely cost 10 percent or 20 percent more than they do now. Consumers benefit from international trade and the resulting international division of labor.

At this point you might wonder whether foreign iPod production prevents the United States from benefiting from its own innovation. How much of the value added from iPod manufacturing goes to foreign producers and not to the iPod's U.S. inventors? Of course, even if all of the value added went to foreign workers, U.S. consumers would still benefit from the low cost of an iPod. But is a low retail price the only benefit that U.S. residents receive?

A study by economists Greg Linden, Kenneth Kraemer, and Jason Dedrick shows that a large part of the retail price of an iPod is ultimately received by U.S. residents.[2] For iPods sold in the United States through a retailer other than Apple, 41 percent of the value added is generated by U.S. firms other than Apple, including distributors, retailers, and component manufacturers with domestic production facilities. Another 45 percent of the value added goes to Apple, the company that designed the iPod and owns the intellectual property rights. These are not just corporate earnings, since Apple has a large team of in-house engineers, designers, and executives whose salaries are paid with Apple's revenues.

The example of the iPod illustrates that international trade contributes to value added in the United States as well as low prices for U.S. consumers.

The iPod story is not unusual. Other products confirm the same pattern of widely shared benefits from trade. For example, Hewlett-Packard's laptop computers are assembled in low-wage countries like China and Brazil. Nevertheless, over half of the value added from the production of these laptops accrues to residents of the United States.

> **Though international trade achieves a more efficient allocation of resources . . . in any given instance, trade will produce some winners and some losers.**

This doesn't mean that everybody gains from trade. Though international trade achieves a more efficient allocation of resources and creates potential gains for society as a whole, in any given instance, trade will produce some winners and some losers. We can see this by going back to the issue of U.S.-China trade. When we discussed the gains from exploiting comparative advantage, we talked of the typical U.S. worker. In practice, of course, the United States isn't inhabited by "typical" U.S. workers, but by some U.S. workers with high levels of skill, and others with low levels of skill and a comparative advantage in assembly. International trade causes routine assembly jobs to move to developing countries like China, and as a result, there are many fewer assembly jobs performed in the United States today than three decades ago. If they can no longer find assembly jobs, those U.S. workers with a comparative advantage in assembly are made worse off by the outsourcing of assembly jobs to countries like China. This is illustrated by our Evidence-Based Economics feature in Chapter 23, which showed how workers in areas specializing in products competing with Chinese imports have experienced employment losses.

When considering the consequences of opening a country to free international trade, it is important to recognize that within that country there will be winners and losers. The efficiencies achieved by exploiting comparative advantage and specialization are so great that the winners will be far more numerous than the losers. In principle, the winners could compensate the losers so that everyone would be better off as a result of free trade. In practice, however, this is usually not possible, because it is hard for the government to identify how much each person has gained or lost as a consequence of international trade. Hence, the government can't compensate the losers with targeted individual subsidies. With imperfect targeting or no compensating redistribution by the government, many people do end up on the losing side of the ledger. Nevertheless, because many more end up on the winning side, open international trade still tends to be favored by economists.

How We Trade

To realize the gains from comparative advantage and specialization, the United States and China need to trade goods and services. This takes the form of *imports* and *exports*. Recall from Chapter 19 that imports refer to the goods and services that are produced abroad and sold domestically, and exports are the goods and services that are produced domestically and sold abroad. Thus exports from the United States to China are China's imports from the United States.

In theory it is possible for a country not to have any exports or imports. Such a country that doesn't trade—that is, does not have any imports or exports—is said to be a **closed economy**. Today, not a single country has an entirely closed economy, but North Korea, a totalitarian dictatorship with mostly closed borders, comes the closest.

A **closed economy** does not trade with the rest of the world.

An **open economy** trades freely with the rest of the world.

An **open economy** allows international trade, and in most countries such trade amounts to a significant share of GDP. For example, in 2012, the United Kingdom's imports equaled 34 percent of GDP, double the import share in the United States. But neither country could compete with Hong Kong and Singapore, which each had 2012 imports equaling about 200 percent of GDP. Hong Kong and Singapore have such large import shares since many of their imports are later re-exported with only modest value added domestically. For example, if a country imports $200 of electronic parts and assembles them into a $250 smart phone, then the value added is just $50. In this illustrative example, imports are 4 times the level of GDP (because only value added is counted in GDP). If the assembled phone is later exported, then exports ($250) are 5 times the level of value added.

28.1

28.2

28.3

Exhibit 28.5 U.S. Imports and Exports as a Share of GDP from 1929 to 2013

The U.S. economy has become more open over the last 80 years, with its share of imports to GDP rising from around 4 percent to around 16 percent.

Source: Bureau of Economic Analysis, National Income and Product Accounts.

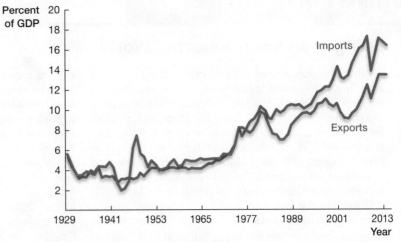

Exhibit 28.5 depicts the evolution of U.S. imports and exports as a share of GDP since 1929. In 1950, imports amounted to 4 percent of GDP. In 2013, the import share was 16 percent. Economically speaking, the United States is now more closely linked to the rest of the world than at any other period in U.S. history.

The increase in imports and exports as a share of GDP is not confined to the United States. Most major economies in the world have been trading more over the last 50 years. Exhibit 28.6 plots the evolution of imports as a share of GDP for Germany, China, India, and the world average, as well as the United States.

Trade Barriers: Tariffs

Because international trade creates winners and losers, there are some opponents to trade. As a result, most countries, including the United States, impose a host of *trade barriers* that reduce their imports. The most common restrictions are tariffs, which are special taxes levied only on imports.

The average U.S. tariff on all imported products was 2.8 percent in 2011, down from over 5 percent in 1990. The average 2011 tariff of 2.8 percent masked an enormous amount of variation across industries. In recent years, the average U.S. tariff on agricultural products has been 62 percent. Tariffs on tobacco have run to approximately 90 percent, while tariffs on sugar have been even higher, sometimes exceeding 100 percent. Such tariffs naturally

Exhibit 28.6 The Ratio of Imports to GDP in Four Large Economies and in the Total World Economy

Most major economies, including the United States, have been trading more over the last 50 years. This is a reflection of the process of globalization, which has generated a steady increase in the value of international trade flows relative to GDP.

Source: Bureau of Economic Analysis, National Income and Product Accounts; and World Bank DataBank: World Development Indicators.

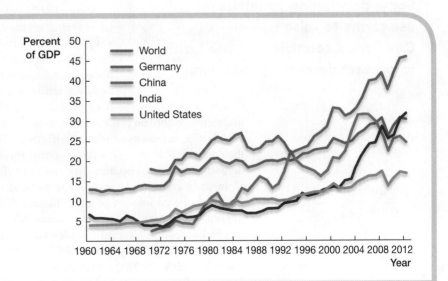

LETTING THE DATA SPEAK

Living in an Interconnected World

Given the importance of specialization and comparative advantage, the world is highly interconnected through imports and exports. The first and most obvious facet of this interconnection is the array of goods and services we consume. Look at the shelves of your local Walmart and you will find an enormous number of items made in China, Mexico, and Brazil. Two-thirds of the goods sold in Walmart are imported. For example, Walmart annually imports over $30 billion worth of goods from China.

Check out the geography of trade whenever you go shopping. You'll be amazed at the range of countries that manufacture the goods you buy. You may think of Pakistan only as a hotbed of political and religious unrest on the border of Afghanistan. Pakistan also happens to manufacture *half* of the world's hand-stitched soccer balls. Pakistan is also an important exporter of textiles and clothing. Look at the latest fashions on display at Banana Republic or Old Navy, and you will see that much of this clothing is produced in India, Indonesia, Turkey, and Vietnam.

Many people mistakenly believe that international trade can only flow in goods. Services, however, are also getting into the act. In 2013, the United States imported $453 billion in services and exported $682 billion in services. The next time you call a computer company for advice about removing a virus or upgrading software, ask the technician where he or she is located. There's a good chance you are speaking to someone in India, where service representatives carefully hone American accents and adopt American names during working hours. Carol Miller might be Bhumika Chaturvedi.

Many of the services that now flow across international boundaries are very sophisticated. The United States exports entertainment services—music and movies—and financial services—financial advice given by a New York investment bank to an oil exploration company in Brazil.

Even medical services can be traded internationally. An Indian radiologist—a physician specializing in reading X-rays—earns one-eighth of a U.S. radiologist's income. So an Indian radiologist has a lower opportunity cost of time than a U.S. radiologist. There is a small group of Indian teleradiologists who read X-rays for hospitals in the United States, United Kingdom, and Singapore. Here's how it works. A patient who is a resident of the United Kingdom has an X-ray taken at a U.K. hospital. The images are uploaded to a teleradiologist in Bangalore, India. The teleradiologist examines the X-ray for abnormalities, like tumors, writes a report, and then sends it back to the patient's U.K. physician.

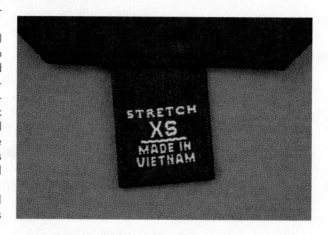

> Some developing countries use tariffs to raise revenue. . . . Developed countries . . . use tariffs to protect domestic producers.

discourage international trade. Due to tariffs and trade barriers, U.S. sugar imports have fallen 80 percent over the last 30 years.

Some *developing* countries use tariffs to raise revenue, because they don't have well-functioning tax systems and can more easily tax imports that flow through a few urban ports than they can tax domestic economic activity that is widely geographically dispersed. On the other hand, *developed* countries overwhelmingly use tariffs to protect domestic producers. In fact, some tariffs are set at such a high level that they block imports completely and therefore raise no revenue since there are no imports to tax. Powerful domestic producers lobby governments to impose tariffs that will drive out foreign competition and increase the domestic industry's profits. Of course, this benefit to the domestic industry is a cost to domestic consumers, because they end up paying higher prices.

In some cases, trade wars create comical inefficiencies. In the 1960s, Germany and France restricted imports of U.S. chickens. The U.S. retaliated with a punitive tariff on imports of European light trucks. Today, Mercedes-Benz assembles light trucks at a factory in Dusseldorf, Germany and tests the trucks to verify that they drive properly. Then Mercedes-Benz partially disassembles the trucks by removing the engines, bumpers, driveshafts, fuel tanks, and exhaust systems. The trucks are exported to the United States, where Mercedes-Benz doesn't need to pay the U.S. tariff, because the trucks aren't fully assembled. At a warehouse in South Carolina, the disassembled parts are screwed on again.[3]

Tariffs and Votes

In March 2002, President George W. Bush imposed 8 percent to 30 percent tariffs on steel imports. The move was widely viewed as a political decision to shore up support among industrial states that might switch party allegiance in the November midterm election. If you ran for office, would you do the same thing, even if you believe in the benefits of trade?

The U.S. trade representative, Robert B. Zoellick, even admitted during a speech in Brazil that political calculations had motivated the new tariffs: "We are committed to moving forward with free trade, but, like Brazil, we have to manage political support for free trade at home. We have to create coalitions." The administration maintained the tariffs despite a flood of world-wide criticism and threats among many countries to erect punitive tariffs in response. One month after the U.S. election, the administration reversed itself and removed the tariffs.[4]

28.2 The Current Account and the Financial Account

In 2013, U.S. imports amounted to $2,746 billion. Of this amount, $456 billion was imported from China. In most years, approximately 1/7th of U.S. imports come from China.

In 2013, the United States exported goods and services worth $2,271 billion. That year, U.S. exports to China were $157 billion. Approximately 1/20th of U.S. exports go to China.

To some pundits, the fact that the United States imports more from China than it exports to China is a sign of a serious problem. However, there is no reason to expect that U.S. exports to China should equal U.S. imports from China, in the same way that there is no reason to expect your own purchases from the grocery store to equal the grocery store owner's purchases from you. If you own a Ford dealership and the grocery store owner loves Cadillacs, then you'll never get a dollar of her business. But that's OK as long as there are other people who are interested in buying your Fords.

That's generally the way that markets and exchanges work. There is no need to sell our goods and services to the same people from whom we buy goods and services. Now apply that idea to a national economy. There is nothing necessarily wrong with the fact that the United States as a whole sells relatively little *to* China and still buys a lot *from* China. There are other countries, like Brazil, to which the United States sells lots of stuff and from which the United States buys relatively little. These facts lead us to the observation that trade between two specific countries—also referred to as bilateral trade—will rarely be balanced. This does not imply that there is absolutely *nothing* wrong with the United States–China trade relationship, but these arguments do imply that a bilateral trade imbalance is not necessarily a bad thing.

Trade Surpluses and Trade Deficits

There is another important sense in which trade can be imbalanced. Sometimes a country imports more or less than it exports to the world as a whole. We'll see that even this imbalance can also be socially desirable, though it depends on the reasons for the trade imbalance.

When a country as a whole imports more from abroad than it exports abroad, the country runs a trade deficit. This is a case of spending on imports more than the country earns from exports. Exports minus imports is defined as **net exports** or the **trade balance**. When the trade balance is positive, it is referred to as a **trade surplus**. When the trade balance is negative, it is called a **trade deficit**. In 2013, U.S. net exports were negative, so the United States ran a trade deficit:

$$\text{Net exports} = \text{Exports} \quad - \quad \text{Imports}$$
$$= \$2{,}271 \text{ billion} - \$2{,}746 \text{ billion} = -\$475 \text{ billion}.$$

Net exports are the value of the country's exports minus the value of its imports. Net exports are also known as the **trade balance**.

A **trade surplus** is an excess of exports over imports and is thus the name given to the trade balance when it is positive.

A **trade deficit** is an excess of imports over exports and is thus the name given to the trade balance when it is negative.

International Financial Flows

It might appear that knowing the value of the trade balance is sufficient for understanding how payments flow from one country to another. However, a complete understanding of international financial flows requires more details. We need to study *all* the sources of payments from foreign residents to domestic residents, and all the sources of payments from domestic residents to foreign residents. Trade flows represent only *one* source of these financial payments.

The international accounting system is built upon the concept of residency, not the concept of citizenship. In this accounting system, domestic *residents* are people who reside in the United States, whether or not they are U.S. citizens. So a Japanese citizen living in the United States is defined as a domestic resident of the United States in the official international trade accounts. Residents of foreign countries—we'll call them "foreigners"—are people who reside outside the United States (some of whom are U.S. citizens living abroad).

Income-Based Payments from Foreigners   Let's start with income-based payments from foreigners. There are three ways that domestic residents receive income-based payments from foreigners:

1. Receiving payments from the sale of goods and services to foreigners—*exports*
2. Receiving income from assets that the domestic resident owns in foreign countries—*factor payments from foreigners*
3. Receiving transfers from individuals who reside abroad or from foreign governments—*transfers from foreigners*

Recall that *exports* are the goods and services that domestic residents produce and then sell in foreign countries. When a foreign resident receives these goods and services, he directly or indirectly makes a payment to the domestic resident who produced them.

Factor payments from foreigners represent the payments that domestic residents receive from assets owned in foreign countries. For example, if a U.S. resident owns stock in Tata Steel, one of the largest companies in India, and Tata Steel pays a dividend, that dividend payment would count as a factor payment from abroad. Likewise, if a U.S. company owns a plant in China and that plant generates earnings, those earnings would count as a factor payment from abroad. Or, if a U.S. engineer who *resides* in the United States spends a day working in Turin, Italy, where she consults for Fiat, the payment that she receives from Fiat would count as a factor payment from abroad. In this consulting example, the relevant factor of production is human capital.

Transfers from foreigners are "gifts" from foreign residents or foreign governments. For example, following Hurricane Katrina in 2005, China sent 104 tons of emergency supplies to New Orleans, including tents and generators, valued at $5 million. All told, foreign governments and citizens of foreign countries sent hundreds of millions of dollars of aid to support the victims of Hurricane Katrina; contributions like these are transfers from abroad.

Income-Based Payments to Foreigners   There are also similar types of financial flows that move in the opposite direction. We now list all of the sources of income-based payments *to* foreigners:

1. Making payments to foreigners in return for their goods and services—*imports*
2. Paying income on assets that foreign residents own in the domestic economy—*factor payments to foreigners*
3. Making transfers to individuals who reside abroad or to foreign governments—*transfers to foreigners*

Imports are the goods and services that foreigners produce and then sell to domestic residents. *Factor payments to foreigners* represent the payments made to foreigners who own assets in the domestic economy. *Transfers to foreigners* are "gifts," which include foreign aid from the U.S. government, donations from U.S. citizens to foreign charitable organizations, and remittances from legal and illegal residents of the United States. For example, a Mexican citizen who permanently resides in the United States and periodically transfers money back to family members in Mexico is making a transfer to foreigners. In this case, the transfer is just the money that is sent to family members in Mexico, and not the total earnings that the Mexican citizen receives for work that she does in the United States.

The Workings of the Current Account and the Financial Account

The **current account** is the sum of net exports, net factor payments from abroad, and net transfers from abroad.

The **current account** adds together these different sources of payments into and out of a country. It consists of the sum of net exports, net factor payments from abroad, and net transfers from abroad.

$$\text{Net exports} = (\text{Payments from abroad for exports})$$
$$- (\text{Payments to foreigners for imports})$$

$$\text{Net factor payments from abroad} = (\text{Factor payments from abroad})$$
$$- (\text{Factor payments to foreigners})$$

$$\text{Net transfers from abroad} = (\text{Transfers from abroad}) - (\text{Transfers to foreigners})$$

The current account is the net flow of payments made to domestic residents from foreign residents.

$$\text{Current Account} = (\text{Net exports}) + (\text{Net factor payments from abroad})$$
$$+ (\text{Net transfers from abroad}).$$

It is important to bear in mind that any of these net flows could be *negative,* which would correspond to a net flow of payments *to* foreign residents. In fact, in 2013, the United States did run a current account deficit of $379 billion. In other words, U.S. residents paid foreigners $379 billion more than foreigners paid U.S. residents.

Exhibit 28.7 breaks down the current account deficit for the United States in 2013 into its three components. The current account is shown in the top box. We'll discuss the bottom box—the financial account—a bit later. Focusing on the top box, we can see that trade in goods and services led to net payments of $475 billion to foreigners. Factor payments led to net payments of $229 billion from foreigners to U.S. residents. Finally, net transfer payments led to net payments to foreigners of $133 billion. Adding these up, and remembering to use a negative sign when net payments are made to foreigners, we come up with a total current account *deficit* of $379 billion.

MyEconLab Real-time data

	Payments from Foreigners	Payments to Foreigners	Net Payments
Trade in goods and services	2,271	2,746	−475
Factor payments	789	560	229
Transfer payments			−133
Current account			−379
Financial account			379

Exhibit 28.7 The Current Account and the Financial Account of the United States in 2013 (in Billions of 2013 Dollars)

The current account (top box in red) is the sum of net exports, net factor payments from abroad, and net transfers from abroad. (The U.S. government does not break down transfer payments into gross flows, so only the net flow is reported here.) The financial account mirrors the current account and represents the change in IOUs resulting from current account transactions.

Source: Bureau of Economic Analysis, National Income and Product Accounts.

What are the consequences of running a current account deficit? When U.S. residents make $379 billion of net payments to foreigners, the payments are made in U.S. dollars. These dollars enable the foreign residents to buy U.S. assets, which can be exchanged for U.S. goods and services at some point in the future.

To understand what this means in practice, consider a simple current account transaction that we illustrate in Exhibit 28.8. Suppose a U.S. consumer decides to buy a Chinese laptop that costs $1,000. In effect, the U.S. consumer gives the Chinese laptop manufacturer $1,000. In the U.S. current account, this amount would show up as a $1,000 payment to foreigners. Exhibit 28.8 illustrates this current account transaction by showing the purchase of the $1,000 laptop.

Now suppose that there is *no* offsetting transaction in which China buys goods and services from the United States, so the $1,000 payment can be thought of as a current account deficit. Instead of importing $1,000 of goods and services from the United States, China saves the $1,000, thereby preserving that purchasing power for *future* purchases of goods and services. For example, the Chinese company could use the $1,000 to buy a specific U.S. asset from U.S. residents, for instance a U.S. Treasury bond. This is the case depicted in the circular flow of Exhibit 28.8.

Let's summarize the flows in Exhibit 28.8. At the end of the international transactions depicted here, the United States has one new laptop and owns one less Treasury bond. In the current account, the U.S. has imported goods worth $1,000. In the **financial account**, the U.S. has transferred to China a Treasury bond worth $1,000. The financial account is defined as the increase in domestic assets held by foreigners minus the increase in foreign assets held domestically. The financial account is just the accounting system that records the asset purchases that domestic residents and foreigners make. The financial account is defined so that *the net flows in the financial account offset the net flows in the current account.* (To keep the analysis simple, we have omitted a few other details in the accounting rules.)

The following two equations give the definition of the financial account and describe its relationship with the current account:

$$\text{Financial account} = (\text{Increase in domestic assets held by foreigners})$$
$$- (\text{Increase in foreign assets held domestically}).$$

$$(\text{Current account}) + (\text{Financial account}) = 0.$$

When foreigners receive net payments in the current account, they can buy any type of U.S. asset in the financial account. In the example that we already discussed, they bought U.S. Treasury bonds. But they could also just hold the payment in dollars (in a bank account) as a claim against the United States. In either case, the current account deficit is exactly offset by a financial account surplus.

The **financial account** is the increase in domestic assets held by foreigners minus the increase in foreign assets held domestically.

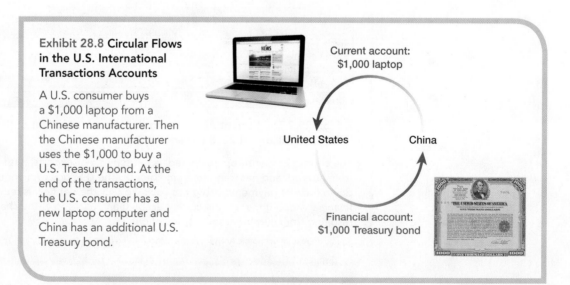

Exhibit 28.8 Circular Flows in the U.S. International Transactions Accounts

A U.S. consumer buys a $1,000 laptop from a Chinese manufacturer. Then the Chinese manufacturer uses the $1,000 to buy a U.S. Treasury bond. At the end of the transactions, the U.S. consumer has a new laptop computer and China has an additional U.S. Treasury bond.

Current account: $1,000 laptop

United States   China

Financial account: $1,000 Treasury bond

Now we are ready to reconsider Exhibit 28.7, which shows the current account for the United States in 2013. As required by the accounting identities, the financial account perfectly offsets the current account. In 2013, foreigners received $379 billion in net payments in the current account, corresponding to a current account deficit. In return, the financial account indicates that U.S. residents gave foreigners $379 billion in assets (including dollar-denominated deposits).

This isn't necessarily bad news for U.S. residents. It was a trade. Residents of the United States got Sony TV sets, Louis Vuitton handbags, BMWs, and hundreds of thousands of other imported goods and services. Foreigners obtained bank deposits and other assets worth $379 billion from residents of the United States.

When a country runs a current account deficit, it is analogous to what takes place when a single household spends more than it earns. To fund this extra spending, the household either borrows or spends down assets that had previously been accumulated. For example, suppose you spend $1,000 more than you earn from all sources, including labor income, asset income, and transfers. If you already have some assets in the bank, say $3,000 in your checking account, you could finance the extra $1,000 of consumption by running down those assets so that at the end of the year you would have only $2,000 left in your checking account. Or if you do not have such assets to spend down, you could borrow. If you start without any assets and without any debt, you would borrow $1,000, so your net asset position would become −$1,000. Notice that regardless of what your asset position was at the beginning, you are financing your $1,000 shortfall by reducing your asset position by $1,000—either from $3,000 to $2,000 or from zero to −$1,000.

> **Just like an individual household, an entire country can only spend more than it earns if it finds a way to fund the extra spending.**

The situation is identical for a country, which must also finance its net exports by running down its assets or borrowing. This fact highlights a central concept in international accounting: just like an individual household, an entire country can only spend more than it earns if it finds a way to fund the extra spending. The country must either sell assets to foreigners or borrow from foreigners. Hence, current account deficits must match financial account flows. In other words, when a country makes net purchases of goods and services from foreigners, the country must make net asset sales to foreigners to pay the bill.

28.3 International Trade, Technology Transfer, and Economic Growth

International trade benefits countries not just through specialization and comparative advantage. It is also a conduit for the transfer of technology from more advanced to less advanced economies, thus contributing to an increase in the recipient's productive capacity (recall the discussion in Chapter 20 on the importance of technology for productivity and living standards).

The interplay between international trade and technology transfer is illustrated by China's economic development. When the founding father of Communist China, Mao Zedong, died in 1976, Chinese PPP-adjusted GDP per capita was $882 in 2005 dollars. Under Mao, China was organized as a planned economy, so state officials decided how to allocate almost all economic resources. Free markets were banned, international travel was forbidden, international trade was very low by comparison to most other countries, and citizens could not own land or businesses. The Chinese state owned all of the important types of physical capital. From an economic perspective, human capital was also controlled by the Chinese government, because people could not choose where to work and did not receive wages that were commensurate with their value added. The economic consequences of these policies were disastrous, leading to mass starvation under Mao's leadership. Approximately 30 million people died from malnutrition during the Great Famine of 1958–1961.

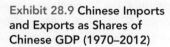

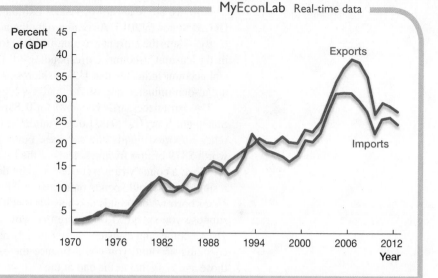

Exhibit 28.9 Chinese Imports and Exports as Shares of Chinese GDP (1970–2012)

China has transitioned from a largely closed economy in the 1970s to an open economy today.

Source: World Bank DataBank: World Development Indicators.

In 1978, two years after Mao's death, Deng Xiaoping became the next powerful leader of China. Under Deng, China began to liberalize the economy, including opening the country to international trade. Exhibit 28.9 plots Chinese imports and exports as shares of GDP since 1970. Under Mao's leadership in the early 1970s, exports represented less than 5 percent of GDP. Over the last 10 years, the export share of the Chinese economy has averaged over 30 percent. Chinese growth over the last 20 years has often been described as "export-led growth."

China achieved an average annual growth rate of real GDP per capita of 6.6 percent between 1979 and 2012. At this pace, Chinese real GDP per capita has *doubled* approximately once every 11 years, implying more than three doublings since 1979. Consequently, Chinese real GDP per capita has increased by more than a factor of $2 \times 2 \times 2 = 8$ since 1979! By comparison, it takes about 40 years for U.S. real GDP per capita to double.

China's spectacular growth is largely due to the shift from central planning—in other words, state control of the economy—towards a market economy. Opening to trade in goods and services was just one part of that transition. Farmers and family businesses were allowed to make their own decisions, own private property, and keep the profits from their economic activity. State-owned industries were privatized and China, which previously banned all kinds of foreign capital inflows, became a major destination for foreign investment. Along the way, China improved its technology greatly, enabling its citizens to work in modern factories, which now export to markets around the world.

Foreign direct investment refers to investments by foreign individuals and companies in domestic firms and businesses. To qualify as foreign *direct* investment, this capital flow must generate a large ownership stake in a local firm for the foreign investors. For example, foreign direct investment in China occurs when a foreign company opens a factory in China. It would also count as foreign direct investment if the Chinese factory were jointly owned by the foreign company and some local Chinese

Foreign direct investment refers to investments by foreign individuals and companies in domestic firms and businesses. To qualify as foreign direct investment, these flows need to generate a large foreign ownership stake in the domestic business.

Technology transfer creates one more type of cross-country interdependence.

investors or a local Chinese company. China receives more foreign direct investment than any other country in the world.

Foreign direct investment is a major conduit for technology transfer, though in most cases this transfer is not the goal of the foreign firm that is making the investment. When a UK company becomes part of a joint venture or opens a factory in China, it brings its know-how and technology to the country. This type of technology transfer enables recipient countries to improve their productivity.

Technology transfer creates one more type of cross-country interdependence. Countries are not only trading goods and services and having their firms and banks borrow from and lend to each other but they are also technologically interlinked. Innovations and technological improvements in one country will ultimately improve productivity in all countries. Moreover, the more interaction there is between these countries, in particular through foreign direct investment, the faster these improvements will migrate from one to the other. Such transfers are particularly beneficial for countries that start out technologically less advanced, as China did in the late 1970s.

28.1

28.2

28.3

LETTING THE DATA SPEAK

From IBM to Lenovo

In 1980, almost no families had a computer at home. Personal computers did exist, but they were expensive, hard to use, and were primarily used by technology hobbyists and science geeks. The internet did not exist. The kind of entertainment one could get from a computer was a game like Pong. The game of Tetris wouldn't even be invented until 1984.

Between 1980 and 1990, the personal computer reached the mainstream, thanks to gradually improving technology as well as successful marketing. The big bang

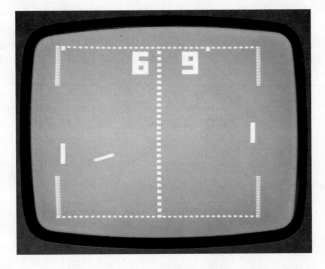

was the introduction of the IBM-PC (model 5150) in 1981. This computer was so successful that it quickly became the industry standard. By the mid-1990s, no self-respecting college student in the developed world still wrote term papers on a typewriter.

The first generation of IBM-PCs was manufactured with mostly U.S. parts and assembled in a U.S. plant. However, even the first IBM-PC had a Japanese monitor. Over time, foreign components came to dominate the business. Mass production of hard disks began in Japan and Korea in the 1980s. Eventually, almost all of the key components of the personal computer were manufactured outside of the United States. Eventually, the final assembly also shifted to foreign factories.

Today, IBM is completely out of the business of manufacturing and selling personal computers. The end of IBM's involvement occurred in 2005, when IBM sold its successful laptop business to Lenovo, its Chinese manufacturing partner. So what did IBM do after abandoning its old line of business? IBM did very well by recognizing that its highly skilled U.S. labor force had higher value added—that is, a *comparative advantage*—in providing consulting services rather than in manufacturing machines that low-wage workers could assemble. Today, IBM remains a highly profitable company. Each year it sells proximately $100 billion in consulting and technical services to companies around the world. It has over 400,000 employees, and the company is worth approximately $200 billion.

Evidence-Based Economics

Q: Are companies like Nike harming workers in Vietnam?

Working on a Vietnamese farm is tough. Wages are very low—approximately $1–$3 per *day* for unskilled labor.[5] And the working conditions are miserable. The physical labor on a Vietnamese farm is grueling and injuries are common. Benefits like health insurance or pension plans don't exist in the agricultural sector. If you are injured on the job and can't work the next day, you don't get paid. Some children work in the agricultural sector because their families can't afford to send them to school and need the meager income that the children can earn.

Unskilled workers in the factories that manufacture Nike products earn little more than the Vietnamese minimum wage, which is $4–$5 per day depending on the location of the factory.[6] But this is greater than the wage they would earn in the largely unregulated agri-

cultural sector. Some of the factory workers also have free access to rudimentary health clinics. But working conditions are terrible—cramped, noisy, hot rooms, filled with dangerous chemicals. As in the agricultural sector, the factories offer no job security. Sick or injured employees lose their jobs and do not receive unemployment benefits. Working in a factory that makes Nike shoes is a nightmare by the standards of workers in the developed world.

Defenders of free markets emphasize the gains from international trade. At the moment, many Vietnamese workers, with limited human capital and limited access to modern technology, have a comparative advantage in assembly jobs—like work in sneaker and clothing factories. Preventing them from working in these jobs reduces their income. Defenders of free trade point to the agricultural sector and say that Nike is doing a good thing by giving agricultural workers an alternative job that increases their pay. The factory job provides reliable income and therefore does not depend on the timing of seasonal rains or whether the harvest happens to be good or bad. Famines occur when agricultural production fails, often because of a long stretch of bad weather. Famines generally don't occur in factory towns. Finally, when Nike's subcontractors use foreign direct investment to build new sneaker factories, this facilitates the transfer of new technology to Vietnam.

On the other hand, critics of the factory sweatshops point out that the factory jobs don't even measure up to the jobs that the *worst-off* workers hold in developed countries. A low-wage worker in the United States earns over $50 per day. An unskilled factory worker in Vietnam earns less than a tenth of that wage. The Vietnam factory wouldn't even come close to passing a U.S. safety inspection. Moreover, many of the factory workers are underage, just like the workers in the agricultural sector.

Almost everyone agrees with these facts. But there is a great deal of disagreement about what should be done. Is it possible for Nike to continue to buy shoes from suppliers in Vietnam but require those suppliers to pay higher wages?

Suppose that U.S. consumers boycotted Nike's products because of the work arrangements at the factories that supply Nike with sneakers. The protestors would like Nike's subcontractors to pay the factory workers more and to improve working conditions in those factories. In principle, such improvements could be implemented without necessitating a very large increase in Nike's sneaker prices.

Would there be unintended negative consequences if Nike paid its subcontractors more and forced them to pass these extra funds on to the workers? Perhaps Nike would lose business because of the need to (modestly) raise its sneaker prices. If Nike does lose some customers, Nike might end up reducing its sneaker purchases from the Vietnamese subcontractors, leading some of its suppliers to shut down. In this case, some of the workers that the U.S. protestors were trying to help might actually be hurt. Perhaps Nike would improve conditions at the existing factories in Vietnam, but the subcontractors would stop building *new* factories in Vietnam, thereby preventing other agricultural workers from transitioning to the relatively well-paid manufacturing sector. Consumers in the United States would like to see the lives of Vietnamese families improve, but it's not clear what would happen if Nike and its subcontractors were forced to raise the wages of workers in Vietnamese sneaker factories.

Though it is not clear what would happen if Nike were forced to pay its Vietnamese workers more, it is clear that globalization in general has been an enormous force for good in Vietnam. Like Deng Xiaoping, who initiated market and trade reforms in China after decades of strict central planning, Nguyen Van Linh pursued a similar policy in Vietnam starting in 1988 (two years after he came to power). As a result of these Vietnamese reforms, trade rapidly expanded, with exports rising from 10 percent of GDP to 75 percent of GDP today. Since the reforms were passed, real GDP per capita has grown at a rate of 5.5 percent (1988–2013), more than a doubling from the pre-reform growth rate.[7] Poverty has fallen precipitously if it is measured with the poverty line of one (U.S.) dollar per day. In 1993, nearly 60 percent of the Vietnamese population fell below that standard of living, but by 2006 (the most recent data available) "only" 16 percent of the population consumed less than a dollar-per-day.[8]

Economists believe that sustained growth is one of the key factors that reduces child labor. Exhibit 28.10 shows that there is a strong negative correlation between child labor and GDP per capita: fewer children are forced to, or choose to, work in countries with higher GDP per capita. Consistent with Exhibit 28.10, rising levels of income in Vietnam have coincided with a sharp fall in child labor, and much of the decline in child labor is credited to Vietnam's opening to trade.[9]

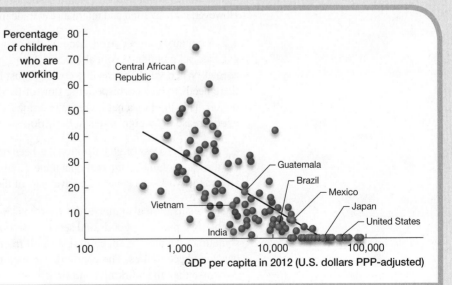

Exhibit 28.10 The Relationship Between GDP per Capita and Child Labor (the Fraction of Children Ages 7–14 Who Are Working)

There is a strong negative relationship between GDP per capita and child labor, which is measured as the percentage of children between the ages of 7 and 14 who are working.

Source: Jean Fares and Dhushyanth Raju (2007). "Child Labor Across the Developing World: Patterns and Correlations," World Development Report, The World Bank.

Evidence-Based Economics (Continued)

Question

Are companies like Nike harming workers in the developing world?

Answer

The Vietnamese workers that make Nike's sneakers are paid extremely low wages and work in conditions that are unsafe by the standards of developed countries. However, the next best alternative for many of the workers that produce Nike's sneakers, which is work in the agricultural sector, appears to be even worse.

Data

Agricultural and factory wages in Vietnam, as well as data on trade, growth, poverty, and child labor-force participation.

Caveat

Nike could improve the quality of life of the workers who manufacture its products if it forced its subcontractors to raise the workers' wages.

Summary

* The process of globalization has produced a highly interconnected world.

* International trade enables us to exploit specialization and comparative advantage. Comparative advantage arises when a person or country has a lower opportunity cost of production than another person or country.

* Some individuals are made worse off by international trade, especially low-skilled workers in *developed* countries who lose their jobs to foreign producers. However, globalization and international trade improve the well-being of most people.

* A country runs a current account deficit when it has a negative sum of net exports, net payments from abroad for factor payments, and net transfers from abroad. When this happens, the country must have a financial account surplus, as there needs to be a corresponding flow of funds that pays for the current account deficit. This implies a net increase in domestic assets held by foreigners and/or a net decrease in foreign assets held by domestic residents.

* A rapid process of globalization has been underway for several decades, increasing the total volume of international trade. Consequently, consumers and workers around the world can better take advantage of the gains from international trade.

* Globalization also makes the enormous inequities across nations more visible. We purchase goods and services produced and assembled by workers, sometimes even children, earning a small fraction of the wages of workers in developed economies. The conditions in factories in the developing world are far worse than the working conditions in developed countries. Nevertheless, globalization usually improves the well-being of most of the low-paid factory workers in foreign countries. Their alternative opportunities for employment are usually worse than these factory jobs in the traded goods sector.

Key Terms

gains from specialization *p. 665*
absolute advantage *p. 666*
comparative advantage *p. 666*
closed economy *p. 670*

open economy *p. 670*
net exports or the trade balance *p. 673*
trade surplus *p. 673*
trade deficit *p. 673*

current account *p. 675*
financial account *p. 676*
foreign direct investment *p. 678*

Questions

All questions are available in MyEconLab *for practice and instructor assignment.*

1. How does comparative advantage differ from absolute advantage?

2. How does trade allow buyers and sellers to exploit gains from specialization?

3. Engaging in trade increases overall economic efficiency. Does this also imply that everyone in an economy gains from trade equally?

4. Explain the following terms:
   a. Open economy
   b. Closed economy
   c. Imports
   d. Exports
   e. Tariffs

5. Has trade been increasing or decreasing over the past few decades? What could explain why the ratio of imports to GDP in the United States fell sharply after 1929 before rebounding shortly thereafter?

6. How is the trade balance defined? When is a country said to be running a trade deficit or a trade surplus?

7. The international accounting system maintains a clear distinction between residency and citizenship.
   a. Who would be considered a domestic resident of the United States, according to the international accounting system?
   b. Suppose a U.S. citizen lives and works in Nigeria. Would he be considered a "foreigner" or a domestic resident in the U.S. international transactions accounts?

8. List the sources of income-based payments that domestic residents make to foreigners and the ways that domestic residents can receive income-based payments from foreigners.

9. What does the current account include? Explain each of its components.

10. What is included in a country's financial account? How is the financial account related to the current account?

11. What is foreign direct investment? Explain with an example. How does foreign direct investment benefit the recipient country?

12. Are multinational companies harming factory workers in the developing world by hiring them at low wages?

Problems

All problems are available in MyEconLab *for practice and instructor assignment.*

1. The economist Alan Blinder said that any economist who mows his own lawn probably has not understood the concept of comparative advantage. Would you agree with Professor Blinder?

2. You and your roommate are enrolled in the same course: Postmodern Deconstruction of Postmodern Deconstructionism. The course requires a term paper. Since the professor encourages collaboration on the paper, you decide to work on it together, "trading" tasks.

   In 8 hours, you can type 18 pages, whereas your roommate can type only 10. If you do outlining instead of typing, in the same 8 hours you could produce 6 summary outlines of the course readings, while your roommate could produce only 2.

   a. Who has the absolute advantage in typing? In outlining? Explain your answers.

   b. Who should do the typing, and who should do the outlining? Explain.

3. Suppose that the United States and Chile are the only two countries in the world, and that labor is the only productive input. In the United States, a worker can produce 15 bushels of corn or 10 barrels of oil per day. In Chile, a worker can produce 5 bushels of corn or 5 barrels of oil per day.

   a. Which country has the absolute advantage in the production of oil? Of corn? Explain.

   b. Explain in words what comparative advantage means. Which country has the comparative advantage in the production of oil? Of corn?

   c. If free trade is allowed, which commodity will the United States import? Which commodity will Chile import? Explain.

4. Assume that an American worker can produce 5 cars per year or 10 tons of grain per year, whereas a Japanese worker can produce 15 cars per year or 5 tons of grain per year. Assume labor is the only input used in car and grain production.

   a. Which country has the absolute advantage in producing cars? In producing grain?

   b. For the United States, what is the opportunity cost of producing a car? What is the opportunity cost of a ton of grain? Show how you arrived at your numbers.

   c. For Japan, what is the opportunity cost of producing a car? What is the opportunity cost of producing a ton of grain? Show how you arrived at your numbers.

   d. If free trade is allowed, which country will import cars? Which country will import grain? Explain.

5. David Ricardo, the British political economist, used the example of two commodities—wine and cloth—produced by England and Portugal to explain trade. The following table shows the number of labor hours it would take England and Portugal to produce one unit each of wine and cloth:

	Portugal	England
Wine	80	120
Cloth	90	100

   Portugal can produce both wine and cloth using fewer labor hours than England. A group of Mercantilists, who believe that nations build their wealth by exporting more than they import, suggest that Portugal has nothing to gain from trading with England. Would you agree? Explain your answer.

6. Tire production in the United States has been on the decline, in both absolute and relative terms. Imported tires are replacing most of the domestically manufactured tires in the market. Trade unions in the United States have claimed that over 7,000 jobs have been lost due to Chinese tire imports. You read a blog post that uses this example to say that this is exactly why countries should not engage in free trade; cheaper imports will flood the domestic market and unemployment in the country will increase. Do you think the blogger's conclusions are entirely correct? Explain.

7. In his book *Where the Right Went Wrong*, commentator and politician Patrick "Pat" Buchanan says that trade between China and the United States must be reciprocal—"If America is to buy 30 percent of China's exports, Beijing must give preference in its purchases to goods made in the USA." According to him, the United States loses the "trade war" unless its imports from China are matched by China's imports of U.S. goods. Based on your understanding of bilateral trade deficits, identify the flaw in Pat Buchanan's reasoning.

8. Suppose the following table shows data on transactions between the United States and the rest of the world for the month of May 2013. Assuming the list is exhaustive, use the information given to fill in the table showing the current and financial accounts for May 2013.

U.S. aid to earthquake-hit Haiti	$8,000,000
Payments made to Indian software companies for services rendered by workers in India to U.S. customers	$850,000
Payments made to U.S. producers for ethanol exports	$3,000,000
Dividend payment from Walmart in China to a U.S. resident	$10,500
Salary earned by a team of IT consultants from the UK who were working in the U.S. for a few days	$120,000
Sale of U.S. Treasury bonds from U.S. Treasury to foreign governments	$15,000,000
Remittances from U.S. residents to other family members in Mexico	$30,000
Payments made to Chinese producers for steel imports	$8,000,000
Purchases of foreign assets by the U.S. government	$1,040,500
A U.S. citizen, who is a resident of Dubai, sends money to a charity in the United States	$30,000

Current and Financial Account for May, 2013

	Payments from Foreigners	Payments to Foreigners	Net Payments
Trade in goods and services			
Factor payments			
Net transfer payments			
Current account			
	Increase in domestic assets held by foreigners	Increase in foreign assets held domestically	
Net sales to foreigners			
Financial account			

9. Recall the national income accounting identity (in Chapter 19): $Y = C + I + G + X - M$, where $X - M$ is net exports, given by exports − imports. We have seen from the chapter that net exports is equivalent to the trade balance, but not to the current account. Hence, aggregate expenditure does not include the current account balance.

   Discuss why the entire current account is not included in the calculation of GDP.

10. Throughout the 1950s and 1960s, many poor countries pursued a policy called "import-substituting industrialization," or ISI for short. India, and many nations in Africa and Latin America, closed themselves off to trade in order to promote the development of domestic industries.

As noted in the *Economist* article "Grinding the Poor" (September 27, 2001), "[o]n the whole, ISI failed; almost everywhere, trade has been good for growth." The article discusses how growth was disappointing in countries that pursued ISI. Nations that were open to trade—primarily in Asia—grew much more rapidly.

Based on the discussion in the chapter, speculate on why ISI was ultimately a failure and why integration with the global economy promotes economic growth and development.

11. Foreign direct investment (FDI) in several sectors in India is still heavily regulated. After much debate, the government of India recently relaxed restrictions on FDI in the retail sector. For purported reasons like national security and possible job losses, many sectors of the economy such as defense, nuclear power, and oil refining are not fully open to foreign direct investment. Suppose you are hired to serve on the government's Working Group on Foreign Direct Investment. What would you suggest to the government? Defend your position.

12. The coffee market is one of the most globalized and volatile commodity markets in existence. In terms of the value of trade, it is second only to oil. Coffee is produced in over seventy countries, primarily lower-income nations in Latin American, Africa, and Asia. In recent years, a movement has developed supporting "fair trade coffee," which seeks to better the conditions and increase the incomes of coffee producers in poor countries.

Read the following online sources and list the main arguments for and against the fair trade coffee movement, as delineated in the articles. Comment on any similarities you see between fair trade coffee policy and the case of Nike in Vietnam (as discussed in the chapter's Evidence-Based Economics feature).

"The Fair Trade Debate," in Wikipedia: http://en.wikipedia.org/wiki/Fair_trade_debate

"Coffee," from Fair Trade International: http://www.fairtrade.net/coffee.html

"Fair Trade Coffee Enthusiasts Should Confront Reality," from the Cato Institute: http://object.cato.org/sites/cato.org/files/serials/files/cato-journal/2007/1/cj27n1-9.pdf

"The Pros and Cons of Fair Trade Coffee" from the Organic Consumers Association: http://www.organicconsumers.org/articles/article_4738.cfm

29 Open Economy Macroeconomics

How did George Soros make $1 billion?

George Soros, one of the world's most renowned investors, challenged the central bank of England in the summer of 1992. In essence, he bet everything he had that the British currency, the pound, would lose value relative to other currencies. Starting in September, the pound plummeted in value. Soros made approximately $1 billion of profits for himself and his investors. How did Soros know that the pound was about to collapse?

CHAPTER **OUTLINE**

KEY IDEAS

☀ The nominal exchange rate is the rate at which one country's currency can be exchanged for the currency of another country.

☀ In a flexible exchange rate system, the nominal exchange rate is determined by supply and demand in the foreign exchange market.

☀ Fixed or managed exchange rates are controlled by the government.

☀ The real exchange rate is the ratio of the prices (for example, all converted to dollars) of a basket of goods and services in two countries and thus influences net exports from one country to the other.

☀ A decline in net exports reduces labor demand and GDP and might cause unemployment.

29.1 Exchange Rates

In the previous chapter, we saw that economies around the world are linked through trade and investment. For example, the United States imported about $456 billion of goods and services from China in 2013. But *how* does this trade take place? After all, almost all transactions in the United States are in U.S. dollars, while most transactions in China are in the Chinese currency, the *yuan*, also called the *renminbi*.

Many countries have their own currencies for use in economic transactions: the United Kingdom has the pound, Japan the yen, Mexico the peso, and India the rupee, among others. An exception to the use of a national currency is the euro, a currency used by twenty-four European countries (as of January 1, 2015). The euro, first introduced in 1999, is the second-most-traded currency after the U.S. dollar.

Nominal Exchange Rates

Walmart sells toys imported from China. How does Walmart decide whether to purchase the toys from China rather than purchasing similar toys from some U.S. toy manufacturer?

To answer this question, we need to understand the concept of the *nominal exchange rate*. The **nominal exchange rate** is the price of one country's currency in units of another country's currency. Specifically, the nominal exchange rate is the number of units of foreign currency that can be purchased with one unit of domestic currency. Sometimes you'll see the nominal exchange rate, referred to simply as the "exchange rate" (which is what we did in Chapter 20). In the current chapter, we often use the full name, *nominal* exchange rate, to distinguish the nominal exchange rate from another type of exchange rate that we will discuss later in the chapter.

In the following equation, the nominal exchange rate is represented by the symbol *e*:

> The **nominal exchange rate** is the rate at which one currency can be traded for another.

$$e = \frac{\text{Units of foreign currency}}{1 \text{ Unit of domestic currency}}.$$

For instance, if the yuan-dollar exchange rate is 6.05 yuan per dollar, then a person holding 1 dollar can exchange the dollar for 6.05 yuan.

$$e = 6.05 \text{ Yuan per dollar} = \frac{6.05 \text{ Yuan}}{1 \text{ Dollar}}.$$

Exhibit 29.1 The Nominal Exchange Rates e and 1/e

The nominal exchange rates e and 1/e for several major currencies on January 2, 2014.

Source: Federal Reserve Board of Governors.

	British Pound Versus Dollar	Euro Versus Dollar	Mexican New Peso Versus Dollar	Swiss Franc Versus Dollar	Yuan Versus Dollar
e	0.61	0.73	13.12	0.90	6.05
1/e	1.64	1.37	0.08	1.11	0.17

All Chinese currency features a portrait of Mao Zedong, the first leader of modern China.

The higher the value of e, the more units of foreign currency a dollar buys. When a nominal exchange rate goes up, we say that the domestic currency is *appreciating* against the foreign currency. When a nominal exchange rate goes down, we say that the domestic currency is *depreciating* against the foreign currency.

We can also use the yuan-dollar exchange rate to calculate the value of 1 yuan in terms of dollars. When the yuan-dollar exchange rate is e, the number of units of dollars that can be purchased with 1 yuan is $1/e$. Put differently, 1 yuan is worth $1/e = 1/6.05 = 0.17$ dollars.

Notice that the appreciation of a currency—a rise in e—always has a flip side. When the dollar appreciates against the yuan, implying that e is rising, the yuan is depreciating against the dollar, implying that $1/e$ is falling.

Exhibit 29.1 shows e and $1/e$ for some key currencies on January 2, 2014. The above discussion and Exhibit 29.1 clarify that both e (yuan per dollar) and $1/e$ (dollars per yuan) convey the same information. In newspapers, you will see exchange rates sometimes expressed as yuan per dollar or euros per dollar and at other times as dollars per yuan or dollars per euro. In this chapter, to avoid confusion, we will stick to the definition above of the exchange rate, e, expressing it as the number of units of foreign currency that can be purchased by one unit of domestic currency, such as yuan per dollar or euros per dollar.

Now let's return to Walmart's *sourcing* decision—should Walmart purchase toys from a Chinese or a U.S. manufacturer? Walmart needs to decide whether a toy sold by a Chinese manufacturer at a unit price of 20 yuan is less expensive than an identical toy sold by a competing U.S. manufacturer at a unit price of $5 (we are ignoring transportation costs for simplicity). To implement this comparison, Walmart makes the yuan and dollar prices comparable by using the nominal exchange rate. For example, on January 2, 2014, the yuan-dollar exchange rate was 6.05, so the dollar price of the Chinese-manufactured toy was

$$\text{Dollar cost} = \text{Yuan cost} \times \frac{\text{Dollars}}{\text{Yuan}}$$
$$= \text{Yuan cost} \times \frac{1}{e}$$
$$= 20 \times \frac{1}{6.05}$$
$$= \$3.31.$$

As you can see, the dollar price of the Chinese-manufactured toy is just over $3, which is less than the $5 price of the U.S.-manufactured toy, so it is less expensive to purchase the toy from the Chinese manufacturer.

Flexible, Managed, and Fixed Exchange Rates

Exhibit 29.2 shows historical movements in two nominal exchange rates: the yuan-dollar and the euro-dollar nominal exchange rates. Both nominal exchange rates vary over time. However, the yuan-dollar exchange rate has had long periods in which it doesn't move, followed

Exhibit 29.2 Yuan-Dollar and Euro-Dollar Exchange Rates from 1999 to January 2014

The yuan-dollar exchange rate is managed by the Chinese government, so its rate is either held fixed or slowly allowed to drift in one direction. The euro-dollar exchange rate floats freely, so its path is set by market forces that fluctuate from day to day.

Source: Federal Reserve Bank of St. Louis.

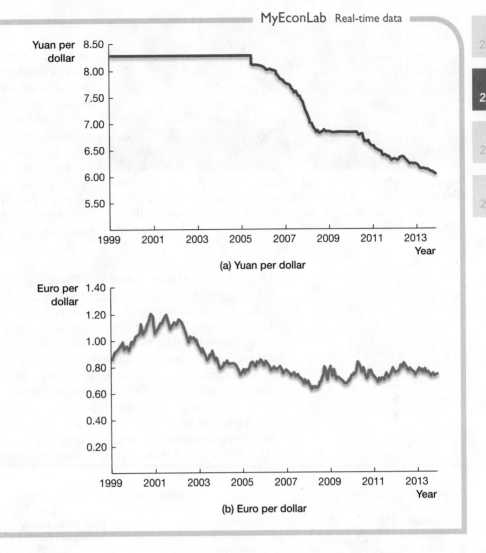

(a) Yuan per dollar

(b) Euro per dollar

If the government does not intervene in the foreign exchange market, then the country has a **flexible exchange rate,** which is also referred to as a **floating exchange rate.**

If the government fixes a value for the exchange rate and intervenes to maintain that value, then the country has a **fixed exchange rate.**

If the government intervenes actively to influence the exchange rate, then the country has a **managed exchange rate.**

by short periods in which it mostly moves down. For example, the yuan-dollar exchange rate was constant—8.28 yuan per dollar—from late 1998 to 2005. Likewise, the yuan-dollar exchange rate was nearly constant at 6.82 yuan per dollar between mid-2008 and mid-2010.

The euro-dollar exchange rate fluctuates much more than the yuan-dollar exchange rate because the euro-dollar exchange rate is determined with little or no government intervention. Each day the exchange rate moves up and down as market forces change. This is referred to as a **flexible exchange rate**, or a **floating exchange rate**.

On the other hand, a government could fix a value for the exchange rate and intervene to maintain that value. In this case, the country has a **fixed exchange rate**.

There is also a middle case. The yuan-dollar exchange rate is not flexible or fixed but is instead a **managed exchange rate**: the Chinese government influences its movement. Managed exchange rates change, but those movements tend to be relatively smooth. For example, the Chinese government has allowed the yuan to slowly appreciate against the dollar since 2005.

We'll explain why a country might adopt a managed or a fixed exchange rate later in the chapter. For now, we only note that there are many reasons, among them the belief that managed or fixed exchange rates provide more economic stability and might facilitate international trade.

29.2 The Foreign Exchange Market

The **foreign exchange market** is the global financial market in which currencies are traded and nominal exchange rates are determined.

The **foreign exchange market** is the global financial market in which currencies are traded and nominal exchange rates are determined. To illustrate the role of this market, suppose Air China would like to add five Boeing Dreamliners, each costing $200 million, to its aircraft fleet. To do this, it needs to pay the Boeing Company in dollars. So Air China will go to the foreign exchange market to buy (demand) a total of $1 billion (= 5 × $200 million), offering yuan in

Boeing's Dreamliner costs $200 million per plane. If a Chinese airline tries to buy one, it will need to exchange (e × $200 million) on the foreign exchange market to obtain $200 million. At an exchange rate of e = 6.05 yuan per dollar, that amounts to 1,210 million yuan.

return. Because the yuan-dollar exchange rate is $e = 6.05$, this means Air China will be paying 6.05 billion yuan in exchange of dollars.

As with other markets, the supply and demand curves determine the equilibrium price, which is the equilibrium exchange rate in the foreign exchange market. Exhibit 29.3 illustrates the supply and demand curves in the foreign exchange market. The horizontal axis represents the quantity of dollars available for transactions in the foreign exchange market. We'll use the yuan-dollar exchange rate on the vertical axis to represent the value or "price" of a dollar: how many yuan a dollar will buy. Recall that we are expressing the nominal exchange rate as units of foreign currency per U.S. dollar.

In panel (a) of Exhibit 29.3, the dollar demand curve represents the relationship between the quantity of dollars demanded and the exchange rate. The demand curve represents traders who are trying to buy dollars in the foreign exchange market with yuan. So, Air China's demand for dollars is reflected in this demand curve. Of course, millions of other economic agents will also be trying to obtain dollars by selling yuan. All of these agents make up the dollar demand curve.

To understand why the demand curve for dollars in exchange for yuan is downward-sloping, consider an *appreciation* of the dollar—in other words, a *depreciation* of the yuan. A dollar appreciation would move the exchange rate from A to B in panel (a) of Exhibit 29.3. The dollar appreciation implies that each dollar buys more yuan, that each yuan buys fewer dollars, and that the price of each Boeing aircraft is now greater in yuan. The Chinese airline's revenues are paid (largely) in yuan, so the relevant price for Air China is the price of the Boeing Dreamliner in yuan. The higher yuan-denominated price for the Dreamliner leads Air China to reduce the quantity of Dreamliners demanded. This implies that the quantity of

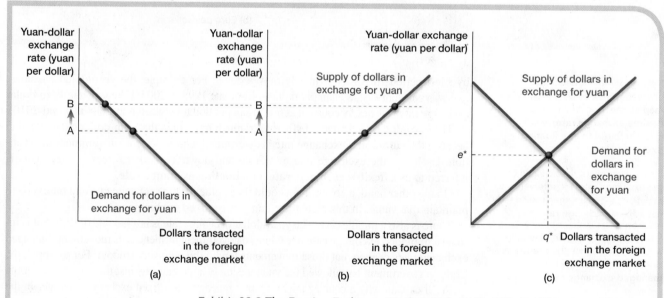

(a)   (b)   (c)

Exhibit 29.3 **The Foreign Exchange Market under a Flexible Exchange Rate Regime**

The demand for dollars in exchange for yuan in panel (a) is downward-sloping because a dollar appreciation (a movement from A to B) increases the price of U.S. goods faced by Chinese firms and consumers, reducing the quantity of goods they demand and thereby reducing the quantity of dollars they demand. The supply of dollars in exchange for yuan in panel (b) is upward-sloping because a dollar appreciation (a movement from A to B) increases the quantity of goods purchased by U.S. buyers from Chinese producers, thus raising the dollar earnings of Chinese producers and the quantity of dollars that they supply to the foreign exchange market. The intersection of the demand and supply curves in panel (c) gives the equilibrium exchange rate in a flexible exchange rate regime.

dollars demanded will fall—with fewer aircraft demanded, fewer dollars will be demanded. We've just shown how an appreciation of the dollar leads to a reduction in the quantity of dollars demanded. Examples like this imply that the demand curve is downward-sloping, as shown in the exhibit.

The dollar supply curve, shown in panel (b) of Exhibit 29.3, represents the relationship between the quantity of dollars supplied and the exchange rate. Traders who are trying to obtain yuan by selling dollars are represented by this dollar supply curve. For example, Chinese manufacturers that export their products are often paid in dollars and they need to exchange these dollars into yuan so they can pay their workers and suppliers. All of the millions of households and firms supplying dollars in exchange for yuan make up the dollar supply curve.

The reason that the supply curve (for dollars in exchange for yuan) slopes up is related to the reason that the demand curve (for dollars in exchange for yuan) slopes down. When the dollar appreciates (yuan depreciates) and we move from exchange rate A to exchange rate B, each dollar buys more yuan. This implies that the prices of all Chinese products, such as the toys produced by Chinese manufacturers, become less expensive in U.S. dollars—recall that when we draw supply (or demand) curves, we are holding constant all other prices, such as the yuan-denominated price of toys manufactured in China. Because an appreciation of the dollar enables U.S. consumers to pay fewer dollars for each good they import from China, U.S. consumers and companies increase their purchases of Chinese goods. This implies greater dollar revenues for Chinese firms, and thus a greater quantity of dollars supplied by them to the foreign exchange market. To sum up, a rising yuan-dollar exchange rate leads to a greater quantity of dollars supplied, so the supply curve is upward-sloping.

The equilibrium exchange rate under a flexible exchange rate regime is given by the foreign exchange equilibrium, which corresponds to the exchange rate that equates the quantity supplied and the quantity demanded. This intersection of the supply and demand curves is shown in panel (c) of Exhibit 29.3 at quantity q^* and price (yuan-dollar exchange rate) e^*. As we have already noted, the yuan-dollar exchange rate is not flexible but managed, so panel (c) shows what the yuan-dollar exchange rate would be if there were no Chinese government intervention. In fact, the Chinese government has been slowly reducing the scope of its foreign exchange market interventions, leading the yuan-dollar market to move closer to the situation that would arise under a flexible exchange rate regime like that in panel (c).

What happens to the equilibrium exchange rate if Air China unexpectedly faces a higher demand for air travel in China? Air China would need more aircraft. For example, its demand curve for aircraft would shift so that, at unchanged prices, it would now demand 10 Dreamliners instead of 5. In this case, again keeping prices including the exchange rate fixed, Air China's demand for dollars would increase by 5 × $200 million = $1 billion. In terms of Exhibit 29.3, this corresponds to a $1 billion rightward shift of the dollar demand curve, as illustrated in Exhibit 29.4.

Exhibit 29.4 The Foreign Exchange Market After a Rightward Shift in the Dollar Demand Curve

Increased demand for Boeing aircraft from Air China causes a rightward shift of the demand for dollars in exchange for yuan. This raises the equilibrium nominal exchange rate from e^* to e^{**}.

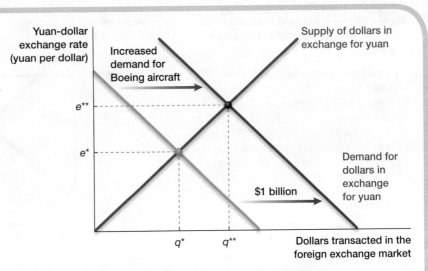

Under a flexible exchange rate, the rightward shift in the dollar demand curve causes the equilibrium yuan-dollar exchange rate to increase, implying that a dollar will now buy more yuan. Using the terminology we introduced earlier we can see that, with flexible exchange rates, in response to the increased demand for Boeing aircraft, the dollar would appreciate against the yuan or, equivalently, the yuan would depreciate against the dollar.

How Do Governments Intervene in the Foreign Exchange Market?

How does equilibrium work when an exchange rate is not flexible? If a government attempts to control the value of its exchange rate through a managed or fixed exchange rate system, we say that the exchange rate is being "pegged" by the government.

Though this may no longer be the case, Chinese authorities have historically chosen an exchange rate that makes the yuan substantially *undervalued* relative to the dollar. By implication this means that the dollar is somewhat *overvalued* relative to the yuan. Exhibit 29.5 illustrates the yuan-dollar foreign exchange market and reveals what it means for the yuan to be undervalued and the dollar to be overvalued. The exchange rate is pegged at the level shown by the solid purple line. The dollar is overvalued because the dollar is worth more yuan than it would have been under a flexible exchange rate regime. The flexible equilibrium is still represented by e^*. The pegged exchange rate is *above* the market-clearing price at the intersection of the supply and demand curves.

At the exchange rate corresponding to the peg, the quantity supplied exceeds the quantity demanded. If the Chinese authorities simply announce the peg and do nothing else, the forces of supply and demand will lower the yuan-dollar exchange rate below the peg. Recall that the supply curve represents the quantity of dollars supplied to the yuan-dollar foreign exchange market at a particular yuan-dollar exchange rate. If that quantity supplied exceeds the quantity demanded at a particular yuan-dollar exchange rate, there will be an excess supply of dollars, which will drive down the price of dollars. In other words, the price of dollars—the exchange rate—will fall, so the dollar will depreciate against the yuan. This process will lower the yuan-dollar exchange rate from the peg toward the market-clearing price at the intersection of the supply and demand curves.

This analysis shows that simply *announcing* a target exchange rate will have little or no effect on the exchange rate that will prevail in the foreign exchange market. Because the quantity of dollars supplied exceeds the quantity of dollars demanded at the pegged yuan-dollar exchange rate, Chinese authorities would need to soak up this excess supply by buying dollars and selling yuan. Exhibit 29.5 shows that to maintain the peg above the

> **Simply announcing a target exchange rate will have little or no effect on the exchange rate that will prevail in the foreign exchange market.**

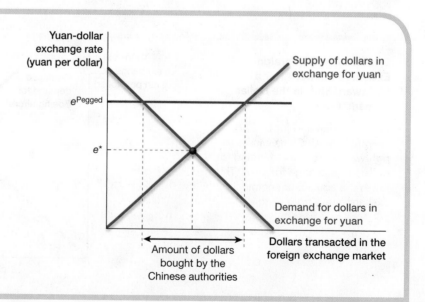

Exhibit 29.5 The Foreign Exchange Market Under a Pegged Exchange Rate That Overvalues the Dollar Relative to the Yuan

To support an overvalued dollar (or equivalently an undervalued yuan), the Chinese government would need to soak up the excess supply of dollars by buying dollars in exchange for yuan. The quantity of dollars that must be purchased is given by the difference between the quantity of dollars supplied and the quantity of dollars demanded at the pegged exchange rate.

market-clearing exchange rate—in other words, to keep the dollar overvalued—Chinese authorities would have to continuously purchase dollars and sell yuan.

In fact, this is exactly what they have been doing. Between 1990 and 2013, the Chinese central bank increased its holdings of foreign reserves from about $30 billion to more than $3,800 billion. Most of these reserves are in dollars, but the Chinese central bank has bought other currencies as well. The analysis in Exhibit 29.5 shows why dollar purchases were necessary, given the fact that the yuan has been pegged to the dollar at exchange rates that overvalued the dollar and therefore undervalued the yuan.

Later in this chapter we'll explain why the Chinese government has gone to all this trouble: an overvalued dollar (undervalued yuan) increase the net exports of China.

Defending an Overvalued Exchange Rate

Exhibit 29.5 makes it look easy to defend a fixed exchange rate. The Chinese authorities bought dollars, building up their dollar reserves. In exchange, the Chinese authorities supplied yuan. This was simple to achieve because a country with a national currency, like the Chinese yuan, has the right to print or electronically create as many units of that currency as it wants. So, at least in the short run, defending an *undervalued* yuan appears feasible. However, it is not as easy to defend an exchange rate when your currency is *overvalued*.

In many cases, countries try to peg their exchange rate at a level that overvalues their *own* currency. To see why a country might do so, let's consider the example of Mexico and analyze the peso-dollar exchange rate, with the convention that the exchange rate is measured in pesos per dollar. Why would the Mexican government want the peso to be overvalued and the dollar to be undervalued?

Most countries regularly borrow from foreign lenders. In developing countries like Mexico, these loans are typically denominated in dollars. So the Mexican borrowers receive dollars when they take out their loans and pay back dollars, not pesos, at the end of the loan period. To work through a numerical example, imagine that Mexican borrowers, including the Mexican government and Mexican companies, owe $1 billion to U.S. banks. If the peso-dollar exchange rate is 10, meaning that 10 pesos purchase one dollar, then Mexican borrowers need 10 billion pesos to pay back their dollar-denominated debts.

Now suppose that at the exchange rate of 10 pesos per dollar, the dollar is undervalued and that its market-clearing price under a flexible exchange rate regime would be 20 pesos per dollar instead. What would happen if the Mexican government allowed the *undervalued* dollar to appreciate, which is equivalent to allowing the *overvalued* peso to depreciate? This situation would have several implications, one of which is that Mexican borrowers would now need to give up 20 billion pesos instead of just 10 billion pesos to pay back their debts of $1 billion. Allowing the dollar to appreciate, and hence the peso to depreciate, has suddenly doubled the number of pesos that are needed to pay back the dollar-denominated debts of Mexican borrowers.

Having an overvalued peso also has other benefits for Mexico. An undervalued dollar—hence, an overvalued peso—lowers the cost that Mexican consumers pay in pesos to import goods from the United States. Consequently, the Mexican government can keep prices and inflation low by keeping the dollar undervalued and the peso overvalued. For example, suppose that an iPhone costs $400 to import into Mexico. If the Mexican exchange rate is 10 pesos per dollar, then the local cost will be 4,000 pesos. This is a lower iPhone price (in pesos) than if the peso-dollar exchange rate rises to 20 pesos per dollar. In that case, the local cost of the iPhone doubles to 8,000 pesos. Price increases like this raise the overall inflation rate in Mexico.

Another reason that countries maintain an overvalued exchange rate is because a fall in the value of a currency is often perceived as a failure of government policies. A currency that is depreciating (sometimes confusingly called a "weak currency") is at times perceived to be a sign of a weak government or a weak country. This perception can be a problem for incumbent politicians in democratic countries. For this reason, officials at the U.S. Treasury Department frequently repeat the mantra that they support a "strong dollar policy." The American public doesn't like to hear politicians associate anything "weak" with the United States, including its currency. However, as we have learned, a "weak" currency is exactly what the non-democratic Chinese government has pursued for decades.

Exhibit 29.6 The Foreign Exchange Market Under a Pegged Exchange Rate That Undervalues the Dollar Relative to the Peso

To maintain an undervalued dollar, which is the same thing as an overvalued peso, the Mexican government needs to supply dollars to purchase pesos. The quantity of dollars that must be supplied is given by the difference between the quantity of dollars demanded and the quantity of dollars supplied at the pegged exchange rate.

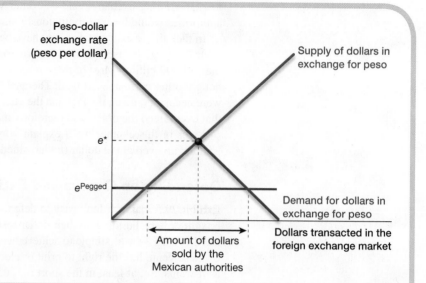

Whatever their motivations, many governments have intervened in the foreign exchange market to maintain an overvalued national currency. But overvaluation is also costly, as we will discuss below. In addition, overvalued currencies are much harder to defend than undervalued ones. Exhibit 29.6 plots the situation for an *overvalued* peso, which implies an *undervalued* dollar. Exhibit 29.6 is very similar to Exhibit 29.5, except that the solid purple line corresponding to the peg value is now *below* the market-clearing price, e^*, at the intersection of the supply and demand curves (again marked with the dotted line in the exhibit). Thus the peso-dollar exchange rate is below what it would have been under a flexible exchange rate regime, and in particular, the dollar is worth fewer pesos than it would be at the market-clearing price. Hence, the dollar is undervalued and the peso is overvalued.

Exhibit 29.6 illustrates how the Mexican authorities would in principle defend an overvalued peso (and thus keep the dollar undervalued). This exhibit differs from Exhibit 29.5, where the quantity of dollars supplied *exceeded* the quantity of dollars demanded. In Exhibit 29.6, the quantity of dollars supplied falls short of the quantity of dollars demanded. To maintain the peso-dollar exchange rate at the value corresponding to the peg, the Mexican authorities have to sell dollars and purchase pesos. The Mexican authorities can certainly do this if they have substantial dollar reserves. But how long can they keep up this policy?

In the situation depicted in Exhibit 29.5, the Chinese authorities can print or electronically create as many yuan as they want, so they could perpetually supply yuan to buy dollars if they wished. Likewise, Mexican authorities can create as many *pesos* as they want, but sustaining an *overvalued* peso relative to the dollar does not rely on the creation of more pesos. Instead, the Mexican authorities need to keep selling dollars to sustain an overvalued peso. Because they can't create new dollars, the Mexican authorities have to use their pre-existing dollar reserves, which are limited. If the quantity of dollars they need to supply exceeds their reserves, they won't be able to sustain an overvalued peso. At the moment it becomes clear that their dollar reserves are going to run out, defending the overvalued peso becomes impossible. Whatever their public announcements, the Mexican authorities will then have to give up the peg and allow the peso to depreciate and the dollar to appreciate, which implies that the number of pesos per dollar—the peso-dollar exchange rate—will rise.

This discussion highlights the observation that overvalued exchange rates can be defended for a while—as long as the dollar reserves of the country defending the exchange rate last. But this scenario cannot continue indefinitely. If the peso-dollar exchange rate is too low relative to what supply and demand dictate—meaning that the dollar is undervalued and the peso is overvalued—there will continue to be an excess demand for dollars, and this excess demand will keep draining the dollar reserves of the Mexican authorities who are trying to defend the overvalued peso.

> **Market pressure often pushes prices in financial markets, including exchange rates, back to their market-clearing levels, no matter what the government tries to do.**

CHOICE & CONSEQUENCE

Fixed Exchange Rates and Corruption

Some developing countries with fixed exchange rates announce an *official* exchange rate that overvalues their local currency and then ration who gets the privilege of exchanging the local currency for dollars at the overvalued exchange rate. In particular, the situation has some similarities to Exhibit 29.6, which depicts an undervalued dollar and, by implication, an overvalued foreign currency. As in Exhibit 29.6, at the official pegged exchange rate the supply of dollars falls short of the demand for dollars, but, with rationing, some of the demand for dollars will *not* be met by the government. The government will pick and choose who gets to sell the local currency at the price that undervalues dollars and overvalues the local currency. In cases like this, a *black market*—the name for the underground market, in this case for dollars—comes into existence. A black market is part of the broader underground economy, which includes all transactions that are hidden from the government. The exchange rate on the black market, which is determined by supply and demand, will be less favorable to sellers of local currency than the official pegged exchange rate.

For instance, in Venezuela in 2009, the official exchange rate was 2.15 bolivares to the dollar, but the black market exchange rate was roughly 5 bolivares to the dollar. Hence, a Venezuelan who wanted to sell 1,000 bolivares in exchange for dollars would get 1,000/2.15 = $465 at the official exchange rate, but only 1,000/5 = $200 at the black market exchange rate. As you can see in this case, everybody with bolivares would have liked to purchase dollars at the more advantageous official rate. But the Venezuelan government did not allow this and simply refused to sell dollars at the official exchange rate to all Venezuelans who asked to buy dollars with bolivares. Those who are denied dollars have to either make do without the dollars or pay the much higher price for dollars on the black market—in this case the black market rate was more than twice as high.

To further complicate matters, many people who receive dollars at the official exchange rate are likely to turn around and sell them at the much higher black market rate. Such black market sales are illegal, but in most cases the black market transactions are prosecuted only if they are conducted by political enemies of the government. Can you see who benefits from the system?

Not surprisingly, many governments maintain overvalued exchange rates as a way of rewarding friends, cronies, and themselves. They can benefit directly from having access to the official and artificially cheap dollars. The system ultimately collapses, however, because it is inefficient. But while it lasts, politicians and their buddies make billions in profits.

Market pressure often pushes prices in financial markets, including exchange rates, back to their market-clearing levels, no matter what the government tries to do. In some cases, this pressure works gradually. In other cases, like the example we discuss in our Evidence-Based Economics feature, the pressure ends up generating explosive fallout.

Evidence-Based Economics

Q: How did George Soros make $1 billion?

From 1990 to 1992 the British pound had an exchange rate that was pegged against the German mark, the currency that Germany used before its current currency, the euro. The mark-pound exchange rate was initially pegged at a value that required little government intervention. However, in 1992, changing market forces put pressure on the British pound to depreciate. During the summer of 1992, the British authorities spent about $24 billion of foreign currency reserves to defend the pegged value of the pound. The British authorities were running low on foreign currency reserves when a new wave of pound sales hit the market on September 16, 1992. At the end of that day, the British authorities gave up trying to prop up its currency and accepted a sharp depreciation, as shown in Exhibit 29.7. This day came to be known as Black Wednesday.

Exhibit 29.7 The Mark-Pound Exchange Rate (Marks per Pound) from January 1991 to December 1992

Changes in economic conditions during 1992 implied that the British pound had become overvalued. British authorities spent their foreign currency reserves trying to defend their overvalued currency, leading to a sharp decline in their reserves in August and especially in early September 1992. On September 16, they gave up on their attempts to prop up the British pound, allowing a sharp depreciation.

Source: Federal Reserve Board of Governors.

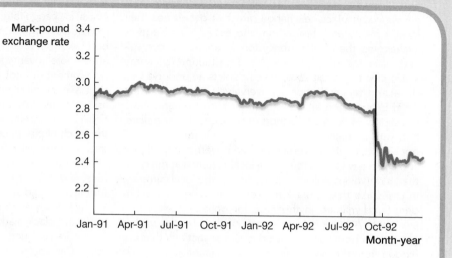

Journalists referred to George Soros as "the man who broke the Bank of England." He bet against the pound in 1992 and made $1 billion when the pound subsequently fell in value.

The events leading up to Black Wednesday yielded winners and losers. The winners were the currency traders, especially George Soros. He had bet against the pound by borrowing about $10 billion worth of pounds and then using those pounds to purchase German marks. Following Black Wednesday, the German mark became more valuable relative to the pound and, consequently, the $10 billion of pound-denominated debts that Soros owed were cheaper to pay off with appreciated marks. Soros is believed to have made over $1 billion of profits on these transactions. These trading profits benefited Soros and the investors in his hedge fund.

In making these investments, Soros was employing basic economic reasoning. He understood that the British government was running out of foreign currency reserves, like German marks, in the summer of 1992. Soros was able to generate billions of dollars of additional sales of the British government's foreign currency reserves—Soros used pounds to buy $10 billion worth of marks on the foreign exchange market—which helped force the British authorities' hand. Soros's pound sales and mark purchases accelerated the pace of the British government's reserve losses, convincing the government that it couldn't resist the tide of pound selling.

The losers from Black Wednesday included the British government, which suffered enormous losses because it spent billions of dollars of foreign currency reserves to prop up the pound. By selling foreign currency reserves that would subsequently appreciate against the pound, the British government ended up with trading losses of approximately $6 billion worth of pounds.

Question

How did George Soros make $1 billion?

Answer

George Soros bet against an overvalued British pound just before the pound depreciated. Soros borrowed pounds and then used those pounds to buy German marks. On September 16, 1992, a day that came to be known as Black Wednesday, the British authorities succumbed to market pressure and devalued the pound. At this moment, Soros's investments in German marks became more valuable than his pound-denominated debts. Soros was able to forecast the pound's depreciation because British foreign currency reserves were rapidly running down during the summer of 1992.

Data

Exchange rate and reserves data.

Caveat

George Soros and other speculators have made many bets against currencies they thought were overvalued, but these bets have not all been successful because authorities can sometimes successfully defend overvalued exchange rates.

29.3 The Real Exchange Rate and Exports

So far we've focused on the nominal exchange rate. That's the exchange rate that you read about in the newspaper each day and is also the exchange rate that equates quantity supplied and quantity demanded in the foreign exchange market. However, it is a different exchange rate—the so-called real exchange rate—that is actually crucial for the macroeconomy and for trade. We now define the concept of the real exchange rate and explain why it plays such an important role in influencing trade flows.

From the Nominal to the Real Exchange Rate

As we have seen, for its sourcing decisions Walmart compares the costs of domestic manufacturers and foreign manufacturers, adjusting for the exchange rate. For example, holding quality fixed, Walmart compares the implied dollar price of the toy manufactured in China to the dollar price of a similar toy manufactured in the United States. In essence, Walmart is interested in the following ratio:

$$\frac{\text{Dollar price of U.S. toy}}{\text{Dollar price of Chinese toy}}.$$

If this ratio is greater than 1, U.S. toys are more expensive than Chinese toys and Walmart buys from the Chinese supplier. On the other hand, if this ratio is less than 1, a U.S. toy is less expensive than a Chinese toy and Walmart buys from the U.S. supplier.

This ratio incorporates two different kinds of information: the prices of the toys in their respective domestic currencies and the yuan-dollar exchange rate that enables Walmart to convert yuan prices to dollar prices. The numerator is just the price that U.S. suppliers quote Walmart. If the U.S. manufacturer will supply toys to Walmart at $5 per toy, then $5 is the numerator.

To calculate the dollar price of the Chinese toy, we need to take the Chinese price (in yuan) and multiply it by the number of dollars per yuan. Recall that e is the yuan-dollar nominal exchange rate, defined as the number of yuan per dollar. The number of dollars per yuan is given by $1/e$. Thus the dollar price of Chinese toys can be calculated as

$$\text{Dollar price of Chinese toy} = (\text{Yuan price of Chinese toy}) \times \frac{\text{Dollars}}{\text{Yuan}}$$
$$= (\text{Yuan price of Chinese toy}) \times \frac{1}{e}.$$

For example, if a Chinese toy has a price of 20 yuan and the nominal exchange rate is 6.05 yuan per dollar, then the dollar price of the Chinese toy is 20/6.05 = $3.31 per toy.

Let's put these pieces together. We can now rewrite our initial ratio this way:

$$\frac{\text{Dollar price of U.S. toy}}{\text{Dollar price of Chinese toy}} = \frac{\text{Dollar price of U.S. toy}}{(\text{Yuan price of Chinese toy}) \times \frac{1}{e}}$$
$$= \frac{\text{Dollar price of U.S. toy} \times e}{\text{Yuan price of Chinese toy}}.$$

This ratio represents the relative price, adjusted for the exchange rate, of U.S. and Chinese toys. All companies make these calculations when sourcing their products.

Because this ratio is at the heart of every firm's sourcing decisions, economists have developed a special name for it. We define this ratio for a general basket of goods and services and refer to it as the *real exchange rate*. The **real exchange rate** for the United States is defined as the ratio of the dollar price of a basket of goods and services in the United States divided by the *dollar* price of the *same* basket of goods and services in a foreign country, for instance, China. Echoing the previous derivation for the toy example, the overall real exchange rate for the United States and China is written as:

The **real exchange rate** is defined as the ratio of the dollar price of a basket of goods and services in the United States, divided by the dollar price of the same basket of goods and services in a foreign country.

$$\frac{\text{Dollar price of U.S. basket}}{\text{Dollar price of Chinese basket}} = \frac{(\text{Dollar price of U.S. basket}) \times e}{\text{Yuan price of Chinese basket}}.$$

The dollar price of a U.S. basket refers to the price of a basket of goods and services in the United States. The yuan price of a Chinese basket is the price of the *same* basket in China. By using the nominal exchange rate, we make the U.S. basket, priced in dollars, and the Chinese basket, priced in yuan, comparable.

Co-Movement Between the Nominal and the Real Exchange Rates

The previous equation makes it clear that the real exchange rate depends partially on the nominal exchange rate and partially on the ratio of U.S. prices and Chinese prices. If U.S. and Chinese prices don't respond to a change in the nominal exchange rate, then the real exchange rate should move proportionally with the nominal exchange rate. This is indeed the case in the short run but not necessarily in the long run.

Let's first consider the short-run consequences of a change in the nominal exchange rate. Exhibit 29.8 plots both the nominal exchange rate between British pounds and U.S. dollars (pounds per dollar, normalized to 100 in 1950, in blue) and the real exchange rate between the two currencies (dollar prices in the United States

In most circumstances the nominal and real exchange rates appreciate and depreciate together.

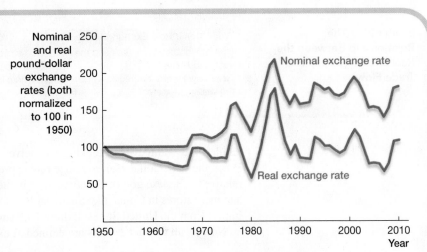

Exhibit 29.8 The Nominal and the Real Pound-Dollar Exchange Rates from 1950 to 2010

This exhibit plots the nominal exchange rate between British pounds and U.S. dollars (pounds per dollar, in blue) and the real exchange rate between the two currencies (dollar prices in the United States divided by dollar prices in the United Kingdom, in red). The pound and the dollar were pegged until 1966, so the nominal exchange rate was constant from 1950 to 1966. However, the real exchange rate fell from 1950 to 1966 because prices were rising faster in the United Kingdom than they were in the United States. After 1967, the nominal and the real exchange rates seem to move up and down together: when the nominal pound-dollar exchange rate rises so that the dollar appreciates, so does the real pound-dollar exchange rate. Over the entire period, the real exchange rate keeps falling further behind the nominal exchange rate because the UK inflation rate has been slightly greater on average than the U.S. inflation rate. Note that both exchange rates are normalized to equal 100 in 1950 (every observation is divided by the value of the same series in 1950 and the result is multiplied by 100).

Source: Alan Heston, Robert Summers, and Bettina Aten, Penn World Table Version 7.1, Center for International Comparisons of Production, Income and Prices at the University of Pennsylvania, July 2012.

divided by dollar prices in the United Kingdom, also normalized to 100 in 1950, in red). The exhibit reveals that, in the short run, the nominal pound-dollar exchange rate moves almost in lockstep with the real exchange rate. In other words, in most circumstances the nominal and real exchange rates appreciate and depreciate together.

However, the exhibit also shows that there are movements in the real exchange rate that are not associated with changes in the nominal exchange rate. This is easiest to see from 1950 to 1966, when the nominal exchange rate was pegged between the two countries. With the nominal exchange rate temporarily *fixed*, movements in the real exchange rate derive solely from different amounts of inflation in the United States and the United Kingdom. During this period, UK inflation was higher than U.S. inflation, causing the ratio of U.S. prices to UK prices to fall. With a fixed nominal exchange rate, a higher inflation rate in the United Kingdom relative to the United States implies that the real exchange rate fell from 1950 to 1966.

Movements in the real exchange rate arising from differences in the U.S. and UK inflation rates have also occurred after 1966 (when the two currencies started floating against one another), but these inflation effects are easy to miss when you look at the exhibit. For floating currencies with modest levels of inflation, most of the year-to-year movement in the real exchange rate derives from movement in the nominal exchange rate and not from cross-country differences in the rate of inflation.

The Real Exchange Rate and Net Exports

The real exchange rate is the key determinant of whether Walmart is stocking its U.S. store shelves with U.S. or Chinese products and whether Shanghai Bailian—a Chinese big-box

Exhibit 29.9 The Relationship Between the Real Exchange Rate and Trade Flows	Yuan-Dollar Real Exchange Rate	China	United States
	Goes up (dollar appreciates and the yuan depreciates)	Import less from United States Export more to United States	Export less to China Import more from China
	Goes down (dollar depreciates and the yuan appreciates)	Import more from United States Export less to United States	Export more to China Import less from China

retailer like Walmart—is stocking its shelves (in China) with U.S. or Chinese products. When the yuan-dollar real exchange rate appreciates, U.S. goods become more expensive relative to Chinese goods, so more stores in the United States prefer to import from China and more stores in China, like Shanghai Bailian, prefer to buy local products rather than to import from the United States. Exhibit 29.9 summarizes these optimizing decisions.

Now recall that net exports are defined as exports minus imports:

$$\text{Net exports} = \text{Exports} - \text{Imports}.$$

Exhibit 29.10 plots the *net exports curve*, denoted by $NX(E)$, which shows the relationship between net exports and the real exchange rate, denoted as E. This relationship is downward-sloping because when the yuan-dollar real exchange rate appreciates (implying a higher value of E), U.S. exports to China tend to fall and U.S. imports from China tend to increase.

Exhibit 29.10 The Real Exchange Rate (E) and Net Exports

When its real exchange rate appreciates, a country imports more from other countries and exports less to other countries, reducing its net exports. This relationship is shown by the downward-sloping net exports curve, denoted by $NX(E)$. For instance, when the real exchange rate rises from E^* to E_1, net exports fall from 0 to NX_1 < 0. Conversely, when the real exchange rate falls from E^* to E_2, net exports rise from 0 to $NX_2 > 0$.

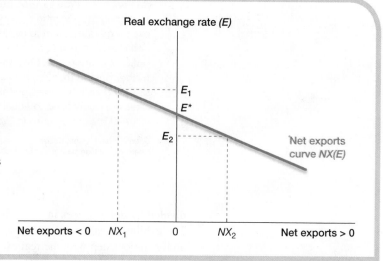

Notice also that there is a particular value of the real exchange rate, marked as E^* in Exhibit 29.10, where net exports are equal to zero. When the real exchange rate is above E^*, net exports are negative (a trade deficit), and when the real exchange rate is below E^*, net exports are positive (a trade surplus). The real exchange rate usually can't stay far above E^*, because large permanent trade deficits tend to be unsustainable. A large permanent trade deficit leads to an ever-rising debt to foreign countries. At some point, foreign countries will get nervous that this debt won't be repaid. When that happens, they will start selling their U.S. assets, driving down the nominal dollar exchange rate, which causes E to fall toward E^*.

29.4 GDP in the Open Economy

We now analyze the macroeconomic implications of changes in the real exchange rate. Let's focus on an appreciation of the real exchange rate. To understand the consequences of this change, let's return to the national income accounting identity, which was introduced in Chapter 19:

$$Y = C + I + G + X - M.$$

LETTING THE DATA SPEAK

Why Have Chinese Authorities Kept the Yuan Undervalued?

Our discussion of the yuan-dollar nominal exchange rate, which is illustrated in Exhibit 29.5, implies that the yuan has been historically undervalued (and the dollar has been overvalued). To hold down the value of the yuan (and thereby prop up the value of the dollar), the Chinese authorities have sold yuan and purchased dollars (about $2 trillion).

Why would the Chinese authorities try to keep the dollar overvalued? Exhibit 29.10 provides the answer: an overvalued real dollar exchange rate implies greater net exports from China to the United States. Chinese authorities have been supporting an overvalued dollar in order to boost Chinese exports. A consequence of the overvalued yuan-dollar real exchange rate—an exchange rate above the equivalent of E^* in Exhibit 29.10—is the large trade deficit that the United States runs with China.

Exhibit 29.11 shows that this trade deficit was approximately $300 billion in 2013. Export growth has been a key pillar of China's growth strategy since the 1980s.

This strategy might boost the rate of Chinese growth, but it does come with costs for China, not to mention the rest of the world. An undervalued Chinese yuan hurts Chinese workers by lowering their buying power because it makes their imports from the rest of the world more expensive. In addition, an undervalued Chinese yuan creates diplomatic problems with China's trading partners. Higher Chinese exports to the United States distort economic activity in the United States by crowding out industries that compete with Chinese manufacturers. This situation creates considerable friction between the United States and China.

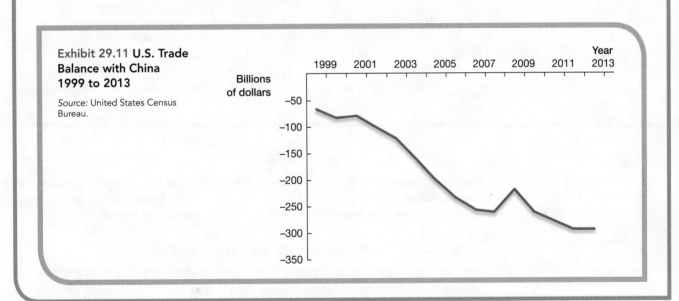

Exhibit 29.11 U.S. Trade Balance with China 1999 to 2013

Source: United States Census Bureau.

Here Y represents GDP, I represents investment (in plants, equipment, and residential construction), C represents consumption, G represents government expenditure, and $X - M$ represents net exports (all for the U.S. economy).

The appreciation of the real exchange rate reduces net exports and causes a decline in GDP—holding all else equal, a decline in $X - M$ on the right-hand side of the national income accounting identity reduces Y or GDP. We can trace out these macroeconomic implications using the labor supply and labor demand diagram introduced in Chapter 23 and used for the analysis of macroeconomic fluctuations in Chapters 26 and 27. Exhibit 29.12 presents the model with downward wage rigidity.

To illustrate how GDP responds to the changes in net exports, suppose that the dollar appreciates and net exports decline. In particular, the foreign demand for certain U.S. products—let's say machine tools—declines because the appreciation of the dollar has made these goods more expensive for foreigners. This decline in demand for machine tools implies that machine-tool producers will shift their labor demand to the left. As shown in Exhibit 29.12, the leftward shift of labor demand induced by the appreciation of the dollar will translate into lower employment and a new pool of unemployed workers.

We also need to consider multiplier effects, which were introduced in Chapter 26. For instance, job losses in an export industry will cause unemployment, and the newly

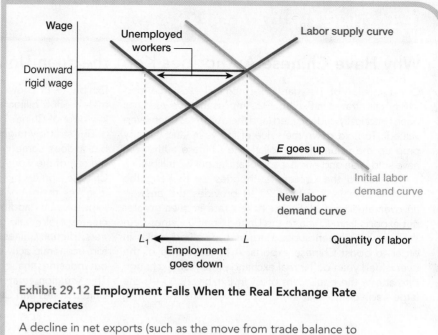

Exhibit 29.12 Employment Falls When the Real Exchange Rate Appreciates

A decline in net exports (such as the move from trade balance to NX_1 in Exhibit 29.10) reduces the demand for the goods and services supplied by certain domestic producers, and this reduces labor demand. With downward rigid wages, the lower labor demand translates into unemployment.

unemployed workers will reduce consumption, thereby affecting other industries. In this way, a decline in net exports might have spillover effects, leading to a larger aggregate economic contraction than the direct effect of the reduction in net exports.

Interest Rates, Exchange Rates, and Net Exports

We just explained that an appreciation of the real exchange rate will reduce GDP. Now we explain how expansionary monetary policy can reverse this contraction by lowering the real exchange rate and increasing net exports.

Imagine that we start from the real exchange rate E_1, as drawn in Exhibit 29.10. Assume that the domestic interest rate falls as the result of expansionary monetary policy. Such a decrease will cause foreigners—say, Europeans—to reduce their holdings of U.S. assets (because with a lower interest rate, the rate of return on U.S. assets relative to foreign assets has declined, making them less attractive). But to do so they need to exchange dollars for euros, and thus there will be a greater supply of dollars from Europeans. The greater supply of U.S. dollars will shift the dollar supply curve to the right in the foreign exchange market. Because the dollar-euro exchange rate is flexible, this greater supply of dollars will lead to a depreciation of the dollar relative to the euro.

In Exhibit 29.10, this depreciation means moving toward a lower real exchange rate, say from E_1 to E^*, which increases net exports from $NX_1 < 0$ to $NX = 0$. In summary, a decrease in U.S. interest rates causes a depreciation of the U.S. dollar, a depreciation in the dollar real exchange rate, and an increase in U.S. net exports.

On the other hand, contractionary monetary policy will have the opposite impact. When the Fed raises the domestic interest rate, this makes U.S. assets more appealing, which causes foreigners to increase their holdings of U.S. assets. Their increased purchases of U.S. assets cause a rightward shift in the demand curve for dollars, raising the equilibrium nominal exchange rate. This in turn causes the real exchange rate to appreciate, reducing net exports.

Summing up, the Fed can increase net exports by lowering domestic interest rates or can lower net exports by raising domestic interest rates.

> The Fed can increase net exports by lowering domestic interest rates or can lower net exports by raising domestic interest rates.

Revisiting Black Wednesday

With the help of this discussion, we can revisit the British experience in the early 1990s. As we discussed in the Evidence-Based Economics feature, the British pound came to be overvalued relative to the German mark and this overvaluation eventually led to the sharp depreciation of the pound on Black Wednesday.

The scenario depicted in Exhibits 29.10 and 29.12 reflects the situation of the British economy during 1991 and 1992. The overvalued pound was reducing British GDP. The British economy was effectively at real exchange rate E_1 in Exhibit 29.10 and the corresponding point with employment given by L_1 in Exhibit 29.12.

You might be wondering why the British authorities thought that they could defend the pound despite its overvaluation. The answer is that they believed that the overvaluation was temporary.

The British authorities' optimistic beliefs were not entirely groundless. We have so far explained how a nominal exchange rate depreciation can eliminate overvaluation of a currency. But there is *another* solution that can occur whether or not a country has a flexible exchange rate. Due to the lower net exports shown in Exhibit 29.10, domestic firms might cut their prices to become more competitive, and this would reduce the ratio of domestic prices to foreign prices. Recall that the real exchange rate is

$$E = \frac{(\text{Domestic prices}) \times e}{\text{Foreign prices}}.$$

A falling ratio of domestic to foreign prices (holding e fixed) would correspond to a falling real exchange rate, boosting net exports, raising labor demand, and increasing GDP.

In 1992, the British authorities anticipated that British prices *would* fall relative to the prices of their trading partners and that this would eliminate the overvaluation of the pound because more foreign countries would choose to import goods from the United Kingdom (shifting the demand curve for the pound to the right). However, such domestic price adjustments take a long time to occur, something the British authorities didn't realize at first. By the time they learned this lesson the overvalued pound had already depressed British net exports and caused a severe recession. As the real exchange rate was showing little sign of improvement and British foreign reserves were running out, the stage was set for Black Wednesday and the sharp depreciation of the pound's nominal exchange rate.

Consistent with the models discussed in this chapter, the depreciation of the pound on Black Wednesday led to a decline in the pound's real exchange rate, an expansion of British net exports, and a corresponding increase in the aggregate level of economic activity. In fact, the British economy did so well after Black Wednesday, growing on average at 3.6 percent per year during the next 3 years, that some commentators switched to calling the day that Soros broke the pound "White Wednesday." Pegging the pound to the mark had been damaging the UK economy. Letting market forces determine the price of the pound turned out to be the best policy after all.

LETTING THE DATA SPEAK

The Costs of Fixed Exchange Rates

Both Europe and the United States were plunged into recession during the 2007–2009 financial crisis. The economic contraction and its aftermath have been worse in Europe, as you can see in Exhibit 29.13. In 2013, U.S. real GDP was 7.6 percent *above* its 2007 pre-crisis level. In 2013, eurozone real GDP was still 0.3 percent *below* its 2007 pre-crisis level.

Many economists believe that the greater severity and duration of the economic crisis in Europe has in part been due to the inability of European exchange rates to adjust. Since January 1, 1999, major European economies (excluding the United Kingdom) have been part of the eurozone, which means that they use a single currency, the euro. This is referred to as a *currency union*, a form of fixed exchange rate, in which, by using the same currency, all of these economies are pegging their exchange rates to each other.

As we have seen, when the exchange rate can change, countries can devalue their currencies and thus increase their net exports, stimulating the economy. This is not possible when a country is a member of a currency union (unless the common currency itself is devalued).

Compounding this problem, there is the mismatch between the needs of different European economies. Germany has been doing relatively well compared to the rest of Europe. In 2013, German real GDP was 5.9 percent above its 2007 pre-crisis level. Many other eurozone economies have done much less well. The aggregate real GDP of Greece, Ireland, Italy, Portugal, and Spain, was 7.2 percent *lower* in 2013 than it was in 2007.

If these countries had independent monetary authorities, they might have adopted highly expansionary monetary policies, stimulating their economies and reducing their real exchange rates. This would have increased their net exports and boosted demand for labor. However, the eurozone currency union has necessitated a one-size-fits-all monetary policy, which has ended up being insufficiently expansionary for Greece, Ireland, Italy, Portugal, and Spain.

Exhibit 29.13 Real GDP Set to 100 in 2007

This exhibit plots the path of real GDP in four economic regions: the United States, Germany, the entire eurozone, and a subset of eurozone economies that were particularly hard hit by the financial crisis (Greece, Ireland, Italy, Portugal, and Spain). All of the data is normalized to 100 in 2007 to simplify comparisons. This is done by dividing all of the real GDP observations for a specific country by the value of real GDP for that country in 2007 and then multiplying by 100.

Sources: World Bank Databank and International Monetary Fund World Economic Outlook Database.

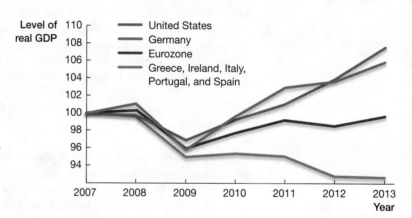

Summary

✹ The nominal exchange rate is the number of units of foreign currency per unit of domestic currency. The real exchange rate, on the other hand, gives the ratio of the dollar price of a basket of goods and services purchased in the United States to the dollar price of the *same* basket purchased in a foreign country.

✹ The nominal exchange rate is determined by the supply and demand for a currency in the foreign exchange market. When a Chinese producer sells goods to a U.S. firm and receives dollars, the Chinese firm converts the dollars to the

Chinese currency, the yuan, in the foreign exchange market. This is equivalent to demanding yuan and supplying dollars in the foreign exchange market. On the other hand, a Chinese firm that imports from the United States would be doing the opposite in the foreign exchange market: supplying yuan and demanding dollars with which it will pay its U.S. trading partners.

☀ When a country has a flexible exchange rate, changes in the supply and demand for a currency lead to fluctuations in the nominal exchange rate. Many countries, however, manage or fix exchange rates and therefore peg their currencies to another currency, such as the dollar. Under managed or fixed exchange rates, fluctuations in the supply and demand for the currency do not necessarily lead to fluctuations in the exchange rate.

☀ Though managed or fixed exchange rate systems might appear more stable at first, when the exchange rates they generate are out of line with market forces, these systems can lead to sudden changes in the exchange rate. In the process, they create huge profit opportunities, like the one exploited by the financier George Soros when he bet that the British pound would be allowed to depreciate.

☀ The real exchange rate is a key price for the economy in part because it determines net exports. A real exchange rate greater than 1 implies that U.S. goods and services are more expensive than foreign goods and services. Thus a real exchange rate above 1 discourages exports and encourages imports, reducing net exports.

☀ A fall in net exports lowers GDP and shifts the labor demand curve to the left.

☀ Domestic interest rates influence the real exchange rate. A fall in domestic interest rates reduces the appeal of U.S. assets to foreign investors, lowering both the nominal and the real exchange rates. The resulting rise in net exports shifts the labor demand curve to the right and increases GDP.

Key Terms

nominal exchange rate *p. 687*
flexible exchange rate, or floating exchange rate *p. 689*

fixed exchange rate *p. 689*
managed exchange rate *p. 689*

foreign exchange market *p. 689*
real exchange rate *p. 698*

Questions

All questions are available in MyEconLab *for practice and instructor assignment.*

1. How is the nominal exchange rate between two currencies defined?

2. When is a currency said to appreciate or depreciate?

3. Distinguish among flexible, fixed, and managed exchange rates.

4. What does the demand curve for dollars show? Why does the demand curve for dollars slope downward?

5. What does the supply curve for dollars show? Why does the supply curve for dollars slope upward?

6. What does it mean to say that, at an exchange rate of 1 USD = 60 INR, the U.S. dollar is overvalued and the Indian rupee is undervalued?

7. Why might a country peg its exchange rate at a level that overvalues its own currency?

8. How did George Soros benefit from the overvaluation of the British pound?

9. How is the real exchange rate for the United States calculated?

10. How does a change in a country's real exchange rate affect its net exports?

11. All else being equal, explain how an increase in the real interest rate can affect a country's net exports, labor demand, and level of employment.

12. The economy of Freedonia is currently faced with negative net exports and high unemployment. Explain two measures that the Freedonian central bank could take to increase net exports and lower unemployment.

Problems

All problems are available in MyEconLab for practice and instructor assignment.
Problems marked 🌐 *update with real-time data.*

1. Suppose that the country Argonia follows a flexible exchange rate regime. The exchange rate between the Argonian dollar (AGD) and the U.S. dollar (USD) is currently 1 AGD = 3 USD.

   a. Use a graph to show the equilibrium in the foreign exchange market with the U.S. dollar-Argonian dollar exchange rate on the vertical axis and the quantity of Argonian dollars on the horizontal axis.

   b. Suppose that the global demand for apricots grown in Argonia increases sharply. Other things being unchanged, how would this affect the value of the Argonian dollar? Use the graph to explain.

2. Recall from Chapter 20 that the Big Mac index is used as a rough measure of purchasing power parity across countries. *The Economist* magazine recently included the Vietnamese dong (VND) in its calculation of the Big Mac index. A Big Mac costs $4.62 in the United States but only 60,000 dong or $2.84 in Vietnam (at the current exchange rate). What does this data suggest about the value of the real exchange rate of the U.S. dollar vs. the Vietnamese dong? Is the real exchange rate likely to be greater than or less than one?

3. As discussed in the chapter, Venezuela has an official exchange rate as well as a black market exchange rate. The following chart shows the official nominal exchange rate between the Venezuelan bolivar (VEF) and the US dollar (USD).

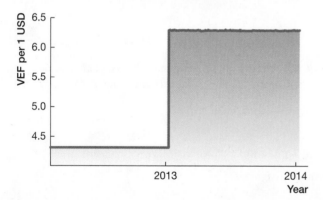

   The Venezuelan authorities increased the value of the VEF/USD nominal exchange rate from 4.3 VEF per dollar to 6.3 VEF per dollar in February 2013. However, in January 2014, buyers and sellers in the black market were exchanging the bolivar for the dollar at a rate of 79 VEF per dollar, leading commentators to believe that the official exchange rate of the VEF is highly overvalued.

   a. Assuming the black market exchange rate reflects what the equilibrium exchange rate would be, use a graph to show the overvalued official exchange rate and the equilibrium exchange rate in the market for VEF. The vertical axis should be expressed as VEF per dollar.

   b. Why might the Venezuelan government choose to maintain an overvalued official exchange rate?

4. The Evidence-Based Economics feature in the chapter discusses how George Soros's hedge fund made money by betting on the devaluation of the British pound. Interestingly, Soros also made money betting against the Thai baht.

   In 1997, the baht had been continually falling against the U.S. dollar. The Bank of Thailand attempted to defend its overvalued exchange rate—the Thai baht (THB) was pegged to the U.S. dollar at a rate of 25 THB per U.S. dollar. Explain how each of the following factors made it difficult for the Thai authorities to continue to defend their exchange rate, leading to a sharp devaluation.

   a. The government's reserves of U.S. dollars fell to a 2-year low in 1997.

   b. A very high level of corporate debt in Thailand was denominated in U.S. dollars.

5. Using the net exports curve and the labor demand and labor supply curve, explain how a fall in the real exchange rate can lead to an increase in employment in a country.

6. Econia trades with its neighbors, the countries of Governmentia and Sociologia. In Econia, the currency is called the econ; in Governmentia, the currency is called the gov; and in Sociologia, the currency is the soc.

   Nominal exchange rates follow:

   200 econ = 1 gov

   1 soc = ¼ gov

   100 econ = 1 soc

   A good that is produced and consumed in all three countries is the Mack Burger. The price of Macks in the three countries is as follows: 1 Mack costs 2 govs in Governmentia, 16 socs in Sociologia, and 600 econ in Econia.

   a. From the perspective of Governmentia, calculate the real exchange rate in Mack Burgers between Governmentia and Sociologia, using the nominal exchange rates and prices listed above. Explain in words what the number you calculated means.

   b. If these three currencies can be freely traded so that their exchange rates are flexible or floating, can the nominal exchange rates listed above persist over time? Why or why not? [Hint: Show that currency traders could make unlimited profits if they could trade at these exchange rates.]

   c. The economy of Econia enters a period of deflation. What will happen as a result of this to the current account in Governmentia, Econia's main trading partner, in the short run? Assume nominal exchange rates are constant in the short run. Explain fully.

7. *Challenge Problem*: The beautiful, mythical country of Coloradial uses the teo as its currency, and the gritty, post-industrial country of Oheo uses the eren. Exactly 1 year ago, you could get 100 teos in exchange for 5 erens in the foreign exchange market. Since then, though, the real interest rate in Coloradial has increased, while staying constant in Oheo.

a. All other things being equal, would you expect the eren to have appreciated or depreciated with respect to the teo? Explain your reasoning.

b. Assume that the change in the value of the eren with respect to the teo (appreciation or depreciation depending on your previous answer) was 50 percent. What is the current nominal exchange rate expressed in teos/eren?

c. One year ago, you borrowed 100,000 teos from a Coloradial bank at a rate of 3 percent per year. You then traded the 100,000 teos for erens at the nominal exchange rate that prevailed at the time (100 teos = 5 erens), and invested those erens in Oheo at 5 percent interest.

After the year was over, your intention was to exchange the erens back for teos, repay the loan to the Coloradial bank, and keep a tidy profit. (This strategy is called a "carry trade" and at various times has been popular with foreign exchange traders.)

  i. How much would you have made on this strategy if the interest rates did not change *and* if the exchange rate had not changed from 100 teos = 5 erens?

  ii. What will be your profit (or loss) on the trade given the changes in the exchange rate you found in parts (a) and (b)? (Assume the interest rate you paid to the Coloradial bank was fixed in your loan agreement, and so did not change.)

8. The graph below shows the Japanese yen per U.S. dollar exchange rate between 2008 and 2014. The table that follows shows the real interest rates in these two countries during the same period.

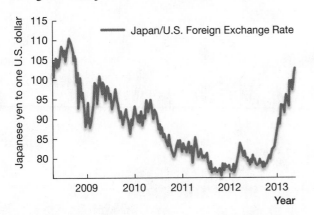

Real Interest rate in the United States and Japan

Year	2009	2010	2011	2012	2013
United States	2.5	2	1.3	1.5	1.7
Japan	2.2	3.8	3.4	2.3	1.9

What could explain why the U.S. dollar depreciated vis-à-vis the Japanese yen between 2008 and 2013? Explain your answer with the help of the information given in the table.

9. Over the last 10 years, the dollar has depreciated vis-à-vis the euro.

a. Suppose that in the short run the Fed wanted both to defend the dollar (that is, stop its decline and/or cause it to appreciate) and stimulate investment. Based on what you have learned in this chapter and in Chapter 27, discuss whether the Fed can achieve both of these goals simultaneously through monetary policy?

b. Suppose instead that the European Central Bank (ECB) conducts expansionary monetary policy. What is the short-run effect, if any, of this policy on the euro/dollar nominal exchange rate and on the real exchange rate between the United States and the European Monetary Union. In your answer about what happens to the real exchange rate, state any assumptions you are making.

10. Thailand and Taiwan are both rapidly growing economies in East and Southeast Asia that trade actively with other countries.

a. Suppose rice wine is the only good produced in Thailand and Taiwan. A bottle of wine costs 100 bhat in Thailand and 200 NT (New Taiwan dollars) in Taiwan. The nominal exchange rate is 0.5 bhat per NT. Calculate the real exchange rate from Thailand's perspective (that is, using Thailand as the "domestic" economy). Show your work. Intuitively, what does this number represent?

b. The Taiwanese trade balance (its current account) with the rest of the world is initially running neither a deficit nor a surplus. Taiwan alone experiences an economic boom and its real interest rate rises at the same time. Thoroughly explain the mechanisms by which the Taiwanese current account is affected by its boom and the increase in its real interest rate.

c. Assume that the change in the value of the bhat/NT exchange rate was 50 percent, which, depending on your answer in part (b), was either appreciation or depreciation. What is the current nominal exchange rate expressed in bhat/NT? Show your work.

11. Imagine that there are two economies in the world: Bostonia and New Yorkland. Bostonia's currency is the sock and New Yorkland's is the yank. Despite the long-standing rivalry between their citizens, Bostonia and New Yorkland are trading partners.

The Central Bank of New Yorkland decides to conduct contractionary monetary policy. Explain the short-run effect, if any, on the following:

a. The yank/sock nominal exchange rate

b. New Yorkland's net exports

c. Bostonia's net exports

d. GDP in New Yorkland recently plummeted. At first, the citizens in Bostonia cheered, happy to see their rivals taken down a notch. But then an economist (always a killjoy) asserts that the fall in New Yorkland's GDP is likely to hurt Bostonia's GDP in the short run. Could the economist be correct? Why or why not?

12. Recall the discussion in "Letting the Data Speak" regarding differences in the recovery of various members of the Eurozone from the recession of 2007–2009. Based on the discussion in this chapter and previous chapters, explain why the adoption of a single currency, like the Euro, would hamper the ability of an individual country to respond to a downturn in its economy.

Endnotes

Chapter 2

1 Philip Oreopoulos, "Estimating Average and Local Treatment Effects of Education when Compulsory Schooling Laws Really Matter," *American Economic Review* 96, no. 1 (2006): 152–175.

2 Sally Sadoff, Steven D. Levitt, and John A. List, "The Effect of Performance-Based Incentives on Educational Achievement: Evidence from a Randomized Experiment," University of Chicago Working Paper (2011).

Chapter 3

1 James Frew and Beth Wilson, "Apartment Rents and Locations in Portland, Oregon: 1992–2002," *Journal of Real Estate Research* 29, no. 2 (2007): 201–217.

Chapter 4

1 Fred Ferretti, "The Way We Were: A Look Back at the Late Great Gas Shortage," *New York Times,* April 15, 1974, p. 386.

2 Stephanie McCrummen and Aymar Jean, "17 Hurt as Computer Sale Turns into Stampede. Source: http://www.washingtonpost.com/wp-dyn/content/article/2005/08/16/AR2005081600738.htm," *Washington Post*, August 17, 2005.

Chapter 5

1 Kevin G. Volpp, Andrea G. Levy, David A. Asch, Jesse A. Berlin, John J. Murphy, Angela Gomez, Harold Sox, Jingsan Zhu, and Caryn Lerman, "A Randomized Controlled Trial of Financial Incentives for Smoking Cessation," *Cancer Epidemiol. Biomakers Prev.* 15, no. 1 (January 2006): 8–12.

2 Kate Cahill and Rafael Perera, "Competitions and Incentives for Smoking Cessation," *Cochrane Database of Systematic Reviews* 3 (2008): 1–36.

3 George Baltas, "Modelling Category Demand in Retail Chains," *Journal of the Operational Research Society* 56, no. 11 (2005): 1258–1264; Frank J. Chaloupka, Michael Grossman, and Henry Saffer, "The Effects of Price on Alcohol Consumption and Alcohol-Related Problems," *Alcohol Research and Health* 26, no. 1 (2002): 22–34; Craig A. Gallet and John A. List, "Cigarette Demand: A Meta-Analysis of Elasticities," *Health Economics* 12, no. 10 (2003): 821–835; Thomas F. Hogarty and Kenneth G. Elzinga, "The Demand for Beer," *The Review of Economics and Statistics* 54, no. 2 (1972): 195–198; Fred Kuchler, Abebayehu Tegene, and J. Michael Harris, "Taxing Snack Foods: Manipulating Diet Quality or Financing Information Programs?" *Applied Economic Perspectives and Policy* 27, no. 1 (2005): 4–20; and USDA Economic Research Service Commodity and Food Elasticities Database, July 5, 2012, http://www.ers.usda.gov/data-products/commodity-and-food-elasticities.aspx#.UsYKP_RDvW1.

4 Angus Deaton, "Estimation of Own- and Cross-Price Elasticities from Household Survey Data," *Journal of Econometrics* 36, no. 1 (1987): 7–30; Edwin T. Fujii, Mohammed Khaled, and James Mak, "An Almost Ideal Demand System for Visitor Expenditures," *Journal of Transport Economics and Policy* (1985): 161–171; and Tatiana Andreyeva, Michael W. Long, and Kelly D. Brownell, "The Impact of Food Prices on Consumption: A Systematic Review of Research on the Price Elasticity of Demand for Food." *American Journal of Public Health* 100, no. 2 (2010): 216–222.

5 Oskar R. Harmon, "The Income Elasticity of Demand for Single-Family Owner-Occupied Housing: An Empirical Reconciliation," *Journal of Urban Economics* 24, no. 2 (1988): 173–185; Livio Di Matteo, "The Income Elasticity of Health Care Spending," *The European Journal of Health Economics* 4, no. 1 (2003): 20–29; Bengt Kristrom, and Pere Riera, "Is the Income Elasticity of Environmental Improvements Less Than One?" *Environmental and Resource Economics* 7, no. 1 (1996): 45–55; E. Raphael Branch, "Short Run Income Elasticity of Demand for Residential Electricity Using Consumer Expenditure Survey Data," *The Energy Journal* 4 (1993): 111–122; Jonathan E. Hughes, Christopher R. Knittel, and Daniel Sperling, "Evidence of a Shift in the Short-Run Price Elasticity of Gasoline Demand," *NBER Working Paper 12530* (2006); Laura Blanciforti and Richard Green, "An Almost Ideal Demand System Incorporating Habits: An Analysis of Expenditures on Food and Aggregate Commodity Groups," *The Review of Economics and Statistics* 65, no. 3 (1983): 511–515; Howarth E. Bouis, "The Effect of Income on Demand for Food in Poor Countries: Are Our Food Consumption Databases Giving Us Reliable Estimates?" *Journal of Development Economics* 44, no. 1 (1994): 199–226; Neil Paulley, Richard Balcombe, Roger Mackett, Helena Titheridge, John Preston, Mark Wardman, Jeremy Shires, and Peter White, "The Demand for Public Transport: The Effects of Fares, Quality of Service, Income and Car Ownership," *Transport Policy* 13, no. 4 (2006): 295–306; Arthur Van Soest and Peter Kooreman, "A Micro-Econometric Analysis of Vacation Behaviour," *Journal of Applied Econometrics* 2, no. 3 (1987): 215–226; Bertrand Melenberg and Arthur Van Soest, "Parametric and Semi-parametric Modelling of Vacation Expenditures," *Journal of Applied Econometrics* 11, no. 1 (1996): 59–76; and Eric S. Belsky, Xiao Di Zhu, and Dan McCue, "Multiple-Home Ownership and the Income Elasticity of Housing Demand" (Joint Center for Housing Studies, Graduate School of Design [and] John F. Kennedy School of Government, Harvard University, 2006).

6 Tatiana Andreyeva, Michael W. Long, and Kelly D. Brownell, "The Impact of Food Prices on Consumption: A Systematic Review of Research on the Price Elasticity of Demand for Food," *American Journal of Public Health* 100, no. 2 (2010): 216–222.

Chapter 6

1 This actually happened to one of the authors.

2 Adam Malecek, "Wisconsin Cheeseman Closing," Sun Prairie Channel3000.com, January 20th, 2011, http://sunprairie.channel3000.com/content/wisconsin-cheeseman-closing.

3 Alec Brandon, John List, and Michael Price, "The Effects of Ethanol Subsidies on Producers" (working paper, University of Chicago.

Chapter 7

1 Adam Smith, *The Wealth of Nations* (1776).

2 Vernon Smith, "Microeconomic Systems as an Experimental Science," *American Economic Review* 72, no. 5 (1982): 923–955.

3 Steven Horwitz, "Wal-Mart to the Rescue: Private Enterprise's Response to Hurricane Katrina," *The Independent Review* 13, no. 4 (2009): 511–528.

4 Friedrich A. Hayek, "The Use of Knowledge in Society," *American Economic Review* 35, no. 4 (1945): 519–530."

5 This box is based on Mark Albright, "Kmart's Blue Light Back On," *Tampa Bay Times,* May 16, 2007, http://www.sptimes.com/2007/05/16/Business/Kmart_s_blue_light_ba.shtml.

Chapter 8

1 Fair Trade Labelling Organizations International: Annual Report 2009–10.

2 Hal Weitzman, "The Bitter Cost of 'Fair Trade' Coffee," *Financial Times*, September 8, 2006.

3 Paul Krugman, "Growing World Trade: Causes and Consequences," *Brookings Papers on Economic Activity*, Economic Studies Program, The Brookings Institute, 26(1995): 327–377; and Robert Z. Lawrence, Matthew J. Slaughter, Robert E. Hall, Steven J. Davis, and Robert H. Topel "International Trade and American Wages in the 1980s: Giant Sucking Sound or Small Hiccup?" *Brookings Papers on Economic Activity*, Microeconomics, 2(1993): 161–226.

4 Robert Z. Lawrence, "Slow Real Wage Growth and U.S. Income Inequality: Is Trade to Blame?" (Is Free Trade Still Optimal in the 21st Century?, International Business School at Brandeis University, 2007)

5 Paul Krugman, "Trade and Wages, Reconsidered," *Brookings Papers on Economic Activity* (2008): 103–154.

Chapter 9

1 This is a true story; we withhold identities to protect the professor.

2 Bryan L. Boulier, Tejwant S. Datta, and Robert S. Goldfarb, "Vaccination Externalities," *The B.E. Journal of Economic Analysis & Policy* 7, no. 1 (2007).

3 Kenneth Y. Chay and Michael Greenstone, "Does Air Quality Matter? Evidence from the Housing Market," *NBER Working Paper 6826* (1998).

4 David H. Folz and Jacqueline N. Giles, "Municipal Experience with 'Pay-as-You-Throw' Policies: Findings from a National Survey," *State and Local Government Review* 34, no. 2 (2002): 105–115.

5 Joseph M. Sulock, "The Free Rider and Voting Paradox 'Games'," *Journal of Economic Education* 21, no. 1 (1990): 65–69.

6 Garrett Hardin, "The Tragedy of the Commons," *Science* 162, no. 3859 (1968): 1243–1248; and William Forster Lloyd, *Two Lectures on the Checks to Population* (1833).

7 Elinor Ostrom, *Governing the Commons: The Evolution of Institutions for Collective Action* (Cambridge University Press, 1990).

8 Peter J. Deadman, Edella Schlager, and Randy Gimblett, "Simulating Common Pool Resource Management Experiments with Adaptive Agents Employing Alternate Communication Routines," *Journal of Artificial Societies and Social Simulation* 3, no. 2 (2000): 22.

9 Jonathan Leape, "The London Congestion Charge," *Journal of Economic Perspectives* 20, no. 4 (2006): 157–176.

10 Hybrid vehicles emit less pollution and this was the reason for the tax break. This is an excellent example of the trade-off inherent in using a tax policy to achieve less congestion and less pollution.

Chapter 10

1 See William Niskanen, "The Peculiar Economics of Bureaucracy," *American Economic Review* 58, no. 2 (1968): 293–305.

2 Arthur M. Okun, *Equality and Efficiency, the Big Tradeoff* (Brookings Institution Press, 1975).

3 Ritva Reinikka and Jakob Svensson, "Local Capture: Evidence from a Central Government Transfer Program in Uganda," *Quarterly Journal of Economics* 119, no. 2 (2004): 679–705.

4 The data come from a 1987 U.S. Department of Justice report.

5 Barry Bosworth and Gary Burtless, "Effects of Tax Reform on Labor Supply, Investment, and Saving," *Journal of Economic Perspectives* 6, no. 1 (1992): 3–25.

6 There are, of course, exceptions to this. For a summary of elasticities in the literature, see Blundell and MaCurdy (1999). Blundell and MaCurdy (1999), Saez, Slemrod, and Giertz (2012), and Goolsbee (2000) conclude that the elasticity on hours supplied is close to zero for men; Richard Blundell and Thomas MaCurdy, "Labor Supply: A Review of Alternative Approaches," in *Handbook of Labor Economics* (Vol. 3C), eds. O. Ashenfelter and D. Card (Holland: Elsevier North, 1999); Emmanuel Saez, Joel Slemrod, and Seth H. Giertz, "The Elasticity of Taxable Income with Respect to Marginal Tax Rates: A Critical Review," *Journal of Economic Literature* 50, no. 1 (2012): 3-50; and Austan Goolsbee, "What Happens When You Tax the Rich? Evidence from Executive Compensation," *Journal of Political Economy* 108, no. 2 (2000): 352–378.

7 Martin Feldstein, "The Effect of Marginal Tax Rates on Taxable Income: A Panel Study of the 1986 Tax Reform Act," *The Journal of Political Economy* 103, no. 3 (1995): 551–572; and Gerald E. Auten and Robert Carroll, "Behavior of the Affluent and the 1986 Tax Reform Act," in *Proceedings of the 87th Annual Conference on Taxation of the National Tax Association* (1995): 7–12.

8 Jonathan M. Karpoff, "Public Versus Private Initiative in Arctic Exploration: The Effects of Incentives and Organizational Structure," *Journal of Political Economy* 109, no. 1 (2001): 38–78.

Chapter 11

1 Gerald S. Oettinger, "An Empirical Analysis of the Daily Labor Supply of Stadium Vendors," *Journal of Political Economy* 107, no. 2 (1999): 360–392.

2 Joshua Angrist, "The Economic Returns to Schooling in the West Bank and Gaza Strip," *American Economic Review* 85, no. 5 (1995): 1065–1087.

3 Gary S. Becker, *The Economics of Discrimination* (University of Chicago Press, 1957).

4 Claudia Goldin and Cecilia Rouse, "Orchestrating Impartiality: The Impact of 'Blind' Auditions on Female Musicians," *American Economic Review* 90, no. 4 (2000): 715–741.

5 Marianne Bertrand and Sendhil Mullainathan, "Are Emily and Greg More Employable Than Lakisha and Jamal? A Field Experiment on Labor Market Discrimination," *American Economic Review* 94, no. 4 (2004): 991–1013.

6 Kerwin Charles and Jonathan Guryan, "Prejudice and Wages: An Empirical Assessment of Becker's The Economics of Discrimination," *Journal of Political Economy* 116, no. 5 (2008): 773–809.

7 For one attempt at doing so using a field experiment, see John A. List, "The Nature and Extent of Discrimination in the Marketplace: Evidence from the Field," *Quarterly Journal of Economics*, 119, no. 1 (2004): 49–89. This study uses a series of field experiments to show that women, the elderly, and African Americans receive higher price quotes in the sportscard market due to statistical discrimination.

Chapter 12

1 Malcolm Gladwell, *Blink: The Power of Thinking Without Thinking* (Hachette Book Group USA, 2007).

2 The expiration of the Claritin patent was to occur on June 19, 2000. However, Schering-Plough requested, and was awarded, a 2-year extension. This extended the patent until June 19, 2002, when it expired.

3 Uri Gneezy, John A. List, and Michael K. Price, "Toward an Understanding of Why People Discriminate: Evidence from a Series of Natural Field Experiments," *NBER Working Paper 17855* (2012).

4 Petra Moser, "How Do Patent Laws Influence Innovation? Evidence from Nineteenth-Century World's Fairs," *American Economic Review* 95, no. 4 (2005): 1214–1236.

5 Heidi Williams, "Intellectual Project Rights and Innovation: Evidence from the Human Genome," *Journal of Political Economy* 121, no. 1 (2013): 1–27.

6 Philippe Aghion, Nick Bloom, Richard Blundell, Rachel Griffith, and Peter Howitt, "Competition and Innovation: An Inverted-U Relationship," *Quarterly Journal of Economics* 120, no. 2 (2005): 701–728.

Chapter 13

1 John F. Nash, Jr., "Non-cooperative Games," Ph.D. thesis, Mathematics Department, Princeton University (1950).

2 Pierre-Andre Chiappori, Steven D. Levitt, and Timothy Groseclose, "Testing Mixed-Strategy Equilibria When Players Are Heterogeneous: The Case of Penalty Kicks in Soccer," *American Economic Review* 92, no. 4 (2002): 1138–1151.

3 Mark Walker and John Wooders, "Minimax Play at Wimbledon," *American Economic Review* 91, no. 5 (2001): 1521–1538.

4 John A. List, "The Behavioralist Meets the Market: Measuring Social Preferences and Reputation Effects in Actual Transactions," *Journal of Political Economy* 114, no. 1 (2006): 1–37.

Chapter 14

1 Austan Goolsbee and Chad Syverson, "How Do Incumbents Respond to the Threat of Entry? Evidence from the Major Airlines," *Quarterly Journal of Economics* 123, no. 4 (2008): 1611–1633.

2 John E. Kwoka, Jr., "Advertising and the Price and Quality of Optometric Services," *American Economic Review* 74, no. 1 (1984): 211–216.

3 Timothy F. Bresnahan and Peter C. Reiss, "Entry and Competition in Concentrated Markets," *Journal of Political Economy* 99, no. 5 (1991): 977–1009.

4 Martin Dufwenberg and Uri Gneezy, "Price Competition and Market Concentration: An Experimental Study," *International Journal of Industrial Organization* 18, no. 1 (2000): 7–22.

Chapter 15

1 Daniel Read and Barbara van Leeuwen, "Predicting Hunger: The Effects of Appetite and Delay on Choice," *Organizational Behavior and Human Decision Processes* 76, no. 2 (1998): 189–205.

2 On an actual roulette wheel in the United States, the expected loss per spin is 5.3 percent of the bet you make.

3 Daniel Kahneman and Amos Tversky, "Prospect Theory: An Analysis of Decision under Risk," *Econometrica* 47, no. 2 (1979): 263–292.

Chapter 16

1 Michael A. Spence, "Job Market Signaling," *Quarterly Journal of Economics* 87, no. 3 (1973): 355–374.

2 George A. Akerlof, "The Market for 'Lemons': Quality Uncertainty and the Market Mechanism," *Quarterly Journal of Economics* 84, no. 3 (1970): 488–500.

3 Michael D. Pratt and George E. Hoffer, "Test of the Lemons Model: Comment," *American Economic Review* 74, no. 4 (1984): 798–800.

4 Winand Emons and George Sheldon, "The Market for Used Cars: A New Test of the Lemons Model," *Discussion Paper Series 26353*, Hamburg Institute of International Economics (2002).

5 Sean B. Carroll, *Making of the Fittest* (New York: W. W. Norton & Company, 2007).

6 Frank T. McDermott, John C. Lane, G. A. Brazenor, and Elizabeth A. Debney, "The Effectiveness of Bicyclist Helmets: A Study of 1710 Casualties," *Journal of Trauma and Acute Care Surgery* 34, no. 6 (1993): 834–845.

7 Ian Walker, "Drivers Overtaking Bicyclists: Objective Data on the Effects of Riding Position, Helmet Use, Vehicle Type and Apparent Gender," *Accident Analysis and Prevention* 39, no. 2 (2007): 417–425.

8 This discussion draws on Daniel M. G. Raff and Lawrence H. Summers, "Did Henry Ford Pay Efficiency Wages?" *Journal of Labor Economics* 5, no. 4 (1987): S57–86.

9 Roland G. Fryer, Jr., Steven D. Levitt, John A. List, and Sally Sadoff, "Enhancing the Efficacy of Teacher Incentives through Loss Aversion: A Field Experiment," *NBER Working Paper 18237* (2012).

10 Brian A. Jacob and Steven D. Levitt, "Rotten Apples: An Investigation of the Prevalence and Predictors of Teacher Cheating," *Quarterly Journal of Economics* 118, no. 3 (2003): 843–877.

11 David M. Cutler and Sarah J. Reber, "Paying for Health Insurance: The Trade-Off Between Competition and Adverse Selection," *Quarterly Journal of Economics* 113, no. 2 (1998): 433–466.

12 Amitabh Chandra, Jonathan Gruber, and Robin McKnight, "The Importance of the Individual Mandate—Evidence from Massachusetts," *New England Journal of Medicine* 364, no. 4 (2011): 293–295.

13 Alan B. Krueger and Andreas Mueller, "Job Search and Unemployment Insurance: New Evidence from Time Use Data," *Journal of Public Economics* 94, no. 3 (2010): 298–307.

14 David Card, Raj Chetty, and Andrea Weber, "The Spike at Benefit Exhaustion: Leaving the Unemployment System or Starting a New Job?" *American Economic Review* 97, no. 2 (2007): 113–118.

15 Gary S. Becker, "Crime and Punishment: An Economic Approach," *Journal of Political Economy* 76, no. 2 (1968): 169–217.; Gary S. Becker and George J. Stigler, "Law Enforcement, Malfeasance, and Compensation of Enforcers," *Journal of Legal Studies* 3, no. 1 (1974): 1–18.

Chapter 17

1 Recent research by Einav, Farronato, Levin, and Sundaresan shows that, on eBay, the fraction of items sold in auctions fell from about 80 percent at the beginning of 2008 to less than 30 percent in 2011, with a corresponding increase in the fraction of items sold with posted prices; Liran Einav, Chiara Farronato, Jonathan D. Levin, and Neel Sundaresan "Sales Mechanisms in Online Markets: What Happened to Internet Auctions?" *NBER Working Paper 19021* (2013).

2 Alvin E. Roth and Axel Ockenfels, "Last-Minute Bidding and the Rules for Ending Second-Price Auctions: Evidence from eBay and Amazon Auctions on the Internet," *American Economic Review* 92, no. 4 (2002): 1093–1103.

3 Sean Gray and David H. Reiley, "Measuring the Benefits to Sniping on eBay: Evidence from a Field Experiment," *Journal of Economics and Management* 9, no. 2 (2013): 137–152.

4 William Vickrey, "Counterspeculation, Auctions, and Competitive Sealed Tenders," *Journal of Finance* 16, no. 1 (1961): 8–37.

5 David Lucking-Reiley, "Using Field Experiments to Test Equivalence Between Auction Formats: Magic on the Internet," *American Economic Review* 89, no. 5 (1999): 1063–1080.

6 Shelly J. Lundberg, Robert A. Pollak, and Terence J. Wales, "Do Husbands and Wives Pool Their Resources? Evidence from the United Kingdom Child Benefit," *Journal of Human Resources* 32, no. 3 (1996): 463–480.

7 Nancy Qian, "Missing Women and the Price of Tea in China: The Effect of Sex-Specific Earnings on Sex Imbalance," *Quarterly Journal of Economics* 123, no. 3 (2008): 1251–1285.

8 Erwin Bulte, John A. List, and Qin Tu, "Battle of the Sexes: How Sex Ratios Affect Female Bargaining Power," Working Paper (2012).

Chapter 18

1 Charles T. Clotfelter, "The Impact of Tax Reform on Charitable Giving: A 1989 Perspective," *NBER Working Paper 3273* (1990).

2 Stefano DellaVigna, John A. List, and Ulrike Malmendier, "Testing for Altruism and Social Pressure in Charitable Giving," *Quarterly Journal of Economics* 127, no. 1 (2012): 1–56.

3 These results are reported in John A. List, "Friend or Foe? A Natural Experiment of the Prisoner's Dilemma," *The Review of Economics and Statistics* 88, no. 3 (2006): 463–471.

4 Iris Bohnet and Bruno S. Frey, "Social Distance and Other-Regarding Behavior in Dictator Games: Comment," *American Economic Review* 89, no. 1 (1999): 335–339.

5 Steffen Andersen, Seda Ertac, Uri Gneezy, Moshe Hoffman, and John A. List, "Stakes Matter in Ultimatum Games," *American Economic Review* 101, no. 7 (2011): 3427–3439.

6 Kenneth J. Arrow, "Gifts and Exchanges," *Philosophy & Public Affairs* 1, no. 4 (1972): 343–362.

7 See Peter J. Richerson and Robert Boyd, *Not by Genes Alone: How Culture Transformed Human Evolution* (University of Chicago Press, 2008); and Elliott Sober and David Sloan Wilson, eds., *Unto Others: The Evolution and Psychology of Unselfish Behavior*, no. 218 (Harvard University Press, 1999).

8 David Sloan Wilson and Edward O. Wilson, "Rethinking the Theoretical Foundation of Sociobiology," *Quarterly Review of Biology* 82, no. 4 (2007): 327–348.

9 Gerald Marwell and Ruth E. Ames, "Economists Free Ride, Does Anyone Else? Experiments on the Provision of Public Goods, IV," *Journal of Public Economics* 15, no. 3 (1981): 295–310; John R. Carter and Michael D. Irons, "Are Economists Different, and If So, Why?" *Journal of Economic Perspectives* 5, no. 2 (1991): 171–177; and Robert H. Frank, Thomas Gilovich, and Dennis T. Regan, "Does Studying Economics Inhibit Cooperation?" *Journal of Economic Perspectives* 7, no. 2 (1993): 159–171.

10 Oriana Bandiera and Imran Rasul, "Social Networks and Technology Adoption in Northern Mozambique," *Economic Journal* 116, no. 514 (2006): 869–902.

11 Bruce Sacerdote, "Peer Effects with Random Assignment: Results for Dartmouth Roommates," *Quarterly Journal of Economics* 116, no. 2 (2001): 681–704.

12 Scott E. Carrell, Mark Hoekstra, and James E. West, "Is Poor Fitness Contagious? Evidence from Randomly Assigned Friends," *Journal of Public Economics* 95, no. 7–8 (2011): 657–663.

13 John B. Horrigan, Kelly Garrett, and Paul Resnick, *The Internet and Democratic Debate* (Washington, D. C.: Pew Internet & American Life Project, 2004).

Chapter 19

1 This is based on a population of 316.4 million in 2013 as reported by the Census Bureau: http://www.census.gov/population/international/data/countryrank/rank.php

2 Daniel Kahneman and Alan B. Krueger, "Developments in the Measurement of Subjective Well-Being," *The Journal of Economic Perspectives* 20.1 (2006): 3–24.

3 Betsey Stevenson and Justin Wolfers, "Economic Growth and Subjective Well-Being: Reassessing the Easterlin Paradox" Brookings Papers on Economic Activity, Spring 2008.

Chapter 21

1 William D. Nordhaus, "Do Real-Output and Real-Wage Measures Capture Reality? The History of Light Suggests Not," Cowles Foundation Discussion Papers 1078, Cowles Foundation for Research in Economics, 1994.

2 Thomas R. Malthus, *An Essay on the Principle of Population* (1798).

3 Emmanuel Saez and Thomas Piketty, "Income Inequality in the United States, 1913–1998," *Quarterly Journal of Economics* 118, no. 1 (2003): 1–39.

4 Daron Acemoglu and Simon Johnson, "Disease and Development: The Effect of Life Expectancy on Economic Growth," *Journal of Political Economy* 115, no. 6 (2007): 925–985.

5 Robert M. Solow, "A Contribution to the Theory of Economic Growth," *Quarterly Journal of Economics* 70, no. 1 (1956): 65–94; and Trevor W. Swan, "Economic Growth and Capital Accumulation," *Economic Record* 32, no. 2 (1956): 334–361.

Chapter 22

1 Charles-Louis de Secondat Montesquieu, *The Spirit of the Laws, Book XIV*, Chapter 2, 230–235, [1748] 1989.

2 Alfred Marshall, *Principles of Economics, Book IV: The Agents of Production*, Chapter 5 (1890).

3 Jeffrey Sachs, "Tropical Underdevelopment," *NBER Working Paper* 8119 (2001).

4 Max Weber, *The Protestant Ethic and the Spirit of Capitalism* (New York: Routledge, [1905] 2001).

5 Samuel P. Huntington, "The Clash of Civilizations?" *Foreign Affairs* (1993): 22–49.

6 Lawrence E. Harrison and Samuel P. Huntington, *Culture Matters: How Values Shape Human Progress* (New York: Basic Books, 2000).

7 Douglass North, *Institutions, Institutional Change and Economic Performance* (Cambridge: Cambridge University Press, 1990).

8 Tim Culpan, "Taiwan's iPads are Free. The Cases Cost $1,000," *Businessweek Magazine*, October 7, 2010.

9 Adam Smith, *The Wealth of Nations* (1776).

10 Daron Acemoglu and James A. Robinson, *Why Nations Fail: the Origins of Power, Prosperity and Poverty* (New York: Crown Publishers, 2012).

11 Joseph A. Schumpeter, *Capitalism, Socialism, and Democracy* (1942).

12 Joel Mokyr, *The Enlightened Economy: An Economic History of Britain 1700–1850* (New Haven: Yale University Press, 2010).

13 Ritva Reinikka and Jakob Svensson, "Local Capture: Evidence from a Central Government Transfer Program in Uganda," *Quarterly Journal of Economics.* 119, no. 2 (2004): 679–705.

Chapter 23

1 Anna Richey-Allen, "The Pain of Unemployment," *New York Times*, October 31, 2010.

2 Alan Krueger and Andreas Mueller, "Job Search and Job Finding in a Period of Mass Unemployment: Evidence from High-Frequency Longitudinal Data," Princeton University, Industrial Relations Section Working Paper 562 (2011).

3 Nathan Hipsman, "Downward Nominal Wage Rigidity: A Double-Density Model," Harvard University Working Paper (2012).

4 David H. Autor, David Dorn, and Gordon H. Hanson, "The China Syndrome: Local Labor Market Effects of Import Competition in the United States," *American Economic Review* 103, no. 6 (2013).

Chapter 24

1 Irving Fisher, "Appreciation and Interest: A Study of the Influence of Monetary Appreciation and Depreciation on the Rate of Interest with Applications to the Bimetallic Controversy and the Theory of Interest," *Publications of the American Economic Association* 11, no. 4 (1896): 331–442.

2 Eugene F. Fama, "Efficient Capital Markets: A Review of Theory and Empirical Work," *Journal of Finance* 25, no. 2 (1970): 383–417.

3 Robert J. Shiller, *Irrational Exuberance* (Princeton University Press, 2005).

Chapter 26

1 Before 1947, U.S. GDP data are only available on an annual basis. Because the 1945 recession occurred within a single year, we don't know how much real GDP declined, but we can estimate it using the annual data. From 1944 to 1946, real GDP fell by 12.7 percent.

2 Kathryn M. Dominguez, Ray C. Fair, and Matthew D. Shapiro, "Forecasting the Depression: Harvard versus Yale," *American Economic Review* 78, no. 4 (1988): 595–612.

3 Arthur M. Okun, "Potential GNP: Its Measurement and Significance," 1963, reprinted as *Cowles Foundation Paper* 190.

4 Arthur C. Pigou, *Industrial Fluctuations*, New York: Macmillan, 1929.

5 Finn E. Kydland and Edward C. Prescott, "Time to Build and Aggregate Fluctuations" *Econometrica* 50, no. 6 (1982): 1345–1370.

6 John M. Keynes, *The General Theory of Employment, Interest and Money*, Palgrave Macmillan, 1936.

7 Milton Friedman and Anna J. Schwartz, *A Monetary History of the United States*, 1867–1960, Princeton University Press, 1963.

Chapter 27

1 William L. Silber, *Volcker: The Triumph of Persistence*, New York: Bloomsbury Press, 2012.

2 Bank of England, Financial Stability Report, June 2014 Issue no. 35, http://www.bankofengland.co.uk/publications/Documents/fsr/2014/fsrfull1406.pdf.

3 John B. Taylor, "Discretion Versus Policy Rules in Practice," in *Carnegie-Rochester Conference Series on Public Policy* 39 (1993): 195–214.

4 Christina Romer and Jared Bernstein, "The Job Impact of the American Recovery and Reinvestment Act." January 9, 2009.

5 Romer and Bernstein, "Job Impact."

6 Valerie A. Ramey, "Identifying Government Spending Shocks: It's All in the Timing," *Quarterly Journal of Economics* 126, no. 1 (2011): 1–50.

Chapter 28

1 Greg Linden, Kenneth Kraemer, and Jason Dedrick, "Who Captures Value in a Global Innovation Network?: The Case of Apple's iPod," *Communications of the ACM* 52, no. 3 (2009): 140–144.

2 Linden, Kraemer, and Dedrick, "Who Captures Value."

3 Jack Ewing, "The Disassembly Line," *New York Times*, July 15, 2014, B1.

4 Jennifer L. Rich, "U.S. Admits That Politics Was Behind Steel Tariffs," *New York Times*, March 14, 2002, at http://www.nytimes.com/2002/03/14/business/us-admits-that-politics-was-behind-steel-tariffs.html.

5 Dalila Cervantes-Godoy and Joe Dewbre, "Economic Importance of Agriculture for Sustainable Development and Poverty Reduction: The Case Study of Vietnam," OECD: 2010.

6 Ben Bland, "Vietnam's Factories Grapple with Growing Unrest," *Financial Times*, January 19, 2012, For the 2014 minimum wage data, see http://www.amchamvietnam.com/30442612/vietnams-2014-minimum-wage-adjustment-shows-moderation-15-increase-vs-17-5-increase-in-2012/

7 Penn World Tables. Alan Heston, Robert Summers and Bettina Aten, Penn World Table Version 7.1, Center for International Comparisons of Production, Income and Prices at the University of Pennsylvania, Nov 2012.

8 Cervantes-Godoy and Dewbre "Economic Importance."

9 Eric V. Edmonds and Nina Pavcnik, "International Trade and Child Labor: Cross-Country Evidence," *Journal of International Economics* 68, no. 1 (2006): 115–140.

Glossary

Absolute advantage Absolute advantage is the ability of an individual, firm, or country to produce more of a certain good than other competing producers, given the same amount of resources.

Accounting profits Accounting profits are equal to total revenue minus explicit costs.

Adverse selection In a market with adverse selection, one agent in a transaction knows about a hidden characteristic of a good and decides whether to participate in the transaction on the basis of this information.

Aggregate production function An aggregate production function describes the relationship between the aggregate output of a nation and its factors of production.

Aggregation The process of adding up individual behaviors is referred to as aggregation.

Animal spirits Animal spirits are psychological factors that lead to changes in the mood of consumers or businesses, thereby affecting consumption, investment, and GDP.

Antitrust policy Antitrust policy aims to regulate and prevent anticompetitive pricing.

Arc elasticity The arc elasticity is a method of calculating elasticities that measures at the mid-point of the demand range.

Asymmetric information In a market with asymmetric information, the information available to sellers and buyers differs.

Auction An auction is a market process in which potential buyers bid on a good and the highest bidder receives the good.

Automatic stabilizers Automatic stabilizers are components of the government budget that automatically adjust to smooth out economic fluctuations.

Average fixed cost (AFC) Average fixed cost is the total fixed cost divided by the total output.

Average tax rate The average tax rate for a household is given by total taxes paid divided by total income.

Average total cost (ATC) Average total cost is the total cost divided by the total output.

Average variable cost (AVC) Average variable cost is the total variable cost divided by the total output.

Average The mean, or average, is the sum of all the different values divided by the number of values.

Backward induction Backward induction is the procedure of solving an extensive-form game by first considering the last mover's decision in order to deduce the decisions of all previous movers.

Bank reserves Official bank reserves consist of vault cash and deposits at the Federal Reserve Bank.

Bank run A bank run occurs when a bank experiences an extraordinarily large volume of withdrawals driven by a concern that the bank will run out of liquid assets with which to pay withdrawals.

Bar chart A bar chart uses bars of different heights or lengths to indicate the properties of different groups.

Bargaining power Bargaining power describes the relative power an individual has in negotiations with another individual.

Barriers to entry Barriers to entry provide a seller with protection from potential competitors entering the market.

Behavioral economics Behavioral economics jointly analyzes the economic and psychological factors that explain human behavior.

Best response A strategy of a player is a best response to the strategies of the others in the game if, taking the other players' strategy as given, it gives her greater payoffs than any other strategy she has available.

Bilateral negotiation A bilateral negotiation is a market mechanism in which a single seller and a single buyer privately negotiate with bids and asks.

Budget constraint A budget constraint shows the bundles of goods or services that a consumer can choose given her limited budget.

Budget deficit A budget deficit occurs when tax revenues do not cover government spending.

Budget set A budget set is the set of all possible bundles of goods and services that can be purchased with a consumer's income.

Budget surplus A budget surplus occurs when tax revenues exceed government spending.

Capital income Capital income is any form of payment that derives from owning physical or financial capital.

Cartel A cartel is a formal organization of producers who agree on anticompetitive actions.

Catch-up growth Catch-up growth refers to a growth process whereby relatively poorer nations increase their incomes by taking advantage of knowledge and technologies already invented in other, technologically more advanced countries.

Causation Causation occurs when one thing directly affects another through a cause-and-effect relationship.

Central bank The central bank is the government institution that monitors financial institutions, controls certain key interest rates, and indirectly controls the money supply. These activities constitute monetary policy.

Closed economy A closed economy does not trade with the rest of the world.

Club good A club good is non-rival but excludable.

Coase Theorem The Coase Theorem states that private bargaining will result in an efficient allocation of resources.

Collective bargaining Collective bargaining refers to contract negotiations between firms and labor unions.

Collusion Collusion occurs when firms conspire to set the quantity they produce or the prices they charge.

Command-and-control regulation Command-and-control regulation either directly restricts the level of production or mandates the use of certain technologies.

Commitment Commitment refers to the ability to choose and stick with an action that might later be costly.

Common pool resource goods Common pool resource goods are a class of goods that are rival and non-excludable.

Comparative advantage Comparative advantage is the ability of an individual, firm, or country to produce a certain good at a lower opportunity cost than other producers.

Comparative statics Comparative statics is the comparison of economic outcomes before and after some economic variable is changed.

Compensating wage differentials Compensating wage differentials are wage premiums paid to attract workers to otherwise undesirable occupations.

Competitive equilibrium price The competitive equilibrium price equates quantity supplied and quantity demanded.

Competitive equilibrium quantity The competitive equilibrium quantity is the quantity that corresponds to the competitive equilibrium price.

Competitive equilibrium The competitive equilibrium is the crossing point of the supply curve and the demand curve.

Complements Two goods are complements when the fall in the price of one, leads to a right shift in the demand curve for the other.

Compound interest equation The compound interest equation or future value equation calculates the future value of an investment with interest rate r that leaves all interest payments in the account until the final withdrawal in year T.

Constant returns to scale Constant returns to scale occur when average total cost does not change as the quantity produced changes.

Consumer Price Index (CPI) The Consumer Price Index is 100 times the ratio of the cost of buying a basket of consumer goods using 2013 prices divided by the cost of buying the same basket of consumer goods using base-year prices.

Consumer sovereignty Consumer sovereignty is the view that choices made by a consumer reflect his or her true preferences, and outsiders, including the government, should not interfere with these choices.

Consumer surplus Consumer surplus is the difference between the willingness to pay and the price paid for the good.

Consumption Consumption is the market value of consumption goods and consumption services that are bought by domestic households.

Contractionary fiscal policy Contractionary fiscal policy uses lower government expenditure and higher taxes to reduce the growth rate of real GDP.

Contractionary monetary policy Contractionary monetary policy slows down growth in bank reserves, raises interest rates, reduces borrowing, slows down growth in the money supply, and reduces the rate of inflation.

Coordination problem When the interests of economic agents coincide, a coordination problem of bringing the agents together to trade arises.

Copyright A copyright is an exclusive right granted by the government to the creator of a literary or artistic work.

Corporate income taxes Corporate income taxes are taxes paid by firms to the government from their profits.

Corrective subsidies Corrective subsidies or, Pigouvian subsidies, are designed to induce agents who produce positive externalities to increase quantity toward the socially optimal level.

Corrective tax A Pigouvian tax or, a corrective tax, is a tax designed to induce agents who produce negative externalities to reduce quantity toward the socially optimal level.

Correlation A correlation means that there is a mutual relationship between two things.

Corruption Corruption refers to the misuse of public funds or the distortion of the allocation of resources for personal gain.

Cost of production The cost of production is what a firm must pay for its inputs.

Cost-Benefit analysis Cost-Benefit analysis is a calculation that adds up costs and benefits using a common unit of measurement, like dollars.

Countercyclical fiscal policy Countercyclical fiscal policy, which is passed by the legislative branch and signed into law by the executive branch, aims to reduce economic fluctuations by manipulating government expenditures and taxes.

Countercyclical monetary policy Countercyclical monetary policy, which is conducted by the central bank (in the United States, the Fed), attempts to reduce economic fluctuations by manipulating bank reserves and interest rates.

Countercyclical policies Countercyclical policies attempt to reduce the intensity of economic fluctuations and smooth the growth rates of employment, GDP, and prices.

Creative destruction Creative destruction refers to the process in which new technologies replace old ones, new businesses replace existing businesses, and new skills make old ones redundant.

Credit Credit refers to the loans that the debtor receives.

Credit demand curve The credit demand curve is the schedule that reports the relationship between the quantity of credit demanded and the real interest rate.

Credit market The credit market is where borrowers obtain funds from savers.

Credit supply curve The credit supply curve is the schedule that reports the relationship between the quantity of credit supplied and the real interest rate.

Cross-price elasticity of demand Cross-price elasticity of demand measures the percentage change in quantity demanded of a good due to a percentage change in another good's price.

Crowding out Crowding out occurs when rising government expenditure partially or even fully displaces expenditures by households and firms.

Culture hypothesis The culture hypothesis claims that different values and cultural beliefs fundamentally cause the differences in prosperity around the world.

Current account The current account is the sum of net exports, net factor payments from abroad, and net transfers from abroad.

Cyclical unemployment Cyclical unemployment is the deviation of the actual unemployment rate from the natural rate of unemployment.

Data Data are facts, measurements, or statistics that describe the world.

Deadweight loss Deadweight loss is the decrease in social surplus from a market distortion.

Debtors Debtors, or borrowers, are economic agents who borrow funds.

Deflation The deflation rate is the rate of decrease of a price index.

Demand curve shifts The demand curve shifts when the quantity demanded changes at a given price.

Demand curve The demand curve plots the quantity demanded at different prices. A demand curve plots the demand schedule.

Demand deposits Demand deposits are funds that depositors can access on demand by withdrawing money from the bank, writing checks, or using their debit cards.

Demand schedule A demand schedule is a table that reports the quantity demanded at different prices, holding all else equal.

Demographic transition The demographic transition refers to the decline in fertility and number of children per family that many societies undergo as they transition from agriculture to industry.

Dependent variable A dependent variable is a variable whose value depends on another variable.

Depression Although there is no consensus on the definition, the term depression is typically used to describe a prolonged recession with an unemployment rate of 20 percent or more.

Differentiated products Differentiated products refer to goods that are similar but are not perfect substitutes.

Diminishing marginal benefit As you consume more of a good, your willingness to pay for an additional unit declines.

Direct regulation Direct regulation, or command-and-control regulation, refers to direct actions by the government to control the amount of a certain activity.

Discount weight A discount weight multiplies delayed utils to translate them into current utils.

Diseconomies of scale Diseconomies of scale occur when average total cost rises as the quantity produced increases.

Dominant strategy equilibrium A combination of strategies is a dominant strategy equilibrium if each strategy is a dominant strategy.

Dominant strategy A dominant strategy is one best response to every possible strategy of the other player(s).

Double oral auction A double oral auction is a market where sellers orally state asks and buyers orally state offers.

Downward wage rigidity Downward wage rigidity arises when workers resist a cut in their wage.

Duopoly Duopoly refers to a two-firm industry.

Dutch auction A Dutch auction is an open-outcry auction in which the price decreases until a bidder stops the auction. The bidder who stops the auction wins the item and pays his bid.

Dynamic equilibrium A dynamic equilibrium traces out the behavior of the economy over time.

Economic agent An economic agent is an individual or a group that makes choices.

Economic expansions Economic expansions are the periods between recessions. Accordingly, an economic expansion begins at the end of one recession and continues until the start of the next recession.

Economic fluctuations Short-run changes in the growth of GDP are referred to as economic fluctuations or business cycles.

Economic growth Economic growth, or growth, is the increase in GDP per capita of an economy.

Economic institutions Economic institutions are the aspects of the society's rules that concern economic transactions.

Economic profits Economic profits are equal to total revenue minus both explicit and implicit costs.

Economics Economics is the study of how agents choose to allocate scarce resources and how those choices affect society.

Economies of scale Economies of scale occur when average total cost falls as the quantity produced increases.

Efficiency of production Efficiency of production refers to the ability of an economy to produce the maximal amount of output from a given amount of factors of production and knowledge.

Efficiency wages Efficiency wages are wages above the lowest pay that workers would accept; employers use them to increase motivation and productivity.

Efficient price An efficient price, or socially optimal price, is a price set at marginal cost.

Elastic demand Goods that have elastic demand have a price elasticity of demand greater than 1.

Elasticity Elasticity is the measure of sensitivity of one variable to a change in another.

Empirical evidence Empirical evidence is a set of facts established by observation and measurement.

Empiricism Empiricism is analysis that uses data. Economists use data to test theories and to determine what is causing things to happen in the world.

Employed A person holding a full-time or part-time paid job is employed.

English auction An English auction is an open-outcry auction in which the price increases until there is only one standing bid. That bidder wins the item and pays his bid.

Equilibrium Equilibrium is the situation in which everyone is simultaneously optimizing, so nobody would benefit personally by changing his or her own behavior.

Equity Equity is concerned with the distribution of resources across society.

Equity-efficiency trade-off The equity-efficiency trade-off refers to the trade-off between ensuring an equitable allocation of resources (equity) and increasing social surplus or total output (efficiency).

Excess demand When the market price is below the competitive equilibrium price, quantity demanded exceeds quantity supplied, creating excess demand.

Excess supply When the market price is above the competitive equilibrium price, quantity supplied exceeds quantity demanded, creating excess supply.

Excise taxes Excise taxes are taxes paid when purchasing a specific good.

Exit Exit is a long-run decision to leave the market.

Expansionary fiscal policy Expansionary fiscal policy uses higher government expenditure and lower taxes to increase the growth rate of real GDP.

Expansionary monetary policy Expansionary monetary policy increases the quantity of bank reserves and lowers interest rates.

Expected real interest rate The expected real interest rate is the nominal interest rate minus the expected rate of inflation.

Expected value Expected value is the sum of all possible outcomes or values, each weighted by its probability of occurring.

Experiment An experiment is a controlled method of investigating causal relationships among variables.

Exponential growth Exponential growth refers to a situation in which the growth process can be described by an approximately constant growth rate of a variable such as GDP or GDP per capita.

Export An export is any good that is produced domestically but sold abroad.

Exports Exports are the market value of all domestically produced goods and services that are purchased by households, firms, and governments in foreign countries.

Extensive-form game An extensive-form game is a representation of games that specifies the order of play.

Externality An externality occurs when an economic activity has either a spillover cost or a spillover benefit on a bystander.

Extractive economic institutions Extractive economic institutions do not protect private property rights, do not uphold contracts, and interfere with the workings of markets. They also erect significant entry barriers into businesses and occupations.

Factors of production Factors of production are the inputs to the production process.

Fairness Fairness is the willingness of individuals to sacrifice their own well-being to either improve upon the well-being of others or to punish those who they perceive as behaving unkindly.

Fair-returns price A fair-returns price is a price set at average total cost.

Federal funds market equilibrium The point where the supply and demand curves cross in the federal funds market is the federal funds market equilibrium.

Federal funds market The federal funds market refers to the market where banks obtain overnight loans of reserves from one another.

Federal funds rate The federal funds rate is the interest rate that banks charge each other for overnight loans in the federal funds market. The funds being lent are reserves at the Federal Reserve Bank.

Federal Reserve Bank The Federal Reserve Bank, or the Fed, is the name of the central bank in the United States.

Fertility Fertility refers to the number of children per adult or per woman of childbearing age.

Fiat money Fiat money refers to something that is used as legal tender by government decree and is not backed by a physical commodity, like gold or silver.

Financial account The financial account is the increase in domestic assets held by foreigners minus the increase in foreign assets held domestically.

Financial intermediaries Financial intermediaries channel funds from suppliers of financial capital to users of financial capital.

Firm A firm is any business entity that produces and sells goods or services.

First-degree price discrimination Perfect price discrimination, also known as first-degree price discrimination, occurs when a firm charges each buyer exactly his or her willingness to pay.

First-mover advantage A game has a first-mover advantage when the first player to act in a sequential game gets a benefit from doing so.

Fixed cost A fixed cost is the cost of fixed factors of production, which a firm must pay even if it produces zero output.

Fixed exchange rate If the government sets a long-run value for the exchange rate and intervenes to maintain that value, then the country has a fixed exchange rate.

Fixed factor of production A fixed factor of production is an input that cannot be changed in the short run.

Flexible exchange rate If the government does not intervene in the foreign exchange market, then the country has a flexible exchange rate, which is also referred to as a floating exchange rate.

Foreign direct investment Foreign direct investment refers to investments by foreign individuals and companies in domestic firms and businesses. To qualify as foreign direct investment, these flows need to generate a large foreign ownership stake in the domestic business.

Foreign exchange market The foreign exchange market is the global financial market in which currencies are traded and nominal exchange rates are determined.

Free entry There is free entry into an industry when entry is unfettered by any special legal or technical barriers.

Free exit There is free exit from an industry when exit is unfettered by any special legal or technical barriers.

Free trade Free trade is the ability to trade without hindrance or encouragement from the government.

Free-rider problem A free-rider problem occurs when an individual who has no incentive to pay for a good does not pay for that good because nonpayment does not prevent consumption.

Frictional unemployment Frictional unemployment refers to unemployment that arises because workers have imperfect information about available jobs and need to engage in a time-consuming process of job search.

Fundamental causes of prosperity Fundamental causes of prosperity are factors that are at the root of the differences in the proximate causes of prosperity.

Future value equation The compound interest equation or future value equation calculates the future value of an investment with interest rate r that leaves all interest payments in the account until the final withdrawal in year T.

Future value The sum of principal and interest is referred to as future value.

Gains from specialization Gains from specialization are the economic gains that society can obtain by having some individuals, regions, or countries specialize in the production of certain goods and services.

Game theory Game theory is the study of strategic interactions.

Game tree A game tree is an extensive-form representation of a game.

GDP deflator The GDP deflator is 100 times the ratio of nominal GDP to real GDP in the same year. It is a measure of how prices of goods and services produced in a country have risen since the base year.

Geography hypothesis The geography hypothesis claims that differences in geography, climate, and ecology are ultimately responsible for the major differences in prosperity observed across the world.

Globalization Globalization is the shift toward more open, integrated economies that participate in foreign trade and investment.

Government expenditure Government expenditure is the market value of government purchases of goods and services.

Government failures Government failures refer to inefficiencies caused by a government's interventions.

Great Depression The Great Depression refers to the severe contraction that started in 1929, reaching a low point for real GDP in 1933. The period of below-trend real GDP did not end until the buildup to World War II in the late 1930s.

Grim strategy A grim strategy is a plan by one player to price a good at marginal cost forever if the other cheats on their agreement.

Gross domestic product (GDP) Gross domestic product (GDP) is the market value of final goods and services produced in a country in a given period of time.

Gross national product (GNP) Gross national product is the market value of production generated by the factors of production—both capital and labor—possessed or owned by the residents of a particular nation.

Growth rate The growth rate is the change in a quantity, for example, GDP per capita, between two dates, relative to the baseline (beginning of period) quantity.

Herding Herding is a behavior of individuals who conform to the decisions of others.

Herfindahl-Hirschman Index The Herfindahl-Hirschman Index is a measure of market concentration to estimate the degree of competition within an industry.

Hidden actions There are hidden actions if one side takes actions that are relevant for, but not observed by, the other party.

Hidden characteristics There are hidden characteristics if one side observes something about the good being transacted that is both relevant for and not observed by the other party.

Holding all else equal Holding all else equal implies that everything else in the economy is held constant. The Latin phrase *ceteris paribus* means "with other things the same" and is sometimes used in economic writing to mean the same thing as "holding all else equal."

Homogeneous products Homogeneous products refer to goods that are identical, and so are perfect substitutes.

Human capital Human capital is each person's stock of skills for producing output or economic value.

Hypotheses Hypotheses are predictions (typically generated by a model) that can be tested with data.

Identity Two variables are related by an identity when the two variables are defined in a way that makes them mathematically identical.

Import An import is any good that is produced abroad but sold domestically.

Imports Imports are the market value of all foreign-produced goods and services that are sold to domestic households, domestic firms, and the domestic government.

Impure altruism Impure altruism is a motivation solely to help oneself feel good.

Incentive problem When the optimizing actions of two economic agents are not aligned, these agents face an incentive problem.

Inclusive economic institutions Inclusive economic institutions protect private property, uphold law and order, allow and enforce private contracts, and allow free entry into new lines of business and occupations.

Income (or GDP) per worker Income (or GDP) per worker is defined as GDP divided by the number of people in employment.

Income effect An income effect is a consumption change that results when a price change moves the consumer to a lower or higher indifference curve.

Income elasticity of demand The income elasticity of demand measures the percentage change in quantity demanded due to a percentage change in income.

Income per capita Income per capita is income per person. This is calculated by dividing a nation's aggregate income by the number of people in the country.

Income (or GDP) per capita Income per capita or GDP per capita is GDP divided by total population.

Independent variable An independent variable is a variable whose value does not depend on another variable; in an experiment it is manipulated by the experimenter.

Independent When two random outcomes are independent, knowing about one outcome does not help you predict the other outcome.

Indifference curve An indifference curve is the set of bundles that provide an equal level of satisfaction for the consumer.

Indoctrination Indoctrination is the process by which agents imbue society with their ideology or opinion.

Industrial Revolution Industrial Revolution is the term used for describing the series of innovations and their implementation in the production process that started to take place at the end of the eighteenth century in Britain.

Inelastic demand Goods that have inelastic demand have a price elasticity of demand less than 1.

Inferior good For an inferior good, an increase in income causes the demand curve to shift to the left (holding the good's price fixed), or in other words, causes consumers to buy less of the good.

Inflation expectations Economic agents' inflation expectations are their beliefs about future inflation rates.

Inflation rate The rate of increase in prices is the inflation rate. It is calculated as the year-over-year percentage increase in a price index.

Information cascade An information cascade occurs when people make the same decisions as others, ignoring their own private information.

Input An input is a good or service used to produce another good or service.

Insolvent A bank becomes insolvent when the value of the bank's assets is less than the value of its liabilities.

Institutions hypothesis The institutions hypothesis claims that differences in institutions—that is, in the way societies have organized themselves and shaped the incentives of individuals and businesses—are at the root of the differences in prosperity across the world.

Institutions Institutions are the formal and informal rules governing the organization of a society, including its laws and regulations.

Interest Interest is the payment received for temporarily giving up the use of money.

Interest rate The interest rate (also referred to as the nominal interest rate), i, is the annual cost of a one-dollar loan, so $i \times L$ is the annual cost of an $\$L$ loan.

Internalizing the externality When an agent accounts for the full costs and benefits of his actions, he is internalizing the externality.

Investment Investment is the market value of new physical capital that is bought by domestic households and domestic firms.

Job search Job search refers to the activities that workers undertake to find appropriate jobs.

Key resources Key resources are materials that are essential for the production of a good or service.

Labor demand curve The labor demand curve depicts the relationship between the quantity of labor demanded and the wage. The value of the marginal product of labor is also the labor demand curve, because they both show how the quantity of labor demanded varies with the wage.

Labor force participation rate The labor force participation rate is the percentage of potential workers that are in the labor force.

Labor force The labor force is the sum of all employed and unemployed workers.

Labor income Labor income is any form of payment that compensates people for their work.

Labor supply curve The labor supply curve represents the relationship between the quantity of labor supplied and the wage.

Labor-complementary technology Labor-complementary technology is a type of technology that complements existing labor inputs, increasing the marginal product of labor.

Labor-saving technology Labor-saving technology is a type of technology that substitutes for existing labor inputs, reducing the marginal product of labor.

Land Land includes the solid surface of the earth and natural resources.

Law of demand In almost all cases, the quantity demanded rises when the price falls (holding all else equal).

Law of Diminishing Marginal Product The Law of Diminishing Marginal Product states that the marginal contribution of a factor of production to output diminishes when we increase the quantity used of that factor of production (holding all others constant).

Law of Diminishing Returns The Law of Diminishing Returns states that successive increases in inputs eventually lead to less additional output.

Law of Supply In almost all cases, the quantity supplied rises when the price rises (holding all else equal).

Legal market power Legal market power occurs when a firm obtains market power through barriers to entry created not by the firm itself, but by the government.

Liquidity Liquidity refers to funds available for immediate payment. To express the same concept a slightly different way, funds are liquid if they are immediately available for payment.

Long run The long run is a period of time when all of a firm's inputs can be varied.

Long-term real interest rate The long-term real interest rate is the long-term nominal interest rate minus the long-term inflation rate.

Loss aversion Loss aversion is the idea that people psychologically weight a loss more heavily than they psychologically weight a gain.

Macroeconomics Macroeconomics is the study of the economy as a whole. Macroeconomists study economy-wide phenomena, like the growth rate of a country's total economic output, the inflation rate, or the unemployment rate.

Malthusian cycle The Malthusian cycle refers to the preindustrial pattern in which increases in aggregate income lead to an expanding population, which in turn reduces income per capita and puts downward pressure on population.

Managed exchange rate If the government intervenes actively to influence the exchange rate, then the country has a managed exchange rate.

Marginal analysis Marginal analysis is a cost-benefit calculation that studies the difference between a feasible alternative and the next feasible alternative.

Marginal cost Marginal cost is the change in total cost associated with producing one more unit of output or moving from one feasible alternative to the next feasible alternative.

Marginal product Marginal product is the change in total output associated with using one more unit of input.

Marginal revenue Marginal revenue is the change in total revenue associated with producing one more unit of output.

Marginal tax rate The marginal tax rate refers to how much of the last dollar earned is paid out in tax.

Market A market is a group of economic agents who are trading a good or service, and the rules and arrangements for trading.

Market demand curve The market demand curve is the sum of the individual demand curves of all the potential buyers. It plots the relationship between the total quantity demanded and the market price, holding all else equal.

Market power Market power relates to the ability of sellers to affect prices.

Market price If all sellers and all buyers face the same price, it is referred to as the market price.

Market supply curve The market supply curve is the sum of the individual supply curves of all the potential sellers. It plots the relationship between the total quantity supplied and the market price, holding all else equal.

Market-based regulatory approach A market-based regulatory approach internalizes externalities by harnessing the power of market forces.

Market-clearing wage We refer to the competitive equilibrium wage as the market-clearing wage. At this wage, every worker that wants a job can find one: the quantity of labor demanded matches the quantity of labor supplied.

Maturity Maturity refers to the time until debt must be repaid.

Maturity transformation Maturity transformation is the process by which banks take short-maturity liabilities and invest in long-maturity assets (long-term investments).

Mean The mean, or average, is the sum of all the different values divided by the number of values.

Medium of exchange A medium of exchange is an asset that can be traded for goods and services.

Microeconomics Microeconomics is the study of how individuals, households, firms, and governments make choices, and how those choices affect prices, the allocation of resources, and the well-being of other agents.

Mixed strategy A mixed strategy involves choosing different actions randomly.

Model A model is a simplified description, or representation, of the world. Sometimes, economists will refer to a model as a *theory*. These terms are often used interchangeably.

Monetary policy The central bank is the government institution that monitors financial institutions, controls certain key interest rates, and indirectly controls the money supply. These activities constitute monetary policy.

Money Money is the asset that people use to make and receive payments when buying and selling goods and services.

Money supply The money supply adds together currency in circulation, checking accounts, savings accounts, travelers' checks, and money market accounts. This is sometimes referred to as M2.

Monopolistic competition Monopolistic competition is the market structure that applies when there are many competing firms and products are differentiated.

Monopoly Monopoly is an industry structure in which only one seller provides a good or service that has no close substitutes.

Moral hazard Moral hazard is another term for actions that are taken by one party but are relevant for and not observed by the other party in the transaction.

Movement along the demand curve If a good's own price changes and its demand curve hasn't shifted, the own price change produces a movement along the demand curve.

Movement along the supply curve If a good's own price changes and its supply curve hasn't shifted, the own price change produces a movement along the supply curve.

Multipliers Multipliers refer to economic mechanisms that amplify the initial impact of a shock.

Nash equilibrium A strategy combination is a Nash equilibrium if each strategy is a best response to the strategies of others.

National income accounting identity The national income accounting identity, $Y = C + I + G + X - M$, decomposes GDP into consumption + investment + government expenditure + exports - imports.

National income accounts National income accounts measure the level of aggregate economic activity in a country.

National Income and Product Accounts (NIPA) The National Income and Product Accounts is the system of national income accounts that is used by the U.S. government.

Natural experiment A natural experiment is an empirical study in which some process—out of the control of the experimenter—has assigned subjects to control and treatment groups in a random or nearly random way.

Natural market power Natural market power occurs when a firm obtains market power through barriers to entry created by the firm itself.

Natural monopoly A natural monopoly is a market in which one firm can provide a good or service at a lower cost than two or more firms.

Natural rate of unemployment The natural rate of unemployment is the rate around which the actual rate of unemployment fluctuates.

Negative correlation Negative correlation implies that two variables tend to move in opposite directions.

Negatively related Two variables are negatively related if the variables move in the opposite direction.

Net exports Net exports are the value of the country's exports minus the value of its imports. Net exports are also known as the trade balance.

Net importer A net importer means that imports are worth more than exports over a given time period.

Net present value The net present value of a project is the present value of the benefits minus the present value of the costs.

Network externalities Network externalities occur when a product's value increases as more consumers begin to use it.

Nominal exchange rate The nominal exchange rate is the rate at which one currency can be traded for another.

Nominal GDP Nominal GDP is the total value of production (final goods and services) using current market prices.

Nominal wages Actual wages are also called nominal wages, which distinguishes them from wages adjusted for inflation, or real wages. To calculate real wages, economists divide nominal wages by a measure of overall prices, for example the Consumer Price Index (CPI).

Non-excludable good Once a non-excludable good is produced, it is not possible to exclude people from using the good.

Non-rival good A non-rival good is a good whose consumption by one person does not prevent consumption by others.

Normal good For a normal good, an increase in income causes the demand curve to shift to the right (holding the good's price fixed), or in other words, causes consumers to buy more of the good.

Normative economics Normative economics is an analysis that prescribes what an individual or society ought to do.

North American Free Trade Agreement The North American Free Trade Agreement (NAFTA) is an agreement signed by Canada, Mexico, and the United States to create a trilateral trade bloc and reduce trade barriers among the three countries.

Okun's Law Okun's law says that the year-to-year change in the rate of unemployment is equal to $-\frac{1}{2} \times (g - 3\%)$, where g represents the annual growth rate of real GDP, in percentage points.

Oligopoly Oligopoly is the market structure that applies when there are few firms competing.

Omitted variable An omitted variable is something that has been left out of a study that, if included, would explain why two variables that are in the study are correlated.

One dollar a day per person poverty line The one dollar a day per person poverty line is a measure of absolute poverty used by economists and other social scientists to compare the extent of poverty across countries.

Open economy An open economy trades freely with the rest of the world.

Open outcry auction An open outcry auction is an auction in which bids are public.

Open market operations If the Fed wishes to increase the level of reserves that private banks hold, it offers to buy government bonds from the private banks, and in return it gives the private banks more electronic reserves. If the Fed wishes to decrease the level of reserves, it offers to sell government bonds to the private banks and in return the private banks give back some of their reserves. By buying or selling government bonds, the Fed shifts the vertical supply curve in the federal funds market and thereby controls the level of reserves. These transactions are referred to as open market operations.

Opportunity cost Opportunity cost is the best alternative use of a resource.

Optimization in differences Optimization in differences calculates the *change* in net benefits when a person switches from one alternative to another and then uses these marginal comparisons to choose the best alternative.

Optimization in levels Optimization in levels calculates the *total* net benefit of different alternatives and then chooses the best alternative.

Optimization Trying to choose the best feasible option given the available information, is optimization.

Optimum The optimum is the best feasible choice. In other words, the optimum is the optimal choice.

Pareto efficient An outcome is Pareto efficient if no individual can be made better off without making someone else worse off.

Patent A patent is the privilege granted to an individual or company by the government, which gives him or her the sole right to produce and sell a good.

Paternalism Paternalism is the view that consumers do not always know what is best for them, and the government should encourage or induce them to change their actions.

Payoff matrix A payoff matrix represents the payoffs for each action players can take.

Payroll tax A payroll tax (also known as social insurance tax) is a tax on the wages of workers.

Pecuniary externality A pecuniary externality occurs when a market transaction affects other people only through market prices.

Peer effects Peer effects are the influence of the decisions of others on our own choices.

Perfect price discrimination Perfect price discrimination, also known as first-degree price discrimination, occurs when a firm charges each buyer exactly his or her willingness to pay.

Perfectly competitive market In a perfectly competitive market, (1) sellers all sell an identical good or service, and (2) any individual buyer or any individual seller isn't powerful enough on his or her own to affect the market price of that good or service.

Perfectly elastic demand A very small increase in price causes consumers to stop using goods that have perfectly elastic demand.

Perfectly inelastic demand Quantity demanded is unaffected by prices of goods with perfectly inelastic demand.

Physical capital Physical capital is any good, including machines and buildings, used for production.

Physical capital stock The physical capital stock of an economy is the value of equipment, structures and other non-labor inputs used in production.

Pie chart A pie chart is a circular chart split into segments, with each showing the percentages of parts relative to the whole.

Pigouvian subsidies Corrective subsidies or, Pigouvian subsidies, are designed to induce agents who produce positive externalities to increase quantity toward the socially optimal level.

Pigouvian tax A Pigouvian tax or, a corrective tax, is a tax designed to induce agents who produce negative externalities to reduce quantity toward the socially optimal level.

Political creative destruction Political creative destruction refers to the process in which economic growth destabilizes existing regimes and reduces the political power of rulers.

Political institutions Political institutions are the aspects of the society's rules that concern the allocation of political power and the constraints on the exercise of political power.

Positive correlation A positive correlation implies that two variables tend to move in the same direction.

Positive economics Positive economics is analysis that generates objective descriptions or predictions about the world that can be verified with data.

Positively related Two variables are positively related if the variables move in the same direction.

Potential workers Potential workers includes everyone in the general population with three exceptions: children under 16 years of age, people on active duty in the military, and institutionalized people, like those in nursing homes or jail.

Present value The present value of a future payment is the amount of money that would need to be invested today to produce that future payment. In other words, the present value is the discounted value of the future payment.

Price ceiling A price ceiling is a cap or maximum price of a market good.

Price control A price control is a government restriction on the price of a good or service.

Price discrimination Price discrimination occurs when firms charge different consumers different prices for the same good or service.

Price elasticity of demand The price elasticity of demand measures the percentage change in quantity demanded of a good due to a percentage change in its price.

Price elasticity of supply Price elasticity of supply is the measure of how responsive quantity supplied is to price changes.

Price floor A price floor is a lower limit on the price of a market good.

Price-maker A price-maker is a seller that sets the price of a good.

Price-taker A price-taker is a buyer or seller who accepts the market price—buyers can't bargain for a lower price and sellers can't bargain for a higher price.

Principal Principal is the amount of an original investment.

Principal-agent relationship In a principal-agent relationship, the principal designs a contract specifying the payments to the agent as a function of his or her performance, and the agent takes an action that influences performance and thus the payoff of the principal.

Principle of optimization at the margin The principle of optimization at the margin states that an optimal feasible alternative has the property that moving to it makes you better off and moving away from it makes you worse off.

Private property rights Private property rights mean that individuals can own businesses and assets and their ownership is secure.

Private provision of public goods Private provision of public goods takes place when private citizens make contributions to the production or maintenance of a public good.

Probability A probability is the frequency with which something occurs.

Producer surplus Producer surplus is the difference between the market price and the marginal cost curve.

Production possibilities curve A production possibilities curve shows the relationship between the maximum production of one good for a given level of production of another good.

Production Production is the process by which the transformation of inputs to outputs occurs.

Productivity Productivity refers to the value of goods and services that a worker generates for each hour of work.

Profits The profits of a firm are equal to its revenues minus its costs.

Progressive tax system A progressive tax system involves higher tax rates on those earning higher incomes.

Property right A property right gives someone ownership of a property or resources.

Proportional tax system In a proportional tax system, households pay the same percentage of their incomes in taxes regardless of their income level.

Protectionism Protectionism is the idea that free trade can be harmful, and government intervention is necessary to control trade.

Proximate causes of prosperity Proximate causes of prosperity are high levels of factors such as human capital, physical capital, and technology that result in a high level of GDP per capita.

Public good A public good is both non-rival and non-excludable.

Purchasing power parity (PPP) The purchasing power parity (PPP) constructs the cost of a representative bundle of commodities in each country and uses these relative costs for comparing income across countries.

Pure altruism Pure altruism is a motivation solely to help others.

Pure strategy A pure strategy involves always choosing one particular action for a situation.

Quantity demanded Quantity demanded is the amount of a good that buyers are willing to purchase at a given price.

Quantity supplied Quantity supplied is the amount of a good or service that sellers are willing to sell at a given price.

Quantity theory of money The quantity theory of money assumes a constant ratio of money supply to nominal GDP.

Random If something is risky, then it is said to have a component that is random.

Randomization Randomization is the assignment of subjects by chance, rather than by choice, to a treatment group or control group.

Real business cycle theory Real business cycle theory is the school of thought that emphasizes the role of changes in technology in causing economic fluctuations.

Real exchange rate The real exchange rate is defined as the ratio of the dollar price of a basket of goods and services in the United States, divided by the dollar price of the same basket of goods and services in a foreign country.

Real GDP growth Real GDP growth is the growth rate of real GDP.

Real GDP Real GDP is the total value of production (final goods and services), using market prices from a specific base year to determine the value of each unit that is produced.

Real interest rate The real interest rate is given by the nominal interest rate minus the inflation rate.

Real wage The real wage is the nominal wage divided by a price index, like the consumer price index (CPI).

Realized real interest rate The realized real interest rate is the nominal interest rate minus the realized rate of inflation.

Receipts Tax revenues, or receipts, are the money a government collects through a tax.

Recessions Recessions are periods (lasting at least two quarters) in which aggregate economic output falls.

Regressive tax system A regressive tax system involves lower tax rates on those earning higher incomes.

Regulation Regulation refers to actions by the federal or local government directed at influencing market outcomes, such as the quantity traded of a good or service, its price, or its quality and safety.

Rental price The rental price of a good is the cost of using a good for some specific period of time.

Research and development (R&D) Research and development (R&D) refers to the activities directed at improving scientific knowledge, generating new innovations, or implementing existing knowledge in production in order to improve the technology of a firm or an economy.

Reservation value Reservation value is the price at which a trading partner is indifferent between making the trade and not doing so.

Residual demand curve The residual demand curve is the demand that is not met by other firms and depends on the prices of all firms in the industry.

Revenue equivalence theorem The revenue equivalence theorem states that under certain assumptions, the four auction types are expected to raise the same revenues.

Revenue Revenue is the amount of money the firm brings in from the sale of its outputs.

Reverse causality Reverse causality occurs when we mix up the direction of cause and effect.

Risk averse Consider a person choosing between two investments with the same expected rate of return but one investment has a fixed return and the other investment has a risky return. When people are risk averse, they prefer the investment with the fixed return.

Risk neutral Consider a person choosing between two investments with the same expected rate of return but one investment has a fixed return and the other investment has a risky return. When people are risk neutral, they don't care about the level of risk and are therefore indifferent between the two investments.

Risk seeking Consider a person choosing between two investments with the same expected rate of return but one investment has a fixed return and the other investment has a risky return. When people are risk seeking, they prefer the investment with the risky return.

Risk Risk exists when an outcome is not known with certainty in advance.

Sales taxes Sales taxes are paid by a buyer, as a percentage of the sale price of an item.

Saving rate The saving rate designates the fraction of income that is saved.

Scarce resources Scarce resources are things that people want, where the quantity that people want exceeds the quantity that is available.

Scarcity Scarcity is the situation of having unlimited wants in a world of limited resources.

Scatter plot A scatter plot displays the relationship between two variables as plotted points of data.

Scientific method The scientific method is the name for the ongoing process that economists and other scientists use to (1) develop models of the world and (2) test those models with data.

Sealed bid auction A sealed bid auction is an auction in which bids are private so that no bidder knows the bid of any other participant.

Sealed bid first-price auction A sealed bid first-price auction is an auction in which bidders privately submit bids at the same time. The highest bidder wins the item and pays an amount equal to her bid.

Sealed bid second-price auction A sealed bid second-price auction is an auction in which bidders privately submit bids at the same time. The highest bidder wins the item and pays an amount equal to the second-highest bid.

Second-degree price discrimination Second-degree price discrimination occurs when consumers are charged different prices based on characteristics of their purchase.

Securities Securities are financial contracts. For example, securities may allocate ownership rights of a company (stocks), or promise payments to lenders (bonds).

Seignorage Government revenue obtained from printing currency is called seignorage.

Self-fulfilling prophecy A self-fulfilling prophecy is a situation in which the expectations of an event (such as a left shift in labor demand in the future) induce actions that lead to that event.

Sentiments Sentiments include changes in expectations about future economic activity, changes in uncertainty facing firms and households, and fluctuations in animal spirits. Changes in sentiments lead to changes in household consumption and firm investment.

Short run The short run is a period of time when only some of a firm's inputs can be varied.

Shutdown Shutdown is a short-run decision to not produce anything during a specific period.

Signaling Signaling refers to an action that an individual with private information takes in order to convince others about his information.

Simultaneous move games In simultaneous move games, players pick their actions at the same time.

Skill-biased technological changes Skill-biased technological changes increase the productivity of skilled workers relative to that of unskilled workers.

Slope The slope is the change in the value of the variable plotted on the vertical axis divided by the change in the value of the variable plotted on the horizontal axis.

Social insurance tax A payroll tax (also known as social insurance tax) is a tax on the wages of workers.

Social surplus Social surplus is the sum of consumer surplus and producer surplus.

Socially optimal price An efficient price, or socially optimal price, is a price set at marginal cost.

Solvent A bank is solvent when the value of the bank's assets is greater than the value of its liabilities.

Specialization Specialization is the result of workers developing a certain skill set in order to increase total productivity.

Statistical discrimination Statistical discrimination occurs when expectations cause people to discriminate against a certain group.

Steady-state equilibrium A steady-state equilibrium is an economic equilibrium in which the physical capital stock remains constant over time.

Stockholders' equity Stockholders' equity is the difference between a bank's total assets and total liabilities.

Store of value A store of value is an asset that enables people to transfer purchasing power into the future.

Strategies Strategies comprise a complete plan describing how a player will act.

Structural unemployment Structural unemployment arises when the quantity of labor supplied persistently exceeds the quantity of labor demanded.

Subsidy A subsidy is a payment or tax break used as an incentive for an agent to complete an activity.

Subsistence level The subsistence level is the minimum level of income per person that is generally necessary for the individual to obtain enough calories, shelter, and clothing to survive.

Substitutes Two goods are substitutes when the fall in the price of one leads to a left shift in the demand curve for the other.

Substitution effect A substitution effect is a consumption change that results when a price change moves the *consumer along a given indifference curve.*

Sunk costs Sunk costs are costs that, once committed, can never be recovered and should not affect current and future production decisions.

Supply curve shifts The supply curve shifts when the quantity supplied changes at a given price.

Supply curve The supply curve plots the quantity supplied at different prices. A supply curve plots the supply schedule.

Supply schedule A supply schedule is a table that reports the quantity supplied at different prices, holding all else equal.

Sustained growth Sustained growth refers to a growth process where GDP per capita grows at a positive and relatively steady rate for long periods of time.

Tariffs Tariffs are taxes levied on goods and services transported across political boundaries.

Taste-based discrimination Taste-based discrimination occurs when people's preferences cause them to discriminate against a certain group.

Tax incidence Tax incidence refers to how the burden of taxation is distributed.

Tax revenues Tax revenues, or receipts, are the money a government collects through a tax.

Technological change Technological change is the process of new technologies and new goods and services being invented, introduced, and used in the economy, enabling the economy to achieve a higher level of GDP for given levels of physical capital stock and total efficiency units of labor.

Technology An economy with better technology uses its labor and capital more efficiently and achieves higher productivity.

Terms of trade The terms of trade is the negotiated exchange rate of goods for goods.

Third-degree price discrimination Third-degree price discrimination occurs when price varies based on a customer's attributes.

Time series graph A time series graph displays data at different points in time.

Total cost Total cost is the sum of variable and fixed costs.

Total efficiency units of labor Total efficiency units of labor is the product of the total number of workers in the economy and the average human capital of each worker.

Trade deficit A trade deficit is an excess of imports over exports and is thus the name given to the trade balance when it is negative.

Trade surplus A trade surplus is an excess of exports over imports and is thus the name given to the trade balance when it is positive.

Trade-off An economic agent faces a trade-off when the agent needs to give up one thing to get something else.

Tragedy of the commons The tragedy of the commons results when common pool resources are dramatically overused.

Transaction costs Transaction costs are the costs of making an economic exchange.

Transfer payments Transfer payments occur when the government gives part of its tax revenue to some individual or group.

Unemployed A worker is officially unemployed if he or she does not have a job, has actively looked for work in the prior four weeks, and is currently available for work.

Unemployment rate The unemployment rate is the fraction of the labor force that is unemployed.

Unit elastic demand Goods that have unit elastic demand have a price elasticity of demand equal to 1.

Unit of account A unit of account is a universal yardstick that is used for expressing the worth (price) of different goods and services.

Unitary model A unitary model of the household assumes that a family maximizes their happiness under a budget constraint that pools all of their income, wealth, and time.

Utility In economics, utility is a measure of satisfaction or happiness that comes from consuming a good or service.

Utils Utils are individual units of utility.

Value added Production-based accounting measures each firm's value added, which is the firm's sales revenue minus the firm's purchases of intermediate products from other firms.

Value of marginal product of labor The value of marginal product of labor is the contribution of an additional worker to a firm's revenues.

Value of marginal product of physical capital The value of marginal product of physical capital is the contribution of an additional unit of physical capital to a firm's revenues.

Variable A variable is a factor that is likely to change or vary.

Variable cost A variable cost is the cost of variable factors of production, which change along with a firm's output.

Variable factor of production A variable factor of production is an input that can be changed in the short run.

Wage rigidity Wage rigidity refers to the condition in which the market wage is held above the competitive equilibrium level that would clear the labor market.

Welfare state The welfare state refers to the set of insurance, regulation, and transfer programs operated by the government, including unemployment benefits, pensions, and government-run and financed healthcare.

Willingness to accept Willingness to accept is the lowest price that a seller is willing to get paid to sell an extra unit of a good. Willingness to accept is the same as the marginal cost of production.

Willingness to pay Willingness to pay is the highest price that a buyer is willing to pay for an extra unit of a good.

World price A world price is the prevailing price of a good on the world market.

Zero correlation Zero correlation implies that two variables have movements that are not related.

Zero-sum game In a zero-sum game, one player's loss is another's gain, so the sum of the payoffs is zero.

Credits

Index

Note: Key terms and the page on which they are defined appear in **boldface**. Page numbers with the letter n indicate content appears in a footnote.

A

Aalsmeer, Holland, 61, 62
A Beautiful Mind, 305, 319
absolute advantage, 175–177, **176,** 665–669, **666**
accounting profit, 123, 134–135
adaptive expectations, 603
adverse selection, 368–370, **369,** 378–379
advertising, decisions about, 334
Affordable Care Act, 272, 369–370, 378–379, 382
Afghanistan, 457, 459, 462, 470, 672
aggregate activity. *See* national income accounts
aggregate income. *See* income, aggregate
aggregate production function, 463
    economic growth and, 487
    mathematics of, 476–477
    overview, 462–465
    Solow growth model, 503–511
aggregation, 65
agriculture, prosperity and, 529
Air China, 689–690
airline price wars, 329
Akerlof, George, 372, 383
Albright, Mark, 161
Alcoa, 278
altruism, 408
Amazon.com, 388
American Association of University Women (AAUW), 272
American Economic Review, 334
American International Group (AIG), 645
American Recovery and Reinvestment Act (2009), 651–658
anecdotal data, 25–26
Angrist, Joshua, 261
animal spirits, 620
antitrust policy, 292–293, 338–339
apartments, decisions about
    location and cost, 53–55
    optimization in differences, 50–53
    optimization in levels, 46–49
Apple, Inc., 322, 516, 665–670

arbitrage, 289
arc elasticities, 103
Archer Daniels Midland (ADM), 332
Argentina
    economic development, 527–528
    economic institutions of, 519
    GDP and life satisfaction, 443
    income per capita, 457
    income per worker, 459
    inflation, 588, 589
artificially scare goods, 212, 213
ask prices, 163
asset bubbles, 578, 629–633, 648
asset management companies, 570
asset price fluctuations, banks and, 578
assets, bank balance sheets, 570–574
asymmetric information, 367–371
    Choice & Consequence, 371
    Evidence-Based Economics, car values, 372–373
    government policy and, 378–381
Aten, Bettina, 481, 497
auctions. *See also* bargaining
    Evidence-Based Economics, eBay, 394–395
    Letting the Data Speak, sniping, 388
    open-outcry Dutch auctions, 389–390
    open-outcry English auctions, 387–389
    overview, **385**–387
    revenue equivalence theorem, 393
    sealed bid auctions, 390–393
    types of, 387
Australia, 457, 459, 527–528
Austria, 519–520
automatic stabilizers, 651
automobile manufacturing, Choice & Consequence, 130
Autor, David, 553–554
average, 25
average fixed cost (AFC), 118–120, **119**
average growth rates, 510–511
average tax rate, 59, **231,** 232
average total cost (ATC), 119
    cost of doing business, 118–120
    cost structures, firm differences, 142–143
    firm market entry and exit, 131–134
    invisible hand, firms, 148–152
    invisible hand, industries, 152–154

long run, profits and, 133–134
    monopolistic competition, 334–335
    natural monopolies, 278–279
    profits and, 123–124
    short-run and long-run supply, 129–131
    subsidies, effects of, 135–138
average variable cost (AVC), 118–120, **119,** 127
Azerbaijan, 519

B

backward induction, 311, **312**
Bahrain, 524
baht, 706
balance sheet
    banks, 570–574
    Federal Reserve, 642–644
Banana Republic, 672
Bandiera, Oriana, 419
bank failures, 631–633
Bank of Japan (BOJ), 607
bank reserves, 571, 594–600
bank run, 574–575
banks. *See also* central bank
    asset price fluctuations and, 578
    balance sheet of, 570–574
    credit markets and, 569–572
    regulation and solvency of, 575–577, 594
    role of, 572–574
    too big to fail, 577
    Troubled Asset Relief Program (TARP), 659
Barbados, 459, 526
bar charts, 36
bargaining. *See also* auctions
    Coase Theorem and, 398–399
    Evidence-Based Economics, household spending, 399–400
    Letting the Data Speak, sex ratios, 401
    overview, 395–396
    Ultimatum Game, 396–398, 410–414
bargaining power, 396
barriers to entry, 276
barter, 606
Becker, Gary, 380–381
Belarus, 524
Benin, 443
Bertrand, Joseph Louis François, 325

movement along a supply curve, **74**

Mozilla Firefox, 279

MSB (marginal social benefit), 202–205

MSC (marginal social cost), 201–202

Mugabe, Robert, 534

Mullainathan, Sendhil, 269

multipliers, 619–627, **620,** 701–702

Myanmar, 519, 524

N

NAFTA (North American Free Trade Agreement), 191–192, 469

Nash, John, 305, 319

Nash equilibrium, 306

  Dutch auction bids, 390

  finding, 305–307

  oligopolies, 326–327

  oligopoly with differentiated products, 328

  tragedy of the commons, 308–309

  zero-sum games, 309–310

National Bureau of Economic Research (NBER), 557

National Flood Insurance Program, 373

national income accounting identity, 435

national income accounts, 429. *See also* gross domestic product (GDP)

  circular flows, 431–432

  Evidence-Based Economics, U.S. GDP, 436–437

  expenditures, 434–435

  income, 438–439

  items not measured by, 439–444

  overview of, 429–430

  production, 432–434

  real *vs.* nominal GDP, 444–450

National Income and Product Accounts (NIPA), 429

national security, free trade and, 188

natural experiment, 29

natural market power, 277

natural monopoly, 279

natural rate of unemployment, 551–552

natural resources

  common pool resource goods, 218–220

  free trade, opposition to, 188–189

  land, 267–268, 464

  production possibilities curve and, 181

  trade between countries, 187–188

  tragedy of the commons, 219–220, 308–309

negative correlation, 27

negative externalities, 441–442

negatively related, 64

negotiation, bilateral, 164–165

Nelson, Bill, 141

net exports, **673**–677

net exports curve, 699–700

net importer, 182

net present value, 354–355

network externalities, 278

Nicaragua, 459, 486, 589

Niger, 459

Nigeria, 497, 498, 527–528

Nike, 569, 575, 664

Nikolai I, 524

Niskanen, William, 234

Nogales, Mexico and Texas, 534

nominal exchange rate, 687–688

nominal GDP, 444–445, 586–588

nominal interest rate, 562–563, 564, 565

nominal wages, 627–628

non-excludable good, 212–213

non-rival good, 212–215

Nordhaus, William D., 490, 501

normal good, 68, 69, 105–106

normative economics, 5–6. *See also* cost-benefit analysis

North, Douglass, 515–516

North American Free Trade Agreement (NAFTA), 191–192, 469

Northern Rock, 560, 575, 581

North Korea, 158–159, 516–519, 524, 670

Norway, 443, 473

O

Obama, Barack, 245, 272, 653–654, 655

Obamacare, 272, 369–370, 378–379, 382

Ockenfels, Axel, 388

offshoring, costs and benefits of, 669–670

oil imports, 183

Okun, Arthur, 237, 618–619

Okun's Law, 618–619

Old Navy, 672

oligopoly, 323

  collusion, 329–332

  differentiated products model, 327–328

  Evidence-Based Economics, competitive markets, 340–342

  homogeneous products model, 325–327

  invisible hand and, 337–339

  Letting the Data Speak, 329, 331

  oligopolist's problem, 325

  overview of, 322–325, 339–340

omitted variable, 27, 28

one dollar a day per person poverty line, 460–462

OPEC (Organization of the Petroleum Exporting Countries), 331

open economy, 670–671

open market operations, 598–600

open outcry auction, 387–390, 394

opportunity cost of time

  labor supply curve, 544–546

  unemployment and, 540–541

opportunity costs, 8–9

  absolute and comparative advantage, 665–669

  budget constraint and, 89–90

  charitable giving and taxes, 407

  comparative advantage and, 174–178

  economic institutions and, 519–523

  economic *vs.* accounting profits, 134–135

  Facebook, cost of, 10–12

  housing prices, 55

  labor supply shifters, 259–261

  leisure-labor trade-off, 256–261

  optimization in levels, 47

  present value and discounting, 353–355

  production possibilities and, 173–174, 179–180

  savings, 565–566

  terms of trade and, 177–178

optimization, 6–10

  buying decisions, 90–93

  housing costs and location, 53–55

  indifference curves, 111–113

  leisure-labor trade-off, 256–261

  Principle of Optimization at the Margin, 52

  profits, 123–124

  shut down, 126–127

  skill development, 45

  social surplus, 147–148

  supply curve shifts, 74–75

  types of, 43–45

  willingness to accept, 72

optimization in differences, 44–45, 50–53

optimization in levels, 44–49

optimum, 47

optometry, advertising for, 334

Oreopoulos, Philip, 30

Ostrom, Elinor, 220

outsourcing, costs and benefits of, 669–670

Owen, Robert, 524

P

Page, Larry, 278

Pakistan, 443, 459, 519, 672

Pareto efficiency, 148, 289–291

patents, 525

patents, 276

  expiration of, 287–288

  monopolies, benefits of, 294–295

  monopolies and, 274–275

  monopolist's problem, 280–282

paternalism, 245–246

Patient Protection and Affordable Care Act (ACA), 272, 369–370, 378–379, 382